Complete Solutions Guide
to accompany
Chemistry
Seventh Edition

Steven S. Zumdahl
Susan Arena Zumdahl

Thomas J. Hummel
Steven S. Zumdahl
Susan Arena Zumdahl

University of Illinois at Urbana-Champaign

HOUGHTON MIFFLIN COMPANY   Boston   New York

Publisher and Editor-in-Chief: Charles Hartford
Executive Editor: Richard Stratton
Development Editor: Rebecca Berardy Schwartz
Assistant Editor: Liz Hogan
Senior Project Editor: Cathy Brooks
Editorial Assistant: Susan Miscio
Senior Marketing Manager: Katherine Greig
Market Assistant: Naveen Hariprasad

Printed in the U.S.A.

ISBN-10: 0-618-52852-0
ISBN-13: 978-0-618-52852-3

1 2 3 4 5 6 7 8 9-POO-10 09 08 07 06

TABLE OF CONTENTS

TO THE STUDENT: HOW TO USE THIS GUIDE

Solutions to all of the end of chapter questions and exercises are in this manual. This "Solutions Guide" can be very valuable if you use it properly. The way <u>NOT</u> to use it is to look at an exercise in the book and then immediately check the solution, often saying to yourself, "That's easy, I can do it." Developing problem solving skills takes practice. Don't look up a solution to a problem until you have tried to work it on your own. If you are completely stuck, see if you can find a similar problem in the Sample Exercises in the chapter. Only look up the solution as a last resort. If you do this for a problem, look for a similar problem in the end of chapter exercises and try working it. The more problems you do, the easier chemistry becomes. It is also in your self interest to try to work as many problems as possible. Most exams that you will take in chemistry will involve a lot of problem solving. If you have worked several problems similar to the ones on an exam, you will do much better than if the exam is the first time you try to solve a particular type of problem. No matter how much you read and study the text, or how well you think you understand the material, you don't really understand it until you have taken the information in the text and applied the principles to problem solving. You will make mistakes, but the good students learn from their mistakes.

In this manual we have worked problems as in the textbook. We have shown intermediate answers to the correct number of significant figures and used the rounded answer in later calculations. Thus, some of your answers may differ slightly from ours. When we have not followed this convention, we have usually noted this in the solution. The most common exception is when working with the natural logarithm (ln) function, where we usually carried extra significant figures in order to reduce round-off error. In addition, we tried to use constants and conversion factors reported to at least one more significant figure as compared to numbers given in the problem. The practice of carrying one extra significant figure in constants helps minimize round-off error.

We are grateful to Claire O. Szoke for her outstanding effort in preparing the manuscript for this manual. We also thank Linda C. Bush for her careful and thorough accuracy review of the Solutions Guide.

TJH
SSZ
SAZ

v

CHAPTER ONE

CHEMICAL FOUNDATIONS

For Review

1. a. Law versus theory: A law is a concise statement or equation that summarizes observed behavior. A theory is a set of hypotheses that gives an overall explanation of some phenomenon. A law summarizes what happens; a theory (or model) attempts to explain why it happens.

    b. Theory versus experiment: A theory is an explanation of why things behave the way they do, while an experiment is the process of observing that behavior. Theories attempt to explain the results of experiments and are, in turn, tested by further experiments.

    c. Qualitative versus quantitative: A qualitative observation only describes a quality while a quantitative observation attaches a number to the observation. Examples: Qualitative observations: The water was hot to the touch. Mercury was found in the drinking water. Quantitative observations: The temperature of the water was 62°C. The concentration of mercury in the drinking water was 1.5 ppm.

    d. Hypothesis versus theory: Both are explanations of experimental observation. A theory is a set of hypotheses that has been tested over time and found to still be valid, with (perhaps) some modifications.

2. No, it is useful whenever a systematic approach of observation and hypothesis testing can be used.

3. a. No.   b. Yes   c. Yes

    Only statements b and c can be determined from experiment.

4. Volume readings are estimated to one decimal place past the markings on the glassware. The assumed uncertainty is ±1 in the estimated digit. For glassware a, the volume would be estimated to the tenths place since the markings are to the ones place. A sample reading would be 4.2 with an uncertainty of ±0.1. This reading has two significant figures. For glassware b, 10.52 ±0.01 would be a sample reading and the uncertainty; this reading has four significant figures. For glassware c, 18 ±1 would be a sample reading and the uncertainty, with the reading having two significant figures.

5. Accuracy: How close a measurement or series of measurements are to an accepted or true value.

    Precision: How close a series of measurements of the same thing are to each other. The results, average = 14.91 ± 0.03%, are precise (close to each other) but are not accurate (not close to the true value).

6.   In both sets of rules, the lease precise number determines the number of significant figures in the final result. For multiplication/division, the number of significant figures in the result is the same as the number of significant figures in the least precise number used in the calculation. For addition/subtraction, the result has the same number of decimal places as the least precise number used in the calculation (not necessarily the number with the fewest significant figures).

7.   Consider gold with a density of 19.32 g/cm^3. The two conversion factors are:

$$\frac{19.32 \, \text{g}}{1 \, \text{cm}^3} \quad \text{or} \quad \frac{1 \, \text{cm}^3}{19.32 \, \text{g}}$$

Use the first form when converting from the volume of gold in cm^3 to the mass of gold and use the second form when converting from mass of gold to volume of gold. When using conversion factors, concentrate on the units crossing off.

8.   To convert from Celsius to Kelvin, a constant number of 273 is added to the Celsius temperature. Because of this, $\Delta T(^{\circ}\text{C}) = \Delta T(\text{K})$. When converting from Fahrenheit to Celsius, one conversion that must occur is to multiply the Fahrenheit temperature by a factor less than one (5/9). Therefore, the Fahrenheit scale is more expansive than the Celsius scale, and 1°F would correspond to a smaller temperature change than 1°C or 1K.

9.   Chemical changes involve the making and breaking of chemical bonds. Physical changes do not. The identity of a substance changes after a chemical change, but not after a physical change.

10.   Many techniques of chemical analysis require relatively pure samples. Thus, a separation step often is necessary to remove materials that will interfere with the analytical measurement.

Questions

17   A law summarizes what happens, e.g., law of conservation of mass in a chemical reaction or the ideal gas law, PV = nRT. A theory (model) is an attempt to explain why something happens. Dalton's atomic theory explains why mass is conserved in a chemical reaction. The kinetic molecular theory explains why pressure and volume are inversely related at constant temperature and moles of gas present as well as explaining the other mathematical relationships summarized in PV = nRT.

18.   The fundamental steps are:
        1. making observations
        2. formulating hypotheses
        3. performing experiments to test the hypotheses

The key to the scientific method is performing experiments to test hypotheses. If after the test of time, the hypotheses seem to account satisfactorily for some aspect of natural behavior, then the set of tested hypotheses turn into a theory (model). However, scientists continue to perform experiments to refine or replace existing theories.

19.   A qualitative observation expresses what makes something what it is; it does not involve a number, e.g., the air we breathe is a mixture of gases, ice is less dense than water, rotten milk stinks.

The SI units are mass in kilograms, length in meters, and volume in the derived units of m^3. The assumed uncertainty in a number is ± 1 in the last significant figure of the number. The precision of an instrument is related to the number of significant figures associated with an experimental reading on that instrument. Different instruments for measuring mass, length, or volume have varying degrees of precision. Some instruments only give a few significant figures for a measurement while others will give more significant figures.

20.   Precision: reproducibility; Accuracy: the agreement of a measurement with the true value.

a.   imprecise and inaccurate data: 12.32 cm, 9.63 cm, 11.98 cm, 13.34 cm

b.   precise but inaccurate data: 8.76 cm, 8.79 cm, 8.72 cm, 8.75 cm

c.   precise and accurate data: 10.60 cm, 10.65 cm, 10.63 cm, 10.64 cm

Data can be imprecise if the measuring device is imprecise as well as if the user of the measuring device has poor skills. Data can be inaccurate due to a systematic error in the measuring device or with the user. For example, a balance may read all masses as weighing 0.2500 g too high or the user of a graduated cylinder may read all measurements 0.05 mL too low.

A set of measurements which are imprecise implies that all the numbers are not close to each other. If the numbers aren't reproducible, then all of the numbers can't be very close to the true value. Some say that if the average of imprecise data gives the true value, then it is accurate data; a better description is that the data takers are extremely lucky.

21.   Significant figures are the digits we associate with a number. They contain all of the certain digits and the first uncertain digit (the first estimated digit). What follows is one thousand indicated to varying numbers of significant figures: 1000 or 1×10^3 (1 S.F.); 1.0×10^3 (2 S.F.); 1.00×10^3 (3 S.F.); 1000. or 1.000×10^3 (4 S.F.).

To perform the calculation, the addition/subtraction significant figure rule is applied to 1.5 – 1.0. The result of this is the one significant figure answer of 0.5. Next, the multiplication/division rule is applied to 0.5/0.50. A one significant figure number divided by a two significant figure number yields an answer with one significant figure (answer = 1).

22.   The volume per mass is the reciprocal of the density (1/density). The volume per mass conversion factor has units of cm^3/g and is useful when converting from the mass of an object to its volume in cm^3.

23.   Straight line equation: $y = mx + b$ where m is the slope of the line and b is the y-intercept. For the T_F vs. T_C plot:

$T_F = (9/5)T_C + 32$
$y =\ \ m\ \ x\ +\ b$

The slope of the plot is 1.8 (= 9/5) and the y-intercept is 32°F.

For the T_C vs. T_K plot:

$$T_C = T_K - 273$$
$$y = m\,x + b$$

The slope of the plot is one and the y-intercept is $-273\,°C$.

24. a. coffee; saltwater; the air we breathe ($N_2 + O_2$ + others); brass (Cu + Zn)

b. book; human being; tree; desk

c. sodium chloride (NaCl); water (H_2O); glucose ($C_6H_{12}O_6$); carbon dioxide (CO_2)

d. nitrogen (N_2); oxygen (O_2); copper (Cu); zinc (Zn)

e. boiling water; freezing water; melting a popsicle; dry ice subliming

f. Elecrolysis of molten sodium chloride to produce sodium and chlorine gas; the explosive reaction between oxygen and hydrogen to produce water; photosynthesis which converts H_2O and CO_2 into $C_6H_{12}O_6$ and O_2; the combustion of gasoline in our car to produce CO_2 and H_2O

Exercises

Significant Figures and Unit Conversions

25. a. exact   b. inexact

c. exact   d. inexact (π has an infinite number of decimal places.)

26. a. one significant figure (S.F.). The implied uncertainty is ±1000 pages. More significant figures should be added if a more precise number is known.

b. two S.F.   c. four S.F.

d. two S.F.   e. infinite number of S.F. (exact number)   f. one S.F.

27. a. $\underline{6.07} \times 10^{-15}$; 3 S.F.   b. $0.00\underline{3840}$; 4 S.F.   c. $\underline{17.00}$; 4 S.F.

d. $\underline{8} \times 10^8$; 1 S.F.   e. $\underline{463.8052}$; 7 S.F.   f. $\underline{3}00$; 1 S.F.

g. $\underline{301}$; 3 S.F.   h. $\underline{300.}$; 3 S.F.

28. a. $\underline{1}00$; 1 S.F.   b. $\underline{1.0} \times 10^2$; 2 S.F.   c. $\underline{1.00} \times 10^3$; 3 S.F.

d. $\underline{100.}$; 3 S.F.   e. $0.00\underline{48}$; 2 S.F.   f. $0.00\underline{480}$; 3 S.F.

g. $\underline{4.80} \times 10^{-3}$; 3 S.F.   h. $\underline{4.800} \times 10^{-3}$; 4 S.F.

29. When rounding, the last significant figure stays the same if the number after this significant figure is less than 5 and increases by one if the number is greater than or equal to 5.

a. 3.42×10^{-4} b. 1.034×10^4 c. 1.7992×10^1 d. 3.37×10^5

30.   a. 5×10^2 b. 4.8×10^2 c. 4.80×10^2 d. 4.800×10^2

31.   For addition and/or subtraction, the result has the same number of decimal places as the number in the calculation with the fewest decimal places. When the result is rounded to the correct number of significant figures, the last significant figure stays the same if the number after this significant figure is less than 5 and increases by one if the number is greater than or equal to 5. The underline shows the last significant figure in the intermediate answers.

a. $212.2 + 26.7 + 402.09 = 640.\underline{9}9 = 641.0$

b. $1.0028 + 0.221 + 0.10337 = 1.32\underline{7}17 = 1.327$

c. $52.331 + 26.01 - 0.9981 = 77.3\underline{4}29 = 77.34$

d. $2.01 \times 10^2 + 3.014 \times 10^3 = 2.01 \times 10^2 + 30.14 \times 10^2 = 32.1\underline{5} \times 10^2 = 3215$

When the exponents are different, it is easiest to apply the addition/subtraction rule when all numbers are based on the same power of 10.

e. $7.255 - 6.8350 = 0.42 = 0.420$ (first uncertain digit is in the third decimal place).

32.   For multiplication and/or division, the result has the same number of significant figures as the number in the calculation with the fewest significant figures.

a. $\dfrac{0.102 \times 0.0821 \times 273}{1.01} = \underline{2.26}35 = 2.26$

b. $0.14 \times 6.022 \times 10^{23} = \underline{8.4}31 \times 10^{22} = 8.4 \times 10^{22}$; Since 0.14 only has two significant figures, the result should only have two significant figures.

c. $4.0 \times 10^4 \times 5.021 \times 10^{-3} \times 7.34993 \times 10^2 = \underline{1.4}76 \times 10^5 = 1.5 \times 10^5$

d. $\dfrac{2.00 \times 10^6}{3.00 \times 10^{-7}} = \underline{6.66}67 \times 10^{12} = 6.67 \times 10^{12}$

33.   a. Here, apply the multiplication/division rule first; then apply the addition/subtraction rule to arrive at the one decimal place answer. We will generally round off at intermediate steps in order to show the correct number of significant figures. However, you should round off at the end of all the mathematical operations in order to avoid round-off error. The best way to do calculations is to keep track of the correct number of significant figures during intermediate steps, but round off at the end. For this problem, we underlined the last significant figure in the intermediate steps.

$$\dfrac{2.526}{3.1} + \dfrac{0.470}{0.623} + \dfrac{80.705}{0.4326} = 0.8\underline{1}48 + 0.75\underline{4}4 + 186.\underline{5}58 = 188.1$$

b. Here, the mathematical operation requires that we apply the addition/subtraction rule first, then apply the multiplication/division rule.

$$\dfrac{6.404 \times 2.91}{18.7 - 17.1} = \dfrac{6.404 \times 2.91}{1.\underline{6}} = 12$$

c. $6.071 \times 10^{-5} - 8.2 \times 10^{-6} - 0.521 \times 10^{-4} = 60.71 \times 10^{-6} - 8.2 \times 10^{-6} - 52.1 \times 10^{-6}$
$$= 0.\underline{4}1 \times 10^{-6} = 4 \times 10^{-7}$$

d. $\dfrac{3.8 \times 10^{-12} + 4.0 \times 10^{-13}}{4 \times 10^{12} + 6.3 \times 10^{13}} = \dfrac{38 \times 10^{-13} + 4.0 \times 10^{-13}}{4 \times 10^{12} + 63 \times 10^{12}} = \dfrac{4\underline{2} \times 10^{-13}}{6\underline{7} \times 10^{12}} = 6.3 \times 10^{-26}$

e. $\dfrac{9.5 + 4.1 + 2.8 + 3.175}{4} = \dfrac{19.\underline{5}75}{4} = 4.89 = 4.9$

Uncertainty appears in the first decimal place. The average of several numbers can only be as precise as the least precise number. Averages can be exceptions to the significant figure rules.

f. $\dfrac{8.925 - 8.905}{8.925} \times 100 = \dfrac{0.020\underline{}}{8.925} \times 100 = 0.22$

34.   a. $6.022 \times 10^{23} \times 1.05 \times 10^{2} = 6.32 \times 10^{25}$

b. $\dfrac{6.6262 \times 10^{-34} \times 2.998 \times 10^{8}}{2.54 \times 10^{-9}} = 7.82 \times 10^{-17}$

c. $1.285 \times 10^{-2} + 1.24 \times 10^{-3} + 1.879 \times 10^{-1}$
$$= 0.1285 \times 10^{-1} + 0.0124 \times 10^{-1} + 1.879 \times 10^{-1} = 2.020 \times 10^{-1}$$

When the exponents are different, it is easiest to apply the addition/subtraction rule when all numbers are based on the same power of 10.

d. $1.285 \times 10^{-2} - 1.24 \times 10^{-3} = 1.285 \times 10^{-2} - 0.124 \times 10^{-2} = 1.161 \times 10^{-2}$

e. $\dfrac{(1.00866 - 1.00728)}{6.02205 \times 10^{23}} = \dfrac{0.00138}{6.02205 \times 10^{23}} = 2.29 \times 10^{-27}$

f. $\dfrac{9.875 \times 10^{2} - 9.795 \times 10^{2}}{9.875 \times 10^{2}} \times 100 = \dfrac{0.080 \times 10^{2}}{9.875 \times 10^{2}} \times 100 = 8.1 \times 10^{-1}$

g. $\dfrac{9.42 \times 10^{2} + 8.234 \times 10^{2} + 1.625 \times 10^{3}}{3} = \dfrac{0.942 \times 10^{3} + 0.824 \times 10^{3} + 1.625 \times 10^{3}}{3}$
$$= 1.130 \times 10^{3}$$

35.   a. $8.43 \text{ cm} \times \dfrac{1 \text{ m}}{100 \text{ cm}} \times \dfrac{1000 \text{ mm}}{\text{m}} = 84.3 \text{ mm}$ b. $2.41 \times 10^{2} \text{ cm} \times \dfrac{1 \text{ m}}{100 \text{ cm}} = 2.41 \text{ m}$

c. $294.5 \text{ nm} \times \dfrac{1 \text{ m}}{1 \times 10^{9} \text{ nm}} \times \dfrac{100 \text{ cm}}{\text{m}} = 2.945 \times 10^{-5} \text{ cm}$

d. $1.445 \times 10^4 \text{ m} \times \dfrac{1 \text{ km}}{1000 \text{ m}} = 14.45 \text{ km}$ e. $235.3 \text{ m} \times \dfrac{1000 \text{ mm}}{\text{m}} = 2.353 \times 10^5 \text{ mm}$

f. $903.3 \text{ nm} \times \dfrac{1 \text{ m}}{1 \times 10^9 \text{ nm}} \times \dfrac{1 \times 10^6 \ \mu\text{m}}{\text{m}} = 0.9033 \ \mu\text{m}$

36.   a. $1 \text{ Tg} \times \dfrac{1 \times 10^{12} \text{ g}}{\text{Tg}} \times \dfrac{1 \text{ kg}}{1000 \text{ g}} = 1 \times 10^9 \text{ kg}$

b. $6.50 \times 10^2 \text{ Tm} \times \dfrac{1 \times 10^{12} \text{ m}}{\text{Tm}} \times \dfrac{1 \times 10^9 \text{ nm}}{\text{m}} = 6.50 \times 10^{23} \text{ nm}$

c. $25 \text{ fg} \times \dfrac{1 \text{ g}}{1 \times 10^{15} \text{ fg}} \times \dfrac{1 \text{ kg}}{1000 \text{ g}} = 25 \times 10^{-18} \text{ kg} = 2.5 \times 10^{-17} \text{ kg}$

d. $8.0 \text{ dm}^3 \times \dfrac{1 \text{ L}}{\text{dm}^3} = 8.0 \text{ L}$ $(1 \text{ L} = 1 \text{ dm}^3 = 1000 \text{ cm}^3 = 1000 \text{ mL})$

e. $1 \text{ mL} \times \dfrac{1 \text{ L}}{1\,000 \text{ mL}} \times \dfrac{1 \times 10^6 \ \mu\text{L}}{\text{L}} = 1 \times 10^3 \ \mu\text{L}$

f. $1 \ \mu\text{g} \times \dfrac{1 \text{ g}}{1 \times 10^6 \ \mu\text{g}} \times \dfrac{1 \times 10^{12} \text{ pg}}{\text{g}} = 1 \times 10^6 \text{ pg}$

37.   a. Appropriate conversion factors are found in Appendix 6. In general, the number of significant figures we use in the conversion factors will be one more than the number of significant figures from the numbers given in the problem. This is usually sufficient to avoid round-off error.

$3.91 \text{ kg} \times \dfrac{1 \text{ lb}}{0.4536 \text{ kg}} = 8.62 \text{ lb}; \ 0.62 \text{ lb} \times \dfrac{16 \text{ oz}}{\text{lb}} = 9.9 \text{ oz}$

Baby's weight = 8 lb and 9.9 oz or to the nearest ounce, 8 lb and 10. oz.

$51.4 \text{ cm} \times \dfrac{1 \text{ in}}{2.54 \text{ cm}} = 20.2 \text{ in} \approx 20 \ 1/4 \text{ in} = \text{baby's height}$

b. $25,000 \text{ mi} \times \dfrac{1.61 \text{ km}}{\text{mi}} = 4.0 \times 10^4 \text{ km}; \ 4.0 \times 10^4 \text{ km} \times \dfrac{1000 \text{ m}}{\text{km}} = 4.0 \times 10^7 \text{ m}$

c. $V = 1 \times w \times h = 1.0 \text{ m} \times \left(5.6 \text{ cm} \times \dfrac{1 \text{ m}}{100 \text{ cm}} \right) \times \left(2.1 \text{ dm} \times \dfrac{1 \text{ m}}{10 \text{ dm}} \right) = 1.2 \times 10^{-2} \text{ m}^3$

$$1.2 \times 10^{-2} \text{ m}^3 \times \left(\frac{10 \text{ dm}}{\text{m}} \right)^3 \times \frac{1 \text{ L}}{\text{dm}^3} = 12 \text{ L}$$

$$12 \text{ L} \times \frac{1000 \text{ cm}^3}{\text{L}} \times \left(\frac{1 \text{ in}}{2.54 \text{ cm}} \right)^3 = 730 \text{ in}^3; \ \ 730 \text{ in}^3 \times \left(\frac{1 \text{ ft}}{12 \text{ in}} \right)^3 = 0.42 \text{ ft}^3$$

38.   a. $908 \text{ oz} \times \dfrac{1 \text{ lb}}{16 \text{ oz}} \times \dfrac{0.4536 \text{ kg}}{\text{lb}} = 25.7 \text{ kg}$

   b. $12.8 \text{ L} \times \dfrac{1 \text{ qt}}{0.9463 \text{ L}} \times \dfrac{1 \text{ gal}}{4 \text{ qt}} = 3.38 \text{ gal}$

   c. $125 \text{ mL} \times \dfrac{1 \text{ L}}{1000 \text{ mL}} \times \dfrac{1 \text{ qt}}{0.9463 \text{ L}} = 0.132 \text{ qt}$

   d. $2.89 \text{ gal} \times \dfrac{4 \text{ qt}}{1 \text{ gal}} \times \dfrac{1 \text{ L}}{1.057 \text{ qt}} \times \dfrac{1000 \text{ mL}}{1 \text{ L}} = 1.09 \times 10^4 \text{ mL}$

   e. $4.48 \text{ lb} \times \dfrac{453.6 \text{ g}}{1 \text{ lb}} = 2.03 \times 10^3 \text{ g}$

   f. $550 \text{ mL} \times \dfrac{1 \text{ L}}{1000 \text{ mL}} \times \dfrac{1.06 \text{ qt}}{\text{L}} = 0.58 \text{ qt}$

39.   a. $1.25 \text{ mi} \times \dfrac{8 \text{ furlongs}}{\text{mi}} = 10.0 \text{ furlongs}; \ \ 10.0 \text{ furlongs} \times \dfrac{40 \text{ rods}}{\text{furlong}} = 4.00 \times 10^2 \text{ rods}$

   $$4.00 \times 10^2 \text{ rods} \times \frac{5.5 \text{ yd}}{\text{rod}} \times \frac{36 \text{ in}}{\text{yd}} \times \frac{2.54 \text{ cm}}{\text{in}} \times \frac{1 \text{ m}}{100 \text{ cm}} = 2.01 \times 10^3 \text{ m}$$

   $$2.01 \times 10^3 \text{ m} \times \frac{1 \text{ km}}{1000 \text{ m}} = 2.01 \text{ km}$$

   b.   Let's assume we know this distance to ± 1 yard. First convert 26 miles to yards.

   $$26 \text{ mi} \times \frac{5280 \text{ ft}}{\text{mi}} \times \frac{1 \text{ yd}}{3 \text{ ft}} = 45,760. \text{ yd}$$

   $$26 \text{ mi} + 385 \text{ yd} = 45,760. \text{ yd} + 385 \text{ yd} = 46,145 \text{ yards}$$

   $$46,145 \text{ yard} \times \frac{1 \text{ rod}}{5.5 \text{ yd}} = 8390.0 \text{ rods}; \ \ 8390.0 \text{ rods} \times \frac{1 \text{ furlong}}{40 \text{ rods}} = 209.75 \text{ furlongs}$$

   $$46,145 \text{ yard} \times \frac{36 \text{ in}}{\text{yd}} \times \frac{2.54 \text{ cm}}{\text{in}} \times \frac{1 \text{ m}}{100 \text{ cm}} = 42,195 \text{ m}; \ \ 42,195 \text{ m} \times \frac{1 \text{ km}}{1000 \text{ m}} = 42.195 \text{ km}$$

40.   a. $1 \text{ ha} \times \dfrac{10,000 \text{ m}^2}{\text{ha}} \times \left(\dfrac{1 \text{ km}}{1000 \text{ m}}\right)^2 = 1 \times 10^{-2} \text{ km}^2$

      b. $5.5 \text{ acre} \times \dfrac{160 \text{ rod}^2}{\text{acre}} \times \left(\dfrac{5.5 \text{ yd}}{\text{rod}} \times \dfrac{36 \text{ in}}{\text{yd}} \times \dfrac{2.54 \text{ cm}}{\text{in}} \times \dfrac{1 \text{ m}}{100 \text{ cm}}\right)^2 = 2.2 \times 10^4 \text{ m}^2$

        $2.2 \times 10^4 \text{ m}^2 \times \dfrac{1 \text{ ha}}{1 \times 10^4 \text{ m}^2} = 2.2 \text{ ha}; \ 2.2 \times 10^4 \text{ m}^2 \times \left(\dfrac{1 \text{ km}}{1000 \text{ m}}\right)^2 = 0.022 \text{ km}^2$

      c.   Area of lot $= 120 \text{ ft} \times 75 \text{ ft} = 9.0 \times 10^3 \text{ ft}^2$

        $9.0 \times 10^3 \text{ ft}^2 \times \left(\dfrac{1 \text{ yd}}{3 \text{ ft}} \times \dfrac{1 \text{ rod}}{5.5 \text{ yd}}\right)^2 \times \dfrac{1 \text{ acre}}{160 \text{ rod}^2} = 0.21 \text{ acre}; \ \dfrac{\$6,500}{0.21 \text{ acre}} = \dfrac{\$31,000}{\text{acre}}$

        We can use our result from (b) to get the conversion factor between acres and ha (5.5 acre = 2.2 ha.). Thus, 1 ha = 2.5 acre.

        $0.21 \text{ acre} \times \dfrac{1 \text{ ha}}{2.5 \text{ acre}} = 0.084 \text{ ha}$; The price is: $\dfrac{\$6,500}{0.084 \text{ ha}} = \dfrac{\$77,000}{\text{ha}}$

41.   a. $1 \text{ troy lb} \times \dfrac{12 \text{ troy oz}}{\text{troy lb}} \times \dfrac{20 \text{ pw}}{\text{troy oz}} \times \dfrac{24 \text{ grains}}{\text{pw}} \times \dfrac{0.0648 \text{ g}}{\text{grain}} \times \dfrac{1 \text{ kg}}{1000 \text{ g}} = 0.373 \text{ kg}$

        $1 \text{ troy lb} = 0.373 \text{ kg} \times \dfrac{2.205 \text{ lb}}{\text{kg}} = 0.822 \text{ lb}$

      b. $1 \text{ troy oz} \times \dfrac{20 \text{ pw}}{\text{troy oz}} \times \dfrac{24 \text{ grains}}{\text{pw}} \times \dfrac{0.0648 \text{ g}}{\text{grain}} = 31.1 \text{ g}$

        $1 \text{ troy oz} = 31.1 \text{ g} \times \dfrac{1 \text{ carat}}{0.200 \text{ g}} = 156 \text{ carats}$

      c. $1 \text{ troy lb} = 0.373 \text{ kg}; \ 0.373 \text{ kg} \times \dfrac{1000 \text{ g}}{\text{kg}} \times \dfrac{1 \text{ cm}^3}{19.3 \text{ g}} = 19.3 \text{ cm}^3$

42.   a. $1 \text{ grain ap} \times \dfrac{1 \text{ scruple}}{20 \text{ grain ap}} \times \dfrac{1 \text{ dram ap}}{3 \text{ scruples}} \times \dfrac{3.888 \text{ g}}{\text{dram ap}} = 0.06480 \text{ g}$

        From the previous question, we are given that 1 grain troy = 0.0648 g = 1 grain ap. So, the two are the same.

      b. $1 \text{ oz ap} \times \dfrac{8 \text{ dram ap}}{\text{oz ap}} \times \dfrac{3.888 \text{ g}}{\text{dram ap}} \times \dfrac{1 \text{ oz troy *}}{31.1 \text{ g}} = 1.00 \text{ oz troy}$ *See Exercise 41b.

c. $5.00 \times 10^2 \text{ mg} \times \dfrac{1 \text{ g}}{1000 \text{ mg}} \times \dfrac{1 \text{ dram ap}}{3.888 \text{ g}} \times \dfrac{3 \text{ scruples}}{\text{dram ap}} = 0.386 \text{ scruple}$

$0.386 \text{ scruple} \times \dfrac{20 \text{ grains ap}}{\text{scruple}} = 7.72 \text{ grains ap}$

d. $1 \text{ scruple} \times \dfrac{1 \text{ dram ap}}{3 \text{ scruples}} \times \dfrac{3.888 \text{ g}}{\text{dram ap}} = 1.296 \text{ g}$

43. $\text{warp } 1.71 = \left(5.00 \times \dfrac{3.00 \times 10^8 \text{ m}}{\text{s}}\right) \times \dfrac{1.094 \text{ yd}}{\text{m}} \times \dfrac{60 \text{ s}}{\text{min}} \times \dfrac{60 \text{ min}}{\text{hr}} \times \dfrac{1 \text{ knot}}{2000 \text{ yd / hr}}$

$= 2.95 \times 10^9 \text{ knots}$

$\left(5.00 \times \dfrac{3.00 \times 10^8 \text{ m}}{\text{s}}\right) \times \dfrac{1 \text{ km}}{1000 \text{ m}} \times \dfrac{1 \text{ mi}}{1.609 \text{ km}} \times \dfrac{60 \text{ s}}{\text{min}} \times \dfrac{60 \text{ min}}{\text{hr}} = 3.36 \times 10^9 \text{ mi/hr}$

44. $\dfrac{100. \text{ m}}{9.77 \text{ s}} = 10.2 \text{ m/s}; \quad \dfrac{100. \text{ m}}{9.77 \text{ s}} \times \dfrac{1 \text{ km}}{1000 \text{ m}} \times \dfrac{60 \text{ s}}{\text{min}} \times \dfrac{60 \text{ min}}{\text{hr}} = 36.8 \text{ km/hr}$

$\dfrac{100. \text{ m}}{9.77 \text{ s}} \times \dfrac{1.0936 \text{ yd}}{\text{m}} \times \dfrac{3 \text{ ft}}{\text{yd}} = 33.6 \text{ ft/s}; \quad \dfrac{33.6 \text{ ft}}{\text{s}} \times \dfrac{1 \text{ mi}}{5280 \text{ ft}} \times \dfrac{60 \text{ s}}{\text{min}} \times \dfrac{60 \text{ min}}{\text{hr}} = 22.9 \text{ mi/hr}$

$1.00 \times 10^2 \text{ yd} \times \dfrac{1 \text{ m}}{1.0936 \text{ yd}} \times \dfrac{9.77 \text{ s}}{100. \text{ m}} = 8.93 \text{ s}$

45. $\dfrac{65 \text{ km}}{\text{hr}} \times \dfrac{0.6214 \text{ mi}}{\text{km}} = 40.4 = 40. \text{ mi/hr}$

To the correct number of significant figures, 65 km/hr does not violate a 40. mi/hr speed limit.

46. $112 \text{ km} \times \dfrac{0.6214 \text{ mi}}{\text{km}} \times \dfrac{1 \text{ hr}}{65 \text{ mi}} = 1.1 \text{ hr} = 1 \text{ hr and 6 min}$

$112 \text{ km} \times \dfrac{0.6214 \text{ mi}}{\text{km}} \times \dfrac{1 \text{ gal}}{28 \text{ mi}} \times \dfrac{3.785 \text{ L}}{\text{gal}} = 9.4 \text{ L of gasoline}$

47. $\dfrac{\$17.25 \text{ U.S.}}{8.21 \text{ gal}} \times \dfrac{\$1.00 \text{ Canadian}}{\$0.82 \text{ U.S.}} \times \dfrac{1 \text{ gal}}{3.7854 \text{ L}} = \$0.68 \text{ Canadian/L}$

48. $1.5 \text{ teaspoons} \times \dfrac{80. \text{ mg acet}}{0.50 \text{ teaspoon}} = 240 \text{ mg acetaminophen}$

$$\frac{240 \text{ mg acet}}{24 \text{ lb}} \times \frac{1 \text{ lb}}{0.454 \text{ kg}} = 22 \text{ mg acetaminophen/kg}$$

$$\frac{240 \text{ mg acet}}{35 \text{ lb}} \times \frac{1 \text{ lb}}{0.454 \text{ kg}} = 15 \text{ mg acetaminophen/kg}$$

The range is from 15 mg to 22 mg acetaminophen per kg of body weight.

Temperature

49.   a. $T_C = \frac{5}{9}(T_F - 32) = \frac{5}{9}(-459°C - 32) = -273°C$; $T_K = T_C + 273 = -273°C + 273 = 0 \text{ K}$

       b. $T_C = \frac{5}{9}(-40.°F - 32) = -40.°C$; $T_K = -40.°C + 273 = 233 \text{ K}$

       c. $T_C = \frac{5}{9}(68°F - 32) = 20.°C$; $T_K = 20.°C + 273 = 293 \text{ K}$

       d. $T_C = \frac{5}{9}(7 \times 10^7 °F - 32) = 4 \times 10^7 °C$; $T_K = 4 \times 10^7 °C + 273 = 4 \times 10^7 \text{ K}$

50.   96.1°F ± 0.2°F; First, convert 96.1°F to °C. $T_C = \frac{5}{9}(T_F - 32) = \frac{5}{9}(96.1 - 32) = 35.6°C$

       A change in temperature of 9°F is equal to a change in temperature of 5°C. So the uncertainty is:

$$\pm 0.2°F \times \frac{5°C}{9°F} = \pm 0.1°C. \text{ Thus, } 96.1 \pm 0.2°F = 35.6 \pm 0.1°C$$

51.   a. $T_F = \frac{9}{5} \times T_C + 32 = \frac{9}{5} \times 39.2°C + 32 = 102.6°F$ (Note: 32 is exact.)

            $T_K = T_C + 273.2 = 39.2 + 273.2 = 312.4 \text{ K}$

       b. $T_F = \frac{9}{5} \times (-25) + 32 = -13°F$; $T_K = -25 + 273 = 248 \text{ K}$

       c. $T_F = \frac{9}{5} \times (-273) + 32 = -459°F$; $T_K = -273 + 273 = 0 \text{ K}$

       d. $T_F = \frac{9}{5} \times 801 + 32 = 1470°F$; $T_K = 801 + 273 = 1074 \text{ K}$

52.   a. $T_C = T_K - 273 = 233 - 273 = -40.°C$

            $T_F = \frac{9}{5} \times T_C + 32 = \frac{9}{5} \times (-40.) + 32 = -40.°F$

       b. $T_C = 4 - 273 = -269°C$; $T_F = \frac{9}{5} \times (-269) + 32 = -452°F$

       c. $T_C = 298 - 273 = 25°C$; $T_F = \frac{9}{5} \times 25 + 32 = 77°F$

d. $T_C = 3680 - 273 = 3410°C;$ $T_F = \dfrac{9}{5} \times 3410 + 32 = 6170°F$

Density

53. $mass = 350\ lb \times \dfrac{453.6\ g}{lb} = 1.6 \times 10^5\ g;$ $V = 1.2 \times 10^4\ in^3 \times \left(\dfrac{2.54\ cm}{in}\right)^3 = 2.0 \times 10^5\ cm^3$

$density = \dfrac{mass}{volume} = \dfrac{1 \times 10^5\ g}{2.0 \times 10^5\ cm^3} = 0.80\ g/cm^3$

Because the material has a density less than water, it will float in water.

54. $V = \dfrac{4}{3}\pi r^3 = \dfrac{4}{3} \times 3.14 \times (0.50\ cm)^3 = 0.52\ cm^3;$ $d = \dfrac{2.0\ g}{0.52\ cm^3} = 3.8\ g/cm^3$

The ball will sink.

55. $V = \dfrac{4}{3}\pi r^3 = \dfrac{4}{3} \times 3.14 \times \left(7.0 \times 10^5\ km \times \dfrac{1000\ m}{km} \times \dfrac{100\ cm}{m}\right)^3 = 1.4 \times 10^{33}\ cm^3$

$density = \dfrac{mass}{volume} = \dfrac{2 \times 10^{36}\ kg \times \dfrac{1000\ g}{kg}}{1.4 \times 10^{33}\ cm^3} = 1.4 \times 10^6\ g/cm^3 = 1 \times 10^6\ g/cm^3$

56. $V = l \times w \times h = 2.9\ cm \times 3.5\ cm \times 10.0\ cm = 1.0 \times 10^2\ cm^3$

$d = density = \dfrac{615.0\ g}{1.0 \times 10^2\ cm^3} = \dfrac{6.2\ g}{cm^3}$

57. $5.0\ carat \times \dfrac{0.200\ g}{carat} \times \dfrac{1\ cm^3}{3.51\ g} = 0.28\ cm^3$

58. $2.8\ mL \times \dfrac{1\ cm^3}{mL} \times \dfrac{3.51\ g}{cm^3} \times \dfrac{1\ carat}{0.200\ g} = 49\ carats$

59. $V = 21.6\ mL - 12.7\ mL = 8.9\ mL;$ $density = \dfrac{33.42\ g}{8.9\ mL} = 3.8\ g/mL = 3.8\ g/cm^3$

60. $5.25\ g \times \dfrac{1\ cm^3}{10.5\ g} = 0.500\ cm^3 = 0.500\ mL$

The volume in the cylinder will rise to 11.7 mL (11.2 mL + 0.500 mL = 11.7 mL).

61.   a.   Both have the same mass of 1.0 kg.

b.   1.0 mL of mercury; Mercury has a greater density than water. Note: 1 mL = 1 cm^3

$1.0\ mL \times \dfrac{13.6\ g}{mL} = 14\ g$ of mercury; $1.0\ mL \times \dfrac{0.998\ g}{mL} = 1.0\ g$ of water

   c.   Same; Both represent 19.3 g of substance.

$$19.3 \text{ mL} \times \frac{0.9982 \text{ g}}{\text{mL}} = 19.3 \text{ g of water}; \quad 1.00 \text{ mL} \times \frac{19.32 \text{ g}}{\text{mL}} = 19.3 \text{ g of gold}$$

   d.   1.0 L of benzene (880 g vs 670 g)

$$75 \text{ mL} \times \frac{8.96 \text{ g}}{\text{mL}} = 670 \text{ g of copper}; \quad 1.0 \text{ L} \times \frac{1000 \text{ mL}}{\text{L}} \times \frac{0.880 \text{ g}}{\text{mL}} = 880 \text{ g of benzene}$$

62.   Volume of lake $= 100 \text{ mi}^2 \times \left(\frac{5280 \text{ ft}}{\text{mi}} \right)^2 \times 20 \text{ ft} = 6 \times 10^{10} \text{ ft}^3$

$$6 \times 10^{10} \text{ ft}^3 \times \left(\frac{12 \text{ in}}{\text{ft}} \times \frac{2.54 \text{ cm}}{\text{in}} \right)^3 \times \frac{1 \text{ mL}}{\text{cm}^3} \times \frac{0.4 \text{ μg}}{\text{mL}} = 7 \times 10^{14} \text{ μg mercury}$$

$$7 \times 10^{14} \text{ μg} \times \ \times \frac{1 \text{ g}}{10^6 \text{ μg}} \times \frac{1 \text{ kg}}{10^3 \text{ g}} = 7 \times 10^5 \text{ kg of mercury}$$

63.   a.   1.0 kg feather; Feathers are less dense than lead.

   b.   100 g water; Water is less dense than gold.   c. Same; Both volumes are 1.0 L.

64.   a. $H_2(g)$: $V = 25.0 \text{ g} \times \dfrac{1 \text{ cm}^3}{0.000084 \text{ g}} = 3.0 \times 10^5 \text{ cm}^3$ [$H_2(g)$ = hydrogen gas]

   b. $H_2O(l)$: $V = 25.0 \text{ g} \times \dfrac{1 \text{ cm}^3}{0.9982 \text{ g}} = 25.0 \text{ cm}^3$ [$H_2O(l)$ = water]

   c. $Fe(s)$: $V = 25.0 \text{ g} \times \dfrac{1 \text{ cm}^3}{7.87 \text{ g}} = 3.18 \text{ cm}^3$ [$Fe(s)$ = iron]

Notice the huge volume of the gaseous H_2 sample as compared to the liquid and solid samples. The same mass of gas occupies a volume that is over 10,000 times larger than the liquid sample. Gases are indeed mostly empty space.

65. $V = 1.00 \times 10^3 \text{ g} \times \dfrac{1 \text{ cm}^3}{22.57 \text{ g}} = 44.3 \text{ cm}^3$

   $44.3 \text{ cm}^3 = 1 \times w \times h = 4.00 \text{ cm} \times 4.00 \text{ cm} \times h, \ h = 2.77 \text{ cm}$

66. $V = 22 \text{ g} \times \dfrac{1 \text{ cm}^3}{8.96 \text{ g}} = 2.5 \text{ cm}^3$; $V = \pi r^2 \times l$ where l = length of the wire

   $2.5 \text{ cm}^3 = \pi \times \left(\dfrac{0.25 \text{ mm}}{2} \right)^2 \times \left(\dfrac{1 \text{ cm}}{10 \text{ mm}} \right)^2 \times l, \ l = 5.1 \times 10^3 \text{ cm} = 170 \text{ ft}$

Classification and Separation of Matter

67.   A gas has molecules that are very far apart from each other while a solid or liquid has molecules that are very close together. An element has the same type of atom, whereas a compound contains two or more different elements. Picture i represents an element that exists as two atoms bonded together (like H_2 or O_2 or N_2). Picture iv represents a compound (like CO, NO, or HF). Pictures iii and iv contain representations of elements that exist as individual atoms (like Ar, Ne, or He).

    a.   Picture iv represents a gaseous compound. Note that pictures ii and iii also contain a gaseous compound, but they also both have a gaseous element present.

    b.   Picture vi represents a mixture of two gaseous elements.

    c.   Picture v represents a solid element.

    d.   Pictures ii and iii both represent a mixture of a gaseous element and a gaseous compound.

68.   Solid: rigid; has a fixed volume and shape; slightly compressible

Liquid: definite volume but no specific shape; assumes shape of the container; slightly compressible

Gas: no fixed volume or shape; easily compressible

Pure substance: has constant composition; can be composed of either compounds or elements

Element: substances that cannot be decomposed into simpler substances by chemical or physical means.

Compound: a substance that can be broken down into simpler substances (elements) by chemical processes.

Homogeneous mixture: a mixture of pure substances that has visibly indistinguishable parts.

Heterogeneous mixture: a mixture of pure substances that has visibly distinguishable parts.
Solution: a homogeneous mixture; can be a solid, liquid or gas

Chemical change: a given substance becomes a new substance or substances with different properties and different composition.

Physical change: changes the form (g, l, or s) of a substance but does no change the chemical composition of the substance.

69.   Homogeneous: Having visibly indistinguishable parts (the same throughout).
Heterogeneous: Having visibly distinguishable parts (not uniform throughout).

    a.   heterogeneous (Due to hinges, handles, locks, etc.)

b. homogeneous (hopefully; If you live in a heavily polluted area, air may be heterogeneous.)

c. homogeneous   d. homogeneous (hopefully, if not polluted)

e. heterogeneous   f. heterogeneous

70.   a. pure   b. mixture   c. mixture   d. pure   e. mixture (copper and zinc)

f. pure   g. mixture   h. mixture   i. pure

Iron and uranium are elements. Water and table salt are compounds. Water is H_2O and table salt is NaCl. Compounds are composed of two or more elements.

71.   A physical change is a change in the state of a substance (solid, liquid and gas are the three states of matter); a physical change does not change the chemical composition of the substance. A chemical change is a change in which a given substance is converted into another substance having a different formula (composition).

a. Vaporization refers to a liquid converting to a gas, so this is a physical change. The formula (composition) of the moth ball does not change.

b. This is a chemical change since hydrofluoric acid (HF) is reacting with glass (SiO_2) to form new compounds which wash away.

c. This is a physical change since all that is happening is the conversion of liquid alcohol to gaseous alcohol. The alcohol formula (C_2H_5OH) does not change.

d. This is a chemical change since the acid is reacting with cotton to form new compounds.

72.   a. Distillation separates components of a mixture, so the orange liquid is a mixture (has an average color of the yellow liquid and the red solid). Distillation utilizes boiling point differences to separate out the components of a mixture. Distillation is a physical change because the components of the mixture do not become different compounds or elements.

b. Decomposition is a type of chemical reaction. The crystalline solid is a compound, and decomposition is a chemical change where new substances are formed.

c. Tea is a mixture of tea compounds dissolved in water. The process of mixing sugar into tea is a physical change. Sugar doesn't react with the tea compounds, it just makes the solution sweeter.

Additional Exercises

73. $15.6 \text{ g} \times \dfrac{1 \text{ capsule}}{0.65 \text{ g}} = 24 \text{ capsules}$

74. $126 \text{ gal} \times \dfrac{4 \text{ qt}}{\text{gal}} \times \dfrac{1 \text{ L}}{1.057 \text{ qt}} = 477 \text{ L}$

75.   Total volume = $\left(200.\,\text{m} \times \dfrac{100\,\text{cm}}{\text{m}}\right) \times \left(300.\,\text{m} \times \dfrac{100\,\text{cm}}{\text{m}}\right) \times 4.0\,\text{cm} = 2.4 \times 10^9\,\text{cm}^3$

Vol. of topsoil covered by 1 bag = $\left[10.\,\text{ft}^2 \times \left(\dfrac{12\,\text{in}}{\text{ft}}\right)^2 \times \left(\dfrac{2.54\,\text{cm}}{\text{in}}\right)^2\right] \times \left(1.0\,\text{in} \times \dfrac{2.54\,\text{cm}}{\text{in}}\right)$

$$= 2.4 \times 10^4\,\text{cm}^3$$

$2.4 \times 10^9\,\text{cm}^3 \times \dfrac{1\,\text{bag}}{2.4 \times 10^4\,\text{cm}^3} = 1.0 \times 10^5\,\text{bags topsoil}$

76.   a.   No; If the volumes were the same, then the gold idol would have a much greater mass because gold is much more dense than sand.

b.   Mass = $1.0\,\text{L} \times \dfrac{1000\,\text{cm}^3}{\text{L}} \times \dfrac{19.32\,\text{g}}{\text{cm}^3} \times \dfrac{1\,\text{kg}}{1000\,\text{g}} = 19.32\,\text{kg}\,(= 42.59\,\text{lb})$

It wouldn't be easy to play catch with the idol because it would have a mass of over 40 pounds.

77. $18.5\,\text{cm} \times \dfrac{10.0°\text{F}}{5.25\,\text{cm}} = 35.2°\text{F increase};\ T_{\text{final}} = 98.6 + 35.2 = 133.8°\text{F}$

$T_c = 5/9\,(133.8 - 32) = 56.56°\text{C}$

78. $\text{mass}_{\text{benzene}} = 58.80\,\text{g} - 25.00\,\text{g} = 33.80\,\text{g};\ V_{\text{benzene}} = 33.80\,\text{g} \times \dfrac{1\,\text{cm}^3}{0.880\,\text{g}} = 38.4\,\text{cm}^3$

$V_{\text{solid}} = 50.0\,\text{cm}^3 - 38.4\,\text{cm}^3 = 11.6\,\text{cm}^3;\ \ \text{density} = \dfrac{25.00\,\text{g}}{11.6\,\text{cm}^3} = 2.16\,\text{g/cm}^3$

79.   a.   Volume × density = mass; the orange block is more dense. Because mass (orange) > mass (blue) and because volume (orange) < volume (blue), the density of the orange block must be greater to account for the larger mass of the orange block.

b.   Which block is more dense cannot be determined. Because mass (orange) > mass (blue) and because volume (orange) > volume (blue), the density of the orange block may or may not be larger than the blue block. If the blue block is more dense, its density cannot be so large that its mass is larger than the orange block's mass.

c.   The blue block is more dense. Because mass (blue) = mass (orange) and because volume (blue) < volume (orange), the density of the blue block must be larger in order to equate the masses.

d.   The blue block is more dense. Because mass (blue) > mass (orange) and because the volumes are equal, the density of the blue block must be larger in order to give the blue block the larger mass.

80.   Circumference = c = 2π r; $V = \dfrac{4\pi r^3}{3} = \dfrac{4\pi}{3}\left(\dfrac{c}{2\pi}\right)^3 = \dfrac{c^3}{6\pi^2}$

Largest density = $\dfrac{5.25\ \text{oz}}{\dfrac{(9.00\ \text{in})^3}{6\pi^2}} = \dfrac{5.25\ \text{oz}}{12.3\ \text{in}^3} = \dfrac{0.427\ \text{oz}}{\text{in}^3}$

Smallest density = $\dfrac{5.00\ \text{oz}}{\dfrac{(9.25\ \text{in})^3}{6\pi^2}} = \dfrac{5.00\ \text{oz}}{13.4\ \text{in}^3} = \dfrac{0.73\ \text{oz}}{\text{in}^3}$

Maximum range is: $\dfrac{(0.373 - 0.427)\ \text{oz}}{\text{in}^3}$ or 0.40 ± 0.03 oz/in^3 (Uncertainty in 2nd decimal place.)

81. $V = V_{\text{final}} - V_{\text{initial}};\ \ d = \dfrac{28.90\ \text{g}}{9.8\ \text{cm}^3 - 6.4\ \text{cm}^3} = \dfrac{28.90\ \text{g}}{3.4\ \text{cm}^3} = 8.5\ \text{g/cm}^3$

$d_{\text{max}} = \dfrac{\text{mass}_{\text{max}}}{V_{\text{min}}}$;   We get V_{min} from 9.7 cm^3 - 6.5 cm^3 = 3.2 cm^3.

$d_{\text{max}} = \dfrac{28.93\ \text{g}}{3.2\ \text{cm}^3} = \dfrac{9.0\ \text{g}}{\text{cm}^3}$; $d_{\text{min}} = \dfrac{\text{mass}_{\text{min}}}{V_{\text{max}}} = \dfrac{28.87\ \text{g}}{9.9\ \text{cm}^3 - 6.3\ \text{cm}^3} = \dfrac{8.0\ \text{g}}{\text{cm}^3}$

The density is: 8.5 ± 0.5 g/cm^3.

Challenge Problems

82.   In general, glassware is estimated to one place past the markings.

a.   128.7 mL glassware   b.   18 mL glassware   c.   23.45 mL glassware

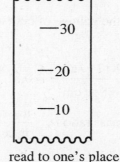

read to tenth's place   read to one's place   read to two decimal places

128.7 + 18 + 23.45 = 170.15 = 170. (Due to 18, the sum would be only known to the ones place.)

83.   a. $\dfrac{2.70 - 2.64}{2.70} \times 100 = 2\%$ b. $\dfrac{|16.12 - 16.48|}{16.12} \times 100 = 2.2\%$

        c. $\dfrac{1.000 - 0.9981}{1.000} \times 100 = \dfrac{0.002}{1.000} \times 100 = 0.2\%$

84.   a. At some point in 1982, the composition of the metal used in minting pennies was changed because the mass changed during this year (assuming the volume of the pennies were constant).

        b. It should be expressed as 3.08 ± 0.05 g. The uncertainty in the second decimal place will swamp any effect of the next decimal places.

85.   Heavy pennies (old): mean mass = 3.08 ± 0.05 g

    Light pennies (new): mean mass = $\dfrac{(2.467 + 2.545 + 2.518)}{3} = 2.51 \pm 0.04$ g

Because we are assuming that volume is additive, let's calculate the volume of 100. g of each type of penny then calculate the density of the alloy. For 100. g of the old pennies, 95 g will be Cu (copper) and 5 g will be Zn (zinc).

$$V = 95 \text{ g Cu} \times \frac{1 \text{ cm}^3}{8.96 \text{ g}} + 5 \text{ g Zn} \times \frac{1 \text{ cm}^3}{7.14 \text{ g}} = 11.3 \text{ cm}^3 \text{ (carrying one extra sig. fig.)}$$

Density of old pennies $= \dfrac{100. \text{ g}}{11.3 \text{ cm}^3} = 8.8 \text{ g/cm}^3$

For 100. g of new pennies, 97.6 g will be Zn and 2.4 g will be Cu.

$$V = 2.4 \text{ g Cu} \times \frac{1 \text{ cm}^3}{8.96 \text{ g}} + 97.6 \text{ g Zn} \times \frac{1 \text{ cm}^3}{7.14 \text{ g}} = 13.94 \text{ cm}^3 \text{ (carrying one extra sig. fig.)}$$

Density of new pennies $= \dfrac{100. \text{ g}}{13.94 \text{ cm}^3} = 7.17 \text{ g/cm}^3$

$d = \dfrac{\text{mass}}{\text{volume}}$; Because the volume of both types of pennies are assumed equal, then:

$$\frac{d_{new}}{d_{old}} = \frac{\text{mass}_{new}}{\text{mass}_{old}} = \frac{7.17 \text{ g} / \text{cm}^3}{8.8 \text{ g} / \text{cm}^3} = 0.81$$

The calculated average mass ratio is: $\dfrac{\text{mass}_{new}}{\text{mass}_{old}} = \dfrac{2.51 \text{ g}}{3.08 \text{ g}} = 0.815$

To the first two decimal places, the ratios are the same. If the assumptions are correct, then we can reasonably conclude that the difference in mass is accounted for by the difference in alloy used.

86.   a.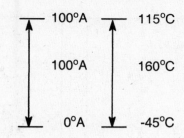

A change in temperature of 160°C equals a change in temperature of 100°A.

So, $\dfrac{160°C}{100°A}$ is our unit conversion for a degree change in temperature.

At the freezing point: $0°A = -45°C$

Combining the two pieces of information:

$$T_A = (T_C + 45°C) \times \frac{100°A}{160°C} = (T_C + 45°C) \times \frac{5°A}{8°C} \text{ or } T_C = T_A \times \frac{8°C}{5°A} - 45°C$$

b. $T_C = (T_F - 32) \times \dfrac{5}{9}$; $T_C = T_A \times \dfrac{8}{5} - 45 = (T_F - 32) \times \dfrac{5}{9}$

$$T_F - 32 = \frac{9}{5} \times \left[T_A \times \frac{8}{5} - 45 \right] = T_A \times \frac{72}{25} - 81, \ T_F = T_A \times \frac{72°F}{25°A} - 49°F$$

c. $T_C = T_A \times \dfrac{8}{5} - 45$ and $T_C = T_A$; So, $T_C = T_C \times \dfrac{8}{5} - 45$, $\dfrac{3 \times T_C}{5} = 45$, $T_C = 75°C = 75°A$

d. $T_C = 86°A \times \dfrac{8°A}{5°C} - 45°C = 93°C$; $T_F = 86°A \times \dfrac{72°F}{25°A} - 49°F = 199°F = 2.0 \times 10^2 °F$

e. $T_A = (45°C + 45°C) \times \dfrac{5°A}{8°C} = 56°A$

87.   Let x = mass of copper and y = mass of silver.

$105.0 \text{ g} = x + y$ and $10.12 \text{ mL} = \dfrac{x}{8.96} + \dfrac{y}{10.5}$; Solving:

$$\left(10.12 = \frac{x}{8.96} + \frac{105.0 - x}{10.5} \right) \times 8.96 \times 10.5, \ 952.1 = 10.5 \, x + 940.8 - 8.96 \, x$$

(carrying 1 extra significant figure)

$11.3 = 1.54 \, x$, $x = 7.3 \text{ g}$; mass %Cu $= \dfrac{7.3 \text{ g}}{105.0 \text{ g}} \times 100 = 7.0\% \text{ Cu}$

88.   a.

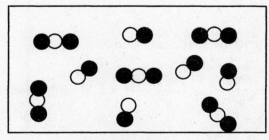

2 compounds

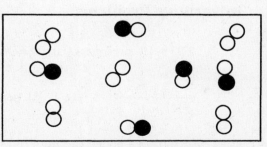

compound and element (diatomic)

b.

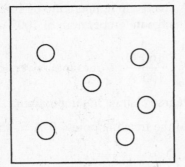 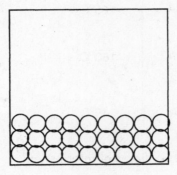 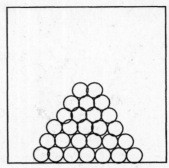

gas element (monoatomic)

atoms/molecules far apart;
random order; takes volume
of container

liquid element

atoms/molecules close
together; somewhat
ordered arrangement;
takes volume of container

solid element

atoms/molecules
close together;
ordered arrangement;
has its own volume

89.   a.   One possibility is that rope B is not attached to anything and rope A and rope C are
            connected via a pair of pulleys and/or gears.

       b.   Try to pull rope B out of the box. Measure the distance moved by C for a given
            movement of A. Hold either A or C firmly while pulling on the other.

90.   The bubbles of gas is air in the sand that is escaping; methanol and sand are not reacting.
       We will assume that the mass of trapped air is insignificant.

       mass of dry sand = 37.3488 g − 22.8317 g = 14.5171 g

       mass of methanol = 45.2613 g − 37.3488 g = 7.9125 g

       Volume of sand particles (air absent) = volume of sand and methanol − volume of methanol

       Volume of sand particles (air absent) = 17.6 mL − 10.00 mL = 7.6 mL

       density of dry sand (air present) = $\dfrac{14.5171\,\text{g}}{10.0\,\text{mL}}$ = 1.45 g/mL

       density of methanol = $\dfrac{7.9125\,\text{g}}{10.00\,\text{mL}}$ = 0.7913 g/mL

       density of sand particles (air absent) = $\dfrac{14.5171\,\text{g}}{7.6\,\text{mL}}$ = 1.9 g/mL

Integrative Problems

91. 2.97×10^8 persons × 0.0100 = 2.97×10^6 persons contributing

       $\dfrac{\$4.75 \times 10^8}{2.97 \times 10^6 \text{ persons}}$ = \$160./person; $\dfrac{\$160.}{\text{person}} \times \dfrac{20 \text{ nickels}}{\$1}$ = 3.20×10^3 nickels/person

       $\dfrac{\$160.}{\text{person}} \times \dfrac{1 \text{ pound sterling}}{\$1.869}$ = 85.6 pounds sterling/person

92. $\dfrac{22610\ kg}{m^3} \times \dfrac{1000\ g}{kg} \times \dfrac{1\ m^3}{1 \times 10^6\ cm^3} = 22.61\ g/cm^3$

volume of block = 10.0 cm × 8.0 cm × 9.0 cm = 720 cm^3; $\dfrac{22.61\ g}{cm^3} \times 720\ cm^3 = 1.6 \times 10^4\ g$

93.   At 200.0 °F: $T_C = \dfrac{5}{9}$ (200.0 °F – 32 °F) = 93.33 °C; T_K = 93.33 + 273.15 = 366.48 K

At – 100.0 °F: $T_C = \dfrac{5}{9}$ (– 100.0 °F – 32 °F) = –73.33 °C; T_K = –73.33 °C + 273.15

= 199.82 K

ΔT(°C) = [93.33 °C– (–73.33 °C)] = 166.66 °C; ΔT(K) = [366.48 K – 199.82 K]

= 166.66 K

The "300 Club" name only works for the Fahrenheit scale; it does not hold true for the Celsius and Kelvin scales.

Marathon Problem

94.   a. $V_{gold} = \pi r^2 h = 3.14 \times (0.25/2\ in)^2 \times 1.5\ in \times \left(\dfrac{2.54\ cm}{in}\right)^3 = 1.2\ cm^3$

d_{gold} (at 86 °F) = $\dfrac{23.1984\ g}{1.2\ cm^3} = 19\ g/cm^3$

b.   Calculate the density of the liquid at 86°F, then determine the density at 40.°F.

mass$_{liquid}$ = 79.16 g – 73.47 g = 5.69 g

volume$_{final}$ = 8.5 cm^3 = V_{gold} + V_{liquid}, V_{liquid} = 8.5 cm^3 – 1.2 cm^3 = 7.3 cm^3

d_{liquid} (at 86 °F) = $\dfrac{5.69\ g}{7.3\ cm^3}$ = 0.78 g/cm^3

The density will increase by 1.0 % for every 10. °C drop in temperature. The temperature drop is 86 – 40. = 46 °F. Because 1°F is equivalent to 5/9°C, the temperature drop in °C equals 46(5/9) = 26°C. Because there is a 1% increase in density for every 10.°C drop in temperature, there will be a 2.6% increase in density for the 26°C temperature drop.

density$_{liquid}$ (at 40.°C) = 1.026 × 0.78 g/cm^3 = 0.80 g/cm^3

CHAPTER TWO

ATOMS, MOLECULES, AND IONS

For Review

1. a. Atoms have mass and are neither destroyed nor created by chemical reactions. Therefore, mass is neither created nor destroyed by chemical reactions. Mass is conserved.

    b. The composition of a substance depends on the number and kinds of atoms that form it.

    c. Compounds of the same elements differ only in the numbers of atoms of the elements forming them, i.e., NO, N_2O, NO_2.

2. Deflection of cathode rays by magnetic and electric fields led to the conclusion that they were negatively charged. The cathode ray was produced at the negative electrode and repelled by the negative pole of the applied electric field.

3. J. J. Thomson discovered electrons. Henri Becquerel discovered radioactivity. Lord Rutherford proposed the nuclear model of the atom. Dalton's original model proposed that atoms were indivisible particles (that is, atoms had no internal structure). Thomson and Becquerel discovered subatomic particles, and Rutherford's model attempted to describe the internal structure of the atom composed of these subatomic particles. In addition, the existence of isotopes, atoms of the same element but with different mass, had to be included in the model.

4. If the plum pudding model were correct (a diffuse positive charge with electrons scattered throughout), then alpha particles should have traveled through the thin foil with very minor deflections in their path. This was not the case as a few of the alpha particles were deflected at very large angles. Rutherford reasoned that the large deflections of these alpha particles could be caused only by a center of concentrated positive charge that contains most of the atom's mass (the nuclear model of the atom).

5. The proton and neutron have similar mass with the mass of the neutron slightly larger than that of the proton. Each of these particles has a mass approximately 1800 times greater than that of an electron. The combination of the protons and the neutrons in the nucleus makes up the bulk of the mass of an atom, but the electrons make the greatest contribution to the chemical properties of the atom.

6. The atomic number of an element is equal to the number of protons in the nucleus of an atom of that element. The mass number is the sum of the number of protons plus neutrons in the nucleus. The atomic mass is the actual mass of a particular isotope (including electrons). As we will see in Chapter Three, the average mass of an atom is taken from a measurement made on a large number of atoms. The average atomic mass value is listed in the periodic table.

7. A family is a set of elements in the same vertical column. A family is also called a group. A period is a set of elements in the same horizontal row.

8. $AlCl_3$, aluminum chloride; $CrCl_3$, chromium(III) chloride; ICl_3, iodine trichloride; $AlCl_3$ and $CrCl_3$ are ionic compounds following the rules for naming ionic compounds. The major difference is that $CrCl_3$ contains a transition metal (Cr) which generally exhibits two or more stable charges when in ionic compounds. We need to indicate which charged ion we have in the compound. This is generally true whenever the metal in the ionic compound is a transition metal. ICl_3 is made from only nonmetals and is a covalent compound. Predicting formulas for covalent compounds is extremely difficult. Because of this, we need to indicate the number of each nonmetal in the binary covalent compound. The exception is when there is only one of the first species present in the formula; when this is the case, mono is not used (it is assumed).

9.   When in ionic compounds, the metals in groups 1A, 2A, and aluminum form +1, +2, and +3 charged ions, respectively. The nonmetals in the groups 5A, 6A, and 7A form −3, −2, and −1 charged ions, respectively, when in ionic compounds. The correct formulas are A_2S where A is an alkali metal, B_3N_2 where B is an alkaline earth metal, and AlC_3 where C is a halogen.

10.   The polyatomic ions and acids in this problem are not named in the text. However, they are all related to other ions and acids named in the text which contain a same group element. Since $HClO_4$ is perchloric acid, $HBrO_4$ is perbromic acid. Since ClO_3^- is the chlorate ion, KIO_3 is potassium iodate. Since ClO_2^- is the chlorite ion, $NaBrO_2$ is sodium bromite. And finally, since $HClO$ is hypochlorous acid, HIO is hypoiodous acid.

Questions

14.   Some elements exist as molecular substances. That is, hydrogen normally exists as H_2 molecules, not single hydrogen atoms. The same is true for N_2, O_2, F_2, Cl_2, etc.

15.   A compound will always contain the same numbers (and types) of atoms. A given amount of hydrogen will react only with a specific amount of oxygen. Any excess oxygen will remain unreacted.

16.   The halogens have a high affinity for electrons, and one important way they react is to form anions of the type X^-. The alkali metals tend to give up electrons easily and in most of their compounds exist as M^+ cations. Note: These two very reactive groups are only one electron away (in the periodic table) from the least reactive family of elements, the noble gases.

17.   Law of conservation of mass: mass is neither created nor destroyed. The mass before a chemical reaction always equals the mass after a chemical reaction.

      Law of definite proportion: a given compound always contains exactly the same proportion of elements by mass. Water is always 1 g H for every 8 g oxygen.

      Law of multiple proportions: When two elements form a series of compounds, the ratios of the mass of the second element that combine with one gram of the first element can always be reduced to small whole numbers: For CO_2 and CO discussed in section 2.2, the mass ratios of oxygen that react with 1 g of carbon in each compound are in a 2:1 ratio.

18.   a.   The smaller parts are electrons and the nucleus. The nucleus is broken down into protons and neutrons which can be broken down into quarks. For our purpose, electrons, neutrons, and protons are the key smaller parts of an atom.

b. All atoms of hydrogen have 1 proton in the nucleus. Different isotopes of hydrogen have 0, 1, or 2 neutrons in the nucleus. Because we are talking about atoms, this implies a neutral charge which dictates 1 electron present for all hydrogen atoms. If charged ions were included, then different ions/atoms of H could have different numbers of electrons.

c. Hydrogen atoms always have 1 proton in the nucleus and helium atoms always have 2 protons in the nucleus. The number of neutrons can be the same for a hydrogen atom and a helium atom. Tritium, ^3H, and ^4He both have 2 neutrons. Assuming neutral atoms, then the number of electrons will be 1 for hydrogen and 2 for helium.

d. Water (H_2O) is always 1 g hydrogen for every 8 g of O present, while H_2O_2 is always 1 g hydrogen for every 16 g of O present. These are distinctly different compounds, each with its own unique relative number and types of atoms present.

e. A chemical equation involves a reorganization of the atoms. Bonds are broken between atoms in the reactants, and new bonds are formed in the products. The number and types of atoms between reactants and products does not change. Because atoms are conserved in a chemical reaction, mass is conserved.

19. J. J. Thomson's study of cathode-ray tubes led him to postulate the existence of negatively charged particles which we now call electrons. Ernest Rutherford and his alpha bombardment of metal foil experiments led him to postulate the nuclear atom − an atom with a tiny dense center of positive charge (the nucleus) with electrons moving about the nucleus at relatively large distances away.

20. The atom is composed of a tiny dense nucleus containing most of the mass of the atom. The nucleus itself is composed of neutrons and protons. Neutrons have a mass slightly larger than that of a proton and have no charge. Protons, on the other hand, have a +1 relative charge as compared to the −1 charged electrons; the electrons move about the nucleus at relatively large dis-tances. The volume of space that the electrons move about is so large, as compared to the nucleus, that we say an atom is mostly empty space.

21. The number and arrangement of electrons in an atom determines how the atom will react with other atoms. The electrons determine the chemical properties of an atom. The number of neutrons present determines the isotope identity.

22. a. A molecule has no overall charge (an equal number of electrons and protons are present). Ions, on the other and, have extra electrons added or removed to form anions (negatively charged ions) or cations (positively charged ions).

b. The sharing of electrons between atoms is a covalent bond. An ionic bond is the force of attraction between two oppositely charged ions.

c. A molelcule is a collection of atoms held together by covalent bonds. A compound is composed of two or more different elements having constant composition. Covalent and/or ionic bonds can hold the atoms together in a compound. Another difference is that molecules do not necessarily have to be compounds. H_2 is two hydrogen atoms held together by a covalent bond. H_2 is a molecule, but it is not a compound; H_2 is a diatomic element.

d.   An anion is a negatively charged ion, e.g., Cl^-, O^{2-}, and SO_4^{2-} are all anions. A cation is a posively charged ion, e.g., Na^+, Fe^{3+}, and NH_4^+ are all cations.

23.   Statements a and b are true. Counting over in the periodic table, element 118 will be the next noble gas (a nonmetal). For statement c, hydrogen has mostly nonmetallic properties. For statement d, a family of elements is also known as a group of elements. For statement e, two items are incorrect. When a metal reacts with a nonmetal, an ionic compound is produced and the formula of the compound would be AX_2 (alkaline earth metals form +2 ions and halogens form -1 ions in ionic compounds). The correct statement would be: When an alkaline earth metal, A, reacts with a halogen, X, the formula of the ionic compound formed should be AX_2.

24.   a.   Dinitrogen monoxide is correct. N and O are both nonmetals resulting in a covalent compound. We need to use the covalent rules of nomenclature. The other two names are for ionic compounds.

b.   Copper(I) oxide is correct. With a metal in a compound, we have an ionic compound. Because copper, like most transition metals, forms at least a couple of different stable charged ions in compounds, we must indicate the charge on copper in the name. Copper oxide could be CuO or Cu_2O, hence why we must give the charge of most transition metal compounds. Dicopper monoxide is the name if this were a covalent compound.

c.   Lithium oxide is correct. Lithium forms +1 charged ions in stable ionic compounds. Because lithium is assumed to form +1 ions in compounds, we do not need to indicate the charge of the metal ion in the compound. Dilithium monoxide would be the name if Li_2O was a covalent compound (a compound composed of only nonmetals).

Exercises

Development of the Atomic Theory

25.   a.   The composition of a substance depends on the numbers of atoms of each element making up the compound (on the formula of the compound) and not on the composition of the mixture from which it was formed.

b.   Avogadro's hypothesis implies that volume ratios are equal to molecule ratios at constant temperature and pressure. $H_2(g) + Cl_2(g) \rightarrow 2\ HCl(g)$. From the balanced equation (2 molecules of HCl are produced per molecule of H_2 or Cl_2 reacted), the volume of HCl produced will be twice the volume of H_2 (or Cl_2) reacted.

26.   From Avogadro's hypothesis, volume ratios are equal to molecule ratios at constant temperature and pressure. Therefore, we can write a balanced equation using the volume data, $Cl_2 + 3\ F_2 \rightarrow 2\ X$. Two molecules of X contain 6 atoms of F and two atoms of Cl. The formula of X is ClF_3 for a balanced equation.

27.   Hydrazine: 1.44×10^{-1} g H/g N; Ammonia: 2.16×10^{-1} g H/g N

Hydrogen azide: 2.40×10^{-2} g H/g N

Let's try all of the ratios:

$$\frac{0.144}{0.0240} = 6.00; \quad \frac{0.216}{0.0240} = 9.00; \quad \frac{0.216}{0.144} = 1.50 = \frac{3}{2}$$

All the masses of hydrogen in these three compounds can be expressed as simple whole number ratios. The g H/g N in hydrazine, ammonia, and hydrogen azide are in the ratios 6:9:1.

28. The law of multiple proportions does not involve looking at the ratio of the mass of one element with the total mass of the compounds. We can show this supports the law of multiple proportions by comparing the mass of carbon that combines with 1.0 g of oxygen in each compound:

Compound 1:   27.2 g C and 72.8 g O   (100.0 - 27.2 = mass O)
Compound 2:   42.9 g C and 57.1 g O   (100.0 - 42.9 = mass O)

Reduce this ratio so that each is compared to 1.0 g oxygen:

Compound 1: $\dfrac{27.2 \text{ g C}}{72.8 \text{ g O}} = 0.374$ g C/g O

Compound 2: $\dfrac{42.9 \text{ g C}}{57.1 \text{ g O}} = 0.751$ g C/g O

$\dfrac{0.751}{0.374} = \dfrac{2}{1}$; This supports the law of multiple proportions.

29. To get the atomic mass of H to be 1.00, we divide the mass of hydrogen that reacts with 1.00 g of oxygen by 0.126, i.e., $\dfrac{0.216}{0.216} = 1.00$. To get Na, Mg and O on the same scale, we do the same division.

Na: $\dfrac{2.875}{0.126} = 22.8$; Mg: $\dfrac{1.500}{0.216} = 11.9$; O: $\dfrac{1.00}{0.216} = 7.94$

	H	O	Na	Mg
Relative Value	1.00	7.94	22.8	11.9
Accepted Value	1.008	16.00	22.99	24.31

The atomic masses of O and Mg are incorrect; the atomic masses of H and Na are close to the values in the periodic table. Something must be wrong about the assumed formulas of the compounds. It turns out the correct formulas are H_2O, Na_2O, and MgO. The smaller discrepancies result from the error in the atomic mass of H.

30. If the formula is InO, then one atomic mass of In would combine with one atomic mass of O, or:

$$\frac{A}{16.00} = \frac{4.784 \text{ g In}}{1.000 \text{ g O}} , \quad A = \text{atomic mass of In} = 76.54$$

If the formula is In_2O_3, then two times the atomic mass of In will combine with three times the atomic mass of O, or:

$$\frac{2A}{(3)16.00} = \frac{4.784 \text{ g In}}{1.000 \text{ g O}} , \quad A = \text{atomic mass of In} = 114.8$$

The latter number is the atomic mass of In used in the modern periodic table.

The Nature of the Atom

31.   Density of hydrogen nucleus (contains one proton only):

$$V_{nucleus} = \frac{4}{3}\pi r^3 = \frac{4}{3}(3.14)(5 \times 10^{-14} \text{ cm})^3 = 5 \times 10^{-40} \text{ cm}^3$$

$$d = \frac{1.67 \times 10^{-24} \text{ g}}{5 \times 10^{-40} \text{ cm}^3} = 3 \times 10^{15} \text{ g/cm}^3$$

Density of H-atom (contains one proton and one electron):

$$V_{atom} = \frac{4}{3}(3.14)(1 \times 10^{-8} \text{ cm})^3 = 4 \times 10^{-24} \text{ cm}^3$$

$$d = \frac{1.67 \times 10^{-24} \text{ g} + 9 \times 10^{-28} \text{ g}}{4 \times 10^{-24} \text{ cm}^3} = 0.4 \text{ g/cm}^3$$

32.   Because electrons move about the nucleus at an average distance of about 1×10^{-8} cm, the diameter of an atom will be about 2×10^{-8} cm. Let's set up a ratio:

$$\frac{\text{diameter of nucleus}}{\text{diameter of atom}} = \frac{1 \text{ mm}}{\text{diameter of model}} = \frac{1 \times 10^{-13} \text{ cm}}{2 \times 10^{-8} \text{ cm}} , \quad \text{Solving:}$$

diameter of model = 2×10^5 mm = 200 m

33. $5.93 \times 10^{-18} \text{ C} \times \dfrac{1 \text{ electron charge}}{1.602 \times 10^{-19} \text{ C}} = 37$ negative (electron) charges on the oil drop

34.   First, divide all charges by the smallest quantity, 6.40×10^{-13}.

$$\frac{2.56 \times 10^{-12}}{6.40 \times 10^{-13}} = 4.00; \quad \frac{7.68}{0.640} = 12.0; \quad \frac{3.84}{0.640} = 6.00$$

Because all charges are whole number multiples of 6.40×10^{-13} zirkombs, the charge on one electron could be 6.40×10^{-13} zirkombs. However, 6.40×10^{-13} zirkombs could be the charge of two electrons (or three electrons, etc.). All one can conclude is that the charge of an electron is 6.40×10^{-13} zirkombs or an integer fraction of 6.40×10^{-13} zirkombs.

35.   sodium–Na; radium–Ra; iron–Fe; gold–Au; manganese–Mn; lead–Pb

36.   fluorine–F; chlorine–Cl; bromine–Br; sulfur–S; oxygen–O; phosphorus–P

37.   Sn–tin; Pt–platinum; Hg–mercury; Mg–magnesium; K–potassium; Ag–silver

38.   As–arsenic; I–iodine; Xe–xenon; He–helium; C–carbon; Si–silicon

39.   a. Metals: Mg, Ti, Au, Bi, Ge, Eu, Am. Nonmetals: Si, B, At, Rn, Br.

        b. Si, Ge, B, At. The elements at the boundary between the metals and the nonmetals are: B, Si, Ge, As, Sb, Te, Po, At. Aluminum has mostly properties of metals.

40.   a. The noble gases are He, Ne, Ar, Kr, Xe, and Rn (helium, neon, argon, krypton, xenon, and radon). Radon has only radioactive isotopes. In the periodic table, the whole number enclosed in parentheses is the mass number of the longest-lived isotope of the element.

        b. promethium (Pm) and technetium (Tc)

41.   a. Six; Be, Mg, Ca, Sr, Ba, Ra   b. Five; O, S, Se, Te, Po

        c. Four; Ni, Pd, Pt, Uun   d. Six; He, Ne, Ar, Kr, Xe, Rn

42.   a. Five; F, Cl, Br, I, and At   b. Six; Li, Na, K, Rb, Cs, Fr
                                                       (H is not considered an alkali metal.)

        c. 14; Ce, Pr, Nd, Pm, Sm, Eu, Gd, Tb, Dy, Ho, Er, Tm, Yb, and Lu

        d. 40; All elements in the block defined by Sc, Zn, Uub, and Ac are transition metals.

43.   a. $^{79}_{35}$Br: 35 protons, $79 - 35 = 44$ neutrons. Since the charge of the atom is neutral,

            the number of protons = the number of electrons = 35.

        b. $^{81}_{35}$Br: 35 protons, 46 neutrons, 35 electrons

c. $^{239}_{94}$Pu: 94 protons, 145 neutrons, 94 electrons

d. $^{133}_{55}$Cs: 55 protons, 78 neutrons, 55 electrons

e. $^{3}_{1}$H: 1 proton, 2 neutrons, 1 electron

f. $^{56}_{26}$Fe: 26 protons, 30 neutrons, 26 electrons

44. a. $^{235}_{92}$U: 92 p, 143 n, 92 e   b. $^{13}_{6}$C: 6 p, 7 n, 6 e   c. $^{57}_{26}$Fe: 26 p, 31 n, 26 e

d. $^{208}_{82}$Pb: 82 p, 126 n, 82 e   e. $^{86}_{37}$Rb: 37 p, 49 n, 37 e   f. $^{41}_{20}$Ca: 20 p, 21 n, 20 e

45. a. Element 8 is oxygen. A = mass number = 9 + 8 = 17; $^{17}_{8}$O

b. Chlorine is element 17. $^{37}_{17}$Cl   c. Cobalt is element 27. $^{60}_{27}$Co

d. Z = 26; A = 26 + 31 = 57; $^{57}_{26}$Fe   e. Iodine is element 53. $^{131}_{53}$I

f. Lithium is element 3. $^{7}_{3}$Li

46. a. Cobalt is element 27. A = mass number = 27 + 31 = 58; $^{58}_{27}$Co

b. $^{10}_{5}$B   c. $^{23}_{12}$Mg   d. $^{132}_{53}$I   e. $^{19}_{9}$F   f. $^{65}_{29}$Cu

47. Atomic number = 63 (Eu); Charge = +63 - 60 = +3; Mass number = 63 + 88 = 151;

Symbol: $^{151}_{63}$Eu^{3+}

Atomic number = 50 (Sn); Mass number = 50 + 68 = 118; Net charge = +50 - 48 = +2; The symbol is $^{118}_{50}$Sn^{2+}.

48. Atomic number = 16 (S); Charge = +16 - 18 = -2; Mass number = 16 + 18 = 34;
Symbol: $^{34}_{16}$S^{2-}

Atomic number = 16 (S); Charge = +16 - 18 = -2; Mass number = 16 + 16 = 32;
Symbol: $^{32}_{16}$S^{2-}

49.

Symbol	Number of protons in nucleus	Number of neutrons in nucleus	Number of electrons	Net charge
$^{238}_{92}U$	92	146	92	0
$^{40}_{20}Ca^{2+}$	20	20	18	2+
$^{51}_{23}V^{3+}$	23	28	20	3+
$^{89}_{39}Y$	39	50	39	0
$^{79}_{35}Br^{-}$	35	44	36	1−
$^{31}_{15}P^{3-}$	15	16	18	3−

50.

Symbol	Number of protons in nucleus	Number of neutrons in nucleus	Number of electrons	Net charge
$^{53}_{26}Fe^{2+}$	26	27	24	2+
$^{59}_{26}Fe^{3+}$	26	33	23	3+
$^{210}_{85}At^{-}$	85	125	86	1−
$^{27}_{13}Al^{3+}$	13	14	10	3+
$^{128}_{52}Te^{2-}$	52	76	54	2−

51.   a.   transition metals   b.   alkaline earth metals   c.   alkali metals

d.   noble gases   e.   halogens

52.   Carbon is a nonmetal. Silicon and germanium are metalloids. Tin and lead are metals. Thus, metallic character increases as one goes down a family in the periodic table. The metallic character decreases from left to right.

53.   In ionic compounds, metals lose electrons to form cations, and nonmetals gain electrons to form anions. Group 1A, 2A and 3A metals form stable +1, +2 and +3 charged cations, respectively. Group 5A, 6A and 7A nonmetals form −3, −2 and -1 charged anions, respectively.

    a.   Lose 2 e^- to form Ra^{2+}.   b.   Lose 3 e^- to form In^{3+}.   c.   Gain 3 e^- to form P^{3-}.

    d.   Gain 2 e^- to form Te^{2-}.   e.   Gain 1 e^- to form Br^-.   f.   Lose 1 e^- to form Rb^+.

54.   See Exercise 53 for a discussion of charges various elements form when in ionic compounds.

    a.   Element 13 is Al. Al forms +3 charged ions in ionic compounds. Al^{3+}

    b. Se^{2-} c. Ba^{2+} d. N^{3-} e. Fr^+ f. Br^-

Nomenclature

55.   a.   sodium bromide   b.   rubidium oxide

    c.   calcium sulfide   d.   aluminum iodide

    e. SrF_2 f. Al_2Se_3

    g. K_3N h. Mg_3P_2

56.   a.   mercury(I) oxide   b.   iron(III) bromide

    c.   cobalt(II) sulfide   d.   titanium(IV) chloride

    e. Sn_3N_2 f. CoI_3

    g.   HgO   h. CrS_3

57.   a.   cesium fluoride   b.   lithium nitride

    c.   silver sulfide (Silver only forms stable +1 ions in compounds so no Roman numerals are needed.)

    d.   manganese(IV) oxide   e.   titanium(IV) oxide   f.   strontium phosphide

58.   a. $ZnCl_2$ (Zn only forms stable +2 ions in compounds so no Roman numerals are needed.)

    b. SnF_4 c. Ca_3N_2 d. Al_2S_3

    e. Hg_2Se f.   AgI (Ag only forms stable +1 ions in compounds.)

59.   a.   barium sulfite   b.   sodium nitrite

    c.   potassium permanganate   d.   potassium dichromate

60.   a. $Cr(OH)_3$ b. $Mg(CN)_2$

    c. $Pb(CO_3)_2$ d. $NH_4C_2H_3O_2$

61.   a.   dinitrogen tetroxide   b.   iodine trichloride

    c.   sulfur dioxide   d.   diphosphorus pentasulfide

62.   a. B_2O_3 b. AsF_5

       c. N_2O d. SCl_6

63.   a.   copper(I) iodide   b.   copper(II) iodide   c.   cobalt(II) iodide

       d.   sodium carbonate   e.   sodium hydrogen carbonate or sodium bicarbonate

       f.   tetrasulfur tetranitride   g.   sulfur hexafluoride   h.   sodium hypochlorite

       i.   barium chromate   j.   ammonium nitrate

64.   a.   acetic acid   b.   ammonium nitrite   c.   cobalt(III) sulfide

       d.   iodine monochloride   e.   lead(II) phosphate   f.   potassium iodate

       g.   sulfuric acid   h.   strontium nitride   i.   aluminum sulfite

       j.   tin(IV) oxide   k.   sodium chromate   l.   hypochlorous acid

65.   a. SF_2 b. SF_6 c. NaH_2PO_4

       d. Li_3N e. $Cr_2(CO_3)_3$ f. SnF_2

       g. $NH_4C_2H_3O_2$ h. NH_4HSO_4 i. $Co(NO_3)_3$

       j. Hg_2Cl_2; Mercury(I) exists as Hg_2^{2+} ions.   k. $KClO_3$ l.   NaH

66.   a. CrO_3 b. S_2Cl_2 c. NiF_2

       d. K_2HPO_4 e.   AlN

       f. NH_3 (Nitrogen trihydride is the systematic name.)   g. MnS_2

       h. $Na_2Cr_2O_7$ i. $(NH_4)_2SO_3$ j. CI_4

67.   a. Na_2O b. Na_2O_2 c.   KCN

       d. $Cu(NO_3)_2$ e. $SeBr_4$ f. HIO_2

       g. PbS_2 h.   CuCl   i.   GaAs (Predict Ga^{3+} and As^{3-} ions.)

       j.   CdSe (Cadmium only forms +2 charged ions in compounds.)

       k.   ZnS (Zinc only forms +2 charged ions in compounds.)

       l. HNO_2 m. P_2O_5

68.   a. $(NH_4)_2HPO_4$ b. Hg_2S c. SiO_2

       d. Na_2SO_3 e. $Al(HSO_4)_3$ f. NCl_3

       g.   HBr   h. $HBrO_2$ i. $HBrO_4$

       j.   KHS   k. CaI_2 l. $CsClO_4$

69.   a.   nitric acid, HNO_3 b.   perchloric acid, $HClO_4$ c.   acetic acid, $HC_2H_3O_2$

       d.   sulfuric acid, H_2SO_4 e.   phosphoric acid, H_3PO_4

70.   a. Iron forms +2 and +3 charged ions; we need to include a Roman numeral for iron. Iron(III) chloride is correct.

        b. This is a covalent compound so use the covalent rules. Nitrogen dioxide is correct.

        c. Calcium forms only +2 ions in ionic compounds; no Roman numeral is needed. Calcium oxide is correct.

        d. This is an ionic compound so use the ionic rules. Aluminum sulfide is correct.

        e. This is an ionic compound so use the ionic rules. Mg is magnesium. Magnesium acetate is correct.

        f. Because phosphate has a −3 charge, the charge on iron is +3. Iron(III) phosphate is correct.

        g. This is a covalent compound so use the covalent rules. Diphosphorus pentasulfide is correct.

        h. Because each sodium is +1 charged, we have the O_2^{2-} (peroxide) ion present. Sodium peroxide is correct. Note that sodium oxide would be Na_2O.

        i. HNO_3 is nitric acid, not nitrate acid. Nitrate acid does not exist.

        j. H_2S is hydrosulfuric acid or dihydrogen sulfide or just hydrogen sulfide (common name). H_2SO_4 is sulfuric acid.

Additional Exercises

71.   Yes, 1.0 g H would react with 37.0 g ^{37}Cl and 1.0 g H would react with 35.0 g ^{35}Cl.

        No, the mass ratio of H/Cl would always be 1 g H/37 g Cl for ^{37}Cl and 1 g H/35 g Cl for ^{35}Cl. As long as we had pure ^{37}Cl or pure ^{35}Cl, the above ratios will always hold. If we have a mixture (such as the natural abundance of chlorine), the ratio will also be constant as long as the composition of the mixture of the two isotopes does not change.

72.   a. False. Neutrons have no charge; therefore, all particles in a nucleus are not charged.
        b. False. The atom is best described as having a tiny dense nucleus containing most of the mass of the atom with the electrons moving about the nucleus at relatively large distances away; so much so that an atom is mostly empty space.
        c. False. The mass of the nucleus makes up most of the mass of the entire atom
        d. True.
        e. False. The number of protons in a neutral atom must equal the number of electrons.

73.   From the Na_2X formula, X has a −2 charge. Since 36 electrons are present, X has 34 p, 79 − 34 = 45 neutrons, and is selenium.

        a. True. Nonmetals bond together using covalent bonds and are called covalent compounds.

      b.   False. The isotope has 34 protons.

      c.   False. The isotope has 45 neutrons.

      d.   False. The identity is selenium, Se.

74.   a. Fe^{2+}: 26 protons (Fe is element 26.); protons – electrons = charge, $26 - 2 = 24$ electrons; FeO is the formula since the oxide ion has a –2 charge.

      b. Fe^{3+}: 26 protons; 23 electrons; Fe_2O_3 c. Ba^{2+}: 56 protons; 54 electrons; BaO

      d. Cs^+: 55 protons; 54 electrons; Cs_2O e. S^{2-}: 16 protons; 18 electrons; Al_2S_3

      f. P^{3-}: 15 protons; 18 electrons; AlP   g. Br^- 35 protons; 36 electrons; $AlBr_3$

      h. N^{3-}: 7 protons; 10 electrons; AlN

75.   a. $Pb(C_2H_3O_2)_2$: lead(II) acetate   b. $CuSO_4$: copper(II) sulfate

      c.   CaO: calcium oxide   d. $MgSO_4$: magnesium sulfate

      e. $Mg(OH)_2$: magnesium hydroxide   f. $CaSO_4$: calcium sulfate

      g. N_2O: dinitrogen monoxide or nitrous oxide

76.   a.   This is element 52, tellurium. Te forms stable –2 charged ions (like other oxygen family members).

      b.   Rubidium. Rb, element 37, forms stable +1 charged ions.

      c.   Argon. Ar is element 18.   d.   Astatine. At is element 85.

77.   From the XBr_2 formula, the charge on element X is +2. Therefore, the element has 88 protons, which identifies it as radium, Ra. $230 - 88 = 142$ neutrons

78.   Because this is a relatively small number of neutrons, the number of protons will be very close to the number of neutrons present. The heavier elements have significantly more neutrons than protons in their nuclei. Because this element forms anions, it is a nonmetal and will be a halogen since they form stable –1 charged ions in ionic compounds. From the halogens listed, chlorine, with an average atomic mass of 35.45, fits the data. The two isotopes are ^{35}Cl and ^{37}Cl, and the number of electrons in the –1 ion is 18. Note that since the atomic mass of chlorine listed in the periodic table is closer to 35 than 37, we can assume that ^{35}Cl is the more abundant isotope. This is discussed in Chapter 3.

79.   a. Ca^{2+} and N^{3-}: Ca_3N_2, calcium nitride   b. K^+ and O^{2-}: K_2O, potassium oxide

      c. Rb^+ and F^-: RbF, rubidium fluoride   d. Mg^{2+} and S^{2-}: MgS, magnesium sulfide

      e. Ba^{2+} and I^-: BaI_2, barium iodide   f. Al^{3+} and Se^{2-}: Al_2Se_3, aluminum selenide

g. Cs^+ and P^{3-}: Cs_3P, cesium phosphide

h. In^{3+} and Br^-: $InBr_3$, indium(III) bromide. In also forms In^+ ions, but one would predict In^{3+} ions from its position in the periodic table.

80.   These compounds are similar to phosphate (PO_4^{3-}) compounds. Na_3AsO_4 contains Na^+ ions and AsO_4^{3-} ions. The name would be sodium arsenate. H_3AsO_4 is analogous to phosphoric acid, H_3PO_4. H_3AsO_4 would be arsenic acid. $Mg_3(SbO_4)_2$ contains Mg^{2+} ions and SbO_4^{3-} ions, and the name would be magnesium antimonate.

81.   A compound will always have a constant composition by mass. From the initial data given, the mass ratio of H:S:O in sulfuric acid is:

$$\frac{2.02}{2.02}:\frac{32.07}{2.02}:\frac{64.00}{2.02} = 1:15.9:31.7$$

If we have 7.27 g H, then we will have $7.27 \times 15.9 = 116$ g S and $7.27 \times 31.7 = 230.$ g O in the second sample of H_2SO_4.

82.   Mass is conserved in a chemical reaction.

chromium(III) oxide + aluminum $\rightarrow$ chromium + aluminum oxide

mass: 34.0 g   12.1 g   23.3 g   ?

mass aluminum oxide produced = $(34.0 + 12.1) - 23.3 = 22.8$ g

Challenge Problems

83.   Copper(Cu), silver (Ag) and gold(Au) make up the coinage metals.

84.   Because the gases are at the same temperature and pressure, the volumes are directly related to the number of molecules present. Let's consider hydrogen and oxygen to be monatomic gases, and that water has   the simplest possible formula (HO). We have the equation:
H + O $\rightarrow$ HO

But, the volume ratios are also the molecule ratios, which correspond to coefficients in the equation:
2H + O $\rightarrow$ 2HO

Because atoms cannot be created nor destroyed in a chemical reaction, this is not possible. To correct this, we can make oxygen a diatomic molecule:
2H + O_2 $\rightarrow$ 2HO

This does not require hydrogen to be diatomic. Of course, if we know water has the formula H_2O, we get:
2H + O_2 $\rightarrow$ $2H_2O$.

The only way to balance this is to make hydrogen diatomic:
$2H_2 + O_2 \rightarrow 2H_2O$

85. Avogadro proposed that equal volumes of gases (at constant temperature and pressure) contain equal numbers of molecules. In terms of balanced equations, Avogadro's hypothesis implies that volume ratios will be identical to molecule ratios. Assuming one molecule of octane reacting, then 1 molecule of C_xH_y produces 8 molecules of CO_2 and 9 molecules of H_2O. $C_xH_y + O_2 \rightarrow 8\ CO_2 + 9\ H_2O$. Because all the carbon in octane ends up as carbon in CO_2, octane contains 8 atoms of C. Similarly, all hydrogen in octane ends up as hydrogen in H_2O, so one molecule of octane contains $9 \times 2 = 18$ atoms of H. Octane formula = C_8H_{18} and the ratio of C:H = 8:18 or 4:9.

86. From Figure 2.14 of the text, the average diameter of the nucleus is $\sim 10^{-13}$ cm and the average diameter of the volume where the electrons roam about is $\sim 10^{-8}$ cm.

$$\frac{10^{-8}\ \text{cm}}{10^{-13}\ \text{cm}} = 10^5;\quad \frac{1\ \text{mile}}{1\ \text{grape}} = \frac{5280\ \text{ft}}{1\ \text{grape}} = \frac{63,360\ \text{in}}{1\ \text{grape}}$$

Because the grape needs to be 10^5 times smaller than a mile, the diameter of the grape is $63,360/1 \times 10^5 = \sim 0.6$ in. This is reasonable.

87. Compound I: $\dfrac{14.0\ \text{g R}}{3.00\ \text{g Q}} = \dfrac{4.67\ \text{g R}}{1.00\ \text{g Q}}$; Compound II: $\dfrac{7.00\ \text{g R}}{4.50\ \text{g Q}} = \dfrac{1.56\ \text{g R}}{1.00\ \text{g Q}}$

The ratio of the masses of R that combine with 1.00 g Q is: $\dfrac{4.67}{1.56} = 2.99 \approx 3$

As expected from the law of multiple proportions, this ratio is a small whole number.

Because Compound I contains three times the mass of R per gram of Q as compared to Compound II (RQ), the formula of Compound I should be R_3Q.

88. The alchemists were incorrect. The solid residue must have come from the flask.

89. a. Both compounds have C_2H_6O as the formula. Because they have the same formula, their mass percent composition will be identical. However, these are different compounds with different properties since the atoms are bonded together differently. These compounds are called isomers of each other.

  b. When wood burns, most of the solid material in wood is converted to gases, which escape. The gases produced are most likely CO_2 and H_2O.

  c. The atom is not an indivisible particle, but is instead composed of other smaller particles, e.g., electrons, neutrons, protons.

  d. The two hydride samples contain different isotopes of either hydrogen and/or lithium. Although the compounds are composed of different isotopes, their properties are similar because different isotopes of the same element have similar properties (except, of course, their mass).

90.   Let X_a = formula for the atom/molecule X, Y_B = formula for the atom/molecule Y, X_cY_d = formula of compound I between X and Y, and X_eY_f = formula of compound II between X and Y. Using the volume data, the following would be the balanced equations for the production of the two compounds.

$$X_a + 2\,Y_b \rightarrow 2\,X_cY_d; \ \ 2\,X_a + Y_b \rightarrow 2\,X_eY_f$$

From the balanced equations, a = 2c = e and b = d = 2f.

Substituting into the balanced equation:

$$X_{2c} + 2\,Y_{2f} \rightarrow 2\,X_cY_{2f}$$

$$2\,X_{2c} + Y_{2f} \rightarrow 2\,X_{2c}Y_f$$

For simplest formulas, assume c = f = 1. So:

$$X_2 + 2\,Y_2 \rightarrow 2\,XY_2 \text{ and } 2\,X_2 + Y_2 \rightarrow 2\,X_2Y$$

Compound I = XY_2: if X has relative mass of 1.00, $\dfrac{1.00}{1.00 + 2y} = 0.3043$, y = 1.14

Compound II = X_2Y: if X has relative mass of 1.00, $\dfrac{2.00}{2.00 + y} = 0.6364$, y = 1.14

The relative mass of Y is 1.14 times that of X. So if X has an atomic mass of 100, then Y will have an atomic mass of 114.

Integrated Problems

91.   The systematic name of Ta_2O_5 is tantalum(V) oxide. Tantalum is a transition metal and requires a Roman numeral. Sulfur is in the same group as oxygen and its most common ion is S^{2-}. Therefore, the formula of the sulfur analogue would be Ta_2S_5.

Total number of protons in Ta_2O_5:

    Ta, Z = 73, so 73 protons × 2 = 146 protons; O, Z = 8, so 8 protons × 5 = 40 protons

    Total protons = 186 protons

Total number of protons in Ta_2S_5:

    Ta, Z = 73, so 73 protons × 2 = 146 protons; S, Z = 16, so 16 protons × 5 = 80 protons

    Total protons = 226 protons

Proton difference between Ta_2S_5 and Ta_2O_5: 226 protons − 186 protons = 40 protons

92.   The cation has 51 protons and 48 electrons. The number of protons corresponds to the atomic number. Thus, this is element 51, antimony. There are 3 fewer electrons than protons. Therefore, the charge on the cation is 3+. The anion has one-third of the number of protons in the cation which corresponds to 17 protons; this is element 17, chlorine. The number of electrons in this anion of chlorine is 17+1 = 18 electrons. The anion must have a charge of 1−.

         The formula of the compound formed between Sb^{3+} and Cl^- is $SbCl_3$. The name of the compound is antimony(III) chloride. The Roman numeral is used to indicate the charge on Sb because the predicted charge is not obvious from the periodic table.

93.   Number of electrons in the unknown ion:

$$2.55 \times 10^{-26} \text{ g} \times \frac{1 \text{ kg}}{1000 \text{ g}} \times \frac{1 \text{ electron}}{9.11 \times 10^{-31} \text{ kg}} = 28 \text{ electrons}$$

         Number of protons in the unknown ion:

$$5.34 \times 10^{-23} \text{ g} \times \frac{1 \text{ kg}}{1000 \text{ g}} \times \frac{1 \text{ proton}}{1.67 \times 10^{-27} \text{ kg}} = 32 \text{ protons}$$

         Therefore this ion has 32 protons and 28 electrons. This is element number 32, germanium (Ge). The charge is +4 because four electrons have been lost from a neutral germanium atom.

         The number of electrons in the unknown atom:

$$3.92 \times 10^{-26} \text{ g} \times \frac{1 \text{ kg}}{1000 \text{ g}} \times \frac{1 \text{ electron}}{9.11 \times 0^{-31} \text{ kg}} = 43 \text{ electrons}$$

         In a neutral atom, the number of protons and electrons is the same. Therefore, this is element 43, technetium (Tc).

         The number of neutrons in the technetium atom:

$$9.35 \times 10^{-23} \text{ g} \times \frac{1 \text{ kg}}{1000 \text{ g}} \times \frac{1 \text{ proton}}{1.67 \times 10^{-27} \text{ kg}} = 56 \text{ neutrons}$$

         The mass number is the sum of the protons and neutrons. In this atom, the mass number is 43 protons + 56 neutrons = 99. Thus, this atom and its mass number is ^{99}Tc.

Marathon Problem

94.   a.   For each set of data, divide the larger number by the smaller number to determine relative masses.

$$\frac{0.602}{0.295} = 2.04, \quad A = 2.04 \text{ when } B = 1.00$$

$$\frac{0.401}{0.172} = 2.33, \quad C = 2.33 \text{ when } B = 1.00$$

$$\frac{0.374}{0.320} = 1.17, \quad C = 1.17 \text{ when } A = 1.00$$

To determine whole numbers, multiply the results by 3.

Data set 1: A = 6.1 and B = 3.0
Data set 2: C = 7.0 and B = 3.0
Data set 3: C = 3.5 and A = 3.0 or C = 7.0 and A = 6.0

Assuming 6.0 for the relative mass of A, then the relative masses would be A = 6.0, B = 3.0, and C = 7.0 (if simplest formulas are assumed).

b. Gas volumes are proportional to how many molecules are present. There are many possible correct answers for the balanced equations. One such solution that fits the gas volume data is:

$$6\,A_2 + B_4 \; \longrightarrow \; 4\,A_3B$$
$$B_4 + 4\,C_3 \; \longrightarrow \; 4\,BC_3$$
$$3\,A_2 + 2\,C_3 \; \longrightarrow \; 6\,AC$$

In any correct set of reactions, the calculated mass data must match the mass data given initially in the problem. Here, the new table of relative masses would be:

$$\frac{6\,(\text{mass } A_2)}{\text{mass } B_4} = \frac{0.602}{0.295}, \; \text{mass } A_2 = 0.340 \text{ mass } B_4$$

$$\frac{4\,(\text{mass } C_3)}{\text{mass } B_4} = \frac{0.401}{0.172}, \; \text{mass } C_3 = 0.583 \text{ mass } B_4$$

$$\frac{2\,(\text{mass } C_3)}{3\,(\text{mass } A_2)} = \frac{0.374}{0.320}, \; \text{mass } A_2 = 0.570 \text{ mass } C_3$$

Assume some relative mass number for any of the masses. We will assume mass B = 3.0, so mass B_4 = 4(3.0) = 12.

mass C_3 = 0.583(12) = 7.0, mass C = 7.0/3

mass A_2 = 0.570(7.0) = 4.0, mass A = 4.0/2 = 2.0

When we assume a relative mass for B = 3.0, then A = 2.0 and C = 7.0/3. The relative masses having all whole numbers would be A = 6.0, B = 9.0 and C = 7.0.

Note: Any set of balanced reactions that confirms the initial mass data is correct. This is just one possibility.

CHAPTER THREE

STOICHIOMETRY

For Review

1. Counting by weighing utilizes the average mass of a particular unit of substance. For marbles, a large sample size will contain many different individual masses for the various marbles. However, the large sample size will have an average mass so that the marbles behave as if each individual marble has that average mass. This assumption is valid as long as the sample size is large. When a large sample of marbles is weighed, one divides the total mass of marbles by the average mass of a marble and this will equal the number of marbles present. For atoms, because we can't count individual atoms, we "count" the atoms by weighing them and convert the mass in grams to the quantity of atoms in the sample. The mole scale of atoms is a huge number (6.022×10^{23} atoms = 1 mol), so the assumption that a weighable sample size behaves as a bunch of atoms each with an average mass is valid and very useful.

2. The masses of all the isotopes are relative to a specific standard. The standard is one atom of the carbon-12 isotope weighing exactly 12.0000 amu. One can determine from experiment how much heavier or lighter any specific isotope is than ^{12}C. From this information, we assign an atomic mass value to that isotope. For example, experiment tells one that ^{16}O is about 4/3 heavier than ^{12}C, so a mass of 4/3(12.00) = 16.00 amu is assigned to ^{16}O.

3. The two major isotopes of boron are ^{10}B and ^{11}B. The listed mass of 10.81 is the average mass of a very large number of boron atoms.

4. There are several ways to do this. The three conversion factors to use are Avogadro's number, the molar mass, and the chemical formula. Two ways to use these conversions to convert grams of aspirin to number of H atoms are given below:

    molar mass aspirin = 9(12.01) + 8(1.008) + 4(16.00) = 180.15 g/mol

    $$1.00 \text{ g } C_9H_8O_4 \times \frac{1 \text{ mol } C_9H_8O_4}{180.15 \text{ g } C_9H_8O_4} \times \frac{8 \text{ mol H}}{\text{mol } C_9H_8O_4} \times \frac{6.022 \times 10^{23} \text{ atoms H}}{\text{mol H}}$$
    $$= 2.67 \times 10^{22} \text{ H atoms}$$

    or

    $$1.00 \text{ g } C_9H_8O_4 \times \frac{1 \text{ mol } C_9H_8O_4}{180.15 \text{ g } C_9H_8O_4} \times \frac{6.022 \times 10^{23} \text{ molecules } C_9H_8O_4}{\text{mol } C_9H_8O_4} \times$$
    $$\frac{8 \text{ atoms H}}{\text{molecule } C_9H_8O_4} = 2.67 \times 10^{22} \text{ H atoms}$$

    Of course, the answer is the same no matter the order of the conversion factors.

5. $C_xH_yO_z$ + oxygen $\rightarrow$ x CO_2 + y/2 H_2O

From the equation above, the only reactant that contains carbon is the unknown compound and the only product that contains carbon is CO_2. From the mass of CO_2 produced, one can calculate the mass of C present which is also the mass of C in $C_xH_yO_z$. Similarly, all the hydrogen in the unknown compound ends up as hydrogen in water. From the mass of H_2O produced, one can calculate the mass of H in $C_xH_yO_z$. Once the mass of C and H are known, the remainder of the compound is oxygen. From the mass of C, H, and O in the compound, one can then go on to determine the empirical formula.

6.   The molecular formula tells us the actual number of atoms of each element in a molecule (or formula unit) of a compound. The empirical formula tells only the simplest whole number ratio of atoms of each element in a molecule. The molecular formula is a whole number multiple of the empirical formula. If that multiplier is one, the molecular and empirical formulas are the same. For example, both the molecular and empirical formulas of water are H_2O. For hydrogen peroxide, the empirical formula is OH; the molecular formula is H_2O_2.

7.   The product of the reaction has two A atoms bonded to a B atom for a formula of A_2B. The initial reaction mixture contains 4 A_2 and 8 AB molecules and the final reaction mixture contains 8 A_2B molecules. The reaction is:

$$8 \ AB(g) + 4 \ A_2(g) \rightarrow 8 \ A_2B(g)$$

Using the smallest whole numbers, the balanced reaction is:

$$2 \ AB(g) + A_2(g) \rightarrow 2 \ A_2B(g)$$

$$2.50 \text{ mol } A_2 \times \frac{2 \text{ mol } A_2B}{\text{mol } A_2} = 5.00 \text{ mol } A_2B$$

The atomic mass of each A atom is 40.0/2 = 20.0 amu and the atomic mass of each B atom is 30.0 − 20.0 = 10.0 amu. The mass of A_2B = 2(20.0) + 10.0 = 50.0 amu.

$$15.0 \text{ g AB} \times \frac{1 \text{ mol AB}}{30.0 \text{ g AB}} \times \frac{1 \text{ mol } A_2}{2 \text{ mol AB}} \times \frac{40.0 \text{ g } A_2}{\text{mol } A_2} = 10.0 \text{ g } A_2$$

From the law of conservation of mass, the mass of product is:

$$10.0 \text{ g } A_2 + 15.0 \text{ g AB} = 25.0 \text{ g } A_2B$$

or by stoichiometric calculation.

$$15.0 \text{ g AB} \times \frac{1 \text{ mol AB}}{30.0 \text{ g AB}} \times \frac{1 \text{ mol } A_2B}{\text{mol AB}} \times \frac{50.0 \text{ g } A_2B}{\text{mol } A_2B} = 25.0 \text{ g } A_2B$$

or

$$10.0 \text{ g } A_2 \times \frac{1 \text{ mol } A_2}{40.0 \text{ g } A_2} \times \frac{2 \text{ mol } A_2B}{\text{mol } A_2} \times \frac{50.0 \text{ g } A_2B}{\text{mol } A_2B} = 25.0 \text{ g } A_2B$$

Generally, there are several ways to correctly do a stoichiometry problem. You should choose the method you like best.

8.   A limiting reactant problem gives you initial masses of at least two of the reactants and then asks for the amount of product that can form. Because one doesn't know which reactant runs out first and hence determines the mass of product formed, this is a more difficult problem. The first step in solving the problem is to figure which reactant runs out first (is limiting).

The strategy outlined in the text is to calculate the mole ratio of reactants actually present and compare this mole ratio to that required from the balanced reaction. Whichever ratio is larger allows one to deduce the identity of the limiting reactant and can, in turn, be used to calculate the amount of product formed. Another strategy is to pick one of the reactants and then calculate the mass of the other reactant required to react with it. By comparing the calculated mass to the actual mass present in the problem, one can deduce the identity of the limiting reactant and go on to solve the problem. A third common strategy is to assume each reactant is limiting and then calculate for each reactant the amount of product that could form. This gives two or more possible answers. The correct answer is the mass of product that is smallest. Even though there is enough of the other reactant to form more product, once the smaller amount of product is formed, the limiting reactant has run out.

9.   Balanced reaction: $2 SO_2(g) + O_2(g) \rightarrow 2 SO_3(g)$

We have 6 SO_2 and 6 O_2 molecules present. If all six of the SO_2 molecules react, then 3 molecules of O_2 will react producing 6 molecules of SO_3. These numbers were determined using the balanced reaction. Since 6 molecules of O_2 are present, and only 3 react when the SO_2 reacts completely, SO_2 is limiting. The product mixture will contain $6 - 6 = 0$ SO_2 molecules, $6 - 3 = 3$ O_2 molecules in excess, and 6 molecules of SO_3 formed.

$$96.0 \text{ g } SO_2 \times \frac{1 \text{ mol } SO_2}{64.07 \text{ g } SO_2} \times \frac{1 \text{ mol } O_2}{2 \text{ mol } SO_2} \times \frac{32.00 \text{ g } O_2}{\text{mol } O_2} = 24.0 \text{ g } O_2$$

Because 32.0 g O_2 are actually present, O_2 is in excess and SO_2 is the limiting reactant. Note that if the calculated amount of O_2 was greater than 32.0 g, then we would have deduced that O_2 is limiting. Solving the rest of the problem:

$$96.0 \text{ g SO}_2 \times \frac{1 \text{ mol SO}_2}{64.07 \text{ g SO}_2} \times \frac{2 \text{ mol SO}_3}{2 \text{ mol SO}_2} \times \frac{80.07 \text{ g SO}_3}{\text{mol SO}_3} = 120. \text{ g SO}_3$$

10.   Side reactions may occur. For example, in the combustion of CH_4 (methane) to CO_2 and H_2O, some CO may also form. Also, reactions only go part way to completion, instead reaching a state of equilibrium where both reactants and products are present (see Ch. 13).

Questions

19.
isotope	mass	abundance
^{12}C	12.0000 amu	98.89%
^{13}C	13.034 amu	1.11%

average mass $= 0.9889\,(12.0000) + 0.0111(13.034) = 12.01$ amu

From the relative abundances, there would be 9889 atoms of ^{12}C and 111 atoms of ^{13}C in the 10,000 atom sample. The average mass of carbon is independent of the sample size; it will always be 12.01 amu.

total mass $= 10{,}000 \text{ atoms} \times \dfrac{12.01 \text{ amu}}{\text{atom}} = 1.201 \times 10^5$ amu

For one mol of carbon (6.0221×10^{23} atoms C), the average mass would still be 12.01 amu.

The number of ^{12}C atoms would be $0.9889\,(6.0221 \times 10^{23}) = 5.955 \times 10^{23}$ atoms ^{12}C and the number of ^{13}C atoms would be $0.0111\,(6.0221 \times 10^{23}) = 6.68 \times 10^{21}$ atoms ^{13}C.

total mass $= 6.0221 \times 10^{23} \text{ atoms} \times \dfrac{12.01 \text{ amu}}{\text{atom}} = 7.233 \times 10^{24}$ amu

total mass in g $= 6.0221 \times 10^{23} \text{ atoms} \times \dfrac{12.01 \text{ amu}}{\text{atom}} \times \dfrac{1 \text{ g}}{6.0221 \times 10^{23} \text{ amu}} = 12.01$ g/mol

By using the carbon-12 standard to define the relative masses of all of the isotopes as well as to define the number of things in a mole, then each element's average atomic mass in units of grams is the mass of a mole of that element as it is found in nature.

20.   Consider a sample of glucose, $C_6H_{12}O_6$. The molar mass of glucose is 180.16 g/mol. The chemical formula allows one to convert from molecules of glucose to atoms of carbon, hydrogen, or oxygen present and vice versa. The chemical formula also gives the mole relationship in the formula. One mol of glucose contains 6 mol C, 12 mol H, and 6 mol O. Thus, mole conversions between molecules and atoms are possible using the chemical formula. The molar mass allows one to convert between mass and moles of compound and Avogadro's number (6.022×10^{23}) allows one to convert between moles of compound and number of molecules.

21.   Avogadro's number of dollars $= \dfrac{6.022 \times 10^{23} \text{ dollars}}{\text{mol dollars}}$

$$\dfrac{1 \text{ mol dollars} \times \dfrac{6.022 \times 10^{23} \text{ dollars}}{\text{mol dollars}}}{6 \times 10^{9} \text{ people}} = 1 \times 10^{14} \text{ dollars/person}$$

1 trillion $= 1,000,000,000,000 = 1 \times 10^{12}$; Each person would have 100 trillion dollars.

22.   The molar mass is the mass of 1 mol of the compound. The empirical mass is the mass of 1 mol of the empirical formula. The molar mass is a whole number multiple of the empirical mass. The masses are the same when the molecular formula = empirical formula, and the masses are different when the two formulas are different. When different, the empirical mass must be multiplied by the same whole number used to convert the empirical formula to the molecular formula. For example, $C_6H_{12}O_6$ is the molecular formula for glucose and CH_2O is the empirical formula. The whole number multiplier is 6. This same factor of 6 is the multiplier used to equate the empirical mass (30 g/mol) of glucose to the molar mass (180 g/mol).

23.   The mass percent of a compound is a constant no matter what amount of substance is present. Compounds always have constant composition.

24.   A balanced reaction starts with the correct formulas of the reactants and products. The co-efficients necessary to balance the reaction give molecule relationships as well as mole relationships between reactants and products. The state (phase) of the reactants and products is also given. Finally, special reaction conditions are sometimes listed above or below the arrow. These can include special catalysts used and/or special temperatures required for a reaction to occur.

25.   The specific information needed is mostly the coefficients in the balanced equation and the molar masses of the reactants and products. For percent yield, we would need the actual yield of the reaction and the amounts of reactants used.

a.   mass of CB produced $= 1.00 \times 10^{4}$ molecules $A_2B_2 \times$

$$\dfrac{1 \text{ mol } A_2B_2}{6.022 \times 10^{23} \text{ molecules } A_2B_2} \times \dfrac{2 \text{ mol CB}}{1 \text{ mol } A_2B_2} \times \dfrac{\text{molar mass of CB}}{\text{mol CB}}$$

b.   atoms of A produced $= 1.00 \times 10^{4}$ molecules $A_2B_2 \times \dfrac{2 \text{ atoms A}}{1 \text{ molecule } A_2B_2}$

c.   mol of C reacted $= 1.00 \times 10^{4}$ molecules $A_2B_2 \times \dfrac{1 \text{ mol } A_2B_2}{6.022 \times 10^{23} \text{ molecules } A_2B_2} \times$

$$\dfrac{2 \text{ mol C}}{1 \text{ mol } A_2B_2}$$

d.   % yield $= \dfrac{\text{actual mass}}{\text{theoretical mass}} \times 100$; The theoretical mass of CB produced was calculated in part a. If the actual mass of CB produced is given, then the percent yield can be determined for the reaction using the % yield equation.

26.   One method is to determine the actual mole ratio of XY to Y_2 present and compare this ratio to the required 2:1 mole ratio from the balanced equation. Which ratio is larger will allow one to deduce the limiting reactant. Once the identity of the limiting reactant is known, then one can calculate the amount of product formed. A second method would be to pick one of the reactants and then calculate how much of the other reactant would be required to react with it all. How the answer compares to the actual amount of that reactant present allows one to deduce the identity of the limiting reactant. Once the identity is known, one would take the limiting reactant and convert it to mass of product formed.

When each reactant is assumed limiting and the amount of product is calculated, there are two possible answers (assuming two reactants). The correct answer (the amount of product that could be produced) is always the smaller number. Even though there is enough of the other reactant to form more product, once the small quantity is reached, the limiting reactant runs out and the reaction cannot continue.

Exercises

Atomic Masses and the Mass Spectrometer

27.   A = 0.0140(203.973) + 0.2410(205.9745) + 0.2210(206.9759) + 0.5240(207.9766)

A = 2.86 + 49.64 + 45.74 + 109.0 = 207.2 amu; From the periodic table, the element is Pb.

28.   A = 0.0800(45.95269) + 0.0730(46.951764) + 0.7380(47.947947) + 0.0550(48.947841) +

0.0540(49.944792) = 47.88 amu

This is element Ti (titanium).

29.   Let A = mass of ^{185}Re:

186.207 = 0.6260(186.956) + 0.3740(A), 186.207 − 117.0 = 0.3740(A)

A = $\dfrac{69.2}{0.3740}$ = 185 amu (A = 184.95 amu without rounding to proper significant figures.)

30.   abundance ^{28}Si = 100.00 −(4.70 + 3.09) = 92.21%; From the periodic table, the average atomic mass of Si is 28.09 amu.

28.09 = 0.9221(27.98) + 0.0470 (atomic mass ^{29}Si) + 0.0309(29.97)

atomic mass ^{29}Si = 29.01

The mass of ^{29}Si is actually a little less than 29 amu. There are other isotopes of silicon that are considered when determining the 28.09 amu average atomic mass of Si listed in the atomic table.

31.   There are three peaks in the mass spectrum, each 2 mass units apart. This is consistent with two isotopes, differing in mass by two mass units. The peak at 157.84 corresponds to a Br_2 molecule composed of two atoms of the lighter isotope. This isotope has mass equal to

157.84/2 or 78.92. This corresponds to ^{79}Br. The second isotope is ^{81}Br with mass equal to 161.84/2 = 80.92. The peaks in the mass spectrum correspond to $^{79}Br_2$, $^{79}Br^{81}Br$, and $^{81}Br_2$ in order of increasing mass. The intensities of the highest and lowest mass tell us the two isotopes are present in about equal abundance. The actual abundance is 50.69% ^{79}Br and 49.31% ^{81}Br. The calculation of the abundance from the mass spectrum is beyond the scope of this text.

32.   GaAs can be either $^{69}GaAs$ or $^{71}GaAs$. The mass spectrum for GaAs will have 2 peaks at 144 (= 69 + 75) and 146 (= 71 + 75) with intensities in the ratio of 60:40 or 3:2.

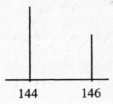

144   146

Ga$_2$As$_2$ can be $^{69}Ga_2As_2$, $^{69}Ga^{71}GaAs_2$, or $^{71}Ga_2As_2$. The mass spectrum will have 3 peaks at 288, 290, and 292 with intensities in the ratio of 36:48:16 or 9:12:4. We get this ratio from the following probability table:

	^{69}Ga (0.60)	^{71}Ga (0.40)
^{69}Ga (0.60)	0.36	0.24
^{71}Ga (0.40)	0.24	0.16

288   290   292

Moles and Molar Masses

33.   When more than one conversion factor is necessary to determine the answer, we will usually put all the conversion factors into one calculation instead of determining intermediate answers. This method reduces round-off error and is a time saver.

$$500. \text{ atoms Fe} \times \frac{1 \text{ mol Fe}}{6.022 \times 10^{23} \text{ atoms Fe}} \times \frac{55.85 \text{ g Fe}}{\text{mol Fe}} = 4.64 \times 10^{-20} \text{ g Fe}$$

34. $$500.0 \text{ g Fe} \times \frac{1 \text{ mol Fe}}{55.85 \text{ g Fe}} = 8.953 \text{ mol Fe}$$

$$8.953 \text{ mol Fe} \times \frac{6.022 \times 10^{23} \text{ atoms Fe}}{\text{mol Fe}} = 5.391 \times 10^{24} \text{ atoms Fe}$$

35. $1.00 \text{ carat} \times \dfrac{0.200 \text{ g C}}{\text{carat}} \times \dfrac{1 \text{ mol C}}{12.01 \text{ g C}} \times \dfrac{6.022 \times 10^{23} \text{ atoms C}}{\text{mol C}} = 1.00 \times 10^{22} \text{ atoms C}$

36. $5.0 \times 10^{21} \text{ atoms C} \times \dfrac{1 \text{ mol C}}{6.022 \times 10^{23} \text{ atoms C}} = 8.3 \times 10^{-3} \text{ mol C}$

        $8.3 \times 10^{-3} \text{ mol C} \times \dfrac{12.01 \text{ g C}}{\text{mol C}} = 0.10 \text{ g C}$

37. Al_2O_3: $2(26.98) + 3(16.00) = 101.96 \text{ g/mol}$

        Na_3AlF_6: $3(22.99) + 1(26.98) + 6(19.00) = 209.95 \text{ g/mol}$

38.   HFC – 134a, CH_2FCF_3: $2(12.01) + 2(1.008) + 4(19.00) = 102.04 \text{ g/mol}$

        HCFC –124, $CHClFCF_3$: $2(12.01) + 1(1.008) + 1(35.45) + 4(19.00) = 136.48 \text{ g/mol}$

39.   a.   The formula is NH_3. $14.01 \text{ g/mol} + 3(1.008 \text{ g/mol}) = 17.03 \text{ g/mol}$

        b.   The formula is N_2H_4. $2(14.01) + 4(1.008) = 32.05 \text{ g/mol}$

        c. $(NH_4)_2Cr_2O_7$: $2(14.01) + 8(1.008) + 2(52.00) + 7(16.00) = 252.08 \text{ g/mol}$

40.   a.   The formula is P_4O_6. $4(30.97 \text{ g/mol}) + 6(16.00 \text{ g/mol}) = 219.88 \text{ g/mol}$

        b. $Ca_3(PO_4)_2$: $3(40.08) + 2(30.97) + 8(16.00) = 310.18 \text{ g/mol}$

        c. Na_2HPO_4: $2(22.99) + 1(1.008) + 1(30.97) + 4(16.00) = 141.96 \text{ g/mol}$

41.   a. $1.00 \text{ g } NH_3 \times \dfrac{1 \text{ mol } NH_3}{17.03 \text{ g } NH_3} = 0.0587 \text{ mol } NH_3$

        b. $1.00 \text{ g } N_2H_4 \times \dfrac{1 \text{ mol } N_2H_4}{32.05 \text{ g } N_2H_4} = 0.0312 \text{ mol } N_2H_4$

        c. $1.00 \text{ g } (NH_4)_2Cr_2O_7 \times \dfrac{1 \text{ mol } (NH_4)_2Cr_2O_7}{252.08 \text{ g } (NH_4)_2Cr_2O_7} = 3.97 \times 10^{-3} \text{ mol } (NH_4)_2Cr_2O_7$

42.   a. $1.00 \text{ g } P_4O_6 \times \dfrac{1 \text{ mol } P_4O_6}{219.88 \text{ g}} = 4.55 \times 10^{-3} \text{ mol } P_4O_6$

        b. $1.00 \text{ g } Ca_3(PO_4)_2 \times \dfrac{1 \text{ mol } Ca_3(PO_4)_2}{310.18 \text{ g}} = 3.22 \times 10^{-3} \text{ mol } Ca_3(PO_4)_2$

        c. $1.00 \text{ g } Na_2HPO_4 \times \dfrac{1 \text{ mol } Na_2HPO_4}{141.96 \text{ g}} = 7.04 \times 10^{-3} \text{ mol } Na_2HPO_4$

43.   a. $5.00 \text{ mol NH}_3 \times \dfrac{17.03 \text{ g NH}_4}{\text{mol NH}_3} = 85.2 \text{ g NH}_3$

     b. $5.00 \text{ mol N}_2\text{H}_4 \times \dfrac{32.05 \text{ g N}_2\text{H}_4}{\text{mol N}_2\text{H}_4} = 160. \text{ g N}_2\text{H}_4$

     c. $5.00 \text{ mol (NH}_4)_2\text{Cr}_2\text{O}_7 \times \dfrac{252.08 \text{ g (NH}_4)_2\text{Cr}_2\text{O}_7}{1 \text{ mol (NH}_4)_2\text{Cr}_2\text{O}_7} = 1260 \text{ g (NH}_4)_2\text{Cr}_2\text{O}_7$

44.   a. $5.00 \text{ mol P}_4\text{O}_6 \times \dfrac{219.88 \text{ g}}{1 \text{ mol P}_4\text{O}_6} = 1.10 \times 10^3 \text{ g P}_4\text{O}_6$

     b. $5.00 \text{ mol Ca}_3(\text{PO}_4)_2 \times \dfrac{310.18 \text{ g}}{\text{mol Ca}_3(\text{PO}_4)_2} = 1.55 \times 10^3 \text{ g Ca}_3(\text{PO}_4)_2$

     c. $5.00 \text{ mol Na}_2\text{HPO}_4 \times \dfrac{141.96 \text{ g}}{\text{mol Na}_2\text{HPO}_4} = 7.10 \times 10^2 \text{ g Na}_2\text{HPO}_4$

45.   Chemical formulas give atom ratios as well as mol ratios.

     a. $5.00 \text{ mol NH}_3 \times \dfrac{1 \text{ mol N}}{\text{mol NH}_3} \times \dfrac{14.01 \text{ g N}}{\text{mol N}} = 70.1 \text{ g N}$

     b. $5.00 \text{ mol N}_2\text{H}_4 \times \dfrac{2 \text{ mol N}}{\text{mol N}_2\text{H}_4} \times \dfrac{14.01 \text{ g N}}{\text{mol N}} = 140. \text{ g N}$

     c. $5.00 \text{ mol (NH}_4)_2\text{Cr}_2\text{O}_7 \times \dfrac{2 \text{ mol N}}{\text{mol (NH}_4)_2\text{Cr}_2\text{O}_7} \times \dfrac{14.01 \text{ g N}}{\text{mol N}} = 140. \text{ g N}$

46.   a. $5.00 \text{ mol P}_4\text{O}_6 \times \dfrac{4 \text{ mol P}}{\text{mol P}_4\text{O}_6} \times \dfrac{30.97 \text{ g P}}{\text{mol P}} = 619 \text{ g P}$

     b. $5.00 \text{ mol Ca}_3(\text{PO}_4)_2 \times \dfrac{2 \text{ mol P}}{\text{mol Ca}_3(\text{PO}_4)_2} \times \dfrac{30.97 \text{ g P}}{\text{mol P}} = 310. \text{ g P}$

     c. $5.00 \text{ mol Na}_2\text{HPO}_4 \times \dfrac{1 \text{ mol P}}{\text{mol Na}_2\text{HPO}_4} \times \dfrac{30.97 \text{ g P}}{\text{mol P}} = 155 \text{ g P}$

47.   a. $1.00 \text{ g NH}_3 \times \dfrac{1 \text{ mol NH}_3}{17.03 \text{ g NH}_3} \times \dfrac{6.022 \times 10^{23} \text{ molecules NH}_3}{\text{mol NH}_3} = 3.54 \times 10^{22} \text{ molecules NH}_3$

     b. $1.00 \text{ g N}_2\text{H}_4 \times \dfrac{1 \text{ mol N}_2\text{H}_4}{32.05 \text{ g N}_2\text{H}_4} \times \dfrac{6.022 \times 10^{23} \text{ molecules N}_2\text{H}_4}{\text{mol N}_2\text{H}_4}$

$$= 1.88 \times 10^{22} \text{ molecules N}_2\text{H}_4$$

c. $1.00 \text{ g } (NH_4)_2Cr_2O_7 \times \dfrac{1 \text{ mol } (NH_4)_2Cr_2O_7}{252.08 \text{ g } (NH_4)_2Cr_2O_7}$

$\times \dfrac{6.022 \times 10^{23} \text{ formula units } (NH_4)_2Cr_2O_7}{\text{mol } (NH_4)_2Cr_2O_7} = 2.39 \times 10^{21} \text{ formula units } (NH_4)_2Cr_2O_7$

48.   a. $1.00 \text{ g } P_4O_6 \times \dfrac{1 \text{ mol } P_4O_6}{219.88 \text{ g}} \times \dfrac{6.022 \times 10^{23} \text{ molecules}}{\text{mol } P_4O_6} = 2.74 \times 10^{21} \text{ molecules } P_4O_6$

b. $1.00 \text{ g } Ca_3(PO_4)_2 \times \dfrac{1 \text{ mol } Ca_3(PO_4)_2}{310.18 \text{ g}} \times \dfrac{6.022 \times 10^{23} \text{ formula units}}{\text{mol } Ca_3(PO_4)_2}$

$= 1.94 \times 10^{21} \text{ formula units } Ca_3(PO_4)_2$

c. $1.00 \text{ g } Na_2HPO_4 \times \dfrac{1 \text{ mol } Na_2HPO_4}{141.96 \text{ g}} \times \dfrac{6.022 \times 10^{23} \text{ formula units}}{\text{mol } Na_2HPO_4}$

$= 4.24 \times 10^{21} \text{ formula units } Na_2HPO_4$

49.   Using answers from Exercise 47:

a. $3.54 \times 10^{22} \text{ molecules } NH_3 \times \dfrac{1 \text{ atom N}}{\text{molecule } NH_3} = 3.54 \times 10^{22} \text{ atoms N}$

b. $1.88 \times 10^{22} \text{ molecules } N_2H_4 \times \dfrac{2 \text{ atoms N}}{\text{molecule } N_2H_4} = 3.76 \times 10^{22} \text{ atoms N}$

c. $2.39 \times 10^{21} \text{ formula units } (NH_4)_2Cr_2O_7 \times \dfrac{2 \text{ atoms N}}{\text{formula unit } (NH_4)_2Cr_2O_7}$

$= 4.78 \times 10^{21} \text{ atoms N}$

50.   Using answers from Exercise 48:

a. $2.74 \times 10^{21} \text{ molecules } P_4O_6 \times \dfrac{4 \text{ atoms P}}{\text{molecule } P_4O_6} = 1.10 \times 10^{22} \text{ atoms P}$

b. $1.94 \times 10^{21} \text{ formula units } Ca_3(PO_4)_2 \times \dfrac{2 \text{ atoms P}}{\text{formula unit } Ca_3(PO_4)_2} = 3.88 \times 10^{21} \text{ atoms P}$

c. $4.24 \times 10^{21} \text{ formula units } Na_2HPO_4 \times \dfrac{1 \text{ atom P}}{\text{formula unit } Na_2HPO_4} = 4.24 \times 10^{21} \text{ atoms P}$

51.   Molar mass of $C_6H_8O_6 = 6(12.01) + 8(1.008) + 6(16.00) = 176.12 \text{ g/mol}$

$500.0 \text{ mg} \times \dfrac{1 \text{ g}}{1000 \text{ mg}} \times \dfrac{1 \text{ mol}}{176.12 \text{ g}} = 2.839 \times 10^{-3} \text{ mol}$

$$2.839 \times 10^{-3} \text{ mol} \times \frac{6.022 \times 10^{23} \text{ molecules}}{\text{mol}} = 1.710 \times 10^{21} \text{ molecules}$$

52.   a. $9(12.01) + 8(1.008) + 4(16.00) = 180.15$ g/mol

       b. $500. \text{ mg} \times \dfrac{1 \text{ g}}{1000 \text{ mg}} \times \dfrac{1 \text{ mol}}{180.15 \text{ g}} = 2.78 \times 10^{-3} \text{ mol}$

$$2.78 \times 10^{-3} \text{ mol} \times \frac{6.022 \times 10^{23} \text{ molecules}}{\text{mol}} = 1.67 \times 10^{21} \text{ molecules}$$

53.   a. $150.0 \text{ g Fe}_2\text{O}_3 \times \dfrac{1 \text{ mol}}{159.70 \text{ g}} = 0.9393 \text{ mol Fe}_2\text{O}_3$

       b. $10.0 \text{ mg NO}_2 \times \dfrac{1 \text{ g}}{1000 \text{ mg}} \times \dfrac{1 \text{ mol}}{46.01 \text{ g}} = 2.17 \times 10^{-4} \text{ mol NO}_2$

       c. $1.5 \times 10^{16} \text{ molecules BF}_3 \times \dfrac{1 \text{ mol}}{6.02 \times 10^{23} \text{ molecules}} = 2.5 \times 10^{-8} \text{ mol BF}_3$

54.   a. $20.0 \text{ mg C}_8\text{H}_{10}\text{N}_4\text{O}_2 \times \dfrac{1 \text{ g}}{1000 \text{ mg}} \times \dfrac{1 \text{ mol}}{194.20 \text{ g}} = 1.03 \times 10^{-4} \text{ mol C}_8\text{H}_{10}\text{N}_4\text{O}_2$

       b. $2.72 \times 10^{21} \text{ molecules C}_2\text{H}_5\text{OH} \times \dfrac{1 \text{ mol}}{6.022 \times 10^{23} \text{ molecules}}$

$$= 4.52 \times 10^{-3} \text{ mol C}_2\text{H}_5\text{OH}$$

       c. $1.50 \text{ g CO}_2 \times \dfrac{1 \text{ mol}}{44.01 \text{ g}} = 3.41 \times 10^{-2} \text{ mol CO}_2$

55.   a.   A chemical formula gives atom ratios as well as mole ratios. We will use both ideas to show how these conversion factors can be used.

          Molar mass of $C_2H_5O_2N = 2(12.01) + 5(1.008) + 2(16.00) + 14.01 = 75.07$ g/mol

$$5.00 \text{ g C}_2\text{H}_5\text{O}_2\text{N} \times \frac{1 \text{ mol C}_2\text{H}_2\text{O}_2\text{N}}{75.07 \text{ g C}_2\text{H}_2\text{O}_2\text{N}} \times \frac{6.022 \times 10^{23} \text{ molecules C}_2\text{H}_5\text{O}_2\text{N}}{\text{mol C}_2\text{H}_2\text{O}_2\text{N}} \times$$

$$\frac{1 \text{ atom N}}{\text{molecule C}_2\text{H}_2\text{O}_2\text{N}} = 4.01 \times 10^{22} \text{ atoms N}$$

       b.   Molar mass of $Mg_3N_2 = 3(24.31) + 2(14.01) = 100.95$ g/mol

$$5.00 \text{ g Mg}_3\text{N}_2 \times \frac{1 \text{ mol Mg}_3\text{N}_2}{100.95 \text{ g Mg}_3\text{N}_2} \times \frac{6.022 \times 10^{23} \text{ formula units Mg}_3\text{N}_2}{\text{mol Mg}_3\text{N}_2} \times \frac{2 \text{ atoms N}}{\text{mol Mg}_3\text{N}_2}$$

$$= 5.97 \times 10^{22} \text{ atoms N}$$

c.   Molar mass of $Ca(NO_3)_2 = 40.08 + 2(14.01) + 6(16.00) = 164.10$ g/mol

$$5.00 \text{ g Ca}(NO_3)_2 \times \frac{1 \text{ mol Ca}(NO_3)_2}{164.10 \text{ g Ca}(NO_3)_2} \times \frac{2 \text{ mols N}}{\text{mol Ca}(NO_3)_2} \times \frac{6.022 \times 10^{23} \text{ atoms N}}{\text{mol N}}$$

$$= 3.67 \times 10^{22} \text{ atoms N}$$

d.   Molar mass of $N_2O_4 = 2(14.01) + 4(16.00) = 92.02$ g/mol

$$5.00 \text{ g N}_2O_4 \times \frac{1 \text{ mol N}_2O_4}{92.02 \text{ g N}_2O_4} \times \frac{2 \text{ mol N}}{\text{mol N}_2O_4} \times \frac{6.022 \times 10^{23} \text{ atoms N}}{\text{mol N}}$$

$$= 6.54 \times 10^{22} \text{ atoms N}$$

56. $4.24 \text{ g C}_6H_6 \times \dfrac{1 \text{ mol}}{78.11 \text{ g}} = 5.43 \times 10^{-2} \text{ mol C}_6H_6$

$5.43 \times 10^{-2} \text{ mol C}_6H_6 \times \dfrac{6.022 \times 10^{23} \text{ molecules}}{\text{mol}} = 3.27 \times 10^{22} \text{ molecules C}_6H_6$

Each molecule of C_6H_6 contains 6 atoms C + 6 atoms H = 12 total atoms.

$3.27 \times 10^{22} \text{ molecules C}_6H_6 \times \dfrac{12 \text{ atoms total}}{\text{molecule}} = 3.92 \times 10^{23} \text{ atoms total}$

$0.224 \text{ mol H}_2O \times \dfrac{18.02 \text{ g}}{\text{mol}} = 4.04 \text{ g H}_2O$

$0.224 \text{ mol H}_2O \times \dfrac{6.022 \times 10^{23} \text{ molecules}}{\text{mol}} = 1.35 \times 10^{23} \text{ molecules H}_2O$

$1.35 \times 10^{23} \text{ molecules H}_2O \times \dfrac{3 \text{ atoms total}}{\text{molecule}} = 4.05 \times 10^{23} \text{ atoms total}$

$2.71 \times 10^{22} \text{ molecules CO}_2 \times \dfrac{1 \text{ mol}}{6.022 \times 10^{23} \text{ molecules}} = 4.50 \times 10^{-2} \text{ mol CO}_2$

$4.50 \times 10^{-2} \text{ mol CO}_2 \times \dfrac{44.01 \text{ g}}{\text{mol}} = 1.98 \text{ g CO}_2$

$2.71 \times 10^{22} \text{ molecules CO}_2 \times \dfrac{3 \text{ atoms total}}{\text{molecule CO}_2} = 8.13 \times 10^{22} \text{ atoms total}$

$3.35 \times 10^{22} \text{ atoms total} \times \dfrac{1 \text{ molecule}}{6 \text{ atoms total}} = 5.58 \times 10^{21} \text{ molecules CH}_3OH$

$5.58 \times 10^{21} \text{ molecules CH}_3OH \times \dfrac{1 \text{ mol}}{6.022 \times 10^{23} \text{ molecules}} = 9.27 \times 10^{-3} \text{ mol CH}_3OH$

$$9.27 \times 10^{-3} \text{ mol } CH_3OH \times \frac{32.04 \text{ g}}{\text{mol}} = 0.297 \text{ g } CH_3OH$$

57.   a. $14 \text{ mol C} \left(\dfrac{12.01 \text{ g}}{\text{mol C}} \right) + 18 \text{ mol H} \left(\dfrac{1.008 \text{ g}}{\text{mol H}} \right) + 2 \text{ mol N} \left(\dfrac{14.01 \text{ g}}{\text{mol N}} \right) + 5 \text{ mol O} \left(\dfrac{16.00 \text{ g}}{\text{mol O}} \right)$

$$= 294.30 \text{ g/mol}$$

b. $10.0 \text{ g aspartame} \times \dfrac{1 \text{ mol}}{294.30 \text{ g}} = 3.40 \times 10^{-2} \text{ mol}$

c. $1.56 \text{ mol} \times \dfrac{294.30 \text{ g}}{\text{mol}} = 459 \text{ g}$

d. $5.0 \text{ mg} \times \dfrac{1 \text{ g}}{1000 \text{ mg}} \times \dfrac{1 \text{ mol}}{294.30 \text{ g}} \times \dfrac{6.02 \times 10^{23} \text{ molecules}}{\text{mol}} = 1.0 \times 10^{19} \text{ molecules}$

e.   The chemical formula tells us that 1 molecule of aspartame contains two atoms of N. The chemical formula also says that 1 mol of aspartame contains two mol of N.

$$1.2 \text{ g aspartame} \times \frac{1 \text{ mol aspartame}}{294.30 \text{ g aspartame}} \times \frac{2 \text{ mol N}}{\text{mol aspartame}} \times \frac{6.02 \times 10^{23} \text{ atoms N}}{\text{mol N}}$$

$$= 4.9 \times 10^{21} \text{ atoms of nitrogen}$$

f. $1.0 \times 10^{9} \text{ molecules} \times \dfrac{1 \text{ mol}}{6.02 \times 10^{23} \text{ molecules}} \times \dfrac{294.30 \text{ g}}{\text{mol}} = 4.9 \times 10^{-13} \text{ g or } 490 \text{ fg}$

g. $1 \text{ molecule aspartame} \times \dfrac{1 \text{ mol}}{6.022 \times 10^{23} \text{ molecules}} \times \dfrac{294.30 \text{ g}}{\text{mol}} = 4.887 \times 10^{-22} \text{ g}$

58.   a. $2(12.01) + 3(1.008) + 3(35.45) + 2(16.00) = 165.39 \text{ g/mol}$

b. $500.0 \text{ g} \times \dfrac{1 \text{ mol}}{165.39 \text{ g}} = 3.023 \text{ mol}$ c. $2.0 \times 10^{-2} \text{ mol} \times \dfrac{165.39 \text{ g}}{\text{mol}} = 3.3 \text{ g}$

d. $5.0 \text{ g } C_2H_3Cl_3O_2 \times \dfrac{1 \text{ mol}}{165.39 \text{ g}} \times \dfrac{6.02 \times 10^{23} \text{ molecules}}{\text{mol}} \times \dfrac{3 \text{ atoms Cl}}{\text{molecule}}$

$$= 5.5 \times 10^{22} \text{ atoms of chlorine}$$

e. $1.0 \text{ g Cl} \times \dfrac{1 \text{ mol Cl}}{35.45 \text{ g}} \times \dfrac{1 \text{ mol } C_2H_3Cl_3O_2}{3 \text{ mol Cl}} \times \dfrac{165.39 \text{ g } C_2H_3Cl_3O_2}{\text{mol } C_2H_3Cl_3O_2} = 1.6 \text{ g chloral hydrate}$

f. $500 \text{ molecules} \times \dfrac{1 \text{ mol}}{6.022 \times 10^{23} \text{ molecules}} \times \dfrac{165.39 \text{ g}}{\text{mol}} = 1.373 \times 10^{-19} \text{ g}$

Percent Composition

59.   a. $C_3H_4O_2$: Molar mass = 3(12.01) + 4(1.008) + 2(16.00) = 36.03 + 4.032 + 32.00 = 72.06 g/mol

$$\%C = \frac{36.03 \text{ g C}}{72.06 \text{ g compound}} \times 100 = 50.00\% \text{ C}; \quad \%H = \frac{4.032 \text{ g H}}{72.06 \text{ g compound}} \times 100$$

$$= 5.595\% \text{ H}$$

$$\%O = 100.00 - (50.00 + 5.595) = 44.41\% \text{ O or } \%O = \frac{32.00 \text{ g}}{72.06 \text{ g}} \times 100 = 44.41\% \text{ O}$$

b. $C_4H_6O_2$: Molar mass = 4(12.01) + 6(1.008) + 2(16.00) = 48.04 + 6.048 + 32.00

$$= 86.09 \text{ g/mol}$$

$$\%C = \frac{48.04 \text{ g}}{86.09 \text{ g}} \times 100 = 55.80\% \text{ C}; \quad \%H = \frac{6.048 \text{ g}}{86.09 \text{ g}} \times 100 = 7.025\% \text{ H}$$

$$\%O = 100.00 - (55.80 + 7.025) = 37.18\% \text{ O}$$

c. C_3H_3N: Molar mass = 3(12.01) + 3(1.008) + 1(14.01) = 36.03 + 3.024 + 14.01

$$= 53.06 \text{ g/mol}$$

$$\%C = \frac{36.03 \text{ g}}{53.06 \text{ g}} \times 100 = 67.90\% \text{ C}; \quad \%H = \frac{3.024 \text{ g}}{53.06 \text{ g}} \times 100 = 5.699\% \text{ H}$$

$$\%N = \frac{14.01 \text{ g}}{53.06 \text{ g}} \times 100 = 26.40\% \text{ N or } \%N = 100.00 - (67.90 + 5.699) = 26.40\% \text{ N}$$

60.   molar mass = 20(12.01) + 29(1.008) + 19.00 + 3(16.00) = 336.43 g/mol

$$\%C = \frac{20(12.01) \text{ g C}}{336.43 \text{ g compound}} \times 100 = 71.40\% \text{ C}$$

$$\%H = \frac{29(1.008) \text{ g H}}{336.43 \text{ g compound}} \times 100 = 8.689\% \text{ H}$$

$$\%F = \frac{19.00 \text{ g F}}{336.43 \text{ g compound}} \times 100 = 5.648\% \text{ F}$$

$$\%O = 100.00 - (71.40 + 8.689 + 5.648) = 14.26\% \text{ O or:}$$

$$\%O = \frac{3(16.00) \text{ g O}}{336.43 \text{ g compound}} \times 100 = 14.27\% \text{ O}$$

61.   a.   NO: $\%N = \dfrac{14.01 \text{ g N}}{30.01 \text{ g NO}} \times 100 = 46.68\% \text{ N}$

b. NO_2: $\%N = \dfrac{14.01\,g\,N}{46.01\,g\,NO_2} \times 100 = 30.45\%\,N$

c. N_2O_4: $\%N = \dfrac{28.02\,g\,N}{92.02\,g\,N_2O_4} \times 100 = 30.45\%\,N$

d. N_2O: $\%N = \dfrac{28.02\,g\,N}{44.02\,g\,N_2O} \times 100 = 63.65\%\,N$

The order from lowest to highest mass percentage of nitrogen is: $NO_2 = N_2O_4 < NO < N_2O$.

62. $C_8H_{10}N_4O_2$: molar mass = 8(12.01) + 10(1.008) + 4(14.01) + 2(16.00) = 194.20 g/mol

$\%C = \dfrac{8(12.01)\,g\,C}{194.20\,g\,C_8H_{10}N_4O_2} \times 100 = \dfrac{96.08}{194.20} \times 100 = 49.47\%\,C$

$C_{12}H_{22}O_{11}$: molar mass = 12(12.01) + 22(1.008) + 11(16.00) = 342.30 g/mol

$\%C = \dfrac{12(12.01)\,g\,C}{342.30\,g\,C_{12}H_{22}O_{11}} \times 100 = 42.10\%\,C$

C_2H_5OH: molar mass = 2(12.01) + 6(1.008) + 1(16.00) = 46.07 g/mol

$\%C = \dfrac{2(12.01)\,g\,C}{46.07\,g\,C_2H_5OH} \times 100 = 52.14\%\,C$

The order from lowest to highest mass percentage of carbon is: sucrose ($C_{12}H_{22}O_{11}$) < caffeine ($C_8H_{10}N_4O_2$) < ethanol (C_2H_5OH)

63.   There are many valid methods to solve this problem. We will assume 100.00 g of compound, then determine from the information in the problem how many mol of compound equals 100.00 g of compound. From this information, we can determine the mass of one mol of compound (the molar mass) by setting up a ratio. Assuming 100.00 g cyanocobalamin:

$$\text{mol cyanocobalamin} = 4.34\,g\,Co \times \dfrac{1\,mol\,Co}{58.93\,g\,Co} \times \dfrac{1\,mol\,cyanocobalamin}{mol\,Co}$$

$$= 7.36 \times 10^{-2}\,\text{mol cyanocobalamin}$$

$$\dfrac{x\,\text{g cyanocobalamin}}{1\,\text{mol cyanocobalamin}} = \dfrac{100.00\,g}{7.36 \times 10^{-2}\,mol}, \quad x = \text{molar mass} = 1360\,\text{g/mol}$$

64.   There are 0.390 g Cu for every 100.00 g of fungal laccase. Assuming 100.00 g fungal laccase:

$$\text{mol fungal laccase} = 0.390 \text{ g Cu} \times \frac{1 \text{ mol Cu}}{63.55 \text{ g Cu}} \times \frac{1 \text{ mol fungal laccase}}{4 \text{ mol Cu}} = 1.53 \times 10^{-3} \text{ mol}$$

$$\frac{x \text{ g fungal laccase}}{1 \text{ mol fungal laccase}} = \frac{100.00 \text{ g}}{1.53 \times 10^{-3} \text{ mol}}, \ x = \text{molar mass} = 6.54 \times 10^4 \text{ g/mol}$$

Empirical and Molecular Formulas

65.   a.   Molar mass of CH_2O = 1 mol C $\left(\dfrac{12.01 \text{ g C}}{\text{mol C}} \right)$ + 2 mol H $\left(\dfrac{1.008 \text{ g H}}{\text{mol H}} \right)$

$$+ 1 \text{ mol O} \left(\frac{16.00 \text{ g O}}{\text{mol O}} \right) = 30.03 \text{ g/mol}$$

$$\%C = \frac{12.01 \text{ g C}}{30.03 \text{ g CH}_2\text{O}} \times 100 = 39.99\% \text{ C}; \ \%H = \frac{2.016 \text{ g H}}{30.03 \text{ g CH}_2\text{O}} \times 100 = 6.713\% \text{ H}$$

$$\%O = \frac{16.00 \text{ g O}}{30.03 \text{ g CH}_2\text{O}} \times 100 = 53.28\% \text{ O} \ \text{ or } \%O = 100.00 - (39.99 + 6.713) = 53.30\%$$

   b.   Molar Mass of $C_6H_{12}O_6$ = 6(12.01) + 12(1.008) + 6(16.00) = 180.16 g/mol

$$\%C = \frac{76.06 \text{ g C}}{180.16 \text{ g C}_6\text{H}_{12}\text{O}_6} \times 100 = 40.00\%; \ \%H = \frac{12.(1.008) \text{ g}}{180.16 \text{ g}} \times 100 = 6.714\%$$

$$\%O = 100.00 - (40.00 + 6.714) = 53.29\%$$

   c.   Molar mass of $HC_2H_3O_2$ = 2(12.01) + 4(1.008) + 2(16.00) = 60.05 g/mol

$$\%C = \frac{24.02 \text{ g}}{60.05 \text{ g}} \times 100 = 40.00\%; \ \ \%H = \frac{4.032 \text{ g}}{60.05 \text{ g}} \times 100 = 6.714\%$$

$$\%O = 100.00 - (40.00 + 6.714) = 53.29\%$$

66.   All three compounds have the same empirical formula, CH_2O, and different molecular formulas. The composition of all three in mass percent is also the same (within rounding differences). Therefore, elemental analysis will give us only the empirical formula.

67.   a.   The molecular formula is N_2O_4. The smallest whole number ratio of the atoms (the empirical formula) is NO_2.

   b.   Molecular formula: C_3H_6; empirical formula = CH_2

   c.   Molecular formula: P_4O_{10}; empirical formula = P_2O_5

   d.   Molecular formula: $C_6H_{12}O_6$; empirical formula = CH_2O

68.   a.   SNH: Empirical formula mass = 32.07 + 14.01 + 1.008 = 47.09 g

$$\frac{188.35\ g}{47.09\ g} = 4.000;\ \text{So the molecular formula is } (SNH)_4 \text{ or } S_4N_4H_4.$$

b. $NPCl_2$: Empirical formula mass = 14.01 + 30.97 + 2(35.45) = 115.88 g/mol

$$\frac{347.64\ g}{115.88\ g} = 3.0000;\ \text{Molecular formula is } (NPCl_2)_3 \text{ or } N_3P_3Cl_6.$$

c. CoC_4O_4: 58.93 + 4(12.01) + 4(16.00) = 170.97 g/mol

$$\frac{341.94\ g}{170.97\ g} = 2.0000;\ \text{Molecular formula: } Co_2C_8O_8$$

d.   SN: 32.07 + 14.01 = 46.08 g/mol; $\dfrac{184.32\ g}{46.08\ g} = 4.000$; Molecular formula: S_4N_4

69.   Out of 100.00 g of adrenaline, there are:

$$56.79\ g\ C \times \frac{1\ mol\ C}{12.01\ g\ C} = 4.729\ mol\ C;\ \ 6.56\ g\ H \times \frac{1\ mol\ H}{1.008\ g\ H} = 6.51\ mol\ H$$

$$28.37\ g\ O \times \frac{1\ mol\ O}{16.00\ g\ O} = 1.773\ mol\ O;\ \ 8.28\ g\ N \times \frac{1\ mol\ N}{14.01\ g\ N} = 0.591\ mol\ N$$

Dividing each mol value by the smallest number:

$$\frac{4.729}{0.591} = 8.00;\ \ \frac{6.51}{0.591} = 11.0;\ \ \frac{1.773}{0.591} = 3.00;\ \ \frac{0.591}{0.591} = 1.00$$

This gives adrenaline an empirical formula of $C_8H_{11}O_3N$.

70.   Assuming 100.00 g of nylon-6:

$$63.68\ g\ C \times \frac{1\ mol\ C}{12.01\ g\ C} = 5.302\ mol\ C;\ \ \ 12.38\ g\ N \times \frac{1\ mol\ N}{14.01\ g\ N} = 0.8837\ mol\ N$$

$$9.80\ g\ H \times \frac{1\ mol\ H}{1.008\ g\ H} = 9.72\ mol\ H;\ \ 14.14\ g\ O \times \frac{1\ mol\ O}{16.00\ g\ O} = 0.8838\ mol\ O$$

Dividing each mol value by the smallest number:

$$\frac{5.302}{0.8837} = 6.000;\ \ \frac{9.72}{0.8837} = 11.0$$

The empirical formula for nylon-6 is $C_6H_{11}NO$

71.   Compound I: mass O = 0.6498 g Hg_xO_y – 0.6018 g Hg = 0.0480 g O

$$0.6018 \text{ g Hg} \times \frac{1 \text{ mol Hg}}{200.6 \text{ g Hg}} = 3.000 \times 10^{-3} \text{ mol Hg}$$

$$0.0480 \text{ g O} \times \frac{1 \text{ mol O}}{16.00 \text{ g O}} = 3.00 \times 10^{-3} \text{ mol O}$$

The mol ratio between Hg and O is 1:1, so the empirical formula of compound I is HgO.

Compound II: mass Hg = 0.4172 g Hg_xO_y – 0.016 g O = 0.401 g Hg

$$0.401 \text{ g Hg} \times \frac{1 \text{ mol Hg}}{200.6 \text{ g Hg}} = 2.00 \times 10^{-3} \text{ mol Hg}; \quad 0.016 \text{ g O} \times \frac{1 \text{ mol O}}{16.00 \text{ g O}}$$
$$= 1.0 \times 10^{-3} \text{ mol O}$$

The mol ratio between Hg and O is 2:1, so the empirical formula is Hg_2O.

72. $$1.121 \text{ g N} \times \frac{1 \text{ mol N}}{14.01 \text{ g N}} = 8.001 \times 10^{-2} \text{ mol N}; \quad 0.161 \text{ g H} \times \frac{1 \text{ mol H}}{1.008 \text{ g H}} = 1.60 \times 10^{-1} \text{ mol H}$$

$$0.480 \text{ g C} \times \frac{1 \text{ mol C}}{12.01 \text{ g C}} = 4.00 \times 10^{-2} \text{ mol C}; \quad 0.640 \text{ g O} \times \frac{1 \text{ mol O}}{16.00 \text{ g O}} = 4.00 \times 10^{-2} \text{ mol O}$$

Dividing all mol values by the smallest number:

$$\frac{8.001 \times 10^{-2}}{4.00 \times 10^{-2}} = 2.00; \quad \frac{1.60 \times 10^{-1}}{4.00 \times 10^{-2}} = 4.00; \quad \frac{4.00 \times 10^{-2}}{4.00 \times 10^{-2}} = 1.00$$

Empirical formula = N_2H_4CO

73.   Out of 100.0 g, there are:

$$69.6 \text{ g S} \times \frac{1 \text{ mol S}}{32.07 \text{ g S}} = 2.17 \text{ mol S}; \quad 30.4 \text{ g N} \times \frac{1 \text{ mol N}}{14.01 \text{ g N}} = 2.17 \text{ mol N}$$

Empirical formula is SN since mol values are in a 1:1 mol ratio.

The empirical formula mass of SN is ~ 46 g. Because 184/46 = 4.0, the molecular formula is S_4N_4.

74.   Assuming 100.0 g of compound:

$$26.7 \text{ g P} \times \frac{1 \text{ mol P}}{30.97 \text{ g P}} = 0.862 \text{ mol P}; \quad 12.1 \text{ g N} \times \frac{1 \text{ mol N}}{14.01 \text{ g N}} = 0.864 \text{ mol N}$$

$$61.2 \text{ g Cl} \times \frac{1 \text{ mol Cl}}{35.45 \text{ g Cl}} = 1.73 \text{ mol Cl}$$

$$\frac{1.73}{0.862} = 2.01; \text{ Empirical formula} = PNCl_2$$

The empirical formula mass is ~31.0 + 14.0 + 2(35.5) = 116

$$\frac{\text{molar mass}}{\text{empirical formula mass}} = \frac{580}{116} = 5; \text{ molecular formula} = (PNCl_2)_5 = P_5N_5Cl_{10}$$

75.   Assuming 100.00 g of compound (mass hydrogen = 100.00 g - 49.31 g C - 43.79 g O
       = 6.90 g H):

$$49.31 \text{ g C} \times \frac{1 \text{ mol C}}{12.01 \text{ g C}} = 4.106 \text{ mol C}; \ 6.90 \text{ g H} \times \times \frac{1 \text{ mol H}}{1.008 \text{ g H}} = 6.85 \text{ mol H}$$

$$43.79 \text{ g O} \times \frac{1 \text{ mol O}}{16.00 \text{ g O}} = 2.737 \text{ mol O}$$

Dividing all mole values by 2.737 gives:

$$\frac{4.106}{2.737} = 1.500; \ \frac{6.85}{2.737} = 2.50; \ \frac{2.737}{2.737} = 1.000$$

Since a whole number ratio is required, the empirical formula is $C_3H_5O_2$.

The empirical formula mass is: 3(12.01) + 5(1.008) +2(16.00) = 73.07 g/mol

$$\frac{\text{molar mass}}{\text{empirical formula mass}} = \frac{146.1}{73.07} = 1.999; \text{ molecular formula} = (C_3H_5O_2)_2 = C_6H_{10}O_4$$

76.   Assuming 100.00 g of compound (mass oxygen = 100.00 g – 41.39 g C – 3.47 g H
                                                                        = 55.14 g O):

$$41.39 \text{ g C} \times \frac{1 \text{ mol C}}{12.01 \text{ g C}} = 3.446 \text{ mol C}; \ 3.47 \text{ g H} \times \frac{1 \text{ mol H}}{1.008 \text{ g H}} = 3.44 \text{ mol H}$$

$$55.14 \text{ g O} \times \frac{1 \text{ mol O}}{16.00 \text{ g O}} = 3.446 \text{ mol O}$$

All are the same mol values so the empirical formula is CHO. The empirical formula mass is
12.01 + 1.008 + 16.00 = 29.02 g/mol.

$$\text{molar mass} = \frac{15.0 \text{ g}}{0.129 \text{ mol}} = 116 \text{ g/mol}$$

$$\frac{\text{molar mass}}{\text{empirical mass}} = \frac{116}{29.02} = 4.00; \text{ molecular formula} = (CHO)_4 = C_4H_4O_4$$

77.   When combustion data are given, it is assumed that all the carbon in the compound ends up as carbon in CO_2 and all the hydrogen in the compound ends up as hydrogen in H_2O. In the sample of propane combusted, the moles of C and H are:

$$\text{mol C} = 2.641 \text{ g CO}_2 \times \frac{1 \text{ mol CO}_2}{44.01 \text{ g CO}_2} \times \frac{1 \text{ mol C}}{\text{mol CO}_2} = 0.06001 \text{ mol C}$$

$$\text{mol H} = 1.442 \text{ g H}_2\text{O} \times \frac{1 \text{ mol H}_2\text{O}}{18.02 \text{ g H}_2\text{O}} \times \frac{2 \text{ mol H}}{\text{mol H}_2\text{O}} = 0.1600 \text{ mol H}$$

$$\frac{\text{mol H}}{\text{mol C}} = \frac{0.1600}{0.06001} = 2.666$$

Multiplying this ratio by three gives the empirical formula of C_3H_8.

78.   This compound contains nitrogen, and one way to determine the amount of nitrogen in the compound is to calculate composition by mass percent. We assume that all of the carbon in 33.5 mg CO_2 came from the 35.0 mg of compound and all of the hydrogen in 41.1 mg H_2O came from the 35.0 mg of compound.

$$3.35 \times 10^{-2} \text{ g CO}_2 \times \frac{1 \text{ mol CO}_2}{44.01 \text{ g CO}_2} \times \frac{1 \text{ mol C}}{\text{mol CO}_2} \times \frac{12.01 \text{ g C}}{\text{mol C}} = 9.14 \times 10^{-3} \text{ g C}$$

$$\%\text{C} = \frac{9.14 \times 10^{-3} \text{ g C}}{3.50 \times 10^{-2} \text{ g compound}} \times 100 = 26.1\% \text{ C}$$

$$4.11 \times 10^{-2} \text{ g H}_2\text{O} \times \frac{1 \text{ mol H}_2\text{O}}{18.02 \text{ g H}_2\text{O}} \times \frac{2 \text{ mol H}}{\text{mol H}_2\text{O}} \times \frac{1.008 \text{ g H}}{\text{mol H}} = 4.60 \times 10^{-3} \text{ g H}$$

$$\%\text{H} = \frac{4.60 \times 10^{-3} \text{ g H}}{3.50 \times 10^{-2} \text{ g compound}} \times 100 = 13.1\% \text{ H}$$

The mass percent of nitrogen is obtained by difference:

$$\%\text{N} = 100.0 - (26.1 + 13.1) = 60.8\% \text{ N}$$

Now perform the empirical formula determination by first assuming 100.0 g of compound. Out of 100.0 g of compound, there are:

$$26.1 \text{ g C} \times \frac{1 \text{ mol C}}{12.01 \text{ g C}} = 2.17 \text{ mol C}; \quad 13.1 \text{ g H} \times \frac{1 \text{ mol H}}{1.008 \text{ g H}} = 13.0 \text{ mol H}$$

$$60.8 \text{ g N} \times \frac{1 \text{ mol N}}{14.01 \text{ g N}} = 4.34 \text{ mol N}$$

Dividing all mol values by 2.17 gives: $\frac{2.17}{2.17} = 1.00$; $\frac{13.0}{2.17} = 5.99$; $\frac{4.34}{2.17} = 2.00$

The empirical formula is CH_6N_2.

79.   The combustion data allow determination of the amount of hydrogen in cumene. One way to determine the amount of carbon in cumene is to determine the mass percent of hydrogen in the compound from the data in the problem; then determine the mass percent of carbon by difference (100.0 - mass %H = mass %C).

$$42.8 \text{ mg H}_2\text{O} \times \frac{1 \text{ g}}{1000 \text{ mg}} \times \frac{2.016 \text{ g H}}{18.02 \text{ g H}_2\text{O}} \times \frac{1000 \text{ mg}}{\text{g}} = 4.79 \text{ mg H}$$

$$\%\text{H} = \frac{4.79 \text{ mg H}}{47.6 \text{ mg cumene}} \times 100 = 10.1\% \text{ H}; \quad \%\text{C} = 100.0 - 10.1 = 89.9\% \text{ C}$$

Now solve this empirical formula problem. Out of 100.0 g cumene, we have:

$$89.9 \text{ g C} \times \frac{1 \text{ mol C}}{12.01 \text{ g C}} = 7.49 \text{ mol C}; \quad 10.1 \text{ g H} \times \frac{1 \text{ mol H}}{1.008 \text{ g H}} = 10.0 \text{ mol H}$$

$$\frac{10.0}{7.49} = 1.34 \approx \frac{4}{3}, \text{ i.e., mol H to mol C are in a 4:3 ratio. Empirical formula} = \text{C}_3\text{H}_4$$

Empirical formula mass $\approx 3(12) + 4(1) = 40$ g/mol

The molecular formula is $(\text{C}_3\text{H}_4)_3$ or C_9H_{12} since the molar mass will be between 115 and 125 g/mol (molar mass $\approx 3 \times 40$ g/mol = 120 g/mol).

80.   First, we will determine composition by mass percent:

$$16.01 \text{ mg CO}_2 \times \frac{1 \text{ g}}{1000 \text{ mg}} \times \frac{12.01 \text{ g C}}{44.01 \text{ g CO}_2} \times \frac{1000 \text{ mg}}{\text{g}} = 4.369 \text{ mg C}$$

$$\%\text{C} = \frac{4.369 \text{ mg C}}{10.68 \text{ mg compound}} \times 100 = 40.91\% \text{ C}$$

$$4.37 \text{ mg H}_2\text{O} \times \frac{1 \text{ g}}{1000 \text{ mg}} \times \frac{2.016 \text{ g H}}{18.02 \text{ g H}_2\text{O}} \times \frac{1000 \text{ mg}}{\text{g}} = 0.489 \text{ mg H}$$

$$\%\text{H} = \frac{0.489 \text{ mg}}{10.68 \text{ mg}} \times 100 = 4.58\% \text{ H}; \quad \%\text{O} = 100.00 - (40.91 + 4.58) = 54.51\% \text{ O}$$

So, in 100.00 g of the compound, we have:

$$40.91 \text{ g C} \times \frac{1 \text{ mol C}}{12.01 \text{ g C}} = 3.406 \text{ mol C}; \quad 4.58 \text{ g H} \times \frac{1 \text{ mol H}}{1.008 \text{ g H}} = 4.54 \text{ mol H}$$

$$54.51 \text{ g O} \times \frac{1 \text{ mol O}}{16.00 \text{ g O}} = 3.407 \text{ mol O}$$

Dividing by the smallest number: $\frac{4.54}{3.406} = 1.33 \approx \frac{4}{3}$; the empirical formula is $\text{C}_3\text{H}_4\text{O}_3$.

The empirical formula mass of $C_3H_4O_3$ is $\approx 3(12) + 4(1) + 3(16) = 88$ g.

Because $\dfrac{176.1}{88} = 2.0$, the molecular formula is $C_6H_8O_6$.

Balancing Chemical Equations

81.   When balancing reactions, start with elements that appear in only one of the reactants and one of the products, then go on to balance the remaining elements.

   a. $C_6H_{12}O_6(s) + O_2(g) \rightarrow CO_2(g) + H_2O(g)$

        Balance C atoms: $C_6H_{12}O_6 + O_2 \rightarrow 6\ CO_2 + H_2O$

        Balance H atoms: $C_6H_{12}O_6 + O_2 \rightarrow 6\ CO_2 + 6\ H_2O$

        Lastly, balance O atoms: $C_6H_{12}O_6(s) + 6\ O_2(g) \rightarrow 6\ CO_2(g) + 6\ H_2O(g)$

   b. $Fe_2S_3(s) + HCl(g) \rightarrow FeCl_3(s) + H_2S(g)$

        Balance Fe atoms: $Fe_2S_3 + HCl \rightarrow 2\ FeCl_3 + H_2S$

        Balance S atoms: $Fe_2S_3 + HCl \rightarrow 2\ FeCl_3 + 3\ H_2S$

        There are 6 H and 6 Cl on right, so balance with 6 HCl on left:

           $Fe_2S_3(s) + 6\ HCl(g) \rightarrow 2\ FeCl_3(s) + 3\ H_2S(g)$.

   c. $CS_2(l) + NH_3(g) \rightarrow H_2S(g) + NH_4SCN(s)$

        C and S balanced; balance N:

           $CS_2 + 2\ NH_3 \rightarrow H_2S + NH_4SCN$

        H is also balanced. So: $CS_2(l) + 2\ NH_3(g) \rightarrow H_2S(g) + NH_4SCN(s)$

82.   One of the most important parts to this problem is writing out correct formulas. If the formulas are incorrect, then the balanced reaction is incorrect.

   a. $C_2H_5OH(l) + 3\ O_2(g) \rightarrow 2\ CO_2(g) + 3\ H_2O(g)$

   b. $3\ Pb(NO_3)_2(aq) + 2\ Na_3PO_4(aq) \rightarrow Pb_3(PO_4)_2(s) + 6\ NaNO_3(aq)$

   c. $Zn(s) + 2\ HCl(aq) \rightarrow ZnCl_2(aq) + H_2(g)$

   d. $Sr(OH)_2(aq) + 2\ HBr(aq) \rightarrow 2H_2O(l) + SrBr_2(aq)$

83.   a. $3\ Ca(OH)_2(aq) + 2\ H_3PO_4(aq) \rightarrow 6\ H_2O(l) + Ca_3(PO_4)_2(s)$

b. $Al(OH)_3(s) + 3\ HCl(aq) \rightarrow AlCl_3(aq) + 3\ H_2O(l)$

c. $2\ AgNO_3(aq) + H_2SO_4(aq) \rightarrow Ag_2SO_4(s) + 2\ HNO_3(aq)$

84.   a. $2\ KO_2(s) + 2\ H_2O(l) \rightarrow 2\ KOH(aq) + O_2(g) + H_2O_2(aq)$ or

$4\ KO_2(s) + 6\ H_2O(l) \rightarrow 4\ KOH(aq) + O_2(g) + 4\ H_2O_2(aq)$

b. $Fe_2O_3(s) + 6\ HNO_3(aq) \rightarrow 2\ Fe(NO_3)_3(aq) + 3\ H_2O(l)$

c. $4\ NH_3(g) + 5\ O_2(g) \rightarrow 4\ NO(g) + 6\ H_2O(g)$

d. $PCl_5(l) + 4\ H_2O(l) \rightarrow H_3PO_4(aq) + 5\ HCl(g)$

e. $2\ CaO(s) + 5\ C(s) \rightarrow 2\ CaC_2(s) + CO_2(g)$

f. $2\ MoS_2(s) + 7\ O_2(g) \rightarrow 2\ MoO_3(s) + 4\ SO_2(g)$

g. $FeCO_3(s) + H_2CO_3(aq) \rightarrow Fe(HCO_3)_2(aq)$

85.   a.   The formulas of the reactants and products are $C_6H_6(l) + O_2(g) \rightarrow CO_2(g) + H_2O(g)$. To balance this combustion reaction, notice that all of the carbon in C_6H_6 has to end up as carbon in CO_2 and all of the hydrogen in C_6H_6 has to end up as hydrogen in H_2O. To balance C and H, we need 6 CO_2 molecules and 3 H_2O molecules for every 1 molecule of C_6H_6. We do oxygen last. Because we have 15 oxygen atoms in 6 CO_2 molecules and 3 H_2O molecules, we need 15/2 O_2 molecules in order to have 15 oxygen atoms on the reactant side.

$C_6H_6(l) + \dfrac{15}{2} O_2(g) \rightarrow 6\ CO_2(g) + 3\ H_2O(g)$; Multiply by two to give whole numbers.

$2\ C_6H_6(l) + 15\ O_2(g) \rightarrow 12\ CO_2(g) + 6\ H_2O(g)$

b.   The formulas of the reactants and products are $C_4H_{10}(g) + O_2(g) \rightarrow CO_2(g) + H_2O(g)$.

$C_4H_{10}(g) + \dfrac{13}{2} O_2(g) \rightarrow 4\ CO_2(g) + 5\ H_2O(g)$; Multiply by two to give whole numbers.

$2\ C_4H_{10}(g) + 13\ O_2(g) \rightarrow 8\ CO_2(g) + 10\ H_2O(g)$

c. $C_{12}H_{22}O_{11}(s) + 12\ O_2(g) \rightarrow 12\ CO_2(g) + 11\ H_2O(g)$

d. $2\ Fe(s) + \dfrac{3}{2} O_2(g) \rightarrow Fe_2O_3(s)$;   For whole numbers: $4\ Fe(s) + 3\ O_2(g) \rightarrow 2\ Fe_2O_3(s)$

e. $2\ FeO(s) + \dfrac{1}{2} O_2(g) \rightarrow Fe_2O_3(s)$;   For whole numbers, multiply by two.

$4\ FeO(s) + O_2(g) \rightarrow 2\ Fe_2O_3(s)$

86.   a. $16\ Cr(s) + 3\ S_8(s) \rightarrow 8\ Cr_2S_3(s)$

b. $2\ NaHCO_3(s) \rightarrow Na_2CO_3(s) + CO_2(g) + H_2O(g)$

c. $2\ KClO_3(s) \rightarrow 2\ KCl(s) + 3\ O_2(g)$

d. $2\ Eu(s) + 6\ HF(g) \rightarrow 2\ EuF_3(s) + 3\ H_2(g)$

87.   a. $SiO_2(s) + C(s) \rightarrow Si(s) + CO(g)$

Balance oxygen atoms: $SiO_2 + C \rightarrow Si + 2\ CO$

Balance carbon atoms: $SiO_2(s) + 2\ C(s) \rightarrow Si(s) + 2\ CO(g)$

b. $SiCl_4(l) + Mg(s) \rightarrow Si(s) + MgCl_2(s)$

Balance Cl atoms: $SiCl_4 + Mg \rightarrow Si + 2\ MgCl_2$

Balance Mg atoms: $SiCl_4(l) + 2\ Mg(s) \rightarrow Si(s) + 2\ MgCl_2(s)$

c. $Na_2SiF_6(s) + Na(s) \rightarrow Si(s) + NaF(s)$

Balance F atoms: $Na_2SiF_6 + Na \rightarrow Si + 6\ NaF$

Balance Na atoms: $Na_2SiF_6(s) + 4\ Na(s) \rightarrow Si(s) + 6\ NaF(s)$

88. $CaSiO_3(s) + 6\ HF(aq) \rightarrow CaF_2(aq) + SiF_4(g) + 3\ H_2O(l)$

Reaction Stoichiometry

89.   The stepwise method to solve stoichiometry problems is outlined in the text. Instead of calculating intermediate answers for each step, we will combine conversion factors into one calculation. This practice reduces round-off error and saves time.

$Fe_2O_3(s) + 2\ Al(s) \rightarrow 2\ Fe(l) + Al_2O_3(s)$

$$15.0\ \text{g Fe} \times \frac{1\ \text{mol Fe}}{55.85\ \text{g Fe}} = 0.269\ \text{mol Fe};\ \ 0.269\ \text{mol Fe} \times \frac{2\ \text{mol Al}}{2\ \text{mol Fe}} \times \frac{26.98\ \text{g Al}}{\text{mol Al}} = 7.26\ \text{g Al}$$

$$0.269\ \text{mol Fe} \times \frac{1\ \text{mol Fe}_2\text{O}_3}{2\ \text{mol Fe}} \times \frac{159.70\ \text{g Fe}_2\text{O}_3}{\text{mol Fe}_2\text{O}_3} = 21.5\ \text{g Fe}_2\text{O}_3$$

$$0.269\ \text{mol Fe} \times \frac{1\ \text{mol Al}_2\text{O}_3}{2\ \text{mol Fe}} \times \frac{101.96\ \text{g Al}_2\text{O}_3}{\text{mol Al}_2\text{O}_3} = 13.7\ \text{g Al}_2\text{O}_3$$

90. $10\ KClO_3(s) + 3\ P_4(s) \rightarrow 3\ P_4O_{10}(s) + 10\ KCl(s)$

$$52.9\ \text{g KClO}_3 \times \frac{1\ \text{mol KClO}_3}{122.55\ \text{g KClO}_3} \times \frac{3\ \text{mol P}_4\text{O}_{10}}{10\ \text{mol KClO}_3} \times \frac{283.88\ \text{g P}_4\text{O}_{10}}{\text{mol P}_4\text{O}_{10}} = 36.8\ \text{g P}_4\text{O}_{10}$$

91. $1.000 \text{ kg Al} \times \dfrac{1000 \text{ g Al}}{\text{kg Al}} \times \dfrac{1 \text{ mol Al}}{26.98 \text{ g Al}} \times \dfrac{3 \text{ mol NH}_4\text{ClO}_4}{3 \text{ mol Al}} \times \dfrac{117.49 \text{ g NH}_4\text{ClO}_4}{\text{mol NH}_4\text{ClO}_4} = 4355 \text{ g}$

92.   a. $\text{Ba(OH)}_2 \bullet 8\text{H}_2\text{O(s)} + 2 \text{ NH}_4\text{SCN(s)} \rightarrow \text{Ba(SCN)}_2\text{(s)} + 10 \text{ H}_2\text{O(l)} + 2 \text{ NH}_3\text{(g)}$

       b. $6.5 \text{ g Ba(OH)}_2 \bullet 8\text{H}_2\text{O} \times \dfrac{1 \text{ mol Ba(OH)}_2 \bullet 8\text{H}_2\text{O}}{315.4 \text{ g}} = 0.0206 \text{ mol} = 0.021 \text{ mol}$

       $0.021 \text{ mol Ba(OH)}_2 \bullet 8\text{H}_2\text{O} \times \dfrac{2 \text{ mol NH}_4\text{SCN}}{1 \text{ mol Ba(OH)}_2 \bullet 8\text{H}_2\text{O}} \times \dfrac{76.13 \text{ g NH}_4\text{SCN}}{\text{mol NH}_4\text{SCN}}$

       $= 3.2 \text{ g NH}_4\text{SCN}$

93. $1.0 \times 10^4 \text{ kg waste} \times \dfrac{3.0 \text{ g NH}_4^+}{100 \text{ kg waste}} \times \dfrac{1000 \text{ g}}{\text{kg}} \times \dfrac{1 \text{ mol NH}_4^+}{18.04 \text{ g NH}_4^+} \times \dfrac{1 \text{ mol C}_5\text{H}_7\text{O}_2\text{N}}{55 \text{ mol NH}_4^+} \times$

       $\dfrac{113.12 \text{ g C}_5\text{H}_7\text{O}_2\text{N}}{\text{mol C}_5\text{H}_7\text{O}_2\text{N}} = 3.4 \times 10^4 \text{ g tissue if all NH}_4^+ \text{ converted}$

Since only 95% of the NH_4^+ ions react:

   mass of tissue = $(0.95) (3.4 \times 10^4 \text{ g}) = 3.2 \times 10^4 \text{ g}$ or 32 kg bacterial tissue

94. $1.0 \times 10^3 \text{ g phosphorite} \times \dfrac{75 \text{ g Ca}_3(\text{PO}_4)_2}{100 \text{ g phosphorite}} \times \dfrac{1 \text{ mol Ca}_3(\text{PO}_4)_2}{310.18 \text{ g Ca}_3(\text{PO}_4)_2} \times$

       $\dfrac{1 \text{ mol P}_4}{2 \text{ mol Ca}_3(\text{PO}_4)_2} \times \dfrac{123.88 \text{ g P}_4}{\text{mol P}_4} = 150 \text{ g P}_4$

95.   a. $1.00 \times 10^2 \text{ g C}_7\text{H}_6\text{O}_3 \times \dfrac{1 \text{ mol C}_7\text{H}_6\text{O}_3}{138.12 \text{ g C}_7\text{H}_6\text{O}_3} \times \dfrac{1 \text{ mol C}_4\text{H}_6\text{O}_3}{1 \text{ mol C}_7\text{H}_6\text{O}_3} \times \dfrac{102.09 \text{ g C}_4\text{H}_6\text{O}_3}{1 \text{ mol C}_4\text{H}_6\text{O}_3}$

       $= 73.9 \text{ g C}_4\text{H}_6\text{O}_3$

       b. $1.00 \times 10^2 \text{ g C}_7\text{H}_6\text{O}_3 \times \dfrac{1 \text{ mol C}_7\text{H}_6\text{O}_3}{138.12 \text{ g C}_7\text{H}_6\text{O}_3} \times \dfrac{1 \text{ mol C}_9\text{H}_8\text{O}_4}{1 \text{ mol C}_7\text{H}_6\text{O}_3} \times \dfrac{180.15 \text{ g C}_9\text{H}_8\text{O}_4}{\text{mol C}_9\text{H}_8\text{O}_4}$

       $= 1.30 \times 10^2 \text{ g aspirin}$

96. $2 \text{ LiOH(s)} + \text{CO}_2\text{(g)} \rightarrow \text{Li}_2\text{CO}_3\text{(aq)} + \text{H}_2\text{O(l)}$

The total volume of air exhaled each minute for the 7 astronauts is $7 \times 20. = 140$ L/min.

$25,000 \text{ g LiOH} \times \dfrac{1 \text{ mol LiOH}}{23.95 \text{ g LiOH}} \times \dfrac{1 \text{ mol CO}_2}{2 \text{ mol LiOH}} \times \dfrac{44.01 \text{ g CO}_2}{\text{mol CO}_2} \times \dfrac{100 \text{ g air}}{4.0 \text{ g CO}_2} \times$

$\dfrac{1 \text{ mL air}}{0.0010 \text{ g air}} \times \dfrac{1 \text{ L}}{1000 \text{ mL}} \times \dfrac{1 \text{ min}}{140 \text{ L air}} \times \dfrac{1 \text{ hr}}{60 \text{ min}} = 68 \text{ hr} = 2.8 \text{ days}$

Limiting Reactants and Percent Yield

97.   The product formed in the reaction is NO_2; the other species present in the product represent-tation is excess O_2. Therefore, NO is the limiting reactant. In the pictures, 6 NO molecules react with 3 O_2 molecules to form 6 NO_2 molecules.

$$6\ NO(g) + 3\ O_2(g)\ \rightarrow\ 6\ NO_2(g)$$

For smallest whole numbers, the balanced reaction is:

$$2\ NO(g) + O_2(g)\ \rightarrow\ 2\ NO_2(g)$$

98.   In the following table, we have listed three rows of information. The Initial row is the number of molecules present initially, the Change row is the number of molecules that react to reach completion, and the Final row is the number of molecules present at completion. To determine the limiting reactant, let's calculate how much of one reactant is necessary to react with the other.

$$10\ \text{molecules}\ O_2\ \times\ \frac{4\ \text{molecules}\ NH_3}{5\ \text{molecules}\ O_2}\ = 8\ \text{molecules}\ NH_3\ \text{to react with all of the}\ O_2$$

Because we have 10 molecules of NH_3 and only 8 molecules of NH_3 are necessary to react with all of the O_2, O_2 is limiting.

$$4\ NH_3(g)\quad +\quad 5\ O_2(g)\quad \rightarrow\quad 4\ NO(g)\quad +\quad 6\ H_2O(g)$$

	NH_3	O_2	NO	H_2O
Initial	10 molecules	10 molecules	0	0
Change	-8 molecules	-10 molecules	$+8$ molecules	$+12$ molecules
Final	2 molecules	0	8 molecules	12 molecules

The total number of molecules present after completion = 2 molecules NH_3 + 0 molecules O_2 + 8 molecules NO + 12 molecules H_2O = 22 molecules total.

99. $1.50\ g\ BaO_2\ \times\ \dfrac{1\ mol\ BaO_2}{169.3\ g\ BaO_2} = 8.86\ \times\ 10^{-3}\ mol\ BaO_2$

$25.0\ mL\ \times\ \dfrac{0.0272\ g\ HCl}{mL}\ \times\dfrac{1\ mol\ HCl}{36.46\ g\ HCl} = 1.87 \times 10^{-2}\ mol\ HCl$

The required mole ratio from the balanced reaction is 2 mol HCl to 1 mol BaO_2. The actual ratio is:

$$\frac{1.87\times10^{-2}\ mol\ HCl}{8.86\times10^{-3}\ mol\ BaO_2} = 2.11$$

Because the actual mole ratio is larger than the required mole ratio, the denominator (BaO_2) is the limiting reagent.

$$8.86 \times 10^{-3} \text{ mol BaO}_2 \times \frac{1 \text{ mol H}_2\text{O}_2}{\text{mol BaO}_2} \times \frac{34.02 \text{ g H}_2\text{O}_2}{\text{mol H}_2\text{O}_2} = 0.301 \text{ g H}_2\text{O}_2$$

The amount of HCl reacted is:

$$8.86 \times 10^{-3} \text{ mol BaO}_2 \times \frac{2 \text{ mol HCl}}{\text{mol BaO}_2} = 1.77 \times 10^{-2} \text{ mol HCl}$$

excess mol HCl = 1.87×10^{-2} mol − 1.77×10^{-2} mol = 1.0×10^{-3} mol HCl

mass of excess HCl = 1.0×10^{-3} mol HCl $\times \dfrac{36.46 \text{ g HCl}}{\text{mol HCl}} = 3.6 \times 10^{-2}$ g HCl

100. $Ca_3(PO_4)_2 + 3 \text{ H}_2\text{SO}_4 \rightarrow 3 \text{ CaSO}_4 + 2 \text{ H}_3\text{PO}_4$

$$1.0 \times 10^3 \text{ g Ca}_3(\text{PO}_4)_2 \times \frac{1 \text{ mol Ca}_3(\text{PO}_4)_2}{310.18 \text{ g Ca}_3(\text{PO}_4)_2} = 3.2 \text{ mol Ca}_3(\text{PO}_4)_2$$

$$1.0 \times 10^3 \text{ g conc. H}_2\text{SO}_4 \times \frac{98 \text{ g H}_2\text{SO}_4}{100 \text{ g conc. H}_2\text{SO}_4} \times \frac{1 \text{ mol H}_2\text{SO}_4}{98.09 \text{ g H}_2\text{SO}_4} = 10. \text{ mol H}_2\text{SO}_4$$

The required mole ratio from the balanced equation is 3 mol H_2SO_4 to 1 mol $Ca_3(PO_4)_2$. The

actual ratio is: $\dfrac{10. \text{ mol H}_2\text{SO}_4}{3.2 \text{ mol Ca}_3(\text{PO}_4)_2} = 3.1$

This is larger than the required mole ratio, so $Ca_3(PO_4)_2$ (the denominator), is the limiting reagent.

$$3.2 \text{ mol Ca}_3(\text{PO}_4)_2 \times \frac{3 \text{ mol CaSO}_4}{\text{mol Ca}_3(\text{PO}_4)_2} \times \frac{136.15 \text{ CaSO}_4}{\text{mol CaSO}_4} = 1300 \text{ g CaSO}_4 \text{ produced}$$

$$3.2 \text{ mol Ca}_3(\text{PO}_4)_2 \times \frac{2 \text{ mol H}_3\text{PO}_4}{\text{mol Ca}_3(\text{PO}_4)_2} \times \frac{97.99 \text{ g H}_3\text{PO}_4}{\text{mol H}_3\text{PO}_4} = 630 \text{ g H}_3\text{PO}_4 \text{ produced}$$

101.   An alternative method to solve limiting reagent problems is to assume each reactant is limiting and calculate how much product could be produced from each reactant. The reactant that produces the smallest amount of product will run out first and is the limiting reagent.

$$5.00 \times 10^6 \text{ g NH}_3 \times \frac{1 \text{ mol NH}_3}{17.03 \text{ g NH}_3} \times \frac{2 \text{ mol HCN}}{2 \text{ mol NH}_3} = 2.94 \times 10^5 \text{ mol HCN}$$

$$5.00 \times 10^6 \text{ g O}_2 \times \frac{1 \text{ mol O}_2}{32.00 \text{ g O}_2} \times \frac{2 \text{ mol HCN}}{3 \text{ mol O}_2} = 1.04 \times 10^5 \text{ mol HCN}$$

$$5.00 \times 10^6 \text{ g CH}_4 \times \frac{1 \text{ mol CH}_4}{16.04 \text{ g CH}_4} \times \frac{2 \text{ mol HCN}}{2 \text{ mol CH}_4} = 3.12 \times 10^5 \text{ mol HCN}$$

O_2 is limiting because it produces the smallest amount of HCN. Although more product could be produced from NH_3 and CH_4, only enough O_2 is present to produce 1.04×10^5 mol HCN.

The mass of HCN produced is:

$$1.04 \times 10^5 \text{ mol HCN} \times \frac{27.03 \text{ g HCN}}{\text{mol HCN}} = 2.81 \times 10^6 \text{ g HCN}$$

$$5.00 \times 10^6 \text{ g O}_2 \times \frac{1 \text{ mol O}_2}{32.00 \text{ g O}_2} \times \frac{6 \text{ mol H}_2\text{O}}{3 \text{ mol O}_2} \times \frac{18.02 \text{ g H}_2\text{O}}{1 \text{ mol H}_2\text{O}} = 5.63 \times 10^6 \text{ g H}_2\text{O}$$

102.   We will use the strategy utilized in the previous problem to solve this limiting reactant problem.

If C_3H_6 is limiting:

$$15.0 \text{ g C}_3\text{H}_6 \times \frac{1 \text{ mol C}_3\text{H}_6}{42.08 \text{ g C}_3\text{H}_6} \times \frac{2 \text{ mol C}_3\text{H}_3\text{N}}{2 \text{ mol C}_3\text{H}_6} \times \frac{53.06 \text{ g C}_3\text{H}_3\text{N}}{\text{mol C}_3\text{H}_3\text{N}} = 18.9 \text{ g C}_3\text{H}_3\text{N}$$

If NH_3 is limiting:

$$5.00 \text{ g NH}_3 \times \frac{1 \text{ mol NH}_3}{17.03 \text{ g NH}_3} \times \frac{2 \text{ mol C}_3\text{H}_3\text{N}}{2 \text{ mol NH}_3} \times \frac{53.06 \text{ g C}_3\text{H}_3\text{N}}{\text{mol C}_3\text{H}_3\text{N}} = 15.6 \text{ g C}_3\text{H}_3\text{N}$$

If O_2 is limiting:

$$10.0 \text{ g O}_2 \times \frac{1 \text{ mol O}_2}{32.00 \text{ g O}_2} \times \frac{2 \text{ mol C}_3\text{H}_3\text{N}}{3 \text{ mol O}_2} \times \frac{53.06 \text{ g C}_3\text{H}_3\text{N}}{\text{mol C}_3\text{H}_3\text{N}} = 11.1 \text{ g C}_3\text{H}_3\text{N}$$

O_2 produces the smallest amount of product, thus O_2 is limiting and 11.1 g C_3H_3N can be produced.

103. $C_7H_6O_3 + C_4H_6O_3 \rightarrow C_9H_8O_4 + HC_2H_3O_2$

$$1.50 \text{ g C}_7\text{H}_6\text{O}_3 \times \frac{1 \text{ mol C}_7\text{H}_6\text{O}_3}{138.12 \text{ g C}_7\text{H}_6\text{O}_3} = 1.09 \times 10^{-2} \text{ mol C}_7\text{H}_6\text{O}_3$$

$$2.00 \text{ g C}_4\text{H}_6\text{O}_3 \times \frac{1 \text{ mol C}_4\text{H}_6\text{O}_3}{102.09 \text{ g C}_4\text{H}_6\text{O}_3} = 1.96 \times 10^{-2} \text{ mol C}_4\text{H}_6\text{O}_3$$

$C_7H_6O_3$ is the limiting reagent because the actual moles of $C_7H_6O_3$ present are below the required 1:1 mol ratio. The theoretical yield of aspirin is:

$$1.09 \times 10^{-2} \text{ mol C}_7\text{H}_6\text{O}_3 \times \frac{1 \text{ mol C}_9\text{H}_8\text{O}_4}{\text{mol C}_7\text{H}_6\text{O}_3} \times \frac{180.15 \text{ g C}_9\text{H}_8\text{O}_4}{\text{mol C}_9\text{H}_8\text{O}_4} = 1.96 \text{ g C}_9\text{H}_8\text{O}_4$$

$$\% \text{ yield} = \frac{1.50 \text{ g}}{1.96 \text{ g}} \times 100 = 76.5\%$$

104.   a. $1142 \text{ g } C_6H_5Cl \times \dfrac{1 \text{ mol } C_6H_5Cl}{112.55 \text{ g } C_6H_5Cl} = 10.1 \text{ mol } C_6H_5Cl$

$485 \text{ g } C_2HOCl_3 \times \dfrac{1 \text{ mol } C_2HOCl_3}{147.38 \text{ g } C_2HOCl_3} = 3.29 \text{ mol } C_2HOCl_3$

From the balanced equation, the required mole ratio is $\dfrac{2 \text{ mol } C_6H_5Cl}{1 \text{ mol } C_2HOCl_3} = 2$. The actual

mole ratio present is $\dfrac{10.1 \text{ mol } C_6H_5Cl}{3.29 \text{ mol } C_2HOCl_3} = 3.07$. The actual mole ratio is greater than

the required mole ratio, so the denominator of actual mole ratio (C_2HOCl_3) is limiting.

$3.29 \text{ mol } C_2HOCl_3 \times \dfrac{1 \text{ mol } C_{14}H_9Cl_5}{\text{mol } C_2HOCl_3} \times \dfrac{354.46 \text{ g } C_{14}H_9Cl_5}{\text{mol } C_{14}H_9Cl_5} = 1170 \text{ g } C_{14}H_9Cl_5 \text{ (DDT)}$

   b. C_2HOCl_3 is limiting and C_6H_5Cl is in excess.

   c. $3.29 \text{ mol } C_2HOCl_3 \times \dfrac{2 \text{ mol } C_6H_5Cl}{\text{mol } C_2HOCl_3} \times \dfrac{112.55 \text{ g } C_6H_5Cl}{\text{mol } C_6H_5Cl} = 741 \text{ g } C_6H_5Cl \text{ reacted}$

$1142 \text{ g} - 741 \text{ g} = 401 \text{ g } C_6H_5Cl \text{ in excess}$

   d. $\% \text{ yield} = \dfrac{200.0 \text{ g DDT}}{1170 \text{ g DDT}} \times 100 = 17.1\%$

105. $2.50 \text{ metric tons } Cu_3FeS_3 \times \dfrac{1000 \text{ kg}}{\text{metric ton}} \times \dfrac{1000 \text{ g}}{\text{kg}} \times \dfrac{1 \text{ mol } Cu_3FeS_3}{342.71 \text{ g}} \times \dfrac{3 \text{ mol Cu}}{1 \text{ mol } Cu_3FeS_3} \times \dfrac{63.55 \text{ g}}{\text{mol Cu}}$

$= 1.39 \times 10^6 \text{ g Cu (theoretical)}$

$1.39 \times 10^6 \text{ g Cu (theoretical)} \times \dfrac{86.3 \text{ g Cu (actual)}}{100. \text{ g Cu (theoretical)}} = 1.20 \times 10^6 \text{ g Cu} = 1.20 \times 10^3 \text{ kg Cu}$

$= 1.20 \text{ metric tons Cu (actual)}$

106. $P_4(s) + 6 F_2(g) \longrightarrow 4 PF_3(g)$; The theoretical yield of PF_3 is:

$120. \text{ g } PF_3 \text{ (actual)} \times \dfrac{100.0 \text{ g } PF_3 \text{ (theoretical)}}{78.1 \text{ g } PF_3 \text{ (actual)}} = 154 \text{ g } PF_3 \text{ (theoretical)}$

$154 \text{ g } PF_3 \times \dfrac{1 \text{ mol } PF_3}{87.97 \text{ g } PF_3} \times \dfrac{6 \text{ mol } F_2}{4 \text{ mol } PF_3} \times \dfrac{38.00 \text{ g } F_2}{\text{mol } F_2} = 99.8 \text{ g } F_2$

$99.8 \text{ g } F_2$ are needed to produce an actual PF_3 yield of 78.1%.

Additional Exercises

107.   molar mass $XeF_n = \dfrac{0.368 \text{ g } XeF_n}{9.03 \times 10^{20} \text{ molecules } XeF_n \times \dfrac{1 \text{ mol } XeF_n}{6.022 \times 10^{23} \text{ molecules}}} = 245$ g/mol

245 g $= 131.3$ g $+ n(19.00$ g$)$, $n = 5.98$; formula $= XeF_6$

108.   In one hour, the 1000. kg of wet cereal produced contains 580 kg H_2O and 420 kg of cereal. We want the final product to contain 20.% H_2O. Let $x =$ mass of H_2O in final product.

$$\frac{x}{420 + x} = 0.20, \ x = 84 + 0.20 \, x, \ x = 105 \approx 110 \text{ kg } H_2O$$

The amount of water to be removed is $580 - 110 = 470$ kg/hr.

109. $2 \, H_2(g) + O_2(g) \rightarrow 2 \, H_2O(g)$

a. $50 \text{ molecules } H_2 \times \dfrac{1 \text{ molecule } O_2}{2 \text{ molecules } H_2} = 25 \text{ molecules } O_2$

Stoichiometric mixture. Neither is limiting.

b. $100 \text{ molecules } H_2 \times \dfrac{1 \text{ molecule } O_2}{2 \text{ molecules } H_2} = 50 \text{ molecules } O_2$;

O_2 is limiting since only 40 molecules O_2 are present.

c.   From b, 50 molecules of O_2 will react completely with 100 molecules of H_2. We have 100 molecules (an excess) of O_2. So, H_2 is limiting.

d. $0.50 \text{ mol } H_2 \times \dfrac{1 \text{ mol } O_2}{2 \text{ mol } H_2} = 0.25 \text{ mol } O_2$; H_2 is limiting because 0.75 mol O_2 are present.

e. $0.80 \text{ mol } H_2 \times \dfrac{1 \text{ mol } O_2}{2 \text{ mol } H_2} = 0.40 \text{ mol } O_2$; H_2 is limiting because 0.75 mol O_2 are present.

f. $1.0 \text{ g } H_2 \times \dfrac{1 \text{ mol } H_2}{2.016 \text{ g } H_2} \times \dfrac{1 \text{ mol } O_2}{2 \text{ mol } H_2} = 0.25 \text{ mol } O_2$

Stoichiometric mixture, neither is limiting.

g. $5.00 \text{ g } H_2 \times \dfrac{1 \text{ mol } H_2}{2.016 \text{ g } H_2} \times \dfrac{1 \text{ mol } O_2}{2 \text{ mol } H_2} \times \dfrac{32.00 \text{ g } O_2}{\text{mol } O_2} = 39.7 \text{ g } O_2$

H_2 is limiting because 56.00 g O_2 are present.

110. $2 \text{ tablets} \times \dfrac{0.262 \text{ g } C_7H_5BiO_4}{\text{tablet}} \times \dfrac{1 \text{ mol } C_7H_5BiO_4}{362.11 \text{ g } C_7H_5BiO_4} \times \dfrac{1 \text{ mol Bi}}{1 \text{ mol } C_7H_5BiO_4} \times \dfrac{209.0 \text{ g Bi}}{\text{mol Bi}}$

$= 0.302$ g Bi consumed

111.   Empirical formula mass = 12.01 + 1.008 = 13.02 g/mol; Because 104.14/13.02 = 7.998 ≈ 8, the molecular formula for styrene is $(CH)_8 = C_8H_8$.

$$2.00 \text{ g } C_8H_8 \times \frac{1 \text{ mol } C_8H_8}{104.14 \text{ g } C_8H_8} \times \frac{8 \text{ mol } H}{\text{mol } C_8H_8} \times \frac{6.002 \times 10^{23} \text{ atoms } H}{\text{mol } H} = 9.25 \times 10^{22} \text{ atoms } H$$

112. $$41.98 \text{ mg } CO_2 \times \frac{12.01 \text{ mg } C}{44.01 \text{ mg } CO_2} = 11.46 \text{ mg } C; \quad \%C = \frac{11.46 \text{ mg}}{19.81 \text{ mg}} \times 100 = 57.85\% \text{ C}$$

$$6.45 \text{ mg } H_2O \times \frac{2.016 \text{ mg } H}{18.02 \text{ mg } H_2O} = 0.722 \text{ mg } H; \quad \%H = \frac{0.772 \text{ mg}}{19.81 \text{ mg}} \times 100 = 3.64\% \text{ H}$$

%O = 100.00 - (57.85 + 3.64) = 38.51% O

Out of 100.00 g terephthalic acid, there are:

$$57.85 \text{ g } C \times \frac{1 \text{ mol } C}{12.01 \text{ g } C} = 4.817 \text{ mol } C; \quad 3.64 \text{ g } H \times \frac{1 \text{ mol } H}{1.008 \text{ g } H} = 3.61 \text{ mol } H$$

$$38.51 \text{ g } O \times \frac{1 \text{ mol } O}{16.00 \text{ g } O} = 2.407 \text{ mol } O$$

$$\frac{4.817}{2.407} = 2.001; \quad \frac{3.61}{2.407} = 1.50; \quad \frac{2.407}{2.407} = 1.000$$

The C:H:O mole ratio is 2:1.5:1 or 4:3:2. Empirical formula: $C_4H_3O_2$

Mass of $C_4H_3O_2 \approx 4(12) + 3(1) + 2(16) = 83$

$$\text{Molar mass} = \frac{41.5 \text{ g}}{0.250 \text{ mol}} = 166 \text{ g/mol}; \quad \frac{166}{83} = 2; \text{ Molecular formula: } C_8H_6O_4$$

113. $$17.3 \text{ g } H \times \frac{1 \text{ mol } H}{1.008 \text{ g } H} = 17.2 \text{ mol } H; \quad 82.7 \text{ g } C \times \frac{1 \text{ mol } C}{12.01 \text{ g } C} = 6.89 \text{ mol } C$$

$$\frac{17.2}{6.89} = 2.50; \text{ The empirical formula is } C_2H_5.$$

The empirical formula mass is ~29 g, so two times the empirical formula would put the compound in the correct range of the molar mass. Molecular formula = $(C_2H_5)_2 = C_4H_{10}$

$$2.59 \times 10^{23} \text{ atoms } H \times \frac{1 \text{ molecule } C_4H_{10}}{10 \text{ atoms } H} \times \frac{1 \text{ mol } C_4H_{10}}{6.022 \times 10^{23} \text{ molecules}} = 4.30 \times 10^{-2} \text{ mol } C_4H_{10}$$

$$4.30 \times 10^{-2} \text{ mol } C_4H_{10} \times \frac{58.12 \text{ g}}{\text{mol } C_4H_{10}} = 2.50 \text{ g } C_4H_{10}$$

114.   Assuming 100.00 g E_3H_8:

$$mol\ E = 8.73\ g\ H \times \frac{1\ mol\ H}{1.008\ g\ H} \times \frac{3\ mol\ E}{8\ mol\ H} = 3.25\ mol\ E$$

$$\frac{x\ g\ E}{1\ mol\ E} = \frac{91.27\ g\ E}{3.25\ mol\ E}\ ,\ \ x = molar\ mass\ of\ E = 28.1\ g/mol;\ \ atomic\ mass\ of\ E = 28.1\ amu$$

115.   Mass of H_2O = 0.755 g $CuSO_4 \cdot xH_2O$ - 0.483 g $CuSO_4$ = 0.272 g H_2O

$$0.483\ g\ CuSO_4 \times \frac{1\ mol\ CuSO_4}{159.62\ g\ CuSO_4} = 0.00303\ mol\ CuSO_4$$

$$0.272\ g\ H_2O \times \frac{1\ mol\ H_2O}{18.02\ g\ H_2O} = 0.0151\ mol\ H_2O$$

$$\frac{0.0151\ mol\ H_2O}{0.00303\ g\ CuSO_4} = \frac{4.98\ mol\ H_2O}{1\ mol\ CuSO_4};\ \ Compound\ formula = CuSO_4 \cdot 5\ H_2O,\ \ x = 5$$

116.   a.   Only acrylonitrile contains nitrogen. If we have 100.00 g of polymer:

$$8.80\ g\ N \times \frac{1\ mol\ C_3H_3N}{14.01\ g\ N} \times \frac{53.06\ g\ C_3H_3N}{1\ mol\ C_3H_3N} = 33.3\ g\ C_3H_3N$$

$$\%\ C_3H_3N = \frac{33.3\ g\ C_3H_3N}{100.00\ g\ polymer} = 33.3\%\ C_3H_3N$$

Only butadiene in the polymer reacts with Br_2:

$$0.605\ g\ Br_2 \times \frac{1\ mol\ Br_2}{159.80\ g\ Br_2} \times \frac{1\ mol\ C_4H_6}{mol\ Br_2} \times \frac{54.09\ g\ C_4H_6}{mol\ C_4H_6} = 0.205\ g\ C_4H_6$$

$$\%\ C_4H_6 = \frac{0.205\ g}{1.20\ g} \times 100 = 17.1\%\ C_4H_6$$

b.   If we have 100.0 g of polymer:

$$33.3\ g\ C_3H_3N \times \frac{1\ mol\ C_3H_3N}{53.06\ g} = 0.628\ mol\ C_3H_3N$$

$$17.1\ g\ C_4H_6 \times \frac{1\ mol\ C_4H_6}{54.09\ g\ C_4H_6} = 0.316\ mol\ C_4H_6$$

$$49.6\ g\ C_8H_8 \times \frac{1\ mol\ C_8H_8}{104.14\ g\ C_8H_8} = 0.476\ mol\ C_8H_8$$

Dividing by 0.316: $\dfrac{0.628}{0.316} = 1.99;\ \ \dfrac{0.316}{0.316} = 1.00;\ \ \dfrac{0.476}{0.316} = 1.51$

This is close to a mol ratio of 4:2:3. Thus, there are 4 acrylonitrile to 2 butadiene to 3 styrene molecules in the polymer or $(A_4B_2S_3)_n$.

117. $1.20 \text{ g CO}_2 \times \dfrac{1 \text{ mol CO}_2}{44.01 \text{ g}} \times \dfrac{1 \text{ mol C}}{\text{mol CO}_2} \times \dfrac{1 \text{ mol C}_{24}\text{H}_{30}\text{N}_3\text{O}}{24 \text{ mol C}} \times \dfrac{376.51 \text{ g}}{\text{mol C}_{24}\text{H}_{30}\text{N}_3\text{O}}$

$= 0.428 \text{ g C}_{24}\text{H}_{30}\text{N}_3\text{O}$

$\dfrac{0.428 \text{ g C}_{24}\text{H}_{30}\text{N}_3\text{O}}{1.00 \text{ g sample}} \times 100 = 42.8\% \text{ C}_{24}\text{H}_{30}\text{N}_3\text{O}$

118.   a. $CH_4(g) + 4 \text{ S}(s) \rightarrow CS_2(l) + 2 \text{ H}_2S(g)$ or $2 \text{ CH}_4(g) + S_8(s) \rightarrow 2 \text{ CS}_2(l) + 4 \text{ H}_2S(g)$

b. $120. \text{ g CH}_4 \times \dfrac{1 \text{ mol CH}_4}{16.04 \text{ g CH}_4} = 7.48 \text{ mol CH}_4$; $120. \text{ g S} \times \dfrac{1 \text{ mol S}}{32.07 \text{ g S}} = 3.74 \text{ mol S}$

The required S to CH_4 mole ratio is 4:1. The actual S to CH_4 mol ratio is:

$\dfrac{3.74 \text{ mol S}}{7.48 \text{ mol CH}_4} = 0.500$

This is well below the required ratio so sulfur is the limiting reagent.

The theoretical yield of CS_2 is: $3.74 \text{ mol S} \times \dfrac{1 \text{ mol CS}_2}{4 \text{ mol S}} \times \dfrac{76.15 \text{ g CS}_2}{\text{mol CS}_2} = 71.2 \text{ g CS}_2$

The same amount of CS_2 would be produced using the balanced equation with S_8.

119. $126 \text{ g B}_5\text{H}_9 \times \dfrac{1 \text{ mol}}{63.12 \text{ g}} = 2.00 \text{ mol B}_5\text{H}_9$; $192 \text{ g O}_2 \times \dfrac{1 \text{ mol}}{32.00 \text{ g}} = 6.00 \text{ mol O}_2$

$\dfrac{\text{mol O}_2}{\text{mol B}_5\text{H}_9} \text{ (actual)} = \dfrac{6.00}{2.00} = 3.00$

The required mol O_2 to mol B_5H_9 ratio is 12/2 = 6. The actual mole ratio is less than the required mole ratio, thus the numerator (O_2) is limiting.

$6.00 \text{ mol O}_2 \times \dfrac{9 \text{ mol H}_2\text{O}}{12 \text{ mol O}_2} \times \dfrac{18.02 \text{ g H}_2\text{O}}{\text{mol H}_2\text{O}} = 81.1 \text{ g H}_2\text{O}$

120. $25.0 \text{ g Ag}_2\text{O} \times \dfrac{1 \text{ mol}}{231.8 \text{ g}} = 0.108 \text{ mol Ag}_2\text{O}$

$50.0 \text{ g C}_{10}\text{H}_{10}\text{N}_4\text{SO}_2 \times \dfrac{1 \text{ mol}}{250.29 \text{ g}} = 0.200 \text{ mol C}_{10}\text{H}_{10}\text{N}_4\text{SO}_2$

$\dfrac{\text{mol C}_{10}\text{H}_{10}\text{N}_4\text{SO}_2}{\text{mol Ag}_2\text{O}} \text{ (actual)} = \dfrac{0.200}{0.108} = 1.85$

The actual mole ratio is less than the required mole ratio (2), so $C_{10}H_{10}N_4SO_2$ is limiting.

$$0.200 \text{ mol } C_{10}H_{10}N_4SO_2 \times \frac{2 \text{ mol } AgC_{10}H_9N_4SO_2}{2 \text{ mol } C_{10}H_{10}N_4SO_2} \times \frac{357.18 \text{ g}}{\text{mol } AgC_{10}H_9N_4SO_2}$$

$$= 71.4 \text{ g } AgC_{10}H_9N_4SO_2 \text{ produced}$$

121. $453 \text{ g Fe} \times \dfrac{1 \text{ mol Fe}}{55.85 \text{ g Fe}} \times \dfrac{1 \text{ mol } Fe_2O_3}{2 \text{ mol Fe}} \times \dfrac{159.70 \text{ g } Fe_2O_3}{\text{mol } Fe_2O_3} = 648 \text{ g } Fe_2O_3$

mass $\% Fe_2O_3 = \dfrac{648 \text{ g } Fe_2O_3}{752 \text{ g ore}} \times 100 = 86.2\%$

122.   a.   Mass of Zn in alloy = $0.0985 \text{ g } ZnCl_2 \times \dfrac{65.38 \text{ g Zn}}{136.28 \text{ g } ZnCl_2} = 0.0473 \text{ g Zn}$

$\%Zn = \dfrac{0.0473 \text{ g Zn}}{0.5065 \text{ g brass}} \times 100 = 9.34\% \text{ Zn}; \quad \%Cu = 100.00 - 9.34 = 90.66\% \text{ Cu}$

b.   The Cu remains unreacted. After filtering, washing, and drying, the mass of the unreacted copper could be measured.

123.   Assuming one mol of vitamin A (286.4 g vitamin A):

$$\text{mol C} = 286.4 \text{ g vitamin A} \times \frac{0.8386 \text{ g C}}{\text{g vitamin A}} \times \frac{1 \text{ mol C}}{12.01 \text{ g C}} = 20.00 \text{ mol C}$$

$$\text{mol H} = 286.4 \text{ g vitamin A} \times \frac{0.1056 \text{ g H}}{\text{g vitamin A}} \times \frac{1 \text{ mol H}}{1.008 \text{ g H}} = 30.00 \text{ mol H}$$

Since one mol of vitamin A contains 20 mol C and 30 mol H, the molecular formula of vitamin A is $C_{20}H_{30}E$. To determine E, let's calculate the molar mass of E.

$286.4 \text{ g} = 20(12.01) + 30(1.008) + \text{molar mass E}, \quad \text{molar mass E} = 16.0 \text{ g/mol}$

From the periodic table, E = oxygen and the molecular formula of vitamin A is $C_{20}H_{30}O$.

Challenge Problems

124. $\dfrac{\text{atoms } ^{85}Rb}{\text{atoms } ^{87}Rb} = 2.591$; Assuming 100 atoms, let x = number of ^{85}Rb atoms and $100 - x$ = number of ^{87}Rb atoms.

$\dfrac{x}{100 - x} = 2.591, \quad x = 259.1 - 2.591x, \quad x = \dfrac{259.1}{3.591} = 72.15\% \ ^{85}Rb$

$0.7215 (84.9117) + 0.2785 (A) = 85.4678, \quad A = \dfrac{85.4678 - 61.26}{0.2785} = 86.92 \text{ amu}$

$$= \text{atomic mass of } ^{87}Rb$$

125.   First, we will determine composition in mass percent. We assume all the carbon in the 0.213 g CO_2 came from 0.157 g of the compound and that all the hydrogen in the 0.0310 g H_2O came from the 0.157 g of the compound.

$$0.213 \text{ g } CO_2 \times \frac{12.01 \text{ g C}}{44.01 \text{ g } CO_2} = 0.0581 \text{ g C}; \quad \%C = \frac{0.0581 \text{ g C}}{0.1571 \text{ g compound}} \times 100 = 37.0\% \text{ C}$$

$$0.0310 \text{ g } H_2O \times \frac{2.016 \text{ g H}}{18.02 \text{ g } H_2O} = 3.47 \times 10^{-3} \text{ g H}; \quad \%H = \frac{3.47 \times 10^{-3} \text{ g}}{0.157 \text{ g}} = 2.21\% \text{ H}$$

We get %N from the second experiment:

$$0.0230 \text{ g } NH_3 \times \frac{14.01 \text{ g N}}{17.03 \text{ g } NH_3} = 1.89 \times 10^{-2} \text{ g N}$$

$$\%N = \frac{1.89 \times 10^{-2} \text{ g}}{0.103 \text{ g}} \times 100 = 18.3\% \text{ N}$$

The mass percent of oxygen is obtained by difference:

$$\%O = 100.00 - (37.0 + 2.21 + 18.3) = 42.5\%$$

So out of 100.00 g of compound, there are:

$$37.0 \text{ g C} \times \frac{1 \text{ mol C}}{12.01 \text{ g C}} = 3.08 \text{ mol C}; \quad 2.21 \text{ g H} \times \frac{1 \text{ mol H}}{1.008 \text{ g H}} = 2.19 \text{ mol H}$$

$$18.3 \text{ g N} \times \frac{1 \text{ mol N}}{14.01 \text{ g N}} = 1.31 \text{ mol N}; \quad 42.5 \text{ g O} \times \frac{1 \text{ mol O}}{16.00 \text{ g O}} = 2.66 \text{ mol O}$$

The last, and often the hardest part, is to find simple whole number ratios. Divide all mole values by the smallest number:

$$\frac{3.08}{1.31} = 2.35; \quad \frac{2.19}{1.31} = 1.67; \quad \frac{1.31}{1.31} = 1.00; \quad \frac{2.66}{1.31} = 2.03$$

Multiplying all these ratios by 3 gives an empirical formula of $C_7H_5N_3O_6$.

126. $$1.0 \times 10^6 \text{ kg } HNO_3 \times \frac{1000 \text{ g } HNO_3}{\text{kg } HNO_3} \times \frac{1 \text{ mol } HNO_3}{63.02 \text{ g } HNO_3} = 1.6 \times 10^7 \text{ mol } HNO_3$$

We need to get the relationship between moles of HNO_3 and moles of NH_3. We have to use all 3 equations.

$$\frac{2 \text{ mol } HNO_3}{3 \text{ mol } NO_2} \times \frac{2 \text{ mol } NO_2}{2 \text{ mol } NO} \times \frac{4 \text{ mol } NO}{4 \text{ mol } NH_3} = \frac{16 \text{ mol } HNO_3}{24 \text{ mol } NH_3}$$

Thus, we can produce 16 mol HNO_3 for every 24 mol NH_3 we begin with:

$$1.6 \times 10^7 \text{ mol HNO}_3 \times \frac{24 \text{ mol NH}_3}{16 \text{ mol HNO}_3} \times \frac{17.03 \text{ g NH}_3}{\text{mol NH}_3} = 4.1 \times 10^8 \text{ g or } 4.1 \times 10^5 \text{ kg}$$

This is an oversimplified answer. In practice, the NO produced in the third step is recycled back continuously into the process in the second step. If this is taken into consideration, then the conversion factor between mol NH_3 and mol HNO_3 turns out to be 1:1, i.e., 1 mol of NH_3 produces 1 mol of HNO_3. Taking into consideration that NO is recycled back gives an answer of 2.7×10^5 kg NH_3 reacted.

127.   The two relevant equations are:

$$4 \text{ FeO(s)} + O_2(g) \rightarrow 2 \text{ Fe}_2O_3(s) \text{ and } 4 \text{ Fe}_3O_4(s) + O_2(g) \rightarrow 6 \text{ Fe}_2O_3(s)$$

Let x = mass FeO, so 5.430 - x = mass Fe_3O_4. The mol of each are:

$$\text{moles FeO} = \frac{x}{71.85} \text{ and moles Fe}_3O_4 = \frac{5.430 - x}{231.55}$$

Thus, moles Fe_2O_3 is:

$$\left(\frac{x}{71.85} \times \frac{2 \text{ moles Fe}_2O_3}{4 \text{ moles FeO}} \right) + \left(\frac{5.430 - x}{231.35} \times \frac{6 \text{ moles Fe}_2O_3}{4 \text{ moles Fe}_3O_4} \right)$$

and mass Fe_2O_3 is:

$$159.70 \text{ g/mol} \left[\left(\frac{x}{71.85} \times \frac{2}{4} \right) + \left(\frac{5.430 - x}{231.35} \times \frac{6}{4} \right) \right] = 5.779 \text{ g}$$

Solving: x = 2.10 g; Thus, the mixture is $\dfrac{2.10 \text{ g}}{5.430 \text{ g}} \times 100 = 38.7\%$ FeO by mass.

128. $2 \text{ C}_2H_6(g) + 7 O_2(g) \rightarrow 4 \text{ CO}_2(g) + 6 \text{ H}_2O(l); \text{ C}_3H_8(g) + 5 O_2(g) \rightarrow 3 \text{ CO}_2(g) + 4 \text{ H}_2O(l)$
    30.07 g/mol   44.09 g/mol

Let x = mass C_2H_6, so 9.780 − x = mass C_3H_8. Use the balanced reaction to set up an equation for the mol of O_2 required.

$$\frac{x}{30.07} \times \frac{7}{2} + \frac{9.780 - x}{44.09} \times \frac{5}{1} = 1.120 \text{ mol O}_2$$

Solving: x = 3.7 g C_2H_6 ; $\dfrac{3.7 \text{ g}}{9.780 \text{ g}} \times 100 = 38\%$ C_2H_6 by mass

129.   The two relevant equations are:

$$\text{Zn(s)} + 2 \text{ HCl(aq)} \rightarrow \text{ZnCl}_2(aq) + H_2(g) \text{ and Mg(s)} + 2 \text{ HCl(aq)} \rightarrow \text{MgCl}_2(aq) + H_2(g)$$

Let x = mass Mg, so 10.00 − x = mass Zn.

From the balanced equations, moles H_2 = moles Zn + moles Mg.

$$\text{mol } H_2 = 0.5171 \text{ g } H_2 \times \frac{1 \text{ mol } H_2}{2.016 \text{ g } H_2} = 0.2565 \text{ mol } H_2$$

Thus, $0.2565 = \dfrac{x}{24.31} + \dfrac{10.00 - x}{65.38}$; Solving, $x = 4.008$ g Mg.

$$\frac{4.008 \text{ g}}{10.00 \text{ g}} \times 100 = 40.08\% \text{ Mg}$$

130. Let M = unknown element

$$\text{mass }\%M = \frac{\text{mass M}}{\text{total mass compound}} \times 100 = \frac{2.077}{3.708} \times 100 = 56.01\% \text{ M}$$

$100.00 - 56.01 = 43.99\%$ O

Assuming 100.00 g compound:

$$43.99 \text{ g O} \times \frac{1 \text{ mol O}}{16.00 \text{ g O}} = 2.749 \text{ mol O}$$

If MO is the formula of the oxide, then M has a molar mass = $\dfrac{56.01 \text{ g M}}{2.749 \text{ mol M}} = 20.37$ g/mol. This is too low for the molar mass. We must have fewer moles of M than mol O present in the formula. Some possibilities are MO_2, M_2O_3, MO_3, etc. It is a guessing game as to which to try. Let's assume an MO_2 formula. Then the molar mass of M is:

$$\frac{56.01 \text{ g M}}{2.749 \text{ mol O} \times \dfrac{1 \text{ mol M}}{2 \text{ mol O}}} = 40.75 \text{ g/mol}$$

This is close to calcium but calcium forms an oxide having the CaO formula, not CaO_2.

If MO_3 is assumed to be the formula then the molar mass of M calculates to be 61.12 g/mol which is too large. Therefore, the mol O to mol M ratio must be between 2 and 3. Some reasonable possibilities are 2.25, 2.33, 2.5, 2.67, 2.75 (these are reasonable since they will lead to whole number formulas). Trying a mol O to mol M ratio of 2.5 to 1 gives a molar mass of:

$$\frac{56.01 \text{ g M}}{2.749 \text{ mol O} \times \dfrac{1 \text{ mol M}}{2.5 \text{ mol O}}} = 50.94 \text{ g/mol}.$$

This is the molar mass of vanadium and V_2O_5 is a reasonable formula for an oxide of vanadium. The other choices for the O:M mol ratios between 2 and 3 do not give as reasonable results. Therefore, M is vanadium and the formula is V_2O_5.

131.   We know water is a product, so one of the elements in the compound is hydrogen.

$$X_aH_b + O_2 \rightarrow H_2O + ?$$

To balance the H atoms, the mole ratio between $X_aH_b : H_2O = \dfrac{2}{b}$.

$$\text{mol compound} = \frac{1.39\,g}{62.09\,g/mol} = 0.0224\,mol; \quad \text{mol } H_2O = \frac{1.21\,g}{18.02\,g/mol} = 0.0671\,mol$$

$$\frac{2}{b} = \frac{0.0224}{0.0671} \text{ and } b = 6; \quad X_aH_6 \text{ has a molar mass of 62.09 g/mol.}$$

$$62.09 = a \times \text{molar mass of } X + 6 \times 1.008, \quad a \times \text{molar mass of } X = 56.04$$

Some possible identities for X could be Fe (a = 1), Si (a = 2), N (a = 4), Li (a = 8). N fits the data best so N_4H_6 is the formula.

132.   The balanced equation is: $2\,Sc(s) + 2x\,HCl(aq) \rightarrow 2\,ScCl_x(aq) + x\,H_2(g)$

The mol ratio of $Sc : H_2 = \dfrac{2}{x}$.

$$\text{moles Sc} = 2.25\,g\,Sc \times \frac{1\,mol\,Sc}{44.96\,g\,Sc} = 0.0500\,mol\,Sc$$

$$\text{mol } H_2 = 0.1502\,g\,H_2 \times \frac{1\,mol\,H_2}{2.016\,g\,H_2} = 0.07450\,mol\,H_2$$

$$\frac{2}{x} = \frac{0.0500}{0.07450}, \quad x = 3; \quad \text{The formula is } ScCl_3.$$

133.   Total mass of copper used:

$$10{,}000\,\text{boards} \times \frac{(8.0\,cm \times 16.0\,cm \times 0.060\,cm)}{\text{board}} \times \frac{8.96\,g}{cm^3} = 6.9 \times 10^5\,g\,Cu$$

Amount of Cu removed = $0.80 \times 6.9 \times 10^5\,g = 5.5 \times 10^5\,g\,Cu$

$$5.5 \times 10^5\,g\,Cu \times \frac{1\,mol\,Cu}{63.55\,g\,Cu} \times \frac{1\,mol\,Cu(NH_3)_4Cl_2}{mol\,Cu} \times \frac{202.59\,g\,Cu(NH_3)_4Cl_2}{mol\,Cu(NH_3)_4Cl_2}$$

$$= 1.8 \times 10^6\,g\,Cu(NH_3)_4Cl_2$$

$$5.5 \times 10^5\,g\,Cu \times \frac{1\,mol\,Cu}{63.55\,g\,Cu} \times \frac{4\,mol\,NH_3}{mol\,Cu} \times \frac{17.03\,g\,NH_3}{mol\,NH_3} = 5.9 \times 10^5\,g\,NH_3$$

134.   a. From the reaction stoichiometry we would expect to produce 4 mol of acetaminophen for every 4 mol of $C_6H_5O_3N$ reacted. The actual yield is 3 moles of acetaminophen compared to a theoretical yield of 4 moles of acetaminophen. Solving for percent yield by mass (where M = molar mass acetaminophen):

$$\% \text{ yield} = \frac{3 \text{ mol} \times M}{4 \text{ mol} \times M} \times 100 = 75\%$$

b. The product of the percent yields of the individual steps must equal the overall yield, 75%.

$(0.87) (0.98) (x) = 0.75, \; x = 0.88;$ Step III has a % yield = 88%.

135. 10.00 g XCl_2 + excess $Cl_2 \rightarrow$ 12.55 g XCl_4; 2.55 g Cl reacted with XCl_2 to form XCl_4. XCl_4 contains 2.55 g Cl and 10.00 g XCl_2. From mol ratios, 10.00 g XCl_2 must also contain 2.55 g Cl; mass X in XCl_2 = 10.00 – 2.55 = 7.45 g X.

$$2.55 \text{ g Cl} \times \frac{1 \text{ mol Cl}}{35.45 \text{ g Cl}} \times \frac{1 \text{ mol } XCl_2}{2 \text{ mol Cl}} \times \frac{1 \text{ mol X}}{\text{mol } XCl_2} = 3.60 \times 10^{-2} \text{ mol X}$$

So, 3.60×10^{-2} mol X has a mass equal to 7.45 g X. The molar mass of X is:

$$\frac{7.45 \text{ g X}}{3.60 \times 10^{-2} \text{ mol X}} = 207 \text{ g/mol X}; \; \text{Atomic mass} = 207 \text{ amu so X is Pb.}$$

136. 4.000 g $M_2S_3 \rightarrow$ 3.723 g MO_2

There must be twice as many mol of MO_2 as mol of M_2S_3 in order to balance M in the reaction. Setting up an equation for 2 mol MO_2 = mol M_2S_3 where A = molar mass M:

$$2 \left(\frac{4.000 \text{ g}}{2A + 3(32.07)} \right) = \frac{3.723 \text{ g}}{A + 2(16.00)}, \; \frac{8.000}{2A + 96.21} = \frac{3.723}{A + 32.00}$$

8.000 A + 256.0 = 7.446 A + 358.2, 0.554 A = 102.2, A = 184 g/mol; atomic mass = 184 amu

137. Consider the case of aluminum plus oxygen. Aluminum forms Al^{3+} ions; oxygen forms O^{2-} anions. The simplest compound of the two elements is Al_2O_3. Similarly, we would expect the formula of any group 6A element with Al to be Al_2X_3. Assuming this, out of 100.00 g of compound there are 18.56 g Al and 81.44 g of the unknown element, X. Let's use this information to determine the molar mass of X which will allow us to identify X from the periodic table.

$$18.56 \text{ g Al} \times \frac{1 \text{ mol Al}}{26.98 \text{ g Al}} \times \frac{3 \text{ mol X}}{2 \text{ mol Al}} = 1.032 \text{ mol X}$$

81.44 g of X must contain 1.032 mol of X.

$$\text{The molar mass of X} = \frac{81.44 \text{ g X}}{1.032 \text{ mol X}} = 78.91 \text{ g/mol X.}$$

From the periodic table, the unknown element is selenium and the formula is Al_2Se_3.

138. $NaCl(aq) + Ag^+(aq) \rightarrow AgCl(s);$ $KCl(aq) + Ag^+(aq) \rightarrow AgCl(s)$

$$8.5904 \text{ g AgCl} \times \frac{1 \text{ mol AgCl}}{143.4 \text{ g AgCl}} \times \frac{1 \text{ mol Cl}^-}{1 \text{ mol AgCl}} = 5.991 \times 10^{-2} \text{ mol Cl}^-$$

The molar masses of NaCl and KCl are 58.44 and 74.55 g/mol, respectively.

Let x = mass NaCl and y = mass KCl:

$$x + y = 4.000 \text{ g}; \quad \frac{x}{58.44} + \frac{y}{74.55} = 5.991 \times 10^{-2} \text{ total mol Cl}^- \text{ or } 1.276\, x + y = 4.466$$

Solving using simultaneous equations:

$$\begin{aligned} 1.276\ x + y &= 4.466 \\ -x - y &= -4.000 \\ \hline 0.276\ x &= 0.466, \quad x = 1.69 \text{ g NaCl and } y = 2.31 \text{ g KCl} \end{aligned}$$

$$\%NaCl = \frac{1.69 \text{ g}}{4.00 \text{ g}} \times 100 = 42.3\% \text{ NaCl}; \quad \%KCl = 57.7\%$$

139.   The balanced equations are:

$$4 NH_3(g) + 5 O_2(g) \rightarrow 4 NO(g) + 6 H_2O(g) \text{ and } 4 NH_3(g) + 7 O_2(g) \rightarrow 4 NO_2(g)$$
$$+ 6 H_2O(g)$$

Let $4x$ = number of mol of NO formed, and let $4y$ = number of mol of NO_2 formed. Then:

$$4x\ NH_3 + 5x\ O_2 \rightarrow 4x\ NO + 6x\ H_2O \text{ and } 4y\ NH_3 + 7y\ O_2 \rightarrow 4y\ NO_2 + 6y\ H_2O$$

All the NH_3 reacted, so $4x + 4y = 2.00$. $10.00 - 6.75 = 3.25$ mol O_2 reacted, so $5x + 7y = 3.25$.

Solving by the method of simultaneous equations:

$$\begin{aligned} 20\ x + 28\ y &= 13.0 \\ -20\ x - 20\ y &= -10.0 \\ \hline 8\ y &= 3.0, \quad y = 0.38; \quad 4x + 4 \times 0.38 = 2.00, \quad x = 0.12 \end{aligned}$$

mol NO = $4x = 4 \times 0.12 = 0.48$ mol NO formed

140. $C_xH_yO_z + \text{oxygen} \rightarrow x\ CO_2 + y/2\ H_2O$

$$\text{mass \%C in aspirin} = \frac{2.20 \text{ g } CO_2 \times \dfrac{1 \text{ mol } CO_2}{44.01 \text{ g } CO_2} \times \dfrac{1 \text{ mol C}}{\text{mol } CO_2} \times \dfrac{12.01 \text{ g C}}{\text{mol C}}}{1.00 \text{ g aspirin}} = 60.0\% \text{ C}$$

$$\text{mass \%H in aspirin} = \frac{0.400 \text{ g } H_2O \times \dfrac{1 \text{ mol } H_2O}{18.02 \text{ g } H_2O} \times \dfrac{2 \text{ mol H}}{\text{mol } H_2O} \times \dfrac{1.008 \text{ g H}}{\text{mol H}}}{1.00 \text{ g aspirin}} = 4.48\% \text{ H}$$

mass %O = 100.00 − (60.0 + 4.48) = 35.5% O

Assuming 100.00 g aspirin:

$$60.0 \text{ g C} \times \frac{1 \text{ mol C}}{12.01 \text{ g C}} = 5.00 \text{ mol C}; \quad 4.48 \text{ g H} \times \frac{1 \text{ mol H}}{1.008 \text{ g H}} = 4.44 \text{ mol H}$$

$$35.5 \text{ g O} \times \frac{1 \text{ mol O}}{16.00 \text{ g O}} = 2.22 \text{ mol O}$$

Dividing by the smallest number: $\frac{5.00}{2.22} = 2.25; \quad \frac{4.44}{2.22} = 2.00$

Empirical formula = $(C_{2.25} H_{2.00}O)_4 = C_9H_8O_4$

Empirical mass ≈ 9(12) + 8(1) + 4(16) = 180 g/mol; This is in the 170 − 190 g/mol range so the molecular formula is also $C_9H_8O_4$.

Balance the aspirin synthesis reaction to determine the formula for salicylic acid.

$C_aH_bO_c + C_4H_6O_3 \rightarrow C_9H_8O_4 + C_2H_4O_2$, $C_aH_bO_c$ = salicylic acid = $C_7H_6O_3$

Integrative Problems

141. a. $1.05 \times 10^{-20} \text{ g Fe} \times \frac{1 \text{ mol Fe}}{55.85 \text{ g Fe}} \times \frac{6.022 \times 10^{23} \text{ atoms Fe}}{\text{mol Fe}} = 113 \text{ atoms Fe}$

      b. The total number of platinum atoms is 14 × 20 = 280 atoms (exact number). The mass of these atoms is:

$$280 \text{ atoms Pt} \times \frac{1 \text{ mol Pt}}{6.022 \times 10^{23} \text{ atoms Pt}} \times \frac{195.1 \text{ g Pt}}{\text{mol Pt}} = 9.071 \times 10^{-20} \text{ g Pt}$$

      c. $9.071 \times 10^{-20} \text{ g Ru} \times \frac{1 \text{ mol Ru}}{101.1 \text{ g Ru}} \times \frac{6.022 \times 10^{23} \text{ atoms Ru}}{\text{mol Ru}} = 540.3 = 540 \text{ atoms Ru}$

142. Assuming 100.00 g of tetrodotoxin:

$$41.38 \text{ g C} \times \frac{1 \text{ mol C}}{12.01 \text{ g C}} = 3.445 \text{ mol C}; \quad 13.16 \text{ g N} \times \frac{1 \text{ mol N}}{14.01 \text{ g N}} = 0.9393 \text{ mol N}$$

$$5.37 \text{ g H} \times \frac{1 \text{ mol H}}{1.008 \text{ g H}} = 5.33 \text{ mol H}; \quad 40.09 \text{ g O} \times \frac{1 \text{ mol O}}{16.00 \text{ g O}} = 2.506 \text{ mol O}$$

Divide by the smallest number:

$$\frac{3.445}{0.9393} = 3.668; \quad \frac{5.33}{0.9393} = 5.67; \quad \frac{2.506}{0.9393} = 2.668$$

To get whole numbers for each element, multiply through by 3.

empirical formula = $(C_{3.668}H_{5.67}NO_{2.668})_3$ = $C_{11}H_{17}N_3O_8$

The mass of the empirical formula is 319.3 g/mol.

$$\text{molar mass tetrodotoxin} = \frac{1.59 \times 10^{-21} \text{ g}}{3 \text{ molecules} \times \dfrac{1 \text{ mol}}{6.022 \times 10^{23} \text{ molecules}}} = 319 \text{ g/mol}$$

Because the empirical mass and molar mass are the same, the molecular formula is the same as the empirical formula, $C_{11}H_{17}N_3O_8$.

$$165 \text{ lb} \times \frac{1 \text{ kg}}{2.2046 \text{ lb}} \times \frac{10. \, \mu\text{g}}{\text{kg}} \times \frac{1 \times 10^{-6} \text{ g}}{\mu\text{g}} \times \frac{1 \text{ mol}}{319.3 \text{ g}} \times \frac{6.022 \times 10^{23} \text{ molecules}}{1 \text{ mol}}$$

$$= 1.4 \times 10^{18} \text{ molecules tetrodotoxin is the } LD_{50} \text{ dosage}$$

143. $$\text{molar mass X}_2 = \frac{0.105 \text{ g}}{8.92 \times 10^{20} \text{ molecules} \times \dfrac{1 \text{ mol}}{6.022 \times 10^{23} \text{ molecules}}} = 70.9 \text{ g/mol}$$

The mass of X = 1/2(70.9 g/mol) = 35.5 g/mol. This is the element chlorine.

Assuming 100.00 g of MX_3 compound:

$$54.47 \text{ g Cl} \times \frac{1 \text{ mol}}{35.45 \text{ g}} = 1.537 \text{ mol Cl}$$

$$1.537 \text{ mol Cl} \times \frac{1 \text{ mol M}}{3 \text{ mol Cl}} = 0.5123 \text{ mol M}$$

$$\text{molar mass M} = \frac{45.53 \text{ g M}}{0.5123 \text{ mol M}} = 88.87 \text{ g/mol M}$$

M is the element yttrium (Y) and the name of YCl_3 is yttrium(III) chloride.

The balanced equation is: $2 \text{ Y} + 3 \text{ Cl}_2 \rightarrow 2 \text{ YCl}_3$

Assuming Cl_2 is limiting:

$$1.00 \text{ g Cl}_2 \times \frac{1 \text{ mol Cl}_2}{70.90 \text{ g Cl}_2} \times \frac{2 \text{ mol YCl}_3}{3 \text{ mol Cl}_2} \times \frac{195.26 \text{ g YCl}_3}{1 \text{ mol YCl}_3} = 1.84 \text{ g YCl}_3$$

Assuming Y is limiting:

$$1.00 \text{ g Y} \times \frac{1 \text{ mol Y}}{88.91 \text{ g Y}} \times \frac{2 \text{ mol YCl}_3}{2 \text{ mol Y}} \times \frac{195.26 \text{ g YCl}_3}{1 \text{ mol YCl}_3} = 2.20 \text{ g YCl}_3$$

Cl_2 is the limiting reagent and the theoretical yield is 1.84 g YCl_3.

144. $2 \text{ As} + 4 \text{ AsI}_3 \rightarrow 3 \text{ As}_2\text{I}_4$

Volume of As cube = $(3.00 \text{ cm})^3 = 27.0 \text{ cm}^3$

$$27.0 \text{ cm}^3 \times \frac{5.72 \text{ g As}}{\text{cm}^3} \times \frac{1 \text{ mol As}}{74.92 \text{ g As}} = 2.06 \text{ mol As}$$

$$1.01 \times 10^{24} \text{ molecules AsI}_3 \times \frac{1 \text{ mol AsI}_3}{6.022 \times 10^{23} \text{ molecules AsI}_3} = 1.68 \text{ mol AsI}_3$$

From the balanced equation, we need twice the number of moles of AsI_3 as As to react. Because the mole of AsI_3 present are less than the mole of As present, AsI_3 is limiting.

$$1.68 \text{ mol AsI}_3 \times \frac{3 \text{ mol As}_2\text{I}_4}{4 \text{ mol AsI}_3} \times \frac{657.44 \text{ g As}_2\text{I}_4}{2 \text{ mol As}_2\text{I}_4} = 828 \text{ g As}_2\text{I}_4$$

$$0.756 = \frac{\text{actual yield}}{828 \text{ g}}, \text{ actual yield} = 0.756 \times 828 \text{ g} = 626 \text{ g As}_2\text{I}_4$$

Marathon Problems

145.   To solve the limiting reagent problem, we must determine the formulas of all the compounds so we can get a balanced reaction.

a.   40 million trillion = $40 \times 10^6 \times 10^{12} = 4.000 \times 10^{19}$ (assuming 4 S.F.)

$$4.000 \times 10^{19} \text{ molecules A} \times \frac{1 \text{ mol A}}{6.0221 \times 10^{23} \text{ molecules A}} = 6.642 \times 10^{-5} \text{ mol A}$$

$$\text{Molar mass of A} = \frac{4.26 \times 10^{-3} \text{ g A}}{6.642 \times 10^{-5} \text{ mol A}} = 64.1 \text{ g/mol}$$

Mass of carbon in one mol of A is:

$$64.1 \text{ g A} \times \frac{37.5 \text{ g C}}{100.0 \text{ g A}} = 24.0 \text{ g carbon} = 2 \text{ mol carbon in substance A}$$

The remainder of the molar mass (64.1 g - 24.0 g = 40.1 g) is due to the alkaline earth metal. From the periodic table, calcium has a molar mass of 40.08 g/mol. The formula of substance A is CaC_2.

b. 5.36 g H + 42.5 g O = 47.9 g; Substance B only contains H and O. Determining the empirical formula of B:

$$5.36 \text{ g H} \times \frac{1 \text{ mol H}}{1.008 \text{ g H}} = 5.32 \text{ mol H}; \quad \frac{5.32}{2.66} = 2.00$$

$$42.5 \text{ g O} \times \frac{1 \text{ mol O}}{16.00 \text{ g O}} = 2.66 \text{ mol O}; \quad \frac{2.66}{2.66} = 1.00$$

Empirical formula = H_2O; The molecular formula of substance B could be H_2O, H_4O_2, H_6O_3, etc. The most reasonable choice is water (H_2O) for substance B.

c. Substance C + O_2 → CO_2 + H_2O; Substance C must contain carbon and hydrogen, and may contain oxygen. Determining the mass of carbon and hydrogen in substance C:

$$33.8 \text{ g CO}_2 \times \frac{1 \text{ mol CO}_2}{44.01 \text{ g CO}_2} \times \frac{1 \text{ mol C}}{\text{mol CO}_2} \times \frac{12.01 \text{ g C}}{\text{mol C}} = 9.22 \text{ g carbon}$$

$$6.92 \text{ g H}_2\text{O} \times \frac{1 \text{ mol H}_2\text{O}}{18.02 \text{ g H}_2\text{O}} \times \frac{2 \text{ mol H}}{\text{mol H}_2\text{O}} \times \frac{1.008 \text{ g H}}{\text{mol H}} = 0.774 \text{ g hydrogen}$$

9.22 g carbon + 0.774 g hydrogen = 9.99 g; Substance C initially weighed 10.0 g, so there is no oxygen present in substance C. Determining the empirical formula for substance C:

$$9.22 \text{ g} \times \frac{1 \text{ mol C}}{12.01 \text{ g C}} = 0.768 \text{ mol carbon}$$

$$0.774 \text{ g H} \times \frac{1 \text{ mol H}}{1.008 \text{ g H}} = 0.768 \text{ mol hydrogen}$$

mol C/mol H = 1.00; The empirical formula is CH which has an empirical formula mass ≈ 13. The mass spectrum data indicates a molar mass of 26 g/mol, thus the molecular formula for substance C is C_2H_2.

d. Substance D is $Ca(OH)_2$.

Now we can answer the question. The balanced equation is:

$$CaC_2(s) + 2 \text{ H}_2O(l) \rightarrow C_2H_2(g) + Ca(OH)_2(aq)$$

$$45.0 \text{ g CaC}_2 \times \frac{1 \text{ mol CaC}_2}{64.10 \text{ g CaC}_2} = 0.702 \text{ mol CaC}_2$$

$$23.0 \text{ g H}_2\text{O} \times \frac{1 \text{ mol H}_2\text{O}}{18.02 \text{ g H}_2\text{O}} = 1.28 \text{ mol H}_2\text{O}$$

$$\frac{\text{mol H}_2\text{O}}{\text{mol CaC}_2} = \frac{1.28}{0.702} = 1.82$$

Because the actual mole ratio present is smaller than the required 2:1 mole ratio from the balanced equation, H_2O is limiting.

$$1.28 \text{ mol H}_2\text{O} \times \frac{1 \text{ mol C}_2\text{H}_2}{2 \text{ mol H}_2\text{O}} \times \frac{26.04 \text{ g C}_2\text{H}_2}{\text{mol C}_2\text{H}_2} = 16.7 \text{ g C}_2\text{H}_2 = \text{mass of product C}$$

146. a. i.   If the molar mass of A is greater than the molar mass of B, then we cannot determine the limiting reactant, because, while we have a smaller number of moles of A, we also need fewer moles of A (from the balanced reaction).

   ii.   If the molar mass of B is greater than the molar mass of A, then B is the limiting reactant because we have a smaller number of moles of B and we need more B (from the balanced reaction).

b. $A + 5 B \rightarrow 3 CO_2 + 4 H_2O$

   To conserve mass : $44.01 + 5(B) = 3(44.01) + 4(18.02)$; solving: B = 32.0 g/mol

   Because it is diatomic, the best choice for B is O_2.

c. We can solve this without mass percent data simply by balancing the equation:

   $A + 5 O_2 \rightarrow 3 CO_2 + 4 H_2O$

   A must be C_3H_8. This is also the empirical formula.

   Note: $\dfrac{3(12.01)}{3(12.01) + 8(1.008)} \times 100 = 81.71\%$. So this checks.

CHAPTER FOUR

TYPES OF CHEMICAL REACTIONS AND SOLUTION STOICHIOMETRY

For Review

1. Soluble ionic compounds break apart into their separate ions when in solution. KBr(aq) really means K^+(aq) + Br^-(aq). The hydration process for ions has the partial negative end of the polar water molecules surrounding and stabilizing the cations in solution. Here, many water molecules would align themselves so the oxygen end of water aligns with the K^+ ions. The negative ions are stabilized in water by having the partial positive end of the polar water molecules surround the anions in solution. Here, many water molecules would align themselves so the hydrogen end of water aligns with the Br^- ion. All this is assumed when (aq) is placed after an ionic compound.

    C_2H_5OH is a covalent compound and does not break up into ions when dissolved in water. C_2H_5OH is a polar covalent compound which means it has a partial negative end and a partial positive end. The hydration process for polar covalent solutes in water is again to have the opposite charged parts of the solute and solvent align themselves. Here, the hydrogens of many water molecules align with the partial negative end of C_2H_5OH and the oxygens of many water molecules align with the partial positive end of C_2H_5OH. This is the hydration process for polar covalent compounds and is always assumed when (aq) is listed after a covalent compound. Note: at this point, you are not able to predict the partial negative and partial positive ends for polar covalent compounds.

2. The electrolyte designation refers to how well the dissolved solute breaks up into ions. Strong electrolytes fully break up into ions when in water, weak electrolytes only partially break up into ions (less than 5% usually), and nonelectrolytes do not break up into ions when they dissolve in water. The conductivity apparatus illustrated in Figure 14.4 is one way to experimentally determine the type of electrolyte. As illustrated, a bright light indicates many charge carriers (ions) are present and the solute is a strong electrolyte. A dim light indicates few ions are present so the solute is a weak electrolyte, and no light indicates no ions are present so the solute is a nonelectrolyte.

3. The electrolyte designation refers to what happens to a substance when it dissolves in water, i.e., does it produce a lot of ions or a few ions or no ions when the substance dissolves. A weak electrolyte is a substance that only partially dissociates in water to produce only a few ions. Solubility refers to how much substance can dissolve in a solvent. "Slightly soluble" refers to substances that dissolve only to a small extent, whether it is an electrolyte or a nonelectrolyte. A weak electrolyte may be very soluble in water, or it may be slightly soluble. Acetic acid is an example of a weak electrolyte that is very soluble in water.

4.   Consider a 0.25 M solution of NaCl. The two ways to write 0.25 M as conversion factors are:

$$\frac{0.25 \text{ mol NaCl}}{\text{L}} \quad \text{or} \quad \frac{1 \text{ L}}{0.25 \text{ mol NaCl}}$$

Use the first conversion factor when converting from volume of NaCl solution (in liters) to mol NaCl and use the second conversion factor when converting from mol NaCl to volume of NaCl solution.

5.   Dilution refers to a method used to prepare solutions. In a dilution, one starts with a certain amount of a more concentrated solution; water is then added to a specific new volume forming a solution which has a lower concentration (it is diluted). The quantity that is constant in a dilution is the moles of solute between the concentrated solution and the dilute solution. The difference between the two solutions is that we have the same number of solute particles occupying a larger volume of water; the new solution is less concentrated. Molarity (mol/L) × volume (L) gives mol of solute. M_1V_1 = mol of solute in the concentrated solution. M_2V_2 = mol of solute in the diluted solution. Since the mol of solute are constant between the two solutions, $M_1V_1 = M_2V_2$ for dilution problems.

6.   In the first set of beakers, Pb^{2+} reacts with Br^- to form $PbBr_2(s)$ (from the solubility rules). The Na^+ and NO_3^- ions are spectator ions. There are 6 Na^+, 6 Br^-, 3 Pb^{2+} and 6 NO_3^- ions present initially. $Pb^{2+}(aq) + 2 Br^-(aq) \rightarrow PbBr_2(s)$. The 3 Pb^{2+} ions will react with 6 Br^- ions to form 3 formula units of the $PbBr_2$ precipitate. The ions remaining in solution will be 6 Na^+ ions and 6 NO_3^- ions floating about in solution with three formula units of $PbBr_2$ settled on the bottom as the precipitate.

In the second set of beakers, Al^{3+} reacts with OH^- to form $Al(OH)_3(s)$ (from the solubility rules). There are 3 Al^{3+} ions, 9 Cl^- ions, 6 OH^- ions and 6 K^+ ions present initially. $Al^{3+}(aq) + 3 OH^-(aq) \rightarrow Al(OH)_3(s)$. The 6 OH^- ions will react with two of the three Al^{3+} ions to form 2 formula units of the $Al(OH)_3$ precipitate. One Al^{3+} ion is in excess. Also remaining in solution are the K^+ and Cl^- spectator ions. Therefore, your drawing should show 1 Al^{3+} ion, 9 Cl^- ions, and 6 K^+ ions in solution with 2 $Al(OH)_3$ formula units shown as the precipitate.

7.   The formula equation keeps all of the ions together in nice, neutral formulas. This is not how soluble ionic compounds are present in solution. Soluble ionic compounds (indicated with aq) exist as separate ions in solution; only the precipitate has the ions together. So in the complete ionic equation, the soluble ionic compounds are shown as separate ions and the precipitate is shown as staying together. In the net ionic equation, we get rid of the ions that did nothing but balance the charge. These ions are called spectator ions. In the net ionic equation, only the ions that come together to form the precipitate are shown. In the following balanced equations, the formula equation is written first, the complete ionic equation is second, and the net ionic equation is third.

$$2 \text{ NaBr(aq)} + Pb(NO_3)_2(aq) \rightarrow PbBr_2(s) + 2 \text{ NaNO}_3(aq)$$

$$2 \text{ Na}^+(aq) + 2 \text{ Br}^-(aq) + Pb^{2+}(aq) + 2NO_3^-(aq) \rightarrow PbBr_2(s) + 2 \text{ Na}^+(aq) + 2 \text{ NO}_3^-(aq)$$

$$Pb^{2+}(aq) + 2 \text{ Br}^-(aq) \rightarrow PbBr_2(s)$$

$$AlCl_3(aq) + 3\ KOH(aq) \rightarrow Al(OH)_3(s) + 3\ KCl(aq)$$

$$Al^{3+}(aq) + 3\ Cl^-(aq) + 3\ K^+(aq) + 3\ OH^-(aq) \rightarrow Al(OH)_3(s) + 3\ K^+(aq) + 3\ Cl^-(aq)$$

$$Al^{3+}(aq) + 3\ OH^-(aq) \rightarrow Al(OH)_3(s)$$

8.   An acid-base reaction involves the transfer of a H^+ ion from an acid to a base. The H^+ ion is just a proton; an electron is removed from neutral hydrogen to form H^+. Acid-base reactions are commonly called proton transfer reactions. The acid is the proton donor and the base is the proton acceptor.

The strong bases are (by the solubility rules) LiOH, NaOH, KOH, RbOH, CsOH, $Ca(OH)_2$, $Sr(OH)_2$ and $Ba(OH)_2$. When OH^- from these strong bases react with H^+ (a proton), water is formed [$H^+(aq) + OH^-(aq) \rightarrow H_2O(l)$].

Titration: a technique in which one solution is used to analyze another.

Stoichiometric point: when exactly enough of one solution has been added to react completely with the other solution.

Neutralization: a term used for acid-base reactions referring to the added OH^- reacting with (neutralizing) the protons from the acid. It can be reversed; the added protons neutralizing the OH^- ions from the base. Either way, the neutralization reaction is: $H^+(aq) + OH^-(aq) \rightarrow H_2O(l)$.

Standardization: the experimental procedure of running a controlled acid-base reaction in order to determine the concentration of a specific solution.

9.   Oxidation: a loss of electrons

Reduction: a gain of electrons.

Oxidizing agent: a reactant that accepts electrons from another reactant.

Reducing agent: a reactant that donates electrons to another reactant

The best way to identify a redox reaction is to assign oxidation states to all elements in the reaction. If elements show a change in oxidation states when going from reactants to products, then the reaction is a redox reaction. No change in oxidation states indicates the reaction is not a redox reaction. Note that the element oxidized shows an increase in oxidation state and the element reduced shows a decrease in oxidation state.

10.   Half-reactions: the two parts of an oxidation-reduction reaction, one representing oxidation, the other reduction.

Overall charge must be balanced in any chemical reaction. We balance the charge in the half-reactions by adding electrons to either the reactant side (reduction half-reaction) or the product side (oxidation half-reaction). In the overall balanced equation, the number of electrons lost by the oxidation half-reaction has to exactly equal the number of electrons gained in the reduction half-reaction. Since electrons lost = electrons gained, then electrons will not appear in the overall balanced equation.

See Section 4.10 for a flow chart summarizing the half-reaction method for balancing redox reactions in acidic or basic solution. In all cases, the redox reaction must be mass balanced as well as charge balanced. Mass balance means that we have the same number and types of atoms on both sides of the equation; charge balance means that the overall net charge on each side of the reaction is the same.

Questions

9.   a.   Polarity is a term applied to covalent compounds. Polar covalent compounds have an unequal sharing of electrons in bonds that results in unequal charge distribution in the overall molecule. Polar molecules have a partial negative end and a partial positive end. These are not full charges like in ionic compounds, but are charges much smaller in magnitude. Water is a polar molecule and dissolves other polar solutes readily. The oxygen end of water (the partial negative end of the polar water molecule) aligns with the partial positive end of the polar solute while the hydrogens of water (the partial positive end of the polar water molecule) align with the partial negative end of the solute. These opposite charge attractions stabilize polar solutes in water. This process is called hydration. Nonpolar solutes do not have permanent partial negative and partial positive ends; nonpolar solutes are not stabilized in water and do not dissolve.

         b.   KF is a soluble ionic compound so it is a strong electrolyte. KF(aq) actually exists as separate hydrated K^+ ions and hydrated F^- ions in solution: $C_6H_{12}O_6$ is a polar covalent molecule that is a nonelectrolyte. $C_6H_{12}O_6$ is hydrated as described in part a.

         c.   RbCl is a soluble ionic compound so it exists as separate hydrated Rb^+ ions and hydrated Cl^- ions in solution. AgCl is an insoluble ionic compound so the ions stay together in solution and fall to the bottom of the container as a precipitate.

         d. HNO_3 is a strong acid and exists as separate hydrated H^+ ions and hydrated NO_3^- ions in solution. CO is a polar covalent molecule and is hydrated as explained in part a.

10.   One mol of NaOH dissolved in 1.00 L of solution will produce 1.00 M NaOH. First, weigh out 40.00 g of NaOH (1.000 mol). Next add some water to a 1-L volumetric flask (an instrument that is precise to 1.000 L). Dissolve the NaOH in the flask, add some more water, mix, add more water, mix, etc., until water has been added to 1.000 L mark of the volumetric flask. The result is 1.000 L of a 1.000 M NaOH solution. Since we know the volume to four significant figures as well as the mass, then the molarity will be known to four significant figures. This is good practice, if you need a three significant figure molarity, your measurements should be taken to four significant figures.

        When you need to dilute a more concentrated solution with water to prepare a solution, again make all measurements to four significant figures to insure three significant figures in the molarity. Here, we need to cut the molarity in half from 2.00 M to 1.00 M. We would start with one mole of NaOH from the concentrated solution. This would be 500.0 mL of 2.00 M NaOH. Add this to a 1-L volumetric flask with addition of more water and mixing until the 1.000 L mark is reached. The resulting solution would be 1.00 M.

11.   Use the solubility rules in Table 4.1. Some soluble bromides by rule 2 would be NaBr, KBr, and NH_4Br (there are others). The insoluble bromides by rule 3 would be AgBr, $PbBr_2$, and Hg_2Br_2. Similar reasoning is used for the other parts to this problem.

Sulfates: Na_2SO_4, K_2SO_4, and $(NH_4)_2SO_4$ (and others) would be soluble and $BaSO_4$, $CaSO_4$, and $PbSO_4$ (or Hg_2SO_4) would be insoluble.

Hydroxides: NaOH, KOH, $Ca(OH)_2$ (and others) would be soluble and $Al(OH)_3$, $Fe(OH)_3$, and $Cu(OH)_2$ (and others) would be insoluble.

Phosphates: Na_3PO_4, K_3PO_4, $(NH_4)_3PO_4$ (and others) would be soluble and Ag_3PO_4, $Ca_3(PO_4)_2$, and $FePO_4$ (and others) would be insoluble.

Lead: $PbCl_2$, $PbBr_2$, PbI_2, $Pb(OH)_2$, $PbSO_4$, and PbS (and others) would be insoluble. $Pb(NO_3)_2$ would be a soluble Pb^{2+} salt.

12. $Pb(NO_3)_2(aq) + 2\ KI(aq) \rightarrow PbI_2(s) + 2\ KNO_3(aq)$ formula equation

$Pb^{2+}(aq) + 2\ NO_3^-(aq) + 2\ K^+(aq) + 2\ I^-(aq) \rightarrow PbI_2(s) + 2\ K^+(aq) + 2\ NO_3^-(aq)$

complete ionic equation

The 1.0 mol of Pb^{2+} ions would react with the 2.0 mol of I^- ions to form 1.0 mol of the PbI_2 precipitate. Even though the Pb^{2+} and I^- ions are removed, the spectator ions K^+ and NO_3^- are still present. The solution above the precipitate will conduct electricity as there are plenty of charge carriers present in solution.

13.   The Brønsted-Lowry definitions are best for our purposes. An acid is a proton donor and a base is a proton acceptor. A proton is an H^+ ion. Neutral hydrogen has 1 electron and 1 proton, so an H^+ ion is just a proton. An acid-base reaction is the transfer of an H^+ ion (a proton) from an acid to a base.

14.   The acid is a diprotic acid, H_2A, meaning that it has two H^+ ions in the formula to donate to a base. The reaction is: $H_2A(aq) + 2\ NaOH(aq) \rightarrow 2\ H_2O(l) + Na_2A(aq)$ where A^{2-} is what is left over from the acid formula when the two protons (H^+ ions) are reacted.

For the HCl reaction, the base has the ability to accept two protons. The most common examples are $Ca(OH)_2$, $Sr(OH)_2$, and $Ba(OH)_2$. A possible reaction would be: $2\ HCl(aq) + Ca(OH)_2(aq) \rightarrow 2\ H_2O(l) + CaCl_2(aq)$.

15.   a.   The species reduced is the element that gains electrons. The reducing agent causes reduc-duction to occur by itself being oxidized. The reducing agent generally refers to the entire formula of the compound/ion that contains the element oxidized.

b.   The species oxidized is the element that loses electrons. The oxidizing agent causes oxidation to occur by itself being reduced. The oxidizing agent generally refers to the entire formula of the compound/ion that contains the element reduced.

c.   For simple binary ionic compounds, the actual charge on the ions are the oxidation states. For covalent compounds, nonzero oxidation states are imaginary charges the elements would have if they were held together by ionic bonds (assuming the bond is between two different nonmetals). Nonzero oxidation states for elements in covalent compounds are not actual charges. Oxidation states for covalent compounds are a bookkeeping method to keep track of electrons in a reaction.

16.   Mass balance indicates that we have the same number and type of atoms on both sides of the equation (so that mass is conserved). Similarly, net charge must also be conserved. We cannot have a build up of charge on one side of the reaction or the other. In redox-reactions, electrons are used to balance the net charge between reactants and products.

Exercises

Aqueous Solutions: Strong and Weak Electrolytes

17.   a. $NaBr(s) \rightarrow Na^+(aq) + Br^-(aq)$ b. $MgCl_2(s) \rightarrow Mg^{2+}(aq) + 2\,Cl^-(aq)$

Your drawing should show equal number of Na^+ and Br^- ions.

Your drawing should show twice the number of Cl^- ions as Mg^{2+} ions.

c. $Al(NO_3)_3(s) \rightarrow Al^{3+}(aq) + 3\,NO_3^-(aq)$ d. $(NH_4)_2SO_4(s) \rightarrow 2\,NH_4^+(aq) + SO_4^{2-}(aq)$

For e-i, your drawings should show equal numbers of the cations and anions present as each salt is a 1:1 salt. The ions present are listed in the following dissolution reactions.

e. $NaOH(s) \rightarrow Na^+(aq) + OH^-(aq)$ f. $FeSO_4(s) \rightarrow Fe^{2+}(aq) + SO_4^{2-}(aq)$

g. $KMnO_4(s) \rightarrow K^+(aq) + MnO_4^-(aq)$ h. $HClO_4(aq) \rightarrow H^+(aq) + ClO_4^-(aq)$

i. $NH_4C_2H_3O_2(s) \rightarrow NH_4^+(aq) + C_2H_3O_2^-(aq)$

18.   a. $Ba(NO_3)_2(aq) \rightarrow Ba^{2+}(aq) + 2\,NO_3^-(aq)$;   Picture iv represents the Ba^{2+} and NO_3^- ions present in $Ba(NO_3)_2(aq)$.

      b. $NaCl(aq) \rightarrow Na^+(aq) + Cl^-(aq)$;   Picture ii represents $NaCl(aq)$.

c. $K_2CO_3(aq) \rightarrow 2\,K^+(aq) + CO_3{}^{2-}(aq)$; Picture iii represents $K_2CO_3(aq)$.

d. $MgSO_4(aq) \rightarrow Mg^{2+}(aq) + SO_4{}^{2-}(aq)$; Picture i represents $MgSO_4(aq)$.

$HNO_3(aq) \rightarrow H^+(aq) + NO_3{}^-(aq)$. Picture ii best represents the strong acid HNO_3. Strong acids are strong electrolytes. $HC_2H_3O_2$ only partially dissociates in water; acetic acid is a weak electrolyte. None of the pictures represent weak electrolyte solutions; they all are representations of strong electrolytes.

19. $CaCl_2(s) \rightarrow Ca^{2+}(aq) + 2\,Cl^-(aq)$

20. $MgSO_4(s) \rightarrow Mg^{2+}(aq) + SO_4{}^{2-}(aq)$; $NH_4NO_3(s) \rightarrow NH_4{}^+(aq) + NO_3{}^-(aq)$

Solution Concentration: Molarity

21.   a. $5.623 \text{ g NaHCO}_3 \times \dfrac{1 \text{ mol NaHCO}_3}{84.01 \text{ g NaHCO}_3} = 6.693 \times 10^{-2} \text{ mol NaHCO}_3$

$$M = \frac{6.693 \times 10^{-2} \text{ mol}}{250.0 \text{ mL}} \times \frac{1000 \text{ mL}}{\text{L}} = 0.2677 \; M \text{ NaHCO}_3$$

b. $0.1846 \text{ g K}_2\text{Cr}_2\text{O}_7 \times \dfrac{1 \text{ mol K}_2\text{Cr}_2\text{O}_7}{294.20 \text{ g K}_2\text{Cr}_2\text{O}_7} = 6.275 \times 10^{-4} \text{ mol K}_2\text{Cr}_2\text{O}_7$

$$M = \frac{6.275 \times 10^{-4} \text{ mol}}{500.0 \times 10^{-3} \text{ L}} = 1.255 \times 10^{-3} \; M \text{ K}_2\text{Cr}_2\text{O}_7$$

c. $0.1025 \text{ g Cu} \times \dfrac{1 \text{ mol Cu}}{63.55 \text{ g Cu}} = 1.613 \times 10^{-3} \text{ mol Cu} = 1.613 \times 10^{-3} \text{ mol Cu}^{2+}$

$$M = \frac{1.613 \times 10^{-2} \text{ mol Cu}^{2+}}{200.0 \text{ mL}} \times \frac{1000 \text{ mL}}{\text{L}} = 8.065 \times 10^{-3} \; M \text{ Cu}^{2+}$$

22. $75.0 \text{ mL} \times \dfrac{0.79 \text{ g}}{\text{mL}} \times \dfrac{1 \text{ mol}}{46.07 \text{ g}} = 1.3 \text{ mol C}_2\text{H}_5\text{OH}$; Molarity $= \dfrac{1.3 \text{ mol}}{0.250 \text{ L}} = 5.2 \; M \text{ C}_2\text{H}_5\text{OH}$

23.   a. $M_{\text{Ca(NO}_3)_2} = \dfrac{0.100 \text{ mol Ca(NO}_3)_2}{0.100 \text{ L}} = 1.00 \; M$

$Ca(NO_3)_2(s) \rightarrow Ca^{2+}(aq) + 2\,NO_3{}^-(aq)$; $M_{\text{ca}^{2+}} = 1.00 \; M$; $M_{\text{NO}_3{}^-} = 2(1.00) = 2.00 \; M$

b. $M_{\text{Na}_2\text{SO}_4} = \dfrac{2.5 \text{ mol Na}_2\text{SO}_4}{1.25 \text{ L}} = 2.0 \; M$

$Na_2SO_4(s) \rightarrow 2\ Na^+(aq) + SO_4^{2-}(aq);\ M_{Na^+} = 2(2.0) = 4.0\ M\ ;\ M_{SO_4^{2-}} = 2.0\ M$

c. $5.00\ g\ NH_4Cl \times \dfrac{1\ mol\ NH_4Cl}{53.49\ g\ NH_4Cl} = 0.0935\ mol\ NH_4Cl$

$M_{NH_4Cl} = \dfrac{0.0935\ mol\ NH_4Cl}{0.5000\ L} = 0.187\ M$

$NH_4Cl(s) \rightarrow NH_4^+(aq) + Cl^-(aq);\ M_{NH_4^+} = M_{Cl^-} = 0.187\ M$

d. $1.00\ g\ K_3PO_4 \times \dfrac{1\ mol\ K_3PO_4}{212.27\ g} = 4.71 \times 10^{-3}\ mol\ K_3PO_4$

$M_{K_3PO_4} = \dfrac{4.71 \times 10^{-3}\ mol}{0.2500\ L} = 0.0188\ M$

$K_3PO_4(s) \rightarrow 3\ K^+(aq) + PO_4^{3-}(aq);\ M_{K^+} = 3(0.0188) = 0.0564\ M;\ M_{PO_4^{3-}} = 0.0188\ M$

24. a. $M_{Na_3PO_4} = \dfrac{0.0200\ mol}{0.0100\ L} = 2.00\ M$

$Na_3PO_4(s) \rightarrow 3\ Na^+(aq) + PO_4^{3-}(aq);\ M_{Na^+} = 3(2.00) = 6.00\ M;\ M_{PO_4^{3-}} = 2.00\ M$

b. $M_{Ba(NO_3)_2} = \dfrac{0.300\ mol}{0.6000\ L} = 0.500\ M;$

$Ba(NO_3)_2(s) \rightarrow Ba^{2+}(aq) + 2\ NO_3^-(aq);\ M_{Ba^{2+}} = 0.500\ M;\ M_{NO_3^-} = 2(0.500) = 1.00\ M$

c. $M_{KCl} = \dfrac{1.00\ g\ KCl \times \dfrac{1\ mol\ KCl}{74.55\ g\ KCl}}{0.5000\ L} = 0.0268\ M$

$KCl(s) \rightarrow K^+(aq) + Cl^-(aq);\ M_{K^+} = M_{Cl^-} = 0.0268\ M$

d. $M_{(NH_4)_2SO_4} = \dfrac{132\ g\ (NH_4)_2SO_4 \times \dfrac{1\ mol\ (NH_4)_2SO_4}{132.15\ g}}{1.50\ L} = 0.666\ M$

$(NH_4)_2SO_4(s) \rightarrow 2\ NH_4^+(aq) + SO_4^{2-}(aq)$

$M_{NH_4^+} = 2(0.666) = 1.33\ M;\ M_{SO_4^{2-}} = 0.666\ M$

25. mol solute = volume (L) $\times \left(\dfrac{mol}{L}\right);\ AlCl_3(s) \rightarrow Al^{3+}(aq) + 3\ Cl^-(aq)$

$$\text{mol Cl}^- = 0.1000 \text{ L} \times \frac{0.30 \text{ mol AlCl}_3}{\text{L}} \times \frac{3 \text{ mol Cl}^-}{\text{mol AlCl}_3} = 9.0 \times 10^{-2} \text{ mol Cl}^-$$

$$\text{MgCl}_2(s) \rightarrow \text{Mg}^{2+}(aq) + 2 \text{ Cl}^-(aq)$$

$$\text{mol Cl}^- = 0.0500 \text{ L} \times \frac{0.60 \text{ mol MgCl}_2}{\text{L}} \times \frac{2 \text{ mol Cl}^-}{\text{mol MgCl}_2} = 6.0 \times 10^{-2} \text{ mol Cl}^-$$

$$\text{NaCl}(s) \rightarrow \text{Na}^+(aq) + \text{Cl}^-(aq)$$

$$\text{mol Cl}^- = 0.2000 \text{ L} \times \frac{0.40 \text{ mol NaCl}}{\text{L}} \times \frac{1 \text{ mol Cl}^-}{\text{mol NaCl}} = 8.0 \times 10^{-2} \text{ mol Cl}^-$$

100.0 mL of 0.30 M AlCl$_3$ contains the most moles of Cl$^-$ ions.

26.   NaOH(s) $\rightarrow$ Na$^+$(aq) + OH$^-$(aq), 2 total mol of ions (1 mol Na$^+$ and 1 mol Cl$^-$) per mol NaOH.

$$0.1000 \text{ L} \times \frac{0.100 \text{ mol NaOH}}{\text{L}} \times \frac{2 \text{ mol ions}}{\text{mol NaOH}} = 2.0 \times 10^{-2} \text{ mol ions}$$

$$\text{BaCl}_2(s) \rightarrow \text{Ba}^{2+}(aq) + 2 \text{ Cl}^-(aq), 3 \text{ total mol of Cl}^- \text{ ions per mol BaCl}_2.$$

$$0.0500 \text{ L} \times \frac{0.200 \text{ mol}}{\text{L}} \times \frac{3 \text{ mol ions}}{\text{mol BaCl}_2} = 3.0 \times 10^{-2} \text{ mol ions}$$

$$\text{Na}_3\text{PO}_4(s) \rightarrow 3 \text{ Na}^+(aq) + \text{PO}_4^{3-}(aq), 4 \text{ total mol of ions per mol Na}_3\text{PO}_4.$$

$$0.0750 \text{ L} \times \frac{0.150 \text{ mol Na}_3\text{PO}_4}{\text{L}} \times \frac{4 \text{ mol ions}}{\text{mol Na}_3\text{PO}_4} = 4.50 \times \text{mol } 10^{-2} \text{ ions}$$

75.0 mL of 0.150 M Na$_3$PO$_4$ contains the largest number of ions.

27.   Molar mass of NaOH = 22.99 + 16.00 + 1.008 = 40.00 g/mol

$$\text{Mass NaOH} = 0.2500 \text{ L} \times \frac{0.400 \text{ mol NaOH}}{\text{L}} \times \frac{40.00 \text{ g NaOH}}{\text{mol NaOH}} = 4.00 \text{ g NaOH}$$

28. $$10. \text{ g AgNO}_3 \times \frac{1 \text{ mol AgNO}_3}{169.9 \text{ g}} \times \frac{1 \text{ L}}{0.25 \text{ mol AgNO}_3} = 0.235 \text{ L} = 235 \text{ mL}$$

29.   a. $$2.00 \text{ L} \times \frac{0.250 \text{ mol NaOH}}{\text{L}} \times \frac{40.00 \text{ g NaOH}}{\text{mol NaOH}} = 20.0 \text{ g NaOH}$$

Place 20.0 g NaOH in a 2 L volumetric flask; add water to dissolve the NaOH, and fill to the mark with water, mixing several times along the way.

b. $2.00 \, L \times \dfrac{0.250 \, mol \, NaOH}{L} \times \dfrac{1 \, L \, stock}{1.00 \, mol \, NaOH} = 0.500 \, L$

Add 500. mL of 1.00 M NaOH stock solution to a 2 L volumetric flask; fill to the mark with water, mixing several times along the way.

c. $2.00 \, L \times \dfrac{0.100 \, mol \, K_2CrO_4}{L} \times \dfrac{194.20 \, g \, K_2CrO_4}{mol \, K_2CrO_4} = 38.8 \, g \, K_2CrO_4$

Similar to the solution made in part a, instead using 38.8 g K_2CrO_4.

d. $2.00 \, L \times \dfrac{0.100 \, mol \, K_2CrO_4}{L} \times \dfrac{1 \, L \, stock}{1.75 \, mol \, K_2CrO_4} = 0.114 \, L$

Similar to the solution made in part b, instead using 114 mL of the 1.75 M K$_2$CrO$_4$ stock solution.

30.   a. $1.00 \, L \, solution \times \dfrac{0.50 \, mol \, H_2SO_4}{L} = 0.50 \, mol \, H_2SO_4$

$0.50 \, mol \, H_2SO_4 \times \dfrac{1 \, L}{18 \, mol \, H_2SO_4} = 2.8 \times 10^{-2} \, L$ conc. H$_2$SO$_4$ or 28 mL

Dilute 28 mL of concentrated H$_2$SO$_4$ to a total volume of 1.00 L with water.

b.   We will need 0.50 mol HCl.

$0.50 \, mol \, HCl \times \dfrac{1 \, L}{12 \, mol \, HCl} = 4.2 \times 10^{-2} \, L = 42 \, mL$

Dilute 42 mL of concentrated HCl to a final volume of 1.00 L.

c.   We need 0.50 mol NiCl$_2$.

$0.50 \, mol \, NiCl_2 \times \dfrac{1 \, mol \, NiCl_2 \bullet 6H_2O}{mol \, NiCl_2} \times \dfrac{237.69 \, g \, NiCl_2 \bullet 6H_2O}{mol \, NiCl_2 \bullet 6H_2O}$

$= 118.8 \, g \, NiCl_2 \bullet 6H_2O \approx 120 \, g$

Dissolve 120 g NiCl$_2$•6H$_2$O in water, and add water until the total volume of the solution is 1.00 L.

d. $1.00 \, L \times \dfrac{0.50 \, mol \, HNO_3}{L} = 0.50 \, mol \, HNO_3$

$0.50 \, mol \, HNO_3 \times \dfrac{1 \, L}{16 \, mol \, HNO_3} = 0.031 \, L = 31 \, mL$

Dissolve 31 mL of concentrated reagent in water. Dilute to a total volume of 1.00 L.

e.   We need 0.50 mol Na_2CO_3.

$$0.50 \text{ mol } Na_2CO_3 \times \frac{105.99 \text{ g } Na_2CO_3}{\text{mol}} = 53 \text{ g } Na_2CO_3$$

Dissolve 53 g Na_2CO_3 in water, dilute to 1.00 L.

31. $10.8 \text{ g } (NH_4)_2SO_4 \times \dfrac{1 \text{ mol}}{132.15 \text{ g}} = 8.17 \times 10^{-2} \text{ mol } (NH_4)_2SO_4$

$$\text{Molarity} = \frac{8.17 \times 10^{-2} \text{ mol}}{100.0 \text{ mL}} \times \frac{1000 \text{ mL}}{\text{L}} = 0.817 \ M \ (NH_4)_2SO_4$$

Moles of $(NH_4)_2SO_4$ in final solution:

$$10.00 \times 10^{-3} \text{ L} \times \frac{0.817 \text{ mol}}{\text{L}} = 8.17 \times 10^{-3} \text{ mol}$$

$$\text{Molarity of final solution} = \frac{8.17 \times 10^{-3} \text{ mol}}{(10.00 + 50.00) \text{ mL}} \times \frac{1000 \text{ mL}}{\text{L}} = 0.136 \ M \ (NH_4)_2SO_4$$

$(NH_4)_2SO_4(s) \rightarrow 2 \ NH_4^+(aq) + SO_4^{2-}(aq); \ M_{NH_4^+} = 2(0.136) = 0.272 \ M; \ M_{SO_4^{2-}} = 0.136 \ M$

32. $\text{mol } Na_2CO_3 = 0.0700 \text{ L} \times \dfrac{3.0 \text{ mol } Na_2CO_3}{\text{L}} = 0.21 \text{ mol } Na_2CO_3$

$Na_2CO_3(s) \rightarrow 2 \ Na^+(aq) + CO_3^{2-}(aq); \ \text{mol } Na^+ = 2(0.21) = 0.42 \text{ mol}$

$\text{mol } NaHCO_3 = 0.0300 \text{ L} \times \dfrac{1.0 \text{ mol } NaHCO_3}{\text{L}} = 0.030 \text{ mol } NaHCO_3$

$NaHCO_3(s) \rightarrow Na^+(aq) + HCO_3^-(aq); \ \text{mol } Na^+ = 0.030 \text{ mol}$

$$M_{Na^+} = \frac{\text{total mol } Na^+}{\text{total volume}} = \frac{0.42 \text{ mol} + 0.030 \text{ mol}}{0.0700 \text{ L} + 0.0300 \text{ L}} = \frac{0.45 \text{ mol}}{0.1000 \text{ L}} = 4.5 \ M \ Na^+$$

33. $\text{Stock solution} = \dfrac{10.0 \text{ mg}}{500.0 \text{ mL}} = \dfrac{10.0 \times 10^{-3} \text{ g}}{500.0 \text{ mL}} = \dfrac{2.00 \times 10^{-5} \text{ g steroid}}{\text{mL}}$

$$100.0 \times 10^{-6} \text{ L stock} \times \frac{1000 \text{ mL}}{\text{L}} \times \frac{2.00 \times 10^{-5} \text{ g steroid}}{\text{mL}} = 2.00 \times 10^{-6} \text{ g steroid}$$

This is diluted to a final volume of 100.0 mL.

$$\frac{2.00 \times 10^{-6} \text{ g steroid}}{100.0 \text{ mL}} \times \frac{1000 \text{ mL}}{\text{L}} \times \frac{1 \text{ mol steroid}}{336.43 \text{ g steroid}} = 5.94 \times 10^{-8} \ M \text{ steroid}$$

34.   Stock solution:

$$1.584 \text{ g Mn}^{2+} \times \frac{1 \text{ mol Mn}^{2+}}{54.94 \text{ g Mn}^{2+}} = 2.883 \times 10^{-2} \text{ mol Mn}^{2+}; \quad \frac{2.833 \times 10^{-2} \text{ mol Mn}^{2+}}{1.000 \text{ L}}$$

$$= 2.883 \times 10^{-2} \text{ } M$$

Solution A contains:

$$50.00 \text{ mL} \times \frac{1 \text{ L}}{1000 \text{ mL}} \times \frac{2.833 \times 10^{-2} \text{ mol}}{\text{L}} = 1.442 \times 10^{-3} \text{ mol Mn}^{2+}$$

$$\text{Molarity} = \frac{1.442 \times 10^{-3} \text{ mol}}{1000.0 \text{ mL}} \times \frac{1000 \text{ mL}}{1 \text{ L}} = 1.442 \times 10^{-3} \text{ } M$$

Solution B contains:

$$10.0 \text{ mL} \times \frac{1 \text{ L}}{1000 \text{ mL}} \times \frac{1.442 \times 10^{-3} \text{ mol}}{\text{L}} = 1.442 \times 10^{-5} \text{ mol Mn}^{2+}$$

$$\text{Molarity} = \frac{1.442 \times 10^{-5} \text{ mol}}{0.2500 \text{ L}} = 5.768 \times 10^{-5} M$$

Solution C contains:

$$10.00 \times 10^{-3} \text{ L} \times \frac{5.768 \times 10^{-5} \text{ mol}}{\text{L}} = 5.768 \times 10^{-7} \text{ mol Mn}^{2+}$$

$$\text{Molarity} = \frac{5.768 \times 10^{-7} \text{ mol}}{0.5000 \text{ L}} = 1.154 \times 10^{-6} M$$

Precipitation Reactions

35.   The solubility rules referenced in the following answers are outlined in Table 4.1 of the text.

a. Soluble: most nitrate salts are soluble (Rule 1).

b. Soluble: most chloride salts are soluble except for Ag^+, Pb^{2+}, and Hg_2^{2+} (Rule 3).

c. Soluble: most sulfate salts are soluble except for $BaSO_4$, $PbSO_4$, Hg_2SO_4, and $CaSO_4$ (Rule 4.)

d. Insoluble: most hydroxide salts are only slightly soluble (Rule 5).
Note: we will interpret the phrase "slightly soluble" as meaning insoluble and the phrase "marginally soluble" as meaning soluble. So the marginally soluble hydroxides $Ba(OH)_2$, $Sr(OH)_2$, and $Ca(OH)_2$ will be assumed soluble unless noted otherwise.

e. Insoluble: most sulfide salts are only slightly soluble (Rule 6). Again, "slightly soluble" is interpreted as "insoluble" in problems like these.

f.   Insoluble: Rule 5 (see answer d).

g.   Insoluble: most phosphate salts are only slightly soluble (Rule 6).

36.   The solubility rules referenced in the following answers are from Table 4.1 of the text. The phrase "slightly soluble" is interpreted to mean insoluble and the phrase "marginally soluble" is interpreted to mean soluble.

a.   Soluble (Rule 3)
b.   Soluble (Rule 1)
c.   Inoluble (Rule 4)
d.   Soluble (Rules 2 and 3)
e.   Insoluble (Rule 6)
f.   Insoluble (Rule 5)
g.   Insoluble (Rule 6)
h.   Soluble (Rule 2)

37.   In these reactions, soluble ionic compounds are mixed together. To predict the precipitate, switch the anions and cations in the two reactant compounds to predict possible products; then use the solubility rules in Table 4.1 to predict if any of these possible products are insoluble (are the precipitate). Note that the phrase "slightly soluble" in Table 4.1 is interpreted to mean insoluble and the phrase "marginally soluble" is interpreted to mean soluble.

a.   Possible products = $FeCl_2$ and K_2SO_4; Both salts are soluble so no precipitate forms.

b.   Possible products = $Al(OH)_3$ and $Ba(NO_3)_2$; precipitate = $Al(OH)_3(s)$

c.   Possible products = $CaSO_4$ and $NaCl$; precipitate = $CaSO_4(s)$

d.   Possible products = KNO_3 and NiS; precipitate = $NiS(s)$

38.   Use Table 4.1 to predict the solubility of the possible products.

a.   Possible products = Hg_2SO_4 and $Cu(NO_3)_2$; precipitate = Hg_2SO_4

b.   Possible products = $NiCl_2$ and $Ca(NO_3)_2$; Both salts are soluble so no precipitate forms.

c.   Possible products = KI and $MgCO_3$; precipitate = $MgCO_3$

d.   Possible products = $NaBr$ and $Al_2(CrO_4)_3$; precipitate = $Al_2(CrO_4)_3$

39.   For the following answers, the balanced formula equation is first, followed by the complete ionic equation, then the net ionic equation.

a.   No reaction occurs since all possible products are soluble salts.

b. $2 Al(NO_3)_3(aq) + 3 Ba(OH)_2(aq) \rightarrow 2 Al(OH)_3(s) + 3 Ba(NO_3)_2(aq)$

$2 Al^{3+}(aq) + 6 NO_3^-(aq) + 3 Ba^{2+}(aq) + 6 OH^-(aq) \rightarrow$
$$2 Al(OH)_3(s) + 3 Ba^{2+}(aq) + 6 NO_3^-(aq)$$
$Al^{3+}(aq) + 3 OH^-(aq) \rightarrow Al(OH)_3(s)$

c. $CaCl_2(aq) + Na_2SO_4(aq) \rightarrow CaSO_4(s) + 2 NaCl(aq)$

$Ca^{2+}(aq) + 2 Cl^-(aq) + 2 Na^+(aq) + SO_4^{2-}(aq) \rightarrow CaSO_4(s) + 2 Na^+(aq) + 2 Cl^-(aq)$

$Ca^{2+}(aq) + SO_4^{2-}(aq) \rightarrow CaSO_4(s)$

d. $K_2S(aq) + Ni(NO_3)_2(aq) \rightarrow 2\ KNO_3(aq) + NiS(s)$

$2\ K^+(aq) + S^{2-}(aq) + Ni^{2+}(aq) + 2\ NO_3^-(aq) \rightarrow 2\ K^+(aq) + 2\ NO_3^-(aq) + NiS(s)$

$Ni^{2+}(aq) + S^{2-}(aq) \rightarrow NiS(s)$

40.   a. $Hg_2(NO_3)_2(aq) + CuSO_4(aq) \rightarrow Hg_2SO_4(s) + Cu(NO_3)_2(aq)$

$Hg_2^{2+}(aq) + 2\ NO_3^-(aq) + Cu^{2+}(aq) + SO_4^{2-}(aq) \rightarrow Hg_2SO_4(s) + Cu^{2+}(aq) + 2\ NO_3^-(aq)$

$Hg_2^{2+}(aq) + SO_4^{2-}(aq) \rightarrow Hg_2SO_4(s)$

b.   No reaction occurs since both possible products are soluble.

c. $K_2CO_3(aq) + MgI_2(aq) \rightarrow 2\ KI(aq) + MgCO_3(s)$

$2\ K^+(aq) + CO_3^{2-}(aq) + Mg^{2+}(aq) + 2\ I^-(aq) \rightarrow 2\ K^+(aq) + 2\ I^-(aq) + MgCO_3(s)$

$Mg^{2+}(aq) + CO_3^{2-}(aq) \rightarrow MgCO_3(s)$

d. $3\ Na_2CrO_4(aq) + 2\ Al(Br)_3(aq) \rightarrow 6\ NaBr(aq) + Al_2(CrO_4)_3(s)$

$6\ Na^+(aq) + 3\ CrO_4^{2-}(aq) + 2\ Al^{3+}(aq) + 6\ Br^-(aq) \rightarrow 6\ Na^+(aq) + 6\ Br^-(aq) +$

$$Al_2(CrO_4)_3(s)$$

$2\ Al^{3+}(aq) + 3\ CrO_4^{2-}(aq) \rightarrow Al_2(CrO_4)_3(s)$

41.   a.   When $CuSO_4(aq)$ is added to $Na_2S(aq)$, the precipitate that forms is $CuS(s)$. Therefore, Na^+ (the grey spheres) and SO_4^{2-} (the blue-green spheres) are the spectator ions.

$CuSO_4(aq) + Na_2S(aq) \rightarrow CuS(s) + Na_2SO_4(aq);\ Cu^{2+}(aq) + S^{2-}(aq) \rightarrow CuS(s)$

b.   When $CoCl_2(aq)$ is added to $NaOH(aq)$, the precipitate that forms is $Co(OH)_2(s)$. Therefore, Na^+ (the grey spheres) and Cl^- (the green spheres) are the spectator ions.

$CoCl_2(aq) + 2\ NaOH(aq) \rightarrow Co(OH)_2(s) + 2\ NaCl(aq)$
$Co^{2+}(aq) + 2\ OH^-(aq) \rightarrow Co(OH)_2(s)$

c.   When $AgNO_3(aq)$ is added to $KI(aq)$, the precipitate that forms is $AgI(s)$. Therefore, K^+ (the red spheres) and NO_3^- ((the blue spheres) are the spectator ions.

$AgNO_3(aq) + KI(aq) \rightarrow AgI(s) + KNO_3(aq);\ Ag^+(aq) + I^- (\ (aq) \rightarrow AgI(s)$

42.   There are many acceptable choices for spectator ions. We will generally choose Na^+ and NO_3^- as the spectator ions because sodium salts and nitrate salts are usually soluble in water.

a. $Fe(NO_3)_3(aq) + 3\ NaOH(aq) \rightarrow Fe(OH)_3(s) + 3\ NaNO_3(aq)$

b. $Hg_2(NO_3)_2(aq) + 2\ NaCl(aq) \rightarrow Hg_2Cl_2(s) + 2\ NaNO_3(aq)$

c. $Pb(NO_3)_2(aq) + Na_2SO_4(aq) \rightarrow PbSO_4(s) + 2\ NaNO_3(aq)$

    d. $BaCl_2(aq) + Na_2CrO_4(aq) \rightarrow BaCrO_4(s) + 2\ NaCl(aq)$

43.   a. $(NH_4)_2SO_4(aq) + Ba(NO_3)_2(aq) \rightarrow 2\ NH_4NO_3(aq) + BaSO_4(s)$

        $Ba^{2+}(aq) + SO_4{}^{2-}(aq) \rightarrow BaSO_4(s)$

    b. $Pb(NO_3)_2(aq) + 2\ NaCl(aq) \rightarrow PbCl_2(s) + 2\ NaNO_3(aq)$

        $Pb^{2+}(aq) + 2\ Cl^-(aq) \rightarrow PbCl_2(s)$

    c. Potassium phosphate and sodium nitrate are both soluble in water. No reaction occurs.

    d. No reaction occurs because all possible products are soluble.

    e. $CuCl_2(aq) + 2\ NaOH(aq) \rightarrow Cu(OH)_2(s) + 2\ NaCl(aq)$

        $Cu^{2+}(aq) + 2\ OH^-(aq) \rightarrow Cu(OH)_2(s)$

44.   a. $CrCl_3(aq) + 3\ NaOH(aq) \rightarrow Cr(OH)_3(s) + 3\ NaCl(aq)$

        $Cr^{3+}(aq) + 3\ OH^-(aq) \rightarrow Cr(OH)_3(s)$

    b. $2\ AgNO_3(aq) + (NH_4)_2CO_3(aq) \rightarrow Ag_2CO_3(s) + 2\ NH_4NO_3(aq)$

        $2\ Ag^+(aq) + CO_3{}^{2-}(aq) \rightarrow Ag_2CO_3(s)$

    c. $CuSO_4(aq) + Hg_2(NO_3)_2(aq) \rightarrow Cu(NO_3)_2(aq) + Hg_2SO_4(s)$

        $Hg_2{}^{2+}(aq) + SO_4{}^{2-}(aq) \rightarrow Hg_2SO_4(s)$

    d. No reaction occurs because all possible products (SrI_2 and KNO_3) are soluble.

45.   Because a precipitate formed with Na_2SO_4, the possible cations are Ba^{2+}, Pb^{2+}, $Hg_2{}^{2+}$, and Ca^{2+} (from the solubility rules). Because no precipitate formed with KCl, Pb^{2+} and $Hg_2{}^{2+}$ cannot be present. Because both Ba^{2+} and Ca^{2+} form soluble chlorides and soluble hydroxides, both of these cations could be present. Therefore, the cations could be Ba^{2+} and Ca^{2+} (by the solubility rules in Table 4.1). For students who do a more rigorous study of solubility, Sr^{2+} could also be a possible cation (it forms an insoluble sulfate salt while the chloride and hydroxide salts of strontium are soluble).

46.   Because no precipitates formed upon addition of NaCl or Na_2SO_4, we can conclude that $Hg_2{}^{2+}$ and Ba^{2+} are not present in the sample since Hg_2Cl_2 and $BaSO_4$ are insoluble salts. However, Mn^{2+} may be present since Mn^{2+} does not form a precipitate with either NaCl or Na_2SO_4. A precipitate formed with NaOH; the solution must contain Mn^{2+} because it forms a precipitate with OH^- [$Mn(OH)_2(s)$].

47. $2\ AgNO_3(aq) + Na_2CrO_4(aq) \rightarrow Ag_2CrO_4(s) + 2\ NaNO_3(aq)$

$$0.0750\ L \times \frac{0.100\ \text{mol AgNO}_3}{L} \times \frac{1\ \text{mol Na}_2\text{CrO}_4}{2\ \text{mol AgNO}_3} \times \frac{161.98\ \text{g Na}_2\text{CrO}_4}{\text{mol Na}_2\text{CrO}_4} = 0.607\ \text{g Na}_2\text{CrO}_4$$

48. $2 Na_3PO_4(aq) + 3 Pb(NO_3)_2(aq) \rightarrow Pb_3(PO_4)_2(s) + 6 NaNO_3(aq)$

$$0.1500 \text{ L} \times \frac{0.250 \text{ mol Pb(NO}_3)_2}{\text{L}} \times \frac{2 \text{ mol Na}_3PO_4}{3 \text{ mol Pb(NO}_3)_2} \times \frac{1 \text{ L Na}_3PO_4}{0.100 \text{ mol Na}_3PO_4} = 0.250 \text{ L}$$

$$= 250. \text{ mL Na}_3PO_4$$

49. $Al(NO_3)_3(aq) + 3 KOH(aq) \rightarrow Al(OH)_3(s) + 3 KNO_3(aq)$

$$0.0500 \text{ L} \times \frac{0.200 \text{ mol Al(NO}_3)_3}{\text{L}} = 0.0100 \text{ mol Al(NO}_3)_3$$

$$0.2000 \text{ L} \times \frac{0.100 \text{ mol KOH}}{\text{L}} = 0.0200 \text{ mol KOH}$$

From the balanced equation, 3 mol of KOH are required to react with 1 mol of $Al(NO_3)_3$ (3:1 mole ratio). The actual KOH to $Al(NO_3)_3$ mole ratio present is 0.0200/0.0100 = 2 (2:1). Since the actual mole ratio present is less than the required mole ratio, KOH (the numerator) is the limiting reagent.

$$0.0200 \text{ mol KOH} \times \frac{1 \text{ mol Al(OH)}_3}{3 \text{ mol KOH}} \times \frac{78.00 \text{ g Al(OH)}_3}{\text{mol Al(OH)}_3} = 0.520 \text{ g Al(OH)}_3$$

50.   The balanced equation is: $3 BaCl_2(aq) + Fe_2(SO_4)_3(aq) \rightarrow 3 BaSO_4(s) + 2 FeCl_3(aq)$

$$100.0 \text{ mL BaCl}_2 \times \frac{1 \text{ L}}{1000 \text{ mL}} \times \frac{0.100 \text{ mol BaCl}_2}{\text{L}} = 1.00 \times 10^{-2} \text{ mol BaCl}_2$$

$$100.0 \text{ mL Fe}_2(SO_4)_3 \times \frac{1 \text{ L}}{1000 \text{ mL}} \times \frac{0.100 \text{ mol Fe}_2(SO_4)_3}{\text{L}} = 1.00 \times 10^{-2} \text{ mol Fe}_2(SO_4)_3$$

The required mol $BaCl_2$ to mol $Fe_2(SO_4)_3$ ratio from the balanced reaction is 3:1. The actual mole ratio is 0.0100/0.0100 = 1 (1:1). This is well below the required mole ratio, so $BaCl_2$ is the limiting reagent.

$$0.0100 \text{ mol BaCl}_2 \times \frac{3 \text{ mol BaSO}_4}{3 \text{ mol BaCl}_2} \times \frac{233.4 \text{ g BaSO}_4}{\text{mol BaSO}_4} = 2.33 \text{ g BaSO}_4$$

51. $2 AgNO_3(aq) + CaCl_2(aq) \rightarrow 2 AgCl(s) + Ca(NO_3)_2(aq)$

$$\text{mol AgNO}_3 = 0.1000 \text{ L} \times \frac{0.20 \text{ mol AgNO}_3}{\text{L}} = 0.020 \text{ mol AgNO}_3$$

$$\text{mol CaCl}_2 = 0.1000 \text{ L} \times \frac{0.15 \text{ mol CaCl}_2}{\text{L}} = 0.015 \text{ mol CaCl}_2$$

The required mol $AgNO_3$ to mol $CaCl_2$ ratio is 2:1 (from the balanced equation). The actual mole ratio present is 0.020/0.015 = 1.3 (1.3:1). Therefore, $AgNO_3$ is the limiting reagent.

$$\text{mass AgCl} = 0.020 \text{ mol AgNO}_3 \times \frac{1 \text{ mol AgCl}}{1 \text{ mol AgNO}_3} \times \frac{143.4 \text{ g AgCl}}{\text{mol AgCl}} = 2.9 \text{ g AgCl}$$

The net ionic equation is: $Ag^+(aq) + Cl^-(aq) \rightarrow AgCl(s)$. The ions remaining in solution are the unreacted Cl^- ions and the spectator ions, NO_3^- and Ca^{2+} (all of the Ag^+ is used up in forming AgCl). The moles of each ion present initially (before reaction) can be easily determined from the moles of each reactant. 0.020 mol $AgNO_3$ dissolves to form 0.020 mol Ag^+ and 0.020 mol NO_3^-. 0.015 mol $CaCl_2$ dissolves to form 0.015 mol Ca^{2+} and 2(0.015) = 0.030 mol Cl^-.

mol unreacted $Cl^- = 0.030$ mol Cl^- initially -0.020 mol Cl^- reacted = 0.010 mol Cl^- unreacted

$$M_{Cl^-} = \frac{0.010 \text{ mol Cl}^-}{\text{total volume}} = \frac{0.010 \text{ mol Cl}^-}{0.1000 \text{ L} + 0.1000 \text{ L}} = 0.050 \text{ M Cl}^-$$

The molarity of the spectator ions are:

$$M_{NO_3^-} = \frac{0.20 \text{ mol NO}_3^-}{0.2000 \text{ L}} = 0.10 \text{ M NO}_3^-; \quad M_{Ca^{2+}} = \frac{0.015 \text{ mol Ca}^{2+}}{0.2000 \text{ L}} = 0.075 \text{ M Ca}^{2+}$$

52.   a. $Cu(NO_3)_2(aq) + 2 KOH(aq) \rightarrow Cu(OH)_2(s) + 2 KNO_3(aq)$

Solution A contains 2.00 L × 2.00 mol/L = 4.00 mol $Cu(NO_3)_2$ and solution B contains 2.00 L × 3.00 mol/L = 6.00 mol KOH. Lets assume in our picture that we have 4 formula units of $Cu(NO_3)_2$ (4 Cu^{2+} ions and 8 NO_3^- ions) and 6 formula units of KOH (6 K^+ ions and 6 OH^- ions). With 4 Cu^{2+} ions and 6 OH^- ions present, then OH^- is limiting. One Cu^{2+} ion remains as 3 $Cu(OH)_2(s)$ formula units form as precipitate. The following drawing summarizes the ions that remain in solution and the relative amount of precipitate that forms. Note that K^+ and NO_3^- ions are spectator ions. In the drawing, V_1 is the volume of solution A or B and V_2 is the volume of the combined solutions with $V_2 = 2V_1$. The drawing exaggerates the amount of precipitate that would actually form.

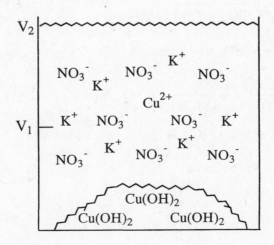

b. The spectator ion concentrations will be one-half of the original spectator ion concentrations in the individual beakers because the volume was doubled. Or using

moles, $M_{K^+} = \dfrac{6.00 \text{ mol K}^+}{4.00 \text{ L}} = 1.50$ M and $M_{NO_3^-} = \dfrac{8.00 \text{ mol NO}_3^-}{4.00 \text{ L}} = 2.00$ M. The

concentration of OH⁻ ions will be zero since OH⁻ is the limiting reagent. From the drawing, the number of Cu^{2+} ions will decrease by a factor of four as the precipitate forms. The volume of solution doubled, thus the concentration of Cu^{2+} ions will decrease by a factor of eight after the two beakers are mixed:

$$M_{Cu^{2+}} = 2.00\left(\dfrac{1}{8}\right) = 0.250\ M$$

Alternately, one could certainly use moles to solve for $M_{Cu^{2+}}$:

$$\text{mol Cu}^{2+}\text{ reacted} = 2.00\text{ L} \times \dfrac{3.00 \text{ mol OH}^-}{\text{L}} \times \dfrac{1 \text{ mol Cu}^{2+}}{2 \text{ mol OH}^-} = 3.00 \text{ mol Cu}^{2+}\text{ reacted}$$

$$\text{mol Cu}^{2+}\text{ present initially} = 2.00\text{ L} \times \dfrac{2.00 \text{ mol Cu}^{2+}}{\text{L}} = 4.00 \text{ mol Cu}^{2+}\text{ present initially}$$

excess Cu^{2+} present after reaction = 4.00 mol − 3.00 mol = 1.00 mol Cu^{2+} excess

$$M_{Cu^{2+}} = \dfrac{1.00 \text{ mol Cu}^{2+}}{2.00\text{ L} + 2.00\text{ L}} = 0.250\ M$$

$$\text{mass of precipitate} = 6.00 \text{ mol KOH} \times \dfrac{1 \text{ mol Cu(OH)}_2}{1 \text{ mol KOH}} \times \dfrac{97.57 \text{ g Cu(OH)}_2}{\text{mol Cu(OH)}_2}$$

$$= 293 \text{ g Cu(OH)}_2$$

53. $M_2SO_4(aq) + CaCl_2(aq) \rightarrow CaSO_4(s) + 2\ MCl(aq)$

$$1.36 \text{ g CaSO}_4 \times \dfrac{1 \text{ mol CaSO}_4}{136.15 \text{ g CaSO}_4} \times \dfrac{1 \text{ mol M}_2SO_4}{\text{mol CaSO}_4} = 9.99 \times 10^{-3} \text{ mol M}_2SO_4$$

From the problem, 1.42 g M_2SO_4 was reacted so:

$$\text{molar mass} = \dfrac{1.42 \text{ g M}_2SO_4}{9.99\times10^{-3} \text{ mol M}_2SO_4} = 142 \text{ g/mol}$$

142 amu = 2(atomic mass M) + 32.07 + 4(16.00), atomic mass M = 23 amu

From periodic table, M = Na (sodium).

54.   a. Na^+, NO_3^-, Cl^-, and Ag^+ ions are present before any reaction occurs. The excess Ag^+ added will remove all of the Cl^- ions present. Therefore, Na^+, NO_3^- and the excess Ag^+ ions will all be present after precipitation of AgCl is complete.

      b. $Ag^+(aq) + Cl^-(aq) \rightarrow AgCl(s)$

      c.   mass NaCl = 0.641 g AgCl $\times \dfrac{1\,mol\,AgCl}{143.4\,g} \times \dfrac{1\,mol\,Cl^-}{mol\,AgCl} \times \dfrac{1\,mol\,NaCl}{mol\,Cl^-} \times \dfrac{58.44\,g}{mol\,NaCl}$

$$= 0.261 \text{ g NaCl}$$

mass %NaCl = $\dfrac{0.261\,g\,NaCl}{1.50\,g\,mixture} \times 100 = 17.4\%$ NaCl

Acid-Base Reactions

55.   All the bases in this problem are ionic compounds containing OH^-. The acids are either strong or weak electrolytes. The best way to determine if an acid is a strong or weak electrolyte is to memorize all the strong electrolytes (strong acids). Any other acid you encounter that is not a strong acid will be a weak electrolyte (a weak acid) and the formula should be left unaltered in the complete ionic and net ionic equations. The strong acids to recognize are HCl, HBr, HI, HNO_3, $HClO_4$ and H_2SO_4. For the following answers, the order of the equations are formula, complete ionic, and net ionic.

      a. $2\,HClO_4(aq) + Mg(OH)_2(s) \rightarrow 2\,H_2O(l) + Mg(ClO_4)_2(aq)$

           $2\,H^+(aq) + 2\,ClO_4^-(aq) + Mg(OH)_2(s) \rightarrow 2\,H_2O(l) + Mg^{2+}(aq) + 2\,ClO_4^-(aq)$

           $2\,H^+(aq) + Mg(OH)_2(s) \rightarrow 2\,H_2O(l) + Mg^{2+}(aq)$

      b. $HCN(aq) + NaOH(aq) \rightarrow H_2O(l) + NaCN(aq)$

           $HCN(aq) + Na^+(aq) + OH^-(aq) \rightarrow H_2O(l) + Na^+(aq) + CN^-(aq)$

           $HCN(aq) + OH^-(aq) \rightarrow H_2O(l) + CN^-(aq)$

      c. $HCl(aq) + NaOH(aq) \rightarrow H_2O(l) + NaCl(aq)$

           $H^+(aq) + Cl^-(aq) + Na^+(aq) + OH^-(aq) \rightarrow H_2O(l) + Na^+(aq) + Cl^-(aq)$

           $H^+(aq) + OH^-(aq) \rightarrow H_2O(l)$

56.   a. $3\,HNO_3(aq) + Al(OH)_3(s) \rightarrow 3\,H_2O(l) + Al(NO_3)_3(aq)$

           $3\,H^+(aq) + 3\,NO_3^-(aq) + Al(OH)_3(s) \rightarrow 3\,H_2O(l) + Al^{3+}(aq) + 3\,NO_3^-(aq)$

           $3\,H^+(aq) + Al(OH)_3(s) \rightarrow 3\,H_2O(l) + Al^{3+}(aq)$

b. $HC_2H_3O_2(aq) + KOH(aq) \rightarrow H_2O(l) + KC_2H_3O_2(aq)$

$HC_2H_3O_2(aq) + K^+(aq) + OH^-(aq) \rightarrow H_2O(l) + K^+(aq) + C_2H_3O_2^-(aq)$

$HC_2H_3O_2(aq) + OH^-(aq) \rightarrow H_2O(l) + C_2H_3O_2^-(aq)$

c. $Ca(OH)_2(aq) + 2 HCl(aq) \rightarrow 2 H_2O(l) + CaCl_2(aq)$

$Ca^{2+}(aq) + 2 OH^-(aq) + 2 H^+(aq) + 2 Cl^-(aq) \rightarrow 2 H_2O(l) + Ca^{2+}(aq) + 2 Cl^-(aq)$

$2 H^+(aq) + 2 OH^-(aq) \rightarrow 2 H_2O(l)$ or $H^+(aq) + OH^-(aq) \rightarrow H_2O(l)$

57.   All the acids in this problem are strong electrolytes (strong acids). The acids to recognize as strong electrolytes are HCl, HBr, HI, HNO_3, $HClO_4$ and H_2SO_4.

a. $KOH(aq) + HNO_3(aq) \rightarrow H_2O(l) + KNO_3(aq)$

$K^+(aq) + OH^-(aq) + H^+(aq) + NO_3^-(aq) \rightarrow H_2O(l) + K^+(aq) + NO_3^-(aq)$

$OH^-(aq) + H^+(aq) \rightarrow H_2O(l)$

b. $Ba(OH)_2(aq) + 2 HCl(aq) \rightarrow 2 H_2O(l) + BaCl_2(aq)$

$Ba^{2+}(aq) + 2 OH^-(aq) + 2 H^+(aq) + 2 Cl^-(aq) \rightarrow 2 H_2O(l) + Ba^{2+}(aq) + 2 Cl^-(aq)$

$2 OH^-(aq) + 2 H^+(aq) \rightarrow 2 H_2O(l)$ or $OH^-(aq) + H^+(aq) \rightarrow H_2O(l)$

c. $3 HClO_4(aq) + Fe(OH)_3(s) \rightarrow 3 H_2O(l) + Fe(ClO_4)_3(aq)$

$3 H^+(aq) + 3 ClO_4^-(aq) + Fe(OH)_3(s) \rightarrow 3 H_2O(l) + Fe^{3+}(aq) + 3 ClO_4^-(aq)$

$3 H^+(aq) + Fe(OH)_3(s) \rightarrow 3 H_2O(l) + Fe^{3+}(aq)$

58.   a. $AgOH(s) + HBr(aq) \rightarrow AgBr(s) + H_2O(l)$

$AgOH(s) + H^+(aq) + Br^-(aq) \rightarrow AgBr(s) + H_2O(l)$

$AgOH(s) + H^+(aq) + Br^-(aq) \rightarrow AgBr(s) + H_2O(l)$

b. $Sr(OH)_2(aq) + 2 HI(aq) \rightarrow 2 H_2O(l) + SrI_2(aq)$

$Sr^{2+}(aq) + 2 OH^-(aq) + 2 H^+(aq) + 2 I^-(aq) \rightarrow 2 H_2O(l) + Sr^{2+}(aq) + 2 I^-(aq)$

$2 OH^-(aq) + 2 H^+(aq) \rightarrow 2 H_2O(l)$ or $OH^-(aq) + H^+(aq) \rightarrow H_2O(l)$

c. $Cr(OH)_3(s) + 3\ HNO_3(aq) \rightarrow 3\ H_2O(l) + Cr(NO_3)_3(aq)$

$Cr(OH)_3(s) + 3\ H^+(aq) + 3\ NO_3^-(aq) \rightarrow 3\ H_2O(l) + Cr^{3+}(aq) + 3\ NO_3^-(aq)$

$Cr(OH)_3(s) + 3\ H^+(aq) \rightarrow 3\ H_2O(l) + Cr^{3+}(aq)$

59.   If we begin with 50.00 mL of 0.200 M NaOH, then:

$$50.00 \times 10^{-3}\,L \times \frac{0.200\ mol}{L} = 1.00 \times 10^{-2}\ mol\ NaOH\ is\ to\ be\ neutralized.$$

a. $NaOH(aq) + HCl(aq) \rightarrow NaCl(aq) + H_2O(l)$

$$1.00 \times 10^{-2}\ mol\ NaOH \times \frac{1\ mol\ HCl}{mol\ NaOH} \times \frac{1\ L}{0.100\ mol} = 0.100\ L\ or\ 100.\ mL$$

b. $HNO_3(aq) + NaOH(aq) \rightarrow H_2O(l) + NaNO_3(aq)$

$$1.00 \times 10^{-2}\ mol\ NaOH \times \frac{1\ mol\ HNO_3}{mol\ NaOH} \times \frac{1\ L}{0.150\ mol\ HNO_3} = 6.67 \times 10^{-2}\ L\ or\ 66.7\ mL$$

c. $HC_2H_3O_2(aq) + NaOH(aq) \rightarrow H_2O(l) + NaC_2H_3O_2(aq)$

$$1.00 \times 10^{-2}\ mol\ NaOH \times \frac{1\ mol\ HC_2H_3O_2}{mol\ NaOH} \times \frac{1\ L}{0.200\ mol\ HC_2H_3O_2} = 5.00 \times 10^{-2}\ L$$

$$= 50.0\ mL$$

60.   We begin with 25.00 mL of 0.200 M HCl or $25.00 \times 10^{-3}\ L \times 0.200\ mol/L$

$$= 5.00 \times 10^{-3}\ mol\ HCl.$$

a. $HCl(aq) + NaOH(aq) \rightarrow H_2O(l) + NaCl(aq)$

$$5.00 \times 10^{-3}\ mol\ HCl \times \frac{1\ mol\ HCl}{mol\ NaOH} \times \frac{1\ L}{0.100\ mol\ NaOH} = 5.00 \times 10^{-2}\ L\ or\ 50.0\ mL$$

b. $2\ HCl(aq) + Ba(OH)_2(aq) \rightarrow 2\ H_2O(l) + BaCl_2(aq)$

$$5.00 \times 10^{-3}\ mol\ HCl \times \frac{1\ mol\ Ba(OH)_2}{2\ mol\ HCl} \times \frac{1\ L}{0.0500\ mol\ Ba(OH)_2} = 5.00 \times 10^{-2}\ L$$

$$= 50.0\ mL$$

c. $HCl(aq) + KOH(aq) \rightarrow H_2O(l) + KCl(aq)$

$$5.00 \times 10^{-3}\ mol\ HCl \times \frac{1\ mol\ KOH}{mol\ HCl} \times \frac{1\ L}{0.250\ mol\ KOH} = 2.00 \times 10^{-2}\ L\ or\ 20.0\ mL$$

61. $Ba(OH)_2(aq) + 2\ HCl(aq) \rightarrow BaCl_2(aq) + 2\ H_2O(l);\ \ H^+(aq) + OH^-(aq) \rightarrow H_2O(l)$

$75.0 \times 10^{-3}\,L \times \dfrac{0.250\ mol\ HCl}{L} = 1.88 \times 10^{-2}\ mol\ HCl = 1.88 \times 10^{-2}\ mol\ H^+ +$

$1.88 \times 10^{-2}\ mol\ Cl^-$

$225.0 \times 10^{-3}\,L \times \dfrac{0.0550\ mol\ Ba(OH)_2}{L} = 1.24 \times 10^{-2}\ mol\ Ba(OH)_2$

$= 1.24 \times 10^{-2}\ mol\ Ba^{2+} + 2.48 \times 10^{-2}\ mol\ OH^-$

The net ionic equation requires a 1:1 mole ratio between OH^- and H^+. The actual mol OH^- to mol H^+ ratio is greater than 1:1 so OH^- is in excess.

Since 1.88×10^{-2} mol OH^- will be neutralized by the H^+, we have $(2.48 - 1.88) \times 10^{-2}$ $= 0.60 \times 10^{-2}$ mol OH^- remaining in excess.

$$M_{OH^-} = \frac{mol\ OH^-\ excess}{total\ volume} = \frac{6.0 \times 10^{-3}\ mol\ OH^-}{0.750\,L + 0.2250\,L} = 2.0 \times 10^{-2}\ M\ OH^-$$

62. HCl and HNO_3 are strong acids; $Ca(OH)_2$ and $RbOH$ are strong bases. The net ionic equation that occurs is $H^+(aq) + OH^-(aq) \rightarrow H_2O(l)$.

$mol\ H^+ = 0.0500\,L \times \dfrac{0.100\ mol\ HCl}{L} \times \dfrac{1\ mol\ H^+}{mol\ HCl} +$

$0.1000\,L \times \dfrac{0.200\ mol\ HNO_3}{L} \times \dfrac{1\ mol\ H^+}{mol\ HNO_3} = 0.00500 + 0.0200 = 0.0250\ mol\ H^+$

$mol\ OH^- = 0.5000\,L \times \dfrac{0.0100\ mol\ Ca(OH)_2}{L} \times \dfrac{2\ mol\ OH^-}{mol\ Ca(OH)_2} +$

$0.2000\,L \times \dfrac{0.100\ mol\ RbOH}{L} \times \dfrac{1\ mol\ OH^-}{mol\ RbOH} = 0.0100 + 0.0200 = 0.0300\ mol\ OH^-$

We have an excess of OH^- so the solution is basic (not neutral). The mol of excess OH^- = 0.0300 mol OH^- initially − 0.0250 mol OH^- reacted (with H^+) = 0.0050 mol OH^- excess.

$$M_{OH^-} = \frac{0.0050\ mol\ OH^-}{(0.0500 + 0.1000 + 0.5000 + 0.2000)\,L} = \frac{0.0050\ mol}{0.8500\,L} = 5.9 \times 10^{-3}\ M$$

63. $HCl(aq) + NaOH(aq) \rightarrow H_2O(l) + NaCl(aq)$

$24.16 \times 10^{-3}\,L\ NaOH \times \dfrac{0.106\ mol\ NaOH}{L\ NaOH} \times \dfrac{1\ mol\ HCl}{mol\ NaOH} = 2.56 \times 10^{-3}\ mol\ HCl$

Molarity of $HCl = \dfrac{2.56 \times 10^{-3}\ mol}{25.00 \times 10^{-3}\ L} = 0.102\ M\ HCl$

64. $2 HNO_3(aq) + Ca(OH)_2(aq) \rightarrow 2 H_2O(l) + Ca(NO_3)_2(aq)$

$$35.00 \times 10^{-3} \text{ L HNO}_3 \times \frac{0.0500 \text{ mol HNO}_3}{\text{L HNO}_3} \times \frac{1 \text{ mol Ca(OH)}_2}{2 \text{ mol HNO}_3} \times \frac{1 \text{ L Ca(OH)}_2}{0.0200 \text{ mol Ca(OH)}_2}$$

$$= 0.0438 \text{ L} = 43.8 \text{ mL Ca(OH)}_2$$

65.   KHP is a monoprotic acid: $NaOH(aq) + KHP(aq) \rightarrow H_2O(l) + NaKP(aq)$

$$\text{Mass KHP} = 0.02046 \text{ L NaOH} \times \frac{0.1000 \text{ mol NaOH}}{\text{L NaOH}} \times \frac{1 \text{ mol KHP}}{\text{mol NaOH}} \times \frac{204.22 \text{ g KHP}}{\text{mol KHP}}$$

$$= 0.4178 \text{ g KHP}$$

66. $NaOH(aq) + KHP(aq) \rightarrow NaKP(aq) + H_2O(l)$

$$0.1082 \text{ g KHP} \times \frac{1 \text{ mol KHP}}{204.22 \text{ g KHP}} \times \frac{1 \text{ mol NaOH}}{\text{mol KHP}} = 5.298 \times 10^{-4} \text{ mol NaOH}$$

There are 5.298×10^{-4} mol of sodium hydroxide in 34.67 mL of solution. Therefore, the concentration of sodium hydroxide is:

$$\frac{5.298 \times 10^{-4} \text{ mol}}{34.67 \times 10^{-3} \text{ L}} = 1.528 \times 10^{-2} \text{ M NaOH}$$

Oxidation-Reduction Reactions

67.   Apply the rules in Table 4.2.

a. $KMnO_4$ is composed of K^+ and MnO_4^- ions. Assign oxygen a value of -2, which gives manganese a $+7$ oxidation state since the sum of oxidation states for all atoms in MnO_4^- must equal the -1 charge on MnO_4^-. K, $+1$; O, -2; Mn, $+7$.

b.   Assign O a -2 oxidation state, which gives nickel a $+4$ oxidation state. Ni, $+4$; O, -2.

c. $Na_4Fe(OH)_6$ is composed of Na^+ cations and $Fe(OH)_6^{4-}$ anions. $Fe(OH)_6^{4-}$ is composed of an iron cation and 6 OH^- anions. For an overall anion charge of -4, iron must have a $+2$ oxidation state. As is usually the case in compounds, assign O a -2 oxidation state and H a $+1$ oxidation state. Na, $+1$; Fe, $+2$; O, -2; H, $+1$.

d. $(NH_4)_2HPO_4$ is made of NH_4^+ cations and HPO_4^{2-} anions. Assign $+1$ as the oxidation state of H and -2 as the oxidation state of O. In NH_4^+, $x + 4(+1) = +1$, $x = -3 =$ oxidation state of N. In HPO_4^{2-}, $+1 + y + 4(-2) = -2$, $y = +5 =$ oxidation state of P.

e.   O, -2; P, $+3$ f.   O, -2; Fe, $+ 8/3$

g.   O, -2; F, -1; Xe, $+6$ h.   F, -1; S, $+4$

i.   O, -2; C, $+2$ j.   H, $+1$; O, -2; C, 0

68   a. UO_2^{2+}: O, -2; For U, $x + 2(-2) = +2$, $x = \underline{+6}$

      b. As_2O_3: O, -2; For As, $2(x) + 3(-2) = 0$, $x = \underline{+3}$

      c. $NaBiO_3$: Na, +1; O, -2; For Bi, $+1 + x + 3(-2) = 0$, $x = \underline{+5}$

      d. As_4: As, 0

      e. $HAsO_2$: assign H = +1 and O = -2; For As, $+1 + x + 2(-2) = 0$, $x = \underline{+3}$

      f. $Mg_2P_2O_7$: Composed of Mg^{2+} ions and $P_2O_7^{4-}$ ions. Oxidation states are:

           Mg, +2; O, -2; P, +5

      g. $Na_2S_2O_3$: Composed of Na^+ ions and $S_2O_3^{2-}$ ions.   Na, +1; O, -2; S, +2

      h. Hg_2Cl_2: Hg, +1; Cl, -1

      i. $Ca(NO_3)_2$: Composed of Ca^{2+} ions and NO_3^- ions.   Ca, +2; O, -2; N, +5

69.   a.   -3   b.   -3   c. $2(x) + 4(+1) = 0$, $x = -2$
      d.   +2   e.   +1   f.   +4
      g.   +3   h.   +5   i.   0

70.   a. $SrCr_2O_7$: composed of Sr^{2+} and $Cr_2O_7^{2-}$ ions. Sr, +2; O, -2; Cr, $2x + 7(-2) = -2$, $x = +6$

      b.   Cu, +2; Cl, -1   c.   O, 0   d.   H, +1; O, -1

      e. Mg^{2+} and CO_3^{2-} ions present. Mg, +2; O, -2; C, +4;   f.   Ag, 0

      g. Pb^{2+} and SO_3^{2-} ions present. Pb, +2; O, -2; S, +4;   h.   O, -2; Pb, +4

      i. Na^+ and $C_2O_4^{2-}$ ions present. Na, +1; O, -2; C, $2x + 4(-2) = -2$, x = +3

      j.   O, -2; C, +4

      k.   Ammonium ion has a +1 charge (NH_4^+) and sulfate ion has a -2 charge (SO_4^{2-}).
           Therefore, the oxidation state of cerium must be +4 (Ce^{4+}). H, +1; N, -3; O, -2; S, +6

      l.   O, -2; Cr, +3

71.   To determine if the reaction is an oxidation-reduction reaction, assign oxidation numbers. If
      the oxidation numbers change for some elements, then the reaction is a redox reaction. If the
      oxidation numbers do not change, then the reaction is not a redox reaction. In redox
      reactions, the species oxidized (called the reducing agent) shows an increase in oxidation
      numbers and the species reduced (called the oxidizing agent) shows a decrease in oxidation
      numbers.

	Redox?	Oxidizing Agent	Reducing Agent	Substance Oxidized	Substance Reduced
a.	Yes	Ag^+	Cu	Cu	Ag^+
b.	No	–	–	–	–
c.	No	–	–	–	–
d.	Yes	$SiCl_4$	Mg	Mg	$SiCl_4$ (Si)
e.	No	–	–	–	–

In b, c, and e, no oxidation numbers change.

72.   The species oxidized shows an increase in oxidation numbers and is called the reducing agent. The species reduced shows a decrease in oxidation numbers and is called the oxidizing agent. The pertinent oxidation numbers are listed by the substance oxidized and the substance reduced.

	Redox?	Oxidizing Agent	Reducing Agent	Substance Oxidized	Substance Reduced
a.	Yes	H_2O	CH_4	CH_4 (C, -4 → +2)	H_2O (H, +1 → 0)
b	Yes	$AgNO_3$	Cu	Cu (0 → +2)	$AgNO_3$ (Ag, +1 → 0)
c.	Yes	HCl	Zn	Zn (0 → +2)	HCl (H, +1 → 0)

d.   No; There is no change in any of the oxidation numbers.

73.   Use the method of half-reactions described in Section 4.10 of the text to balance these redox reactions. The first step always is to separate the reaction into the two half-reactions, then balance each half-reaction separately.

a. $Zn \rightarrow Zn^{2+} + 2\,e^-$ $2e^- + 2\,HCl \rightarrow H_2 + 2\,Cl^-$

Adding the two balanced half-reactions:
   $Zn(s) + 2\,HCl(aq) \rightarrow H_2(g) + Zn^{2+}(aq) + 2\,Cl^-(aq)$

$\qquad\qquad\qquad\qquad\qquad\qquad\qquad\qquad 2\,Cl^-(aq)$

b. $3\,I^- \rightarrow I_3^- + 2e^-$ $ClO^- \rightarrow Cl^-$
$\qquad\qquad\qquad\qquad\qquad\qquad\qquad 2e^- + 2H^+ + ClO^- \rightarrow Cl^- + H_2O$

Adding the two balanced half-reactions so electrons cancel:

   $3\,I^-(aq) + 2\,H^+(aq) + ClO^-(aq) \rightarrow I_3^-(aq) + Cl^-(aq) + H_2O(l)$

c. $As_2O_3 \rightarrow H_3AsO_4$ $NO_3^- \rightarrow NO + 2\,H_2O$
   $As_2O_3 \rightarrow 2\,H_3AsO_4$ $4\,H^+ + NO_3^- \rightarrow NO + 2\,H_2O$
   Left 3 – O; Right 8 – O $(3\,e^- + 4\,H^+ + NO_3^- \rightarrow NO + 2\,H_2O) \times 4$

Right hand side has 5 extra O.
Balance the oxygen atoms first using H_2O, then balance H using H^+, and finally balance charge using electrons. This gives:

$$(5 \; H_2O + As_2O_3 \rightarrow 2 \; H_3AsO_4 + 4 \; H^+ + 4 \; e^-) \times 3$$

Common factor is a transfer of 12 e^-. Add half-reactions so electrons cancel.

$$12 \; e^- + 16 \; H^+ + 4 \; NO_3^- \rightarrow 4 \; NO + 8 \; H_2O$$
$$15 \; H_2O + 3 \; As_2O_3 \rightarrow 6 \; H_3AsO_4 + 12 \; H^+ + 12 \; e^-$$

$$7 \; H_2O(l) + 4 \; H^+(aq) + 3 \; As_2O_3(s) + 4 \; NO_3^-(aq) \rightarrow 4 \; NO(g) + 6 \; H_3AsO_4(aq)$$

d. $(2 \; Br \rightarrow Br_2 + 2 \; e^-) \times 5$ $\qquad\qquad MnO_4^- \rightarrow Mn^{2+} + 4 \; H_2O$
$\qquad\qquad\qquad\qquad\qquad\qquad\qquad (5 \; e^- + 8 \; H^+ + MnO_4^- \rightarrow Mn^{2+} + 4 \; H_2O) \times 2$

Common factor is a transfer of 10 e^-.

$$10 \; Br^- \rightarrow 5 \; Br_2 + 10 \; e^-$$
$$10 \; e^- + 16 \; H^+ + 2 \; MnO_4^- \rightarrow 2 \; Mn^{2+} + 8 \; H_2O$$

$$16 \; H^+(aq) + 2 \; MnO_4^-(aq) + 10 \; Br^-(aq) \rightarrow 5 \; Br_2(l) + 2 \; Mn^{2+}(aq) + 8 \; H_2O(l)$$

e. $CH_3OH \rightarrow CH_2O$ $\qquad\qquad\qquad\qquad\qquad Cr_2O_7^{2-} \rightarrow 2 \; Cr^{3+}$
$(CH_3OH \rightarrow CH_2O + 2 \; H^+ + 2 \; e^-) \times 3 \qquad 14 \; H^+ + Cr_2O_7^{2-} \rightarrow 2 \; Cr^{3+} + 7 \; H_2O$
$\qquad\qquad\qquad\qquad\qquad\qquad\qquad 6 \; e^- + 14 \; H^+ + Cr_2O_7^{2-} \rightarrow 2 \; Cr^{3+} + 7 \; H_2O$

Common factor is a transfer of 6 e^-.

$$3 \; CH_3OH \rightarrow 3 \; CH_2O + 6 \; H^+ + 6 \; e^-$$
$$6 \; e^- + 14 \; H^+ + Cr_2O_7^{2-} \rightarrow 2 \; Cr^{3+} + 7 \; H_2O$$

$$8 \; H^+(aq) + 3 \; CH_3OH(aq) + Cr_2O_7^{2-}(aq) \rightarrow 2 \; Cr^{3+}(aq) + 3 \; CH_2O(aq) + 7 \; H_2O(l)$$

74. a. $(Cu \rightarrow Cu^{2+} + 2 \; e^-) \times 3$ $\qquad\qquad\qquad NO_3^- \rightarrow NO + 2 \; H_2O$
$\qquad\qquad\qquad\qquad\qquad\qquad (3 \; e^- + 4 \; H^+ + NO_3^- \rightarrow NO + 2 \; H_2O) \times 2$

Adding the two balanced half-reactions so electrons cancel:

$$3 \; Cu \rightarrow 3 \; Cu^{2+} + 6 \; e^-$$
$$6 \; e^- + 8 \; H^+ + 2 \; NO_3^- \rightarrow 2 \; NO + 4 \; H_2O$$

$$3 \; Cu(s) + 8 \; H^+(aq) + 2 \; NO_3^-(aq) \rightarrow 3 \; Cu^{2+}(aq) + 2 \; NO(g) + 4 \; H_2O(l)$$

b. $(2 \; Cl^- \rightarrow Cl_2 + 2 \; e^-) \times 3$ $\qquad\qquad\qquad Cr_2O_7^{2-} \rightarrow 2 \; Cr^{3+} + 7 \; H_2O$
$\qquad\qquad\qquad\qquad\qquad\qquad 6 \; e^- + 14 \; H^+ + Cr_2O_7^{2-} \rightarrow 2 \; Cr^{3+} + 7 \; H_2O$

Add the two half-reactions with six electrons transferred:

$$6 \; Cl^- \rightarrow 3 \; Cl_2 + 6 \; e^-$$
$$6 \; e^- + 14 \; H^+ + Cr_2O_7^{2-} \rightarrow 2 \; Cr^{3+} + 7 \; H_2O$$

$$14 \; H^+(aq) + Cr_2O_7^{2-}(aq) + 6 \; Cl^-(aq) \rightarrow 3 \; Cl_2(g) + 2 \; Cr^{3+}(aq) + 7 \; H_2O(l)$$

c. $\qquad$ $Pb \rightarrow PbSO_4$ $\qquad\qquad\qquad\qquad\qquad$ $PbO_2 \rightarrow PbSO_4$

$Pb + H_2SO_4 \rightarrow PbSO_4 + 2\,H^+$ $\qquad\qquad$ $PbO_2 + H_2SO_4 \rightarrow PbSO_4 + 2\,H_2O$

$Pb + H_2SO_4 \rightarrow PbSO_4 + 2\,H^+ + 2\,e^-$ $\qquad$ $2\,e^- + 2\,H^+ + PbO_2 + H_2SO_4 \rightarrow PbSO_4 + 2\,H_2O$

Add the two half-reactions with two electrons transferred:

$$2\,e^- + 2\,H^+ + PbO_2 + H_2SO_4 \rightarrow PbSO_4 + 2\,H_2O$$
$$Pb + H_2SO_4 \rightarrow PbSO_4 + 2\,H^+ + 2\,e^-$$

$$\overline{Pb(s) + 2\,H_2SO_4(aq) + PbO_2(s) \rightarrow 2\,PbSO_4(s) + 2\,H_2O(l)}$$

This is the reaction that occurs in an automobile lead-storage battery.

d. $\qquad\qquad\qquad$ $Mn^{2+} \rightarrow MnO_4^-$

$(4\,H_2O + Mn^{2+} \rightarrow MnO_4^- + 8\,H^+ + 5\,e^-) \times 2$

$$NaBiO_3 \rightarrow Bi^{3+} + Na^+$$
$$6\,H^+ + NaBiO_3 \rightarrow Bi^{3+} + Na^+ + 3\,H_2O$$
$$(2\,e^- + 6\,H^+ + NaBiO_3 \rightarrow Bi^{3+} + Na^+ + 3\,H_2O) \times 5$$

$$8\,H_2O + 2\,Mn^{2+} \rightarrow 2\,MnO_4^- + 16\,H^+ + 10\,e^-$$
$$10\,e^- + 30\,H^+ + 5\,NaBiO_3 \rightarrow 5\,Bi^{3+} + 5\,Na^+ + 15\,H_2O$$

$$\overline{8\,H_2O + 30\,H^+ + 2\,Mn^{2+} + 5\,NaBiO_3 \rightarrow 2\,MnO_4^- + 5\,Bi^{3+} + 5\,Na^+ + 15\,H_2O + 16\,H^+}$$

Simplifying:

$$14\,H^+(aq) + 2\,Mn^{2+}(aq) + 5\,NaBiO_3(s) \rightarrow 2\,MnO_4^-(aq) + 5\,Bi^{3+}(aq) + 5\,Na^+(aq) +$$
$$7\,H_2O(l)$$

e. $\qquad\qquad$ $H_3AsO_4 \rightarrow AsH_3$ $\qquad\qquad\qquad$ $(Zn \rightarrow Zn^{2+} + 2\,e^-) \times 4$

$\qquad\qquad$ $H_3AsO_4 \rightarrow AsH_3 + 4\,H_2O$

$8\,e^- + 8\,H^+ + H_3AsO_4 \rightarrow AsH_3 + 4\,H_2O$

$$8\,e^- + 8\,H^+ + H_3AsO_4 \rightarrow AsH_3 + 4\,H_2O$$
$$4\,Zn \rightarrow 4\,Zn^{2+} + 8\,e^-$$

$$\overline{8\,H^+(aq) + H_3AsO_4(aq) + 4\,Zn(s) \rightarrow 4\,Zn^{2+}(aq) + AsH_3(g) + 4\,H_2O(l)}$$

75. Use the same method as with acidic solutions. After the final balanced equation, convert H^+ to OH^- as described in section 4.10 of the text. The extra step involves converting H^+ into H_2O by adding equal moles of OH^- to each side of the reaction. This converts the reaction to a basic solution while still keeping it balanced.

a. $\qquad\qquad$ $Al \rightarrow Al(OH)_4^-$ $\qquad\qquad\qquad$ $MnO_4^- \rightarrow MnO_2$

$\qquad$ $4\,H_2O + Al \rightarrow Al(OH)_4^- + 4\,H^+$ $\qquad$ $3\,e^- + 4\,H^+ + MnO_4^- \rightarrow MnO_2 + 2\,H_2O$

$4\,H_2O + Al \rightarrow Al(OH)_4^- + 4\,H^+ + 3\,e^-$

$$4 \text{ H}_2\text{O} + \text{Al} \rightarrow \text{Al(OH)}_4^- + 4 \text{ H}^+ + 3 \text{ e}^-$$
$$3 \text{ e}^- + 4 \text{ H}^+ + \text{MnO}_4^- \rightarrow \text{MnO}_2 + 2 \text{ H}_2\text{O}$$

$$2 \text{ H}_2\text{O(l)} + \text{Al(s)} + \text{MnO}_4^-(\text{aq}) \rightarrow \text{Al(OH)}_4^-(\text{aq}) + \text{MnO}_2(\text{s})$$

H^+ doesn't appear in the final balanced reaction, so we are done.

b. $\text{Cl}_2 \rightarrow \text{Cl}^-$ $\text{Cl}_2 \rightarrow \text{OCl}^-$

    $2 \text{ e}^- + \text{Cl}_2 \rightarrow 2 \text{ Cl}^-$ $2 \text{ H}_2\text{O} + \text{Cl}_2 \rightarrow 2 \text{ OCl}^- + 4 \text{ H}^+ + 2 \text{ e}^-$

$$2 \text{ e}^- + \text{Cl}_2 \rightarrow 2 \text{ Cl}^-$$
$$2 \text{ H}_2\text{O} + \text{Cl}_2 \rightarrow 2 \text{ OCl}^- + 4 \text{ H}^+ + 2 \text{ e}^-$$

$$2 \text{ H}_2\text{O} + 2 \text{ Cl}_2 \rightarrow 2 \text{ Cl}^- + 2 \text{ OCl}^- + 4 \text{ H}^+$$

Now convert to a basic solution. Add 4 OH^- to both sides of the equation. The 4 OH^- will react with the 4 H^+ on the product side to give 4 H_2O. After this step, cancel identical species on both sides (2 H_2O). Applying these steps gives: 4 OH^- + 2 $\text{Cl}_2 \rightarrow$ 2 Cl^- + 2 OCl^- + 2 H_2O, which can be further simplified to:

$$2 \text{ OH}^-(\text{aq}) + \text{Cl}_2(\text{g}) \rightarrow \text{Cl}^-(\text{aq}) + \text{OCl}^-(\text{aq}) + \text{H}_2\text{O(l)}$$

c. $\text{NO}_2^- \rightarrow \text{NH}_3$ $\text{Al} \rightarrow \text{AlO}_2^-$

   $6 \text{ e}^- + 7 \text{ H}^+ + \text{NO}_2^- \rightarrow \text{NH}_3 + 2 \text{ H}_2\text{O}$ $(2 \text{ H}_2\text{O} + \text{Al} \rightarrow \text{AlO}_2^- + 4 \text{ H}^+ + 3 \text{ e}^-) \times 2$

Common factor is a transfer of 6 e^-.

$$6\text{e}^- + 7 \text{ H}^+ + \text{NO}_2^- \rightarrow \text{NH}_3 + 2 \text{ H}_2\text{O}$$
$$4 \text{ H}_2\text{O} + 2 \text{ Al} \rightarrow 2 \text{ AlO}_2^- + 8 \text{ H}^+ + 6 \text{ e}^-$$

$$\text{OH}^- + 2 \text{ H}_2\text{O} + \text{NO}_2^- + 2 \text{ Al} \rightarrow \text{NH}_3 + 2 \text{ AlO}_2^- + \text{H}^+ + \text{OH}^-$$

Reducing gives: $\text{OH}^-(\text{aq}) + \text{H}_2\text{O(l)} + \text{NO}_2^-(\text{aq}) + 2 \text{ Al(s)} \rightarrow \text{NH}_3(\text{g}) + 2 \text{ AlO}_2^-(\text{aq})$

76.   a. $\text{Cr} \rightarrow \text{Cr(OH)}_3$ $\text{CrO}_4^{2-} \rightarrow \text{Cr(OH)}_3$

   $3 \text{ H}_2\text{O} + \text{Cr} \rightarrow \text{Cr(OH)}_3 + 3 \text{ H}^+ + 3 \text{ e}^-$ $3 \text{ e}^- + 5 \text{ H}^+ + \text{CrO}_4^{2-} \rightarrow \text{Cr(OH)}_3 + \text{H}_2\text{O}$

$$3 \text{ H}_2\text{O} + \text{Cr} \rightarrow \text{Cr(OH)}_3 + 3 \text{ H}^+ + 3 \text{ e}^-$$
$$3 \text{ e}^- + 5 \text{ H}^+ + \text{CrO}_4^{2-} \rightarrow \text{Cr(OH)}_3 + \text{H}_2\text{O}$$

$$2 \text{ OH}^- + 2 \text{ H}^+ + 2 \text{ H}_2\text{O} + \text{Cr} + \text{CrO}_4^{2-} \rightarrow 2 \text{ Cr(OH)}_3 + 2 \text{ OH}^-$$

Two OH^- were added above to each side to convert to a basic solution. The two OH^- react with the 2 H^+ on the reactant side to produce 2 H_2O. The overall balanced equation is:

$$4 \text{ H}_2\text{O(l)} + \text{Cr(s)} + \text{CrO}_4^{2-}(\text{aq}) \rightarrow 2 \text{ Cr(OH)}_3(\text{s}) + 2 \text{ OH}^-(\text{aq})$$

b. $S^{2-} \rightarrow S$ $MnO_4^- \rightarrow MnS$

$(S^{2-} \rightarrow S + 2 \, e^-) \times 5$ $MnO_4^- + S^{2-} \rightarrow MnS$

$(5 \, e^- + 8 \, H^+ + MnO_4^- + S^{2-} \rightarrow MnS + 4 \, H_2O) \times 2$

Common factor is a transfer of 10 e^-.

$$5 \, S^{2-} \rightarrow 5 \, S + 10 \, e^-$$
$$10 \, e^- + 16 \, H^+ + 2 \, MnO_4^- + 2 \, S^{2-} \rightarrow 2 \, MnS + 8 \, H_2O$$

$16 \, OH^- + 16 \, H^+ + 7 \, S^{2-} + 2 \, MnO_4^- \rightarrow 5 \, S + 2 \, MnS + 8 \, H_2O + 16 \, OH^-$

$16 \, H_2O + 7 \, S^{2-} + 2 \, MnO_4^- \rightarrow 5 \, S + 2 \, MnS + 8 \, H_2O + 16 \, OH^-$

Reducing gives: $8 \, H_2O(l) + 7 \, S^{2-}(aq) + 2 \, MnO_4^-(aq) \rightarrow 5 \, S(s) + 2 \, MnS(s) + 16 \, OH^-(aq)$

c. $CN^- \rightarrow CNO^-$

$(H_2O + CN^- \rightarrow CNO^- + 2 \, H^+ + 2 \, e^-) \times 3$

$MnO_4^- \rightarrow MnO_2$

$(3 \, e^- + 4 \, H^+ + MnO_4^- \rightarrow MnO_2 + 2 \, H_2O) \times 2$

Common factor is a transfer of 6 electrons.

$$3 \, H_2O + 3 \, CN^- \rightarrow 3 \, CNO^- + 6 \, H^+ + 6 \, e^-$$
$$6 \, e^- + 8 \, H^+ + 2 \, MnO_4^- \rightarrow 2 \, MnO_2 + 4 \, H_2O$$

$2 \, OH^- + 2 \, H^+ + 3 \, CN^- + 2 \, MnO_4^- \rightarrow 3 \, CNO^- + 2 \, MnO_2 + H_2O + 2 \, OH^-$

Reducing gives:

$H_2O(l) + 3 \, CN^-(aq) + 2 \, MnO_4^-(aq) \rightarrow 3 \, CNO^-(aq) + 2 \, MnO_2(s) + 2 \, OH^-(aq)$

77. $NaCl + H_2SO_4 + MnO_2 \rightarrow Na_2SO_4 + MnCl_2 + Cl_2 + H_2O$

We could balance this reaction by the half-reaction method or by inspection. Let's try inspection. To balance Cl^-, we need 4 NaCl:

$4 \, NaCl + H_2SO_4 + MnO_2 \rightarrow Na_2SO_4 + MnCl_2 + Cl_2 + H_2O$

Balance the Na^+ and SO_4^{2-} ions next:

$4 \, NaCl + 2 \, H_2SO_4 + MnO_2 \rightarrow 2 \, Na_2SO_4 + MnCl_2 + Cl_2 + H_2O$

On the left side: 4-H and 10-O; On the right side: 8-O not counting H_2O

We need 2 H_2O on the right side to balance H and O:

$4 \, NaCl(aq) + 2 \, H_2SO_4(aq) + MnO_2(s) \rightarrow 2 \, Na_2SO_4(aq) + MnCl_2(aq) + Cl_2(g) + 2 \, H_2O(l)$

78. $Au + HNO_3 + HCl \rightarrow AuCl_4^- + NO$

Only deal with ions that are reacting (omit H^+): $Au + NO_3^- + Cl^- \rightarrow AuCl_4^- + NO$

The balanced half-reactions are:

$Au + 4\ Cl^- \rightarrow AuCl_4^- + 3\ e^-$ $3\ e^- + 4\ H^+ + NO_3^- \rightarrow NO + 2\ H_2O$

Adding the two balanced half-reactions:

$Au(s) + 4\ Cl^-(aq) + 4\ H^+(aq) + NO_3^-(aq) \rightarrow AuCl_4^-(aq) + NO(g) + 2\ H_2O(l)$

Additional Exercises

79.   Only statement b is true. A concentrated solution can also contain a nonelectrolyte dissolved in water, e.g., concentrated sugar water. Acids are either strong or weak electrolytes. Some ionic compounds are not soluble in water so they are not labeled as a specific type of electrolyte.

80. $\text{mol } CaCl_2 \text{ present} = 0.230\ \text{L } CaCl_2 \times \dfrac{0.275\ \text{mol } CaCl_2}{\text{L } CaCl_2} = 6.33 \times 10^{-2}\ \text{mol } CaCl_2$

The volume of $CaCl_2$ solution after evaporation is:

$6.33 \times 10^{-2}\ \text{mol } CaCl_2 \times \dfrac{1\ \text{L } CaCl_2}{1.10\ \text{mol } CaCl_2} = 5.75 \times 10^{-2}\ \text{L} = 57.5\ \text{mL } CaCl_2$

Volume H_2O evaporated = 230. mL − 57.5 mL = 173 mL H_2O evaporated

81.   There are other possible correct choices for most of the following answers. We have listed only three possible reactants in each case.

a. $AgNO_3$, $Pb(NO_3)_2$, and $Hg_2(NO_3)_2$ would form precipitates with the Cl^- ion.
       $Ag^+(aq) + Cl^-(aq) \rightarrow AgCl(s)$; $Pb^{2+}(aq) + 2\ Cl^-(aq) \rightarrow PbCl_2(s)$;
       $Hg_2^{2+}(aq) + 2\ Cl^-(aq) \rightarrow Hg_2Cl_2(s)$

b. Na_2SO_4, Na_2CO_3, and Na_3PO_4 would form precipitates with the Ca^{2+} ion.
       $Ca^{2+}(aq) + SO_4^{2-}(aq) \rightarrow CaSO_4(s)$; $Ca^{2+}(aq) + CO_3^{2-}(aq) \rightarrow CaCO_3(s)$
       $3\ Ca^{2+}(aq) + 2\ PO_4^{3-}(aq) \rightarrow Ca_3(PO_4)_2(s)$

c. $NaOH$, Na_2S, and Na_2CO_3 would form precipitates with the Fe^{3+} ion.
       $Fe^{3+}(aq) + 3\ OH^-(aq) \rightarrow Fe(OH)_3(s)$; $2\ Fe^{3+}(aq) + 3\ S^{2-}(aq) \rightarrow Fe_2S_3(s)$;
       $2\ Fe^{3+}(aq) + 3\ CO_3^{2-}(aq) \rightarrow Fe_2(CO_3)_3(s)$

d. $BaCl_2$, $Pb(NO_3)_2$, and $Ca(NO_3)_2$ would form precipitates with the SO_4^{2-} ion.
       $Ba^{2+}(aq) + SO_4^{2-}(aq) \rightarrow BaSO_4(s)$; $Pb^{2+}(aq) + SO_4^{2-}(aq) \rightarrow PbSO_4(s)$;
       $Ca^{2+}(aq) + SO_4^{2-}(aq) \rightarrow CaSO_4(s)$

e. Na_2SO_4, NaCl, and NaI would form precipitates with the Hg_2^{2+} ion.
$Hg_2^{2+}(aq) + SO_4^{2-}(aq) \rightarrow Hg_2SO_4(s)$; $Hg_2^{2+}(aq) + 2\ Cl^-(aq) \rightarrow Hg_2Cl_2(s)$;
$Hg_2^{2+}(aq) + 2\ I^-(aq) \rightarrow Hg_2I_2(s)$

f. NaBr, Na_2CrO_4, and Na_3PO_4 would form precipitates with the Ag^+ ion.
$Ag^+(aq) + Br^-(aq) \rightarrow AgBr(s)$; $2\ Ag^+(aq) + CrO_4^{2-}(aq) \rightarrow Ag_2CrO_4(s)$;
$3\ Ag^+(aq) + PO_4^{3-}(aq) \rightarrow Ag_3PO_4(s)$

82. a. $MgCl_2(aq) + 2\ AgNO_3(aq) \rightarrow 2\ AgCl(s) + Mg(NO_3)_2(aq)$

$$0.641\ g\ AgCl \times \frac{1\ mol\ AgCl}{143.4\ g\ AgCl} \times \frac{1\ mol\ MgCl_2}{2\ mol\ AgCl} \times \frac{95.21\ g\ MgCl_2}{mol\ MgCl_2} = 0.213\ g\ MgCl_2$$

$$\frac{0.213\ g\ MgCl_2}{1.50\ g\ mixture} \times 100 = 14.2\%\ MgCl_2$$

b. $0.213\ g\ MgCl_2 \times \dfrac{1\ mol\ MgCl_2}{95.21\ g\ MgCl_2} \times \dfrac{2\ mol\ AgNO_3}{mol\ MgCl_2} \times \dfrac{1\ L}{0.500\ mol\ AgNO_3} \times \dfrac{1000\ mL}{1\ L}$

$$= 8.95\ mL\ AgNO_3$$

83. $XCl_2(aq) + 2\ AgNO_3(aq) \rightarrow 2\ AgCl(s) + X(NO_3)_2(aq)$

$$1.38\ g\ AgCl \times \frac{1\ mol}{143.4\ g} \times \frac{1\ mol\ XCl_2}{2\ mol\ AgCl} = 4.81 \times 10^{-3}\ mol\ XCl_2$$

$$\frac{1.00\ g\ XCl_2}{4.91\times10^{-3}\ mol\ XCl_2} = 208\ g/mol; \quad x + 2(35.45) = 208,\ x = 137\ g/mol$$

The metal X is barium (Ba).

84. Use aluminum in the formulas to convert from mass of $Al(OH)_3$ to mass of $Al_2(SO_4)_3$ in the mixture.

$$0.107\ g\ Al(OH)_3 \times \frac{1\ mol\ Al(OH)_3}{78.00\ g} \times \frac{1\ mol\ Al^{3+}}{mol\ Al(OH)_3} \times \frac{1\ mol\ Al_2(SO_4)_3}{2\ mol\ Al^{3+}} \times$$

$$\frac{342.17\ g\ Al_2(SO_4)_3}{mol\ Al_2(SO_4)_3} = 0.235\ g\ Al_2(SO_4)_3$$

mass % $Al_2(SO_4)_3 = \dfrac{0.235\ g}{1.45\ g} \times 100 = 16.2\%$

85. All the sulfur in $BaSO_4$ came from the saccharin. The conversion from $BaSO_4$ to saccharin utilizes the molar masses of each compound.

$$0.5032 \text{ g BaSO}_4 \times \frac{32.07 \text{ g S}}{233.4 \text{ g BaSO}_4} \times \frac{183.19 \text{ g saccharin}}{32.07 \text{ g S}} = 0.3949 \text{ g saccharin}$$

$$\frac{\text{Avg. mass}}{\text{Tablet}} = \frac{0.3949 \text{ g}}{10 \text{ tablets}} = \frac{3.949 \times 10^{-2} \text{ g}}{\text{tablet}} = \frac{39.49 \text{ mg}}{\text{tablet}}$$

$$\text{Avg. mass \%} = \frac{0.3949 \text{ g saccharin}}{0.5894 \text{ g}} \times 100 = 67.00\% \text{ saccharin by mass}$$

86.   a. $Fe^{3+}(aq) + 3 \; OH^-(aq) \rightarrow Fe(OH)_3(s)$

$Fe(OH)_3$: $55.85 + 3(16.00) + 3(1.008) = 106.87$ g/mol

$$0.107 \text{ g Fe(OH)}_3 \times \frac{55.85 \text{ g Fe}}{106.87 \text{ g Fe(OH)}_3} = 0.0559 \text{ g Fe}$$

b. $Fe(NO_3)_3$: $55.85 + 3(14.01) + 9(16.00) = 241.86$ g/mol

$$0.0559 \text{ g Fe} \times \frac{241.86 \text{ g Fe(NO}_3)_3}{55.85 \text{ g Fe}} = 0.242 \text{ g Fe(NO}_3)_3$$

c.   Mass % $Fe(NO_3)_3 = \dfrac{0.242 \text{ g}}{0.456 \text{ g}} \times 100 = 53.1\%$

87. $Cr(NO_3)_3(aq) + 3 \; NaOH(aq) \rightarrow Cr(OH)_3(s) + 3 \; NaNO_3(aq)$

$$2.06 \text{ g Cr(OH)}_3 \times \frac{1 \text{ mol Cr(OH)}_3}{103.02 \text{ g}} \times \frac{3 \text{ mol NaOH}}{1 \text{ mol Cr(OH)}_3} = 6.00 \times 10^{-2} \text{ mol NaOH to form ppt}$$

$NaOH(aq) + HCl(aq) \rightarrow NaCl(aq) + H_2O(l)$

$$0.1000 \text{ L} \times \frac{0.400 \text{ mol HCl}}{\text{L}} \times \frac{1 \text{ mol NaOH}}{\text{mol HCl}} = 4.00 \times 10^{-2} \text{ mol NaOH to react with HCl}$$

$$M_{\text{NaOH}} = \frac{6.00 \times 10^{-2} \text{ mol} + 4.00 \times 10^{-2} \text{ mol}}{0.0500 \text{ L}} = 2.00 \; M \text{ NaOH}$$

88.   a.   Perchloric acid reacted with potassium hydroxide is a possibility.

$HClO_4(aq) + KOH(aq) \rightarrow H_2O(l) + KClO_4(aq)$

b.   Nitric acid reacted with cesium hydroxide is a possibility.

$HNO_3(aq) + CsOH(aq) \rightarrow H_2O(l) + CsNO_3(aq)$

c.   Hydroiodic acid reacted with calcium hydroxide is a possibility.

$2 \; HI(aq) + Ca(OH)_2(aq) \rightarrow 2 \; H_2O(l) + CaI_2(aq)$

89. $HC_2H_3O_2(aq) + NaOH(aq) \rightarrow H_2O(l) + NaC_2H_3O_2(aq)$

a. 16.58×10^{-3} L soln $\times \dfrac{0.5062 \text{ mol NaOH}}{\text{L soln}} \times \dfrac{1 \text{ mol acetic acid}}{\text{mol NaOH}}$

$$= 8.393 \times 10^{-3} \text{ mol acetic acid}$$

Concentration of acetic acid $= \dfrac{8.393 \times 10^{-3} \text{ mol}}{0.01000 \text{ L}} = 0.8393 \, M$

b.   If we have 1.000 L of solution: total mass $= 1000.$ mL $\times \dfrac{1.006 \text{ g}}{\text{mL}} = 1006$ g

Mass of $HC_2H_3O_2 = 0.8393$ mol $\times \dfrac{60.05 \text{ g}}{\text{mol}} = 50.40$ g

Mass % acetic acid $= \dfrac{50.40 \text{ g}}{1006 \text{ g}} \times 100 = 5.010\%$

90. $Mg(s) + 2 HCl(aq) \rightarrow MgCl_2(aq) + H_2(g)$

3.00 g Mg $\times \dfrac{1 \text{ mol Mg}}{24.31 \text{ g Mg}} \times \dfrac{2 \text{ mol HCl}}{\text{mol Mg}} \times \dfrac{1 \text{ L}}{5.0 \text{ mol HCl}} = 0.049$ L $= 49$ mL HCl

91.   Let HA = unknown acid; $HA(aq) + NaOH(aq) \rightarrow NaA(aq) + H_2O(l)$

mol HA present $= 0.0250$ L $\times \dfrac{0.500 \text{ mol NaOH}}{\text{L}} \times \dfrac{1 \text{ mol HA}}{1 \text{ mol NaOH}} = 0.0125$ mol HA

$\dfrac{x \text{ g HA}}{\text{mol HA}} = \dfrac{2.20 \text{ g HA}}{0.0125 \text{ mol HA}}$ $x =$ molar mass of HA $= 176$ g/mol

Empirical formula weight $\approx 3(12) + 4(1) + 3(16) = 88$ g/mol

$176/88 = 2.0$, so the molecular formula is $(C_3H_4O_3)_2 = C_6H_8O_6$.

92.   We get the empirical formula from the elemental analysis. Out of 100.00 g carminic acid there are:

53.66 g C $\times \dfrac{1 \text{ mol C}}{12.01 \text{ g C}} = 4.468$ mol C;   4.09 g H $\times \dfrac{1 \text{ mol H}}{1.008 \text{ g H}} = 4.06$ mol H

42.25 g O $\times \dfrac{1 \text{ mol O}}{16.00 \text{ g C}} = 2.641$ mol O

Dividing the moles by the smallest number gives:

$\dfrac{4.468}{2.641} = 1.692$; $\dfrac{4.06}{2.641} = 1.54$

These numbers don't give obvious mole ratios. Let's determine the mol C to mol H ratio.

$$\frac{4.468}{4.06} = 1.10 = \frac{11}{10}$$

So let's try $\dfrac{4.06}{10} = 0.406$ as a common factor: $\dfrac{4.468}{0.406} = 11.0$; $\quad \dfrac{4.06}{0.406} = 10.0$; $\quad \dfrac{2.641}{0.406} = 6.50$

Therefore, $C_{22}H_{20}O_{13}$ is the empirical formula.

We can get the molar mass from the titration data.

$$18.02 \times 10^{-3}\,L \times \frac{0.0406\;mol\;NaOH}{L} \times \frac{1\;mol\;carminic\;acid}{mol\;NaOH} = 7.32 \times 10^{-4}\;mol\;carminic\;acid$$

$$Molar\;mass = \frac{0.3602\;g}{7.32 \times 10^{-4}\;mol} = \frac{492\;g}{mol}$$

The empirical formula mass of $C_{22}H_{20}O_{13} \approx 22(12) + 20(1) + 13(16) = 492\;g$.

Therefore, the molecular formula of carminic acid is also $C_{22}H_{20}O_{13}$.

93.   Strong bases contain the hydroxide ion, OH^-. The reaction that occurs is $H^+ + OH^- \rightarrow H_2O$.

$$0.0120\;L \times \frac{0.150\;mol\;H^+}{L} \times \frac{1\;mol\;OH^-}{mol\;H^+} = 1.80 \times 10^{-3}\;mol\;OH^-$$

The 30.0 mL of the unknown strong base contains 1.80×10^{-3} mol OH^-.

$$\frac{1.8 \times 10^{-3}\;mol\;OH^-}{0.0300\;L} = 0.0600\;M\;OH^-$$

The unknown base concentration is one-half the concentration of OH^- ions produced from the base, so the base must contain 2 OH^- in each formula unit. The three soluble strong bases that have 2 OH^- ions in the formula are $Ca(OH)_2$, $Sr(OH)_2$, and $Ba(OH)_2$. These are all possible identities for the strong base.

94.   a. $Al(s) + 3\;HCl(aq) \rightarrow AlCl_3(aq) + 3/2\;H_2(g)$ or $2\;Al(s) + 6\;HCl(aq) \rightarrow 2\;AlCl_3(aq) +$

$$3\;H_2(g)$$

Hydrogen is reduced (goes from the +1 oxidation state to the 0 oxidation state) and aluminum Al is oxidized ($0 \rightarrow +3$).

b.   Balancing S is most complicated since sulfur is in both products. Balance C and H first, then worry about S.

$CH_4(g) + 4\;S(s) \rightarrow CS_2(l) + 2\;H_2S(g)$

Sulfur is reduced ($0 \rightarrow -2$) and carbon is oxidized ($-4 \rightarrow +4$).

c. Balance C and H first, then balance O.

$$C_3H_8(g) + 5\ O_2(g) \rightarrow 3\ CO_2(g) + 4\ H_2O(l)$$

Oxygen is reduced ($0 \rightarrow -2$) and carbon is oxidized ($-8/3 \rightarrow +4$).

d. Although this reaction is mass balanced, it is not charge balanced. We need 2 mol of silver on each side to balance the charge.

$$Cu(s) + 2\ Ag^+(aq) \rightarrow 2\ Ag(s) + Cu^{2+}(aq)$$

Silver is reduced ($+1 \rightarrow 0$) and copper is oxidized ($0 \rightarrow +2$).

95. $Mn + HNO_3 \rightarrow Mn^{2+} + NO_2$

$$Mn \rightarrow Mn^{2+} + 2\ e^- \qquad\qquad HNO_3 \rightarrow NO_2$$
$$HNO_3 \rightarrow NO_2 + H_2O$$
$$(e^- + H^+ + HNO_3 \rightarrow NO_2 + H_2O) \times 2$$

$$Mn \rightarrow Mn^{2+} + 2\ e^-$$
$$\underline{2\ e^- + 2\ H^+ + 2\ HNO_3 \rightarrow 2\ NO_2 + 2\ H_2O}$$

$$2\ H^+(aq) + Mn(s) + 2\ HNO_3(aq) \rightarrow Mn^{2+}(aq) + 2\ NO_2(g) + 2\ H_2O(l)$$

$Mn^{2+} + IO_4^- \rightarrow MnO_4^- + IO_3^-$

$$(4\ H_2O + Mn^{2+} \rightarrow MnO_4^- + 8\ H^+ + 5\ e^-) \times 2 \qquad (2\ e^- + 2\ H^+ + IO_4^- \rightarrow IO_3^- + H_2O) \times 5$$

$$8\ H_2O + 2\ Mn^{2+} \rightarrow 2\ MnO_4^- + 16\ H^+ + 10\ e^-$$
$$\underline{10\ e^- + 10\ H^+ + 5\ IO_4^- \rightarrow 5\ IO_3^- + 5\ H_2O}$$

$$3\ H_2O(l) + 2\ Mn^{2+}(aq) + 5\ IO_4^-(aq) \rightarrow 2\ MnO_4^-(aq) + 5\ IO_3^-(aq) + 6\ H^+(aq)$$

Challenge Problems

96.   a. 5.0 ppb Hg in water $= \dfrac{5.0\ \text{ng Hg}}{\text{g soln}} \times \dfrac{5.0 \times 10^{-9}\ \text{g Hg}}{\text{mL soln}}$

$$\frac{5.0 \times 10^{-9}\ \text{g Hg}}{\text{mL soln}} \times \frac{1\ \text{mol Hg}}{200.6\ \text{g Hg}} \times \frac{1000\ \text{mL}}{\text{L}} = 2.5 \times 10^{-8}\ M\ \text{Hg}$$

b. $\dfrac{1.0 \times 10^{-9}\ \text{g CHCl}_3}{\text{mL}} \times \dfrac{1\ \text{mol CHCl}_3}{119.37\ \text{g CHCl}_3} \times \dfrac{1000\ \text{mL}}{\text{L}} = 8.4 \times 10^{-9}\ M\ \text{CHCl}_3$

c. $10.0 \text{ ppm As} = \dfrac{10.0\ \mu g\ As}{g\ soln} \times \dfrac{10.0 \times 10^{-6}\ g\ As}{mL\ soln}$

$\dfrac{10.0 \times 10^{-6}\ g\ As}{mL\ soln} \times \dfrac{1\ mol\ As}{74.92\ g\ As} \times \dfrac{1000\ mL}{L} = 1.33 \times 10^{-4}\ M\ As$

d. $\dfrac{0.10 \times 10^{-6}\ g\ DDT}{mL} \times \dfrac{1\ mol\ DDT}{354.46\ g\ DDT} \times \dfrac{1000\ mL}{L} = 2.8 \times 10^{-7}\ M\ DDT$

97. a. $0.308\ g\ AgCl \times \dfrac{35.45\ g\ Cl}{143.4\ g\ AgCl} = 0.0761\ g\ Cl;\ \%Cl = \dfrac{0.761\ g}{0.256\ g} \times 100 = 29.7\%\ Cl$

Cobalt(III) oxide, Co_2O_3: $2(58.93) + 3(16.00) = 165.86\ g/mol$

$0.145\ g\ Co_2O_3 \times \dfrac{117.86\ g\ Co}{165.86\ g\ Co_2O_3} = 0.103\ g\ Co;\ \%Co = \dfrac{0.103\ g}{0.416\ g} \times 100 = 24.8\%\ Co$

The remainder, $100.0 - (29.7 + 24.8) = 45.5\%$, is water.

Assuming 100.0 g of compound:

$45.5\ g\ H_2O \times \dfrac{2.016\ g\ H}{18.02\ g\ H_2O} = 5.09\ g\ H;\ \%H = \dfrac{5.09\ g\ H}{100.0\ g\ compound} \times 100 = 5.09\%\ H$

$45.5\ g\ H_2O \times \dfrac{16.00\ g\ O}{18.02\ g\ H_2O} = 40.4\ g\ O;\ \%O = \dfrac{40.4\ g\ O}{100.0\ g\ compound} \times 100 = 40.4\%\ O$

The mass percent composition is 24.8% Co, 29.7% Cl, 5.09% H and 40.4% O.

b. Out of 100.0 g of compound, there are:

$24.8\ g\ Co \times \dfrac{1\ mol\ Co}{58.93\ g\ Co} = 0.421\ mol\ Co;\ 29.7\ g\ Cl \times \dfrac{1\ mol\ Cl}{35.45\ g\ Cl} = 0.838\ mol\ Cl$

$5.09\ g\ H \times \dfrac{1\ mol\ H}{1.008\ g\ H} = 5.05\ mol\ H;\ 40.4\ g\ O \times \dfrac{1\ mol\ O}{16.00\ g\ O} = 2.53\ mol\ O$

Dividing all results by 0.421, we get $CoCl_2 \cdot 6H_2O$ for the formula.

c. $CoCl_2 \cdot 6H_2O(aq) + 2\ AgNO_3(aq) \rightarrow 2\ AgCl(s) + Co(NO_3)_2(aq) + 6\ H_2O(l)$

$CoCl_2 \cdot 6H_2O(aq) + 2\ NaOH(aq) \rightarrow Co(OH)_2(s) + 2\ NaCl(aq) + 6\ H_2O(l)$

$Co(OH)_2 \rightarrow Co_2O_3$ This is an oxidation-reduction reaction. Thus, we also need to include an oxidizing agent. The obvious choice is O_2.

$4\ Co(OH)_2(s) + O_2(g) \rightarrow 2\ Co_2O_3(s) + 4\ H_2O(l)$

98.   a. $C_{12}H_{10-n}Cl_n + n\ Ag^+ \rightarrow n\ AgCl$; molar mass (AgCl) = 143.4 g/mol

molar mass (PCB) = 12(12.01) + (10 − n) (1.008) + n(35.45) = 154.20 + 34.44 n

Because n mol AgCl are produced for every 1 mol PCB reacted, n(143.4) grams of AgCl will be produced for every (154.20 + 34.44 n) grams of PCB reacted.

$$\frac{\text{mass of AgCl}}{\text{mass of PCB}} = \frac{143.3\,n}{154.20 + 34.44\,n}\ \text{or}\ \text{mass}_{AgCl}\,(154.20 + 34.44\,n) = \text{mass}_{PCB}\,(143.4\,n)$$

b.   0.4791 (154.20 + 34.44 n) = 0.1947 (143.4 n), 73.88 + 16.50 n = 27.92 n

73.88 = 11.42 n, n = 6.469

99.   a. $2\ AgNO_3(aq)\ +\ K_2CrO_4(aq)\ \rightarrow\ Ag_2CrO_4(s) + 2\ KNO_3(aq)$

Molar mass: 169.9 g/mol   194.20 g/mol   331.8 g/mol

The molar mass of Ag_2CrO_4 is 331.8 g/mol, so one mol of precipitate was formed.

We have equal masses of $AgNO_3$ and K_2CrO_4. Since the molar mass of $AgNO_3$ is less than that of K_2CrO_4, then we have more mol of $AgNO_3$ present. However, we will not have twice the mol of $AgNO_3$ present as compared to K_2CrO_4 as required by the balanced reaction; this is because the molar mass of $AgNO_3$ is nowhere near one-half the molar mass of K_2CrO_4. Therefore, $AgNO_3$ is limiting.

$$\text{mass AgNO}_3 = 1.000\ \text{mol Ag}_2\text{CrO}_4 \times \frac{2\ \text{mol AgNO}_3}{\text{mol Ag}_2\text{CrO}_4} \times \frac{169.9\ \text{g}}{\text{mol AgNO}_3} = 339.8\ \text{g AgNO}_3$$

Because equal masses of reactants are present, 339.8 g K_2CrO_4 were present initially.

$$M_{K^+} = \frac{\text{mol K}^+}{\text{total volume}} = \frac{339.8\ \text{g K}_2\text{CrO}_4 \times \dfrac{1\ \text{mol K}_2\text{CrO}_4}{194.20\ \text{g}} \times \dfrac{2\ \text{mol K}^+}{\text{mol K}_2\text{CrO}_4}}{0.5000\ \text{L}} = 7.000\ M\ \text{K}^+$$

b. $\text{mol CrO}_4{}^{2-}$ present initially $= 339.8\ \text{g K}_2\text{CrO}_4 \times \dfrac{1\ \text{mol K}_2\text{CrO}_4}{194.20\ \text{g}} \times \dfrac{1\ \text{mol CrO}_4{}^{2-}}{\text{mol K}_2\text{CrO}_4} = 1.750\ \text{mol CrO}_4{}^{2-}$

$\text{mol CrO}_4{}^{2-}$ in precipitate $= 1.000\ \text{mol Ag}_2\text{CrO}_4 \times \dfrac{1\ \text{mol CrO}_4{}^{2-}}{\text{mol Ag}_2\text{CrO}_4} = 1.000\ \text{mol CrO}_4{}^{2-}$

$$M_{CrO_4{}^{2-}} = \frac{\text{excess mol CrO}_4{}^{2-}}{\text{total volume}} = \frac{1.750\ \text{mol} - 1.000\ \text{mol}}{0.5000\ \text{L} + 0.5000\ \text{L}} = \frac{0.750\ \text{mol}}{1.0000\ \text{L}} = 0.750\ M$$

100.   Molar masses: KCl, 39.10 + 35.45 = 74.55 g/mol; KBr, 39.10 + 79.90 = 119.00 g/mol

AgCl, 107.9 + 35.45 = 143.4 g/mol; AgBr, 107.9 + 79.90 = 187.8 g/mol

Let x = number of moles of KCl in mixture and y = number of moles of KBr in mixture. Since $Ag^+ + Cl^- \rightarrow AgCl$ and $Ag^+ + Br^- \rightarrow AgBr$, then x = moles AgCl and y = moles AgBr.

Setting up two equations:

0.1024 g = $74.55\,x + 119.0\,y$ and 0.1889 g = $143.4\,x + 187.8\,y$

Multiply the first equation by $\dfrac{187.8}{119.0}$ and subtract from the second.

$$
\begin{aligned}
0.1889 &= 143.4\,x + 187.8\,y \\
-0.1616 &= -117.7\,x - 187.8\,y \\
\hline
0.0273 &= 25.7\,x, \qquad x = 1.06 \times 10^{-3}\text{ mol KCl}
\end{aligned}
$$

1.06×10^{-3} mol KCl $\times \dfrac{74.55 \text{ g KCl}}{\text{mol KCl}} = 0.0790$ g KCl

% KCl = $\dfrac{0.0790 \text{ g}}{0.1024 \text{ g}} \times 100 = 77.1\%$, % KBr = $100.0 - 77.1 = 22.9\%$

101.   0.298 g $BaSO_4 \times \dfrac{96.07 \text{ g SO}_4^{2-}}{233.4 \text{ g BaSO}_4} = 0.123$ g SO_4^{2-}; % sulfate = $\dfrac{0.123 \text{ g SO}_4^{2-}}{0.205 \text{ g}} = 60.0\%$

Assume we have 100.0 g of the mixture of Na_2SO_4 and K_2SO_4. There are:

60.0 g $SO_4^{2-} \times \dfrac{1 \text{ mol}}{96.07 \text{ g}} = 0.625$ mol SO_4^{2-}

There must be $2 \times 0.625 = 1.25$ mol of +1 cations to balance the -2 charge of SO_4^{2-}.

Let x = number of moles of K^+ and y = number of moles of Na^+; then $x + y = 1.25$.

The total mass of Na^+ and K^+ must be 40.0 g in the assumed 100.0 g of mixture. Setting up an equation:

x mol $K^+ \times \dfrac{39.10 \text{ g}}{\text{mol}} + y$ mol $Na^+ \times \dfrac{22.99 \text{ g}}{\text{mol}} = 40.0$ g

So, we have two equations with two unknowns: $x + y = 1.25$ and $39.10\,x + 22.99\,y = 40.0$

$x = 1.25 - y,$ so $39.10(1.25 - y) + 22.99\,y = 40.0$

$48.9 - 39.10\,y + 22.99\,y = 40.0,\ -16.11\,y = -8.9$

$y = 0.55$ mol Na^+ and $x = 1.25 - 0.55 = 0.70$ mol K^+

Therefore:

$$0.70 \text{ mol K}^+ \times \frac{1 \text{ mol K}_2\text{SO}_4}{2 \text{ mol K}^+} = 0.35 \text{ mol K}_2\text{SO}_4; \ 0.35 \text{ mol K}_2\text{SO}_4 \times \frac{174.27 \text{ g}}{\text{mol}}$$

$$= 61 \text{ g K}_2\text{SO}_4$$

We assumed 100.0 g, therefore the mixture is 61% $K_2\text{SO}_4$ and 39% $Na_2\text{SO}_4$.

102.   a.   Let x = mass of Mg, so 10.00 − x = mass of Zn. $Ag^+(aq) + Cl^-(aq) \rightarrow AgCl(s)$.

From the given balanced equations, there is a 2:1 mole ratio between mol Mg and mol Cl^-. The same is true for Zn. Because mol Ag^+ = mol Cl^- present, one can set-up an equation relating mol Cl^- present to mol Ag^+ added.

$$\text{x g Mg} \times \frac{1 \text{ mol Mg}}{24.31 \text{ g Mg}} \times \frac{2 \text{ mol Cl}^-}{\text{mol Mg}} + (10.00 - \text{x}) \text{ g Zn} \times \frac{1 \text{ mol Zn}}{65.38 \text{ g Zn}} \times \frac{2 \text{ mol Cl}^-}{\text{mol Zn}}$$

$$= 0.156 \text{ L} \times \frac{3.00 \text{ mol Ag}^+}{\text{L}} \times \frac{1 \text{ mol Cl}^-}{\text{mol Ag}^+} = 0.468 \text{ mol Cl}^-$$

$$\frac{2\text{x}}{24.31} + \frac{2(10.00 - \text{x})}{65.38} = 0.468, \ 24.31 \times 65.38 \left(\frac{2\text{x}}{24.31} + \frac{20.00 - 2\text{x}}{65.38} = 0.468 \right)$$

130.8 x + 486.2 − 48.62 x = 743.8 (carrying 1 extra S.F.)

$$82.2 \text{ x} = 257.6, \ \text{x} = 3.13 \text{ g Mg}; \ \%\text{Mg} = \frac{3.13 \text{ g Mg}}{10.00 \text{ g mixture}} \times 100 = 31.3\% \text{ Mg}$$

b. $0.156 \text{ L} \times \dfrac{3.00 \text{ mol Ag}^+}{\text{L}} \times \dfrac{1 \text{ mol Cl}^-}{\text{mol Ag}^+} = 0.468 \text{ mol Cl}^- = 0.468 \text{ mol HCl added}$

$$M_{\text{HCl}} = \frac{0.648 \text{ mol}}{0.0780 \text{ L}} = 6.00 \ M \text{ HCl}$$

103. $Pb^{2+}(aq) + 2 Cl^-(aq) \rightarrow PbCl_2(s)$
                             3.407 g

$$3.407 \text{ g PbCl}_2 \times \frac{1 \text{ mol PbCl}_2}{278.1 \text{ g PbCl}_2} \times \frac{1 \text{ mol Pb}^{2+}}{1 \text{ mol PbCl}_2} = 0.01225 \text{ mol Pb}^{2+}$$

$$\frac{0.01225 \text{ mol}}{2.00 \times 10^{-3} \text{ L}} = 6.13 \ M \text{ Pb}^{2+} \text{ (evaporated concentration)}$$

$$\text{original concentration} = \frac{0.0800 \text{ L} \times 6.13 \text{ mol}/\text{L}}{0.100 \text{ L}} = 4.90 \ M$$

104.   moles $CuSO_4 = 87.7 \text{ mL} \times \dfrac{1 \text{ L}}{1000 \text{ mL}} \times \dfrac{0.500 \text{ mol}}{\text{L}} = 0.0439 \text{ mol}$

moles $Fe = 2.00 \text{ g} \times \dfrac{1 \text{ mol Fe}}{55.85 \text{ g}} = 0.0358 \text{ mol}$

The two possible reactions are:

I. $CuSO_4(aq) + Fe(s) \rightarrow Cu(s) + FeSO_4(aq)$

II. $3 CuSO_4(aq) + 2 Fe(s) \rightarrow 3 Cu(s) + Fe_2(SO_4)_3(aq)$

If reaction I occurs, Fe is limiting and we can produce:

$0.0358 \text{ mol Fe} \times \dfrac{1 \text{ mol Cu}}{\text{mol Fe}} \times \dfrac{63.55 \text{ g Cu}}{\text{mol Cu}} = 2.28 \text{ g Cu}$

If reaction II occurs, $CuSO_4$ is limiting and we can produce:

$0.0439 \text{ mol } CuSO_4 \times \dfrac{3 \text{ mol Cu}}{3 \text{ mol } CuSO_4} \times \dfrac{63.55 \text{ g Cu}}{\text{mol Cu}} = 2.79 \text{ g Cu}$

Assuming 100% yield, reaction I occurs because it fits the data best.

105. $0.2750 \text{ L} \times 0.300 \text{ mol/L} = 0.0825 \text{ mol H}^+$; Let y = volume (L) delivered by Y and z = volume (L) delivered by Z.

$H^+(aq) + OH^-(aq) \rightarrow H_2O(l)$; $\underbrace{y(0.150 \text{ mol/L}) + z(0.250 \text{ mol/L})}_{\text{mol OH}^-} = 0{,}9725 \text{ mol H}^+$

$0.2750 \text{ L} + y + z = 0.655 \text{ L}$,   y + z = 0.380,   z = 0.380 − y

y(0.150) + (0.380 − y)(0.250) = 0.0825, Solving: y = 0.125 L, z = 0.255 L

flow rates: Y $\rightarrow \dfrac{125 \text{ mL}}{60.65 \text{ min}} = 2.06 \text{ mL/min}$ and Z $\rightarrow \dfrac{255 \text{ mL}}{60.65 \text{ min}} = 4.20 \text{ mL/min}$

106.   a. $H_3PO_4(aq) + 3 NaOH(aq) \rightarrow 3 H_2O(l) + Na_3PO_4(aq)$

b. $3 H_2SO_4(aq) + 2 Al(OH)_3(s) \rightarrow 6 H_2O(l) + Al_2(SO_4)_3(aq)$

c. $H_2Se(aq) + Ba(OH)_2(aq) \rightarrow 2 H_2O(l) + BaSe(s)$

d. $H_2C_2O_4(aq) + 2 NaOH(aq) \rightarrow 2 H_2O(l) + Na_2C_2O_4(aq)$

107. $2 H_3PO_4(aq) + 3 Ba(OH)_2(aq) \rightarrow 6 H_2O(l) + Ba_3(PO_4)_2(s)$

$$0.01420 \text{ L} \times \frac{0.141 \text{ mol } H_3PO_4}{\text{L}} \times \frac{3 \text{ mol } Ba(OH)_2}{2 \text{ mol } H_3PO_4} \times \frac{1 \text{ L } Ba(OH)_2}{0.0521 \text{ mol } Ba(OH)_2} = 0.0576 \text{ L}$$

$$= 57.6 \text{ mL } Ba(OH)_2$$

108. $$35.08 \text{ mL NaOH} \times \frac{1 \text{ L}}{1000 \text{ mL}} \times \frac{2.12 \text{ mol NaOH}}{\text{L NaOH}} \times \frac{1 \text{ mol } H_2SO_4}{2 \text{ mol NaOH}} = 3.72 \times 10^{-2} \text{ mol } H_2SO_4$$

$$\text{Molarity} = \frac{3.72 \times 10^{-2} \text{ mol}}{10.00 \text{ mL}} \times \frac{1000 \text{ mL}}{\text{L}} = 3.72 \ M \ H_2SO_4$$

109.   a. $MgO(s) + 2 HCl(aq) \rightarrow MgCl_2(aq) + H_2O(l)$

$Mg(OH)_2(s) + 2 HCl(aq) \rightarrow MgCl_2(aq) + 2 H_2O(l)$

$Al(OH)_3(s) + 3 HCl(aq) \rightarrow AlCl_3(aq) + 3 H_2O(l)$

b.   Let's calculate the number of moles of HCl neutralized per gram of substance. We can get these directly from the balanced equations and the molar masses of the substances.

$$\frac{2 \text{ mol HCl}}{\text{mol MgO}} \times \frac{1 \text{ mol MgO}}{40.31 \text{ g MgO}} = \frac{4.962 \times 10^{-2} \text{ mol HCl}}{\text{g MgO}}$$

$$\frac{2 \text{ mol HCl}}{\text{mol } Mg(OH)_2} \times \frac{1 \text{ mol } Mg(OH)_2}{58.33 \text{ g } Mg(OH)_2} = \frac{3.429 \times 10^{-2} \text{ mol HCl}}{\text{g } Mg(OH)_2}$$

$$\frac{3 \text{ mol HCl}}{\text{mol } Al(OH)_3} \times \frac{1 \text{ mol } Al(OH)_3}{78.00 \text{ g } Al(OH)_3} = \frac{3.846 \times 10^{-2} \text{ mol HCl}}{\text{g } Al(OH)_3}$$

Therefore, one gram of magnesium oxide would neutralize the most 0.10 M HCl.

110.   Let H_2A = formula for diprotic acid

$H_2A(aq) + 2 NaOH(aq) \rightarrow 2 H_2O(l) + Na_2A(aq)$

$$\text{mol } H_2A = 0.1375 \text{ L} \times \frac{0.750 \text{ mol NaOH}}{\text{L}} \times \frac{1 \text{ mol } H_2A}{2 \text{ mol NaOH}} = 0.0516 \text{ mol}$$

$$\text{molar mass of } H_2A = \frac{6.50 \text{ g}}{0.0516 \text{ mol}} = 126 \text{ g/mol}$$

111. $$\text{mol } C_6H_8O_7 = 0.250 \text{ g } C_6H_8O_7 \times \frac{1 \text{ mol } C_6H_8O_7}{192.12 \text{ g } C_6H_8O_7} = 1.30 \times 10^{-3} \text{ mol } C_6H_8O_7$$

Let H_xA represent citric acid where x is the number of acidic hydrogens. The balanced neutralization reaction is:

$$H_xA(aq) + x\ OH^-(aq) \rightarrow x\ H_2O(l) + A^{x-}(aq)$$

$$\text{mol }OH^-\text{ reacted} = 0.0372\ L \times \frac{0.105\text{ mol }OH^-}{L} = 3.91 \times 10^{-3}\text{ mol }OH^-$$

$$x = \frac{\text{mol }OH^-}{\text{mol citric acid}} = \frac{3.91 \times 10^{-3}\text{ mol}}{1.30 \times 10^{-3}\text{ mol}} = 3.01$$

Therefore, the general acid formula for citric acid is H_3A, meaning that citric acid has three acidic hydrogens per citric acid molecule (citric acid is a triprotic acid).

112.   a.   HCl(aq) dissociates to $H^+(aq) + Cl^-(aq)$. For simplicity let's use H^+ and Cl^- separately.

$$H^+ \rightarrow H_2 \qquad\qquad\qquad\qquad\qquad Fe \rightarrow HFeCl_4$$
$$(2\ H^+ + 2\ e^- \rightarrow H_2) \times 3 \qquad\qquad (H^+ + 4\ Cl^- + Fe \rightarrow HFeCl_4 + 3\ e^-) \times 2$$

$$6\ H^+ + 6\ e^- \rightarrow 3\ H_2$$
$$\underline{2\ H^+ + 8\ Cl^- + 2\ Fe \rightarrow 2\ HFeCl_4 + 6\ e^-}$$

$$8\ H^+ + 8\ Cl^- + 2\ Fe \rightarrow 2\ HFeCl_4 + 3\ H_2$$

or $8\ HCl(aq) + 2\ Fe(s) \rightarrow 2\ HFeCl_4(aq) + 3\ H_2(g)$

b.

$$IO_3^- \rightarrow I_3^- \qquad\qquad\qquad\qquad\qquad I^- \rightarrow I_3^-$$
$$3\ IO_3^- \rightarrow I_3^- \qquad\qquad\qquad (3\ I^- \rightarrow I_3^- + 2\ e^-) \times 8$$
$$3\ IO_3^- \rightarrow I_3^- + 9\ H_2O$$
$$16\ e^- + 18\ H^+ + 3\ IO_3^- \rightarrow I_3^- + 9\ H_2O$$

$$16\ e^- + 18\ H^+ + 3\ IO_3^- \rightarrow I_3^- + 9\ H_2O$$
$$\underline{24\ I^- \rightarrow 8\ I_3^- + 16\ e^-}$$

$$18\ H^+ + 24\ I^- + 3\ IO_3^- \rightarrow 9\ I_3^- + 9\ H_2O$$

Reducing: $6\ H^+(aq) + 8\ I^-(aq) + IO_3^-(aq) \rightarrow 3\ I_3^-(aq) + 3\ H_2O(l)$

c. $(Ce^{4+} + e^- \rightarrow Ce^{3+}) \times 97$

$$Cr(NCS)_6^{4-} \rightarrow Cr^{3+} + NO_3^- + CO_2 + SO_4^{2-}$$
$$54\ H_2O + Cr(NCS)_6^{4-} \rightarrow Cr^{3+} + 6\ NO_3^- + 6\ CO_2 + 6\ SO_4^{2-} + 108\ H^+$$

Charge on left -4. Charge on right $= +3 + 6(-1) + 6(-2) + 108(+1) = +93$. Add 97 e^- to the right, then add the two balanced half-reactions with a common factor of 97 e^- transferred.

$$54 \ H_2O + Cr(NCS)_6^{4-} \rightarrow Cr^{3+} + 6 \ NO_3^- + 6 \ CO_2 + 6 \ SO_4^{2-} + 108 \ H^+ + 97 \ e^-$$

$$97 \ e^- + 97 \ Ce^{4+} \rightarrow 97 \ Ce^{3+}$$

$$97 \ Ce^{4+}(aq) + 54 \ H_2O(l) + Cr(NCS)_6^{4-}(aq) \rightarrow 97 \ Ce^{3+}(aq) + Cr^{3+}(aq) + 6 \ NO_3^-(aq) +$$

$$6 \ CO_2(g) + 6 \ SO_4^{2-}(aq) + 108 \ H^+(aq)$$

This is very complicated. A check of the net charge is a good check to see if the equation is balanced. Left: charge = 97(+4) − 4 = +384. Right: charge = 97(+3) + 3 + 6(−1) + 6(−2) + 108(+1) = +384. The reaction is also mass balanced.

d. $CrI_3 \rightarrow CrO_4^{2-} + IO_4^-$ $Cl_2 \rightarrow Cl^-$

$(16 \ H_2O + CrI_3 \rightarrow CrO_4^{2-} + 3 \ IO_4^- + 32 \ H^+ + 27 \ e^-) \times 2$ $(2 \ e^- + Cl_2 \rightarrow 2 \ Cl^-) \times 27$

Common factor is a transfer of 54 e^-.

$$54 \ e^- + 27 \ Cl_2 \rightarrow 54 \ Cl^-$$

$$32 \ H_2O + 2 \ CrI_3 \rightarrow 2 \ CrO_4^{2-} + 6 \ IO_4^- + 64 \ H^+ + 54 \ e^-$$

$$32 \ H_2O + 2 \ CrI_3 + 27 \ Cl_2 \rightarrow 54 \ Cl^- + 2 \ CrO_4^{2-} + 6 \ IO_4^- + 64 \ H^+$$

Add 64 OH^- to both sides and convert 64 H^+ into 64 H_2O.

$$64 \ OH^- + 32 \ H_2O + 2 \ CrI_3 + 27 \ Cl_2 \rightarrow 54 \ Cl^- + 2 \ CrO_4^{2-} + 6 \ IO_4^- + 64 \ H_2O$$

Reducing gives:

$$64 \ OH^-(aq) + 2 \ CrI_3(s) + 27 \ Cl_2(g) \rightarrow 54 \ Cl^-(aq) + 2 \ CrO_4^{2-}(aq) + 6 \ IO_4^-(aq) +$$

$$32 \ H_2O(l)$$

e. $Ce^{4+} \rightarrow Ce(OH)_3$

$(e^- + 3 \ H_2O + Ce^{4+} \rightarrow Ce(OH)_3 + 3 \ H^+) \times 61$

$$Fe(CN)_6^{4-} \rightarrow Fe(OH)_3 + CO_3^{2-} + NO_3^-$$

$$Fe(CN)_6^{4-} \rightarrow Fe(OH)_3 + 6 \ CO_3^{2-} + 6 \ NO_3^-$$

There are 39 extra O atoms on right. Add 39 H_2O to left, then add 75 H^+ to right to balance H^+.

$$39 \ H_2O + Fe(CN)_6^{4-} \rightarrow Fe(OH)_3 + 6 \ CO_3^{2-} + 6 \ NO_3^- + 75 \ H^+$$

$$\text{net charge} = -4 \qquad\qquad \text{net charge} = +57$$

Add 61 e^- to the right; then add the two balanced half-reactions with a common factor of 61 e^- transferred.

$$39 \ H_2O + Fe(CN)_6^{4-} \rightarrow Fe(OH)_3 + 6 \ CO_3^{2-} + 6 \ NO_3^- + 75 \ H^+ + 61 \ e^-$$

$$61 \ e^- + 183 \ H_2O + 61 \ Ce^{4+} \rightarrow 61 \ Ce(OH)_3 + 183 \ H^+$$

$$222 \ H_2O + Fe(CN)_6^{4-} + 61 \ Ce^{4+} \rightarrow 61 \ Ce(OH)_3 + Fe(OH)_3 + 6 \ CO_3^{2-} + 6 \ NO_3^- + 258 \ H^+$$

Adding 258 OH⁻ to each side then reducing gives:

$$258 \, OH^-(aq) + Fe(CN)_6{}^{4-}(aq) + 61 \, Ce^{4+}(aq) \rightarrow 61 \, Ce(OH)_3(s) + Fe(OH)_3(s) +$$

$$6 \, CO_3{}^{2-}(aq) + 6 \, NO_3{}^-(aq) + 36 \, H_2O(l)$$

f.
$$Fe(OH)_2 \rightarrow Fe(OH)_3 \qquad\qquad\qquad H_2O_2 \rightarrow H_2O$$
$$(H_2O + Fe(OH)_2 \rightarrow Fe(OH)_3 + H^+ + e^-) \times 2 \qquad 2 \, e^- + 2 \, H^+ + H_2O_2 \rightarrow 2 \, H_2O$$

$$2 \, H_2O + 2 \, Fe(OH)_2 \rightarrow 2 \, Fe(OH)_3 + 2 \, H^+ + 2 \, e^-$$
$$\underline{2 \, e^- + 2 \, H^+ + H_2O_2 \rightarrow 2 \, H_2O}$$

$$2 \, H_2O + 2 \, H^+ + 2 \, Fe(OH)_2 + H_2O_2 \rightarrow 2 \, Fe(OH)_3 + 2 \, H_2O + 2 \, H^+$$

Reducing gives: $2 \, Fe(OH)_2(s) + H_2O_2(aq) \rightarrow 2 \, Fe(OH)_3(s)$

113.   mol KHP used $= 0.4016 \, g \times \dfrac{1 \, mol}{204.22 \, g} = 1.967 \times 10^{-3}$ mol KHP

One mole of NaOH reacts completely with one mole of KHP, therefore the NaOH solution contains 1.967×10^{-3} mol NaOH.

Molarity of NaOH $= \dfrac{1.967 \times 10^{-3} \, mol}{25.06 \times 10^{-3} \, L} = \dfrac{7.849 \times 10^{-2} \, mol}{L}$

Maximum molarity $= \dfrac{1.967 \times 10^{-3} \, mol}{25.01 \times 10^{-3} \, L} = \dfrac{7.865 \times 10^{-2} \, mol}{L}$

Minimum molarity $= \dfrac{1.967 \times 10^{-3} \, mol}{25.11 \times 10^{-3} \, L} = \dfrac{7.834 \times 10^{-2} \, mol}{L}$

We can express this as $0.07849 \pm 0.00016 \, M$. An alternative is to express the molarity as $0.0785 \pm 0.0002 \, M$. The second way shows the actual number of significant figures in the molarity. The advantage of the first method is that it shows that we made all of our individual measurements to four significant figures.

Integrative Problems

114.   a.   Assume 100.00 g of material.

$$42.23 \, g \, C \times \dfrac{1 \, mol \, C}{12.01 \, g \, C} = 3.516 \, mol \, C; \;\; 55.66 \, g \, F \times \dfrac{1 \, mol \, F}{19.00 \, g \, F} = 2.929 \, mol \, F$$

$$2.11 \, g \, B \times \dfrac{1 \, mol \, B}{10.81 \, g \, B} = 0.195 \, mol \, B$$

Dividing by the smallest number: $\dfrac{3.516}{0.195} = 18.0$; $\dfrac{2.929}{0.195} = 15.0$

The empirical formula is $C_{18}F_{15}B$.

b. $0.3470\ L \times \dfrac{0.01267\ mol}{L} = 4.396 \times 10^{-3}\ mol\ BARF$

molar mass of BARF $= \dfrac{2.251\ g}{4.396 \times 10^{-3}\ mol} = 512.1\ g/mol$

The empirical formula mass of BARF is 511.99 g. Therefore, the molecular formula is the same as the empirical formula, $C_{18}F_{15}B$.

115. $3\ (NH_4)_2CrO_4(aq) + 2\ Cr(NO_2)_3(aq) \rightarrow 6\ NH_4NO_2(aq) + Cr_2(CrO_4)_3(s)$

$0.203\ L \times \dfrac{0.307\ mol}{L} = 6.23 \times 10^{-2}\ mol\ (NH_4)_2CrO_4$

$0.137\ L \times \dfrac{0.269\ mol}{L} = 3.69 \times 10^{-2}\ mol\ Cr(NO_2)_3$

$\dfrac{0.0623\ mol}{0.0369\ mol} = 1.69$ (actual); The balanced reaction requires a $3/2 = 1.5$ mol ratio between

$(NH_4)_2CrO_4$ and $Cr(NO_2)_3$. Actual > required, so $Cr(NO_2)_3$ (the denominator) is limiting.

$3.69 \times 10^{-2}\ mol\ Cr(NO_2)_3 \times \dfrac{1\ mol\ Cr_2(CrO_4)_3}{2\ mol\ Cr(NO_2)_3} \times \dfrac{452.00\ g\ Cr_2(CrO_4)_3}{1\ mol\ Cr_2(CrO_4)_3} = 8.34\ g\ Cr_2(CrO_4)_3$

$0.880 = \dfrac{actual\ yield}{8.34\ g}$, actual yield $= (8.34\ g)(0.880) = 7.34\ g\ Cr_2(CrO_4)_3$ isolated

116. The unbalanced reaction is: $VO^{2+} + MnO_4^- \rightarrow V(OH)_4^+ + Mn^{2+}$

This is a redox reaction in acidic solution and must be balanced accordingly. The two half-reactions to balance are: $VO^{2+} \rightarrow V(OH)_4^+$ and $MnO_4^- \rightarrow Mn^{2+}$

Balancing by the half-reaction method gives:

$MnO_4^-(aq) + 5\ VO^{2+}(aq) + 11\ H_2O(l) \rightarrow 5\ V(OH)_4^+(aq) + Mn^{2+}(aq) + 2\ H^+(aq)$

$0.02645\ L \times \dfrac{0.02250\ mol\ MnO_4^-}{L} \times \dfrac{5\ mol\ VO^{2+}}{mol\ MnO_4^-} \times \dfrac{1\ mol\ V}{mol\ VO^{2+}} \times \dfrac{50.94\ g\ V}{mol\ V} = 0.1516\ g\ V$

$0.581 = \dfrac{0.1516\ g\ V}{mass\ of\ ore\ sample}$, $0.1516/0.581 = 0.261\ g$ ore sample

The oxidation states of the elements in the various ions are:

$$VO^{2+}: O, -2; \ V, \ x + (-2) = +2, \ x = +4$$

$$MnO_4^-: O, -2; \ Mn, \ x + 4(-2) = -1, \ x = +7$$

$$V(OH)_4^+: O, -2, H, +1; \ V, \ x + 4(-2) + 4(+1) = +1, \ x = +5$$

$$Mn^{2+}: Mn, +2$$

MnO_4^- has the transition metal with the highest oxidation state (+7).

117. X^{2-} contains 36 electrons, so X^{2-} has 34 protons which identifies X as selenium (Se). The name of H_2Se would be hydroselenic acid following the conventions described in Chapter 2.

$$H_2Se(aq) + 2 \ OH^-(aq) \rightarrow Se^{2-}(aq) + 2 \ H_2O(l)$$

$$0.0356 \ L \times \frac{0.175 \ mol \ OH^-}{L} \times \frac{1 \ mol \ H_2Se}{2 \ mol \ OH^-} \times \frac{80.98 \ g \ H_2Se}{mol \ H_2Se} = 0.252 \ g \ H_2Se$$

Marathon Problems

118. $$moles \ BaSO_4 = 0.2327 \ g \times \frac{1 \ mol}{233.4 \ g} = 9.970 \times 10^{-4} \ mol \ BaSO_4$$

The moles of the sulfate salt is dependent on the formula of the salt. The general equation is:

$$M_x(SO_4)_y(aq) + y \ Ba^{2+}(aq) \rightarrow y \ BaSO_4(s) + x \ M^{z+}$$

Depending on the value of y, the mole ratio between the unknown sulfate salt and $BaSO_4$ varies. For example if Pat thinks the formula is $TiSO_4$, the equation becomes:

$$TiSO_4(aq) + Ba^{2+}(aq) \rightarrow BaSO_4(s) + Ti^{2+}(aq)$$

Because there is a 1:1 mole ratio between mol $BaSO_4$ and mol $TiSO_4$, you need 9.970×10^{-4} mol of $TiSO_4$. Since 0.1472 g of salt was used, the compound would have a molar mass of (assuming the $TiSO_4$ formula):

$$0.1472 \ g/9.970 \times 10^{-4} \ mol = 147.6 \ g/mol$$

From atomic masses in the periodic table, the molar mass of $TiSO_4$ is 143.95 g/mol. From just these data, $TiSO_4$ seems reasonable.

Chris thinks the salt is sodium sulfate, which would have the formula Na_2SO_4. The equation is:

$$Na_2SO_4(aq) + Ba^{2+}(aq) \rightarrow BaSO_4(s) + 2 \ Na^+(aq)$$

As with $TiSO_4$, there is a 1:1 mole ratio between mol $BaSO_4$ and mol Na_2SO_4. For sodium sulfate to be a reasonable choice, it must have a molar mass of about 147.6 g/mol. Using atomic masses, the molar mass of Na_2SO_4 is 142.05 g/mol. Thus, Na_2SO_4 is also reasonable.

Randy, who chose gallium, deduces that gallium should have a +3 charge (since it is in column 3A) and the formula of the sulfate would be $Ga_2(SO_4)_3$. The equation would be:

$$Ga_2(SO_4)_3(aq) + 3\,Ba^{2+}(aq) \rightarrow 3\,BaSO_4(s) + 2\,Ga^{3+}(aq)$$

The calculated molar mass of $Ga_2(SO_4)_3$ would be:

$$\frac{0.1472\text{ g Ga}_2(SO_4)_3}{9.970\times10^{-4}\text{ mol BaSO}_4} \times \frac{3\text{ mol BaSO}_4}{\text{mol Ga}_2(SO_4)_3} = 442.9 \text{ g/mol}$$

Using atomic masses, the molar mass of $Ga_2(SO_4)_3$ is 427.65 g/mol. Thus, $Ga_2(SO_4)_3$ is also reasonable.

Looking in references, sodium sulfate (Na_2SO_4) exists as a white solid with orthorhombic crystals, while gallium sulfate $Ga_2(SO_4)_3$ is a white powder. Titanium sulfate exists as a green powder, but its formula is $Ti_2(SO_4)_3$. Because this has the same formula as gallium sulfate, the calculated molar mass should be around 443 g/mol. However, the molar mass of $Ti_2(SO_4)_3$ is 383.97 g/mol. It is unlikely, then, that the salt is titanium sulfate.

To distinguish between Na_2SO_4 and $Ga_2(SO_4)_3$, one could dissolve the sulfate salt in water and add NaOH. Ga^{3+} would form a precipitate with the hydroxide while Na_2SO_4 would not. References confirm that gallium hydroxide is insoluble in water.

119. a.   Compound A = $M(NO_3)_x$; In 100.00 g compound: $8.246\text{ g N} \times \dfrac{48.00\text{ g O}}{14.01\text{ g N}} = 28.25 \text{ g O}$

Thus, the mass of nitrate in the compound = 8.246 + 28.25 g = 36.50 g if x = 1.

If x = 1: mass of M = 100.00 − 36.50 g = 63.60 g

$$\text{mol M} = \text{mol N} = \frac{8.246\text{ g}}{14.01\text{ g/mol}} = 0.5886 \text{ mol}$$

$$\text{molar mass of metal M} = \frac{63.50\text{ g}}{0.5886\text{ mol}} = 107.9 \text{ g/mol (This is silver, Ag.)}$$

If x = 2: mass of M = 100.00 − 2(36.50) = 27.00 g

$$\text{mol M} = \tfrac{1}{2}\text{ mol N} = \frac{0.5886\text{ mol}}{2} = 0.2943 \text{ mol}$$

$$\text{molar mass of metal M} = \frac{27.00\text{ g}}{0.2943\text{ mol}} = 91.74 \text{ g/mol}$$

This is close to Zr, but Zr does not form stable +2 ions in solution; it forms stable +4 ions. Since we cannot have x = 3 or more nitrates (3 nitrates would have a mass greater than 100.00 g), compound A must be $AgNO_3$.

Compound B: K_2CrO_x is the formula. This salt is composed of K^+ and CrO_x^{2-} ions. Using oxidation states, $6 + x(-2) = -2$, $x = 4$. Compound B is K_2CrO_4 (potassium chromate).

b.   The reaction is:

$$2\ AgNO_3(aq) + K_2CrO_4(aq) \rightarrow Ag_2CrO_4(s) + 2\ KNO_3(aq)$$

The blood red precipitate is $Ag_2CrO_4(s)$.

c.   331.8 g Ag_2CrO_4 formed; this is equal to the molar mass of Ag_2CrO_4, so 1 mol of precipitate formed. From the balanced reaction, we need 2 mol $AgNO_3$ to react with 1 mol K_2CrO_4 to produce 1 mol (331.8 g) of Ag_2CrO_4.

$$2.000\ \text{mol AgNO}_3\ \times\ \frac{169.9\ \text{g}}{\text{mol}} = 339.8\ \text{g AgNO}_3$$

$$1.000\ \text{mol K}_2\text{CrO}_4 \times \frac{194.2\ \text{g}}{\text{mol}} = 194.2\ \text{g K}_2\text{CrO}_4$$

The problem says we have equal masses of reactants. Our two choices are 339.8 g $AgNO_3$ + 339.8 g K_2CrO_4 or 194.2 g $AgNO_3$ + 194.2 g K_2CrO_4. If we assume the 194.2 g quantities are correct, then when 194.2 g K_2CrO_4 (1 mol) reacts, 339.8 g $AgNO_3$ (2.0 mol) must be present to react with all of the K_2CrO_4. We only have 194.2 g $AgNO_3$ present; this cannot be correct. Instead of K_2CrO_4 limiting, $AgNO_3$ must be limiting and we have reacted 339.8 g $AgNO_3$ and 339.8 g K_2CrO_4.

Solution A: $\dfrac{2.000\ \text{mol Ag}^+}{0.5000\ \text{L}} = 4.000\ M\ \text{Ag}^+$; $\dfrac{2.000\ \text{mol NO}_3^-}{0.5000\ \text{L}} = 4.000\ M\ \text{NO}_3^-$.

Solution B: $339.8\ \text{g K}_2\text{CrO}_4 \times \dfrac{1\ \text{mol}}{194.2\ \text{g}} = 1.750\ \text{mol K}_2\text{CrO}_4$

$\dfrac{2 \times 1.750\ \text{mol K}^+}{0.5000\ \text{L}} = 7.000\ M\ \text{K}^+$; $\dfrac{1.750\ \text{mol CrO}_4^{2-}}{0.5000\ \text{L}} = 3.500\ M\ \text{CrO}_4^{2-}$

d.   After the reaction, moles of K^+ and moles of NO_3^- remain unchanged because they are spectator ions. Because Ag^+ is limiting, its concentration will be $0\ M$ after precipitation is complete.

$$2\ Ag^+(aq)\ +\ CrO_4^{2-}(aq)\ \rightarrow\ Ag_2CrO_4(s)$$

Initial	2.000 mol	1.750 mol	0
Change	−2.000 mol	−1.000 mol	+1.000 mol
After rxn	0	0.750 mol	1.000 mol

$M_{K^+} = \dfrac{2 \times 1.750\ \text{mol}}{1.0000\ \text{L}} = 3.500\ M\ \text{K}^+$; $M_{NO_3^-} = \dfrac{2.000\ \text{mol}}{1.0000\ \text{L}} = 2.000\ M\ \text{NO}_3^-$

$M_{CrO_4^{2-}} = \dfrac{0.750\ \text{mol}}{1.0000\ \text{L}} = 0.750\ M\ \text{CrO}_4^{2-}$; $M_{Ag^+} = 0\ M$ (the limiting reagent)

CHAPTER FIVE

GASES

For Review

1.   See Fig. 5.2 for an illustration of a barometer. A barometer initially starts with a full column of mercury which is tipped upside down and placed in a dish of mercury. The mercury in the column drops some, then levels off. The height of the column of mercury is a measure of the atmospheric pressure. Here, there are two opposite processes occurring. The weight of the mercury in the column is producing a force downward; this results in mercury wanting to flow out of the column. However, there is an opposing force keeping mercury in the column. The opposing force is that of the atmospheric gas particles colliding with the surface of the mercury in the dish; this results in mercury being pushed up into the column. When the two opposing processes are equal in strength to each other, the level of mercury in the column stays constant. The height of mercury in the column supported by the atmosphere is then a measure of pressure of the atmosphere.

See Fig. 5.3 for an illustration of a simple manometer. A manometer also has two opposing forces going against each other. There is the force exerted by the gas molecules in the flask. The opposing force is on the other side of the mercury filled U tube; it is the force exerted by atmospheric gases. The difference in height of the mercury in the U tube is a measure of the difference in pressure between the gas in the flask and the atmosphere. By measuring the height difference of mercury, one can determine how much greater than or less than the gas pressure in the flask is to the atmospheric pressure.

2.   Boyle's law: P is inversely proportional to V at constant n and T. Mathematically, $PV = k =$ constant. The plot to make to show a linear relationship is V vs. 1/P. The resulting linear plot has positive slope equal to the value of k, and the y-intercept is the origin.

Charles's law: V is directly proportional to T at constant P and n. Mathematically: $V = bT$ where b = constant. The plot to make to show a linear relationship is V vs. T. The slope of the line is equal to b, and the y-intercept is the origin if the temperature is in Kelvin.

Avogadro's law: V is directly proportional to n at constant P and T. Mathematically: $V = an$ where a = constant. A plot of V vs. n gives a line with a positive slope equal to the a constant value, and the y-intercept is the origin.

3.   Boyles' law: T and n are constant. $PV = nRT = $ constant, $PV = $ constant

Charles's law: P and n are constant. $PV = nRT$, $V = \left(\dfrac{nR}{P} \right) T = $ (constant) T

Avogadro's law: V and T are constant. $PV = nRT$, $V = \left(\dfrac{RT}{P} \right) n = $ (constant) n

P and n relationship at constant V and T: $PV = nRT$, $P = \left(\dfrac{RT}{V}\right) n = \text{(constant) } n$

P is directly proportional to n at constant V and T.

P and T relationship at constant V and n. $PV = nRT$, $P = \left(\dfrac{nR}{V}\right) T = \text{(constant) } T$

P is directly proportional to T at constant V and n.

4.   a.   Heating the can will increase the pressure of the gas inside the can, $P \propto T$ when V and n are constant. As the pressure increases, it may be enough to rupture the can.

b.   As you draw a vacuum in your mouth, atmospheric pressure pushing on the surface of the liquid forces the liquid up the straw.

c.   The external atmospheric pressure pushes on the can. Since there is no opposing pressure from the air inside, the can collapses.

d.   How "hard" the tennis ball is depends on the difference between the pressure of the air inside the tennis ball and atmospheric pressure. A "sea level" ball will be much "harder" at high altitude since the external pressure is lower at high altitude. A "high altitude" ball will be "soft" at sea level.

5.   Rigid container (constant volume): As reactants are converted to products, the moles of gas particles present decrease by one-half. As n decreases, the pressure will decrease (by one-half). Density is the mass per unit volume. Mass is conserved in a chemical reaction, so the density of the gas will not change since mass and volume do not change.

Flexible container (constant pressure): Pressure is constant since the container changes volume in order to keep a constant pressure. As the moles of gas particles decrease by a factor of 2, the volume of the container will decrease (by one-half). We have the same mass of gas in a smaller volume, so the gas density will increase (is doubled).

6.   Boyle's law: $P \propto 1/V$ at constant n and T

In the kinetic molecular theory (KMT), P is proportional to the collision frequency which is proportional to $1/V$. As the volume increases there will be fewer collisions per unit area with the walls of the container and pressure will decrease (Boyle's law).

Charles's law: $V \propto T$ at constant n and P

When a gas is heated to a higher temperature, the velocities of the gas molecules increase and thus hit the walls of the container more often and with more force. In order to keep the pressure constant, the volume of the container must increase (this increases surface area which decreases the number of collisions per unit area which decreases the pressure). Therefore, volume and temperature are directly related at constant n and P (Charles's law).

Avogadro's law: $V \propto n$ at constant P and T

As gas is added to a container (n increases), there will be an immediate increase in the number of gas particle collisions with the walls of the container. This results in an increase in pressure in the container. However, the container is such that it wants to keep the pressure constant. In order to keep pressure constant, the volume of the container increases in order to reduce the collision frequency which reduces the pressure. V is directly related to n at constant P and T.

Dalton's law of partial pressure: $P_{tot} = P_1 + P_2 + P_3 + \ldots$

The KMT assumes that gas particles are volumeless and that they exert no interparticle forces on each other. Gas molecules all behave the same way. Therefore, a mixture of gases behaves as one big gas sample. You can concentrate on the partial pressures of the individual components of the mixture or you can collectively group all of the gases together to determine the total pressure. One mole of an ideal gas behaves the same whether it is a pure gas or a mixture of gases.

P vs. n relationship at constant V and T. From question 3, this is a direct relationship. As gas is added to a container, there will be an increase in the collision frequency, resulting in an increase in pressure. P and n are directly related at constant V and T.

P vs. T relationship at constant V and n. From question 3, this is a direct relationship. As the temperature of the gas sample increases, the gas molecules move with a faster average velocity. This increases the gas collision frequency as well as increases the force of each gas particle collision. Both of these result in an increase in pressure. Pressure and temperature are directly related at constant V and n.

7.   a.   At constant temperature, the average kinetic energy of the He gas sample will equal the average kinetic energy of the Cl_2 gas sample. In order for the average kinetic energies to be the same, the smaller He atoms must move at a faster average velocity as compared to Cl_2. Therefore, plot A, with the slower average velocity, would be for the Cl_2 sample, and plot B would be for the He sample. Note the average velocity in each plot is a little past the top of the peak.

      b.   As temperature increases, the average velocity of a gas will increase. Plot A would be for $O_2(g)$ at 273 K and plot B, with the faster average velocity, would be for $O_2(g)$ at 1273 K.

            Because a gas behaves more ideally at higher temperatures, $O_2(g)$ at 1273 K would behave most ideally.

8.   Method 1: molar mass $= \dfrac{dRT}{P}$

      Determine the density of a gas at a measurable temperature and pressure, then use the above equation to determine the molar mass.

      Method 2: $\dfrac{\text{effusion rate for gas 1}}{\text{effusion rate for gas 2}} = \sqrt{\dfrac{(\text{molar mass})_2}{(\text{molar mass})_1}}$

      Determine the effusion rate of the unknown gas relative to some known gas; then use Graham's law of effusion (the above equation) to determine the molar mass.

9.   The pressure measured for real gases is too low as compared to ideal gases. This is due to the attractions gas particles do have for each other; these attractions "hold" them back from hitting the container walls as forcefully. To make up for this slight decrease in pressure for real gases, a factor is added to the measured pressure. The measured volume is too large. A fraction of the space of the container volume is taken up by the volume of gas of the molecules themselves. Therefore, the actual volume available to real gas molecules is slightly less than the container volume. A term is subtracted from the container volume to correct for the volume taken up by real gas molecules.

10.   The kinetic molecular theory assumes that gas particles do not exert forces on each other and that gas particles are volumeless. Real gas particles do exert attractive forces for each other, and real gas particles do have volumes. A gas behaves most ideally at low pressures and high temperatures. The effect of attractive forces is minimized at high temperatures since the gas particles are moving very rapidly. At low pressure, the container volume is relatively large (P and V are inversely related) so the volume of the container taken up by the gas particles is negligible.

Questions

16.   Molecules in the condensed phases (liquids and solids) are very close together. Molecules in the gaseous phase are very far apart. A sample of gas is mostly empty space. Therefore, one would expect 1 mol of $H_2O(g)$ to occupy a huge volume as compared to 1 mol of $H_2O(l)$.

17.   The column of water would have to be 13.6 times taller than a column of mercury. When the pressure of the column of liquid standing on the surface of the liquid is equal to the pressure of air on the rest of the surface of the liquid, then the height of the column of liquid is a measure of atmospheric pressure. Because water is 13.6 times less dense than mercury, the column of water must be 13.6 times longer than that of mercury to match the force exerted by the columns of liquid standing on the surface.

18.   A bag of potato chips is a constant pressure container. The volume of the bag increases or decreases in order to keep the internal pressure equal to the external (atmospheric) pressure. The volume of the bag increased because the external pressure decreased. This seems reasonable as atmospheric pressure is lower at higher altitudes than at sea level. We ignored n (moles) as a possibility because the question said to concentrate on external conditions. It is possible that a chemical reaction occurred that would increase the number of gas molecules inside the bag. This would result in a larger volume for the bag of potato chips. The last factor to consider is temperature. During ski season, one would expect the temperature of Lake Tahoe to be colder than Los Angeles. A decrease in T would result in a decrease in the volume of the potato chip bag. This is the exact opposite of what actually happened; so apparently the temperature effect is not dominant.

19.   The P versus 1/V plot is incorrect. The plot should be linear with <u>positive</u> slope and a y-intercept of zero. PV = k so P = k(1/V). This is in the form of the straight-line equation y = mx + b. The y-axis is pressure and the x-axis is 1/V.

20.   The decrease in temperature causes the balloon to contract (V and T are directly related). Because weather balloons do expand, the effect of the decrease in pressure must be dominant.

21.   d = (molar mass) P/RT; Density is directly proportional to the molar mass of a gas. Helium, with the smallest molar mass of all the noble gases, will have the smallest density.

22.   Rigid container: As temperature is increases, the gas molecules move with a faster average velocity. This results in more frequent and more forceful collisions resulting in an increase in pressure. Density = mass/volume; The moles of gas are constant and the volume of the container is constant, so density must be temperature independent (density is constant).

Flexible container: The flexible container is a constant pressure container. Therefore, the internal pressure will be unaffected by an increase in temperature. The density of the gas, however, will be affected because the container volume is affected. As T increases, there is an immediate increase in P inside the container. The container expands its volume to reduce the internal pressure back to the external pressure. We have the same mass of gas in a larger volume. Gas density will decrease in the flexible container as T increases.

23.   No; At any nonzero Kelvin temperature, there is a distribution of kinetic energies. Similarly, there is a distribution of velocities at any nonzero Kelvin temperature. The reason there is a distribution of energies at any specific temperature is because there is a distribution of gas particle velocities at any T.

24.   a.   Containers ii, iv, vi, and viii have volumes twice that of containers i, iii, v, and vii. Containers iii, iv, vii, and viii have twice the number of molecules present as compared to containers i, ii, v, and vi. The container with the lowest pressure will be the one which has the fewest moles of gas present in the largest volume (containers ii and vi both have the lowest P). The smallest container with the most mol of gas present will have the highest pressure (containers iii and vii both have the highest P). All the other containers (i, iv, v and viii) will have the same pressure between the two extremes. The order is: ii = vi < i = iv = v = viii < iii = vii.

b.   All have the same average kinetic energy since the temperature is the same in each container. Only temperature determines the average kinetic energy.

c.   The least dense gas will be container ii since it has the fewest of the lighter Ne atoms present in the largest volume. Container vii has the most dense gas since the largest number of the heavier Ar atoms are present in the smallest volume. To figure out the ordering for the other containers, we will calculate the relative density of each. In the table below, m_1 equals the mass of Ne in container i, V_1 equals the volume of container i, and d_1 equals the density of the gas in container i.

Container	i	ii	iii	iv	v	vi	vii	viii
mass, volume	m_1, V_1	$m_1, 2V_1$	$2m_1, V_1$	$2m_1, 2V_1$	$2m_1, V_1$	$2m_1, 2V_1$	$4m_1, V_1$	$4m_1, 2V_1$
density $\left(\dfrac{mass}{volume}\right)$	$\dfrac{m_1}{V_1} = d_1$	$\dfrac{m_1}{2V_1} = \dfrac{1}{2}d_1$	$\dfrac{2m_1}{V_1} = 2d_1$	$\dfrac{2m_1}{2V_1} = d_1$	$\dfrac{2m_1}{V_1} = 2d_1$	$\dfrac{2m_1}{2V_1} = d_1$	$\dfrac{4m_1}{V_1} = 4d_1$	$\dfrac{4m_1}{2V_1} = 2d_1$

From the table, the order of gas density is: ii < i = iv = vi < iii = v = viii < vii

d. $\mu_{rms} = (3\ RT/M)^{1/2}$; the root mean square velocity only depends on the temperature and the molar mass. Since T is constant, the heavier argon molecules will have the slower root mean square velocity as compared to the neon molecules. The order is:

v = vi = vii = viii < i = ii = iii = iv.

25. $2\ NH_3(g) \rightarrow N_2(g) + 3\ H_2(g)$: As reactants are converted into products, we go from 2 moles of gaseous reactants to 4 moles of gaseous products (1 mol N_2 + 3 mol H_2). Because the mol of gas doubles as reactants are converted into products, the volume of the gases will double (at constant P and T).

$PV = nRT$, $P = \left(\dfrac{RT}{V}\right)$ n = (constant) n; Pressure is directly related to n at constant T and V.

As the reaction occurs, the moles of gas will double so the pressure will double. Because 1 mol of N_2 is produced for every 2 mol of NH_3 reacted, $P_{N_2} = 1/2\ P^o_{NH_3}$. Due to the 3 to 2 mol ratio in the balanced equation, $P_{H_2} = 3/2\ P^o_{NH_3}$.

Note: $P_{tot} = P_{H_2} + P_{N_2} = 3/2\ P^o_{NH_3} + 1/2\ P^o_{NH_3} = 2\ P^o_{NH_3}$. As said earlier, the total pressure will double from the initial pressure of NH_3 as the reactants are completely converted into products.

26. Statements a, c, and e are true. For statement b, if temperature is constant, then the average kinetic energy will be constant no matter what the identity of the gas ($KE_{ave} = 3/2\ RT$). For statement d, as T increases, the average velocity of the gas molecules increases. When gas molecules are moving faster, the effect of interparticle interactions is minimized. For statement f, the KMT predicts that P is directly related to T at constant V and n. As T increases, the gas molecules move faster on average, resulting in more frequent and more forceful collisions. This leads to an increase in P.

Exercises

Pressure

27. a. $4.8\ atm \times \dfrac{760\ mm\ Hg}{atm} = 3.6 \times 10^3\ mm\ Hg$ b. $3.6 \times 10^3\ mm\ Hg \times \dfrac{1\ torr}{mm\ Hg}$

$= 3.6 \times 10^3\ torr$

c. $4.8\ atm \times \dfrac{1.013 \times 10^5\ Pa}{atm} = 4.9 \times 10^5\ Pa$ d. $4.8\ atm \times \dfrac{14.7\ psi}{atm} = 71\ psi$

28. a. $2200\ psi \times \dfrac{1\ atm}{14.7\ psi} = 150\ atm$

b. $150\ atm \times \dfrac{1.013 \times 10^5\ Pa}{atm} \times \dfrac{1\ MPa}{1. \times 10^6\ Pa} = 15\ MPa$

c. $150 \text{ atm} \times \dfrac{760 \text{ torr}}{\text{atm}} = 1.1 \times 10^5 \text{ torr}$

29. $6.5 \text{ cm} \times \dfrac{10 \text{ mm}}{\text{cm}} = 65 \text{ mm Hg} = 65 \text{ torr}; \ 65 \text{ torr} \times \dfrac{1 \text{ atm}}{760 \text{ torr}} = 8.6 \times 10^{-2} \text{ atm}$

$8.6 \times 10^{-2} \text{ atm} \times \dfrac{1.013 \times 10^5 \text{ Pa}}{\text{atm}} = 8.7 \times 10^3 \text{ Pa}$

30. $20.0 \text{ in Hg} \times \dfrac{2.54 \text{ cm}}{\text{in}} \times \dfrac{10 \text{ mm}}{\text{cm}} = 508 \text{ mm Hg} = 508 \text{ torr}; \ 508 \text{ torr} \times \dfrac{1 \text{ atm}}{760 \text{ torr}} = 0.668 \text{ atm}$

31.   If the levels of Hg in each arm of the manometer are equal, the pressure in the flask is equal to atmospheric pressure. When they are unequal, the difference in height in mm will be equal to the difference in pressure in mm Hg between the flask and the atmosphere. Which level is higher will tell us whether the pressure in the flask is less than or greater than atmospheric.

a. $P_{flask} < P_{atm}$; $P_{flask} = 760. - 118 = 642 \text{ mm Hg} = 642 \text{ torr}$; $642 \text{ torr} \times \dfrac{1 \text{ atm}}{760 \text{ torr}}$

$= 0.845 \text{ atm}$

$0.845 \text{ atm} \times \dfrac{1.013 \times 10^5 \text{ Pa}}{\text{atm}} = 8.56 \times 10^4 \text{ Pa}$

b. $P_{flask} > P_{atm}$; $P_{flask} = 760. \text{ torr} + 215 \text{ torr} = 975 \text{ torr}$; $975 \text{ torr} \times \dfrac{1 \text{ atm}}{760 \text{ torr}} = 1.28 \text{ atm}$

$1.28 \text{ atm} \times \dfrac{1.013 \times 10^5 \text{ Pa}}{\text{atm}} = 1.30 \times 10^5 \text{ Pa}$

c. $P_{flask} = 635 - 118 = 517 \text{ torr}$; $P_{flask} = 635 + 215 = 850. \text{ torr}$

32.   a.   The pressure is proportional to the mass of the fluid. The mass is proportional to the volume of the column of fluid (or to the height of the column assuming the area of the column of fluid is constant).

$d = \dfrac{\text{mass}}{\text{volume}}$; In this case, the volume of silicon oil will be the same as the volume of Hg in Exercise 5.31.

$V = \dfrac{m}{d}$; $V_{Hg} = V_{oil}$, $\dfrac{m_{Hg}}{d_{Hg}} = \dfrac{m_{oil}}{d_{oil}}$, $m_{oil} = \dfrac{m_{Hg} d_{oil}}{d_{Hg}}$

Because P is proportional to the mass of liquid:

$P_{oil} = P_{Hg}\left(\dfrac{d_{oil}}{d_{Hg}}\right) = P_{Hg}\left(\dfrac{1.30}{13.6}\right) = 0.0956 \ P_{Hg}$

This conversion applies only to the column of liquid.

$$P_{flask} = 760. \text{ torr} - (118 \times 0.0956) \text{ torr} = 760. - 11.3 = 749 \text{ torr}$$

$$749 \text{ torr} \times \frac{1 \text{ atm}}{760 \text{ torr}} = 0.986 \text{ atm}; \quad 0.986 \text{ atm} \times \frac{1.013 \times 10^5 \text{ Pa}}{\text{atm}} = 9.99 \times 10^4 \text{ Pa}$$

$$P_{flask} = 760. \text{ torr} + (215 \times 0.0956) \text{ torr} = 760. + 20.6 = 781 \text{ torr}$$

$$781 \text{ torr} \times \frac{1 \text{ atm}}{760 \text{ torr}} = 1.03 \text{ atm}; \quad 1.03 \text{ atm} \times \frac{1.013 \times 10^5 \text{ Pa}}{\text{atm}} = 1.04 \times 10^5 \text{ Pa}$$

    b.   If we are measuring the same pressure, the height of the silicon oil column would be 13.6 ÷ 1.30 = 10.5 times the height of a mercury column. The advantage of using a less dense fluid than mercury is in measuring small pressures. The quantity measured (length) will be larger for the less dense fluid. Thus, the measurement will be more precise.

Gas Laws

33.   At constant n and T, PV = nRT = constant, $P_1V_1 = P_2V_2$; At sea level, P = 1.00 atm = 760. mm Hg.

$$V_2 = \frac{P_1 V_1}{P_2} = \frac{760. \text{ mm} \times 2.0 \text{ L}}{500. \text{ mm Hg}} = 3.0 \text{ L}$$

The balloon will burst at this pressure since the volume must expand beyond the 2.5 L limit of the balloon.

Note: To solve this problem, we did not have to convert the pressure units into atm; the units of mm Hg canceled each other. In general, only convert units if you have to. Whenever the gas constant R is not used to solve a problem, pressure and volume units must only be consistent, and not necessarily in units of atm and L. The exception is temperature which must <u>always</u> be converted to the Kelvin scale.

34.   The pressure exerted on the balloon is constant and the moles of gas present is constant. From Charles's law, $V_1/T_1 = V_2/T_2$ at constant P and n.

$$V_2 = \frac{V_1 T_2}{T_1} = \frac{700. \text{ mL} \times 100. \text{ K}}{(273.2 + 20.0) \text{ K}} = 239 \text{ mL}$$

As expected, as the temperature decreased, the volume decreased.

35.   At constant T and P, Avogadro's law holds.

$$\frac{V_1}{n_1} = \frac{V_2}{n_2}, \quad n_2 = \frac{V_2 n_1}{V_1} = \frac{20. \text{ L} \times 0.50 \text{ mol}}{11.2 \text{ L}} = 0.89 \text{ mol}$$

As expected, as V increases, n increases.

36.   As NO_2 is converted completely into N_2O_4, the moles of gas present will decrease by one-half (from the 2:1 mol ratio in the balanced equation). Using Avogadro's law,

$$\frac{V_1}{n_1} = \frac{V_2}{n_2}, \quad V_2 = V_1 \times \frac{n_2}{n_1} = 25.0 \text{ mL} \times \frac{1}{2} = 12.5 \text{ mL}$$

$N_2O_4(g)$ will occupy one-half the original volume of $NO_2(g)$. This is expected since the mol of gas present decrease by one-half when NO_2 is converted into N_2O_4.

37.   a. $PV = nRT$, $V = \dfrac{nRT}{P} = \dfrac{2.00 \text{ mol} \times \dfrac{0.08206 \text{ L atm}}{\text{mol K}} \times (155 + 273) \text{ K}}{5.00 \text{ atm}} = 14.0 \text{ L}$

       b. $PV = nRT$, $n = \dfrac{PV}{RT} = \dfrac{0.300 \text{ atm} \times 2.00 \text{ L}}{\dfrac{0.08206 \text{ L atm}}{\text{mol K}} \times 155 \text{ K}} = 4.72 \ 10^{-2} \text{ mol}$

       c. $PV = nRT$, $T = \dfrac{PV}{nR} = \dfrac{4.47 \text{ atm} \times 25.0 \text{ L}}{2.01 \text{ mol} \times \dfrac{0.08206 \text{ L atm}}{\text{mol K}}} = 678 \text{ K} = 405°C$

       d. $PV = nRT$, $P = \dfrac{nRT}{V} = \dfrac{10.5 \text{ mol} \times \dfrac{0.08206 \text{ L atm}}{\text{mol K}} \times (273 + 75) \text{ K}}{2.25 \text{ L}} = 133 \text{ atm}$

38.   a. $P = 7.74 \times 10^3 \text{ Pa} \times \dfrac{1 \text{ atm}}{1.013 \times 10^5 \text{ Pa}} = 0.0764 \text{ atm};$ $T = 25 + 273 = 298 \text{ K}$

       $PV = nRT$, $n = \dfrac{PV}{RT} = \dfrac{0.0764 \text{ atm} \times 0.0122 \text{ L}}{\dfrac{0.08206 \text{ L atm}}{\text{mol K}} \times 298 \text{ K}} = 3.81 \times 10^{-5} \text{ mol}$

       b. $PV = nRT$, $P = \dfrac{nRT}{V} = \dfrac{0.421 \text{ mol} \times \dfrac{0.08206 \text{ L atm}}{\text{mol K}} \times 223 \text{ K}}{0.0430 \text{ L}} = 179 \text{ atm}$

       c. $V = \dfrac{nRT}{P} = \dfrac{4.4 \times 10^{-2} \text{ mol} \times \dfrac{0.08206 \text{ L atm}}{\text{mol K}} \times (331 + 273) \text{ K}}{455 \text{ torr} \times \dfrac{1 \text{ atm}}{760 \text{ torr}}} = 3.6 \text{ L}$

d. $T = \dfrac{PV}{nR} = \dfrac{\left(745 \text{ mm Hg} \times \dfrac{1 \text{ atm}}{760 \text{ mm Hg}}\right) \times 11.2 \text{ L}}{0.401 \text{ mol} \times \dfrac{0.08206 \text{ L atm}}{\text{mol K}}} = 334 \text{ K} = 61°C$

39. $n = \dfrac{PV}{RT} = \dfrac{135 \text{ atm} \times 200.0 \text{ L}}{\dfrac{0.08206 \text{ L atm}}{\text{mol K}} \times (273 + 24) \text{ K}} = 1.11 \times 10^3 \text{ mol}$

For He: $1.11 \times 10^3 \text{ mol} \times \dfrac{4.003 \text{ g He}}{\text{mol}} = 4.44 \times 10^3 \text{ g He}$

For H_2: $1.11 \times 10^3 \text{ mol} \times \dfrac{2.016 \text{ g He}}{\text{mol}} = 2.24 \times 10^3 \text{ g H}_2$

40. $\dfrac{PV}{nT} = R$; For a gas at two conditions:

$\dfrac{P_1 V_1}{n_1 T_1} = \dfrac{P_2 V_2}{n_2 T_2}$; Since n and V are constant: $\dfrac{P_1}{T_1} = \dfrac{P_2}{T_2}$

$T_2 = \dfrac{P_2 T_1}{P_1} = \dfrac{2500 \text{ torr} \times 294.2 \text{ K}}{758 \text{ torr}} = 970 \text{ K} = 7.0 \times 10^2 °C$

41.   a. $PV = nRT$; $175 \text{ g Ar} \times \dfrac{1 \text{ mol Ar}}{39.95 \text{ g Ar}} = 4.38 \text{ mol Ar}$

$T = \dfrac{PV}{nR} = \dfrac{10.0 \text{ atm} \times 2.50 \text{ L}}{4.38 \text{ mol} \times \dfrac{0.08206 \text{ L atm}}{\text{mol K}}} = 69.6 \text{ K}$

b. $PV = nRT$, $P = \dfrac{nRT}{V} = \dfrac{4.38 \text{ mol} \times \dfrac{0.08206 \text{ L atm}}{\text{mol K}} \times 255 \text{ K}}{2.50 \text{ L}} = 32.3 \text{ atm}$

42. $0.050 \text{ mL} \times \dfrac{1.149 \text{ g}}{\text{mL}} \times \dfrac{1 \text{ mol O}_2}{32.00 \text{ g}} = 1.8 \times 10^{-3} \text{ mol O}_2$

$V = \dfrac{nRT}{P} = \dfrac{1.8 \times 10^{-3} \text{ mol} \times \dfrac{0.08206 \text{ L atm}}{\text{mol K}} \times 310. \text{ K}}{1.0 \text{ atm}} = 4.6 \times 10^{-2} \text{ L} = 46 \text{ mL}$

43.   For a gas at two conditions: $\dfrac{P_1V_1}{n_1T_1} = \dfrac{P_2V_2}{n_2T_2}$

Because V is constant: $\dfrac{P_1}{n_1T_1} = \dfrac{P_2}{n_2T_2}$, $n_2 = \dfrac{n_1P_2T_1}{P_1T_2}$

$$n_2 = \frac{1.50 \text{ mol} \times 800.\text{ torr} \times 298\text{ K}}{400.\text{ torr} \times 323\text{ K}} = 2.77 \text{ mol}$$

mol of gas added = $n_2 - n_1$ = 2.77 − 1.50 = 1.27 mol

For two condition problems, units for P and V just need to be the same units for both conditions, not necessarily atm and L. The unit conversions from other P or V units would cancel when applied to both conditions. However, temperature always must be converted to the Kelvin scale. The temperature conversions between other units and Kelvin will not cancel each other.

44.   PV = nRT, n is constant. $\dfrac{PV}{T} = nR = $ constant, $\dfrac{P_1V_1}{T_1} = \dfrac{P_2V_2}{T_2}$

$V_2 = 1.040\, V_1$, so $\dfrac{V_1}{V_2} = \dfrac{1.000}{1.040}$

$$P_2 = \frac{P_1V_1T_2}{V_2T_1} = 100.\text{ psi} \times \frac{1.000}{1.040} \times \frac{(273+58)\text{ K}}{(273+19)\text{ K}} = 109 \text{ psi}$$

45.   At two conditions: $\dfrac{P_1V_1}{n_1T_1} = \dfrac{P_2V_2}{n_2T_2}$;   All gases follow the ideal gas law. The identity of the gas in container B is unimportant as long as we know the mol of gas.

$$\frac{P_B}{P_A} = \frac{V_A\,n_b\,T_b}{V_B\,n_a\,T_a} = \frac{1.0\text{ L} \times 2.0\text{ mol} \times 560.\text{ K}}{2.0\text{ L} \times 1.0\text{ mol} \times 280.\text{ K}} = 2.0$$

The pressure of the gas in container B is twice the pressure of the gas in container A.

46.   a.   At constant n and V, $\dfrac{P_1}{T_1} = \dfrac{P_2}{T_2}$, $P_2 = \dfrac{P_1T_2}{T_1} = 40.0\text{ atm} \times \dfrac{318\text{ K}}{273\text{ K}} = 46.6 \text{ atm}$

b. $\dfrac{P_1}{T_1} = \dfrac{P_2}{T_2}$, $T_2 = \dfrac{T_1P_2}{P_1} = 273\text{ K} \times \dfrac{150.\text{ atm}}{40.0\text{ atm}} = 1.02 \times 10^3 \text{ K}$

c. $T_2 = \dfrac{T_1P_2}{P_1} = 273\text{ K} \times \dfrac{25.0\text{ atm}}{40.0\text{ atm}} = 171 \text{ K}$

47. $$\frac{PV}{T} = nR = \text{constant}, \quad \frac{P_1 V_1}{T_1} = \frac{P_2 V_2}{T_2}$$

$$P_2 = \frac{P_1 V_1 T_2}{V_2 T_1} = 7.10. \text{ torr} \times \frac{5.0 \times 10^2 \text{ mL}}{25 \text{ mL}} \times \frac{(273 + 820.) \text{ K}}{(273 + 30.) \text{ K}} = 5.1 \times 10^4 \text{ torr}$$

48. $PV = nRT$, V constant; $\dfrac{nT}{P} = \dfrac{V}{R}$ = constant ; $\dfrac{n_1 T_1}{P_1} = \dfrac{n_2 T_2}{P_2}$; mol × molar mass = mass

$$\frac{n_1 \,(\text{molar mass})\, T_1}{P_1} = \frac{n_2 \,(\text{molar mass})\, T_2}{P_2}, \quad \frac{\text{mass}_1 \times T_1}{P_1} = \frac{\text{mass}_2 \times T_2}{P_2}$$

$$\text{mass}_2 = \frac{\text{mass}_1 \times T_1 P_2}{T_2 P_1} = \frac{1.00 \times 10^3 \text{ g} \times 291 \text{ K} \times 650. \text{ psi}}{299 \text{ K} \times 2050. \text{ psi}} = 309 \text{ g Ar remains}$$

49. $PV = nRT$, n is constant. $\dfrac{PV}{T} = nR = \text{constant}, \quad \dfrac{P_1 V_1}{T_1} = \dfrac{P_2 V_2}{T_2}$, $V_2 = \dfrac{V_1 P_1 T_2}{V_2 T_1}$

$$V_2 = 1.00 \text{ L} \times \frac{760. \text{torr}}{220. \text{ torr}} \times \frac{(273 - 31) \text{ K}}{(273 + 23) \text{ K}} = 2.82 \text{ L}; \quad \Delta V = 2.82 - 1.00 = 1.82 \text{ L}$$

50. $PV = nRT$, P is constant. $\dfrac{nT}{V} = \dfrac{P}{R} = \text{constant}, \quad \dfrac{n_1 T_1}{V_1} = \dfrac{n_2 T_2}{V_2}$

$$\frac{n_2}{n_1} = \frac{T_1 V_2}{T_2 V_1} = \frac{294 \text{ K}}{335 \text{ K}} \times \frac{4.20 \times 10^3 \text{ m}^3}{4.00 \times 10^3 \text{ m}^3} = 0.921$$

Gas Density, Molar Mass, and Reaction Stoichiometry

51. STP: $T = 273$ K and $P = 1.00$ atm; At STP, the molar volume of a gas is 22.42 L.

$$2.00 \text{ L } O_2 \times \frac{1 \text{ mol } O_2}{22.42 \text{ L}} \times \frac{4 \text{ mol Al}}{3 \text{ mol } O_2} \times \frac{26.98 \text{ g Al}}{\text{mol Al}} = 3.21 \text{ g Al}$$

52. $CO_2(s) \rightarrow CO_2(g)$; $4.00 \text{ g } CO_2 \times \dfrac{1 \text{ mol } CO_2}{44.01 \text{ g } CO_2} = 9.09 \times 10^{-2} \text{ mol } CO_2$

At STP, the molar volume of a gas is 22.42 L. $9.09 \times 10^{-2} \text{ mol } CO_2 \times \dfrac{22.42 \text{ L}}{\text{mol } CO_2} = 2.04 \text{ L}$

53. $2 \text{ NaN}_3(s) \rightarrow 2 \text{ Na}(s) + 3 \text{ N}_2(g)$

$$n_{N_2} = \frac{PV}{RT} = \frac{1.00 \text{ atm} \times 70.0 \text{ L}}{\dfrac{0.08206 \text{ L atm}}{\text{mol K}} \times 273 \text{ K}} = 3.12 \text{ mol } N_2 \text{ needed to fill air bag.}$$

$$\text{mass NaN}_3 \text{ reacted} = 3.12 \text{ mol } N_2 \times \frac{2 \text{ mol NaN}_3}{3 \text{ mol } N_2} \times \frac{65.02 \text{ g NaN}_3}{\text{mol NaN}_3} = 135 \text{ g NaN}_3$$

54.   Since the solution is 50.0% H_2O_2 by mass, the mass of H_2O_2 decomposed is 125/2 = 62.5 g.

$$62.5 \text{ g } H_2O_2 \times \frac{1 \text{ mol } H_2O_2}{34.02 \text{ g } H_2O_2} \times \frac{1 \text{ mol } O_2}{2 \text{ mol } H_2O_2} = 0.919 \text{ mol } O_2$$

$$V = \frac{nRT}{P} = \frac{0.919 \text{ mol} \times \dfrac{0.08206 \text{ L atm}}{\text{mol K}} \times 300. \text{ K}}{746 \text{ torr} \times \dfrac{1 \text{ atm}}{760 \text{ torr}}} = 23.0 \text{ L } O_2$$

55. $$n_{H_2} = \frac{PV}{RT} = \frac{1.0 \text{ atm} \times \left[4800 \text{ m}^3 \times \left(\dfrac{100 \text{ cm}}{\text{m}} \right)^3 \times \dfrac{1 \text{ L}}{1000 \text{ cm}^3} \right]}{\dfrac{0.08206 \text{ L atm}}{\text{mol K}} \times 273 \text{ K}} = 2.1 \times 10^5 \text{ mol}$$

2.1×10^5 mol H_2 are in the balloon. This is 80.% of the total amount of H_2 that had to be generated:

0.80 (total mol H_2) = 2.1×10^5, total mol H_2 = 2.6×10^5 mol H_2

$$2.6 \times 10^5 \text{ mol } H_2 \times \frac{1 \text{ mol Fe}}{\text{mol } H_2} \times \frac{55.85 \text{ g Fe}}{\text{mol Fe}} = 1.5 \times 10^7 \text{ g Fe}$$

$$2.6 \times 10^5 \text{ mol } H_2 \times \frac{1 \text{ mol } H_2SO_4}{\text{mol } H_2} \times \frac{98.09 \text{ g } H_2SO_4}{\text{mol } H_2SO_4} \times \frac{100 \text{ g reagent}}{98 \text{ g } H_2SO_4}$$

$$= 2.6 \times 10^7 \text{ g of } 98\% \text{ sulfuric acid}$$

56. $$5.00 \text{ g S} \times \frac{1 \text{ mol S}}{32.07 \text{ g}} = 0.156 \text{ mol S}$$

0.156 mol S will react with 0.156 mol O_2 to produce 0.156 mol SO_2. More O_2 is required to convert SO_2 into SO_3.

$$0.156 \text{ mol } SO_2 \times \frac{1 \text{ mol } O_2}{2 \text{ mol } SO_2} = 0.0780 \text{ mol } O_2$$

Total mol O_2 reacted = 0.156 + 0.0780 = 0.234 mol O_2

$$V = \frac{nRT}{P} = \frac{0.234 \text{ mol} \times \dfrac{0.08206 \text{ L atm}}{\text{mol K}} \times 623 \text{ K}}{5.25 \text{ atm}} = 2.28 \text{ L } O_2$$

57. $CH_3OH + 3/2 O_2 \rightarrow CO_2 + 2 H_2O$ or $2 CH_3OH(l) + 3 O_2(g) \rightarrow 2 CO_2(g) + 4 H_2O(g)$

$$50.0 \text{ mL} \times \frac{0.850 \text{ g}}{\text{mL}} \times \frac{1 \text{ mol}}{32.04 \text{ g}} = 1.33 \text{ mol } CH_3OH(l) \text{ available}$$

$$n_{O_2} = \frac{PV}{RT} = \frac{2.00 \text{ atm} \times 22.8 \text{ L}}{\dfrac{0.08206 \text{ L atm}}{\text{mol K}} \times 300. \text{ K}} = 1.85 \text{ mol } O_2 \text{ available}$$

$$1.33 \text{ mol CH}_3\text{OH} \times \frac{3 \text{ mol } O_2}{2 \text{ mol CH}_3\text{OH}} = 2.00 \text{ mol } O_2$$

2.00 mol O_2 are required to react completely with all of the CH_3OH available. We only have 1.85 mol O_2, so O_2 is limiting.

$$1.85 \text{ mol } O_2 \times \frac{4 \text{ mol H}_2\text{O}}{3 \text{ mol } O_2} = 2.47 \text{ mol H}_2\text{O}$$

58.   For ammonia (in one minute):

$$n_{NH_3} = \frac{PV}{RT} = \frac{90. \text{ atm} \times 500. \text{ L}}{\dfrac{0.08206 \text{ L atm}}{\text{mol K}} \times 496 \text{ K}} = 1.1 \times 10^3 \text{ mol NH}_3$$

NH_3 flows into the reactor at a rate of 1.1×10^3 mol/min.

For CO_2 (in one minute):

$$n_{CO_2} = \frac{PV}{RT} = \frac{45 \text{ atm} \times 600. \text{ L}}{\dfrac{0.08206 \text{ L atm}}{\text{mol K}} \times 496 \text{ K}} = 6.6 \times 10^2 \text{ mol CO}_2$$

CO_2 flows into the reactor at 6.6×10^2 mol/min.

To react completely with 1.1×10^3 mol NH_3/min, we need:

$$\frac{1.1 \times 10^3 \text{ mol NH}_3}{\text{min}} \times \frac{1 \text{ mol CO}_2}{2 \text{ mol NH}_3} = 5.5 \times 10^2 \text{ mol CO}_2/\text{min}$$

Since 660 mol CO_2/min are present, ammonia is the limiting reagent.

$$\frac{1.1 \times 10^3 \text{ mol NH}_3}{\text{min}} \times \frac{1 \text{ mol urea}}{2 \text{ mol urea}} \times \frac{60.06 \text{ g urea}}{\text{mol urea}} = 3.3 \times 10^4 \text{ g urea/min}$$

59.   a. $CH_4(g) + NH_3(g) + O_2(g) \rightarrow HCN(g) + H_2O(g)$; Balancing H first, then O, gives:

$$CH_4 + NH_3 + \frac{3}{2}O_2 \rightarrow HCN + 3 H_2O \text{ or } 2 CH_4(g) + 2 NH_3(g) + 3 O_2(g) \rightarrow$$

$$2 HCN(g) + 6 H_2O(g)$$

       b. $PV = nRT$, T and P constant; $\dfrac{V_1}{n_1} = \dfrac{V_2}{n_2}$, $\dfrac{V_1}{V_2} = \dfrac{n_1}{n_2}$

The volumes are all measured at constant T and P, so the volumes of gas present are directly proportional to the moles of gas present (Avogadro's law). Because Avogadro's law applies, the balanced reaction gives mole relationships as well as volume relationships. Therefore, 2 L of CH_4, 2 L of NH_3 and 3 L of O_2 are required by the balanced equation for the production of 2 L of HCN. The actual volume ratio is 20.0 L CH_4:20.0 L NH_3:20.0 L O_2 (or 1:1:1). The volume of O_2 required to react with all of the CH_4 and NH_3 present is 20.0 L ×(3/2) = 30.0 L. Since only 20.0 L of O_2 are present, O_2 is the limiting reagent. The volume of HCN produced is:

$$20.0 \text{ L } O_2 \times \frac{2 \text{ L HCN}}{3 \text{ L } O_2} = 13.3 \text{ L HCN}$$

60.   Since P and T are constant, V and n are directly proportional. The balanced equation requires 2 L of H_2 to react with 1 L of CO (2:1 volume ratio due to 2:1 mole ratio in the balanced equation). The actual volume ratio present in one minute is 16.0 L/25.0 L = 0.640 (0.640:1). Because the actual volume ratio present is smaller than the required volume ratio, H_2 is the limiting reactant. The volume of CH_3OH produced at STP will be one-half the volume of H_2 reacted due to the 1:2 mol ratio in the balanced equation. In one minute, 16.0 L/2 = 8.00 L CH_3OH are produced (theoretical yield).

$$n_{CH_3OH} = \frac{PV}{RT} = \frac{1.00 \text{ atm} \times 8.00 \text{ L}}{\dfrac{0.08206 \text{ L atm}}{\text{mol K}} \times 273 \text{ K}} = 0.357 \text{ mol } CH_3OH \text{ in one minute}$$

$$0.357 \text{ mol } CH_3OH \times \frac{32.04 \text{ g } CH_3OH}{\text{mol } CH_3OH} = 11.4 \text{ g } CH_3OH \text{ (theoretical yield per minute)}$$

$$\% \text{ yield} = \frac{\text{actual yield}}{\text{theoretical yield}} \times 100 = \frac{5.30 \text{ g}}{11.4 \text{ g}} = 46.5\% \text{ yield}$$

61. $\text{molar mass} = \dfrac{dRT}{P}$ where d = density of gas in units of g/L

$$\text{molar mass} = \frac{3.164 \text{ g/L} \times \dfrac{0.08206 \text{ L atm}}{\text{mol K}} \times 273.2 \text{ K}}{1.000 \text{ atm}} = 70.98 \text{ g/mol}$$

The gas is diatomic, so the atomic mass = 70.93/2 = 35.47. This is chlorine and the identity of the gas is Cl_2.

62. $P \times (\text{molar mass}) = dRT, \quad d = \dfrac{\text{mass}}{\text{volume}}, \quad P \times (\text{molar mass}) = \dfrac{\text{mass}}{V} \times RT$

$$\text{Molar mass} = \frac{\text{mass} \times RT}{PV} = \frac{0.800 \text{ g} \times \dfrac{0.08206 \text{ L atm}}{\text{mol K}} \times 373 \text{ K}}{\left(750. \text{ torr} \times \dfrac{1 \text{ atm}}{760 \text{ torr}}\right) \times 0.256 \text{ L}} \times 373 \text{ K} = 96.9 \text{ g/mol}$$

Mass of CHCl $\approx$ 12.0 + 1.0 + 35.5 = 48.5; $\dfrac{96.9}{48.5}$ = 2.00; Molecular formula is $C_2H_2Cl_2$.

63. $d_{UF_6} = \dfrac{P \times (\text{molar mass})}{RT} = \dfrac{\left(745 \text{ torr} \times \dfrac{1 \text{ atm}}{760 \text{ torr}}\right) \times 352.0 \text{ g/mol}}{\dfrac{0.08206 \text{ L atm}}{\text{mol K}} \times 333 \text{ K}} = 12.6 \text{ g/L}$

64. $d = P \times (\text{molar mass})/RT$; We need to determine the average molar mass of air. We get this by using the mol fraction information to determine the weighted value for the molar mass. If we have 1.000 mol of air:

average molar mass = $0.78 \text{ mol N}_2 \times \dfrac{28.02 \text{ g N}_2}{\text{mol N}_2} + 0.21 \text{ mol O}_2 \times \dfrac{32.00 \text{ g O}_2}{\text{mol O}_2} +$

$0.010 \text{ mol Ar} \times \dfrac{39.95 \text{ g Ar}}{\text{mol Ar}} = 28.98 = 29 \text{ g}$

$d_{air} = \dfrac{1.00 \text{ atm} \times 29 \text{ g/mol}}{\dfrac{0.08206 \text{ L atm}}{\text{mol K}} \times 273 \text{ K}} = 1.3 \text{ g/L}$

Partial Pressure

65. $P_{CO_2} = \dfrac{nRT}{V} = \dfrac{\left(7.8 \text{ torr} \times \dfrac{1 \text{ mol}}{44.01 \text{ g}}\right) \times \dfrac{0.08206 \text{ L atm}}{\text{mol K}} \times 300. \text{ K}}{4.0 \text{ L}} = 1.1 \text{ atm}$

With air present, the partial pressure of CO_2 will still be 1.1 atm. The total pressure will be the sum of the partial pressures, $P_{total} = P_{CO_2} + P_{air}$.

$P_{total} = 1.1 \text{ atm} + \left(740 \text{ torr} \times \dfrac{1 \text{ atm}}{760 \text{ torr}}\right) = 1.1 + 0.97 = 2.1 \text{ atm}$

66. $n_{H_2} = 1.00 \text{ g H}_2 \times \dfrac{1 \text{ mol H}_2}{2.016 \text{ g H}_2} = 0.496 \text{ mol H}_2$; $n_{He} = 1.00 \text{ g He} \times \dfrac{1 \text{ mol He}}{4.003 \text{ g He}}$

$= 0.250 \text{ mol He}$

$P_{H_2} = \dfrac{n_{H_2} \times RT}{V} = \dfrac{0.496 \text{ mol} \times \dfrac{0.08206 \text{ L atm}}{\text{mol K}} \times (273 + 27) \text{ K}}{1.00 \text{ L}} = 12.2 \text{ atm}$

$P_{He} = \dfrac{n_{He} \times RT}{V} = 6.15 \text{ atm}$; $P_{total} = P_{H_2} + P_{He} = 12.2 \text{ atm} + 6.15 \text{ atm} = 18.4 \text{ atm}$

67.   Use the relationship $P_1V_1 = P_2V_2$ for each gas, since T and n for each gas are constant.

For H_2: $P_2 = \dfrac{P_1V_1}{V_2} = 475 \text{ torr} \times \dfrac{2.00 \text{ L}}{3.00 \text{ L}} = 317 \text{ torr}$

For N_2: $P_2 = 0.200 \text{ atm} \times \dfrac{1.00 \text{ L}}{3.00 \text{ L}} = 0.0667 \text{ atm}; \ \ 0.0667 \text{ atm} \times \dfrac{760 \text{ torr}}{\text{atm}} = 50.7 \text{ torr}$

$P_{total} = P_{H_2} + P_{N_2} = 317 + 50.7 = 368 \text{ torr}$

68.   For H_2: $P_2 = \dfrac{P_1V_1}{V_2} = 360. \text{ torr} \times \dfrac{2.00 \text{ L}}{3.00 \text{ L}} = 240. \text{ torr}$

$P_{TOT} = P_{H_2} + P_{N_2}, \ P_{N_2} = P_{TOT} - P_{H_2} = 320. \text{ torr} - 240. \text{ torr} = 80. \text{ torr}$

For N_2: $P_1 = \dfrac{P_2V_2}{V_1} = 80. \text{ torr} \times \dfrac{3.00 \text{ L}}{1.00 \text{ L}} = 240 \text{ torr}$

69.   a.   mol fraction $CH_4 = \chi_{CH_4} = \dfrac{P_{CH_4}}{P_{total}} = \dfrac{0.175 \text{ atm}}{0.175 \text{ atm} + 0.250 \text{ atm}} = 0.412$

$\chi_{O_2} = 1.000 - 0.412 = 0.588$

b. $PV = nRT, \ n_{total} = \dfrac{P_{total} \times V}{RT} = \dfrac{0.425 \text{ atm} \times 10.5 \text{ L}}{\dfrac{0.08206 \text{ L atm}}{\text{mol K}} \times 338 \text{ K}} = 0.161 \text{ mol}$

c. $\chi_{CH_4} = \dfrac{n_{CH_4}}{n_{total}}, \ n_{CH_4} = \chi_{CH_4} \times n_{total} = 0.412 \times 0.161 \text{ mol} = 6.63 \times 10^{-2} \text{ mol } CH_4$

$6.63 \times 10^{-2} \text{ mol } CH_4 \times \dfrac{16.04 \text{ g } CH_4}{\text{mol } CH_4} = 1.06 \text{ g } CH_4$

$n_{O_2} = 0.588 \times 0.161 \text{ mol} = 9.47 \times 10^{-2} \text{ mol } O_2; \ 9.47 \times 10^{-2} \text{ mol } O_2 \times \dfrac{32.00 \text{ g } O_2}{\text{mol } O_2}$

$= 3.03 \text{ g } O_2$

70.   If we had 100.0 g of the gas, we would have 50.0 g He and 50.0 g Xe.

$\chi_{He} = \dfrac{n_{He}}{n_{He} + n_{Xe}} = \dfrac{\dfrac{50.0 \text{ g}}{4.003 \text{ g/mol}}}{\dfrac{50.0 \text{ g}}{4.003 \text{ g/mol}} + \dfrac{50.0 \text{ g}}{131.3 \text{ g/mol}}} = \dfrac{12.5 \text{ mol He}}{12.5 \text{ mol He} + 0.381 \text{ mol Xe}} = 0.970$

$P_{He} = \chi_{He}P_{total} = 0.970 \times 600. \text{ torr} = 582 \text{ torr}; \ P_{Xe} = 600. - 582 = 18 \text{ torr}$

71. $P_{TOT} = P_{H_2} + P_{H_2O}$, $1.032 \text{ atm} = P_{H_2} + 32 \text{ torr} \times \dfrac{1 \text{ atm}}{760 \text{ torr}}$, $P_{H_2} = 1.032 - 0.042 = 0.990 \text{ atm}$

$$n_{H_2} = \frac{P_{H_2} V}{RT} = \frac{0.990 \text{ atm} \times 0.240 \text{ L}}{\dfrac{0.08206 \text{ L atm}}{\text{mol K}} \times 303 \text{ K}} = 9.56 \times 10^{-3} \text{ mol H}_2$$

$$9.56 \times 10^{-3} \text{ mol H}_2 \times \frac{1 \text{ mol Zn}}{\text{mol H}_2} \times \frac{65.38 \text{ g Zn}}{\text{mol Zn}} = 0.625 \text{ g Zn}$$

72.   To calculate the volume of gas, we can use P_{total} and n_{total} $(V = n_{tot}RT/P_{tot})$ or we can use P_{He} and n_{He} $(V = n_{He}RT/P_{He})$. Since n_{H_2O} is unknown, we will use P_{He} and n_{He}.

$P_{He} + P_{H_2O} = 1.00 \text{ atm} = 760. \text{ torr} = P_{He} + 23.8 \text{ torr}$, $P_{He} = 736 \text{ torr}$

$$n_{He} = 0.586 \text{ g} \times \frac{1 \text{ mol}}{4.003 \text{ g}} = 0.146 \text{ mol He}$$

$$V = \frac{n_{He}RT}{P_{He}} = \frac{0.146 \text{ mol} \times \dfrac{0.08206 \text{ L atm}}{\text{mol K}} \times 298 \text{ K}}{736 \text{ torr} \times \dfrac{1 \text{ atm}}{760 \text{ torr}}} = 3.69 \text{ L}$$

73. $2 \text{ NaClO}_3(s) \rightarrow 2 \text{ NaCl}(s) + 3 \text{ O}_2(g)$

$P_{total} = P_{O_2} + P_{H_2O}$, $P_{O_2} = P_{total} - P_{H_2O} = 734 \text{ torr} - 19.8 \text{ torr} = 714 \text{ torr}$

$$n_{O_2} = \frac{P_{O_2} \times V}{RT} = \frac{\left(714 \text{ torr} \times \dfrac{1 \text{ atm}}{760 \text{ torr}} \right) \times 0.0572 \text{ L}}{\dfrac{0.08206 \text{ L atm}}{\text{mol K}} \times (273 + 22) \text{ K}} = 2.22 \times 10^{-3} \text{ mol O}_2$$

Mass $NaClO_3$ decomposed $= 2.22 \times 10^{-3} \text{ mol O}_2 \times \dfrac{2 \text{ mol NaClO}_3}{3 \text{ mol O}_2} \times \dfrac{106.44 \text{ g NaClO}_3}{\text{mol NaClO}_3}$

$$= 0.158 \text{ g NaClO}_3$$

Mass % $NaClO_3 = \dfrac{0.158 \text{ g}}{0.8765 \text{ g}} \times 100 = 18.0\%$

74.   10.10 atm - 7.62 atm = 2.48 atm is the pressure of the amount of F_2 reacted.

PV = nRT, V and T are constant. $\dfrac{P}{n} = \text{constant}$, $\dfrac{P_1}{n_1} = \dfrac{P_2}{n_2}$ or $\dfrac{P_1}{P_2} = \dfrac{n_1}{n_2}$

$$\frac{\text{moles F}_2 \text{ reacted}}{\text{moles Xe reacted}} = \frac{2.48 \text{ atm}}{1.24 \text{ atm}} = 2.00; \text{ So: } \text{Xe} + 2 \text{ F}_2 \rightarrow \text{XeF}_4$$

75. $2 \, HN_3(g) \rightarrow 3 \, N_2(g) + H_2(g)$; At constant V and T, P is directly proportional to n. In the reaction, we go from 2 moles of gaseous reactants to 4 moles of gaseous products. Since moles doubled, the final pressure will double ($P_{tot} = 6.0$ atm). Similarly, from the 2:1 mole ratio between HN_3 and H_2, the partial pressure of H_2 will be $3.0/2 = 1.5$ atm. The partial pressure of N_2 will be $3/2 \, (3.0 \text{ atm}) = 4.5$ atm. This is from the 2:3 mole ratio between HN_3 and N_2.

76. $$150 \text{ g } (CH_3)_2N_2H_2 \times \frac{1 \text{ mol } (CH_3)_2N_2H_2}{60.10 \text{ g}} \times \frac{3 \text{ mol } N_2}{\text{mol } (CH_3)_2N_2H_2} = 7.5 \text{ mol } N_2 \text{ produced}$$

$$P_{N_2} = \frac{nRT}{V} = \frac{7.5 \text{ mol} \times \dfrac{0.08206 \text{ L atm}}{\text{mol K}} \times 300. \text{ K}}{250 \text{ L}} = 0.74 \text{ atm}$$

We could do a similar calculation for P_{H_2O} and P_{CO_2} and then calculate P_{total} ($= P_{N_2} + P_{H_2O} + P_{CO_2}$). Or we can recognize that 9 total mol of gaseous products form. This is 3 times the mol of N_2 produced. Therefore, P_{tot} will be 3 times larger than P_{N_2}. $P_{tot} = 3 \times P_{N_2} = 3 \times 0.74$ atm $= 2.2$ atm

Kinetic Molecular Theory and Real Gases

77. $KE_{avg} = 3/2 \, RT$; The average kinetic energy depends only on temperature. At each temperature, CH_4 and N_2 will have the same average KE. For energy units of joules (J), use R = 8.3145 J/mol•K. To determine average KE per molecule, divide by Avogadro's number, 6.022×10^{23} molecules/mol.

at 273 K: $KE_{avg} = \dfrac{3}{2} \times \dfrac{8.3145 \text{ J}}{\text{mol K}} \times 273 \text{ K} = 3.40 \times 10^3 \text{ J/mol} = 5.65 \times 10^{-21} \text{ J/molecule}$

at 546 K: $KE_{avg} = \dfrac{3}{2} \times \dfrac{8.3145 \text{ J}}{\text{mol K}} \times 546 \text{ K} = 6.81 \times 10^3 \text{ J/mol} = 1.13 \times 10^{-20} \text{ J/molecule}$

78. $n_{Ar} = \dfrac{228 \text{ g}}{39.95 \text{ g/mol}} = 5.71 \text{ mol Ar}; \quad \chi_{CH_4} = \dfrac{n_{CH_4}}{n_{CH_4} + n_{Ar}} = 0.650 = \dfrac{n_{CH_4}}{n_{CH_4} + 5.71}$

$0.650 \, (n_{CH_4} + 5.71) = n_{CH_4}, \quad 3.71 = 0.350 \, n_{CH_4}, \quad n_{CH_4} = 10.6 \text{ mol } CH_4$

$KE_{avg} = \dfrac{3}{2} RT$ for 1 mol

$KE_{total} = (10.6 + 5.71) \text{ mol} \times 3/2 \times 8.3145 \text{ J/mol•K} \times 298 \text{ K} = 6.06 \times 10^4 \text{ J} = 60.6 \text{ kJ}$

79. $u_{rms} = \left(\dfrac{3RT}{M}\right)^{1/2}$, $R = \dfrac{8.3145\ J}{mol\ K}$ and M = molar mass in kg = 1.604×10^{-2} kg/mol for CH_4

For CH_4 at 273 K: $u_{rms} = \left(\dfrac{\dfrac{3 \times 8.3145\ J}{mol\ K} \times 273\ K}{1.604 \times 10^{-2}\ kg/mol}\right)^{1/2} = 652$ m/s

Similarly, u_{rms} for CH_4 at 546 K is 921 m/s.

For N_2 at 273 K: $u_{rms} = \left(\dfrac{\dfrac{3 \times 8.3145\ J}{mol\ K} \times 273\ K}{2.802 \times 10^{-2}\ kg/mol}\right)^{1/2} = 493$ m/s

Similarly, for N_2 at 546 K, $u_{rms} = 697$ m/s.

80. $u_{rms} = \left(\dfrac{3RT}{M}\right)^{1/2}$; $\dfrac{u_{UF_6}}{u_{He}} = \dfrac{\left(\dfrac{3RT_{UF_6}}{M_{UF_6}}\right)^{1/2}}{\left(\dfrac{3RT_{He}}{M_{He}}\right)^{1/2}} = \left(\dfrac{M_{He}T_{UF_6}}{M_{UF_6}T_{He}}\right)^{1/2}$

We want the root mean square velocities to be equal, and this occurs when $M_{He}T_{UF_6} = M_{UF_6}T_{He}$. The ratio of the temperatures is:

$$\dfrac{T_{UF_6}}{T_{He}} = \dfrac{M_{UF_6}}{M_{He}} = \dfrac{352.0}{4.003} = 87.93$$

The heavier UF_6 molecules would need a temperature 87.93 times that of the He atoms in order for the root mean square velocities to be equal.

81.

	a	b	c	d
avg. KE	inc	dec	same (KE $\propto$ T)	same
avg. velocity	inc	dec	same ($\frac{1}{2}$ mv^2 = KE $\propto$ T)	same
coll. freq wall	inc	dec	inc	inc

Average kinetic energy and average velocity depend on T. As T increases, both average kinetic energy and average velocity increase. At constant T, both average kinetic energy and average velocity are constant. The collision frequency is proportional to the average velocity (as velocity increases it takes less time to move to the next collision) and to the quantity n/V (as molecules per volume increase, collision frequency increases).

82.   V, T, and P are all constant, so n must be constant. Because we have equal mol of gas in each container, gas B molecules must be heavier than gas A molecules.

a.   Both gas samples have the same number of molecules present (n is constant).

b.   Since T is constant, KE_{ave} must be the same for both gases (KE_{ave} = 3/2 RT).

c.   The lighter gas A molecules will have the faster average velocity.

d.   The heavier gas B molecules do collide more forcefully, but gas A molecules, with the faster average velocity, collide more frequently. The end result is that P is constant between the two containers.

83.   a.   They will all have the same average kinetic energy since they are all at the same temperature.

b.   Flask C; H_2 has the smallest molar mass. At constant T, the lightest molecules are the fastest (on the average). This must be true in order for the average kinetic energies to be constant.

84.   a.   All the gases have the same average kinetic energy since they are all at the same temperature.

b.   At constant T, the lighter the gas molecule, the faster the average velocity.

Xe (131.3 g/mol) < Cl_2 (70.90 g/mol) < O_2 (32.00 g/mol) < H_2 (2.016 g/mol)
slowest   fastest

c.   At constant T, the lighter H_2 molecules have a faster average velocity than the heavier O_2 molecules. As temperature increases, the average velocity of the gas molecules increases. Separate samples of H_2 and O_2 can only have the same average velocities if the temperature of the O_2 sample is greater than the temperature of the H_2 sample.

85.   Graham's law of effusion: $\dfrac{Rate_1}{Rate_2} = \left(\dfrac{M_2}{M_1}\right)^{1/2}$

Let Freon-12 = gas 1 and Freon-11 = gas 2:

$$\frac{1.07}{1.00} = \left(\frac{137.4}{M_1}\right)^{1/2}, \ 1.14 = \frac{137.4}{M_1}, \ M_1 = 121 \text{ g/mol}$$

The molar mass of CF_2Cl_2 is equal to 121 g/mol, so Freon-12 is CF_2Cl_2.

86. $\dfrac{Rate_1}{Rate_2} = \left(\dfrac{M_2}{M_1}\right)^{1/2}$; $Rate_1 = \dfrac{24.0 \text{ mL}}{min}$; $Rate_2 = \dfrac{47.8 \text{ mL}}{min}$, $M_2 = \dfrac{16.04 \text{ g}}{mol}$ and $M_1 = ?$

$$\frac{24.0}{47.8} = \left(\frac{16.04}{M_1}\right)^{1/2} = 0.502, \ 16.04 = (0.502)^2 \times M_1, \ M_1 = \frac{16.04}{0.252} = \frac{63.7 \text{ g}}{\text{mol}}$$

87. $$\frac{\text{Rate}_1}{\text{Rate}_2} = \left(\frac{M_2}{M_1}\right)^{1/2}, \quad \frac{\text{Rate}(^{12}C^{17}O)}{\text{Rate}(^{12}C^{18}O)} = \left(\frac{30.0}{29.0}\right)^{1/2} = 1.02$$

$$\frac{\text{Rate}(^{12}C^{16}O)}{\text{Rate}(^{12}C^{18}O)} = \left(\frac{30.0}{28.0}\right)^{1/2} = 1.04$$

The relative rates of effusion of $^{12}C^{16}O$: $^{12}C^{17}O$: $^{12}C^{18}O$ are 1.04: 1.02: 1.00.

Advantage: CO_2 isn't as toxic as CO.

Major disadvantages of using CO_2 instead of CO:

1. Can get a mixture of oxygen isotopes in CO_2.

2. Some species, e.g., $^{12}C^{16}O^{18}O$ and $^{12}C^{17}O_2$, would effuse (gaseously diffuse) at about the same rate since the masses are about equal. Thus, some species cannot be separated from each other.

88. $$\frac{\text{Rate}_1}{\text{Rate}_2} = \left(\frac{M_2}{M_1}\right)^{1/2}, \text{ where } M = \text{molar mass; Let Gas (1)} = \text{He, Gas (2)} = Cl_2:$$

$$\frac{\dfrac{1.0 \text{ L}}{4.5 \text{ min}}}{\dfrac{1.0 \text{ L}}{t}} = \left(\frac{70.90}{4.003}\right)^{1/2}, \quad \frac{t}{4.5 \text{ min}} = 4.209, \ t = 19 \text{ min}$$

89.   a. $$P = \frac{nRT}{V} = \frac{0.5000 \text{ mol} \times \dfrac{0.08206 \text{ L atm}}{\text{mol K}} \times (25.0 + 273.2) \text{ K}}{1.0000 \text{ L}} = 12.24 \text{ atm}$$

b. $$\left[P + a\left(\frac{n}{V}\right)^2\right] \times (V - nb) = nRT; \text{ For } N_2: \ a = 1.39 \text{ atm L}^2/\text{mol}^2 \text{ and } b = 0.0391 \text{ L/mol}$$

$$\left[P + 1.39\left(\frac{0.5000}{1.0000}\right)^2 \text{ atm}\right] \times (1.0000 \text{ L} - 0.5000 \times 0.0391 \text{ L}) = 12.24 \text{ L atm}$$

$$(P + 0.348 \text{ atm}) \times (0.9805 \text{ L}) = 12.24 \text{ L atm}$$

$$P = \frac{12.24 \text{ L atm}}{0.9805 \text{ L}} - 0.348 \text{ atm} = 12.48 - 0.348 = 12.13 \text{ atm}$$

c. The ideal gas law is high by 0.11 atm or $\dfrac{0.11}{12.13} \times 100 = 0.91\%$.

90. a. $P = \dfrac{nRT}{V} = \dfrac{0.5000 \text{ mol} \times \dfrac{0.08206 \text{ L atm}}{\text{mol K}} \times 298.2 \text{ K}}{10.000 \text{ L}} = 1.224 \text{ atm}$

b. $\left[P + a\left(\dfrac{n}{V}\right)^2\right] \times (V - nb) = nRT$; For N_2: a = 1.39 atm L^2/mol^2 and b = 0.0391 L/mol

$\left[P + 1.39\left(\dfrac{0.5000}{10.000}\right)^2 \text{ atm}\right] \times (10.000 \text{ L} - 0.5000 \times 0.0391 \text{ L}) = 12.24 \text{ L atm}$

(P + 0.00348 atm) × (10.000 L - 0.0196 L) = 12.24 L atm

$P + 0.00348 \text{ atm} = \dfrac{12.24 \text{ L atm}}{9.980 \text{ L}} = 1.226 \text{ atm},\ P = 1.226 - 0.00348 = 1.223 \text{ atm}$

c. The results agree to ± 0.001 atm (0.08%).

d. In Exercise 5.89, the pressure is relatively high and there is a significant disagreement. In 5.90, the pressure is around 1 atm, and both gas law equations show better agreement. The ideal gas law holds best at relatively low pressures.

Atmospheric Chemistry

91. $\chi_{He} = 5.24 \times 10^{-6}$ from Table 5.4. $P_{He} = \chi_{He} \times P_{total} = 5.24 \times 10^{-6} \times 1.0 \text{ atm} = 5.2 \times 10^{-6} \text{ atm}$

$\dfrac{n}{V} = \dfrac{P}{RT} = \dfrac{5.2 \times 10^{-6} \text{ atm}}{\dfrac{0.08206 \text{ L atm}}{\text{mol K}} \times 298 \text{ K}} = 2.1 \times 10^{-7} \text{ mol He/L}$

$\dfrac{2.1 \times 10^{-7} \text{ atm}}{\text{L}} \times \dfrac{1 \text{ L}}{1000 \text{ cm}^3} \times \dfrac{6.022 \times 10^{23} \text{ atoms}}{\text{mol}} = 1.3 \times 10^{14} \text{ atoms He/cm}^3$

92. At 15 km, T ≈ -50°C and P = 0.1 atm. Use $\dfrac{P_1 V_1}{T_1} = \dfrac{P_2 V_2}{T_2}$ since n is constant.

$V_2 = \dfrac{V_1 P_1 T_2}{P_2 T_1} = \dfrac{1.0 \text{ L} \times 1.00 \text{ atm} \times 223 \text{ K}}{0.1 \text{ atm} \times 298 \text{ K}} = 7 \text{ L}$

93. $N_2(g) + O_2(g) \rightarrow 2\ NO(g)$, automobile combustion or formed by lightning

$2\ NO(g) + O_2(g) \rightarrow 2\ NO_2(g)$, reaction with atmospheric O_2

$2 NO_2(g) + H_2O(l) \rightarrow HNO_3(aq) + HNO_2(aq)$, reaction with atmospheric H_2O

$S(s) + O_2(g) \rightarrow SO_2(g)$, combustion of coal

$2 SO_2(g) + O_2(g) \rightarrow 2SO_3(g)$, reaction with atmospheric O_2

$H_2O(l) + SO_3(g) \rightarrow H_2SO_4(aq)$, reaction with atmospheric H_2O

94. $2 HNO_3(aq) + CaCO_3(s) \rightarrow Ca(NO_3)_2(aq) + H_2O(l) + CO_2(g)$

        $H_2SO_4(aq) + CaCO_3(s) \rightarrow CaSO_4(aq) + H_2O(l) + CO_2(g)$

Additional Exercises

95.   a. $PV = nRT$ b. $P = \left(\dfrac{nR}{V}\right) \times T$ c. $T = \left(\dfrac{P}{nR}\right) \times V$

            $PV = $ constant $P = $ constant $\times T$ $T = $ constant $\times V$

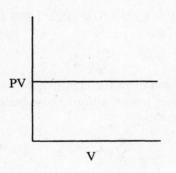

d. $PV = nRT$ e. $P = \dfrac{nRT}{V}$ f. $\dfrac{PV}{T} = nR$

    $PV = $ constant $P = $ constant $\times \dfrac{1}{V}$ $\dfrac{PV}{T} = $ constant

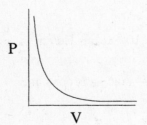   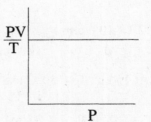

96.   At constant T and P, Avogadro's law applies; that is, equal volumes contain equal moles of molecules. In terms of balanced equations, we can say that mole ratios and volume ratios between the various reactants and products will be equal to each other. $Br_2 + 3 F_2 \rightarrow 2 X$; Two moles of X must contain two moles of Br and 6 moles of F; X must have the formula BrF_3.

97. 14.1×10^2 in Hg $\bullet$ in$^3 \times \dfrac{2.54\,\text{cm}}{\text{in}} \times \dfrac{10\,\text{mm}}{1\,\text{cm}} \times \dfrac{1\,\text{atm}}{760\,\text{mm}} \times \left(\dfrac{2.54\,\text{cm}}{\text{in}}\right)^3 \times \dfrac{1\,\text{L}}{1000\,\text{cm}^3}$

$$= 0.772 \text{ atm L}$$

Boyle's law: $PV = k$ where $k = nRT$; From Sample Exercise 5.3, the k values are around 22 atm L. Because $k = nRT$, we can assume that Boyle's data and sample Exercise 5.3 data were taken at different temperatures and/or had different sample sizes (different mol).

98.   Since the container is flexible, P is assumed constant. The moles of gas present are also constant.

$$\frac{P_1 V_1}{n_1 T_1} = \frac{P_2 V_2}{n_2 T_2},\ \frac{V_1}{T_1} = \frac{V_2}{T_2};\ V_{\text{sphere}} = 4/3\ \pi r^3$$

$$V_2 = \frac{V_1 T_2}{T_1},\ 4/3\ \pi(r_2)^3 = \frac{4/3\ \pi(1.00\,\text{cm})^3 \times 361\,\text{K}}{280.\,\text{K}}$$

$$r_2^3 = \frac{361\,\text{K}}{280.\,\text{K}} = 1.29,\ r_2 = (1.29)^{1/3} = 1.09\,\text{cm} = \text{radius of sphere after heating}$$

99. $Mn(s) + x\,HCl(g) \rightarrow MnCl_x(s) + \dfrac{x}{2}\,H_2(g)$

$$n_{H_2} = \frac{PV}{RT} = \frac{0.951\,\text{atm} \times 3.22\,\text{L}}{\dfrac{0.08206\,\text{L atm}}{\text{mol K}} \times 373\,\text{K}} = 0.100 \text{ mol } H_2$$

mol Cl in compound = mol HCl = $0.100 \text{ mol } H_2 \times \dfrac{x\,\text{mol Cl}}{\dfrac{x}{2}\,\text{mol } H_2} = 0.200 \text{ mol Cl}$

$$\frac{\text{mol Cl}}{\text{mol Mn}} = \frac{0.200\,\text{mol Cl}}{2.747\,\text{g Mn} \times \dfrac{1\,\text{mol Mn}}{54.94\,\text{g Mn}}} = \frac{0.200\,\text{mol Cl}}{0.05000\,\text{mol Mn}} = 4.00$$

The formula of compound is $MnCl_4$.

100. $2\,H_2(g) + O_2(g) \rightarrow 2\,H_2O(g)$; Because P and T are constant, volume ratios will equal mol ratios ($V_f/V_i = n_f/n_i$). Let x = mol H_2 = mol O_2 present initially. H_2 will be limiting since a 2:1 H_2 to O_2 mole ratio is required by the balanced equation, but only a 1:1 mole ratio is present. Therefore, no H_2 will be present after the reaction goes to completion. However, excess $O_2(g)$ will be present as well as the $H_2O(g)$ produced.

mol O_2 reacted = x mol $H_2 \times \dfrac{1\,\text{mol } O_2}{2\,\text{mol } H_2} = x/2 \text{ mol } O_2$

mol O_2 remaining = x mol O_2 initially $- x/2$ mol O_2 reacted = $x/2$ mol O_2

mol H_2O produced = x mol H_2 $\times$ $\dfrac{2 \text{ mol } H_2O}{2 \text{ mol } H_2}$ = x mol H_2O

Total mol gas initially = x mol H_2 + x mol O_2 = $2x$

Total mol gas after reaction = $x/2$ mol O_2 + x mol H_2O = $1.5\,x$

$$\frac{n_f}{n_i} = \frac{V_f}{V_i} = \frac{1.5\,x}{2\,x} = \frac{1.5}{2} = 0.75; \quad V_f/V_i = 0.75{:}1 \text{ or } 3{:}4$$

101. We will apply Boyle's law to solve. $PV = nRT = \text{contstant}$, $P_1V_1 = P_2V_2$

Let condition (1) correspond to He from the tank that can be used to fill balloons. We must leave 1.0 atm of He in the tank, so P_1 = 200. atm - 1.00 = 199 atm and V_1 = 15.0 L. Condition (2) will correspond to the filled balloons with P_2 = 1.00 atm and V_2 = N(2.00 L) where N is the number of filled balloons, each at a volume of 2.00 L.

199 atm $\times$ 15.0 L = 1.00 atm $\times$ N(2.00 L), N = 1492.5; We can't fill 0.5 of a balloon, so N = 1492 balloons or to 3 significant figures, 1490 balloons.

102. mol of He removed = $\dfrac{PV}{RT}$ = $\dfrac{1.00 \text{ atm} \times 1.75 \times 10^{-3} \text{ L}}{\dfrac{0.08206 \text{ L atm}}{\text{mol K}} \times 298 \text{ K}}$ = 7.16×10^{-5} mol

In the original flask, 7.16 10^{-5} mol of He exerted a partial pressure of 1.960 - 1.710 = 0.250 atm.

$$V = \frac{nRT}{P} = \frac{7.16 \times 10^{-5} \text{ mol} \times 0.08206 \times 298 \text{ K}}{0.250 \text{ atm}} = 7.00 \times 10^{-3} \text{ L} = 7.00 \text{ mL}$$

103. For O_2, n and T are constant, so $P_1V_1 = P_2V_2$.

$$P_1 = \frac{P_2V_2}{V_1} = 785 \text{ torr} \times \frac{1.94 \text{ L}}{2.00 \text{ L}} = 761 \text{ torr} = P_{O_2}$$

$P_{tot} = P_{O_2} + P_{H_2O}$, P_{H_2O} = 785 - 761 = 24 torr

104. $PV = nRT$, V and T are constant. $\dfrac{P_1}{n_1} = \dfrac{P_2}{n_2}$ or $\dfrac{P_1}{P_2} = \dfrac{n_1}{n_2}$

When V and T are constant, pressure is directly proportional to moles of gas present, and pressure ratios are identical to mole ratios.

At 25°C: $2 H_2(g) + O_2(g) \rightarrow 2 H_2O(l)$; $H_2O(l)$ is produced.

The balanced equation requires 2 mol H_2 for every mol O_2 reacted. The same ratio (2:1) holds true for pressure units. The actual pressure ratio present is 2 atm H_2 to 3 atm O_2, well below the required 2:1 ratio. Therefore, H_2 is the limiting reactant. The only gas present at 25°C after the reaction goes to completion will be the excess O_2.

$$P_{O_2} \text{ (reacted)} = 2.00 \text{ atm } H_2 \times \frac{1 \text{ atm } O_2}{2 \text{ atm } H_2} = 1.00 \text{ atm } O_2$$

$$P_{O_2} \text{ (excess)} = P_{O_2} \text{ (initially)} - P_{O_2} \text{ (reacted)} = 3.00 \text{ atm} - 1.00 \text{ atm} = 2.00 \text{ atm } O_2 = P_{\text{total}}$$

At 125°C: $2 H_2(g) + O_2(g) \rightarrow 2 H_2O(g)$; $H_2O(g)$ is produced.

The major difference in the problem is that gaseous water is now a product, which will increase the total pressure.

$$P_{H_2O} \text{ (produced)} = 2.00 \text{ atm } H_2 \times \frac{2 \text{ atm } H_2O}{2 \text{ atm } H_2} = 2.00 \text{ atm } H_2O$$

$$P_{\text{total}} = P_{O_2} \text{ (excess)} + P_{H_2O} \text{ (produced)} = 2.00 \text{ atm } O_2 + 2.00 \text{ atm } H_2O = 4.00 \text{ atm}$$

105. $1.00 \times 10^3 \text{ kg Mo} \times \dfrac{1000 \text{ g}}{\text{kg}} \times \dfrac{1 \text{ mol Mo}}{95.94 \text{ g Mo}} = 1.04 \times 10^4 \text{ mol Mo}$

$1.04 \times 10^4 \text{ mol Mo} \times \dfrac{1 \text{ mol MoO}_3}{\text{mol Mo}} \times \dfrac{7/2 \text{ mol O}_2}{\text{mol MoO}_3} = 3.64 \times 10^4 \text{ mol O}_2$

$$V_{O_2} = \frac{n_{O_2} RT}{P} = \frac{3.64 \times 10^4 \text{ mol} \times \dfrac{0.08206 \text{ L atm}}{\text{mol K}} \times 290. \text{ K}}{1.00 \text{ atm}} = 8.66 \times 10^5 \text{ L of } O_2$$

$8.66 \times 10^5 \text{ L } O_2 \times \dfrac{100 \text{ L air}}{21 \text{ L } O_2} = 4.1 \times 10^6 \text{ L air}$

$1.04 \times 10^4 \text{ mol Mo} \times \dfrac{3 \text{ mol } H_2}{\text{mol Mo}} = 3.12 \times 10^4 \text{ mol } H_2$

$$V_{H_2} = \frac{3.12 \times 10^4 \text{ mol} \times \dfrac{0.08206 \text{ L atm}}{\text{mol K}} \times 290. \text{ K}}{1.00 \text{ atm}} = 7.42 \times 10^5 \text{ L of } H_2$$

106. For NH_3: $P_2 = \dfrac{P_1 V_1}{V_2} = 0.500 \text{ atm} \times \dfrac{2.00 \text{ L}}{3.00 \text{ L}} = 0.333 \text{ atm}$

For O_2: $P_2 = \dfrac{P_1 V_1}{V_2} = 1.50 \text{ atm} \times \dfrac{1.00 \text{ L}}{3.00 \text{ L}} = 0.500 \text{ atm}$

After the stopcock is opened, V and T will be constant, so $P \propto n$. The balanced equation requires:

$$\frac{n_{O_2}}{n_{NH_3}} = \frac{P_{O_2}}{P_{NH_3}} = \frac{5}{4} = 1.25$$

The actual ratio present is: $\dfrac{P_{O_2}}{P_{NH_3}} = \dfrac{0.500 \text{ atm}}{0.333 \text{ atm}} = 1.50$

The actual ratio is larger than the required ratio, so NH_3 in the denominator is limiting. Because equal moles of NO will be produced as NH_3 that reacts, the partial pressure of NO produced is 0.333 atm (the same as P_{NH_3} reacted).

107. $750. \text{ mL juice} \times \dfrac{12 \text{ mL } C_2H_5OH}{100 \text{ mL juice}} = 90. \text{ mL } C_2H_5OH \text{ present}$

$90. \text{ mL } C_2H_5OH \times \dfrac{0.79 \text{ g } C_2H_5OH}{\text{mL } C_2H_5OH} \times \dfrac{1 \text{ mol } C_2H_5OH}{46.07 \text{ g } C_2H_5OH} \times \dfrac{2 \text{ mol } CO_2}{2 \text{ mol } C_2H_5OH}$

$= 1.5 \text{ mol } CO_2$

The CO_2 will occupy (825 − 750. =) 75 mL not occupied by the liquid (headspace).

$$P_{CO_2} = \dfrac{n_{CO_2} \times RT}{V} = \dfrac{1.5 \text{ mol} \times \dfrac{0.08206 \text{ L atm}}{\text{mol K}} \times 298 \text{ K}}{75 \times 10^{-3} \text{ L}} = 490 \text{ atm}$$

Actually, enough CO_2 will dissolve in the wine to lower the pressure of CO_2 to a much more reasonable value.

108.   If Be^{3+}, the formula is $Be(C_5H_7O_2)_3$ and the molar mass $\approx 13.5 + 15(12) + 21(1) + 6(16)$ = 311 g/mol.

If Be^{2+}, the formula is $Be(C_5H_7O_2)_2$ and the molar mass $\approx 9.0 + 10(12) + 14(1) + 4(16)$ = 207 g/mol.

Data Set I (molar mass = dRT/P and d = mass/V):

$$\text{molar mass} = \dfrac{\text{mass} \times RT}{PV} = \dfrac{0.2022 \text{ g} \times \dfrac{0.08206 \text{ L atm}}{\text{mol K}} \times 286 \text{ K}}{\left(765.2 \text{ torr} \times \dfrac{1 \text{ atm}}{760 \text{ torr}}\right) \times 22.6 \times 10^{-3} \text{ L}} = 209 \text{ g/mol}$$

Data Set II:

$$\text{molar mass} = \dfrac{\text{mass} \times RT}{PV} = \dfrac{0.2224 \text{ g} \times \dfrac{0.08206 \text{ L atm}}{\text{mol K}} \times 290. \text{ K}}{\left(764.6 \text{ torr} \times \dfrac{1 \text{ atm}}{760 \text{ torr}}\right) \times 26.0 \times 10^{-3} \text{ L}} = 202 \text{ g/mol}$$

These results are close to the expected value of 207 g/mol for $Be(C_5H_7O_2)_2$. Thus, we conclude from these data that beryllium is a divalent element with an atomic mass of 9.0 amu.

109. $P_{total} = P_{N_2} + P_{H_2O}$, $P_{N_2} = 726$ torr $- 23.8$ torr $= 702$ torr $\times \dfrac{1 \text{ atm}}{760 \text{ torr}} = 0.924$ atm

$$PV = nRT, \quad n_{N_2} = \frac{P_{N_2} \times V}{RT} = \frac{0.924 \text{ atm} \times 31.9 \times 10^{-3} \text{ L}}{\dfrac{0.08206 \text{ L atm}}{\text{mol K}} \times 298 \text{ K}} = 1.20 \times 10^{-3} \text{ mol N}_2$$

Mass of N in compound $= 1.20 \times 10^{-3}$ mol $\times \dfrac{28.02 \text{ g N}_2}{\text{mol}} = 3.36 \times 10^{-2}$ g

$\% \text{ N} = \dfrac{3.36 \times 10^{-2} \text{ g}}{0.253 \text{ g}} \times 100 = 13.3\% \text{ N}$

110. 33.5 mg $CO_2 \times \dfrac{12.01 \text{ mg C}}{44.01 \text{ mg CO}_2} = 9.14$ mg C; $\%C = \dfrac{9.14 \text{ mg}}{35.0 \text{ mg}} \times 100 = 26.1\%$ C

41.1 mg $H_2O \times \dfrac{2.016 \text{ mg H}}{18.02 \text{ mg H}_2O} = 4.60$ mg H; $\%H = \dfrac{4.60 \text{ mg}}{35.0 \text{ mg}} \times 100 = 13.1\%$H

$$n_{N_2} = \frac{P_{N_2} \times V}{RT} = \frac{\dfrac{740.}{760} \text{ atm} \times 35.6 \times 10^{-3} \text{ L}}{\dfrac{0.08206 \text{ L atm}}{\text{mol K}} \times 298 \text{ K}} = 1.42 \times 10^{-3} \text{ mol N}_2$$

1.42×10^{-3} mol $N_2 \times \dfrac{28.02 \text{ g N}_2}{\text{mol N}_2} = 3.98 \times 10^{-2}$ g nitrogen $= 39.8$ mg nitrogen

$\% \text{ N} = \dfrac{39.8 \text{ mg}}{65.2 \text{ mg}} \times 100 = 61.0\% \text{ N}$

Or we can get % N by difference: % N $= 100.0 - (26.1 + 13.1) = 60.8\%$

Out of 100.0 g:

26.1 g C $\times \dfrac{1 \text{ mol}}{12.01 \text{ g}} = 2.17$ mol C; $\dfrac{2.17}{2.17} = 1.00$

13.1 g H $\times \dfrac{1 \text{ mol}}{1.008 \text{ g}} = 13.0$ mol H; $\dfrac{13.0}{2.17} = 5.99$

60.8 g N $\times \dfrac{1 \text{ mol}}{14.01 \text{ g}} = 4.34$ mol N; $\dfrac{4.34}{2.17} = 2.00$

Empirical formula is CH_6N_2.

$$\frac{\text{Rate}_1}{\text{Rate}_2} = \left(\frac{M}{39.95}\right)^{1/2} = \frac{26.4}{24.6} = 1.07, \ M = (1.07)^2 \times 39.95 = 45.7 \text{ g/mol}$$

Empirical formula mass of $CH_6N_2 \approx 12 + 6 + 2(14) = 46$. Thus, molecular formula is also CH_6N_2.

111. $0.2766 \text{ g CO}_2 \times \dfrac{12.01 \text{ g C}}{44.01 \text{ g CO}_2} = 7.548 \times 10^{-2} \text{ g C}; \ \% \text{ C} = \dfrac{7.548 \times 10^{-2} \text{ g}}{0.1023 \text{ g}} \times 100 = 73.78\% \text{ C}$

$0.0991 \text{ g H}_2\text{O} \times \dfrac{2.016 \text{ g H}}{18.02 \text{ g H}_2\text{O}} = 1.11 \times 10^{-2} \text{ g H}; \ \% \text{ H} = \dfrac{1.11 \times 10^{-2} \text{ g}}{0.1023 \text{ g}} \times 100 = 10.9\% \text{ H}$

$PV = nRT, \ n_{N_2} = \dfrac{PV}{RT} = \dfrac{1.00 \text{ atm} \times 27.6 \times 10^{-3} \text{ L}}{\dfrac{0.08206 \text{ L atm}}{\text{mol K}} \times 273 \text{ K}} = 1.23 \times 10^{-3} \text{ mol N}_2$

$1.23 \times 10^{-3} \text{ mol N}_2 \times \dfrac{28.02 \text{ g N}_2}{\text{mol N}_2} = 3.45 \times 10^{-2} \text{ g nitrogen}$

$\% \text{ N} = \dfrac{3.45 \times 10^{-2} \text{ g}}{0.4831 \text{ g}} \times 100 = 7.14\% \text{ N}$

$\% \text{ O} = 100.00 - (73.78 + 10.9 + 7.14) = 8.2\% \text{ O}$

Out of 100.00 g of compound, there are:

$73.78 \text{ g C} \times \dfrac{1 \text{ mol}}{12.01 \text{ g}} = 6.143 \text{ mol C}; \ 7.14 \text{ g N} \times \dfrac{1 \text{ mol}}{14.01 \text{ g}} = 0.510 \text{ mol N}$

$10.9 \text{ g H} \times \dfrac{1 \text{ mol}}{1.008 \text{ g}} = 10.8 \text{ mol H}; \ 8.2 \text{ g O} \times \dfrac{1 \text{ mol}}{16.00 \text{ g}} = 0.51 \text{ mol O}$

Dividing all values by 0.51 gives an empirical formula of $C_{12}H_{21}NO$.

$$\text{Molar mass} = \frac{dRT}{P} = \frac{\dfrac{4.02 \text{ g}}{\text{L}} \times \dfrac{0.08206 \text{ L atm}}{\text{mol K}} \times 400. \text{ K}}{256 \text{ torr} \times \dfrac{1 \text{ atm}}{760 \text{ torr}}} = 392 \text{ g/mol}$$

Empirical formula mass of $C_{12}H_{21}NO \approx 195$ g/mol; $\dfrac{392}{195} \approx 2$

Thus, the molecular formula is $C_{24}H_{42}N_2O_2$.

112.   At constant T, the lighter the gas molecules, the faster the average velocity. Therefore, the pressure will increase initially because the lighter H_2 molecules will effuse into container A faster than air will escape. However, the pressures will eventually equalize once the gases have had time to mix thoroughly.

113.   The van der Waals constant b is a measure of the size of the molecule. Thus, C_3H_8 should have the largest value of b since it has the largest molar mass (size). The values of a are: H_2, 0.244 L^2 atm/mol^2; CO_2, 3.59; N_2, 1.39; CH_4, 2.25. Because a is a measure of interparticle attractions, the attractions are greatest for CO_2.

Challenge Problems

114.   PV = nRT, V and T are constant. $\dfrac{P_1}{n_1} = \dfrac{P_2}{n_2}$, $\dfrac{P_2}{P_1} = \dfrac{n_2}{n_1}$

We will do this limiting reagent problem using an alternative method. Let's calculate the partial pressure of C_3H_3N that can be produced from each of the starting materials assuming each reactant is limiting. The reactant that produces the smallest amount of product will run out first and is the limiting reagent.

$$P_{C_3H_3N} = 0.500 \text{ MPa } C_3H_6 \times \frac{2 \text{ MPa } C_3H_3N}{2 \text{ MPa } C_3H_6} = 0.500 \text{ MPa if } C_3H_6 \text{ is limiting.}$$

$$P_{C_3H_3N} = 0.800 \text{ MPa } NH_3 \times \frac{2 \text{ MPa } C_3H_3N}{2 \text{ MPa } NH_3} = 0.800 \text{ MPa if } NH_3 \text{ is limiting.}$$

$$P_{C_3H_3N} = 1.500 \text{ MPa } O_2 \times \frac{2 \text{ MPa } C_3H_3N}{3 \text{ MPa } O_2} = 1.000 \text{ MPa if } O_2 \text{ is limiting.}$$

Thus, C_3H_6 is limiting. Although more product could be produced from NH_3 and O_2, there is only enough C_3H_6 to produce 0.500 MPa of C_3H_3N. The partial pressure of C_3H_3N after the reaction is:

$$0.500 \times 10^6 \text{ Pa} \times \frac{1 \text{ atm}}{1.013 \times 10^5 \text{ Pa}} = 4.94 \text{ atm}$$

$$n = \frac{PV}{RT} = \frac{4.94 \text{ atm} \times 150. \text{ L}}{\dfrac{0.08206 \text{ L atm}}{\text{mol K}} \times 298 \text{ K}} = 30.3 \text{ mol } C_3H_3N$$

$$30.3 \text{ mol} \times \frac{53.06 \text{ g}}{\text{mol}} = 1.61 \times 10^3 \text{ g } C_3H_3N \text{ can be produced.}$$

115. $BaO(s) + CO_2(g) \rightarrow BaCO_3(s)$; $CaO(s) + CO_2(g) \rightarrow CaCO_3(s)$

$$n_i = \frac{P_i V}{RT} = \text{initial moles of } CO_2 = \frac{\dfrac{750.}{760}\,\text{atm}\times 1.50\,\text{L}}{\dfrac{0.08206\,\text{L atm}}{\text{mol K}}\times 303.2\ \text{K}} = 0.0595\ \text{mol } CO_2$$

$$n_f = \frac{P_f V}{RT} = \text{final moles of } CO_2 = \frac{\dfrac{230.}{760}\,\text{atm}\times 1.50\,\text{L}}{\dfrac{0.08206\,\text{L atm}}{\text{mol K}}\times 303.2\ \text{K}} = 0.0182\ \text{mol } CO_2$$

$0.0595 - 0.0182 = 0.0413$ mol CO_2 reacted

Since each metal reacts 1:1 with CO_2, the mixture contains 0.0413 mol of BaO and CaO. The molar masses of BaO and CaO are 153.3 g/mol and 56.08 g/mol, respectively.

Let x = mass of BaO and y = mass of CaO, so:

$$x + y = 5.14\ \text{g and } \frac{x}{153.3} + \frac{y}{56.08} = 0.0413\ \text{mol}$$

Solving by simultaneous equations:

$$\begin{array}{rl} x + 2.734\,y = & 6.33 \\ \underline{-x \qquad -y =} & \underline{-5.14} \\ 1.734\,y = & 1.19 \end{array}$$

$y = 0.686$ g CaO and $5.14 - y = x = 4.45$ g BaO

$$\%BaO = \frac{4.45\ \text{g BaO}}{5.14\ \text{g}} \times 100 = 86.6\%\ BaO;\ \ \%CaO = 100.0 - 86.6 = 13.4\%\ CaO$$

116. $Cr(s) + 3\ HCl(aq) \rightarrow CrCl_3(aq) + 3/2\ H_2(g);\ \ Zn(s) + 2\ HCl(aq) \rightarrow ZnCl_2(aq) + H_2(g)$

$$\text{mol } H_2 \text{ produced} = n = \frac{PV}{RT} = \frac{\left(750.\ \text{torr}\times\dfrac{1\ \text{atm}}{760\ \text{torr}}\right)\times 0.225\ \text{L}}{\dfrac{0.08206\,\text{L atm}}{\text{mol K}}\times(273+27)\ \text{K}} = 9.02\times 10^{-3}\ \text{mol } H_2$$

9.02×10^{-3} mol H_2 = mol H_2 from Cr reaction + mol H_2 from Zn reaction

From the balanced equation: 9.02×10^{-3} mol H_2 = mol Cr $\times$ (3/2) + mol Zn $\times$ 1

Let x = mass of Cr and y = mass of Zn, then:

$$x + y = 0.362\ \text{g and } 9.02\times 10^{-3} = \frac{1.5\,x}{52.00} + \frac{y}{65.38}$$

We have two equations and two unknowns. Solving by simultaneous equations:

$$9.02 \times 10^{-3} = 0.02885\,x + 0.01530\,y$$
$$\underline{-0.01530 \times 0.362 = -0.01530\,x - 0.01530\,y}$$

$$3.48 \times 10^{-3} = 0.01355\,x \qquad\qquad x = \text{mass Cr} = \frac{3.48 \times 10^{-3}}{0.01355} = 0.257 \text{ g}$$

$$y = \text{mass Zn} = 0.362 \text{ g} - 0.257 \text{ g} = 0.105 \text{ g Zn}; \quad \text{mass \%Zn} = \frac{0.105 \text{ g}}{0.362 \text{ g}} \times 100 = 29.0\% \text{ Zn}$$

117.   Assuming 1.000 L of the hydrocarbon (C_xH_y), then the volume of products will be 4.000 L and the mass of products ($H_2O + CO_2$) will be:

$$1.391 \text{ g/L} \times 4.000 \text{ L} = 5.564 \text{ g products}$$

$$\text{moles } C_xH_y = n_{C_xH_y} = \frac{PV}{RT} = \frac{0.959 \text{ atm} \times 1.000 \text{ L}}{\dfrac{0.08206 \text{ L atm}}{\text{mol K}} \times 298 \text{ K}} = 0.0392 \text{ mol}$$

$$\text{moles products} = n_p = \frac{PV}{RT} = \frac{1.51 \text{ atm} \times 4.000 \text{ L}}{\dfrac{0.08206 \text{ L atm}}{\text{mol K}} \times 375 \text{ K}} = 0.196 \text{ mol}$$

$$C_xH_y + \text{oxygen} \longrightarrow x\,CO_2 + y/2\,H_2O$$

Setting up two equations:

$$0.0392x + 0.0392(y/2) = 0.196 \text{ (mol of products)}$$

$$0.0392x(44.01 \text{ g/mol}) + 0.0392(y/2)(18.02 \text{ g/mol}) = 5.564 \text{ g (mass of products)}$$

Solving: $x = 2$ and $y = 6$, so the formula of the hydrocarbon is C_2H_6.

118.   Let n = mol SO_2 = mol O_2 and z = mol He.

a. $\dfrac{P \bullet MM}{RT}$ where MM = molar mass

$$1.924 \text{ g/L} = \frac{1.000 \text{ atm} \times MM}{\dfrac{0.08206 \text{ L atm}}{\text{mol K}} \times 273.2 \text{ K}}, \quad MM_{mixture} = 43.13 \text{ g/mol}$$

Assuming 1.000 total mol of mixture is present, then: $n + n + z = 1.000$ and:

$$64.07 \text{ g/mol} \times n + 32.00 \text{ g/mol} \times n + 4.003 \text{ g/mol} \times z = 43.13 \text{ g}$$

$$2n + z = 1.000 \text{ and } 96.07n + 4.003z = 43.13$$

Solving: n = 0.4443 mol and z = 0.1114 mol

Thus, χ_{He} = 0.1114 mol/1.000 mol = 0.1114

b. $SO_2(g) + O_2(g) \rightarrow 2\, SO_3(g)$

Initially, assume 0.4443 mol SO_2, 0.444 mol O_2 and 0.1114 mol He. Because SO_2 is limiting, we end with 0.2222 mol O_2, 0.4443 mol SO_3, and 0.1114 mol He in the gaseous product mixture. Thus, n_{init} = 1.0000 mol and n_{final} = 0.7779 mol.

$d = \dfrac{m}{V}$, but mass is constant. Thus, $d \propto \dfrac{mass}{V}$ and $V \propto n$, so, $d \propto \dfrac{1}{n}$.

$\dfrac{n_1}{n_2} = \dfrac{1.0000}{0.7779} = \dfrac{d_2}{d_1}$, $d_2 = \left(\dfrac{1.0000}{0.7779}\right) \times 1.924$ g/L, d_2 = 2.473 g/L

119. a. The reaction is: $CH_4(g) + 2\, O_2(g) \rightarrow CO_2(g) + 2\, H_2O(g)$

$PV = nRT$, $\dfrac{PV}{n} = RT =$ constant, $\dfrac{P_{CH_4} V_{CH_4}}{n_{CH_4}} = \dfrac{P_{air} V_{air}}{n_{air}}$

The balanced equation requires 2 mol O_2 for every mol of CH_4 that reacts. For three times as much oxygen, we would need 6 mol O_2 per mol of CH_4 reacted ($n_{O_2} = 6\, n_{CH_4}$). Air is 21% mol percent O_2, so $n_{O_2} = 0.21\, n_{air}$. Therefore, the moles of air we would need to delivery the excess O_2 are:

$n_{O_2} = 0.21\, n_{air} = 6\, n_{CH_4}$, $n_{air} = 29\, n_{CH_4}$, $\dfrac{n_{air}}{n_{CH_4}} = 29$

In one minute:

$V_{air} = V_{CH_4} \times \dfrac{n_{air}}{n_{CH_4}} \times \dfrac{P_{CH_4}}{P_{air}} = 200.\, L \times 29 \times \dfrac{1.50\ atm}{1.00\ atm} = 8.7 \times 10^3$ L air/min

b. If x moles of CH_4 were reacted, then 6 x mol O_2 were added, producing 0.950 x mol CO_2 and 0.050 x mol of CO. In addition, 2 x mol H_2O must be produced to balance the hydrogens.

$CH_4(g) + 2\, O_2(g) \rightarrow CO_2(g) + 2\, H_2O(g)$; $CH_4(g) + 3/2\, O_2(g) \rightarrow CO(g) + 2\, H_2O(g)$

Amount O_2 reacted:

0.950 x mol $CO_2 \times \dfrac{2\ mol\ O_2}{mol\ CO_2} = 1.90\ x$ mol O_2

0.050 x mol $CO \times \dfrac{1.5\ mol\ O_2}{mol\ CO} = 0.075\ x$ mol O_2

Amount of O_2 left in reaction mixture = 6.00 x - 1.90 x - 0.075 x = 4.03 x mol O_2

$$\text{Amount of } N_2 = 6.00 \, x \text{ mol } O_2 \times \frac{79 \text{ mol } N_2}{21 \text{ mol } O_2} = 22.6 \, x \approx 23 \, x \text{ mol } N_2$$

The reaction mixture contains:

$$0.950 \, x \text{ mol } CO_2 + 0.050 \, x \text{ mol } CO + 4.03 \, x \text{ mol } O_2 + 2.00 \, x \text{ mol } H_2O +$$

$$23 \, x \text{ mol } N_2 = 30. \, x \text{ total mol of gas}$$

$$\chi_{CO} = \frac{0.050 \, x}{30. \, x} = 0.017; \quad \chi_{CO_2} = \frac{0.950 \, x}{30. \, x} = 0.032; \quad \chi_{O_2} = \frac{4.03 \, x}{30. \, x} = 0.13$$

$$\chi_{H_2O} = \frac{2.00 \, x}{30. \, x} = 0.067; \quad \chi_{N_2} = \frac{23 \, x}{30. \, x} = 0.77$$

120.   The reactions are:

$$C(s) + 1/2 \, O_2(g) \rightarrow CO(g) \text{ and } C(s) + O_2(g) \rightarrow CO_2(g)$$

$$PV = nRT, \quad P = n\left(\frac{RT}{V}\right) = n \text{ (constant)}$$

Since the pressure has increased by 17.0%, the number of moles of gas has also increased by 17.0%.

$$n_{final} = 1.170 \, n_{initial} = 1.170 \, (5.00) = 5.85 \text{ mol gas} = n_{O_2} + n_{CO} + n_{CO_2}$$

$$n_{CO} + n_{CO_2} = 5.00 \quad \text{(balancing moles of C). Solving by simultaneous equations:}$$

$$\begin{aligned}
n_{O_2} + n_{CO} + n_{CO_2} &= 5.85 \\
-(n_{CO} + n_{CO_2} &= 5.00) \\
\hline
n_{O_2} \qquad\qquad\qquad &= 0.85
\end{aligned}$$

If all C was converted to CO_2, no O_2 would be left. If all C was converted to CO, we would get 5 mol CO and 2.5 mol excess O_2 in the reaction mixture. In the final mixture, mol of CO equals twice the mol O_2 present ($n_{CO} = 2 \, n_{O_2}$).

$$n_{CO} = 2 \, n_{O_2} = 1.70 \text{ mol CO}; \quad 1.70 + n_{CO_2} = 5.00, \quad n_{CO_2} = 3.30 \text{ mol } CO_2$$

$$\chi_{CO} = \frac{1.70}{5.85} = 0.291; \quad \chi_{CO_2} = \frac{3.30}{5.85} = 0.564; \quad \chi_{O_2} = \frac{0.85}{5.85} = 0.145 \approx 0.15$$

121.   a.   Volume of hot air: $V = \dfrac{4}{3}\pi r^3 = \dfrac{4}{3}\pi(2.50 \text{ m})^3 = 65.4 \text{ m}^3$

(Note: radius = diameter/2 = 5.00/2 = 2.50 m)

$$65.4 \text{ m}^3 \left(\frac{10 \text{ dm}}{\text{m}}\right)^3 \times \frac{1 \text{ L}}{\text{dm}^3} = 6.54 \times 10^4 \text{ L}$$

$$n = \frac{PV}{RT} = \frac{\left(754 \text{ torr} \times \dfrac{1 \text{ atm}}{760 \text{ torr}}\right) \times 6.54 \times 10^4 \text{ L}}{\dfrac{0.08206 \text{ L atm}}{\text{mol K}} \times (273 + 65) \text{ K}} = 2.31 \times 10^3 \text{ mol air}$$

Mass of hot air $= 2.31 \times 10^3 \text{ mol} \times \dfrac{29.0 \text{ g}}{\text{mol}} = 6.70 \times 10^4 \text{ g}$

Mass of air displaced:

$$n = \frac{PV}{RT} = \frac{\dfrac{745}{760} \text{ atm} \times 6.54 \times 10^4 \text{ L}}{\dfrac{0.08206 \text{ L atm}}{\text{mol K}} \times (273 + 21) \text{ K}} = 2.66 \times 10^3 \text{ mol air}$$

Mass $= 2.66 \times 10^3 \text{ mol} \times \dfrac{29.0 \text{ g}}{\text{mol}} = 7.71 \times 10^4 \text{ g of air displaced}$

Lift $= 7.71 \times 10^4 \text{ g} - 6.70 \times 10^4 \text{ g} = 1.01 \times 10^4 \text{ g}$

b.   Mass of air displaced is the same, 7.71×10^4 g. Moles of He in balloon will be the same as moles of air displaced, 2.66×10^3 mol, since P, V and T are the same.

Mass of He $= 2.66 \times 10^3 \text{ mol} \times \dfrac{4.003 \text{ g}}{\text{mol}} = 1.06 \times 10^4 \text{ g}$

Lift $= 7.71 \times 10^4 \text{ g} - 1.06 \times 10^4 \text{ g} = 6.65 \times 10^4 \text{ g}$

c.   Mass of hot air:

$$n = \frac{PV}{RT} = \frac{\dfrac{630.}{760} \text{ atm} \times 6.54 \times 10^4 \text{ L}}{\dfrac{0.08206 \text{ L atm}}{\text{mol K}} \times 338 \text{ K}} = 1.95 \times 10^3 \text{ mol air}$$

$$1.95 \times 10^3 \text{ mol} \times \frac{29.0 \text{ g}}{\text{mol}} = 5.66 \times 10^4 \text{ g of hot air}$$

Mass of air displaced:

$$n = \frac{PV}{RT} = \frac{\dfrac{630.}{760}\,atm \times 6.54 \times 10^4\,L}{\dfrac{0.08206\,L\,atm}{mol\,K} \times 294\,K} = 2.25 \times 10^3\,mol\,air$$

$$2.25 \times 10^3\,mol \times \frac{29.0\,g}{mol} = 6.53 \times 10^4\,g\;of\;air\;displaced$$

Lift $= 6.53 \times 10^4\,g - 5.66 \times 10^4\,g = 8.7 \times 10^3\,g$

122.   a.   When the balloon is heated, the balloon will expand (P and n remain constant). The mass of the balloon is the same but the volume increases, so the density of the argon in the balloon decreases. When the density is less than that of air, the balloon will rise.

b.   Assuming the balloon has no mass, when the density of the argon = the density of air, the balloon will float in air. Above this temperature, the balloon will rise.

$$d_{air} = \frac{P \bullet MM_{air}}{RT}\quad where\;MM_{air} = average\;molar\;mass\;of\;air$$

$MM_{air} = 0.790 \times 28.02\,g/mol + 0.210 \times 32.00\,g/mol = 28.9\,g/mol$

$$d_{air} = \frac{1.00\,atm \times 28.9\,g/mol}{\dfrac{0.08206\,L\,atm}{mol\,K} \times 298\,K} = 1.18\,g/L$$

$$d_{argon} = \frac{1.00\,atm \times 39.95\,g/mol}{\dfrac{0.08206\,L\,atm}{mol\,K} \times T} = 1.18\,g/L,\;\;T = 413\,K$$

Heat the Ar above 413 K or 140.°C and the balloon would float.

123.   a.   Average molar mass of air $= 0.790 \times 28.02\,g/mol + 0.210 \times 32.00\,g/mol = 28.9\,g/mol$; molar mass of helium = 4.003 g/mol

A given volume of air at a given set of conditions has a larger density than helium at those conditions. We need to heat the air to greater than 25°C to lower the air density (by driving air out of the hot air balloon) until the density is the same as that for helium (at 25°C and 1.00 atm).

b.   To provide the same lift as the helium balloon (assume V = 1.00 L), the mass of air in the hot air balloon (V = 1.00 L) must be the same as that in the helium balloon. Let MM = molar mass:

$$P \cdot MM = dRT, \quad mass = \frac{MM \cdot PV}{RT}, \quad \text{Solving: mass He} = 0.164 \text{ g}$$

$$\text{mass air} = 0.164 \text{ g} = \frac{28.9 \text{ g/mol} \times 1.00 \text{ atm} \times 1.00 \text{ L}}{\frac{0.08206 \text{ L atm}}{\text{mol K}} \times T}, \quad T = 2150 \text{ K (a very high temp)}$$

124. $\left(P + \dfrac{an^2}{V^2}\right) \times (V - nb) = nRT, \quad PV + \dfrac{an^2 V}{V^2} - nbP - \dfrac{an^3 b}{V^2} = nRT$

$$PV + \frac{an^2}{V} - nbP - \frac{an^3 b}{V^2} = nRT$$

At low P and high T, the molar volume of a gas will be relatively large. The an^2/V and an^3b/V^2 terms become negligible because V is large. Since nb is the actual volume of the gas molecules themselves, then nb << V and the −nbP term is negligible compared to PV. Thus PV = nRT.

125. a. If we have 1.0×10^6 L of air, then there are 3.0×10^2 L of CO.

$$P_{CO} = \chi_{CO} \times P_{total}; \quad \chi_{CO} = \frac{V_{CO}}{V_{total}} \text{ since } V \propto n; \quad P_{CO} = \frac{3.0 \times 10^2 \text{ L}}{1.0 \times 10^6 \text{ L}} \times 628 \text{ torr} = 0.19 \text{ torr}$$

b. $n_{CO} = \dfrac{P_{CO} \times V}{RT}$; Assuming 1.0 cm^3 of air = 1.0 mL = 1.0×10^{-3} L:

$$n_{CO} = \frac{\frac{0.19}{760} \text{ atm} \times 1.0 \times 10^{-3} \text{ L}}{\frac{0.08206 \text{ L atm}}{\text{mol K}} \times 273 \text{ K}} = 1.1 \times 10^{-8} \text{ mol CO}$$

$$1.1 \times 10^{-8} \text{ mol} \times \frac{6.022 \times 10^{23} \text{ molecules}}{\text{mol}} = 6.6 \times 10^{15} \text{ molecules CO in the 1.0 cm}^3 \text{ of air}$$

126. a. Initially, $P_{N_2} = P_{H_2} = 1.00$ atm and the total pressure is 2.00 atm ($P_{tot} = P_{N_2} + P_{H_2}$). The total pressure after reaction will also be 2.00 atm since we have a constant pressure container. Since V and T are constant before the reaction takes place, there must be equal moles of N_2 and H_2 present initially. Let x = mol N_2 = mol H_2 that are present initially. From the balanced equation, $N_2(g) + 3 H_2(g) \rightarrow 2 NH_3(g)$, H_2 will be limiting since three times as many mol of H_2 are required to react as compared to mol of N_2.

After the reaction occurs, none of the H_2 remains (it is the limiting reagent).

$$\text{mol NH}_3 \text{ produced} = x \text{ mol H}_2 \times \frac{2 \text{ mol NH}_3}{3 \text{ mol H}_2} = 2x/3$$

$$\text{mol N}_2 \text{ reacted} = x \text{ mol H}_2 \times \frac{1 \text{ mol N}_2}{3 \text{ mol H}_2} = x/3$$

mol N_2 remaining = x mol N_2 present initially - $x/3$ mol N_2 reacted = $2x/3$ mol N_2 remaining

After the reaction goes to completion, equal mol of $N_2(g)$ and $NH_3(g)$ are present ($2x/3$). Since equal mol are present, then the partial pressure of each gas must be equal ($P_{N_2} = P_{NH_3}$).

$P_{tot} = 2.00 \text{ atm} = P_{N_2} + P_{NH_3}$;   Solving $P_{N_2} = 1.00 \text{ atm} = P_{NH_3}$

b. $V \propto n$ since P and T are constant. The mol of gas present initially are:

$$n_{N_2} + n_{H_2} = x + x = 2x \text{ mol}$$

After reaction, the mol of gas present are:

$$n_{N_2} + n_{NH_3} = \frac{2x}{3} + \frac{2x}{3} = 4x/3 \text{ mol}$$

$$\frac{V_{after}}{V_{initial}} = \frac{n_{after}}{n_{initial}} = \frac{4x/3}{2x} = \frac{2}{3}$$

The volume of the container will be two-thirds the original volume so:

$$V = 2/3(15.0 \text{ L}) = 10.0 \text{ L}$$

Integrative Problems

127.   The redox equation must be balanced first using the half-reaction method. The two half-reactions to balance are: $NO_3^- \rightarrow NO$ and $UO^{2+} \rightarrow UO_2^{2+}$; The balanced equation is:

$$2 \text{ H}^+(aq) + 2 \text{ NO}_3^-(aq) + 3 \text{ UO}^{2+}(aq) \rightarrow 3 \text{ UO}_2^{2+}(aq) + 2 \text{ NO}(g) + \text{H}_2\text{O}(l)$$

$$n_{NO} = \frac{PV}{RT} = \frac{1.5 \text{ atm} \times 0.255 \text{ L}}{\dfrac{0.08206 \text{ L atm}}{\text{mol K}} \times 302 \text{ K}} = 0.015 \text{ mol NO}$$

$$0.015 \text{ mol NO} \times \frac{3 \text{ mol UO}^{2+}}{2 \text{ mol NO}} = 0.023 \text{ mol UO}^{2+}$$

128.   a. $156 \text{ mL} \times \dfrac{1.34 \text{ g}}{\text{mL}} = 209 \text{ g HSiCl}_3 = $ actual yield of HSiCl_3

$$n_{HCl} = \frac{PV}{RT} = \frac{10.0 \text{ atm} \times 15.0 \text{ L}}{\dfrac{0.08206 \text{ L atm}}{\text{mol K}} \times 308 \text{ K}} = 5.93 \text{ mol HCl}$$

$$5.93 \text{ mol HCl} \times \frac{1 \text{ mol HSiCl}_3}{3 \text{ mol HCl}} \times \frac{135.45 \text{ g HSiCl}_3}{1 \text{ mol HSiCl}_3} = 268 \text{ g HSiCl}_3$$

$$\% \text{ yield} = \frac{\text{actual yield}}{\text{theoretical yield}} \times 100 = \frac{209 \text{ g}}{268 \text{ g}} \times 100 = 78.0\%$$

   b. $209 \text{ g HiSCl}_3 \times \dfrac{1 \text{ mol HSiCl}_3}{135.45 \text{ g HSiCl}_3} \times \dfrac{1 \text{ mol SiH}_4}{4 \text{ mol HSiCl}_3} = 0.386 \text{ mol SiH}_4$

This is the theoretical yield. If the percent yield is 93.1%, then the actual yield is:

$$0.386 \text{ mol SiH}_4 \times 0.931 = 0.359 \text{ mol SiH}_4$$

$$V_{SiH_4} = \frac{nRT}{P} = \frac{0.359 \text{ mol} \times \dfrac{0.08206 \text{ L atm}}{\text{mol K}} \times 308 \text{ K}}{10.0 \text{ atm}} = 0.907 \text{ L} = 907 \text{ mL SiH}_4$$

129. ThF_4, $232.0 + 4(19.00) = 308.0 \text{ g/mL}$

$$d = \frac{\text{molar mass} \times P}{RT} = \frac{308.0 \text{ g/mol} \times 2.5 \text{ atm}}{\dfrac{0.08206 \text{ L atm}}{\text{mol K}} \times (1680 + 273) \text{ K}} = 4.8 \text{ g/L}$$

The gas with the lower mass will effuse faster. Molar mass of $\text{ThF}_4 = 308.0$ g/mol; molar mass of $\text{UF}_3 = 238.0 + 3(19.00) = 295.0$. Therefore, UF_3 will effuse faster.

$$\frac{\text{rate of effusion of UF}_3}{\text{rate of effusion of ThF}_4} = \sqrt{\frac{\text{molar mass of ThF}_4}{\text{molar mass of UF}_3}} = \sqrt{\frac{308.0 \text{ g/mol}}{295.0 \text{ g/mol}}} = 1.02$$

UF_3 effuses 1.02 times faster than ThF_4.

130.   The partial pressures can be determined by using the mole fractions.

$P_{methane} = P_{tot} \times \chi_{methane} = 1.44 \text{ atm} \times 0.915 = 1.32 \text{ atm}$; $P_{ethane} = 1.44 - 1.32 = 0.12 \text{ atm}$

Determining the number of mol of natural gas combusted:

$$n_{natural\ gas} = \frac{PV}{RT} = \frac{1.44\ atm \times 15.00\ L}{\dfrac{0.08206\ L\ atm}{mol\ K} \times 293\ K} = 0.898\ mol\ natural\ gas$$

$$n_{methane} = n_{natural\ gas} \times \chi_{methane} = 0.898\ mol \times 0.915 = 0.822\ mol\ methane$$

$$n_{ethane} = 0.898 - 0.822 = 0.076\ mol\ ethane$$

$$CH_4(g) + 2\ O_2(g) \rightarrow CO_2(g) + 2\ H_2O(l);\quad 2\ C_2H_6 + 7\ O_2(g) \rightarrow 4\ CO_2(g) + 6\ H_2O(l)$$

$$0.822\ mol\ CH_4 \times \frac{2\ mol\ H_2O}{1\ mol\ CH_4} \times \frac{18.02\ g\ H_2O}{mol\ H_2O} = 29.6\ g\ H_2O$$

$$0.076\ mol\ C_2H_6 \times \frac{6\ mol\ H_2O}{2\ mol\ C_2H_6} \times \frac{18.02\ g\ H_2O}{mol\ H_2O} = 4.1\ g\ H_2O$$

The total mass of H_2O produced = 29.6 g + 4.1 g = 33.7 g H_2O

Marathon Problem

131.   We must determine the identities of element A and compound B in order to answer the questions. Use the first set of data to determine the identity of element A.

Mass N_2 = 659.452 g - 658.572 g = 0.880 g N_2

$$0.880\ g\ N_2 \times \frac{1\ mol\ N_2}{28.02\ g\ N_2} = 0.0314\ mol\ N_2$$

$$V = \frac{nRT}{P} = \frac{0.0314\ mol \times \dfrac{0.08206\ L\ atm}{mol\ K} \times 288\ K}{790.\ torr \times \dfrac{1\ atm}{760\ torr}} = 0.714\ L$$

$$moles\ of\ A = n = \frac{\left(745\ torr \times \dfrac{1\ atm}{760\ torr}\right) \times 0.714\ L}{\dfrac{0.08206\ L\ atm}{mol\ K} \times (273 + 26)\ K} = 0.0285\ mol\ A$$

Mass of A = 660.59 - 658.572 g = 2.02 g A

$$Molar\ mass\ of\ A = \frac{202\ g\ A}{0.0285\ mol\ A} = 70.9\ g/mol$$

The only element that is a gas at 26°C and 745 torr and has a molar mass close to 70.9 g/mol is chlorine = Cl_2 = element A.

The remainder of the information is used to determine the formula of compound B. Assuming 100.00 g of B:

$$85.6 \text{ g C} \times \frac{1 \text{ mol C}}{12.01 \text{ g C}} = 7.13 \text{ mol C}; \quad \frac{7.13}{7.13} = 1.00$$

$$14.4 \text{ g H} \times \frac{1 \text{ mol H}}{1.008 \text{ g H}} = 14.3 \text{ mol H}; \quad \frac{14.3}{7.13} = 2.01$$

Empirical formula of B = CH_2; Molecular formula = C_xH_{2x} where x is a whole number.

The balanced combustion reaction of C_xH_{2x} with O_2 is:

$$C_xH_{2x}(g) + 3x/2 \, O_2(g) \rightarrow x \, CO_2(g) + x \, H_2O(l)$$

To determine the formula of C_xH_{2x}, we need to determine the actual moles of all species present.

Mass of CO_2 + H_2O produced = 846.7 g - 765.3 g = 81.4 g

From the balanced equation, mol CO_2 = mol H_2O = x, so:

$$81.4 \text{ g} = x \text{ mol } CO_2 \times \frac{44.01 \text{ g } CO_2}{\text{mol } CO_2} + x \text{ mol } H_2O \times \frac{18.02 \text{ g } H_2O}{\text{mol } H_2O}, \quad x = 1.31 \text{ mol}$$

$$\text{mol } O_2 \text{ reacted} = 1.31 \text{ mol } CO_2 \times \frac{1.5 \text{ mol } O_2}{\text{mol } CO_2} = 1.97 \text{ mol } O_2$$

From the data, we can calculate moles excess O_2 since only $O_2(g)$ remains after the combustion reaction has gone to completion.

$$n_{O_2} = \frac{PV}{RT} = \frac{6.02 \text{ atm} \times 10.68 \text{ L}}{\dfrac{0.08206 \text{ L atm}}{\text{mol K}} \times (273 + 22) \text{ K}} = 2.66 \text{ mol excess } O_2$$

mol O_2 present initially = 1.97 mol + 2.66 mol = 4.63 mol O_2

$$\text{Total mol gaseous reactants before reaction} = \frac{PV}{RT} = \frac{11.98 \text{ atm} \times 10.68 \text{ L}}{\dfrac{0.08206 \text{ L atm}}{\text{mol K}} \times 295 \text{ K}}$$

$$= 5.29 \text{ mol total}$$

mol C_xH_{2x} = 5.29 mol total - 4.63 mol O_2 = 0.66 mol C_xH_{2x}

Summarizing:

$$0.66 \text{ mol } C_xH_{2x} + 1.97 \text{ mol } O_2 \rightarrow 1.31 \text{ mol } CO_2 + 1.31 \text{ mol } H_2O$$

Dividing all quantities by 0.66 gives:

$$C_xH_{2x} + 3\ O_2 \rightarrow 2\ CO_2 + 2\ H_2O$$

To balance the equation, C_xH_{2x} must be C_2H_4 = compound B.

a.   Now we can answer the questions. The reaction is:

$$C_2H_4(g) + Cl_2(g) \rightarrow C_2H_4Cl_2(g)$$
$$B\quad +\quad A\qquad\qquad C$$

$$mol\ Cl_2 = n = \frac{PV}{RT} = \frac{1.00\ atm \times 10.0\ L}{\dfrac{0.08206\ L\ atm}{mol\ K} \times 273K} = 0.446\ mol\ Cl_2$$

$$mol\ C_2H_4 = n = \frac{PV}{RT} = \frac{1.00\ atm \times 8.60\ L}{\dfrac{0.08206\ L\ atm}{mol\ K} \times 273K} = 0.384\ mol\ C_2H_4$$

A 1:1 mol ratio is required by the balanced reaction, so C_2H_4 is limiting.

$$Mass\ C_2H_4Cl_2\ produced = 0.384\ mol\ C_2H_4 \times \frac{1\ mol\ C_2H_4Cl_2}{mol\ C_2H_4} \times \frac{98.95\ g}{mol\ C_2H_4Cl_2}$$
$$= 38.0\ g\ C_2H_4Cl_2$$

b.   excess mol Cl_2 = 0.446 mol Cl_2 - 0.384 mol Cl_2 reacted = 0.062 mol Cl_2

$$P_{total} = \frac{n_{total}RT}{V}\ ;\ \ n_{total} = 0.384\ mol\ C_2H_4Cl_2\ produced + 0.062\ mol\ Cl_2\ excess = 0.446\ mol$$

$$V = 10.0\ L + 8.60\ L = 18.6\ L$$

$$P_{total} = \frac{0.446\ mol \times \dfrac{0.08206\ L\ atm}{mol\ K} \times 273K}{18.6\ L} = 0.537\ atm$$

CHAPTER SIX

THERMOCHEMISTRY

For Review

1. Potential energy: energy due to position or composition

    Kinetic energy: energy due to motion of an object

    Path-dependent function: a property that depends on how the system gets from the initial state to the final state; a property that is path-dependent

    State function: a property that is independent of the pathway

    System: that part of the universe on which attention is to be focused

    Surroundings: everything in the universe surrounding a thermodynamic system

2. Plot a represents an exothermic reaction. In an exothermic process, the bonds in the product molecules are stronger (on average) than those in the reactant molecules. The net result is that the quantity of energy $\Delta(PE)$ is transferred to the surroundings as heat when reactants are converted to products.

    For an endothermic process, energy flows into the system from the surroundings as heat to increase the potential energy of the system. In an endothermic process, the products have higher potential energy (weaker bonds on average) than the reactants.

3. First law of thermodynamics: the energy of universe is constant. A system can change its internal energy by flow of work, heat, or both ($\Delta E = q + w$). Whenever a property is added to the system from the surroundings, the sign is positive; whenever a property is added to the surroundings by the system, the sign is negative.

4. As a gas expands, the system does work on the surroundings so w is negative. When a gas contracts, the surroundings do work on the system so w is positive. $H_2O(l) \rightarrow H_2O(g)$; To boil water, heat must be added so q is positive. The molar volume of a gas is huge compared to the molar volume of a liquid. As a liquid converts to a gas, the system will expand its volume, performing work on the surroundings; w is negative.

5. $q_P = \Delta H$; $q_V = \Delta E$; A coffee-cup calorimeter is at constant (atmospheric) pressure. The heat released or gained at constant pressure is ΔH. A bomb calorimeter is at constant volume. The heat released or gained at constant volume is ΔE.

6.   The specific heat capacities are: 0.89 J/°C•g (Al) and 0.45 J/°C•g (Fe)
        Al would be the better choice. It has a higher heat capacity and a lower density than Fe.
        Using Al, the same amount of heat could be dissipated by a smaller mass, keeping the mass
        of the amplifier down.

7.   In calorimetry, heat flow is determined into or out of the surroundings. Because $\Delta E_{univ} = 0$ by
        the first law of thermodynamics, $\Delta E_{sys} = -\Delta E_{surr}$; what happens to the surroundings is the
        exact opposite of what happens to the system. To determine heat flow, we need to know the
        heat capacity of the surroundings, the mass of the surroundings that accepts/donates the heat,
        and the change in temperature. If we know these quantities, q_{surr} can be calculated and then
        equated to q_{sys} ($-q_{surr} = q_{sys}$). For an endothermic reaction, the surroundings (the calorimeter
        contents) donates heat to the system. This is accompanied by a decrease in temperature of the
        surroundings. For an exothermic reaction, the system donates heat to the surroundings (the
        calorimeter) so temperature increases.

8.   Hess's law: in going from a particular set of products, the change in enthalpy is the same
        whether the reaction takes place in one step or in a series of steps (ΔH is path independent).
        When a reaction is reversed, the sign of ΔH is also reversed but the magnitude is the same. If
        the coefficients in a balanced reaction are multiplied by a number, the value of ΔH is
        multiplied by the same number while the sign is unaffected.

9.   Standard enthalpy of formation: the change in enthalpy that accompanies the formation of
        one mole of a compound from its elements with all substances in their standard states. The
        standard state for a compound has the following conventions:

        a.   gaseous substances are at a pressure of exactly 1 atm.

        b.   for a pure substance in a condensed state (liquid or solid), the standard state is the pure
             liquid or solid.

        c.   for a substance present in solution, the standard state is a concentration of exactly 1 M.

        The standard state of an element is the form in which the element exists under conditions of
        1 atm and 25°C. ΔH_f^o values for elements in their standard state are, by definition, equal to
        zero.

        Step 1: reactants → elements in standard states $\Delta H_1 = -\sum n_r \Delta H_f^o (\text{reactants})$

        Step 2: elements in standard state → products $\Delta H_2 = \sum n_p \Delta H_f^o (\text{products})$

        _____

                        reactants → products $\Delta H_{reaction}^o = \Delta H_1 + \Delta H_2$

                              $\Delta H_{reaction}^o = \sum n_p \Delta H_f^o (\text{products}) - \sum n_r \Delta H_f^o (\text{reactants})$

10.   Three problems are: there is only a finite amount of fossil fuels, fossil fuels can be expensive,
        and the combustion and exploration of fossil fuels can add pollution to the biosphere whose
        effects may not be reversible. Some alternative fuels are syngas from coal, hydrogen from the
        breakdown of water, and ethanol from the fermentation of sugar.

Questions

9.   Path-dependent functions for a trip from Chicago to Denver are those quantities that depend on the route taken. One can fly directly from Chicago to Denver or one could fly from Chicago to Atlanta to Los Angeles and then to Denver. Some path-dependent quantities are miles traveled, fuel consumption of the airplane, time traveling, airplane snacks eaten, etc. State functions are path independent; they only depend on the initial and final states. Some state functions for an airplane trip from Chicago to Denver would be longitude change, latitude change, elevation change, and overall time zone change.

10.   Products have a lower potential energy than reactants when the bonds in the products are stronger (on average) than in the reactants. This occurs generally in exothermic processes. Products have a higher potential energy than reactants when the reactants have the stronger bonds (on average). This is typified by endothermic reactions.

11. $2 C_8H_{18}(l) + 25 O_2(g) \rightarrow 16 CO_2(g) + 18 H_2O(g)$; All combustion reactions are exothermic; they all release heat to the surroundings so q is negative. To determine the sign of w, concentrate on the moles of gaseous reactants versus the moles of gaseous products. In this combustion reaction, we go from 25 moles of reactant gas molecules to $16 + 18 = 34$ moles of product gas molecules. As reactants are converted to products, an expansion will occur. When a gas expands, the system does work on the surroundings and w is negative.

12. $\Delta H = \Delta E + P\Delta V$ at constant P; From the strict definition of enthalpy, the difference between ΔH and ΔE is the quantity $P\Delta V$. Thus, when a system at constant P can do pressure-volume work, then $\Delta H \neq \Delta E$. When the system cannot do PV work, then $\Delta H = \Delta E$ at constant pressure. An important way to differentiate ΔH from ΔE is to concentrate on q, the heat flow; the heat flow by a system at constant pressure equals ΔH and the heat flow by a system at constant volume equals ΔE.

13.
$$CH_4(g) + 2 O_2(g) \rightarrow CO_2(g) + 2 H_2O(l) \qquad\qquad \Delta H = -891 \text{ kJ}$$
$$CH_4(g) + 2 O_2(g) \rightarrow CO_2(g) + 2 H_2O(g) \qquad\qquad \Delta H = -803 \text{ kJ}$$

$$H_2O(l) + 1/2\ CO_2(g) \rightarrow 1/2\ CH_4(g) + O_2(g) \qquad \Delta H_1 = -1/2(-891 \text{ kJ})$$
$$1/2\ CH_4(g) + 2 O_2(g) \rightarrow 1/2\ CO_2(g) + H_2O(g) \qquad \Delta H_2 = 1/2(-803 \text{ kJ})$$

$$H_2O(l) \rightarrow H_2O(g) \qquad\qquad\qquad \Delta H = \Delta H_1 + \Delta H_2 = 44 \text{ kJ}$$

The enthalpy of vaporization of water is 44 kJ/mol.

14.   The zero point for ΔH_f° values are elements in their standard state. All substances are measured in relationship to this zero point.

15.   Fossil fuels contain carbon; the incomplete combustion of fossil fuels produces $CO(g)$ instead of $CO_2(g)$. This occurs when the amount of oxygen reacting is not sufficient to convert all the carbon to CO_2. Carbon monoxide is a poisonous gas to humans.

16.   Advantages: H_2 burns cleanly (less pollution) and gives a lot of energy per gram of fuel.

         Disadvantages: Expensive and gas storage and safety issues

Exercises

Potential and Kinetic Energy

17. $KE = \dfrac{1}{2}mv^2$; Convert mass and velocity to SI units. $1\,J = \dfrac{1\,kg\,m^2}{s^2}$

Mass $= 5.25\,oz \times \dfrac{1\,lb}{16\,oz} \times \dfrac{1\,kg}{2.205\,lb} = 0.149\,kg$

Velocity $= \dfrac{1.0 \times 10^2\,mi}{hr} \times \dfrac{1\,hr}{60\,min} \times \dfrac{1\,min}{60\,s} \times \dfrac{1760\,yd}{mi} \times \dfrac{1\,m}{1.094\,yd} = \dfrac{45\,m}{s}$

$KE = \dfrac{1}{2}\,mv^2 = \dfrac{1}{2} \times 0.149\,kg \times \left(\dfrac{45\,m}{s}\right)^2 = 150\,J$

18. $KE = \dfrac{1}{2}\,mv^2 = \dfrac{1}{2} \times \left(1.0 \times 10^{-5}\,g \times \dfrac{1\,kg}{1000\,g}\right) \times \left(\dfrac{2.0 \times 10^5\,cm}{sec} \times \dfrac{1\,m}{100\,cm}\right)^2 = 2.0 \times 10^{-2}\,J$

19. $KE = \dfrac{1}{2}\,mv^2 = \dfrac{1}{2} \times 2.0\,kg \times \left(\dfrac{1.0\,m}{s}\right)^2 = 1.0\,J$; $KE = \dfrac{1}{2}\,mv^2 = \dfrac{1}{2} \times 1.0\,kg \times \left(\dfrac{2.0\,m}{s}\right)^2$
$= 2.0\,J$

The 1.0 kg object with a velocity of 2.0 m/s has the greater kinetic energy.

20.   Ball A: $PE = mgz = 2.00\,kg \times \dfrac{9.81\,m}{s^2} \times 10.0\,m = \dfrac{196\,kg\,m^2}{s^2} = 196\,J$

At Point I: All of this energy is transferred to Ball B. All of B's energy is kinetic energy at this point. $E_{total} = KE = 196\,J$. At point II, the sum of the total energy will equal 196 J.

At Point II: $PE = mgz = 4.00\,kg \times \dfrac{9.81\,m}{s^2} \times 3.00\,m = 118\,J$

$KE = E_{total} - PE = 196\,J - 118\,J = 78\,J$

Heat and Work

21   a. $\Delta E = q + w = -47\,kJ + 88\,kJ = 41\,kJ$

b. $\Delta E = 82 - 47 = 35\,kJ$ c. $\Delta E = 47 + 0 = 47\,kJ$

d.   When the surroundings deliver work to the system, $w > 0$. This is the case for a.

22.   Step 1: $\Delta E_1 = q + w = 72\ J + 35\ J = 107\ J$;   Step 2: $\Delta E_2 = 35\ J - 72\ J = -37\ J$

        $\Delta E_{overall} = \Delta E_1 + \Delta E_2 = 107\ J - 37\ J = 70.\ J$

23. $\Delta E = q + w$;   Work is done by the system on the surroundings in a gas expansion; w is negative.

        $300.\ J = q - 75\ J$, $q = 375\ J$ of heat transferred to the system

24.   a. $\Delta E = q + w = -23\ J + 100.\ J = 77\ J$

        b. $w = -P\ \Delta V = -1.90\ atm\ (2.80\ L - 8.30\ L) = 10.5\ L\ atm \times \dfrac{101.3\ J}{L\ atm} = 1060\ J$

             $\Delta E = q + w = 350.\ J + 1060 = 1410\ J$

        c. $w = -P\ \Delta V = -1.00\ atm\ (29.1\ L - 11.2\ L) = -17.9\ L\ atm \times \dfrac{101.3\ J}{L\ atm} = -1810\ J$

             $\Delta E = q + w = 1037\ J - 1810\ J = -770\ J$

25. $w = -P\Delta V$;   We need the final volume of the gas. Since T and n are constant, $P_1 V_1 = P_2 V_2$.

        $$V_2 = \frac{V_1\ P_1}{P_2} = \frac{10.0\ L\ (15.0\ atm)}{2.00\ atm} = 75.0\ L$$

        $w = -P\Delta V = -2.00\ atm\ (75.0\ L - 10.0\ L) = -130.\ L\ atm \ \times \dfrac{101.3\ J}{L\ atm} \times \dfrac{1\ kJ}{1000\ J}$

        $$= -13.2\ kJ = work$$

26. $w = -210.\ J = -P\Delta V$, $-210\ J = -P\ (25\ L - 10.\ L)$, $P = 14\ atm$

27.   In this problem $q = w = -950.\ J$

        $-950.\ J \times \dfrac{1\ L\ atm}{101.3\ J} = -9.38\ L\ atm$ of work done by the gases.

        $w = -P\Delta V$, $-9.38\ L\ atm = \dfrac{-650.}{760}\ atm \times (V_f - 0.040\ L)$, $V_f - 0.040 = 11.0\ L$, $V_f = 11.0\ L$

28. $\Delta E = q + w$, $-102.5\ J = 52.5\ J + w$, $w = -155.0\ J \times \dfrac{1\ L\ atm}{101.3\ J} = -1.530\ L\ atm$

        $w = -P\Delta V$, $-1.530\ L\ atm = -0.500\ atm\ \times \Delta V$, $\Delta V = 3.06\ L$

        $\Delta V = V_f - V_i$, $3.06\ L = 58.0\ L - V_i$, $V_i = 54.9\ L = initial\ volume$

29. q = molar heat capacity × mol × $\Delta T = \dfrac{20.8 \text{ J}}{°\text{C mol}} \times 39.1 \text{ mol} \times (38.0 - 0.0)\ °\text{C} = 30{,}900 \text{ J}$

$$= 30.9 \text{ kJ}$$

$w = -P\Delta V = -1.00 \text{ atm} \times (998 \text{ L} - 876 \text{ L}) = -122 \text{ L atm} \times \dfrac{101.3 \text{ J}}{\text{L atm}} = -12{,}400 \text{ J} = -12.4 \text{ kJ}$

$\Delta E = q + w = 30.9 \text{ kJ} + (-12.4 \text{ kJ}) = 18.5 \text{ kJ}$

30. $H_2O(g) \rightarrow H_2O(l);\ \ \Delta E = q + w;\ \ q = -40.66 \text{ kJ};\ \ w = -P\Delta V$

Volume of 1 mol $H_2O(l)$ = 1 mol $H_2O(l) \times \dfrac{18.02 \text{ g}}{\text{mol}} \times \dfrac{1 \text{ cm}^3}{0.996 \text{ g}} = 18.1 \text{ cm}^3 = 18.1 \text{ mL}$

$w = -P\Delta V = -1.00 \text{ atm} \times (0.0181 \text{ L} - 30.6 \text{ L}) = 30.6 \text{ L atm} \times \dfrac{101.3 \text{ J}}{\text{L atm}} = 3.10 \times 10^3 \text{ J}$

$$= 3.10 \text{ kJ}$$

$\Delta E = q + w = -40.66 \text{ kJ} + 3.10 \text{ kJ} = -37.56 \text{ kJ}$

Properties of Enthalpy

31.   This is an endothermic reaction so heat must be absorbed in order to convert reactants into products. The high temperature environment of internal combustion engines provides the heat.

32.   One should try to cool the reaction mixture or provide some means of removing heat since the reaction is very exothermic (heat is released). The $H_2SO_4(aq)$ will get very hot and possibly boil unless cooling is provided.

33.   a.   Heat is absorbed from the water (it gets colder) as KBr dissolves, so this is an endothermic process.

        b.   Heat is released as CH_4 is burned, so this is an exothermic process.

        c.   Heat is released to the water (it gets hot) as H_2SO_4 is added, so this is an exothermic process.

        d.   Heat must be added (absorbed) to boil water, so this is an endothermic process.

34.   a.   The combustion of gasoline releases heat, so this is an exothermic process.

        b. $H_2O(g) \rightarrow H_2O(l);$ Heat is released when water vapor condenses, so this is an exothermic process.

        c.   To convert a solid to a gas, heat must be absorbed, so this is an endothermic process.

        d.   Heat must be added (absorbed) in order to break a bond, so this is an endothermic process.

35. $4 Fe(s) + 3 O_2(g) \rightarrow 2 Fe_2O_3(s)$ $\Delta H = -1652$ kJ; Note that 1652 kJ of heat are released when
       4 mol Fe react with 3 mol O_2 to produce 2 mol Fe_2O_3.

   a. 4.00 mol Fe $\times \dfrac{-1652 \text{ kJ}}{4 \text{ mol Fe}} = -1650$ kJ; 1650 kJ of heat released

   b. 1.00 ml $Fe_2O_3 \times \dfrac{-1652 \text{ kJ}}{2 \text{ mol Fe}_2\text{O}_3} = -826$ kJ; 826 kJ of heat released

   c. 1.00 g Fe $\times \dfrac{1 \text{ mol Fe}}{55.85 \text{ g}} \times \dfrac{-1652 \text{ kJ}}{4 \text{ mol Fe}} = -7.39$ kJ; 7.39 kJ of heat released

   d. 10.0 g Fe $\times \dfrac{1 \text{ mol Fe}}{55.85 \text{ g}} = 0.179$ mol Fe; 2.00 g $O_2 \times \dfrac{1 \text{ mol O}_2}{32.00 \text{ g}} = 0.0625$ mol O_2

       0.179 mol Fe/0.0625 mol O_2 = 2.86; The balanced equation requires a 4 mol Fe/3 mol O_2
       = 1.33 mol ratio. O_2 is limiting since the actual mol Fe/mol O_2 ratio is greater than the
       required mol ratio.

       0.0625 mol $O_2 \times \dfrac{-1652 \text{ kJ}}{3 \text{ mol O}_2} = -34.4$ kJ; 34.4 kJ of heat released

36.   a. 1.00 mol $H_2O \times \dfrac{-572 \text{ kJ}}{2 \text{ mol H}_2\text{O}} = -286$ kJ; 286 kJ of heat released

   b. 4.03 g $H_2 \times \dfrac{1 \text{ mol H}_2}{2.016 \text{ g H}_2} \times \dfrac{-572 \text{ kJ}}{2 \text{ mol H}_2} = -572$ kJ; 572 kJ of heat released

   c. 186 g $O_2 \times \dfrac{1 \text{ mol O}_2}{32.00 \text{ g O}_2} \times \dfrac{-572 \text{ kJ}}{\text{mol O}_2} = -3320$ kJ; 3320 kJ of heat released

   d. $n_{H_2} = \dfrac{PV}{RT} = \dfrac{1.0 \text{ atm} \times 2.0 \times 10^8 \text{ L}}{\dfrac{0.08206 \text{ L atm}}{\text{mol K}} \times 298 \text{ K}} = 8.2 \times 10^6$ mol H_2

       8.2×10^6 mol $H_2 \times \dfrac{-572 \text{ kJ}}{2 \text{ mol H}_2\text{O}} = -2.3 \times 10^9$ kJ; 2. 3 $\times 10^9$ kJ of heat released

37.   From Sample Exercise 6.3, q = 1.3×10^8 J. Since the heat transfer process is only 60.%
       efficient, the total energy required is: 1.3×10^8 J $\times \dfrac{100. \text{ J}}{60. \text{ J}} = 2.2 \times 10^8$ J

       mass $C_3H_8 = 2.2 \times 10^8$ J $\times \dfrac{1 \text{ mol C}_3\text{H}_8}{2221 \times 10^3 \text{ J}} \times \dfrac{44.09 \text{ g C}_3\text{H}_8}{\text{mol C}_3\text{H}_8} = 4.4 \times 10^3$ g C_3H_8

38.   a. $1.00 \text{ g CH}_4 \times \dfrac{1 \text{ mol CH}_4}{16.04 \text{ g CH}_4} \times \dfrac{-891 \text{ kJ}}{\text{mol CH}_4} = -55.5 \text{ kJ}$

     b. $n = \dfrac{PV}{RT}, \quad \dfrac{\dfrac{740.}{760} \text{ atm} \times 1.00 \times 10^3 \text{ L}}{\dfrac{0.08206 \text{ L atm}}{\text{mol K}} \times 298 \text{ K}} = 39.8 \text{ mol CH}_4$

         $39.8 \text{ mol} \times \dfrac{-891 \text{ kJ}}{\text{mol}} = -3.55 \times 10^4 \text{ kJ}$

39.   When a liquid is converted into gas, there is an increase in volume. The 2.5 kJ/mol quantity is the work done by the vaporization process in pushing back the atmosphere.

40. $\Delta H = \Delta E + P\Delta V$; From this equation, $\Delta H > \Delta E$ when $\Delta V > 0$, $\Delta H < \Delta E$ when $\Delta V < 0$, and $\Delta H = \Delta E$ when $\Delta V = 0$. Concentrate on the moles of gaseous products versus the moles of gaseous reactants to predict ΔV for a reaction.

     a.   There are 2 moles of gaseous reactants converting to 2 moles of gaseous products so $\Delta V = 0$. For this reaction, $\Delta H = \Delta E$.

     b.   There are 4 moles of gaseous reactants converting to 2 moles of gaseous products so $\Delta V < 0$ and $\Delta H < \Delta E$.

     c.   There are 9 moles of gaseous reactants converting to 10 moles of gaseous products so $\Delta V > 0$ and $\Delta H > \Delta E$.

Calorimetry and Heat Capacity

41.   Specific heat capacity is defined as the amount of heat necessary to raise the temperature of one gram of substance by one degree Celsius. Therefore, $H_2O(l)$ with the largest heat capacity value requires the largest amount of heat for this process. The amount of heat for $H_2O(l)$ is:

$$\text{energy} = s \times m \times \Delta T = \dfrac{4.18 \text{ J}}{\text{g }^\circ\text{C}} \times 25.0 \text{ g} \times (37.0^\circ\text{C} - 15.0^\circ\text{C}) = 2.30 \times 10^3 \text{ J}$$

The largest temperature change when a certain amount of energy is added to a certain mass of substance will occur for the substance with the smallest specific heat capacity. This is Hg(l), and the temperature change for this process is:

$$\Delta T = \dfrac{\text{energy}}{s \times m} = \dfrac{10.7 \text{ kJ} \times \dfrac{1000 \text{ J}}{\text{kJ}}}{\dfrac{0.14 \text{ J}}{\text{g }^\circ\text{C}} \times 550. \text{ g}} = 140^\circ\text{C}$$

42.   a. s = specific heat capacity = $\dfrac{0.24\,\text{J}}{\text{g}\,°\text{C}} = \dfrac{0.24\,\text{J}}{\text{g}\,\text{K}}$ since $\Delta T(\text{K}) = \Delta T(°\text{C})$.

energy = $s \times m \times \Delta T = \dfrac{0.24\,\text{J}}{\text{g}\,°\text{C}} \times 150.0\,\text{g} \times (298\,\text{K} - 273\,\text{K}) = 9.0 \times 10^2\,\text{J}$

b.   molar heat capacity = $\dfrac{0.24\,\text{J}}{\text{g}\,°\text{C}} \times \dfrac{107.9\,\text{g Ag}}{\text{mol Ag}} = \dfrac{26\,\text{J}}{\text{mol}\,°\text{C}}$

c. $1250\,\text{J} = \dfrac{0.24\,\text{J}}{\text{g}\,°\text{C}} \times m \times (15.2°\text{C} - 12.0°\text{C})$, $m = \dfrac{1250}{0.24 \times 3.2} = 1.6 \times 10^3\,\text{g Ag}$

43. s = specific heat capacity = $\dfrac{q}{m \times \Delta T} = \dfrac{133\,\text{J}}{5.00\,\text{g} \times (55.1 - 25.2)°\text{C}} = 0.890\,\text{J/°C•g}$

From Table 6.1, the substance is aluminum.

44. $s = \dfrac{585\,\text{J}}{125.6\,\text{g} \times (53.5 - 20.0)\,°\text{C}} = 0.139\,\text{J/g}•°\text{C}$

Molar heat capacity = $\dfrac{0.139\,\text{J}}{\text{g}\,°\text{C}} \times \dfrac{200.6\,\text{g}}{\text{mol Hg}} = \dfrac{27.9\,\text{J}}{\text{mol}\,°\text{C}}$

45. | Heat loss by hot water | = | Heat gain by cooler water |

The magnitude of heat loss and heat gain are equal in calorimetry problems. The only difference is the sign (positive or negative). To avoid sign errors, keep all quantities positive and, if necessary, deduce the correct signs at the end of the problem. Water has a specific heat capacity = s = 4.18 J/°C•g = 4.18 J/K•g (ΔT in °C = ΔT in K).

Heat loss by hot water = $s \times m \times \Delta T = \dfrac{4.18\,\text{J}}{\text{g}\,\text{K}} \times 50.0\,\text{g} \times (330.\,\text{K} - T_f)$

Heat gain by cooler water = $\dfrac{4.18\,\text{J}}{\text{g}\,\text{K}} \times 30.0\,\text{g} \times (T_f - 280.\,\text{K})$;   Heat loss = Heat gain, so:

$\dfrac{209\,\text{J}}{\text{K}} \times (330.\,\text{K} - T_f) = \dfrac{125\,\text{J}}{\text{K}} \times (T_f - 280.\,\text{K})$, $6.90 \times 10^4 - 209\,T_f = 125\,T_f - 3.50 \times 10^4$

$334\,T_f = 1.040 \times 10^5$, $T_f = 311\,\text{K}$

Note that the final temperature is closer to the temperature of the more massive hot water, which is as it should be.

46.   Heat loss by hot water = heat gain by cold water; Keeping all quantities positive to avoid sign errors:

$$\frac{4.18\ J}{g\ °C} \times m_{hot} \times (55.0\ °C - 37.0°C) = \frac{4.18\ J}{g\ °C} \times 90.0\ g \times (37.0\ °C - 22.0°C)$$

$$m_{hot} = \frac{90.0\ g \times 15.0\ °C}{18.0\ °C} = 75.0\ g\ \text{hot water needed}$$

47.   Heat loss by Al + heat loss by Fe = heat gain by water;   Keeping all quantities positive to avoid sign error:

$$\frac{0.89\ J}{g\ °C} \times 5.00\ g\ Al \times (100.0°C - T_f) + \frac{0.45\ J}{g\ °C} \times 10.00\ g\ Fe \times (100.0 - T_f)$$

$$= \frac{4.18\ J}{g\ °C} \times 97.3\ g\ H_2O \times (T_f - 22.0°C)$$

$$4.5(100.0 - T_f) + 4.5(100.0 - T_f) = 407(T_f - 22.0),\ \ 450 - 4.5\ T_f + 450 - 4.5\ T_f$$

$$= 407\ T_f - 8950$$

$$416\ T_f = 9850,\ \ T_f = 23.7°C$$

48.   heat released to water $= 5.0\ g\ H_2 \times \dfrac{120.\ J}{g\ H_2} + 10.\ g\ \text{methane} \times \dfrac{50.\ J}{g\ \text{methane}} = 1.10 \times 10^3\ J$

heat gain by water $= 1.10 \times 10^3\ J = \dfrac{4.18\ J}{g\ °C} \times 50.0\ g \times \Delta T$

$$\Delta T = 5.26°C,\ \ 5.26°C = T_f - 25.0°C,\ T_f = 30.3°C$$

49.   Heat gain by water = heat loss by metal = $s \times m \times \Delta T$ where s = specific heat capacity.

Heat gain $= \dfrac{4.18\ J}{g\ °C} \times 150.0\ g \times (18.3°C - 15.0°C) = 2100\ J$

A common error in calorimetry problems is sign errors. Keeping all quantities positive helps eliminate sign errors.

heat loss $= 2100\ J = s \times 150.0\ g \times (75.0°C - 18.3°C),\ \ s = \dfrac{2100\ J}{150.0\ g \times 56.7\ °C} = 0.25\ J/g•°C$

50.   Heat gain by water = heat loss by Cu;   Keeping all quantities positive to avoid sign errors:

$$\frac{4.18\ J}{g\ °C} \times \text{mass} \times (24.9°C - 22.3°C) = \frac{0.20\ J}{g\ °C} \times 110.\ g\ Cu \times (82.4°C - 24.9°C)$$

$$11 \times \text{mass} = 1300,\ \ \text{mass} = 120\ g\ H_2O$$

51. 50.0×10^{-3} L $\times$ 0.100 mol/L = 5.00×10^{-3} mol of both $AgNO_3$ and HCl are reacted. Thus, 5.00×10^{-3} mol of AgCl will be produced since there is a 1:1 mole ratio between reactants.

Heat lost by chemicals = Heat gained by solution

Heat gain = $\dfrac{4.18 \text{ J}}{\text{g }^\circ\text{C}} \times 100.0 \text{ g} \times (23.40 - 22.60)^\circ\text{C} = 330$ J

Heat loss = 330 J; This is the heat evolved (exothermic reaction) when 5.00×10^{-3} mol of AgCl is produced. So q = -330 J and ΔH (heat per mol AgCl formed) is negative with a value of:

$$\Delta H = \dfrac{-330 \text{ J}}{5.00 \times 10^{-3} \text{ mol}} \times \dfrac{1 \text{ kJ}}{1000 \text{ J}} = -66 \text{ kJ/mol}$$

Note: Sign errors are common with calorimetry problems. However, the correct sign for ΔH can easily be determined from the ΔT data, i.e., if ΔT of the solution increases, then the reaction is exothermic since heat was released, and if ΔT of the solution decreases, then the reaction is endothermic since the reaction absorbed heat from the water. For calorimetry problems, keep all quantities positive until the end of the calculation, then decide the sign for ΔH. This will help eliminate sign errors.

52. $NH_4NO_3(s) \rightarrow NH_4^+(aq) + NO_3^-(aq)$ ΔH = ?; mass of solution = 75.0 g + 1.60 g = 76.6 g

Heat lost by solution = Heat gained as NH_4NO_3 dissolves. To help eliminate sign errors, we will keep all quantities positive (q and ΔT), then deduce the correct sign for ΔH at the end of the problem. Here, since temperature decreases as NH_4NO_3 dissolves, heat is absorbed as NH_4NO_3 dissolves, so it is an endothermic process (ΔH is positive).

Heat loss by solution = $\dfrac{4.18 \text{ J}}{\text{g }^\circ\text{C}} \times 76.6 \text{ g} \times (25.00 - 23.34)^\circ\text{C} = 532$ J = heat gain as NH_4NO_3 dissolves

$$\Delta H = \dfrac{532 \text{ J}}{1.60 \text{ g } NH_4NO_3} \times \dfrac{80.05 \text{ g } NH_4NO_3}{\text{mol } NH_4NO_3} \times \dfrac{1 \text{ kJ}}{1000 \text{ J}} = 26.6 \text{ kJ/mol } NH_4NO_3 \text{ dissolving}$$

53.   Since ΔH is exothermic, the temperature of the solution will increase as $CaCl_2(s)$ dissolves. Keeping all quantities positive:

Heat loss as $CaCl_2$ dissolves = 11.0 g $CaCl_2$ $\times$ $\dfrac{1 \text{ mol } CaCl_2}{110.98 \text{ g } CaCl_2} \times \dfrac{81.5 \text{ kJ}}{\text{mol } CaCl_2} = 8.08$ kJ

Heat gain by solution = 8.08×10^3 J = $\dfrac{4.18 \text{ J}}{\text{g }^\circ\text{C}} \times (125 + 11.0) \text{ g} \times (T_f - 25.0^\circ\text{C})$

$T_f - 25.0^\circ\text{C} = \dfrac{8.08 \times 10^3}{4.18 \times 136} = 14.2^\circ\text{C}$, $T_f = 14.2^\circ\text{C} + 25.0^\circ\text{C} = 39.2^\circ\text{C}$

54.　　$0.100 \text{ L} \times \dfrac{0.500 \text{ mol HCl}}{\text{L}} = 5.00 \times 10^{-2} \text{ mol HCl}$

$0.300 \text{ L} \times \dfrac{0.100 \text{ mol Ba(OH)}_2}{\text{L}} = 3.00 \times 10^{-2} \text{ mol Ba(OH)}_2$

To react with all the HCl present, $5.00 \times 10^{-2}/2 = 2.50 \times 10^{-2}$ mol Ba(OH)$_2$ are required. Since 3.00×10^{-2} mol Ba(OH)$_2$ are present, HCl is the limiting reactant.

$5.00 \times 10^{-2} \text{ mol HCl} \times \dfrac{118 \text{ kJ}}{2 \text{ mol HCl}} = 2.95 \text{ kJ of heat is evolved by reaction.}$

Heat gain by solution $= 2.95 \times 10^3 \text{ J} = \dfrac{4.18 \text{ J}}{\text{g }^\circ\text{C}} \times 400.0 \text{ g} \times \Delta T$

$\Delta T = 1.76^\circ\text{C} = T_f - T_i = T_f - 25.0^\circ\text{C}, \ T_f = 26.8^\circ\text{C}$

55.　　a.　heat gain by calorimeter = heat loss by CH$_4$ = $6.79 \text{ g CH}_4 \times \dfrac{1 \text{ mol CH}_4}{16.04 \text{ g}} \times \dfrac{802 \text{ kJ}}{\text{mol}}$

$= 340. \text{ kJ}$

heat capacity of calorimeter $= \dfrac{340. \text{ kJ}}{10.8 \ ^\circ\text{C}} = 31.5 \text{ kJ/}^\circ\text{C}$

b.　heat loss by C$_2$H$_2$ = heat gain by calorimeter $= 16.9^\circ\text{C} \times \dfrac{31.5 \text{ kJ}}{^\circ\text{C}} = 532 \text{ kJ}$

$\Delta E_{comb} = \dfrac{-532 \text{ kJ}}{12.6 \text{ g C}_2\text{H}_2} \times \dfrac{26.04 \text{ g}}{\text{mol C}_2\text{H}_2} = -1.10 \times 10^3 \text{ kJ/mol}$

56.　　Heat gain by calorimeter $= \dfrac{1.56 \text{ kJ}}{^\circ\text{C}} \times 3.2^\circ\text{C} = 5.0 \text{ kJ} = $ heat loss by quinine

Heat loss = 5.0 kJ, which is the heat evolved (exothermic reaction) by the combustion of 0.1964 g of quinone.

$\Delta E_{comb} = \dfrac{-5.0 \text{ kJ}}{0.1964 \text{ g}} = -25 \text{ kJ/g}; \qquad \Delta E_{comb} = \dfrac{-25 \text{ kJ}}{\text{g}} \times \dfrac{108.09 \text{ g}}{\text{mol}} = -2700 \text{ kJ/mol}$

Hess's Law

57.　　Information given:

$$C(s) + O_2(g) \rightarrow CO_2(g) \qquad \Delta H = -393.7 \text{ kJ}$$
$$CO(g) + 1/2 \ O_2(g) \rightarrow CO_2(g) \qquad \Delta H = -283.3 \text{ kJ}$$

Using Hess's Law:

$$2\ C(s) + 2\ O_2(g) \rightarrow 2\ CO_2(g) \qquad \Delta H_1 = 2(-393.7\ kJ)$$
$$2\ CO_2(g) \rightarrow 2\ CO(g) + O_2(g) \qquad \Delta H_2 = -2(-283.3\ kJ)$$

$$\overline{2\ C(s) + O_2(g) \rightarrow 2\ CO(g) \qquad \Delta H = \Delta H_1 + \Delta H_2 = -220.8\ kJ}$$

Note: The enthalpy change for a reaction that is reversed is the negative quantity of the enthalpy change for the original reaction. If the coefficients in a balanced reaction are multiplied by an integer, the value of ΔH is multiplied by the same integer while the sign stays the same.

58. $C_4H_4(g) + 5\ O_2(g) \rightarrow 4\ CO_2(g) + 2\ H_2O(l) \qquad \Delta H_{comb} = -2341\ kJ$
       $C_4H_8(g) + 6\ O_2(g) \rightarrow 4\ CO_2(g) + 4\ H_2O(l) \qquad \Delta H_{comb} = -2755\ kJ$
       $H_2(g) + 1/2\ O_2(g) \rightarrow H_2O(l) \qquad \Delta H_{comb} = -286\ kJ$

By convention, $H_2O(l)$ is produced when enthalpies of combustion are given and, since per mole quantities are given, the combustion reaction refers to 1 mole of that quantity reacting with $O_2(g)$.

Using Hess's Law to solve:

$$C_4H_4(g) + 5\ O_2(g) \rightarrow 4\ CO_2(g) + 2\ H_2O(l) \qquad \Delta H_1 = -2341\ kJ$$
$$4\ CO_2(g) + 4\ H_2O(l) \rightarrow C_4H_8(g) + 6\ O_2(g) \qquad \Delta H_2 = -\ (-2755\ kJ)$$
$$2\ H_2(g) + O_2(g) \rightarrow 2\ H_2O(l) \qquad \Delta H_3 = 2(-286\ kJ)$$

$$\overline{C_4H_4(g) + 2\ H_2(g) \rightarrow C_4H_8(g) \qquad \Delta H = \Delta H_1 + \Delta H_2 + \Delta H_3 = -158\ kJ}$$

59. $2\ N_2(g) + 6\ H_2(g) \rightarrow 4\ NH_3(g) \qquad \Delta H = -4(46\ kJ)$
       $6\ H_2O(g) \rightarrow 6\ H_2(g) + 3\ O_2(g) \qquad \Delta H = -3(-484\ kJ)$

$$\overline{2\ N_2(g) + 6\ H_2O(g) \rightarrow 3\ O_2(g) + 4\ NH_3(g) \qquad \Delta H = 1268\ kJ}$$

No, since the reaction is very endothermic (requires a lot of heat), it would not be a practical way of making ammonia due to the high energy costs.

60. $ClF + 1/2\ O_2 \rightarrow 1/2\ Cl_2O + 1/2\ F_2O \qquad \Delta H = 1/2\ (167.4\ kJ)$
       $1/2\ Cl_2O + 3/2\ F_2O \rightarrow ClF_3 + O_2 \qquad \Delta H = -1/2\ (341.4\ kJ)$
       $F_2 + 1/2\ O_2 \rightarrow F_2O \qquad \Delta H = 1/2\ (-43.4\ kJ)$

$$\overline{ClF(g) + F_2(g) \rightarrow ClF_3 \qquad \Delta H = -108.7\ kJ}$$

61. $NO + O_3 \rightarrow NO_2 + O_2 \qquad \Delta H = -199\ kJ$
       $3/2\ O_2 \rightarrow O_3 \qquad \Delta H = -1/2(-427\ kJ)$
       $O \rightarrow 1/2\ O_2 \qquad \Delta H = -1/2(495\ kJ)$

$$\overline{NO(g) + O(g) \rightarrow NO_2(g) \qquad \Delta H = -233\ kJ}$$

62. $\qquad$
$C_6H_4(OH)_2 \rightarrow C_6H_4O_2 + H_2$	$\Delta H = 177.4 \text{ kJ}$
$H_2O_2 \rightarrow H_2 + O_2$	$\Delta H = -(-191.2 \text{ kJ})$
$2 H_2 + O_2 \rightarrow 2 H_2O(g)$	$\Delta H = 2(-241.8 \text{ kJ})$
$2 H_2O(g) \rightarrow 2 H_2O(l)$	$\Delta H = 2(-43.8 \text{ kJ})$

$C_6H_4(OH)_2(aq) + H_2O_2(aq) \rightarrow C_6H_4O_2(aq) + 2 H_2O(l)$ $\Delta H = -202.6 \text{ kJ}$

63.
$CaC_2 \rightarrow Ca + 2 C$	$\Delta H = -(-62.8 \text{ kJ})$
$CaO + H_2O \rightarrow Ca(OH)_2$	$\Delta H = -653.1 \text{ kJ}$
$2 CO_2 + H_2O \rightarrow C_2H_2 + 5/2 O_2$	$\Delta H = -(-1300. \text{ kJ})$
$Ca + 1/2 O_2 \rightarrow CaO$	$\Delta H = -635.5 \text{ kJ}$
$2 C + 2 O_2 \rightarrow 2 CO_2$	$\Delta H = 2(-393.5 \text{ kJ})$

$CaC_2(s) + 2 H_2O(l) \rightarrow Ca(OH)_2(aq) + C_2H_2(g)$ $\Delta H = -713 \text{ kJ}$

64.
$P_4O_{10} \rightarrow P_4 + 5 O_2$	$\Delta H = -(-2967.3 \text{ kJ})$
$10 PCl_3 + 5 O_2 \rightarrow 10 Cl_3PO$	$\Delta H = 10(-285.7 \text{ kJ})$
$6 PCl_5 \rightarrow 6 PCl_3 + 6 Cl_2$	$\Delta H = -6(-84.2 \text{ kJ})$
$P_4 + 6 Cl_2 \rightarrow 4 PCl_3$	$\Delta H = -1225.6$

$P_4O_{10}(s) + 6 PCl_5(g) \rightarrow 10 Cl_3PO(g)$ $\Delta H = -610.1 \text{ kJ}$

Standard Enthalpies of Formation

65. The change in enthalpy that accompanies the formation of one mole of a compound from its elements, with all substances in their standard states, is the standard enthalpy of formation for a compound. The reactions that refer to ΔH_f° are:

$Na(s) + 1/2 Cl_2(g) \rightarrow NaCl(s); \quad H_2(g) + 1/2 O_2(g) \rightarrow H_2O(l)$

$6 C(graphite, s) + 6 H_2(g) + 3 O_2(g) \rightarrow C_6H_{12}O_6(s)$

$Pb(s) + S(rhombic, s) + 2 O_2(g) \rightarrow PbSO_4(s)$

66. a. aluminum oxide = Al_2O_3; $2 Al(s) + 3/2 O_2(g) \rightarrow Al_2O_3(s)$

b. $C_2H_5OH(l) + 3 O_2(g) \rightarrow 2 CO_2(g) + 3 H_2O(l)$

c. $NaOH(aq) + HCl(aq) \rightarrow H_2O(l) + NaCl(aq)$

d. $2 C(graphite, s) + 3/2 H_2(g) + 1/2 Cl_2(g) \rightarrow C_2H_3Cl(g)$

e. $C_6H_6(l) + 15/2 O_2(g) \rightarrow 6 CO_2(g) + 3 H_2O(l)$

Note: ΔH_{comb} values assume one mole of compound combusted.

f. $NH_4Br(s) \rightarrow NH_4^+(aq) + Br^-(aq)$

67.   In general: $\Delta H° = \sum n_p \Delta H°_{f, \text{products}} - \sum n_r \Delta H°_{f, \text{reactants}}$ and all elements in their standard state have $\Delta H°_f = 0$ by definition.

a.   The balanced equation is: $2\ NH_3(g) + 3\ O_2(g) + 2\ CH_4(g) \rightarrow 2\ HCN(g) + 6\ H_2O(g)$

$\Delta H° = [\ 2\ \text{mol HCN} \times \Delta H°_{f,\ HCN} + 6\ \text{mol}\ H_2O(g) \times \Delta H°_{f,\ H_2O}]$

$- [2\ \text{mol}\ NH_3 \times \Delta H°_{f,\ NH_3} + 2\ \text{mol}\ CH_4 \times \Delta H°_{f,\ CH_4}]$

$\Delta H° = [2(135.1) + 6(-242)] - [2(-46) + 2(-75)] = -940.\ kJ$

b. $Ca_3(PO_4)_2(s) + 3\ H_2SO_4(l) \rightarrow 3\ CaSO_4(s) + 2\ H_3PO_4(l)$

$$\Delta H° = \left[3\ \text{mol}\ CaSO_4\left(\frac{-1433\ kJ}{mol}\right) + 2\ \text{mol}\ H_3PO_4\ (l)\left(\frac{-1267\ kJ}{mol}\right)\right]$$

$$- \left[1\ \text{mol}\ Ca_3(PO_4)_2\left(\frac{-4126\ kJ}{mol}\right) + 3\ \text{mol}\ H_2SO_4\ (l)\left(\frac{-814\ kJ}{mol}\right)\right]$$

$\Delta H° = -6833\ kJ - (-6568\ kJ) = -265\ kJ$

c. $NH_3(g) + HCl(g) \rightarrow NH_4Cl(s)$

$\Delta H° = [1\ \text{mol}\ NH_4Cl \times \Delta H°_{f,\ NH_4Cl}] - [1\ \text{mol}\ NH_3 \times \Delta H°_{f,\ NH_3} + 1\ \text{mol}\ HCl \times \Delta H°_{f,\ HCl}]$

$$\Delta H° = \left[1\ \text{mol}\left(\frac{-314\ kJ}{mol}\right)\right] - \left[1\ \text{mol}\left(\frac{-46\ kJ}{mol}\right) + 1\ \text{mol}\left(\frac{-92\ kJ}{mol}\right)\right]$$

$\Delta H° = -314\ kJ + 138\ kJ = -176\ kJ$

68.   a.   The balanced equation is: $C_2H_5OH(l) + 3\ O_2(g) \rightarrow 2\ CO_2(g) + 3\ H_2O(g)$

$$\Delta H° = \left[2\ \text{mol}\left(\frac{-393.5\ kJ}{mol}\right) + 3\ \text{mol}\left(\frac{-242\ kJ}{mol}\right)\right] - \left[1\ \text{mol}\left(\frac{-278\ kJ}{mol}\right)\right]$$

$\Delta H° = = -1513\ kJ - (-278\ kJ) = -1235\ kJ$

b. $SiCl_4(l) + 2\ H_2O(l) \rightarrow SiO_2(s) + 4\ HCl(aq)$

Since $HCl(aq)$ is $H^+(aq) + Cl^-(aq)$, then $\Delta H°_f = 0 - 167 = -167\ kJ/mol$.

$$\Delta H^\circ = \left[4 \text{ mol}\left(\frac{-167 \text{ kJ}}{\text{mol}}\right) + 1 \text{ mol}\left(\frac{-911 \text{ kJ}}{\text{mol}}\right) \right] - \left[1 \text{ mol}\left(\frac{-687 \text{ kJ}}{\text{mol}}\right) + 2 \text{ mol}\left(\frac{-286 \text{ kJ}}{\text{mol}}\right) \right]$$

$$\Delta H^\circ = -1579 \text{ kJ} - (-1259 \text{ kJ}) = -320. \text{ kJ}$$

c. $MgO(s) + H_2O(l) \rightarrow Mg(OH)_2(s)$

$$\Delta H^\circ = \left[1 \text{ mol}\left(\frac{-925 \text{ kJ}}{\text{mol}}\right) \right] - \left[1 \text{ mol}\left(\frac{-602 \text{ kJ}}{\text{mol}}\right) + 1 \text{ mol}\left(\frac{-286 \text{ kJ}}{\text{mol}}\right) \right]$$

$$\Delta H^\circ = -925 \text{ kJ} - (-888 \text{ kJ}) = -37 \text{ kJ}$$

69. a. $4 NH_3(g) + 5 O_2(g) \rightarrow 4 NO(g) + 6 H_2O(g);$ $\Delta H^\circ = \sum n_p \Delta H^\circ_{f,\text{ products}} - \sum n_r \Delta H^\circ_{f,\text{ reactants}}$

$$\Delta H^\circ = \left[4 \text{ mol}\left(\frac{90. \text{ kJ}}{\text{mol}}\right) + 6 \text{ mol}\left(\frac{-242 \text{ kJ}}{\text{mol}}\right) \right] - \left[4 \text{ mol}\left(\frac{-46 \text{ kJ}}{\text{mol}}\right) \right] = -908 \text{ kJ}$$

$2 NO(g) + O_2(g) \rightarrow 2 NO_2(g)$

$$\Delta H^\circ = \left[2 \text{ mol}\left(\frac{34 \text{ kJ}}{\text{mol}}\right) \right] - \left[2 \text{ mol}\left(\frac{90. \text{ kJ}}{\text{mol}}\right) \right] = -112 \text{ kJ}$$

$3 NO_2(g) + H_2O(l) \rightarrow 2 HNO_3(aq) + NO(g)$

$$\Delta H^\circ = \left[2 \text{ mol}\left(\frac{-207 \text{ kJ}}{\text{mol}}\right) + 1 \text{ mol}\left(\frac{90. \text{ kJ}}{\text{mol}}\right) \right] - \left[3 \text{ mol}\left(\frac{34 \text{ kJ}}{\text{mol}}\right) + 1 \text{ mol}\left(\frac{-286 \text{ kJ}}{\text{mol}}\right) \right]$$

$$= -140. \text{ kJ}$$

Note: All ΔH°_f values are assumed ± 1 kJ.

b. $12 NH_3(g) + 15 O_2(g) \rightarrow 12 NO(g) + 18 H_2O(g)$
$12 NO(g) + 6 O_2(g) \rightarrow 12 NO_2(g)$
$12 NO_2(g) + 4 H_2O(l) \rightarrow 8 HNO_3(aq) + 4 NO(g)$
$4 H_2O(g) \rightarrow 4 H_2O(l)$

$12 NH_3(g) + 21 O_2(g) \rightarrow 8 HNO_3(aq) + 4 NO(g) + 14 H_2O(g)$

The overall reaction is exothermic since each step is exothermic.

70. $4 Na(s) + O_2(g) \rightarrow 2 Na_2O(s),$ $\Delta H^\circ = 2 \text{ mol} \times \frac{-416 \text{ kJ}}{\text{mol}} = -832 \text{ kJ}$

$$2 \text{ Na(s)} + 2 \text{ H}_2\text{O(l)} \rightarrow 2 \text{ NaOH(aq)} + \text{H}_2\text{(g)}$$

$$\Delta H^\circ = \left[2 \text{ mol} \left(\frac{-470 \text{ kJ}}{\text{mol}} \right) \right] - \left[2 \text{ mol} \left(\frac{-286 \text{ kJ}}{\text{mol}} \right) \right] = -368 \text{ kJ}$$

$$2 \text{ Na(s)} + \text{CO}_2\text{(g)} \rightarrow \text{Na}_2\text{O(s)} + \text{CO(g)}$$

$$\Delta H^\circ = \left[1 \text{ mol} \left(\frac{-416 \text{ kJ}}{\text{mol}} \right) + 1 \text{ mol} \left(\frac{-110.5. \text{ kJ}}{\text{mol}} \right) \right] - \left[1 \text{ mol} \left(\frac{-393.5 \text{ kJ}}{\text{mol}} \right) \right] = -133 \text{ kJ}$$

In both cases, sodium metal reacts with the "extinguishing agent." Both reactions are exothermic and each reaction produces a flammable gas, H_2 and CO, respectively.

71. $$3 \text{ Al(s)} + 3 \text{ NH}_4\text{ClO}_4\text{(s)} \rightarrow \text{Al}_2\text{O}_3\text{(s)} + \text{AlCl}_3\text{(s)} + 3 \text{ NO(g)} + 6 \text{ H}_2\text{O(g)}$$

$$\Delta H^\circ = \left[6 \text{ mol} \left(\frac{-242 \text{ kJ}}{\text{mol}} \right) + 3 \text{ mol} \left(\frac{90. \text{ kJ}}{\text{mol}} \right) + 1 \text{ mol} \left(\frac{-704 \text{ kJ}}{\text{mol}} \right) + 1 \text{ mol} \left(\frac{-1676 \text{ kJ}}{\text{mol}} \right) \right]$$

$$- \left[3 \text{ mol} \left(\frac{-295 \text{ kJ}}{\text{mol}} \right) \right] = -2677 \text{ kJ}$$

72. $$5 \text{ N}_2\text{O}_4\text{(l)} + 4 \text{ N}_2\text{H}_3\text{CH}_3\text{(l)} \rightarrow 12 \text{ H}_2\text{O(g)} + 9 \text{ N}_2\text{(g)} + 4 \text{ CO}_2\text{(g)}$$

$$\Delta H^\circ = \left[12 \text{ mol} \left(\frac{-242 \text{ kJ}}{\text{mol}} \right) + 4 \text{ mol} \left(\frac{-393.5 \text{ kJ}}{\text{mol}} \right) \right]$$

$$- \left[5 \text{ mol} \left(\frac{-20. \text{ kJ}}{\text{mol}} \right) + 4 \text{ mol} \left(\frac{54 \text{ kJ}}{\text{mol}} \right) \right] = -4594 \text{ kJ}$$

73. $$2 \text{ ClF}_3\text{(g)} + 2 \text{ NH}_3\text{(g)} \rightarrow \text{N}_2\text{(g)} + 6 \text{ HF(g)} + \text{Cl}_2\text{(g)} \quad \Delta H^\circ = -1196 \text{ kJ}$$

$$\Delta H^\circ = [6 \ \Delta H^\circ_{f, \text{HF}}] - [2 \ \Delta H^\circ_{f, \text{ClF}_3} + 2 \ \Delta H^\circ_{f, \text{NH}_3}]$$

$$-1196 \text{ kJ} = 6 \text{ mol} \left(\frac{-271 \text{ kJ}}{\text{mol}} \right) - 2 \ \Delta H^\circ_{f, \text{ClF}_3} - 2 \text{ mol} \left(\frac{-46 \text{ kJ}}{\text{mol}} \right)$$

$$-1196 \text{ kJ} = -1626 \text{ kJ} - 2 \ \Delta H^\circ_{f, \text{ClF}_3} + 92 \text{ kJ}, \ \Delta H^\circ_{f, \text{ClF}_3} = \frac{(-1626 + 92 + 1196) \text{ kJ}}{2 \text{ mol}} = \frac{-169 \text{ kJ}}{\text{mol}}$$

74. $$\text{C}_2\text{H}_4\text{(g)} + 3 \text{ O}_2\text{(g)} \rightarrow 2 \text{ CO}_2\text{(g)} + 2 \text{ H}_2\text{O(l)} \quad \Delta H^\circ = -1411.1 \text{ kJ}$$

$$\Delta H^\circ = -1411.1 \text{ kJ} = 2(-393.5) \text{ kJ} + 2(-285.8) \text{ kJ} - \Delta H^\circ_{f, \text{C}_2\text{H}_4}$$

$$-1411.1 \text{ kJ} = -1358.6 \text{ kJ} - \Delta H^\circ_{f, \text{C}_2\text{H}_4}, \ \Delta H^\circ_{f, \text{C}_2\text{H}_4} = 52.5 \text{ kJ/mol}$$

Energy Consumption and Sources

75. $C_2H_5OH(l) + 3 O_2(g) \rightarrow 2 CO_2(g) + 3 H_2O(l)$

$\Delta H° = [2 (-393.5 \text{ kJ}) + 3(-286 \text{ kJ})] - (-278 \text{ kJ}) = -1367 \text{ kJ/mol ethanol}$

$$\frac{-1367 \text{ kJ}}{\text{mol}} \times \frac{1 \text{ mol}}{46.07 \text{ g}} = -29.67 \text{ kJ/g}$$

76. $CH_3OH(l) + 3/2 O_2(g) \rightarrow CO_2(g) + 2 H_2O(l)$

$\Delta H° = [-393.5 \text{ kJ} + 2(-286 \text{ kJ})] - (-239 \text{ kJ}) = -727 \text{ kJ/mol } CH_3OH$

$$\frac{-727 \text{ kJ}}{\text{mol}} \times \frac{1 \text{ mol}}{32.04 \text{ g}} = -22.7 \text{ kJ/g vs. } -29.67 \text{ kJ/g for ethanol}$$

Ethanol has a slightly higher fuel value than methanol.

77. $C_3H_8(g) + 5 O_2(g) \rightarrow 3 CO_2(g) + 4 H_2O(l)$

$\Delta H° = [3(-393.5 \text{ kJ}) + 4(-286 \text{ kJ})] - [-104 \text{ kJ}] = -2221 \text{ kJ/mol } C_3H_8$

$$\frac{-2221 \text{ kJ}}{\text{mol}} \times \frac{1 \text{ mol}}{44.09 \text{ g}} = \frac{-50.37 \text{ kJ}}{\text{mol}} \text{ vs. } -47.7 \text{ kJ/g for octane (Sample Exercise 6.11)}$$

The fuel values are close. An advantage of propane is that it burns more cleanly. The boiling point of propane is $-42°C$. Thus, it is more difficult to store propane and there are extra safety hazards associated with using high pressure compressed gas tanks.

78. 1 mole of $C_2H_2(g)$ and 1 mole of $C_4H_{10}(g)$ have equivalent volumes at the same T and P.

$$\frac{\text{enthalpy of combustion per volume of } C_2H_2}{\text{enthalpy of combustion per volume of } C_4H_{10}} = \frac{\text{enthalpy of combustion per mol of } C_2H_2}{\text{enthalpy of combustion per mol of } C_4H_{10}}$$

$$\frac{\text{enthalpy of combustion per volume of } C_2H_2}{\text{enthalpy of combustion per volume of } C_4H_{10}} = \frac{\dfrac{-49.9 \text{ kJ}}{\text{g } C_2H_2} \times \dfrac{26.04 \text{ g } C_2H_2}{\text{mol } C_2H_2}}{\dfrac{-49.5 \text{ kJ}}{\text{g } C_4H_{10}} \times \dfrac{58.12 \text{ g } C_4H_{10}}{\text{mol } C_4H_{10}}} = 0.452$$

More than twice the volume of acetylene is needed to furnish the same energy as a given volume of butane.

79. The molar volume of a gas at STP is 22.42 L (from Chapter 5).

$$4.19 \times 10^6 \text{ kJ} \times \frac{1 \text{ mol } CH_4}{891 \text{ kJ}} \times \frac{22.42 \text{ L } CH_4}{\text{mol } CH_4} = 1.05 \times 10^5 \text{ L } CH_4$$

80.   Mass of H_2O = 1.00 gal $\times \dfrac{3.785\,L}{gal} \times \dfrac{1000\,mL}{L} \times \dfrac{1.00\,g}{mL}$ = 3790 g H_2O

Energy required (theoretical) = s $\times$ m $\times \Delta T = \dfrac{4.18\,J}{g\,^\circ C} \times$ 3790 g $\times$ 10.0 $^\circ C$ = 1.58 $\times 10^5$ J

For the actual (80.0% efficient) process, more than this quantity of energy is needed since heat is always lost in any transfer of energy. The energy required is:

$$1.58 \times 10^5\,J = \dfrac{100.\,J}{80.0\,J} = 1.98 \times 10^5\,J$$

Mass of C_2H_2 = 1.98 $\times 10^5$ J $\times \dfrac{1\,mol\,C_2H_2}{1300.\times 10^3\,J} \times \dfrac{26.04\,g\,C_2H_2}{mol\,C_2H_2}$ = 3.97 g C_2H_2

Additional Exercises

81.   a.   2 $SO_2(g)$ + $O_2(g) \rightarrow$ 2 $SO_3(g)$ (w = $-P\Delta V$); Because the volume of the piston apparatus decreased as reactants were converted to products, w is positive (w > 0).

b. $COCl_2(g) \rightarrow CO(g)$ + $Cl_2(g)$; Because the volume increased, w is negative (w < 0).

c. $N_2(g)$ + $O_2(g) \rightarrow$ 2 NO(g); Because the volume did not change, no PV work is done (w = 0).

In order to predict the sign of w for a reaction, compare the coefficients of all the product gases in the balanced equation to the coefficients of all the reactant gases. When a balanced reaction has more mol of product gases than mol of reactant gases (as in b), the reaction will expand in volume (ΔV positive), and the system does work on the surroundings. When a balanced reaction has a decrease in the mol of gas from reactants to products (as in a), the reaction will contract in volume (ΔV negative), and the surroundings will do compression work on the system. When there is no change in the mol of gas from reactants to products (as in c), $\Delta V = 0$ and w = 0.

82.   w = $-P\Delta V$; Δn = mol gaseous products - mol gaseous reactants. Only gases can do PV work (we ignore solids and liquids). When a balanced reaction has more mol of product gases than mol of reactant gases (Δn positive), the reaction will expand in volume (ΔV positive) and the system will do work on the surroundings. For example, in reaction c, $\Delta n = 2 - 0 = 2$ mol, and this reaction would do expansion work against the surroundings. When a balanced reaction has a decrease in the mol of gas from reactants to products (Δn negative), the reaction will contract in volume (ΔV negative) and the surroundings will do compression work on the system, e.g., reaction a where $\Delta n = 0 - 1 = -1$. When there is no change in the mol of gas from reactants to products, $\Delta V = 0$ and w = 0, e.g., reaction b where $\Delta n = 2 - 2 = 0$.

When $\Delta V > 0$ ($\Delta n > 0$), then w < 0 and system does work on the surroundings (c and e).

When $\Delta V < 0$ ($\Delta n < 0$), then w > 0 and the surroundings do work on the system (a and d).

When $\Delta V = 0$ ($\Delta n = 0$), then w = 0 (b).

83. $\Delta E_{overall} = \Delta E_{step\ 1} + \Delta E_{step\ 2}$; This is a cyclic process which means that the overall initial state and final state are the same. Since ΔE is a state function, $\Delta E_{overall} = 0$ and $\Delta E_{step\ 1} = -\Delta E_{step\ 2}$.

$\Delta E_{step\ 1} = q + w = 45\ J + (-10.\ J) = 35\ J$

$\Delta E_{step\ 2} = -\Delta E_{step\ 1} = -35\ J = q + w,\ -35\ J = -60\ J + w,\ w = 25\ J$

84. $2\ K(s) + 2\ H_2O(l) \rightarrow 2\ KOH(aq) + H_2(g),\quad \Delta H^{\circ} = 2(-481\ kJ) - 2(-286\ kJ) = -390.\ kJ$

$5.00\ g\ K \times \dfrac{1\ mol\ K}{39.10\ g\ K} \times \dfrac{-390.\ kJ}{2\ mol\ K} = -24.9\ kJ;$

24.9 kJ of heat is released upon reaction of 5.00 g K.

$24{,}900\ J = \dfrac{4.18\ J}{g\ ^{\circ}C} \times (1.00 \times 10^3\ g) \times \Delta T,\ \Delta T = \dfrac{24{,}900}{4.18 \times 1.00 \times 10^3} = 5.96^{\circ}C$

Final temperature $= 24.0 + 5.96 = 30.0^{\circ}C$

85. $HCl(aq) + NaOH(aq) \rightarrow H_2O(l) + NaCl(aq)\ \ \Delta H = -56\ kJ$

$0.2000\ L \times \dfrac{0.400\ mol\ HCl}{L} = 8.00 \times 10^{-2}\ mol\ HCl$

$0.1500\ L \times \dfrac{0.500\ mol\ NaOH}{L} = 7.50 \times 10^{-2}\ mol\ NaOH$

Because the balanced reaction requires a 1:1 mole ratio between HCl and NaOH, and because fewer moles of NaOH are actually present as compared to HCl, NaOH is the limiting reagent.

$7.50 \times 10^{-2}\ mol\ NaOH \times \dfrac{-56\ kJ}{mol\ NaOH} = -4.2\ kJ;\ 4.2\ kJ$ of heat is released.

86. $Na_2SO_4(aq)_2 + Ba(NO_3)_2(aq) \rightarrow BaSO_4(s) + 2\ NaNO_3(aq)\quad \Delta H = ?$

$1.00\ L \times \dfrac{2.00\ mol}{L} = 2.00\ mol\ Na_2SO_4;\ \ 2.00\ L \times \dfrac{0.750\ mol}{L} = 1.50\ mol\ Ba(NO_3)_2$

The balanced equation requires a 1:1 mole ratio between Na_2SO_4 and $Ba(NO_3)_2$. Because we have fewer moles of $Ba(NO_3)_2$ present, it is limiting and 1.50 mol $BaSO_4$ will be produced [there is a 1:1 mole ratio between $Ba(NO_3)_2$ and $BaSO_4$].

heat gain by solution = heat loss by reaction

mass of solution $= 3.00\ L \times \dfrac{1000\ mol}{1\ L} \times \dfrac{2.00\ g}{mL} = 6.00 \times 10^3\ g$

heat gain by solution = $\dfrac{6.37\ J}{g\ °C}$ × 6.00 × 10^3 g × (42.0 − 30.0)°C = 4.59 × 10^5 J

Because the solution gained heat, the reaction is exothermic;   q = −4.59 × 10^5 J for the reaction.

$$\Delta H = \dfrac{-4.59 \times 10^5\ J}{1.50\ mol\ BaSO_4} = -3.06 \times 10^5\ J/mol = -306\ kJ/mol$$

87. $q_{surr} = q_{solution} + q_{cal}$;   We normally assume q_{cal} is zero (no heat gain/loss by the calorimeter). However, if the calorimeter has a nonzero heat capacity, then some of the heat absorbed by the endothermic reaction came from the calorimeter. If we ignore q_{cal}, then q_{surr} is too small giving a calculated ΔH value which is less positive (smaller) than it should be.

88.   The specific heat of water is 4.18 J/g•°C, which is equal to 4.18 kJ/kg•°C.

We have 1.00 kg of H_2O, so: 1.00 kg × $\dfrac{4.18\ J}{kg\ °C}$ = 4.18 kJ/°C

This is the portion of the heat capacity that can be attributed to H_2O.

Total heat capacity = $C_{cal} + C_{H_2O}$, C_{cal} = 10.84 − 4.18 = 6.66 kJ/°C

89.   Heat released = 1.056 g × 26.42 kJ/g = 27.90 kJ = Heat gain by water and calorimeter

Heat gain = 27.90 kJ = $\dfrac{4.18\ J}{kg\ °C}$ × 0.987 kg × ΔT + $\dfrac{6.66\ kJ}{°C}$ × ΔT

27.90 = (4.13 + 6.66) ΔT = 10.79 ΔT, ΔT = 2.586°C

2.586°C = T_f − 23.32°C, T_f = 25.91°C

90.   To avoid fractions, let's first calculate ΔH for the reaction:

6 FeO(s) + 6 CO(g) → 6 Fe(s) + 6 CO$_2$(g)

6 FeO + 2 CO$_2$ → 2 Fe$_3$O$_4$ + 2 CO	$\Delta H°$ = −2(18 kJ)
2 Fe$_3$O$_4$ + CO$_2$ → 3 Fe$_2$O$_3$ + CO	$\Delta H°$ = − (−39 kJ)
3 Fe$_2$O$_3$ + 9 CO → 6 Fe + 9 CO$_2$	$\Delta H°$ = 3(−23 kJ)

6 FeO(s) + 6 CO(g) → 6 Fe(s) + 6 CO$_2$(g) $\Delta H°$ = −66 kJ

So for: FeO(s) + CO(g) → Fe(s) + CO$_2$(g) $\Delta H° = \dfrac{-66\ kJ}{6} = -11$ kJ

91.   a. $\Delta H°$ = 3 mol (227 kJ/mol) − 1 mol (49 kJ/mol) = 632 kJ

b.   Since 3 C$_2$H$_2$(g) is higher in energy than C$_6$H$_6$(l), acetylene will release more energy per gram when burned in air.

92.
$$I(g) + Cl(g) \rightarrow ICl(g) \qquad \Delta H = -(211.3 \text{ kJ})$$
$$1/2 \ Cl_2(g) \rightarrow Cl(g) \qquad \Delta H = 1/2(242.3 \text{ kJ})$$
$$1/2 \ I_2(g) \rightarrow I(g) \qquad \Delta H = 1/2(151.0 \text{ kJ})$$
$$1/2 \ I_2(s) \rightarrow 1/2 \ I_2(g) \qquad \Delta H = 1/2(62.8 \text{ kJ})$$

$$1/2 \ I_2(s) + 1/2 \ Cl_2(g) \rightarrow ICl(g) \qquad \Delta H = 16.8 \text{ kJ/mol} = \Delta H^\circ_{f, \ ICl}$$

93. a. $C_2H_4(g) + O_3(g) \rightarrow CH_3CHO(g) + O_2(g)$, $\Delta H^\circ = -166 \text{ kJ} - [143 \text{ kJ} + 52 \text{ kJ}] = -361 \text{ kJ}$

b. $O_3(g) + NO(g) \rightarrow NO_2(g) + O_2(g)$, $\Delta H^\circ = 34 \text{ kJ} - [90. \text{ kJ} + 143 \text{ kJ}] = -199 \text{ kJ}$

c. $SO_3(g) + H_2O(l) \rightarrow H_2SO_4(aq)$, $\Delta H^\circ = -909 \text{ kJ} - [-396 \text{ kJ} + (-286 \text{ kJ})] = -227 \text{ kJ}$

d. $2 \ NO(g) + O_2(g) \rightarrow 2 \ NO_2(g)$, $\Delta H^\circ = 2(34) \text{ kJ} - 2(90.) \text{ kJ} = -112 \text{ kJ}$

Challenge Problems

94.   Only when there is a volume change can PV work be done. In pathway 1 (steps 1 + 2), only the first step does PV work (step 2 has a constant volume of 30.0 L). In pathway 2 (steps 3 + 4), only step 4 does PV work (step 3 has a constant volume of 10.0 L).

Pathway 1: $w = -P\Delta V = -2.00 \text{ atm} (30.0 \text{ L} - 10.0 \text{ L}) = -40.0 \text{ L atm} \times \dfrac{101.3 \text{ J}}{\text{L atm}}$
$$= -4.05 \times 10^3 \text{ J}$$

Pathway 2: $w = -P\Delta V = -1.00 \text{ atm} (30.0 \text{ L} - 10.0 \text{ L}) = -20.0 \text{ L atm} \times \dfrac{101.3 \text{ J}}{\text{L atm}}$
$$= -2.03 \times 10^3 \text{ J}$$

Note: The sign is (−) because the system is doing work on the surroundings (an expansion).

We get different values of work for the two pathways; both pathways have the same initial and final states. Because w depends on the pathway, work cannot be a state function.

95.   a. $C_{12}H_{22}O_{11}(s) + 12 \ O_2(g) \rightarrow 12 \ CO_2(g) + 11 \ H_2O(l)$

b.   A bomb calorimeter is at constant volume, so heat released = $q_v = \Delta E$:

$$\Delta E = \frac{-24.00 \text{ kJ}}{1.46 \text{ g}} \times \frac{342.30 \text{ g}}{\text{mol}} = -5630 \text{ kJ/mol } C_{12}H_{22}O_{11}$$

c. $PV = nRT$; At constant P and T, $P\Delta V = RT\Delta n$ where Δn = mol gaseous products − mol gaseous reactants.

$$\Delta H = \Delta E + P\Delta V = \Delta E + RT\Delta n$$

For this reaction, $\Delta n = 12 - 12 = 0$, so $\Delta H = \Delta E = -5630 \text{ kJ/mol}$.

96.   Energy needed = $\dfrac{20.\times10^3 \text{ g C}_{12}\text{H}_{22}\text{O}_{11}}{\text{hr}} \times \dfrac{1 \text{ mol C}_{12}\text{H}_{22}\text{O}_{11}}{342.30 \text{ g C}_{12}\text{H}_{22}\text{O}_{11}} \times \dfrac{5640 \text{ kJ}}{\text{mol}} = 3.3 \times 10^5 \text{ kJ/hr}$

Energy from sun = 1.0 kW/m^2 = 1000 W/m^2 = $\dfrac{1000 \text{ J}}{\text{s m}^2} = \dfrac{1.0 \text{ kJ}}{\text{s m}^2}$

$10{,}000 \text{ m}^2 \times \dfrac{1.0 \text{ kJ}}{\text{s m}^2} \times \dfrac{60 \text{ s}}{\text{min}} \times \dfrac{60 \text{ min}}{\text{hr}} = 3.6 \times 10^7 \text{ kJ/hr}$

% efficiency = $\dfrac{\text{Energy used per hour}}{\text{Total energy per hour}} \times 100 = \dfrac{3.3 \times 10^5 \text{ kJ}}{3.6 \times 10^7 \text{ kJ}} = 0.92\%$

97.   Energy used in 8.0 hours = 40. kWh = $\dfrac{40.0 \text{ kJ hr}}{\text{s}} \times \dfrac{3600 \text{ s}}{\text{hr}} = 1.4 \times 10^5 \text{ kJ}$

Energy from the sun in 8.0 hours = $\dfrac{1.0 \text{ kJ}}{\text{s m}^2} \times \dfrac{60 \text{ s}}{\text{min}} \times \dfrac{60 \text{ min}}{\text{hr}} \times 8.0 \text{ hr} = 2.9 \times 10^4 \text{ kJ/m}^2$

Only 13% of the sunlight is converted into electricity:

$0.13 \times (2.9 \times 10^4 \text{ kJ/m}^2) \times \text{Area} = 1.4 \times 10^5 \text{ kJ}, \quad \text{Area} = 37 \text{ m}^2$

98.   a. $2 \text{ HNO}_3(aq) + \text{Na}_2\text{CO}_3(s) \rightarrow 2 \text{ NaNO}_3(aq) + \text{H}_2\text{O}(l) + \text{CO}_2(g)$

$\Delta H° = [2(-467 \text{ kJ}) + (-286 \text{ kJ}) + (-393.5 \text{ kJ})] - [2(-207 \text{ kJ}) + (-1131 \text{ kJ})] = -69 \text{ kJ}$

$2.0 \times 10^4 \text{ gallons} \times \dfrac{4 \text{ qt}}{\text{gal}} \times \dfrac{946 \text{ mL}}{\text{qt}} \times \dfrac{1.42 \text{ g}}{\text{mL}} = 1.1 \times 10^8 \text{ g of concentrated nitric}$
acid solution

$1.1 \times 10^8 \text{ g solution} \times \dfrac{70.0 \text{ g HNO}_3}{100.0 \text{ g solution}} = 7.7 \times 10^7 \text{ g HNO}_3$

$7.7 \times 10^7 \text{ g HNO}_3 \times \dfrac{1 \text{ mol}}{63.02 \text{ g}} \times \dfrac{1 \text{ mol Na}_2\text{CO}_3}{2 \text{ mol HNO}_3} \times \dfrac{105.99 \text{ g Na}_2\text{CO}_3}{\text{mol Na}_2\text{CO}_3}$
$= 6.5 \times 10^7 \text{ g Na}_2\text{CO}_3$

There are $(7.7 \times 10^7/63.02)$ mol of HNO$_3$ from the previous calculation. There are 69 kJ of heat evolved for every two moles of nitric acid neutralized. Combining these two results:

$7.7 \times 10^7 \text{ g HNO}_3 \times \dfrac{1 \text{ mol HNO}_3}{63.02 \text{ g HNO}_3} \times \dfrac{-69 \text{ kJ}}{2 \text{ mol HNO}_3} = -4.2 \times 10^7 \text{ kJ}$

b.   They feared the heat generated by the neutralization reaction would vaporize the unreacted nitric acid, causing widespread airborne contamination.

99. $$400 \text{ kcal} \times \frac{4.18 \text{ kJ}}{\text{kcal}} = 1.7 \times 10^3 \text{ kJ} \approx 2 \times 10^3 \text{ kJ}$$

$$PE = mgz = \left(180 \text{ lb} \times \frac{1 \text{ kg}}{2.205 \text{ lb}}\right) \times \frac{9.81 \text{ m}}{\text{s}^2} \times \left(8 \text{ in} \times \frac{2.54 \text{ cm}}{\text{in}} \times \frac{1 \text{ m}}{100 \text{ cm}}\right) = 160 \text{ J} \approx 200 \text{ J}$$

200 J of energy are needed to climb one step. The total number of steps to climb are:

$$2 \times 10^6 \text{ J} \times \frac{1 \text{ step}}{200 \text{ J}} = 1 \times 10^4 \text{ steps}$$

100. $H_2(g) + 1/2 \, O_2(g) \rightarrow H_2O(l) \quad \Delta H^\circ = \Delta H^\circ_{f, H_2O(l)} = -285.8 \text{ kJ}$; We want the reverse reaction:

$$H_2O(l) \rightarrow H_2(g) + 1/2 \, O_2(g) \quad \Delta H^\circ = 285.8 \text{ kJ}$$

$w = -P\Delta V$; Because $PV = nRT$, at constant T and P, $P\Delta V = RT\Delta n$ where $\Delta n = \text{mol gaseous}$ products – mol gaseous reactants. Here, $\Delta n = (1 \text{ mol } H_2 + 0.5 \text{ mol } O_2) - (0) = 1.5 \text{ mol}$

$$\Delta E^\circ = \Delta H^\circ - P\Delta V = \Delta H^\circ - \Delta nRT$$

$$\Delta E^\circ = 285.8 \text{ kJ} - 1.50 \text{ mol} \times 8.3145 \text{ J/mol} \cdot \text{K} \times 298 \text{ K} \times \frac{1 \text{ kJ}}{1000 \text{ J}}$$

$$\Delta E^\circ = 285.8 \text{ kJ} - 3.72 \text{ kJ} = 282.1 \text{ kJ}$$

101. There are five parts to this problem. We need to calculate:

1. q required to heat $H_2O(s)$ from $-30.\degree C$ to $0\degree C$; use the specific heat capacity of $H_2O(s)$

2. q required to convert 1 mol $H_2O(s)$ at $0\degree C$ into 1 mol $H_2O(l)$ at $0\degree C$; use ΔH_{fusion}

3. q required to heat $H_2O(l)$ from $0\degree C$ to $100.\degree C$; use the specific heat capacity of $H_2O(l)$

4. q required to convert 1 mol $H_2O(l)$ at $100.\degree C$ into 1 mol $H_2O(g)$ at $100.\degree C$; use $\Delta H_{vaporization}$

5. q required to heat $H_2O(g)$ from $100.\degree C$ to $140.\degree C$; use the specific heat capacity of $H_2O(g)$

We will sum up the heat required for all five parts and this will be the total amount of heat required to convert 1.00 mol of $H_2O(s)$ at $-30.\degree C$ to $H_2O(g)$ at $140.\degree C$. ($q_{total} = q_1 + q_2 + q_3 + q_4 + q_5$). The molar mass of H_2O is 18.02 g/mol.

$$q_1 = 2.03 \text{ J/}\degree C \cdot g \times 18.02 \text{ g} \times [0 - (-30.)]\degree C = 1.1 \times 10^3 \text{ J}$$

$$q_2 = 1.00 \text{ mol} \times 6.02 \times 10^3 \text{ J/mol} = 6.02 \times 10^3 \text{ J}$$

$$q_3 = 4.18 \text{ J/}\degree C \cdot g \times 18.02 \text{ g} \times (100. - 0)\degree C = 7.53 \times 10^3 \text{ J}$$

$$q_4 = 1.00 \text{ mol} \times 40.7 \times 10^4 \text{ J/mol} = 4.07 \times 10^4 \text{ J}$$

$$q_5 = 2.02 \text{ J/}°\text{C}\bullet\text{g} \times 18.02 \text{ g} \times (140. - 100.) = 1.5 \times 10^3 \text{ J}$$

$$q_{\text{total}} = q_1 + q_2 + q_3 + q_4 + q_5 = 5.68 \times 10^4 \text{ J} = 56.9 \text{ kJ}$$

102.   When a mixture of ice and water exists, the temperature of the mixture remains at 0°C until all of the ice has melted. Because an ice water mixture exists at the end of the process, the temperature remains at 0°C. All of the energy released by the element goes to convert ice into water. The energy required to do this is related to $\Delta H_{\text{fusion}} = 6.02 \text{ kJ/mol}$ (from Exercise 101).

heat loss by element = heat gain by ice cubes at 0°C

$$\text{heat gain} = 109.5 \text{ g H}_2\text{O} \times \frac{1 \text{ mol H}_2\text{O}}{18.02 \text{ g}} \times \frac{6.02 \text{ kJ}}{\text{mol H}_2\text{O}} = 36.6 \text{ kJ}$$

$$\text{specific heat of element} = \frac{q}{\text{mass} \times \Delta T} = \frac{36,600 \text{ J}}{500.0 \text{ g} \times (195 - 0)°\text{C}} = 0.375 \text{ J/}°\text{C}\bullet\text{g}$$

Integrative Problems

103. $$N_2(g) + 2 O_2(g) \rightarrow 2 NO_2(g) \qquad \Delta H = 67.7 \text{ kJ}$$

$$n_{N_2} = \frac{PV}{RT} = \frac{3.50 \text{ atm} \times 0.250 \text{ L}}{\dfrac{0.08206 \times \text{L atm}}{\text{mol K}} \times 373 \text{ K}} = 2.86 \times 10^{-2} \text{ mol N}_2$$

$$n_{O_2} = \frac{PV}{RT} = \frac{3.50 \text{ atm} \times 0.450 \text{ L}}{\dfrac{0.08206 \times \text{L atm}}{\text{mol K}} \times 373 \text{ K}} = 5.15 \times 10^{-2} \text{ mol O}_2$$

The balanced equation requires a 2:1 O_2 to N_2 mole ratio. The actual mole ratio is $5.15 \times 10^{-2} / 2.86 \times 10^{-2} = 1.80$; Because the actual mole ratio < required mole ratio, O_2 in the numerator is limiting.

$$5.15 \times 10^{-2} \text{ mol O}_2 \times \frac{2 \text{ mol NO}_2}{2 \text{ mol O}_2} = 5.15 \times 10^{-2} \text{ mol NO}_2$$

$$5.15 \times 10^{-2} \text{ mol NO}_2 \times \frac{67.7 \text{ kJ}}{2 \text{ mol NO}_2} = 1.74 \text{ kJ}$$

104.   a. $4 CH_3NO_2(l) + 3 O_2(g) \rightarrow 4 CO_2(g) + 2 N_2(g) + 6 H_2O(g)$

$$\Delta H^°_{\text{rxn}} = -1288.5 \text{ kJ} = [4 \text{ mol}(-393.5 \text{ kJ/mol}) + 6 \text{ mol}(-242 \text{ kJ/mol})] -$$

$$[4 \text{ mol}(\Delta H^°_{f, CH_3NO_2})]$$

Solving: $\Delta H^°_{f, CH_3NO_2} = -434 \text{ kJ/mol}$

b. $P_{tot} = 950.$ torr $\times \dfrac{1\,atm}{760\,torr} = 1.25$ atm; $P_{N_2} = P_{tot} \times \chi_{N_2} = 1.25$ atm $\times 0.134$

$$= 0.168\,atm$$

$$n_{N_2} = \dfrac{0.168\,atm \times 15.0\,L}{\dfrac{0.08206\,L\,atm}{mol\,K} \times 373\,K} = 0.0823\,mol\,N_2$$

$$0.0823\,mol\,N_2 \times \dfrac{28.02\,g\,N_2}{1\,mol\,N_2} = 2.31\,g\,N_2$$

105.   heat loss by U = heat gain by heavy water;   vol of cube = (cube edge)^3

mass of heavy water = 1.00×10^3 mL $\times \dfrac{1.11\,g}{mL} = 1110$ g

heat gain by heavy water = $\dfrac{4.211\,J}{g\,°C} \times 1110$ g $\times (28.5 - 25.5)°C = 1.4 \times 10^4$ J

heat loss by U = 1.4×10^4 J = $\dfrac{0.117\,J}{g\,°C} \times$ mass $\times (200.0 - 28.5)°C$,   mass = 7.0×10^2 g U

7.0×10^2 g U $\times \dfrac{1\,cm^3}{19.05\,g} = 37$ cm^3;   cube edge = $(37\,cm^3)^{1/3} = 3.3$ cm

Marathon Problems

106. $X \rightarrow CO_2(g) + H_2O(l) + O_2(g) + A(g)$ $\Delta H = -1893$ kJ/mol   (unbalanced)

To determine X, we must determine the moles of X reacted, the identity of A and the moles of A produced. For the reaction at constant P ($\Delta H = q$):

$$-q_{H_2O} = q_{rxn} = -4.184\,J/°C \cdot g \times 1.000 \times 10^4\,g \times (29.52 - 25.00)\,°C \times 1\,kJ/1000\,J$$

$q_{rxn} = -189.1$ kJ (carrying extra sig. figs.)

Since $\Delta H = -1893$ kJ/mol for the decomposition reaction and since only -189.1 kJ of heat was released for this reaction, then 189.1 kJ $\times$ 1 mol X/1893 kJ = 0.100 mol X was reacted.

Molar mass of X = $\dfrac{22.7\,g\,X}{0.100\,mol\,X} = 227$ g/mol

From the problem, 0.100 mol X produced 0.300 mol CO_2, 0.250 mol H_2O and 0.025 mol O_2. Therefore, 1.00 mol X produces 3.00 mol CO_2, 2.50 mol H_2O and 0.25 mol O_2.

$$1.00 \text{ mol X} = 227 \text{ g} = 3.00 \text{ mol CO}_2 \left(\frac{44.01 \text{ g}}{\text{mol}} \right) + 2.50 \text{ mol H}_2\text{O} \left(\frac{18.02 \text{ g}}{\text{mol}} \right)$$

$$+ 0.25 \text{ mol} \left(\frac{32.00 \text{ g}}{\text{mol}} \right) + (\text{mass of A})$$

mass of A in 1.00 mol X = 227 g − 132.0 g − 45.05 g − 8.00 g = 42 g A

To determine A, we need the moles of A produced. The total moles of gases produced can be determined from the gas law data provided in the problem. Since $H_2O(l)$ is a product, we need to subtract P_{H_2O} (the vapor pressure of H_2O) from the total pressure.

$$n_{total} = \frac{PV}{RT} ; \quad P_{total} = P_{gases} + P_{H_2O} , \quad P_{gases} = 778 \text{ torr} - 31 \text{ torr} = 747 \text{ torr}$$

$$V = \text{height} \times \text{area}; \quad \text{area} = \pi r^2; \quad V = 59.8 \text{ cm } (\pi) (8.00 \text{ cm})^2 \left(\frac{1 \text{ L}}{1000 \text{ cm}^3} \right) = 12.0 \text{ L}$$

T = 273.15 + 29.52 = 302.67 K

$$n_{total} = \frac{PV}{RT} = \frac{\left(747 \text{ torr} \times \dfrac{1 \text{ atm}}{760 \text{ torr}} \right) \times 12.0 \text{ L}}{\dfrac{0.08206 \text{ L atm}}{\text{K mol}} \times 302.67 \text{ K}} = 0.475 \text{ mol} = \text{mol CO}_2 + \text{mol O}_2 + \text{mol A}$$

mol A = 0.475 mol − 0.300 mol CO_2 − 0.025 mol O_2 = 0.150 mol A

Since 0.100 mol X reacted, then 1.00 mol X would produce 1.50 mol A which from a previous calculation represents 42 g A.

$$\text{Molar mass of A} = \frac{42 \text{ g A}}{1.50 \text{ mol A}} = 28 \text{ g/mol}$$

Since A is a gaseous element, the only element that is a gas and has this molar mass is $N_2(g)$. Thus, A = $N_2(g)$

a.   Now we can determine the formula of X.

   X → 3 $CO_2(g)$ + 2.5 $H_2O(l)$ + 0.25 $O_2(g)$ + 1.5 $N_2(g)$. For a balanced reaction, X = $C_3H_5N_3O_9$, which, for your information, is nitroglycerine.

b. $w = -P\Delta V = -778 \text{ torr} \times \dfrac{1 \text{ atm}}{760 \text{ torr}} \times (12.0 \text{ L} - 0) = -12.3 \text{ L atm}$

   $-12.3 \text{ L atm} \times \dfrac{101.3 \text{ J}}{\text{L atm}} = -1250 \text{ J} = -1.25 \text{ kJ}, \quad w = -1.25 \text{ kJ}$

c. $\Delta E = q + w$, where $q = \Delta H$ since at constant pressure. For 1 mol of X decomposed:

$$w = -1.25 \text{ kJ}/0.100 \text{ mol} = -12.5 \text{ kJ/mol}; \quad \Delta E = \Delta H - P\Delta V \text{ and } w = -P\Delta V$$

$$\Delta E = \Delta H + w = -1893 \text{ kJ/mol} + (-12.5 \text{ kJ/mol}) = -1906 \text{ kJ/mol}$$

ΔH_f^o for $C_3H_5N_3O_9$ can be estimated from standard enthalpies of formation data and assuming $\Delta H_{rxn} = \Delta H_{rxn}^o$. For the balanced reaction given in part a:

$$\Delta H_{rxn}^o = -1893 \text{ kJ} = [3 \, \Delta H_{f,CO_2}^o + 2.5 \, \Delta H_{f,H_2O}^o] - [\Delta H_{f,C_3H_5N_3O_9}^o]$$

$$-1893 \text{ kJ} = [3 \, (-393.5) \text{ kJ} + 2.5 \, (-286) \text{ kJ}] - \Delta H_{f,C_3H_5N_3O_9}^o$$

$$\Delta H_{f,C_3H_5N_3O_9}^o = -2.5 \text{ kJ/mol} = -3 \text{ kJ/mol}$$

107. $C_xH_y + \left(\dfrac{2x + y/2}{2}\right) O_2 \rightarrow x \, CO_2 + y/2 \, H_2O$

$$[-393.5x + y/2 \, (-242)] - \Delta H_{C_xH_y}^o = -2044.5, \quad -393.5x - 121y - \Delta H_{C_xH_y} = -2044.5$$

$$d_{gas} = \frac{P \bullet MM}{RT} \quad \text{where MM = average molar mass of } CO_2/H_2O \text{ mixture}$$

$$0.751 \text{ g/L} = \frac{1.00 \text{ atm} \times MM}{\dfrac{0.08206 \text{ L atm}}{K \text{ mol}} \times 473 \text{ K}}, \quad MM \text{ of } CO_2/H_2O \text{ mixture = 29.1 g/mol}$$

Let a = mol CO_2 and 1.00 − a = mol H_2O (assuming 1.00 total mol of mixture)

44.01 a + (1.00 − a) × 18.02 = 29.1; Solving: a = 0.426 mol CO_2 , mol H_2O = 0.574

Thus: $\dfrac{0.574}{0.426} = \dfrac{\frac{y}{2}}{x}, \dfrac{y}{x} = 2.69, \ y = 2.69 \ x$

For whole numbers, multiply by three which gives y = 8, x = 3. Note that y = 16, x = 6 is possible, along with other combinations. Because the hydrocarbon has a lower density than Kr, the molar mass of C_xH_y must be less than the molar mass of Kr (83.80 g/mol). Only C_3H_8 works.

$$-2044.5 = -393.5(3) - 121(8) - \Delta H_{C_3H_8}^o, \ \Delta H_{C_3H_8}^o = -104 \text{ kJ/mol}$$

CHAPTER SEVEN

ATOMIC STRUCTURE AND PERIODICITY

For Review

1. Wavelength: the distance between two consecutive peaks or troughs in a wave

   Frequency: the number of waves (cycles) per second that pass a given point in space

   Photon energy: the discrete units by which all electromagnetic radiation transmits energy; EMR can be viewed as a stream of "particles" called photons. Each photon has a unique quantum of energy associated with it; the photon energy is determined by the frequency (or wavelength) of the specific EMR.

   Speed of travel: all electromagnetic radiation travels at the same speed, c, the speed of light; $c = 2.9979 \times 10^8$ m/s

   $\lambda\nu = c$, $E = h\nu = hc/\lambda$: From these equations, wavelength and frequency are inversely related, photon energy and frequency are directly related, and photon energy and wavelength are inversely related. Thus, the EMR with the longest wavelength has the lowest frequency and least energetic photons. The EMR with the shortest wavelength has the highest frequency and most energetic photons. Using Figure 7.2 to determine the wavelengths, the order is:

   wavelength: gamma rays < ultraviolet < visible < microwaves

   frequency: microwaves < visible < ultraviolet < gamma rays

   photon energy: microwaves < visible < ultraviolet < gamma rays

   speed: all travel at the same speed, c, the speed of light

2. The Bohr model assumes that the electron in hydrogen can orbit the nucleus at specific distances from the nucleus. Each orbit has a specific energy associated with it. Therefore, the electron in hydrogen can only have specific energies; not all energies are allowed. The term quantized refers to the allowed energy levels for the electron in hydrogen.

   The great success of the Bohr model is that it could explain the hydrogen emission spectrum. The electron in H, moves about the allowed energy levels by absorbing or emitting certain photons of energy. The photon energies absorbed or emitted must be exactly equal to the energy difference between any two allowed energy levels. Because not all energies are allowed in hydrogen (energy is quantized), then not all energies of EMR are absorbed/emitted.

The Bohr model predicted the exact wavelengths of light that would be emitted for a hydrogen atom. Although the Bohr model has great success for hydrogen and other 1 electron ions, it does not explain emission spectra for elements/ions having more than one electron. The fundamental flaw is that we cannot know the exact motion of an electron as it moves about the nucleus; therefore, well defined circular orbits are not appropriate.

3. Planck's discovery that heated bodies give off only certain frequencies of light and Einstein's study of the photoelectric effect support the quantum theory of light. The wave-particle duality is summed up by saying all matter exhibits both particulate and wave properties. Electromagnetic radiation, which was thought to be a pure waveform, transmits energy as if it has particulate properties. Conversely, electrons, which were thought to be particles, have a wavelength associated with them. This is true for all matter. Some evidence supporting wave properties of matter are:

    1. Electrons can be diffracted like light.

    2. The electron microscope uses electrons in a fashion similar to the way in which light is used in a light microscope.

    However, wave properties of matter are only important for small particles with a tiny mass, e.g., electrons. The wave properties of larger particles are not significant.

4. Four scientists whose work was extremely important to the development of the quantum mechanical model were Niels Bohr, Louis deBroglie, Werner Heisenberg, and Erwin Schrödinger. The Bohr model of the atom presented the idea of quantized energy levels for electrons in atoms. DeBroglie came up with the relationship between mass and wavelength, supporting the idea that all matter (especially tiny particles like electrons) exhibits wave properties as well as the classic properties of matter. Heisenberg is best known for his uncertainty principle which states there is a fundamental limitation to just how precisely we can know both the position and the momentum of a particle at a given time. If we know one quantity accurately, we cannot absolutely determine the other. The uncertainty principle, when applied to electrons, forbids well-defined circular orbits for the electron in hydrogen, as presented in the Bohr model. When we talk about the location of an electron, we can only talk about the probability of where the electron is located. Schrödinger put the ideas presented by the scientists of the day into a mathematical equation. He assumed wave motion for the electron. The solutions to this complicated mathematical equation give allowed energy levels for the electrons. These solutions are called wave functions, ψ, and the allowed energy levels are often referred to as orbitals. In addition, the square of the wave function (ψ^2) indicates the probability of finding an electron near a particular point in space. When we talk about the shape of an orbital, we are talking about a surface that encompasses where the electron is located 90% of the time. The key is we can only talk about probabilities when referencing electron location.

5. Quantum numbers give the allowed solutions to Schrödinger equation. Each solution is an allowed energy level called a wave function or an orbital. Each wave function solution is described by three quantum numbers, n, ℓ, and m_ℓ. The physical significance of the quantum numbers are:

    n: Gives the energy (it completely specifies the energy only for the H atom or ions with one electron) and the relative size of the orbitals.

ℓ: Gives the type (shape) of orbital.

m_ℓ: Gives information about the direction in which the orbital is pointing.

The specific rules for assigning values to the quantum numbers n, ℓ, and m_ℓ are covered in Section 7.6. In Section 7.8, the spin quantum number m_s is discussed. Since we cannot locate electrons, we cannot see if they are spinning. The spin is a convenient model. It refers to the ability of the two electrons that can occupy any specific orbital to produce two different oriented magnetic moments.

6.   The 2p orbitals differ from each other in the direction in which they point in space. The 2p and 3p orbitals differ from each other in their size, energy and number of nodes. A nodal surface in an atomic orbital is a surface in which the probability of finding an electron is zero.

The 1p, 1d, 2d, 1f, 2f, and 3f orbitals are not allowed solutions to the Schrödinger equation. For n = 1, $\ell \neq$ 1, 2, 3, etc., so 1p, 1d, and 1f orbitals are forbidden. For n = 2, $\ell \neq$ 2, 3, 4, etc., so 2d and 2f orbitals are forbidden. For n = 3, $\ell \neq$ 3, 4, 5, etc., so 3f orbitals are forbidden.

The penetrating term refers to the fact that there is a higher probability of finding a 4s electron closer to the nucleus than a 3d electron. This leads to a lower energy for the 4s orbital relative to the 3d orbitals in polyelectronic atoms and ions.

7.   The four blocks are the s, p, d, and f blocks. The s block contains the alkali and alkaline earth metals (Groups 1A and 2A). The p block contains the elements in Groups 3A, 4A, 5A, 6A, 7A, and 8A. The d block contains the transition metals. The f block contains the inner transition metals. The energy ordering is obtained by sequentially following the atomic numbers of the elements through the periodic table while keeping track of the various blocks you are transversing. The periodic table method for determining energy ordering is illustrated in Figure 7.27.

The Aufbau principle states that as protons are added one by one to the nucleus to build up the elements, electrons are similarly added to hydrogenlike orbitals. The main assumptions are that all atoms have the same types of orbitals and that the most stable electron configuration, the ground state, has the electrons occupying the lowest energy levels first. Hund's rule refers to adding electrons to degenerate (same energy) orbitals. The rule states that the lowest energy configuration for an atom is the one having the maximum number of unpaired electrons allowed by the Pauli exclusion principle. The Pauli exclusion principle states that in a given atom, no two electrons can have the same four quantum numbers. This corresponds to having only two electrons in any one orbital and they must have opposite "spins".

The two major exceptions to the predicted electron configurations for elements 1-36 are Cr and Cu. The expected electron configurations for each are:

Cr: [Ar]$4s^2 3d^4$ and Cu: [Ar]$4s^2 3d^9$

The actual electron configurations are:

Cr: [Ar]$4s^1 3d^5$ and Cu: [Ar]$4s^1 3d^{10}$

8.   Valence electrons are the electrons in the outermost principle quantum level of an atom (those electrons in the highest n value orbitals). The electrons in the lower n value orbitals are all inner core or just core electrons. The key is that the outer most electrons are the valence electrons. When atoms interact with each other, it will be the outermost electrons that are involved in these interactions. In addition, how tightly the nucleus holds these outermost electrons determines atomic size, ionization energy and other properties of atoms. Elements in the same group have similar valence electron configurations and, as a result, have similar chemical properties.

9.   Ionization energy: $P(g) \rightarrow P^+(g) + e^-$; electron affinity: $P(g) + e^- \rightarrow P^-(g)$

Across a period, the positive charge from the nucleus increases as protons are added. The number of electrons also increase, but these outer electrons do not completely shield the increasing nuclear charge from each other. The general result is that the outer electrons are more strongly bound as one goes across a period which results in larger ionization energies (and smaller size).

Aluminum is out of order because the electrons in the filled 3s orbital shield some of the nuclear charge from the 3p electron. Hence, the 3p electron is less tightly bound than a 3s electron, resulting in a lower ionization energy for aluminum as compared to magnesium. The ionization energy of sulfur is lower than phosphorus because of the extra electron-electron repulsions in the doubly occupied sulfur 3p orbital. These added repulsions, which are not present in phosphorus, make it slightly easier to remove an electron from sulfur as compared to phosphorus.

As successive electrons are removed, the net positive charge on the resultant ion increases. This increase in positive charge binds the remaining electrons more firmly, and the ionization energy increases.

The electron configuration for Si is $1s^2 2s^2 2p^6 3s^2 3p^2$. There is a large jump in ionization energy when going from the removal of valence electrons to the removal of core electrons. For silicon, this occurs when the fifth electron is removed since we go from the valence electrons in $n = 3$ to the core electrons in $n = 2$. There should be another big jump when the thirteenth electron is removed, i.e., when a 1s electron is removed.

10.   Both trends are a function of how tightly the outermost electrons are held by the positive charge in the nucleus. An atom where the outermost electrons are held tightly will have a small radius and a large ionization energy. Conversely, an atom where the outermost electrons are held weakly will have a large radius and a small ionization energy. The trends of radius and ionization energy should be opposite of each other.

Electron affinity is the energy change associated with the addition of an electron to a gaseous atom. Ionization energy is the energy it takes to remove an electron from a gaseous atom. Because electrons are always attracted to the positive charge of the nucleus, energy will always have to be added to break the attraction and remove the electron from a neutral charged atom. Ionization energies are always endothermic for neutral charged atoms. Adding an electron is more complicated. The added electron will be attracted to the nucleus; this attraction results in energy being released. However, the added electron will encounter the other electrons which results in electron-electron repulsions; energy must be added to overcome these repulsions. Which of the two opposing factors dominates determines whether the overall electron affinity for an element is exothermic or endothermic.

Questions

15.   The equations relating the terms are $v\lambda = c$, $E = hv$, and $E = hc/\lambda$. From the equations, wavelength and frequency are inversely related, photon energy and frequency are directly related, and photon energy and wavelength are inversely related. The unit of 1 Joule (J) = 1 kg m^2/s^2. This is why you must change mass units to kg when using the deBroglie equation.

16.   The photoelectric effect refers to the phenomenon in which electrons are emitted from the surface of a metal when light strikes it. The light must have a certain minimum frequency (energy) in order to remove electrons from the surface of a metal. Light having a frequency below the minimum results in no electrons being emitted, while light at or higher than the minimum frequency does cause electrons to be emitted. For light having a frequency higher than the minimum frequency, the excess energy is transferred into kinetic energy for the emitted electron. Albert Einstein explained the photoelectric effect by applying quantum theory.

17.   Sample Exercise 7.3 calculates the deBroglie wavelength of a ball and of an electron. The ball has a wavelength on the order of 10^{-34} m. This is incredibly short and, as far as the wave-particle duality is concerned, the wave properties of large objects are insignificant. The electron, with its tiny mass, also has a short wavelength; on the order of 10^{-10} m. However, this wavelength is significant as it is on the same order as the spacing between atoms in a typical crystal. For very tiny objects like electrons, the wave properties are important. The wave properties must be considered, along with the particle properties, when hypothesizing about the electron motion in an atom.

18.   The Bohr model was an important step in the development of the current quantum mechanical model of the atom. The idea that electrons can only occupy certain, allowed energy levels is illustrated nicely (and relatively easily). We talk about the Bohr model to present the idea of quantized energy levels.

19.   For the radial probability distribution, the space around the hydrogen nucleus is cut-up into a series of thin spherical shells. When the total probability of finding the electron in each spherical shell is plotted versus the distance from the nucleus, we get the radial probability distribution graph. The plot initially shows a steady increase with distance from the nucleus, reaches a maximum, then shows a steady decrease. Even though it is likely to find an electron near the nucleus, the volume of the spherical shell close to the nucleus is tiny, resulting in a low radial probability. The maximum radial probability distribution occurs at a distance of 5.29×10^{-2} nm from the nucleus; the electron is most likely to be found in the volume of the shell centered at this distance from the nucleus. The 5.29×10^{-2} nm distance is the exact radius of innermost ($n = 1$) orbit in the Bohr model.

20.   The width of the various blocks in the periodic table is determined by the number of electrons that can occupy the specific orbital(s). In the s block, we have 1 orbital ($\ell = 0$, $m_\ell = 0$) which can hold two electrons; the s block is 2 elements wide. For the f block, there are 7 degenerate f orbitals ($\ell = 3$, $m_\ell = -3, -2, -1, 0, 1, 2, 3$), so the f block is 14 elements wide. The g block

corresponds to $\ell = 4$. The number of degenerate g orbitals is 9. This comes from the 9 possible m_ℓ values when $\ell = 4$ ($m_\ell = -4, -3, -2, -1, 0, 1, 2, 3, 4$). With 9 orbitals, each orbital holding two electrons, the g block would be 18 elements wide. The h block has $\ell = 5$, $m_\ell = -5, -4, -3, -2, -1, 0, 1, 2, 3, 4, 5$. With 11 degenerate h orbitals, the h block would be 22 elements wide.

21.   If one more electron is added to a half-filled subshell, electron-electron repulsions will increase since two electrons must now occupy the same atomic orbital. This may slightly decrease the stability of the atom. Hence, half-filled subshells minimize electron-electron repulsions.

22.   Size decreases from left to right and increases going down the periodic table. So, going one element right and one element down would result in a similar size for the two elements diagonal to each other. The ionization energies will be similar for the diagonal elements since the periodic trends also oppose each other. Electron affinities are harder to predict, but atoms with similar size and ionization energy should also have similar electron affinities.

23.   The valence electrons are strongly attracted to the nucleus for elements with large ionization energies. One would expect these species to readily accept another electron and have very exothermic electron affinities. The noble gases are an exception; they have a large IE but have an endothermic EA. Noble gases have a stable arrangement of electrons. Adding an electron disrupts this stable arrangement, resulting in unfavorable electron affinities.

24.   Electron-electron repulsions become more important when we try to add electrons to an atom. From the standpoint of electron-electron repulsions, larger atoms would have more favorable (more exothermic) electron affinities. Considering only electron-nucleus attractions, smaller atoms would be expected to have the more favorable (more exothermic) EA's. These trends are exactly the opposite of each other. Thus, the overall variation in EA is not as great as ionization energy in which attractions to the nucleus dominate.

25.   For hydrogen and one-electron ions (hydrogenlike ions), all atomic orbitals with the same n value have the same energy. For polyatomic atoms/ions, the energy of the atomic orbitals also depends on ℓ. Because there are more nondegenerate energy levels for polyatomic atoms/ions as compared to hydrogen, there are many more possible electronic transitions resulting in more complicated line spectra.

26.   Each element has a characteristic spectrum because each element has unique energy levels. Thus, the presence of the characteristic spectral lines of an element confirms its presence in any particular sample.

27.   Yes, the maximum number of unpaired electrons in any configuration corresponds to a minimum in electron-electron repulsions.

28.   The electron is no longer part of that atom. The proton and electron are completely separated.

29.   Ionization energy is for removal of the electron from the atom in the gas phase. The work function is for the removal of an electron from the solid.

   $M(g) \rightarrow M^+(g) + e^-$ ionization energy; $M(s) \rightarrow M^+(s) + e^-$ work function

30. Li^+ ions are the smallest of the alkali metal cations and will be most strongly attracted to the water molecules.

Exercises

Light and Matter

31. $\nu\lambda = c, \ \nu = \dfrac{c}{\lambda} = \dfrac{2.998\times10^8 \text{ m/s}}{660 \text{ nm}\times\dfrac{1\text{ m}}{1\times10^9 \text{ nm}}} = 4.5\times10^{14} \text{ s}^{-1}$

32. $99.5 \text{ MHz} = 99.5\times10^6 \text{ Hz} = 99.5\times10^6 \text{ s}^{-1}; \ \ \lambda = \dfrac{c}{\nu} = \dfrac{2.998\times10^8 \text{ m/s}}{99.5\times10^6 \text{ s}^{-1}} = 3.01 \text{ m}$

33. $\nu = \dfrac{c}{\lambda} = \dfrac{3.00\times10^8 \text{ m/s}}{1.0\times10^{-2}\text{ m}} = 3.0\times10^{10} \text{ s}^{-1}$

$E = h\nu = 6.63\times10^{-34} \text{ J s}\times3.0\times10^{10} \text{ s}^{-1} = 2.0\times10^{-23} \text{ J/photon}$

$\dfrac{2.0\times10^{-23} \text{ J}}{\text{photon}} \times \dfrac{6.01\times10^{23} \text{ photons}}{\text{mol}} = 12 \text{ J/mol}$

34. $E = h\nu = \dfrac{hc}{\lambda} = \dfrac{6.63\times10^{-34} \text{ J s}\times3.00\times10^8 \text{ m/s}}{25 \text{ nm}\times\dfrac{1\text{ m}}{1\times10^9 \text{ nm}}} = 8.0\times10^{-18} \text{ J/photon}$

$\dfrac{8.0\times10^{-18} \text{ J}}{\text{photon}} \times \dfrac{6.02\times10^{23} \text{ photons}}{\text{mol}} = 4.8\times10^6 \text{ J/mol}$

35.   The wavelength is the distance between consecutive wave peaks. Wave a shows 4 wavelengths and wave b shows 8 wavelengths.

Wave a: $\lambda = \dfrac{1.6\times10^{-3} \text{ m}}{4} = 4.0\times10^{-4} \text{ m}$

Wave b: $\lambda = \dfrac{1.6\times10^{-3} \text{ m}}{8} = 2.0\times10^{-4} \text{ m}$

Wave a has the longer wavelength. Frequency and photon energy are both inversely proportional to wavelength, thus wave b will have the higher frequency and larger photon energy because it has the shorter wavelength.

$\nu = \dfrac{c}{\lambda} = \dfrac{3.00\times10^8 \text{ m/s}}{2.0\times10^{-4} \text{ m}} = 1.5\times10^{12} \text{ s}^{-1}$

$$E = \frac{hc}{\lambda} = \frac{6.63 \times 10^{-34} \text{ J s} \times 3.00 \times 10^8 \text{ m/s}}{2.0 \times 10^{-4} \text{ m}} = 9.9 \times 10^{-22} \text{ J}$$

Both waves are examples of electromagnetic radiation, so both waves travel at the same speed, c, the speed of light. From Figure 7.2 of the text, both of these waves represent infrared electromagnetic radiation.

36.   Referencing figure 7.2 of the text, 2.12×10^{-10} m electromagnetic radiation is X-rays.

$$\lambda = \frac{c}{v} = \frac{2.9979 \times 10^8 \text{ m/s}}{107.1 \times 10^6 \text{ s}^{-1}} = 2.799 \text{ m}$$

From the wavelength calculated above, 107.1 MHz electromagnetic radiation is FM radiowaves.

$$\lambda = \frac{hc}{E} = \frac{6.626 \times 10^{-34} \text{ J s} \times 2.998 \times 10^8 \text{ m/s}}{3.97 \times 10^{-19} \text{ J}} = 5.00 \times 10^{-7} \text{ m}$$

The 3.97×10^{-19} J/photon electromagnetic radiation is visible (green) light.

The photon energy and frequency order will be the exact opposite of the wavelength ordering because E and v are both inversely related to λ. From the calculated wavelengths above, the order of photon energy and frequency are:

FM radiowaves < visible (green) light < X-rays
longest λ shortest λ
lowest v highest v
smallest E   largest E

37. $$E_{photon} = \frac{hc}{\lambda} = \frac{6.626 \times 10^{-34} \text{ J s} \times 2.998 \times 10^8 \text{ m/s}}{150. \text{ nm} \times \dfrac{1 \text{ m}}{1 \times 10^9 \text{ nm}}} = 1.32 \times 10^{-18} \text{ J}$$

$$1.98 \times 10^5 \text{ J} \times \frac{1 \text{ photon}}{1.32 \times 10^{-18} \text{ J}} \times \frac{1 \text{ atom C}}{\text{photon}} = 1.50 \times 10^{23} \text{ atoms C}$$

38.   a. $$\lambda = \frac{c}{v} = \frac{3.00 \times 10^8 \text{ m/s}}{6.0 \times 10^{13} \text{ s}^{-1}} = 5.0 \times 10^{-6} \text{ m}$$

b.   From Figure 7.2, this is infrared EMR.

c. $E = hv = 6.63 \times 10^{-34} \text{ J s} \times 6.0 \times 10^{13} \text{ s}^{-1} = 4.0 \times 10^{-20} \text{ J/photon}$

$$\frac{4.0 \times 10^{-20} \text{ J}}{\text{photon}} \times \frac{6.0221 \times 10^{23} \text{ photons}}{\text{mol}} = 2.4 \times 10^4 \text{ J/mol}$$

d. Frequency and photon energy are directly related (E = hv). Because 5.4×10^{13} s^{-1} EMR has a lower frequency than 6.0×10^{13} s^{-1} EMR, the 5.4×10^{13} s^{-1} EMR will have less energetic photons.

39.   The energy needed to remove a single electron is:

$$\frac{279.7 \text{ kJ}}{\text{mol}} \times \frac{1 \text{ mol}}{6.0221 \times 10^{23}} = 4.645 \times 10^{-22} \text{ kJ} = 4.645 \times 10^{-19} \text{ J}$$

$$E = \frac{hc}{\lambda}, \ \lambda = \frac{hc}{E} = \frac{6.6261 \times 10^{-34} \text{ J s} \times 2.9979 \times 10^{8} \text{ m/s}}{4.645 \times 10^{-19} \text{ J}} = 4.277 \times 10^{-7} \text{ m} = 427.7 \text{ nm}$$

40. $$\frac{208.4 \text{ kJ}}{\text{mol}} \times \frac{1 \text{ mol}}{6.0221 \times 10^{23}} = 3.461 \times 10^{-22} \text{ kJ} = 3.461 \times 10^{-19} \text{ J to remove one electron}$$

$$E = \frac{hc}{\lambda}, \ \lambda = \frac{hc}{E} = \frac{6.6261 \times 10^{-34} \text{ J s} \times 2.9979 \times 10^{8} \text{ m/s}}{3.461 \times 10^{-19} \text{ J}} = 5.739 \times 10^{-7} \text{ m} = 573.9 \text{ nm}$$

41.   a.   10.% of speed of light = $0.10 \times 3.00 \times 10^{8}$ m/s = 3.0×10^{7} m/s

$$\lambda = \frac{h}{mv}, \ \lambda = \frac{6.63 \times 10^{-34} \text{ J s}}{9.11 \times 10^{-31} \text{ kg} \times 3.0 \times 10^{7} \text{ m/s}} = 2.4 \times 10^{-11} \text{ m} = 2.4 \times 10^{-2} \text{ nm}$$

Note: For units to come out, the mass must be in kg since $1 \text{ J} = \dfrac{1 \text{ kg m}^2}{\text{s}^2}$

b. $$\lambda = \frac{h}{mv} = \frac{6.63 \times 10^{-34} \text{ J s}}{0.055 \text{ kg} \times 35 \text{ m/s}} = 3.4 \times 10^{-34} \text{ m} = 3.4 \times 10^{-25} \text{ nm}$$

This number is so small that it is insignificant. We cannot detect a wavelength this small. The meaning of this number is that we do not have to worry about the wave properties of large objects.

42.   a. $$\lambda = \frac{h}{mv} = \frac{6.626 \times 10^{-34} \text{ J s}}{1.675 \times 10^{-27} \text{ kg} \times (0.0100 \times 2.998 \times 10^{8} \text{ m/s})} = 1.32 \times 10^{-13} \text{ m}$$

b. $$\lambda = \frac{h}{mv}, \ v = \frac{h}{\lambda m} = \frac{6.626 \times 10^{-34} \text{ J s}}{75 \times 10^{-12} \text{ m} \times 1.675 \times 10^{-27} \text{ kg}} = 5.3 \times 10^{3} \text{ m/s}$$

43. $$\lambda = \frac{h}{mv}, \ m = \frac{h}{\lambda v} = \frac{6.63 \times 10^{-34} \text{ J s}}{1.5 \times 10^{-15} \text{ m} \times (0.90 \times 3.00 \times 10^{8} \text{ m/s})} = 1.6 \times 10^{-27} \text{ kg}$$

This particle is probably a proton or a neutron.

44. $\lambda = \dfrac{h}{mv}$, $v = \dfrac{h}{\lambda m}$; For $\lambda = 1.0 \times 10^2$ nm $= 1.0 \times 10^{-7}$ m:

$$v = \frac{6.63 \times 10^{-34} \text{ J s}}{9.11 \times 10^{-31} \text{ kg} \times 1.0 \times 10^{-7} \text{ m}} = 7.3 \times 10^3 \text{ m/s}$$

For $\lambda = 1.0$ nm $= 1.0 \times 10^{-9}$ m: $v = \dfrac{6.63 \times 10^{-34} \text{ J s}}{9.11 \times 10^{-31} \text{ kg} \times 1.0 \times 10^{-9} \text{ m}} = 7.3 \times 10^5 \text{ m/s}$

Hydrogen Atom: The Bohr Model

45.   For the H atom (Z = 1): $E_n = -2.178 \times 10^{-18}$ J/n^2; For a spectral transition, $\Delta E = E_f - E_i$:

$$\Delta E = -2.178 \times 10^{-18} \text{ J} \left(\frac{1}{n_f^2} - \frac{1}{n_i^2} \right)$$

where n_i and n_f are the levels of the initial and final states, respectively. A positive value of ΔE always corresponds to an absorption of light, and a negative value of ΔE always corresponds to an emission of light.

a. $\Delta E = -2.178 \times 10^{-18} \text{ J} \left(\dfrac{1}{2^2} - \dfrac{1}{3^2} \right) = -2.178 \times 10^{-18} \text{ J} \left(\dfrac{1}{4} - \dfrac{1}{9} \right)$

$\Delta E = -2.178 \times 10^{-18} \text{ J} \times (0.2500 - 0.1111) = -3.025 \times 10^{-19} \text{ J}$

The photon of light must have precisely this energy (3.025×10^{-19} J).

$|\Delta E| = E_{photon} = h\nu = \dfrac{hc}{\lambda}$ or $\lambda = \dfrac{hc}{|\Delta E|} = \dfrac{6.6261 \times 10^{-34} \text{ J s} \times 2.9979 \times 10^8 \text{ m/s}}{3.025 \times 10^{-19} \text{ J}}$

$$= 6.567 \times 10^{-7} \text{ m} = 656.7 \text{ nm}$$

From Figure 7.2, this is visible electromagnetic radiation (red light).

b. $\Delta E = -2.178 \times 10^{-18} \text{ J} \left(\dfrac{1}{2^2} - \dfrac{1}{4^2} \right) = -4.084 \times 10^{-19} \text{ J}$

$\lambda = \dfrac{hc}{|\Delta E|} = \dfrac{6.6261 \times 10^{-34} \text{ J s} \times 2.9979 \times 10^8 \text{ m/s}}{4.084 \times 10^{-19} \text{ J}} = 4.864 \times 10^{-7} \text{ m} = 486.4 \text{ nm}$

This is visible electromagnetic radiation (green-blue light).

c. $\Delta E = -2.178 \times 10^{-18} \, J \left(\dfrac{1}{1^2} - \dfrac{1}{2^2} \right) = -1.634 \times 10^{-18} \, J$

$$\lambda = \frac{6.6261 \times 10^{-34} \, J\,s \times 2.9979 \times 10^8 \, m/s}{1.634 \times 10^{-18} \, J} = 1.216 \times 10^{-7} \, m = 121.6 \, nm$$

This is ultraviolet electromagnetic radiation.

46.   a. $\Delta E = -2.178 \times 10^{-18} \, J \left(\dfrac{1}{3^2} - \dfrac{1}{4^2} \right) = -1.059 \times 10^{-19} \, J$

$$\lambda = \frac{hc}{|\Delta E|} = \frac{6.6261 \times 10^{-34} \, J\,s \times 2.9979 \times 10^8 \, m/s}{1.059 \times 10^{-19} \, J} = 1.876 \times 10^{-6} \, m = 1876 \, nm$$

From Figure 7.2, this is infrared electromagnetic radiation.

b. $\Delta E = -2.178 \times 10^{-18} \, J \left(\dfrac{1}{4^2} - \dfrac{1}{5^2} \right) = -4.901 \times 10^{-20} \, J$

$$\lambda = \frac{hc}{|\Delta E|} = \frac{6.6261 \times 10^{-34} \, J\,s \times 2.9979 \times 10^8 \, m/s}{4.901 \times 10^{-20} \, J} = 4.053 \times 10^{-6} \, m$$

$$= 4053 \, nm \, (infrared)$$

c. $\Delta E = -2.178 \times 10^{-18} \, J \left(\dfrac{1}{3^2} - \dfrac{1}{5^2} \right) = -1.549 \times 10^{-19} \, J$

$$\lambda = \frac{hc}{|\Delta E|} = \frac{6.6261 \times 10^{-34} \, J\,s \times 2.9979 \times 10^8 \, m/s}{1.549 \times 10^{-19} \, J} = 1.282 \times 10^{-6} \, m$$

$$= 1282 \, nm \, (infrared)$$

47.

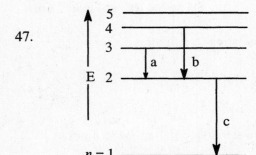

a. $3 \rightarrow 2$

b. $4 \rightarrow 2$

c. $2 \rightarrow 1$

Energy levels are not to scale.

48.

$$5 \quad \downarrow b$$
$$4$$
$$\downarrow a \qquad \downarrow c$$
$$3$$

$$E \quad 2 \underline{\hspace{3cm}}$$

$$n = 1 \underline{\hspace{3cm}}$$

a. $4 \rightarrow 3$

b. $5 \rightarrow 4$

c. $5 \rightarrow 3$

Energy levels are not to scale.

49. $\Delta E = -2.178 \times 10^{-18} \text{ J} \left(\dfrac{1}{n_f^2} - \dfrac{1}{n_i^2} \right) = -2.178 \times 10^{-18} \text{ J} \left(\dfrac{1}{5^2} - \dfrac{1}{1^2} \right) = 2.091 \times 10^{-18} \text{ J} = E_{photon}$

$$\lambda = \frac{hc}{E} = \frac{6.6261 \times 10^{-34} \text{ J s} \times 2.9979 \times 10^8 \text{ m/s}}{2.091 \times 10^{-18} \text{ J}} = 9.500 \times 10^{-8} \text{ m} = 95.00 \text{ nm}$$

Because wavelength and energy are inversely related, visible light ($\lambda \approx 400 - 700$ nm) is not energetic enough to excite an electron in hydrogen from $n = 1$ to $n = 5$.

$$\Delta E = -2.178 \times 10^{-18} \text{ J} \left(\frac{1}{6^2} - \frac{1}{2^2} \right) = 4.840 \times 10^{-19} \text{ J}$$

$$\lambda = \frac{hc}{E} = \frac{6.6261 \times 10^{-34} \text{ J s} \times 2.9979 \times 10^8 \text{ m/s}}{4.840 \times 10^{-18} \text{ J}} = 4.104 \times 10^{-7} \text{ m} = 410.4 \text{ nm}$$

Visible light with $\lambda = 410.4$ nm will excite an electron from the $n = 2$ to the $n = 6$ energy level.

50.   a.   False; It takes less energy to ionize an electron from $n = 3$ than from the ground state.

b.   True

c.   False; The energy difference from $n = 3 \rightarrow n = 2$ is less than the energy difference from $n = 3 \rightarrow n = 1$, thus, the wavelength is larger for $n = 3 \rightarrow n = 2$ than for $n = 3 \rightarrow n = 1$.

d.   True

e.   False; $n = 2$ is the first excited state and $n = 3$ is the second excited state.

51.   Ionization from $n = 1$ corresponds to the transition $n_i = 1 \rightarrow n_f = \infty$ where $E_\infty = 0$.

$$\Delta E = E_\infty - E_1 = -E_1 = 2.178 \times 10^{-18} \left(\frac{1}{1^2} \right) = 2.178 \times 10^{-18} \text{ J} = E_{photon}$$

$$\lambda = \frac{hc}{E} = \frac{6.6261 \times 10^{-34} \text{ J s} \times 2.9979 \times 10^8 \text{ m/s}}{2.178 \times 10^{-18} \text{ J}} = 9.120 \times 10^{-8} \text{ m} = 91.20 \text{ nm}$$

To ionize from $n = 2$, $\Delta E = E_\infty - E_2 = -E_2 = 2.178 \times 10^{-18} \left(\dfrac{1}{2^2}\right) = 5.445 \times 10^{-19}$ J

$$\lambda = \frac{6.6261 \times 10^{-34} \text{ J s} \times 2.9979 \times 10^8 \text{ m/s}}{5.445 \times 10^{-19} \text{ J}} = 3.648 \times 10^{-7} \text{ m} = 364.8 \text{ nm}$$

52. $\Delta E = E_\infty - E_n = -E_n = 2.178 \times 10^{-18} \text{ J} \left(\dfrac{1}{n^2}\right)$

$$E_{photon} = \frac{hc}{\lambda} = \frac{6.626 \times 10^{-34} \text{ J s} \times 2.9979 \times 10^8 \text{ m/s}}{1460 \times 10^{-9} \text{ m}} = 1.36 \times 10^{-19} \text{ J}$$

$E_{photon} = \Delta E = 1.36 \times 10^{-19}$ J $= 2.178 \times 10^{-18} \left(\dfrac{1}{n^2}\right)$, $n^2 = 16.0$, $n = 4$

53. $|\Delta E| = E_{photon} = h\nu = 6.662 \times 10^{-34}$ J s $\times 6.90 \times 10^{14}$ s$^{-1} = 4.57 \times 10^{-19}$ J

$\Delta E = -4.57 \times 10^{-19}$ J because we have an emission.

-4.57×10^{-19} J $= E_n - E_5 = -2.178 \times 10^{-18}$ J $\left(\dfrac{1}{n^2} - \dfrac{1}{5^2}\right)$,

$\dfrac{1}{n^2} - \dfrac{1}{25} = 0.210$, $\dfrac{1}{n^2} = 0.250$, $n^2 = 4$, $n = 2$

The electronic transition is from $n = 5$ to $n = 2$.

54. $|\Delta E| = E_{photon} = \dfrac{hc}{\lambda} = \dfrac{6.6261 \times 10^{-34} \text{ J s} \times 2.9979 \times 10^8 \text{ m/s}}{397.2 \times 10^{-9} \text{ m}} = 10^{-19} = 5.001 \times 10^{-19}$ J

$\Delta E = -5.001 \times 10^{-19}$ J because we have an emission.

-5.001×10^{-19} J $= E_2 - E_n = -2.178 \times 10^{-18}$ J $\left(\dfrac{1}{2^2} - \dfrac{1}{n^2}\right)$

$0.2296 = \dfrac{1}{4} - \dfrac{1}{n^2}$, $\dfrac{1}{n^2} = 0.0204$, $n = 7$

Quantum Mechanics, Quantum Numbers, and Orbitals

55.   a. $\Delta(mv) = m\Delta v = 9.11 \times 10^{-31}$ kg $\times 0.100$ m/s $= \dfrac{9.11 \times 10^{-32} \text{ kg m}}{s}$

$$\Delta(mv) \bullet \Delta x \geq \frac{h}{4\pi}, \quad \Delta x = \frac{h}{4\pi\Delta(mv)} = \frac{6.626\times10^{-34} \text{ J s}}{4\times3.142\times(9.11 \times 10^{-32} \text{ kg m/s})}$$

$$= 5.79 \times 10^{-4} \text{ m}$$

b. $\Delta x = \dfrac{h}{4\pi\Delta(mv)} = \dfrac{6.626\times10^{-34} \text{ J s}}{4\times3.142\times0.145 \text{ kg} \times0.100 \text{ m/s}} = 3.64 \times 10^{-33} \text{ m}$

c.   The diameter of an H atom is roughly 1.0×10^{-8} cm. The uncertainty in position is much larger than the size of the atom.

d.   The uncertainty is insignificant compared to the size of a baseball.

56.   Units of $\Delta E \bullet \Delta t = J \times s$, the same as the units of Planck's constant.

$$\text{Units of } \Delta(mv) \bullet \Delta x = kg \times \frac{m}{s} \times m = \frac{kg \ m^2}{s} = \frac{kg \ m^2}{s^2} \times s = J \times s$$

57. $n = 1, 2, 3, \dots ; \quad \ell = 0, 1, 2, \dots (n - 1); \quad m_\ell = -\ell \dots -2, -1, 0, 1, 2, \dots +\ell$

58.   1p: $n = 1, \ell = 1$ is not possible; 3f: $n = 3, \ell = 3$ is not possible; 2d: $n = 2, \ell = 2$ is not possible; In all three incorrect cases, $n = \ell$. The maximum value ℓ can have is $n - 1$, not n.

59.   b.   For $\ell = 3$, m_ℓ can range from -3 to +3; thus +4 is not allowed.

c. n cannot equal zero.   d. ℓ cannot be a negative number.

60.   a.   For $n = 3$, $\ell = 3$ is not possible.

d. m_s cannot equal -1.

e. ℓ cannot be a negative number.

f.   For $\ell = 1$, m_ℓ cannot equal 2.

61. ψ^2 gives the probability of finding the electron at that point.

62.   The diagrams of the orbitals in the text give only 90% probabilities of where the electron may reside. We can never be 100% certain of the location of the electrons due to Heisenburg's uncertainty principle.

Polyelectronic Atoms

63.   5p: three orbitals; $3d_{z^2}$: one orbital; 4d: five orbitals

n = 5: $\ell = 0$ (1 orbital), $\ell = 1$ (3 orbitals), $\ell = 2$ (5 orbitals), $\ell = 3$ (7 orbitals),

$\ell = 4$ (9 orbitals)

Total for n = 5 is 25 orbitals.

n = 4: $\ell = 0$ (1), $\ell = 1$ (3), $\ell = 2$ (5), $\ell = 3$ (7); Total for n = 4 is 16 orbitals.

64.   1p, 0 electrons ($\ell \neq 1$ when n = 1); $6d_{x^2-y^2}$, 2 electrons (specifies one atomic orbital); 4f, 14 electrons (7 orbitals have 4f designation); $7p_y$, 2 electrons (specifies one atomic orbital); 2s, 2 electrons (specifies one atomic orbital); n = 3, 18 electrons (3s, 3p and 3d orbitals are possible; there are one 3s orbital, three 3p orbitals and five 3d orbitals).

65.   a.   n = 4: ℓ can be 0, 1, 2, or 3. Thus we have s (2 e⁻), p (6 e⁻), d (10 e⁻) and f (14 e⁻) orbitals present. Total number of electrons to fill these orbitals is 32.

b.   n = 5, $m_\ell = +1$: For n = 5, ℓ = 0, 1, 2, 3, 4. For ℓ = 1, 2, 3, 4, all can have $m_\ell = +1$. Four distinct orbitals, thus 8 electrons.

c.   n = 5, $m_s = +1/2$: For n = 5, ℓ = 0, 1, 2, 3, 4. Number of orbitals = 1, 3, 5, 7, 9 for each value of ℓ, respectively. There are 25 orbitals with n = 5. They can hold 50 electrons and 25 of these electrons can have $m_s = +1/2$.

d.   n = 3, ℓ = 2: These quantum numbers define a set of 3d orbitals. There are 5 degenerate 3d orbitals which can hold a total of 10 electrons.

e.   n = 2, ℓ = 1: These define a set of 2p orbitals. There are 3 degenerate 2p orbitals which can hold a total of 6 electrons.

66.   a.   It is impossible to have n = 0. Thus, no electrons can have this set of quantum numbers.

b.   The four quantum numbers completely specify a single electron in a 2p orbital.

c.   n = 3, $m_s = +1/2$: 3s, 3p and 3d orbitals all have n = 3. These nine orbitals can each hold one electron with $m_s = +1/2$; 9 electrons can have these quantum numbers

d.   n = 2, ℓ = 2: This combination is not possible ($\ell \neq 2$ for n = 2). Zero electrons in an atom can have these quantum numbers.

e.   n = 1, $\ell = 0$, $m_\ell = 0$: These define a 1s orbital which can hold 2 electrons.

67.   a.   Na: $1s^2 2s^2 2p^6 3s^1$; Na has 1 unpaired electron.

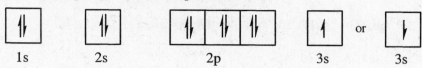

b.   Co: $1s^2 2s^2 2p^6 3s^2 3p^6 4s^2 3d^7$; Co has 3 unpaired electrons.

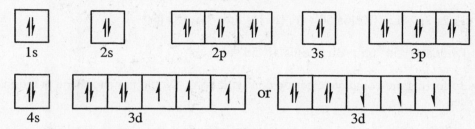

c.   Kr: $1s^2 2s^2 2p^6 3s^2 3p^6 4s^2 3d^{10} 4p^6$; Kr has 0 unpaired electrons.

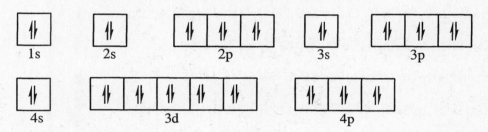

68.   The two exceptions are Cr and Cu.

Cr: $1s^2 2s^2 2p^6 3s^2 3p^6 4s^1 3p^5$; Cr has 6 unpaired electrons.

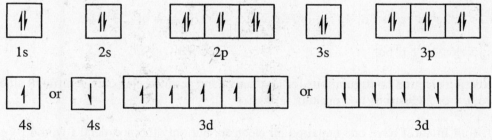

Cu: $1s^2 2s^2 2p^6 3s^2 3p^6 4s^1 3d^{10}$; Cu has 1 unpaired electron.

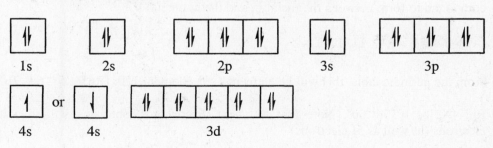

69.   Si: $1s^22s^22p^63s^23p^2$ or $[Ne]3s^23p^2$; Ga: $1s^22s^22p^63s^23p^64s^23d^{10}4p^1$ or $[Ar]4s^23d^{10}4p^1$

As: $[Ar]4s^23d^{10}4p^3$; Ge: $[Ar]4s^23d^{10}4p^2$; Al: $[Ne]3s^23p^1$; Cd: $[Kr]5s^24d^{10}$

S: $[Ne]3s^23p^4$; Se: $[Ar]4s^23d^{10}4p^4$

70.   Cu: $[Ar]4s^23d^9$ (using periodic table), $[Ar]4s^13d^{10}$ (actual)

O: $1s^22s^22p^4$; La: $[Xe]6s^25d^1$; Y: $[Kr]5s^24d^1$; Ba: $[Xe]6s^2$

Tl: $[Xe]6s^24f^{14}5d^{10}6p^1$; Bi: $[Xe]6s^24f^{14}5d^{10}6p^3$

71.   The following are complete electron configurations. Noble gas shorthand notation could also be used.

Sc: $1s^22s^22p^63s^23p^64s^23d^1$; Fe: $1s^22s^22p^63s^23p^64s^23d^6$

P: $1s^22s^22p^63s^23p^3$; Cs: $1s^22s^22p^63s^23p^64s^23d^{10}4p^65s^24d^{10}5p^66s^1$

Eu: $1s^22s^22p^63s^23p^64s^23d^{10}4p^65s^24d^{10}5p^66s^24f^65d^1$*

Pt: $1s^22s^22p^63s^23p^64s^23d^{10}4p^65s^24d^{10}5p^66s^24f^{14}5d^8$*

Xe: $1s^22s^22p^63s^23p^64s^23d^{10}4p^65s^24d^{10}5p^6$; Br: $1s^22s^22p^63s^23p^64s^23d^{10}4p^5$

*Note: These electron configurations were predicted using only the periodic table.
The actual electron configurations are: Eu: $[Xe]6s^24f^7$ and Pt: $[Xe]6s^14f^{14}5d^9$

72.   Cl: $1s^22s^22p^63s^23p^5$ or $[Ne]3s^23p^5$ Sb: $[Kr]5s^24d^{10}5p^3$

Sr: $1s^22s^22p^63s^23p^64s^23d^{10}4p^65s^2$ or $[Kr]5s^2$ W: $[Xe]6s^24f^{14}5d^4$

Pb: $[Xe]6s^24f^{14}5d^{10}6p^2$ Cf: $[Rn]7s^25f^{10}$

Predicting electron configurations for lanthanide and actinide elements is difficult since they have 0, 1 or 2 electrons in d orbitals.

73.   a.   Both In and I have one unpaired 5p electron, but only the nonmetal I would be expected to form a covalent compound with the nonmetal F. One would predict an ionic compound to form between the metal In and the nonmetal F.

      I: $[Kr]5s^24d^{10}5p^5$ ⇅ ⇅ ↑
                              5p

      b.   From the periodic table, this will be element 120. Element 120: $[Rn]7s^25f^{14}6d^{10}7p^68s^2$

      c.   Rn: $[Xe]6s^24f^{14}5d^{10}6p^6$; Note that the next discovered noble gas will also have 4f electrons (as well as 5f electrons).

d. This is chromium, which is an exception to the predicted filling order. Cr has 6 unpaired electrons and the next most is 5 unpaired electrons for Mn.

Cr: $[Ar]4s^13d^5$ ⇅ ↑ ↑ ↑ ↑ ↑
   $\underset{4s}{}$ $\underset{3d}{}$

74.   a. As: $1s^22s^22p^63s^23p^64s^23d^{10}4p^3$

b. Element 116 will be below Po in the periodic table: $[Rn]7s^25f^{14}6d^{10}7p^4$

c. Ta: $[Xe]6s^24f^{14}5d^3$ or Ir: $[Xe]6s^24f^{14}5d^7$

d. At: $[Xe]6s^24f^{14}5d^{10}6p^5$. Note that element 117 (when it is discovered) will also have electrons in the 6p atomic orbitals (as well as electrons in the 7p atomic orbitals).

75.   Hg: $1s^22s^22p^63s^23p^64s^23d^{10}4p^65s^24d^{10}5p^66s^24f^{14}5d^{10}$

a. From the electron configuration for Hg, we have $3s^2$, $3p^6$, and $3d^{10}$ electrons; 18 total electrons with $n = 3$.

b. $3d^{10}$, $4d^{10}$, $5d^{10}$; 30 electrons are in d atomic orbitals.

c. $2p^6$, $3p^6$, $4p^6$, $5p^6$; Each set of np orbitals contain one p_z atomic orbital. Because we have 4 sets of np orbitals and two electrons can occupy the p_z orbital, there are $4(2) = 8$ electrons in p_z atomic orbitals.

d. All the electrons are paired in Hg, so one-half of the electrons are spin-up ($m_s = +1/2$) and the other half are spin-down ($m_s = -1/2$). 40 electrons have spin-up.

76.   Element 115, Uup, is in Group 5A under Bi (bismuth):

Uup: $1s^22s^22p^63s^23p^64s^23d^{10}4p^65s^24d^{10}5p^66s^24f^{14}5d^{10}6p^67s^25f^{14}6d^{10}7p^3$

a. $5s^2$, $5p^6$, $5d^{10}$, and $5f^{14}$; 32 electrons have $n = 5$ as one of their quantum numbers

b. $\ell = 3$ are f orbitals. $4f^{14}$ and $5f^{14}$ are the f orbitals used. They are all filled so 28 electrons have $\ell = 3$.

c. p, d, and f orbitals all have one of the degenerate orbitals with $m_\ell = 1$. There are 6 orbitals with $m_\ell = 1$ for the various p orbitals used; there are 4 orbitals with $m_\ell = 1$ for the various d orbitals used; and there are 2 orbitals with $m_\ell = 1$ for the various f orbitals used. We have a total of $6 + 4 + 2 = 12$ orbitals with $m_\ell = 1$. Eleven of these orbitals are filled with 2 electrons, and the 7p orbitals are only half-filled. The number of electrons with $m_\ell = 1$ is $11 \times (2\ e^-) + 1 \times (1\ e^-) = 23$ electrons.

d. The first 112 electrons are all paired; one-half of these electrons (56 e^-) will have $m_s = -1/2$. The 3 electrons in the 7p orbitals singly occupy each of the three degenerate 7p orbitals; the three electrons are spin parallel, so the 7p electrons either have $m_s = +1/2$ or $m_s = -1/2$. Therefore, either 56 electrons have $m_s = -1/2$ or 59 electrons have $m_s = -1/2$.

77.   B: $1s^2 2s^2 2p^1$

	n	ℓ	m_ℓ	m_s
1s	1	0	0	+1/2
1s	1	0	0	−1/2
2s	2	0	0	+1/2
2s	2	0	0	−1/2
2p*	2	1	−1	+1/2

*This is only one of several possibilities for the 2p electron. The 2p electron in B cold have $m_\ell = -1$, 0 or +1, and $m_s = +1/2$ or $-1/2$, for a total of six possibilities.

N: $1s^2 2s^2 2p^3$

	n	ℓ	m_ℓ	m_s
1s	1	0	0	+1/2
1s	1	0	0	−1/2
2s	2	0	0	+1/2
2s	2	0	0	−1/2
2p	2	1	-1	+1/2
2p	2	1	0	+1/2
2p	2	1	+1	+1/2

(Or all 2p electrons could have $m_s = -1/2$.)

78.   Ti : $[Ar]4s^2 3d^2$

	n	ℓ	m_ℓ	m_s
4s	4	0	0	+1/2
4s	4	0	0	−1/2
3d	3	2	−2	+1/2
3d	3	2	−1	+1/2

Only one of 10 possible combinations of m_ℓ and m_s for the first d electron. For the ground state, the second d electron should be in a different orbital with spin parallel; 4 possibilities.

79.   O: $1s^2 2s^2 2p_x^2 2p_y^2$ (↑↓ ↑↓ _); There are no unpaired electrons in this oxygen atom. This configuration would be an excited state, and in going to the more stable ground state (↑↓ ↑ ↑), energy would be released.

80.   The number of unpaired electrons is in parentheses.

a. excited state of boron   (1)   b. ground state of neon   (0)

B ground state: $1s^2 2s^2 2p^1$ (1)   Ne ground state: $1s^2 2s^2 2p^6$

  c. exited state of fluorine   (3)   d. excited state of iron   (6)

  F ground state: $1s^2 2s^2 2p^5$ (1)   Fe ground state: $[Ar]4s^2 3d^6$ (4)

$\underset{2p}{\uparrow\downarrow\ \ \uparrow\downarrow\ \ \uparrow}$ $\underset{3d}{\uparrow\downarrow\ \uparrow\ \uparrow\ \uparrow\ \uparrow}$

81. None of the s block elements have 2 unpaired electrons. In the p block, the elements with either $ns^2 np^2$ or $ns^2 np^4$ valence electron configurations have 2 unpaired electrons. For elements 1-36, these are elements C, Si, and Ge (with $ns^2 np^2$), and element O, S, and Se (with $ns^2 np^4$). For the d block, the elements with configurations nd^2 or nd^8 have two unpaired electrons. For elements 1-36, these are Ti ($3d^2$) and Ni ($3d^8$). A total of 8 elements from the first 36 elements have two unpaired electrons in the ground state.

82. The s block elements with ns^1 for a valence electron configuration have one unpaired electrons. These are elements H, Li, Na, and K for the first 36 elements. The p block elements with $ns^2 np^1$ or $ns^2 np^5$ valence electron configurations have one unpaired electron. These are elements B, Al, and Ga ($ns^2 np^1$) and elements F, Cl, and Br ($ns^2 np^5$) for the first 36 elements. In the d block, Sc ($[Ar]4s^2 3d^1$) and Cu ($[Ar]4s^1 3d^{10}$) each have one unpaired electron. A total of 12 elements from the first 36 elements have one unpaired electron in the ground state.

83. We get the number of unpaired electrons by examining the incompletely filled subshells. The paramagnetic substances have unpaired electrons, and the ones with no unpaired electrons are not paramagnetic (they are called diamagnetic).

Li: $1s^2 2s^1$ $\underset{2s}{\uparrow}$; Paramagnetic with 1 unpaired electron.

N: $1s^2 2s^2 2p^3$ $\underset{2p}{\uparrow\ \uparrow\ \uparrow}$; Paramagnetic with 3 unpaired electrons.

Ni: $[Ar]4s^2 3d^8$ $\underset{3d}{\uparrow\downarrow\ \uparrow\downarrow\ \uparrow\downarrow\ \uparrow\ \uparrow}$; Paramagnetic with 2 unpaired electrons.

Te: $[Kr]5s^2 4d^{10} 5p^4$ $\underset{5p}{\uparrow\downarrow\ \uparrow\ \uparrow}$; Paramagnetic with 2 unpaired electrons.

Ba: $[Xe]6s^2$ $\underset{6s}{\uparrow\downarrow}$; Not paramagnetic since no unpaired electrons.

Hg: $[Xe]6s^2 4f^{14} 5d^{10}$ $\underset{5d}{\uparrow\downarrow\ \uparrow\downarrow\ \uparrow\downarrow\ \uparrow\downarrow\ \uparrow\downarrow}$; Not paramagnetic since no unpaired electrons.

84. We get the number of unpaired electrons by examining the incompletely filled subshells.

O: $[He]2s^2 2p^4$ $2p^4$: $\uparrow\downarrow\ \uparrow\ \uparrow$ two unpaired e^-

O^+: $[He]2s^2 2p^3$ $2p^3$: $\uparrow\ \uparrow\ \uparrow$ three unpaired e^-

O^-: $[He]2s^2 2p^5$ $2p^5$: $\uparrow\downarrow\ \uparrow\downarrow\ \uparrow$ one unpaired e^-

Os: $[Xe]6s^2 4f^{14} 5d^6$ $5d^6$: $\uparrow\downarrow\ \uparrow\ \uparrow\ \uparrow\ \uparrow$ four unpaired e^-

Zr: $[Kr]5s^24d^2$ $4d^2$:   ↑ ↑ __ __ __   two unpaired e⁻

S: $[Ne]3s^23p^4$ $3p^4$:   ↑↓ ↑ ↑   two unpaired e⁻

F: $[He]2s^22p^5$ $2p^5$:   ↑↓ ↑↓ ↑   one unpaired e⁻

Ar: $[Ne]3s^23p^6$ $3p^6$ ↑↓ ↑↓ ↑↓   zero unpaired e⁻

The Periodic Table and Periodic Properties

85.   Size (radii) decreases left to right across the periodic table, and size increases from top to bottom of the periodic table.

     a.   S < Se < Te   b.   Br < Ni < K   c.   F < Si < Ba

86.   a.   Be < Na < Rb   b.   Ne < Se < Sr   c.   O < P < Fe; All follow the general radii trend.

87.   The ionization energy trend is the opposite of the radii trend; ionization energy (IE), in general, increases left to right across the periodic table and decreases from top to bottom of the periodic table.

     a.   Te < Se < S   b.   K < Ni < Br   c.   Ba < Si < F

88.   a.   Rb < Na < Be   b.   Sr < Se < Ne   c.   Fe < P < O ; All follow the general IE trend.

89.   a.   He   b.   Cl

     c.   Element 117 is the next halogen to be discovered (under At), element 119 is the next alkali metal to be discovered (under Fr), and element 120 is the next alkaline earth metal to be discovered (under Ra). From the general radii trend, the halogen (element 117) will be the smallest.

     d.   Si

     e. Na^+. This ion has the fewest electrons as compared to the other sodium species present. Na^+ has the smallest amount of electron-electron repulsions, which makes it the smallest ion with the largest ionization energy.

90.   a.   Ba   b.   K

     c.   O; In general, group 6A elements have a lower ionization energy than neighboring group 5A elements. This is an exception to the general ionization energy trend across the periodic table.

d. S^{2-}; This ion has the most electrons as compared to the other sulfur species present. S^{2-} has the largest amount of electron-electron repulsions which leads to S^{2-} having the largest size and smallest ionization energy.

e. Cs; This follows the general ionization energy trend.

91.   a. Sg: $[Rn]7s^25f^{14}6d^4$ b. W   c. SgO_3 or Sg_2O_3 and SgO_4^{2-} or $Sg_2O_7^{2-}$
                                                    (similar to Cr; Sg = 106)

92.   a. Uus will have 117 electrons. $[Rn]7s^25f^{14}6d^{10}7p^5$

       b. It will be in the halogen family and most similar to astatine, At.

       c. Uus should form -1 charged anions like the other halogens.

          NaUus, $Mg(Uus)_2$, $C(Uus)_4$, $O(Uus)_2$

       d. Assuming Uus is like the other halogens: $UusO^-$, $UusO_2^-$, $UusO_3^-$, $UusO_4^-$

93.   As: $[Ar]4s^23d^{10}4p^3$; Se: $[Ar]4s^23d^{10}4p^4$; The general ionization energy trend predicts that Se should have a higher ionization energy than As. Se is an exception to the general ionization energy trend. There are extra electron-electron repulsions in Se because two electrons are in the same 4p orbital, resulting in a lower ionization energy for Se than predicted.

94.   Expected order from IE trend: Be < B < C < N < O

       B and O are exceptions to the general IE trend. The IE of O is lower because of the extra electron-electron repulsions present when two electrons are paired in the same orbital. This makes it slightly easier to remove an electron from O as compared to N. B is an exception because of the smaller penetrating ability of the 2p electron in B as compared to the 2s electrons in Be. The smaller penetrating ability makes it slightly easier to remove an electron from B as compared to Be. The correct IE ordering taking into account the two exceptions is: B < Be < C < O < N.

95.   a. More favorable EA: C and Br; The electron affinity trend is very erratic. Both N and Ar have positive EA values (unfavorable) due to their electron configurations (see text for detailed explanation).

       b. Higher IE: N and Ar (follows the IE trend)

       c. Larger size: C and Br (follows the radii trend)

96.   a. More favorable EA: K and Cl; Mg has a positive EA value, and F has a more positive EA value than expected from its position relative to Cl.

       b. Higher IE: Mg and F   c. Larger radius: K and Cl

97.   Al(-44), Si(-120), P(-74), S(-200.4), Cl(-348.7); Based on the increasing nuclear charge, we would expect the electron affinity (EA) values to become more exothermic as we go from left to right in the period. Phosphorus is out of line. The reaction for the EA of P is:

$$P(g) + e^- \rightarrow P^-(g)$$

$$[Ne]3s^23p^3 \qquad [Ne]3s^23p^4$$

The additional electron in P^- will have to go into an orbital that already has one electron. There will be greater repulsions between the paired electrons in P^-, causing the EA of P to be less favorable than predicted based solely on attractions to the nucleus.

98.   Electron-electron repulsions are much greater in O^- than in S^- because the electron goes into a smaller 2p orbital vs. the larger 3p orbital in sulfur. This results in a more favorable (more exothermic) EA for sulfur.

99.   The electron affinity trend is very erratic. In general, EA becomes more positive in going down a group and EA becomes more negative from left to right across a period (with many exceptions).

a.   I < Br < F < Cl; Cl is most exothermic (F is an exception).

b.   N < O < F; F is most exothermic.

100.   O; The electron-electron repulsions will be much more severe for $O^- + e^- \rightarrow O^{2-}$ than for $O + e^- \rightarrow O^-$.

101.   a. $Se^{3+}(g) \rightarrow Se^{4+}(g) + e^-$ b. $S^-(g) + e^- \rightarrow S^{2-}(g)$

c. $Fe^{3+}(g) + e^- \rightarrow Fe^{2+}(g)$ d. $Mg(g) \rightarrow Mg^+(g) + e^-$

102.   a.   The electron affinity of Mg^{2+} is ΔH for $Mg^{2+}(g) + e^- \rightarrow Mg^+(g)$. This is just the reverse of the second ionization energy for Mg, or $EA(Mg^{2+}) = -IE_2(Mg) = -1445$ kJ/mol (Table 7.5).

b.   IE of Cl^- is ΔH for $Cl^-(g) \rightarrow Cl(g) + e^-$. $IE(Cl^-) = -EA(Cl) = 348.7$ kJ/mol (Table 7.7)

c. $Cl^+(g) + e^- \rightarrow Cl(g) \qquad \Delta H = -IE_1(Cl) = -1255$ kJ/mol $= EA(Cl^+)$

d. $Mg^-(g) \rightarrow Mg(g) + e^- \quad \Delta H = -EA(Mg) = -230$ kJ/mol $= IE(Mg^-)$

Alkali Metals

103.   It should be potassium peroxide, K_2O_2; stable ionic compounds of potassium have K^+ ions, not K^{2+} ions.

104.   a. Li_3N; lithium nitride   b.   NaBr; sodium bromide   c. K_2S; potassium sulfide

105. $v = \dfrac{c}{\lambda} = \dfrac{2.9979 \times 10^8 \text{ m/s}}{455.5 \times 10^{-9} \text{ m}} = 6.582 \times 10^{14} \text{s}^{-1}$

$E = hv = 6.6261 \times 10^{-34} \text{ J s} \times 6.582 \times 10^{14} \text{s}^{-1} = 4.361 \times 10^{-19} \text{ J}$

106. For 589.0 nm: $v = \dfrac{c}{\lambda} = \dfrac{2.9979 \times 10^8 \text{ m/s}}{589.0 \times 10^{-9} \text{ m}} = 5.090 \times 10^{14} \text{s}^{-1}$

$E = hv = 6.6261 \times 10^{-34} \text{ J s} \times 5.090 \times 10^{14} \text{s}^{-1} = 3.373 \times 10^{-19} \text{ J}$

For 589.6 nm: $v = c/\lambda = 5.085 \times 10^{14} \text{s}^{-1}$; $E = hv = 3.369 \times 10^{-19} \text{ J}$

The energies in kJ/mol are:

$$3.373 \times 10^{-19} \text{ J} \times \frac{1 \text{ kJ}}{1000 \text{ J}} \times \frac{6.0221 \times 10^{23}}{\text{mol}} = 203.1 \text{ kJ/mol}$$

$$3.369 \times 10^{-19} \text{ J} \times \frac{1 \text{ kJ}}{1000 \text{ J}} \times \frac{6.0221 \times 10^{23}}{\text{mol}} = 202.9 \text{ kJ/mol}$$

107. Yes; the ionization energy general trend is to decrease down a group, and the atomic radius trend is to increase down a group. The data in Table 7.8 confirm both of these general trends.

108. It should be element #119 with the ground state electron configuration: $[Rn]7s^2 5f^{14} 6d^{10} 7p^6 8s^1$

109. a. $6 \text{ Li}(s) + N_2(g) \rightarrow 2 \text{ Li}_3N(s)$ \qquad b. $2 \text{ Rb}(s) + S(s) \rightarrow Rb_2S(s)$

110. a. $2 \text{ Cs}(s) + 2 \text{ H}_2O(l) \rightarrow 2 \text{ CsOH}(aq) + H_2(g)$ \qquad b. $2 \text{ Na}(s) + Cl_2(g) \rightarrow 2 \text{ NaCl}(s)$

Additional Exercises

111. $E = \dfrac{310 \text{ kJ}}{\text{mol}} \times \dfrac{1 \text{ mol}}{6.022 \times 10^{23}} = 5.15 \times 10^{-22} \text{ kJ} = 5.15 \times 10^{-19} \text{ J}$

$E = \dfrac{hc}{\lambda}$, $\lambda = \dfrac{hc}{E} = \dfrac{6.626 \times 10^{-34} \text{ J s} \times 2.998 \times 10^8 \text{ m/s}}{5.15 \times 10^{-19} \text{ J}} = 3.86 \times 10^{-7} \text{ m} = 386 \text{ nm}$

112. Energy to make water boil = $s \times m \times \Delta T = \dfrac{4.18 \text{ J}}{\text{g } ^\circ\text{C}} \times 50.0 \text{ g} \times 75.0 ^\circ\text{C} = 1.57 \times 10^4 \text{ J}$

$E_{photon} = \dfrac{hc}{\lambda} = \dfrac{6.626 \times 10^{-34} \text{ J s} \times 2.998 \times 10^8 \text{ m/s}}{9.75 \times 10^{-2} \text{ m}} = 2.04 \times 10^{-24} \text{ J}$

$$1.57 \times 10^4 \text{ J} \times \frac{1 \sec}{750. \text{ J}} = 20.9 \sec; \quad 1.57 \times 10^4 \text{ J} \times \frac{1 \text{ photon}}{2.04 \times 10^{-24} \text{ J}} = 7.70 \times 10^{27} \text{ photons}$$

113. $$60 \times 10^6 \text{ km} \times \frac{1000 \text{ m}}{\text{km}} \times \frac{1 \text{ s}}{3.00 \times 10^8 \text{ m}} = 200 \text{ s} \quad \text{(about 3 minutes)}$$

114. $$\lambda = \frac{hc}{E} = \frac{6.626 \times 10^{-34} \text{ J s} \times 2.998 \times 10^8 \text{ m/s}}{3.59 \times 10^{-19} \text{ J}} = 5.53 \times 10^{-7} \text{ m} \times \frac{100 \text{ cm}}{\text{m}} = 5.53 \times 10^{-5} \text{ cm}$$

From the spectrum, $\lambda = 5.53 \times 10^{-5}$ cm is greenish-yellow light.

115. $$\Delta E = -R_H \left(\frac{1}{n_f^2} - \frac{1}{n_i^2} \right) = -2.178 \times 10^{-18} \text{ J} \left(\frac{1}{2^2} - \frac{1}{6^2} \right) = -4.840 \times 10^{-19} \text{ J}$$

$$\lambda = \frac{hc}{|\Delta E|} = \frac{6.6261 \times 10^{-34} \text{ J s} \times 2.9979 \times 10^8 \text{ m/s}}{4.840 \times 10^{-19} \text{ J}} = 4.104 \times 10^{-7} \text{ m} \times \frac{100 \text{ cm}}{\text{m}}$$

$$= 4.104 \times 10^{-5} \text{ cm}$$

From the spectrum, $\lambda = 4.104 \times 10^{-5}$ cm is violet light, so the $n = 6$ to $n = 2$ visible spectrum line is violet.

116.   Exceptions: Cr, Cu, Nb, Mo, Tc, Ru, Rh, Pd, Ag, Pt, Au; The elements Tc, Ru, Rh, Pd and Pt do not correspond to the supposed extra stability of half-filled and filled subshells.

117.   a.   True for H only.   b.   True for all atoms.   c.   True for all atoms.

118. $n = 5$; $m_\ell = -4, -3, -2, -1, 0, 1, 2, 3, 4$; 18 electrons

119.   When the p and d orbital functions are evaluated at various points in space, the results sometimes have positive values and sometimes have negative values. The term phase is often associated with the + and − signs. For example, a sine wave has alternating positive and negative phases. This is analogous to the positive and negative values (phases) in the p and d orbitals.

120.   He: $1s^2$; Ne: $1s^2 2s^2 2p^6$; Ar: $1s^2 2s^2 2p^6 3s^2 3p^6$; Each peak in the diagram corresponds to a subshell with different values of n. Corresponding subshells are closer to the nucleus for heavier elements because of the increased nuclear charge.

121.   The general ionization energy trend is for ionization energy to increase going left to right across the periodic table. However, one of the exceptions to this trend occurs between groups 2A and 3A. Between these two groups, group 3A elements usually have a lower ionization energy than group 2A elements. Therefore, Al should have the lowest first ionization energy value, followed by Mg, with Si having the largest ionization energy. Looking at the values for the first ionization energy in the graph, the green plot is Al, the blue plot is Mg, and the red plot is Si.

Mg (the blue plot) is the element with the huge jump between I_2 and I_3. Mg has two valence electrons, so the third electron removed is an inner core electron. Inner core electrons are always much more difficult to remove compared to valence electrons since they are closer to the nucleus, on average, than the valence electrons.

122.   a. The 4+ ion contains 20 electrons. Thus, the electrically neutral atom will contain 24 electrons. The atomic number is 24.

   b. The ground state electron configuration of the ion must be: $1s^2 2s^2 2p^6 3s^2 3p^6 4s^0 3d^2$; There are 6 electrons in s orbitals.

   c. 12   d. 2

   e. From the mass, this is the isotope $^{50}_{24}$Cr. There are 26 neutrons in the nucleus.

   f. $1s^2 2s^2 2p^6 3s^2 3p^6 4s^1 3d^5$ is the ground state electron configuration for Cr. Cr is an exception to the normal filling order.

123.   Valence electrons are easier to remove than inner core electrons. The large difference in energy between I_2 and I_3 indicates that this element has two valence electrons. This element is most likely an alkaline earth metal since alkaline earth metal elements all have two valence electrons.

124.   All oxygen family elements have $ns^2 np^4$ valence electron configurations, so this nonmetal is from the oxygen family.

   a. 2 + 4 = 6 valence electrons

   b. O, S, Se and Te are the nonmetals from the oxygen family (Po is a metal).

   c. Because oxygen family nonmetals form -2 charged ions in ionic compounds, K_2X would be the predicted formula where X is the unknown nonmetal.

   d. From the size trend, this element would have a smaller radius than barium.

   e. From the ionization energy trend, this element would have a smaller ionization energy than fluorine.

125.   a.

$$Na(g) \rightarrow Na^+(g) + e^- \qquad IE_1 = 495 \text{ kJ}$$
$$Cl(g) + e^- \rightarrow Cl^-(g) \qquad EA = -348.7 \text{ kJ}$$

_____

$$Na(g) + Cl(g) \rightarrow Na^+(g) + Cl^-g) \qquad \Delta H = 146 \text{ kJ}$$

   b.

$$Mg(g) \rightarrow Mg^+(g) + e^- \qquad IE_1 = 735 \text{ kJ}$$
$$F(g) + e^- \rightarrow F^-(g) \qquad EA = -327.8 \text{ kJ}$$

_____

$$Mg(g) + F(g) \rightarrow Mg^+(g) + F^-(g) \qquad \Delta H = 407 \text{ kJ}$$

c.
$$Mg^+(g) \rightarrow Mg^{2+}(g) + e^- \qquad IE_2 = 1445 \text{ kJ}$$
$$F(g) + e^- \rightarrow F^-(g) \qquad EA = -327.8 \text{ kJ}$$

$$Mg^+(g) + F(g) \rightarrow Mg^{2+}(g) + F^-(g) \qquad \Delta H = 1117 \text{ kJ}$$

d.   From parts b and c we get:

$$Mg(g) + F(g) \rightarrow Mg^+(g) + F^-(g) \qquad \Delta H = 407 \text{ kJ}$$
$$Mg^+(g) + F(g) \rightarrow Mg^{2+}(g) + F^-(g) \qquad \Delta H = 1117 \text{ kJ}$$

$$Mg(g) + 2 F(g) \rightarrow Mg^{2+}(g) + 2 F^-(g) \qquad \Delta H = 1524 \text{ kJ}$$

Challenge Problems

126. $E_{photon} = \dfrac{hc}{\lambda} = \dfrac{6.6261 \times 10^{-34} \text{ J s} \times 2.9979 \times 10^8 \text{ m/s}}{253.4 \times 10^{-9} \text{ m}} = 7.839 \times 10^{-19} \text{ J}; \ \Delta E = 7.839 \times 10^{-19} \text{ J}$

The general energy equation for one-electron ions is $E_n = -2.178 \times 10^{-18} \text{ J} (Z^2)/n^2$ where Z = atomic number.

$$\Delta E = -2.178 \times 10^{-18} \text{ J} (Z)^2 \left(\frac{1}{n_f^2} - \frac{1}{n_i^2} \right), \ Z = 4 \text{ for Be}^{3+}$$

$$\Delta E = -7.839 \times 10^{-19} \text{ J} = -2.178 \times 10^{-18} (4)^2 \left(\frac{1}{n_f^2} - \frac{1}{5^2} \right)$$

$$\frac{7.839 \times 10^{-19}}{2.178 \times 10^{-18} \times 16} + \frac{1}{25} = \frac{1}{n_f^2}, \ \frac{1}{n_f^2} = 0.06249, \ n_f = 4$$

This emission line corresponds to the $n = 5 \rightarrow n = 4$ electronic transition.

127.   a.   Because wavelength is inversely proportional to energy, the spectral line to the right of B (at a longer wavelength) represents the lowest possible energy transition; this is $n = 4$ to $n = 3$. The B line represents the next lowest energy transition, which is $n = 5$ to $n = 3$ and the A line corresponds to the $n = 6$ to $n = 3$ electronic transition.

b.   This spectrum is for a one-electron ion, thus $E_n = -2.178 \times 10^{-18} \text{ J} (Z^2/n^2)$. To determine ΔE and, in turn, the wavelength of spectral line A, we must determine Z, the atomic number of the one-electron species. Use spectral line B data to determine Z.

$$\Delta E_{5 \rightarrow 3} = -2.178 \times 10^{-18} \text{ J} (Z)^2 \left(\frac{1}{3^2} - \frac{1}{5^2} \right) = -2.178 \times 10^{-18} \text{ J} \left(\frac{Z^2}{3^2} - \frac{Z^2}{5^2} \right)$$

$$\Delta E_{5 \rightarrow 3} = -2.178 \times 10^{-18} \left(\frac{16 Z^2}{9 \times 25} \right)$$

$$E = \frac{hc}{\lambda} = \frac{6.6261 \times 10^{-34} \text{ J s} \times 2.9979 \times 10^8 \text{ m/s}}{142.5 \times 10^{-9} \text{ m}} = 1.394 \times 10^{-18} \text{ J}$$

Because an emission occurs, $\Delta E_{5 \rightarrow 3} = -1.394 \times 10^{-18}$ J.

$$\Delta E = -1.394 \times 10^{-18} \text{ J} = -2.178 \times 10^{-18} \text{ J} \left(\frac{16 Z^2}{9 \times 25} \right), \quad Z^2 = 9.001, \quad Z = 3; \text{ The ion is Li}^{2+}.$$

Solving for the wavelength of line A:

$$\Delta E_{6 \rightarrow 3} = -2.178 \times 10^{-18} \text{ } (3)^2 \left(\frac{1}{3^2} - \frac{1}{6^2} \right) = -1.634 \times 10^{-18} \text{ J}$$

$$\lambda = \frac{hc}{|\Delta E|} = \frac{6.6261 \times 10^{-34} \text{ J s} \times 2.9979 \times 10^8 \text{ m/s}}{1.634 \times 10^{-18} \text{ J}} = 1.216 \times 10^{-7} \text{ m} = 121.6 \text{ nm}$$

128.   For hydrogen: $\Delta E = -2.178 \times 10^{-18} \text{ J} \left(\frac{1}{2^2} - \frac{1}{5^2} \right) = -4.574 \times 10^{-19}$ J

For a similar blue light emission, He$^+$ will need about the same ΔE value.

For He$^+$: $E_n = -2.178 \times 10^{-18}$ J (Z^2/n^2) where $Z = 2$:

$$\Delta E = -4.574 \times 10^{-19} \text{ J} = -2.178 \times 10^{-18} \text{ J} \left(\frac{2^2}{n_f^2} - \frac{2^2}{4^2} \right)$$

$$0.2100 = \frac{4}{n_f^2} - \frac{4}{16}, \quad 0.4600 = \frac{4}{n_f^2}, \quad n_f = 2.949$$

The transition from $n = 4$ to $n = 3$ for He$^+$ should emit similar colored blue light as the $n = 5$ to $n = 2$ hydrogen transition; both these transitions correspond to very nearly the same energy change.

129.   For $r = a_o$ and $\theta = 0°$ ($Z = 1$ for H):

$$\psi_{2p_z} = \frac{1}{4(2\pi)^{1/2}} \left(\frac{1}{5.29 \times 10^{-11}} \right)^{3/2} (1) \text{ } e^{-1/2} \cos 0 = 1.57 \times 10^{14}; \quad \psi^2 = 2.46 \times 10^{28}$$

For $r = a_o$ and $\theta = 90°$, $\psi_{2p_z} = 0$ since $\cos 90° = 0$; $\psi^2 = 0$

There is no probability of finding an electron in the 2p$_z$ orbital with $\theta = 0°$. As expected, the xy plane, which corresponds to $\theta = 0°$, is a node for the 2p$_z$ atomic orbital.

130.   a.   Each orbital could hold 3 electrons.

b.   The first period corresponds to $n = 1$ which can only have 1s orbitals. The 1s orbital could hold 3 electrons, hence the first period would have three elements. The second period corresponds to $n = 2$, which has 2s and 2p orbitals. These four orbitals can each hold three electrons. A total of 12 elements would be in the second period.

c.   15   d.   21

131.   a.   1st period: $p = 1$, $q = 1$, $r = 0$, $s = \pm 1/2$ (2 elements)

2nd period: $p = 2$, $q = 1$, $r = 0$, $s = \pm 1/2$ (2 elements)

3rd period: $p = 3$, $q = 1$, $r = 0$, $s = \pm 1/2$ (2 elements)

$p = 3$, $q = 3$, $r = -2$, $s = \pm 1/2$ (2 elements)

$p = 3$, $q = 3$, $r = 0$, $s = \pm 1/2$ (2 elements)

$p = 3$, $q = 3$, $r = +2$, $s = \pm 1/2$ (2 elements)

4th period: $p = 4$; q and r values are the same as with $p = 3$ (8 total elements)

1							2
3							4
5	6	7	8	9	10	11	12
13	14	15	16	17	18	19	20

b.   Elements 2, 4, 12 and 20 all have filled shells and will be least reactive.

c.   Draw similarities to the modern periodic table.

XY could be X^+Y^-, $X^{2+}Y^{2-}$ or $X^{3+}Y^{3-}$. Possible ions for each are:

X^+ could be elements 1, 3, 5 or 13; Y^- could be 11 or 19.

X^{2+} could be 6 or 14; Y^{2-} could be 10 or 18.

X^{3+} could be 7 or 15; Y^{3-} could be 9 or 17.

Note: X^{4+} and Y^{4-} ions probably won't form.

XY_2 will be $X^{2+}(Y^-)_2$; See above for possible ions.

X_2Y will be $(X^+)_2Y^{2-}$ See above for possible ions.

XY_3 will be $X^{3+}(Y^-)_3$; See above for possible ions.

X_2Y_3 will be $(X^{3+})_2(Y^{2-})_3$; See above for possible ions.

    d. $p = 4$, $q = 3$, $r = -2$, $s = \pm 1/2$ (2)

          $p = 4$, $q = 3$, $r = 0$, $s = \pm 1/2$ (2)

          $p = 4$, $q = 3$, $r = +2$, $s = \pm 1/2$ (2)

          A total of 6 electrons can have $p = 4$ and $q = 3$.

    e. $p = 3$, $q = 0$, $r = 0$: This is not allowed; q must be odd. Zero electrons can have these quantum numbers.

    f. $p = 6$, $q = 1$, $r = 0$, $s = \pm 1/2$ (2)

          $p = 6$, $q = 3$, $r = -2, 0, +2$; $s = \pm 1/2$ (6)

          $p = 6$, $q = 5$, $r = -4, -2, 0, +2, +4$; $s = \pm 1/2$ (10)

          Eighteen electrons can have $p = 6$.

132.   The third IE refers to the following process: $E^{2+} \rightarrow E^{3+} + e^{-}$ $\Delta H = IE_3$. The electron configurations for the +2 charged ions of Na to Ar are:

Na^{2+}:	$1s^2 2s^2 2p^5$	Al^{2+}:	$[Ne]3s^1$
Mg^{2+}:	$1s^2 2s^2 2p^6$	Si^{2+}:	$[Ne]3s^2$
		P^{2+}:	$[Ne]3s^2 3p^1$
		S^{2+}:	$[Ne]3s^2 3p^2$
		Cl^{2+}:	$[Ne]3s^2 3p^3$
		Ar^{2+}:	$[Ne]3s^2 3p^4$

IE_3 for sodium and magnesium should be extremely large as compared to the others because $n = 2$ electrons are much more difficult to remove than $n = 3$ electrons. Between Na^{2+} and Mg^{2+}, one would expect to have the same trend as seen with $IE_1(F)$ versus $IE_1(Ne)$; these neutral atoms have identical electron configurations to Na^{2+} and Mg^{2+}. Therefore the $1s^2 2s^2 2p^5$ ion (Na^{2+}) should have a lower ionization energy than the $1s^2 2s^2 2p^6$ ion (Mg^{2+}).

The remaining 2+ ions (Al^{2+} to Ar^{2+}) should follow the same trend as the neutral atoms having the same electron configurations. The general IE trend predicts an increase from $[Ne]3s^1$ to $[Ne]3s^2 3p^4$. The exceptions occur between $[Ne]3s^2$ to $[Ne]3s^2 3p^1$ and between $[Ne]3s^2 3p^3$ and $[Ne]3s^2 3p^4$. $[Ne]3s^2 3p^1$ is out of order because of the small penetrating ability of the 3p electron as compared to the 3s electrons. $[Ne]3s^2 3p^4$ is out of order because of the extra electron-electron repulsions present when two electrons are paired in the same orbital. Therefore, the correct ordering for Al^{2+} to Ar^{2+} should be $Al^{2+} < P^{2+} < Si^{2+} < S^{2+} < Ar^{2+} < Cl^{2+}$ where P^{2+} and Ar^{2+} are out of line for the same reasons that Al and S are out of line in the general ionization energy trend for neutral atoms.

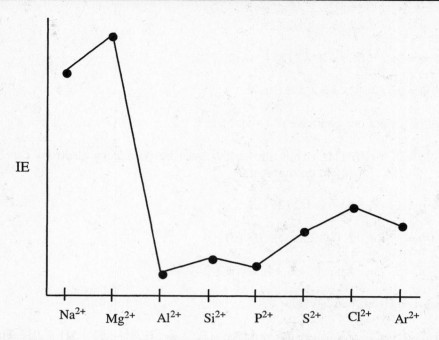

Note: The actual numbers in Table 7.5 support most of this plot. No IE_3 is given for Na^{2+}, so you cannot check this. The only deviation from our discussion is IE_3 for Ar^{2+} which is greater than IE_3 for Cl^{2+} instead of less than.

133.   The ratios for Mg, Si, P, Cl, and Ar are about the same. However, the ratios for Na, Al, and S are higher. For Na, the second IE is extremely high because the electron is taken from $n = 2$ (the first electron is taken from $n = 3$). For Al, the first electron requires a bit less energy than expected due to the fact it is a 3p electron versus a 3s electron. For S, the first electron requires a bit less energy than expected due to electrons being paired in one of the p orbitals.

134.   Size also decreases going across a period. Sc & Ti and Y & Zr are adjacent elements. There are 14 elements (the lanthanides) between La and Hf, making Hf considerable smaller.

135.   a. As we remove succeeding electrons, the electron being removed is closer to the nucleus, and there are fewer electrons left repelling it. The remaining electrons are more strongly attracted to the nucleus, and it takes more energy to remove these electrons; successive ionization energies should increase.

    b. Al : $1s^2 2s^2 2p^6 3s^2 3p^1$; For I_4, we begin by removing an electron with $n = 2$. For I_3, we remove an electron with $n = 3$. In going from $n = 3$ to $n = 2$, there is a big jump in ionization energy because the $n = 2$ electrons (inner core electrons) are much closer to the nucleus on average than $n = 3$ electrons (valence electrons). Since the $n = 2$ electrons are closer to the nucleus, they are held more tightly and require a much larger amount of energy to remove them compared to the $n = 3$ electrons.

    c. Al^{4+}; The electron affinity for Al^{4+} is ΔH for the reaction:

$$Al^{4+}(g) + e^- \rightarrow Al^{3+}(g)   \Delta H = -I_4 = -11,600 \text{ kJ/mol}$$

d. The greater the number of electrons, the greater the size.

Size trend: $Al^{4+} < Al^{3+} < Al^{2+} < Al^{+} < Al$

136.   None of the noble gases and no subatomic particles had been discovered when Mendeleev published his periodic table. Thus, there was not an element out of place in terms of reactivity. There was no reason to predict an entire family of elements. Mendeleev ordered his table by mass; he had no way of knowing there were gaps in atomic numbers (they hadn't been discovered yet).

137. $m = \dfrac{h}{\lambda v} = \dfrac{6.626 \times 10^{-34} \text{ kg m}^2/\text{s}}{3.31 \times 10^{-15} \text{ m} \times (0.0100 \times 2.998 \times 10^8 \text{ m/s})} = 6.68 \times 10^{-26} \text{ kg/atom}$

$\dfrac{6.68 \times 10^{-26} \text{ kg}}{\text{atom}} \times \dfrac{6.022 \times 10^{23} \text{ atoms}}{1 \text{ mol}} \times \dfrac{1000 \text{ g}}{1 \text{ kg}} = 40.2 \text{ g/mol}$

The element is calcium, Ca.

Integrated Problems

138.   a. $v = \dfrac{E}{h} = \dfrac{7.52 \times 10^{-19} \text{ J}}{6.626 \times 10^{-34} \text{ J s}} = 1.13 \times 10^{15} \text{ s}^{-1}$

$\lambda = \dfrac{c}{v} = \dfrac{2.998 \times 10^8 \text{ m/s}}{1.13 \times 10^{15} \text{ s}^{-1}} = 2.65 \times 10^{-7} \text{ m} = 265 \text{ nm}$

b. E_{photon} and λ are inversely related ($E = hc/\lambda$). Any wavelength of EMR less than or equal to 265 nm ($\lambda \leq 265$) will have sufficient energy to eject an electron. So, yes 259 nm EMR will eject an electron.

c.   This is the electron configuration for copper, Cu, an exception to the expected filling order.

139.   a.   An atom of francium has 87 protons and 87 electrons. Francium is an alkali metal and forms stable 1+ cations in ionic compounds. This cation would have 86 electrons.

Therefore, the electron configurations will be:

Fr: $[Rn]7s^1$; Fr^+: $[Rn] = [Xe]6s^2 4f^{14} 5d^{10} 6p^6$

b. $1.0 \text{ oz Fr} \times \dfrac{1 \text{ lb}}{16 \text{ oz}} \times \dfrac{1 \text{ kg}}{2.205 \text{ lb}} \times \dfrac{1000 \text{ g}}{1 \text{ kg}} \times \dfrac{1 \text{ mol Fr}}{223 \text{ g Fr}} \times \dfrac{6.02 \times 10^{23} \text{ atoms}}{1 \text{ mol Fr}}$

$= 7.7 \times 10^{22} \text{ atoms Fr}$

c. ^{223}Fr is element 87, so it has $223 - 87 = 136$ neutrons.

$$136 \text{ neutrons} \times \frac{1.67493 \times 10^{-27} \text{ kg}}{1 \text{ neutron}} \times \frac{1000 \text{ g}}{1 \text{ kg}} = 2.27790 \times 10^{-22} \text{ g neutrons}$$

140.   a. $[Kr]5s^2 4d^{10}5p^6 = Xe$; $[Kr]5s^2 4d^{10}5p^1 = In$; $[Kr]5s^2 4d^{10}5p^3 = Sb$

From the general radii trend, the increasing size order is Xe < Sb < In.

b. $[Ne]3s^2 3p^5 = Cl$; $[Ar]4s^2 3d^{10}4p^3 = As$; $[Ar]4s^2 3d^{10}4p^5 = Br$

From the general IE trend, the decreasing IE order is: Cl > Br > As.

Marathon Problem

141.   a.   Let λ = wavelength corresponding to the energy difference between the excited state, $n = ?$, and the ground state, $n = 1$. Use the information in part a to first solve for the energy difference, $\Delta E_{1 \to n}$, and then solve for the value of n. From the problem, $\lambda = (\lambda_{radio}/3.00 \times 10^7)$.

$$\Delta E_{1 \to n} = \frac{hc}{\lambda} = \frac{hc}{(\lambda_{radio}/3.00 \times 10^7)}, \quad \lambda_{radio} = \frac{hc \times 3.00 \times 10^7}{\Delta E_{1 \to n}}$$

$$\lambda_{radio} = \frac{c}{\nu_{radio}} = \frac{c}{97.1 \times 10^6 \text{ s}^{-1}} ; \quad \text{Equating the two } \lambda_{radio} \text{ expressions gives:}$$

$$\frac{c}{97.1 \times 10^6 \text{ s}^{-1}} = \frac{hc \times 3.00 \times 10^7}{\Delta E_{1 \to n}}, \quad \Delta E_{1 \to n} = h \times 3.00 \times 10^7 \times 97.1 \times 10^6$$

$$\Delta E_{1 \to n} = 6.626 \times 10^{-34} \text{ J s} \times 3.00 \times 10^7 \times 97.1 \times 10^6 \text{ s}^{-1} = 1.93 \times 10^{-18} \text{ J}$$

Now we can solve for the n value of the excited state.

$$\Delta E_{1 \to n} = 1.93 \times 10^{-18} \text{ J} = -2.178 \times 10^{-18} \left(\frac{1}{n^2} - \frac{1}{1^2} \right)$$

$$\frac{1}{n^2} = \frac{-1.93 \times 10^{-18} + 2.178 \times 10^{-18}}{2.178 \times 10^{-18}} = 0.11, \quad n = 3 = \text{energy level of the excited state}$$

b.   From de Broglie's equation:

$$\lambda = \frac{h}{mv} = \frac{6.626 \times 10^{-34} \text{ J s}}{9.109 \times 10^{-31} \text{ kg} \times 570. \text{ m/s}} = 1.28 \times 10^{-6} \text{ m}$$

Let $n = V$ = principal quantum number of the valence shell of element X. The electronic transition in question will be from $n = V$ to $n = 3$ (as determined in part a).

$$\Delta E_{n \to 3} = -2.178 \times 10^{-18} \left(\frac{1}{3^2} - \frac{1}{n^2} \right)$$

$$|\Delta E_{n \to 3}| = \frac{hc}{\lambda} = \frac{6.626 \times 10^{-34} \text{ J s} \times 2.998 \times 10^8 \text{ m/s}}{1.28 \times 10^{-6} \text{ m}} = 1.55 \times 10^{-19} \text{ J}$$

$$\Delta E_{n \to 3} = -1.55 \times 10^{-19} \text{ J} = -2.178 \times 10^{-18} \text{ J} \left(\frac{1}{9} - \frac{1}{n^2} \right)$$

$$\frac{1}{n^2} = \frac{-1.55 \times 10^{-19} + 2.178 \times 10^{-18} \left(\frac{1}{9} \right)}{1.28 \times 10^{-6} \text{ m}} = 0.040, \; n = 5$$

Thus, V = 5 = the principal quantum number for the valence shell of element X, that is, element X is in the fifth period (row) of the periodic table (element X = Rb – Xe).

c.   For $n = 2$, we can have 2s and 2p orbitals. None of the 2s orbitals have $m_\ell = -1$ and only one of the 2p orbitals has $m_\ell = -1$. In this one 2p atomic orbital, only one electron can have $m_s = -1/2$. Thus, only one unpaired electron exists in the ground state for element X. From period 5 elements, X could be Rb, Y, Ag, In or I since all of these elements only have one unpaired electron in the ground state.

d.   Element 120 will be the next alkaline earth metal discovered. Alkaline earth metals form 2+ charged ions in stable ionic compounds.

Thus, the angular momentum quantum number (ℓ) for the subshell of X which contains the unpaired electron is 2, which means the unpaired electron is in the d subshell. Although Y and Ag are both d-block elements, only Y has one unpaired electron in the d-block. Silver is an exception to the normal filling order; Ag has the unpaired electron in the 5s orbital. The ground state electron configurations are:

Y: $[Kr]5s^2 4d^1$ and Ag: $[Kr]5s^1 4d^{10}$

Element X is yttrium (Y).

CHAPTER EIGHT

BONDING: GENERAL CONCEPTS

For Review

1. Electronegativity is the ability of an atom in a molecule to attract electrons to itself. Electronegativity is a bonding term. Electron affinity is the energy change when an electron is added to a substance. Electron affinity deals with isolated atoms in the gas phase.

    A covalent bond is a sharing of electron pair(s) in a bond between two atoms. An ionic bond is a complete transfer of electrons from one atom to another to form ions. The electrostatic attraction of the oppositely charged ions is the ionic bond.

    A pure covalent bond is an equal sharing of shared electron pair(s) in a bond. A polar covalent bond is an unequal sharing.

    Ionic bonds form when there is a large difference in electronegativity between the two atoms bonding together. This usually occurs when a metal with a small electronegativity is bonded to a nonmetal having a large electronegativity. A pure covalent bond forms between atoms having identical or nearly identical eletronegativities. A polar covalent bond forms when there is an intermediate electronegativity difference. In general, nonmetals bond together by forming covalent bonds, either pure covalent or polar covalent.

    Ionic bonds form due to the strong electrostatic attraction between two oppositely charged ions. Covalent bonds form because the shared electrons in the bond are attracted to two different nuclei, unlike the isolated atoms where electrons are only attracted to one nuclei. The attraction to another nuclei overrides the added electron-electron repulsions.

2. Anions are larger than the neutral atom and cations are smaller than the neutral atom. For anions, the added electrons increase the electron-electron repulsions. To counteract this, the size of the electron cloud increases, placing the electrons further apart from one another. For cations, as electrons are removed, there are fewer electron-electron repulsions and the electron cloud can be pulled closer to the nucleus.

    Isoelectronic: same number of electrons. Two variables, the number of protons and the number of electrons, determine the size of an ion. Keeping the number of electrons constant, we only have to consider the number of protons to predict trends in size. The ion with the most protons attracts the same number of electrons most strongly resulting in a smaller size.

3. Lattice energy: the change in energy that takes place when separated gaseous ions are packed together to form an ionic solid. The reason ionic compounds form is the extremely favorable lattice energy value (large and negative). Looking at Figure 8.11, there are many processes that occur when forming an ionic compound from the elements in their standard state. Most of these processes (if not all) are unfavorable (endothermic). However, the large, exothermic lattice energy value dominates and the ionic compound forms.

The lattice energy follows Coulomb's law ($E \propto Q_1Q_2/r$). Because MgO has ions with +2 and -2 charges, it will have a more favorable lattice energy than NaF where the charge on the ions are -1 and $+1$. The reason MgO has +2 and -2 charged ions and not +1 and -1 charged ions is that lattice energy is more favorable as the charges increase. However, there is a limit to the magnitude of the charges. To form $Mg^{3+}O^{3-}$, the ionization energy would be extremely unfavorable for Mg^{2+} since an inner core ($n = 2$) electron is being removed. The same is true for the electron affinity of O^{2-}; it would be very unfavorable as the added electron goes into the $n = 3$ level. The lattice energy would certainly be more favorable for $Mg^{3+}O^{3-}$, but the unfavorable ionization energy and electron affinity would dominate making $Mg^{3+}O^{3-}$ energetically unfavorable overall. In general, ionic compounds want large charges, but only up to the point where valence electrons are removed or added. When we go beyond the valence shell, the energies become very unfavorable.

4.   When reactants are converted into products, reactant bonds are broken and product bonds are formed. Thus, ΔH for a reaction should be the energy it takes to break the reactant bonds minus the energy released when bonds are formed. Bond energies give good estimates for gas phase reactions, but give poor estimates when solids or liquids are present. This is because bond energy calculations ignore the attractive forces holding solids and liquids together. Gases have the molecules very far apart and they have minimal (assumed zero) attractive forces. This is not true for solids and liquids where the molecules are very close together. Attractive forces in substances are discussed in Chapter 10.

For an exothermic reaction, stronger bonds are formed in the products as compared to the strength of the bonds broken in the reactants so energy is released. For endothermic reactions, the product bonds are weaker overall and energy must be absorbed.

As the number of bonds increase, bond strength increases and bond length decreases.

5.   Nonmetals, which form covalent bonds, have valence electrons in the s and p orbitals. Since there are 4 total s and p orbitals, there is room for only 8 valence electrons (the octet rule). The valence shell for hydrogen is just the 1s orbital. This orbital can hold 2 electrons, so hydrogen follows the duet rule.

Drawing Lewis structures is mostly trial and error. The first step is to sum the valence electrons available. Next, attach the bonded atoms with a single bond. This is called the skeletal structure. In general, the atom listed first in a compound is called the central atom; all other atoms listed after the first atom are attached (bonded) to this central atom. If the skeletal structure is something different, we will generally give you hints to determine how the atoms are attached. The final step in drawing Lewis structures is to arrange the remaining electrons around the various atoms to satisfy the octet rule for all atoms (duet role for H).

Be and B are the usual examples for molecules that have fewer than 8 electrons. BeH_2 and BH_3 only have 4 and 6 total valence electrons, respectively; it is impossible to satisfy the octet rule for BeH_2 and BH_3 because fewer than 8 electrons are present.

All row three and heavier nonmetals can have more than 8 electrons around them, but only if they have to. Always satisfy the octet rule when you can; exceptions to the octet rule occur when there are no other options. Of the molecules listed in review question 10, KrF_2, IF_3, SF_4,

XeF_4, PF_5, IF_5, and SCl_6 are all examples of central atoms having more than 8 electrons. In all cases, exceptions occur because they have to.

The octet rule cannot be satisfied when there is an odd number of valence electrons. There must be an unpaired electron somewhere in the molecule and molecules do not like unpaired electrons. In general, odd electron molecules are very reactive; they react to obtain an even number of valence electrons. NO_2 is a good example. NO_2 has 17 valence electrons; when two NO_2 molecules react, N_2O_4, which has 34 valence electrons forms. The octet rule can be satisfied for N_2O_4.

6.   Resonance occurs when more than one valid Lewis structure can be drawn for a particular molecule. A common characteristic of resonance structures is a multiple bond(s) that moves from one position to another. We say the electrons in the multiple bond(s) are delocalized in the molecule. This helps us rationalize why the bonds in a molecule that exhibit resonance are all equivalent in length and strength. Any one of the resonance structures indicates different types of bonds within that molecule. This is not correct, hence none of the individual resonance structures are correct. We think of the actual structure as an average of all the resonance structures; again this helps explain the equivalent bonds within the molecule that experiment tells us we have.

7.   Formal charge: a made up charge assigned to an atom in a molecule or polyatomic ion derived from a specific set of rules. The equation to calculate formal charge is:

FC = (number of valence electrons of the free atom) −
                (number of valence electrons assigned to the atom in the molecule)

The assigned electrons are all of the lone pair electrons plus one-half of the bonding electrons.

Formal charge can be utilized when more than one nonequivalent resonance structure can be drawn for a molecule. The best structure, from a formal charge standpoint, is the structure that has the atoms in the molecule with a formal charge of zero. For organic compounds, carbon has 4 valence electrons and needs 4 more electrons to satisfy the octet rule. Carbon does this by forming 4 bonds to other atoms and by having no lone pairs of electrons. Any carbon with 4 bonds and no lone pairs has a formal charge of zero. Hydrogen needs just 1 more electron to obtain the He noble gas electron configuration. Hydrogen is always attached with a single bond to one other atom. N has 5 valence electrons for a formal charge of zero, N will form 3 bonds to other atom(s) for 6 electrons, and the remaining 2 electrons are a lone pair on N. Oxygen will have a formal charge of zero when it is attached to other atom(s) with 2 bonds and has 2 lone pairs. The halogens obtain a formal charge of zero by forming 1 bond to another atom as well as having 3 lone pairs.

8.   VSEPR = Valence Shell Electron-Pair Repulsion model. The main postulate is that the structure around a given atom is determined principally by minimizing electron-pair repulsion. Electrons don't like each other, so a molecule adopts a geometry to place the electron pairs about a central atom as far apart as possible. The five base geometries and bond angles are:

Number of bonded atoms plus
lone pairs about a central atom   Geometry   Bond Angle(s)

	Geometry	Bond Angle(s)
2	linear	180°
3	trigonal planar	120°
4	tetrahedral	109.5°
5	trigonal bipyramid	90°, 120°
6	octahedral	90°

To discuss deviations from the predicted VSEPR bond angles, let us examine CH_4, NH_3, and H_2O. CH_4 has the true 109.5° bond angles, but NH_3 (107.3°) and H_2O (104.5°) do not. CH_4 does not have any lone pairs of electrons about the central atom, while H_2O and NH_3 do. These lone pair electrons require more room than bonding electrons, which tends to compress the angles between the bonding pairs. The bond angle for H_2O is the smallest because oxygen has two lone pairs on the central atom; the bond angle is compressed more than in NH_3 where N has only one lone pair. So, in general, lone pairs compress the bond angles to a value slightly smaller than predicted by VSEPR.

9.   The two general requirements for a polar molecule are:

1. polar bonds
2. a structure such that the bond dipoles of the polar bonds do not cancel.

CF_4, 4 + 4(7) = 32 valence electrons XeF_4, 8 + 4(7) = 36 e⁻

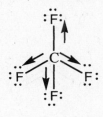

tetrahedral, 109.5°   square planar, 90°

SF_4, 6 + 4(7) = 34 e⁻

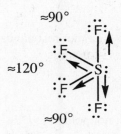

see-saw, ≈90°, ≈120°

The arrows indicate the individual bond dipoles in the three molecules (the arrows point to the more electronegative atom in the bond which will be the partial negative end of the bond dipole). All three of these molecules have polar bonds. To determine the polarity of the overall molecule, we sum the effect of all of the individual bond dipoles. In CF_4, the fluorines are symmetrically arranged about the central carbon atom. The net result is for all of the individual C–F bond dipoles to cancel each other out giving a nonpolar molecule. In XeF_4, the 4 Xe–F bond dipoles are also symmetrically arranged and XeF_4 is also nonpolar. The individual bond dipoles cancel out when summed together. In SF_4, we also have 4 polar bonds. But in SF_4, the bond dipoles are not symmetrically arranged and they do not cancel each other out. SF_4 is polar. It is the positioning of the lone pair that disrupts the symmetry in SF_4.

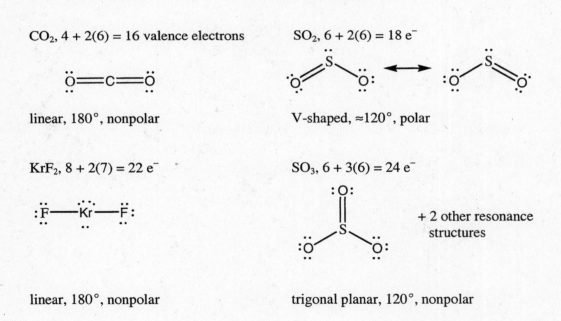

CO_2, $4 + 2(6) = 16\ e^-$

CO_2 is nonpolar because the individual bond dipoles cancel each other out, but COS is polar. By replacing an O with a less electronegative S atom, the molecule is not symmetric any more. The individual bond dipoles do not cancel since the C–S bond dipole is smaller than the C–O bond dipole resulting in a polar molecule.

10.   To predict polarity, draw in the individual bond dipoles, then sum up the net effect of the bond dipoles on each other. If the net effect is to have the bond dipoles cancel each other out, then the molecule is nonpolar. If the net effect of the bond dipoles is to not cancel each other out, then the molecule will have a partial positive end and a partial negative end (the molecule is polar). This is called a dipole moment or a polar molecule.

CO_2, $4 + 2(6) = 16$ valence electrons

linear, 180°, nonpolar

SO_2, $6 + 2(6) = 18\ e^-$

V-shaped, ≈120°, polar

KrF_2, $8 + 2(7) = 22\ e^-$

linear, 180°, nonpolar

SO_3, $6 + 3(6) = 24\ e^-$

+ 2 other resonance
structures

trigonal planar, 120°, nonpolar

NF_3, $5 + 3(7) = 26$ e$^-$

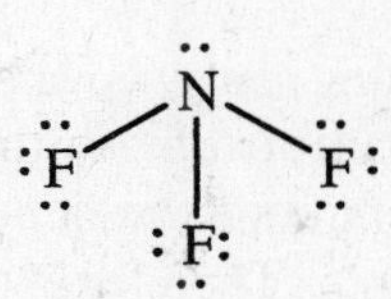

trigonal pyramid, $< 109.5°$, polar

The bond angles will be somewhat
less than $109.5°$ due to the lone
pair on the central nitrogen atom
needing more space.

CF_4, $4 + 4(7) = 32$ e$^-$

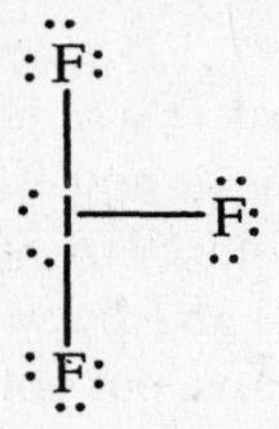

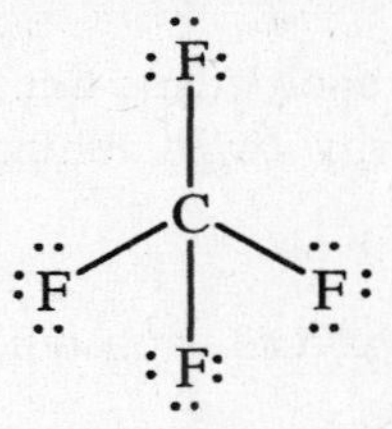

tetrahedral, $109.5°$, nonpolar

XeF_4, $8 + 4(7) = 36$ e$^-$

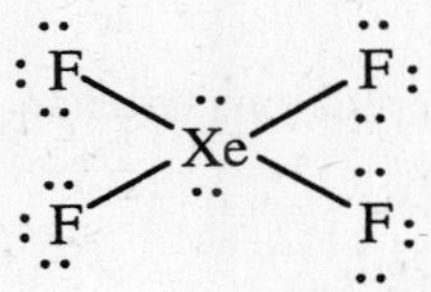

square planar, $90°$, nonpolar

IF_5, $7 + 5(7) = 42$ e$^-$

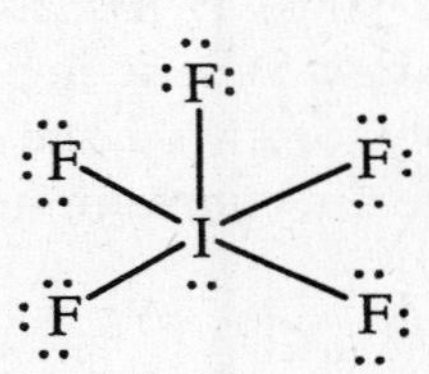

square pyramid, $\approx 90°$, polar

IF_3, $7 + 3(7) = 28$ e$^-$

T-shaped, ≈ 90, polar

SF_4, $6 + 4(7) = 34$ e$^-$

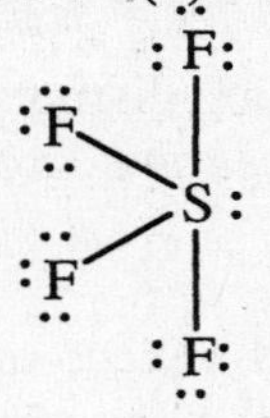

see-saw, $\approx 90°$ and $\approx 120°$, polar

PF_5, $5 + 5(7) = 40$ e$^-$

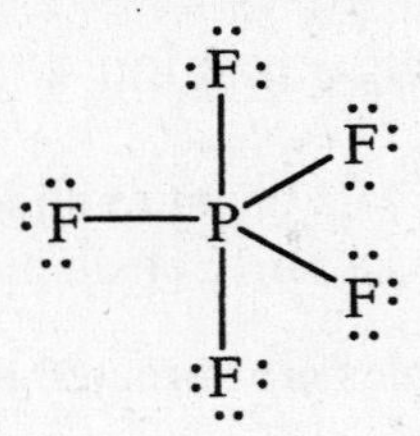

trigonal bipyramid,
$90°$ and $120°$, nonpolar

SCl_6, $6 + 6(7) = 48$ e$^-$

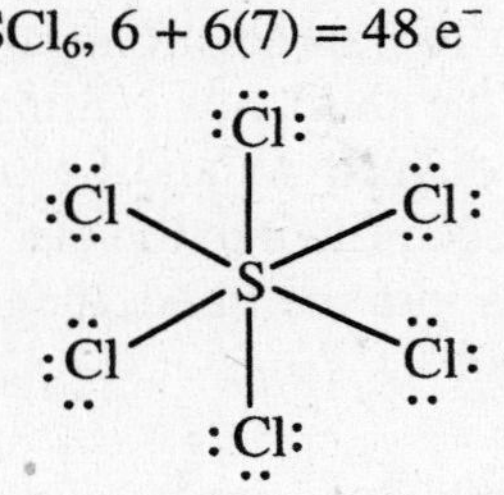

octahedral, $90°$, nonpolar

Questions

13.   Of the compounds listed, P_2O_5 is the only compound containing only covalent bonds. $(NH_4)_2SO_4$, $Ca_3(PO_4)_2$, K_2O, and KCl are all compounds composed of ions so they exhibit ionic bonding. The ions in $(NH_4)_2SO_4$ are NH_4^+ and SO_4^{2-}. Covalent bonds exist between the N and H atoms in NH_4^+ and between the S and O atoms in SO_4^{2-}. Therefore, $(NH_4)_2SO_4$ contains both ionic and covalent bonds. The same is true for $Ca_3(PO_4)_2$. The bonding is ionic between the Ca^{2+} and PO_4^{3-} ions and covalent between the P and O atoms in PO_4^{3-}. Therefore, $(NH_4)_2SO_4$ and $Ca_3(PO_4)_2$ are the compounds with both ionic and covalent bonds.

14.   Ionic solids are held together by strong electrostatic forces which are omnidirectional.

     i.   For electrical conductivity, charged species must be free to move. In ionic solids the charged ions are held rigidly in place. Once the forces are disrupted (melting or dissolution), the ions can move about (conduct).

     ii.   Melting and boiling disrupts the attractions of the ions for each other. Because these electrostatic forces are strong, it will take a lot of energy (high temperature) to accomplish this.

     iii.   If we try to bend a piece of material, the ions must slide across each other. For an ionic solid the following might happen:

            strong attraction   strong repulsion

        Just as the layers begin to slide, there will be very strong repulsions causing the solid to snap across a fairly clean plane.

     iv.   Polar molecules are attracted to ions and can break up the lattice.

These properties and their correlation to chemical forces will be discussed in detail in Chapters 10 and 11.

15.   Electronegativity increases left to right across the periodic table and decreases from top to bottom. Hydrogen has an electronegativity value between B and C in the second row, and identical to P in the third row. Going further down the periodic table, H has an electronegativity value between As and Se (row 4) and identical to Te (row 5). It is important to know where hydrogen fits into the electronegativity trend, especially for rows 2 and 3. If you know where H fits into the trend, then you can predict bond dipole directions for nonmetals bonded to hydrogen.

16.   linear structure (180° bond angle)

       $\ddot{\text{S}}\!=\!\!=\!\!=\!\text{C}\!=\!\!=\!\!=\!\ddot{\text{O}}$ $\ddot{\text{O}}\!=\!\!=\!\!=\!\text{C}\!=\!\!=\!\!=\!\ddot{\text{O}}$

       polar, bond dipoles do not cancel   nonpolar, bond dipoles cancel

trigonal planar structure (120° bond angle)

polar, bond dipoles do not cancel   nonpolar, bond dipoles cancel

tetrahedral structure (109.5° bond angles)

polar, bond dipoles do not cancel   nonpolar, bond dipoles cancel

17.   For ions, concentrate on the number of protons and the number of electrons present. The species whose nucleus holds the electrons most tightly will be smallest. For example, anions are larger than the neutral atom. The anion has more electrons held by the same number of protons in the nucleus. These electrons will not be held as tightly, resulting in a bigger size for the anion as compared to the neutral atom. For isoelectronic ions, the same number of electrons are held by different numbers of protons in the various ions. The ion with the most protons holds the electrons tightest and is smallest in size.

18.   Two other factors that must be considered are the ionization energy needed to produce more positively charged ions and the electron affinity needed to produce more negatively charged ions. The favorable lattice energy more than compensates for the unfavorable ionization energy of the metal and for the unfavorable electron affinity of the nonmetal, as long as electrons are added to or removed from the valence shell. Once the valence shell is full, the ionization energy required to remove another electron is extremely unfavorable; the same is true for electron affinity when an electron is added to a higher n shell. These two quantities are so unfavorable after the valence shell is complete, that they overshadow the favorable lattice energy and the higher charged ionic compounds do not form.

19.   Fossil fuels contain a lot of carbon and hydrogen atoms. Combustion of fossil fuels (reaction with O_2) produces CO_2 and H_2O. Both these compounds have very strong bonds. Because strong bonds are formed, combustion reactions are very exothermic.

20.   Statements a and c are true. For statement a, XeF_2 has 22 valence electrons and it is impossible to satisfy the octet rule for all atoms with this number of electrons. The best Lewis structure is:

For statement c, NO^+ has 10 valence electrons, while NO^- has 12 valence electrons. The Lewis structures are:

$$\left[\ :N\equiv O:\ \right]^+ \qquad \left[\ \ddot{N}=\ddot{O}\ \right]^-$$

Because a triple bond is stronger than a double bond, NO^+ has a stronger bond.

For statement b, SF_4 has 5 electron pairs around the sulfur in the best Lewis structure; it is an exception to the octet rule. Because OF_4 has the same number of valence electrons as SF_4, OF_4 would also have to be an exception to the octet rule. However, Row 2 elements like O never have more than 8 electrons around them, so OF_4 does not exist. For statement d, two resonance structures can be drawn for ozone:

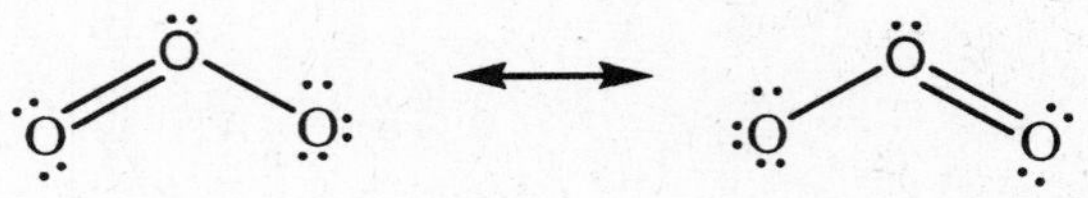

When resonance structures can be drawn, the actual bond lengths and strengths are all equal to each other. Even though each Lewis structure implies the two O−O bonds are different, this is not the case in real life. In real life, both of the O−O bonds are equivalent. When resonance structures can be drawn, you can think of the bonding as an average of all of the resonance structures.

21. CO_2, $4 + 2(6) = 16$ valence electrons

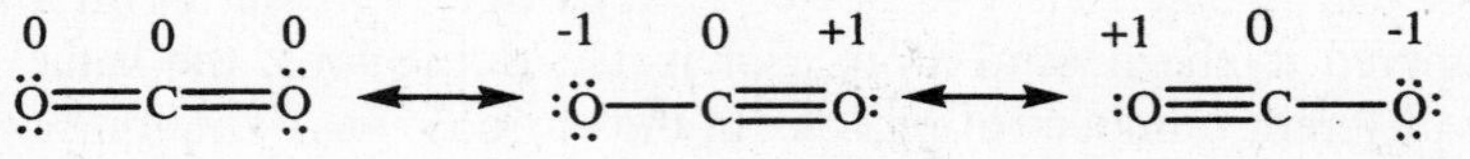

The formal charges are shown above the atoms in the three Lewis structures. The best Lewis structure for CO_2 from a formal charge standpoint is the first structure having each oxygen double bonded to carbon. This structure has a formal charge of zero on all atoms (which is preferred). The other two resonance structures have nonzero formal charges on the oxygens making them less reasonable. For CO_2, we usually ignore the last two resonance structures and think of the first structure as the true Lewis structure for CO_2.

22.   Only statement c is true. The bond dipoles in CF_4 and KrF_4 are arranged in a manner that they all cancel each other out, making them nonpolar molecules (CF_4 has a tetrahedral molecular structure while KrF_4 has a square planar molecular structure). In SeF_4, the bond dipoles in this see-saw molecule do not cancel each other out, so SeF_4 is polar. For statement a, all the molecules have either a trigonal planar geometry or a trigonal bipyramid geometry; both of which have 120° bond angles. However, $XeCl_2$ has three lone pairs and two bonded fluorine atoms around it. $XeCl_2$ has a linear molecular structure with a 180° bond angle. With three lone pairs, we no longer have a 120° bond angle in $XeCl_2$. For statement b, SO_2 has a V-shaped molecular structure with a bond angle of about 120°. CS_2 is linear with a 180° bond angle and SCl_2 is V-shaped but with a ≈109.5 bond angle. The three compounds do not have the same bond angle. For statement d, central atoms adopt a geometry to minimize electron repulsions, not maximize them.

Exercises

Chemical Bonds and Electronegativity

23.   The general trend for electronegativity is:
        1) increase as we go from left to right across a period and
        2) decrease as we go down a group

        Using these trends, the expected orders are:

        a. C < N < O   b. Se < S < Cl   c. Sn < Ge < Si   d. Tl < Ge < S

24.   a. Rb < K < Na   b. Ga < B < O   c. Br < Cl < F   d. S < O < F

25.   The most polar bond will have the greatest difference in electronegativity between the two
        atoms. From positions in the periodic table, we would predict:

        a. Ge–F   b. P–Cl   c. S–F   d. Ti–Cl

26.   a. Sn–H   b. Tl–Br   c. Si–O   d. O–F

27.   The general trends in electronegativity used in Exercises 8.23 and 8.25 are only rules of
        thumb. In this exercise, we use experimental values of electronegativities and can begin to
        see several exceptions. The order of EN from Figure 8.3 is:

        a. C (2.5) < N (3.0) < O (3.5)   same as predicted

        b. Se (2.4) < S (2.5) < Cl (3.0)   same

        c. Si = Ge = Sn (1.8)   different

        d. Tl (1.8) = Ge (1.8) < S (2.5)   different

        Most polar bonds using actual EN values:

        a. Si–F and Ge–F have equal polarity (Ge–F predicted).

        b. P–Cl (same as predicted)

        c. S–F (same as predicted)   d. Ti–Cl (same as predicted)

28.   The order of EN from Figure 8.3 is:

        a. Rb (0.8) = K (0.8) < Na (0.9), different   b. Ga (1.6) < B (2.0) < O (3.5), same

        c. Br (2.8) < Cl (3.0) < F (4.0), same   d. S (2.5) < O (3.5) < F (4.0), same

Most polar bonds using actual EN values:

a. C–H most polar (Sn–H predicted)

b. Al–Br most polar (Tl–Br predicted).   c. Si–O (same as predicted).

d. Each bond has the same polarity, but the bond dipoles point in opposite directions. Oxygen is the positive end in the O–F bond dipole, and oxygen is the negative end in the O–Cl bond dipole. (O–F predicted.)

29.   Use the electronegativity trend to predict the partial negative end and the partial positive end of the bond dipole (if there is one). To do this, you need to remember that H has electronegativity between B and C and identical to P. Answers b, d, and e are incorrect. For d (Br_2), the bond between two Br atoms will be a pure covalent bond where there is equal sharing of the bonding electrons and no dipole moment. For b and e, the bond polarities are reversed. In Cl–I, the more electronegative Cl atom will be the partial negative end of the bond dipole with I having the partial positive end. In O–P, the more electronegative oxygen will be the partial negative end of the bond dipole with P having the partial positive end. In the following, we used arrows to indicate the bond dipole. The arrow always points to the partial negative end of a bond dipole (which always is the most electronegative atom in the bond).

$$\overleftarrow{Cl \text{——} I} \qquad \overleftarrow{O \text{——} P}$$

30.   See Exercise 8.29 for a discussion on bond dipoles. We will use arrows to indicate the bond dipoles. The arrow always points to the partial negative end of the bond dipole which will always be to the more electronegative atom. The tail of the arrow indicates the partial positive end of the bond dipole.

a. $\overrightarrow{C \text{——} O}$

b.   P–H is a pure covalent (nonpolar) bond since P and H have identical electronegativities.

c. $\overrightarrow{H \text{——} Cl}$

d. $\overleftarrow{Br \text{——} Te}$

e. $\overrightarrow{Se \text{——} S}$ The actual electronegativity difference between Se and S is so small that this bond is probably best characterized as a pure covalent bond having no bond dipole.

31.   Electronegativity values increase from left to right across the periodic table. The order of electronegativities for the atoms from smallest to largest electronegativity will be H = P < C < N < O < F. The most polar bond will be F–H since it will have the largest difference in electronegativities, and the least polar bond will be P–H since it will have the smallest difference in electronegativities ($\Delta EN = 0$). The order of the bonds in decreasing polarity will be F–H > O–H > N–H > C–H > P–H.

32.   Ionic character is proportional to the difference in electronegativity values between the two elements forming the bond. Using the trend in electronegativity, the order will be:

$$Br\text{–}Br < N\text{–}O < C\text{–}F < Ca\text{–}O < K\text{–}F$$

least   most
ionic character   ionic character

Note that Br–Br, N–O and C–F bonds are all covalent bonds since the elements are all non-metals. The Ca–O and K–F bonds are ionic as is generally the case when a metal forms a bond with a nonmetal.

Ions and Ionic Compounds

33. Fr^+: $[Xe]6s^24f^{14}5d^{10}6p^6 = [Rn]$; Be^{2+}: $1s^2 = [He]$; P^{3-}: $[Ne]3s^23p^6 = [Ar]$

Cl^-: $[Ne]3s^23p^6 = [Ar]$; Se^{2-}: $[Ar]4s^23d^{10}4p^6 = [Kr]$

34.   a. Mg^{2+}: $1s^22s^22p^6$; K^+: $1s^22s^22p^63s^23p^6$; Al^{3+}: $1s^22s^22p^6$

        b. N^{3-}, O^{2-} and F^-: $1s^22s^22p^6$; Te^{2-}: $[Kr]5s^24d^{10}5p^6$

35.   a. Sc^{3+}: [Ar]   b. Te^{2-}: [Xe]   c. Ce^{4+}: [Xe] and Ti^{4+}: [Ar]   d. Ba^{2+}: [Xe]

All of these ions have the noble gas electron configuration shown in brackets.

36.   a. Cs_2S is composed of Cs^+ and S^{2-}. Cs^+ has the same electron configuration as Xe, and S^{2-} has the same configuration as Ar.

        b. SrF_2; Sr^{2+} has the Kr electron configuration and F^- has the Ne configuration.

        c. Ca_3N_2; Ca^{2+} has the Ar electron configuration and N^{3-} has the Ne configuration.

        d. $AlBr_3$; Al^{3+} has the Ne electron configuration and Br^- has the Kr configuration.

37.   There are many possible ions with 54 electrons. Some are: Sb^{3-}, Te^{2-}, I^-, Cs^+, Ba^{2+} and La^{3+}. In terms of size, the ion with the most protons will hold the electrons the tightest and will be the smallest. The largest ion will be the ion with the fewest protons. The size trend is:

$$La^{3+} < Ba^{2+} < Cs^+ < I^- < Te^{2-} < Sb^{3-}$$
smallest   largest

38.   All of these ions have 18 e^-; the smallest ion (Sc^{3+}) has the most protons attracting the 18 e^- and the largest ion has the fewest protons (S^{2-}). The order in terms of increasing size is: $Sc^{3+} < Ca^{2+} < K^+ < Cl^- < S^{2-}$. In terms of the atom size indicated in the question:

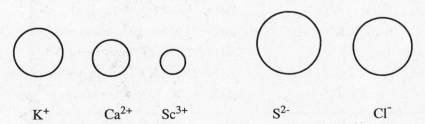

K⁺   Ca²⁺   Sc³⁺   S²⁻   Cl⁻

39.   a. $Cu > Cu^+ > Cu^{2+}$ b. $Pt^{2+} > Pd^{2+} > Ni^{2+}$ c. $O^{2-} > O^- > O$

d. $La^{3+} > Eu^{3+} > Gd^{3+} > Yb^{3+}$ e. $Te^{2-} > I^- > Cs^+ > Ba^{2+} > La^{3+}$

For answer a, as electrons are removed from an atom, size decreases. Answers b and d follow the radii trend. For answer c, as electrons are added to an atom, size increases. Answer e follows the trend for an isoelectronic series, i.e., the smallest ion has the most protons.

40.   a. $V > V^{2+} > V^{3+} > V^{5+}$ b. $Cs^+ > Rb^+ > K^+ > Na^+$ c. $Te^{2-} > I^- > Cs^+ > Ba^{2+}$

d. $P^{3-} > P^{2-} > P^- > P$ e. $Te^{2-} > Se^{2-} > S^{2-} > O^{2-}$

41.   a. Al^{3+} and S^{2-} are the expected ions. The formula of the compound would be Al_2S_3 (aluminum sulfide).

b. K^+ and N^{3-}; K_3N, potassium nitride

c. Mg^{2+} and Cl^-; $MgCl_2$, magnesium chloride

d. Cs^+ and Br^-; CsBr, cesium bromide

42.   a. Ga^{3+} and I^-; GaI_3, gallium iodide   b. Na^+ and O^{2-}; Na_2O, sodium oxide or Na^+ and O_2^{2-}; Na_2O_2, sodium peroxide

c. Sr^{2+} and F^-; SrF_2, strontium fluoride   d. Ca^{2+} and P^{3-}; Ca_3P_2, calcium phosphide

43.   Lattice energy is proportional to Q_1Q_2/r where Q is the charge of the ions and r is the distance between the ions. In general, charge effects on lattice energy are much greater than size effects.

a. NaCl; Na^+ is smaller than K^+.   b. LiF; F^- is smaller than Cl^-.

c. MgO; O^{2-} has a greater charge than OH^-.   d. $Fe(OH)_3$; Fe^{3+} has a greater charge than Fe^{2+}.

e. Na_2O; O^{2-} has a greater charge than Cl^-.   f. MgO; The ions are smaller in MgO.

44.   a. LiF; Li^+ is smaller than Cs^+.   b. NaBr; Br^- is smaller than I^-.

c. BaO; O^{2-} has a greater charge than Cl^-.   d. $CaSO_4$; Ca^{2+} has a greater charge than Na^+.

e. K_2O; O^{2-} has a greater charge than F^-.   f. Li_2O; The ions are smaller in Li_2O.

45.

$K(s) \rightarrow K(g)$	$\Delta H = $ 64 kJ (sublimation)
$K(g) \rightarrow K^+(g) + e^-$	$\Delta H = $ 419 kJ (ionization energy)
$1/2\ Cl_2(g) \rightarrow Cl(g)$	$\Delta H = $ 239/2 kJ (bond energy)
$Cl(g) + e^- \rightarrow Cl^-(g)$	$\Delta H = -349$ kJ (electron affinity)
$K^+(g) + Cl^-(g) \rightarrow KCl(s)$	$\Delta H = -690.$ kJ (lattice energy)

$K(s) + 1/2\ Cl_2(g) \rightarrow KCl(s)$	$\Delta H_f^\circ = -437$ kJ/mol

46.

$Mg(s) \rightarrow Mg(g)$	$\Delta H = 150. \text{ kJ}$	(sublimation)
$Mg(g) \rightarrow Mg^+(g) + e^-$	$\Delta H = 735 \text{ kJ}$	(IE_1)
$Mg^+(g) \rightarrow Mg^{2+}(g) + e^-$	$\Delta H = 1445 \text{ kJ}$	(IE_2)
$F_2(g) \rightarrow 2 F(g)$	$\Delta H = 154 \text{ kJ}$	(BE
$2 F(g) + 2 e^- \rightarrow 2 F^-(g)$	$\Delta H = 2(-328) \text{ kJ}$	(EA)
$Mg^{2+}(g) + 2 F^-(g) \rightarrow MgF_2(s)$	$\Delta H = -3916 \text{ kJ}$	(LE)

$$Mg(s) + F_2(g) \rightarrow MgF_2(s) \qquad \Delta H_f^\circ = -2088 \text{ kJ/mol}$$

47.   From the data given, it takes less energy to produce $Mg^+(g) + O^-(g)$ than to produce $Mg^{2+}(g) + O^{2-}(g)$. However, the lattice energy for $Mg^{2+}O^{2-}$ will be much more exothermic than that for Mg^+O^- due to the greater charges in $Mg^{2+}O^{2-}$. The favorable lattice energy term dominates and $Mg^{2+}O^{2-}$ forms.

48.

$Na(g) \rightarrow Na^+(g) + e^-$	$\Delta H = IE_1 = 495 \text{ kJ}$ (Table 7.5)
$F(g) + e^- \rightarrow F^-(g)$	$\Delta H = EA = -327.8 \text{ kJ}$ (Table 7.7)

$$Na(g) + F(g) \rightarrow Na^+(g) + F^-(g) \qquad \Delta H = 167 \text{ kJ}$$

The described process is endothermic. What we haven't accounted for is the extremely favorable lattice energy. Here, the lattice energy is a large negative (exothermic) value, making the overall formation of NaF a favorable exothermic process.

49.   Use Figure 8.11 as a template for this problem.

$Li(s) \rightarrow Li(g)$	$\Delta H_{sub} = ?$
$Li(g) \rightarrow Li^+(g) + e^-$	$\Delta H = 520. \text{ kJ}$
$1/2 I_2(g) \rightarrow I(g)$	$\Delta H = 151/2 \text{ kJ}$
$I(g) + e^- \rightarrow I^-(g)$	$\Delta H = -295 \text{ kJ}$
$Li^+(g) + I^-(g) \rightarrow LiI(s)$	$\Delta H = -753 \text{ kJ}$

$$Li(s) + 1/2 I_2(g) \rightarrow LiI(s) \qquad \Delta H = -272 \text{ kJ}$$

$\Delta H_{sub} + 520. + 151/2 - 295 - 753 = -272$, $\Delta H_{sub} = 181 \text{ kJ}$

50.   Let us look at the complete cycle for Na_2S.

$2 Na(s) \rightarrow 2 Na(g)$	$2 \Delta H_{sub, Na} = 2(109) \text{ kJ}$
$2 Na(g) \rightarrow 2 Na^+(g) + 2 e^-$	$2 IE = 2(495) \text{ kJ}$
$S(s) \rightarrow S(g)$	$\Delta H_{sub, S} = 277 \text{ kJ}$
$S(g) + e^- \rightarrow S^-(g)$	$EA_1 = -200. \text{ kJ}$
$S^-(g) + e^- \rightarrow S^{2-}(g)$	$EA_2 = ?$
$2 Na^+(g) + S^{2-}(g) \rightarrow Na_2S$	$LE = -2203 \text{ kJ}$

$$2 Na(s) + S(s) \rightarrow Na_2S(s) \qquad \Delta H_f^\circ = -365 \text{ kJ}$$

$\Delta H_f^\circ = 2\,\Delta H_{sub,\,Na} + 2\,IE + \Delta H_{sub,\,S} + EA_1 + EA_2 + LE,\ -365 = -918 + EA_2,\ EA_2 = 553\ kJ$

For each salt: $\Delta H_f^\circ = 2\,\Delta H_{sub,\,M} + 2\,IE + 277 - 200. + LE + EA_2$

K_2S: $\ -381 = 2(90.) + 2(419) + 277 - 200. - 2052 + EA_2,\ EA_2 = 576\ kJ$

Rb_2S: $-361 = 2(82) + 2(409) + 277 - 200. - 1949 + EA_2,\ EA_2 = 529\ kJ$

Cs_2S: $-360. = 2(78) + 2(382) + 277 - 200. - 1850. + EA_2,\ EA_2 = 493\ kJ$

We get values from 493 to 576 kJ.

The mean value is: $\dfrac{553 + 576 + 529 + 493}{4} = 538\ kJ$

We can represent the results as $EA_2 = 540 \pm 50\ kJ$.

51. Ca^{2+} has a greater charge than Na^+, and Se^{2-} is smaller than Te^{2-}. The effect of charge on the lattice energy is greater than the effect of size. We expect the trend from most exothermic to least exothermic to be:

$\quad\quad CaSe\ >\ CaTe\ >\ Na_2Se\ >\ Na_2Te$

$\quad\quad (-2862)\quad (-2721)\quad (-2130)\quad (-2095)\quad$ This is what we observe.

52. Lattice energy is proportional to the charge of the cation times the charge of the anion, Q_1Q_2.

Compound	Q_1Q_2	Lattice Energy
$FeCl_2$	$(+2)(-1) = -2$	-2631 kJ/mol
$FeCl_3$	$(+3)(-1) = -3$	-5359 kJ/mol
Fe_2O_3	$(+3)(-2) = -6$	$-14{,}744$ kJ/mol

Bond Energies

53. a. $H\!-\!H + Cl\!-\!Cl \longrightarrow 2\,H\!-\!Cl$

Bonds broken: Bonds formed:

$\quad$ 1 H $-$ H (432 kJ/mol)$\quad\quad\quad$ 2 H $-$ Cl (427 kJ/mol)

$\quad$ 1 Cl $-$ Cl (239 kJ/mol)

$\Delta H = \Sigma D_{broken} - \Sigma D_{formed},\ \Delta H = 432\ kJ + 239\ kJ - 2(427)\ kJ = -183\ kJ$

b. $N\!\equiv\!N + 3\,H\!-\!H \longrightarrow 2\,H\!-\!N\!-\!H$
$\quad\quad\quad\quad\quad\quad\quad\quad\quad\quad\quad\quad\quad\ |$
$\quad\quad\quad\quad\quad\quad\quad\quad\quad\quad\quad\quad\quad\ H$

Bonds broken: Bonds formed:

     1 N ≡ N (941 kJ/mol)   6 N − H (391 kJ/mol)
     3 H − H (432 kJ/mol)

ΔH = 941 kJ + 3(432) kJ − 6(391) kJ = −109 kJ

54.   Sometimes some of the bonds remain the same between reactants and products. To save time, only break and form bonds that are involved in the reaction.

a.

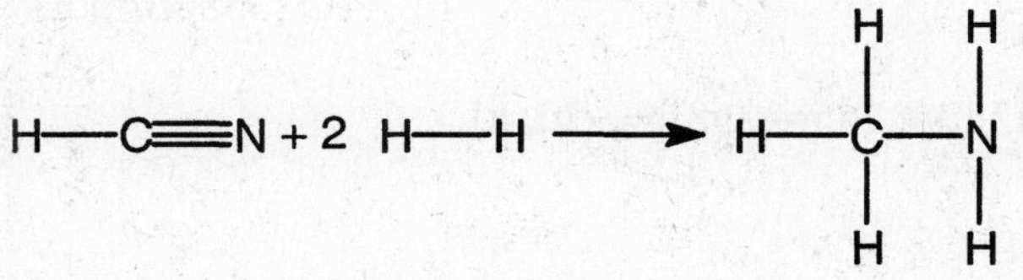

Bonds broken: Bonds formed:

    1 C ≡ N (891 kJ/mol)   1 C − N (305 kJ/mol)
    2 H − H (432 kJ/mol)   2 C − H (413 kJ/mol)
                                                    2 N − H (391 kJ/mol)

ΔH = 891 kJ + 2(432 kJ) - [305 kJ + 2(413 kJ) + 2(391 kJ)] = -158 kJ

b.

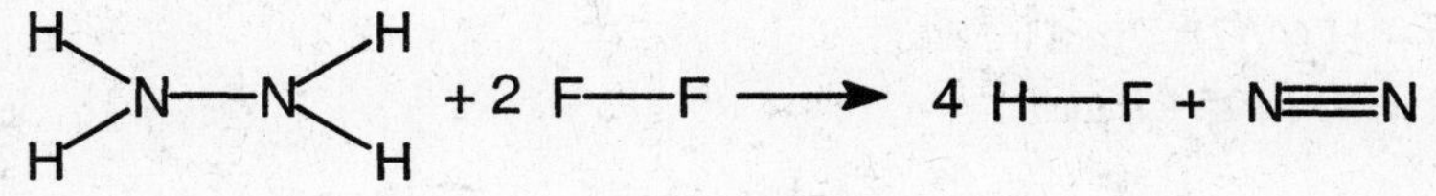

Bonds broken: Bonds formed:

    1 N − N (160. kJ/mol)   4 H − F (565 kJ/mol)
    4 N − H (391 kJ/mol)   1 N ≡ N (941 kJ/mol)
    2 F − F (154 kJ/mol)

ΔH = 160. kJ + 4(391 kJ) + 2(154 kJ) − [4(565 kJ) + 941 kJ] = −1169 kJ

55.

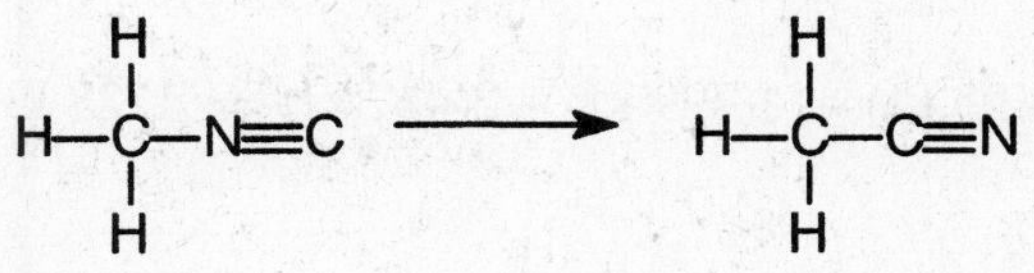

Bonds broken: 1 C − N (305 kJ/mol)   Bonds formed: 1 C − C (347 kJ/mol)

ΔH = ΣD$_{broken}$ − ΣD$_{formed}$,   ΔH = 305 − 347 = −42 kJ

Note: Sometimes some of the bonds remain the same between reactants and products. To save time, only break and form bonds that are involved in the reaction.

56.

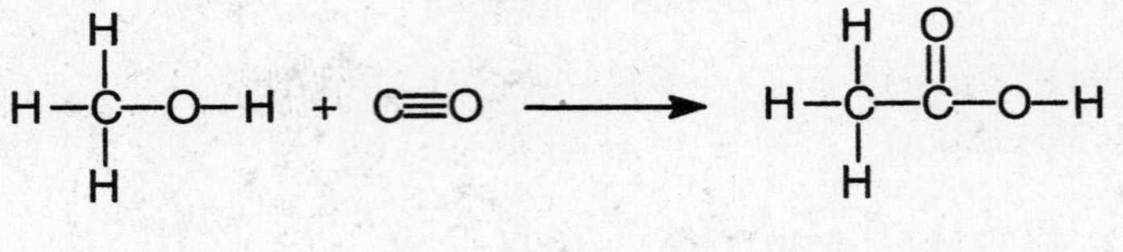

Bonds broken:

1 C ≡ O (1072 kJ/mol)
1 C − O (358 kJ/mol)

Bonds formed:

1 C − C (347 kJ/mol)
1 C = O (745 kJ/mol)
1 C − O (358 kJ/mol)

$\Delta H = 1072 + 358 - [347 + 745 + 358] = -20. \text{ kJ}$

57.

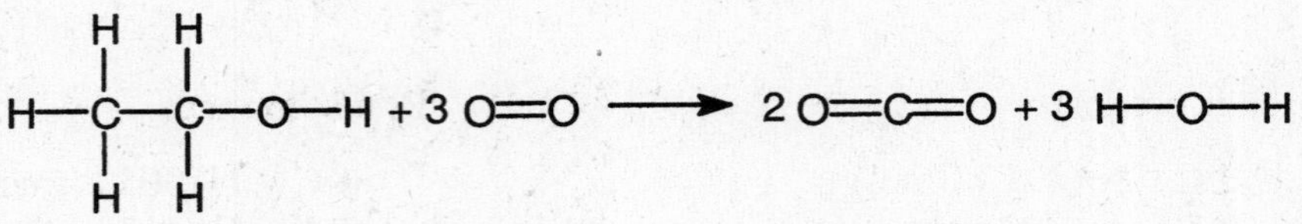

Bonds broken:

5 C − H (413 kJ/mol)
1 C − C (347 kJ/mol)
1 C − O (358 kJ/mol)
1 O − H (467 kJ/mol)
3 O = O (495 kJ/mol)

Bonds formed:

2 × 2 C = O (799 kJ/mol)
3 × 2 O − H (467 kJ/mol)

$\Delta H = 5(413 \text{ kJ}) + 347 \text{ kJ} + 358 \text{ kJ} + 467 \text{ kJ} + 3(495 \text{ kJ}) - [4(799 \text{ kJ}) + 6(467 \text{ kJ})]$

$$= -1276 \text{ kJ}$$

58. $H−C \equiv C−H + 5/2 \; O = O \rightarrow 2 \; O = C = O + H−O−H$

Bonds broken:

2 C−H (413 kJ/mol)
1 C ≡ C (839 kJ/mol)
5/2 O = O (495 kJ/mol)

Bonds formed:

2 × 2 C=O (799 kJ/mol)
2 O−H (467 kJ/mol)

$\Delta H = 2(413 \text{ kJ}) + 839 \text{ kJ} + 5/2 \; (495 \text{ kJ}) - [4(799 \text{ kJ}) + 2(467 \text{ kJ}] = -1228 \text{ kJ}$

59.

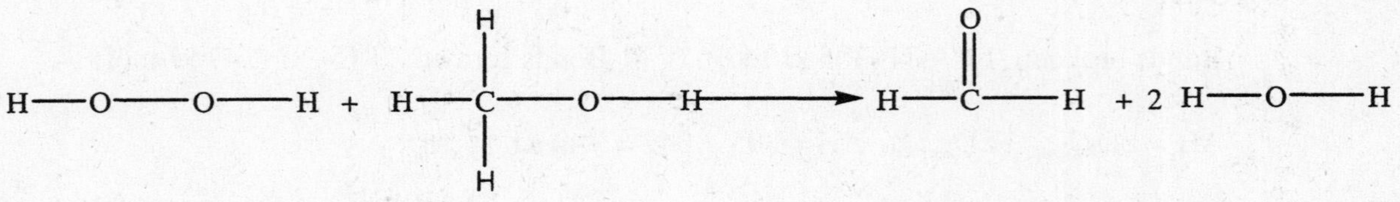

Bonds broken: Bonds formed:

    3 O–H (467 kJ/mol)   1 C=O (745 kJ/mol); This is not CO_2.

    1 O–O (146 kJ/mol)   2 × 2 O–H (467 kJ/mol)

    1 C–H (413 kJ/mol)

    1 C–O (358 kJ/mol)

$$\Delta H = 3(467 \text{ kJ}) + 146 \text{ kJ} + 413 \text{ kJ} + 358 \text{ kJ} - [745 \text{ kJ} + 4(467 \text{ kJ})] = -295 \text{ kJ}$$

60.

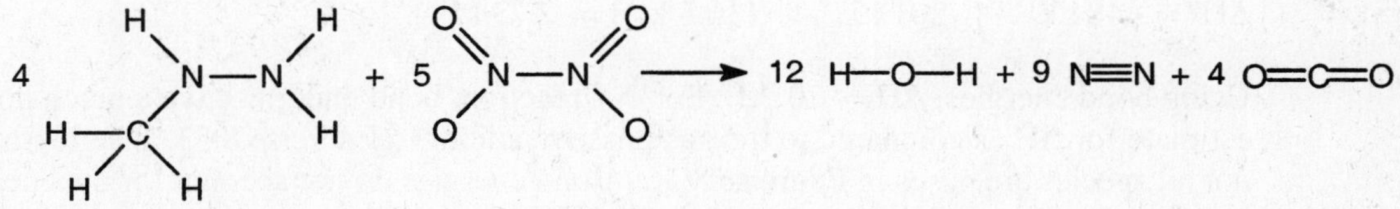

Bonds broken: Bonds formed:

    9 N – N (160. kJ/mol)   24 O – H (467 kJ/mol)

    4 N – C (305 kJ/mol)   9 N ≡ N (941 kJ/mol)

    12 C – H (413 kJ/mol)   8 C = O (799 kJ/mol)

    12 N – H (391 kJ/mol)

    10 N = O (607 kJ/mol)

    10 N – O   (201 kJ/mol)

$$\Delta H = 9(160.) + 4(305) + 12(413) + 12(391) + 10(607) + 10(201)$$

$$-[24(467) + 9(941) + 8(799)]$$

$$\Delta H = 20{,}388 \text{ kJ} - 26{,}069 \text{ kJ} = -5681 \text{ kJ}$$

61.

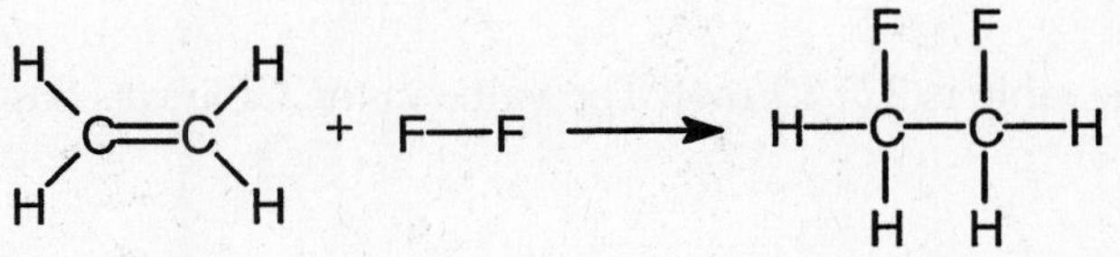

$$\Delta H = -549 \text{ kJ}$$

Bonds broken: Bonds formed:

    1 C = C (614 kJ/mol)   1 C – C (347 kJ/mol)

    1 F – F (154 kJ/mol)   2 C – F (D_{CF})

$$\Delta H = -549 \text{ kJ} = 614 \text{ kJ} + 154 \text{ kJ} - [347 \text{ kJ} + 2 D_{CF}], \ 2 D_{CF} = 970., \ D_{CF} = 485 \text{ kJ/mol}$$

62.   Let x = bond energy for A_2, then 2x = bond energy for AB.

$$\Delta H = -285 \text{ kJ} = x + 432 \text{ kJ} - [2(2x)], \ 3x = 717, \ x = 239 \text{ kJ/mol}$$

The bond energy for A_2 is 239 kJ/mol.

63.   a. $\Delta H° = 2 \, \Delta H°_{f,HCl} = 2$ mol (-92 kJ/mol) $= -184$ kJ ($= -183$ kJ from bond energies)

       b. $\Delta H° = 2 \, \Delta H°_{f,NH_3} = 2$ mol (-46 kJ/mol) $= -92$ kJ ($= -109$ kJ from bond energies)

Comparing the values for each reaction, bond energies seem to give a reasonably good estimate of the enthalpy change for a reaction. The estimate is especially good for gas phase reactions.

64. $CH_3OH(g) + CO(g) \rightarrow CH_3COOH(l)$

      $\Delta H° = -484$ kJ $- [(-201$ kJ$) + (-110.5$ kJ$)] = -173$ kJ

Using bond energies, $\Delta H = -20.$ kJ. For this reaction, bond energies give a much poorer estimate for ΔH as compared to the gas phase reactions in Exercise 8.53. The reason is that not all species are gases in Exercise 8.56. Bond energies do not account for the energy changes that occur when liquids and solids form instead of gases. These energy changes are due to intermolecular forces and will be discussed in Chapter 10.

65.   a.   Using SF_4 data: $SF_4(g) \rightarrow S(g) + 4 \, F(g)$

          $\Delta H° = 4 \, D_{SF} = 278.8 + 4 \, (79.0) - (-775) = 1370.$ kJ

          $D_{SF} = \dfrac{1370. \, kJ}{4 \, mol \, SF \, bonds} = 342.5$ kJ/mol

          Using SF_6 data: $SF_6(g) \rightarrow S(g) + 6 \, F(g)$

          $\Delta H° = 6 \, D_{SF} = 278.8 + 6 \, (79.0) - (-1209) = 1962$ kJ

          $D_{SF} = \dfrac{1962. \, kJ}{6 \, mol} = 327.0$ kJ/mol

       b.   The S $-$ F bond energy in the table is 327 kJ/mol. The value in the table was based on the S $-$ F bond in SF_6.

       c.   S(g) and F(g) are not the most stable forms of the elements at 25°C. The most stable forms are $S_8(s)$ and $F_2(g)$; $\Delta H°_f = 0$ for these two species.

66. $NH_3(g) \rightarrow N(g) + 3 \, H(g)$; $\Delta H° = 3 \, D_{NH} = 472.7 + 3(216.0) - (-46.1) = 1166.8$ kJ

     $D_{NH} = \dfrac{1166.8 \, kJ}{3 \, mol \, NH \, bonds} = 388.93$ kJ/mol ≈ 389 kJ/mol

     $D_{calc} = 389$ kJ/mol as compared to 391 kJ/mol in the table. There is good agreement.

Lewis Structures and Resonance

67.   Drawing Lewis structures is mostly trial and error. However, the first two steps are always the same. These steps are 1) count the valence electrons available in the molecule/ion, and 2) attach all atoms to each other with single bonds (called the skeletal structure). Unless noted otherwise, the atom listed first is assumed to be the atom in the middle (called the central atom) and all other atoms in the formula are attached to this atom. The most notable exceptions to the rule are formulas which begin with H, e.g., H_2O, H_2CO, etc. Hydrogen can never be a central atom since this would require H to have more than two electrons. In these compounds, the atom listed second is assumed to be the central atom.

After counting valence electrons and drawing the skeletal structure, the rest is trial and error. We place the remaining electrons around the various atoms in an attempt to satisfy the octet rule (or duet rule for H). Keep in mind that practice makes perfect. After practicing you can (and will) become very adept at drawing Lewis structures.

a.   HCN has $1 + 4 + 5 = 10$ valence

| Skeletal structure | Lewis structure |

b. PH_3 has $5 + 3(1) = 8$ valence electrons.

| Skeletal structure | Lewis structure |

c. $CHCl_3$ has $4 + 1 + 3(7) = 26$ valence electrons.

| Skeletal structure | Lewis structure |

d. NH_4^+ has $5 + 4(1) - 1 = 8$ valence electrons.

Note: Subtract valence electrons for positive charged ions.

Lewis structure

e. H_2CO has $2(1) + 4 + 6 = 12$ valence electrons.

f. SeF_2 has $6 + 2(7) = 20$ valence electrons.

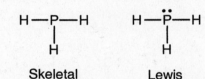

g. CO_2 has $4 + 2(6) = 16$ valence electrons

h. O_2 has $2(6) = 12$ valence electrons.

i.   HBr has 1 + 7 = 8 valence electrons.

H—B̈r:

68.   a. $POCl_3$ has 5 + 6 + 3(7) = 32 valence electrons.

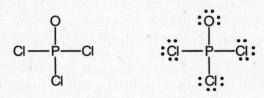

Skeletal structure	Lewis structure

This structure uses all 32 e⁻ while satisfying the octet rule for all atoms. This is a valid Lewis structure.

SO_4^{2-} has 6 + 4(6) + 2 = 32 valence electrons.

Note: A negatively charged ion will have additional electrons to those that come from the valence shell of the atoms.

XeO_4, 8 + 4(6) = 32 e⁻ PO_4^{3-}, 5 + 4(6) + 3 = 32 e⁻

ClO_4^- has 7 + 4(6) + 1 = 32 valence electrons

Note: All of these species have the same number of atoms and the same number of valence electrons. They also have the same Lewis structure.

b. NF_3 has $5 + 3(7) = 26$ valence electrons. SO_3^{2-}, $6 + 3(6) + 2 = 26$ e$^-$

Skeletal   Lewis
structure   structure

PO_3^{3-}, $5 + 3(6) + 3 = 26$ e$^-$ ClO_3^-, $7 + 3(6) + 1 = 26$ e$^-$

Note: Species with the same number of atoms and valence electrons have similar Lewis structures.

c. ClO_2^- has $7 + 2(6) + 1 = 20$ valence

Skeletal structure   Lewis structure

SCl_2, $6 + 2(7) = 20$ e$^-$ PCl_2^-, $5 + 2(7) + 1 = 20$ e$^-$

Note: Species with the same number of atoms and valence electrons have similar Lewis structures.

d.   Molecules ions that have the same number of valence electrons and the same number of atoms will have similar Lewis structures.

69. BeH_2, $2 + 2(1) = 4$ valence electrons BH_3, $3 + 3(1) = 6$ valence electrons

H——Be——H

70.   a. NO_2, $5 + 2(6) = 17\ e^-$ N_2O_4, $2(5) + 4(6) = 34\ e^-$

plus others

                                               plus other resonance structures

b. BH_3, $3 + 3(1) = 6\ e^-$ NH_3, $5 + 3(1) = 8\ e^-$

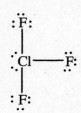

BH_3NH_3, $6 + 8 = 14\ e^-$

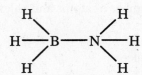

In reaction a, NO_2 has an odd number of electrons so it is impossible to satisfy the octet rule. By dimerizing to form N_2O_4, the odd electron on two NO_2 molecules can pair up, giving a species whose Lewis structure can satisfy the octet rule. In general, odd electron species are very reactive. In reaction b, BH_3 is electron deficient. Boron has only six electrons around it. By forming BH_3NH_3, the boron atom satisfies the octet rule by accepting a lone pair of electrons from NH_3 to form a fourth bond.

71. PF_5, $5 + 5(7) = 40$ valence electrons SF_4, $6 + 4(7) = 34\ e^-$

ClF_3, $7 + 3(7) = 28\ e^-$ Br_3^-, $3(7) + 1 = 22\ e^-$

Row 3 and heavier nonmetals can have more than 8 electrons around them when they have to. Row 3 and heavier elements have empty d orbitals which are close in energy to valence s and p orbitals. These empty d orbitals can accept extra electrons.

For example, P in PF_5 has its five valence electrons in the 3s and 3p orbitals. These s and p orbitals have room for 3 more electrons, and if it has to, P can use the empty 3d orbitals for any electrons above 8.

72. SF_6, $6 + 6(7) = 48$ e$^-$ ClF_5, $7 + 5(7) = 42$ e$^-$

XeF_4, $8 + 4(7) = 36$ e$^-$

73.   a. NO_2^- has $5 + 2(6) + 1 = 18$ valence electrons. The skeletal structure is: O—N—O

To get an octet about the nitrogen and only use 18 e$^-$, we must form a double bond to one of the oxygen atoms.

Since there is no reason to have the double bond to a particular oxygen atom, we can draw two resonance structures. Each Lewis structure uses the correct number of electrons and satisfies the octet rule, so each is a valid Lewis structure. Resonance structures occur when you have multiple bonds that can be in various positions. We say the actual structure is an average of these two resonance structures.

NO_3^- has $5 + 3(6) + 1 = 24$ valence electrons. We can draw three resonance structures for NO_3^-, with the double bond rotating among the three oxygen atoms.

N_2O_4 has $2(5) + 4(6) = 34$ valence electrons. We can draw four resonance structures for N_2O_4.

b. OCN^- has $6 + 4 + 5 + 1 = 16$ valence electrons. We can draw three resonance structures for OCN^-.

SCN^- has $6 + 4 + 5 + 1 = 16$ valence electrons. Three resonance structures can be drawn.

N_3^- has $3(5) + 1 = 16$ valence electrons. As with OCN^- and SCN^-, three different resonance structures can be drawn.

74.   Ozone: O_3 has $3(6) = 18$ valence electrons.

Sulfur dioxide: SO_2 has $6 + 2(6) = 18$ valence electrons.

Sulfur trioxide: SO_3 has $6 + 3(6) = 24$ valence electrons.

75.   Benzene has $6(4) + 6(1) = 30$ valence electrons. Two resonance structures can be drawn for benzene. The actual structure of benzene is an average of these two resonance structures, that is, all carbon-carbon bonds are equivalent with a bond length and bond strength somewhere between a single and a double bond.

76.   Borazine ($B_3N_3H_6$) has $3(3) + 3(5) + 6(1) = 30$ valence electrons. The possible resonance structures are similar to those of benzene in Exercise 8.75.

77.   We will use a hexagon to represent the six-member carbon ring, and we will omit the 4 hydrogen atoms and the three lone pairs of electrons on each chlorine. If no resonance existed, we could draw 4 different molecules:

If the double bonds in the benzene ring exhibit resonance, then we can draw only three different dichlorobenzenes. The circle in the hexagon represents the delocalization of the three double bonds in the benzene ring (see Exercise 8.75).

With resonance, all carbon-carbon bonds are equivalent. We can't distinguish between a single and double bond between adjacent carbons that have a chlorine attached. That only 3 isomers are observed supports the concept of resonance.

78. CO_3^{2-} has $4 + 3(6) + 2 = 24$ valence electrons.

Three resonance structures can be drawn for CO_3^{2-}. The actual structure for CO_3^{2-} is an average of these three resonance structures. That is, the three C–O bond lengths are all equivalent, with a length somewhere between a single and a double bond. The actual bond length of 136 pm is consistent with this resonance view of CO_3^{2-}.

79.

N_2 (10 e$^-$): $:N{\equiv}N:$ Triple bond between N and N.

N_2F_4 (38 e$^-$):   Single bond between N and N.

N_2F_2 (24 e$^-$): $:\!\ddot{F}\!-\!N\!=\!N\!-\!\ddot{F}\!:$ Double bond between N and N.

As the number of bonds increase between two atoms, bond strength increases and bond length decreases. From the Lewis structure, the shortest to longest N-N bonds are: $N_2 < N_2F_2 < N_2F_4$.

80.   The Lewis structures for the various species are:

CO (10 e⁻):   :C≡O: Triple bond between C and O.

CO_2 (16 e⁻):   Ö=C=Ö   Double bond between C and O.

CO_3^{2-} (24 e⁻):

Average of 1 1/3 bond between C and O in CO_3^{2-}.

CH_3OH (14 e⁻):

Single bond between C and O.

As the number of bonds increases between two atoms, bond length decreases and bond strength increases. With this in mind, then:

longest → shortest   C – O bond: $CH_3OH > CO_3^{2-} > CO_2 > CO$

weakest → strongest C – O bond: $CH_3OH < CO_3^{2-} < CO_2 < CO$

Formal Charge

81.   See Exercise 8.68a for the Lewis structures of $POCl_3$, SO_4^{2-}, ClO_4^- and PO_4^{3-}. Formal charge = [number of valence electrons on free atom] - [number of lone pair electrons on atom + 1/2 (number of shared electrons of atom)].

a. $POCl_3$: P, FC = 5 – 1/2(8) = +1   b. SO_4^{2-}: S, FC = 6 – 1/2(8) = +2

c. ClO_4^-: Cl, FC = 7 – 1/2(8) = +3   d. PO_4^{3-}: P, FC = 5 – 1/2(8) = +1

e. SO_2Cl_2, 6 + 2(6) + 2(7) = 32 e⁻   f. XeO_4, 8 + 4(6) = 32 e⁻

S, FC = 6 – 1/2(8) = +2   Xe, FC = 8 – 1/2(8) = +4

g. ClO_3^-, $7 + 3(6) + 1 = 26$ e$^-$

$$\left[\quad :\ddot{O}-\ddot{Cl}-\ddot{O}: \atop :\ddot{O}: \quad \right]^-$$

Cl, FC = $7 - 2 - 1/2(6) = +2$

h. NO_4^{3-}, $5 + 4(6) + 3 = 32$ e$^-$

$$\left[\quad :\ddot{O}: \atop :\ddot{O}-N-\ddot{O}: \atop :\ddot{O}: \quad \right]^{3-}$$

N, FC = $5 - 1/2(8) = +1$

82. For SO_4^{2-}, ClO_4^-, PO_4^{3-} and ClO_3^-, only one of the possible resonance structures is drawn.

a. Must have five bonds to P to minimize formal charge of P. The best choice is to form a double bond to O since this will give O a formal charge of zero and single bonds to Cl for the same reason.

$$:\ddot{O}: \atop :\ddot{Cl}-P-\ddot{Cl}: \atop :\ddot{Cl}: \qquad P, FC = 0$$

b. Must form six bonds to S to minimize formal charge of S.

$$\left[\quad :\ddot{O}: \atop :\ddot{O}-S-\ddot{O}: \atop :\ddot{O}: \quad \right]^{2-} \qquad S, FC = 0$$

c. Must form seven bonds to Cl to minimize formal charge.

$$\left[\quad :\ddot{O}: \atop \ddot{O}=\ddot{Cl}=\ddot{O} \atop :\ddot{O}: \quad \right]^- \qquad Cl, FC = O$$

d. Must form five bonds to P to to minimize formal charge.

$$\left[\quad :\ddot{O}: \atop :\ddot{O}-P-\ddot{O}: \atop :\ddot{O}: \quad \right]^{3-} \qquad P, FC = 0$$

e.

$$:\ddot{O}: \atop :\ddot{Cl}-S-\ddot{Cl}: \atop :\ddot{O}: \qquad \begin{matrix} S, \ FC = 0 \\ Cl, \ FC = 0 \\ O, \ FC = 0 \end{matrix}$$

f.

$$:\ddot{O}: \atop \ddot{O}=\ddot{Xe}=\ddot{O} \atop :\ddot{O}: \qquad Xe, FC = 0$$

g.

$$\left[\quad \ddot{O}=\ddot{Cl}=\ddot{O} \atop :\ddot{O}: \quad \right]^- \qquad Cl, FC = 0$$

h.   We can't. The following structure has a zero formal charge for N:

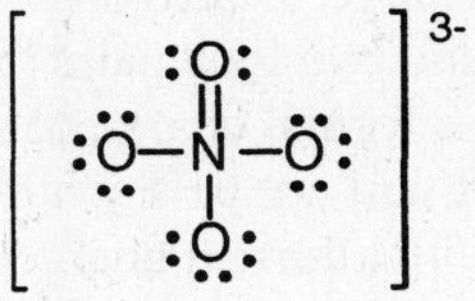

But N does not expand its octet. We wouldn't expect this resonance form to exist.

83. O_2F_2 has $2(6) + 2(7) = 26$ valence e⁻. The formal charge and oxidation number of each atom is below the Lewis structure of O_2F_2.

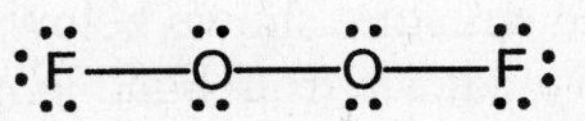

Formal Charge   0   0   0   0

Oxid. Number   -1   +1   +1   -1

Oxidation numbers are more useful when accounting for the reactivity of O_2F_2. We are forced to assign +1 as the oxidation number for oxygen. Oxygen is very electronegative, and +1 is not a stable oxidation state for this element.

84.   OCN⁻ has $6 + 4 + 5 + 1 = 16$ valence electrons.

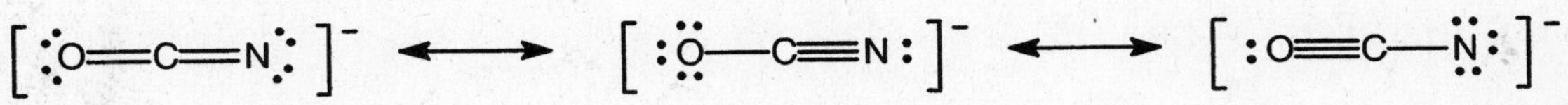

Formal
charge   0   0   -1   -1   0   0   +1   0   -2

Only the first two resonance structures should be important. The third places a positive formal charge on the most electronegative atom in the ion and a –2 formal charge on N.

CNO⁻ will also have 16 valence electrons.

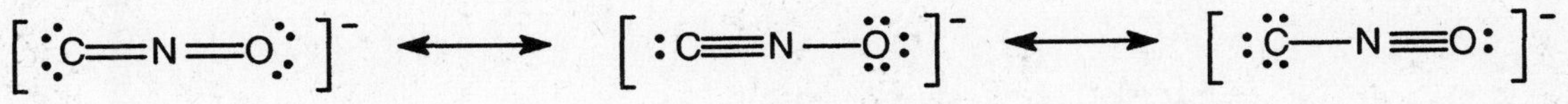

Formal
charge   -2   +1   0   -1   +1   -1   -3   +1   +1

All of the resonance structures for fulminate (CNO⁻) involve greater formal charges than in cyanate (OCN⁻), making fulminate more reactive (less stable).

85.   SCl, 6 + 7 = 13; the formula could be SCl (13 valence electrons), S_2Cl_2 (26 valence electrons), S_3Cl_3 (39 valence electrons), etc. For a formal charge of zero on S, we will need each sulfur in the Lewis structure to have two bonds to it and two lone pairs [FC = 6 – 4 – 1/2(4) = 0]. Cl will need one bond and three lone pairs for a formal charge of zero [FC = 7 – 6 – 1/2(2) = 0]. Since chlorine wants only one bond to it, it will not be a central atom here. With this in mind, only S_2Cl_2 can have a Lewis structure with a formal charge of zero on all atoms. The structure is:

$$:\ddot{C}l\!-\!\!-\!\!\ddot{S}\!-\!\!-\!\!\ddot{S}\!-\!\!-\!\!\ddot{C}l:$$

86.   The nitrogen-nitrogen bond length of 112 pm is between a double (120 pm) and a triple (110 pm) bond. The nitrogen-oxygen bond length of 119 pm is between a single (147 pm) and a double bond (115 pm). The third resonance structure shown below doesn't appear to be as important as the other two since there is no evidence from bond lengths for a nitrogen-oxygen triple bond or a nitrogen-nitrogen single bond as in the third resonance form. We can adequately describe the structure of N_2O using the resonance forms:

$$\ddot{N}\!=\!\!=\!N\!=\!\!=\!\ddot{O} \quad\longleftrightarrow\quad :N\!\equiv\!N\!-\!\ddot{O}:$$

Assigning formal charges for all 3 resonance forms:

$$\ddot{N}\!=\!\!=\!N\!=\!\!=\!\ddot{O} \quad\longleftrightarrow\quad :N\!\equiv\!N\!-\!\ddot{O}: \quad\longleftrightarrow\quad :\ddot{N}\!-\!N\!\equiv\!O:$$
$$\;-1\quad +1\quad\; 0 \qquad\qquad\quad 0\quad +1\quad -1 \qquad\qquad\quad -2\quad +1\quad +1$$

For:

$$\left(\ddot{\underset{\cdot\cdot}{N}}\!=\!\!=\right),\ \text{FC} = 5 - 4 - 1/2(4) = -1$$

$$\left(=\!\!=\!N\!=\!\!=\right),\ \text{FC} = 5 - 1/2(8) = +1 ,\ \text{Same for}\ \left(\equiv\!N\!-\!\right)\ \text{and}\ \left(-\!N\!\equiv\right)$$

$$\left(:\ddot{N}\!-\!\right),\ \text{FC} = 5 - 6 - 1/2(2) = -2 ;\ \left(:N\!\equiv\right),\ \text{FC} = 5 - 2 - 1/2(6) = 0$$

$$\left(=\!\!=\!\ddot{O}\right),\ \text{FC} = 6 - 4 - 1/2(4) = 0 ;\ \left(-\!\ddot{O}:\right),\ \text{FC} = 6 - 6 - 1/2(2) = -1$$

$$\left(\equiv\!O:\right),\ \text{FC} = 6 - 2 - 1/2(6) = +1$$

We should eliminate N–N≡O since it has a formal charge of +1 on the most electronegative element (O). This is consistent with the observation that the N–N bond is between a double and triple bond and that the N–O bond is between a single and double bond.

Molecular Structure and Polarity

87.   The first step always is to draw a valid Lewis structure when predicting molecular structure. When resonance is possible, only one of the possible resonance structures is necessary to predict the correct structure because all resonance structures give the same structure. The Lewis structures are in Exercises 8.67 and 8.73. The structures and bond angles for each follow.

8.67   a. HCN: linear, 180°   b. PH_3: trigonal pyramid, < 109.5°

        c. $CHCl_3$: tetrahedral, 109.5°   d. NH_4^+: tetrahedral, 109.5°

        e. H_2CO: trigonal planar, 120°   f. SeF_2: V-shaped or bent, < 109.5°

        g. CO_2: linear, 180°   h and i. O_2 and HBr are both linear, but
                                                            there is no bond angle in either.

Note: PH_3 and SeF_2 both have lone pairs of electrons on the central atom which result in bond angles that are something less than predicted from a tetrahedral arrangement (109.5°). However, we cannot predict the exact number. For the solutions manual, we will insert a less than sign to indicate this phenomenon. For bond angles equal to 120°, the lone pair phenomenon isn't as significant as compared to smaller bond angles. For these molecules, e.g., NO_2^-, we will insert an approximate sign in front of the 120° to note that there may be a slight distortion from the VSEPR predicted bond angle.

8.73   a. NO_2^-: V-shaped, ≈ 120°; NO_3^-: trigonal planar, 120°

            N_2O_4: trigonal planar, 120° about both N atoms

        b. OCN^-, SCN^- and N_3^- are all linear with 180° bond angles.

88.   See Exercises 8.68 and 8.74 for the Lewis structures.

8.68   a. All are tetrahedral; 109.5°

        b. All are trigonal pyramid; < 109.5°

        c. All are V-shaped; < 109.5°

8.74 O_3 and SO_2 are V-shaped (or bent) with a bond angle ≈ 120°. SO_3 is trigonal planar with 120° bond angles.

89.   From the Lewis structures (see Exercise 8.71), Br_3^- would have a linear molecular structure, ClF_3 would have a T-shaped molecular structure and SF_4 would have a see-saw molecular structure. For example, consider ClF_3 (28 valence electrons):

The central Cl atom is surrounded by 5 electron pairs, which requires a trigonal bipyramid geometry. Since there are 3 bonded atoms and 2 lone pairs of electrons about Cl, we describe the molecular structure of ClF_3 as T-shaped with predicted bond angles of about 90°. The actual bond angles would be slightly less than 90° due to the stronger repulsive effect of the lone pair electrons as compared to the bonding electrons.

90.   From the Lewis structures (see Exercise 8.72), XeF_4 would have a square planar molecular structure, and ClF_5 would have a square pyramid molecular structure.

91.   a. SeO_3, $6 + 3(6) = 24$ e⁻

SeO₃ has a trigonal planar molecular structure with all bond angles equal to 120°. Note that any one of the resonance structures could be used to predict molecular structure and bond angles.

b. SeO_2, $6 + 2(6) = 18$ e⁻

SeO_2 has a V-shaped molecular structure. We would expect the bond angle to be approximately 120° as expected for trigonal planar geometry.

Note: Both of these structures have three effective pairs of electrons about the central atom. All of the structures are based on a trigonal planar geometry, but only SeO₃ is described as having a trigonal planar structure. Molecular structure always describes the relative positions of the atoms.

92.   a. PCl_3 has $5 + 3(7) =$ 26 valence electrons.

Trigonal pyramid; all angles are < 109.5°.

b. SCl_2 has $6 + 2(7) =$ 20 valence electrons.

V-shaped; angle is < 109.5°.

c. SiF_4 has $4 + 4(7) = 32$ valence electrons.

Tetrahedral; all angles are 109.5°.

Note: There are 4 pairs of electrons about the central atom in each case in this exercise. All of the structures are based on a tetrahedral geometry, but only SiF_4 has a tetrahedral structure. We consider only the relative positions of the atoms when describing the molecular structure.

93.   a. $XeCl_2$ has $8 + 2(7) = 22$ valence electrons.

$$:\ddot{Cl} - \underset{\cdot\cdot}{Xe} - \ddot{Cl}:$$

$$180°$$

There are 5 pairs of electrons about the central Xe atom. The structure will be based on a trigonal bipyramid geometry. The most stable arrangement of the atoms in $XeCl_2$ is a linear molecular structure with a 180° bond angle.

b. ICl_3 has $7 + 3(7) = 28$ valence electrons.

$:\ddot{Cl}:$ ≈90°

$:\ddot{I} - \ddot{Cl}:$

$:\ddot{Cl}:$ ≈90°

T-shaped; The ClICl angles are ≈ 90°. Since the lone pairs will take up more space, the ClICl bond angles will probably be slightly less than 90°.

c. TeF_4 has $6 + 4(7) = 34$
valence electrons.

≈ 120° ⟶

≈ 90°

See-saw or teeter-totter
or distorted tetrahedron

d. PCl_5 has $5 + 5(7) = 40$
valence electrons.

90°

120° ⟶

Trigonal bipyramid

All of the species in this exercise have 5 pairs of electrons around the central atom. All of the structures are based on a trigonal bipyramid geometry, but only in PCl_5 are all of the pairs bonding pairs. Thus, PCl_5 is the only one we describe as a trigonal bipyramid molecular structure. Still, we had to begin with the trigonal bipyramid geometry to get to the structures of the others.

94.   a. ICl_5, $7 + 5(7) = 42$ e⁻

≈ 90°

90° ⟵

90°

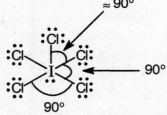

Square pyramid, ≈ 90° bond angles

b. $XeCl_4$, $8 + 4(7) = 36$ e⁻

90°

90°

Square planar, 90° bond angles

c. $SeCl_6$ has $6 + 6(7) = 48$ valence electrons.

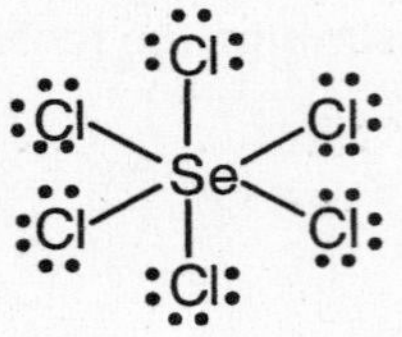

Octahedral, 90° bond angles

Note: All these species have 6 pairs of electrons around the central atom. All three structures are based on the octahedron, but only $SeCl_6$ has an octahedral molecular structure.

95. SeO_3 and SeO_2 both have polar bonds but only SeO_2 has a dipole moment. The three bond dipoles from the three polar Se–O bonds in SeO_3 will all cancel when summed together. Hence, SeO_3 is nonpolar since the overall molecule has no resulting dipole moment. In SeO_2, the two Se–O bond dipoles do not cancel when summed together, hence SeO_2 has a dipole moment (is polar). Since O is more electronegative than Se, the negative end of the dipole moment is between the two O atoms, and the positive end is around the Se atom. The arrow in the following illustration represents the overall dipole moment in SeO_2. Note that to predict polarity for SeO_2, either of the two resonance structures can be used.

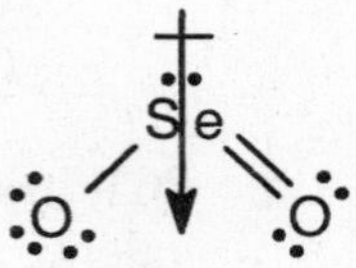

96.   All have polar bonds; in SiF_4 the individual bond dipoles cancel when summed together, and in PCl_3 and SCl_2 the individual bond dipoles do not cancel. Therefore, SiF_4 has no dipole moment (is nonpolar), and PCl_3 and SCl_2 have dipole moments (are polar). For PCl_3, the negative end of the dipole moment is between the more electronegative chlorine atoms and the positive end is around P. For SCl_2, the negative end is between the more electronegative Cl atoms, and the positive end of the dipole moment is around S.

97.   All have polar bonds, but only TeF_4 and ICl_3 have dipole moments. The bond dipoles from the five P–Cl bonds in PCl_5 cancel each other when summed together, so PCl_5 has no dipole moment. The bond dipoles in $XeCl_2$ also cancel:

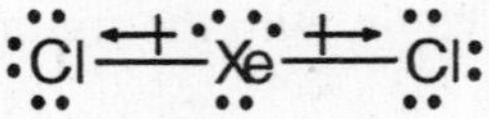

Since the bond dipoles from the two Xe–Cl bonds are equal in magnitude but point in opposite directions, they cancel each other and $XeCl_2$ has no dipole moment (is nonpolar). For TeF_4 and ICl_3, the arrangement of these molecules is such that the individual bond dipoles do <u>not</u> all cancel, so each has an overall dipole moment (is polar).

98.   All have polar bonds, but only ICl_5 has an overall dipole moment. The six bond dipoles in $SeCl_6$ all cancel each other, so $SeCl_6$ has no dipole moment. The same is true for $XeCl_4$:

When the four bond dipoles are added together, they all cancel each other, resulting in $XeCl_4$ having no overall dipole moment (is nonpolar). ICl_5 has a structure where the individual bond dipoles do <u>not</u> all cancel, hence ICl_5 has a dipole moment (is polar)

99.   Molecules which have an overall dipole moment are called polar molecules, and molecules which do not have an overall dipole moment are called nonpolar molecules.

a. OCl_2, $6 + 2(7) = 20$ e$^-$ KrF_2, $8 + 2(7) = 22$ e$^-$

V-shaped, polar; OCl_2 is polar because the two O–Cl bond dipoles don't cancel each other. The resultant dipole moment is shown in the drawing.

Linear, nonpolar; The molecule is nonpolar because the two Kr–F bond dipoles cancel each other.

BeH_2, $2 + 2(1) = 4$ e$^-$ SO_2, $6 + 2(6) = 18$ e$^-$

Linear, nonpolar; Be–H bond dipoles are equal and point in opposite directions. They cancel each other. BeH_2 is nonpolar.

V-shaped, polar; The S–O bond dipoles do not cancel, so SO_2 is polar (has a dipole moment). Only one resonance structure is shown.

Note: All four species contain three atoms. They have different structures because the number of lone pairs of electrons around the central atom is different in each case. Polarity can only be predicted on an individual basis.

b. SO_3, $6 + 3(6) = 24 e^-$ NF_3, $5 + 3(7) = 26 e^-$

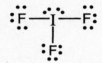

Trigonal planar, nonpolar; Bond dipoles   Trigonal pyramid, polar; Bond dipoles do
cancel. Only one resonance structure is   not cancel.
shown.

IF_3 has $7 + 3(7) = 28$ valence electrons.

T-shaped, polar; bond dipoles do not cancel.

Note: Each molecule has the same number of atoms, but the structures are different because
of differing numbers of lone pairs around each central atom.

c. CF_4, $4 + 4(7) = 32 e^-$ SeF_4, $6 + 4(7) = 34 e^-$

Tetrahedral, nonpolar;   See-saw, polar;
Bond dipoles cancel.   Bond dipoles do not cancel.

KrF_4, $8 + 4(7) = 36$ valence electrons

Square planar, nonpolar;
Bond dipoles cancel.

Again, each molecule has the same number of atoms, but a different structure
because of differing numbers of lone pairs around the central atom.

d. IF_5, $7 + 5(7) = 42$ e⁻

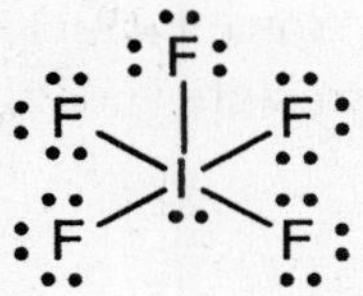

AsF₅, $5 + 5(7) = 40$ e⁻

Square pyramid, polar;
Bond dipoles do not cancel.

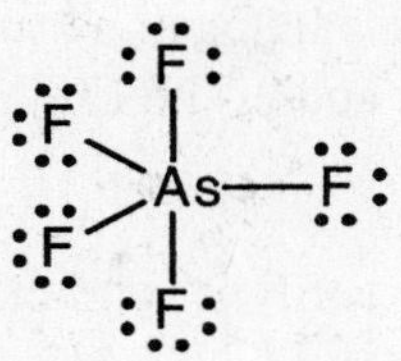

Trigonal bipyramid, nonpolar;
Bond dipoles cancel.

Yet again, the molecules have the same number of atoms, but different structures
because of the presence of differing numbers of lone pairs.

100.   a.   b.

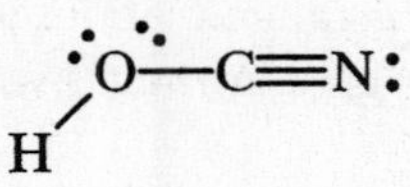

Polar; The bond dipoles do
not cancel.

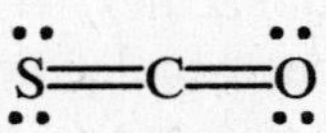

Polar; The C–O bond is a more polar
bond than the C–S bond. So the two
bond dipoles do not cancel each other.

c.   d.

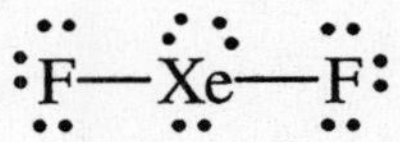

Nonpolar; The two Xe–F bond
dipoles cancel each other.

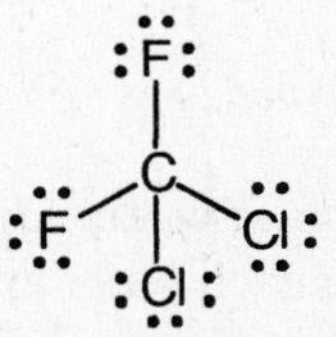

Polar; All the bond dipoles are not
equivalent, and they don't cancel each
other.

e.   f.

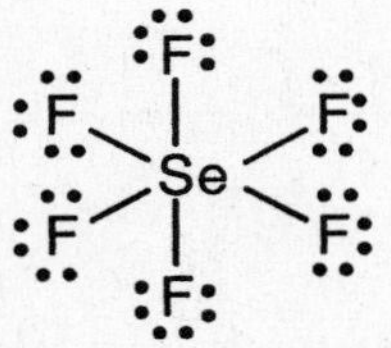

Nonpolar; The six Se–F bond
dipoles cancel each other.

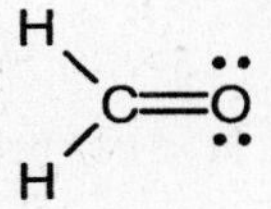

Polar; The bond dipoles are not
equivalent, and they don't cancel
each other.

101. EO_3^- is the formula of the ion. The Lewis structure has 26 valence electrons. Let x = number
of valence electrons of element E.

$26 = x + 3(6) + 1$, $x = 7$ valence electrons

Element E is a halogen because halogens have 7 valence electrons. Some possible identities are F, Cl, Br and I. The EO_3^- ion has a trigonal pyramid molecular structure with bond angles $< 109.5°$.

102.   The formula is EF_2O^{2-} and the Lewis structure has 28 valence electrons.

$28 = x + 2(7) + 6 + 2$, $x = 6$ valence electrons for element E

Element E must belong to the group 6A elements because E has 6 valence electrons. E must also be a row 3 or heavier element since this ion has more than 8 electrons around the central E atom (row 2 elements never have more than 8 electrons around them). Some possible identities for E are S, Se and Te. The ion has a T-shaped molecular structure with bond angles of $\approx 90°$.

103.   All these molecules have polar bonds that are symmetrically arranged about the central atoms. In each molecule, the individual bond dipoles cancel to give no net overall dipole moment, so they are all nonpolar.

104. XeF_2Cl_2, $8 + 2(7) + 2(7) = 36$ e$^-$

polar   nonpolar

The two possible structures for XeF_2Cl_2 are above. In the first structure, the F atoms are 90° apart from each other and the Cl atoms are also 90° apart. The individual bond dipoles would not cancel in this molecule, so this molecule is polar. In the second possible structure, the F atoms are 180° apart as are the Cl atoms. Here, the bond dipoles are symmetrically arranged so they do cancel out each other, and this molecule is nonpolar. Therefore, measurement of the dipole moment would differentiate between the two compounds. These are different compounds and not resonance structures.

Additional Exercises

105.   a.   Radius: $N^+ < N < N^-$; IE: $N^- < N < N^+$

N^+ has the fewest electrons held by the 7 protons in the nucleus, while N^- has the most electrons held by the 7 protons. The 7 protons in the nucleus will hold the electrons most tightly in N^+ and least tightly in N^-. Therefore, N^+ has the smallest radius with the largest ionization energy (IE) and N^- is the largest species with the smallest IE.

b.   Radius: $Cl^+ < Cl < Se < Se^-$; IE: $Se^- < Se < Cl < Cl^+$

The general trends tell us that Cl has a smaller radius than Se and a larger IE than Se. Cl^+, with fewer electron-electron repulsions than Cl, will be smaller than Cl and have a larger IE. Se^-, with more electron-electron repulsions than Se, will be larger than Se and have a smaller IE.

c.   Radius: $Sr^{2+} < Rb^+ < Br^-$; IE: $Br^- < Rb^+ < Sr^{2+}$

These ions are isoelectronic. The species with the most protons (Sr^{2+}) will hold the electrons most tightly and will have the smallest radius and largest IE.   The ion with the fewest protons (Br^-) will hold the electrons least tightly and will have the largest radius and smallest IE.

106.   a. $Na^+(g) + Cl^-(g) \rightarrow NaCl(s)$ b. $NH_4^+(g) + Br^-(g) \rightarrow NH_4Br(s)$

c. $Mg^{2+}(g) + S^{2-}(g) \rightarrow MgS(s)$ d. $O_2(g) \rightarrow 2\ O(g)$

107.   a.

$$HF(g) \rightarrow H(g) + F(g) \qquad \Delta H = 565\ kJ$$
$$H(g) \rightarrow H^+(g) + e^- \qquad \Delta H = 1312\ kJ$$
$$F(g) + e^- \rightarrow F^-(g) \qquad \Delta H = -327.8\ kJ$$

$$HF(g) \rightarrow H^+(g) + F^-(g) \qquad \Delta H = 1549\ kJ$$

b.

$$Cl(g) \rightarrow H(g) + Cl(g) \qquad \Delta H = 427\ kJ$$
$$H(g) \rightarrow H^+(g) + e^- \qquad \Delta H = 1312\ kJ$$
$$I(g) + e^- \rightarrow Cl^-(g) \qquad \Delta H = -348.7\ kJ$$

$$HCl(g) \rightarrow H^+(g) + Cl^-(g) \qquad \Delta H = 1390.\ kJ$$

c.

$$HI(g) \rightarrow H(g) + I(g) \qquad \Delta H = 295\ kJ$$
$$H(g) \rightarrow H^+(g) + e^- \qquad \Delta H = 1312\ kJ$$
$$I(g) + e^- \rightarrow I^-(g) \qquad \Delta H = -295.2\ kJ$$

$$HI(g) \rightarrow H^+(g) + I^-(g) \qquad \Delta H = 1312\ kJ$$

d.

$$H_2O(g) \rightarrow OH(g) + H(g) \qquad \Delta H = 467\ kJ$$
$$H(g) \rightarrow H^+(g) + e^- \qquad \Delta H = 1312\ kJ$$
$$OH(g) + e^- \rightarrow OH^-(g) \qquad \Delta H = -180.\ kJ$$

$$H_2O(g) \rightarrow H^+(g) + OH^-(g) \qquad \Delta H = 1599\ kJ$$

108. CO_3^{2-} has $4 + 3(6) + 2 = 24$ valence electrons.

HCO_3^- has $1 + 4 + 3(6) + 1 = 24$ valence electrons.

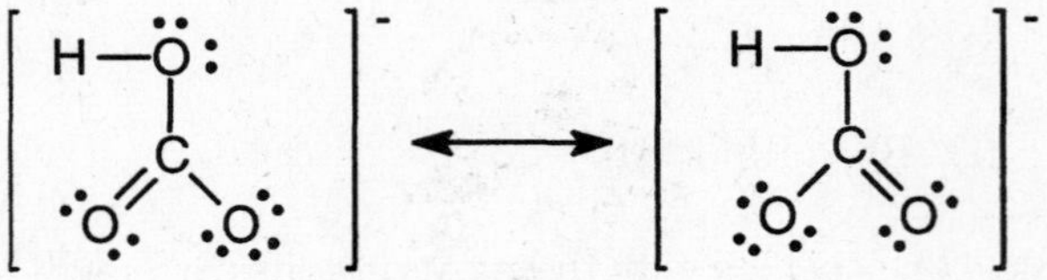

H_2CO_3 has $2(1) + 4 + 3(6) = 24$ valence electrons.

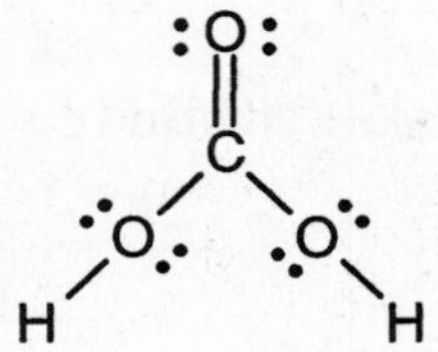

The Lewis structures for the reactants and products are:

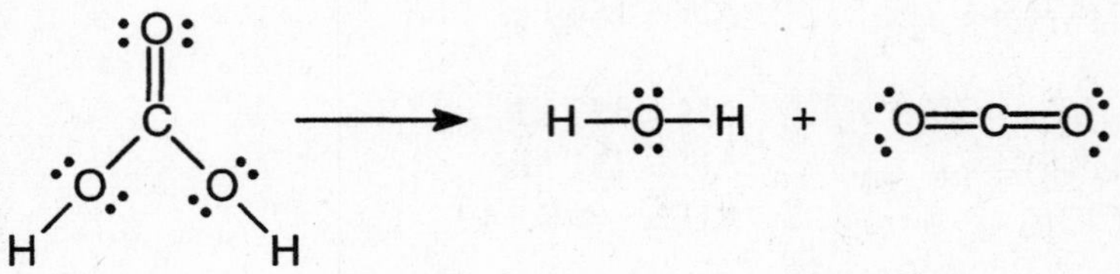

Bonds broken:	Bonds formed:
2 C–O (358 kJ/mol)	1 C=O (799 kJ/mol)
1 O–H (467 kJ/mol)	1 O–H (467 kJ/mol)

$\Delta H = 2(358) + 467 - [799 + 467] = -83$ kJ; The carbon-oxygen double bond is stronger than two carbon-oxygen single bonds, hence CO_2 and H_2O are more stable than H_2CO_3.

109.   The stable species are:

a.   NaBr: In $NaBr_2$, the sodium ion would have a $+2$ charge assuming each bromine has a -1 charge. Sodium doesn't form stable Na^{2+} ionic compounds.

b. ClO_4^-: ClO_4 has 31 valence electrons so it is impossible to satisfy the octet rule for all atoms in ClO_4. The extra electron from the -1 charge in ClO_4^- allows for complete octets for all atoms.

c. XeO_4: We can't draw a Lewis structure that obeys the octet rule for SO_4 (30 electrons), unlike XeO_4 (32 electrons).

d. SeF_4: Both compounds require the central atom to expand its octet. O is too small and doesn't have low energy d orbitals to expand its octet (which is true for all row 2 elements).

110.   a.   All have 24 valence electrons and the same number of atoms in the formula. All have the same resonance Lewis structures; the structures are all trigonal planar with 120° bond angles. The Lewis structures for NO_3^- and CO_3^{2-} will be the same as the three SO_3 Lewis structures shown below.

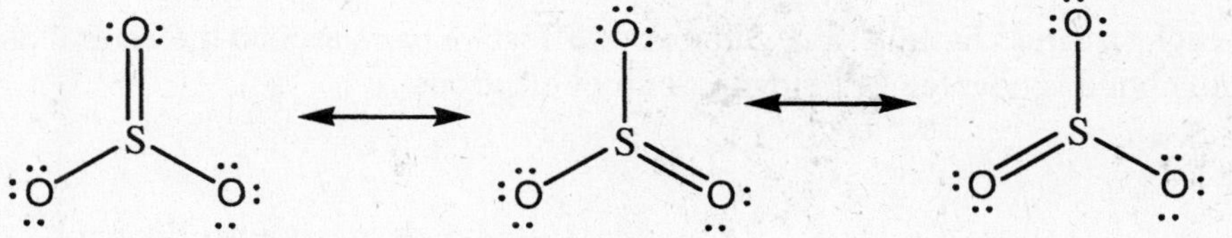

        b.   All have 18 valence electrons and the same number of atoms. All have the same resonance Lewis structures; the molecular structures are all V-shaped with ≈120° bond angles. O_3 and SO_2 have the same two Lewis structures as is shown for NO_2^-.

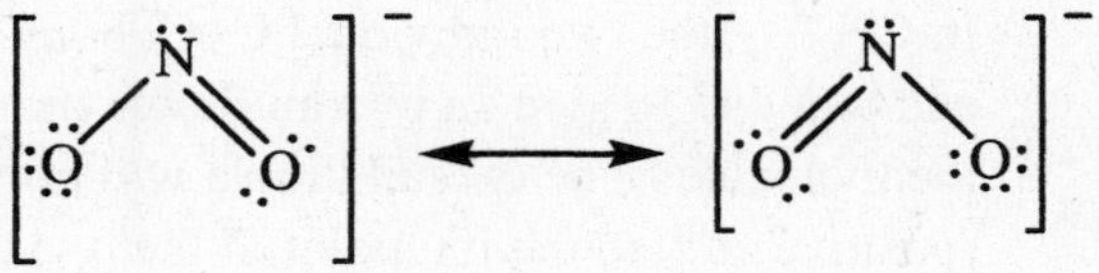

111.   a. $XeCl_4$, 8 + 4(7) = 36 e$^-$ $XeCl_2$, 8 + 2(7) = 22 e$^-$

        square planar, 90°, nonpolar   linear, 180°, nonpolar

        Both compounds have a central Xe atom that does not satisfy the octet rule. Both are nonpolar because the Xe–Cl bond dipoles are arranged in such a manner that they all cancel each other. The last item is that both have 180° bond angles. Although we haven't emphasized this, the bond angle between the Cl atoms on the diagonal in $XeCl_4$ are 180° apart from each other.

        b.   We didn't draw the Lewis structures, but all are polar covalent compounds. The bond dipoles do not cancel out each other when summed together. The reason the bond dipoles are not symmetrically arranged in these compounds is that they all have at least one lone pair of electrons on the central atom which disrupts the symmetry. Note that there are molecules that have lone pairs and are nonpolar, e.g., $XeCl_4$ and $XeCl_2$ in the previous problem. A lone pair on a central atom does not guarantee a polar molecule.

112.   The general structure of the trihalide ions is:

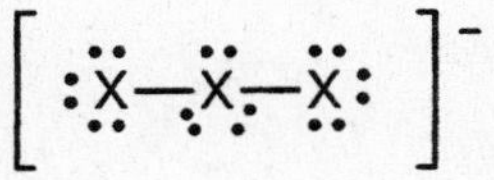

Bromine and iodine are large enough and have low energy, empty d-orbitals to accommodate the expanded octet. Fluorine is small, its valence shell contains only 2s and 2p orbitals (4 orbitals) and it does not expand its octet. The lowest energy d orbitals in F are 3d orbitals; they are too high in energy, as compared to the 2s and 2p orbitals, to be used in bonding.

113.   Yes, each structure has the same number of effective pairs around the central atom. (A multiple bond is counted as a single group of electrons.)

114.   a.

The C–H bonds are assumed nonpolar since the electronegativities of C and H are about equal.

$\delta+$ $\delta-$
C–Cl is the charge distribution for each C–Cl bond. In CH_2Cl_2, the two individual C–Cl bond dipoles add together to give an overall dipole moment for the molecule. The overall dipole will point from C (positive end) to the midpoint of the two Cl atoms (negative end).

In $CHCl_3$, the C–H bond is essentially nonpolar. The three C–Cl bond dipoles in $CHCl_3$ add together to give an overall dipole moment for the molecule. The overall dipole will have the negative end at the midpoint of the three chlorines and the positive end around the carbon.

CCl_4 is nonpolar. CCl_4 is a tetrahedral molecule where all four C–Cl bond dipoles cancel when added together. Let's consider just the C and two of the Cl atoms. There will be a net dipole pointing in the direction of the middle of the two Cl atoms.

There will be an equal and opposite dipole arising from the other two Cl atoms. Combining:

The two dipoles cancel and CCl_4 is nonpolar.

b. CO_2 is nonpolar. CO_2 is a linear molecule with two equivalence bond dipoles that cancel. N_2O is polar since the bond dipoles do not cancel.

c. NH_3 is polar. The 3 N–H bond dipoles add together to give a net dipole in the direction of the lone pair. We would predict PH_3 to be nonpolar on the basis of electronegativitity, i.e., P–H bonds are nonpolar. However, the presence of the lone pair makes the PH_3 molecule slightly polar. The net dipole is in the direction of the lone pair and has a magnitude about one third that of the NH_3 dipole.

115. TeF_5^- has $6 + 5(7) + 1 = 42$ valence electrons.

The lone pair of electrons around Te exerts a stronger repulsion than the bonding pairs of electrons. This pushes the four square planar F's away from the lone pair and reduces the bond angles between the axial F atom and the square planar F atoms.

Challenge Problems

116. | | (IE − EA) | (IE − EA)/502 | EN (text) | 2006/502 = 4.0 |
|---|---|---|---|---|
| F | 2006 kJ/mol | 4.0 | 4.0 | |
| Cl | 1604 | 3.2 | 3.0 | |
| Br | 1463 | 2.9 | 2.8 | |
| I | 1302 | 2.6 | 2.5 | |

The values calculated from IE and EA show the same trend (and agree fairly closely) to the values given in the text.

117.   The reaction is:

$$1/2 \ I_2(g) + 1/2 \ Cl_2(g) \rightarrow ICl(g) \qquad \Delta H_f^o = ?$$

Using Hess's law:

$1/2 \ I_2(s) \rightarrow 1/2 \ I_2(g)$	$\Delta H = 1/2 \ (62 \ kJ)$	[Appendix 4]
$1/2 \ I_2(g) \rightarrow I(g)$	$\Delta H = 1/2 \ (149 \ kJ)$	[Table 8.4]
$1/2 \ Cl_2(g) \rightarrow Cl(g)$	$\Delta H = 1/2 \ (239 \ kJ)$	[Table 8.4]
$I(g) + Cl(g) \rightarrow ICl(g)$	$\Delta H = -208 \ kJ$	[Table 8.4]

$$1/2 \ I_2(s) + 1/2 \ Cl_2(g) \rightarrow ICl(g) \qquad \Delta H = 17 \ kJ$$

118. | | |
|---|---|
| $2 \ Li^+(g) + 2 \ Cl^-(g) \rightarrow 2 \ LiCl(s)$ | $\Delta H = 2(-829 \ kJ)$ |
| $2 \ Li(g) \rightarrow 2 \ Li^+(g) + 2 \ e^-$ | $\Delta H = 2(520. \ kJ)$ |
| $2 \ Li(s) \rightarrow 2 \ Li(g)$ | $\Delta H = 2(166 \ kJ)$ |
| $2 \ HCl(g) \rightarrow 2 \ H(g) + 2 \ Cl(g)$ | $\Delta H = 2(427 \ kJ)$ |
| $2 \ Cl(g) + 2 \ e^- \rightarrow 2 \ Cl^-(g)$ | $\Delta H = 2(-349 \ kJ)$ |
| $2 \ H(g) \rightarrow H_2(g)$ | $\Delta H = -(432 \ kJ)$ |

$$2 \ Li(s) + 2 \ HCl(g) \rightarrow 2LiCl(s) + H_2(g) \qquad \Delta H = -562 \ kJ$$

119.   See Fig. 8.11 for data supporting MgO as an ionic compound. Note that the lattice energy is large enough to overcome all of the other processes (removing 2 electrons from Mg, etc.). The bond energy for O_2 (247 kJ/mol) and the electron affinity for O (737 kJ/mol) are the same when making CO. However, the energy needed to ionize carbon to form a C^{2+} ion must be too large. Fig. 7.30 shows that the first ionization energy for carbon is about 400 kJ/mol greater than the first IE for magnesium. If all other numbers were equal, the overall energy change would be down from ~ −600 kJ/mol to ~ −200 kJ/mol (see Fig. 8.11). It is not unreasonable to assume that the second ionization energy for carbon is more than 200 kJ/mol greater than the second ionization energy of magnesium. This would make ΔH_f^o for CO a positive number (if it were ionic). One doesn't expect CO to be ionic as the energetics would be unfavorable.

120.   a.   1)   removing an electron from the metal: IE, positive ($\Delta H > 0$)
           2)   adding an electron to the nonmetal: EA, often negative ($\Delta H < 0$)
           3)   allowing the metal cation and nonmetal anion to come together: LE, negative
                ($\Delta H < 0$)

       b.   Often, the sign of the sum of the first two processes is positive (or unfavorable). This is especially true due to the fact that we must also vaporize the metal and often break a bond on a diatomic gas.

            For example, the ionization energy for Na is +495 kJ/mol and the electron affinity for F is -328 kJ/mol. Overall, the change is +167 kJ/mol (unfavorable).

       c.   For an ionic compound to form, the sum must be negative (exothermic).

       d.   The lattice energy must be favorable enough to overcome the endothermic process of forming the ions, i.e., the lattice energy must be a large, negative quantity.

       e.   While Na_2Cl (or $NaCl_2$) would have a greater lattice energy than NaCl, the energy to make a Cl^{2-} ion (or Na^{2+} ion) must be larger (more unfavorable) than what would be gained by the larger lattice energy. The same argument can be made for MgO compared to MgO_2 or Mg_2O. The energy to make the ions is too unfavorable or the lattice energy is not favorable enough and the compounds do not form.

121.   As the halogen atoms get larger, it becomes more difficult to fit three halogen atoms around the small nitrogen atom, and the NX_3 molecule becomes less stable.

122.   a.   I.

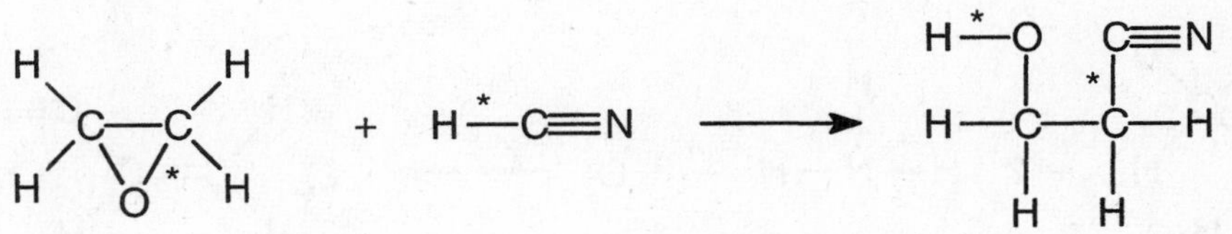

            Bonds broken (*):   Bonds formed (*):

                1 C–O (358 kJ)   1 O–H (467 kJ)
                1 H–C (413 kJ)   1 C–C (347 kJ)

            ΔH_I = 358 kJ + 413 kJ – [467 kJ + 347 kJ] = –43 kJ

       II.

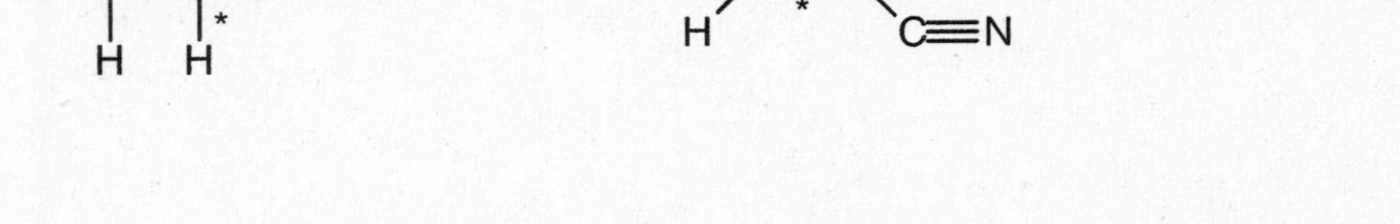

Bonds broken (*):   Bonds formed (*):

    1 C–O (358 kJ/mol)   1 H–O (467 kJ/mol)
    1 C–H (413 kJ/mol)   1 C=C (614 kJ/mol)
    1 C–C (347 kJ/mol)

ΔH_{II} = 358 kJ + 413 kJ + 347 kJ - [467 kJ + 614 kJ] = 37 kJ

$\Delta H_{overall}$ = ΔH_I + ΔH_{II} = -43 kJ + 37 kJ = -6 kJ

b.

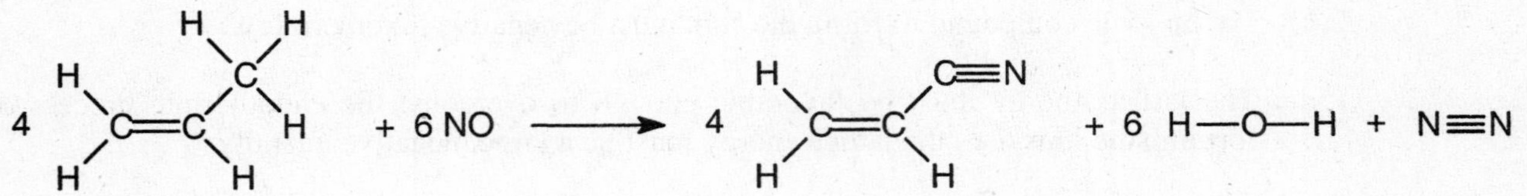

Bonds broken: Bonds formed:

    4 × 3 C–H (413 kJ/mol)   4 C≡N (891 kJ/mol)
    6 N=O (630. kJ/mol)   6 × 2 H–O (467 kJ/mol)
                      1 N≡N (941 kJ/mol)

ΔH = 12(413) + 6(630.) - [4(891) + 12(467) + 941] = -1373 kJ

c.

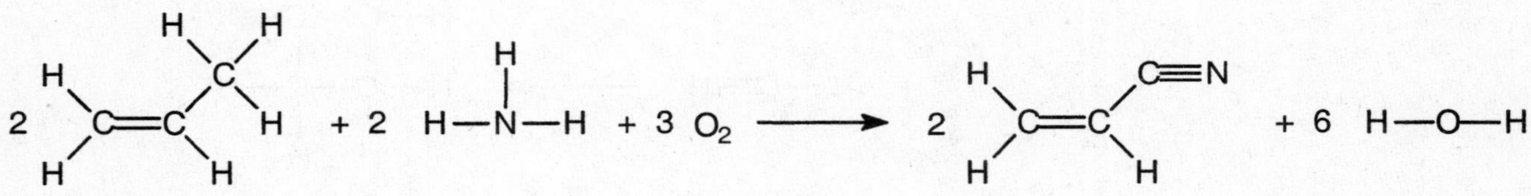

Bonds broken: Bonds formed:

    2 × 3 C–H (413 kJ/mol)   2 C≡N (891 kJ/mol)
    2 × 3 N–H (391 kJ/mol)   6 × 2 O–H (467 kJ/mol)
       3 O=O (495 kJ/mol)

ΔH = 6(413) + 6(391) + 3(495) - [2(891) + 12(467)] = -1077 kJ

d.   Because both reactions are highly exothermic, the high temperature is not needed to provide energy. It must be necessary for some other reason. The reason is to increase the speed of the reaction. This is discussed in Chapter 12 on kinetics.

123.   a.   i. $C_6H_6N_{12}O_{12} \rightarrow 6\ CO + 6\ N_2 + 3\ H_2O + 3/2\ O_2$

The NO_2 groups are assumed to have one N–O single bond and one N=O double bond and each carbon atom has one C–H single bond. We must break and form all bonds.

Bonds broken: Bonds formed:

    3 C–C (347 kJ/mol)   6 C≡O (1072 kJ/mol)

    6 C–H (413 kJ/mol)   6 N≡N (941 kJ/mol)

  12 C–N (305 kJ/mol)   6 H–O (467 kJ/mol)

    6 N–N (160. kJ/mol)   3/2 O=O (495 kJ/mol)

    6 N–O (201 kJ/mol) $\Sigma D_{formed} = 15{,}623$ kJ

    6 N=O (607 kJ/mol)

    $\Sigma D_{broken} = 12{,}987$ kJ

$\Delta H = \Sigma D_{broken} - \Sigma D_{formed} = 12{,}987$ kJ $- 15{,}623$ kJ $= -2636$ kJ

ii. $C_6H_6N_{12}O_{12} \rightarrow 3\ CO + 3\ CO_2 + 6\ N_2 + 3\ H_2O$

Note: The bonds broken will be the same for all three reactions.

Bonds formed:

    3 C≡O (1072 kJ/mol)

    6 C=O (799 kJ/mol)

    6 N≡N (941 kJ/mol)

    6 H–O (467 kJ/mol)

    $\Sigma D_{formed} = 16{,}458$ kJ

$\Delta H = 12{,}987$ kJ $- 16{,}458$ kJ $= -3471$ kJ

iii. $C_6H_6N_{12}O_{12} \rightarrow 6\ CO_2 + 6\ N_2 + 3\ H_2$

Bonds formed:

  12 C=O (799 kJ/mol)

    6 N≡N (941 kJ/mol)

    3 H–H (432 kJ/mol)

    $\Sigma D_{formed} = 16{,}530.$ kJ

$\Delta H = 12{,}987$ kJ $- 16{,}530.$ kJ $= -3543$ kJ

b.   Reaction iii yields the most energy per mole of CL-20 so it will yield the most energy per kg.

$$\frac{-3543\ kJ}{mol} \times \frac{1\ mol}{438.23\ g} \times \frac{1000\ g}{kg} = -8085\ kJ/kg$$

124.   If we can draw resonance forms for the anion after the loss of H^+, we can argue that the extra stability of the anion causes the proton to be more readily lost, i.e., makes the compound a better acid.

a.

b.

c.

In all 3 cases, extra resonance forms can be drawn for the anion that are not possible when the H^+ is present, which leads to enhanced stability.

125.   PAN ($H_3C_2NO_5$) has $3(1) + 2(4) + 5 + 5(6) = 46$ valence electrons.

Skeletal structure with complete octets about oxygen atoms (46 electrons used).

This structure has used all 46 electrons, but there are only six electrons around one of the carbon atoms and the nitrogen atom. Two unshared pairs must become shared; we must form two double bonds.

(this form not important by formal charge arguments)

126.

127.   a. $BrFI_2$, $7 + 7 + 2(7) = 28$ e$^-$; Two possible structures exist; each has a T-shaped molecular structure.

90° bond angles between I atoms   180° bond angles between I atoms

b. XeO_2F_2, $8 + 2(6) + 2(7) = 34$ e⁻; Three possible structures exist; each has a see-saw molecular structure.

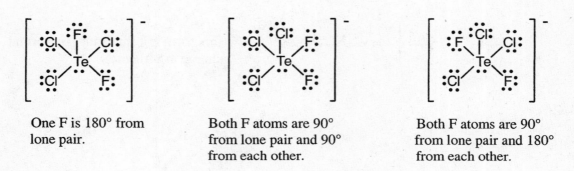

| 90° bond angle between O atoms | 180° bond angle between O atoms | 120° bond angle between O atoms |

c. $TeF_2Cl_3^-$; $6 + 2(7) + 3(7) + 1 = 42$ e⁻; Three possible structures exist; each has a square pyramid molecular structure.

One F is 180° from lone pair.

Both F atoms are 90° from lone pair and 90° from each other.

Both F atoms are 90° from lone pair and 180° from each other.

128.   For carbon atoms to have a formal charge of zero, each C atom must satisfy the octet rule by forming four bonds (with no lone pairs). For nitrogen atoms to have a formal charge of zero, each N atom must satisfy the octet rule by forming three bonds and have one lone pair of electrons. For oxygen atoms to have a formal charge of zero, each O atom must satisfy the octet rule by forming two bonds and have two lone pairs of electrons. With these bonding requirements in mind, the Lewis structure of histidine, where all atoms have a formal charge of zero, is:

We would expect 120° bond angles about the carbon atom labeled 1 and ~109.5° bond angles about the nitrogen atom labeled 2. The nitrogen bond angles are slightly smaller than 109.5° due to the lone pair on nitrogen.

129.

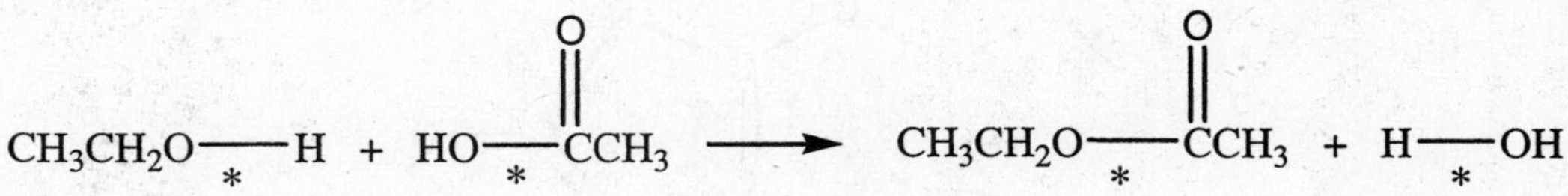

Bonds broken (*):

  O–H
  C–O

Bonds formed (*)

  O–H
  C–O

We make the same bonds that we have to break in order to convert reactants into products. Therefore, we would predict $\Delta H = 0$ for this reaction using bond energies. This is probably not a great estimate for this reaction because this is not a gas phase reaction where bond energies work best.

130.   The skeletal structure of caffeine is:

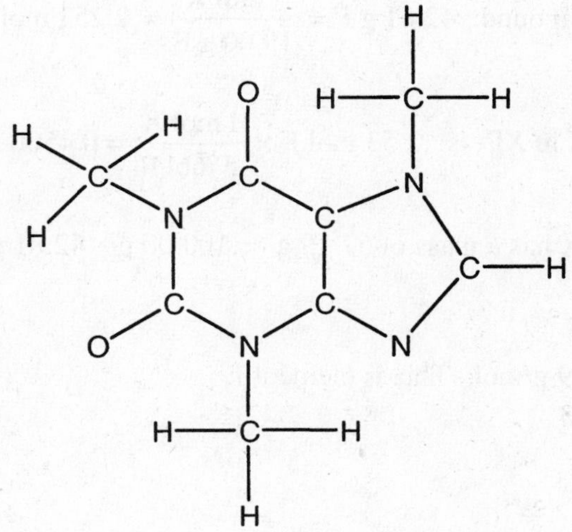

For a formal charge of zero on all atoms, the bonding requirements are:

a. four bonds and no lone pairs for each carbon atom
b. three bonds and one lone pair for each nitrogen atom
c. two bonds and two lone pairs for each oxygen atom
d. one bond and no lone pairs for each hydrogen atom

Following these guidelines gives a Lewis structure that has a formal charge of zero for all of the atoms in the molecule. The Lewis structure is:

Integrative Problems

131.   Assuming 100.00 g of compound: $42.81 \text{ g F} = \dfrac{1 \text{ mol X}}{19.00 \text{ g F}} = 2.253 \text{ mol F}$

The number of moles of X in XF_5 is: $2.53 \text{ mol F} \times \dfrac{1 \text{ mol X}}{5 \text{ mol F}} = 0.4506 \text{ mol X}$

This number of moles of X has a mass of 57.19 g (= 100.00 g – 42.81 g). The molar mass of X is:

$$\dfrac{57.19 \text{ g X}}{0.4506 \text{ mol X}} = 126.9 \text{ g/mol}; \text{This is element I.}$$

IF_5, $7 + 5(7) = 42 \text{ e}^-$

The molecular structure is square pyramid.

132.   If X^{2-} has a configuration of $[Ar]4s^2 3d^{10} 4p^6$, then X must have a configuration with two fewer electrons, $[Ar]4s^2 3d^{10} 4p^4$. This is element Se.

$SeCN^-$, $6 + 4 + 5 + 1 = 16 \, e^-$

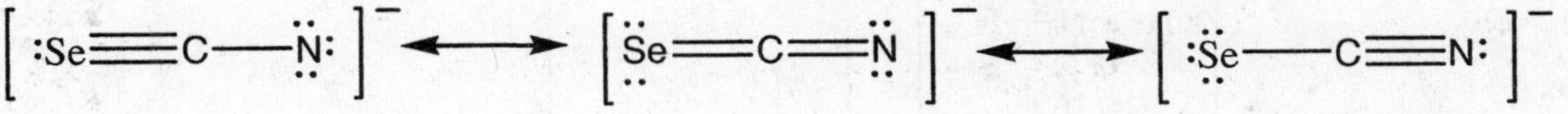

$$\left[:Se \equiv C - \ddot{N}: \right]^- \longleftrightarrow \left[\ddot{Se} = C = \ddot{N} \right]^- \longleftrightarrow \left[:\ddot{Se} - C \equiv N: \right]^-$$

133.   The elements are identified by their electron configurations:

[Ar]$4s^1 3d^5$ = Cr;   [Ne]$3s^2 3p^3$ = P;   [Ar]$4s^2 3d^{10} 4p^3$ = As;   [Ne]$3s^2 3p^5$ = Cl

Following the electronegativity trend, the order is Cr < As < P < Cl.

Marathon Problem

134.   <u>Compound A</u>: This compound is a strong acid (part g). HNO_3 is a strong acid and is available in concentrated solutions of 16 *M* (part c). The highest possible oxidation state of nitrogen is +5, and in HNO_3, the oxidation state of nitrogen is +5 (part b). Therefore, compound A is most likely HNO_3. The Lewis structures for HNO_3 are:

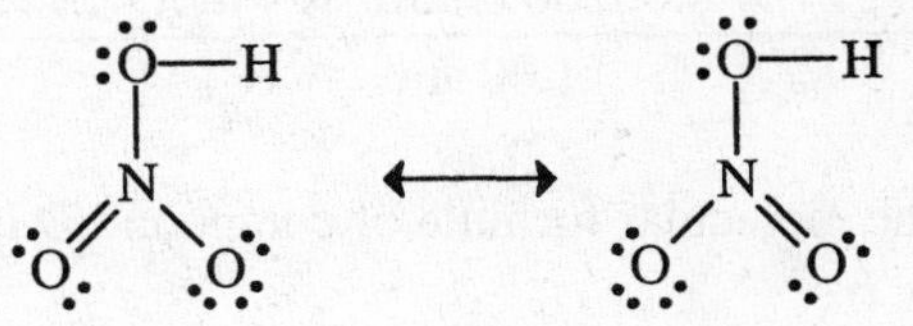

<u>Compound B</u>: This compound is basic (part g) and has one nitrogen (part b). The formal charge of zero (part b) tells us that there are three bonds and one lone pair to the nitrogen. Assuming compound B is monobasic, then the data in part g tells us that the molar mass of B is 33.0 g/mol (21.98 mL of 1.000 *M* HCl = 0.02198 mol HCl, thus there are 0.02198 mol of B; 0.726 g/0.02198 mol = 33.0 g/mol). Because this number is rather small, it limits the possibilities. That is, there is one nitrogen, and the remainder of the atoms are O and H. Since the molar mass of B is 33.0 g/mol, then only one O oxygen atom can be present. The N and O atoms have a combined molar mass of 30.0 g/mol; the rest is made up of hydrogens (3 H atoms), giving the formula NH_3O. From the list of K_b values for weak bases in Appendix 5.3 of the text, compound B is most likely NH_2OH. The Lewis structure is:

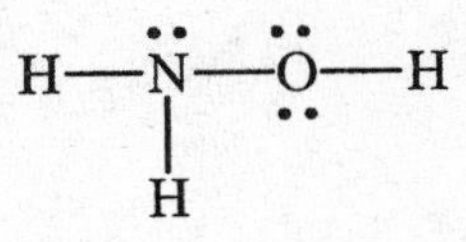

<u>Compound C</u>: From parts a and f and assuming compound A is HNO_3 , then compound C contains the nitrate ion, NO_3^-. Because part b tells us that there are two nitrogens, the other ion needs to have one N and some H's. In addition, compound C must be a weak acid (part g), which must be due to the other ion since NO_3^- has no acidic properties. Also, the nitrogen atom in the other ion must have an oxidation state of -3 (part b) and a formal charge of +1. The ammonium ion fits the data. Thus, compound C is most likely NH_4NO_3. A Lewis structure is:

Note: Two more resonance structures can be drawn for NO_3^-.

Compound D: From part f, this compound has one less oxygen atom than compound C, thus NH_4NO_2 is a likely formula. Data from part e confirms this. Assuming 100.0 g of compound, we have:

    43.7 g N × 1 mol/14.01 g = 3.12 mol N
    50.0 g O × 1 mol/16.00 g = 3.12 mol O
     6.3 g H × 1 mol/1.008 g = 6.3 mol H

There is a 1:1:2 mole ratio of N:O:H. The empirical formula is NOH_2, which has an empirical formula mass of 32.0 g/mol.

$$\text{Molar mass} = \frac{dRT}{P} = \frac{2.86\,g/L \times 0.08206\,L\,atm/K \bullet mol \times 273\,K}{1.00\,atm} = 64.1\ g/mol$$

For a correct molar mass, the molecular formula of compound D is $N_2O_2H_4$ or NH_4NO_2. A Lewis structure is:

Note: One more resonance structure for NO_2^- can be drawn.

Compound E: A basic solution (part g) which is commercially available at 15 M (part c) is ammonium hydroxide, NH_4OH. This is also consistent with the information given in parts b and d. The Lewis structure for NH_4OH is:

CHAPTER NINE

COVALENT BONDING: ORBITALS

For Review

1. The valence orbitals of the nonmetals are the s and p orbitals. The lobes of the p orbitals are 90° and 180° apart from each other. If the p orbitals were used to form bonds, then all bonds should be 90° or 180°. This is not the case. In order to explain the observed geometry (bond angles) that molecules exhibit, we need to make up (hybridize) orbitals that point to where the bonded atoms and lone pairs are located. We know the geometry; we hybridize orbitals to explain the geometry.

    Sigma bonds have shared electrons in the area centered on a line joining the atoms. The orbitals that overlap to form the sigma bonds must overlap head to head or end to end. The hybrid orbitals about a central atom always are directed at the bonded atoms. Hybrid orbitals will always overlap head to head to form sigma bonds.

2.

geometry	hybridization	unhybridized p atomic orbitals
linear	sp	2
trigonal planar	sp^2	1
tetrahedral	sp^3	0

    The unhybridized p atomic orbitals are used to form π bonds. Two unhybridized p atomic orbitals each from a different atom overlap side to side, resulting in a shared electron pair occupying the space above and below the line joining the atoms (the internuclear axis).

3. H_2S, $2(1) + 6 = 8\ e^-$ CH_4, $4 + 4(1) = 8\ e^-$

    H_2CO, $2(1) + 4 + 6 = 12\ e^-$ HCN, $1 + 4 + 5 = 10\ e^-$

H_2S and CH_4 both have four effective pairs of electrons about the central atom. Both central atoms will be sp^3 hybridized. For H_2S, two of the sp^3 hybrid orbitals are occupied by lone pairs. The other two sp^3 hybrid orbitals overlap with 1s orbitals from hydrogen to form the 2 S–H sigma bonds. For CH_4, the four C–H bonds are formed by overlap of the sp^3 hybrid orbitals from carbon with 1s orbitals on H.

H_2CO has a trigonal planar geometry, so carbon is sp^2 hybridized. Two of the sp^2 hybrid orbitals overlap with hydrogen 1s orbitals to form the two C–H sigma bonds. The third sp^2 hybrid orbital is used to form the sigma bond in the double bond by overlapping head to head with an sp^2 hybrid orbital from oxygen. The second bond in the double bond is a π bond. The unhybridized p atomic orbital on carbon will overlap with a parallel p atomic orbital on O to form the π bond.

HCN has a linear geomtry, so carbon is sp hybridized. HCN has one C–H sigma bond, one C–N sigma bond and two C–N π bonds. The C–H sigma bond is formed from sp–1s orbital overlap. The C–N sigma bond is formed from an sp hybrid orbital on carbon overlapping with an sp^2 hybrid orbital from nitrogen. The π bonds are formed from the two unhybridized p atomic orbitals from carbon overlapping with two unhybridized p atomic orbitals from N. Each π bond is formed from the p orbitals overlapping side to side. Because the p orbitals used must be perpendicular to each other, the π bonds must be in two different planes that are perpendicular to each other and perpendicular to the internuclear axis.

4.   Molecules having trigonal bipyramid geometry have five pairs of electrons around the central atom. We need five hybrid orbitals to account for the location of these five sets of electrons. We use the valence s and the three degenerate p valence atomic orbitals for four of the five orbitals; the fifth is an empty d orbital close in energy to the valence atomic orbitals. We call this hybridization dsp^3. For octahedral geometry, we need six hybrid orbitals to account for the locations of six pairs of electrons about the central atom. We use the s and three p valence atomic orbitals along with two empty d orbitals. We mix these six atomic orbitals together and come up with six hybrid orbitals which point to the vertices of an octahedron.

PF_5 and SF_4 both have five pairs of electrons about the central atoms so both exhibit dsp^3 hybridization to account for the trigonal bipyramid arrangement of electron pairs. In PF_5, the five pairs of electrons are bonding electrons in the five P–F sigma bonds. Overlap of the dsp^3 hybrid orbitals from phosphorus with the appropriate orbitals on each F atom go to form the sigma bonds. SF_4 has four S–F bonds and a lone pair of electrons about the sulfur. Four of the sulfur dsp^3 hybrid orbitals overlap with appropriate orbitals on the fluorines to form the four S–F sigma bonds, the fifth dsp^3 hybrid orbital holds the lone pair of electrons on the sulfur.

SF_6 and IF_5 both have six pairs of electrons about the central atoms so both exhibit d^2sp^3 hybridization to account for the octahedral geometries of electron pairs. In SF_6, the six d^2sp^3 hybrid orbitals overlap with appropriate orbitals from F to form the six S–F sigma bonds. In IF_5, five of the six d^2sp^3 hybrid orbitals go to form the five I–F sigma bonds with the sixth d^2sp^3 holding the lone pair of electrons on iodine.

5.   The electrons in sigma bonding molecular orbtials are attracted to two nuclei, which is a lower, more stable energy arrangement for the electrons than in separate atoms. In sigma antibonding molecular orbitals, the electrons are mainly outside the space between the nuclei, which is a higher, less stable energy arrangement than in the separated atoms.

6.   See Fig. 9.32 for the 2s σ bonding and σ antibonding molecular orbitals and see Fig. 9.34 for the 2p σ bonding, σ antibonding, π bonding, and π antibonding molecular orbitals.

7.   Bond energy is directly proportional to bond order. Bond length is inversely proportional to bond order. Bond energy and bond length can be measured; bond order is calculated from the molecular orbital energy diagram (bond order is the difference between the number of bonding electrons and the number of antibonding electrons divided by two).

Paramagnetic: a kind of induced magnetism, associated with unpaired electrons, that causes a substance to be attracted into an inducing magnetic field. Diamagnetic: a type of induced magnetism, associated with paired electrons, that causes a substance to be repelled from the inducing magnetic field. The key is that paramagnetic substances have unpaired electrons in the molecular orbital diagram while diamagnetic substances have only paired electrons in the MO diagram.

To determine the type of magnetism, measure the mass of a substance in the presence and absence of a magnetic field. A substance with unpaired electrons will be attracted by the magnetic field, giving an apparent increase in mass in the presence of the field. A greater number of unpaired electrons will give a greater attraction and a greater observed mass increase. A diamagnetic species will not be attracted by a magnetic field and will not show a mass increase (a slight mass decrease is observed for diamagnetic species).

8.   a. H_2 has two valence electrons to put in the MO diagram for H_2 while He_2 has 4 valence electrons.

H_2: $(\sigma_{1s})^2$ Bond order = B.O. = $(2-0)/2 = 1$
He_2: $(\sigma_{1s})^2(\sigma_{1s}*)^2$ B.O. = $(2-2)/2 = 0$

H_2 has a nonzero bond order so MO theory predicts it will exist. The H_2 molecule is stable with respect to the two free H atoms. He_2 has a bond order of zero so it should not form. The He_2 molecule is not more stable than the two free He atoms.

b.   See Fig. 9.39 for the MO energy-level diagrams of B_2, C_2, N_2, O_2, and F_2. B_2 and O_2 have unpaired electrons in their electron configuration so they are predicted to be paramagnetic. C_2, N_2 and F_2 have no unpaired electrons in the MO diagrams; they are all diamagnetic.

c.   From the MO energy diagram in Fig. 9.39, N_2 maximizes the number of electrons in the lower energy bonding orbitals and has no electrons in the antibonding 2p molecular orbitals. N_2 has the highest possible bond order of three so it should be a very strong (stable) bond.

d. NO^+ has $5 + 6 - 1 = 10$ valence electrons to place in the MO diagram and NO^- has $5 + 6 + 1 = 12$ valence electrons. The MO diagram for these two ions is assumed to be the same as that used for N_2.

NO^+: $(\sigma_{2s})^2(\sigma_{2s}*)^2(\pi_{2p})^4(\sigma_{2p})^2$ B.O. = $(8-2)/2 = 3$
NO^-: $(\sigma_{2s})^2(\sigma_{2s}*)^2(\pi_{2p})^4(\sigma_{2p})^2(\pi_{2p}*)^2$ B.O. = $(8-4)/2 = 2$

NO^+ has a larger bond order than NO^- , so NO^+ should be more stable than NO^-.

9.   In HF, it is assumed that the hydrogen 1s atomic orbital overlaps with a fluorine 2p orbital to form the bonding molecular orbital. The specific 2p orbital used in forming the bonding MO is the p orbital on the internuclear axis. This p orbital will overlap head to head with the hydrogen 1s orbital forming a sigma bonding and a sigma antibonding MO. In the MO diagram, the unpaired H 1s electron and the unpaired fluorine 2p electron fill the σ bonding MO. No electrons are in the antibonding orbital. Therefore, HF has a bond order of $(2-0)/2 = 1$ and it should (and does) form.

We also use the MO diagram to explain the polarity of the H–F bond. The fluorine 2p orbitals are assumed lower in energy than the hydrogen 1s orbital because F is more electronegative. Because the σ bonding MO is closer in energy to the fluorine 2p atomic orbitals, we say the bonding orbital has more fluorine 2p character than hydrogen 1s character. With more fluorine 2p character, the electrons in the bonding orbital will have a greater probability of being closer to F. This leads to a partial negative charge on F and a partial positive charge on H.

10.   Molecules that exhibit resonance have delocalized π bonding. This is a fancy way of saying that the π electrons are not permanently stationed between two specific atoms, but instead can roam about over the surface of a molecule. We use the concept of delocalized π electrons to explain why molecules that exhibit resonance have equal bonds in terms of strength. Because the π electrons can roam about over the entire surface of the molecule, the π electrons are shared by all of the atoms in the molecule giving rise to equal bond strengths.

The classic example of delocalized π electrons is benzene, C_6H_6. Fig. 9.47 and 9.48 show the π molecular orbital system for benzene. Each carbon in benzene is sp^2 hybridized, leaving one unhybridized p atomic orbital. All six of the carbon atoms in benzene have an unhybridized p orbital pointing above and below the planar surface of the molecule. Instead of just two unhybridized p orbitals overlapping, we say all six of the unhybridized p orbitals overlap resulting in delocalized π electrons roaming about above and below the entire surface of the benzene molecule.

O_3, $6 + 2(6) = 18$ e⁻

Ozone has a delocalized π system. Here the central atom is sp^2 hybridized. The unhybridized p atomic orbital on the central oxygen will overlap with parallel p orbitals on each adjacent O atom. All three of these p orbitals overlap together resulting in the π electrons moving about above and below the surface of the O_3 molecule. With the delocalized π electrons, the O-O bond lengths in O_3 are equal (and not different as each individual Lewis structure indicates).

Questions

7.   In hybrid orbital theory, some or all of the valence atomic orbitals of the central atom in a molecule are mixed together to form hybrid orbitals; these hybrid orbitals point to where the bonded atoms and lone pairs are oriented. The sigma bonds are formed from the hybrid

orbitals overlapping head to head with an appropriate orbital from the bonded atom. The π bonds in hybrid orbital theory are formed from unhybridized p atomic orbitals. The p orbitals overlap side to side to form the π bond where the π electrons occupy the space above and below a line joining the atoms (the internuclear axis). Assuming the z-axis is the internuclear axis, then the p_z atomic orbital will always be hybridized whether the hybridization is sp, sp^2, sp^3, dsp^3 or d^2sp^3. For sp hybridization, the p_x and p_y atomic orbitals are unhybridized; they are used to form two π bonds to the bonded atom(s). For sp^2 hybridization, either the p_x or p_y atomic orbital is hybridized (along with the s and p_z orbitals); the other p orbital is used to form a π bond to a bonded atom. For sp^3 hybridization, the s and all of the p orbitals are hybridized; no unhybridized p atomic orbitals are present, so no π bonds form with sp^3 hybridization. For dsp^3 and d^2sp^3 hybridization, we just mix in one or two d orbitals into the hybridization process. Which specific d orbitals are used is not important to our discussion.

8. The MO theory is a mathematical model. The allowed electron energy levels (molecular orbitals) in a molecule are solutions to the mathematical problem. The square of the solutions gives the shapes of the molecular orbitals. A sigma bond is an allowed energy level where the greatest electron probability is between the nuclei forming the bond. Valence s orbitals form sigma bonds, and if the z-axis is the internuclear axis, then valence p_z orbitals also form sigma bonds. For a molecule like HF, a sigma bonding MO results from the combination of the H 1s orbital and the F $2p_z$ atomic orbital.

For π bonds, the electron density lies above and below the internuclear axis. The π bonds are formed when p_x orbitals are combined (side to side overlap) and when p_y orbitals are combined.

9. We use d orbitals when we have to, i.e., we use d orbitals when the central atom on a molecule has more than eight electrons around it. The d orbitals are necessary to accommodate the electrons over eight. Row 2 elements never have more than eight electrons around them so they never hybridize d orbitals. We rationalize this by saying there are no d orbitals close in energy to the valence 2s and 2p orbitals (2d orbitals are forbidden energy levels). However, for row 3 and heavier elements, there are 3d, 4d, 5d, etc. orbitals which will be close in energy to the valence s and p orbitals. It is row 3 and heavier nonmetals that hybridize d orbitals when they have to.

For phosphorus, the valence electrons are in 3s and 3p orbitals. Therefore, 3d orbitals are closest in energy and are available for hybridization. Arsenic would hybridize 4d orbitals to go with the valence 4s and 4p orbitals while iodine would hybridize 5d orbitals since the valence electrons are in $n = 5$.

10. Rotation occurs in a bond as long as the orbitals that go to form that bond still overlap when the atoms are rotating. Sigma bonds, with the head to head overlap, remain unaffected by rotating the atoms in the bonds. Atoms which are bonded together by only a sigma bond (single bond) exhibit this rotation phenomenon. The π bonds, however, cannot be rotated. The p orbitals must be parallel to each other to form the π bond. If we try to rotate the atoms in a π bond, the p orbitals would no longer have the correct alignment necessary to overlap. Because π bonds are present in double and triple bonds, (a double bond is composed of 1 σ and 1 π bond and a triple bond is always 1 σ and 2 π bonds), the atoms in a double or triple bond cannot rotate (unless the bond is broken).

11.   Bonding and antibonding molecular orbitals are both solutions to the quantum mechanical treatment of the molecule. Bonding orbitals form when in-phase orbitals combine to give constructive interference. This results in enhanced electron probability located between the two nuclei. The end result is that a bonding MO is lower in energy than the atomic orbitals from which it is composed. Antibonding orbitals form when out-of-phase orbitals combine. The mismatched phases produce destructive interference leading to a node of electron probability between the two nuclei. With electron distribution pushed to the outside, the energy of an antibonding orbital is higher than the energy of the atomic orbitals from which it is composed.

12.   From experiment, B_2 is paramagnetic. If the σ_{2p} MO is lower in energy than the two degenerate π_{2p} MOs, the electron configuration for B_2 would have all electrons paired. Experiment tells us we must have unpaired electrons. Therefore, the MO diagram is modified to have the π_{2p} orbitals lower in energy than the σ_{2p} orbitals. This gives two unpaired electrons in the electron configuration for B_2 and explains the paramagnetic properties of B_2. The model allowed for s and p orbitals to mix, which shifted the energy of the σ_{2p} orbital to above that of the π_{2p} orbitals.

13.   The localized electron model does not deal effectively with molecules containing unpaired electrons. We can draw all of the possible structures for NO with its odd number of valence electrons, but still not have a good feel for whether the bond in NO is weaker or stronger than the bond in NO^-. MO theory can handle odd electron species without any modifications. In addition, hybrid orbital theory does not predict that NO^- is paramagnetic. The MO theory correctly makes this prediction.

14. NO_3^-, $5 + 3(6) + 1 = 24$ e$^-$

When resonance structures can be drawn, it is usually due to a multiple bond that can be in different positions. This is the case for NO_3^-. Experiment tells us that the three N–O bonds are equivalent. To explain this, we say the π electrons are delocalized in the molecule. For NO_3^-, the π bonding system is composed of an unhybridized p atomic orbital from all the atoms in NO_3^-. These p orbitals are oriented perpendicular to the plane of the atoms in NO_3^-. The π bonding system consists of all of the perpendicular p orbitals overlapping forming a diffuse electron cloud above and below the entire surface of the NO_3^- ion. Instead of having the π electrons situated above and below two specific nuclei, we think of the π electrons in NO_3^- as extending over the entire surface of the molecule (hence the term delocalized). See Fig. 9.49 for an illustration of the π bonding system in NO_3^-.

Exercises

The Localized Electron Model and Hybrid Orbitals

15. H_2O has $2(1) + 6 = 8$ valence electrons.

H₂O has a tetrahedral arrangement of the electron pairs about the O atom that requires sp^3 hybridization. Two of the four sp^3 hybrid orbitals are used to form bonds to the two hydrogen atoms and the other two sp^3 hybrid orbitals hold the two lone pairs of oxygen. The two O–H bonds are formed from overlap of the sp^3 hybrid orbitals on oxygen with the 1s atomic orbitals on the hydrogen atoms.

16. CCl_4 has $4 + 4(7) = 32$ valence electrons.

CCl_4 has a tetrahedral arrangement of the electron pairs about the carbon atom which requires sp^3 hybridization. The four sp^3 hybrid orbitals on carbon are used to form the four bonds to chlorine. The chlorine atoms also have a tetrahedral arrangement of electron pairs and we will assume that they are also sp^3 hybridized. The C–Cl sigma bonds are all formed from overlap of sp^3 hybrid orbitals on carbon with sp^3 hybrid orbitals from each chlorine atom.

17. H_2CO has $2(1) + 4 + 6 = 12$ valence electrons.

The central carbon atom has a trigonal planar arrangement of the electron pairs which requires sp^2 hybridization. The two C–H sigma bonds are formed from overlap of the sp^2 hybrid orbitals on carbon with the hydrogen 1s atomic orbitals. The double bond between carbon and oxygen consists of one σ and one π bond. The oxygen atom, like the carbon atom, also has a trigonal planar arrangement of the electrons which requires sp^2 hybridization. The σ bond in the double bond is formed from overlap of a carbon sp^2 hybrid orbital with an oxygen sp^2 hybrid orbital. The π bond in the double bond is formed from overlap of the unhybridized p atomic orbitals. Carbon and oxygen each have one unhybridized p atomic orbital which are parallel to each other. When two parallel p atomic orbitals overlap, a π bond results.

18. C_2H_2 has $2(4) + 2(1) = 10$ valence electrons.

H —— C≡C —— H

Each carbon atom in C_2H_2 is sp hybridized since each carbon atom is surrounded by two effective pairs of electrons, i.e., each carbon atom has a linear arrangement of electrons. Because each carbon atom is sp hybridized, each carbon atom has two unhybridized p atomic orbitals. The two C–H sigma bonds are formed from overlap of carbon sp hybrid orbitals with hydrogen 1s atomic orbitals. The triple bond is composed of one σ bond and two π bonds. The sigma bond between the carbon atoms is formed from overlap of sp hybrid orbitals on each carbon atom. The two π bonds of the triple bond are formed from parallel overlap of the two unhybridized p atomic orbitals on each carbon.

19.   Ethane, C_2H_6, has $2(4) + 6(1) = 14$ valence electrons.

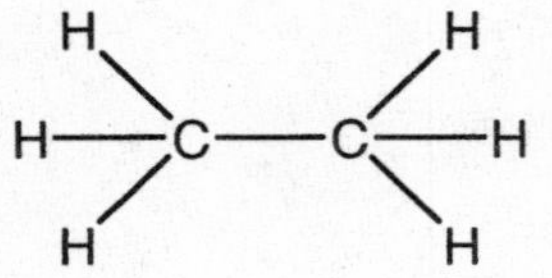

The carbon atoms are sp^3 hybridized. The six C–H sigma bonds are formed from overlap of the sp^3 hybrid orbitals on C with the 1s atomic orbitals from the hydrogen atoms. The carbon-carbon sigma bond is formed from overlap of an sp^3 hybrid orbital on each C atom.

Ethanol, C_2H_6O has $2(4) + 6(1) + 6 = 20$ e$^-$

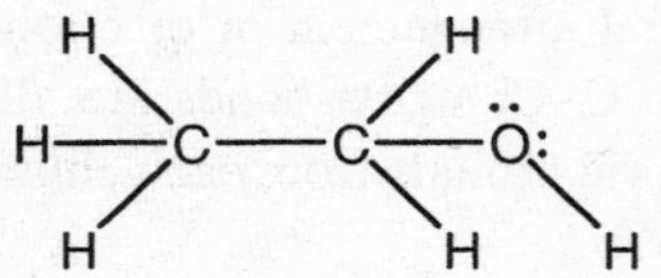

The two C atoms and the O atom are sp^3 hybridized. All bonds are formed from overlap with these sp^3 hybrid orbitals. The C–H and O–H sigma bonds are formed from overlap of sp^3 hybrid orbitals with hydrogen 1s atomic orbitals. The C–C and C–O sigma bonds are formed from overlap of the sp^3 hybrid orbitals on each atom.

20.   HCN, $1 + 4 + 5 = 10$ valence electrons

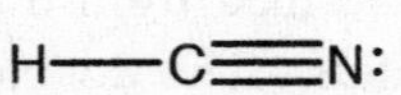

H —— C≡≡N:

Assuming N is hybridized, both C and N atoms are sp hybridized. The C–H σ bond is formed from overlap of a carbon sp^3 hybrid orbital with a hydrogen 1s atomic orbital. The triple bond is composed of one σ bond and two π bonds. The sigma bond is formed from head to head overlap of the sp hybrid orbitals from the C and N atoms. The two π bonds in the triple bond are formed from overlap of the two unhybridized p atomic orbitals on each C and N atom. $COCl_2$, $4 + 6 + 2(7) = 24$ valence electrons

Assuming all atoms are hybridized, the carbon and oxygen atoms are sp^2 hybridized, and the two chlorine atoms are sp^3 hybridized. The two C–Cl σ bonds are formed from overlap of sp^2 hybrids from C with sp^3 hybrid orbitals from Cl. the double bond between the carbon and oxygen atoms consists of one σ and one π bond. The σ bond in the double bond is formed from head to head overlap of an sp^2 orbital from carbon with an sp^2 hybrid orbital from oxygen. The π bond is formed from parallel overlap of the unhybridized p atomic orbitals on each atom of C and O.

21.   See Exercises 8.67 and 8.73 for the Lewis structures. To predict the hybridization, first determine the arrangement of electron pairs about each central atom using the VSEPR model; then utilize the information in Figure 9.24 of the text to deduce the hybridization required for that arrangement of electron pairs.

      8.67   a.   HCN; C is sp hybridized.   b. PH_3; P is sp^3 hybridized.

             c. $CHCl_3$; C is sp^3 hybridized.   d. NH_4^+; N is sp^3 hybridized.

             e. H_2CO; C is sp^2 hybridized.   f. SeF_2; Se is sp^3 hybridized.

             g. CO_2; C is sp hybridized.   h. O_2; Each O atom is sp^2 hybridized.

             i.   HBr; Br is sp^3 hybridized.

      8.73   a.   The central N atom is sp^2 hybridized in NO_2^- and NO_3^-. In N_2O_4, both central N atoms are sp^2 hybridized.

             b.   In OCN$^-$ and SCN$^-$, the central carbon atoms in each ion are sp hybridized and in N_3^-, the central N atom is also sp hybridized.

22.   See Exercises 8.68 and 8.74 for the Lewis structures.

      8.68   a.   All the central atoms are sp^3 hybridized.

             b.   All the central atoms are sp^3 hybridized.

             c.   All the central atoms are sp^3 hybridized.

      8.74   In O_3 and in SO_2, the central atoms are sp^2 hybridized and in SO_3, the central sulfur atom is also sp^2 hybridized.

23.   All exhibit dsp^3 hybridization. See Exercise 8.71 for the Lewis structures. All of these molecules/ions have a trigonal bipyramid arrangement of electron pairs about the central atom; all have central atoms with dsp^3 hybridization.

24.   See Exercise 8.72 for the Lewis structures. All of these molecules have an octahedral arrangement of electron pairs about the central atom; all have central atoms with d^2sp^3 hybridization.

25.   The molecules in Exercise 8.91 all have a trigonal planar arrangement of electron pairs about
       the central atom so all have central atoms with sp^2 hybridization. The molecules in Exercise
       8.92 all have a tetrahedral arrangement of electron pairs about the central atom so all have
       central atoms with sp^3 hybridization. See Exercises 8.91 and 8.92 for the Lewis structures.

26.   The molecules in Exercise 8.93 all have central atoms with dsp^3 hybridization since all are
       based on the trigonal bipyramid arrangement of electron pairs. The molecules in Exercise
       8.94 all have central atoms with d^2sp^3 hybridization since all are based on the octahedral
       arrangement of electron pairs. See Exercises 8.93 and 8.94 for the Lewis structures.

27.   a.   b.

       tetrahedral sp^3 trigonal pyramid sp^3
       109.5°   nonpolar   < 109.5°   polar

       The angles in NF_3 should be slightly less than 109.5° because the lone pair requires more
       space than the bonding pairs.

       c.   d.

       V-shaped sp^3 trigonal planar sp^2
       < 109.5°   polar   120°   nonpolar

       e.   f.

       linear   sp   see-saw
       180°   nonpolar   a. ≈ 120°, b. ≈ 90°
                                                            dsp^3 polar

g.

trigonal bipyramid   dsp³
a. 90°, b. 120°   nonpolar

h.

:F—Kr—F:

linear   dsp³
120°   nonpolar

i.

square planar   d²sp³
90°   nonpolar

j.

octahedral   d²sp³
90°   nonpolar

k.

square pyramid   d²sp³
≈90°   polar

l.

T-shaped   dsp³
≈ 90°   polar

28.   a.

V-shaped, sp², 120°

Only one resonance form is shown. Resonance does not change the position of the atoms. We can predict the geometry and hybridization from any one of the resonance structures.

b.

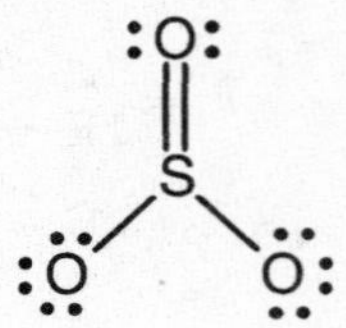

plus two other resonance structures
trigonal planar, 120°, sp^2

c.

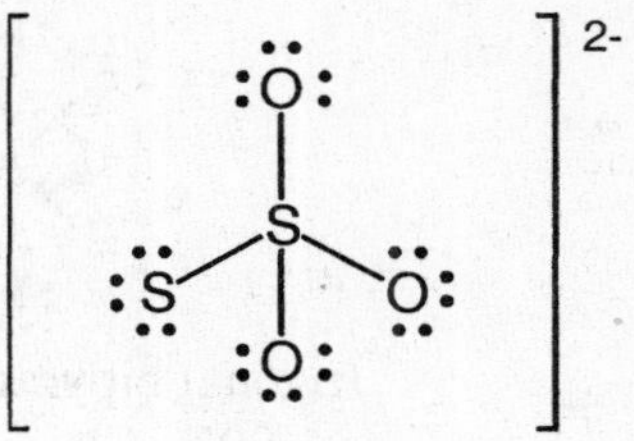

tetrahedral, 109.5°, sp^3

d.

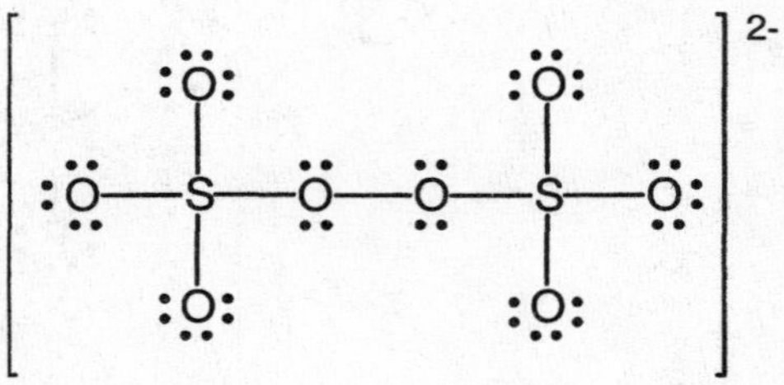

Tetrahedral geometry about each S, 109.5°,
sp^3 hybrids; V-shaped arrangement about
peroxide O's, ≈109.5°, sp^3 hybrids

e.

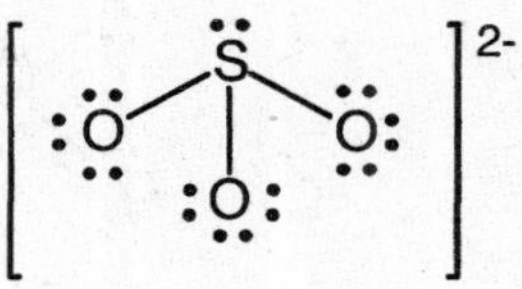

trigonal pyramid, < 109.5°, sp^3

f.

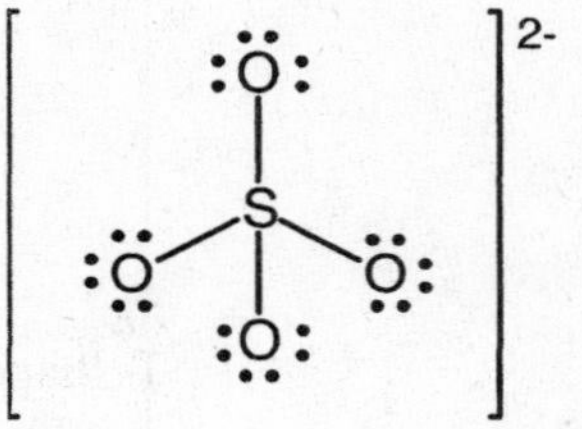

tetrahedral, 109.5°, sp^3

g.

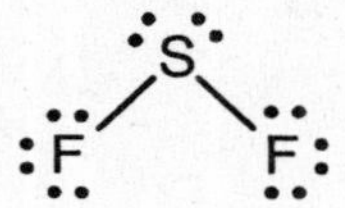

V-shaped, < 109.5°, sp^3

h.

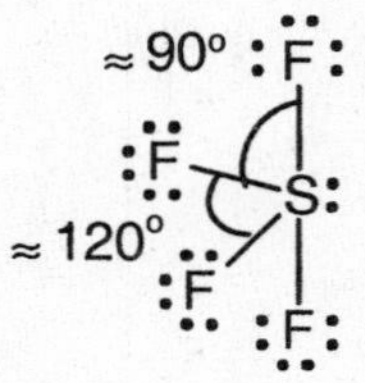

see-saw, ≈ 90° and ≈ 120°, dsp^3

i.

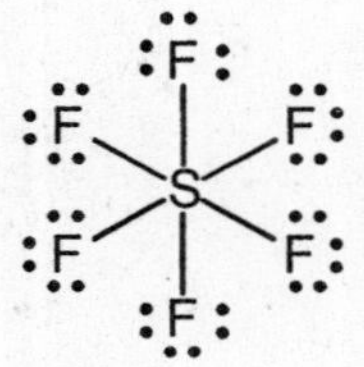

octahedral, 90°, d^{2}sp^3

j.   k.

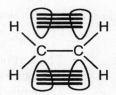

a) ≈ 109.5°   b) ≈ 90°   c) ≈ 120°

See-saw about S atom with one lone pair (dsp³);

bent about S atom with two lone pairs (sp³)

trigonal bipyramid,
90° and 120°, dsp³

29.

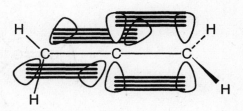

For the p-orbitals to properly line up to form the π bond, all six atoms are forced into the same plane. If the atoms were not in the same plane, the π bond could not form since the p-orbitals would no longer be parallel to each other.

30.   No, the CH₂ planes are mutually perpendicular to each other. The center C atom is sp hybridized and is involved in two π-bonds. The p-orbitals used to form each π bond must be perpendicular to each other. This forces the two CH₂ planes to be perpendicular.

31.   To complete the Lewis structures, just add lone pairs of electrons to satisfy the octet rule for the atoms with fewer than eight electrons.

Biacetyl ($C_4H_6O_2$) has $4(4) + 6(1) + 2(6) = 34$ valence electrons.

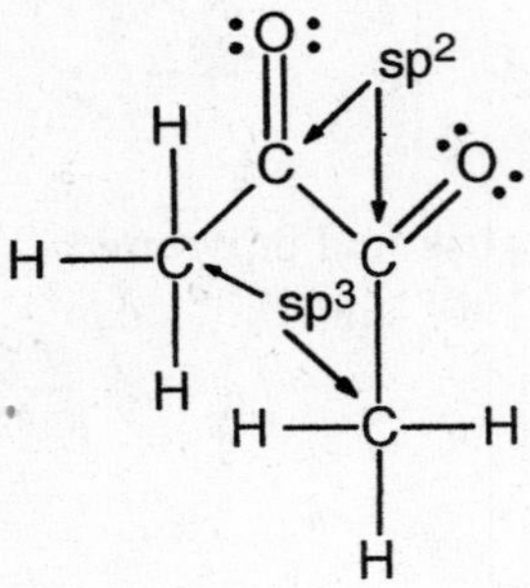

All CCO angles are 120°. The six atoms are not in the same plane because of free rotation about the carbon- carbon single (sigma) bonds. There are 11 σ and 2 π bonds in biacetyl.

Acetoin ($C_4H_8O_2$) has $4(4) + 8(1) + 2(6) = 36$ valence electrons.

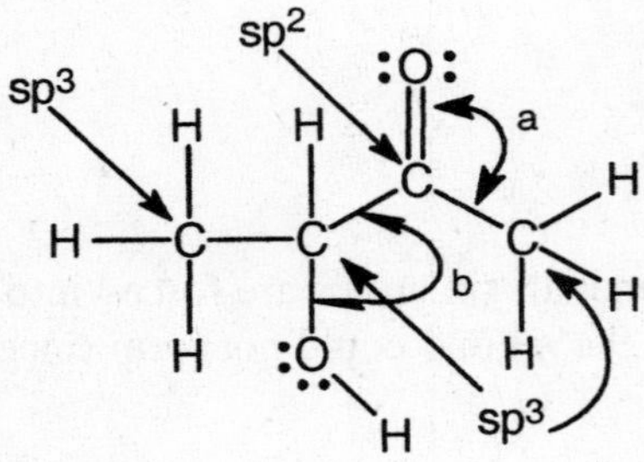

The carbon with the doubly-bonded O is sp^2 hybridized. The other 3 C atoms are sp^3 hybridized. Angle a = 120° and angle b = 109.5°. There are 13 σ and 1 π bonds in acetoin.

Note: All single bonds are σ bonds, all double bonds are one σ and one π bond, and all triple bonds are one σ and two π bonds.

32.   Acrylonitrile: C_3H_3N has $3(4) + 3(1) + 5 = 20$ valence electrons.

a.   120°

b.   120°

c.   180°

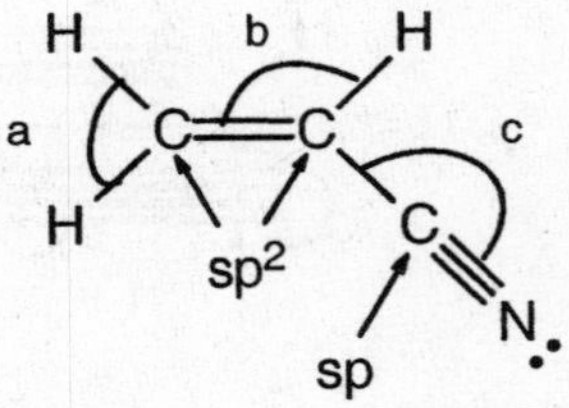

6 σ and 3 π bonds

All atoms of acrylonitrile lie in the same plane. The π bond in the double bond dictates that the C and H atoms are all in the same plane, and the triple bond dictates that N is in the same plane with the other atoms.

Methyl methacrylate ($C_5H_8O_2$) has $5(4) + 8(1) + 2(6) = 40$ valence electrons.

d. 120°

e. 120°

f. ≈109.5°

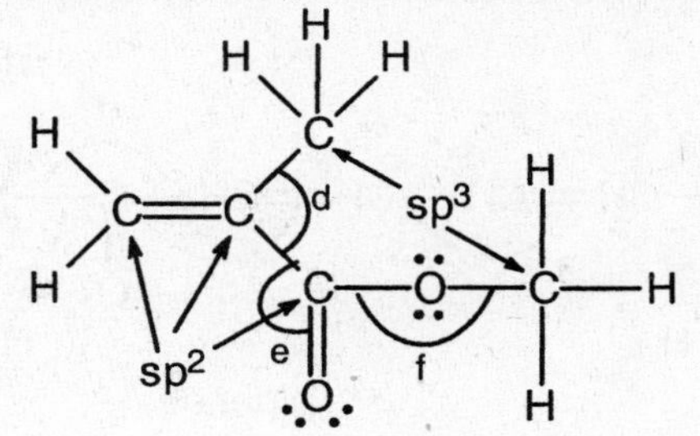

14 σ and 2 π bonds

33.   To complete the Lewis structure, just add lone pairs of electrons to satisfy the octet rule for the atoms that have fewer than eight electrons.

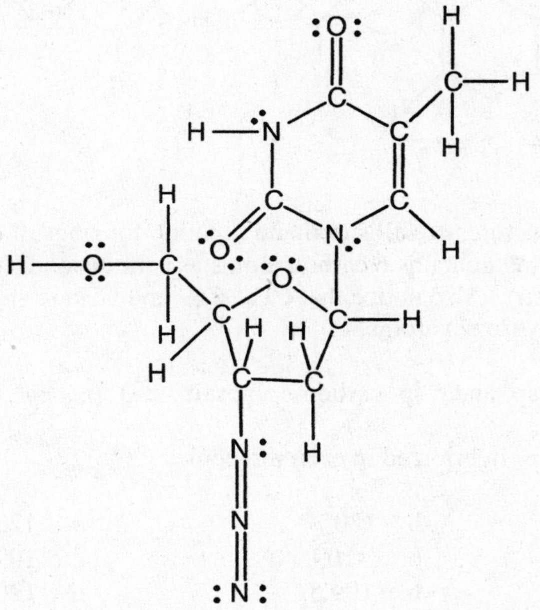

a. 6   b. 4   c. The center N in −N=N=N group

d. 33 σ   e. 5 π bonds   f. 180°

g. < 109.5°   h. sp³

34.   a. Piperine and capsaicin are molecules classified as organic compounds, i.e., compounds based on carbon. The majority of Lewis structures for organic compounds have all atoms with zero formal charge. Therefore, carbon atoms in organic compounds will usually form four bonds, nitrogen atoms will form three bonds and complete the octet with one lone pair of electrons, and oxygen atoms will form two bonds and complete the octet with two lone pairs of electrons. Using these guidelines, the Lewis structures are:

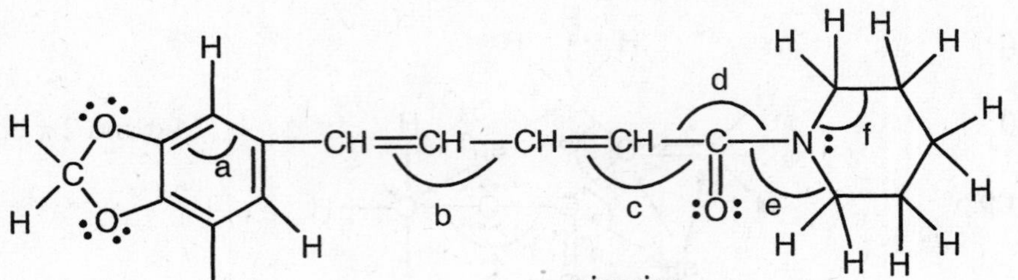

piperine

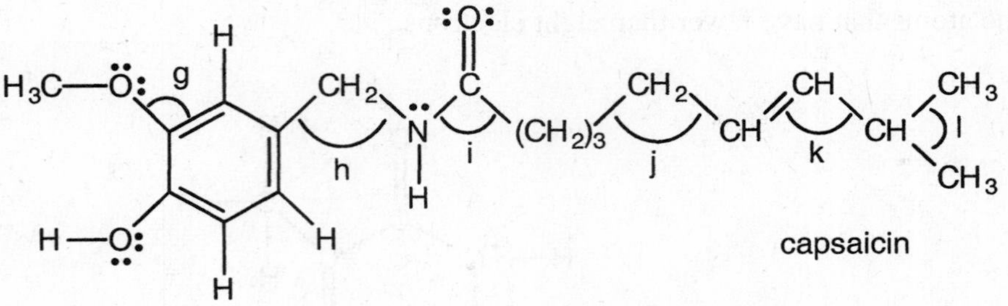

capsaicin

Note: The ring structures are all shorthand notation for rings of carbon atoms. In piperine, the first ring contains 6 carbon atoms and the second ring contains 5 carbon atoms (plus nitrogen). Also notice that CH_3, CH_2 and CH are shorthand for carbon atoms singly bonded to hydrogen atoms.

b. piperine: 0 sp, 11 sp^2 and 6 sp^3 carbons; capsaicin: 0 sp, 9 sp^2, and 9 sp^3 carbons

c. The nitrogens are sp^3 hybridized in each molecule.

d.
a. 120°	b. 120°	c. 120°
d. 120°	e. ≈109.5°	f. 109.5°
g. 120°	h. 109.5°	i. 120°
j. 109.5°	k. 120°	l. 109.5°

The Molecular Orbital Model

35. If we calculate a non-zero bond order for a molecule, then we predict that it can exist (is stable).

a. H_2^+: $(\sigma_{1s})^1$ B.O. = (1–0)/2 = 1/2, stable

     H_2: $(\sigma_{1s})^2$ B.O. = (2–0)/2 = 1, stable

     H_2^-: $(\sigma_{1s})^2(\sigma_{1s}*)^1$ B.O. = (2–1)/2 = 1/2, stable

     H_2^{2-}: $(\sigma_{1s})^2(\sigma_{1s}*)^2$ B.O. = (2–2)/2 = 0, not stable

b. He_2^{2+}: $(\sigma_{1s})^2$ B.O. = (2–0)/2 = 1, stable

     He_2^+: $(\sigma_{1s})^2(\sigma_{1s}*)^1$ B.O. = (2–1)/2 = 1/2, stable

     He_2: $(\sigma_{1s})^2(\sigma_{1s}*)^2$ B.O. = (2–2)/2 = 0, not stable

36.   a. N_2^{2-}: $(\sigma_{2s})^2(\sigma_{2s}*)^2(\pi_{2p})^4(\sigma_{2p})^2(\pi_{2p}*)^2$ B.O. = (8–4)/2 = 2, stable

             O_2^{2-}: $(\sigma_{2s})^2(\sigma_{2s}*)^2(\sigma_{2p})^2(\pi_{2p})^4(\pi_{2p}*)^4$ B.O. = (8–6)/2 = 1, stable

             F_2^{2-}: $(\sigma_{2s})^2(\sigma_{2s}*)^2(\sigma_{2p})^2(\pi_{2p})^4(\pi_{2p}*)^4(\sigma_{2p}*)^2$ B.O. = (8–8)/2 = 0, not stable

       b. Be_2: $(\sigma_{2s})^2(\sigma_{2s}*)^2$ B.O. = (2–2)/2 = 0, not stable

             B_2: $(\sigma_{2s})^2(\sigma_{2s}*)^2(\pi_{2p})^2$ B.O. = (4–2)/2 = 1, stable

             Ne_2: $(\sigma_{2s})^2(\sigma_{2s}*)^2(\sigma_{2p})^2(\pi_{2p})^4(\pi_{2p}*)^4(\sigma_{2p}*)^2$ B.O. = (8–8)/2 = 0, not stable

37.   The electron configurations are:

       a. Li_2: $(\sigma_{2s})^2$ B.O. = (2–0)/2 = 1, diamagnetic (0 unpaired e^-)

       b. C_2: $(\sigma_{2s})^2(\sigma_{2s}*)^2(\pi_{2p})^4$ B.O. = (6–2)/2 = 2, diamagnetic (0 unpaired e^-)

       c. S_2: $(\sigma_{3s})^2(\sigma_{3s}*)^2(\sigma_{3p})^2(\pi_{3p})^4(\pi_{3p}*)^2$ B.O. = (8–4)/2 = 2, paramagnetic (2 unpaired e^-)

38.   There are 14 valence electrons in the MO electron configuration. Also, the valence shell is
       n=3. Some possibilities from row 3 having 14 valence electrons are Cl_2, SCl^-, S_2^{2-}, and Ar_2^{2+}.

39. O_2: $(\sigma_{2s})^2(\sigma_{2s}^*)^2(\sigma_{2p})^2(\pi_{2p})^4(\pi_{2p}^*)^2$ B.O. = (8 – 4)/2 = 2

       N_2: $(\sigma_{2s})^2(\sigma_{2s}^*)^2(\pi_{2p})^4(\sigma_{2p})^2$ B.O. = (8 – 2)/2 = 3

       In O_2, an antibonding electron is removed which will increase the bond order to
       2.5 [= (8–3)/2]. The bond order increases as an electron is removed, so the bond strengthens.
       In N_2, a bonding electron is removed which decreases the bond order to 2.5 = [(7 – 2)/2], so
       the bond strength weakens.

40.   The electron configurations are:

             F_2^+: $(\sigma_{2s})^2(\sigma_{2s}*)^2(\sigma_{2p})^2(\pi_{2p})^4(\pi_{2p}*)^3$ B.O. = (8–5)/2 = 1.5; 1 unpaired e^-

             F_2: $(\sigma_{2s})^2(\sigma_{2s}*)^2(\sigma_{2p})^2(\pi_{2p})^4(\pi_{2p}*)^4$ B.O. = (8–6)/2 = 1;   0 unpaired e^-

             F_2^-: $(\sigma_{2s})^2(\sigma_{2s}*)^2(\sigma_{2p})^2(\pi_{2p})^4(\pi_{2p}*)^4(\sigma_{2p}*)^1$ B.O. = (8–7)/2 = 0.5; 1 unpaired e^-

       From the calculated bond orders, the order of bond lengths should be: $F_2^+ < F_2 < F_2^-$

41. N_2: $(\sigma_{2s})^2(\sigma_{2s}^*)^2(\pi_{2p})^4(\pi_{2p})^2$ B.O. = (8 – 2)/2 = 3

       We need to decrease the bond order from 3 to 2.5. There are two ways to do this. One is to
       add an electron to form N_2^-. This added electron goes into one of the π_{2p}^* orbitals giving a
       bond order = (8 – 3)/2 = 2.5. We could also remove a bonding electron to form N_2^+. The bond
       order for N_2^+ is also 2.5 [= (7 – 2)/2].

42.   Considering only the twelve valence electrons in O_2, the MO models would be:

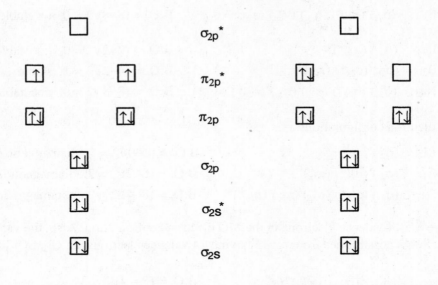

              O_2 ground state   Arrangement of electrons consistent
                                              with the Lewis structure (double bond
                                              and no unpaired electrons).

It takes energy to pair electrons in the same orbital. Thus, the structure with no unpaired
electrons is at a higher energy; it is an excited state.

43.   The electron configurations are (assuming the same orbital order as that for N_2):

a. CO: $(\sigma_{2s})^2(\sigma_{2s}*)^2(\pi_{2p})^4(\sigma_{2p})^2$ B.O. = (8-2)/2 = 3, diamagnetic
b. CO^+: $(\sigma_{2s})^2(\sigma_{2s}*)^2(\pi_{2p})^4(\sigma_{2p})^1$ B.O. = (7-2)/2 = 2.5, paramagnetic
c. CO^{2+}: $(\sigma_{2s})^2(\sigma_{2s}*)^2(\pi_{2p})^4$ B.O. = (6-2)/2 = 2, diamagnetic

Since bond order is directly proportional to bond energy and inversely proportional to bond
length, then:

     shortest → longest bond length: $CO < CO^+ < CO^{2+}$

     smallest → largest bond energy: $CO^{2+} < CO^+ < CO$

44.   The electron configurations are (assuming the same orbital order as that for N_2):

a. NO^+: $(\sigma_{2s})^2(\sigma_{2s}*)^2(\pi_{2p})^4(\sigma_{2p})^2$ B.O. = (8-2)/2 = 3, diamagnetic
b. NO: $(\sigma_{2s})^2(\sigma_{2s}*)^2(\pi_{2p})^4(\sigma_{2p})^2(\pi_{2p}*)^1$ B.O. = (8-3)/2 = 2.5, paramagnetic
c. NO^-: $(\sigma_{2s})^2(\sigma_{2s}*)^2(\pi_{2p})^4(\sigma_{2p})^2(\pi_{2p}*)^2$ B.O. = (8-4)/2 = 2, paramagnetic

     shortest → longest bond length: $NO^+ < NO < NO^-$

     smallest → largest bond energy: $NO^- < NO < NO^+$

45. H_2: $(\sigma_{1s})^2$

B_2: $(\sigma_{2s})^2(\sigma_{2s}*)^2(\pi_{2p})^2$

C_2^{2-}: $(\sigma_{2s})^2(\sigma_{2s}*)^2(\pi_{2p})^4(\sigma_{2p})^2$

OF: $(\sigma_{2s})^2(\sigma_{2s}*)^2(\sigma_{2p})^2(\pi_{2p})^4(\pi_{2p}*)^3$

The bond strength will weaken if the electron removed comes from a bonding orbital. Of the molecules listed, H_2, B_2, and C_2^{2-} would be expected to have their bond strength weaken as an electron is removed. OF has the electron removed from an antibonding orbital, so its bond strength increases.

46. CN: $(\sigma_{2s})^2(\sigma_{2s}*)^2(\pi_{2p})^4(\sigma_{2p})^1$

NO: $(\sigma_{2s})^2(\sigma_{2s}*)^2(\pi_{2p})^4(\sigma_{2p})^2(\pi_{2p}*)^1$

O_2^{2+}: $(\sigma_{2s})^2(\sigma_{2s}*)^2(\sigma_{2p})^2(\pi_{2p})^4$

N_2^{2+}: $(\sigma_{2s})^2(\sigma_{2s}*)^2(\pi_{2p})^4$

If the added electron goes into a bonding orbital, the bond order would increase, making the species more stable and more likely to form. Between CN and NO, CN would most likely form CN^- since the bond order increases (unlike NO^- where the added electron goes into an antibonding orbital). Between O_2^{2+} and N_2^{2+}, N_2^+ would most likely form since the bond order increases (unlike O_2^+ as ccompared to O_2^{2+}).

47.   The two types of overlap that result in bond formation for p orbitals are in-phase side to side overlap (π bond) and in-phase head to head overlap (σ bond).

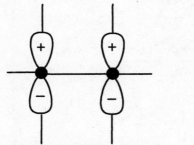

π_{2p} (in-phase; the signs match up)

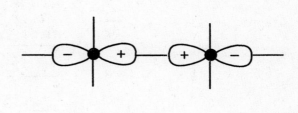

σ_{2p} (in-phase; the signs match up)

48.

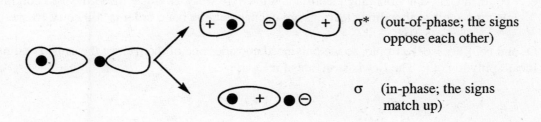

$\sigma*$ (out-of-phase; the signs oppose each other)

σ (in-phase; the signs match up)

These molecular orbitals are sigma MOs since the electron density is cylindrically symmetric about the internuclear axis.

49.   a.   The electron density would be closer to F on the average. The F atom is more electronegative than the H atom, and the 2p orbital of F is lower in energy than the 1s orbital of H.

b.   The bonding MO would have more fluorine 2p character since it is closer in energy to the fluorine 2p atomic orbital.

c.   The antibonding MO would place more electron density closer to H and would have a greater contribution from the higher energy hydrogen 1s atomic orbital.

50.   a.   The antibonding MO will have more hydrogen 1s character because the hydrogen 1s atomic orbital is closer in energy to the antibonding MO.

b.   No, the net overall overlap is zero. The p_x orbital does not have proper symmetry to overlap with a 1s orbital. The $2p_x$ and $2p_y$ orbitals are called nonbonding orbitals.

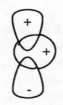

c.

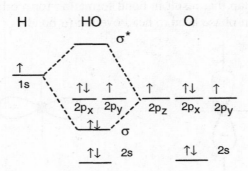

d.   Bond order = $(2 - 0)/2 = 1$; Note: The 2s, $2p_x$, and $2p_y$ electrons have no effect on the bond order.

e.   To form OH^+, a nonbonding electron is removed from OH. Since the number of bonding electrons and antibonding electrons are unchanged, the bond order is still equal to one.

51. O_3 and NO_2^- are isoelectronic, so we only need consider one of them since the same bonding ideas apply to both. The Lewis structures for O_3 are:

For each of the two resonance forms, the central O atom is sp^2 hybridized with one unhybridized p atomic orbital. The sp^2 hybrid orbitals are used to form the two sigma bonds to the central atom. The localized electron view of the π bond utilizes unhybridized p atomic orbitals. The π bond resonates between the two positions in the Lewis structures:

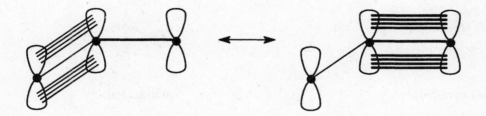

In the MO picture of the π bond, all three unhybridized p-orbitals overlap at the same time, resulting in π electrons that are delocalized over the entire surface of the molecule. This is represented as:

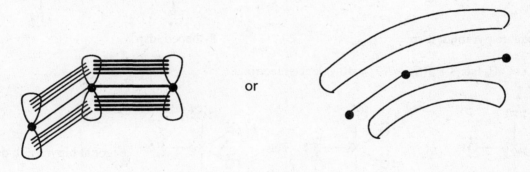

or

52.   The Lewis structures for CO_3^{2-} are (24 e^-):

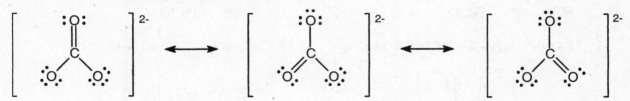

In the localized electron view, the central carbon atom is sp^2 hybridized; the sp^2 hybrid orbitals are used to form the three sigma bonds in CO_3^{2-}. The central C atom also has one unhybridized p atomic orbital which overlaps with another p atomic orbital from one of the oxygen atoms to form the π bond in each resonance structure. This localized π bond moves (resonates) from one position to another. In the molecular orbital model for CO_3^{2-}, all four atoms in CO_3^{2-} have a p atomic orbital which is perpendicular to the plane of the ion. All four of these p orbitals overlap at the same time to form a delocalized π bonding system where the π electrons can roam above and below the entire surface of the ion. The π molecular orbital system for CO_3^{2-} is analogous to that for NO_3^- which is shown in Figure 9.49 of the text.

Additional Exercises

53. a. XeO_3, $8 + 3(6) = 26 \, e^-$

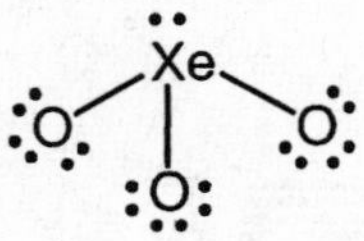

b. XeO_4, $8 + 4(6) = 32 \, e^-$

trigonal pyramid; sp^3

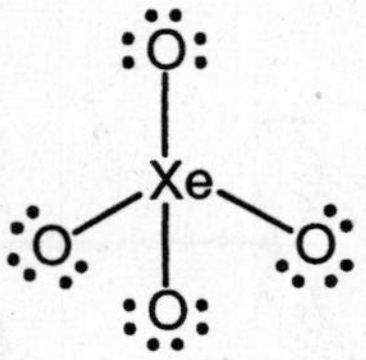

tetrahedral; sp^3

c. $XeOF_4$, $8 + 6 + 4(7) = 42 \, e^-$

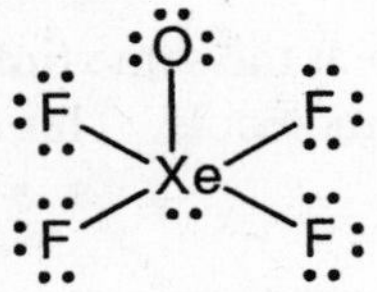

d. $XeOF_2$, $8 + 6 + 2(7) = 28 \, e^-$

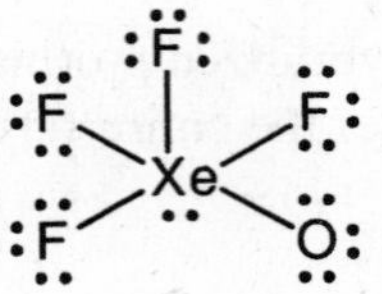

or

square pyramid; d^2sp^3

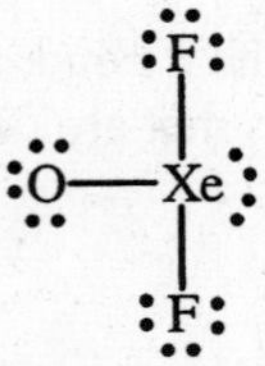

or

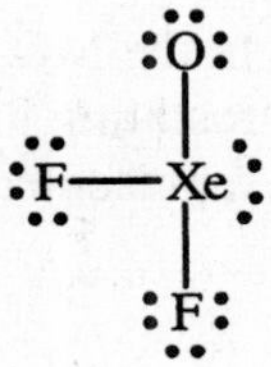

T-shaped; dsp^3

e. XeO_3F_2 has $8 + 3(6) + 2(7) = 40$ valence electrons.

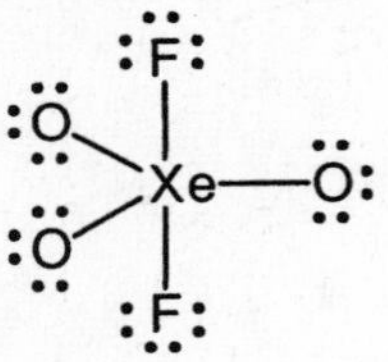

or 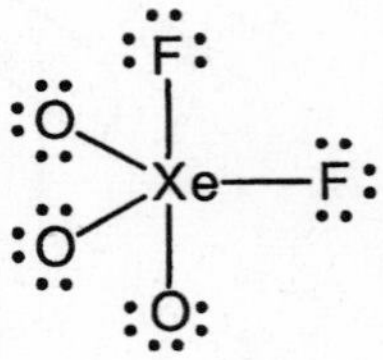   or 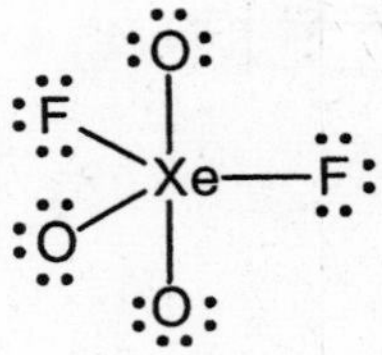   trigonal bipyramid; dsp^3

54. $FClO_2 + F^- \rightarrow F_2ClO_2^-$

$F_3ClO + F^- \rightarrow F_4ClO^-$

$F_2ClO_2^-$, $2(7) + 7 + 2(6) + 1 = 34 \, e^-$

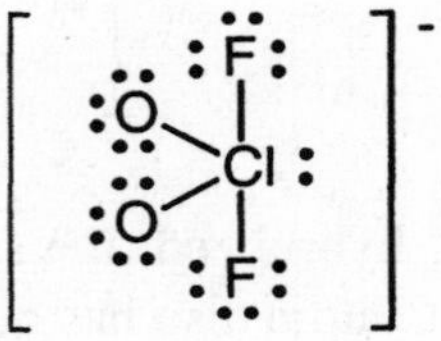

F_4ClO^-, $4(7) + 7 + 6 + 1 = 42 \, e^-$

see-saw, dsp^3

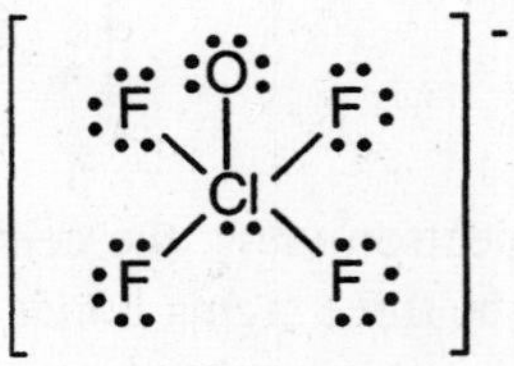

square pyramid, d^2sp^3

Note: Similar to Exercises 9.53 c, d and e, $F_2ClO_2^-$ has two additional Lewis structures that are possible, and F_4ClO^- has one additional Lewis structure that is possible. The predicted hybridization is unaffected.

$F_3ClO \rightarrow F^- + F_2ClO^+$ $F_3ClO_2 \rightarrow F^- + F_2ClO_2^+$

F_2ClO^+, $2(7) + 7 + 6 - 1 = 26$ e$^-$ $F_2ClO_2^+$, $2(7) + 7 + 2(6) - 1 = 32$ e$^-$

trigonal pyramid, sp^3 tetrahedral, sp^3

55.   For carbon, nitrogen, and oxygen atoms to have formal charge values of zero, each C atom will form four bonds to other atoms and have no lone pairs of electrons, each N atom will form three bonds to other atoms and have one lone pair of electrons, and each O atom will form two bonds to other atoms and have two lone pairs of electrons. Following these bonding requirements gives the following two resonance structures for vitamin B$_6$:

a.   21 σ bonds; 4 π bonds (The electrons in the 3 π bonds in the ring are delocalized.)

b.   angles a, c, and g: ≈ 109.5°; angles b, d, e and f: ≈ 120°

c.   6 sp^2 carbons; the 5 carbon atoms in the ring are sp^2 hybridized, as is the carbon with the double bond to oxygen.

d.   4 sp^3 atoms; the 2 carbons which are not sp^2 hybridized are sp^3 hybridized, and the oxygens marked with angles a and c are sp^3 hybridized.

e.   Yes, the π electrons in the ring are delocalized. The atoms in the ring are all sp^2 hybridized. This leaves a p orbital perpendicular to the plane of the ring from each atom. Overlap of all six of these p orbitals results in a π molecular orbital system where the electrons are delocalized above and below the plane of the ring (similar to benzene in Figure 9.48 of the text).

56.   We rotated the molecule about some single bonds from the structure given in the question. Following the bonding guidelines outlined in Exercise 9.55, a Lewis structure for aspartame is:

Another resonance structure could be drawn having the double bonds in the benzene ring moved over one position.

Atoms which have trigonal planar geometry of electron pairs are assumed to have sp^2 hybridization and atoms with tetrahedral geometry of electron pairs are assumed to have sp^3 hybridization. All the N atoms have tetrahedral geometry so they are all sp^3 hybridized (no sp^2 hybridization). The oxygens double bonded to carbon atoms are sp^2 hybridized; the other two oxygens with two single bonds are sp^3 hybridized. For the carbon atoms, the six carbon atoms in the benzene ring are sp^2 hybridized and the three carbons double bonded to oxygen are also sp^2 hybridized (tetrahedral geometry). Answering the questions:

- 9 sp^2 hybridized C and N atoms (9 from Cs and 0 from Ns)
- 7 sp^3 hybridized C and O atoms (5 from Cs and 2 from Os)
- 39 σ bonds and 6 π bonds (this includes the 3 π bonds in the benzene ring that are delocalized)

57.

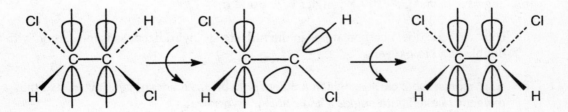

In order to rotate about the double bond, the molecule must go through an intermediate stage where the π bond is broken while the sigma bond remains intact. Bond energies are 347 kJ/mol for C–C and 614 kJ/mol for C=C. If we take the single bond as the strength of the σ bond, then the strength of the π bond is (614 – 347 =) 267 kJ/mol. In theory, 267 kJ/mol must be supplied to rotate about a carbon-carbon double bond.

58.   CO, 4 + 6 = 10 e⁻;   CO₂, 4 + 2(6) = 16 e⁻;   C₃O₂, 3(4) + 2(6) = 24 e⁻

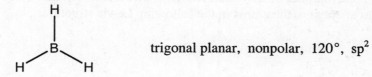

There is no molecular structure for the diatomic CO molecule. The carbon in CO is sp hybridized. CO_2 is a linear molecule, and the central carbon atom is sp hybridized. C_3O_2 is a linear molecule with all of the central carbon atoms exhibiting sp hybridization.

59.   a. BH_3 has 3 + 3(1) = 6 valence electrons.

trigonal planar, nonpolar, 120°, sp^2

b. N_2F_2 has 2(5) + 2(7) = 24 valence electrons.

Can also be:

V-shaped about both Ns;
≈120° about both Ns;
Both Ns: sp^2

polar   nonpolar

These are distinctly different molecules.

c. C_4H_6 has 4(4) + 6(1) = 22 valence electrons.

All Cs are trigonal planar with 120° bond angles and sp^2 hybridization. Because C and H have about equal electronegativities, the C–H bonds are essentially nonpolar so the molecule is nonpolar. All neutral compounds composed of only C and H atoms are nonpolar.

d. ICl_3 has 7 + 3(7) = 28 valence electrons.

T-shaped polar
a. ≈ 90°, dsp^3

60.   a.   Yes, both have 4 sets of electrons about the P. We would predict a tetrahedral structure for both. See part d for the Lewis structures.

b.   The hybridization is sp^3 for each P since both structures are tetrahedral.

c.   P has to use one of its d orbitals to form the π bond since the p orbitals are all used to form the hybrid orbitals.

d.   Formal charge = number of valence electrons of an atom − [(number of lone pair electrons) + 1/2 (number of shared electrons)]. The formal charges calculated for the O and P atoms are next to the atoms in the following Lewis structures.

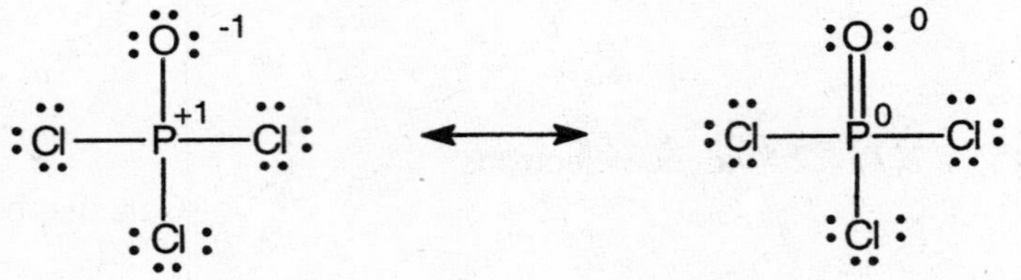

In both structures, the formal charges of the Cl atoms are all zeros. The structure with the P=O bond is favored on the basis of formal charge since it has a zero formal charge for all atoms.

61.   a.   The Lewis structures for NNO and NON are:

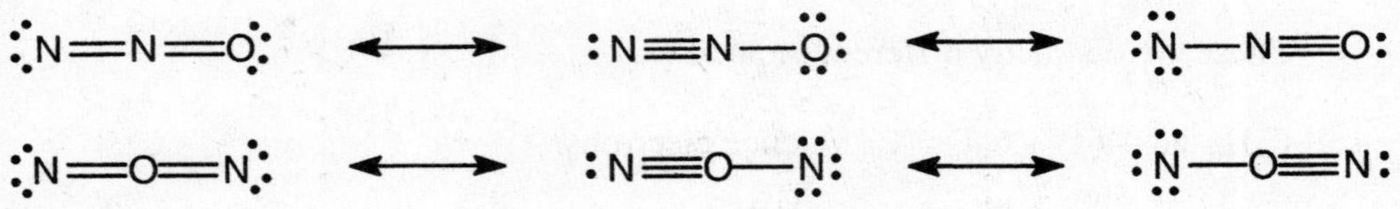

The NNO structure is correct. From the Lewis structures, we would predict both NNO and NON to be linear. However, we would predict NNO to be polar and NON to be nonpolar. Since experiments show N_2O to be polar, NNO is the correct structure.

b.   Formal chare = number of valence electrons of atoms - [(number of lone pair electrons) + 1/2 (number of shared electrons)].

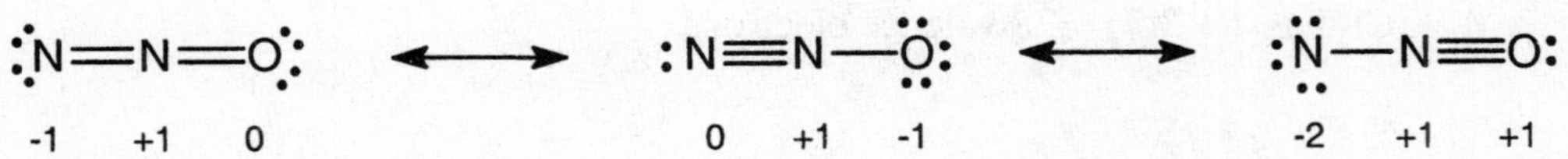

The formal charges for the atoms in the various resonance structures are below each atom. The central N is sp hybridized in all of the resonance structures. We can probably ignore the third resonance structure on the basis of the relatively large formal charges as compared to the first two resonance structures.

c.   The sp hybrid orbitals on the center N overlap with atomic orbitals (or hybrid orbitals) on the other two atoms to form the two sigma bonds. The remaining two unhybridized p orbitals on the center N overlap with two p orbitals on the peripheral N to form the two π bonds.

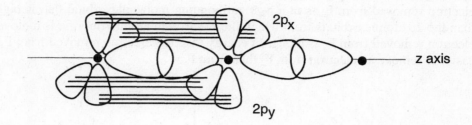

62.   Lewis structures:

NO$^+$: $\left[\; :N\equiv O: \;\right]$ NO$^-$: $\left[\; \ddot{N}\!=\!\ddot{O} \;\right]^-$

NO: $\ddot{N}\!=\!\ddot{O}$ or $\ddot{N}\!=\!\ddot{O}$ + others

Note: Lewis structures do not handle odd numbered electron species very well.

M.O. model:

NO$^+$: $(\sigma_{2s})^2(\sigma_{2s}*)^2(\pi_{2p})^4(\sigma_{2p})^2$, B.O. = 3, 0 unpaired e$^-$ (diamagnetic)

NO: $(\sigma_{2s})^2(\sigma_{2s}*)^2(\pi_{2p})^4(\sigma_{2p})^2(\pi_{2p}*)^1$, B.O. = 2.5, 1 unpaired e$^-$ (paramagnetic)

NO$^-$: $(\sigma_{2s})^2(\sigma_{2s}*)^2(\pi_{2p})^4(\sigma_{2p})^2(\pi_{2p}*)^2$ B.O. = 2, 2 unpaired e$^-$ (paramagnetic)

The two models give the same results only for NO$^+$ (a triple bond with no unpaired electrons). Lewis structures are not adequate for NO and NO$^-$. The MO model gives a better representation for all three species. For NO, Lewis structures are poor for odd electron species. For NO$^-$, both models predict a double bond, but only the MO model correctly predicts that NO$^-$ is paramagnetic.

63.   N$_2$ (ground state): $(\sigma_{2s})^2(\sigma_{2s}*)^2(\pi_{2p})^4(\sigma_{2p})^2$, B.O. = 3, diamagnetic (0 unpaired e$^-$)

N$_2$ (1st excited state): $(\sigma_{2s})^2(\sigma_{2s}*)^2(\pi_{2p})^4(\sigma_{2p})^1(\pi_{2p}*)^1$

B.O. = (7 −3)/2 = 2, paramagnetic (2 unpaired e$^-$)

The first excited state of N$_2$ should have a weaker bond and should be paramagnetic.

64.   C$_2{}^{2-}$ has 10 valence electrons. The Lewis structure predicts sp hybridization for each carbon with two unhybridized p orbitals on each carbon.

$\left[\; :C\equiv C: \;\right]^{2-}$ sp hybrid orbitals form the σ bond, and the two unhybridized p atomic orbitals from each carbon form the two π bonds.

MO: $(\sigma_{2s})^2(\sigma_{2s}*)^2(\pi_{2p})^4(\sigma_{2p})^2$, B.O. = (8 − 2)/2 = 3

Both give the same picture, a triple bond composed of one σ and two π-bonds. Both predict the ion will be diamagnetic. Lewis structures deal well with diamagnetic (all electrons paired) species. The Lewis model cannot really predict magnetic properties.

65. F_2: $(\sigma_{2s})^2(\sigma_{2s}*)^2(\sigma_{2p})^2(\pi_{2p})^4(\pi_{2p}*)^4$; F_2 should have a lower ionization energy than F. The electron removed from F_2 is in a $\pi_{2p}*$ antibonding molecular orbital that is higher in energy than the 2p atomic orbitals from which the electron in atomic fluorine is removed. Since the electron removed from F_2 is higher in energy than the electron removed from F, it should be easier to remove an electron from F_2 than from F.

66.

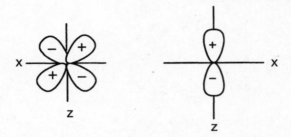

The orbitals overlap side to side so when the orbitals are in-phase, a π bonding molecular orbital would form.

67.   Side to side in-phase overlap of these d-orbitals would produce a π bonding molecular orbital. There would be no probability of finding an electron on the axis joining the two nuclei, which is characteristic of π MOs.

68.   Molecule A has a tetrahedral arrangement of electron pairs since it is sp^3 hybridized. Molecule B has 6 electron pairs about the central atom so it is d^2sp^3 hybridized. Molecule C has two σ and two π bonds to the central atom so it either has two double bonds to the central atom (like in CO_2) or one triple bond and one single bond (like in HCN). Molecule C is consistent with a linear arrangement of electron pairs exhibiting sp hybridization. There are many correct possibilities for each molecule; an example of each is:

Molecule A: CH_4 Molecule B: XeF_4 Molecule C: CO_2 or HCN

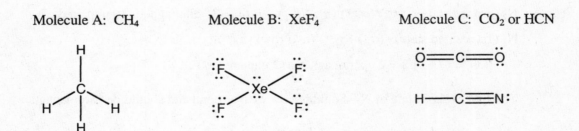

Challenge Problems

69.

The three C atoms each bonded to three H atoms are sp^3 hybridized (tetrahedral geometry); the other five C atoms with trigonal planar geometry are sp^2 hybridized. The one N atom with the double bond is sp^2 hybridized and the other three N atoms are sp^3 hybridized. The answers to the questions are:

- 6 C and N atoms are sp^2 hybridized
- 6 C and N atoms are sp^3 hybridized
- 0 C and N atoms are sp hybridized (linear geometry)
- 25 σ bonds and 4 π bonds

70.   Benzoic acid, $C_7H_6O_2$ has $7(4) + 6(1) + + 2(6) = 46$ valence electrons.

The circle in the ring indicates the delocalized π bonding in the benzene ring. The two benzene resonance Lewis structures have three alternating double bonds in the ring (see Fig. 9.46).

The six carbons in the ring and the carbon bonded to the ring are all sp^2 hybridized. The five C–H sigma bonds are formed from overlap of the sp^2 hybridized carbon atoms with hydrogen 1s atomic orbitals. The seven C–C σ bonds are formed from head to head overlap of sp^2 hybrid orbitals from each carbon. The C–O single bond is formed from overlap of an sp^2 hybrid orbital on carbon with an sp^3 hybrid orbital from oxygen. The C–O σ bond in the double bond is formed from overlap of carbon sp^2 hybrid orbital with an oxygen sp^2 orbital. The π bond in the C–O double bond is formed from overlap of parallel p unhybridized atomic orbitals from C and O. The delocalized π bonding system in the ring is formed from overlap of all six unhybridized p atomic orbitals from the six carbon atoms. See Fig. 9.48 for delocalized π bonding system in the benzene ring.

71.   a.   No, some atoms are in different places. Thus, these are not resonance structures; they are different compounds.

       b.   For the first Lewis structure, all nitrogens are sp^3 hybridized and all carbons are sp^2 hybridized. In the second Lewis structure, all nitrogens and carbons are sp^2 hybridized.

       c.   For the reaction:

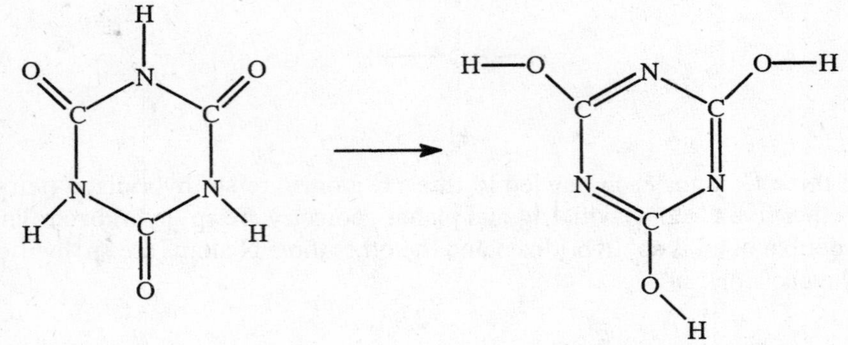

Bonds broken:

3 C=O (745 kJ/mol)

3 C–N (305 kJ/mol)

3 N–H (391 kJ/mol)

Bonds formed:

3 C=N (615 kJ/mol)

3 C–O (358 kJ/mol)

3 O–H (467 kJ/mol)

$\Delta H = 3(745) + 3(305) + 3(391) - [3(615) + 3(358) + 3(467)]$

$\Delta H = 4323 \text{ kJ} - 4320 \text{ kJ} = 3 \text{ kJ}$

The bonds are slightly stronger in the first structure with the carbon-oxygen double bonds since ΔH for the reaction is positive. However, the value of ΔH is so small that the best conclusion is that the bond strengths are comparable in the two structures.

72.   The complete Lewis structure follows. All but two of the carbon atoms are sp^3 hybridized. The two carbon atoms which contain the double bond are sp^2 hybridized (see *).

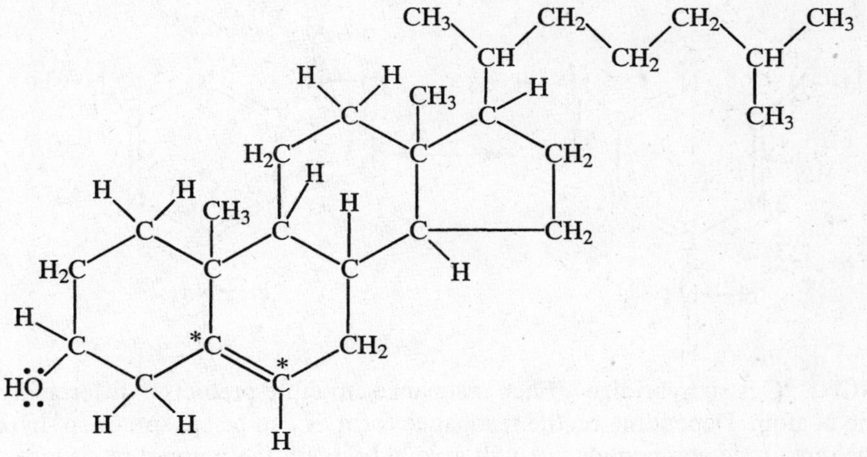

No; most of the carbons are not in the same plane since a majority of carbon atoms exhibit a tetrahedral structure (109.5 bond angles).

73.   a. NCN^{2-} has $5 + 4 + 5 + 2 = 16$ valence electrons.

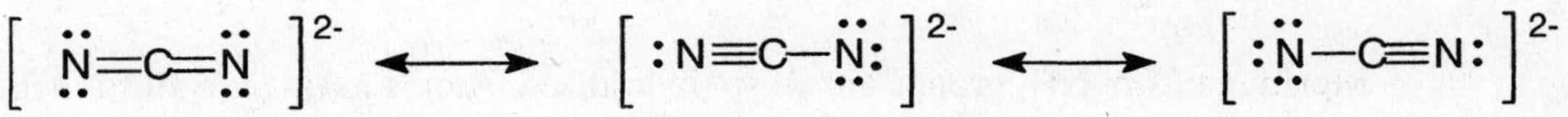

H_2NCN has $2(1) + 5 + 4 + 5 = 16$ valence electrons.

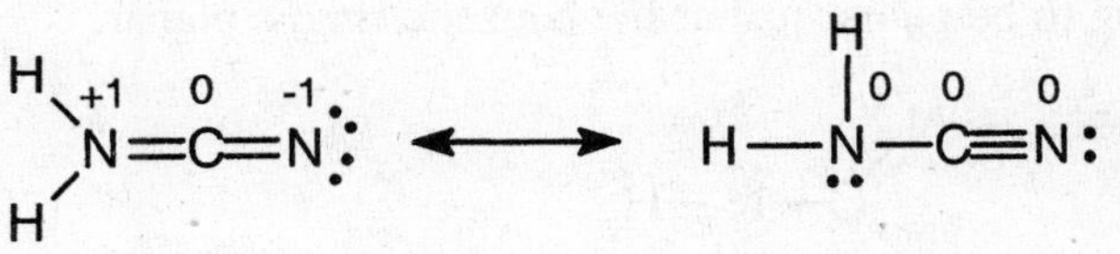

favored by formal charge

$NCNC(NH_2)_2$ has $5 + 4 + 5 + 4 + 2(5) + 4(1) = 32$ valence electrons.

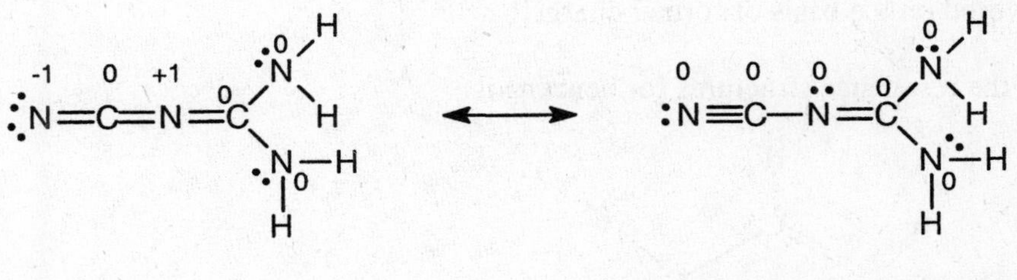

favored by formal charge

Melamine ($C_3N_6H_6$) has 3(4) + 6(5) + 6(1) = 48 valence electrons.

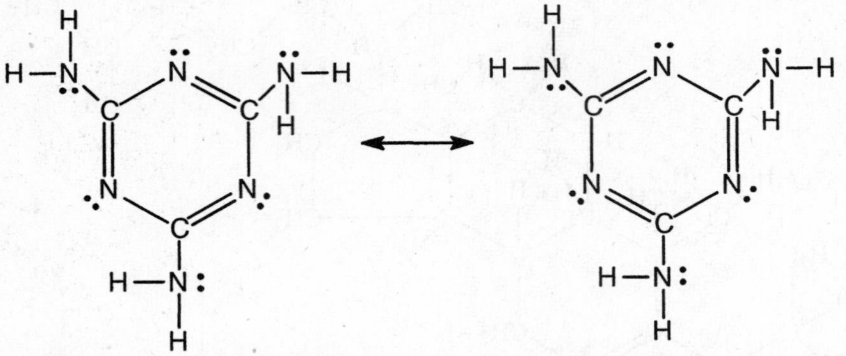

b. NCN^{2-}: C is sp hybridized. Each resonance structure predicts a different hybridization for the N atom. Depending on the resonance form, N can be sp, sp^2, or sp^3 hybridized. For the remaining compounds, we will give hybrids for the favored resonance structures as predicted from formal charge considerations.

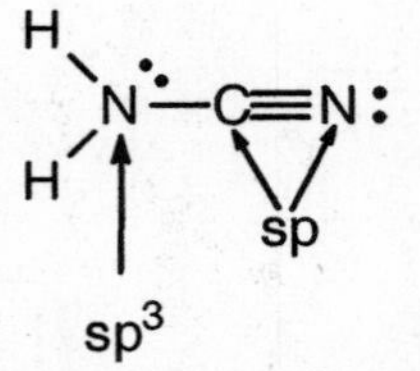

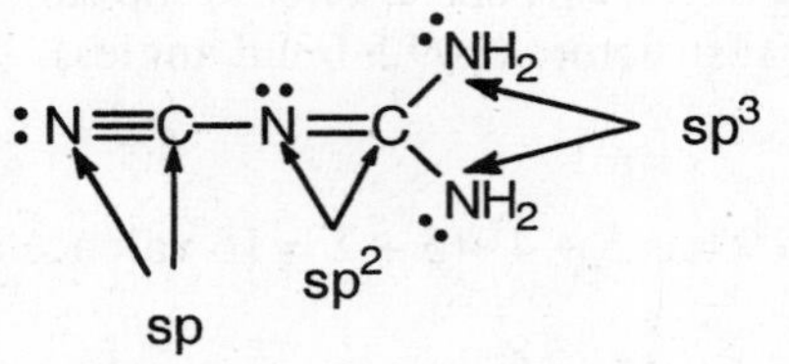

Melamine: N in NH_2 groups are all sp^3 hybridized. Atoms in ring are all sp^2 hybridized.

c. NCN^{2-}: 2 σ and 2 π bonds; H_2NCN: 4 σ and 2 π bonds; dicyandiamide: 9 σ and 3 π bonds; melamine: 15 σ and 3 π bonds

d. The π-system forces the ring to be planar just as the benzene ring is planar.

e. The structure:

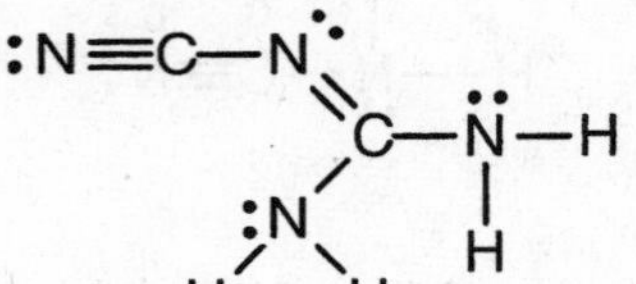

is the most important since it has three different CN bonds. This structure is also favored on the basis of formal charge.

74.   One of the resonance structures for benzene is:

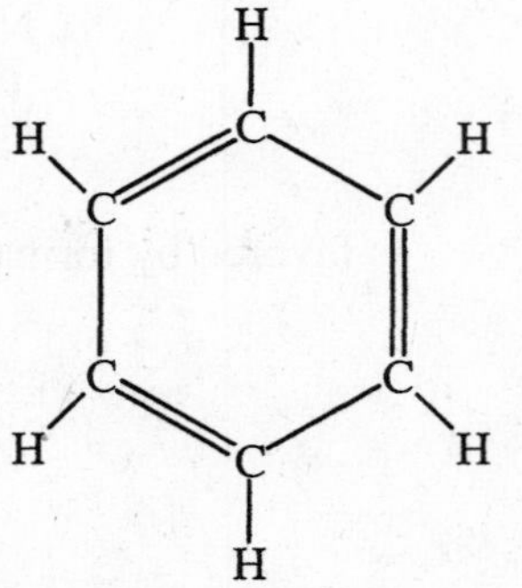

To break $C_6H_6(g)$ into $C(g)$ and $H(g)$ requires the breaking of 6 C–H bonds, 3 C=C bonds and 3 C–C bonds:

$$C_6H_6(g) \rightarrow 6\ C(g) + 6\ H(g) \quad \Delta H = 6\ D_{C-H} + 3\ D_{C=C} + 3\ D_{C-C}$$

$$\Delta H = 6(413\ kJ) + 3(614\ kJ) + 3(347\ kJ) = 5361\ kJ$$

The question asks for ΔH_f° for $C_6H_6(g)$, which is ΔH for the reaction:

$$6\ C(s) + 3\ H_2(g) \rightarrow C_6H_6(g) \quad \Delta H = \Delta H_{f,\ C_6H_6(g)}^\circ$$

To calculate ΔH for this reaction, we will use Hess's law along with the value ΔH_f° for $C(g)$ and the bond energy value for H_2 ($D_{H_2} = 432\ kJ/mol$).

$$
\begin{array}{ll}
6\ C(g) + 6\ H(g) \rightarrow C_6H_6(g) & \Delta H_1 = {}^-5361\ kJ \\
6\ C(s) \rightarrow 6\ C(g) & \Delta H_2 = 6(717\ kJ) \\
3\ H_2(g) \rightarrow 6\ H(g) & \Delta H_3 = 3(432\ kJ)
\end{array}
$$

$$6\ C(s) + 3\ H_2(g) \rightarrow C_6H_6(g) \quad \Delta H = \Delta H_1 + \Delta H_2 + \Delta H_3 = 237\ kJ;\ \Delta H_{f,\ C_6H_6(g)}^\circ = 237\ kJ/mol$$

The experimental ΔH_f° for $C_6H_6(g)$ is more stable (lower in energy) by 154 kJ as compared to ΔH_f° calculated from bond energies ($83 - 237 = {}^-154\ kJ$). This extra stability is related to benzene's ability to exhibit resonance. Two equivalent Lewis structures can be drawn for benzene. The π bonding system implied by each Lewis structure consists of three localized π bonds. This is not correct as all C–C bonds in benzene are equivalent. We say the π electrons in benzene are delocalized over the entire surface of C_6H_6 (see Section 9.5 of the text). The large discrepancy between ΔH_f° values is due to the delocalized π electrons, whose effect was not accounted for in the calculated ΔH_f° value. The extra stability associated with benzene can be called resonance stabilization. In general, molecules that exhibit resonance are usually more stable than predicted using bond energies.

75.   a. $E = \dfrac{hc}{\lambda} = \dfrac{(6.626 \times 10^{-34}\ J\ s)(2.998 \times 10^8\ m/s)}{25 \times 10^{-9}\ m} = 7.9 \times 10^{-18}\ J$

$$7.9 \times 10^{-18}\ J \times \frac{6.022 \times 10^{23}}{mol} \times \frac{1\ kJ}{1000\ J} = 4800\ kJ/mol$$

Using ΔH values from the various reactions, 25 nm light has sufficient energy to ionize N_2 and N and to break the triple bond. Thus, N_2, N_2^+, N, and N^+ will all be present, assuming excess N_2.

b. To produce atomic nitrogen but no ions, the range of energies of the light must be from 941 kJ/mol to just below 1402 kJ/mol.

$$\frac{941\,kJ}{mol}\times\frac{mol}{6.022\times10^{23}}\times\frac{1000\,J}{kJ}=1.56\times10^{-18}\ J/photon$$

$$\lambda=\frac{hc}{E}=\frac{(6.626\times10^{-34}\ J\ s)(2.998\times10^{8}\ m/s)}{1.56\times10^{-18}\ J}=1.27\times10^{-7}\ m=127\ nm$$

$$\frac{1402\,kJ}{mol}\times\frac{mol}{6.0221\times10^{23}}\times\frac{1000\,J}{kJ}=2.328\times10^{-18}\ J/photon$$

$$\lambda=\frac{hc}{E}=\frac{(6.6261\times10^{-34}\ J\ s)(2.9979\times10^{8}\ m/s)}{2.328\times10^{-18}\ J}=8.533\times10^{-8}\ m=85.33\ nm$$

Light with wavelengths in the range of 85.33 nm $< \lambda \le$ 127 nm will produce N but no ions.

c. N_2: $(\sigma_{2s})^2(\sigma_{2s}{*})^2(\pi_{2p})^4(\sigma_{2p})^2$; The electron removed from N_2 is in the σ_{2p} molecular orbital which is lower in energy than the 2p atomic orbital from which the electron in atomic nitrogen is removed. Since the electron removed from N_2 is lower in energy than the electron in N, the ionization energy of N_2 is greater than that for N.

76.   The π bonds between two S atoms and between C and S atoms are not as strong. The orbitals do not overlap with each other as well as the smaller atomic orbitals of C and O overlap.

77.   O=N–Cl: The bond order of the NO bond in NOCl is 2 (a double bond).

        NO: From molecular orbital theory, the bond order of this NO bond is 2.5.

        Both reactions apparently involve only the breaking of the N–Cl bond. However, in the reaction ONCl → NO + Cl, some energy is released in forming the stronger NO bond, lowering the value of ΔH. Therefore, the apparent N–Cl bond energy is artificially low for this reaction. The first reaction involves only the breaking of the N–Cl bond.

78.   The molecular orbitals for BeH_2 are formed from the two hydrogen 1s orbitals and the 2s and one of the 2p orbitals from beryllium. One of the sigma bonding orbitals forms from in phase overlap of the hydrogen 1s orbitals with a 2s orbital from beryllium. Assuming the z-axis is the internuclear axis in the linear BeH_2 molecule, then the $2p_z$ orbital from beryllium has proper symmetry to overlap with the 1s orbitals from hydrogen; the $2p_x$ and $2p_y$ orbitals are nonbonding orbitals since they don't have proper symmetry necessary to overlap with 1s orbitals. The type of bond formed from the $2p_z$ and 1s orbitals is a sigma bond since the orbitals overlap head to head. The MO diagram for BeH_2 is:

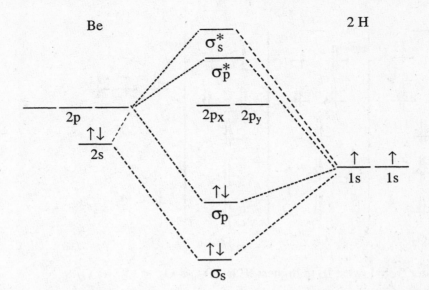

Bond Order = (4 − 0)/2 = 2; The MO diagram predicts BeH_2 to be a stable species and also predicts that BeH_2 is diamagnetic. Note: The σ_s MO is a mixture of the two hydrogen 1s orbitals with the 2s orbital from beryllium and the σ_p MO is a mixture of the two hydrogen 1s orbitals with the $2p_z$ orbital from beryllium. The MOs are not localized between any two atoms; instead, they extend over the entire surface of the three atoms.

79.   a.   The CO bond is polar with the negative end around the more electronegative oxygen atom. We would expect metal cations to be attracted to and bond to the oxygen end of CO on the basis of electronegativity.

b.   :C≡O: FC (carbon) = 4 − 2 − 1/2(6) = −1

FC (oxygen) = 6 − 2 − 1/2(6) = +1

From formal charge, we would expect metal cations to bond to the carbon (with the negative formal charge).

c.   In molecular orbital theory, only orbitals with proper symmetry overlap to form bonding orbitals. The metals that form bonds to CO are usually transition metals, all of which have outer electrons in the d orbitals. The only molecular orbitals of CO that have proper symmetry to overlap with d orbitals are the $\pi_{2p}*$ orbitals, whose shape is similar to the d orbitals (see Figure 9.34). Since the antibonding molecular orbitals have more carbon character (carbon is less electronegative than oxygen), one would expect the bond to form through carbon.

80.

The order from lowest IE to highest IE is: $O_2^- < O_2 < O_2^+ < O$.

The electrons for O_2^-, O_2, and O_2^+ that are highest in energy are in the π_{2p}^* MOs. But for O_2^-, these electrons are paired. O_2^- should have the lowest ionization energy (its paired π_{2p}^* electron is easiest to remove). The species O_2^+ has an overall positive charge, making it harder to remove an electron from O_2^+ than from O_2. The highest energy electrons for O (in the 2p atomic orbitals) are lower in energy than the π_{2p}^* electrons for the other species; O will have the highest ionization energy because it requires a larger quantity of energy to remove an electron from O as compared to the other species.

81.   The electron configurations are:

N_2: $(\sigma_{2s})^2(\sigma_{2s}^*)^2(\pi_{2p})^4(\sigma_{2p})^2$

O_2: $(\sigma_{2s})^2(\sigma_{2s}^*)^2(\sigma_{2p})^2(\pi_{2p})^4(\pi_{2p}^*)^2$

N_2^{2-}: $(\sigma_{2s})^2(\sigma_{2s}^*)^2(\pi_{2p})^4(\sigma_{2p})^2(\pi_{2p}^*)^2$

N_2^-: $(\sigma_{2s})^2(\sigma_{2s}^*)^2(\pi_{2p})^4(\sigma_{2p})^2(\pi_{2p}^*)^1$

O_2^+: $(\sigma_{2s})^2(\sigma_{2s}^*)^2(\sigma_{2p})^2(\pi_{2p})^4(\pi_{2p}^*)^1$

Note: the ordering of the σ_{2p} and π_{2p} orbitals is not important to this question.

The species with the smallest ionization energy has the electron which is easiest to remove. From the MO electron configurations, O_2, N_2^{2-}, N_2^-, and O_2^+ all contain electrons in the same higher energy antibonding orbitals (π_{2p}^*), so they should have electrons that are easier to remove as compared to N_2 which has no π_{2p}^* electrons. To differentiate which has the easiest π_{2p}^* to remove, concentrate on the number of electrons in the orbitals attracted to the number of protons in the nucleus.

N_2^{2-} and N_2^- both have 14 protons in the two nuclei combined. Because N_2^{2-} has more electrons, one would expect N_2^{2-} to have more electron repulsions which translates into having an easier electron to remove. Between O_2 and O_2^+, the electron in O_2 should be easier to remove. O_2 has one more electron than O_2^+, and one would expect the fewer electrons in

O_2^+ to be better attracted to the nuclei (and harder to remove). Between N_2^{2-} and O_2, both have 16 electrons; the difference is the number of protons in the nucleus. Because N_2^{2-} has two fewer protons than O_2, one would expect the N_2^{2-} to have the easiest electron to remove which translates into the smallest ionization energy.

82. F_2: $(\sigma_{2s})^2(\sigma_{2s}^*)^2(\sigma_{2p})^2(\pi_{2p})^4(\pi_{2p}^*)^4$ B.O. $(8-6)/2 = 1$

       F_2^-: $(\sigma_{2s})^2(\sigma_{2s}^*)^2(\sigma_{2p})^2(\pi_{2p})^4(\pi_{2p}^*)^4(\sigma_{2p}^*)^1$ B.O. $= (8-7)/2 = 0.5$

MO theory predicts that F_2 should have a stronger bond than F_2^- because F_2 has the larger bond order. Let's compare the F_2 bond energy in Table 8.4 (154 kJ/mol) to the calculated F_2^- bond energy.

$$F_2^-(g) \rightarrow F(g) + F^-(g) \qquad \Delta H = F_2^- \text{ bond energy}$$

Using Hess's law:

$F_2^-(g) \rightarrow F_2(g) + e^-$	$\Delta H =$	290 kJ (IE for F_2^-)
$F_2(g) \rightarrow 2\,F(g)$	$\Delta H =$	154 kJ (BE for F_2)
$F(g) + e^- \rightarrow F^-(g)$	$\Delta H =$	-327.8 kJ (EA for F from Table 7.7)

$$F_2^-(g) \rightarrow F(g) + F^-(g) \qquad \Delta H = \quad 116 \text{ kJ}$$

As predicted from the MO theory, the bond energy of F_2^- is smaller than the bond energy of F_2.

Integrative Problems

83.   a. Li_2: $(\sigma_{2s})^2$ B.O. $= (2-0)/2 = 1$

            B_2: $(\sigma_{2s})^2(\sigma_{2s}^*)^2(\pi_{2p})^2$ B.O. $= (4-2)/2 = 1$

        Both have a bond order of 1.

    b. B_2 has four more electrons than Li_2 so four electrons must be removed from B_2 to make it isoelectronic with Li_2. The isoelectronic ion is B_2^{4+}.

    c. $1.5 \text{ kg } B_2 \times \dfrac{1000 \text{ g}}{1 \text{ kg}} \times \dfrac{1 \text{ mol } B_2}{21.62 \text{ g } B_2} \times \dfrac{6455 \text{ kJ}}{\text{mol } B_2} = 4.5 \times 10^5 \text{ kJ}$

84.   a.   HF, $1 + 7 = 8 \text{ e}^-$ SbF_5, $5 + 5(7) = 40 \text{ e}^-$

H——F:

linear, sp^3 (if F is hybridized)

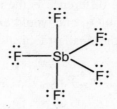

trigonal bipyramid, dsp^3

H_2F^+, $2(1) + 7 - 1 = 8 \text{ e}^-$ SbF_6^-, $5 + 6(7) + 1 = 48 \text{ e}^-$

V-shaped, sp^3

octahedral, d^2sp^3

b. $2.93 \text{ mL} \times \dfrac{0.975 \text{ g HF}}{\text{mL}} \times \dfrac{1 \text{ mol HF}}{20.01 \text{ g HF}} = 0.143 \text{ mol HF}$

$10.0 \text{ mL} \times \dfrac{3.10 \text{ g SbF}_5}{\text{mL}} \times \dfrac{1 \text{ mol SbF}_5}{216.8 \text{ g SbF}_5} = 0.143 \text{ mol SbF}_5$

The balanced equation requires a 2:1 mol ratio between HF and SbF_5. Because we have the same amount (moles) of the reactants, HF is limiting.

$0.143 \text{ mol HF} \times \dfrac{1 \text{ mol } [H_2F]^+ [SbF_6]^-}{2 \text{ mol HF}} \times \dfrac{256.8 \text{ g}}{\text{mol } [H_2F]^+ [SbF_6]^-} = 18.4 \text{ g } [H_2F]^+[SbF_6]^-$

85.   Element X has 36 protons which identifies it as Kr. Element Y has one less electron than Y^-, so the electron configuration of Y is $1s^2 2s^2 2p^5$. This is F.

KrF_3^+, $8 + 3(7) - 1 = 28 \text{ e}^-$

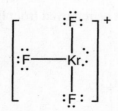   T-shaped, dsp^3

CHAPTER TEN

LIQUIDS AND SOLIDS

For Review

1. Intermolecular forces are the relatively weak forces between molecules that hold the molecules together in the solid and liquid phases. Intramolecular forces are the forces within a molecule. These are the covalent bonds in a molecule. Intramolecular forces (covalent bonds) are much stronger than intermolecular forces.

   Dipole forces are the forces that act between polar molecules. The electrostatic attraction between the positive end of one polar molecule and the negative end of another is the dipole force. Dipole forces are generally weaker than hydrogen bonding. Both of these forces are due to dipole moments in molecules. Hydrogen bonding is given a separate name from dipole forces because hydrogen bonding is a particularly strong dipole force. Any neutral molecule that has a hydrogen covalently bonded to N, O, or F exhibits the relatively strong hydrogen bonding intermolecular forces.

   London dispersion forces are accidental-induced dipole forces. Like dipole forces, London dispersion forces are electrostatic in nature. Dipole forces are the electrostatic forces between molecules having a permanent dipole. London dispersion forces are the electrostatic forces between molecules having an accidental or induced dipole. All covalent molecules (polar and nonpolar) have London dispersion forces, but only polar molecules (those with permanent dipoles) exhibit dipole forces.

   As the size of a molecule increases, the strength of the London dispersion forces increases. This is because, as the electron cloud about a molecule gets larger, it is easier for the electrons to be drawn away from the nucleus. The molecule is said to be more polarizable.

   London dispersion (LD) < dipole-dipole < H bonding < metallic bonding, covalent network, ionic.

   Yes, there is considerable overlap. Consider some of the examples in Exercise 10.98. Benzene (only LD forces) has a higher boiling point than acetone (dipole-dipole forces). Also, there is even more overlap among the stronger forces (metallic, covalent, and ionic).

2. a. Surface tension: the resistance of a liquid to an increase in its surface area.

   b. Viscosity: the resistance of a liquid to flow.

   c. Melting point: the temperature (at constant pressure) where a solid converts entirely to a liquid as long as heat is applied. A more detailed definition is the temperature at which the solid and liquid states have the same vapor pressure under conditions where the total pressure is constant.

    d.   Boiling point: the temperature (at constant pressure) where a liquid converts entirely to a gas as long as heat is applied. The detailed definition is the temperature at which the vapor pressure of the liquid is exactly equal to the external pressure.

    e.   Vapor pressure: the pressure of the vapor over a liquid at equilibrium.

As the strengths of intermolecular forces increase, surface tension, viscosity, melting point and boiling point increase, while vapor pressure decreases.

3.   Solid: rigid; has fixed volume and shape; slightly compressible

Liquid: definite volume but no specific shape; assumes shape of the container; slightly compressible

Gas: no fixed volume or shape; easily compressible

4.   a.   Crystalline solid: Regular, repeating structure

          Amorphous solid: Irregular arrangement of atoms or molecules

    b.   Ionic solid: Made up of ions held together by ionic bonding

          Molecular solid: Made up of discrete covalently bonded molecules held together in the solid phase by weaker forces (LD, dipole, or hydrogen bonds).

    c.   Molecular solid: Discrete, individual molecules

          Network solid: No discrete molecules; A network solid is one large molecule. The forces holding the atoms together are the covalent bonds between atoms.

    d.   Metallic solid: Completely delocalized electrons, conductor of electricity (cations in a sea of electrons)

          Network solid: Localized electrons; Insulator or semiconductor

5.   Lattice: a three-dimensional system of points designating the positions of the centers of the components of a solid (atoms, ions, or molecules)

Unit cell: the smallest repeating unit of a lattice

A simple cubic unit cell has an atom, ion or molecule located at the eight corners of a cube. There is one net atom per simple cubic unit cell. Because the atoms in the cubic unit cell are assumed to touch along the cube edge, cube edge = ℓ = 2r where r = radius of the atom. A body-centered cubic unit cell has an atom, ion or molecule at the eight corners of a cube and one atom, ion, or molecule located at the center of the cube. There are two net atoms per body-centered cubic unit cell. Because the atoms in the cubic unit cell are assumed to touch along the body diagonal of the cube, body diagonal = $\sqrt{3}\,\ell$ = 4r where ℓ = cube edge and r = radius of atom. A face-centered cubic unit cell has an atom, ion, or molecule at the eight corners of a cube and an atom, ion, or molecule located at the six faces of the cube. There are four net atoms per face-centered unit cell. Because the atoms in the cubic unit cell are assumed to touch along the face diagonal of the cube, face diagonal = $\sqrt{2}\ \ell = 4r$.

6.   Closest packing: the packing of atoms (uniform, hard spheres) in a manner that most efficiently uses the available space with the least amount of empty space. The two types of closest packing are hexagonal closest packing and cubic closest packing. In both closest packed arrangements, the atoms (spheres) are packed in layers. The difference between the two closest packed arrangements is the ordering of the layers. Hexagonal closest packing has the third layer directly over the first layer forming a repeating layer pattern of abab...   In cubic closest packing the layer pattern is abcabc...   The unit cell for hexagonal closest packing is a hexagonal prism. See Fig. 10.14 for an illustration of the hexagonal prism unit cell. The unit cell for cubic closest packing is the face-centered cubic unit cell.

7.   Conductor: The energy difference between the filled and unfilled molecular orbitals is minimal. We call this energy difference the band gap. Because the band gap is minimal, electrons can easily move into the conduction bands (the unfilled molecular orbitals).

       Insulator: Large band gap; Electrons do not move from the filled molecular orbitals to the conduction bands since the energy difference is large.

       Semiconductor: Small band gap; The energy difference between the filled and unfilled molecular orbitals is smaller than in insulators, so some electrons can jump into the conduction bands. The band gap, however, is not as small as with conductors, so semiconductors have intermediate conductivity.

   a. As the temperature is increased, more electrons in the filled molecular orbitals have sufficient kinetic energy to jump into the conduction bands (the unfilled molecular orbitals).

   b. A photon of light is absorbed by an electron which then has sufficient energy to jump into the conduction bands.

   c. An impurity either adds electrons at an energy near that of the conduction bands (n-type) or creates holes (unfilled energy levels) at energies in the previously filled molecular orbitals (p-type). Both n-type and p-type semiconductors increase conductivity by creating an easier path for electrons to jump from filled to unfilled energy levels.

In conductors, electrical conductivity is inversely proportional to temperature. Increases in temperature increase the motions of the atoms, which gives rise to increased resistance (decreased conductivity). In a semiconductor, electrical conductivity is directly proportional to temperature. An increase in temperature provides more electrons with enough kinetic energy to jump from the filled molecular orbitals to the conduction bands, increasing conductivity.

To produce an n-type semiconductor, dope Ge with a substance that has more than 4 valence electrons, e.g., a group 5A element. Phosphorus or arsenic are two substances which will produce n-type semiconductors when they are doped into germanium. To produce a p-type semiconductor, dope Ge with a substance that has fewer than 4 valence electrons, e.g., a group 3A element. Gallium or indium are two substances which will produce p-type semi-conductors when they are doped into germanium.

8.   The structures of most binary ionic solids can be explained by the closest packing of spheres. Typically, the larger ions, usually the anions, are packed in one of the closest packing arrangements, and the smaller cations fit into holes among the closest packed anions. There are different types of holes within the closest packed anions which are determined by the number of spheres that form them. Which of the three types of holes are filled usually depends on the relative size of the cation to the anion. Ionic solids will always try to maximize electrostatic attractions among oppositely charged ions and minimize the repulsions among ions with like charges.

The structure of sodium chloride can be described in terms of a cubic closest packed array of Cl^- ions with Na^+ ions in all of the octahedral holes. An octahedral hole is formed between 6 Cl^- anions. The number of octahedral holes is the same as the number of packed ions. So in the face-centered unit cell of sodium chloride, there are 4 net Cl^- ions and 4 net octahedral holes. Because the stoichiometry dictates a 1:1 ratio between the number of Cl^- anions and Na^+ cations, all of the octahedral holes must be filled with Na^+ ions.

In zinc sulfide, the sulfide anions also occupy the lattice points of a cubic closest packing arrangement. But instead of having the cations in octahedral holes, the Zn^{2+} cations occupy tetrahedral holes. A tetrahedral hole is the empty space created when four spheres are packed together. There are twice as many tetrahedral holes as packed anions in the closest packed structure. Therefore, each face-centered unit cell of sulfide anions contains 4 net S^{2-} ions and 8 net tetrahedral holes. For the 1:1 stoichiometry to work out, only one-half of the tetrahedral holes are filled with Zn^{2+} ions. This gives 4 S^{2-} ions and 4 Zn^{2+} ions per unit cell for an empirical formula of ZnS.

9.   a.   Evaporation: process where liquid molecules escape the liquid's surface to form a gas.

b.   Condensation: process where gas molecules hit the surface of a liquid and convert to a liquid.

c.   Sublimation: process where a solid converts directly to a gas without passing through the liquid state.

d.   Boiling: the temperature and pressure at which a liquid completely converts to a gas as long as heat is applied.

e.   Melting: temperature and pressure at which a solid completely converts to a liquid as long as heat is applied.

f.   Enthalpy of vaporization (ΔH_{vap}): the enthalpy change that occurs at the boiling point when a liquid converts into a gas.

g.   Enthalpy of fusion (ΔH_{fus}): the enthalpy change that occurs at the melting point when a solid converts into a liquid.

h. Heating curve: a plot of temperature versus time as heat is applied at a constant rate to some substance.

Fusion refers to a solid converting to a liquid, and vaporization refers to a liquid converting to a gas. Only a fraction of the hydrogen bonds in ice are broken in going from the solid phase to the liquid phase. Most of the hydrogen bonds in water are still present in the liquid phase and must be broken during the liquid to gas phase transition. Thus, the enthalpy of vaporization is much larger than the enthalpy of fusion because more intermolecular forces are broken during the vaporization process.

A volatile liquid is one that evaporates relatively easily. Volatile liquids have large vapor pressures because the intermolecular forces that prevent evaporation are relatively weak.

10.   See Fig. 10.49 and 10.52 for the phase diagrams of H_2O and CO_2. Most substances exhibit only three different phases: solid, liquid, and gas. This is true for H_2O and CO_2. Also typical of phase diagrams is the positive slopes for both the liquid-gas equilibrium line and the solid-gas equilibrium line. This is also true for both H_2O and CO_2. The solid-liquid equilibrium line also generally has a positive slope. This is true for CO_2, but not for H_2O. In the H_2O phase diagram, the slope of the solid-liquid line is negative. The determining factor for the slope of the solid-liquid line is the relative densities of the solid and liquid phases. The solid phase is denser than the liquid phase in most substances; for these substances, the slope of the solid-liquid equilibrium line is positive. For water, the liquid phase is denser than the solid phase which corresponds to a negative sloping solid-liquid equilibrium line. Another difference between H_2O and CO_2 is the normal melting points and normal boiling points. The term normal just dictates a pressure of 1 atm. H_2O has a normal melting point ($0\,^\circ C$) and a normal boiling point ($100\,^\circ C$), but CO_2 does not. At 1 atm pressure, CO_2 only sublimes (goes from the solid phase directly to the gas phase). There are no temperatures at 1 atm for CO_2 where the solid and liquid phases are in equilibrium or where the liquid and gas phases are in equilibrium. There are other differences, but those discussed above are the major ones.

The relationship between melting points and pressure is determined by the slope of the solid-liquid equilibrium line. For most substances (CO_2 included), the positive slope of the solid-liquid line shows a direct relationship between the melting point and pressure. As pressure increases, the melting point increases. Water is just the opposite since the slope of the solid-liquid line in water is negative. Here the melting point of water is inversely related to the pressure.

For boiling points, the positive slope of the liquid-gas equilibrium line indicates a direct relationship between the boiling point and pressure. This direct relationship is true for all substances including H_2O and CO_2.

The critical temperature for a substance is defined as the temperature above which the vapor cannot be liquefied no matter what pressure is applied. The critical temperature, like the boiling point temperature, is directly related to the strength of the intermolecular forces. Since H_2O exhibits relatively strong hydrogen bonding interactions and CO_2 only exhibits London dispersion forces, one would expect a higher critical temperature for H_2O than for CO_2.

Questions

12. $C_{25}H_{52}$ has the stronger intermolecular forces because it has the higher boiling point. Even though $C_{25}H_{52}$ is nonpolar, it is so large that its London dispersion forces are much stronger than the sum of the London dispersion and hydrogen bonding interactions found in H_2O.

13.   Atoms have an approximately spherical shape (on the average). It is impossible to pack spheres together without some empty space among the spheres.

14.   Critical temperature: The temperature above which a liquid cannot exist, i.e., the gas cannot be liquified by increased pressure.

       Critical pressure: The pressure that must be applied to a substance at its critical temperature to produce a liquid.

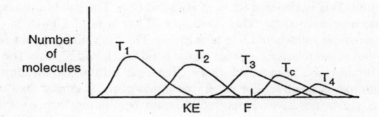

       The kinetic energy distribution changes as one raises the temperature ($T_4 > T_c > T_3 > T_2 > T_1$). At the critical temperature, T_c, all molecules have kinetic energies greater than the intermolecular forces, F, and a liquid can't form. Note: The distributions above are not to scale.

15.   Evaporation takes place when some molecules at the surface of a liquid have enough energy to break the intermolecular forces holding them in the liquid phase. When a liquid evaporates, the molecules that escape have high kinetic energies. The average kinetic energy of the remaining molecules is lower, thus, the temperature of the liquid is lower.

16.   A crystalline solid will have the simpler diffraction pattern because a regular, repeating arrangement is necessary to produce planes of atoms that will diffract the X-rays in regular patterns. An amorphous solid does not have a regular repeating arrangement and will produce a complicated diffraction pattern.

17.   An alloy is a substance that contains a mixture of elements and has metallic properties. In a substitutional alloy, some of the host metal atoms are replaced by other metal atoms of similar size, e.g., brass, pewter, plumber's solder. An interstitial alloy is formed when some of the interstices (holes) in the closest packed metal structure are occupied by smaller atoms, e.g., carbon steels.

18.   Equilibrium: There is no change in composition; the vapor pressure is constant.

       Dynamic: Two processes, vapor $\rightarrow$ liquid and liquid $\rightarrow$ vapor, are both occurring but with equal rates so the composition of the vapor is constant.

19.   a.   As the strength of the intermolecular forces increase, the rate of evaporation decreases.

       b.   As temperature increases, the rate of evaporation increases.

       c.   As surface area increases, the rate of evaporation increases.

20. $C_2H_5OH(l) \rightarrow C_2H_5OH(g)$ is an endothermic process. Heat is absorbed when liquid ethanol vaporizes; the internal heat from the body provides this heat which results in the cooling of the body.

21.   Sublimation will occur allowing water to escape as $H_2O(g)$.

22.   The phase change, $H_2O(g) \rightarrow H_2O(l)$, releases heat that can cause additional damage. Also steam can be at a temperature greater than 100°C.

23.   The strength of intermolecular forces determines relative boiling points. The types of intermolecular forces for covalent compounds are London dispersion forces, dipole forces, and hydrogen bonding. Because the three compounds are assumed to have similar molar mass and shape, the strength of the London dispersion forces will be about equal between the three compounds. One of the compounds will be nonpolar so it only has London dispersion forces. The other two compounds will be polar so they have additional dipole forces and will boil at a higher temperature than the nonpolar compound. One of the polar compounds will have an H covalently bonded to either N, O, or F. This gives rise to the strongest type of covalent intermolecular forces, hydrogen bonding. The compound which hydrogen bonds will have the highest boiling point while the polar compound with no hydrogen bonding will boil at a temperature in the middle of the other compounds.

24.   a.   Both forms of carbon are network solids. In diamond, each carbon atom is surrounded by a tetrahedral arrangement of other carbon atoms to form a huge molecule. Each carbon atom is covalently bonded to four other carbon atoms.

            The structure of graphite is based on layers of carbon atoms arranged in fused six-membered rings. Each carbon atom in a particular layer of graphite is surrounded by three other carbons in a trigonal planar arrangement. This requires sp^2 hybridization. Each carbon has an unhybridized p atomic orbital; all of these p orbitals in each six-membered ring overlap with each other to form a delocalized π electron system.

       b.   Silica is a network solid having an empirical formula of SiO_2. The silicon atoms are singly bonded to four oxygens. Each silicon atom is at the center of a tetrahedral arrangement of oxygen atoms which are shared with other silicon atoms. The structure of silica is based on a network of SiO_4 tetrahedra with shared oxygen atoms, rather than discrete SiO_2 molecules.

            Silicates closely resemble silica. The structure is based on interconnected SiO_4 tetrahedra. However, in contrast to silica, where the O/Si ratio is 2:1, silicates have O/Si ratios greater than 2:1 and contain silicon-oxygen anions. To form a neutral solid silicate, metal cations are needed to balance the charge. In other words, silicates are salts containing metal cations and polyatomic silicon-oxygen anions.

When silica is heated above its melting point and cooled rapidly, an amorphous (disordered) solid called glass results. Glass more closely resembles a very viscous solution than it does a crystalline solid. To affect the properties of glass, several different additives are thrown into the mixture. Some of these additives are Na_2CO_3, B_2O_3, and K_2O, with each compound serving a specific purpose relating to the properties of the glass.

25.   a.   Both CO_2 and H_2O are molecular solids. Both have an ordered array of the individual molecules, with the molecular units occupying the lattice points. A difference within each solid lattice is the strength of the intermolecular forces. CO_2 is nonpolar and only exhibits London dispersion forces. H_2O exhibits the relatively strong hydrogen bonding interactions. The differences in strength is evidenced by the solid phase changes that occur at 1 atm. $CO_2(s)$ sublimes at a relatively low temperature of $-78\,°C$. In sublimation, all of the intermolecular forces are broken. However, $H_2O(s)$ doesn't have a phase change until $0\,°C$, and in this phase change from ice to water, only a fraction of the intermolecular forces are broken. The higher temperature and the fact that only a portion of the intermolecular forces are broken are attributed to the strength of the intermolecular forces in $H_2O(s)$ as compared to $CO_2(s)$.

Related to the intermolecular forces are the relative densities of the solid and liquid phases for these two compounds. $CO_2(s)$ is denser than $CO_2(l)$ while $H_2O(s)$ is less dense than $H_2O(l)$. For $CO_2(s)$, the molecules pack together as close as possible, hence solids are usually more dense than the liquid phase. For H_2O, each molecule has two lone pairs and two bonded hydrogen atoms. Because of the equal number of lone pairs and O–H bonds, each H_2O molecule can form two hydrogen bonding interactions to other H_2O molecules. To keep this symmetric arrangement (which maximizes the hydrogen bonding interactions), the $H_2O(s)$ molecules occupy positions that create empty space in the lattice. This translates into a smaller density for $H_2O(s)$ as compared to $H_2O(l)$.

       b.   Both NaCl and CsCl are ionic compounds with the anions at the lattice points of the unit cells and the cations occupying the empty spaces created by anions (called holes). In NaCl, the Cl^- anions occupy the lattice points of a face-centered unit cell with the Na^+ cations occupying the octahedral holes. Octahedral holes are the empty spaces created by six Cl^- ions. CsCl has the Cl^- ions at the lattice points of a simple cubic unit cell with the Cs^+ cations occupying the middle of the cube.

26.   Because silicon carbide is made from Group 4A elements and because it is extremely hard, one would expect SiC to form a covalent network structure similar to diamond.

27.   The mathematical equation that relates the vapor pressure of a substance to temperature is:

$$\ln P_{vap} = -\frac{\Delta H_{vap}}{R}\left(\frac{1}{T}\right) + C$$
$$\quad y \qquad\qquad m \quad\; x \;+ b$$

As shown above, this equation is in the form of the straight line equation. If one plots $\ln P_{vap}$ vs. $1/T$, the slope of the straight line is $-\Delta H_{vap}/R$. Because ΔH_{vap} is always positive, the slope of the straight line will be negative.

28.   The typical phase diagram for a substance shows three phases and has a positive sloping solid-liquid equilibrium line (water is atypical). A sketch of the phase diagram for I_2 would look like this:

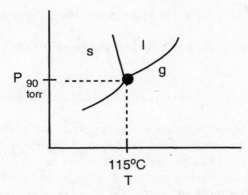

Statements a and e are true. For statement a, the liquid phase is always more dense than the gaseous phase (gases are mostly empty space). For statement e, because the triple point is at 90 torr, the liquid phase cannot exist at any pressure less than 90 torr, no matter what the temperature. For statements b, c, and d, examine the phase diagram to prove to yourself that they are false.

Exercises

Intermolecular Forces and Physical Properties

29.   Ionic compounds have ionic forces. Covalent compounds all have London Dispersion (LD) forces, while polar covalent compounds have dipole forces and/or hydrogen bonding forces. For H bonding forces, the covalent compound must have either a N–H, O–H or F–H bond in the molecule.

a. LD only   b. dipole, LD   c.   H bonding, LD

d. ionic   e. LD only (CH_4 in a nonpolar covalent compound.)

f. dipole, LD   g. ionic

30.   a. ionic

b. LD mostly; C–F bonds are polar, but polymers like teflon are so large the LD forces are the predominant intermolecular forces.

c. LD   d. dipole, LD   e. H bonding, LD

f. dipole, LD   g. LD

31.   a. OCS; OCS is polar and has dipole-dipole forces in addition to London dispersion (LD) forces. All polar molecules have dipole forces. CO_2 is nonpolar and only has LD forces. To predict polarity, draw the Lewis structure and deduce whether the individual bond dipoles cancel.

b. SeO_2; Both SeO_2 and SO_2 are polar compounds, so they both have dipole forces as well as LD forces. However, SeO_2 is a larger molecule, so it would have stronger LD forces.

c. $H_2NCH_2CH_2NH_2$; More extensive hydrogen bonding is possible.

d. H_2CO; H_2CO is polar while CH_3CH_3 is nonpolar. H_2CO has dipole forces in addition to LD forces.

e. CH_3OH; CH_3OH can form relatively strong H bonding interactions, unlike H_2CO.

32.   Ar exists as individual atoms which are held together in the condensed phases by London dispersion forces. The molecule which will have a boiling point closest to Ar will be a nonpolar substance with about the same molar mass as Ar (39.95 g/mol); this same size nonpolar substance will have about equivalent strength of London dispersion forces. Of the choices, only Cl_2 (70.90 g/mol) and F_2 (38.00 g/mol) are nonpolar. Because F_2 has a molar mass closest to that of Ar, one would expect the boiling point of F_2 to be close to that of Ar.

33.   a. Neopentane is more compact than n-pentane. There is less surface area contact among neopentane molecules. This leads to weaker LD forces and a lower boiling point.

      b. HF is capable of H bonding; HCl is not.

      c. LiCl is ionic, and HCl is a molecular solid with only dipole forces and LD forces. Ionic forces are much stronger than the forces for molecular solids.

      d. n-Hexane is a larger molecule, so it has stronger LD forces.

34.   Ethanol, C_2H_6O, has 2(4) + 6(1) + 6 = 20 valence electrons.

Exhibits H-bonding and London dispersion forces.

Dimethyl ether, C_2H_6O, also has 20 valence electrons. It has a Lewis structure of:

Exhibits dipole and London dispersion forces, but no hydrogen bonding since it has no H covalently bonded to the O.

Propane, C_3H_6, has $3(4) + 6(1) = 18$ valence electrons.

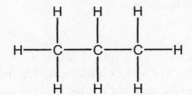

Propane only has relatively nonpolar bonds so it is nonpolar. Propane exhibits only London dispersion forces.

The three compounds have similar molar mass so the strength of the London dispersion forces will be approximately equivalent. Because dimethyl ether has additional dipole forces, it will boil at a higher temperature than propane. The compound with the highest boiling point is ethanol since it exhibits relatively strong hydrogen bonding forces. The correct matching of boiling points is:

ethanol, 78.5°C; dimethyl ether, –23°C; propane, –42.1°C

35.   Boiling points and freezing points are assumed directly related to the strength of the intermolecular forces, while vapor pressure is inversely related to the strength of the intermolecular forces.

   a.   HBr; HBr is polar, while Kr and Cl_2 are nonpolar. HBr has dipole forces unlike Kr and Cl_2.

   b.   NaCl; Ionic forces are much stronger than molecular forces.

   c. I_2; All are nonpolar, so the largest molecule (I_2) will have the strongest LD forces and the lowest vapor pressure.

   d. N_2; Nonpolar and smallest, so has the weakest intermolecular forces.

   e. CH_4; Smallest, nonpolar molecule so has the weakest LD forces.

   f.   HF; HF can form relatively strong H bonding interactions unlike the others.

   g. $CH_3CH_2CH_2OH$; H bonding, unlike the others, so has strongest intermolecular forces.

36.   a. CBr_4; Largest of these nonpolar molecules so has strongest LD forces.

   b. F_2; Ionic forces in LiF are much stronger than the covalent forces in F_2 and HCl. HCl has dipole forces that the nonpolar F_2 does not exhibit; so F_2 has the weakest intermolecular forces and the lowest freezing point.

   c. CH_3CH_2OH; Can form H bonding interactions unlike the others.

   d. H_2O_2; H–O–O–H structure produces stronger H bonding interactions than HF, so has greatest viscosity.

   e. H_2CO; H_2CO is polar so has dipole forces, unlike the other nonpolar covalent compounds.

f. I_2; I_2 has only LD forces while CsBr and CaO have much stronger ionic forces. I_2 has weakest intermolecular forces so has smallest ΔH_{fusion}.

Properties of Liquids

37.   The attraction of H_2O for glass is stronger than the H_2O–H_2O attraction. The miniscus is concave to increase the area of contact between glass and H_2O. The Hg–Hg attraction is greater than the Hg–glass attraction. The miniscus is convex to minimize the Hg–glass contact.

38.   A molecule at the surface of a waterdrop is subject to attractions only by molecules below it and to each side. The effect of this uneven pull on the surface molecules tends to draw them into the body of the liquid and causes the droplet to assume the shape that has the minimum surface area, a sphere.

39.   The structure of H_2O_2 is H–O–O–H, which produces greater hydrogen bonding than water. Long chains of hydrogen–bonded H_2O_2 molecules then get tangled together.

40. CO_2 is a gas at room temperature. As mp and bp increase, the strength of the intermolecular forces also increases. Therefore, the strength of forces is $CO_2 < CS_2 < CSe_2$. From a structural standpoint this is expected. All three are linear, nonpolar molecules. Thus, only London dispersion forces are present. Since the molecules increase in size from $CO_2 < CS_2 < CSe_2$, the strength of the intermolecular forces will increase in the same order.

Structures and Properties of Solids

41. $n\lambda = 2d \sin \theta$, $d = \dfrac{n\lambda}{2\sin \theta} = \dfrac{1 \times 154\,pm}{2 \times \sin 14.22°} = 313\,pm = 3.13 \times 10^{-10}\,m$

42. $d = \dfrac{n\lambda}{2\sin \theta} = \dfrac{2 \times 154\,pm}{2 \times \sin 22.20°} = 408\,pm = 4.08 \times 10^{-10}\,m$

43. $\lambda = \dfrac{2d \sin \theta}{n} = \dfrac{2 \times 1.36 \times 10^{-10}\,m \times \sin 15.0°}{1} = 7.04 \times 10^{-11}\,m = 0.704\,\text{Å}$

44. $n\lambda = 2d \sin \theta$, $d = \dfrac{n\lambda}{2\sin \theta} = \dfrac{1 \times 2.63\,\text{Å}}{2 \times \sin 15.55°} = 4.91\,\text{Å} = 4.91 \times 10^{-10}\,m = 491\,pm$

$\sin \theta = \dfrac{n\lambda}{2d} = \dfrac{2 \times 2.63\,\text{Å}}{2 \times 4.91\,\text{Å}} = 0.536,\ \ \theta = 32.4°$

45.   A cubic closest packed structure has a face-centered cubic unit cell. In a face-centered cubic unit, there are:

$$8\ corners \times \frac{1/8\ atom}{corner} + 6\ faces \times \frac{1/2\ atom}{face} = 4\ atoms$$

The atoms in a face-centered cubic unit cell touch along the face diagonal of the cubic unit cell. Using the Pythagorean formula where l = length of the face diagonal and r = radius of the atom:

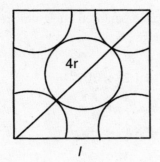

$$l^2 + l^2 = (4r)^2$$

$$2\,l^2 = 16\,r^2$$

$$l = r\sqrt{8}$$

$$l = r\,\sqrt{8} = 197 \times 10^{-12}\,\text{m} \times \sqrt{8} = 5.57 \times 10^{-10}\,\text{m} = 5.57 \times 10^{-8}\,\text{cm}$$

Volume of a unit cell $= l^3 = (5.57 \times 10^{-8}\,\text{cm})^3 = 1.73 \times 10^{-22}\,\text{cm}^3$

Mass of a unit cell $= 4\ \text{Ca atoms} \times \dfrac{1\ \text{mol Ca}}{6.022 \times 10^{23}\ \text{atoms}} \times \dfrac{40.08\ \text{g Ca}}{\text{mol Ca}} = 2.662 \times 10^{-22}\ \text{g Ca}$

$$\text{density} = \dfrac{\text{mass}}{\text{volume}} = \dfrac{2.662 \times 10^{-22}\ \text{g}}{1.73 \times 10^{-22}\ \text{cm}^3} = 1.54\ \text{g/cm}^3$$

46.   There are 4 Ni atoms in each unit cell: For a unit cell:

$$\text{density} = \dfrac{\text{mass}}{\text{volume}} = 6.84\ \text{g/cm}^3 = \dfrac{4\ \text{Ni atoms} \times \dfrac{1\ \text{mol Ni}}{6.022 \times 10^{23}\ \text{atoms}} \times \dfrac{58.69\ \text{g Ni}}{\text{mol Ni}}}{l^3}$$

Solving: $l = 3.85 \times 10^{-8}\,\text{cm}$ = cube edge length

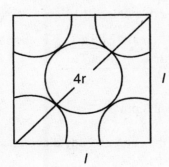

For a face centered cube:

$$(4r)^2 = l^2 + l^2 = 2\,l^2$$

$$r\sqrt{8} = l,\ r = l/\sqrt{8}$$

$$r = 3.85 \times 10^{-8}\,\text{cm}/\sqrt{8}$$

$$r = 1.36 \times 10^{-8}\,\text{cm} = 136\ \text{pm}$$

47.   The unit cell for cubic closest packing is the face-centered unit cell. The volume of a unit cell is:

$$V = l^3 = (492 \times 10^{-10}\,\text{cm})^3 = 1.19 \times 10^{-22}\,\text{cm}^3$$

There are 4 Pb atoms in the unit cell, as is the case for all face-centered cubic unit cells. The mass of atoms in a unit cell is:

$$\text{mass} = 4\ \text{Pb atoms} \times \frac{1\,\text{mol Pb}}{6.022 \times 10^{23}\,\text{atoms}} \times \frac{207.2\,\text{g Pb}}{\text{mol Pb}} = 1.38 \times 10^{-21}\,\text{g}$$

$$\text{density} = \frac{\text{mass}}{\text{volume}} = \frac{1.38 \times 10^{-21}\,\text{g}}{1.19 \times 10^{-22}\,\text{cm}^3} = 11.6\,\text{g/cm}^3$$

From Exercise 45, the relationship between the cube edge length, l, and the radius of an atom in a face-centered unit cell is: $l = r\sqrt{8}$.

$$r = \frac{l}{\sqrt{8}} = \frac{492\,\text{pm}}{\sqrt{8}} = 174\,\text{pm} = 1.74 \times 10^{-10}\,\text{m}$$

48.   A face-centered cubic unit cell contains 4 atoms. For a unit cell:

$$\text{mass of X} = \text{volume} \times \text{density} = (4.09 \times 10^{-8}\,\text{cm})^3 \times 10.5\,\text{g/cm}^3 = 7.18 \times 10^{-22}\,\text{g}$$

$$\text{mol X} = 4\ \text{atoms X} \times \frac{1\,\text{mol X}}{6.022 \times 10^{23}\,\text{atoms}} = 6.642 \times 10^{-24}\,\text{mol X}$$

$$\text{Molar mass} = \frac{7.18 \times 10^{-22}\,\text{g X}}{6.642 \times 10^{-24}\,\text{mol X}} = 108\,\text{g/mol};\ \ \text{The metal is silver (Ag).}$$

49.   For a body-centered unit cell: $8\ \text{corners} \times \dfrac{1/8\ \text{Ti}}{\text{corner}} + \text{Ti at body center} = 2\ \text{Ti atoms}$

All body-centered unit cells have 2 atoms per unit cell. For a unit cell:

$$\text{density} = 4.50\,\text{g/cm}^3 = \frac{2\ \text{atoms Ti} \times \dfrac{1\,\text{mol Ti}}{6.022 \times 10^{23}\,\text{atoms}} \times \dfrac{47.88\,\text{g Ti}}{\text{mol Ti}}}{l^3}$$

Solving: $l = \text{edge length of unit cell} = 3.28 \times 10^{-8}\,\text{cm} = 328\,\text{pm}$

Assume Ti atoms just touch along the body diagonal of the cube, so body diagonal = $4 \times$ radius of atoms = 4r.

The triangle we need to solve is:

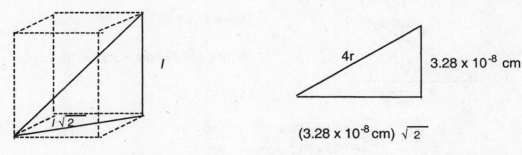

$$(4r)^2 = (3.28 \times 10^{-8}\,cm)^2 + [(3.28 \times 10^{-8}\,cm)\,\sqrt{2}\,]^2, \quad r = 1.42 \times 10^{-8}\,cm = 142\ pm$$

For a body-centered unit cell (bcc), the radius of the atom is related to the cube edge length by: $4r = l\sqrt{3}$ or $l = 4r/\sqrt{3}$.

50.   From Exercise 10.49:

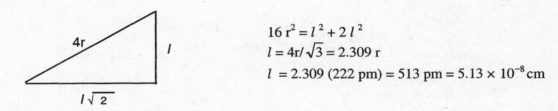

$$16\,r^2 = l^2 + 2\,l^2$$

$$l = 4r/\sqrt{3} = 2.309\ r$$

$$l = 2.309\,(222\ pm) = 513\ pm = 5.13 \times 10^{-8}\,cm$$

In a bcc, there are 2 atoms/unit cell. For a unit cell:

$$density = \frac{mass}{volume} = \frac{2\ atoms\ Ba\ \times\dfrac{1\ mol\ Ba}{6.022\times10^{23}\ atoms}\times\dfrac{137.3\ g\ Ba}{mol\ Ba}}{(5.13\times10^{-8}\ cm)^3} = \frac{3.38\ g}{cm^3}$$

51.   If a face-centered cubic structure, then 4 atoms/unit cell and from Exercise 10.45:

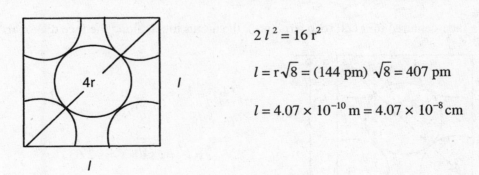

$$2\,l^2 = 16\,r^2$$

$$l = r\sqrt{8} = (144\ pm)\,\sqrt{8} = 407\ pm$$

$$l = 4.07 \times 10^{-10}\,m = 4.07 \times 10^{-8}\,cm$$

$$density = \frac{4\ atoms\ Au\ \times\ \dfrac{1\ mol\ Au}{6.022\times10^{23}\ atoms}\times\dfrac{197.0\ g\ Au}{mol\ Au}}{(4.07\times10^{-8}\ cm)^3} = 19.4\ g/cm^3$$

If a body-centered cubic structure, then 2 atoms/unit cell and from Exercise 10.49:

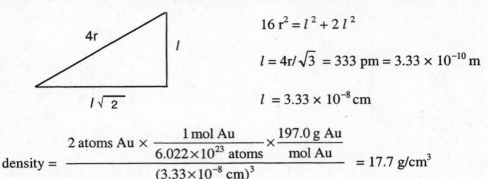

$$16\,r^2 = l^2 + 2\,l^2$$

$$l = 4r/\sqrt{3} = 333 \text{ pm} = 3.33 \times 10^{-10} \text{ m}$$

$$l = 3.33 \times 10^{-8} \text{ cm}$$

$$\text{density} = \frac{2 \text{ atoms Au} \times \dfrac{1 \text{ mol Au}}{6.022 \times 10^{23} \text{ atoms}} \times \dfrac{197.0 \text{ g Au}}{\text{mol Au}}}{(3.33 \times 10^{-8} \text{ cm})^3} = 17.7 \text{ g/cm}^3$$

The measured density is consistent with a face-centered cubic unit cell.

52.   If face-centered cubic:

$$l = r\sqrt{8} = (137 \text{ pm}) \sqrt{8} = 387 \text{ pm} = 3.87 \times 10^{-8} \text{ cm}$$

$$\text{density} = \frac{4 \text{ atoms W} \times \dfrac{1 \text{ mol}}{6.022 \times 10^{23} \text{ atoms}} \times \dfrac{183.9 \text{ g W}}{\text{mol}}}{(3.87 \times 10^{-8} \text{ cm})^3} = 21.1 \text{ g/cm}^3$$

If body-centered cubic:

$$l = \frac{4r}{\sqrt{3}} = \frac{4 \times 137 \text{ pm}}{\sqrt{3}} = 316 \text{ pm} = 3.16 \times 10^{-8} \text{ cm}$$

$$\text{density} = \frac{2 \text{ atoms W} \times \dfrac{1 \text{ mol}}{6.022 \times 10^{23} \text{ atoms}} \times \dfrac{183.9 \text{ g W}}{\text{mol}}}{(3.16 \times 10^{-8} \text{ cm})^3} = 19.4 \text{ g/cm}^3$$

The measured density is consistent with a body-centered unit cell.

53.   In a face-centered unit cell (ccp structure), the atoms touch along the face diagonal:

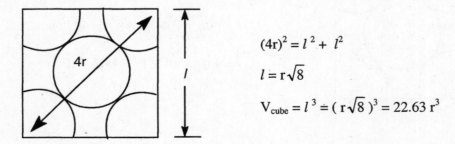

$$(4r)^2 = l^2 + l^2$$

$$l = r\sqrt{8}$$

$$V_{cube} = l^3 = (r\sqrt{8})^3 = 22.63\, r^3$$

There are four atoms in a face-centered cubic cell (see Exercise 10.45). Each atom has a volume of $4/3\ \pi r^3$.

$$V_{atoms} = 4 \times \frac{4}{3}\pi r^3 = 16.76 \; r^3$$

So, $\dfrac{V_{atoms}}{V_{cube}} = \dfrac{16.76 \; r^3}{22.63 \; r^3} = 0.7406$ or 74.06% of the volume of each unit cell is occupied by atoms.

In a simple cubic unit cell, the atoms touch along the cube edge (l):

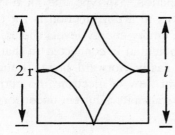

$$2(radius) = 2r = l$$

$$V_{cube} = l^3 = (2r)^3 = 8 \; r^3$$

There is one atom per simple cubic cell (8 corner atoms $\times$ 1/8 atom per corner = 1 atom/unit cell). Each atom has an assumed volume of $4/3 \; \pi r^3$ = volume of a sphere.

$$V_{atom} = \frac{4}{3}\pi r^3 = 4.189 \; r^3$$

So, $\dfrac{V_{atom}}{V_{cube}} = \dfrac{4.189 \; r^3}{8 \; r^3} = = 0.5236$ or 52.36% of the volume of each unit cell is occupied by atoms.

A cubic closest packed structure packs the atoms much more efficiently than a simple cubic structure.

54.   From Exercise 10.49, a body-centered unit cell contains 2 net atoms, and the length of a cube edge (l) is related to the radius of the atom (r) by the equation $l = 4r/\sqrt{3}$.

Volume of unit cell = $l^3 = (4 \; r/\sqrt{3})^3 = 12.32 \; r^3$

Volume of atoms in unit cell = $2 \times \dfrac{4}{3}\pi r^3 = 8.378 \; r^3$

So: $\dfrac{V_{atoms}}{V_{cube}} = \dfrac{8.378 \; r^3}{12.32 \; r^3} = 0.6800 = 68.00\%$ occupied

To determine the radius of the Fe atoms, we need to determine the cube edge length (l).

$$\text{Volume of unit cell} = \left(2 \; \text{Fe atoms} \times \frac{1 \; mol \; Fe}{6.022 \times 10^{23} \; atoms} \times \frac{55.85 \; g \; Fe}{mol \; Fe} \right) \times \frac{1 \; cm^3}{7.86 \; g}$$

$$= 2.36 \times 10^{-23} \; cm^3$$

Volume = $l^3 = 2.36 \times 10^{-23} \; cm^3$, $l = 2.87 \times 10^{-8} \; cm$

$l = 4r/\sqrt{3}$, $r = l\sqrt{3}/4 = 2.87 \times 10^{-8} \; cm \times \sqrt{3}/4 = 1.24 \times 10^{-8} \; cm$

55. Doping silicon with phosphorus produces an n-type semiconductor. The phosphorus adds electrons at energies near the conduction band of silicon. Electrons do not need as much energy to move from filled to unfilled energy levels so conduction increases. Doping silicon with gallium produces a p-type semiconductor. Because gallium has fewer valence electrons than silicon, holes (unfilled energy levels) at energies in the previously filled molecular orbitals are created, which induces greater electron movement (greater conductivity).

56. A rectifier is a device that produces a current that flows in one direction from an alternating current which flows in both directions. In a p-n junction, a p-type and an n-type semi-conductor are connected. The natural flow of electrons in a p-n junction is for the excess electrons in the n-type semiconductor to move to the empty energy levels (holes) of the p-type semiconductor. Only when an external electric potential is connected so that electrons flow in this natural direction will the current flow easily (forward bias). If the external electric potential is connected in reverse of the natural flow of electrons, no current flows through the system (reverse bias). A p-n junction only transmits a current under forward bias, thus converting the alternating current to direct current.

57. In has fewer valence electrons than Se, thus, Se doped with In would be a p-type semiconductor.

58. To make a p-type semiconductor we need to dope the material with atoms that have fewer valence electrons. The average number of valence electrons is four when 50-50 mixtures of group 3A and group 5A elements are considered. We could dope with more of the Group 3A element or with atoms of Zn or Cd. Cadmium is the most common impurity used to produce p-type GaAs semiconductors. To make an n-type GaAs semiconductor, dope with an excess group 5A element or dope with a Group 6A element such as sulfur.

59. $E_{gap} = 2.5$ eV $\times 1.6 \times 10^{-19}$ J/eV $= 4.0 \times 10^{-19}$ J; We want $E_{gap} = E_{light}$, so:

$$\lambda = \frac{hc}{E} = \frac{(6.63 \times 10^{-34} \text{ J s})(3.00 \times 10^{8} \text{ m/s})}{4.0 \times 10^{-19} \text{ J}} = 5.0 \times 10^{-7} \text{ m} = 5.0 \times 10^{2} \text{ nm}$$

60. $$E = \frac{hc}{\lambda} = \frac{(6.63 \times 10^{-34} \text{ J s})(2.998 \times 10^{8} \text{ m/s})}{730. \times 10^{-9} \text{ m}} = 2.72 \times 10^{-19} \text{ J} = \text{energy of band gap}$$

61. a. $8 \text{ corners} \times \dfrac{1/8 \text{ Cl}}{\text{corner}} + 6 \text{ faces} \times \dfrac{1/2 \text{ Cl}}{\text{face}} = 4 \text{ Cl ions}$

$12 \text{ edges} \times \dfrac{1/4 \text{ Na}}{\text{edge}} + 1 \text{ Na at body center} = 4 \text{ Na ions; NaCl is the formula.}$

   b. 1 Cs ion at body center; $8 \text{ corners} \times \dfrac{1/8 \text{ Cl}}{\text{corner}} = 1 \text{ Cl ion; CsCl is the formula.}$

   c. There are 4 Zn ions inside the cube.

$8 \text{ corners} \times \dfrac{1/8 \text{ S}}{\text{corner}} + 6 \text{ faces} \times \dfrac{1/2 \text{ S}}{\text{face}} = 4 \text{ S ions;}$ ZnS is the formula.

d.   8 corners $\times \dfrac{1/8 \, Ti}{corner}$ + 1 Ti at body center = 2 Ti ions

4 faces $\times \dfrac{1/2 \, O}{face}$ + 2 O inside cube = 4 O ions; TiO_2 is the formula.

62.   Both As ions are inside the unit cell. 8 corners $\times \dfrac{1/8 \, Ni}{corner}$ + 4 edges $\times \dfrac{1/4 \, Ni}{edge}$ = 2 Ni ions

The unit cell contains 2 ions of Ni and 2 ions of As which gives a formula of NiAs.

63.   There is one octahedral hole per closest packed anion in a closest packed structure. If half of the octahedral holes are filled, there is a 2:1 ratio of fluoride ions to cobalt ions in the crystal. The formula is CoF_2.

64.   There are 2 tetrahedral holes per closest packed anion. Let f = fraction of tetrahedral holes filled by the cations.

Na_2O: cation to anion ratio = $\dfrac{2}{1} = \dfrac{2f}{1}$, f = 1; All of the tetrahedral holes are filled by Na^+ cations.

CdS: cation to anion ratio = $\dfrac{1}{1} = \dfrac{2f}{1}$, f = $\dfrac{1}{2}$; 1/2 of the tetrahedral holes are filled by Cd^{2+} cations.

ZrI_4: cation to anion ratio = $\dfrac{1}{4} = \dfrac{2f}{1}$, f = $\dfrac{1}{8}$; 1/8 of the tetrahedral holes are filled by Zr^{4+} cations.

65.   In a cubic closest packed array of anions, there are twice the number of tetrahedral holes as anions present and an equal number of octahedral holes as anions present. A cubic closest packed array of sulfide ions will have 4 S^{2-} ions, 8 tetrahedral holes, and 4 octahedral holes. In this structure we have 1/8(8) = 1 Zn^{2+} ion and 1/2(4) = 2 Al^{3+} ions present along with the 4 S^{2-} ions. The formula is $ZnAl_2S_4$.

66.   The two-dimension unit cell is:

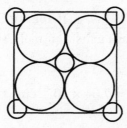

Assuming the anions A are the larger circles, there are 4 anions completely in the unit cell. The corner cations (smaller circles) are shared by 4 different unit cells. Therefore, there is 1 cation in the middle of the unit cell plus 1/4(4) = 1 net cation from the corners. Each unit cell has 2 cations and 4 anions. The empirical formula is MA_2.

67. 8 F⁻ ions at corners × 1/8 F⁻/corner = 1 F⁻ ion per unit cell; Because there is one cubic hole per cubic unit cell, there is a 2:1 ratio of F⁻ ions to metal ions in the crystal if only ½ of the body centers are filled with the metal ions. The formula is MF_2 where M^{2+} is the metal ion.

68. Mn ions at 8 corners: $8(1/8) = 1$ Mn ion; F ions at 12 edges: $12(1/4) = 3$ F ions

Formula is MnF_3. Assuming fluoride is -1 charged, the charge on Mn is +3.

69. From Fig. 10.37, MgO has the NaCl structure containing 4 Mg^{2+} ions and 4 O^{2-} ions per face-centered unit cell.

$$4 \text{ MgO formula units} \times \frac{1 \text{ mol MgO}}{6.022 \times 10^{23} \text{ atoms}} \times \frac{40.31 \text{ g MgO}}{1 \text{ mol MgO}} = 2.678 \times 10^{-22} \text{ g MgO}$$

$$\text{Volume of unit cell} = 2.678 \times 10^{-22} \text{ g MgO} \times \frac{1 \text{ cm}^3}{3.58 \text{ g}} = 7.48 \times 10^{-23} \text{ cm}^3$$

Volume of unit cell = l^3, l = cube edge length; $l = (7.48 \times 10^{-23} \text{ cm}^3)^{1/3} = 4.21 \times 10^{-8}$ cm

For a face-centered unit cell, the O^{2-} ions touch along the face diagonal:

$$\sqrt{2}\, l = 4 r_{O^{2-}}, \quad r_{O^{2-}} = \frac{\sqrt{2} \times 4.21 \times 10^{-8} \text{ cm}}{4} = 1.49 \times 10^{-8} \text{ cm}$$

The cube edge length goes through two radii of the O^{2-} anions and the diameter of the Mg^{2+} cation. So:

$$l = 2 r_{O^{2-}} + 2 r_{Mg^{2+}}, \quad 4.21 \times 10^{-8} \text{ cm} = 2(1.49 \times 10^{-8} \text{ cm}) + 2 r_{Mg^{2+}}, \quad r_{Mg^{2+}} = 6.15 \times 10^{-9} \text{ cm}$$

70. CsCl is a simple cubic array of Cl⁻ ions with Cs⁺ in the middle of each unit cell. There is one Cs⁺ and one Cl⁻ ion in each unit cell. Cs⁺ and Cl⁻ ions touch along the body diagonal.

body diagonal = $2 r_{Cs^+} + 2 r_{Cl^-} = \sqrt{3}\, l$, l = length of cube edge

In each unit cell:

$$\text{mass} = 1 \text{ CsCl formula unit} \left(\frac{1 \text{ mol CsCl}}{6.022 \times 10^{23} \text{ formula units}} \right) \left(\frac{168.4 \text{ g CsCl}}{\text{mol CsCl}} \right)$$
$$= 2.796 \times 10^{-22} \text{ g}$$

$$\text{volume} = l^3 = 2.796 \times 10^{-22} \text{ g CsCl} \times \frac{1 \text{ cm}^3}{3.97 \text{ g CsCl}} = 7.04 \times 10^{-23} \text{ cm}^3$$

$l^3 = 7.04 \times 10^{-23}$ cm³, $l = 4.13 \times 10^{-8}$ cm $= 413$ pm = length of cube edge

$$2 r_{Cs^+} + 2 r_{Cl^-} = \sqrt{3}\, l = \sqrt{3}(413 \text{ pm}) = 715 \text{ pm}$$

The distance between ion centers = $r_{Cs^+} + r_{Cl^-}$ = 715 pm/2 = 358 pm

From ionic radii: r_{Cs^+} = 169 pm and r_{Cl^-} = 181 pm; $r_{Cs^+} + r_{Cl^-}$ = 169 + 181 = 350. pm

The actual distance is 8 pm (2.3%) greater than that calculated from values of ionic radii.

71.   a. CO_2: molecular   b. SiO_2: network   c.   Si: atomic, network

      d. CH_4: molecular   e.   Ru: atomic, metallic   f. I_2: molecular

      g.   KBr: ionic   h. H_2O: molecular   i.   NaOH: ionic

      j.   U: atomic, metallic   k. $CaCO_3$: ionic   l. PH_3: molecular

72.   a.   diamond: atomic, network b. PH_3: molecular   c. H_2: molecular

      d.   Mg: atomic, metallic   e.   KCl: ionic   f.   quartz: network

      g. NH_4NO_3: ionic   h. SF_2: molecular   i.   Ar: atomic, group 8A

      j.   Cu: atomic, metallic   k. $C_6H_{12}O_6$: molecular

73.   a.   The unit cell consists of Ni at the cube corners and Ti at the body center, or Ti at the cube corners and Ni at the body center.

      b.   8 × 1/8 = 1 atom from corners + 1 atom at body center; Empirical formula = NiTi

      c.   Both have a coordination number of 8 (both are surrounded by 8 atoms).

74.   8 corners × $\dfrac{1/8\,Xe}{corner}$ + 1 Xe inside cell = 2 Xe; 8 edges × $\dfrac{1/4\,F}{edge}$ + 2 F inside cell = 4 F

      Empirical formula is XeF_2. This is also the molecular formula.

75.   Structure 1   Structure 2

      8 corners × $\dfrac{1/8\,Ca}{corner}$ = 1 Ca atom   8 corners × $\dfrac{1/8\,Ti}{corner}$ = 1 Ti atom

      6 faces × $\dfrac{1/2\,O}{face}$ = 3 O atoms   12 edges × $\dfrac{1/4\,O}{corner}$ = 3 O atoms

      1 Ti at body center. Formula = $CaTiO_3$ 1 Ca at body center. Formula = $CaTiO_3$

      In the extended lattice of both structures, each Ti atom is surrounded by six O atoms.

76.   With a cubic closest packed array of oxygen ions, we have 4 O^{2-} ions per unit cell. We need to balance the total -8 charge of the anions with a +8 charge from the Al^{3+} and Mg^{2+} cations.

The only combination of ions that gives a +8 charge is 2 Al^{3+} ions and 1 Mg^{2+} ion. The formula is Al_2MgO_4.

There are an equal number of octahedral holes as anions (4) in a cubic closest packed array, and twice the number of tetrahedral holes as anions in a cubic closest packed array. For the stoichiometry to work out, we need 2 Al^{3+} and 1 Mg^{2+} per unit cell. Hence, one-half of the octahedral holes are filled with Al^{3+} ions and one-eighth of the tetrahedral holes are filled with Mg^{2+} ions.

77.   a.   Y: 1 Y in center; Ba: 2 Ba in center

Cu: $8 \text{ corners} \times \dfrac{1/8 \text{ Cu}}{\text{corner}} = 1 \text{ Cu}$, $8 \text{ edges} \times \dfrac{1/4 \text{ Cu}}{\text{edge}} = 2 \text{ Cu}$, total = 3 Cu atoms

O: $20 \text{ edges} \times \dfrac{1/4 \text{ O}}{\text{edge}} = 5 \text{ oxygen}$, $8 \text{ faces} \times \dfrac{1/2 \text{ O}}{\text{face}} = 4 \text{ oxygen}$, total = 9 O atoms

Formula: $YBa_2Cu_3O_9$

b.   The structure of this superconductor material follows the second perovskite structure described in Exercise 10.75. The $YBa_2Cu_3O_9$ structure is three of these cubic perovskite unit cells stacked on top of each other. The oxygen atoms are in the same places, Cu takes the place of Ti, two of the calcium atoms are replaced by two barium atoms, and one Ca is replaced by Y.

c.   Y, Ba, and Cu are the same. Some oxygen atoms are missing.

$12 \text{ edges} \times \dfrac{1/4 \text{ O}}{\text{edge}} = 3 \text{ O}$, $8 \text{ faces} \times \dfrac{1/2 \text{ O}}{\text{face}} = 4 \text{ O}$, total = 7 O atoms

Superconductor formula is $YBa_2Cu_3O_7$.

78.   a.   Structure (a):

Ba: 2 Ba inside unit cell; Tl: $8 \text{ corners} \times \dfrac{1/8 \text{ Tl}}{\text{corner}} = 1 \text{ Tl}$

Cu: $4 \text{ edges} \times \dfrac{1/4 \text{ Cu}}{\text{edge}} = 1 \text{ Cu}$

O: $6 \text{ faces} \times \dfrac{1/2 \text{ O}}{\text{face}} + 8 \text{ edges} \times \dfrac{1/4 \text{ O}}{\text{edge}} = 5 \text{ O}$;   Formula = $TlBa_2CuO_5$

Structure (b):

Tl and Ba are the same as in structure (a).

Ca: 1 Ca inside unit cell; Cu: $8 \text{ edges} \times \dfrac{1/4 \text{ Cu}}{\text{edge}} = 2 \text{ Cu}$

O: $10 \text{ faces} \times \dfrac{1/2 \text{ O}}{\text{face}} + 8 \text{ edges} \times \dfrac{1/4 \text{ O}}{\text{edge}} = 7 \text{ O}$;   Formula = $TlBa_2CaCu_2O_7$

Structure (c):

Tl and Ba are the same, and two Ca are located inside the unit cell.

$$\text{Cu: } 12 \text{ edges} \times \frac{1/4 \text{ Cu}}{\text{edge}} = 3 \text{ Cu}; \quad \text{O: } 14 \text{ faces} \times \frac{1/2 \text{ O}}{\text{face}} + 8 \text{ edges} \times \frac{1/4 \text{ O}}{\text{edge}} = 9 \text{ O}$$

Formula: $TlBa_2Ca_2Cu_3O_9$

Structure (d):   Following similar calculations, formula $= TlBa_2Ca_3Cu_4O_{11}$

b. Structure (a) has one planar sheet of Cu and O atoms, and the number increases by one for each of the remaining structures. The order of superconductivity temperature from lowest to highest temperature is: (a) < (b) < (c) < (d).

c. $TlBa_2CuO_5$: $3 + 2(2) + x + 5(-2) = 0$, $x = +3$
    Only Cu^{3+} is present in each formula unit.

    $TlBa_2CaCu_2O_7$: $3 + 2(2) + 2 + 2(x) + 7(-2) = 0$, $x = +5/2$
    Each formula unit contains 1 Cu^{2+} and 1 Cu^{3+}.

    $TlBa_2Ca_2Cu_3O_9$: $3 + 2(2) + 2(2) + 3(x) + 9(-2) = 0$, $x = +7/3$
    Each formula unit contains 2 Cu^{2+} and 1 Cu^{3+}.

    $TlBa_2Ca_3Cu_4O_{11}$: $3 + 2(2) + 3(2) + 4(x) + 11(-2) = 0$, $x = +9/4$
    Each formula unit contains 3 Cu^{2+} and 1 Cu^{3+}.

d. This superconductor material achieves variable copper oxidation states by varying the numbers of Ca, Cu and O in each unit cell. The mixtures of copper oxidation states are discussed above. The superconductor material in Exercise 10.77 achieves variable copper oxidation states by omitting oxygen at various sites in the lattice.

Phase Changes and Phase Diagrams

79.   If we graph $\ln P_{vap}$ vs $1/T$, the slope of the resulting straight line will be $-\Delta H_{vap}/R$.

P_{vap}	$\ln P_{vap}$	T (Li)	$1/T$	T (Mg)	$1/T$
1 torr	0	1023 K	$9.775 \times 10^{-4} \text{ K}^{-1}$	893 K	$11.2 \times 10^{-4} \text{ K}^{-1}$
10.	2.3	1163	8.598×10^{-4}	1013	9.872×10^{-4}
100.	4.61	1353	7.391×10^{-4}	1173	8.525×10^{-4}
400.	5.99	1513	6.609×10^{-4}	1313	7.616×10^{-4}
760.	6.63	1583	6.317×10^{-4}	1383	7.231×10^{-4}

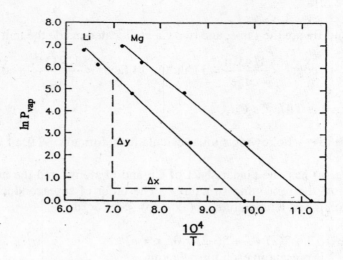

For Li:

We get the slope by taking two points (x, y) that are on the line we draw. For a line:

$$\text{slope} = \frac{\Delta y}{\Delta x} = \frac{y_2 - y_1}{x_2 - x_1}$$

or we can determine the straight line equation using a calculator. The general straight line equation is $y = mx + b$ where $m =$ slope and $b =$ y-intercept.

The equation of the Li line is: $\ln P_{vap} = -1.90 \times 10^4 (1/T) + 18.6$, slope $= -1.90 \times 10^4$ K

Slope $= -\Delta H_{vap}/R$, $\Delta H_{vap} = -\text{slope} \times R = 1.90 \times 10^4$ K $\times 8.3145$ J/K•mol

$\Delta H_{vap} = 1.58 \times 10^5$ J/mol $= 158$ kJ/mol

For Mg:

The equation of the line is: $\ln P_{vap} = -1.67 \times 10^4 (1/T) + 18.7$, slope $= -1.67 \times 10^4$ K

$\Delta H_{vap} = -\text{slope} \times R = 1.67 \times 10^4$ K $\times 8.3145$ J/K•mol,

$\Delta H_{vap} = 1.39 \times 10^5$ J/mol $= 139$ kJ/mol

The bonding is stronger in Li since ΔH_{vap} is larger for Li.

80.   We graph $\ln P_{vap}$ vs $1/T$. The slope of the line equals $-\Delta H_{vap}/R$.

T(K)	$10^3/T$ (K^{-1})	P_{vap} (torr)	ln P_{vap}
273	3.66	14.4	2.67
283	3.53	26.6	3.28
293	3.41	47.9	3.87
303	3.30	81.3	4.40
313	3.19	133	4.89
323	3.10	208	5.34
353	2.83	670.	6.51

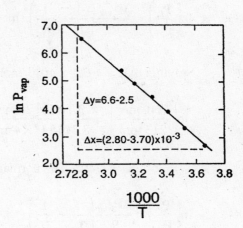

$$\text{slope} = \frac{6.6 - 2.5}{(2.80\times10^{-3} - 3.70\times10^{-3})\ \text{K}^{-1}} = -4600\ \text{K}$$

$$-4600\ \text{K} = \frac{-\Delta H_{vap}}{R} = \frac{-\Delta H_{vap}}{8.3145\ \text{J}/\text{K}\bullet\text{mol}}, \quad \Delta H_{vap} = 38{,}000\ \text{J/mol} = 38\ \text{kJ/mol}$$

To determine the normal boiling point, we can use the following formula:

$$\ln\left(\frac{P_1}{P_2}\right) = \frac{\Delta H_{vap}}{R} = \left(\frac{1}{T_2} - \frac{1}{T_1}\right)$$

At the normal boiling point, the vapor pressure equals 1.00 atm or 760. torr. At 273 K, the vapor pressure is 14.4. torr (from data in the problem).

$$\ln\left(\frac{14.4}{760.}\right) = \frac{38{,}000\ \text{J}/\text{mol}}{8.3145\ \text{J}/\text{K}\bullet\text{mol}}\left(\frac{1}{T_2} - \frac{1}{273\ \text{K}}\right), \quad -3.97 = 4.6\times10^3\ (1/T_2 - 3.66\times10^{-3})$$

$$-8.6\times10^{-4} + 3.66\times10^{-3} = 1/T_2 = 2.80\times10^{-3}, \quad T_2 = 357\ \text{K} = \text{normal boiling point}$$

81.   At 100.°C (373 K), the vapor pressure of H_2O is 1.00 atm = 760. torr.
      For water, $\Delta H_{vap} = 40.7$ kJ/mol.

$$\ln\left(\frac{P_1}{P_2}\right) = \frac{\Delta H_{vap}}{R}\left(\frac{1}{T_2} - \frac{1}{T_1}\right) \text{ or } \ln\left(\frac{P_2}{P_1}\right) = \frac{\Delta H_{vap}}{R}\left(\frac{1}{T_1} - \frac{1}{T_2}\right)$$

$$\ln\left(\frac{520.\ \text{torr}}{760.\ \text{torr}}\right) = \frac{40.7\times10^3\ \text{J}/\text{mol}}{8.3145\ \text{J}/\text{K}\bullet\text{mol}}\left(\frac{1}{373\ \text{K}} - \frac{1}{T_2}\right), \quad -7.75\times10^{-5} = \left(\frac{1}{373\ \text{K}} - \frac{1}{T_2}\right)$$

$$-7.75\times10^{-5} = 2.68\times10^{-3} - \frac{1}{T_2}, \quad \frac{1}{T_2} = 2.76\times10^{-3}, \quad T_2 = \frac{1}{2.76\times10^{-3}} = 362\ \text{K or } 89°C$$

82. $$\ln\left(\frac{P_2}{1.00}\right) = \frac{40.7\times10^3\ \text{J}/\text{mol}}{8.3145\ \text{J}/\text{K}\bullet\text{mol}}\left(\frac{1}{373\ \text{K}} - \frac{1}{623\ \text{K}}\right), \quad \ln P_2 = 5.27, \quad P_2 = e^{5.27} = 194\ \text{atm}$$

83. $\ln\left(\dfrac{P_1}{P_2}\right) = \dfrac{\Delta H_{vap}}{R}\left(\dfrac{1}{T_2} - \dfrac{1}{T_1}\right)$, $\ln\left(\dfrac{836 \text{ torr}}{213 \text{ torr}}\right) = \dfrac{\Delta H_{vap}}{8.3145 \text{ J/K} \bullet \text{mol}}\left(\dfrac{1}{313 \text{ K}} - \dfrac{1}{353 \text{ K}}\right)$

Solving: $\Delta H_{vap} = 3.1 \times 10^4$ J/mol; For the normal boiling point, P = 1.00 atm = 760. torr.

$\ln\left(\dfrac{760. \text{ torr}}{213 \text{ torr}}\right) = \dfrac{3.1 \times 10^4 \text{ J/mol}}{8.3145 \text{ J/K} \bullet \text{mol}}\left(\dfrac{1}{313 \text{ K}} - \dfrac{1}{T_1}\right)$, $\dfrac{1}{313} - \dfrac{1}{T_1} = 3.4 \times 10^{-4}$

$T_1 = 350.$ K = 77°C; The normal boiling point of CCl_4 is 77°C.

84. $\ln\left(\dfrac{P_1}{P_2}\right) = \dfrac{\Delta H_{vap}}{R}\left(\dfrac{1}{T_2} - \dfrac{1}{T_1}\right)$

$P_1 = 760.$ torr, $T_1 = 56.5°C + 273.2 = 329.7$ K; $P_2 = 630.$ torr, $T_2 = ?$

$\ln\left(\dfrac{760.}{630.}\right) = \dfrac{32.0 \times 10^3 \text{ J/mol}}{8.3145 \text{ J/K} \bullet \text{mol}}\left(\dfrac{1}{T_2} - \dfrac{1}{329.7}\right)$, $0.188 = 3.85 \times 10^3\left(\dfrac{1}{T_2} - 3.033 \times 10^{-3}\right)$

$\dfrac{1}{T_2} - 3.033 \times 10^{-3} = 4.88 \times 10^{-5}$, $\dfrac{1}{T_2} = 3.082 \times 10^{-3}$, $T_2 = 324.5$ K = 51.3°C

$\ln\left(\dfrac{630. \text{ torr}}{P_2}\right) = \dfrac{32.0 \times 10^3 \text{ J/mol}}{8.3145 \text{ J/K} \bullet \text{mol}}\left(\dfrac{1}{298.2} - \dfrac{1}{324.5}\right)$, ln 630. − ln P_2 = 1.05

ln P_2 = 5.40, $P_2 = e^{5.40}$ = 221 torr

85.

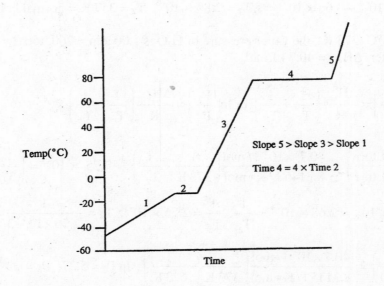

Slope 5 > Slope 3 > Slope 1

Time 4 = 4 × Time 2

86. $X(g, 100.°C) \rightarrow X(g, 75°C)$, $\Delta T = -25°C$

$$q_1 = s_{gas} \times m \times \Delta T = \frac{1.0 \text{ J}}{g \, °C} \times 250. \text{ g} \times (-25°C) = -6300 \text{ J} = -6.3 \text{ kJ}$$

$X(g, 75°C) \rightarrow X(l, 75°C)$, $q_2 = 250. \text{ g} \times \frac{1 \text{ mol}}{75.0 \text{ g}} \times \frac{-20. \text{ kJ}}{\text{mol}} = -67 \text{ kJ}$

$X(l, 75°C) \rightarrow X(l, -15°C)$, $q_3 = \frac{2.5 \text{ J}}{g \, °C} \times 250. \text{ g} \times (-90.°C) = -56,000 \text{ J} = -56 \text{ kJ}$

$X(l, -15°C) \rightarrow X(s, -15°C)$, $q_4 = 250. \text{ g} \times \frac{1 \text{ mol}}{75.0 \text{ g}} \times \frac{-5.0 \text{ kJ}}{\text{mol}} = -17 \text{ kJ}$

$X(s, -15°C) \rightarrow X(s, -50.°C)$, $q_5 = \frac{3.0 \text{ J}}{g \, °C} \times 250. \text{ g} \times (-35°C) = -26,000 \text{ J} = -26 \text{ kJ}$

$q_{total} = q_1 + q_2 + q_3 + q_4 + q_5 = -6.3 - 67 - 56 - 17 - 26 = -172 \text{ kJ}$

87. $H_2O(s, -20.°C) \rightarrow H_2O(s, 0°C)$, $\Delta T = 20.°C$

$$q_1 = s_{ice} \times m \times \Delta T = \frac{2.03 \text{ J}}{g \, °C} \times 5.00 \times 10^2 \text{ g} \times 20.°C = 2.0 \times 10^4 \text{ J} = 20. \text{ kJ}$$

$H_2O(s, 0°C) \rightarrow H_2O(l, 0°C)$, $q_2 = 5.00 \times 10^2 \text{ g } H_2O \times \frac{1 \text{ mol}}{18.02 \text{ g}} \times \frac{6.02 \text{ kJ}}{\text{mol}} = 167 \text{ kJ}$

$H_2O(l, 0°C) \rightarrow H_2O(l, 100.°C)$, $q_3 = \frac{4.2 \text{ J}}{g \, °C} \times 5.00 \times 10^2 \text{ g} \times 100.°C = 2.1 \times 10^5 \text{ J} = 210 \text{ kJ}$

$H_2O(l, 100.°C) \rightarrow H_2O(g, 100.°C)$, $q_4 = 5.00 \times 10^2 \text{ g} \times \frac{1 \text{ mol}}{18.02 \text{ g}} \times \frac{40.7 \text{ kJ}}{\text{mol}} = 1130 \text{ kJ}$

$H_2O(g, 100.°C) \rightarrow H_2O(g, 250.°C)$, $q_5 = \frac{2.0 \text{ J}}{g \, °C} \times 5.00 \times 10^2 \text{ g} \times 150.°C = 1.5 \times 10^5 \text{ J}$

$$= 150 \text{ kJ}$$

$q_{total} = q_1 + q_2 + q_3 + q_4 + q_5 = 20. + 167 + 210 + 1130 + 150 = 1680 \text{ kJ}$

88. $H_2O(g, 125°C) \rightarrow H_2O(g, 100.°C)$, $q_1 = 2.0 \text{ J/g} \bullet °C \times 75.0 \text{ g} \times (-25°C) = -3800 \text{ J} = -3.8 \text{ kJ}$

$H_2O(g, 100.°C) \rightarrow H_2O(l, 100.°C)$, $q_2 = 75.0 \text{ g} \times \frac{1 \text{ mol}}{18.02 \text{ g}} \times \frac{-40.7 \text{ kJ}}{\text{mol}} = -169 \text{ kJ}$

$H_2O(l, 100.°C) \rightarrow H_2O(l, 0°C)$, $q_3 = 4.2 \text{ J/g} \bullet °C \times 75.0 \text{ g} \times (-100.°C) = -32,000 \text{ J} = -32 \text{ kJ}$

To convert $H_2O(g)$ at 125°C to $H_2O(l)$ at 0°C requires $(-3.8 \text{ kJ} - 169 \text{ kJ} - 32 \text{ kJ} =) -205 \text{ kJ}$ of heat removed. To convert from $H_2O(l)$ at 0°C to $H_2O(s)$ at 0°C requires:

$$q_4 = 75.0 \text{ g} \times \frac{1 \text{ mol}}{18.02 \text{ g}} \times \frac{-6.02 \text{ kJ}}{\text{mol}} = -25 \text{ kJ}$$

This amount of energy puts us over the -215 kJ limit (-205 kJ - 25 kJ = -230. kJ). Therefore, a mixture of $H_2O(s)$ and $H_2O(l)$ will be present at 0°C when 215 kJ of heat are removed from the gas sample.

89.   Total mass H_2O = 18 cubes $\times \dfrac{30.0 \text{ g}}{\text{cube}} = 540.$ g; 540. g $H_2O \times \dfrac{1 \text{ mol } H_2O}{18.02 \text{ g}} = 30.0$ mol H_2O

Heat removed to produce ice at -5.0°C:

$$\frac{4.18 \text{ J}}{\text{g} \,^\circ\text{C}} \times 540. \text{ g} \times 22.0 \,^\circ\text{C} + \frac{6.02 \times 10^3 \text{ J}}{\text{mol}} \times 30.0 \text{ mol} + \frac{2.03 \text{ J}}{\text{g} \,^\circ\text{C}} \times 540. \text{ g} \times 5.0 \,^\circ\text{C}$$

$$4.97 \times 10^4 \text{ J} + 1.81 \times 10^5 \text{ J} + 5.5 \times 10^3 \text{ J} = 2.36 \times 10^5 \text{ J}$$

$$2.36 \times 10^5 \text{ J} \times \frac{1 \text{ g CF}_2\text{Cl}_2}{158 \text{ J}} = 1.49 \times 10^3 \text{ g CF}_2\text{Cl}_2 \text{ must be vaporized.}$$

90.   Heat released = 0.250 g Na $\times \dfrac{1 \text{ mol}}{22.99 \text{ g}} \times \dfrac{368 \text{ kJ}}{2 \text{ mol}} = 2.00$ kJ

To melt 50.0 g of ice requires: 50.0 g ice $\times \dfrac{1 \text{ mol } H_2O}{18.02 \text{ g}} \times \dfrac{6.02 \text{ kJ}}{\text{mol}} = 16.7$ kJ

The reaction doesn't release enough heat to melt all of the ice. The temperature will remain at 0°C.

91.   A: solid   B: liquid   C: vapor

D: solid + vapor   E: solid + liquid + vapor

F: liquid + vapor   G: liquid + vapor   H: vapor

triple point: E   critical point: G

normal freezing point: temperature at which solid - liquid line is at 1.0 atm (see plot below).

normal boiling point: temperature at which liquid - vapor line is at 1.0 atm (see plot below).

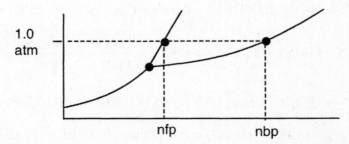

Since the solid-liquid line has a positive slope, the solid phase is denser than the liquid phase.

92.   a.   3

b.   Triple point at 95.31°C: rhombic, monoclinic, gas
       Triple point at 115.18°C: monoclinic, liquid, gas
       Triple point at 153°C: rhombic, monoclinic, liquid

c.   From the phase diagram, the monoclinic solid phase is stable at T = 100°C and P = 1 atm.

d.   Normal melting point = 115.21°C; normal boiling point = 444.6°C; The normal melting and boiling points occur at P = 1.0 atm.

e.   Rhombic is the densest phase since the rhombic-monoclinic equilibrium line has a positive slope and since the solid-liquid lines also have positive slopes.

f.   No; P = 1.0×10^{-5} atm is at a pressure somewhere between the 95.31°C and 115.18°C triple points. At this pressure, the rhombic and gas phases are never in equilibrium with each other, so rhombic sulfur cannot sublime at P = 1.0×10^{-5} atm. However, monoclinic sulfur can sublime at this pressure.

g.   From the phase diagram, we would start off with gaseous sulfur. At 100°C and ~1×10^{-5} atm, S(g) would convert to the solid monoclinic form of sulfur. Finally at 100°C and some large pressure less than 1420 atm, S(s, monoclinic) would convert to the solid rhombic form of sulfur. Summarizing, the phase changes are S(g) → S(monoclinic) → S(rhombic).

93.   a.   two

b.   Higher pressure triple point: graphite, diamond and liquid; Lower pressure triple point: graphite, liquid and vapor

c.   It is converted to diamond (the more dense solid form).

d.   Diamond is more dense, which is why graphite can be converted to diamond by applying pressure.

94.   The following sketch of the Br_2 phase diagram is not to scale. Since the triple point of Br_2 is at a temperature below the freezing point of Br_2, the slope of the solid-liquid line is positive.

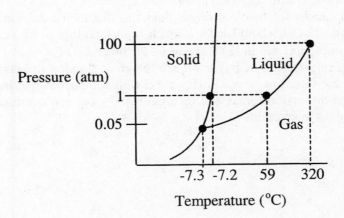

The positive slopes of all the lines indicate that $Br_2(s)$ is more dense than $Br_2(l)$ which is more dense than $Br_2(g)$. At room temperature (~22°C) and 1 atm, $Br_2(l)$ is the stable phase. $Br_2(l)$ cannot exist at a temperature below the triple point temperature of −7.3°C and at a temperature above the critical point temperature of 320°C. The phase changes that occur as temperature is increased at 0.10 atm are solid → liquid → gas.

95.   Because the density of the liquid phase is greater than the density of the solid phase, the slope of the solid-liquid boundary line is negative (as in H_2O). With a negative slope, the melting points increase with a decrease in pressure so the normal melting point of X should be greater than 225°C.

96.

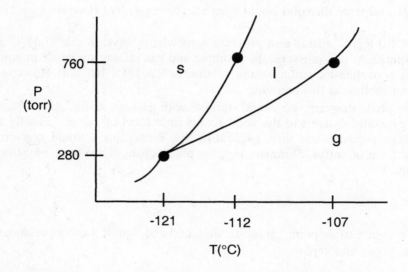

From the three points given, the slope of the s-l boundary line is positive so Xe(s) is more dense than Xe(l). Also, the positive slope of this line tells us that the melting point of Xe increases as pressure increases. The same direct relationship exists for the boiling point of Xe as the l-g boundary line also has a positive slope.

Additional Exercises

97.   Chalk is composed of the ionic compound calcium carbonate ($CaCO_3$). The electrostatic forces in ionic compounds are much stronger than the intermolecular forces in covalent compounds. Therefore, $CaCO_3$ should have a much higher boiling point than the covalent compounds found in motor oil and in H_2O. Motor oil is composed of nonpolar C−C and C−H bonds. The intermolecular forces in motor oil are therefore London dispersion forces. We generally consider these forces to be weak. However, with compounds that have large molar masses, these London dispersion forces add up significantly and can overtake the relatively strong hydrogen bonding interactions in water.

98.   Benzene   Naphthalene

LD forces only   LD forces only

Note: London dispersion forces in molecules like benzene and naphthalene are fairly large. The molecules are flat, and there is efficient surface area contact among molecules. Large surface area contact leads to stronger London dispersion forces.

Carbon tetrachloride (CCl_4) has polar bonds but is a nonpolar molecule. CCl_4 only has LD forces.

In terms of size and shape: $CCl_4 < C_6H_6 < C_{10}H_8$

The strengths of the LD forces are proportional to size and are related to shape. Although CCl_4 is fairly large, its overall spherical shape gives rise to relatively weak LD forces as compared to flat molecules like benzene and naphthalene. The physical properties given in the problem are consistent with the order listed above. Each of the physical properties will increase with an increase in intermolecular forces.

Acetone   Acetic Acid

LD, dipole   LD, dipole, H bonding

Benzoic acid

LD, dipole, H bonding

We would predict the strength of intermolecular forces for the last three molecules to be:

acetone   <   acetic acid   <   benzoic acid

polar   H bonding   H bonding, but large LD forces because of greater size and shape.

This ordering is consistent with the values given for bp, mp, and ΔH_{vap}.

The overall order of the strengths of intermolecular forces based on physical properties are:

acetone $< CCl_4 < C_6H_6 <$ acetic acid $<$ naphthalene $<$ benzoic acid

The order seems reasonable except for acetone and naphthalene. Since acetone is polar, we would not expect it to boil at the lowest temperature. However, in terms of size and shape, acetone is the smallest molecule, and the LD forces in acetone must be very small compared to the other molecules. Naphthalene must have very strong LD forces because of its size and flat shape.

99.   At any temperature, the plot tells us that substance A has a higher vapor pressure than substance B, with substance C having the lowest vapor pressure. Therefore, the substance with the weakest intermolecular forces is A, and the substance with the strongest intermolecular forces is C.

NH_3 can form hydrogen bonding interactions while the others cannot. Substance C is NH_3. The other two are nonpolar compounds with only London dispersion forces. Since CH_4 is smaller than SiH_4, CH_4 will have weaker LD forces and is substance A. Therefore, substance B is SiH_4.

100.   As the electronegativity of the atoms covalently bonded to H increases, the strength of the hydrogen bonding interaction increases.

N $\cdots$ H–N $<$ N $\cdots$ H– O $<$ O $\cdots$ H–O $<$ O $\cdots$ H–F $<$ F $\cdots$ H–F

weakest   strongest

101.   If TiO_2 conducts electricity as a liquid, then it is an ionic solid; if not, then TiO_2 is a network solid.

102.   One B atom and one N atom together have the same number of electrons as two C atoms. The description of physical properties sounds a lot like the properties of graphite and diamond, the two solid forms of carbon. The two forms of BN have structures similar to graphite and diamond.

103. B_2H_6:   This compound contains only nonmetals so it is probably a molecular solid with covalent bonding. The low boiling point confirms this.

       SiO_2:   This is the empirical formula for quartz, which is a network solid.

       CsI: This is a metal bonded to a nonmetal, which generally form ionic solids. The electrical conductivity in aqueous solution confirms this.

       W: Tungsten is a metallic solid as the conductivity data confirms.

104.   In order to set up an equation, we need to know what phase exists at the final temperature. To heat 20.0 g of ice from $-10.0°C$ to $0.0°C$ requires:

$$q = \frac{2.03\,J}{g\,°C} \times 20.0\,g \times 10.0°C = 406\,J$$

To convert ice to water at 0.0°C requires:

$$q = 20.0\,g \times \frac{1\,mol}{18.02} \times \frac{6.02\,kJ}{mol} = 6.68\,kJ = 6680\,J$$

To chill 100.0 g of water from 80.0°C to 0.0° requires:

$$q = \frac{4.18\,J}{g\,°C} \times 100.0\,g \times 80.0°C = 33,400\,J \text{ of heat removed}$$

From the heat values above, the liquid phase exists once the final temperature is reached (a lot more heat is lost when the 100.0 g of water is cooled to 0.0°C than the heat required to convert the ice into water). To calculate the final temperature, we will equate the heat gain by the ice to the heat loss by the water. We will keep all quantities positive in order to avoid sign errors. The heat gain by the ice will be the 406 J required to convert the ice to 0.0°C plus the 6680 J required to convert the ice at 0.0°C into water at 0.0°C plus the heat required to raise the temperature from 0.0°C to the final temperature.

$$\text{heat gain by ice} = 406\,J + 6680\,J + \frac{4.18\,J}{g\,°C} \times 20.0\,g \times (T_f - 0.0°C) = 7.09 \times 10^3 + 83.6\,T_f$$

$$\text{heat loss by water} = \frac{4.18\,J}{g\,°C} \times 100.0\,g \times (80.0°C - T_f) = 3.34 \times 10^4 - 418\,T_f$$

Solving for the final temperature:

$$7.09 \times 10^3 + 83.6\,T_f = 3.34 \times 10^4 - 418\,T_f, \quad 502\,T_f = 2.63 \times 10^4, \quad T_f = 52.4°C$$

105. $1.00\,lb \times \frac{454\,g}{lb} = 454\,g\ H_2O$; A change of 1.00°F is equal to a change of $\frac{5}{9}$ °C.

The amount of heat in J in 1 Btu is: $\dfrac{4.18\,J}{g\,°C} \times 454\,g \times \dfrac{5}{9}\,°C = 1.05 \times 10^3\,J = 1.05\,kJ$

It takes 40.7 kJ to vaporize 1 mol H_2O (ΔH_{vap}). Combining these:

$$\dfrac{1.00 \times 10^4\,Bu}{hr} \times \dfrac{1.05\,kJ}{Btu} \times \dfrac{1\,mol\,H_2O}{40.7\,kJ} = 258\,mol/hr$$

or: $\dfrac{258\,mol}{hr} \times \dfrac{18.02\,g\,H_2O}{mol} = 4650\,g/hr = 4.65\,kg/hr$

106.   The critical temperature is the temperature above which the vapor cannot be liquefied no matter what pressure is applied. Since N_2 has a critical temperature below room temperature (~22°C), it cannot be liquefied at room temperature. NH_3, with a critical temperature above room temperature, can be liquefied at room temperature.

Challenge Problems

107. $\Delta H = q_p = 30.79\,kJ$; $\Delta E = q_p + w$, $w = -P\Delta V$

   $w = -P\Delta V = -1.00\,atm\,(28.90\,L) = -28.9\,L\,atm \times \dfrac{101.3\,J}{L\,atm} = -2930\,J$

   $\Delta E = 30.79\,kJ + (-2.93\,kJ) = 27.86\,kJ$

108. $XeCl_2F_2$, $8 + 2(7) + 2(7) = 36\,e^-$

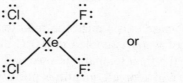   or

   polar (bond dipoles do   nonpolar (bond dipoles
   not each other cancel)   cancel each other)

   These are two possible square planar molecular structures for $XeCl_2F_2$. One structure has the Cl atoms 90° apart, the other has the Cl atoms 180° apart. The structure with the Cl atoms 90° apart is polar; the other structure is nonpolar. The polar structure will have additional dipole forces so it has the stronger intermolecular forces and is the liquid. The gas form of $XeCl_2F_2$ is the nonpolar form having the Cl atoms 180° apart.

109.   A single hydrogen bond in H_2O has a strength of 21 kJ/mol. Each H_2O molecule forms two H bonds. Thus, it should take 42 kJ/mol of energy to break all of the H bonds in water. Consider the phase transitions:

   solid $\xrightarrow{\ 6.0\,kJ\ }$ liquid $\xrightarrow{\ 40.7\,kJ\ }$ vapor $\Delta H_{sub} = \Delta H_{fus} + \Delta H_{vap}$

It takes a total of 46.7 kJ/mol to convert solid H_2O to vapor (ΔH_{sub}). This would be the amount of energy necessary to disrupt all of the intermolecular forces in ice. Thus, $(42 \div 46.7) \times 100 = 90\%$ of the attraction in ice can be attributed to H bonding.

110.   Both molecules are capable of H bonding. However, in oil of wintergreen the hydrogen bonding is <u>intramolecular</u> (within each molecule).

In methyl-4-hydroxybenzoate, the H bonding is <u>intermolecular</u>, resulting in stronger forces between molecules and a higher melting point.

111.   NaCl, $MgCl_2$, NaF, MgF_2 AlF_3 all have very high melting points indicative of strong inter-molecular forces. They are all ionic solids. $SiCl_4$, SiF_4, F_2, Cl_2, PF_5 and SF_6 are nonpolar covalent molecules. Only LD forces are present. PCl_3 and SCl_2 are polar molecules. LD forces and dipole forces are present. In these 8 molecular substances, the intermolecular forces are weak and the melting points low. $AlCl_3$ doesn't seem to fit in as well. From the melting point, there are much stronger forces present than in the nonmetal halides, but they aren't as strong as we would expect for an ionic solid. $AlCl_3$ illustrates a gradual transition from ionic to covalent bonding, from an ionic solid to discrete molecules.

112.   a.   The NaCl unit cell has a face centered cubic arrangement of the anions with cations in the octahedral holes. There are 4 NaCl formula units per unit cell and, since there is a 1:1 ratio of cations to anions in MnO, there would be 4 MnO formula units per unit cell, assuming an NaCl type structure. The CsCl unit cell has a simple cubic structure of anions with the cations in the cubic holes. There is one CsCl formula unit per unit cell, so there would be one MnO formula unit per unit cell if a CsCl structure is observed.

$$\frac{\text{molecules MnO}}{\text{unit cell}} = (4.47 \times 10^{-8} \text{ cm})^3 \times \frac{5.28 \text{ g MnO}}{\text{cm}^3} \times \frac{1 \text{ mol MnO}}{70.94 \text{ g MnO}}$$

$$\times \frac{6.022 \times 10^{23} \text{ molecules MnO}}{\text{mol MnO}_4} = 4.00 \text{ molecules MnO}$$

From the calculation, MnO crystallizes in the NaCl type structure.

b.   From the NaCl structure and assuming the ions touch each other, then ℓ = cube edge length = $2r_{Mn^{2+}} + 2r_{O^{2-}}$.

$\ell = 4.47 \times 10^{-8} \text{ cm} = 2 \ r_{Mn^{2+}} + 2(1.40 \times 10^{-8} \text{ cm})$, $r_{Mn^{2+}} = 8.4 \times 10^{-9} \text{ cm} = 84 \text{ pm}$

113. Out of 100.00 g: $28.31 \text{ g O} \times \dfrac{1 \text{ mol}}{16.00 \text{ g}} = 1.769 \text{ mol O}$; $71.69 \text{ g Ti} \times \dfrac{1 \text{ mol}}{47.88 \text{ g}} = 1.497 \text{ mol Ti}$

$\dfrac{1.769}{1.497} = 1.182$; $\dfrac{1.497}{1.769} = 0.8462$; The formula is $TiO_{1.182}$ or $Ti_{0.8462}O$.

For $Ti_{0.8462}O$, let $x = Ti^{2+}$ per mol O^{2-} and $y = Ti^{3+}$ per mol O^{2-}. Setting up two equations and solving:

$x + y = 0.8462$ (mass balance) and $2x + 3y = 2$ (charge balance); $2x + 3(0.8462 - x) = 2$

$x = 0.539 \text{ mol Ti}^{2+}/\text{mol O}^{2-}$ and $y = 0.307 \text{ mol Ti}^{3+}/\text{mol O}^{2-}$

$\dfrac{0.539}{0.8462} \times 100 = 63.7\%$ of the titanium ions are Ti^{2+} and 36.3% are Ti^{3+} (a 1.75:1 ion ratio).

114. First we need to get the empirical formula of spinel. Assume 100.0 g of spinel.

$37.9 \text{ g Al} \times \dfrac{1 \text{ mol Al}}{26.98 \text{ g Al}} = 1.40 \text{ mol Al}$

The mole ratios are 2:1:4.

$17.1 \text{ g Mg} \times \dfrac{1 \text{ mol Mg}}{24.31 \text{ g Mg}} = 0.703 \text{ mol Mg}$

Empirical Formula = Al_2MgO_4

$45.0 \text{ g O} \times \dfrac{1 \text{ mol O}}{16.00 \text{ g O}} = 2.81 \text{ mol O}$

Assume each unit cell contains an integral value (n) of Al_2MgO_4 formula units. Each Al_2MgO_4 formula unit has a mass of: $24.31 + 2(26.98) + 4(16.00) = 142.27$ g/mol

$\text{density} = \dfrac{n \text{ formula units} \times \dfrac{1 \text{ mol}}{6.022 \times 10^{23} \text{ atoms}} \times \dfrac{142.27 \text{ g}}{\text{mol}}}{(8.09 \times 10^{-8} \text{ cm})^3} = \dfrac{3.57 \text{ g}}{\text{cm}^3}$, Solving: n = 8.00

Each unit cell has 8 formula units of Al_2MgO_4 or 16 Al^{3+}, 8 Mg^{2+} and 32 O^{2-} ions.

115. $\dfrac{\text{density}_{Mn}}{\text{density}_{Cu}} = \dfrac{\text{mass}_{Mn} \times \text{volume}_{Cu}}{\text{volume}_{Mn} \times \text{mass}_{Cu}} = \dfrac{\text{mass}_{Mn}}{\text{mass}_{Cu}} \times \dfrac{\text{volume}_{Cu}}{\text{volume}_{Mn}}$

The type of cubic cell formed is not important; only that Cu and Mn crystallize in the same type of cubic unit cell is important. Each cubic unit cell has a specific relationship between the cube edge length, l, and the radius, r. In all cases $l \propto r$. Therefore, $V \propto l^3 \propto r^3$. For the mass ratio, we can use the molar masses of Mn and Cu since each unit cell must contain the same number of Mn and Cu atoms. Solving:

$$\frac{\text{density}_{Mn}}{\text{density}_{Cu}} = \frac{\text{mass}_{Mn}}{\text{mass}_{Cu}} \times \frac{\text{volume}_{Cu}}{\text{volume}_{Mn}} = \frac{54.94\,\text{g}/\text{mol}}{63.55\,\text{g}/\text{mol}} \times \frac{(r_{Cu})^3}{(1.056\,r_{Cu})^3}$$

$$\frac{\text{density}_{Mn}}{\text{density}_{Cu}} = 0.8645 \times \left(\frac{1}{1.056}\right)^3 = 0.7341$$

$$\text{density}_{Mn} = 0.7341 \times \text{density}_{Cu} = 0.7341 \times 8.96\,\text{g/cm}^3 = 6.58\,\text{g/cm}^3$$

116. a. The arrangement of the layers are:

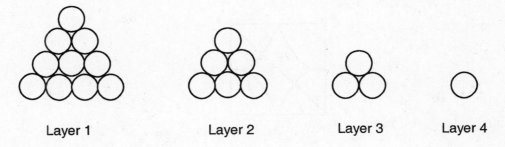

Layer 1   Layer 2   Layer 3   Layer 4

A total of 20 cannon balls will be needed.

b. The layering alternates abcabc which is cubic closest packing.

c. tetrahedron

117.

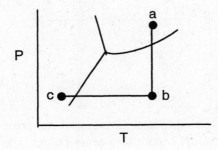

As P is lowered, we go from a to b on the phase diagram. The water boils. The boiling of water is endothermic and the water is cooled (b →c), forming some ice. If the pump is left on, the ice will sublime until none is left. This is the basis of freeze drying.

118. $w = -P\Delta V$;   Assume a constant P of 1.00 atm.

$$V_{373} = \frac{nRT}{P} = \frac{1.00\,(0.8206)\,(373)}{1.00} = 30.6\,\text{L for one mol of water vapor}$$

Since the density of $H_2O(l)$ is 1.00 g/cm^3, 1.00 mol of $H_2O(l)$ occupies 18.0 cm^3 or 0.0180 L.

$w = -1.00\,\text{atm}\,(30.6\,\text{L} - 0.0180\,\text{L}) = -30.6\,\text{L atm}$

$w = -30.6\,\text{L atm} \times 101.3\,\text{J/L}\bullet\text{atm} = -3.10 \times 10^3\,\text{J} = -3.10\,\text{kJ}$

$\Delta E = q + w = 40.7\ kJ - 3.10\ kJ = 37.6\ kJ$

$\dfrac{37.6}{40.7} \times 100 = 92.4\%$ of the energy goes to increase the internal energy of the water.

The remainder of the energy (7.6%) goes to do work against the atmosphere.

119.   For a cube: $(body\ diagonal)^2 = (face\ diagonal)^2 + (cube\ edge\ length)^2$

In a simple cubic structure, the atoms touch on cube edge so the cube edge = 2 r where r = radius of sphere.

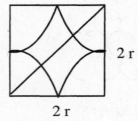

2 r

face diagonal $= \sqrt{(2\,r)^2 + (2\,r)^2} = \sqrt{4\,r^2 + 4\,r^2} = r\sqrt{8} = 2\sqrt{2}\ r$

body diagonal $= \sqrt{(2\sqrt{2}\,r)^2 + (2\,r)^2} = \sqrt{12\,r^2} = 2\sqrt{3}\ r$

The diameter of the hole = body diagonal − 2 radius of atoms at corners.

diameter $= 2\sqrt{3}\ r - 2\,r$; Thus, the radius of the hole is: $\dfrac{2\sqrt{3}\,r - 2\,r}{2} = \left(\dfrac{2\sqrt{3}-2}{2}\right)r$

The volume of the hole is: $\dfrac{4}{3}\pi\left[\left(\dfrac{2\sqrt{3}-2}{2}\right)r\right]^3$

120. C_2H_6O, $2(4) + 6(1) + 6 = 20\ e^-$; Determining the two possible structures is trial and error. Because hydrogen is always attached with a single bond, H cannot be a central atom. The two possible structures having two bonds and two lone pairs for O are:

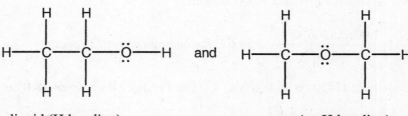

liquid (H-bonding)   gas (no H-bonding)

The first structure with the –OH bond is capable of forming hydrogen bonding; the other structure is not. Therefore, the liquid (which has the stronger intermolecular forces) is the first structure and the gas is the second structure.

Integrative Problems

121.   molar mass XY = $\dfrac{19.0\,g}{0.132\,mol}$ = 144 g/mol

X: [Kr] $5s^2 4d^{10}$; This is cadmium, Cd.

molar mass Y = 144 − 112.4 = 32 g/mol; Y is sulfur, S.

The semiconductor is CdS. The dopant has the electron configuration of bromine, Br. Because Br has one more valence electron than S, doping with Br will produce an n-type semiconductor.

122.   Assuming 100.00 g of MO_2:

$$23.72\,g\,O \times \frac{1\,mol\,O}{16.00\,g\,O} = 1.483\,mol\,O$$

$$1.483\,mol\,O \times \frac{1\,mol\,M}{2\,mol\,O} = 0.7415\,mol\,M$$

100.00 g − 23.72 g = 76.28 g M

$$molar\,mass\,M = \frac{76.28\,g}{0.7415\,mol} = 102.9\,g/mol$$

From the periodic table element M is rhodium, Rh.

The unit cell for cubic closest packing is face-centered cubic (4 atoms/unit cell). The atoms for fcc are assumed to touch along the face diagonal of the cube so face diagonal = 4 r. The distance between the centers of touching Rh atoms will be the distance of 2 r where r = radius of Rh atom.

face diagonal = $\sqrt{2}\ l$, where l = cube edge

face diagonal = 4 r = 2 × 269.0 × 10^{-12} m = 5.380 × 10^{-10} m

$\sqrt{2}\ l$ = 4 r = 5.38 × 10^{-10} m, $l = \dfrac{5.38 \times 10^{-10}\,m}{\sqrt{2}}$ = 3.804 × 10^{-10} m = 3.804 × 10^{-8} cm

$$density = \frac{4\,atoms\,Rh \times \dfrac{1\,mol\,Rh}{6.0221 \times 10^{23}\,atoms} \times \dfrac{102.9\,g\,Rh}{mol\,Rh}}{(3.804 \times 10^{-8}\,cm)^3} = 12.42\,g/cm^3$$

123. $\ln\left(\dfrac{P_1}{P_2}\right) = \dfrac{\Delta H_{vap}}{R}\left(\dfrac{1}{T_2} - \dfrac{1}{T_1}\right);\quad \Delta H_{vap} = \dfrac{296\,J}{g} \times \dfrac{200.6\,g}{mol} = 5.94 \times 10^4\ J/mol\ Hg$

$$\ln\left(\dfrac{2.56\times10^{-3}\ torr}{P_2}\right) = \dfrac{5.94\times10^4\ J/mol}{8.3145\times10^4\ J/K \bullet mol}\left(\dfrac{1}{573\ K} - \dfrac{1}{298.2\ K}\right)$$

$$\ln\left(\dfrac{2.56\times10^{-3}\ torr}{P_2}\right) = -11.5,\quad P_2 = 2.56\times10^{-3}\ torr/e^{-11.5} = 253\ torr$$

$$n = \dfrac{PV}{RT} = \dfrac{\left(253\ torr \times \dfrac{1\,atm}{760\,torr}\right)\times15.0\,L}{\dfrac{0.08206\ L\ atm}{K\ mol}\times573\ K} = 0.106\ mol\ Hg$$

$$0.106\ mol\ Hg \times \dfrac{6.022\times10^{23}\ atoms\ Hg}{mol\ Hg} = 6.38\times10^{22}\ atoms\ Hg$$

Marathon Problem

124. $q = s \times m \times \Delta T$; heat loss by metal = heat gain by calorimeter. The change in temperature for the calorimeter is: $\Delta T = 25.2°C \pm 0.2°C - 25.0°C \pm 0.2°C$. Including the error limits, ΔT can range from $0.0°C$ to $0.4°C$. Because the temperature change can be $0.0°C$, there is no way that the calculated heat capacity has any meaning.

The density experiment is also not conclusive.

$$d = \dfrac{4\,g}{0.42\ cm^3} = 10\ g/cm^3\ (1\ significant\ figure)$$

$$d_{high} = \dfrac{5\,g}{0.40\ cm^3} = 12.5\ g/cm^3 = 10\ g/cm^3\ to\ 1\ sig\ fig$$

$$d_{low} = \dfrac{3\,g}{0.44\ cm^3} = 7\ g/cm^3$$

From Table 1.5, the density of copper is $8.96\ g/cm^3$. The results from this experiment cannot be used to distinguish between a density of $8.96\ g/cm^3$ and $9.2\ g/cm^3$.

The crystal structure determination is more conclusive. Assuming the metal is copper:

$$volume\ of\ unit\ cell = (600.\ pm)^3\left(\dfrac{1\times10^{-10}\ cm}{1\,pm}\right)^3 = 2.16\times10^{-22}\ cm^3$$

$$\text{Cu mass in unit cell} = 4 \text{ atoms} \times \frac{1 \text{ mol Cu}}{6.022 \times 10^{23} \text{ atoms}} \times \frac{63.55 \text{ g Cu}}{\text{mol Cu}} = 4.221 \times 10^{-22} \text{ g Cu}$$

$$d = \frac{\text{mass}}{\text{volume}} = \frac{4.221 \times 10^{-22} \text{ g}}{2.16 \times 10^{-22} \text{ cm}^3} = 1.95 \text{ g/cm}^3$$

Because the density of Cu is 8.96 g/cm^3, then one can assume this metal is not copper. If the metal is not Cu, then it must be kryptonite (as the question reads). Because we don't know the molar mass of kryptonite, we cannot confirm that the calculated density would be close to 9.2 g/cm^3.

To improve the heat capacity experiment, a more precise balance is a must and a more precise temperature reading is needed. Also, a larger piece of the metal should be used so that ΔT of the calorimeter has more significant figures. For the density experiment, we would need a more precise balance and a more precise way to determine the volume. Again, a larger piece of metal would help in order to insure more significant figures in the volume.

CHAPTER ELEVEN

PROPERTIES OF SOLUTIONS

For Review

1. Mass percent: the percent by mass of the solute in the solution.

    Mole fraction: the ratio of the number of moles of a given component to the total number of moles of solution.

    Molarity: the number of moles of solute per liter of solution.

    Molality: the number of moles of solute per kilogram of solvent.

    Volume is temperature dependent, whereas mass and the number of moles are not. Only molarity has a volume term so only molarity is temperature dependent.

2. $KF(s) \rightarrow K^+(aq) + F^-(aq)$ $\Delta H = \Delta H_{soln}$; $K^+(g) + Cl^-(g) \rightarrow K^+(aq) + F^-(aq)$ $\Delta H = \Delta H_{hyd}$

    $$\begin{array}{ll} KF(s) \rightarrow K^+(g) + F^-(g) & \Delta H_1 = -\Delta H_{LE} \\ K^+(g) + F^-(g) \rightarrow K^+(aq) + F^-(aq) & \Delta H_2 = \Delta H_{hyd} \end{array}$$

    $$KF(s) \rightarrow K^+(aq) + F^-(aq) \qquad \Delta H = \Delta H_{soln} = -\Delta H_{LE} + \Delta H_{hyd}$$

    It is true that ΔH_1 and ΔH_2 have large magnitudes for their values; however, the signs are opposite (ΔH_1 is large and positive because it is the reverse of the lattice energy and ΔH_2, the hydration energy, is large and negative). These two ΔH values basically cancel out each other giving a ΔH_{soln} value close to zero.

3. "Like dissolves like" refers to the nature of the intermolecular forces. Polar solutes and ionic solutes dissolve in polar solvents because the types of intermolecular forces present in solute and solvent are similar. When they dissolve, the strength of the intermolecular forces in solution are about the same as in pure solute and pure solvent. The same is true for nonpolar solutes in nonpolar solvents. The strength of the intermolecular forces (London dispersion forces) are about the same in solution as in pure solute and pure solvent. In all cases of like dissolves like, the magnitude of ΔH_{soln} is either a small positive number (endothermic) or a small negative number (exothermic). For polar solutes in nonpolar solvents and vice versa, ΔH_{soln} is a very large, unfavorable value (very endothermic). Because the energetics are so unfavorable, polar solutes do not dissolve in nonpolar solvents and vice versa.

4. Structure effects refer to solute and solvent having similar polarities in order for solution formation to occur. Hydrophobic solutes are mostly nonpolar substances that are "water-fearing." Hydrophilic solutes are mostly polar or ionic substances that are "water-loving."

Pressure has little effect on the solubilities of solids or liquids; it does significantly affect the solubility of a gas. Henry's law states that the amount of a gas dissolved in a solution is directly proportional to the pressure of the gas above the solution (C = kP). The equation for Henry's law works best for dilute solutions of gases that do not dissociate in or react with the solvent. HCl(g) does not follow Henry's law because it dissociates into $H^+(aq)$ and $Cl^-(aq)$ in solution (HCl is a strong acid). For O_2 and N_2, Henry's law works well since these gases do not react with the water solvent.

An increase in temperature can either increase or decrease the solubility of a solid solute in water. It is true that a solute dissolves more rapidly with an increase in temperature, but the amount of solid solute that dissolves to form a saturated solution can either decrease or increase with temperature. The temperature effect is difficult to predict for solid solutes. However, the temperature effect for gas solutes is easier to predict as the solubility of a gas typically decreases with increasing temperature.

5. Raoult's law: $P_{soln} = \chi_{solvent} P^o_{solvent}$; When a solute is added to a solvent, the vapor pressure of a solution is lowered from that of the pure solvent. The quantity $\chi_{solvent}$, the mole fraction of solvent, is the fraction that the solution vapor pressure is lowered.

For the experiment illustrated in Fig. 11.9, the beaker of water will stop having a net transfer of water molecules out of the beaker when the equilibrium vapor pressure, $P^o_{H_2O}$, is reached. This can never happen. The beaker with the solution wants an equilibrium vapor pressure of P_{H_2O}, which is less than $P^o_{H_2O}$. When the vapor pressure over the solution is above P_{H_2O}, a net transfer of water molecules into the solution will occur in order to try to reduce the vapor pressure to P_{H_2O}. The two beakers can never obtain the equilibrium vapor pressure they want. The net transfer of water molecules from the beaker of water to the beaker of solution stops after all of the water has evaporated.

If the solute is volatile, then we can get a transfer of both the solute and solvent back and forth between the beakers. A state can be reached in this experiment where both beakers have the same solute concentration and hence the same vapor pressure. When this state is reached, no net transfer of solute or water molecules occurs between the beakers so the levels of solution remain constant.

When both substances in a solution are volatile, then Raoult's law applies to both. The total vapor pressure above the solution is the equilibrium vapor pressure of the solvent plus the equilibrium vapor pressure of the solute. Mathematically:

$$P_{TOT} = P_A + P_B = \chi_A P^o_A + \chi_B P^o_B$$

where A is either the solute or solvent and B is the other one.

6. An ideal liquid-liquid solution follows Raoult's law:

$$P_{TOT} = \chi_A P^o_A + \chi_B P^o_B$$

A nonideal liquid-liquid solution does not follow Raoult's law, either giving a total pressure greater than predicted by Raoult's law (positive deviation) or less than predicted (negative deviation).

In an ideal solution, the strength of the intermolecular forces in solution are equal to the strength of the intermolecular forces in pure solute and pure solvent. When this is true, ΔH_{soln} = 0 and ΔT_{soln} = 0. For positive deviations from Raoult's law, the solution has weaker intermolecular forces in solution than in pure solute and pure solvent. Positive deviations have $\Delta H_{soln} > 0$ (are endothermic) and $\Delta T_{soln} < 0$. For negative deviations, the solution has stronger intermolecular forces in solution than in pure solute or pure solvent. Negative deviations have $\Delta H_{soln} < 0$ (are exothermic) and $\Delta T_{soln} > 0$. Examples of each type of solution are:

ideal:	benzene-toluene
positive deviations:	ethanol-hexane
negative deviations:	acetone-water

7.   Colligative properties are properties of a solution that depend only on the number, not the identity, of the solute particles. A solution of some concentration of glucose ($C_6H_{12}O_6$) has the same colligative properties as a solution of sucrose ($C_{12}H_{22}O_{11}$) having the same concentration.

A substance freezes when the vapor pressure of the liquid and solid are identical to each other. Adding a solute to a substance lowers the vapor pressure of the liquid. A lower temperature is needed to reach the point where the vapor pressures of the solution and solid are identical. Hence, the freezing point is depressed when a solution forms.

A substance boils when the vapor pressure of the liquid equals the external pressure. Because a solute lowers the vapor pressure of the liquid, a higher temperature is needed to reach the point where the vapor pressure of the liquid equals the external pressure. Hence, the boiling point is elevated when a solution forms.

The equation to calculate the freezing point depression or boiling point elevation is:

$\Delta T = Km$

where K is the freezing point or boiling point constant for the solvent and m is the molality of the solute. Table 11.5 lists the K values for several solvents. The solvent which shows the largest change in freezing point for a certain concentration of solute is camphor; it has the largest K_f value. Water, with the smallest K_b value, will show the smallest increase in boiling point for a certain concentration of solute.

To calculate molar mass, you need to know the mass of the unknown solute, the mass and identity of solvent used, and the change in temperature (ΔT) of the freezing or boiling point of the solution. Since the mass of unknown solute is known, one manipulates the freezing point data to determine the number of moles of solute present. Once the mass and moles of solute are known, one can determine the molar mass of the solute. To determine the moles of solute present, one determines the molality of the solution from the freezing point data and multiplies this by the kilograms of solvent present; this equals the moles of solute present.

8.   Osmotic pressure: the pressure that must be applied to a solution to stop osmosis; osmosis is the flow of solvent into the solution through a semipermeable membrane. The equation to calculate osmotic pressure, π, is:

$\pi = MRT$

where M is the molarity of the solution, R is the gas constant, and T is the Kelvin temperature. The molarity of a solution approximately equals the molality of the solution when 1 kg solvent ≈ 1 L solution. This occurs for dilute solutions of water since $d_{H_2O} = 1.00$ g/cm^3.

With addition of salt or sugar, the osmotic pressure inside the fruit cells (and bacteria) is less than outside the cell. Water will leave the cells which will dehydrate bacteria present, causing them to die.

Dialysis allows the transfer of solvent and small solute molecules through a membrane. To purify blood, the blood is passed through a cellophane tube (the semipermeable membrane); this cellophane tube is immersed in a dialyzing solution which contains the same concentrations of ions and small molecules as in blood, but has none of the waste products normally removed by the kidney. As blood is passed through the dialysis machine, the unwanted waste products pass through the cellophane membrane, cleansing the blood.

Desalination is the removal of dissolved salts from an aqueous solution. Here, a solution is subjected to a pressure greater than the osmotic pressure and reverse osmosis occurs, i.e., water passes from the solution through the semipermeable membrane back into pure water. Desalination plants can turn sea-water with its high salt content into drinkable water.

9.   A strong electrolyte completely dissociates into ions in solution, a weak electrolyte only partially dissociates into ions in solution, and a nonelectrolyte does not dissociate into ions when dissolved in solution. Colligative properties depend on the total number of solute particles in solution. By measuring a property such as freezing point depression, boiling point elevation, or osmotic pressure, we can determine the number of solute particles present from the solute and thus characterize the solute as a strong, weak, or nonelectrolyte.

The van't Hoff factor, i, is the number of moles of particles (ions) produced for every mol of solute dissolved. For NaCl, i = 2 since Na$^+$ and Cl$^-$ are produced in water; for Al(NO$_3$)$_3$, i = 4 since Al^{3+} and 3 NO$_3^-$ ions are produced when Al(NO$_3$)$_3$ dissolves in water. In real life, the van't Hoff factor is rarely the value predicted by the number of ions a salt dissolves into; i is generally something less than the predicted number of ions. This is due to a phenomenon called ion pairing where at any instant a small percentage of oppositely charged ions pair up and act like a single solute particle. Ion pairing occurs most when the concentration of ions is large. Therefore, dilute solutions behave most ideally; here i is close to that determined by the number of ions in a salt.

10.   A colloidal dispersion is a suspension of particles in a dispersing medium. See Table 11.7 for some examples of different types of colloids.

Both solutions and colloids have suspended particles in some medium. The major difference between the two is the size of the particles. A colloid is a suspension of relatively large particles as compared to a solution. Because of this, colloids will scatter light while solutions will not. The scattering of light by a colloidal suspension is called the Tyndall effect.

Coagulation is the destruction of a colloid by the aggregation of many suspended particles to form a large particle that settles out of solution.

Solution Review

9. $$\dfrac{585\ \text{g C}_3\text{H}_7\text{OH} \times \dfrac{1\ \text{mol C}_3\text{H}_7\text{OH}}{60.09\ \text{g C}_3\text{H}_7\text{OH}}}{1.00\ \text{L}} = 9.74\ M$$

10. $1.28\ \text{g CaCl}_2 \times \dfrac{1\ \text{mol CaCl}_2}{110.98\ \text{g CaCl}_2} \times \dfrac{1\ \text{L}}{0.580\ \text{mol CaCl}_2} \times \dfrac{1000\ \text{mL}}{\text{L}} = 19.9\ \text{mL}$

11. $\text{mol Na}_2\text{CO}_3 = 0.0700\ \text{L} \times \dfrac{3.0\ \text{mol Na}_2\text{CO}_3}{\text{L}} = 0.21\ \text{mol Na}_2\text{CO}_3$

   $\text{Na}_2\text{CO}_3(s) \rightarrow 2\ \text{Na}^+(aq) + \text{CO}_3{}^{2-}(aq);\ \ \text{mol Na}^+ = 2(0.21) = 0.42\ \text{mol}$

   $\text{mol NaHCO}_3 = 0.0300\ \text{L} \times \dfrac{1.0\ \text{mol NaHCO}_3}{\text{L}} = 0.030\ \text{mol NaHCO}_3$

   $\text{NaHCO}_3(s) \rightarrow \text{Na}^+(aq) + \text{HCO}_3{}^-(aq);\ \ \text{mol Na}^+ = 0.030\ \text{mol}$

   $M_{\text{Na}^+} = \dfrac{\text{total mol Na}^+}{\text{total volume}} = \dfrac{0.42\ \text{mol} + 0.030\ \text{mol}}{0.0700\ \text{L} + 0.030\ \text{L}} = \dfrac{0.45\ \text{mol}}{0.1000\ \text{L}} = 4.5\ M\ \text{Na}^+$

12.   a. $\text{HNO}_3(l) \rightarrow \text{H}^+(aq) + \text{NO}_3{}^-(aq)$ b. $\text{Na}_2\text{SO}_4(s) \rightarrow 2\ \text{Na}^+(aq) + \text{SO}_4{}^{2-}(aq)$

   c. $\text{Al(NO}_3)_3(s) \rightarrow \text{Al}^{3+}(aq) + 3\ \text{NO}_3{}^-(aq)$ d. $\text{SrBr}_2(s) \rightarrow \text{Sr}^{2+}(aq) + 2\ \text{Br}^-(aq)$

   e. $\text{KClO}_4(s) \rightarrow \text{K}^+(aq) + \text{ClO}_4{}^-(aq)$ f. $\text{NH}_4\text{Br}(s) \rightarrow \text{NH}_4{}^+(aq) + \text{Br}^-(aq)$

   g. $\text{NH}_4\text{NO}_3(s) \rightarrow \text{NH}_4{}^+(aq) + \text{NO}_3{}^-(aq)$ h. $\text{CuSO}_4(s) \rightarrow \text{Cu}^{2+}(aq) + \text{SO}_4{}^{2-}(aq)$

   i. $\text{NaOH}(s) \rightarrow \text{Na}^+(aq) + \text{OH}^-(aq)$

Questions

13.   As the temperature increases, the gas molecules will have a greater average kinetic energy. A greater fraction of the gas molecules in solution will have kinetic energy greater than the attractive forces between the gas molecules and the solvent molecules. More gas molecules will escape to the vapor phase and the solubility of the gas will decrease.

14.   Henry's law is obeyed most accurately for dilute solutions of gases that do not dissociate in or react with the solvent. NH_3 is a weak base and reacts with water by the following reaction:

   $\text{NH}_3(aq) + \text{H}_2\text{O}(l) \rightarrow \text{NH}_4{}^+(aq) + \text{OH}^-(aq)$

   O_2 will bind to hemoglobin in the blood. Due to these reactions in the solvent, $NH_3(g)$ in water and $O_2(g)$ in blood do not follow Henry's law.

15   Because the solute is volatile, both the water and solute will transfer back and forth between the two beakers. The volume in each beaker will become constant when the concentrations of solute in the beakers are equal to each other. Because the solute is less volatile than water, one would expect there to be a larger net transfer of water molecules into the right beaker than the net transfer of solute molecules into the left beaker. This results in a larger solution volume in the right beaker when equilibrium is reached, i.e., when the solute concentration is identical in each beaker.

16.   Solutions of A and B have vapor pressures less than ideal (see Figure 11.13 of the text), so this plot shows negative deviations from Rault's law. Negative deviations occur when the intermolecular forces are stronger in solution than in pure solvent and solute. This results in an exothermic enthalpy of solution. The only statement that is false is e. A substance boils when the vapor pressure equals the external pressure. Since $\chi_B = 0.6$ has a lower vapor pressure at the temperature of the plot than either pure A or pure B, then one would expect this solution to require the highest temperature in order for the vapor pressure to reach the external pressure. Therefore, the solution with $\chi_B = 0.6$ will have a higher boiling point than either pure A or pure B. (Note that because $P°_B > P°_A$, B is more volatile than A, and B will have a lower boiling point temperature than A).

17.   No, the solution is not ideal. For an ideal solution, the strength of intermolecular forces in solution is the same as in pure solute and pure solvent. This results in $\Delta H_{soln} = 0$ for an ideal solution. ΔH_{soln} for methanol/water is not zero. Because $\Delta H_{soln} < 0$ (heat is released), this solution shows a negative deviation from Raoult's law.

18.   The micelles form so the ionic ends of the detergent molecules, the SO_4^- ends, are exposed to the polar water molecules on the outside, while the nonpolar hydrocarbon chains from the detergent molecules are hidden from the water by pointing toward the inside of the micelle. Dirt, which is basically nonpolar, is stabilized in the nonpolar interior of the micelle and is washed away.

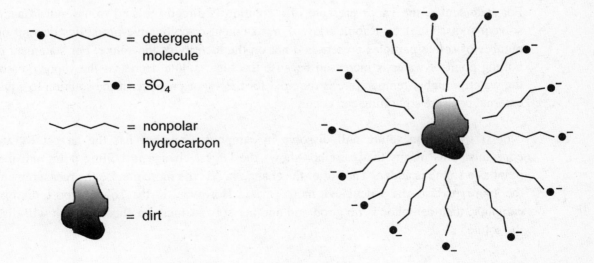

19.   Normality is the number of equivalents per liter of solution. For an acid or a base, an equivalent is the mass of acid or base that can furnish 1 mol of protons (if an acid) or accept 1

mol of protons (if a base). A proton is an H^+ ion. Molarity is defined as the moles of solute per liter of solution. When the number of equivalents equals the number of moles of solute, then normality = molarity. This is true for acids which only have one acidic proton in them and for bases that accept only one proton per formula unit. Examples of acids where equivalents = moles solute are HCl, HNO_3, HF, and $HC_2H_3O_2$. Examples of bases where equivalents = moles solute are NaOH, KOH, and NH_3. When equivalents ≠ moles solute, then normality ≠ molarity. This is true for acids that donate more than one proton (H_2SO_4, H_3PO_4, H_2CO_3, etc.) and for bases that react with more than one proton per formula unit [$Ca(OH)_2$, $Ba(OH)_2$, $Sr(OH)_2$, etc.].

20. It is true that the sodium chloride lattice must be broken in order to dissolve in water, but a lot of energy is released when the water molecules hydrate the Na^+ and Cl^- ions. These two processes have relatively large values for the amount of energy associated with them, but they are opposite in sign. The end result is they basically cancel each other out resulting in a ΔH_{soln} ≈ 0. So energy is not the reason why ionic solids like NaCl are so soluble in water. The answer lies in nature's tendency toward the higher probability of the mixed state. Processes, in general, are favored that result in an increase in disorder because the disordered state is the easiest (most probable) state to achieve. The tendency of processes to increase disorder will be discussed in Chapter 16 when entropy, S, is introduced.

21. Only statement b is true. A substance freezes when the vapor pressure of the liquid and solid are the same. When a solute is added to water, the vapor pressure of the solution at 0°C is less than the vapor pressure of the solid and the net result is for any ice present to convert to liquid in order to try to equalize the vapor pressures (which never can occur at 0°C). A lower temperature is needed to equalize the vapor pressure of water and ice, hence the freezing point is depressed.

For statement a, the vapor pressure of a solution is directly related to the mole fraction of solvent (not solute) by Raoult's law. For statement c, colligative properties depend on the number of solute particles present and not on the identity of the solute. For statement d, the boiling point of water is increased because the sugar solute decreases the vapor pressure of the water; a higher temperature is required for the vapor pressure of the solution to equal the external pressure so boiling can occur.

22. This is true if the solute will dissolve in camphor. Camphor has the largest K_b and K_f constants. This means that camphor shows the largest change in boiling point and melting point as a solute is added. The larger the change in ΔT, the more precise the measurement and the more precise the calculated molar mass. However, if the solute won't dissolve in camphor, then camphor is no good and another solvent must be chosen which will dissolve the solute.

23. Isotonic solutions are those which have identical osmotic pressures. Crenation and hemolysis refer to phenomena that occur when red blood cells are bathed in solutions having a mismatch in osmotic pressures inside and outside the cell. When red blood cells are in a solution having a higher osmotic pressure than that of the cells, the cells shrivel as there is a net transfer of

water out of the cells. This is called crenation. Hemolysis occurs when the red blood cells are bathed in a solution having lower osmotic pressure than that inside the cell. Here, the cells rupture as there is a net transfer of water to into the red blood cells.

24.   Ion pairing is a phenomenon that occurs in solution when oppositely charged ions aggregate and behave as a single particle. For example, when NaCl is dissolved in water, one would expect sodium chloride to exist as separate hydrated Na^+ ions and Cl^- ions. A few ions, however, stay together as NaCl and behave as just one particle. Ion pairing increases in a solution as the ion concentration increases (as the molality increases).

Exercises

Concentration of Solutions

25.   Because the density of water is 1.00 g/mL, 100.0 mL of water has a mass of 100. g.

$$\text{density} = \frac{\text{mass}}{\text{volume}} = \frac{10.0 \text{ g H}_3\text{PO}_4 + 100. \text{ g H}_2\text{O}}{104 \text{ mL}} = 1.06 \text{ g/mL} = 1.06 \text{ g/cm}^3$$

$$\text{mol H}_3\text{PO}_4 = 10.0 \text{ g} \times \frac{1 \text{ mol}}{97.99 \text{ g}} = 0.102 \text{ mol H}_3\text{PO}_4$$

$$\text{mol H}_2\text{O} = 100. \text{ g} \times \frac{1 \text{ mol}}{18.02 \text{ g}} = 5.55 \text{ mol H}_2\text{O}$$

$$\text{mole fraction of H}_3\text{PO}_4 = \frac{0.102 \text{ mol H}_3\text{PO}_4}{(0.102 + 5.55) \text{ mol}} = 0.0180$$

$$\chi_{\text{H}_2\text{O}} = 1.000 - 0.0180 = 0.9820$$

$$\text{molarity} = \frac{0.102 \text{ mol H}_3\text{PO}_4}{0.104 \text{ L}} = 0.981 \text{ mol/L}$$

$$\text{molality} = \frac{0.102 \text{ mol H}_3\text{PO}_4}{0.100 \text{ kg}} = 1.02 \text{ mol/kg}$$

26. $$\text{molality} = \frac{40.0 \text{ g EG}}{60.0 \text{ g H}_2\text{O}} \times \frac{1000 \text{ g}}{\text{kg}} \times \frac{1 \text{ mol EG}}{62.07 \text{ g}} = 10.7 \text{ mol/kg}$$

where EG = ethylene glycol $(C_2H_6O_2)$

$$\text{molarity} = \frac{40.0 \text{ g EG}}{100.0 \text{ g solution}} \times \frac{1.05 \text{ g}}{\text{cm}^3} \times \frac{1000 \text{ cm}^3}{\text{L}} \times \frac{1 \text{ mol}}{62.07 \text{ g}} = 6.77 \text{ mol/L}$$

$$40.0 \text{ g EG} \times \frac{1 \text{ mol}}{62.07 \text{ g}} = 0.644 \text{ mol EG}; \quad 60.0 \text{ g H}_2\text{O} \times \frac{1 \text{ mol}}{18.02 \text{ g}} = 3.33 \text{ mol H}_2\text{O}$$

$$\chi_{EG} = \frac{0.644}{3.33 + 0.644} = 0.162 = \text{mole fraction ethylene glycol}$$

27.   Hydrochloric acid:

$$\text{molarity} = \frac{38 \text{ g HCl}}{100. \text{ g soln}} \times \frac{1.19 \text{ g soln}}{\text{cm}^3 \text{ soln}} \times \frac{1000 \text{ cm}^3}{\text{L}} \times \frac{1 \text{ mol HCl}}{36.46 \text{ g}} = 12 \text{ mol/L}$$

$$\text{molality} = \frac{38 \text{ g HCl}}{62 \text{ g solvent}} \times \frac{1000 \text{ g}}{\text{kg}} \times \frac{1 \text{ mol HCl}}{36.46 \text{ g}} = 17 \text{ mol/kg}$$

$$38 \text{ g HCl} \times \frac{1 \text{ mol}}{36.46 \text{ g}} = 1.0 \text{ mol HCl}; \quad 62 \text{ g H}_2\text{O} \times \frac{1 \text{ mol}}{18.02 \text{ g}} = 3.4 \text{ mol H}_2\text{O}$$

$$\text{mole fraction of HCl} = \chi_{HCl} = \frac{1.0}{3.4 + 1.0} = 0.23$$

Nitric acid:

$$\frac{70. \text{ g HNO}_3}{100. \text{ g soln}} \times \frac{1.42 \text{ g soln}}{\text{cm}^3 \text{ soln}} \times \frac{1000 \text{ cm}^3}{\text{L}} \times \frac{1 \text{ mol HNO}_3}{63.02 \text{ g}} = 16 \text{ mol/L}$$

$$\frac{70. \text{ g HNO}_3}{30. \text{ g solvent}} \times \frac{1000 \text{ g}}{\text{kg}} \times \frac{1 \text{ mol HNO}_3}{63.02 \text{ g}} = 37 \text{ mol/kg}$$

$$70. \text{ g HNO}_3 \times \frac{1 \text{ mol}}{63.02 \text{ g}} = 1.1 \text{ mol HNO}_3; \quad 30. \text{ g H}_2\text{O} \times \frac{1 \text{ mol}}{18.02 \text{ g}} = 1.7 \text{ mol H}_2\text{O}$$

$$\chi_{HNO_3} = \frac{1.1}{1.7 + 1.1} = 0.39$$

Sulfuric acid:

$$\frac{95 \text{ g H}_2\text{SO}_4}{100. \text{ g soln}} \times \frac{1.84 \text{ g soln}}{\text{cm}^3 \text{ soln}} \times \frac{1000 \text{ cm}^3}{\text{L}} \times \frac{1 \text{ mol H}_2\text{SO}_4}{98.09 \text{ g H}_2\text{SO}_4} = 18 \text{ mol/L}$$

$$\frac{95 \text{ g H}_2\text{SO}_4}{5 \text{ g H}_2\text{O}} \times \frac{1000 \text{ g}}{\text{kg}} \times \frac{1 \text{ mol}}{98.09 \text{ g}} = 194 \text{ mol/kg} \approx 200 \text{ mol/kg}$$

$$95 \text{ g H}_2\text{SO}_4 \times \frac{1 \text{ mol}}{98.09 \text{ g}} = 0.97 \text{ mol H}_2\text{SO}_4; \quad 5 \text{ g H}_2\text{O} \times \frac{1 \text{ mol}}{18.02 \text{ g}} = 0.3 \text{ mol H}_2\text{O}$$

$$\chi_{H_2SO_4} = \frac{0.97}{0.97 + 0.3} = 0.76$$

Acetic Acid:

$$\frac{99 \text{ g HC}_2\text{H}_3\text{O}_2}{100. \text{ g soln}} \times \frac{1.05 \text{ g soln}}{\text{cm}^3 \text{ soln}} \times \frac{1000 \text{ cm}^3}{\text{L}} \times \frac{1 \text{ mol}}{60.05 \text{ g H}} = 17 \text{ mol/L}$$

$$\frac{99 \text{ g HC}_2\text{H}_3\text{O}_2}{1 \text{ g H}_2\text{O}} \times \frac{1000 \text{ g}}{\text{kg}} \times \frac{1 \text{ mol}}{60.05 \text{ g}} = 1600 \text{ mol/kg} \approx 2000 \text{ mol/kg}$$

$$99 \text{ g HC}_2\text{H}_3\text{O}_2 \times \frac{1 \text{ mol}}{60.05 \text{ g}} = 1.6 \text{ mol HC}_2\text{H}_3\text{O}_2; \; 1 \text{ g H}_2\text{O} \times \frac{1 \text{ mol}}{18.02 \text{ g}} = 0.06 \text{ mol H}_2\text{O}$$

$$\chi_{\text{HC}_2\text{H}_3\text{O}_2} = \frac{1.6}{1.6 + 0.06} = 0.96$$

Ammonia:

$$\frac{28 \text{ g NH}_3}{100. \text{ g soln}} \times \frac{0.90 \text{ g}}{\text{cm}^3} \times \frac{1000 \text{ cm}^3}{\text{L}} \times \frac{1 \text{ mol}}{17.03 \text{ g}} = 15 \text{ mol/L}$$

$$\frac{28 \text{ g NH}_3}{72 \text{ g H}_2\text{O}} \times \frac{1000 \text{ g}}{\text{kg}} \times \frac{1 \text{ mol}}{17.03 \text{ g}} = 23 \text{ mol/kg}$$

$$28 \text{ g NH}_3 \times \frac{1 \text{ mol}}{17.03 \text{ g}} = 1.6 \text{ mol NH}_3; \; 72 \text{ g H}_2\text{O} \times \frac{1 \text{ mol}}{18.02 \text{ g}} = 4.0 \text{ mol H}_2\text{O}$$

$$\chi_{\text{NH}_3} = \frac{1.6}{4.0 + 1.6} = 0.29$$

28.   a.   If we use 100. mL (100. g) of H_2O, we need:

$$0.100 \text{ kg H}_2\text{O} \times \frac{2.0 \text{ mol KCl}}{\text{kg}} \times \frac{74.55 \text{ g}}{\text{mol KCl}} = 14.9 \text{ g} = 15 \text{ g KCl}$$

Dissolve 15 g KCl in 100. mL H_2O to prepare a 2.0 m KCl solution. This will give us slightly more than 100 mL, but this will be the easiest way to make the solution. Since we don't know the density of the solution, we can't calculate the molarity and use a volumetric flask to make exactly 100 mL of solution.

b.   If we took 15 g NaOH and 85 g H_2O, the volume would probably be less than 100 mL. To make sure we have enough solution, let's use 100. mL H_2O (100. g). Let x = mass of NaCl.

$$\text{mass \% NaOH} = 15 = \frac{x}{100. + x} \times 100, \quad 1500 + 15\,x = 100.\,x, \; x = 17.6 \text{ g} \approx 18 \text{ g}$$

Dissolve 18 g NaOH in 100. mL H_2O to make a 15% NaOH solution by mass.

c. In a fashion similar to part b, let's use 100. mL CH_3OH. Let x = mass of NaOH.

$$100. \text{ mL } CH_3OH \times \frac{0.79 \text{ g}}{\text{mL}} = 79 \text{ g } CH_3OH$$

$$\text{mass \% NaOH} = 25 = \frac{x}{79 + x} \times 100, \quad 25(79) + 25\,x = 100.\,x, \quad x = 26.3 \text{ g} \approx 26 \text{ g}$$

Dissolve 26 g NaOH in 100. mL CH_3OH.

d. To make sure we have enough solution, let's use 100. mL (100. g) of H_2O. Let x = mol $C_6H_{12}O_6$.

$$100. \text{ g } H_2O \times \frac{1 \text{ mol } H_2O}{18.02 \text{ g}} = 5.55 \text{ mol } H_2O$$

$$\chi_{C_6H_{12}O_6} = 0.10 = \frac{x}{x + 5.55}; \quad 0.10\,x + 0.56 = x, \quad x = 0.62 \text{ mol } C_6H_{12}O_6$$

$$0.62 \text{ mol } C_6H_{12}O_6 \times \frac{180.16 \text{ g}}{\text{mol}} = 110 \text{ g } C_6H_{12}O_6$$

Dissolve 110 g $C_6H_{12}O_6$ in 100. mL of H_2O to prepare a solution with $\chi_{C_6H_{12}O_6} = 0.10$.

29. $25 \text{ mL } C_5H_{12} \times \dfrac{0.63 \text{ g}}{\text{mL}} = 16 \text{ g } C_5H_{12};$ $25 \text{ mL} \times \dfrac{0.63 \text{ g}}{\text{mL}} \times \dfrac{1 \text{ mol}}{72.15 \text{ g}} = 0.22 \text{ mol } C_5H_{12}$

$45 \text{ mL } C_6H_{14} \times \dfrac{0.66 \text{ g}}{\text{mL}} = 30. \text{ g } C_6H_{14};$ $45 \text{ mL} \times \dfrac{0.66 \text{ g}}{\text{mL}} \times \dfrac{1 \text{ mol}}{86.17 \text{ g}} = 0.34 \text{ mol } C_6H_{14}$

$$\text{mass \% pentane} = \frac{\text{mass pentane}}{\text{total mass}} \times 100 = \frac{16 \text{ g}}{16 \text{ g} + 30. \text{ g}} = 35\%$$

$$\chi_{\text{pentane}} = \frac{\text{mol pentane}}{\text{total mol}} = \frac{0.22 \text{ mol}}{0.22 \text{ mol} + 0.34 \text{ mol}} = 0.39$$

$$\text{molality} = \frac{\text{mol pentane}}{\text{kg hexane}} = \frac{0.22 \text{ mol}}{0.030 \text{ kg}} = = 7.3 \text{ mol/kg}$$

$$\text{molarity} = \frac{\text{mol pentane}}{\text{L solution}} = \frac{0.22 \text{ mol}}{25 \text{ mL} + 45 \text{ mL}} \times \frac{1000 \text{ mL}}{1 \text{ L}} = 3.1 \text{ mol/L}$$

30. If there are 100.0 mL of wine:

$$12.5 \text{ mL } C_2H_5OH \times \frac{0.789 \text{ g}}{\text{mL}} = 9.86 \text{ g } C_2H_5OH \text{ and } 87.5 \text{ mL } H_2O \times \frac{1.00 \text{ g}}{\text{mL}} = 87.5 \text{ g } H_2O$$

$$\text{mass \% ethanol} = \frac{9.86}{87.5 + 9.86} \times 100 = 10.1\% \text{ by mass}$$

$$\text{molality} = \frac{9.86 \text{ g } C_2H_5OH}{0.0875 \text{ kg } H_2O} \times \frac{1 \text{ mol}}{46.07 \text{ g}} = 2.45 \text{ mol/kg}$$

31.   If we have 1.00 L of solution:

$$1.37 \text{ mol citric acid} \times \frac{192.12 \text{ g}}{\text{mol}} = 263 \text{ g citric acid } (H_3C_6H_5O_7)$$

$$1.00 \times 10^3 \text{ mL solution} \times \frac{1.10 \text{ g}}{\text{mL}} = 1.10 \times 10^3 \text{ g solution}$$

$$\text{mass \% of citric acid} = \frac{263 \text{ g}}{1.10 \times 10^3 \text{ g}} \times 100 = 23.9\%$$

In 1.00 L of solution, we have 263 g citric acid and $(1.10 \times 10^3 - 263) = 840$ g of H_2O.

$$\text{molality} = \frac{1.37 \text{ mol citric acid}}{0.84 \text{ kg } H_2O} = 1.6 \text{ mol/kg}$$

$$840 \text{ g } H_2O \times \frac{1 \text{ mol}}{18.02 \text{ g}} = 47 \text{ mol } H_2O; \quad \chi_{\text{citric acid}} = \frac{1.37}{47 + 1.37} = 0.028$$

Since citric acid is a triprotic acid, the number of protons citric acid can provide is three times the molarity. Therefore, normality = 3 × molarity:

$$\text{normality} = 3 \times 1.37 \, M = 4.11 \, N$$

32. $\dfrac{1.00 \text{ mol acetone}}{1.00 \text{ kg ethanol}} = 1.00 \text{ molal}; \quad 1.00 \times 10^3 \text{ g } C_2H_5OH \times \dfrac{1 \text{ mol}}{46.07 \text{ g}} = 21.7 \text{ mol } C_2H_5OH$

$$\chi_{\text{acetone}} = \frac{1.00}{1.00 + 21.7} = 0.0441$$

$$1 \text{ mol } CH_3COCH_3 \times \frac{58.08 \text{ g } CH_3COCH_3}{\text{mol } CH_3COCH_3} \times \frac{1 \text{ mL}}{0.788 \text{ g}} = 73.7 \text{ mL } CH_3COCH_3$$

$$1.00 \times 10^3 \text{ g ethanol} \times \frac{1 \text{ mL}}{0.789 \text{ g}} = 1270 \text{ mL}; \quad \text{Total volume} = 1270 + 73.7 = 1340 \text{ mL}$$

$$\text{molarity} = \frac{1.00 \text{ mol}}{1.34 \text{ L}} = 0.746 \, M$$

Energetics of Solutions and Solubility

33.   Using Hess's law:

$$NaI(s) \rightarrow Na^+(g) + I^-(g) \qquad\qquad \Delta H = -\Delta H_{LE} = -(-686 \text{ kJ/mol})$$

$$Na^+(g) + I^-(g) \rightarrow Na^+(aq) + I^-(aq) \qquad \Delta H = \Delta H_{hyd} = -694 \text{ kJ/mol}$$

$$NaI(s) \rightarrow Na^+(aq) + I^-(aq) \qquad\qquad \Delta H_{soln} = -8 \text{ kJ/mol}$$

ΔH_{soln} refers to the heat released or gained when a solute dissolves in a solvent. Here, an ionic compound dissolves in water.

34.   a. $$CaCl_2(s) \rightarrow Ca^{2+}(g) + 2\ Cl^-(g) \qquad \Delta H = -\Delta H_{LE} = -(-2247 \text{ kJ})$$

$$Ca^{2+}(g) + 2\ Cl^-(g) \rightarrow Ca^{2+}(aq) + 2\ Cl^-(aq) \qquad \Delta H = \Delta H_{hyd}$$

$$CaCl_2(s) \rightarrow Ca^{2+}(aq) + 2\ Cl^-(aq) \qquad \Delta H_{soln} = -46 \text{ kJ}$$

$-46 \text{ kJ} = 2247 \text{ kJ} + \Delta H_{hyd},\ \ \Delta H_{hyd} = -2293 \text{ kJ}$

$$CaI_2(s) \rightarrow Ca^{2+}(g) + 2\ I^-(g) \qquad \Delta H = -\Delta H_{LE} = -(-2059 \text{ kJ})$$

$$Ca^{2+}(g) + 2\ I^-(g) \rightarrow Ca^{2+}(aq) + 2\ I^-(aq) \qquad \Delta H = \Delta H_{hyd}$$

$$CaI_2(s) \rightarrow Ca^{2+}(aq) + 2\ I^-(aq) \qquad \Delta H_{soln} = -104 \text{ kJ}$$

$-104 \text{ kJ} = 2059 \text{ kJ} + \Delta H_{hyd},\ \ \Delta H_{hyd} = -2163 \text{ kJ}$

   b. The enthalpy of hydration for $CaCl_2$ is more exothermic than for CaI_2. Any differences must be due to differences in hydration between Cl^- and I^-. Thus, the chloride ion is more strongly hydrated as compared to the iodide ion.

35.   Both $Al(OH)_3$ and NaOH are ionic compounds. Since the lattice energy is proportional to the charge of the ions, the lattice energy of aluminum hydroxide is greater than that of sodium hydroxide. The attraction of water molecules for Al^{3+} and OH^- cannot overcome the larger lattice energy and $Al(OH)_3$ is insoluble. For NaOH, the favorable hydration energy is large enough to overcome the smaller lattice energy and NaOH is soluble.

36.   The dissolving of an ionic solute in water can be thought of as taking place in two steps. The first step, called the lattice energy term, refers to breaking apart the ionic compound into gaseous ions. This step, as indicated in the problem requires a lot of energy and is unfavorable. The second step, called the hydration energy term, refers to the energy released when the separated gaseous ions are stabilized as water molecules surround the ions. Since the interactions between water molecules and ions are strong, a lot of energy is released when ions are hydrated. Thus, the dissolution process for ionic compounds can be thought of as consisting of an unfavorable and a favorable energy term. These two processes basically cancel each other out; so when ionic solids dissolve in water, the heat released or gained is minimal, and the temperature change is minimal.

37.   Water is a polar solvent and dissolves polar solutes and ionic solutes. Carbon tetrachloride (CCl_4) is a nonpolar solvent and dissolves nonpolar solutes (like dissolves like). To predict the polarity of the following molecules, draw the correct Lewis structure and then determine if the individual bond dipoles cancel or not. If the bond dipoles are arranged in such a manner that they cancel each other out, then the molecule is nonpolar. If the bond dipoles do not cancel each other out, then the molecule is polar.

a. KrF_2, $8 + 2(7) = 22$ e⁻

:F—Kr—F:

nonpolar; soluble in CCl_4

b. SF_2, $6 + 2(7) = 20$ e⁻

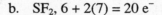

polar; soluble in H_2O

c. SO_2, $6 + 2(6) = 18$ e⁻

    + 1 more

polar; soluble in H_2O

d. CO_2, $4 + 2(6) = 16$ e⁻

Ö=C=Ö

nonpolar; soluble in CCl_4

e. MgF_2 is an ionic compound so it is soluble in water.

f. CH_2O, $4 + 2(1) + 6 = 12$ e⁻

:O:
‖
C
/ \
H   H

polar; soluble in H_2O

g. C_2H_4, $2(4) + 4(1) = 12$ e⁻

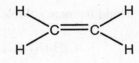

nonpolar (like all compounds made up of only carbon and hydrogen); soluble in CCl_4

38.   a. water   b. water   c. hexane   d. water

39.   Water is a polar molecule capable of hydrogen bonding. Polar molecules, especially molecules capable of hydrogen bonding, and ions are all attracted to water. For covalent compounds, as polarity increases, the attraction to water increases. For ionic compounds, as the charge of the ions increases and/or the size of the ions decreases, the attraction to water increases.

a. CH_3CH_2OH; CH_3CH_2OH is polar while $CH_3CH_2CH_3$ is nonpolar.

b. $CHCl_3$; $CHCl_3$ is polar while CCl_4 is nonpolar.

c. CH_3CH_2OH; CH_3CH_2OH is much more polar than $CH_3(CH_2)_{14}CH_2OH$.

40.   For ionic compounds, as the charge of the ions increases and/or the size of the ions decreases, the attraction to water (hydration) increases.

a. Mg^{2+}; smaller size, higher charge

b. Be^{2+}; smaller

c. Fe^{3+}; smaller size, higher charge

d. F^-; smaller

e. Cl^-; smaller

f. SO_4^{2-}; higher charge

41.   As the length of the hydrocarbon chain increases, the solubility decreases. The $-OH$ end of the alcohols can hydrogen bond with water. The hydrocarbon chain, however, is basically nonpolar and interacts poorly with water. As the hydrocarbon chain gets longer, a greater portion of the molecule cannot interact with the water molecules and the solubility decreases, i.e., the effect of the $-OH$ group decreases as the alcohols get larger.

42.   Benzoic acid is capable of hydrogen bonding, but a significant part of benzoic acid is the non-polar benzene ring which is composed of only carbon and hydrogen. In benzene, a hydrogen bonded dimer forms:

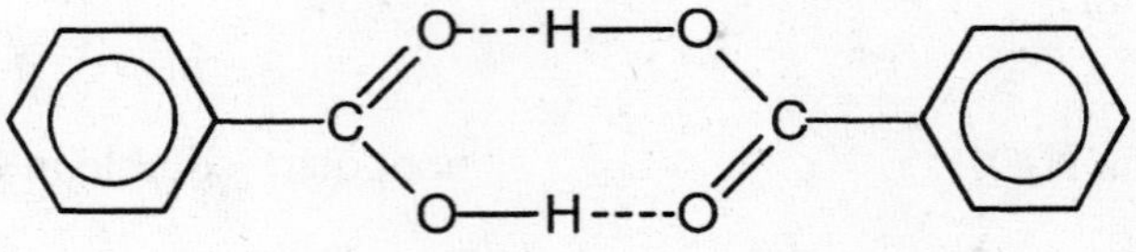

The dimer is relatively nonpolar since the polar part of benzoic acid is hidden in the dimer formation. Thus, benzoic acid is more soluble in benzene than in water due to the dimer formation.

Benzoic acid would be more soluble in 0.1 M NaOH because of the reaction:

$$C_6H_5CO_2H + OH^- \rightarrow C_6H_5CO_2^- + H_2O$$

By removing the proton from benzoic acid, an anion forms, and like all anions, the species becomes more soluble in water.

43. $C = kP$, $\dfrac{8.21 \times 10^{-4} \text{ mol}}{L} = k \times 0.790 \text{ atm}$, $k = 1.04 \times 10^{-3} \text{ mol/L} \cdot \text{atm}$

$C = kP$, $C = \dfrac{1.04 \times 10^{-4} \text{ mol}}{L \text{ atm}} \times 1.10 \text{ atm} = 1.14 \times 10^{-3} \text{ mol/L}$

44.   750. mL grape juice $\times \dfrac{12 \text{ mL } C_2H_5OH}{100. \text{ mL juice}} \times \dfrac{0.79 \text{ g } C_2H_5OH}{mL} \times \dfrac{1 \text{ mol } C_2H_5OH}{46.07 \text{ g}}$

$\times \dfrac{2 \text{ mol } CO_2}{2 \text{ mol } C_2H_5OH} = 1.54 \text{ mol } CO_2$ (carry extra significant figure)

1.54 mol CO_2 = total mol CO_2 = mol $CO_2(g)$ + mol $CO_2(aq)$ = $n_g + n_{aq}$

$$P_{CO_2} = \frac{n_g RT}{V} = \frac{n_g\left(\frac{0.08206 \text{ L atm}}{\text{mol K}}\right)(298 \text{ K})}{75 \times 10^{-3} \text{ L}} = 326 \, n_g$$

$$P_{CO_2} = \frac{C}{k} = \frac{\frac{n_{aq}}{0.750 \text{ L}}}{\frac{3.1 \times 10^{-2} \text{ mol}}{\text{L atm}}} = 43.0 \, n_{aq} = 43.0 \, n_{aq}$$

$P_{CO_2} = 326 \, n_g = 43.0 \, n_{aq}$ and from above $n_{aq} = 1.54 - n_g$; Solving:

$$326 \, n_g = 43.0(1.54 - n_g), \quad 369 \, n_g = 66.2, \quad n_g = 0.18 \text{ mol}$$

$P_{CO_2} = 326(0.18) = 59$ atm in gas phase

$$C = kP_{CO_2} = \frac{3.1 \times 10^{-2} \text{ mol}}{\text{L atm}} \times 59 \text{ atm}, \; C = 1.8 \text{ mol CO}_2/\text{L in wine}$$

Vapor Pressures of Solutions

45. $\text{mol C}_3\text{H}_8\text{O}_3 = 164 \text{ g} \times \dfrac{1 \text{ mol}}{92.09 \text{ g}} = 1.78 \text{ mol C}_3\text{H}_8\text{O}_3$

$\text{mol H}_2\text{O} = 338 \text{ mL} \times \dfrac{0.992 \text{ g}}{\text{mL}} \times \dfrac{1 \text{ mol}}{18.02 \text{ g}} = 18.6 \text{ mol H}_2\text{O}$

$P_{H_2O} = \chi_{H_2O} P^o_{H_2O} = \dfrac{18.6 \text{ mol}}{(1.78 + 18.6) \text{ mol}} \times 54.74 \text{ torr} = 0.913 \times 54.74 \text{ torr} = 50.0 \text{ torr}$

46. $P_{C_2H_5OH} = \chi_{C_2H_5OH} P^o_{C_2H_5OH}; \; \chi_{C_2H_5OH} = \dfrac{\text{mol C}_2\text{H}_5\text{OH solution}}{\text{total mol in solution}}$

$53.6 \text{ g C}_3\text{H}_8\text{O}_3 \times \dfrac{1 \text{ mol C}_3\text{H}_8\text{O}_3}{92.09 \text{ g}} = 0.582 \text{ mol C}_3\text{H}_8\text{O}_3$

$133.7 \text{ g C}_2\text{H}_5\text{OH} \times \dfrac{1 \text{ mol C}_2\text{H}_5\text{OH}}{46.07 \text{ g}} = 2.90 \text{ mol C}_2\text{H}_5\text{OH}; \; \text{total mol} = 0.582 + 2.90$

$$= 3.48 \text{ mol}$$

$113 \text{ torr} = \dfrac{2.90 \text{ mol}}{3.48 \text{ mol}} \times P^o_{C_2H_5OH}, \; P^o_{C_2H_5OH} = 136 \text{ torr}$

47. $P_B = \chi_B P_B^o$, $\chi_B = P_B / P_B^o$ = 0.900 atm/0.930 atm = 0.968

$0.968 = \dfrac{\text{mol benzene}}{\text{total mol}}$; mol benzene = 78.11 g $C_6H_6 \times \dfrac{1\,\text{mol}}{78.11\,\text{g}}$ = 1.000 mol

Let x = mol solute, then: $\chi_B = 0.968 = \dfrac{1.000\,\text{mol}}{1.000 + x}$, $0.968 + 0.968\,x = 1.000$, $x = 0.033$ mol

molar mass = $\dfrac{10.0\,\text{g}}{0.033\,\text{mol}}$ = 303 g/mol $\approx 3.0 \times 10^2$ g/mol

48. 19.6 torr = χ_{H_2O} (23.8 torr), χ_{H_2O} = 0.824; χ_{solute} = 1.000 − 0.824 = 0.176

0.176 is the mol fraction of all the solute particles present. Since NaCl dissolves to produce two ions in solution (Na^+ and Cl^-), 0.176 is the mole fraction of Na^+ and Cl^- ions present (assuming complete dissociation of NaCl).

At 45°C, P_{H_2O} = 0.824 (71.9 torr) = 59.2 torr

49. a. 25 mL $C_5H_{12} \times \dfrac{0.63\,\text{g}}{\text{mL}} \times \dfrac{1\,\text{mol}}{72.15\,\text{g}}$ = 0.22 mol C_5H_{12}

45 mL $C_6H_{14} \times \dfrac{0.66\,\text{g}}{\text{mL}} \times \dfrac{1\,\text{mol}}{86.17\,\text{g}}$ = 0.34 mol C_6H_{14}; total mol = 0.22 + 0.34 = 0.56 mol

$\chi_{pen}^L = \dfrac{\text{mol pentane in solution}}{\text{total mol in solution}} = \dfrac{0.22\,\text{mol}}{0.56\,\text{mol}}$ = 0.39, χ_{hex}^L = 1.00 − 0.39 = 0.61

$P_{pen} = \chi_{pen}^L P_{pen}^o$ = 0.39(511 torr) = 2.0×10^2 torr; P_{hex} = 0.61(150. torr) = 92 torr

$P_{total} = P_{pen} + P_{hex} = 2.0 \times 10^2 + 92$ = 292 torr = 290 torr

b. From Chapter 5 on gases, the partial pressure of a gas is proportional to the number of moles of gas present. For the vapor phase:

$\chi_{pen}^V = \dfrac{\text{mol pentane in vapor}}{\text{total mol vapor}} = \dfrac{P_{pen}}{P_{total}} = \dfrac{2.0 \times 10^2\,\text{torr}}{290\,\text{torr}}$ = 0.69

Note: In the Solutions Guide, we have added V or L to the mole fraction symbol to emphasize the value for which we are solving. If the L or V is omitted, then the liquid phase is assumed.

50. $P_{total} = P_{CH_2Cl_2} + P_{CH_2Br_2}$; $P = \chi^L P^o$; $\chi_{CH_2Cl_2}^L = \dfrac{0.0300\,\text{mol CH}_2\text{Cl}_2}{0.0800\,\text{mol total}}$ = 0.375

P_{total} = 0.375 (133 torr) + (1.000 − 0.375) (11.4 torr) = 49.9 + 7.13 = 57.0 torr

In the vapor: $\chi_{CH_2Cl_2}^V = \dfrac{P_{CH_2Cl_2}}{P_{total}} = \dfrac{49.9 \text{ torr}}{57.0 \text{ torr}} = 0.875$; $\chi_{CH_2Br_2}^V = 1.000 - 0.875 = 0.125$

51. $P_{total} = P_{meth} + P_{prop}$, 174 torr $= \chi_{meth}^L$ (303 torr) $+ \chi_{prop}^L$ (44.6 torr); $\chi_{prop}^L = 1.000 - \chi_{meth}^L$

$174 = 303\ \chi_{meth}^L + (1.000 - \chi_{meth}^L)\ 44.6$, $\dfrac{129}{258} = \chi_{meth}^L = 0.500$; $\chi_{prop}^L = 1.000 - 0.500 = 0.500$

52. $P_{tol} = \chi_{tol}^L P_{tol}^o$; $P_{ben} = \chi_{ben}^L P_{ben}^o$; For the vapor, $\chi_A^V = P_A / P_{total}$. Since the mole fractions of benzene and toluene are equal in the vapor phase, then $P_{tol} = P_{ben}$.

$\chi_{tol}^L P_{tol}^o = \chi_{ben}^L P_{ben}^o = (1.00 - \chi_{tol}^L) P_{ben}^o$, χ_{tol}^L (28 torr) $= (1.00 - \chi_{tol}^L)$ 95 torr

$123\ \chi_{tol}^L = 95$, $\chi_{tol}^L = 0.77$; $\chi_{ben}^L = 1.00 - 0.77 = 0.23$

53.   Compared to H_2O, solution d (methanol/water) will have the highest vapor pressure because methanol is more volatile than water. Both solution b (glucose/water) and solution c (NaCl/water) will have a lower vapor pressure than water by Raoult's law. NaCl dissolves to give Na^+ ions and Cl^- ions; glucose is a nonelectrolyte. Since there are more solute particles in solution c, the vapor pressure of solution c will be the lowest.

54.   Solution d (methanol/water); Methanol is more volatile than water, which will increase the total vapor pressure to a value greater than the vapor pressure of pure water at this temperature.

55. $50.0 \text{ g CH}_3\text{COCH}_3 \times \dfrac{1 \text{ mol}}{58.08 \text{ g}} = 0.861$ mol acetone

$50.0 \text{ g CH}_3\text{OH} \times \dfrac{1 \text{ mol}}{32.04 \text{ g}} = 1.56$ mol methanol

$\chi_{acetone}^L = \dfrac{0.861}{0.861 + 1.56} = 0.356$; $\chi_{methanol}^L = 1.000 - \chi_{acetone}^L = 0.644$

$P_{total} = P_{methanol} + P_{acetone} = 0.644(143 \text{ torr}) + 0.356(271 \text{ torr}) = 92.1 \text{ torr} + 96.5 \text{ torr}$

$$= 188.6 \text{ torr}$$

Because partial pressures are proportional to the moles of gas present, then in the vapor phase:

$\chi_{acetone}^V = \dfrac{P_{acetone}}{P_{total}} = \dfrac{96.5 \text{ torr}}{188.6 \text{ torr}} = 0.512$; $\chi_{methanol}^V = 1.000 - 0.512 = 0.488$

The actual vapor pressure of the solution (161 torr) is less than the calculated pressure assuming ideal behavior (188.6 torr). Therefore, the solution exhibits negative deviations from Raoult's law. This occurs when the solute-solvent interactions are stronger than in pure solute and pure solvent.

56. a. An ideal solution would have a vapor pressure at any mole fraction of H_2O between that of pure propanol and pure water (between 74.0 torr and 71.9 torr). The vapor pressures of the solutions are not between these limits, so water and propanol do not make ideal solutions.

     b. From the data, the vapor pressures of the various solutions are greater than in the ideal solution (positive deviation from Raoult's law). This occurs when the intermolecular forces in solution are weaker than the intermolecular forces in pure solvent and pure solute. This gives rise to endothermic (positive) ΔH_{soln} values.

     c. The interactions between propanol and water molecules are weaker than between the pure substances since this solution exhibits a positive deviation from Raoult's law.

     d. At $\chi_{H_2O} = 0.54$, the vapor pressure is highest as compared to the other solutions. Since a solution boils when the vapor pressure of the solution equals the external pressure, the $\chi_{H_2O} = 0.54$ solution should have the lowest normal boiling point; this solution will have a vapor pressure equal to 1 atm at a lower temperature than the other solutions.

Colligative Properties

57. $\text{molality} = m = \dfrac{\text{mol solute}}{\text{kg solvent}} = \dfrac{27.0\,\text{g N}_2\text{H}_4\text{CO}}{150.0\,\text{g H}_2\text{O}} \times \dfrac{1000\,\text{g}}{\text{kg}} \times \dfrac{1\,\text{mol N}_2\text{H}_4\text{CO}}{60.06\,\text{g N}_2\text{H}_4\text{CO}} = 3.00\ \text{molal}$

$\Delta T_b = K_b m = \dfrac{0.51\,°\text{C}}{\text{molal}} \times 3.00\ \text{molal} = 1.5\,°\text{C}$

The boiling point is raised from 100.0°C to 101.5°C (assuming P = 1 atm).

58. $\Delta T_b = 77.85\,°\text{C} - 76.50\,°\text{C} = 1.35\,°\text{C};\quad m = \dfrac{\Delta T_b}{K_b} = \dfrac{1.35\,°\text{C}}{5.03\,°\text{C kg} / \text{mol}} = 0.268\ \text{mol/kg}$

$\text{mol biomolecule} = 0.0150\ \text{kg solvent} \times \dfrac{0.268\ \text{mol hydrocarbon}}{\text{kg solvent}} = 4.02 \times 10^{-3}\ \text{mol}$

From the problem, 2.00 g biomolecule was used that must contain 4.02×10^{-3} mol biomolecule. The molar mass of the biomolecule is:

$\dfrac{2.00\,\text{g}}{4.02 \times 10^{-3}\ \text{mol}} = 498\ \text{g/mol}$

59. $\Delta T_f = K_f m,\ \ \Delta T_f = 1.50\,°\text{C} = \dfrac{1.86\,°\text{C}}{\text{molal}} \times m,\ \ m = 0.806\ \text{mol/kg}$

$0.200\ \text{kg H}_2\text{O} \times \dfrac{0.806\ \text{mol C}_3\text{H}_8\text{O}_3}{\text{kg H}_2\text{O}} \times \dfrac{92.09\ \text{g C}_3\text{H}_8\text{O}_3}{\text{mol C}_3\text{H}_8\text{O}_3} = 14.8\ \text{g C}_3\text{H}_8\text{O}_3$

60. $\Delta T_f = 25.50°C - 24.59°C = 0.91°C = K_f m$, $m = \dfrac{0.91°C}{9.1°C/molal} = 0.10$ mol/kg

mass $H_2O = 0.0100$ kg t-butanol $\left(\dfrac{0.10 \text{ mol } H_2O}{\text{kg t – butanol}}\right)\left(\dfrac{18.02 \text{ g } H_2O}{\text{mol } H_2O}\right) = 0.018$ g H_2O

61.   molality $= m = \dfrac{50.0 \text{ g } C_2H_6O_2}{50.0 \text{ g } H_2O} \times \dfrac{1000 \text{ g}}{\text{kg}} \times \dfrac{1 \text{ mol}}{62.07 \text{ g}} = 16.1$ mol/kg

$\Delta T_f = K_f m = 1.86°C/molal \times 16.1$ molal $= 29.9°C$; $T_f = 0.0°C - 29.9°C = -29.9°C$

$\Delta T_b = K_b m = 0.51°C/molal \times 16.1$ molal $= 8.2°C$; $T_b = 100.0°C + 8.2°C = 108.2°C$

62. $m = \dfrac{\Delta T_f}{K_f} = \dfrac{25.0°C}{1.86 °C \text{ kg}/mol} = 13.4$ mol $C_2H_6O_2$/kg

Since the density of water is 1.00 g/cm^3, the moles of $C_2H_6O_2$ needed are:

15.0 L $H_2O \times \dfrac{1.00 \text{ kg } H_2O}{\text{L } H_2O} \times \dfrac{13.4 \text{ mol } C_2H_6O_2}{\text{kg } H_2O} = 201$ mol $C_2H_6O_2$

Volume $C_2H_6O_2 = 201$ mol $C_2H_6O_2 \times \dfrac{62.07 \text{ g}}{\text{mol } C_2H_6O_2} \times \dfrac{1 \text{ cm}^3}{1.11 \text{ g}} = 11,200 \text{ cm}^3 = 11.2$ L

$\Delta T_b = K_b m = \dfrac{0.51°C}{molal} \times 13.4$ molal $= 6.8°C$, $T_b = 100.0°C + 6.8°C = 106.8°C$

63. $\Delta T_f = K_f m$, $m = \dfrac{\Delta T_f}{K_f} = \dfrac{0.300°C}{5.12 °C \text{ kg}/mol} = \dfrac{5.86 \times 10^{-2} \text{ mol thyroxine}}{\text{kg benzene}}$

The mol of thyroxine present is:

0.0100 kg benzene $\times \dfrac{5.86 \times 10^{-2} \text{ mol thyroxine}}{\text{kg benzene}} = 5.86 \times 10^{-4}$ mol thyroxine

From the problem, 0.455 g thyroxine were used; this must contain 5.86×10^{-4} mol thyroxine. The molar mass of the thyroxine is:

molar mass $= \dfrac{0.455 \text{ g}}{5.86 \times 10^{-4} \text{ mol}} = 776$ g/mol

64.   empirical formula mass $\approx 7(12) + 4(1) + 16 = 104$ g/mol

$\Delta T_f = K_f m$, $m = \dfrac{\Delta T_f}{K_f} = \dfrac{22.3°C}{40. °C/molal} = 0.56$ molal

$$\text{mol anthraquinone} = 0.0114 \text{ kg solvent} \times \frac{0.56 \text{ mol anthraquinone}}{\text{kg solvent}} = 6.4 \times 10^{-3} \text{ mol}$$

$$\text{molar mass} = \frac{1.32 \text{ g}}{6.4 \times 10^{-3} \text{ mol}} = 210 \text{ g/mol}$$

$$\frac{\text{molar mass}}{\text{empirical formula mass}} = \frac{210}{104} = 2.0; \quad \text{molecular formula} = C_{14}H_8O_2$$

65. a. $M = \dfrac{1.0 \text{ g protein}}{L} \times \dfrac{1 \text{ mol}}{9.0 \times 10^{-4} \text{ g}} = 1.1 \times 10^{-5} \text{ mol/L}; \quad \pi = MRT$

At 298 K: $\pi = \dfrac{1.1 \times 10^{-5} \text{ mol}}{L} \times \dfrac{0.08206 \text{ L atm}}{\text{mol K}} \times 298 \text{ K} \times \dfrac{760 \text{ torr}}{\text{atm}}, \quad \pi = 0.20 \text{ torr}$

Because d = 1.0 g/cm^3, 1.0 L solution has a mass of 1.0 kg. Because only 1.0 g of protein is present per liter of solution, 1.0 kg of H_2O is present and molality equals molarity.

$$\Delta T_f = K_f m = \frac{1.86 \,^\circ\text{C}}{\text{molal}} \times 1.1 \times 10^{-5} \text{ molal} = 2.0 \times 10^{-5} \,^\circ\text{C}$$

b. Osmotic pressure is better for determining the molar mass of large molecules. A temperature change of $10^{-5} \,^\circ\text{C}$ is very difficult to measure. A change in height of a column of mercury by 0.2 mm (0.2 torr) is not as hard to measure precisely.

66. $M = \dfrac{\pi}{RT} = \dfrac{0.74 \text{ torr} \times \dfrac{1 \text{ atm}}{760 \text{ torr}}}{\dfrac{0.08206 \text{ L atm}}{\text{mol K}} \times 300. \text{ K}} = 4.0 \times 10^{-5} \text{ mol/L}$

$$1.00 \text{ L} \times \frac{4.0 \times 10^{-5} \text{ mol}}{L} = 4.0 \times 10^{-5} \text{ mol catalase}$$

$$\text{molar mass} = \frac{10.00 \text{ g}}{4.0 \times 10^{-5} \text{ mol}} = 2.5 \times 10^5 \text{ g/mol}$$

67. $\pi = MRT, \quad M = \dfrac{\pi}{RT} = \dfrac{8.00 \text{ atm}}{\dfrac{0.08206 \text{ L atm}}{\text{mol K}} \times 298 \text{ K}} = 0.327 \text{ mol/L}$

68. $M = \dfrac{\pi}{RT} = \dfrac{15 \text{ atm}}{\dfrac{0.08206 \text{ L atm}}{\text{mol K}} \times 295 \text{ K}} = 0.62 \, M \text{ solute particles}$

This represents the total molarity of the solute particles. NaCl is a soluble ionic compound that breaks up into two ions, Na^+ and Cl^-. Therefore, the concentration of NaCl needed is $0.62/2 = 0.31 \, M$; this NaCl concentration will produce a 0.62 M solute particle solution assuming complete dissociation.

$$1.0 \text{ L} \times \frac{0.31 \text{ mol NaCl}}{\text{L}} \times \frac{58.44 \text{ g NaCl}}{\text{mol NaCl}} = 18.1 \approx 18 \text{ g NaCl}$$

Dissolve 18 g of NaCl in some water and dilute to 1.0 L in a volumetric flask. To get 0.31 ± 0.01 mol/L, we need 18.1 g ± 0.6 g NaCl in 1.00 L solution.

Properties of Electrolyte Solutions

69. $Na_3PO_4(s) \rightarrow 3 \text{ Na}^+(aq) + PO_4^{3-}(aq)$, i = 4.0; $CaBr_2(s) \rightarrow Ca^{2+}(aq) + 2 \text{ Br}^-(aq)$, i = 3.0

$KCl(s) \rightarrow K^+(aq) + Cl^-(aq)$, i = 2.0.

The effective particle concentrations of the solutions are:

4.0(0.010 molal) = 0.040 molal for Na_3PO_4 solution; 3.0(0.020 molal) = 0.060 molal for $CaBr_2$ solution; 2.0(0.020 molal) = 0.040 molal for KCl solution; slightly greater than 0.020 molal for HF solution since HF only partially dissociates in water (it is a weak acid).

a.   The 0.010 m Na_3PO_4 solution and the 0.020 m KCl solution both have effective particle concentrations of 0.040 m (assuming complete dissociation), so both of these solutions should have the same boiling point as the 0.040 m $C_6H_{12}O_6$ solution (a nonelectrolyte).

b. $P = \chi P°$; As the solute concentration decreases, the solvent's vapor pressure increases since χ increases. Therefore, the 0.020 m HF solution will have the highest vapor pressure since it has the smallest effective particle concentration.

c. $\Delta T = K_f m$; The 0.020 m $CaBr_2$ solution has the largest effective particle concentration so it will have the largest freezing point depression (largest ΔT).

70.   The solutions of $C_{12}H_{22}O_{11}$, NaCl and $CaCl_2$ will all have lower freezing points, higher boiling points and higher osmotic pressures than pure water. The solution with the largest particle concentration will have the lowest freezing point, the highest boiling point and the highest osmotic pressure. The $CaCl_2$ solution will have the largest effective particle concentration because it produces three ions per mol of compound.

a.   pure water   b. $CaCl_2$ solution   c. $CaCl_2$ solution

d.   pure water   e. $CaCl_2$ solution

71.   a. $MgCl_2(s) \rightarrow Mg^{2+}(aq) + 2 \text{ Cl}^-(aq)$, i = 3.0 mol ions/mol solute

$\Delta T_f = i K_f m = 3.0 \times 1.86°\text{C/molal} \times 0.050 \text{ molal} = 0.28°\text{C}$; $T_f = -0.28°\text{C}$ (Assuming water freezes at 0.00°C.)

$\Delta T_b = i K_b m = 3.0 \times 0.51°\text{C/molal} \times 0.050 \text{ molal} = 0.077°\text{C}$; $T_b = 100.077°\text{C}$ (Assuming water boils at 100.000°C.)

b. $FeCl_3(s) \rightarrow Fe^{3+}(aq) + 3\ Cl^-(aq)$, i = 4.0 mol ions/mol solute

$\Delta T_f = iK_f m = 4.0 \times 1.86°C/molal \times 0.050\ molal = 0.37°C$; $T_f = -0.37°C$

$\Delta T_b = iK_b m = 4.0 \times 0.51°C/molal \times 0.050\ molal = 0.10°C$; $T_b = 100.10°C$

72. $NaCl(s) \rightarrow Na^+(aq) + Cl^-(aq)$, i = 2.0

$$\pi = iMRT = 2.0 \times \frac{0.10\,mol}{L} \times \frac{0.08206\ L\ atm}{mol\ K} \times 293\ K = 4.8\ atm$$

A pressure greater than 4.8 atm should be applied to insure purification by reverse osmosis.

73. $\Delta T_f = iK_f m$, $i = \dfrac{\Delta T_f}{K_f m} = \dfrac{0.110°C}{1.86°C/molal \times 0.0225\ molal} = 2.63$ for 0.0225 m $CaCl_2$

$i = \dfrac{0.440}{1.86 \times 0.0910} = 2.60$ for 0.0910 m $CaCl_2$; $i = \dfrac{1.330}{1.86 \times 0.278} = 2.57$ for 0.278 m $CaCl_2$

$i_{ave} = (2.63 + 2.60 + 2.57)/3 = 2.60$

Note that i is less than the ideal value of 3.0 for $CaCl_2$. This is due to ion pairing in solution. Also note that as molality increases, i decreases. More ion pairing occurs as the solute concentration increases.

74.   a. $MgCl_2$, i(observed) = 2.7

$\Delta T_f = iK_f m = 2.7 \times 1.86°C/molal \times 0.050\ molal = 0.25°C$; $T_f = -0.25°C$

$\Delta T_b = iK_b m = 2.7 \times 0.51°C/molal \times 0.050\ molal = 0.069°C$; $T_b = 100.069°C$

b. $FeCl_3$, i(observed) = 3.4

$\Delta T_f = iK_f m = 3.4 \times 1.86\ °C/molal \times 0.050\ molal = 0.32°C$; $T_f = -0.32°C$

$\Delta T_b = iK_b m = 3.4 \times 0.51°C/molal \times 0.050\ molal = 0.087°C$; $T_b = 100.087°C$

75.   a. $T_C = 5(T_F - 32)/9 = 5(-29 - 32)/9 = -34°C$; Assuming the solubility of $CaCl_2$ is temperature independent, the molality of a saturated $CaCl_2$ solution is:

$$\frac{74.5\ g\ CaCl_2}{100.0\ g} \times \frac{1000\ g}{kg} \times \frac{1\ mol\ CaCl_2}{110.98\ g\ CaCl_2} = \frac{6.71\ mol\ CaCl_2}{kg\ H_2O}$$

$\Delta T_f = iK_f m = 3.00 \times 1.86°C\ kg/mol \times 6.71\ mol/kg = 37.4°C$

Assuming i = 3.00, a saturated solution of $CaCl_2$ can lower the freezing point of water to −37.4°C. Assuming these conditions, a saturated $CaCl_2$ solution should melt ice at −34°C (−29°F).

b.   From Exercise 11.73, $i_{ave} = 2.60$; $\Delta T_f = iK_f m = 2.60 \times 1.86 \times 6.71 = 32.4°C$

$T_f = -32.4°C$

Assuming $i = 2.60$, a saturated $CaCl_2$ solution will not melt ice at $-34°C(-29°F)$.

76. $\pi = iMRT$, $M = \dfrac{\pi}{iRT} = \dfrac{2.50\ atm}{2.00 \times \dfrac{0.08206\ L\ atm}{K\ mol} \times 298\ K} = 5.11 \times 10^{-2}\ mol/L$

molar mass of compound $= \dfrac{0.500\ g}{0.1000\ L \times \dfrac{5.11 \times 10^{-2}\ mol}{L}} = 97.8\ g/mol$

Additional Exercises

77   a. $NH_4NO_3(s) \rightarrow NH_4^+(aq) + NO_3^-(aq)$ $\Delta H_{soln} = ?$

Heat gain by dissolution process = heat loss by solution; We will keep all quantities positive in order to avoid sign errors. Since the temperature of the water decreased, the dissolution of NH_4NO_3 is endothermic (ΔH is positive). Mass of solution = 1.60 + 75.0 = 76.6 g.

heat loss by solution $= \dfrac{4.18\ J}{g\ °C} \times 76.6\ g \times (25.00°C - 23.34°C) = 532\ J$

$\Delta H_{soln} = \dfrac{532\ J}{1.60\ g\ NH_4NO_3} \times \dfrac{80.05\ g\ NH_4NO_3}{mol\ NH_4NO_3} = 2.66 \times 10^4\ J/mol = 26.6\ kJ/mol$

b.   We will use Hess's law to solve for the lattice energy. The lattice energy equation is:

$NH_4^+(g) + NO_3^-(g) \rightarrow NH_4NO_3(s)$ ΔH = lattice energy

$NH_4^+(g) + NO_3^-(g) \rightarrow NH_4^+(aq) + NO_3^-(aq)$ $\Delta H = \Delta H_{hyd} = -630.\ kJ/mol$

$NH_4^+(aq) + NO_3^-(aq) \rightarrow NH_4NO_3(s)$ $\Delta H = -\Delta H_{soln} = -26.6\ kJ/mol$

$\overline{NH_4^+(g) + NO_3^-(g) \rightarrow NH_4NO_3(s) \qquad\qquad\qquad \Delta H = \Delta H_{hyd} - \Delta H_{soln}}$

$= -657\ kJ/mol$

78.   The main intermolecular forces are: hexane (C_6H_{14}): London dispersion; chloroform ($CHCl_3$): dipole-dipole; London dispersion; methanol (CH_3OH): H bonding; H_2O: H bonding (two places)

There is a gradual change in the nature of the intermolecular forces (weaker to stronger). Each preceding solvent is miscible in its predecessor because there is not a great change in the strengths of the intermolecular forces from one solvent to the next.

79.   a.   Water boils when the vapor pressure equals the pressure above the water. In an open pan, $P_{atm} \approx 1.0$ atm. In a pressure cooker, $P_{inside} > 1.0$ atm, and water boils at a higher temperature. The higher the cooking temperature, the faster the cooking time.

b. Salt dissolves in water forming a solution with a melting point lower than that of pure water ($\Delta T_f = K_f m$). This happens in water on the surface of ice. If it is not too cold, the ice melts. This won't work if the ambient temperature is lower than the depressed freezing point of the salt solution.

c. When water freezes from a solution, it freezes as pure water, leaving behind a more concentrated salt solution. Therefore, the melt of frozen sea ice is pure water.

d. On the CO_2 phase diagram in chapter 10, the triple point is above 1 atm, so $CO_2(g)$ is the stable phase at 1 atm and room temperature. $CO_2(l)$ can't exist at normal atmospheric pressures. Therefore, dry ice sublimes instead of boils. In a fire extinguisher, $P > 1$ atm and $CO_2(l)$ can exist. When CO_2 is released from the fire extinguisher, $CO_2(g)$ forms as predicted from the phase diagram.

e. Adding a solute to a solvent increases the boiling point and decreases the freezing point of the solvent. Thus, the solvent is a liquid over a wider range of temperatures when a solute is dissolved.

80.   A 92 proof ethanol solution is 46% C_2H_5OH by volume. Assuming 100.0 mL of solution:

$$\text{mol ethanol} = 46 \text{ mL } C_2H_5OH \times \frac{0.79 \text{ g}}{\text{mL}} \times \frac{1 \text{ mol } C_2H_5OH}{46.07 \text{ g}} = 0.79 \text{ mol } C_2H_5OH$$

$$\text{molarity} = \frac{0.79 \text{ mol}}{0.1000 \text{ L}} = 7.9 \text{ } M \text{ ethanol}$$

81.   Because partial pressures are proportional to the moles of gas present, then $\chi_{CS_2}^V = P_{CS_2} / P_{tot}$.

$$P_{CS_2} = \chi_{CS_2}^V P_{tot} = 0.855 \text{ (263 torr)} = 225 \text{ torr}$$

$$P_{CS_2} = \chi_{CS_2}^L P_{CS_2}^o, \quad \chi_{CS_2}^L = \frac{P_{CS_2}}{P_{CS_2}^o} = \frac{225 \text{ torr}}{375 \text{ torr}} = 0.600$$

82. $$\pi = MRT = \frac{0.1 \text{ mol}}{L} \times \frac{0.08206 \text{ L atm}}{\text{mol K}} \times 298 \text{ K} = 2.45 \text{ atm} \approx 2 \text{ atm}$$

$$\pi = 2 \text{ atm} \times \frac{760 \text{ mm Hg}}{\text{atm}} \approx 2000 \text{ mm} \approx 2 \text{ m}$$

The osmotic pressure would support a mercury column of ≈ 2 m. The height of a fluid column in a tree will be higher because Hg is more dense than the fluid in a tree. If we assume the fluid in a tree is mostly H_2O, then the fluid has a density of $\approx 1.0 \text{ g/cm}^3$. The density of Hg is 13.6 g/cm^3.

Height of fluid $\approx 2 \text{ m} \times 13.6 \approx 30 \text{ m}$

83.   Out of 100.00 g, there are:

$$31.57 \text{ g C} \times \frac{1 \text{ mol C}}{12.01 \text{ g}} = 2.629 \text{ mol C}; \quad \frac{2.629}{2.629} = 1.000$$

$$5.30 \text{ g H} \times \frac{1 \text{ mol H}}{1.008 \text{ g}} = 5.26 \text{ mol H}; \quad \frac{5.26}{2.629} = 2.00$$

$$63.13 \text{ g O} \times \frac{1 \text{ mol O}}{16.00 \text{ g}} = 3.946 \text{ mol O}; \quad \frac{3.946}{2.629} = 1.501$$

empirical formula: $C_2H_4O_3$; Use the freezing point data to determine the molar mass.

$$m = \frac{\Delta T_f}{K_f} = \frac{5.20\,°C}{1.86\,°C/\text{molal}} = 2.80 \text{ molal}$$

$$\text{mol solute} = 0.0250 \text{ kg} \times \frac{2.80 \text{ mol solute}}{\text{kg}} = 0.0700 \text{ mol solute}$$

$$\text{molar mass} = \frac{10.56 \text{ g}}{0.0700 \text{ mol}} = 151 \text{ g/mol}$$

The empirical formula mass of $C_2H_4O_3$ = 76.05 g/mol. Since the molar mass is about twice the empirical mass, the molecular formula is $C_4H_8O_6$, which has a molar mass of 152.10 g/mol.

Note: We use the experimental molar mass to determine the molecular formula. Knowing this, we calculate the molar mass precisely from the molecular formula using the atomic masses in the periodic table.

84.   a.   As discussed in Figure 11.18 of the text, the water would migrate from right to left. Initially, the level of liquid in the right arm would go down and the level in the left arm would go up. At some point, the rate of solvent transfer would be the same in both directions and the levels of the liquids in the two arms would stabilize. The height difference between the two arms is a measure of the osmotic pressure of the NaCl solution.

        b.   Initially, H_2O molecules will have a net migration into the NaCl side. However, Na^+ and Cl^- ions can now migrate into the H_2O side. Because solute and solvent transfer are both possible, the levels of the liquids will be equal once the rate of solute and solvent transfer is equal in both directions. At this point, the concentration of Na^+ and Cl^- ions will be equal in both chambers and the levels of liquid will be equal.

85.   If ideal, NaCl dissociates completely and i = 2.00. $\Delta T_f = iK_f m$; Assuming water freezes at 0.00°C:

$$1.28°C = 2 \times 1.86°C \text{ kg/mol} \times m, \quad m = 0.344 \text{ mol NaCl/kg } H_2O$$

Assume an amount of solution which contains 1.00 kg of water (solvent).

$$0.344 \text{ mol NaCl} \times \frac{58.44 \text{ g}}{\text{mol}} = 20.1 \text{ g NaCl}; \quad \text{mass \% NaCl} = \frac{20.1 \text{ g}}{1.00 \times 10^3 \text{ g} + 20.1 \text{ g}} \times 100$$

$$= 1.97\%$$

86.   The main factor for stabilization seems to be electrostatic repulsion. The center of a colloid particle is surrounded by a layer of same charged ions, with opposite charged ions forming another charged layer on the outside. Overall, there are equal numbers of charged and oppositely charged ions, so the colloidal particles are electrically neutral. However, since the outer layers are the same charge, the particles repel each other and do not easily aggregate for precipitation to occur.

Heating increases the velocities of the colloidal particles. This causes the particles to collide with enough energy to break the ion barriers, allowing the colloids to aggregate and eventually precipitate out. Adding an electrolyte neutralizes the adsorbed ion layers which allows colloidal particles to aggregate and then precipitate out.

87. $\Delta T = K_f m$, $m = \dfrac{\Delta T}{K_f} = \dfrac{2.79°C}{1.86°C/molal} = 1.50$ molal

a. $\Delta T = K_b m$, $\Delta T = (0.51°C/molal)(1.50 \text{ molal}) = 0.77°C$, $T_b = 100.77°C$

b. $P_{water} = \chi_{water} P^o_{water}$, $\chi_{water} = \dfrac{\text{mol } H_2O}{\text{mol } H_2O + \text{mol solute}}$

Assuming 1.00 kg of water, we have 1.50 mol solute and:

$$\text{mol } H_2O = 1.00 \times 10^3 \text{ g } H_2O \times \dfrac{1 \text{ mol } H_2O}{18.02 \text{ g } H_2O} = 55.5 \text{ mol } H_2O$$

$\chi_{water} = \dfrac{55.5 \text{ mol}}{1.50 + 55.5} = 0.974$; $P_{water} = (0.974)(23.76 \text{ mm Hg}) = 23.1 \text{ mm Hg}$

c.   We assumed ideal behavior in solution formation and assumed i = 1 (no ions form).

Challenge Problems

88.   For the second vapor collected, $\chi^V_{B,2} = 0.714$ and $\chi^V_{T,2} = 0.286$, where $\chi^L_{B,2}$ = mole fraction of benzene in the second solution and $\chi^L_{T,2}$ = mole fraction of toluene in the second solution.

$\chi^L_{B,2} + \chi^L_{T,2} = 1.000$

$\chi^V_{B,2} = 0.714 = \dfrac{P_B}{P_{TOT}} = \dfrac{P_B}{P_B + P_T} = \dfrac{\chi^L_{B,2}(750.0 \text{ torr})}{\chi^L_{B,2}(750.0 \text{ torr}) + (1.000 - \chi^L_{B,2})(300.0 \text{ torr})}$

Solving: $\chi^L_{B,2} = 0.500 = \chi^L_{T,2}$

This second solution came from the vapor collected from the first (initial) solution. So, $\chi^V_{B,1} = \chi^V_{T,1} = 0.500$. Let $\chi^L_{B,1}$ = mole fraction benzene in the first solution and $\chi^L_{T,1}$ = mole fraction of toluene in first solution. $\chi^L_{B,1} + \chi^L_{T,1} = 1.000$

$$\chi_{B,1}^{V} = 0.500 = \frac{P_B}{P_{TOT}} = \frac{P_B}{P_B + P_T} = \frac{\chi_{B,1}^{L}(750.0 \text{ torr})}{\chi_{B,1}^{L}(750.0 \text{ torr}) + (1.000 - \chi_{B,1}^{L})(300.0 \text{ torr})}$$

Solving: $\chi_{B,1}^{L} = 0.286$

The original solution had $\chi_B = 0.286$ and $\chi_T = 0.714$.

89.   For 30.% A by moles in the vapor, $30. = \dfrac{P_A}{P_A + P_B} \times 100$:

$$0.30 = \frac{\chi_A x}{\chi_A x + \chi_B y}, \quad 0.30 = \frac{\chi_A x}{\chi_A x + (1.00 - \chi_A)y}$$

$\chi_A x = 0.30(\chi_A x) + 0.30 y - 0.30 \chi_A y, \quad \chi_A x - 0.30 \chi_A x + 0.30 \chi_A y = 0.30 y$

$$\chi_A(x - 0.30 x + 0.30 y) = 0.30 y, \quad \chi_A = \frac{0.30 y}{0.70 x + 0.30 y}; \quad \chi_B = 1.00 - \chi_A$$

Similarly, if vapor above is 50.% A: $\chi_A = \dfrac{y}{x + y}; \quad \chi_B = 1.00 - \dfrac{y}{x + y}$

If vapor above is 80%A: $\chi_A = \dfrac{0.80 y}{0.20 x + 0.80 y}; \quad \chi_B = 1.00 - \chi_A$

If the liquid solution is 30.%A by moles, $\chi_A = 0.30$.

Thus, $\chi_A^{V} = \dfrac{P_A}{P_A + P_B} = \dfrac{0.30 x}{0.30 x + 0.70 y}$ and $\chi_B^{V} = 1.00 - \dfrac{0.30 x}{0.30 x + 0.70 y}$

If solution is 50.%A: $\chi_A^{V} = \dfrac{x}{x + y}$ and $\chi_B^{V} = 1.00 - \chi_A^{V}$

If solution is 80.%A: $\chi_A^{V} = \dfrac{0.80 x}{0.80 x + 0.20 y}$ and $\chi_B^{V} = 1.00 - \chi_A^{V}$

90. $m = \dfrac{\Delta T}{K_f} = \dfrac{0.406°C}{1.86°C / \text{molal}} = 0.218 \text{ mol/kg}$

$\pi = MRT$ where $M = $ mol/L; We must assume that molarity = molality so we can calculate the osmotic pressure. This is a reasonable assumption for dilute solutions when 1.00 kg of water $\approx$ 1.00 L of solution. Assuming complete dissociation of NaCl, a 0.218 m solution corresponds to 6.37 g NaCl dissolved in 1.00 kg of water. The volume of solution may be a little larger than 1.00 L, but not by much (to three sig figs). The assumption that molarity = molality will be good here.

$\pi = (0.218 \, M)(0.08206 \text{ L atm/K} \bullet \text{mol})(298 \text{ K}) = 5.33 \text{ atm}$

91. $m = \dfrac{\Delta T}{K_f} = \dfrac{0.426°C}{1.86°C / \text{molal}} = 0.229 \text{ molal}$

Let x = mol NaCl in mixture and y = mol $C_{12}H_{22}O_{11}$.

$NaCl(aq) \rightarrow Na^+(aq) + Cl^-(aq)$; In solution, NaCl exists as separate Na^+ and Cl^- ions.

0.229 mol = mol Na^+ + mol Cl^- + mol $C_{12}H_{22}O_{11}$ = x + x + y = 2x + y

The molar mass of NaCl is 58.44 g/mol and the molar mass of $C_{12}H_{22}O_{11}$ = 342.3 g/mol. Setting up another equation for the mass of the mixture:

20.0 g = x(58.44) + y(342.3)

Substituting: 20.0 = 58.44 x + (0.229 – 2x) 342.3

Solving: x = mol NaCl = 0.0932 mol and

y = mol $C_{12}H_{22}O_{11}$ = 0.229 – 2(0.0932) = 0.043 mol

mass NaCl = 0.0932 mol × 58.44 g/mol = 5.45 g NaCl

mass% NaCl = $\dfrac{5.45\,g}{20.0\,g}$ × 100 = 27.3%, mass % $C_{12}H_{22}O_{11}$ = 100.0 – 27.3 = 72.7%

$\chi_{sucrose} = \dfrac{0.043\ mol}{(0.043 + 0.0932)\ mol} = 0.32$

92.   a. $\pi = iMRT$, $iM = \dfrac{\pi}{RT} = \dfrac{7.83\ atm}{\dfrac{0.08206\ L\ atm}{mol\ K} \times 298\ K} = 0.320\ mol/L$

Assuming 1.000 L of solution:

total mol solute particles = mol Na^+ + mol Cl^- + mol NaCl = 0.320 mol

mass solution = 1000. mL × $\dfrac{1.071\,g}{mL}$ = 1071 g solution

mass NaCl in solution = 0.0100 × 1071 g = 10.7 g NaCl

mol NaCl added to solution = 10.7 g × $\dfrac{1\ mol}{58.44\ g}$ = 0.183 mol NaCl

Some of this NaCl dissociates into Na^+ and Cl^- (two mol ions per mol NaCl) and some remains undissociated. Let x = mol undissociated NaCl = mol ion pairs.

mol solute particles = 0.320 mol = 2(0.183 – x) + x

0.320 = 0.366 – x, x = 0.046 mol ion pairs

$$\text{fraction of ion pairs} = \frac{0.046}{0.183} = 0.25, \text{ or } 25\%$$

b. $\Delta T = K_f m$ where $K_f = 1.86$ °C kg/mol; From part a, 1.000 L of solution contains 0.320 mol of solute particles. To calculate the molality of the solution, we need the kg of solvent present in 1.000 L solution.

mass of 1.000 L solution = 1071 g; mass of NaCl = 10.7 g

mass of solvent in 1.000 L solution = 1071 g – 10.7 g = 1060. g

$$\Delta T = 1.86 \text{ °C kg/mol} \times \frac{0.320 \text{ mol}}{1.060 \text{ kg}} = 0.562°C$$

Assuming water freezes at 0.000°C, then $T_f = -0.562$°C.

93. $\chi_{pen}^{V} = 0.15 = \dfrac{P_{pen}}{P_{total}}$; $P_{pen} = \chi_{pen}^{L} P_{pen}^{o} = \chi_{pen}^{L} (511 \text{ torr})$; $P_{total} = P_{pen} + P_{hex} = \chi_{pen}^{L} (511) + \chi_{hex}^{L} (150.)$

Since $\chi_{hex}^{L} = 1.000 - \chi_{pen}^{L}$, then: $P_{total} = \chi_{pen}^{L} (511 \text{ torr}) + (1.000 - \chi_{pen}^{L})(150.) = 150. + 361 \chi_{pen}^{L}$

$\chi_{pen}^{V} = \dfrac{P_{pen}}{P_{total}}$, $0.15 = \dfrac{\chi_{pen}^{L} (511)}{150. + 361 \chi_{pen}^{L}}$, $0.15 (150. + 361 \chi_{pen}^{L}) = 511 \chi_{pen}^{L}$

$23 + 54 \chi_{pen}^{L} = 511 \chi_{pen}^{L}$, $\chi_{pen}^{L} = \dfrac{23}{457} = 0.050$

94.   a. $m = \dfrac{\Delta T_f}{K_f} = \dfrac{1.32°C}{5.12 °C \text{ kg / mol}} = 0.258$ mol/kg

mol unknown $= 0.01560$ kg $\times \dfrac{0.258 \text{ mol unknown}}{\text{kg}} = 4.02 \times 10^{-3}$ mol

molar mass of unknown $= \dfrac{1.22 \text{ g}}{4.02 \times 10^{-3} \text{ mol}} = 303$ g/mol

Uncertainty in temperature $= \dfrac{0.04}{1.32} \times 100 = 3\%$; A 3% uncertainty in 303 g/mol

$= 9$ g/mol.

So, molar mass = 303 ± 9 g/mol.

b.   No, codeine could not be eliminated since its molar mass is in the possible range including the uncertainty.

c.   We would really like the uncertainty to be ± 1 g/mol. We need the freezing point depression to be about 10 times what it was in this problem. Two possibilities are:

1. make the solution ten times more concentrated (may be a solubility problem) or
2. use a solvent with a larger K_f value, e.g., camphor

95. $\Delta T_f = 5.51°C - 2.81°C = 2.70°C; \quad m = \dfrac{\Delta T_f}{K_f} = \dfrac{2.70°C}{5.12°C / molal} = 0.527$ molal

Let x = mass of naphthalene (molar mass = 128.2 g/mol). Then, $1.60 - x$ = mass of anthracene (molar mass = 178.2 g/mol).

$\dfrac{x}{128.2}$ = moles napthalene and $\dfrac{1.60 - x}{178.2}$ = moles anthracene

$\dfrac{0.527 \text{ mol solute}}{\text{kg solvent}} = \dfrac{\dfrac{x}{128.2} + \dfrac{1.60 - x}{178.2}}{0.0200 \text{ kg solvent}}, \quad 1.05 \times 10^{-2} = \dfrac{178.2\,x + 1.60(128.2) - 128.2\,x}{128.2(178.2)}$

$50.0\,x + 205 = 240., \quad 50.0\,x = 35, \quad x = 0.70$ g naphthalene

So mixture is: $\dfrac{0.70 \text{ g}}{1.60 \text{ g}} \times 100 = 44\%$ naphthalene by mass and 56% anthracene by mass

96. $iM = \dfrac{\pi}{RT} = \dfrac{0.3950 \text{ atm}}{\dfrac{0.08206 \text{ L atm}}{\text{mol K}} \times 298.2 \text{ K}} = 0.01614$ mol/L = total ion concentration

$0.01614 \text{ mol/L} = M_{Mg^{2+}} + M_{Na^+} + M_{Cl^-}; \quad M_{Cl^-} = 2\,M_{Mg^{2+}} + M_{Na^+}$ (charge balance)

Combining: $0.01614 = 3\,M_{Mg^{2+}} + 2\,M_{Na^+}$

Let x = mass $MgCl_2$ and y = mass NaCl, then $x + y = 0.5000$ g.

$M_{Mg^{2+}} = \dfrac{x}{95.21}$ and $M_{Na^+} = \dfrac{y}{58.44}$ (Because V = 1.000 L.)

Total ion concentration = $\dfrac{3\,x}{95.21} + \dfrac{2\,y}{58.44} = 0.01614$ mol/L; Rearranging: $3\,x + 3.258\,y$
$$= 1.537$$

Solving by simultaneous equations:

$$3\,x \quad + \quad 3.258\,y \quad = \quad 1.537$$
$$-3\,(x \quad + \qquad y) \quad = \quad -3(0.5000)$$
$$\overline{\qquad\qquad\qquad\qquad\qquad\qquad\qquad\qquad}$$
$$0.258\,y \quad = \quad 0.037, \quad y = 0.14 \text{ g NaCl}$$

mass $MgCl_2$ = 0.5000 g - 0.14 g = 0.36 g; mass % $MgCl_2 = \dfrac{0.36 \text{ g}}{0.5000 \text{ g}} \times 100 = 72\%$

97. $HCO_2H \rightarrow H^+ + HCO_2^-$; Only 4.2% of HCO_2H ionizes. The amount of H^+ or HCO_2^- produced is:

$$0.042 \times 0.10 \, M = 0.0042 \, M$$

The amount of HCO_2H remaining in solution after ionization is:

$$0.10 \, M - 0.0042 \, M = 0.10 \, M$$

The total molarity of species present $= M_{HCO_2H} + M_{H^+} + M_{HCO_2^-}$
$$= 0.10 + 0.0042 + 0.0042 = 0.11 \, M$$

Assuming $0.11 \, M = 0.11$ molal and assuming ample significant figures in the freezing point and boiling point of water at $P = 1$ atm:

$$\Delta T = K_f m = 1.86°C/molal \times 0.11 \text{ molal} = 0.20°C; \quad \text{freezing point} = -0.20°C$$

$$\Delta T = K_b m = 0.51°C/molal \times 0.11 \text{ molal} = 0.056°C; \quad \text{boiling point} = 100.056°C$$

98.   a.   The average values for each ion are:

300. mg Na^+; 15.7 mg K^+; 5.45 mg Ca^{2+}; 388 mg Cl^-; 246 mg lactate, $C_3H_5O_3^-$

Note: Since we can precisely weigh to ± 0.1 mg on an analytical balance, we'll carry extra significant figures and calculate results to ± 0.1 mg.

The only source of lactate is $NaC_3H_5O_3$.

$$246 \text{ mg } C_3H_5O_3^- \times \frac{112.06 \text{ mg } NaC_3H_5O_3}{89.07 \text{ mg } C_3H_5O_3^-} = 309.5 \text{ mg sodium lactate}$$

The only source of Ca^{2+} is $CaCl_2 \cdot 2H_2O$.

$$5.45 \text{ mg } Ca^{2+} \times \frac{147.0 \text{ mg } CaCl_2 \cdot 2H_2O}{40.08 \text{ mg } Ca^{2+}} = 19.99 \text{ or } 20.0 \text{ mg } CaCl_2 \cdot 2H_2O$$

The only source of K^+ is KCl.

$$15.7 \text{ mg } K^+ \times \frac{74.55 \text{ mg } KCl}{39.10 \text{ mg } K^+} = 29.9 \text{ mg } KCl$$

From what we have used already, let's calculate the mass of Na^+ added.

$$309.5 \text{ mg sodium lactate} = 246.0 \text{ mg lactate} + 63.5 \text{ mg } Na^+$$

Thus, we need to add an additional 236.5 mg Na^+ to get the desired 300. mg.

$$236.5 \text{ mg } Na^+ \times \frac{58.44 \text{ mg } NaCl}{22.99 \text{ mg } Na^+} = 601.2 \text{ mg } NaCl$$

Now, let's check the mass of Cl⁻ added:

$$20.0 \text{ mg CaCl}_2\text{•}2\text{H}_2\text{O} \times \frac{70.90 \text{ mg Cl}^-}{147.0 \text{ mg CaCl}_2 \bullet 2\text{H}_2\text{O}} = 9.6 \text{ mg Cl}^-$$

$$20.0 \text{ mg CaCl}_2\text{•}2\text{H}_2\text{O} = 9.6 \text{ mg Cl}^-$$
$$29.9 \text{ mg KCl} - 15.7 \text{ mg K}^+ = 14.2 \text{ mg Cl}^-$$
$$601.2 \text{ mg NaCl} - 236.5 \text{ mg Na}^+ = 364.7 \text{ mg Cl}^-$$

$$\text{Total Cl}^- = 388.5 \text{ mg Cl}^-$$

This is the quantity of Cl⁻ we want (the average amount of Cl⁻).

An analytical balance can weigh to the nearest 0.1 mg. We would use 309.5 mg sodium lactate, 20.0 mg CaCl₂•2H₂O, 29.9 mg KCl and 601.2 mg NaCl.

b. To get the range of osmotic pressure, we need to calculate the molar concentration of each ion at its minimum and maximum values. At minimum concentrations, we have:

$$\frac{285 \text{ mg Na}^+}{100. \text{ mL}} \times \frac{1 \text{ mmol}}{22.99 \text{ mg}} = 0.124 \ M; \quad \frac{14.1 \text{ mg K}^+}{100. \text{ mL}} \times \frac{1 \text{ mmol}}{39.10 \text{ mg}} = 0.00361 \ M$$

$$\frac{4.9 \text{ mg Ca}^{2+}}{100. \text{ mL}} \times \frac{1 \text{ mmol}}{40.08 \text{ mg}} = 0.0012 \ M; \quad \frac{368 \text{ mg Cl}^-}{100. \text{ mL}} \times \frac{1 \text{ mmol}}{35.45 \text{ mg}} = 0.104 \ M$$

$$\frac{231 \text{ mg C}_3\text{H}_5\text{O}_3{}^-}{100. \text{ mL}} \times \frac{1 \text{ mmol}}{89.07 \text{ mg}} = 0.0259 \ M \quad \text{(Note: molarity = mol/L = mmol/mL.)}$$

Total = 0.124 + 0.00361 + 0.0012 + 0.104 + 0.0259 = 0.259 M

$$\pi = MRT = \frac{0.259 \text{ mol}}{L} \times \frac{0.08206 \text{ L atm}}{\text{mol K}} \times 310. \text{ K} = 6.59 \text{ atm}$$

Similarly at maximum concentrations, the concentration of each ion is:

Na⁺: 0.137 M; K⁺: 0.00442 M; Ca²⁺: 0.0015 M; Cl⁻: 0.115 M; C₃H₅O₃⁻: 0.0293 M

The total concentration of all ions is the sum, 0.287 M.

$$\pi = \frac{0.287 \text{ mol}}{L} \times \frac{0.08206 \text{ L atm}}{\text{mol K}} \times 310. \text{ K} = 7.30 \text{ atm}$$

Osmotic pressure ranges from 6.59 atm to 7.30 atm.

99.   a. Assuming MgCO₃(s) does not dissociate, the solute concentration in water is:

$$\frac{560 \ \mu\text{g MgCO}_3(s)}{\text{mL}} = \frac{560 \text{ mg}}{L} = \frac{560 \times 10^{-3} \text{g}}{L} \times \frac{1 \text{ mol MgCO}_3}{84.32 \text{ g}} = 6.6 \times 10^{-3} \text{ mol MgCO}_3/\text{L}$$

An applied pressure of 8.0 atm will purify water up to a solute concentration of:

$$M = \frac{\pi}{RT} = \frac{8.0 \text{ atm}}{\dfrac{0.08206 \text{ L atm}}{\text{mol K}} \times 300.\text{ K}} = \frac{0.32 \text{ mol}}{\text{L}}$$

When the concentration of $MgCO_3(s)$ reaches 0.32 mol/L, the reverse osmosis unit can no longer purify the water. Let V = volume (L) of water remaining after purifying 45 L of H_2O. When V + 45 L of water have been processed, the moles of solute particles will equal:

$$6.6 \times 10^{-3} \text{ mol/L} \times (45 \text{ L} + \text{V}) = 0.32 \text{ mol/L} \times \text{V}$$

Solving: $0.30 = (0.32 - 0.0066) \times \text{V}, \text{V} = 0.96 \text{ L}$

The minimum total volume of water that must be processed is 45 L + 0.96 L = 46 L.

Note: If $MgCO_3$ does dissociate into Mg^{2+} and CO_3^{2-} ions, the solute concentration will increase to 1.3×10^{-2} M and at least 47 L of water must be processed.

b. No; A reverse osmosis system that applies 8.0 atm can only purify water with a solute concentration less than 0.32 mol/L. Salt water has a solute concentration of 2(0.60 M) = 1.20 M ions. The solute concentration of salt water is much too high for this reverse osmosis unit to work.

Integrative Problems

100. $10.0 \text{ mL} \times \dfrac{1 \text{ L}}{1000 \text{ mL}} \times \dfrac{10 \text{ dL}}{1 \text{ L}} \times \dfrac{1.0 \text{ mg}}{1 \text{ dL}} \times \dfrac{1 \text{ g}}{1000 \text{ mg}} \times \dfrac{1 \text{ mol}}{113.14 \text{ g}} = 8.8 \times 10^{-7} \text{ mol } C_4H_7N_3O$

mass of blood = $10.0 \text{ mL} \times \dfrac{1.025 \text{ g}}{\text{mL}} = 10.3 \text{ g}$

molality = $\dfrac{8.8 \times 10^{-7} \text{ mol}}{0.0103 \text{ kg}} = 8.5 \times 10^{-5} \text{ mol/kg}$

$\pi = MRT, M = \dfrac{8.8 \times 10^{-7} \text{ mol}}{0.0100 \text{ L}} = 8.8 \times 10^{-5} \text{ mol/L}$

$\pi = 8.8 \times 10^{-5} \text{ mol/L} \times \dfrac{0.08206 \text{ L atm}}{\text{K mol}} \times 298 \text{ K} = 2.2 \times 10^{-3} \text{ atm}$

101. $\Delta T = imK_f, i = \dfrac{\Delta T}{mK_f} = \dfrac{2.79°C}{\dfrac{0.250 \text{ mol}}{0.500 \text{ kg}} \times \dfrac{1.86°C \text{ kg}}{\text{mol}}} = 3.00$

We have 3 ions in solutions and we have twice as many anions as cations. Therefore, the formula of Q is MCl_2. Assuming 100.00 g compound:

$$38.68 \text{ g Cl} \times \frac{1 \text{ mol Cl}}{35.45 \text{ g}} = 1.091 \text{ mol Cl}$$

$$\text{mol M} = 1.091 \text{ mol Cl} \times \frac{1 \text{ mol M}}{2 \text{ mol Cl}} = 0.5455 \text{ mol M}$$

$$\text{molar mass of M} = \frac{61.32 \text{ g M}}{0.5455 \text{ mol M}} = 112.4 \text{ g/mol}; \quad \text{M is Cd so Q} = CdCl_2.$$

102. $$\text{mass of H}_2\text{O} = 160. \text{ mL} \times \frac{0.995 \text{ g}}{\text{mL}} = 159 \text{ g} = 0.159 \text{ kg}$$

$$\text{mol NaDTZ} = 0.159 \text{ kg} \times \frac{0.378 \text{ mol}}{\text{kg}} = 0.0601 \text{ mol}$$

$$\text{molar mass of NaDTZ} = \frac{38.4 \text{ g}}{0.0601 \text{ mol}} = 639 \text{ g/mol}$$

$$P_{soln} = \chi_{H_2O} P^o_{H_2O}; \quad \text{mol H}_2\text{O} = 159 \text{ g} \times \frac{1 \text{ mol}}{18.02 \text{ g}} = 8.82 \text{ mol}$$

Sodium diatrizoate is a salt because there is a metal (sodium) in the compound. From the short-hand notation for sodium diatrizoate, NaDTZ, we can assume this salt breaks up into Na^+ and DTZ^- ions. So the moles of solute particles are $2(0.0601) = 0.120$ mol solute particles.

$$\chi_{H_2O} = \frac{8.82 \text{ mol}}{0.120 \text{ mol} + 8.82 \text{ mol}} = 0.987; \quad P_{soln} = 0.987 \times 34.1 \text{ torr} = 33.7 \text{ torr}$$

Marathon Problem

103.   a.   From part a information, we can calculate the molar mass of Na_nA and deduce the formula.

$$\text{mol Na}_n\text{A} = \text{mol reducing agent} = 0.01526 \text{ L} \times \frac{0.02313 \text{ mol}}{\text{L}} = 3.530 \times 10^{-4} \text{ mol Na}_n\text{A}$$

$$\text{molar mass of Na}_n\text{A} = \frac{30.0 \times 10^{-3} \text{ g}}{3.530 \times 10^{-4} \text{ mol}} = 85.0 \text{ g/mol}$$

To deduce the formula, we will assume various charges and numbers of oxygens present in the oxyanion, then use the periodic table to see if an element fits the molar mass data.

Assuming n = 1 so the formula is NaA. The molar mass of the oxyanion, A^-, is 85.0 − 23.0 = 62.0 g/mol. The oxyanion part of the formula could be EO^- or EO_2^- or EO_3^- where E is some element. If EO^-, then the molar mass of E is 62.0 − 16.0 = 46.0 g/mol; no element has this molar mass. If EO_2^-, molar mass of E = 62.0 − 32.0 = 30.0 g/mol. Phosphorus is close, but PO_2^- anions are not common. If EO_3^-, molar mass of E = 62.0 − 48.0 = 14.0. Nitrogen has this molar mass and NO_3^- anions are very common. Therefore, NO_3^- is a possible formula for A^-.

Next, we assume Na_2A and Na_3A formulas and go through the same procedure as above. In all cases, no element in the periodic table fits the data. Therefore, we assume the oxyanion is $NO_3^- = A^-$.

b. The crystal data in part b allows determination of the metal, M, in the formula. See Exercise 10.49 for a review of relationships in body-centered cubic cells. In a bcc unit cell, there are 2 atoms per unit cell and the body diagonal of the cubic cell is related to the radius of the metal by the equation $4r = \sqrt{3}\,\ell$ where ℓ = cubic edge length.

$$\ell = \frac{4r}{\sqrt{3}} = \frac{4(1.984\times10^{-8}\text{ cm})}{\sqrt{3}} = 4.582 \times 10^{-8}\text{ cm}$$

volume of unit cell = $\ell^3 = (4.582\times10^{-8})^3 = 9.620 \times 10^{-23}\text{ cm}^3$

mass of M in a unit cell = $9.620 \times 10^{-23}\text{ cm}^3 \times \dfrac{5.243\text{ g}}{\text{cm}^3} = 5.044 \times 10^{-22}\text{ g M}$

mol M in a unit cell = 2 atoms $\times \dfrac{1\text{ mol}}{6.022\times10^{23}\text{ atoms}} = 3.321 \times 10^{-24}\text{ mol M}$

molar mass of M = $\dfrac{5.044\times10^{-22}\text{ g M}}{3.321\times10^{-24}\text{ mol M}} = 151.9$ g/mol

From the periodic table, M is europium, Eu. Given the charge of Eu is +3, then the formula of the salt is $Eu(NO_3)_3 \bullet zH_2O$.

c. Part c data allows determination of the molar mass of $Eu(NO_3)_3 \bullet zH_2O$, from which we can determine z, the number of waters of hydration.

$$\pi = iMRT, \quad iM = \frac{\pi}{RT} = \frac{558\text{ torr}\left(\dfrac{1\text{ atm}}{760\text{ torr}}\right)}{\dfrac{0.08206\text{ L atm}}{\text{mol K}}\times298\text{ K}} = 0.0300\text{ mol/L}$$

The total molarity of solute particles present is 0.0300 M. The solute particles are Eu^{3+} and NO_3^- ions (the waters of hydration are not solute particles). Because each mol of $Eu(NO_3)_3 \bullet zH_2O$ dissolves to form 4 ions (Eu^{3+} + 3 NO_3^-), the molarity of $Eu(NO_3)_3 \bullet zH_2O$ is 0.0300/4 = 0.00750 M.

mol $Eu(NO_3)_3 \bullet zH_2O$ = 0.01000 L $\times \dfrac{0.00750\text{ mol}}{\text{L}} = 7.50 \times 10^{-5}$ mol

molar mass of $Eu(NO_3)_3 \bullet zH_2O$ = $\dfrac{33.45\times10^{-3}\text{ g}}{7.50\times10^{-5}\text{ mol}} = 446$ g/mol

446 g/mol = 152.0 + 3(62.0) + z(18.0), z(18.0) = 108, z = 6.00

The formula for the strong electrolyte is $Eu(NO_3)_3 \bullet 6H_2O$.

CHAPTER TWELVE

CHEMICAL KINETICS

For Review

1.   The reaction rate is defined as the change in concentration of a reactant or product per unit time.   Consider the general reaction:

$$A \rightarrow \text{Products where rate} = \frac{-\Delta[A]}{\Delta t}$$

If we graph [A] vs. t, it would usually look like the dark line in the following plot.

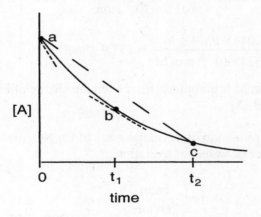

An instantaneous rate is the slope of a tangent line to the graph of [A] vs. t. We can determine the instantaneous rate at any time during the reaction. On the plot, tangent lines at $t \approx 0$ and $t = t_1$ are drawn. The slope of these tangent lines would be the instantaneous rates at $t \approx 0$ and $t = t_1$. We call the instantaneous rate at $t \approx 0$ the initial rate. The average rate is measured over a period of time. For example, the slope of the line connecting points a and c is the average rate of the reaction over the entire length of time 0 to t_2 (average rate $= \Delta[A]/\Delta t$). An average rate is determined over some time period while an instantaneous rate is determined at one specific time. The rate which is largest is generally the initial rate. At $t \approx 0$, the slope of the tangent line is greatest, which means the rate is largest at $t \approx 0$.

The initial rate is used by convention so that the rate of reaction only depends on the forward reaction; at $t \approx 0$, the reverse reaction is insignificant because no products are present yet.

2.   The differential rate law describes the dependence of the rate on the concentration of reactants. The integrated rate law expresses reactant concentrations as a function of time. The differential rate law is generally just called the rate law. The rate constant k is a constant that allows one to equate the rate of a reaction to the concentration of reactants. The order is the exponent that the reactant concentrations are raised to in the rate equation.

3.   The method of initial rates uses the results from several experiments where each experiment is carried out at a different set of initial reactant concentrations and the initial rate is determined. The results of the experiments are compared to see how the initial rate depends on the initial concentrations. If possible, two experiments are compared where only one reactant concentration changes. For these two experiments, any change in the initial rate must be due to the change in that one reactant concentration. The results of the experiments are compared until all of the orders are determined. After the orders are determined, then one can go back to any (or all) of the experiments and set the initial rate equal to the rate law using the concentrations in that experiment. The only unknown is k which is then solved for. The units on k depend on the reactants and orders in the rate law. Because there are many different rate laws, there are many different units for k.

Rate = $k[A]^n$; For a first-order rate law, n = 1. If [A] is tripled, then the rate is tripled. When [A] is quadrupled (increased by a factor of four), and the rate increases by a factor of 16, then A must be second order (4^2 = 16). For a third order reaction, as [A] is doubled, the rate will increase by a factor of 2^3 = 8. For a zero order reaction, the rate is independent of the concentration of A. The only stipulation for zero order reactions is that the reactant or reactants must be present; if they are, then the rate is a constant value (rate = k).

4.   Zero order:

$$\frac{-d[A]}{dt} = k, \quad \int_{[A]_0}^{[A]_t} d[A] = -\int_0^t k\,dt$$

$$[A]\Big|_{[A]_0}^{[A]_t} = -kt\Big|_0^t, \quad [A]_t - [A]_0 = -kt, \quad [A]_t = -kt + [A]_0$$

First order:

$$\frac{-d[A]}{dt} = k[A], \quad \int_{[A]_0}^{[A]_t} \frac{d[A]}{[A]} = -\int_0^t k\,dt$$

$$\ln[A]\Big|_{[A]_0}^{[A]_t} = -kt, \quad \ln[A]_t - \ln[A]_0 = -kt, \quad \ln[A]_t = -kt + \ln[A]_0$$

Second order:

$$\frac{-d[A]}{dt} = k[A]^2, \quad \int_{[A]_0}^{[A]_t} \frac{d[A]}{[A]^2} = -\int_0^t k\,dt$$

$$-\frac{1}{[A]}\Big|_{[A]_0}^{[A]_t} = -kt, \quad -\frac{1}{[A]_t} + \frac{1}{[A]_0} = -kt, \quad \frac{1}{[A]_t} = kt + \frac{1}{[A]_0}$$

5.   The integrated rate laws can be put into the equation for a straight line, y = mx + b where x and y are the x and y axes, m is the slope of the line and b is the y-intercept.

Zero order: $[A] = -kt + [A]$
           $y = mx + b$

A plot of [A] vs. time will be linear with a negative slope equal to $-k$ and a y-intercept equal to [A].

First order: $\ln[A] = -kt + \ln[A]_0$
            $y = mx + b$

A plot of ln[A] vs. time will be linear with a negative slope equal to $-k$ and a y-intercept equal to $\ln[A]_0$.

Second order: $\dfrac{1}{[A]} = kt + \dfrac{1}{[A]_0}$
             $y = mx + b$

A plot of 1/[A] vs. time will be linear with a positive slope equal to k and a y-intercept equal to $1/[A]_0$.

When two or more reactants are studied, only one of the reactants is allowed to change during any one experiment. This is accomplished by having a large excess of the other reactant(s) as compared to the reactant studied; so large that the concentration of the other reactant(s) stays effectively constant during the experiment. The slope of the straight-line plot equals k (or –k) times the other reactant concentrations raised to the correct orders. Once all the orders are known for a reaction, then any (or all) of the slopes can be used to determine k.

6.   At $t = t_{1/2}$, $[A] = 1/2[A]_0$; Plugging these terms into the integrated rate laws yields the following half-life expressions:

zero order   first order   second order

$t_{1/2} = \dfrac{[A]_0}{2\,k}$ $t_{1/2} = \dfrac{\ln 2}{k}$ $t_{1/2} = \dfrac{1}{k[A]_0}$

The first order half-life is independent of concentration, the zero order half-life is directly related to the concentration, and the second order half-life is inversely related to concentration. For a first order reaction, if the first half-life equals 20. s, the second half-life will also be 20. s because the half-life for a first order reaction is concentration independent. The second half-life for a zero order reaction will be 1/2(20.) = 10. s. This is because the half-life for a zero order reaction has a direct relationship with concentration (as the concentration decreases by a factor of 2, the half-life decreases by a factor of 2). For a second order reaction which has an inverse relationship between $t_{1/2}$ and $[A]_0$, the second half-life will be 40. s (twice the first half-life value).

7.   a.   An elementary step (reaction) is one for which the rate law can be written from the molecularity, i.e., from coefficients in the balanced equation.

b. The molecularity is the number of species that must collide to produce the reaction represented by an elementary step in a reaction mechanism.

c. The mechanism of a reaction is the series of proposed elementary reactions that may occur to give the overall reaction. The sum of all the steps in the mechanism gives the balanced chemical reaction.

d. An intermediate is a species that is neither a reactant nor a product but that is formed and consumed in the reaction sequence.

e. The rate-determining step is the slowest elementary reaction in any given mechanism.

For a mechanism to be acceptable, the sum of the elementary steps must give the overall balanced equation for the reaction and the mechanism must give a rate law that agrees with the experimentally determined rate law. A mechanism can never be proven absolutely. We can only say it is possibly correct if it follows the two requirements described above.

Most reactions occur by a series of steps. If most reactions were unimolecular, then most reactions would have a first order overall rate law, which is not the case.

8. The premise of the collision model is that molecules must collide to react, but not all collisions between reactant molecules result in product formation.

a. The larger the activation energy, the slower the rate.

b. The higher the temperature, the more molecular collisions with sufficient energy to convert to products and the faster the rate.

c. The greater the frequency of collisions, the greater the opportunities for molecules to react, and, hence, the greater the rate.

d. For a reaction to occur, it is the reactive portion of each molecule that must be involved in a collision. Only some of all the possible collisions have the correct orientation to convert reactants to products.

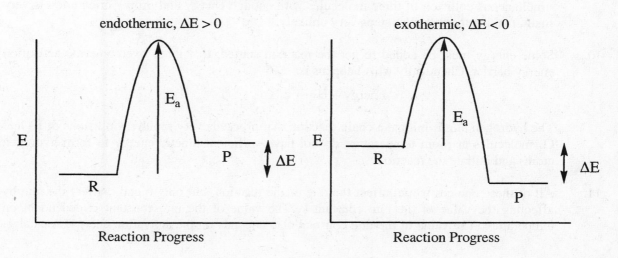

The activation energy for the reverse reaction will be the energy difference between the products and the transition state at the top of the potential energy "hill." For an exothermic reaction, the activation energy for the reverse reaction ($E_{a,r}$) is larger than the activation energy for the forward reaction (E_a), so the rate of the forward reaction will be greater than the rate of the reverse reaction. For an endothermic reaction, $\Delta E_{a,r} < E_a$ so the rate of the forward reaction will be less than the rate of the reverse reaction (with other factors being equal).

9.   Arrhenius equation: $k = Ae^{-E_a/RT}$; $\ln(k) = \dfrac{-E_a}{R}\left(\dfrac{1}{T}\right) + \ln A$

$$y = \quad m \quad x \quad + \quad b$$

The data needed is the value of the rate constant as a function of temperature. One would plot $\ln k$ versus $1/T$ to get a straight line. The slope of the line is equal to $-E_a/R$ and the y-intercept is equal to $\ln(A)$. The R value is 8.3145 J/K•mol. If one knows the rate constant at two different temperatures, then the following equation allows determination of E_a:

$$\ln\left(\frac{k_2}{k_1}\right) = \frac{E_a}{R}\left(\frac{1}{T_1} - \frac{1}{T_2}\right)$$

10.   A catalyst increases the rate of a reaction by providing reactants with an alternate pathway (mechanism) to convert to products. This alternate pathway has a lower activation energy, thus increasing the rate of the reaction.

A homogeneous catalyst is one that is in the same phase as the reacting molecules, and a heterogeneous catalyst is in a different phase than the reactants. The heterogeneous catalyst is usually a solid, although a catalyst in a liquid phase can act as a heterogeneous catalyst for some gas phase reactions. Since the catalyzed reaction has a different mechanism than the uncatalyzed reaction, the catalyzed reaction most likely will have a different rate law.

Questions

9.   In a unimolecular reaction, a single reactant molecule decomposes to products. In a bimolecular reaction, two molecules collide to give products. The probability of the simultaneous collision of three molecules with enough energy and proper orientation is very small, making termolecular steps very unlikely.

10.   Some energy must be added to get the reaction started, that is, to overcome the activation energy barrier. Chemically what happens is:

$$\text{Energy} + H_2 \rightarrow 2\,H$$

The hydrogen atoms initiate a chain reaction that proceeds very rapidly. Collisions of H_2 and O_2 molecules at room temperature do not have sufficient kinetic energy to form hydrogen atoms and initiate the reaction.

11.   All of these choices would affect the rate of the reaction, but only b and c affect the rate by affecting the value of the rate constant k. The value of the rate constant is dependent on temperature. The value of the rate constant also depends on the activation energy. A catalyst

will change the value of k because the activation energy changes. Increasing the concentration (partial pressure) of either H_2 or NO does not affect the value of k, but it does increase the rate of the reaction because both concentrations appear in the rate law.

12.   One experimental method to determine rate laws is the method of initial rates. Several experiments are carried out using different initial concentrations of reactants, and the initial rate is determined for each run. The results are then compared to see how the initial rate depends on the initial concentrations. This allows the orders in the rate law to be determined. The value of the rate constant is determined from the experiments once the orders are known.

The second experimental method utilizes the fact that the integrated rate laws can be put in the form of a straight line equation. Concentration vs. time data is collected for a reactant as a reaction is run. This data is then manipulated and plotted to see which manipulation gives a straight line. From the straight line plot, we get the order of the reactant and the slope of the line is mathematically related to k, the rate constant.

13.   The average rate decreases with time because the reverse reaction occurs more frequently as the concentration of products increase. Initially, with no products present, the rate of the forward reaction is at its fastest; but as time goes on, the rate gets slower and slower since products are converting back into reactants. The instantaneous rate will also decrease with time. The only rate that is constant is the initial rate. This is the instantaneous rate taken at $t \approx 0$. At this time, the amount of products is insignificant and the rate of the reaction only depends on the rate of the forward reaction.

14.   The most common method to experimentally determine the differential rate law is the method of initial rates. Once the differential rate law is determined experimentally, the integrated rate law can be derived. However, sometimes it is more convenient and more accurate to collect concentration versus time data for a reactant. When this is the case, then we do "proof" plots to determine the integrated rate law. Once the integrated rate law is determined, the differential rate law can be determined. Either experimental procedure allows determination of both the integrated and the differential rate; which rate law is determined by experiment and which is derived is usually decided by which data is easiest and most accurately collected.

15. $$\frac{rate_2}{rate_1} = \frac{k[A]_2^x}{k[A]_1^x} = \left(\frac{[A]_2}{[A]_1}\right)^x$$

The rate doubles as the concentration quadruples:

$$2 = (4)^x, \quad x = 1/2$$

The order is 1/2 (the square root of the concentration of reactant).

For a reactant that has an order of -1 and the reactant concentration is doubled:

$$\frac{rate_2}{rate_1} = (2)^{-1} = \frac{1}{2}$$

The rate will decrease by a factor of 1/2 when the reactant concentration is doubled for a -1 order reaction.

16.   A metal catalyzed reaction is dependent on the number of adsorption sites on the metal surface. Once the metal surface is saturated with reactant, the rate of reaction becomes independent of concentration.

17.   Two reasons are:

    a.   The collision must involve enough energy to produce the reaction, i.e., the collision energy must be equal to or exceed the activation energy.

    b.   The relative orientation of the reactants when they collide must allow formation of any new bonds necessary to produce products.

18.   The slope of the $\ln k$ vs. $1/T$ (K) plot is equal to $-E_a/R$. Because E_a for the catalyzed reaction will be smaller than E_a for the uncatalyzed reaction, the slope of the catalyzed plot will be less negative.

Exercises

Reaction Rates

19.   The coefficients in the balanced reaction relate the rate of disappearance of reactants to the rate of production of products. From the balanced reaction, the rate of production of P_4 will be 1/4 the rate of disappearance of PH_3, and the rate of production of H_2 will be 6/4 the rate of disappearance of PH_3. By convention, all rates are given as positive values.

$$\text{Rate} = \frac{-\Delta[PH_3]}{\Delta t} = \frac{(0.0048 \text{ mol}/2.0 \text{ L})}{s} = 2.4 \times 10^{-3} \text{ mol/L·s}$$

$$\frac{\Delta[P_4]}{\Delta t} = -\frac{1}{4}\frac{\Delta[PH_3]}{\Delta t} = 2.4 \times 10^{-3}/4 = 6.0 \times 10^{-4} \text{ mol/L·s}$$

$$\frac{\Delta[H_2]}{\Delta t} = -\frac{6}{4}\frac{\Delta[PH_3]}{\Delta t} = 6(2.4 \times 10^{-3})/4 = 3.6 \times 10^{-3} \text{ mol/L·s}$$

20. $\dfrac{\Delta[H_2]}{\Delta t} = 3\dfrac{\Delta[N_2]}{\Delta t}$ and $\dfrac{\Delta[NH_3]}{\Delta t} = -2\dfrac{\Delta[N_2]}{\Delta t}$;   So, $-\dfrac{1}{3}\dfrac{\Delta[H_2]}{\Delta t} = \dfrac{1}{2}\dfrac{\Delta[NH_3]}{\Delta t}$

    or: $\dfrac{\Delta[NH_3]}{\Delta t} = -\dfrac{2}{3}\dfrac{\Delta[H_2]}{\Delta t}$

Ammonia is produced at a rate equal to 2/3 of the rate of consumption of hydrogen.

21.   a.   average rate $= \dfrac{-\Delta[H_2O_2]}{\Delta t} = \dfrac{-(0.500\ M - 1.000\ M)}{(2.16 \times 10^4\ s - 0)} = 2.31 \times 10^{-5}$ mol/L•s

From the coefficients in the balanced equation:

$$\dfrac{\Delta[O_2]}{\Delta t} = -\dfrac{1}{2}\ \dfrac{\Delta[H_2O_2]}{\Delta t} = 1.16 \times 10^{-5}\ \text{mol/L•s}$$

b. $\dfrac{-\Delta[H_2O_2]}{\Delta t} = \dfrac{-(0.250 - 0.500)\ M}{(4.32 \times 10^4 - 2.16 \times 10^4)\ s} = 1.16 \times 10^{-5}$ mol/L•s

$$\dfrac{\Delta[O_2]}{\Delta t} = 1/2\ (1.16 \times 10^{-5}) = 5.80 \times 10^{-6}\ \text{mol/L•s}$$

Notice that as time goes on in a reaction, the average rate decreases.

22. $0.0120/0.0080 = 1.5$;   Reactant B is used up 1.5 times faster than reactant A. This corresponds to a 3 to 2 mol ratio between B and A in the balanced equation. $0.0160/0.0080 = 2$; Product C is produced twice as fast as reactant A is used up. So the coefficient for C is twice the coefficient for A. A possible balanced equation is: $2A + 3B \rightarrow 4C$

23.   a.   The units for rate are always mol/L•s.   b.   Rate = k; k must have units of mol/L•s.

c.   Rate = k[A], $\dfrac{mol}{L\ s} = k\left(\dfrac{mol}{L}\right)$ d.   Rate = k[A]^2, $\dfrac{mol}{L\ s} = k\left(\dfrac{mol}{L}\right)^2$

k must have units of s^{-1} .   k must have units of L/mol•s.

e. L^2/mol^2•s

24.   Rate = k[Cl]$^{1/2}$[CHCl$_3$], $\dfrac{mol}{L\ s} = k\left(\dfrac{mol}{L}\right)^{1/2}\left(\dfrac{mol}{L}\right)$, k must have units of $L^{1/2}/mol^{1/2}$•s.

Rate Laws from Experimental Data: Initial Rates Method

25.   a.   In the first two experiments, [NO] is held constant and [Cl$_2$] is doubled. The rate also doubled. Thus, the reaction is first order with respect to Cl$_2$. Or mathematically: Rate = k[NO]^x[Cl$_2$]^y

$$\dfrac{0.36}{0.18} = \dfrac{k(0.10)^x(0.20)^y}{k(0.10)^x(0.10)^y} = \dfrac{(0.20)^y}{(0.10)^y}, \ 2.0 = 2.0^y, \ y = 1$$

We can get the dependence on NO from the second and third experiments. Here, as the NO concentration doubles (Cl$_2$ concentration is constant), the rate increases by a factor of four. Thus, the reaction is second order with respect to NO. Or mathematically:

$$\frac{1.45}{0.36} = \frac{k(0.20)^x(0.20)}{k(0.10)^x(0.20)} = \frac{(0.20)^x}{(0.10)^x}, \quad 4.0 = 2.0^x, \quad x = 2; \quad \text{So,} \quad \text{Rate} = k[NO]^2[Cl_2]$$

Try to examine experiments where only one concentration changes at a time. The more variables that change, the harder it is to determine the orders. Also, these types of problems can usually be solved by inspection. In general, we will solve using a mathematical approach, but keep in mind you probably can solve for the orders by simple inspection of the data.

b. The rate constant k can be determined from the experiments. From experiment 1:

$$\frac{0.18 \text{ mol}}{\text{L min}} = k\left(\frac{0.10 \text{ mol}}{\text{L}}\right)^2\left(\frac{0.10 \text{ mol}}{\text{L}}\right), \quad k = 180 \text{ L}^2/\text{mol}^2 \cdot \text{min}$$

From the other experiments:

$$k = 180 \text{ L}^2/\text{mol}^2 \cdot \text{min (2nd exp.)}; \quad k = 180 \text{ L}^2/\text{mol}^2 \cdot \text{min (3rd exp.)}$$

The average rate constant is $k_{mean} = 1.8 \times 10^2 \text{ L}^2/\text{mol}^2 \cdot \text{min}$.

26. a. $\text{Rate} = k[I^-]^x[S_2O_8^{2-}]^y; \quad \dfrac{1.25 \times 10^{-6}}{6.25 \times 10^{-6}} = \dfrac{k(0.080)^x(0.040)^y}{k(0.040)^x(0.040)^y}, \quad 2.00 = 2.0^x, \quad x = 1$

$$\frac{1.25 \times 10^{-6}}{6.25 \times 10^{-6}} = \frac{k(0.080)(0.040)^y}{k(0.080)(0.020)^y}, \quad 2.00 = 2.0^y, \quad y = 1; \quad \text{Rate} = k[I^-][S_2O_8^{2-}]$$

b. For the first experiment:

$$\frac{12.5 \times 10^{-6} \text{ mol}}{\text{L s}} = k\left(\frac{0.080 \text{ mol}}{\text{L}}\right)\left(\frac{0.040 \text{ mol}}{\text{L}}\right); \quad k = 3.9 \times 10^{-3} \text{ L/mol} \cdot \text{s}$$

Each of the other experiments also gives $k = 3.9 \times 10^{-3} \text{ L/mol} \cdot \text{s}$,
so $k_{mean} = 3.9 \times 10^{-3} \text{ L/mol} \cdot \text{s}$.

27. a. $\text{Rate} = k[NOCl]^n$; Using experiments two and three:

$$\frac{2.66 \times 10^4}{6.64 \times 10^3} = k\frac{(2.0 \times 10^{16})^n}{(1.0 \times 10^{16})^n}, \quad 4.01 = 2.0^n, \quad n = 2; \quad \text{Rate} = k[NOCl]^2$$

b. $\dfrac{5.98 \times 10^4 \text{ molecules}}{\text{cm}^3 \text{ s}} = k\left(\dfrac{3.0 \times 10^{16} \text{ molecules}}{\text{cm}^3}\right)^2, \quad k = 6.6 \times 10^{-29} \text{ cm}^3/\text{molecules} \cdot \text{s}$

The other three experiments give (6.7, 6.6 and 6.6) $\times 10^{-29} \text{ cm}^3/\text{molecules} \cdot \text{s}$, respectively.

The mean value for k is $6.6 \times 10^{-29} \text{ cm}^3/\text{molecules} \cdot \text{s}$.

c. $\dfrac{6.6 \times 10^{-29} \text{ cm}^3}{\text{molecules s}} \times \dfrac{1 \text{ L}}{1000 \text{ cm}^3} \times \dfrac{6.022 \times 10^{23} \text{ molecules}}{\text{mol}} = \dfrac{4.0 \times 10^{-8} \text{ L}}{\text{mol s}}$

28. Rate = $k[N_2O_5]^x$; The rate laws for the first two experiments are:

$2.26 \times 10^{-3} = k(0.190)^x$ and $8.90 \times 10^{-4} = k(0.0750)^x$

Dividing: $2.54 = \dfrac{(0.190)^x}{(0.0750)^x} = (2.53)^x$, $x = 1$; Rate = $k[N_2O_5]$

$k = \dfrac{\text{Rate}}{[N_2O_5]} = \dfrac{8.90 \times 10^{-4}\ \text{mol}/\text{L} \bullet \text{s}}{0.0750\ \text{mol}/\text{L}} = 1.19 \times 10^{-2}\ \text{s}^{-1}$; $k_{mean} = 1.19 \times 10^{-2}\ \text{s}^{-1}$

29. a. Rate = $k[Hb]^x[CO]^y$; Comparing the first two experiments, [CO] is unchanged, [Hb] doubles, and the rate doubles. Therefore, $x = 1$ and the reaction is first order in Hb. Comparing the second and third experiments, [Hb] is unchanged, [CO] triples. and the rate triples. Therefore, $y = 1$ and the reaction is first order in CO.

b. Rate = k[Hb][CO]

c. From the first experiment:

$0.619\ \mu\text{mol/L} \bullet \text{s} = k\ (2.21\ \mu\text{mol/L})(1.00\ \mu\text{mol/L})$, $k = 0.280\ \text{L}/\mu\text{mol} \bullet \text{s}$

The second and third experiments give similar k values, so $k_{mean} = 0.280\ \text{L}/\mu\text{mol} \bullet \text{s}$.

d. Rate = k[Hb][CO] = $\dfrac{0.280\ \text{L}}{\mu\text{mol s}} \times \dfrac{3.36\ \mu\text{mol}}{\text{L}} \times \dfrac{2.40\ \mu\text{mol}}{\text{L}} = 2.26\ \mu\text{mol/L} \bullet \text{s}$

30. a. Rate = $k[ClO_2]^x[OH^-]^y$; From the first two experiments:

$2.30 \times 10^{-1} = k(0.100)^x(0.100)^y$ and $5.75 \times 10^{-2} = k(0.0500)^x(0.100)^y$

Dividing the two rate laws: $4.00 = \dfrac{(0.100)^x}{(0.0500)^x} = 2.00^x$, $x = 2$

Comparing the second and third experiments:

$2.30 \times 10^{-1} = k(0.100)(0.100)^y$ and $1.15 \times 10^{-1} = k(0.100)(0.0500)^y$

Dividing: $2.00 = \dfrac{(0.100)^y}{(0.0500)^y} = 2.00^y$, $y = 1$

The rate law is: Rate = $k[ClO_2]^2[OH^-]$

$2.30 \times 10^{-1}\ \text{mol/L} \bullet \text{s} = k(0.100\ \text{mol/L})^2(0.100\ \text{mol/L})$, $k = 2.30 \times 10^2\ \text{L}^2/\text{mol}^2 \bullet \text{s} = k_{mean}$

b. Rate = $k[ClO_2]^2[OH^-] = \dfrac{2.30 \times 10^2\ \text{L}^2}{\text{mol}^2\ \text{s}} \times \left(\dfrac{0.175\ \text{mol}}{\text{L}}\right)^2 \times \dfrac{0.0844\ \text{mol}}{\text{L}} = 0.594\ \text{mol/L} \bullet \text{s}$

Integrated Rate Laws

31.   The first assumption to make is that the reaction is first order because first-order reactions are most common. For a first-order reaction, a graph of ln $[H_2O_2]$ vs time will yield a straight line. If this plot is not linear, then the reaction is not first order and we make another assumption. The data and plot for the first-order assumption follows.

Time (s)	$[H_2O_2]$ (mol/L)	ln H_2O_2]
0	1.00	0.000
120.	0.91	−0.094
300.	0.78	−0.25
600.	0.59	−0.53
1200.	0.37	−0.99
1800.	0.22	−1.51
2400.	0.13	−2.04
3000.	0.082	−2.50
3600.	0.050	−3.00

Note: We carried extra significant figures in some of the ln values in order to reduce round-off error. For the plots, we will do this most of the time when the ln function is involved.

The plot of ln $[H_2O_2]$ vs. time is linear. Thus, the reaction is first order. The rate law and integrated rate law are: Rate = $k[H_2O_2]$ and ln $[H_2O_2]$ = $-kt$ + ln $[H_2O_2]_o$.

We determine the rate constant k by determining the slope of the ln $[H_2O_2]$ vs time plot (slope = $-k$). Using two points on the curve gives:

$$\text{slope} = -k = \frac{\Delta y}{\Delta x} = \frac{0 - (3.00)}{0 - 3600.} = -8.3 \times 10^{-4} \text{ s}^{-1}, \quad k = 8.3 \times 10^{-4} \text{ s}^{-1}$$

To determine $[H_2O_2]$ at 4000. s, use the integrated rate law where at t = 0, $[H_2O_2]_o = 1.00 \, M$.

$$\ln [H_2O_2] = -kt + \ln [H_2O_2]_o \text{ or } \ln\left(\frac{[H_2O_2]}{[H_2O_2]_o}\right) = -kt$$

$$\ln\left(\frac{[H_2O_2]}{1.00}\right) = -8.3 \times 10^{-4} \text{ s}^{-1} \times 4000. \text{ s}, \ \ln [H_2O_2] = -3.3, \ [H_2O_2] = e^{-3.3} = 0.037 \, M$$

32.   a.   Because the ln[A] vs time plot was linear, the reaction is first order in A. The slope of the ln[A] vs. time plot equals $-k$. Therefore, the rate law, the integrated rate law and the rate constant value are:

Rate = k[A]; ln[A] = $-kt$ + ln[A]$_o$; k = 2.97×10^{-2} min^{-1}

b. The half-life expression for a first-order rate law is:

$$t_{1/2} = \frac{\ln 2}{k} = \frac{0.6931}{k}, \quad t_{1/2} = \frac{0.6931}{2.97 \times 10^{-2} \text{ min}^{-1}} = 23.3 \text{ min}$$

c. $2.50 \times 10^{-3} M$ is 1/8 of the original amount of A present, so the reaction is 87.5% complete. When a first-order reaction is 87.5% complete (or 12.5% remains), the reaction has gone through 3 half-lives:

$$100\% \quad \xrightarrow[t_{1/2}]{} \quad 50.0\% \quad \xrightarrow[t_{1/2}]{} \quad 25\% \quad \xrightarrow[t_{1/2}]{} \quad 12.5\%; \quad t = 3 \times t_{1/2} = 3 \times 23.3 \text{ min} = 69.9 \text{ min}$$

Or we can use the integrated rate law:

$$\ln\left(\frac{[A]}{[A]_o}\right) = -kt, \quad \ln\left(\frac{2.50 \times 10^{-3} M}{2.00 \times 10^{-2} M}\right) = -(2.97 \times 10^{-2} \text{ min}^{-1})\,t$$

$$t = \frac{\ln(0.125)}{-2.97 \times 10^{-2} \text{ min}^{-1}} = 70.0 \text{ min}$$

33.   Assume the reaction is first order and see if the plot of ln [NO$_2$] vs. time is linear. If this isn't linear, try the second-order plot of 1/[NO$_2$] vs. time because second-order reactions are the next most common after first-order reactions. The data and plots follow.

Time (s)	[NO$_2$] (M)	ln [NO$_2$]	1/[NO$_2$] (M^{-1})
0	0.500	-0.693	2.00
1.20×10^3	0.444	-0.812	2.25
3.00×10^3	0.381	-0.965	2.62
4.50×10^3	0.340	-1.079	2.94
9.00×10^3	0.250	-1.386	4.00
1.80×10^4	0.174	-1.749	5.75

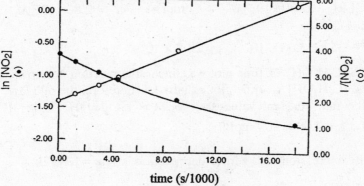

The plot of 1/[NO$_2$] vs. time is linear. The reaction is second order in NO$_2$. The rate law and

integrated rate law are: Rate = k[NO$_2$]^2 and $\dfrac{1}{[NO_2]} = kt + \dfrac{1}{[NO_2]_o}$.

The slope of the plot $1/[NO_2]$ vs. t gives the value of k. Using a couple of points on the plot:

$$\text{slope} = k = \frac{\Delta y}{\Delta x} = \frac{(5.75 - 2.00)\ M^{-1}}{(1.80 \times 10^4 - 0)\ s} = 2.08 \times 10^{-4}\ L/mol \cdot s$$

To determine $[NO_2]$ at 2.70×10^4 s, use the integrated rate law where $1/[NO_2]_o = 1/0.500\ M$ $= 2.00\ M^{-1}$.

$$\frac{1}{[NO_2]} = kt + \frac{1}{[NO_2]_o}, \quad \frac{1}{[NO_2]} = \frac{2.08 \times 10^{-4}\ L}{mol\ s} \times 2.70 \times 10^4\ s + 2.00\ M^{-1}$$

$$\frac{1}{[NO_2]} = 7.62, \quad [NO_2] = 0.131\ M$$

34. a. Because the $1/[A]$ vs. time plot was linear, the reaction is second order in A. The slope of the $1/[A]$ vs. time plot equals the rate constant k. Therefore, the rate law, the integrated rate law and the rate constant value are:

$$\text{Rate} = k[A]^2; \quad \frac{1}{[A]} = kt + \frac{1}{[A]_o}; \quad k = 3.60 \times 10^{-2}\ L/mol \cdot s$$

   b. The half-life expression for a second-order reaction is: $t_{1/2} = \dfrac{1}{k[A]_o}$

For this reaction: $t_{1/2} = \dfrac{1}{3.60 \times 10^{-2}\ L/mol \cdot s \times 2.80 \times 10^{-3}\ mol/L} = 9.92 \times 10^3\ s$

Note: We could have used the integrated rate law to solve for $t_{1/2}$ where $[A] = (2.80 \times 10^{-3}/2)$ mol/L.

   c. Since the half-life for a second-order reaction depends on concentration, we will use the integrated rate law to solve.

$$\frac{1}{[A]} = kt + \frac{1}{[A]_o}, \quad \frac{1}{7.00 \times 10^{-4}\ M} = \frac{3.60 \times 10^{-2}\ L}{mol \cdot s} \times t + \frac{1}{2.80 \times 10^{-3}\ M}$$

$$1.43 \times 10^3 - 357 = 3.60 \times 10^{-2}\ t, \quad t = 2.98 \times 10^4\ s$$

35. a. Because the $[C_2H_5OH]$ vs. time plot was linear, the reaction is zero order in C_2H_5OH. The slope of the $[C_2H_5OH]$ vs. time plot equals -k. Therefore, the rate law, the integrated rate law and the rate constant value are: $\text{Rate} = k[C_2H_5OH]^0 = k$; $[C_2H_5OH] = -kt + [C_2H_5OH]_o$; $k = 4.00 \times 10^{-5}$ mol/L$\cdot$s.

   b. The half-life expression for a zero-order reaction is: $t_{1/2} = [A]_o/2k$.

$$t_{1/2} = \frac{[C_2H_5OH]_o}{2\ k} = \frac{1.25 \times 10^{-2}\ mol/L}{2 \times 4.00 \times 10^{-5}\ mol/L \cdot s} = 156\ s$$

Note: we could have used the integrated rate law to solve for $t_{1/2}$ where $[C_2H_5OH] = (1.25 \times 10^{-2}/2)$ mol/L.

c. $[C_2H_5OH] = -kt + [C_2H_5OH]_o$, $0 \text{ mol/L} = -(4.00 \times 10^{-5} \text{ mol/L} \cdot s)\, t + 1.25 \times 10^{-2} \text{ mol/L}$

$$t = \frac{1.25 \times 10^{-2} \text{ mol/L}}{4.00 \times 10^{-5} \text{ mol/L} \cdot s} = 313 \text{ s}$$

36.   From the data, the pressure of C_2H_5OH decreases at a constant rate of 13 torr for every 100. s. Since the rate of disappearance of C_2H_5OH is not dependent on concentration, the reaction is zero order in C_2H_5OH.

$$k = \frac{13 \text{ torr}}{100. \text{ s}} \times \frac{1 \text{ atm}}{760 \text{ torr}} = 1.7 \times 10^{-4} \text{ atm/s}$$

The rate law and integrated rate law are:

$$\text{Rate} = k = 1.7 \times 10^{-4} \text{ atm/s}; \quad P_{C_2H_5OH} = -kt + 250. \text{ torr} \left(\frac{1 \text{ atm}}{760 \text{ torr}} \right) = -kt + 0.329 \text{ atm}$$

At 900. s: $P_{C_2H_5OH} = -1.7 \times 10^{-4} \text{ atm/s} \times 900. \text{ s} + 0.329 \text{ atm} = 0.176 \text{ atm} = 0.18 \text{ atm} = 130 \text{ torr}$

37.   The first assumption to make is that the reaction is first order. For a first-order reaction, a graph of ln $[C_4H_6]$ vs. t should yield a straight line. If this isn't linear, then try the second-order plot of $1/[C_4H_6]$ vs. t. The data and the plots follow.

Time	195	604	1246	2180	6210 s
$[C_4H_6]$	1.6×10^{-2}	1.5×10^{-2}	1.3×10^{-2}	1.1×10^{-2}	$0.68 \times 10^{-2}\ M$
ln $[C_4H_6]$	-4.14	-4.20	-4.34	-4.51	-4.99
$1/[C_4H_6]$	62.5	66.7	76.9	90.9	$147\ M^{-1}$

Note: To reduce round-off error, we carried extra sig. figs. in the data points.

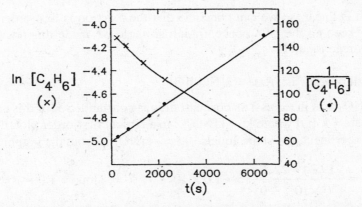

The ln plot is not linear, so the reaction is not first order. Since the second-order plot of $1/[C_4H_6]$ vs. t is linear, we can conclude that the reaction is second order in butadiene. The rate law is:

$$\text{Rate} = k[C_4H_6]^2$$

For a second order reaction, the integrated rate law is: $\dfrac{1}{[C_4H_6]} = kt + \dfrac{1}{[C_4H_6]_o}$

The slope of the straight line equals the value of the rate constant. Using the points on the line at 1000. and 6000. s:

$$k = \text{slope} = \frac{144\,L\,/\,mol - 73\,L\,/\,mol}{6000.\,s - 1000.\,s} = 1.4 \times 10^{-2}\,L/mol \bullet s$$

38.   a.   First, assume the reaction to be first order with respect to O. A graph of ln [O] vs. t should be linear if the reaction is first order in O.

t(s)	[O] (atoms/cm^3)	ln[O]
0	5.0×10^9	22.33
$10. \times 10^{-3}$	1.9×10^9	21.37
$20. \times 10^{-3}$	6.8×10^8	20.34
$30. \times 10^{-3}$	2.5×10^8	19.34

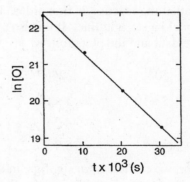

The graph is linear, so we can conclude that the reaction is first order with respect to O. Note: by keeping the NO_2 concentration so large we made this reaction into a pseudo-first-order reaction in O.

b.   The overall rate law is: Rate = $k[NO_2][O]$

Because NO_2 was in excess, its concentration is constant. So for this experiment, the rate law is: Rate = $k'[O]$ where $k' = k[NO_2]$. In a typical first-order plot, the slope equals $-k$. For this experiment, the slope equals $-k' = -k[NO_2]$. From the graph:

$$\text{slope} = \frac{19.34 - 22.33}{(30.\times 10^{-3} - 0)\,s} = -1.0 \times 10^2\,s^{-1},\ \ k' = -\text{slope} = 1.0 \times 10^2\,s^{-1}$$

To determine k, the actual rate constant:

$k' = k[NO_2]$, $1.0 \times 10^2\,s^{-1} = k(1.0 \times 10^{13}\,\text{molecules/cm}^3)$

$k = 1.0 \times 10^{-11}\,\text{cm}^3/\text{molecules} \bullet s$

39.   Because the 1/[A] vs. time plot is linear with a positive slope, the reaction is second order with respect to A. The y-intercept in the plot will equal $1/[A]_o$. Extending the plot, the y-intercept will be about 10, so $1/10 = 0.1\ M = [A]_o$.

40.   The slope of the 1/[A] vs time plot in Exercise 12.39 with equal k.

$$\text{slope} = k = \frac{(60 - 20)\ L\,/\,mol}{(5 - 1)\ s} = 10\ L/mol{\cdot}s$$

a. $\dfrac{1}{[A]} = kt + \dfrac{1}{[A]_o} = \dfrac{10\ L}{mol\ s} \times 9\ s + \dfrac{1}{0.1\ M} = 100,\ \ [A] = 0.01\ M$

b.   For a second-order reaction, the half-life does depend on concentration: $t_{1/2} = \dfrac{1}{k[A]_o}$

First half-life: $t_{1/2} = \dfrac{1}{\dfrac{10\ L}{mol\ s} \times \dfrac{0.1\ mol}{L}} = 1\ s$

Second half-life ($[A]_o$ is now 0.05 M): $t_{1/2} = 1/(10 \times 0.05) = 2\ s$

Third half-life ($[A]_o$ is now 0.025 M): $t_{1/2} = 1/(10 \times 0.025) = 4\ s$

41.   a. $[A] = -kt + [A]_o,\ \ [A] = -(5.0 \times 10^{-2}\ mol/L{\cdot}s)\,t + 1.0 \times 10^{-3}\ mol/L$

b.   The half-life expression for a zero-order reaction is: $t_{1/2} = \dfrac{[A]_o}{2\,k}$

$t_{1/2} = \dfrac{1.0 \times 10^{-3}\ mol\,/\,L}{2 \times 5.0 \times 10^{-2}\ mol/L \bullet s} = 1.0 \times 10^{-2}\ s$

c. $[A] = -5.0 \times 10^{-2}\ mol/L{\cdot}s \times 5.0 \times 10^{-3}\ s + 1.0 \times 10^{-3}\ mol/L = 7.5 \times 10^{-4}\ mol/L$

Because $7.5 \times 10^{-4}\ M$ A remains, $2.5 \times 10^{-4}\ M$ A reacted, which means that $2.5 \times 10^{-4}\ M$ B has been produced.

42. $\ln\left(\dfrac{[A]}{[A]_o}\right) = -kt;\ \ k = \dfrac{\ln 2}{t_{1/2}} = \dfrac{0.6931}{14.3\ d} = 4.85 \times 10^{-2}\ d^{-1}$

If $[A]_o = 100.0$, then after 95.0% completion, $[A] = 5.0$.

$\ln\left(\dfrac{5.0}{100.0}\right) = -4.85 \times 10^{-2}\ d^{-1} \times t,\ \ t = 62\ days$

43.   a.   When a reaction is 75.0% complete (25.0% of reactant remains), this represents two half lives (100% $\rightarrow$ 50% $\rightarrow$ 25%). The first-order half-life expression is: $t_{1/2} = (\ln 2)/k$. Because there is no concentration dependence for a first order half-life: 320. s = two half-lives, $t_{1/2} = 320./2 = 160.$ s. This is both the first half-life, the second half-life, etc.

b. $t_{1/2} = \dfrac{\ln 2}{k}, \quad k = \dfrac{\ln 2}{t_{1/2}} = \dfrac{\ln 2}{160.\,s} = 4.33 \times 10^{-3}\,s^{-1}$

At 90.0% complete, 10.0% of the original amount of the reactant remains, so [A] = $0.100[A]_0$.

$$\ln\left(\dfrac{[A]}{[A]_o}\right) = -kt, \quad \ln\dfrac{0.100[A]_0}{[A]_0} = -(4.33 \times 10^{-3}\,s^{-1})t, \quad t = \dfrac{\ln 0.100}{-4.33 \times 10^{-3}\,s^{-1}} = 532\,s$$

44.   For a first-order reaction, the integrated rate law is: $\ln([A]/[A]_o) = -kt$. Solving for k:

$$\ln\left(\dfrac{0.250\,mol/L}{1.00\,mol/L}\right) = -k \times 120.\,s, \ k = 0.0116\,s^{-1}$$

$$\ln\left(\dfrac{0.350\,mol/L}{2.00\,mol/L}\right) = -0.0116\,s^{-1} \times t, \ t = 150.\,s$$

45.   Comparing experiments 1 and 2, as the concentration of AB is doubled, the initial rate increases by a factor of 4. The reaction is second order in AB.

Rate = $k[AB]^2$, $3.20 \times 10^{-3}\,mol/L \bullet s = k_1(0.200\,M)^2$

$k = 8.00 \times 10^{-2}\,L/mol \bullet s = k_{mean}$

For a second order reaction:

$$t_{1/2} = \dfrac{1}{k[AB]_o} = \dfrac{1}{8.00 \times 10^{-2}\,L/mol \bullet s \times 1.00\,mol/L} = 12.5\,s$$

46.   a.   The integrated rate law for a second-order reaction is: $1/[A] = kt + 1/[A]_o$, and the half-life expression is: $t_{1/2} = 1/k[A]_o$. We could use either to solve for $t_{1/2}$. Using the integrated rate law:

$$\dfrac{1}{(0.900/2)\,mol/L} = k \times 2.00\,s + \dfrac{1}{0.900\,mol/L}, \ k = \dfrac{1.11\,L/mol}{2.00\,s} = 0.555\,L/mol\bullet s$$

b. $\dfrac{1}{0.100\,mol/L} = 0.555\,L/mol\bullet s \times t + \dfrac{1}{0.900\,mol/L}, \ t = \dfrac{8.9\,L/mol}{0.555\,L/mol \bullet s} = 16\,s$

47.   Successive half-lives double as concentration is decreased by one-half. This is consistent with second-order reactions so assume the reaction is second order in A.

$t_{1/2} = \dfrac{1}{k[A]_o}, \ k = \dfrac{1}{t_{1/2}[A]_o} = \dfrac{1}{10.0\,min\,(0.10\,M)} = 1.0\,L/mol\bullet min$

a. $\dfrac{1}{[A]} = kt + \dfrac{1}{[A]_o} = \dfrac{1.0\,L}{mol\,min} \times 80.0\,min + \dfrac{1}{0.10\,M} = 90.\,M^{-1}, \ [A] = 1.1 \times 10^{-2}\,M$

b.   30.0 min = 2 half-lives, so 25% of original A is remaining.

$$[A] = 0.25(0.10 \ M) = 0.025 \ M$$

48.   Because $[B]_o >> [A]_o$, the B concentration is essentially constant during this experiment, so rate = k'[A] where $k' = k[B]^2$. For this experiment, the reaction is a pseudo-first-order reaction in A.

a. $\ln\left(\dfrac{[A]}{[A]_o}\right) = -k't, \ \ln\left(\dfrac{3.8 \times 10^{-3} \ M}{1.0 \times 10^{-2} \ M}\right) = -k' \times 8.0 \ s, \ k' = 0.12 \ s^{-1}$

For the reaction: $k' = k[B]^2, \ k = 0.12 \ s^{-1}/(3.0 \ mol/L)^2 = 1.3 \times 10^{-2} \ L^2/mol^2 \cdot s$

b. $t_{1/2} = \dfrac{\ln 2}{k'} = \dfrac{0.693}{0.12 \ s^{-1}} = 5.8 \ s$

c. $\ln\left(\dfrac{[A]}{1.0 \times 10^{-2} \ M}\right) = -0.12 \ s^{-1} \times 13.0 \ s, \ \dfrac{[A]}{1.0 \times 10^{-2}} = e^{-0.12(13.0)} = 0.21$

$$[A] = 2.1 \times 10^{-3} \ M$$

d. $[A]_{reacted} = 0.010 \ M - 0.0021 \ M = 0.008 \ M$

$$[C]_{reacted} = 0.008 \ M \times \dfrac{2 \ mol \ C}{1 \ mol \ A} = 0.016 \ M \approx 0.02 \ M$$

$[C]_{remaining} = 2.0 \ M - 0.02 \ M = 2.0 \ M$; As expected, the concentration of C basically remains constant during this experiment since $[C]_o >> [A]_o$.

Reaction Mechanisms

49.   For elementary reactions, the rate law can be written using the coefficients in the balanced equation to determine orders.

a.   Rate = $k[CH_3NC]$ b.   Rate = $k[O_3][NO]$

c.   Rate = $k[O_3]$ d.   Rate = $k[O_3][O]$

50.   The observed rate law for this reaction is: Rate = $k[NO]^2[H_2]$. For a mechanism to be plausible, the sum of all the steps must give the overall balanced equation (true for all of the proposed mechanisms in this problem), and the rate law derived from the mechanism must agree with the observed mechanism. In each mechanism (I - III), the first elementary step is the rate-determining step (the slow step), so the derived rate law for each mechanism will be the rate of the first step. The derived rate laws follow:

Mechanism I: Rate = $k[H_2]^2[NO]^2$

Mechanism II: Rate = $k[H_2][NO]$

Mechanism III: Rate = $k[H_2][NO]^2$

Only in Mechanism III does the derived rate law agree with the observed rate law. Thus, only Mechanism III is a plausible mechanism for this reaction.

51.   A mechanism consists of a series of elementary reactions where the rate law for each step can be determined using the coefficients in the balanced equations. For a plausible mechanism, the rate law derived from a mechanism must agree with the rate law determined from experiment. To derive the rate law from the mechanism, the rate of the reaction is assumed to equal the rate of the slowest step in the mechanism.

Because step 1 is the rate-determining step, the rate law for this mechanism is: Rate = $[C_4H_9Br]$. To get the overall reaction, we sum all the individual steps of the mechanism.

Summing all steps gives:

$$C_4H_9Br \rightarrow C_4H_9^+ + Br^-$$
$$C_4H_9^+ + H_2O \rightarrow C_4H_9OH_2^+$$
$$C_4H_9OH_2^+ + H_2O \rightarrow C_4H_9OH + H_3O^+$$

$$\overline{C_4H_9Br + 2\ H_2O\ \rightarrow C_4H_9OH + Br^- + H_3O^+}$$

Intermediates in a mechanism are species that are neither reactants nor products, but that are formed and consumed during the reaction sequence. The intermediates for this mechanism are $C_4H_9^+$ and $C_4H_9OH_2^+$.

52.   Because the rate of the slowest elementary step equals the rate of a reaction:

Rate = rate of step 1 = $k[NO_2]^2$

The sum of all steps in a plausible mechanism must give the overall balanced reaction. Summing all steps gives:

$$NO_2 + NO_2 \rightarrow NO_3 + NO$$
$$NO_3 + CO \rightarrow NO_2 + CO_2$$

$$\overline{NO_2 + CO \rightarrow NO + CO_2}$$

Temperature Dependence of Rate Constants and the Collision Model

53.   In the following plot, R = reactants, P = products, E_a = activation energy and RC = reaction coordinate which is the same as reaction progress. Note for this reaction that ΔE is positive since the products are at a higher energy than the reactants.

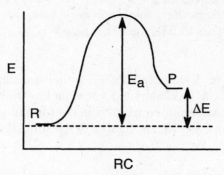

54.   When ΔE is positive, the products are at a higher energy relative to reactants and, when ΔE is negative, the products are at a lower energy relative to reactants.

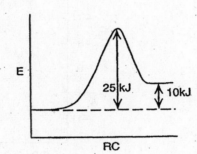

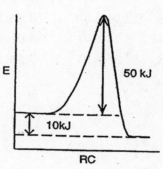

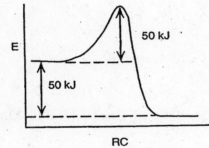

55.

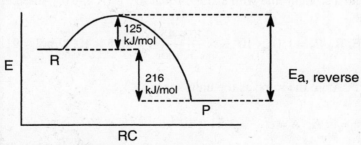

The activation energy for the reverse reaction is:

$E_{a, \text{ reverse}} = 216 \text{ kJ/mol} + 125 \text{ kJ/mol} = 341 \text{ kJ/mol}$

56.   When ΔE is negative, then $E_{a, \text{reverse}} > E_{a, \text{forward}}$ (see energy profile in Exercise 12.55). When ΔE is positive (the products have higher energy than the reactants as represented in the energy profile for Exercise 12.53), then $E_{a, \text{forward}} > E_{a, \text{reverse}}$. Therefore, this reaction has a positive ΔE value.

57.   The Arrhenius equation is: $k = A \exp(-E_a/RT)$ or in logarithmic form, $\ln k = -E_a/RT + \ln A$. Hence, a graph of $\ln k$ vs. $1/T$ should yield a straight line with a slope equal to $-E_a/R$ since the logarithmic form of the Arrhenius equation is in the form of a straight line equation, $y = mx + b$. Note: We carried extra significant figures in the following $\ln k$ values in order to reduce round off error.

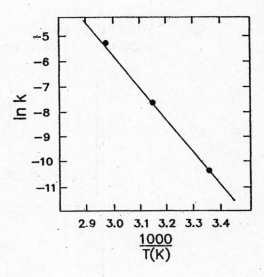

T (K)	1/T (K^{-1})	k (s^{-1})	ln k
338	2.96×10^{-3}	4.9×10^{-3}	-5.32
318	3.14×10^{-3}	5.0×10^{-4}	-7.60
298	3.36×10^{-3}	3.5×10^{-5}	-10.26

$$\text{Slope} = \frac{-10.76 - (-5.85)}{(3.40 \times 10^{-3} - 3.00 \times 10^{-3})\,\text{K}^{-1}} = -1.2 \times 10^4\,\text{K} = -E_a/R$$

$$E_a = -\text{slope} \times R = 1.2 \times 10^4\,\text{K} \times \frac{8.3145\,\text{J}}{\text{K mol}}, \quad E_a = 1.0 \times 10^5\,\text{J/mol} = 1.0 \times 10^2\,\text{kJ/mol}$$

58.   From the Arrhenius equation in logarithmic form ($\ln k = -E_a/RT + \ln A$), a graph of $\ln k$ vs. $1/T$ should yield a straight line with a slope equal to $-E_a/R$ and a y-intercept equal to $\ln A$.

   a.   slope = $-E_a/R$, $E_a = 1.10 \times 10^4\,\text{K} \times \dfrac{8.3145\,\text{J}}{\text{K mol}} = 9.15 \times 10^4\,\text{J/mol} = 91.5\,\text{kJ/mol}$

   b.   The units for A are the same as the units for $k(\text{s}^{-1})$.

          y-intercept = $\ln A$, $A = e^{33.5} = 3.54 \times 10^{14}\,\text{s}^{-1}$

   c. $\ln k = -E_a/RT + \ln A$ or $k = A \exp(-E_a/RT)$

$$k = 3.54 \times 10^{14}\,\text{s}^{-1} \times \exp\left(\frac{-9.15 \times 10^{-4}\,\text{J/mol}}{8.3145\,\text{J/K} \bullet \text{mol} \times 298\,\text{K}}\right) = 3.24 \times 10^{-2}\,\text{s}^{-1}$$

59. $k = A \exp(-E_a/RT)$ or $\ln k = \dfrac{-E_a}{RT} + \ln A$ (the Arrhenius equation)

For two conditions: $\ln\left(\dfrac{k_2}{k_1}\right) = \dfrac{E_a}{R}\left(\dfrac{1}{T_1} - \dfrac{1}{T_2}\right)$ (Assuming A is temperature independent.)

Let $k_1 = 3.52 \times 10^{-7}$ L/mol•s, $T_1 = 555$ K; $k_2 = ?$, $T_2 = 645$ K; $E_a = 186 \times 10^3$ J/mol

$$\ln\left(\dfrac{k_2}{3.52\times10^{-7}}\right) = \dfrac{1.86\times10^5 \text{ J/mol}}{8.3145 \text{ J/mol} \bullet \text{K}}\left(\dfrac{1}{555 \text{ K}} - \dfrac{1}{645 \text{ K}}\right) = 5.6$$

$$\dfrac{k_2}{3.52\times10^{-7}} = e^{5.6} = 270, \quad k_2 = 270(3.52 \times 10^{-7}) = 9.5 \times 10^{-5} \text{ L/mol•s}$$

60.   For two conditions: $\ln\left(\dfrac{k_2}{k_1}\right) = \dfrac{E_a}{R}\left(\dfrac{1}{T_1} - \dfrac{1}{T_2}\right)$ (Assuming A factor is T independent.)

$$\ln\left(\dfrac{8.1\times10^{-2} \text{ s}^{-1}}{4.6\times10^{-2} \text{ s}^{-1}}\right) = \dfrac{E_a}{8.3145 \text{ J/mol} \bullet \text{K}}\left(\dfrac{1}{273 \text{ K}} - \dfrac{1}{293 \text{ K}}\right)$$

$$0.57 = \dfrac{E_a}{83145}(2.5 \times10^{-4}), \quad E_a = 1.9 \times 10^4 \text{ J/mol} = 19 \text{ kJ/mol}$$

61. $\ln\left(\dfrac{k_2}{k_1}\right) = \dfrac{E_a}{R}\left(\dfrac{1}{T_1} - \dfrac{1}{T_2}\right)$; $\dfrac{k_2}{k_1} = 7.00$, $T_1 = 295$ K, $E_a = 54.0 \times 10^3$ J/mol

$$\ln(7.00) = \dfrac{5.0\times10^3 \text{ J/mol}}{8.3145 \text{ J/mol} \bullet \text{K}}\left(\dfrac{1}{295 \text{ K}} - \dfrac{1}{T_2}\right), \quad \dfrac{1}{295 \text{ K}} - \dfrac{1}{T_2} = 3.00 \times 10^{-4}$$

$$\dfrac{1}{T_2} = 3.09 \times10^{-3}, \quad T_2 = 324 \text{ K} = 51°C$$

62. $\ln\left(\dfrac{k_2}{k_1}\right) = \dfrac{E_a}{R}\left(\dfrac{1}{T_1} - \dfrac{1}{T_2}\right)$; Since the rate doubles, then $k_2 = 2\,k_1$.

$$\ln(2.00) = \dfrac{E_a}{8.3145 \text{ J/mol} \bullet \text{K}}\left(\dfrac{1}{298 \text{ K}} - \dfrac{1}{308 \text{ K}}\right), \quad E_a = 5.3 \times 10^4 \text{ J/mol} = 53 \text{ kJ/mol}$$

63. $H_3O^+(aq) + OH^-(aq) \rightarrow 2\,H_2O(l)$ should have the faster rate. H_3O^+ and OH^- will be electro-statically attracted to each other; Ce^{4+} and Hg_2^{2+} will repel each other (so E_a is much larger).

64.   Carbon cannot form the fifth bond necessary for the transition state because of the small atomic size of carbon and because carbon doesn't have low energy d orbitals available to expand the octet.

Catalysts

65.   a.   NO is the catalyst. NO is present in the first step of the mechanism on the reactant side, but it is not a reactant since it is regenerated in the second step.

       b. NO_2 is an intermediate. Intermediates also never appear in the overall balanced equation. In a mechanism, intermediates always appear first on the product side while catalysts always appear first on the reactant side.

       c. $k = A \exp(-E_a/RT)$; $\dfrac{k_{cat}}{k_{un}} = \dfrac{A \exp[-E_a(cat)/RT]}{A \exp[-E(un)/RT]} = \exp\left(\dfrac{E_a(un) - E_a(cat)}{RT}\right)$

            $\dfrac{k_{cat}}{k_{un}} = \exp\left(\dfrac{2100 \text{ J/mol}}{8.3145 \text{ J/mol} \bullet K \times 298 \text{ K}}\right) = e^{0.85} = 2.3$

            The catalyzed reaction is 2.3 times faster than the uncatalyzed reaction at 25°C.

66.   The mechanism for the chlorine catalyzed destruction of ozone is:

$$O_3 + Cl \rightarrow O_2 + ClO \quad (slow)$$
$$ClO + O \rightarrow O_2 + Cl \quad (fast)$$
$$\overline{O_3 + O \rightarrow 2\, O_2}$$

       Because the chlorine atom-catalyzed reaction has a lower activation energy, then the Cl catalyzed rate is faster. Hence, Cl is a more effective catalyst. Using the activation energy, we can estimate the efficiency with which Cl atoms destroy ozone as compared to NO molecules (see Exercise 12.65c).

       At 25°C: $\dfrac{k_{Cl}}{k_{NO}} = \exp\left(\dfrac{-E_a(Cl)}{RT} + \dfrac{E_a(NO)}{RT}\right) = \exp\left(\dfrac{(-2100 + 11,900) \text{ J/mol}}{(8.3145 \times 298) \text{ J/mol}}\right) = e^{3.96} = 52$

       At 25°C, the Cl catalyzed reaction is roughly 52 times faster than the NO catalyzed reaction, assuming the frequency factor A is the same for each reaction.

67.   The reaction at the surface of the catalyst is assumed to follow the steps:

       metal surface

       Thus, CH_2D–CH_2D should be the product. If the mechanism is possible, then the reaction must be:

$$C_2H_4 + D_2 \rightarrow CH_2DCH_2D$$

If we got this product, then we could conclude that this is a possible mechanism. If we got some other product, e.g., CH_3CHD_2, then we would conclude that the mechanism is wrong. Even though this mechanism correctly predicts the products of the reaction, we cannot say conclusively that this is the correct mechanism; we might be able to conceive of other mechanisms that would give the same products as our proposed one.

68.   a.   W, because it has a lower activation energy than the Os catalyst.

        b. $k_w = A_w \exp[-E_a(W)/RT]$; $k_{uncat} = A_{uncat} \exp[-E_a(uncat)/RT]$; Assume $A_w = A_{uncat}$

$$\frac{k_w}{k_{uncat}} = \exp\left(\frac{-E_a(W)}{RT} + \frac{E_a(uncat)}{RT}\right)$$

$$\frac{k_w}{k_{uncat}} = \exp\left(\frac{-163{,}000\,J/mol + 335{,}000\,J/mol}{8.3145\,J/mol \bullet K \times 298\,K}\right) = 1.41 \times 10^{30}$$

The W-catalyzed reaction is approximately 10^{30} times faster than the uncatalyzed reaction.

        c.   Because $[H_2]$ is in the denominator of the rate law, the presence of H_2 decreases the rate of the reaction. For the decomposition to occur, NH_3 molecules must be adsorbed on the surface of the catalyst. If H_2 is also adsorbed on the catalyst surface, then there are fewer sites for NH_3 molecules to be adsorbed and the rate decreases.

69.   Assuming the catalyzed and uncatalyzed reactions have the same form and orders and because concentrations are assumed equal, the rates will be equal when the k values are equal.

$k = A \exp(-E_a/RT)$, $k_{cat} = k_{un}$ when $E_{a,cat}/RT_{cat} = E_{a,un}/RT_{un}$

$$\frac{4.20 \times 10^4\,J/mol}{8.3145\,J/mol \bullet K \times 293\,K} = \frac{7.00 \times 10^4\,J/mol}{8.3145\,J/mol \bullet K \times T_{un}},\ T_{un} = 488\,K = 215°C$$

70.   Rate $= \dfrac{-\Delta[A]}{\Delta t} = k[A]^x$

Assuming the catalyzed and uncatalyzed reaction have the same form and orders and because concentrations are assumed equal, rate $\alpha\ \dfrac{1}{\Delta t}$.

$$\frac{rate_{cat}}{rate_{un}} = \frac{\Delta t_{un}}{\Delta t_{cat}} = \frac{2400\,yr}{\Delta t_{cat}}\ \text{and}\ \frac{rate_{cat}}{rate_{un}} = \frac{k_{cat}}{k_{un}}$$

$$\frac{rate_{cat}}{rate_{un}} = \frac{k_{cat}}{k_{un}} = \frac{A \exp[-E_a(cat)/RT]}{A \exp[-E_a(un)/RT]} = \frac{\exp[-E_a(cat) + E_a(un)]}{RT}$$

$$\frac{k_{cat}}{k_{un}} = \exp\left(\frac{-5.90 \times 10^4 \text{ J/mol} + 1.84 \times 10^5 \text{ J/mol}}{8.3145 \text{ J/mol} \cdot K \times 600. \text{ K}}\right) = 7.62 \times 10^{10}$$

$$\frac{\Delta t_{un}}{\Delta t_{cat}} = \frac{rate_{cat}}{rate_{un}} = \frac{k_{cat}}{k_{un}}, \quad \frac{2400 \text{ yr}}{\Delta t_{cat}} = 7.62 \times 10^{10}, \quad \Delta t_{cat} = 3.15 \times 10^{-8} \text{ yr} \approx 1 \text{ sec}$$

Additional Exercises

71.   Rate = $k[NO]^x[O_2]^y$; comparing the first two experiments, $[O_2]$ is unchanged, [NO] is tripled, and the rate increases by a factor of nine. Therefore, the reaction is second order in NO ($3^2 = 9$). The order of O_2 is more difficult to determine. Comparing the second and third experiments;

$$\frac{3.13 \times 10^{17}}{1.80 \times 10^{17}} = \frac{k(2.50 \times 10^{18})^2(2.50 \times 10^{18})^y}{k(3.00 \times 10^{18})^2(1.00 \times 10^{18})^y}, \quad 1.74 = 0.694 \, (2.50)^y, \quad 2.51 = 2.50^y, \quad y = 1$$

Rate = $k[NO]^2[O_2]$; From experiment 1:

2.00×10^{16} molecules/cm$^3 \cdot$s = k $(1.00 \times 10^{18}$ molecules/cm$^3)^2$ $(1.00 \times 10^{18}$ molecules/cm$^3)$

k = 2.00×10^{-38} cm^6/molecules$^2 \cdot$s = k_{mean}

$$\text{Rate} = \frac{2.00 \times 10^{-38} \text{ cm}^6}{\text{molecules}^2 \cdot \text{s}} \times \left(\frac{6.21 \times 10^{18} \text{ molecules}}{\text{cm}^3}\right)^2 \times \frac{7.36 \times 10^{18} \text{ molecules}}{\text{cm}^3}$$
$$= 5.68 \times 10^{18} \text{ molecules/cm}^3 \cdot \text{s}$$

72.   The pressure of a gas is directly proportional to concentration. Therefore, we can use the pressure data to solve the problem because Rate = $-\Delta[SO_2Cl_2]/\Delta t \propto -\Delta P_{SO_2Cl_2}/\Delta t$.

Assuming a first order equation, the data and plot follow.

Time (hour)	0.00	1.00	2.00	4.00	8.00	16.00
$P_{SO_2Cl_2}$ (atm)	4.93	4.26	3.52	2.53	1.30	0.34
$\ln P_{SO_2Cl_2}$	1.595	1.449	1.258	0.928	0.262	-1.08

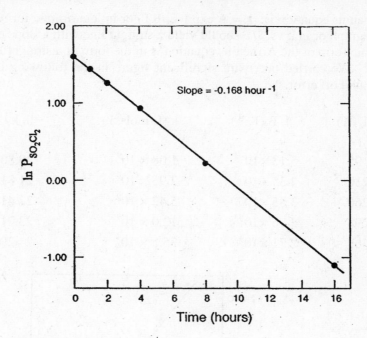

Because the $\ln P_{SO_2Cl_2}$ vs. time plot is linear, the reaction is first order in SO_2Cl_2.

a. Slope of $\ln(P)$ vs. t plot is $-0.168 \, \text{hour}^{-1} = -k$, $k = 0.168 \, \text{hour}^{-1} = 4.67 \times 10^{-5} \, s^{-1}$

Since concentration units don't appear in first-order rate constants, this value of k determined from the pressure data will be the same as if concentration data in molarity units were used.

b. $t_{1/2} = \dfrac{\ln 2}{k} = \dfrac{0.6931}{k} = \dfrac{0.6931}{0.168 \, h^{-1}} = 4.13 \, \text{hour}$

c. $\ln\left(\dfrac{P_{SO_2Cl_2}}{P_o}\right) = -kt = -0.168 \, h^{-1}(20.0 \, h) = -3.36$, $\left(\dfrac{P_{SO_2Cl_2}}{P_o}\right) = e^{-3.36} = 3.47 \times 10^{-2}$

Fraction left = 0.0347 = 3.47%

73.   From 338 K data, a plot of $\ln[N_2O_5]$ vs. t is linear and the slope $= -4.86 \times 10^{-3}$ (plot not included). This tells us the reaction is first order in N_2O_5 with $k = 4.86 \times 10^{-3}$ at 338 K.

From 318 K data, the slope of $\ln[N_2O_5]$ vs t plot is equal to -4.98×10^{-4}, so $k = 4.98 \times 10^{-4}$ at 318 K. We now have two values of k at two temperatures, so we can solve for E_a.

$\ln\left(\dfrac{k_2}{k_1}\right) = \dfrac{E_a}{R}\left(\dfrac{1}{T_1} - \dfrac{1}{T_2}\right)$, $\ln\left(\dfrac{4.86 \times 10^{-3}}{4.98 \times 10^{-4}}\right) = \dfrac{E_a}{8.3145 \, \text{J/mol} \bullet \text{K}}\left(\dfrac{1}{318 \, \text{K}} - \dfrac{1}{338 \, \text{K}}\right)$

$E_a = 1.0 \times 10^5 \, \text{J/mol} = 1.0 \times 10^2 \, \text{kJ/mol}$

74.   The Arrhenius equation is: $k = A \exp(-E_a/RT)$ or in logarithmic form, $\ln k = -E_a/RT + \ln A$. Hence, a graph of $\ln k$ vs. $1/T$ should yield a straight line with a slope equal to $-E_a/R$ since the logarithmic form of the Arrhenius equation is in the form of a straight line equation, $y = mx + b$. Note: We carried one extra significant figure in the following $\ln k$ values in order to reduce round off error.

T (K)	$1/T$ (K^{-1})	k (L/mol•s)	$\ln k$
195	5.13×10^{-3}	1.08×10^{9}	20.80
230.	4.35×10^{-3}	2.95×10^{9}	21.81
260.	3.85×10^{-3}	5.42×10^{9}	22.41
298	3.36×10^{-3}	12.0×10^{9}	23.21
369	2.71×10^{-3}	35.5×10^{9}	24.29

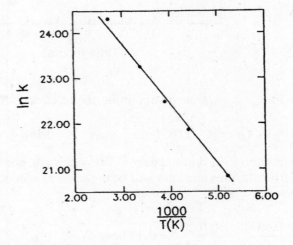

From "eyeballing" the line on the graph:

$$\text{slope} = \frac{20.95 - 23.65}{(5.00 \times 10^{-3} - 3.00 \times 10^{-3})\,K^{-1}} = \frac{-2.70}{2.00 \times 10^{-3}} = -1.35 \times 10^{3}\,K = \frac{-E_a}{R}$$

$$E_a = 1.35 \times 10^{3}\,K \times \frac{8.3145\,J}{K\,mol} = 1.12 \times 10^{4}\,J/mol = 11.2\,kJ/mol$$

From a graphing calculator: slope $= -1.43 \times 10^{3}$ K and $E_a = 11.9$ kJ/mol

75.   At high [S], the enzyme is completely saturated with substrate. Once the enzyme is completely saturated, the rate of decomposition of ES can no longer increase, and the overall rate remains constant.

76. $k = A \exp(-E_a/RT)$; $\dfrac{k_{cat}}{k_{uncat}} = \dfrac{A_{cat}\,\exp(-E_{a,cat}/RT)}{A_{uncat}\,\exp(-E_{a,uncat}/RT)} = \exp\left(\dfrac{E_{a,cat} + E_{a,uncat}}{RT}\right)$

$$2.50 \times 10^3 = \frac{k_{cat}}{k_{uncat}} = \exp\left(\frac{-E_{a,cat} + 5.00 \times 10^4 \, J/mol}{8.3145 \, J/mol \bullet K \times 310. \, K}\right)$$

$$\ln(2.50 \times 10^3) \times 2.58 \times 10^3 \, J/mol = -E_{a,cat} + 5.00 \times 10^4 \, J/mol$$

$$E_{a, cat} = 5.00 \times 10^4 \, J/mol - 2.02 \times 10^4 \, J/mol = 2.98 \times 10^4 \, J/mol = 29.8 \, kJ/mol$$

77.   a.   Because $[A]_o << [B]_o$ or $[C]_o$, the B and C concentrations remain constant at $1.00 \, M$ for this experiment. So: rate $= k[A]^2[B][C] = k'[A]^2$ where $k' = k[B][C]$

For this pseudo-second-order reaction:

$$\frac{1}{[A]} = k't + \frac{1}{[A]_0}, \quad \frac{1}{3.26 \times 10^{-5} \, M} = k'(3.00 \, min) + \frac{1}{1.00 \times 10^{-4} \, M}$$

$$k' = 6890 \, L/mol \bullet min = 115 \, L/mol \bullet s$$

$$k' = k[B][C], \quad k = \frac{k'}{[B][C]} = \frac{115 \, L/mol \bullet s}{(1.00 \, M)(1.00 \, M)} = 115 \, L^3/mol^3 \bullet s$$

b.   For this pseudo-second-order reaction:

$$rate = k'[A]^2, \quad t_{1/2} = \frac{1}{k'[A]_0} = \frac{1}{115 \, L/mol \bullet s \, (1.00 \times 10^{-4} \, mol/L)} = 87.0 \, s$$

c. $$\frac{1}{[A]} = k't + \frac{1}{[A]_0} = 115 \, L/mol \bullet s \times 600. \, s + \frac{1}{1.00 \times 10^{-4} \, mol/L} = 7.90 \times 10^4 \, L/mol,$$

$$[A] = \frac{1}{7.90 \times 10^{-4} \, L/mol} = 1.27 \times 10^{-5} \, mol/L$$

From the stoichiometry in the balanced reaction, 1 mol of B reacts with every 3 mol of A.

amount A reacted $= 1.00 \times 10^{-4} \, M - 1.27 \times 10^{-5} \, M = 8.7 \times 10^{-5} \, M$

amount B reacted $= 8.7 \times 10^{-5} \, mol/L \times 1 \, mol \, B / 3 \, mol \, A = 2.9 \times 10^{-5} \, M$

$[B] = 1.00 \, M - 2.9 \times 10^{-5} \, M = 1.00 \, M$

As we mentioned in part a, the concentration of B (and C) remains constant since the A concentration is so small.

Challenge Problems

78. $$\frac{-d[A]}{dt} = k[A]^3, \quad \int_{[A]_0}^{[A]_t} \frac{d[A]}{[A]^3} = -\int_0^t k \, dt$$

$$\int x^n dx = \frac{x^{n+1}}{n+1}; \text{ So: } -\frac{1}{2[A]^2}\Big|_{[A]_0}^{[A]_t} = -kt, \quad -\frac{1}{2[A]_t^2} + \frac{1}{2[A]_0^2} = -kt$$

For the half-life equation, $[A]_t = 1/2[A]_0$:

$$-\frac{1}{2\left(\frac{1}{2}[A]_0\right)^2} + \frac{1}{2[A]_0^2} = -kt_{1/2}, \quad -\frac{4}{2[A]_0^2} + \frac{1}{2[A]_0^2} = -kt_{1/2}$$

$$-\frac{3}{2[A]_0^2} = -kt_{1/2}, \quad t_{1/2} = \frac{3}{2[A]_0^2 k}$$

The first half-life is $t_{1/2} = 40.$ s and corresponds to going from $[A]_0$ to $1/2[A]_0$. The second half-life corresponds to going from $1/2[A]_0$ to $1/4[A]_0$.

$$\text{First half-life} = \frac{3}{2[A]_0^2 k}; \quad \text{Second half-life} = \frac{3}{2\left(\frac{1}{2}[A]_0\right)^2 k} = \frac{6}{[A]_0^2 k}$$

$$\frac{\text{First half} - \text{life}}{\text{Second half} - \text{life}} = \frac{\dfrac{3}{2[A]_0^2 k}}{\dfrac{6}{[A]_0^2 k}} = 3/12 = 1/4$$

Because the first half-life is 40. s, the second half-life will be one-fourth of this or 10. s.

79. $\text{Rate} = k[I^-]^x[OCl^-]^y[OH^-]^z$; Comparing the first and second experiments:

$$\frac{18.7\times10^{-3}}{9.4\times10^{-3}} = \frac{k(0.0026)^x(0.012)^y(0.10)^z}{k(0.0013)^x(0.012)^y(0.10)^z}, \quad 2.0 = 2.0^x, \quad x = 1$$

Comparing the first and third experiments:

$$\frac{9.4\times10^{-3}}{4.7\times10^{-3}} = \frac{k(0.0013)(0.012)^y(0.10)^z}{k(0.0013)^x(0.0060)^y(0.10)^z}, \quad 2.0 = 2.0^y, \quad y = 1$$

Comparing the first and sixth experiments:

$$\frac{4.8\times10^{-3}}{9.4\times10^{-3}} = \frac{k(0.0013)(0.012)(0.20)^z}{k(0.0013)(0.012)(0.10)^z}, \quad 1/2 = 2.0^z, \quad z = -1$$

$\text{Rate} = \dfrac{k[I^-][OCl^-]}{[OH^-]}$; The presence of OH^- decreases the rate of the reaction.

For the first experiment:

$$\frac{9.4 \times 10^{-3} \text{ mol}}{\text{L s}} = k \frac{(0.0013 \text{ mol/L})(0.012 \text{ mol/L})}{(0.10 \text{ mol/L})} , \quad k = 60.3 \text{ s}^{-1} = 60. \text{ s}^{-1}$$

For all experiments, $k_{mean} = 60. \text{ s}^{-1}$.

80.   For second order kinetics: $\dfrac{1}{[A]} - \dfrac{1}{[A]_o} = kt$ and $t_{1/2} = \dfrac{1}{k[A]_o}$

a. $\dfrac{1}{[A]} = (0.250 \text{ L/mol·s})t + \dfrac{1}{[A]_o}, \quad \dfrac{1}{[A]} = 0.250 \times 180. \text{ s} + \dfrac{1}{1.00 \times 10^{-2} \text{ } M}$

$\dfrac{1}{[A]} = 145 \text{ } M^{-1}, \quad [A] = 6.90 \times 10^{-3} \text{ } M$

Amount of A that reacted = 0.0100   0.00690 = 0.0031 M

$[A_2] = \dfrac{1}{2}(3.1 \times 10^{-3} M) = 1.6 \times 10^{-3} M$

b.   After 3.00 minutes (180. s): $[A] = 3.00 \text{ } [B], \quad 6.90 \times 10^{-3} M = 3.00 \text{ } [B]$

$[B] = 2.30 \times 10^{-3} M$

$\dfrac{1}{[B]} = k_2 t + \dfrac{1}{[B]_o}, \quad \dfrac{1}{2.30 \times 10^{-3} \text{ } M} = k_2(180. \text{ s}) + \dfrac{1}{2.50 \times 10^{-2} \text{ } M}, \quad k_2 = 2.19 \text{ L/mol·s}$

c. $t_{1/2} = \dfrac{1}{k[A]_o} = \dfrac{1}{0.250 \text{ L/mol·s} \times 1.00 \times 10^{-2} \text{ mol/L}} = 4.00 \times 10^2 \text{ s}$

81.   a.   We check for first-order dependence by graphing ln [concentration] vs. time for each set of data. The rate dependence on NO is determined from the first set of data because the ozone concentration is relatively large compared to the NO concentration, so $[O_3]$ is effectively constant.

Time (ms)	[NO] (molecules/cm^3)	ln [NO]
0	6.0×10^8	20.21
100.	5.0×10^8	20.03
500.	2.4×10^8	19.30
700.	1.7×10^8	18.95
1000.	9.9×10^7	18.41

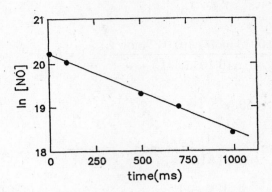

Because ln [NO] vs. t is linear, the reaction is first order with respect to NO.

We follow the same procedure for ozone using the second set of data. The data and plot are:

Time (ms)	$[O_3]$ (molecules/cm^3)	ln $[O_3]$
0	1.0×10^{10}	23.03
50.	8.4×10^{9}	22.85
100.	7.0×10^{9}	22.67
200.	4.9×10^{9}	22.31
300.	3.4×10^{9}	21.95

The plot of ln $[O_3]$ vs. t is linear. Hence, the reaction is first order with respect to ozone.

b.   Rate = k[NO][O$_3$] is the overall rate law.

c.   For NO experiment, Rate = k′[NO] and k′ = −(slope from graph of ln [NO] vs. t).

$$k' = -\text{slope} = -\frac{18.41 - 20.21}{(1000. - 0) \times 10^{-3} \text{ s}} = 1.8 \text{ s}^{-1}$$

For ozone experiment, Rate = k″[O$_3$] and k″ = −(slope from ln [O$_3$] vs. t plot).

$$k'' = -\text{slope} = -\frac{(21.95 - 23.03)}{(300. - 0) \times 10^{-3} \text{ s}} = 3.6 \text{ s}^{-1}$$

d. From NO experiment, Rate = k[NO][O$_3$] = k'[NO] where k' = k[O$_3$].

k' = 1.8 s^{-1} = k(1.0 × 10^{14} molecules/cm^3), k = 1.8 × 10^{-14} cm^3/molecules•s

We can check this from the ozone data. Rate = k"[O$_3$] = k[NO][O$_3$] where k" = k[NO].

k" = 3.6 s^{-1} = k(2.0 × 10^{14} molecules/cm^3), k = 1.8 × 10^{-14} cm^3/molecules•s

Both values of k agree.

82.   On the energy profile to the right, R = reactants, P = products, E$_a$ = activation energy, ΔE = overall energy change for the reaction and I = intermediate.

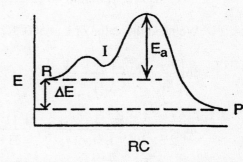

a-d.   See plot to the right.

e. This is a two-step reaction since an intermediate plateau appears between the reactant and the products. This plateau represents the energy of the intermediate. The general reaction mechanism for this reaction is:

R → I
I → P
──────
R → P

In a mechanism, the rate of the slowest step determines the rate of the reaction. The activation energy for the slowest step will be the largest energy barrier that the reaction must over-come. Since the second hump in the diagram is at the highest energy, the second step has the largest activation energy and will be the rate-determining step (the slow step).

83.   a. If the interval between flashes is 16.3 sec, then the rate is:

1 flash/16.3 s = 6.13 × 10^{-2} s^{-1} = k

Interval	k	T
16.3 s	6.13 × 10^{-2} s^{-1}	21.0°C (294.2 K)
13.0 s	7.69 × 10^{-2} s^{-1}	27.8°C (301.0 K)

$\ln\left(\dfrac{k_2}{k_1}\right) = \dfrac{E_a}{R}\left(\dfrac{1}{T_1} - \dfrac{1}{T_2}\right)$; Solving: E$_a$ = 2.5 × 10^4 J/mol = 25 kJ/mol

b. $\ln\left(\dfrac{k}{6.13\times10^{-2}}\right) = \dfrac{2.5\times10^{4}\,\text{J/mol}}{8.3145\,\text{J/mol}\bullet\text{K}}\left(\dfrac{1}{294.2\,\text{K}} - \dfrac{1}{303.2\,\text{K}}\right) = 0.30$

$k = e^{0.30}\times6.13\times10^{-2} = 8.3\times10^{-2}\,\text{s}^{-1}$; Interval = 1/k = 12 seconds

c.

T	Interval	54-2(Intervals)
21.0 °C	16.3 s	21 °C
27.8 °C	13.0 s	28 °C
30.0 °C	12 s	30. °C

This rule of thumb gives excellent agreement to two significant figures.

84.   We need the value of k at 500. K.

$$\ln\left(\dfrac{k_2}{k_1}\right) = \dfrac{E_a}{R}\left(\dfrac{1}{T_1} - \dfrac{1}{T_2}\right)$$

$$\ln\left(\dfrac{k_2}{2.3\times10^{-12}\,\text{L/mol}\bullet\text{s}}\right) = \dfrac{1.11\times10^{5}\,\text{J/mol}}{8.3145\,\text{J/mol}\bullet\text{K}}\left(\dfrac{1}{273\,\text{K}} - \dfrac{1}{500.\,\text{K}}\right) = 22.2$$

$$\dfrac{k_2}{2.3\times10^{-12}} = e^{22.2}, \quad k_2 = 1.0\times10^{-2}\,\text{L/mol}\bullet\text{s}$$

Because the decomposition reaction is an elementary reaction, then the rate law can be written using the coefficients in the balanced equation. For this reaction: Rate = $k[NO_2]^2$. To solve for the time, we must use the integrated rate law for second-order kinetics. The major problem now is converting units so they match. Rearranging the ideal gas law gives n/V = P/RT. Substituting P/RT for concentration units in the second-order integrated rate law equation:

$$\dfrac{1}{[NO_2]} = kt + \dfrac{1}{[NO_2]_o}, \quad \dfrac{1}{P/RT} = kt + \dfrac{1}{P_o/RT}, \quad \dfrac{RT}{P} - \dfrac{RT}{P_o} = kt, \quad t = \dfrac{RT}{k}\left(\dfrac{P_o - P}{P\times P_o}\right)$$

$$t = \dfrac{(0.08206\,\text{L atm/K}\bullet\text{mol})(500.\,\text{K})}{1.0\times10^{-2}\,\text{L/mol}\bullet\text{s}}\times\left(\dfrac{2.5\,\text{atm} - 1.5\,\text{atm}}{1.5\,\text{atm}\times2.5\,\text{atm}}\right) = 1.1\times10^{3}\,\text{s}$$

85.   a.   [B] >> [A] so that [B] can be considered constant over the experiments. (This gives us a pseudo-order rate law equation.)

b.   Note in each data set that successive half-lives double (in expt. 1 the first half-life is 40. sec, the second is 80. sec; in expt. 2 the first half-life is 20. sec, the second is 40. sec). Thus, the reaction is second order in [A] since $t_{1/2}$ for second order reactions is inversely proportional to concentration. Between expt. 1 and expt. 2, we double [B] and the reaction rate doubles, thus it is first order in [B]. The overall rate law equation is rate = $k[A]^2[B]$.

Using $t_{1/2} = \dfrac{1}{k[A]_0}$, we get $k = \dfrac{1}{(40.\text{ s})(10.0 \times 10^{-2}\text{ mol}/\text{L})} = 0.25$ L/mol•s. But this is actually k' where rate $= k'\,[A]^2$ and $k' = k[B]$.

$$k = \frac{k'}{[B]} = \frac{0.25\,\text{L}/\text{mol} \bullet \text{s}}{5.0\,\text{mol}/\text{L}} = 0.050\,\text{L}^2/\text{mol}^2 \bullet \text{s}$$

86.   a.   Rate $= k[H_2]^x[NO]^y$; Looking at the data in experiment 2, notice that the concentration of H_2 is cut in half every 10. sec. Only first-order reactions have a half-life that is independent of concentration. The reaction is first order in H_2. In the data for experiment 1, notice that the half-life is 40. s. This indicates that in going from experiment 1 to experiment 2 where the NO concentration doubled, the rate of reaction increased by a factor of four. This tells us that the reaction is second order in NO.

$$\text{Rate} = k[H_2][NO]^2$$

b.   This reaction is pseudo-first-order in $[H_2]$ as the concentration of NO is so large, it is basically constant.

$$\text{Rate} = k[NO]^2[H_2] = k'[H_2] \text{ where } k' = k[NO]^2$$

For a first-order reaction, the integrated rate law is:

$$\ln\!\left(\frac{[H_2]}{[H_2]_0}\right) = -k't$$

Use any set of data you want to calculate k'. For example, in experiment 1 from 0 to 20. s the concentration of H_2 decreased from 0.010 M to 0.0071 M.

$$\ln\!\left(\frac{0.0071}{0.010}\right) = -k'(20.\text{ s}), \quad k' = 1.7 \times 10^{-2}\text{ s}^{-1}$$

$$k' = k[NO]_2, \quad 1.7 \times 10^{-2}\text{ s}^{-1} = k(10.0\text{ mol/L})^2$$

$$k = 1.7 \times 10^{-4}\text{ L}^2/\text{mol}^2 \bullet \text{s}$$

We get similar values for k using other data from either experiment 1 or experiment 2.

c. $\ln\!\left(\dfrac{[H_2]}{0.010\,M}\right) = -k't = -(1.7 \times 10^{-2}\text{ L}^2/\text{mol}^2 \bullet \text{s}) \times 30.\text{ s}, \quad [H_2] = 6.0 \times 10^{-3}\,M$

87.   Rate $= k[A]^x[B]^y[C]^z$; During the course of experiment 1, [A] and [C] are essentially constant, and Rate $= k'[B]^y$ where $k' = k[A]_0^x[C]_0^z$.

[B] (M)	time (s)	ln[B]	1/[B] (M^{-1})
1.0×10^{-3}	0	-6.91	1.0×10^{3}
2.7×10^{-4}	1.0×10^{5}	-8.22	3.7×10^{3}
1.6×10^{-4}	2.0×10^{5}	-8.74	6.3×10^{3}
1.1×10^{-4}	3.0×10^{5}	-9.12	9.1×10^{3}
8.5×10^{-5}	4.0×10^{5}	-9.37	12×10^{3}
6.9×10^{-5}	5.0×10^{5}	-9.58	14×10^{3}
5.8×10^{-5}	6.0×10^{5}	-9.76	17×10^{3}

A plot of 1/[B] vs. t is linear (plot not included). So the reaction is second order in B and the integrated rate equation from the slope and y-intercept of the straight line in the plot is:

$$1/[B] = (2.7 \times 10^{-2} \text{ L/mol} \cdot \text{s}) \, t + 1.0 \times 10^{3} \text{ L/mol}; \quad k' = 2.7 \times 10^{-2} \text{ L/mol} \cdot \text{s}$$

For experiment 2, [B] and [C] are essentially constant and Rate = $k''[A]^{x}$ where $k'' = k[B]_0^y[C]_0^z = k[B]_0^2[C]_0^z$.

[A] (M)	time (s)	ln[A]	1/[A] (M^{-1})
1.0×10^{-2}	0	-4.61	1.0×10^{2}
8.9×10^{-3}	1.0	-4.72	110
7.1×10^{-3}	3.0	-4.95	140
5.5×10^{-3}	5.0	-5.20	180
3.8×10^{-3}	8.0	-5.57	260
2.9×10^{-3}	10.0	-5.84	340
2.0×10^{-3}	13.0	-6.21	5.0×10^{2}

A plot of ln[A] vs. t is linear. So the reaction is first order in A and the integrated rate law from the slope and y-intercept of the straight line in the plot is:

$$\ln[A] = -(0.123 \text{ s}^{-1}) \, t - 4.61; \quad k'' = 0.123 \text{ s}^{-1}$$

Note: We will carry an extra significant figure in k''.

Experiment 3:   [A] and [B] are constant; Rate = $k'''[C]^{z}$

The plot of [C] vs. t is linear. Thus, z = 0.

The overall rate law is: Rate = $k[A][B]^{2}$

From Experiment 1 (to determine k):

$$k' = 2.7 \times 10^{-2} \text{ L/mol} \cdot \text{s} = k[A]_0^x[C]_0^z = k[A]_o = k(2.0 \ M), \quad k = 1.4 \times 10^{-2} \text{ L}^2/\text{mol}^2 \cdot \text{s}$$

From Experiment 2: $k'' = 0.123 \text{ s}^{-1} = k[B]_0^2$, $k = \dfrac{0.123 \text{ s}^{-1}}{(3.0 \ M)^2} = 1.4 \times 10^{-2} \text{ L}^2/\text{mol}^2 \cdot \text{s}$

Thus, Rate = $k[A][B]^{2}$ and $k = 1.4 \times 10^{-2} \text{ L}^2/\text{mol}^2 \cdot \text{s}$.

88.   a.   Rate $= (k_1 + k_2[H^+])[I^-]^m[H_2O_2]^n$

In all the experiments, the concentration of H_2O_2 is small compared to the concentrations of I^- and H^+. Therefore, the concentrations of I^- and H^+ are effectively constant and the rate law reduces to:

Rate $= k_{obs}[H_2O_2]^n$ where $k_{obs} = (k_1 + k_2[H^+])[I^-]^m$

Since all plots of $\ln[H_2O_2]$ vs. time are linear, the reaction is first order with respect to H_2O_2 ($n = 1$). The slopes of the $\ln[H_2O_2]$ vs. time plots equal $-k_{obs}$ which equals $-(k_1 + k_2[H^+])[I^-]^m$. To determine the order of I^-, compare the slopes of two experiments where I^- changes and H^+ is constant. Comparing the first two experiments:

$$\frac{\text{slope (exp. 2)}}{\text{slope (exp. 1)}} = \frac{-0.360}{-0.120} = \frac{-[k_1 + k_2\,(0.0400\,M)][0.3000\,M)^m}{-[k_1 + k_2\,(0.0400\,M)][0.1000\,M)^m},$$

$$3.00 = \left(\frac{0.3000}{0.1000}\right)^m = (3.000)^m, \quad m = 1$$

The reaction is also first order with respect to I^-.

b.   The slope equation has two unknowns, k_1 and k_2. To solve for k_1 and k_2, we must have two equations. We need to take one of the first set of three experiments and one of the 2nd set of three experiments to generate the two equations in k_1 and k_2.

Experiment 1: slope $= -(k_1 + k_2[H^+])[I^-]$

-0.120 min$^{-1} = -[k_1 + k_2\,(0.0400\,M)]\,0.1000\,M$ or $1.20 = k_1 + k_2\,(0.0400)$

Experiment 4:

-0.0760 min$^{-1} = -[k_1 + k_2\,(0.0200\,M)]\,0.0750\,M$ or $1.01 = k_1 + k_2\,(0.0200)$

Subtracting 4 from 1:

$$1.20 = k_1 + k_2\,(0.0400)$$
$$-1.01 = -k_1 - k_2\,(0.0200)$$

$$\overline{}$$

$0.19 = \qquad k_2\,(0.0200), \quad k_2 = 9.5\ \text{L}^2/\text{mol}^2\cdot\text{min}$

$1.20 = k_1 + 9.5(0.0400), \quad k_1 = 0.82\ \text{L/ mol}\cdot\text{min}$

c.   There are two pathways, one involving H^+ with rate $= k_2[H^+][I^-][H_2O_2]$ and another pathway not involving H^+ with rate $= k_1[I^-][H_2O_2]$. The overall rate of reaction depends on which of these two pathways dominates, and this depends on the H^+ concentration.

Integrative Problems

89. $8.75 \text{ h} \times \dfrac{3600 \text{ s}}{\text{h}} = 3.15 \times 10^4 \text{ s}; \quad k = \dfrac{\ln 2}{t_{1/2}} = \dfrac{\ln 2}{3.15 \times 10^4 \text{ s}} = 2.20 \times 10^{-5} \text{ s}^{-1}$

The partial pressure of a gas is directly related to the concentration in mol/L. So instead of using mol/L as the concentration units in the integrated first order rate law, we can use partial pressures of SO_2Cl_2.

$$\ln\left(\dfrac{P}{P_0}\right) = -kt, \quad \ln\left(\dfrac{P}{791 \text{ torr}}\right) = -(2.20 \times 10^{-5} \text{ s}^{-1})(12.5 \text{ h} \times \dfrac{3600 \text{ s}}{\text{h}})$$

$$P_{SO_2Cl_2} = 294 \text{ torr} \times \dfrac{1 \text{ atm}}{760 \text{ torr}} = 0.387 \text{ atm}$$

$$n = \dfrac{PV}{RT} = \dfrac{0.387 \text{ atm} \times 1.25 \text{ L}}{\dfrac{0.08206 \text{ L atm}}{\text{mol K}} \times 593 \text{ K}} = 9.94 \times 10^{-3} \text{ mol } SO_2Cl_2$$

$$9.94 \times 10^{-3} \text{ mol} \times \dfrac{6.022 \times 10^{23} \text{ molecules}}{\text{mol}} = 5.99 \times 10^{21} \text{ molecules } SO_2Cl_2$$

90. $k = \dfrac{\ln 2}{t_{1/2}} = \dfrac{\ln 2}{667 \text{ s}} = 1.04 \times 10^{-3} \text{ s}^{-1}$

$$[In^+]_0 = \dfrac{2.38 \text{ g InCl} \times \dfrac{1 \text{ mol InCl}}{150.3 \text{ g}} \times \dfrac{1 \text{ mol In}^+}{\text{mol InCl}}}{0.500 \text{ L}} = 0.0317 \text{ mol/L}$$

$$\ln\left(\dfrac{[In^+]}{[In^+]_0}\right) = -kt, \quad \ln\left(\dfrac{[In^+]}{0.0317 \, M}\right) = -(1.04 \times 10^{-3} \text{ s}^{-1}) \times 1.25 \text{ h} \times \dfrac{3600 \text{ s}}{\text{h}}$$

$[In^+] = 2.94 \times 10^{-4} \text{ mol/L}$

The balanced redox reaction is: $3 \, In^+(aq) \rightarrow 2 \, In(s) + In^{3+}(aq)$

$$\text{mol } In^+ \text{ reacted} = 0.500 \text{ L} \times \dfrac{0.0317 \text{ mol}}{\text{L}} - 0.500 \text{ L} \times \dfrac{2.94 \times 10^{-4} \text{ mol}}{\text{L}} = 1.57 \times 10^{-2} \text{ mol } In^+$$

$$1.57 \times 10^{-2} \text{ mol } In^+ \times \dfrac{2 \text{ mol In}}{3 \text{ mol In}^+} \times \dfrac{114.8 \text{ g In}}{\text{mol In}} = 1.20 \text{ g In}$$

91. $\ln\left(\dfrac{k_2}{k_1}\right) = \dfrac{E_a}{R}\left(\dfrac{1}{T_1} - \dfrac{1}{T_2}\right); \quad \ln\left(\dfrac{1.7 \times 10^{-2} \text{ s}^{-1}}{7.2 \times 10^{-4} \text{ s}^{-1}}\right) = \dfrac{E_a}{8.3145 \text{ J/K} \bullet \text{mol}}\left(\dfrac{1}{660. \text{ K}} - \dfrac{1}{720. \text{ K}}\right)$

$E_a = 2.1 \times 10^5 \text{ J/mol}$

For k at 325°C (598 K):

$$\ln\left(\frac{1.7\times10^{-2}\ s^{-1}}{k}\right) = \frac{2.1\times10^5\ J/mol}{8.3145\ J/K\bullet mol}\left(\frac{1}{598\ K} - \frac{1}{720.\ K}\right),\ k = 1.3\ \times\ 10^{-5}\ s^{-1}$$

For three half-lives, we go from 100% → 50% → 25% → 12.5%. After three half-lives, 12.5% of the original amount of C_2H_5I remains. Partial pressures are directly related to gas concentrations in mol/L:

$P_{C_2H_5I}$ = 894 torr × 0.125 = 112 torr after 3 half-lives

Marathon Problem

92.   a.   Rate = $k[CH_3X]^x[Y]^y$; For experiment 1, [Y] is constant so Rate = $k'[CH_3X]^x$ where $k' = k(3.0\ M)^y$.

A plot (not included) of $\ln[CH_3X]$ vs t is linear (x = 1). The integrated rate law is:

$\ln[CH_3X] = -0.93\ t - 3.99;\ k' = 0.93\ h^{-1}$

For Experiment 2, [Y] is again constant with Rate = $k''[CH_3X]^x$ where $k'' = k(4.5\ M)^y$. The ln plot is linear again with an integrated rate law:

$\ln[CH_3X] = -0.93\ t - 5.40;\ k'' = 0.93\ h^{-1}$

Dividing the rate constant values: $\dfrac{k'}{k''} = \dfrac{0.93}{0.93} = \dfrac{k(3.0)^y}{k(4.5)^y}$, $1.0 = (0.67)^y$, y = 0

The reaction is first order in CH_3X and zero order in Y. The overall rate law is:

Rate = $k[CH_3X]$ where k = 0.93 h^{-1} at 25°C.

b. $t_{1/2}$ = (ln 2)/k = 0.6931/(7.88 × $10^8\ h^{-1}$) = 8.80 × 10^{-10} h

c. $\ln\dfrac{k_2}{k_1} = \dfrac{E_a}{R}\left(\dfrac{1}{T_1} - \dfrac{1}{T_2}\right)$, $\ln\left(\dfrac{7.88\times10^8}{0.93}\right) = \dfrac{E_a}{8.3145\ J/K\bullet mol}\left(\dfrac{1}{298\ K} - \dfrac{1}{358\ K}\right)$

E_a = 3.0 × 10^5 J/mol = 3.0 × 10^2 kJ/mol

d.   From part a, the reaction is first order in CH_3X and zero order in Y. From part c, the activation energy is close to the C-X bond energy. A plausible mechanism that explains the results in parts a and c is:

$CH_3X \rightarrow CH_3 + X$ (slow)

$CH_3 + Y \rightarrow CH_3Y$ (fast)

Note: This is a possible mechanism since the derived rate law is the same as the experimental rate law and the sum of the steps give the overall balanced equation.

CHAPTER THIRTEEN

CHEMICAL EQUILIBRIUM

For Review

1. a. The rates of the forward and reverse reactions are equal at equilibrium.

    b. There is no net change in the composition (as long as temperature is constant).

        See Figure 13.5 for an illustration of the concentration vs. time plot for this reaction. In Fig. 13.5, A = H_2, B = N_2, and C = NH_3. Notice how the reactant concentrations decrease with time until they reach equilibrium where the concentrations remain constant. The product concentration increases with time until equilibrium is reached. Also note that H_2 decreases faster than N_2; this is due to the 3:1 mole ratio in the balanced equation. H_2 should be used up three times faster than N_2. Similarly, NH_3 should increase at rate twice the rate of decrease of N_2. This is shown in the plot.

        Reference Figure 13.4 for the reaction rate vs. time plot. As concentrations of reactants decrease, the rate of the forward reaction decreases. Also, as product concentration increases, the rate of the reverse reaction increases. Eventually they reach the point where the rate that reactants are converted into products exactly equals the rate that products are converted into reactants. This is equilibrium and the concentrations of reactants and products do not change.

2. The law of mass action is a general description of the equilibrium condition; it defines the equilibrium constant expression. The law of mass action is based on experimental observation.

    K is a constant; the value (at constant temperature) does not depend on the initial conditions. Table 13.1 illustrates this nicely. Three experiments were run with each experiment having a different initial condition (only reactants present initially, only products present initially, and some of reactants and products present initially). In all three experiments, the value of K calculated is the same in each experiment (as it should be).

    Equilibrium and rates of reaction (kinetics) are independent of each other. A reaction with a large equilibrium constant value may be a fast reaction or a slow reaction. The same is true for a reaction with a small equilibrium constant value. Kinetics is discussed in detail in Chapter 12 of the text.

    The equilibrium constant is a number that tells us the relative concentrations (pressures) of reactants and products at equilibrium. An equilibrium position is a set of concentrations that satisfy the equilibrium constant expression. More than one equilibrium position can satisfy the same equilibrium constant expression.

From Table 13.1, each of the three experiments have different equilibrium positions; that is, each experiment has different equilibrium concentrations. However, when these equilibrium concentrations are inserted into the equilibrium constant expression, each experiment gives the same value for K. The equilibrium position depends on the initial concentrations one starts with. Since there are an infinite number of initial conditions, there are an infinite number of equilibrium positions. However, each of these infinite equilibrium positions will always give the same value for the equilibrium constant (assuming temperature is constant).

3. $2 NOCl(g) \rightleftharpoons 2 NO(g) + Cl_2(g)   K = 1.6 \times 10^{-5}$

The expression for K is the product concentrations divided by the reactant concentrations. When K has a value much less than one, the product concentrations are relatively small and the reactant concentrations are relatively large.

$2 NO(g) \rightleftharpoons N_2(g) + O_2(g)   K = 1 \times 10^{31}$

When K has a value much greater than one, the product concentrations are relatively large and the reactant concentrations are relatively small. In both cases, however, the rate of the forward reaction equals the rate of the reverse reaction at equilibrium (this is a definition of equilibrium).

4.   The difference between K and K_p are the units used to express the amounts of reactants and products present. K is calculated using units of molarity. K_p is calculated using partial pressures in units of atm (usually). Both have the same form; the difference is the units used to determine the values. K_p is only used when the equilibria involves gases; K can be used for gas phase equilibria and for solution equilibria.

$K_p = K(RT)^{\Delta n}$ where Δn = moles gaseous products in the balanced equation – moles gaseous reactants in the balanced equation. $K = K_p$ when $\Delta n = 0$ (when moles of gaseous products = moles of gaseous reactants. $K \neq K_p$ when $\Delta n \neq 0$.

When a balanced equation is multiplied by a factor n, $K_{new} = (K_{original})^n$. So if a reaction is tripled, $K_{new} = K_{original}^3$. If a reaction is reversed, $K_{new} = 1/K_{original}$. Here $K_{p,\,new} = 1/K_{p,\,original}$.

5.   When reactants and products are all in the same phase, these are homogeneous equilibria. Heterogeneous equilibria involve more than one phase. In general, for a homogeneous gas phase equilibria, all reactants and products are included in the K expression. In heterogeneous equilibria, equilibrium does not depend on the amounts of pure solids or liquids present. The amount of solids and liquids present are not included in K expressions; they just have to be present. On the other hand, gases and solutes are always included in K expressions. Solutes have (aq) written after them.

6.   For the gas phase reaction: $aA + bB \rightleftharpoons cC + dD$

the equilibrium constant expression is: $K = \dfrac{[C]^c [D]^d}{[A]^a [B]^b}$

and the reaction quotient has the same form: $Q = \dfrac{[C]^c[D]^d}{[A]^a[B]^b}$

The difference is that in the expression for K we use equilibrium concentrations, i.e., [A], [B], [C], and [D] are all in equilibrium with each other. Any set of concentrations can be plugged into the reaction quotient expression. Typically, we plug initial concentrations into the Q expression and then compare the value of Q to K to see how far we are from equilibrium. If Q = K, the reaction is at equilibrium with these concentrations. If Q ≠ K, then the reaction will have to shift either to products or to reactants to reach equilibrium. For Q > K, the net change in the reaction to get to equilibrium must be a conversion of products into reactants. We say the reaction shifts left to reach elquilibrium. When Q < K, the net change in the reaction to get to equilibrium must be a conversion of reactants into products; the reaction shifts right to reach equilibrium.

7.   The steps to solve equilibrium problems are outlined at the beginning of section 13.6. The ICE table is a convenient way to summarize an equilibrium problem. We make three rows under the balanced reaction. The initials in ICE stand for <u>i</u>nitial, <u>c</u>hange, and <u>e</u>quilibrium. The first step is to fill in the initial row, then deduce the net change that must occur to reach equilibrium. You then define x or 2x or 3x... as the change (molarity or partial pressure) that must occur to reach equilibrium. After defining your x, fill in the change column in terms of x. Finally, sum the initial and change columns together to get the last row of the ICE table; the equilibrium concentrations (or partial pressures). The ICE table again summarizes what must occur for a reaction to reach equilibrium. This is vital in solving equilibrium problems.

8.   The assumption comes from the value of K being much less than 1. For these reactions, the equilibrium mixture will not have a lot of products present; mostly reactants are present at equilibrium. If we define the change that must occur in terms of x as the amount (molarity or partial pressure) of a reactant that must react to reach equilibrium, then x must be a small number because K is a very small number. We want to know the value of x in order to solve the problem, so we don't assume x = 0. Instead, we concentrate on the equilibrium row in the ICE table. Those reactants (or products) have equilibrium concentrations in the form of 0.10 – x or 0.25 + x or 3.5 – 3x, etc., is where an important assumption can be made. The assumption is that because K << 1, x will be small (x << 1) and when we add x or subtract x from some initial concentration, it will make little or no difference. That is, we assume that 0.10 – x ≈ 0.10 or 0.25 + x ≈ 0.25 or 3.5 – 3x ≈ 3.5; we assume that the initial concentration of a substance is equal to the equilibrium concentration. This assumption makes the math much easier, and usually gives a value of x that is well within 5% of the true value of x (we get about the same answer with a lot less work).

We check the assumptions for validity using the 5% rule. From doing a lot of these calculations, it is found that when a assumption like 0.20 – x ≈ 0.20 is made, if x is less than 5% of the number the assumption was made against, then our final answer is within acceptable error limits of the true value of x (as determined when the equation is solved exactly). For our example above (0.20 – x ≈ 0.20), if (x/0.20) × 100 ≤ 5%, then our assumption is valid by the 5% rule. If the error is greater than 5%, then we must solve the equation exactly or use a math trick called the method of successive approximations. See Appendix A1.4 for details regarding the method of successive approximations as well as for a review in solving quadratic equations exactly.

9.   LeChatlier's Principle: if a change is imposed on a system at equilibrium, the position of the equilibrium will shift in the direction that tends to reduce that change.

   a.   When a gaseous (or solute) reactant is added to a reaction at equilibrium, the reaction shifts right to use up some of the added reactant. Adding NOCl causes the equilibrium to shift to the right.

   b.   If a gaseous (or solute) product is added to a system at equilibrium, the reaction shifts left to use up some of the added product. Adding NO(g) causes the equilibrium to shift left.

   c.   Here a gaseous reactant is removed (NOCl), so the reaction shifts left to produce more of the NOCl.

   d.   Here a gaseous product is removed (Cl_2), so the reaction shifts right to produce more of the Cl_2.

   e.   In this reaction, 2 moles of gaseous reactants are converted into 3 moles of gaseous products. If the volume of the container is decreased, the reaction shifts to the side that occupies a smaller volume. Here, the reactions shift left to side with the fewer moles of reactant gases present.

   For all of these changes, the value of K does not change. As long as temperature is constant, the value of K is constant.

   $2 H_2(g) + O_2(g) \rightleftharpoons 2 H_2O(l)$; In this reaction, the amount of water present has no effect on the equilibrium; $H_2O(l)$ just has to be present whether it's 0.0010 grams or 1.0×10^6 grams. The same is true for solids. When solids or liquids are in a reaction, addition or removal of these solids or liquids has no effect on the equilibrium (the reaction remains at equilibrium). Note that for this example, if the temperature is such that $H_2O(g)$ is the product, then the amount of $H_2O(g)$ present does affect the equilibrium.

   A change in volume will change the partial pressure of all reactants and products by the same factor. The shift in equilibrium depends on the number of gaseous particles on each side. An increase in volume will shift the equilibrium to the side with the greater number of particles in the gas phase. A decrease in volume will favor the side with lesser gas phase particles. If there are the same number of gas phase particles on each side of the reaction, a change in volume will not shift the equilibrium.

   When we change the pressure by adding an unreactive gas, we do not change the partial pressures (or concentrations) of any of the substances in equilibrium with each other. This is because the volume of the container did not change. If the partial pressures (and concentrations) are unchanged, the reaction is still at equilibrium.

10.   In an exothermic reaction, heat is a product. When the temperature increases, heat (a product) is added and the reaction shifts left to use up the added heat. For an exothermic reaction, the value of K decreases as temperature increases. In an endothermic reaction, heat is a reactant. Heat (a reactant) is added when the temperature increases and the reaction shifts right to use up the added heat in order to reestablish equilibrium. The value of K increases for an endothermic reaction as temperature increases.

A decrease in temperature corresponds to the removal of heat. Here, the value of K increases as T decreases. This indicates that as heat is removed, more products are produced. Heat must be a product, so this is an exothermic reaction.

Questions

9.   No, equilibrium is a dynamic process. Both reactions:

$$H_2O + CO \rightarrow H_2 + CO_2 \text{ and } H_2 + CO_2 \rightarrow H_2O + CO$$

are occurring, but at equal rates. Thus, ^{14}C atoms will be distributed between CO and CO_2.

10.   No, it doesn't matter from which direction the equilibrium position is reached. Both experiments will give the same equilibrium position since both experiments started with stoichiometric amounts of reactants or products.

11. $H_2O(g) + CO(g) \rightleftharpoons H_2(g) + CO_2(g)$ $K = \dfrac{[H_2][CO_2]}{[H_2O][CO]} = 2.0$

K is a unitless number since there is an equal number of moles of product gases as compared to moles of reactant gases in the balanced equation. Therefore, we can use units of molecules per liter instead of moles per liter to determine K.

We need to start somewhere, so let's assume 3 molecules of CO react. If 3 molecules of CO react, then 3 molecules of H_2O must react, and 3 molecules each of H_2 and CO_2 are formed. We would have 6 – 3 = 3 molecules CO, 8 – 3 = 5 molecules H_2O, 0 + 3 = 3 molecules H_2, and 0 + 3 = 3 molecules CO_2 present. This will be an equilibrium mixture if K = 2.0:

$$K = \frac{\left(\dfrac{3 \text{ molecules } H_2}{L}\right)\left(\dfrac{3 \text{ molecules } CO_2}{L}\right)}{\left(\dfrac{5 \text{ molecules } H_2O}{L}\right)\left(\dfrac{3 \text{ molecules } CO}{L}\right)} = \frac{3}{5}$$

Because this mixture does not give a value of K = 2.0, this is not an equilibrium mixture. Let's try 4 molecules of CO reacting to reach equilibrium.

molecules CO remaining = 6 – 4 = 2 molecules CO;
molecules H_2O remaining = 8 – 4 = 4 molecules H_2O;
molecules H_2 present = 0 + 4 = 4 molecules H_2;
molecules CO_2 present = 0 + 4 = 4 molecules CO_2

$$K = \frac{\left(\dfrac{4 \text{ molecules } H_2}{L}\right)\left(\dfrac{4 \text{ molecules } CO_2}{L}\right)}{\left(\dfrac{4 \text{ molecules } H_2O}{L}\right)\left(\dfrac{2 \text{ molecules } CO}{L}\right)} = 2.0$$

Since K = 2.0 for this reaction mixture, we are at equilibrium.

12.   When equilibrium is reached, there is no net change in the amount of reactants and products present since the rates of the forward and reverse reactions are equal to each other. The first diagram has 4 A_2B molecules, 2 A_2 molecules and 1 B_2 molecule present. The second diagram has 2 A_2B molecules, 4 A_2 molecules, and 2 B_2 molecules. Therefore, the first diagram cannot represent equilibrium since there was a net change in reactants and products. Is the second diagram the equilibrium mixture? That depends on whether there is a net change between reactants and products when going from the second diagram to the third diagram. The third diagram contains the same number and type of molecules as the second diagram, so the second diagram is the first illustration that represents equilibrium.

The reaction container initially contained only A_2B. From the first diagram, 2 A_2 molecules and 1 B_2 molecule are present (along with 4 A_2B molecules). From the balanced reaction, these 2 A_2 molecules and 1 B_2 molecule were formed when 2 A_2B molecules decomposed. Therefore, the initial number of A_2B molecules present equals $4 + 2 = 6$ molecules A_2B.

13.   K and K_p are equilibrium constants as determined by the law of mass action. For K, concentration units of mol/L are used, and for K_p, partial pressures in units of atm are used (generally). Q is called the reaction quotient. Q has the exact same form as K or K_p, but instead of equilibrium concentrations, initial concentrations are used to calculate the Q value. The use of Q is when it is compared to the K value. When $Q = K$ (or when $Q_p = K_p$), the reaction is at equilibrium. When $Q \neq K$, the reaction is not at equilibrium and one can deduce the net change that must occur for the system to get to equilibrium.

14. $H_2(g) + I_2(g) \rightarrow 2\,HI(g)$ $K = \dfrac{[HI]^2}{[H_2][I_2]}$

$H_2(g) + I_2(s) \rightarrow 2\,HI(g)$ $K = \dfrac{[HI]^2}{[H_2]}$ (Solids are not included in K expressions.)

Some property differences are:

a.   the reactions have different K expressions.

b.   for the first reaction, $K = K_p$ (since $\Delta n = 0$), and for the second reaction, $K \neq K_p$ (since $\Delta n \neq 0$).

c.   a change in the container volume will have no effect on the equilibrium for reaction 1, whereas a volume change will effect the equilibrium for reaction 2 (shifts the reaction left or right depending on whether the volume is decreased or increased).

15.   We always try to make good assumptions that simplify the math. In some problems, we can set-up the problem so that the net change, x, that must occur to reach equilibrium is a small number. This comes in handy when you have expressions like $0.12 - x$ or $0.727 + 2x$, etc. When x is small, we can assume that it makes little difference when subtracted from or added to some relatively big number. When this is the case, $0.12 - x \approx 0.12$ and $0.727 + 2x \approx 0.727$, etc. If the assumption holds by the 5% rule, the assumption is assumed valid. The 5% rule refers to x (or 2x or 3x, etc.) that is assumed small compared to some number. If x (or 2x or 3x, etc.) is less than 5% of the number the assumption was made against, then the assumption

will be assumed valid. If the 5% rule fails to work, one can use a math procedure called the method of successive approximations to solve the quadratic or cubic equation. Of course, one could always solve the quadratic or cubic equation exactly. This is generally a last resort (and is usually not necessary).

16.   Only statement e is correct. Addition of a catalyst has no effect on the equilibrium position; the reaction just reaches equilibrium more quickly. Statement a is false for reactants that are either solids or liquids (adding more of these has no effect on the equilibrium). Statement b is false always. If temperature remains constant, then the value of K is constant. Statement c is false for exothermic reactions where an increase in temperature decreases the value of K. For statement d, only reactions which have more reactant gases than product gases will shift left with an increase in container volume. If the moles of gas are equal or if there are more moles of product gases than reactant gases, the reaction will not shift left with an increase in volume.

The Equilibrium Constant

17.   a. $K = \dfrac{[NO]^2}{[N_2][O_2]}$ b. $K = \dfrac{[NO_2]^2}{[N_2O_4]}$

       c. $K = \dfrac{[SiCl_4][H_2]^2}{[SiH_4][Cl_2]^2}$ d. $K = \dfrac{[PCl_3]^2[Br_2]^3}{[PBr_3]^2[Cl_2]^3}$

18.   a. $K_p = \dfrac{P_{NO}^2}{P_{N_2} \times P_{O_2}}$ b. $K_p = \dfrac{P_{NO_2}^2}{P_{N_2O_4}}$

       c. $K_p = \dfrac{P_{SiCl_4} \times P_{H_2}^2}{P_{SiH_4} \times P_{Cl_2}^2}$ d. $K_p = \dfrac{P_{PCl_3}^2 \times P_{Br_2}^3}{P_{PBr_3}^2 \times P_{Cl_2}^3}$

19. $K = 1.3 \times 10^{-2} = \dfrac{[NH_3]^2}{[N_2][H_2]^3}$ for $N_2(g) + 3\,H_2(g) \rightleftharpoons 2\,NH_3(g)$

When a reaction is reversed, then $K_{new} = 1/K_{original}$. When a reaction is multiplied through by a value of n, then $K_{new} = (K_{original})^n$.

     a. $1/2\,N_2(g) + 3/2\,H_2(g) \rightleftharpoons NH_3(g)$ $K' = \dfrac{[NH_3]^2}{[N_2]^{1/2}[H_2]^{3/2}} = K^{1/2} = (1.3 \times 10^{-2})^{1/2} = 0.11$

     b. $2\,NH_3(g) \rightleftharpoons N_2(g) + 3\,H_2(g)$ $K'' = \dfrac{[N_2][H_2]^3}{[NH_3]^2} = \dfrac{1}{K} = \dfrac{1}{1.3 \times 10^{-2}} = 77$

     c. $NH_3(g) \rightleftharpoons 1/2\,N_2(g) + 3/2\,H_2(g)$ $K''' = \dfrac{[N_2]^{1/2}[H_2]^{3/2}}{[NH_3]} = \left(\dfrac{1}{K}\right)^{1/2} = \left(\dfrac{1}{1.3 \times 10^{-2}}\right)^{1/2}$

                                                           $= 8.8$

     d. $2\,N_2(g) + 6\,H_2(g) \rightleftharpoons 4\,NH_3(g)$ $K = \dfrac{[NH_3]^4}{[N_2]^2[H_2]^6} = (K)^2 = (1.3 \times 10^{-2})^2 = 1.7 \times 10^{-4}$

20. $H_2(g) + Br_2(g) \rightleftharpoons 2\,HBr(g)$ $K_p = \dfrac{P_{HBr}^2}{(P_{H_2})(P_{Br_2})} = 3.5 \times 10^4$

a. $HBr \rightleftharpoons 1/2\,H_2 + 1/2\,Br_2$ $K_p' = \dfrac{(P_{H_2})^{1/2}(P_{Br_2})^{1/2}}{P_{HBr}} = \left(\dfrac{1}{K_p}\right)^{1/2} = \left(\dfrac{1}{3.5 \times 10^4}\right)^{1/2}$

$$= 5.3 \times 10^{-3}$$

b. $2\,HBr \rightleftharpoons H_2 + Br_2$ $K_p'' = \dfrac{(P_{H_2})(P_{Br_2})}{P_{HBr}^2} = \dfrac{1}{K_p} = \dfrac{1}{3.5 \times 10^4} = 2.9 \times 10^{-5}$

c. $1/2\,H_2 + 1/2\,Br_2 \rightleftharpoons HBr$ $K_p''' = \dfrac{P_{HBr}}{(P_{H_2})^{1/2}(P_{Br_2})^{1/2}} = (K_p)^{1/2} = 190$

21. $2\,NO(g) + 2\,H_2(g) \rightleftharpoons N_2(g) + 2\,H_2O(g)$ $K = \dfrac{[N_2][H_2O]^2}{[NO]^2[H_2]^2}$

$K = \dfrac{(5.3 \times 10^{-2})(2.9 \times 10^{-3})^2}{(8.1 \times 10^{-3})^2(4.1 \times 10^{-5})^2} = 4.0 \times 10^6$

22. $K = \dfrac{[NCl_3]^2}{[N_2][Cl_2]^3} = \dfrac{(0.19)^2}{(1.4 \times 10^{-3})(4.3 \times 10^{-4})^3} = 3.2 \times 10^{11}$

23. $[NO] = \dfrac{4.5 \times 10^{-3}\ mol}{3.0\ L} = 1.5 \times 10^{-3}\,M;\ \ [Cl_2] = \dfrac{2.4\ mol}{3.0\ L} = 0.80\,M$

$[NOCl] = \dfrac{1.0\ mol}{3.0\ L} = 0.33\,M;\ \ \ K = \dfrac{[NO]^2[Cl_2]}{[NOCl]^2} = \dfrac{(1.5 \times 10^{-3})^2(0.80)}{(0.33)^2} = 1.7 \times 10^{-5}$

24. $[N_2O] = \dfrac{2.00 \times 10^{-2}\ mol}{2.00\ L};\ \ [N_2] = \dfrac{2.80 \times 10^{-4}\ mol}{2.00\ L};\ \ [O_2] = \dfrac{2.5 \times 10^{-5}\ mol}{2.00\ L}$

$K = \dfrac{[N_2O]^2}{[N_2]^2[O_2]} = \dfrac{\left(\dfrac{2.00 \times 10^{-2}}{2.00}\right)^2}{\left(\dfrac{2.80 \times 10^{-4}}{2.00}\right)^2\left(\dfrac{2.50 \times 10^{-5}}{2.00}\right)} = \dfrac{(1.00 \times 10^{-2})^2}{(1.40 \times 10^{-4})^2(1.25 \times 10^{-5})} = 4.08 \times 10^8$

If the given concentrations represent equilibrium concentrations, then they should give a value of $K = 4.08 \times 10^8$.

$\dfrac{(0.200)^2}{(2.00 \times 10^{-4})^2(0.00245)} = 4.08 \times 10^8$

Because the given concentrations when plugged into the equilibrium constant expression give a value equal to K (4.08×10^8), this set of concentrations is a system at equilibrium.

25. $K_p = \dfrac{P_{NO}^2 \times P_{O_2}}{P_{NO_2}^2} = \dfrac{(6.5 \times 10^{-5})^2 (4.5 \times 10^{-5})}{(0.55)^2} = 6.3 \times 10^{-13}$

26. $K_p = \dfrac{P_{NH_3}^2}{P_{N_2} \times P_{H_2}^3} = \dfrac{(3.1 \times 10^{-2})^2}{(0.85)(3.1 \times 10^{-3})^3} = 3.8 \times 10^4$

$\dfrac{(0.167)^2}{(0.525)(0.00761)^3} = 1.21 \times 10^3$

When the given partial pressures are plugged into the K_p expression, the value does not equal the K_p value of 3.8×10^4. Therefore, one can conclude that the given set of partial pressures does not represent a system at equilibrium.

27. $K_p = K(RT)^{\Delta n}$ where Δn = sum of gaseous product coefficients – sum of gaseous reactant coefficients. For this reaction, $\Delta n = 3 - 1 = 2$.

$K = \dfrac{[CO][H_2]^2}{[CH_3OH]} = \dfrac{(0.24)(1.1)^2}{(0.15)} = 1.9$

$K_P = K(RT)^2 = 1.9\,(0.08206\ \text{L/atm/K} \cdot \text{mol} \times 600.\ \text{K})^2 = 4.6 \times 10^3$

28. $K_P = K(RT)^{\Delta n}$, $K = \dfrac{K_p}{(RT)^{\Delta n}}$ $\Delta n = 2 - 3 = -1$; $K = 0.25 \times (0.08206 \times 1100) = 23$

29.   Solids and liquids do not appear in equilibrium expressions. Only gases and dissolved solutes appear in equilibrium expressions.

a. $K = \dfrac{[H_2O]}{[NH_3]^2[CO_2]}$; $K_p = \dfrac{P_{H_2O}}{P_{NH_3}^2 \times P_{CO_2}}$ b. $K = [N_2][Br_2]^3$; $K_p = P_{N_2} \times P_{Br_2}^3$

c. $K = [O_2]^3$; $K_p = P_{O_2}^3$ d. $K = \dfrac{[H_2O]}{[H_2]}$; $K_p = \dfrac{P_{H_2O}}{P_{H_2}}$

30. $K_p = K(RT)^{\Delta n}$ where Δn equals the difference in the sum of the coefficients between gaseous products and gaseous reactants (Δn = mol gaseous products – mol gaseous reactants). When $\Delta n = 0$, then $K_p = K$. In Exercise 13.29, only reaction d has $\Delta n = 0$ so only reaction d has $K_p = K$.

31.   Because solids do not appear in the equilibrium constant expression, $K = 1/[O_2]^3$.

$$[O_2] = \frac{1.0 \times 10^{-3} \, mol}{2.0 \, L}; \quad K = \frac{1}{[O_2]^3} = \frac{1}{\left(\frac{1.0 \times 10^{-3}}{2.0}\right)^3} = \frac{1}{(5.0 \times 10^{-4})^3} = 8.0 \times 10^9$$

32. $K_p = \dfrac{P_{H_2}^4}{P_{H_2O}^4}$; $P_{tot} = P_{H_2O} + P_{H_2}$, $36.3 \, torr = 15.0 \, torr + P_{H_2}$, $P_{H_2} = 21.3 \, torr$

Because 1 atm = 760 torr: $K_P = \dfrac{(21.3 / 760)^4}{(15.0 / 760)^4} = 4.07$

Equilibrium Calculations

33. $2 \, NO(g) \rightleftharpoons N_2(g) + O_2(g)$ $K = \dfrac{[N_2][O_2]}{[NO]^2} = 2.4 \times 10^3$

Use the reaction quotient Q to determine which way the reaction shifts to reach equilibrium. For the reaction quotient, initial concentrations given in a problem are used to calculate the value for Q. If Q < K, then the reaction shifts right to reach equilibrium. If Q > K, then the reaction shifts left to reach equilibrium. If Q = K, then the reaction does not shift in either direction because the reaction is at equilibrium.

a. $[N_2] = \dfrac{2.0 \, mol}{1.0 \, L} = 2.0 \, M$; $[O_2] = \dfrac{2.6 \, mol}{1.0 \, L} = 2.6 \, M$; $[NO] = \dfrac{0.024 \, mol}{1.0 \, L} = 0.024 \, M$

$$Q = \frac{[N_2]_o [O_2]_o}{[NO]_o^2} = \frac{(2.0)(2.6)}{(0.024)^2} = 9.0 \times 10^3$$

Q > K so the reaction shifts left to produce more reactants in order to reach equilibrium.

b. $[N_2] = \dfrac{0.62 \, mol}{2.0 \, L} = 0.31 \, M$; $[O_2] = \dfrac{4.0 \, mol}{2.0 \, L} = 2.0 \, M$; $[NO] = \dfrac{0.032 \, mol}{2.0 \, L} = 0.016 \, M$

$$Q = \frac{(0.31)(2.0)}{(0.016)^2} = 2.4 \times 10^3 = K; \text{ at equilibrium}$$

c. $[N_2] = \dfrac{2.4 \, mol}{3.0 \, L} = 0.80 \, M$; $[O_2] = \dfrac{1.7 \, mol}{3.0 \, L} = 0.57 \, M$; $[NO] = \dfrac{0.060 \, mol}{3.0 \, L} = 0.020 \, M$

$$Q = \frac{(0.80)(0.57)}{(0.020)^2} = 1.1 \times 10^3 < K; \text{ Reaction shifts right to reach equilibrium.}$$

34.   As in Exercise 13.33, determine Q for each reaction, and compare this value to K_p (2.4×10^3) to determine which direction the reaction shifts to reach equilibrium. Note that, for this reaction, $K = K_p$ since $\Delta n = 0$.

a. $Q = \dfrac{P_{N_2} \times P_{O_2}}{P_{NO}^2} = \dfrac{(0.11)(2.0)}{(0.010)^2} = 2.2 \times 10^3$

$Q < K_p$ so the reaction shifts right to reach equilibrium.

b. $Q = \dfrac{(0.36)(0.67)}{(0.078)^2} = 4.0 \times 10^3 > K_p$

Reaction shifts left to reach equilibrium.

c. $Q = \dfrac{(0.51)(0.18)}{(0.0062)^2} = 2.4 \times 10^3 = K_p$; at equilbrium

35. $CaCO_3(s) \rightleftharpoons CaO(s) + CO_2(g)$ $K_p = P_{CO_2} = 1.04$

a. $Q = P_{CO_2}$; We only need the partial pressure of CO_2 to determine Q since solids do not appear in equilibrium expressions (or Q expressions). At this temperature all CO_2 will be in the gas phase. Q = 2.55 so $Q > K_p$; Reaction will shift to the left to reach equilibrium; the mass of CaO will decrease.

b. $Q = 1.04 = K_p$ so the reaction is at equilibrium; mass of CaO will not change.

c. $Q = 1.04 = K_p$ so the reaction is at equilibrium; mass of CaO will not change.

d. $Q = 0.211 < K_p$; The reaction will shift to the right to reach equilibrium; the mass of CaO will increase.

36. $CH_3CO_2H + C_2H_5OH \rightleftharpoons CH_3CO_2C_2H_5 + H_2O$ $K = \dfrac{[CH_3CO_2C_2H_5][H_2O]}{[CH_3CO_2H][C_2H_5OH]} = 2.2$

a. $Q = \dfrac{(0.22)(0.10)}{(0.010)(0.010)} = 220 > K$;   Reaction will shift left to reach equilibrium so the concentration of water will decrease.

b. $Q = \dfrac{(0.22)(0.0020)}{(0.0020)(0.10)} = 2.2 = K$;   Reaction is at equilibrium, so the concentration of water will remain the same.

c. $Q = \dfrac{(0.88)(0.12)}{(0.044)(6.0)} = 0.40 < K$;   Because $Q < K$, the concentration of water will increase because the reaction shifts right to reach equilibrium.

d. $Q = \dfrac{(4.4)(4.4)}{(0.88)(10.0)} = 2.2 = K$;   At equilibrium, so the water concentration is unchanged.

e. $K = 2.2 = \dfrac{(2.0)[H_2O]}{(0.10)(5.0)}$, $[H_2O] = 0.55$ M

f.   Water is a product of the reaction, but it is not the solvent. Thus, the concentration of water must be included in the equilibrium expression since it is a solute in the reaction. Only when water is the solvent do we not include it in the equilibrium expression.

37. $K = \dfrac{[H_2]^2[O_2]}{[H_2O]^2}$, $2.4 \times 10^{-3} = \dfrac{(1.9 \times 10^{-2})^2[O_2]}{(0.11)^2}$, $[O_2] = 0.080\ M$

38. $K_P = \dfrac{P_{NOBr}^2}{P_{NO}^2 \times P_{Br_2}}$, $109 = \dfrac{(0.768)^2}{P_{NO}^2 \times 0.0159}$, $P_{NO} = 0.0583$ atm

39. $SO_2(g) + NO_2(g) \rightleftharpoons SO_3(g) + NO(g)$ $K = \dfrac{[SO_3][NO]}{[SO_2][NO_2]}$

To determine K, we must calculate the equilibrium concentrations. The initial concentrations are:

$$[SO_3]_o = [NO]_o = 0;\quad [SO_2]_o = [NO_2]_o = \frac{2.00\ \text{mol}}{1.00\ \text{L}} = 2.00\ M$$

Next, we determine the change required to reach equilibrium. At equilibrium, [NO] = 1.30 mol/1.00 L = 1.30 M. Since there was zero NO present initially, 1.30 M of SO$_2$ and 1.30 M NO$_2$ must have reacted to produce 1.30 M NO as well as 1.30 M SO$_3$, all required by the balanced reaction. The equilibrium concentration for each substance is the sum of the initial concentration plus the change in concentration necessary to reach equilibrium. The equilibrium concentrations are:

$$[SO_3] = [NO] = 0 + 1.30\ M = 1.30\ M;\quad [SO_2] = [NO_2] = 2.00\ M - 1.30\ M = 0.70\ M$$

We now use these equilibrium concentrations to calculate K:

$$K = \frac{[SO_3][NO]}{[SO_2][NO_2]} = \frac{(1.30)(1.30)}{(0.70)(0.70)} = 3.4$$

40. $S_8(g) \rightleftharpoons 4\ S_2(g)$ $K_P = \dfrac{P_{S_2}^4}{P_{S_8}}$

Initially: $P_{S_8} = 1.00$ atm and $P_{S_2} = 0$ atm

Change: Since 0.25 atm of S$_8$ remain at equilibrium, then 1.00 atm − 0.25 atm = 0.75 atm of S$_8$ must have reacted in order to reach equilibrium. Since there is a 4:1 mol ratio between S$_2$ and S$_8$ (from the balanced reaction), then 4(0.75 atm) = 3.0 atm of S$_2$ must have been produced when the reaction went to equilibrium (moles and pressure are directly related at constant T and V).

Equilibrium: $P_{S_8} = 0.25$ atm, $P_{S_2} = 0 + 3.0$ atm = 3.0 atm; Solving for K_p:

$$K_P = \frac{(3.0)^4}{0.25} = 3.2 \times 10^2$$

41.   When solving equilibrium problems, a common method to summarize all the information in the problem is to set up a table. We call this table the ICE table since it summarizes initial concentrations, changes that must occur to reach equilibrium and equilibrium concentrations (the sum of the initial and change columns). For the change column, we will generally use the variable x, which will be defined as the amount of reactant (or product) that must react to reach equilibrium. In this problem, the reaction must shift right to reach equilibrium because there are no products present initially. Therefore, x is defined as the amount (in units of mol/L) of reactant SO_3 that reacts to reach equilibrium; we use the coefficients in the balanced equation to relate the net change in SO_3 to the net change in SO_2 and O_2. The general ICE table for this problem is:

$$2\ SO_3(g)\ \rightleftharpoons\ 2\ SO_2(g)\ +\ O_2(g) \qquad K = \dfrac{[SO_2]^2[O_2]}{[SO_3]^2}$$

Initial	12.0 mol/3.0 L	0	0
	Let x mol/L of SO_3 react to reach equilibrium		
Change	$-x$ $\rightarrow$	$+x$	$+x/2$
Equil.	$4.0 - x$	x	$x/2$

From the problem, we are told that the equilibrium SO_2 concentration is 3.0 mol/3.0 L = 1.0 M ($[SO_2]_e = 1.0\ M$). From the ICE table, $[SO_2]_e = x$ so $x = 1.0$. Solving for the other equilibrium concentrations: $[SO_3]_e = 4.0 - x = 4.0 - 1.0 = 3.0\ M$; $[O_2] = x/2 = 1.0/2 = 0.50\ M$.

$$K = \dfrac{[SO_2]^2[O_2]}{[SO_3]^2} = \dfrac{(1.0)^2(0.50)}{(3.0)^2} = 0.056$$

Alternate Method: Fractions in the change column can be avoided (if you want) by defining x differently. If we were to let $2x$ mol/L of SO_3 react to reach equilibrium, then the ICE table is:

$$2\ SO_3(g)\ \rightleftharpoons\ 2\ SO_2(g)\ +\ O_2(g) \qquad K = \dfrac{[SO_2]^2[O_2]}{[SO_3]^2}$$

Initial	4.0 M	0	0
	Let $2x$ mol/L of SO_3 react to reach equilibrium		
Change	$-2x$ $\rightarrow$	$+2x$	$+x$
Equil.	$4.0 - 2x$	$2x$	x

Solving: $2x = [SO_2]_e = 1.0\ M$, $x = 0.50\ M$; $[SO_3]_e = 4.0 - 2(0.50) = 3.0\ M$; $[O_2]_e = x$
$$= 0.50\ M$$

These are exactly the same equilibrium concentrations as solved for previously, thus K will be the same (as it must be). The moral of the story is to define x in a manner that is most comfortable for you. Your final answer is independent of how you define x initially.

42. $$2\ NH_3(g)\ \rightleftharpoons\ N_2(g)\ +\ 3\ H_2(g) \qquad K = \dfrac{[N_2]^2[H_2]^3}{[NH_3]^2}$$

Initial	4.0 mol/2.0 L	0	0
	Let $2x$ mol/L of NH_3 react to reach equilibrium		
Change	$-2x$ $\rightarrow$	$+x$	$+3x$
Equil.	$2.0 - 2x$	x	$3x$

From the problem: $[NH_3]_e = 2.0 \text{ mol}/2.0 \text{ L} = 1.0 \, M = 2.0 - 2x, \ x = 0.50 \, M$

$[N_2] = x = 0.50 \, M; \ [H_2] = 3x = 3(0.50 \, M) = 1.5 \, M$

$$K = \frac{[N_2]^2[H_2]^3}{[NH_3]^2} = \frac{(0.50)(1.5)^3}{(1.0)^2} = 1.7$$

43. $3 \, H_2(g) \quad + \quad N_2(g) \ \rightleftharpoons \ 2 \, NH_3(g)$

Initial	$[H_2]_o$	$[N_2]_o$	0

x mol/L of N_2 reacts to reach equilibrium

Change	$-3x$	$-x \quad \rightarrow$	$+2x$
Equil	$[H_2]_o - 3x$	$[N_2]_o - x$	$2x$

From the problem:

$[NH_3]_e = 4.0 \, M = 2x, \ x = 2.0 \, M; \ [H_2]_e = 5.0 \, M = [H_2]_o - 3x; \ [N_2]_e = 8.0 \, M = [N_2]_o - x$

$5.0 \, M = [H_2]_o - 3(2.0 \, M), \ [H_2]_o = 11.0 \, M; \ 8.0 \, M = [N_2]_o - 2.0 \, M, \ [N_2]_o = 10.0 \, M$

44. $N_2(g) \quad + \quad 3 \, H_2(g) \ \rightleftharpoons \ 2 \, NH_3(g)$

Initial	1.00 atm	2.00 atm	0

x atm of N_2 reacts to reach equilibrium

Change	$-x$	$-3x \quad \rightarrow$	$+2x$
equil.	$1.00 - x$	$2.00 - 3x$	$2x$

From set-up: $P_{TOT} = 2.00 \text{ atm} = P_{N_2} + P_{H_2} + P_{NH_3}$

$2.00 \text{ atm} = (1.00 - x) + (2.00 - 3x) + 2x = 3.00 - 2x$

$x = 0.500 \text{ atm}; \ P_{H_2} = 2.00 - 3x = 2.00 - 3(0.500) = 0.50 \text{ atm}$

45. $Q = 1.00$, which is less than K. Reaction shifts to the right to reach equilibrium. Summarizing the equilibrium problem in a table:

$$SO_2(g) \quad + \quad NO_2(g) \rightleftharpoons SO_3(g) \quad + \quad NO(g) \quad K = 3.75$$

Initial	0.800 M	0.800 M	0.800 M	0.800 M

x mol/L of SO_2 reacts to reach equilibrium

Change	$-x$	$-x \quad \rightarrow$	$+x$	$+x$
Equil.	$0.800 - x$	$0.800 - x$	$0.800 + x$	$0.800 + x$

Plug the equilibrium concentrations into the equilibrium constant expression:

$$K = \frac{[SO_3][NO]}{[SO_2][NO_2]} = 3.75 = \frac{(0.800 + x)^2}{(0.800 - x)^2}; \ \text{Take the square root of both sides and solve for } x:$$

$$\frac{0.800+x}{0.800-x} = 1.94, \ 0.800+x = 1.55 - 1.94\,x, \ 2.94\,x = 0.75, \ x = 0.26\,M$$

The equilibrium concentrations are:

$$[SO_3] = [NO] = 0.800 + x = 0.800 + 0.26 = 1.06\,M; \ [SO_2] = [NO_2] = 0.800 - x = 0.54\,M$$

46. $Q = 1.00$, which is less than K. Reaction shifts right to reach equilibrium.

$$H_2(g) \quad + \quad I_2(g) \quad \rightleftharpoons \quad 2\,HI(g) \quad K\,\frac{[HI]^2}{[H_2][I_2]} = 100.$$

Initial	1.00 M	1.00 M	1.00 M
	x mol/L of H_2 reacts to reach equilibrium		
Change	$-x$	$-x \quad \rightarrow$	$+2x$
Equil.	$1.00 - x$	$1.00 - x$	$1.00 + 2x$

$$K = 100. = \frac{(1.00+2x)^2}{(1.00-x)^2}; \text{ Taking the square root of both sides:}$$

$$10.0 = \frac{1.00+2x}{1.00-x}, \ 10.0 - 10.0\,x = 1.00 + 2x, \ 12.0\,x = 9.0, \ x = 0.75\,M$$

$$[H_2] = [I_2] = 1.00 - 0.75 = 0.25\,M; \ [HI] = 1.00 + 2(0.75) = 2.50\,M$$

47.   Because only reactants are present initially, the reaction must proceed to the right to reach equilibrium. Summarizing the problem in a table:

$$N_2(g) \quad + \quad O_2(g) \quad \rightleftharpoons \quad 2\,NO(g) \quad K_p = 0.050$$

Initial	0.80 atm	0.20 atm	0
	x atm of N_2 reacts to reach equilibrium		
Change	$-x$	$-x \quad \rightarrow$	$+2x$
Equil.	$0.80 - x$	$0.20 - x$	$2x$

$$K_p = 0.050 = \frac{P_{NO}^2}{P_{N_2} \times P_{O_2}} = \frac{(2x)^2}{(0.80-x)(0.20-x)}, \ 0.050(0.16 - 1.00\,x + x^2) = 4\,x^2$$

$$4\,x^2 = 8.0 \times 10^{-3} - 0.050\,x + 0.050\,x^2, \ 3.95\,x^2 + 0.050\,x - 8.0 \times 10^{-3} = 0$$

Solving using the quadratic formula (see Appendix 1.4 of the text):

$$x = \frac{-b \pm (b^2 - 4ac)^{1/2}}{2a} = \frac{-0.050 \pm [(0.050)^2 - 4(3.95)(-8.0 \times 10^{-3})]^{1/2}}{2(3.95)}$$

$x = 3.9 \times 10^{-2}$ atm or $x = -5.2 \times 10^{-2}$ atm; Only $x = 3.9 \times 10^{-2}$ atm makes sense (x cannot be negative), so the equilibrium NO partial pressure is:

$$P_{NO} = 2x = 2(3.9 \times 10^{-2} \text{ atm}) = 7.8 \times 10^{-2} \text{ atm}$$

48. $H_2O(g) + Cl_2O(g) \rightleftharpoons 2\ HOCl(g)$ $K = 0.090 = \dfrac{[HOCl]^2}{[H_2O][Cl_2O]}$

a.   The initial concentrations of H_2O and Cl_2O are:

$$\dfrac{1.0\ g\ H_2O}{1.0\ L} \times \dfrac{1\ mol}{18.02\ g} = 5.5 \times 10^{-2}\ mol/L; \quad \dfrac{2.0\ g\ Cl_2O}{1.0\ L} \times \dfrac{1\ mol}{86.90\ g} = 2.3 \times 10^{-2}\ mol/L$$

	$H_2O(g)$	$+$	$Cl_2O(g)$	$\rightleftharpoons$	$2\ HOCl(g)$
Initial	$5.5 \times 10^{-2}\ M$		$2.3 \times 10^{-2}\ M$		0

x mol/L of H_2O reacts to reach equilibrium

| Change | $-x$ | | $-x$ | $\rightarrow$ | $+2x$ |
| Equil. | $5.5 \times 10^{-2} - x$ | | $2.3 \times 10^{-2} - x$ | | $2x$ |

$$K = 0.090 = \dfrac{(2x)^2}{(5.5\times10^{-2} - x)(2.3\times10^{-2} - x)}, \quad 1.14 \times 10^{-4} - 7.02 \times 10^{-3}\,x + 0.090\,x^2 = 4\,x^2$$

$3.91\,x^2 + 7.02 \times 10^{-3}\,x - 1.14 \times 10^{-4} = 0$ (We carried extra significant figures.)

Solving using the quadratic formula:

$$\dfrac{-7.02\times10^{-3} \pm (4.93\times10^{-5} + 1.78\times10^{-3})^{1/2}}{7.82} = 4.6 \times 10^{-3}\ or\ -6.4 \times 10^{-3}$$

A negative answer makes no physical sense; we can't have less than nothing.
So $x = 4.6 \times 10^{-3}\,M$.

$[HOCl] = 2x = 9.2 \times 10^{-3}\,M; \quad [Cl_2O] = 2.3 \times 10^{-2} - x = 0.023 - 0.0046 = 1.8 \times 10^{-2}\,M$

$[H_2O] = 5.5 \times 10^{-2} - x = 0.055 - 0.0046 = 5.0 \times 10^{-2}\,M$

b.

	$H_2O(g)$	$+$	$Cl_2O(g)$	$\rightleftharpoons$	$2\ HOCl(g)$
Initial	0		0		$1.0\ mol/2.0\ L = 0.50\ M$

$2x$ mol/L of HOCl reacts to reach equilibrium

| Change | $+x$ | | $+x$ | $\leftarrow$ | $-2x$ |
| Equil. | x | | x | | $0.50 - 2x$ |

$$K = 0.090 = \dfrac{[HOCl]^2}{[H_2O][Cl_2O]} = \dfrac{(0.50 - 2x)^2}{x^2}$$

The expression is a perfect square, so we can take the square root of each side:

$$0.30 = \dfrac{0.50 - 2x}{x}, \quad 0.30\,x = 0.50 - 2x, \quad 2.30\,x = 0.50$$

$x = 0.217$ (We carried extra significant figures.)

$x = [H_2O] = [Cl_2O] = 0.217 = 0.22\ M;\ [HOCl] = 0.50 - 2x = 0.50 - 0.434 = 0.07\ M$

49. $2\ SO_2(g)$ + $O_2(g)$ $\rightleftharpoons$ $2\ SO_3(g)$ $K_p = 0.25$

Initial	0.50 atm	0.50 atm	0

$2x$ atm of SO_2 reacts to reach equilibrium

Change	$-2x$	$-x$	$\rightarrow$	$+2x$
Equil.	$0.50 - 2x$	$0.50 - x$		$2x$

$$K_p = 0.25 = \frac{P_{SO_3}^2}{P_{SO_2}^2 \times P_{O_2}} = \frac{(2x)^2}{(0.50 - 2x)^2(0.50 - x)}$$

This will give a cubic equation. Graphing calculators can be used to solve this expression. If you don't have a graphing calculator, an alternative method for solving a cubic equation is to use the method of successive approximations (see Appendix 1.4 of the text). The first step is to guess a value for x. Because the value of K is small (K < 1), then not much of the forward reaction will occur to reach equilibrium. This tells us that x is small. Lets guess that $x = 0.050$ atm. Now we take this estimated value for x and substitute it into the equation everywhere that x appears except for one. For equilibrium problems, we will substitute the estimated value for x into the denominator, then solve for the numerator value of x. We continue this process until the estimated value of x and the calculated value of x converge on the same number. This is the same answer we would get if we were to solve the cubic equation exactly. Applying the method of successive approximations and carrying extra significant figures:

$$\frac{4x^2}{[0.50 - 2(0.050)]^2[0.50 - (0.050)]} = \frac{4x^2}{(0.40)^2(0.45)} = 0.25,\ x = 0.067$$

$$\frac{4x^2}{[0.50 - 2(0.067)]^2[0.50 - (0.067)]} = \frac{4x^2}{(0.366)^2(0.433)} = 0.25,\ x = 0.060$$

$$\frac{4x^2}{(0.38)^2(0.44)},\ 0.25,\ x = 0.063;\quad \frac{4x^2}{(0.374)^2(0.437)} = 0.25,\ x = 0.062$$

The next trial gives the same value for $x = 0.062$ atm. We are done except for determining the equilibrium concentrations. They are:

$P_{SO_2} = 0.50 - 2x = 0.50 - 2(0.062) = 0.376 = 0.38$ atm

$P_{O_2} = 0.50 - x = 0.438 = 0.44$ atm; $P_{SO_3} = 2x = 0.124 = 0.12$ atm

50.   a.   The reaction must proceed to products to reach equilibrium. Summarizing the problem in a table where x atm of N_2O_4 reacts to reach equilibrium:

$$N_2O_4(g) \quad \rightleftharpoons \quad 2\,NO_2(g) \qquad K_p = 0.25$$

Initial	4.5 atm		0
Change	$-x$	$\rightarrow$	$+2x$
Equil.	$4.5 - x$		$2x$

$$K_p = \frac{P_{NO_2}^2}{P_{N_2O_4}} = \frac{(2x)^2}{4.5 - x}, \ \ 4x^2 = 1.125 - 0.25\,x, \ \ 4x^2 + 0.25\,x - 1.125 = 0$$

We carried extra significant figures in this expression (as will be typical when we solve an expression using the quadratic formula). Solving using the quadratic formula (Appendix 1.4 of text):

$$x = \frac{-0.25 \pm [(0.25)^2 - 4(4)(-1.125)]^{1/2}}{2(4)} = \frac{-0.25 \pm 4.25}{8}, \ \ x = 0.50 \ \text{(Other value is negative.)}$$

$$P_{NO_2} = 2x = 1.0 \text{ atm}; \ \ P_{N_2O_4} = 4.5 - x = 4.0 \text{ atm}$$

b. The reaction must shift to reactants (shifts left) to reach equilibrium.

$$N_2O_4(g) \quad \rightleftharpoons \quad 2\,NO_2(g)$$

Initial	0		9.0 atm
Change	$+x$	$\leftarrow$	$-2x$
Equil.	x		$9.0 - 2x$

$$K_p = \frac{(9.0 - 2x)^2}{x} = 0.25, \ \ 4x^2 - 36.25\,x + 81 = 0 \ \text{(carrying extra sig. figs.)}$$

Solving using quadratic formula: $x = \dfrac{-(-36.25) \pm [(-36.25)^2 - 4(4)(-81)]^{1/2}}{2(4)}$,

$$x = 4.0 \text{ atm}$$

The other value, 5.1, is impossible. $P_{N_2O_4} = x = 4.0$ atm; $P_{NO_2} = 9.0 - 2x = 1.0$ atm

c. No, we get the same equilibrium position starting with either pure N_2O_4 or pure NO_2 in stoichiometric amounts.

51.   a. The reaction must proceed to products to reach equilibrium since only reactants are present initially. Summarizing the problem in a table:

$$2\,NOCl(g) \quad \rightleftharpoons \quad 2\,NO(g) \quad + \quad Cl_2(g) \qquad K = 1.6 \times 10^{-5}$$

Initial	$\dfrac{2.0\ \text{mol}}{2.0\ \text{L}}$	0	0

$2x$ mol/L of NOCl reacts to reach equilibrium

Change	$-2x$	$\rightarrow$ $+2x$	$+x$
Equil.	$1.0 - 2x$	$2x$	x

$$K = 1.6 \times 10^{-5} = \frac{[NO]^2[Cl_2]}{[NOCl]^2} = \frac{(2x)^2(x)}{(1.0 - 2x)^2}$$

If we assume that $1.0 - 2x \approx 1.0$ (from the small size of K, we know that not a lot of products are present at equilibrium so x is small), then:

$$1.6 \times 10^{-5} = \frac{4x^3}{1.0^2}\ , \quad x = 1.6 \times 10^{-2}\ ;\ \text{Now we must check the assumption.}$$

$$1.0 - 2x = 1.0 - 2(0.016) = 0.97 = 1.0\ \text{(to proper significant figures)}$$

Our error is about 3%, i.e., $2x$ is 3.2% of 1.0 M. Generally, if the error we introduce by making simplifying assumptions is less than 5%, we go no further and the assumption is said to be valid. We call this the 5% rule. Solving for the equilibrium concentrations:

$$[NO] = 2x = 0.032\ M;\ \ [Cl_2] = x = 0.016\ M;\ \ [NOCl] = 1.0 - 2x = 0.97\ M \approx 1.0\ M$$

Note: If we were to solve this cubic equation exactly (a long and tedious process), we would get $x = 0.016$. This is the exact same answer we determined by making a simplifying assumption. We saved time and energy. Whenever K is a very small value, always make the assumption that x is small. If the assumption introduces an error of less than 5%, then the answer you calculated making the assumption will be considered the correct answer.

b.
$$2\,NOCl(g) \quad \rightleftharpoons \quad 2\,NO(g) \quad + \quad Cl_2(g)$$

Initial	1.0 M	1.0 M	0

$2x$ mol/L of NOCl reacts to reach equilibrium

Change	$-2x$	$\rightarrow$ $+2x$	$+x$
Equil.	$1.0 - 2x$	$1.0 + 2x$	x

$$1.6 \times 10^{-5} = \frac{(1.0 + 2x)^2(x)}{(1.0 - 2x)^2} = \frac{(1.0)^2(x)}{(1.0)^2}\ \ \text{(assuming } 2x \ll 1.0)$$

$x = 1.6 \times 10^{-5}$; Assumptions are great ($2x$ is 3.2×10^{-3} % of 1.0).

$[Cl_2] = 1.6 \times 10^{-5}\,M$ and $[NOCl] = [NO] = 1.0\ M$

c. 2 NOCl(g) $\rightleftharpoons$ 2 NO(g) $+$ $\text{Cl}_2\text{(g)}$

Initial	2.0 *M*	0	1.0 *M*

2*x* mol/L of NOCl reacts to reach equilibrium

Change	$-2x$	$\rightarrow$	$+2x$	$+x$
Equil.	$2.0 - 2x$		$2x$	$1.0 + x$

$$1.6 \times 10^{-5} = \frac{(2x)^2(1.0 + x)}{(2.0 - 2x)^2} = \frac{4x^2}{4.0} \quad \text{(assuming } x \ll 1.0\text{)}$$

Solving: $x = 4.0 \times 10^{-3}$; Assumptions good (*x* is 0.4% of 1.0 and 2*x* is 0.4% of 2.0).

$[\text{Cl}_2] = 1.0 + x = 1.0\ M$; $[\text{NO}] = 2(4.0 \times 10^{-3}) = 8.0 \times 10^{-3}\ M$; $[\text{NOCl}] = 2.0\ M$

52. $\text{N}_2\text{O}_4\text{(g)}$ $\rightleftharpoons$ $2 \text{ NO}_2\text{(g)}$ $K = \dfrac{[\text{NO}_2]^2}{[\text{N}_2\text{O}_4]} = 4.0 \times 10^{-7}$

Initial	1.0 mol/10.0 L	0

x mol/L of N_2O_4 reacts to reach equilibrium

Change	$-x$	$\rightarrow$	$+2x$
Equil.	$0.10 - x$		$2x$

$K = \dfrac{[\text{NO}_2]^2}{[\text{N}_2\text{O}_4]} = \dfrac{(2x)^2}{0.10 - x} = 4.0 \times 10^{-7}$; Because K has a small value, assume that *x* is small compared to 0.10 so that $0.10 - x \approx 0.10$. Solving:

$$4.0 \times 10^{-7} \approx \frac{4x^2}{0.10}, \quad 4x^2 = 4.0 \times 10^{-8}, \quad x = 1.0 \times 10^{-4}\ M$$

Checking the assumption by the 5% rule: $\dfrac{x}{0.10} \times 100 = \dfrac{1.0 \times 10^{-4}}{0.10} \times 100 = 0.10\%$

Because this number is less than 5%, we will say that the assumption is valid.

$[\text{N}_2\text{O}_4] = 0.10 - 1.0 \times 10^{-4} = 0.10\ M$; $[\text{NO}_2] = 2x = 2(1.0 \times 10^{-4}) = 2.0 \times 10^{-4}\ M$

53. $2 \text{ CO}_2\text{(g)}$ $\rightleftharpoons$ 2 CO(g) $+$ $\text{O}_2\text{(g)}$ $K = \dfrac{[\text{CO}]^2[\text{O}_2]}{[\text{CO}_2]^2} = 2.0 \times 10^{-6}$

Initial	2.0 mol/5.0 L	0	0

2*x* mol/L of CO_2 reacts to reach equilibrium

Change	$-2x$	$\rightarrow$	$+2x$	$+x$
Equil.	$0.40 - 2x$		$2x$	x

$K = 2.0 \times 10^{-6} = \dfrac{[\text{CO}]^2[\text{O}_2]}{[\text{CO}_2]^2} = \dfrac{(2x)^2(x)}{(0.40 - 2x)^2}$; Assuming $2x \ll 0.40$:

$$2.0 \times 10^{-6} \approx \frac{4x^3}{(0.40)^2}, \; 2.0 \times 10^{-6} = \frac{4x^3}{0.16}, \; x = 4.3 \times 10^{-3} \, M$$

Checking assumption: $\frac{2(4.3 \times 10^{-3})}{0.40} \times 100 = 2.2\%$; Assumption valid by the 5% rule.

$[CO_2] = 0.40 - 2x = 0.40 - 2(4.3 \times 10^{-3}) = 0.39 \, M$

$[CO] = 2x = 2(4.3 \times 10^{-3}) = 8.6 \times 10^{-3} M; \quad [O_2] = x = 4.3 \times 10^{-3} \, M$

54. $\qquad COCl_2(g) \; \rightleftharpoons \; CO(g) \; + \; Cl_2(g) \quad K_p = \dfrac{P_{CO} \times P_{Cl_2}}{P_{COCl_2}} = 6.8 \times 10^{-9}$

Initial	1.0 atm	0	0

x atm of $COCl_2$ reacts to reach equilibrium

Change	$-x$	$\rightarrow$ $+x$	$+x$
Equil.	$1.0 - x$	x	x

$$6.8 \times 10^{-9} = \frac{P_{CO} \times P_{Cl_2}}{P_{CoCl_2}} = \frac{x^2}{1.0 - x} \neq \frac{x^2}{1.0} \quad \text{(Assuming } 1.0 - x \approx 1.0.\text{)}$$

$x = 8.2 \times 10^{-5}$ atm; Assumption good (x is $8.2 \times 10^{-3}\%$ of 1.0).

$P_{COCl_2} = 1.0 - x = 1.0 - 8.2 \times 10^{-5} = 1.0$ atm; $P_{CO} = P_{Cl_2} = x = 8.2 \times 10^{-5}$ atm

55.   This is a typical equilibrium problem except that the reaction contains a solid. Whenever solids and liquids are present, we basically ignore them in the equilibrium problem.

$\qquad NH_4OCONH_2(s) \; \rightleftharpoons \; 2\,NH_3(g) \; + \; CO_2(g) \qquad K_p = 2.9 \times 10^{-3}$

Initial	–	0	0

Some NH_4OCONH_2 decomposes to produce $2x$ atm of NH_3 and x atm of CO_2.

Change	–	$\rightarrow$ $+2x$	$+x$
Equil.	–	$2x$	x

$K_p = 2.9 \times 10^{-3} = P_{NH_3}^2 \times P_{CO_2} = (2x)^2(x) = 4x^3$

$$x = \left(\frac{2.9 \times 10^{-3}}{4} \right)^{1/3} = 9.0 \times 10^{-2} \text{ atm; } P_{NH_3} = 2x = 0.18 \text{ atm; } P_{CO_2} = x = 9.0 \times 10^{-2} \text{ atm}$$

$P_{total} = P_{NH_3} + P_{CO_2} = 0.18 \text{ atm} + 0.090 \text{ atm} = 0.27 \text{ atm}$

56. $NH_4Cl(s) \rightleftharpoons NH_3(g) + HCl(g) \quad K_P = P_{NH_3} \times P_{HCl}$

For this system to reach equilibrium, some of the $NH_4Cl(s)$ decomposes to form equal moles of $NH_3(g)$ and $HCl(g)$ at equilibrium. Because mol HCl = mol NH_3, the partial pressures of each gas must be equal to each other.

At equilibrium: $P_{total} = P_{NH_3} + P_{HCl}$ and $P_{NH_3} = P_{HCl}$

$P_{total} = 4.4$ atm $= 2\,P_{NH_3}$, 2.2 atm $= P_{NH_3} = P_{HCl}$; $K_p = (2.2)(2.2) = 4.8$

Le Chatelier's Principle

57.   a.   No effect; Adding more of a pure solid or pure liquid has no effect on the equilibrium position.

   b.   Shifts left; $HF(g)$ will be removed by reaction with the glass. As $HF(g)$ is removed, the reaction will shift left to produce more $HF(g)$.

   c.   Shifts right; As $H_2O(g)$ is removed, the reaction will shift right to produce more $H_2O(g)$.

58.   When the volume of a reaction container is increased, the reaction itself will want to increase its own volume by shifting to the side of the reaction which contains the most molecules of gas. When the molecules of gas are equal on both sides of the reaction, then the reaction will remain at equilibrium no matter what happens to the volume of the container.

   a.   Reaction shifts left (to reactants) since the reactants contain 4 molecules of gas compared to 2 molecules of gas on the product side.

   b.   Reaction shifts right (to products) since there are more product molecules of gas (2) than reactant molecules (1).

   c.   No change since there are equal reactant and product molecules of gas.

   d.   Reaction shifts right.

   e.   Reaction shifts right to produce more $CO_2(g)$. One can ignore the solids and only concentrate on the gases because gases occupy a relatively large volume compared to solids. We make the same assumption when liquids are present (only worry about the gas molecules).

59.   a.   right   b.   right   c.   no effect; $He(g)$ is neither a reactant nor a product.

   d.   left; The reaction is exothermic; heat is a product:

$$CO(g) + H_2O(g) \rightarrow H_2(g) + CO_2(g) + \text{Heat}$$

   Increasing T will add heat. The equilibrium shifts to the left to use up the added heat.

   e.   no effect; There are equal numbers of gas molecules on both sides of the reaction, so a change in volume has no effect on the equilibrium position.

60.   a.   The moles of SO_3 will increase because the reaction will shift left to use up the added $O_2(g)$.

b.   Increase; Because there are fewer reactant gas molecules than product gas molecules, the reaction shifts left with a decrease in volume.

c.   No effect; The partial pressures of sulfur trioxide, sulfur dioxide, and oxygen are unchanged.

d.   Increase; Heat + 2 SO_3 ⇌ 2 SO_2 + O_2; Decreasing T will remove heat, shifting this endothermic reaction to the left.

e.   Decrease

61.   a.   left   b.   right   c.   left

d.   no effect (reactant and product concentrations are unchanged)

e.   no effect; Since there are equal numbers of product and reactant gas molecules, a change in volume has no effect on this equilibrium position.

f.   right; A decrease in temperature will shift the equilibrium to the right since heat is a product in this reaction (as is true in all exothermic reactions).

62.   a.   shift to left

b.   shift to right;   The reaction is endothermic (heat is a reactant), thus an increase in temperature will shift the equilibrium to the right.

c.   no effect   d.   shift to right

e.   shift to right; Because there are more gaseous product molecules than gaseous reactant molecules, the equilibrium will shift right with an increase in volume.

63.   An endothermic reaction, where heat is a reactant, will shift right to products with an increase in temperature. The amount of $NH_3(g)$ will increase as the reaction shifts right so the smell of ammonia will increase.

64.   As temperature increases, the value of K decreases. This is consistent with an exothermic reaction. In an exothermic reaction, heat is a product and an increase in temperature shifts the equilibrium to the reactant side (as well as lowering the value of K).

Additional Exercises

65. $O(g) + NO(g) \rightleftharpoons NO_2(g)$ $K = 1/6.8 \times 10^{-49} = 1.5 \times 10^{48}$

$NO_2(g) + O_2(g) \rightleftharpoons NO(g) + O_3(g)$ $K = 1/5.8 \times 10^{-34} = 1.7 \times 10^{33}$

_____

$O_2(g) + O(g) \rightleftharpoons O_3(g)$ $K = (1.5 \times 10^{48})(1.7 \times 10^{33}) = 2.6 \times 10^{81}$

66.   a. $N_2(g) + O_2(g) \rightleftharpoons 2\ NO(g)$ $K_p = 1 \times 10^{-31} = \dfrac{P_{NO}^2}{P_{N_2} \times P_{O_2}} = \dfrac{P_{NO}^2}{(0.8)(0.2)}$

$P_{NO} = 1 \times 10^{-16}$ atm; $n_{NO} = \dfrac{PV}{RT} = \dfrac{(1 \times 10^{-16}\ \text{atm})(1.0 \times 10^{-3}\ \text{L})}{\left(\dfrac{0.08206\ \text{L atm}}{\text{mol K}}\right)(298\ \text{K})} = 4 \times 10^{-21}$ mol NO

$\dfrac{4 \times 10^{-21}\ \text{mol NO}}{\text{cm}^3} \times \dfrac{6.02 \times 10^{23}\ \text{molecules}}{\text{mol NO}} = \dfrac{2 \times 10^3\ \text{molecules NO}}{\text{cm}^3}$

b.   There is more NO in the atmosphere than we would expect from the value of K. The answer must lie in the rates of the reaction. At 25°C the rates of both reactions:

$$N_2 + O_2 \rightarrow 2\ NO \text{ and } 2\ NO \rightarrow N_2 + O_2$$

are so slow that they are essentially zero. Very strong bonds must be broken; the activation energy is very high. Nitric oxide is produced in high energy or high temperature environments. In nature, some NO is produced by lightning, and the primary manmade source is from automobiles. The production of NO is endothermic ($\Delta H = +90$ kJ/mol). At high temperatures, K will increase, and the rates of the reaction will also increase, resulting in a higher production of NO. Once the NO gets into a more normal temperature environment, it doesn't go back to N_2 and O_2 because of the slow rate.

67.   a. $2\ AsH_3(g) \quad \rightleftharpoons \quad 2\ As(s) \quad + \quad 3\ H_2(g)$

	2 AsH₃(g)		3 H₂(g)
Initial	392.0 torr	–	0
Equil.	392.0 – 2x	–	3x

Using Dalton's Law of Partial Pressure:

$$P_{total} = 488.0\ \text{torr} = P_{AsH_3} + P_{H_2} = 392.0 - 2x + 3x,\ \ x = 96.0\ \text{torr}$$

$P_{H_2} = 3x = 3(96.0) = 288\ \text{torr} \times \dfrac{1\ \text{atm}}{760\ \text{torr}} = 0.379\ \text{atm}$

b. $P_{AsH_3} = 392.0 - 2(96.0) = 200.0\ \text{torr} \times \dfrac{1\ \text{atm}}{760\ \text{torr}} = 0.2632\ \text{atm}$

$K_p = \dfrac{\left(P_{H_2}\right)^3}{\left(P_{AsH_3}\right)^2} = \dfrac{(0.379)^3}{(0.2632)^2} = 0.786$

68. $FeSCN^{2+}(aq) \quad \rightleftharpoons \quad Fe^{3+}(aq) \quad + \quad SCN^-(aq)$ $K = 9.1 \times 10^{-4}$

	FeSCN²⁺(aq)		Fe³⁺(aq)	SCN⁻(aq)
Initial	2.0 M		0	0
Change	–x	$\rightarrow$	+x	+x
Equil.	2.0 – x		x	x

x mol/L of $FeSCN^{2+}$ reacts to reach equilibrium

$$9.1 \times 10^{-4} = \frac{[Fe^{3+}][SCN^-]}{[FeSCN^{2+}]} = \frac{x^2}{2.0 - x} = \frac{x^2}{2.0} \quad (\text{Assuming } 2.0 - x \approx 2.0.)$$

$x = 4.3 \times 10^{-2} \, M$; Assumption good by the 5% rule (x is 2.2% of 2.0).

$[FeSCN^{2+}] = 2.0 - x = 2.0 - 4.3 \times 10^{-2} = 2.0 \, M$; $[Fe^{3+}] = [SCN^-] = x = 4.3 \times 10^{-2} \, M$

69.   a. $P_{Cl_5} = \dfrac{nRT}{V} = \dfrac{\dfrac{2.450 \text{ g PCl}_5}{208.22 \text{ g}/\text{mol}} \times \dfrac{0.08206 \text{ L atm}}{\text{mol K}} \times 600. \text{ K}}{0.500 \text{ L}} = 1.16 \text{ atm}$

b. $PCl_5(g) \quad \rightleftharpoons \quad PCl_3(g) \quad + \quad Cl_2(g) \qquad K_p = \dfrac{P_{PCl_3} \times P_{Cl_2}}{P_{PCl_5}} = 11.5$

Initial	1.16 atm	0	0
	x atm of PCl$_5$ reacts to reach equilibrium		
Change	$-x$ $\rightarrow$	$+x$	$+x$
Equil.	$1.16 - x$	x	x

$K_p = \dfrac{x^2}{1.16 - x} = 11.5$, $x^2 + 11.5\,x - 13.3 = 0$; Using the quadratic formula: $x = 1.06$ atm

$P_{PCl_5} = 1.16 - 1.06 = 0.10$ atm

c. $P_{PCl_3} = P_{Cl_2} = 1.06$ atm; $P_{PCl_5} = 0.10$ atm

$P_{tot} = P_{PCl_5} + P_{PCl_3} + P_{Cl_2} = 0.10 + 1.06 + 1.06 = 2.22$ atm

d.   Percent dissociation $= \dfrac{x}{1.16} \times 100 = \dfrac{1.06}{1.16} \times 100 = 91.4\%$

70. $SO_2Cl_2(g) \quad \rightleftharpoons \quad Cl_2(g) \quad + \quad SO_2(g)$

Initial	P_0	0	0	P_0 = initial pressure of SO$_2$Cl$_2$
Change	$-x$ $\rightarrow$	$+x$	$+x$	
Equil.	$P_0 - x$	x	x	

$P_{total} = 0.900 \text{ atm} = P_0 - x + x + x = P_0 + x$

$\dfrac{x}{P_0} \times 100 = 12.5$, $P_0 = 8.00\,x$

Solving: $0.900 = P_0 + x = 9.00\,x$, $x = 0.100$ atm

$x = 0.100 \text{ atm} = P_{Cl_2} = P_{SO_2}$; $P_0 - x = 0.800 - 0.100 = 0.700 \text{ atm} = P_{SO_2Cl_2}$

$K_p = \dfrac{P_{Cl_2} \times P_{SO_2}}{P_{SO_2Cl_2}} = \dfrac{(0.100)^2}{0.700} = 1.43 \times 10^{-2} \text{ atm}$

71. $K = \dfrac{[HF]^2}{[H_2][F_2]} = \dfrac{(0.400)^2}{(0.0500)(0.0100)} = 320.$; 0.200 mol F_2/5.00 L = 0.0400 M F_2 added

From LeChatelier's principle, added F_2 causes the reaction to shift right to reestablish equilibrium.

$$H_2(g) \qquad + \qquad F_2(g) \quad \rightleftharpoons \quad 2\ HF(g)$$

Initial	0.0500 M	0.0500 M	0.400 M

x mol/L of F_2 reacts to reach equilibrium

Change	$-x$	$-x$	$\rightarrow$	$+2x$
Equil.	0.0500 $-x$	0.0500 $-x$		0.400 $+ 2x$

$K = 320. = \dfrac{(0.400 + 2x)^2}{(0.500 - x)^2}$;   Taking the square root of the equation:

$17.9 = \dfrac{0.400 + 2x}{0.500 - x}$, $0.895 - 17.9\,x = 0.400 + 2x$, $19.9\,x = 0.495$, $x = 0.0249$ mol/L

[HF] = 0.400 + 2(0.0249) = 0.450 M; [H_2] = [F_2] = 0.0500 - 0.0249 = 0.0251 M

72.   a.   Doubling the volume will decrease all concentrations by a factor of one-half.

$$Q = \dfrac{\frac{1}{2}[FeSCN^{2+}]_{eq}}{\left(\frac{1}{2}[Fe^{3+}]_{eq}\right)\left(\frac{1}{2}[SCN^-]_{eq}\right)} = 2\,K, \ Q > K$$

The reaction will shift to the left to reestablish equilibrium.

b.   Adding Ag^+ will remove SCN^- through the formation of AgSCN(s). The reaction will shift to the left to produce more SCN^-.

c.   Removing Fe^{3+} as $Fe(OH)_3$(s) will shift the reaction to the left to produce more Fe^{3+}.

d.   Reaction will shift to the right as Fe^{3+} is added.

73. $H^+ + OH^- \rightarrow H_2O$; Sodium hydroxide (NaOH) will react with the H^+ on the product side of the reaction. This effectively removes H^+ from the equilibrium, which will shift the reaction to the right to produce more H^+ and CrO_4^{2-}. Because more CrO_4^{2-} is produced, the solution turns yellow.

74. $N_2(g) + 3\ H_2(g) \rightleftharpoons 2\ NH_3(g)$ + heat

a.   This reaction is exothermic, so an increase in temperature will decrease the value of K (see Table 13.3 of text.) This has the effect of lowering the amount of NH_3(g) produced at equilibrium. The temperature increase, therefore, must be for kinetics reasons. As temperature increases, the reaction reaches equilibrium much faster. At low temperatures, this reaction is very slow, too slow to be of any use.

b.   As $NH_3(g)$ is removed, the reaction shifts right to produce more $NH_3(g)$.

c.   A catalyst has no effect on the equilibrium position. The purpose of a catalyst is to speed up a reaction so it reaches equilibrium more quickly.

d.   When the pressure of reactants and products is high, the reaction shifts to the side that has fewer gas molecules. Since the product side contains 2 molecules of gas as compared to 4 molecules of gas on the reactant side, then the reaction shifts right to products at high pressures of reactants and products.

75. $PCl_5(g) \rightleftharpoons PCl_3(g) + Cl_2(g)$ $K = \dfrac{[PCl_3][Cl_2]}{[PCl_5]} = 4.5 \times 10^{-3}$

At equilibrium, $[PCl_5] = 2[PCl_3]$.

$4.5 \times 10^{-3} = \dfrac{[PCl_3][Cl_2]}{2[PCl_3]}$, $[Cl_2] = 2(4.5 \times 10^{-3}) = 9.0 \times 10^{-3}\ M$

76. $CaCO_3(s) \rightleftharpoons CaO(s) + CO_2(g)$ $K_p = 1.16 = P_{CO_2}$

Some of the 20.0 g of $CaCO_3$ will react to reach equilibrium. The amount that reacts is the quantity of $CaCO_3$ required to produce a CO_2 pressure of 1.16 atm (from the K_p expression).

$$n_{CO_2} = \dfrac{P_{CO_2}V}{RT} = \dfrac{1.16\,\text{atm} \times 10.0\,\text{L}}{\dfrac{0.08206\,\text{L atm}}{\text{K mol}} \times 1073\,\text{K}} = 0.132\ \text{mol}\ CO_2$$

mass $CaCO_3$ reacted $= 0.132\ \text{mol}\ CO_2 \times \dfrac{1\ \text{mol}\ CaCO_3}{\text{mol}\ CO_2} \times \dfrac{100.09\ \text{g}}{\text{mol}\ CaCO_3} = 13.2\ \text{g}\ CaCO_3$

mass % $CaCO_3$ reacted $= \dfrac{13.2\ \text{g}}{20.0\ \text{g}} \times 100 = 66.0\%$

77. $PCl_5(g) \rightleftharpoons PCl_3(g) + Cl_2(g)$ $K_p = P_{PCl_3} \times P_{Cl_2} / P_{PCl_5}$

Initial	P_0	0	0	$P_0 =$ initial PCl_5 pressure
Change	$-x$	$\rightarrow$ $+x$	$+x$	
Equil.	$P_0 - x$	x	x	

$P_{total} = P_0 - x + x + x = P_0 + x = 358.7\ \text{torr}$

$$P_0 = \dfrac{n_{PCl_5}RT}{V} = \dfrac{\dfrac{2.4156\ \text{g}}{208.22\ \text{g/mol}} \times \dfrac{0.08206\ \text{L atm}}{\text{K mol}} \times 523.2\ \text{K}}{2.000\ \text{L}} = 0.2490\ \text{atm} = 189.2\ \text{torr}$$

$x = P_{total} - P_0 = 358.7 - 189.2 = 169.5\ \text{torr}$

$P_{PCl_3} = P_{Cl_2} = 169.5 \text{ torr} = 0.2230 \text{ atm}$

$P_{PCl_5} = 189.2 - 169.5 = 19.7 \text{ torr} = 0.0259 \text{ atm}$

$K_p = \dfrac{(0.2230)^2}{0.0259} = 1.92$

78. $5.63 \text{ g } C_5H_6O_3 \times \dfrac{1 \text{ mol } C_5H_6O_3}{114.10 \text{ g}} = 0.0493 \text{ mol } C_5H_6O_3 \text{ initially}$

total mol gas at equilibrium $= n_{TOT} = \dfrac{P_{TOT}V}{RT} = \dfrac{1.63 \text{ atm} \times 2.50 \text{ L}}{\dfrac{0.08206 \text{ L atm}}{\text{K mol}} \times 473 \text{ K}} = 0.105 \text{ mol}$

$$C_5H_6O_3(g) \;\rightleftharpoons\; C_2H_6(g) + 3\,CO(g)$$

Initial	0.0493 mol	0	0

Let x mol $C_5H_6O_3$ react to reach equilibrium

Change	$-x$	$+x$	$+3x$
Equil.	$0.0493 - x$	x	$3x$

$0.105 \text{ mol total} = 0.0493 - x + x + 3x = 0.0493 + 3x, \; x = 0.0186 \text{ mol}$

$K = \dfrac{[C_2H_6][CO]^3}{[C_5H_6O_3]} = \dfrac{\left[\dfrac{0.0186 \text{ mol } C_2H_6}{2.50 \text{ L}}\right]\left[\dfrac{3(0.0186) \text{ mol CO}}{2.50 \text{ L}}\right]^3}{\left[\dfrac{(0.0493 - 0.0186) \text{ mol } C_5H_6O_3}{2.50 \text{ L}}\right]} = 6.74 \times 10^{-6}$

Challenge Problems

79.   There is a little trick we can use to solve this problem in order to avoid solving a cubic equation. Because K for this reaction is very small, the dominant reaction is the reverse reaction. We will let the products react to completion by the reverse reaction, then we will solve the forward equilibrium problem to determine the equilibrium concentrations. Summarizing these steps in a table:

$$2\,NOCl(g) \;\rightleftharpoons\; 2\,NO(g) + Cl_2(g) \qquad K = 1.6 \times 10^{-5}$$

Before	0	2.0 *M*	1.0 *M*	

Let 1.0 mol/L Cl_2 react completely.   (K is small, reactants dominate.)

Change	+2.0	$\leftarrow$ -2.0	-1.0	React completely
After	2.0	0	0	New initial conditions

2x mol/L of NOCl reacts to reach equilibrium

Change	$-2x$	$\rightarrow$ $+2x$	$+x$
Equil.	$2.0 - 2x$	$2x$	x

$K = 1.6 \times 10^{-5} = \dfrac{(2x)^2(x)}{(2.0 - 2x)^2} \approx \dfrac{4x^3}{2.0^2}$ (assuming $2.0 - 2x \approx 2.0$)

$x^3 = 1.6 \times 10^{-5}$, $x = 2.5 \times 10^{-2}$;   Assumption good by the 5% rule ($2x$ is 2.5% of 2.0).

[NOCl] = 2.0 - 0.050 = 1.95 M = 2.0 M; [NO] = 0.050 M; [Cl$_2$] = 0.025 M

Note: If we do not break this problem into two parts (a stoichiometric part and an equilibrium part), we are faced with solving a cubic equation. The set-up would be:

$$2\,NOCl(g) \;\rightleftharpoons\; 2\,NO(g) \;+\; Cl_2(g)$$

Initial	0	2.0 M	1.0 M
Change	+2.0	$\leftarrow$ $-2y$	$-y$
Equil.	$2y$	2.0 - $2y$	1.0 - y

$1.6 \times 10^{-5} = \dfrac{(2.0 - 2y)^2(1.0 - y)}{(2y)^2}$ If we say that y is small to simplify the problem, then:

$1.6 \times 10^{-5} = \dfrac{2.0^2}{4y^2}$;   We get $y = 250$. This is impossible!

To solve this equation, we cannot make any simplifying assumptions; we have to solve a cubic equation. If you don't have a graphing calculator, this is difficult. Alternatively, we can use some chemical common sense and solve the problem as illustrated above.

80.   a. $2\,NO(g) \;+\; Br_2(g) \;\rightleftharpoons\; 2\,NOBr(g)$

Initial	98.4 torr	41.3 torr	0
	2x torr of NO reacts to reach equilibrium		
Change	$-2x$	$-x$ $\rightarrow$	$+2x$
Equil.	98.4 - $2x$	41.3 - x	$2x$

$P_{total} = P_{NO} + P_{Br_2} + P_{NOBr} = (98.4 - 2x) + (41.3 - x) + 2x = 139.7 - x$

$P_{total} = 110.5 = 139.7 - x$, $x = 29.2$ torr; $P_{NO} = 98.4 - 2(29.2) = 40.0$ torr = 0.0526 atm

$P_{Br_2} = 41.3 - 29.2 = 12.1$ torr = 0.0159 atm; $P_{NOBr} = 2(29.2) = 58.4$ torr = 0.0768 atm

$K_p = \dfrac{P_{NOBr}^2}{P_{NO}^2 \times P_{Br_2}} = \dfrac{(0.0768)^2}{(0.0526)^2(0.0159)} = 134$

b. $2\,NO(g) \;+\; Br_2(g) \;\rightleftharpoons\; 2\,NOBr(g)$

Initial	0.30 atm	0.30 atm	0
	2x atm of NO reacts to reach equilibrium		
Change	$-2x$	$-x$ $\rightarrow$	$+2x$
Equil.	0.30 - $2x$	0.30 - x	$2x$

This would yield a cubic equation. For those students without a graphing calculator, a strategy to solve this is to first notice that K_p is pretty large. Since K_p is large, let us approach equilibrium in two steps; assume the reaction goes to completion then solve the back equilibrium problem.

$$2\,NO \quad + \quad Br_2 \quad \rightleftharpoons \quad 2\,NOBr$$

Before	0.30 atm	0.30 atm	0	

Let 0.30 atm NO react completely.

Change	-0.30	-0.15 $\rightarrow$	$+0.30$	React completely
After	0	0.15	0.30	New initial conditions

$2y$ atm of NOBr reacts to reach equilibrium

Change	$+2y$	$+y$ $\leftarrow$	$-2y$
Equil.	$2y$	$0.15 + y$	$0.30 - 2y$

$$\frac{(0.30 - 2y)^2}{(2y)^2(0.15 + y)} = 134, \quad \frac{(0.30 - 2y)^2}{(0.15 + y)} = 134 \times 4y^2 = 536\,y^2$$

If $y \ll 0.15$: $\dfrac{(0.30)^2}{0.15} \approx 536\,y^2$ and $y = 0.034$;   Assumptions are poor (y is 23% of 0.15).

Use 0.034 as approximation for y and solve by successive approximations:

$$\frac{(0.30 - 0.068)^2}{0.15 + 0.034} = 536\,y^2, \quad y = 0.023; \quad \frac{(0.30 - 0.046)^2}{0.15 + 0.023} = 536\,y^2, \quad y = 0.026$$

$$\frac{(0.30 - 0.052)^2}{0.15 + 0.026} = 536\,y^2, \quad y = 0.026$$

So: $P_{NO} = 2y = 0.052$ atm; $P_{Br_2} = 0.15 + y = 0.18$ atm; $P_{NOBr} = 0.30 - 2y = 0.25$ atm

81. $N_2(g) \quad + \quad 3\,H_2(g) \quad \rightleftharpoons \quad 2\,NH_3(g)$

Initial	0	0	P_0	P_0 = initial pressure of NH_3 in atm

$2x$ atm of NH_3 reacts to reach equilibrium

Change	$+x$	$+3x$ $\leftarrow$	$-2x$
Equil.	x	$3x$	$P_0 - 2x$

From problem, $P_0 - 2x = \dfrac{P_0}{2.00}$, so $P_0 = 4.00\,x$

$$K_p = \frac{(4.00\,x - 2x)^2}{(x)(3x)^3} = \frac{(2.00\,x)^2}{(x)(3x)^3} = \frac{4.00\,x^2}{27x^4} = \frac{4.00}{27x^2} = 5.3 \times 10^5, \quad x = 5.3 \times 10^{-4}\,\text{atm}$$

$P_0 = 4.00\,x = 4.00 \times (5.3 \times 10^{-4})$ atm $= 2.1 \times 10^{-3}$ atm

82. $P_4(g) \rightleftharpoons 2 P_2(g)$ $K_p = 0.100 = \dfrac{P_{P_2}^2}{P_{P_4}}$; $P_{P_4} + P_{P_2} = P_{total} = 1.00$ atm, $P_{P_4} = 1.00$ atm $- P_{P_2}$

Let $y = P_{P_2}$ at equilibrium, then $\dfrac{y^2}{1.00 - y} = 0.100$

Solving: $y = 0.270$ atm $= P_{P_2}$; $P_{P_4} = 1.00 - 0.270 = 0.73$ atm

To solve for the fraction dissociated, we need the initial pressure of P_4 (mol $\propto$ pressure).

$$P_4(g) \quad \rightleftharpoons \quad 2 P_2(g)$$

Initial P_0 0 P_0 = initial pressure of P_4 in atm.
         x atm of P_4 reacts to reach equilibrium
Change $-x$ $\rightarrow$ $+2x$
Equil. $P_0 - x$ $2x$

$P_{total} = P_0 - x + 2x = 1.00$ atm $= P_0 + x$

Solving: 0.270 atm $= P_{P_2} = 2x$, $x = 0.135$ atm; $P_0 = 1.00 - 0.135 = 0.87$ atm

Fraction dissociated $= \dfrac{x}{P_0} = \dfrac{0.135}{0.87} = 0.16$ or 16% of P_4 is dissociated to reach equilibrium.

83. $N_2O_4(g) \rightleftharpoons 2 NO_2(g)$ $K_p = \dfrac{P_{NO_2}^2}{P_{N_2O_4}} = \dfrac{(1.20)^2}{0.34} = 4.2$

Doubling the volume decreases each partial pressure by a factor of 2 ($P = nRT/V$).

$P_{NO_2} = 0.600$ atm and $P_{N_2O_4} = 0.17$ atm are the new partial pressures.

$Q = \dfrac{(0.600)^2}{0.17} = 2.1$, so $Q < K$; Equilibrium will shift to the right.

$$N_2O_4(g) \quad \rightleftharpoons \quad 2 NO_2(g)$$

Initial   0.17 atm   0.600 atm
         x atm of N_2O_4 reacts to reach equilibrium
Change $-x$ $\rightarrow$ $+2x$
Equil. $0.17 - x$ $0.600 + 2x$

$K_p = 4.2 = \dfrac{(0.600 + 2x)^2}{(0.17 - x)}$, $4x^2 + 6.6\,x - 0.354 = 0$ (carrying extra sig. figs.)

Solving using the quadratic formula: $x = 0.052$

$P_{NO_2} = 0.600 + 2(0.052) = 0.704$ atm; $P_{N_2O_4} = 0.17 - 0.052 = 0.12$ atm

84.   a. $2 NaHCO_3(s) \rightleftharpoons Na_2CO_3(s) + CO_2(g) + H_2O(g)$

Initial   –   –   0   0

NaHCO$_3$(s) decomposes to form x atm each of $CO_2(g)$ and $H_2O(g)$ at equilibrium.

Change   – $\rightarrow$ – $+x$ $+x$
Equil.   –   – x x

$$0.25 = K_P = P_{CO_2} \times P_{H_2O}, \quad 0.25 = x^2, \quad x = P_{CO_2} = P_{H_2O} = 0.50 \text{ atm}$$

b. $n_{CO_2} = \dfrac{PV}{RT} = \dfrac{(0.50 \text{ atm})(1.00 \text{ L})}{(0.08206 \text{ L atm}/\text{mol} \bullet \text{K})(398 \text{ K})} = 1.5 \times 10^{-2} \text{ mol CO}_2$

Mass of Na_2CO_3 produced:

$$1.5 \times 10^{-2} \text{ mol CO}_2 \times \frac{1 \text{ mol Na}_2\text{CO}_3}{\text{mol CO}_2} \times \frac{105.99 \text{ g Na}_2\text{CO}_3}{\text{mol Na}_2\text{CO}_3} = 1.6 \text{ g Na}_2\text{CO}_3$$

Mass of $NaHCO_3$ reacted:

$$1.5 \times 10^{-2} \text{ mol CO}_2 \times \frac{2 \text{ mol NaHCO}_3}{1 \text{ mol CO}_2} \times \frac{84.01 \text{ g NaHCO}_3}{\text{mol}} = 2.5 \text{ g NaHCO}_3$$

Mass of $NaHCO_3$ remaining = 10.0 – 2.5 = 7.5 g

c. $10.0 \text{ g NaHCO}_3 \times \dfrac{1 \text{ mol NaHCO}_3}{84.01 \text{ g NaHCO}_3} \times \dfrac{1 \text{ mol CO}_2}{2 \text{ mol NaHCO}_3} = 5.95 \times 10^{-2} \text{ mol CO}_2$

When all of the NaHCO$_3$ has been just consumed, we will have 5.95×10^{-2} mol CO$_2$ gas at a pressure of 0.50 atm (from a).

$$V = \frac{nRT}{P} = \frac{(5.95 \times 10^{-2} \text{ mol})(0.08206 \text{ L atm}/\text{mol} \bullet \text{K})(398 \text{ K})}{(0.50 \text{ atm})} = 3.9 \text{ L}$$

85. $SO_3(g) \rightleftharpoons SO_2(g) + 1/2 \, O_2(g)$

Initial P_0 0   0 P_0 = initial pressure of SO$_3$
Change $-x$ $\rightarrow$ $+x$ $+x/2$
Equil. $P_0 - x$ x $x/2$

The average molar mass of the mixture is:

$$\text{average molar mass} = \frac{dRT}{P} = \frac{(1.60 \text{ g}/\text{L})(0.08206 \text{ L atm}/\text{mol} \bullet \text{K})(873 \text{ K})}{1.80 \text{ atm}} = 63.7 \text{ g/mol}$$

The average molar mass is determined by:

$$\text{average molar mass} = \frac{n_{SO_3}\,(80.07\ g/mol) + n_{SO_2}\,(64.07\ g/mol) + n_{O_2}\,(32.00\ g/mol)}{n_{total}}$$

Since χ_A = mol fraction of component A = $n_A/n_{total} = P_A/P_{total}$, then:

$$63.7\ g/mol = \frac{P_{SO_3}\,(80.07) + P_{SO_2}\,(64.07) + P_{O_2}\,(32.00)}{P_{total}}$$

$P_{total} = P_0 - x + x + x/2 = P_0 + x/2 = 1.80\ atm,\ \ P_0 = 1.80 - x/2$

$$63.7 = \frac{(P_0 - x)(80.07) + x(64.07) + \dfrac{x}{2}(32.00)}{1.80}$$

$$63.7 = \frac{(1.80 - 3/2\,x)(80.07) + x(64.07) + \dfrac{x}{2}(32.00)}{1.80}$$

$115 = 144 - 120.1\,x + 64.07\,x + 16.00\,x,\ \ 40.0\,x = 29,\ \ x = 0.73\ atm$

$P_{SO_3} = P_0 - x = 1.80 - 3/2\,x = 0.71\ atm;\ \ P_{SO_2} = 0.73\ atm;\ \ P_{O_2} = x/2 = 0.37\ atm$

$$K_p = \frac{P_{SO_2} \times P_{O_2}^{1/2}}{P_{SO_3}} = \frac{(0.73)(0.37)^{1/2}}{(0.71)} = 0.63$$

86.   The first reaction produces equal amounts of SO_3 and SO_2. Using the second reaction, calculate the SO_3, SO_2 and O_2 partial pressures at equilibrium.

$$SO_3(g) \ \rightleftharpoons\ SO_2(g) \ +\ 1/2\ O_2(g)$$

	$SO_3(g)$	$SO_2(g)$	$1/2\ O_2(g)$	
Initial	P_0	P_0	0	P_0 = initial pressure of SO_3 and SO_2 after first reaction occurs.
Change	$-x \rightarrow$	$+x$	$+x/2$	
Equil.	$P_0 - x$	$P_0 + x$	$x/2$	

$P_{total} = P_0 - x + P_0 + x + x/2 = 2\,P_0 + x/2 = 0.836\ atm$

$P_{O_2} = x/2 = 0.0275\ atm,\ \ x = 0.0550\ atm$

$2\,P_0 + x/2 = 0.836\ atm;\ \ 2\,P_0 = 0.836 - 0.0275 = 0.809\ atm,\ \ P_0 = 0.405\ atm$

$P_{SO_3} = P_0 - x = 0.405 - 0.0550 = 0.350$ atm; $P_{SO_2} = P_0 + x = 0.405 + 0.0550 = 0.460$ atm

For 2 $FeSO_4(s) \rightleftharpoons Fe_2O_3(s) + SO_3(g) + SO_2(g)$:

$K_p = P_{SO_2} \times P_{SO_3} = (0.460)(0.350) = 0.161$

For $SO_3(g) \rightleftharpoons SO_2(g) + 1/2 \ O_2(g)$:

$$K_p = \frac{P_{SO_2} \times P_{O_2}^{1/2}}{P_{SO_3}} = \frac{(0.460)(0.0275)^{1/2}}{0.350} = 0.218$$

87. $O_2 \rightleftharpoons 2\,O$ Assuming exactly 100 O_2 molecules

	O_2	O
Initial	100	0
Change	-83	$+166$
Equil.	17	166

Thus: $\chi_O = \dfrac{166}{183} = 0.9071$ and $\chi_{O_2} = 0.0929$

$P \propto n$, so $P_{O_2} \propto \chi_{O_2}$ and $P_O \propto \chi_O$.

Because $P_{TOTAL} = 1.000$ atm, $P_{O_2} = 0.0929$ atm and $P_O = 0.9071$ atm.

$$K_p = \frac{(0.9071)^2}{0.0929} = 8.857$$

	O_2	O
Initial	x	0
Change	$-y \quad \rightarrow$	$+2y$
Equil.	$x - y$	$2y$

$$\frac{(2y)^2}{x - y} = 8.857; \quad \frac{y}{x} \times 100 = 95.0$$

Solving: x = 0.123 atm and y = 0.117 atm; $P_{total} = 0.240$ atm

88.   a. $N_2O_4(g) \rightleftharpoons 2\,NO_2(g)$

	N_2O_4	NO_2
Initial	x	0
Change	$-0.16x$	$+0.32\,x$
Equil.	$0.84x$	$0.32x$

$0.84x + 0.32x = 1.5$ atm, $x = 1.3$ atm; $K_p = \dfrac{(0.42)^2}{1.1} = 0.16$ atm

b. $N_2O_4 \rightleftharpoons 2\,NO_2$; $x + y = 1.0$ atm; $\dfrac{y^2}{x} = 0.16$

Equil. x y

Solving, $x = 0.67$ atm $(= P_{N_2O_4})$ and $y = 0.33$ atm $(= P_{NO_2})$

c. $N_2O_4 \rightleftharpoons 2\,NO_2$

Initial	P_0	0	P_0 = initial pressure of N_2O_4
Change	$-x$	$+2x$	
Equil.	0.67 atm	0.33 atm	

$x = 0.165$ (using extra sig figs)

$P_0 - x = 0.67$;   Solving: $P_0 = 0.84$ atm; $\dfrac{0.165}{0.84} \times 100 = 20.\%$ dissociated

89. $2\,NOBr\,(g) \rightleftharpoons 2\,NO(g) + Br_2(g)$

Initial	P_0	0	0	P_0 = initial pressure of NOBr
Equil.	$P_0 - 2x$	$2x$	x	Note: $P_{NO} = 2\,P_{Br_2}$

$P_{total} = 0.0515$ atm $= (P_0 - 2x) + (2x) + (x) = P_0 + x$; 0.0515 atm $= P_{NOBr} + 3\,P_{Br_2}$

$$d = \frac{P \times (\text{molar mass})}{RT} = 0.1861 \text{ g/L} = \frac{P_{NOBr}(109.9) + 2\,P_{Br_2}(30.01) + P_{Br_2}(159.8)}{0.08206 \times 298}$$

$4.55 = 109.9\,P_{NOBr} + 219.8\,P_{Br_2}$

Solving using simultaneous equations:

$$\begin{aligned} 0.0515 &= P_{NOBr} + 3\,P_{Br_2} \\ -0.0414 &= -P_{NOBr} - 2.000\,P_{Br_2} \\ \hline 0.0101 &= P_{Br_2} \end{aligned}$$

$P_{Br_2} = 1.01 \times 10^{-2}$ atm; $P_{NO} = 2\,P_{Br_2} = 2.02 \times 10^{-2}$ atm

$P_{NOBr} = 0.0515 - 3(1.01 \times 10^{-2}) = 2.12 \times 10^{-2}$ atm

$$K_p = \frac{P_{Br_2} \times P_{NO}^2}{P_{NOBr}^2} = \frac{(1.01 \times 10^{-2})(2.02 \times 10^{-2})^2}{(2.12 \times 10^{-2})^2} = 9.17 \times 10^{-3}$$

90. $CCl_4(g)$ $\rightleftharpoons$ $C(s)$ + $2\,Cl_2(g)$ $K_p = 0.76 = P^2_{Cl_2}/P_{CCl_4}$

Initial P_0 –   0 P_0 = initial pressure of CCl_4
Change $-x$ $\rightarrow$ – $+2x$
Equil. $P_0 - x$ – $2x$

$P_{total} = P_0 - x + 2x = P_0 + x = 1.20$ atm

$K_p = \dfrac{(2x)^2}{P_0 - x} = 0.76,\ \ 4x^2 = 0.76\,P_0 - 0.76\,x,\ \ P_0 = \dfrac{4x^2 + 0.76\,x}{0.76} = \dfrac{4x^2}{0.76} + x$

Substituting into $P_0 + x = 1.20$:

$\dfrac{4x^2}{0.76} + x + x = 1.20$ atm, $5.3\,x^2 + 2x - 1.20 = 0$; Solving using the quadratic formula:

$x = \dfrac{-2 \pm (4 + 25.4)^{1/2}}{2(5.3)} = 0.32,\ \ P_0 + 0.32\ \text{atm} = 1.20\ \text{atm},\ \ P_0 = 0.88\ \text{atm}$

Integrative Problems

91. $NH_3(g)$ + $H_2S(g)$ $\rightleftharpoons$ $NH_4HS(s)$ $K = 400. = \dfrac{1}{[NH_3][H_2S]}$

Initial $\dfrac{2.00\ \text{mol}}{5.00\ \text{L}}$ $\dfrac{2.00\ \text{mol}}{5.00\ \text{L}}$ –

         x mol/L of NH_3 reacts to reach equilibrium
Change $-x$ $-x$ –
Equil. $0.400 - x$ $0.400 - x$ –

$K = 400. = \dfrac{1}{(0.400 - x)(0.400 - x)},\ \ 0.400 - x = \left(\dfrac{1}{400.}\right)^{1/2} = 0.0500$

$x = 0.350\ M$; mol $NH_4HS(s)$ produced $= 5.00\ \text{L} \times \dfrac{0.350\ \text{mol}\ NH_3}{L} \times \dfrac{1\ \text{mol}\ NH_4HS}{\text{mol}\ NH_3}$

$= 1.75$ mol

Total mol $NH_4HS(s) = 2.00$ mol initially $+ 1.75$ mol produced $= 3.75$ mol total

3.75 mol $NH_4HS\ \times\ \dfrac{51.12\ \text{g}\ NH_4HS}{\text{mol}\ NH_4HS} = 192$ g NH_4HS

$[H_2S]_e = 0.400 \ M - x = 0.400 \ M - 0.350 \ M = 0.050 \ M \ H_2S$

$$P_{H_2S} = \frac{n_{H_2S} \ RT}{V} = \frac{n_{H_2S}}{V} \times RT = \frac{0.050 \ mol}{L} \times \frac{0.08206 \ L \ atm}{K \ mol} \times 308 \ K = 1.3 \ atm$$

92.   See the hint for Exercise 65.

$2 \ C(g) \rightleftharpoons 2 \ A(g) + 2 \ B(g)$ $K_1 = (1/3.50)^2 = 8.16 \times 10^{-2}$

$2 \ A(g) + D(g) \rightleftharpoons C(g)$ $K_2 = 7.10$

_____

$C(g) + D(g) \rightleftharpoons 2 \ B(g)$ $K = K_1 \times K_2 = 0.579$

$K_p = K(RT)^{\Delta n}, \ \ \Delta n = 2 - (1 + 1) = 0;$ Because $\Delta n = 0, \ K_p = K = 0.579.$

$C(g) \quad + \quad D(g) \quad \rightleftharpoons \quad 2 \ B(g)$

Initial   1.50 atm   1.50 atm   0
Equil. $1.50 - x$ $1.50 - x$ $2x$

$$0.579 = K = \frac{(2x)^2}{(1.50 - x)(1.50 - x)} = \frac{(2x)^2}{(1.50 - x)^2}$$

$$\frac{2x}{1.50 - x} = (0.579)^{1/2} = 0.761, \ x = 0.413 \ atm$$

$P_B \ (\text{at equilibrium}) = 2x = 2(0.413) = 0.826 \ atm$

$P_{TOT} = P_C + P_D + P_B = 2(1.50 - 0.413) + 0.826 = 3.00 \ atm$

$$P_B = \chi_B P_{TOT}, \ \ \chi_B = \frac{P_B}{P_{TOT}} = \frac{0.826 \ atm}{3.00 \ atm} = 0.275$$

93.   Assuming 100.00 g naphthalene:

$$93.71 \ C \times \frac{1 \ mol \ C}{12.01 \ g} = 7.803 \ mol \ C$$

$$6.29 \ g \ H \times \frac{1 \ mol \ H}{1.008 \ g} = 6.240 \ mol \ H; \quad \frac{7.803}{6.240} = 1.25$$

empirical formula = $(C_{1.25}H) \times 4 = C_5H_4;$ molar mass = $\dfrac{32.8 \ g}{0.256 \ mol} = 128 \ g/mol$

Because the empirical mass (64.08 g/mol) is one-half of 128, the molecular formula is $C_{10}H_8$.

$$C_{10}H_8(s) \quad \rightleftharpoons \quad C_{10}H_8(g) \qquad K = 4.29 \times 10^{-6} = [C_{10}H_8]$$

Initial	–	0
Equil.	–	x

$$K = 4.29 \times 10^{-6} = [C_{10}H_8] = x$$

mol $C_{10}H_8$ sublimed = 5.00 L $\times 4.29 \times 10^{-6}$ mol/L = 2.15×10^{-5} mol $C_{10}H_8$ sublimed

mol $C_{10}H_8$ initially = 3.00 g $\times \dfrac{1 \, mol \, C_{10}H_8}{128.16 \, g} = 2.34 \times 10^{-2}$ mol $C_{10}H_8$ initially

% $C_{10}H_8$ sublimed = $\dfrac{2.15 \times 10^{-5} \, mol}{2.34 \times 10^{-2} \, mol} \times 100 = 9.19 \times 10^{-2}$ %

Marathon Problem

94. Concentration units involve both moles and volume and since both quantities are changing at the same time, we have a complicated system. Let's simplify the set-up to the problem initially by only worrying about the changes that occur to the moles of each gas.

$$A(g) \quad + \quad B(g) \quad \rightleftharpoons \qquad C(g) \qquad K = 130.$$

Initial	0	0	0.406 mol
	Let x mol of C(g) react to reach equilibrium		
Change	$+x$	$+x$ ←	$-x$
Equil.	x	x	$0.406 - x$

Let V_{eq} = the equilibrium volume of the container, so:

$$[A]_{eq} = [B]_{eq} = \frac{x}{V_{eq}}; \quad [C]_{eq} = \frac{0.406 - x}{V_{eq}}$$

$$K = 130. = \frac{[C]}{[A][B]} = \frac{\dfrac{0.406 - x}{V_{eq}}}{\dfrac{x}{V_{eq}} \times \dfrac{x}{V_{eq}}} = \frac{(0.406 - x)\, V_{eq}}{x^2}$$

From the ideal gas equation: $V = \dfrac{nRT}{P}$

To calculate the equilibrium volume from the ideal gas law, we need the total moles of gas present at equilibrium.

At equilibrium: n_{total} = mol A(g) + mol B(g) + mol C(g) = $x + x + 0.406 - x = 0.406 + x$

Therefore: $V_{eq} = \dfrac{n_{total}RT}{P} = \dfrac{(0.406 + x) \times \dfrac{0.08206 \text{ L atm}}{\text{mol K}} \times 300.0 \text{ K}}{1.00 \text{ atm}}$

$V_{eq} = (0.406 + x)\ 24.6 \text{ L/mol}$

Substituting into the equilibrium expression for V_{eq}:

$K = 130. = \dfrac{(0.406 - x)(0.406 + x)\,24.6}{x^2}$

Solving for x (we will carry one extra significant figure):

$130.\ x^2 = (0.1648 - x^2)\,24.6,\ \ 154.6\,x^2 = 4.054,\ \ x = 0.162 \text{ mol}$

Solving for the volume of the container at equilibrium:

$V_{eq} = \dfrac{(0.406 \text{ mol} + 0.162 \text{ mol}) \times \dfrac{0.08206 \text{ L atm}}{\text{K mol}} \times 300.0 \text{ K}}{1.00 \text{ atm}} = 14.0 \text{ L}$

CHAPTER FOURTEEN

ACIDS AND BASES

For Review

1.   a. Arrhenius acid: produce H^+ in water
      b. Børnsted-Lowry acid: proton (H^+) donor
      c. Lewis acid: electron pair acceptor

The Lewis definition is most general. The Lewis definition can apply to all Arrhenius and Brønsted-Lowry acids; H^+ has an empty 1s orbital and forms bonds to all bases by accepting a pair of electrons from the base. In addition, the Lewis definition incorporates other reactions not typically considered acid-base reactions, e.g., $BF_3(g) + NH_3(g) \rightarrow F_3B-NH_3(s)$. NH_3 is something we usually consider a base and it is a base in this reaction using the Lewis definition; NH_3 donates a pair of electrons to form the N–B bond.

2.   a. The K_a reaction always refers to an acid reacting with water to produce the conjugate base of the acid and the hydronium ion (H_3O^+). For a general weak acid HA, the K_a reaction is:

$$HA(aq) + H_2O(l) \rightleftharpoons A^-(aq) + H_3O^+(aq) \text{ where } A^- = \text{conjugate base of the acid HA}$$

This reaction is often abbreviated as: $HA(aq) \rightleftharpoons H^+(aq) + A^-(aq)$

      b. The K_a equilibrium constant is the equilibrium constant for the K_a reaction of some substance. For the general K_a reaction, the K_a expression is:

$$K_a = \frac{[A^-][H_3O^+]}{[HA]} \text{ or } K_a = \frac{[H^+][A^-]}{[HA]} \quad \text{(for the abbreviated } K_a \text{ reaction)}$$

      c. The K_b reaction always refers to a base reacting with water to produce the conjugate acid of the base and the hydroxide ion (OH^-). For a general base, B, the K_b reaction is:

$$B(aq) + H_2O(l) \rightleftharpoons BH^+(aq) + OH^-(aq) \text{ where } BH^+ = \text{conjugate acid of the base B}$$

      d. The K_b equilibrium constant for the general K_b reaction is: $K_b = \dfrac{[BH^+][OH^-]}{[B]}$

      e. A conjugate acid-base pair consists of two substances related to each other by the donating and accepting of a single proton. The conjugate bases of the acids HCl, HNO_2, $HC_2H_3O_2$ and H_2SO_4 are Cl^-, NO_2^-, $C_2H_3O_2^-$, and HSO_4^-, respectively. The conjugate acids of the bases NH_3, C_5H_5N, and $HONH_2$ are NH_4^+, $C_5H_5NH^+$, and $HONH_3^+$, respectively. Conjugate acid-base pairs only differ by H^+ in their respective formulas.

3.   a.   Amphoteric: a substance that can behave either as an acid or as a base.

      b.   The K_w reaction is also called the autoionization of water reaction. The reaction always occurs when water is present as the solvent. The reaction is:

      $$H_2O(l) + H_2O(l) \rightleftharpoons H_3O^+(aq) + OH^-(aq) \text{ or } H_2O(l) \rightleftharpoons H^+(aq) + OH^-(aq)$$

      c.   The K_w equilibrium constant is also called the ion-product constant or the dissociation constant of water. It is the equilibrium constant for the autoionization reaction of water:

      $$K_w = [H_3O^+][OH^-] \text{ or } K_w = [H^+][OH^-]$$

      At typical solution temperatures of 25°C, $K_w = 1.0 \times 10^{-14}$.

      d.   pH is a mathematical term which is equal to the –log of the H^+ concentration of a solution ($pH = -\log[H^+]$.

      e.   pOH is a mathematical terem which is equal to the –log of the OH^- concentration of a solution ($pOH = -\log[OH^-]$).

      f.   The p of any quantity is the –log of that quantity. So: $pK_w = -\log K_w$. At 25°C, $pK_w = -\log (1.0 \times 10^{-14}) = 14.00$.

      Neutral solution at 25°C: $K_w = 1.0 \times 10^{-14} = [H^+][OH^-]$ and $pH + pOH = 14.00$

      $$[H^+] = [OH^-] = 1.0 \times 10^{-7} \, M; \; pH = pOH = -\log(1.0 \times 10^{-7}) = 7.00$$

      Acidic solution at 25°C:

      $$[H^+] > [OH^-]; [H^+] > 1.0 \times 10^{-7} M; \; [OH^-] < 1.0 \times 10^{-7} \, M; \; pH < 7.00; \; pOH > 7.00$$

      Basic solution at 25°C:

      $$[OH^-] > [H^+]; \; [OH^-] > 1.0 \times 10^{-7} \, M; \; [H^+] < 1.0 \times 10^{-7} \, M; \; pOH < 7.00; \; pH > 7.00$$

      As a solution becomes more acidic, $[H^+]$ increases, so $[OH^-]$ decreases, pH decreases, and pOH increases. As a solution becomes more basic, $[OH^-]$ increases, so $[H^+]$ decreases, pH increases, and pOH decreases.

4.   The K_a value refers to the reaction of an acid reacting with water to produce the conjugate base and H_3O^+. The stronger the acid, the more conjugate base and H_3O^+ produced, and the larger the K_a value.

      Strong acids are basically 100% dissociated in water. Therefore, the strong acids have a $K_a \gg 1$ because the equilibrium position lies far to the right. The conjugate bases of strong acids are terrible bases; much worse than water, so we can ignore their basic properties in water.

Weak acids are only partially dissociated in water. We say that the equilibrium lies far to the left, thus giving values for $K_a < 1$. (We have mostly reactants at equilibrium and few products present). The conjugate bases of weak acids are better bases than water. When we have a solution composed of just the conjugate base of a weak acid in water, the resulting pH is indeed basic (pH > 7.0). In general, as the acid strength increases, the conjugate base strength decreases, or as acid strength decreases, the conjugate base strength increases. They are inversely related.

Base strength is directly related to the K_b value. The larger the K_b value, the more OH^- produced from the K_b reaction, and the more basic the solution (the higher the pH). Weak bases have a $K_b < 1$ and their conjugate acids behave as weak acids in solution. As the strength of the base increases, the strength of the conjugate acid gets weaker; the stronger the base, the weaker the conjugate acid, or the weaker the base, the stronger the conjugate acid.

5.   Strong acids are assumed 100% dissociated in water, and we assume that the amount of H^+ donated by water is negligible. Hence, the equilibrium $[H^+]$ of a strong acid is generally equal to the initial acid concentration ($[HA]_0$). Note that solutions of H_2SO_4 can be different from this as H_2SO_4 is a diprotic acid. Also, when you have very dilute solutions of a strong acid, the H^+ contribution from water by itself must be considered. The strong acids to memorize are HCl, HBr, HI, HNO_3, $HClO_4$, and H_2SO_4.

K_a values for weak acids are listed in Table 14.2 and in Appendix 5 of the text. Because weak acids only partially dissociate in water, we must solve an equilibrium problem to determine how much H^+ is added to water by the weak acid. We write down the K_a reaction, set-up the ICE table, then solve the equilibrium problem. The two assumptions generally made are that acids are less than 5% dissociated in water and that the H^+ contribution from water is negligible.

The 5% rule comes from the assumptions that weak acids are less than 5% dissociated. When this is true, the mathematics of the problem are made much easier. The equilibrium expression we get for weak acids in water generally has the form (assuming an initial acid concentration of 0.10 M):

$$K_a = \frac{x^2}{0.10 - x} \approx \frac{x^2}{0.10}$$

The 5% rule refers to assuming $0.10 - x \approx 0.10$. The assumption is valid if x is less than 5% of the number the assumption was made against ($[HA]_0$). When the 5% rule is valid, solving for x is very straight forward. When the 5% rule fails, we must solve the mathematical expression exactly using the quadratic equation (or your graphing calculator). Even if you do have a graphing calculator, reference Appendix A1.4 to review the quadratic equation. Appendix A1.4 also discusses the method of successive approximations which can also be used to solve quadratic (and cubic) equations.

6.   Strong bases are soluble ionic compounds containing the OH^- anion. Strong bases increase the OH^- concentration in water by just dissolving. Thus, for strong bases like LiOH, NaOH, KOH, RbOH, and CsOH, the initial concentration of the strong base equals the equilibrium $[OH^-]$ of water.

The other strong bases to memorize have +2 charged metal cations. The soluble ones to know are $Ca(OH)_2$, $Sr(OH)_2$, and $Ba(OH)_2$. These are slightly more difficult to solve because they donate 2 moles OH^- for every mole of salt dissolved. Here, the $[OH^-]$ is equal to two times the initial concentration of the soluble alkaline earth hydroxide salt dissolved.

Neutrally charged organic compounds containing at least one nitrogen atom generally behave as weak bases. The nitrogen atom has an unshared pair of electrons around it. This lone pair of electrons is used to form a bond to H^+.

Weak bases only partially react with water to produce OH^-. To determine the amount of OH^- produced by the weak acid (and, in turn, the pH of the solution), we set-up the ICE table using the K_b reaction of the weak base. The typical weak base equilibrium expression is:

$$K_b = \frac{x^2}{0.25 - x} \approx \frac{x^2}{0.25} \quad \text{(assuming } [B]_0 = 0.25 \text{ } M)$$

Solving for x gives us the $[OH^-]$ in solution. We generally assume that weak bases are only 5% reacted with water and that the OH^- contribution from water is negligible. The 5% assumption makes the math easier. By assuming an expression like $0.25 \text{ } M - x \approx 0.25 \text{ } M$, the calculation is very straight forward. The 5% rule applied here is that if $(x/0.25) \times 100$ is less than 5%, the assumption is valid. When the assumption is not valid, then we solve the equilibrium expression exactly using the quadratic equation (or by the method of successive approximations).

7.   Monoprotic acid: an acid with one acidic proton; the general formula for monoprotic acids is HA.

Diprotic acid: an acid with two acidic protons (H_2A)

Triprotic acid: an acid with three acidic protons (H_3A)

$$H_2SO_4(aq) \rightarrow HSO_4^-(aq) + H^+(aq) \qquad K_{a_1} \gg 1; \text{ this is a strong acid.}$$

$$HSO_4^-(aq) \rightleftharpoons SO_4^{2-}(aq) + H^+(aq) \qquad K_{a_2} = 0.012; \text{ this is a weak acid.}$$

When H_2SO_4 is dissolved in water, the first proton is assumed 100% dissociated because H_2SO_4 is a strong acid. After H_2SO_4 dissociates, we have H^+ and HSO_4^- present. HSO_4^- is a weak acid and can donate some more protons to water. To determine the amount of H^+ donated by HSO_4^-, one must solve an equilibrium problem using the K_{a_2} reaction for HSO_4^-.

$$H_3PO_4(aq) \rightleftharpoons H^+(aq) + H_2PO_4^-(aq) \qquad K_{a_1} = 7.5 \times 10^{-3}$$

$$H_2PO_4^-(aq) \rightleftharpoons H^+(aq) + HPO_4^{2-}(aq) \qquad K_{a_2} = 6.2 \times 10^{-8}$$

$$HPO_4^{2-}(aq) \rightleftharpoons H^+(aq) + PO_4^{3-}(aq) \qquad K_{a_3} = 4.8 \times 10^{-13}$$

When H_3PO_4 is added to water, the three acids that are present are H_3PO_4, $H_2PO_4^-$, and HPO_4^{2-}. H_3PO_4, with the largest K_a value, is the strongest of these weak acids. The conjugate bases of the three acids are $H_2PO_4^-$, HPO_4^{2-}, and PO_4^{3-}. Because HPO_4^{2-} is the weakest acid (smallest K_a value), its conjugate base (PO_4^{3-}) will have the largest K_b value and is the strongest base.

See Sample Exercises 14.15-14.17 on the strategies used to solve for the pH of polyprotic acids. The strategy to solve most polyprotic acid solutions is covered in Sample Exercise 14.15. For typical polyprotic acids, $K_{a_1} \gg K_{a_2}$ (and K_{a_3} if a triprotic acid). Because of this, the dominant producer of H^+ in solution is just the K_{a_1} reaction. We set-up the equilibrium problem using the K_{a_1} reaction and solve for H^+. We then assume that the H^+ donated by the K_{a_2} (and K_{a_3} if triprotic) reaction is negligible that is, the H^+ donated by the K_{a_1} reaction is assumed to be the H^+ donated by the entire acid system. This assumption is great when $K_{a_1} \gg K_{a_2}$ (roughly a 1000 fold difference in magnitude).

Sample Exercises 14.16 and 14.17 cover strategies for the other type of polyprotic acid problems. This other type is solutions of H_2SO_4. As discussed above, H_2SO_4 problems are both a strong acid and a weak acid problem in one. To solve for the $[H^+]$, we sometimes must worry about the H^+ contribution from HSO_4. Sample Exercise 13.16 is an example of an H_2SO_4 solution where the HSO_4^- contribution of H^+ can be ignored. Sample Exercise 14.17 illustrates an H_2SO_4 problem where we can't ignore the H^+ contribution from HSO_4^-.

8.   a. H_2O and $CH_3CO_2^-$

       b.   An acid-base reaction can be thought of as a competiton between two opposing bases. Since this equilibrium lies far to the left ($K_a < 1$), $CH_3CO_2^-$ is a stronger base than H_2O.

       c.   The acetate ion is a better base than water and produces basic solutions in water. When we put acetate ion into solution as the only major basic species, the reaction is:

$$CH_3CO_2^- + H_2O \rightleftharpoons CH_3CO_2H + OH^-$$

Now the competition is between $CH_3CO_2^-$ and OH^- for the proton. Hydroxide ion is the strongest base possible in water. The equilibrium above lies far to the left, resulting in a K_b value less than one. Those species we specifically call weak bases ($10^{-14} < K_b < 1$) lie between H_2O and OH^- in base strength. Weak bases are stronger bases than water but are weaker bases than OH^-.

The NH_4^+ ion is a weak acid because it lies between H_2O and H_3O^+ (H^+) in terms of acid strength. Weak acids are better acids than water, thus their aqueous solutions are acidic. They are weak acids because they are not as strong as H_3O^+ (H^+). Weak acids only partially dissociate in water and have K_a values between 10^{-14} and 1.

For a strong acid HX having $K_a = 1 \times 10^6$, the conjugate base, X^-, has $K_b = K_w/K_a$ $= 1.0 \times 10^{-14} / 1 \times 10^6 = 1 \times 10^{-20}$.

The conjugate bases of strong acids have extremely small values for K_b; so small that they are worse bases than water ($K_b \ll K_w$). Therefore, conjugate bases of strong acids have no basic properties in water. They are present, but they only balance charge in solution and nothing else. The conjugate bases of the six strong acids are Cl^-, Br^-, I^-, NO_3^-, ClO_4^-, and HSO_4^-.

Summarizing the acid-base properlties of conjugates:

a. The conjugate base of a weak acid is a weak base ($10^{-14} < K_b < 1$)

b. The conjugate acid of a weak base is a weak acid ($10^{-14} < K_a < 1$)

c. The conjugate base of a strong acid is a worthless base ($K_b \ll 10^{-14}$)

d. The conjugate acid of a strong base is a worthless acid ($K_a \ll 10^{-14}$)

Identifying/recognizing the acid-base properties of conjugates is crucial in order to understand the acid-base properties of salts. The salts we will give you will be salts containing the conjugates discussed above. Your job is to recognize the type of conjugate present, and then use that information to solve an equilibrium problem.

9.   A salt is an ionic compound composed of a cation and an anion.

Weak base anions: these are the conjugate bases of the weak acids having the HA general formula. Table 14.2 lists several HA type acids. Some weak base anions derived from the acids in Table 14.2 are ClO_2^-, F^-, NO_2^-, $C_2H_3O_2^-$, OCl^-, and CN^-.

Garbage anions (those anions with no basic or acidic properties): these are the conjugate bases of the strong acids having the HA general formula. Some neutral anions are Cl^-, NO_3^-, Br^-, I^-, and ClO_4^-.

Weak acid cations: these are the conjugate acids of the weak bases which contain nitrogen. Table 14.3 lists several nitrogen-containing bases. Some weak acid cations derived from the weak bases in Table 14.3 are NH_4^+, $CH_3NH_3^+$, $C_2H_5NH_3^+$, $C_6H_5NH_3^+$, and $C_5H_5NH^+$.

Garbage cations (those cations with no acidic properties or basic properties): the most common ones used are the cations in the strong bases. These are Li^+, Na^+, K^+, Rb^+, Cs^+, Ca^{2+}, Sr^{2+}, and Ba^{2+}.

We mix and match the cations and anions to get what type of salt we want. For a weak base salt, we combine a weak base anion with a garbage cation. Some weak base salts are NaF, KNO_2, $Ca(CN)_2$, and $RbC_2H_3O_2$. To determine the pH of a weak base salt, we write out the K_b reaction for the weak base anion and determine K_b ($= K_w/K_a$). We set-up the ICE table under the K_b reaction, and then solve the equilibrium problem to calculate $[OH^-]$ and, in turn, pH.

For a weak acid salt, we combine a weak acid cation with a garbage anion. Some weak acid salts are NH_4Cl, $C_5H_5NHNO_3$, CH_3NH_3I, and $C_2H_5NH_3ClO_4$. To determine the pH, we write out the K_a reaction for the weak acid cation and determine K_a ($= K_w/K_b$). We set-up the ICE table under the K_a reaction, and then solve the equilibrium problem to calculate $[H^+]$ and, in turn, pH.

For a neutral (pH = 7.0) salt, we combine a garbage cation with a garbage anion. Some examples are $NaCl$, KNO_3, $BaBr_2$, and $Sr(ClO_4)_2$.

For salts that contain a weak acid cation and a weak base anion, we compare the K_a value of the weak acid cation to the K_b value for the weak base anion. When $K_a > K_b$, the salt produces an acidic solution (pH < 7.0). When $K_b > K_a$, the salt produces a basic solution. And when $K_a = K_b$, the salt produces a neutral solution (pH = 7.0).

10.   a.   The weaker the X–H bond in an oxyacid, the stronger the acid.

      b.   As the electronegativity of neighboring atoms increases in an oxyacid, the strength of the acid increases.

      c.   As the number of oxygen atoms increases in an oxyacid, the strength of the acid increases.

In general, the weaker the acid, the stronger the conjugate base and vice versa.

      a.   Because acid strength increases as the X–H bond strength decreases, conjugate base strength will increase as the strength of the X–H bond increases.

      b.   Because acid strength increases as the electronegativity of neighboring atoms increases, conjugate base strength will decrease as the electronegativity of neighboring atoms increases.

      c.   Because acid strength increases as the number of oxygen atoms increases, conjugate base strength decreases as the number of oxygen atoms increases.

Nonmetal oxides form acidic solutions when dissolved in water:

$$SO_3(g) + H_2O(l) \rightarrow H_2SO_4(aq)$$

Metal oxides form basic solutions when dissolved in water:

$$CaO(s) + H_2O(l) \rightarrow Ca(OH)_2$$

Questions

16.   When a strong acid (HX) is added to water, the reaction $HX + H_2O \rightarrow H_3O^+ + X^-$ basically goes to completion. All strong acids in water are completely converted into H_3O^+ and X^-. Thus, no acid stronger than H_3O^+ will remain undissociated in water. Similarly, when a strong base (B) is added to water, the reaction $B + H_2O \rightarrow BH^+ + OH^-$ basically goes to completion. All bases stronger than OH^- are completely converted into OH^- and BH^+. Even though there are acids and bases stronger than H_3O^+ and OH^-, in water these acids and bases are completely converted into H_3O^+ and OH^-.

17.   10.78 (4 S.F.); 6.78 (3 S.F.); 0.78 (2 S.F.); A pH value is a logarithm. The numbers to the left of the decimal point identify the power of ten to which $[H^+]$ is expressed in scientific notation, e.g., $10^{-11}, 10^{-7}$, 10^{-1}. The number of decimal places in a pH value identifies the number of significant figures in $[H^+]$. In all three pH values, the $[H^+]$ should be expressed only to two significant figures because these pH values have only two decimal places.

18.   A Lewis acid must have an empty orbital to accept an electron pair, and a Lewis base must have an unshared pair of electrons.

19.   a.   These are strong acids like HCl, HBr, HI, HNO_3, H_2SO_4 or $HClO_4$.

b.   These are salts of the conjugate acids of the bases in Table 14.3. These conjugate acids are all weak acids. NH_4Cl, $CH_3NH_3NO_3$, and $C_2H_5NH_3Br$ are three examples. Note that the anions used to form these salts (Cl^-, NO_3^-, and Br^-) are conjugate bases of strong acids; this is because they have no acidic or basic properties in water (with the exception of HSO_4^-, which has weak acid properties).

c.   These are strong bases like LiOH, NaOH, KOH, RbOH, CsOH, $Ca(OH)_2$, $Sr(OH)_2$, and $Ba(OH)_2$.

d.   These are salts of the conjugate bases of the neutrally charged weak acids in Table 14.2. The conjugate bases of weak acids are weak bases themselves. Three examples are $NaClO_2$, $KC_2H_3O_2$, and CaF_2. The cations used to form these salts are Li^+, Na^+, K^+, Rb, Cs^+, Ca^{2+}, Sr^{2+}, and Ba^{2+} since these cations have no acidic or basic properties in water. Notice that these are the cations of the strong bases you should memorize.

e.   There are two ways to make a neutral salt. The easiest way is to combine a conjugate base of a strong acid (except for HSO_4^-) with one of the cations from a strong base. These ions have no acidic/basic properties in water so salts of these ions are neutral. Three examples are NaCl, KNO_3, and SrI_2. Another type of strong electrolyte that can produce neutral solutions are salts that contain an ion with weak acid properties combined with an ion of opposite charge having weak base properties. If the K_a for the weak acid ion is equal to the K_b for the weak base ion, then the salt will produce a neutral solution. The most common example of this type of salt is ammonium acetate, $NH_4C_2H_3O_2$. For this salt, K_a for $NH_4^+ = K_b$ for $C_2H_3O_2^- = 5.6 \times 10^{-10}$. This salt at any concentration produces a neutral solution.

20. $K_a \times K_b = K_w$, $-\log (K_a \times K_b) = -\log K_w$

$-\log K_a - \log K_b = -\log K_w$, $pK_a + pK_b = pK_w = 14.00$ (at 25°C)

21.   a. $H_2O(l) + H_2O(l) \rightleftharpoons H_3O^+(aq) + OH^-(aq)$ or

$H_2O(l) \rightleftharpoons H^+(aq) + OH^-(aq)$ $K = K_w = [H^+][OH^-]$

b. $HF(aq) + H_2O(l) \rightleftharpoons F^-(aq) + H_3O^+(aq)$ or

$HF(aq) \rightleftharpoons H+(aq) + F^-(aq)$ $K = K_a = \dfrac{[H^+][F^-]}{[HF]}$

c. $C_5H_5N(aq) + H_2O(l) \rightleftharpoons C_5H_5NH^+(aq) + OH^-(aq)$ $K = K_b = \dfrac{[C_5H_5NH^+][OH^-]}{[C_5H_5N]}$

22.   Only statement a is true (assuming the species is not amphoteric). You cannot add a base to water and get an acidic pH (pH < 7.0). For statement b, you can have negative pH values. This just indicates an $[H^+] > 1.0$ M. For statement c, a dilute solution of a strong acid can have a higher pH than a more concentrated weak acid solution. For statement d, the $Ba(OH)_2$ solution will have an $[OH^-]$ twice of the same concentration of KOH, but this does not correspond to a pOH value twice that of the same concentration of KOH (prove it to yourselves).

23. a. This expression holds true for solutions of strong acids having a concentration greater than 1.0×10^{-6} M. 0.10 M HCl, 7.8 M HNO$_3$, and 3.6×10^{-4} M HClO$_4$ are examples where this expression holds true.

b. This expression holds true for solutions of weak acids where the two normal assumptions hold. The two assumptions are that water does not contribute enough H$^+$ to solution to matter and that the acid is less than 5% dissociated in water (from the assumption that x is small compared to some number). This expression will generally hold true for solutions of weak acids having a K$_a$ value less than 1×10^{-4}, as long as there is a significant amount of weak acid present. Three example solutions are 1.5 M HC$_2$H$_3$O$_2$, 0.10 M HOCl, and 0.72 M HCN.

c. This expression holds true for strong bases that donate 2 OH$^-$ ions per formula unit. As long as the concentration of the base is above 5×10^{-7} M, this expression will hold true. Three examples are 5.0×10^{-3} M Ca(OH)$_2$, 2.1×10^{-4} M Sr(OH)$_2$, and 9.1×10^{-5} M Ba(OH)$_2$.

d. This expression holds true for solutions of weak bases where the two normal assumptions hold. The assumptions are that the OH$^-$ contribution from water is negligible and that and that the base is less than 5% ionized in water (for the 5% rule to hold). For the 5% rule to hold, you generally need bases with K$_b$ < 1×10^{-4} and concentrations of weak base greater than 0.10 M. Three examples are 0.10 M NH$_3$, 0.54 M C$_6$H$_5$NH$_2$, and 1.1 M C$_5$H$_5$N.

24. H$_2$CO$_3$ is a weak acid with $K_{a_1} = 4.3 \times 10^{-7}$ and $K_{a_2} = 5.6 \times 10^{-11}$. The [H$^+$] concentration in solution will be determined from the K_{a_1} reaction since $K_{a_1} \gg K_{a_2}$. Since $K_{a_1} \ll 1$, then the [H$^+$] < 0.10 M; only a small percentage of H$_2$CO$_3$ will dissociate into HCO$_3^-$ and H$^+$. So statement a best describes the 0.10 M H$_2$CO$_3$ solution. H$_2$SO$_4$ is a strong acid and a very good weak acid ($K_{a_1} \gg 1$, $K_{a_2} = 1.2 \times 10^{-2}$). All of the 0.1 M H$_2SO_4$ solution will dissociate into 0.10 M H$^+$ and 0.10 M HSO$_4^-$. However, since HSO$_4^-$ is a good weak acid due to the relatively large K$_a$ value, then some of the 0.10 M HSO$_4^-$ will dissociate into some more H$^+$ and SO$_4^{2-}$. Therefore, the [H$^+$] will be greater than 0.10 M, but will not reach 0.20 since only some of 0.10 M HSO$_4^-$ will dissociate. Statement c is best for a 0.10 M H$_2$SO$_4$ solution.

25. One reason HF is a weak acid is that the H–F bond is unusually strong and is difficult to break. This contributes significantly to the reluctance of the HF molecules to dissociate in water.

26. a. Sulfur reacts with oxygen to produce SO$_2$ and SO$_3$. These sulfur oxides both react with water to produce H$_2$SO$_3$ and H$_2$SO$_4$, respectively. Acid rain can result when sulfur emissions are not controlled. Note that in general, nonmetal oxides react with water to produce acidic solutions.

b. CaO reacts with water to produce Ca(OH)$_2$, a strong base. A gardener mixes lime (CaO) into soil in order to raise the pH of the soil. The effect of adding lime is to add Ca(OH)$_2$. Note that in general, metal oxides react with water to produce basic solutions.

Exercises

Nature of Acids and Bases

27.   a. $HClO_4(aq) + H_2O(l) \rightarrow H_3O^+(aq) + ClO_4^-(aq)$. Only the forward reaction is indicated since $HClO_4$ is a strong acid and is basically 100% dissociated in water. For acids, the dissociation reaction is commonly written without water as a reactant. The common abbreviation for this reaction is: $HClO_4(aq) \rightarrow H^+(aq) + ClO_4^-(aq)$. This reaction is also called the K_a reaction as the equilibrium constant for this reaction is called K_a.

      b.   Propanoic acid is a weak acid, so it is only partially dissociated in water. The dissociation reaction is: $CH_3CH_2CO_2H(aq) + H_2O(l) \rightleftharpoons H_3O^+(aq) + CH_3CH_2CO_2^-(aq)$ or $CH_3CH_2CO_2H(aq) \rightleftharpoons H^+(aq) + CH_3CH_2CO^-(aq)$.

      c. NH_4^+ is a weak acid. Similar to propanoic acid, the dissociation reaction is:

           $NH_4^+(aq) + H_2O(l) \rightleftharpoons H_3O^+(aq) + NH_3(aq)$ or $NH_4^+(aq) \rightleftharpoons H^+(aq) + NH_3(aq)$

28.   The dissociation reaction (the K_a reaction) of an acid in water commonly omits water as a reactant. We will follow this practice. All dissociation reactions produce H^+ and the conjugate base of the acid that is dissociated.

      a. $HCN(aq) \rightleftharpoons H^+(aq) + CN^-(aq)$ $K_a = \dfrac{[H^+][CN^-]}{[HCN]}$

      b. $C_6H_5OH(aq) \rightleftharpoons H^+(aq) + C_6H_5O^-(aq)$ $K_a = \dfrac{[H^+][C_6H_5O^-]}{[C_6H_5OH]}$

      c. $C_6H_5NH_3^+(aq) \rightleftharpoons H^+(aq) + C_6H_5NH_2(aq)$ $K_a = \dfrac{[H^+][C_6H_5NH_2]}{[C_6H_5NH_3^+]}$

29.   An acid is a proton (H^+) donor and a base is a proton acceptor. A conjugate acid-base pair differs by only a proton (H^+).

	Acid	Base	Conjugate Base of Acid	Conjugate Acid of Base
a.	H_2CO_3	H_2O	HCO_3^-	H_3O^+
b.	$C_5H_5NH^+$	H_2O	C_5H_5N	H_3O^+
c.	$C_5H_5NH^+$	HCO_3^-	C_5H_5N	H_2CO_3

30.

	Acid	Base	Conjugate Base of Acid	Conjugate Acid of Base
a.	$Al(H_2O)_6^{3+}$	H_2O	$Al(H_2O)_5(OH)^{2+}$	H_3O^+
b.	$HONH_3^+$	H_2O	$HONH_2$	H_3O^+
c.	$HOCl$	$C_6H_5NH_2$	OCl^-	$C_6H_5NH_3^+$

31.   Strong acids have a $K_a \gg 1$ and weak acids have $K_a < 1$. Table 14.2 in the text lists some K_a values for weak acids. K_a values for strong acids are hard to determine so they are not listed in the text. However, there are only a few common strong acids so if you memorize the strong acids, then all other acids will be weak acids. The strong acids to memorize are HCl, HBr, HI, HNO_3, $HClO_4$ and H_2SO_4.

   a. $HClO_4$ is a strong acid.

   b.   HOCl is a weak acid ($K_a = 3.5 \times 10^{-8}$).

   c. H_2SO_4 is a strong acid.

   d. H_2SO_3 is a weak diprotic acid with K_{a1} and K_{a2} values less than one.

32.   The beaker on the left represents a strong acid in solution; the acid, HA, is 100% dissociated into the H^+ and A^- ions. The beaker on the right represents a weak acid in solution; only a little bit of the acid, HB, dissociates into ions, so the acid exists mostly as undissociated HB molecules in water.

   a. HNO_2: weak acid beaker

   b. HNO_3: strong acid beaker

   c.   HCl: strong acid beaker

   d.   HF: weak acid beaker

   e. $HC_2H_3O_2$: weak acid beaker

33.   The K_a value is directly related to acid strength. As K_a increases, acid strength increases. For water, use K_w when comparing the acid strength of water to other species. The K_a values are:

   $HClO_4$: strong acid ($K_a \gg 1$); $HClO_2$: $K_a = 1.2 \times 10^{-2}$

   NH_4^+: $K_a = 5.6 \times 10^{-10}$; H_2O: $K_a = K_w = 1.0 \times 10^{-14}$

   From the K_a values, the ordering is: $HClO_4 > HClO_2 > NH_4^+ > H_2O$.

34.   Except for water, these are the conjugate bases of the acids in the previous exercise. In general, the weaker the acid, the stronger the conjugate base. ClO_4^- is the conjugate base of a strong acid; it is a terrible base (worse than water). The ordering is: $NH_3 > ClO_2^- > H_2O > ClO_4^-$

35.   a.   HCl is a strong acid and water is a very weak acid with $K_a = K_w = 1.0 \times 10^{-14}$. HCl is a much stronger acid than H_2O.

   b. H_2O, $K_a = K_w = 1.0 \times 10^{-14}$; HNO_2, $K_a = 4.0 \times 10^{-4}$; HNO_2 is a stronger acid than H_2O because K_a for $HNO_2 > K_w$ for H_2O.

   c. HOC_6H_5, $K_a = 1.6 \times 10^{-10}$; HCN, $K_a = 6.2 \times 10^{-10}$; HCN is a stronger acid than HOC_6H_5 because K_a for HCN $> K_a$ for HOC_6H_5.

36.   a. H_2O; The conjugate bases of strong acids are terrible bases ($K_b < 10^{-14}$).

   b. NO_2^-; The conjugate bases of weak acids are weak bases ($10^{-14} < K_b < 1$).

c. $OC_6H_5^-$; For a conjugate acid-base pair, $K_a \times K_b = K_w$. From this relationship, the stronger the acid the weaker the conjugate base (K_b decreases as K_a increases). Because HCN is a stronger acid than HOC_6H_5 (K_a for HCN > K_a for HOC_6H_5), $OC_6H_5^-$ will be a stronger base than CN^-.

Autoionization of Water and the pH Scale

37.   At 25°C, the relationship: $[H^+] [OH^-] = K_w = 1.0 \times 10^{-14}$ always holds for aqueous solutions. When $[H^+]$ is greater than $1.0 \times 10^{-7} M$, the solution is acidic; when $[H^+]$ is less than $1.0 \times 10^{-7} M$, the solution is basic; when $[H^+] = 1.0 \times 10^{-7} M$, the solution is neutral. In terms of $[OH^-]$, an acidic solution has $[OH^-] < 1.0 \times 10^{-7} M$, a basic solution has $[OH^-] > 1.0 \times 10^{-7} M$, and a neutral solution has $[OH^-] = 1.0 \times 10^{-7} M$.

a. $[OH^-] = \dfrac{K_w}{[H^+]} = \dfrac{1.0 \times 10^{-14}}{1.0 \times 10^{-7}} = 1.0 \times 10^{7} M$; The solution is neutral.

b. $[OH^-] = \dfrac{1.0 \times 10^{-14}}{8.3 \times 10^{-16}} = 12 \ M$; The solution is basic.

c. $[OH^-] = \dfrac{1.0 \times 10^{-14}}{12} = 8.3 \times 10^{-16} M$; The solution is acidic.

d. $[OH^-] = \dfrac{1.0 \times 10^{-14}}{5.4 \times 10^{-5}} = 1.9 \times 10^{-10} M$; The solution is acidic.

38.   a. $[H^+] = \dfrac{K_w}{[OH^-]} = \dfrac{1.0 \times 10^{-14}}{1.5} = 6.7 \times 10^{-15} M$; basic

b. $[H^+] = \dfrac{1.0 \times 10^{-14}}{3.6 \times 10^{-15}} = 2.8 \ M$; acidic

c. $[H^+] = \dfrac{1.0 \times 10^{-14}}{1.0 \times 10^{-7}} = 1.0 \times 10^{-7} M$; neutral

d. $[H^+] = \dfrac{1.0 \times 10^{-14}}{7.3 \times 10^{-4}} = 1.4 \times 10^{-11} M$; basic

39.   a.   Because the value of the equilibrium constant increases as the temperature increases, the reaction is endothermic. In endothermic reactions, heat is a reactant so an increase in temperature (heat) shifts the reaction to produce more products and increases K in the process.

b. $H_2O(l) \rightleftharpoons H^+(aq) + OH^-(aq)$ $K_w = 5.47 \times 10^{-14} = [H^+][OH^-]$ at 50.°C

In pure water $[H^+] = [OH^-]$, so $5.47 \times 10^{-14} = [H^+]^2$, $[H^+] = 2.34 \times 10^{-7} M = [OH^-]$

40.   a. $H_2O(l) \rightleftharpoons H^+(aq) + OH^-(aq)$ $K_w = 2.92 \times 10^{-14} = [H^+][OH^-]$

In pure water $[H^+] = [OH^-]$, so $2.92 \times 10^{-14} = [H^+]^2$, $[H^+] = 1.71 \times 10^{-7} M = [OH^-]$

b. $pH = -\log [H^+] = -\log (1.71 \times 10^{-7}) = 6.767$

c. $[H^+] = K_w/[OH^-] = 2.92 \times 10^{-14}/0.10 = 2.9 \times 10^{-13} M$; $pH = -\log (2.9 \times 10^{-13}) = 12.54$

41. $pH = -\log [H^+]$; $pOH = -\log [OH^-]$; At 25°C, $pH + pOH = 14.00$; For Exercise 13.37:

a. $pH = -\log [H^+] = -\log (1.0 \times 10^{-7}) = 7.00$; $pOH = 14.00 - pH = 14.00 - 7.00 = 7.00$

b. $pH = -\log (8.3 \times 10^{-16}) = 15.08$; $pOH = 14.00 - 15.08 = -1.08$

c. $pH = -\log (12) = -1.08$; $pOH = 14.00 - (-1.08) = 15.08$

d. $pH = -\log (5.4 \times 10^{-5}) = 4.27$; $pOH = 14.00 - 4.27 = 9.73$

Note that pH is less than zero when $[H^+]$ is greater than 1.0 M (an extremely acidic solution). For Exercise 13.38:

a. $pOH = -\log [OH^-] = -\log (1.5) = -0.18$; $pH = 14.00 - pOH = 14.00 - (-0.18) = 14.18$

b. $pOH = -\log (3.6 \times 10^{-15}) = 14.44$; $pH = 14.00 - 14.44 = -0.44$

c. $pOH = -\log (1.0 \times 10^{-7}) = 7.00$; $pH = 14.00 - 7.00 = 7.00$

d. $pOH = -\log (7.3 \times 10^{-4}) = 3.14$; $pH = 14.00 - 3.14 = 10.86$

Note that pH is greater than 14.00 when $[OH^-]$ is greater than 1.0 M (an extremely basic solution).

42.   a. $[H^+] = 10^{-pH}$, $[H^+] = 10^{-7.40} = 4.0 \times 10^{-8} M$

$pOH = 14.00 - pH = 14.00 - 7.40 = 6.60$; $[OH^-] = 10^{-pOH} = 10^{-6.60} = 2.5 \times 10^{-7} M$

or $[OH^-] = \dfrac{K_w}{[H^+]} = \dfrac{1.0 \times 10^{-14}}{4.0 \times 10^{-8}} = 2.5 \times 10^{-7} M$; This solution is basic since pH > 7.00.

b. $[H^+] = 10^{-15.3} = 5 \times 10^{-16} M$; $pOH = 14.00 - 15.3 = -1.3$; $[OH^-] = 10^{-(-1.3)} = 20 M$; basic

c. $[H^+] = 10^{-(-1.0)} = 10 M$; $pOH = 14.0 - (-1.0) = 15.0$; $[OH^-] = 10^{-15.0} = 1 \times 10^{-15} M$; acidic

d. $[H^+] = 10^{-3.20} = 6.3 \times 10^{-4} M$; $pOH = 14.00 - 3.20 = 10.80$; $[OH^-] = 10^{-10.80} = 1.6 \times 10^{-11} M$; acidic

e. $[OH^-] = 10^{-5.0} = 1 \times 10^{-5} M$; pH = 14.0 − pOH = 14.0 − 5.0 = 9.0; $[H^+] = 10^{-9.0}$

$= 1 \times 10^{-9} M$; basic

f. $[OH^-] = 10^{-9.60} = 2.5 \times 10^{-5} M$; pH = 14.00 − 9.60 = 4.40; $[H^+] = 10^{-4.40} = 4.0 \times 10^{-5} M$; acidic

43.   a.   pOH = 14.00 − 6.88 = 7.12; $[H^+] = 10^{-6.88} = 1.3 \times 10^{-7} M$

$[OH^-] = 10^{-7.12} = 7.6 \times 10^{-8} M$;   acidic

b. $[H^+] = \dfrac{1.0 \times 10^{-14}}{8.4 \times 10^{-14}} = 0.12 \, M$;   pH = −log(0.12) = 0.92

pOH = 14.00 − 0.92 = 13.08;   acidic

c.   pH = 14.00 − 3.11 = 10.89; $[H^+] = 10^{-10.89} = 1.3 \times 10^{-11} \, M$

$[OH^-] = 10^{-3.11} = 7.8 \times 10^{-4} M$;   basic

d.   pH = −log (1.0×10^{-7}) = 7.00;   pOH = 14.00 − 7.00 = 7.00

$[OH^-] = 10^{-7.00} = 1.0 \times 10^{-7} M$;   neutral

44.   a.   pOH = 14.00 − 9.63 = 4.37; $[H^+] = 10^{-9.63} = 2.3 \times 10^{-10} M$

$[OH^-] = 10^{-4.37} = 4.3 \times 10^{-5} M$;   basic

b. $[H^+] = \dfrac{1.0 \times 10^{-14}}{3.9 \times 10^{-6}} = 2.6 \times 10^{-9} \, M$;   pH = −log (2.6×10^{-9}) = 8.59

pOH = 14.00 − 8.59 = 5.41;   basic

c.   pH = −log (0.027) = 1.57;   pOH = 14.00 − 1.57 = 12.43

$[OH^-] = 10^{-12.43} = 3.7 \times 10^{-13} M$;   acidic

d.   pH = 14.0 − 12.2 = 1.8; $[H^+] = 10^{-1.8} = 2 \times 10^{-2} M$

$[OH^-] = 10^{-12.2} = 6 \times 10^{-13} M$;   acidic

45.   pOH = 14.0 − pH = 14.0 − 2.1 = 11.9; $[H^+] = 10^{-pH} = 10^{-2.1} = 8 \times 10^{-3} M$ (1 sig fig)

$[OH^-] = \dfrac{K_w}{[H^+]} = \dfrac{1.0 \times 10^{-14}}{8 \times 10^{-3}} = 1 \times 10^{-12} M$ or $[OH^-] = 10^{-pOH} = 10^{-11.9} = 1 \times 10^{-12} M$

The sample of gastric juice is acidic since the pH is less than 7.00 at 25°C.

46. $pH = 14.00 - pOH = 14.00 - 5.74 = 8.26$; $[H^+] = 10^{-pH} = 10^{-8.26} = 5.5 \times 10^{-9}\ M$

$$[OH^-] = \frac{K_w}{[H^+]} = \frac{1.0 \times 10^{-14}}{5.5 \times 10^{-9}} = 1.8 \times 10^{-6}\ M \text{ or } [OH^-] = 10^{-pOH} = 10^{-5.74} = 1.8 \times 10^{-6}\ M$$

The solution of baking soda is basic since the pH is greater than 7.00 at 25°C.

Solutions of Acids

47.   All the acids in this problem are strong acids that are always assumed to completely dissociate in water. The general dissociation reaction for a strong acid is: $HA(aq) \rightarrow H^+(aq) + A^-(aq)$ where A^- is the conjugate base of the strong acid HA. For 0.250 M solutions of these strong acids, 0.250 M H^+ and 0.250 M A^- are present when the acids completely dissociate. The amount of H^+ donated from water will be insignificant in this problem since H_2O is a very weak acid.

   a.   Major species present after dissociation = H^+, ClO_4^- and H_2O;

   $pH = -\log [H^+] = -\log (0.250) = 0.602$

   b.   Major species = H^+, NO_3^- and H_2O; pH = 0.602

48.   Strong acids are assumed to completely dissociate in water: $HCl(aq) \rightarrow H^+(aq) + Cl^-(aq)$

   a.   A 0.10 M HCl solution gives 0.10 M H^+ and 0.10 M Cl^- since HCl completely dissociates. The amount of H^+ from H_2O will be insignificant. $pH = -\log [H^+] = -\log (0.10) = 1.00$

   b.   5.0 M H^+ is produced when 5.0 M HCl completely dissociates. The amount of H^+ from H_2O will be insignificant. $pH = -\log (5.0) = -0.70$ (Negative pH values just indicate very concentrated acid solutions).

   c. $1.0 \times 10^{-11}\ M$ H^+ is produced when $1.0 \times 10^{-11}\ M$ HCl completely dissociates. If you take the negative log of 1.0×10^{-11} this gives pH = 11.00. This is impossible! We dissolved an acid in water and got a basic pH. What we must consider in this problem is that water by itself donates $1.0 \times 10^{-7}\ M$ H^+. We can normally ignore the small amount of H^+ from H_2O except when we have a very dilute solution of an acid (as is the case here). Therefore, the pH is that of neutral water (pH = 7.00) since the amount of HCl present is insignificant.

49.   Both are strong acids.

   $0.0500\ L \times 0.050\ mol/L = 2.5 \times 10^{-3}\ mol\ HCl = 2.5 \times 10^{-3}\ mol\ H^+ + 2.5 \times 10^{-3}\ mol\ Cl^-$

   $0.1500\ L \times 0.10\ mol/L = 1.5 \times 10^{-2}\ mol\ HNO_3 = 1.5 \times 10^{-2}\ mol\ H^+ + 1.5 \times 10^{-2}\ mol\ NO_3^-$

   $$[H^+] = \frac{(2.5 \times 10^{-3} + 1.5 \times 10^{-2})\ mol}{0.2000\ L} = 0.088\ M;\quad [OH^-] = \frac{K_w}{[H^+]} = 1.1 \times 10^{-13}\ M$$

   $$[Cl^-] = \frac{2.5 \times 10^{-3}\ mol}{0.2000\ L} = 0.013\ M;\quad [NO_3^-] = \frac{1.5 \times 10^{-2}\ mol}{0.2000\ L} = 0.075\ M$$

50. $90.0 \times 10^{-3}\,L \times \dfrac{5.00\,mol}{L} = 0.450$ mol H^+ from HCl

$30.0 \times 10^{-3}\,L \times \dfrac{8.00\,mol}{L} = 0.240$ mol H^+ from HNO_3

$[H^+] = \dfrac{0.450\,mol + 0.240\,mol}{1.00\,L} = 0.690\,M; \;\; pH = -\log(0.690) = 0.161$

$pOH = 14.000 - 0.161 = 13.839; \;\; [OH^-] = 10^{-13.839} = 1.45 \times 10^{-14}\,M$

51. $[H^+] = 10^{-1.50} = 3.16 \times 10^{-2}\,M$ (carryiung one extra sig fig); $M_1V_1 = M_2V_2$

$V_1 = \dfrac{M_2V_2}{M_1} = \dfrac{3.16 \times 10^{-2}\,mol/L \times 1.6\,L}{12\,mol/L} = 4.2 \times 10^{-3}\,L$

To 4.2 mL of 12 M HCl, add enough water to make 1600 mL of solution. The resulting solution will have $[H^+] = 3.2 \times 10^{-2}\,M$ and pH = 1.50.

52. $[H^+] = 10^{-5.10} = 7.9 \times 10^{-6}\,M; \;\; HNO_3(aq) \rightarrow H^+(aq) + NO_3^-(aq)$

Because HNO_3 is a strong acid, we have a $7.9 \times 10^{-6}\,M\;HNO_3$ solution.

$0.2500\,L \times \dfrac{7.9 \times 10^{-6}\,mol\;HNO_3}{L} \times \dfrac{63.02\,g\;HNO_3}{mol\;HNO_3} = 1.2 \times 10^{-4}\,g\;HNO_3$

53.   a. HNO_2 ($K_a = 4.0 \times 10^{-4}$) and H_2O ($K_a = K_w = 1.0 \times 10^{-14}$) are the major species. HNO_2 is a much stronger acid than H_2O so it is the major source of H^+. However, HNO_2 is a weak acid ($K_a < 1$) so it only partially dissociates in water. We must solve an equilibrium problem to determine $[H^+]$. In the Solutions Guide, we will summarize the initial, change and equilibrium concentrations into one table called the ICE table. Solving the weak acid problem:

	HNO_2	$\rightleftharpoons$	H^+	$+$	NO_2^-
Initial	0.250 M		~0		0
	x mol/L HNO_2 dissociates to reach equilibrium				
Change	$-x$	$\rightarrow$	$+x$		$+x$
Equil.	$0.250 - x$		x		x

$K_a = \dfrac{[H^+][NO_2^-]}{[HNO_2]} = 4.0 \times 10^{-4} = \dfrac{x^2}{0.250 - x}; \;\;$ If we assume $x \ll 0.250$, then:

$4.0 \times 10^{-4} \approx \dfrac{x^2}{0.250}, \;\;\; x = \sqrt{4.0 \times 10^{-4}\,(0.250)} = 0.010\,M$

We must check the assumption: $\dfrac{x}{0.250} \times 100 = \dfrac{0.010}{0.250} \times 100 = 4.0\%$

All the assumptions are good. The H^+ contribution from water (10^{-7} M) is negligible, and x is small compared to 0.250 (percent error = 4.0%). If the percent error is less than 5% for an assumption, we will consider it a valid assumption (called the 5% rule). Finishing the problem: $x = 0.010$ $M = [H^+]$; pH $= -\log(0.010) = 2.00$

b. CH_3CO_2H ($K_a = 1.8 \times 10^{-5}$) and H_2O ($K_a = K_w = 1.0 \times 10^{-14}$) are the major species. CH_3CO_2H is the major source of H^+. Solving the weak acid problem:

$$CH_3CO_2H \rightleftharpoons H^+ + CH_3CO_2^-$$

Initial	0.250 M	~0	0

x mol/L CH_3CO_2H dissociates to reach equilibrium

Change	$-x$	$\rightarrow$	$+x$	$+x$
Equil.	$0.250 - x$		x	x

$$K_a = \frac{[H^+][CH_3CO_2^-]}{[CH_3CO_2H]} = 1.8 \times 10^{-5} = \frac{x^2}{0.250-x} \approx \frac{x^2}{0.250} \quad \text{(assuming } x \ll 0.250\text{)}$$

$x = 2.1 \times 10^{-3}$ M; Checking assumption: $\dfrac{2.1 \times 10^{-3}}{0.250} \times 100 = 0.84\%$. Assumptions good.

$[H^+] = x = 2.1 \times 10^{-3} M$; pH $= -\log(2.1 \times 10^{-3}) = 2.68$

54.   a. HOC_6H_5 ($K_a = 1.6 \times 10^{-10}$) and H_2O ($K_a = K_w = 1.0 \times 10^{-14}$) are the major species. The major equilibrium is the dissociation of HOC_6H_5. Solving the weak acid problem:

$$HOC_6H_5 \rightleftharpoons H^+ + OC_6H_5^-$$

Initial	0.250 M	~0	0

x mol/L HOC_6H_5 dissociates to reach equilibrium

Change	$-x$	$\rightarrow$	$+x$	$+x$
Equil.	$0.250 - x$		x	x

$$K_a = 1.6 \times 10^{-10} = \frac{[H^+][OC_6H_5^-]}{[HOC_6H_5]} = \frac{x^2}{0.250-x} \approx \frac{x^2}{0.250} \quad \text{(assuming } x \ll 0.250\text{)}$$

$x = [H^+] = 6.3 \times 10^{-6}$ M; Checking assumption: x is 2.5×10^{-3}% of 0.250, so assumption is valid by the 5% rule.

pH $= -\log(6.3 \times 10^{-6}) = 5.20$

b. HCN ($K_a = 6.2 \times 10^{-10}$) and H_2O are the major species. HCN is the major source of H^+.

$$HCN \rightleftharpoons H^+ + CN^-$$

Initial	0.250 M	~0	0

x mol/L HCN dissociates to reach equilibrium

Change	$-x$	$\rightarrow$	$+x$	$+x$
Equil.	$0.250 - x$		x	x

$$K_a = 6.2 \times 10^{-10} = \frac{[H^+][CN^-]}{[HCN]} = \frac{x^2}{0.250 - x} \approx \frac{x^2}{0.250} \quad \text{(assuming } x \ll 0.250)$$

$x = [H^+] = 1.2 \times 10^{-5} \ M$; Checking assumption: x is $4.8 \times 10^{-3}\%$ of 0.250

Assumptions good. $pH = -\log (1.2 \times 10^{-5}) = 4.92$

55. $[CH_3COOH]_0 = [HC_2H_3O_2]_0 = \dfrac{0.0560 \text{ g } HC_2H_3O_2 \times \dfrac{1 \text{ mol } HC_2H_3O_2}{60.05 \text{ g}}}{0.05000 \text{ L}} = 1.87 \times 10^{-2} \ M$

$$HC_2H_3O_2 \quad \rightleftharpoons \quad H^+ \quad + \quad C_2H_3O_2^- \qquad K_a = 1.8 \times 10^{-5}$$

Initial	0.0187 M	~0	0

x mol/L $HC_2H_3O_2$ dissociates to reach equilibrium

Change	$-x$	$\rightarrow$ $+x$	$+x$
Equil.	0.0187 $- x$	x	x

$$K_a = 1.8 \times 10^{-5} = \frac{[H^+][C_2H_3O_2^-]}{[HC_3H_3O_2]} = \frac{x^2}{0.0187 - x} \approx \frac{x^2}{0.0187}$$

$x = [H^+] = 5.8 \times 10^{-4} \ M$; $pH = 3.24$ Assumptions good (x is 3.1% of 0.0187).

$[H^+] = [C_2H_3O_2^-] = [CH_3COO^-] = 5.8 \times 10^{-4} \ M$; $[CH_3COOH] = 0.0187 - 5.8 \times 10^{-4}$
$$= 0.0181 \ M$$

56. $HC_3H_5O_2$ ($K_a = 1.3 \times 10^{-5}$) and H_2O ($K_a = K_w = 1.0 \times 10^{-14}$) are the major species present. $HC_3H_5O_2$ will be the dominant producer of H^+ since $HC_3H_5O_2$ is a stronger acid than H_2O. Solving the weak acid problem:

$$HC_3H_5O_2 \quad \rightleftharpoons \quad H^+ \quad + \quad C_3H_5O_2^-$$

Initial	0.100 M	~0	0

x mol/L $HC_3H_5O_2$ dissociates to reach equilibrium

Change	$-x$	$\rightarrow$ $+x$	$+x$
Equil.	0.100 $- x$	x	x

$$K_a = 1.3 \times 10^{-5} = \frac{[H^+][C_3H_5O_2^-]}{[HC_3H_5O_2]} = \frac{x^2}{0.100 - x} \approx \frac{x^2}{0.100}$$

$x = [H^+] = 1.1 \times 10^{-3} M$; $pH = -\log (1.1 \times 10^{-3}) = 2.96$

Assumption follows the 5% rule (x is 1.1% of 0.100).

$[H^+] = [C_3H_5O_2^-] = 1.1 \times 10^{-3} M$; $[OH^-] = K_w/[H^+] = 9.1 \times 10^{-12} M$

$[HC_3H_5O_2] = 0.100 - 1.1 \times 10^{-3} = 0.099 \ M$

$$\text{Percent dissociation} = \frac{[H^+]}{[HC_3H_5O_2]_0} \times 100 = \frac{1.1 \times 10^{-3}}{0.100} = 1.1\%$$

57.   This is a weak acid in water. Solving the weak acid problem:

$$HF \quad \rightleftharpoons \quad H^+ \quad + \quad F^- \qquad K_a = 7.2 \times 10^{-4}$$

Initial	0.020 M	~0	0

x mol/L HF dissociates to reach equilibrium

Change	$-x$	$\rightarrow$ $+x$	$+x$
Equil.	$0.020 - x$	x	x

$$K_a = 7.2 \times 10^{-4} = \frac{[H^+][F^-]}{[HF]} = \frac{x^2}{0.020 - x} \approx \frac{x^2}{0.020} \quad \text{(assuming } x \ll 0.020)$$

$$x = [H^+] = 3.8 \times 10^{-3}\,M; \text{ Check assumptions: } \frac{x}{0.020} \times 100 = \frac{3.8 \times 10^{-3}}{0.020} = 19\%$$

The assumption $x \ll 0.020$ is not good (x is more than 5% of 0.020). We must solve $x^2/(0.020 - x) = 7.2 \times 10^{-4}$ exactly by using either the quadratic formula or by the method of successive approximations (see Appendix 1.4 of text). Using successive approximations, we let 0.016 M be a new approximation for [HF]. That is, in the denominator, try $x = 0.0038$ (the value of x we calculated making the normal assumption), so $0.020 - 0.0038 = 0.016$, then solve for a new value of x in the numerator.

$$\frac{x^2}{0.020 - x} \approx \frac{x^2}{0.016} = 7.2 \times 10^{-4}, \quad x = 3.4 \times 10^{-3}$$

We use this new value of x to further refine our estimate of [HF], i.e., $0.020 - x = 0.020 - 0.0034 = 0.0166$ (carry extra significant figure).

$$\frac{x^2}{0.020 - x} \approx \frac{x^2}{0.0166} = 7.2 \times 10^{-4}, \quad x = 3.5 \times 10^{-3}$$

We repeat until we get an answer that repeats itself. This would be the same answer we would get solving exactly using the quadratic equation. In this case it is: $x = 3.5 \times 10^{-3}$

So: $[H^+] = [F^-] = x = 3.5 \times 10^{-3}\,M; \quad [OH^-] = K_w/[H^+] = 2.9 \times 10^{-12}\,M$

$[HF] = 0.020 - x = 0.020 - 0.0035 = 0.017\,M; \quad pH = 2.46$

Note: When the 5% assumption fails, use whichever method you are most comfortable with to solve exactly. The method of successive approximations is probably fastest when the percent error is less than ~25% (unless you have a calculator that can solve quadratic equations).

58.   Major species: HIO_3, H_2O; Major source of H^+: HIO_3 (a weak acid, $K_a = 0.17$)

$$HIO_3 \rightleftharpoons H^+ + IO_3^-$$

Initial	0.20 M	~0	0

x mol/L HIO_3 dissociates to reach equilibrium

Change	$-x$	$\rightarrow$ $+x$	$+x$
Equil.	0.20 - x	x	x

$$K_a = 0.17 = \frac{x^2}{0.20-x} \approx \frac{x^2}{0.20}, \quad x = 0.18; \quad \text{Check assumption.}$$

Assumption is horrible (x is 90% of 0.20). When the assumption is this poor, it is generally quickest to solve exactly using the quadratic formula (see Appendix 1.4 in text). The method of successive approximations will require many trials to finally converge on the answer. For this problem, 5 trials were required. Using the quadratic formula and carrying extra significant figures:

$$0.17 = \frac{x^2}{0.020-x}, \quad x^2 = 0.17(0.20 - x), \quad x^2 + 0.17x - 0.034 = 0$$

$$x = \frac{-0.17 \pm [(0.17)^2 - 4(1)(-0.034)]^{1/2}}{2(1)} = \frac{-0.17 \pm 0.1406}{2}, \quad x = 0.12 \text{ or } -0.29$$

Only $x = 0.12$ makes sense. $x = 0.12\ M = [H^+]$; pH = $-\log(0.12) = 0.92$

59.   Major species: $HC_2H_2ClO_2$ ($K_a = 1.35 \times 10^{-3}$) and H_2O; Major source of H^+: $HC_2H_2ClO_2$

$$HC_2H_2ClO_2 \rightleftharpoons H^+ + C_2H_2ClO_2^-$$

Initial	0.10 M	~0	0

x mol/L $HC_2H_2ClO_2$ dissociates to reach equilibrium

Change	$-x$	$\rightarrow$ $+x$	$+x$
Equil.	0.10- x	x	x

$$K_a = 1.35 \times 10^{-3} = \frac{x^2}{0.10-x} \approx \frac{x^2}{0.10}, \quad x = 1.2 \times 10^{-2}\ M$$

Checking the assumptions finds that x is 12% of 0.10 which fails the 5% rule. We must solve $1.35 \times 10^{-3} = x^2/(0.10 - x)$ exactly using either the method of successive approximations or the quadratic equation. Using either method gives $x = [H^+] = 1.1 \times 10^{-2}\ M$. pH = $-\log[H^+] = -\log(1.1 \times 10^{-2}) = 1.96$.

60. $$[HC_9H_7O_4] = \frac{2\text{ tablets} \times \dfrac{0.325\text{ g }HC_9H_7O_4}{\text{tablet}} \times \dfrac{1\text{ mol }HC_9H_7O_4}{180.15\text{ g}}}{0.237\text{ L}} = 0.0152\ M$$

$$HC_9H_7O_4 \rightleftharpoons H^+ + C_9H_7O_4^-$$

Initial	$0.0152\ M$	~0	0

x mol/L $HC_9H_7O_4$ dissociates to reach equilibrium

Change	$-x$	$\rightarrow$ $+x$	$+x$
Equil.	$0.0152 - x$	x	x

$$K_a = 3.3 \times 10^{-4} = \frac{[H^+][C_9H_7O_4^-]}{[HC_9H_7O_4]} = \frac{x^2}{0.0152 - x} \approx \frac{x^2}{0.0152},\ x = 2.2 \times 10^{-3}\ M$$

Assumption that $0.0152 - x \approx 0.0152$ fails the 5% rule: $\dfrac{2.2 \times 10^{-3}}{0.0152} \times 100 = 14\%$

Using successive approximations or the quadratic equation gives an exact answer of $x = 2.1 \times 10^{-3}\ M$.

$[H^+] = x = 2.1 \times 10^{-3}\ M;\ \ pH = -\log(2.1 \times 10^{-3}) = 2.68$

61. a. HCl is a strong acid. It will produce $0.10\ M$ H^+. HOCl is a weak acid. Let's consider the equilibrium:

$$HOCl \rightleftharpoons H^+ + OCl^- \qquad K_a = 3.5 \times 10^{-8}$$

Initial	$0.10\ M$	$0.10\ M$	0

x mol/L HOCl dissociates to reach equilibrium

Change	$-x$	$\rightarrow$ $+x$	$+x$
Equil.	$0.10 - x$	$0.10 + x$	x

$$K_a = 3.5 \times 10^{-8} = \frac{[H^+][OCl^-]}{[HOCl]} = \frac{(0.10 + x)(x)}{0.10 - x} \approx x,\ x = 3.5 \times 10^{-8}\ M$$

Assumptions are great (x is $3.5 \times 10^{-5}\%$ of 0.10). We are really assuming that HCl is the only important source of H^+, which it is. The $[H^+]$ contribution from HOCl, x, is negligible. Therefore, $[H^+] = 0.10\ M;\ pH = 1.00$

b. HNO_3 is a strong acid, giving an initial concentration of H^+ equal to $0.050\ M$. Consider the equilibrium:

$$HC_2H_3O_2 \rightleftharpoons H^+ + C_2H_3O_2^- \qquad K_a = 1.8 \times 10^{-5}$$

Initial	$0.50\ M$	$0.050\ M$	0

x mol/L $HC_2H_3O_2$ dissociates to reach equilibrium

Change	$-x$	$\rightarrow$ $+x$	$+x$
Equil.	$0.50 - x$	$0.050 + x$	x

$$K_a = 1.8 \times 10^{-5} = \frac{[H^+][C_2H_3O_2^-]}{[HC_2H_3O_2]} = \frac{(0.050 + x)x}{0.50 - x} \approx \frac{0.050\ x}{0.50}$$

$x = 1.8 \times 10^{-4}$; Assumptions are good (well within the 5% rule).

$[H^+] = 0.050 + x = 0.050\ M$ and $pH = 1.30$

62.   HF and HOC_6H_5 are both weak acids with K_a values of 7.2×10^{-4} and 1.6×10^{-10}, respectively. Since the K_a value for HF is much greater than the K_a value for HOC_6H_5, HF will be the dominant producer of H^+ (we can ignore the amount of H^+ produced from HOC_6H_5 since it will be insignificant).

$$HF \quad \rightleftharpoons \quad H^+ \quad + \quad F^-$$

Initial	1.0 M	~0	0

x mol/L HF dissociates to reach equilibrium

Change	$-x$	$\rightarrow$	$+x$	$+x$
Equil.	$1.0 - x$		x	x

$$K_a = 7.2 \times 10^{-4} = \frac{[H^+][F^-]}{[HF]} = \frac{x^2}{1.0 - x} \approx \frac{x^2}{1.0}$$

$x = [H^+] = 2.7 \times 10^{-2} M$; $\text{pH} = -\log(2.7 \times 10^{-2}) = 1.57$ Assumptions good.

Solving for $[OC_6H_5^-]$ using $HOC_6H_5 \rightleftharpoons H^+ + OC_6H_5^-$ equilibrium:

$$K_a = 1.6 \times 10^{-10} = \frac{[H^+][OC_6H_5^-]}{[HOC_6H_5]} = \frac{(2.7 \times 10^{-2})[OC_6H_5^-]}{1.0}, \quad [OC_6H_5^-] = 5.9 \times 10^{-9} M$$

Note that this answer indicates that only $5.9 \times 10^{-9} M$ HOC_6H_5 dissociates, which indicates that HF is truly the only significant producer of H^+ in this solution.

63.   In all parts of this problem, acetic acid ($HC_2H_3O_2$) is the best weak acid present. We must solve a weak acid problem.

a.
$$HC_2H_3O_2 \quad \rightleftharpoons \quad H^+ \quad + \quad C_2H_3O_2^-$$

Initial	0.50 M	~0	0

x mol/L $HC_2H_3O_2$ dissociates to reach equilibrium

Change	$-x$	$\rightarrow$	$+x$	$+x$
Equil.	$0.50 - x$		x	x

$$K_a = 1.8 \times 10^{-5} = \frac{[H^+][C_2H_3O_2^-]}{[HC_2H_3O_2]} = \frac{x^2}{0.50 - x} \approx \frac{x^2}{0.50}$$

$x = [H^+] = [C_2H_3O_2^-] = 3.0 \times 10^{-3} M$ Assumptions good.

$$\text{Percent dissociation} = \frac{[H^+]}{[HC_2H_3O_2]_0} \times 100 = \frac{3.0 \times 10^{-3}}{0.50} \times 100 = 0.60\%$$

b.   The setups for solutions b and c are similar to solution a except the final equation is slightly different, reflecting the new concentration of $HC_2H_3O_2$.

$$K_a = 1.8 \times 10^{-5} = \frac{x^2}{0.050 - x} \approx \frac{x^2}{0.050}$$

$x = [H^+] = [C_2H_3O_{2^-}] = 9.5 \times 10^{-4}\,M$ Assumptions good.

$$\% \text{ dissociation} = \frac{9.5 \times 10^{-4}}{0.050} \times 100 = 1.9\%$$

c. $K_a = 1.8 \times 10^{-5} = \dfrac{x^2}{0.0050 - x} \approx \dfrac{x^2}{0.0050}$

$x = [H^+] = [C_2H_3O_2^-] = 3.0 \times 10^{-4}\,M$;   Check assumptions.

Assumption that x is negligible is borderline (6.0% error). We should solve exactly. Using the method of successive approximations (see Appendix 1.4 of text):

$$1.8 \times 10^{-5} = \frac{x^2}{0.0050 - 3.0 \times 10^{-4}} = \frac{x^2}{0.0047}\ ,\ x = 2.9 \times 10^{-4}$$

Next trial also gives $x = 2.9 \times 10^{-4}$.

$$\% \text{ dissociation} = \frac{2.9 \times 10^{-4}}{5.0 \times 10^{-3}} \times 100 = 5.8\%$$

d. As we dilute a solution, all concentrations decrease. Dilution will shift the equilibrium to the side with the greater number of particles. For example, suppose we double the volume of an equilibrium mixture of a weak acid by adding water, then:

$$Q = \frac{\left(\dfrac{[H^+]_{eq}}{2}\right)\left(\dfrac{[X^-]_{eq}}{2}\right)}{\left(\dfrac{[HX]_{eq}}{2}\right)} = \frac{1}{2}K_a$$

$Q < K_a$, so the equilibrium shifts to the right or towards a greater percent dissociation.

e. $[H^+]$ depends on the initial concentration of weak acid and on how much weak acid dissociates. For solutions a-c the initial concentration of acid decreases more rapidly than the percent dissociation increases. Thus, $[H^+]$ decreases.

64. a. HNO_3 is a strong acid; it is assumed 100% dissociated in solution.

b.

	HNO_2	$\rightleftharpoons$	H^+	$+$	NO_2^-	$K_a = 4.0 \times 10^{-4}$
Initial	0.20 M		~0		0	

x mol/L HNO_2 dissociates to reach equilibrium

Change	$-x$	$\rightarrow$	$+x$		$+x$
Equil.	$0.20 - x$		x		x

$$K_a = 4.0 \times 10^{-4} = \frac{[H^+][NO_2^-]}{[HNO_2]} = \frac{x^2}{0.20 - x} \approx \frac{x^2}{0.20}$$

$x = [H^+] = [NO_2^-] = 8.9 \times 10^{-3}\,M$; Assumptions good.

$$\% \text{ dissociation} = \frac{[H^+]}{[HNO_2]_0} \times 100 = \frac{8.9 \times 10^{-3}}{0.20} \times 100 = 4.5\%$$

c. $HOC_6H_5 \quad \rightleftharpoons \quad H^+ \quad + \quad OC_6H_5^- \quad K_a = 1.6 \times 10^{-10}$

Initial	0.20 M	~0	0

x mol/L HOC_6H_5 dissociates to reach equilibrium

Change	$-x$	$\rightarrow$ $+x$	$+x$
Equil.	0.20 - x	x	x

$$K_a = 1.6 \times 10^{-10} = \frac{[H^+][OC_6H_5^-]}{[HOC_6H_5]} = \frac{x^2}{0.20 - x} \approx \frac{x^2}{0.20}$$

$x = [H^+] = [OC_6H_5^-] = 5.7 \times 10^{-6}\,M$;   Assumptions good.

$$\% \text{ dissociation} = \frac{5.7 \times 10^{-6}}{0.20} \times 100 = 2.9 \times 10^{-3}\,\%$$

d.   For the same initial concentration, the percent dissociation increases as the strength of the acid increases (as K_a increases).

65.   Let HX symbolize the weak acid. Setup the problem like a typical weak acid equilibrium problem.

$$HX \quad \rightleftharpoons \quad H^+ \quad + \quad X^-$$

Initial	0.15 M	~0	0

x mol/L HX dissociates to reach equilibrium

Change	$-x$	$\rightarrow$ $+x$	$+x$
Equil.	0.15 - x	x	x

If the acid is 3.0% dissociated, then $x = [H^+]$ is 3.0% of 0.15: $x = 0.030 \times (0.15\,M) = 4.5 \times 10^{-3}\,M$. Now that we know the value of x, we can solve for K_a.

$$K_a = \frac{[H^+][X^-]}{[HX]} = \frac{x^2}{0.15 - x} = \frac{(4.5 \times 10^{-3})^2}{0.15 - 4.5 \times 10^{-3}} = 1.4 \times 10^{-4}$$

66.
$$HX \quad \rightleftharpoons \quad H^+ \quad + \quad X^-$$

Initial	I	~0	0

where I = $[HX]_o$

x mol/L HX dissociates to reach equilibrium

Change	$-x$	$\rightarrow$	$+x$	$+x$
Equil.	$I - x$		x	x

From the problem, $x = 0.25(I)$ and $I - x = 0.30\ M$.

$I - 0.25(I) = 0.30\ M$, $I = 0.40\ M$ and $x = 0.25\ (0.40\ M) = 0.10\ M$

$$K_a = \frac{[H^+][X^-]}{[HX]} = \frac{x^2}{I - x} = \frac{(0.10)^2}{0.30} = 0.033$$

67. Setup the problem using the K_a equilibrium reaction for HOCN.

$$HOCN \quad \rightleftharpoons \quad H^+ \quad + \quad OCN^-$$

Initial	0.0100 M	~0	0

x mol/L HOCN dissociates to reach equilibrium

Change	$-x$	$\rightarrow$	$+x$	$+x$
Equil.	$0.0100 - x$		x	x

$$K_a = \frac{[H^+][OCN^-]}{[HOCN]} = \frac{x^2}{0.0100 - x}\ ;\ pH = 2.77:\ x = [H^+] = 10^{-pH} = 10^{-2.77} = 1.7 \times 10^{-3}\ M$$

$$K_a = \frac{(1.7 \times 10^{-3})^2}{0.0100 - 1.7 \times 10^{-3}} = 3.5 \times 10^{-4}$$

68. $HClO_4$ is a strong acid with $[H^+] = 0.040\ M$. This equals the $[H^+]$ in the trichloroacetic acid solution. Now setup the problem using the K_a equilibrium reaction for CCl_3CO_2H.

$$CCl_3CO_2H \quad \rightleftharpoons \quad H^+ \quad + \quad CCl_3CO_2^-$$

Initial	0.050 M	~0	0
Equil.	$0.050 - x$	x	x

$$K_a = \frac{[H^+][CCl_3CO_2^-]}{[CCl_3CO_2H]} = \frac{x^2}{0.050 - x}\ ;\ x = [H^+] = 4.0 \times 10^{-2}\ M$$

$$K_a = \frac{(4.0 \times 10^{-2})^2}{0.050 - (4.0 \times 10^{-2})} = 0.16$$

69. Major species: HCOOH and H_2O; Major source of H^+: HCOOH

$$HCOOH \quad \rightleftharpoons \quad H^+ \quad + \quad HCOO^-$$

Initial	C	~0	0

where C = $[HCOOH]_o$

x mol/L HCOOH dissociates to reach equilibrium

Change	$-x$	$\rightarrow$ $+x$	$+x$
Equil.	$C - x$	x	x

$$K_a = 1.8 \times 10^{-4} = \frac{[H^+][HCOO^-]}{[HCOOH]} = \frac{x^2}{C - x} \text{ where } x = [H^+]$$

$$1.8 \times 10^{-4} = \frac{[H^+]^2}{C - [H^+]}; \quad pH = 2.70, \text{ so: } [H^+] = 10^{-2.70} = 2.0 \times 10^{-3} M$$

$$1.8 \times 10^{-4} = \frac{(2.0 \times 10^{-3})^2}{C - (2.0 \times 10^{-3})}, \quad C - (2.0 \times 10^{-3}) = \frac{4.0 \times 10^{-6}}{1.8 \times 10^{-4}}, \quad C = 2.4 \times 10^{-2} M$$

A 0.024 M formic acid solution will have pH = 2.70.

70. $[HA]_o = \dfrac{1.0 \text{ mol}}{2.0 \text{ L}} = 0.50$ mol/L; Solve using the K_a equilibrium reaction.

$$HA \quad \rightleftharpoons \quad H^+ \quad + \quad A^-$$

Initial	0.50 M	~0	0
Equil.	0.50 – x	x	x

$$K_a = \frac{[H^+][A^-]}{[HA]} = \frac{x^2}{0.50 - x}; \quad \text{In this problem, } [HA] = 0.45 \, M \text{ so:}$$

$$[HA] = 0.45 \, M = 0.50 \, M - x, \quad x = 0.05 \, M; \quad K_a = \frac{(0.05)^2}{0.45} = 6 \times 10^{-3}$$

Solutions of Bases

71.   a. $NH_3(aq) + H_2O(l) \rightleftharpoons NH_4^+(aq) + OH^-(aq)$ $\qquad K_b = \dfrac{[NH_4^+][OH^-]}{[NH_3]}$

        b. $C_5H_5N(aq) + H_2O(l) \rightleftharpoons C_5H_5NH^+(aq) + OH^-(aq)$ $\qquad K_b = \dfrac{[C_5H_5NH^+][OH^-]}{[C_5H_5N]}$

72.   a. $C_6H_5NH_2(aq) + H_2O(l) \rightleftharpoons C_6H_5NH_3^+(aq) + OH^-(aq)$ $\qquad K_b = \dfrac{[C_6H_5NH_3^+][OH^-]}{[C_6H_5NH_2]}$

        b. $(CH_3)_2NH(aq) + H_2O(l) \rightleftharpoons (CH_3)_2NH_2^+(aq) + OH^-(aq)$ $\qquad K_b = \dfrac{[(CH_3)_2NH_2^+][OH^-]}{[(CH_3)_2NH]}$

73. NO_3^-: $K_b \ll K_w$ since HNO_3 is a strong acid. All conjugate bases of strong acids have no base strength. H_2O: $K_b = K_w = 1.0 \times 10^{-14}$; NH_3: $K_b = 1.8 \times 10^{-5}$; C_5H_5N: $K_b = 1.7 \times 10^{-9}$

$NH_3 > C_5H_5N > H_2O > NO_3^-$ (As K_b increases, base strength increases.)

74.   Excluding water, these are the conjugate acids of the bases in the previous exercise. In general, the stronger the base, the weaker the conjugate acid. Note: Even though NH_4^+ and $C_5H_5NH^+$ are conjugate acids of weak bases, they are still weak acids with K_a values between K_w and 1. Prove this to yourself by calculating the K_a values for NH_4^+ and $C_5H_5NH^+$ ($K_a = K_w/K_b$).

$HNO_3 > C_5H_5NH^+ > NH_4^+ > H_2O$

75.   a. $C_6H_5NH_2$ b. $C_6H_5NH_2$ c. OH^- d. CH_3NH_2

The base with the largest K_b value is the strongest base ($K_{b, C_6H_5NH_2} = 3.8 \times 10^{-10}$,

$K_{b, CH_3NH_2} = 4.4 \; 10^{-4}$. OH^- is the strongest base possible in water.

76.   a. $HClO_4$ b. $C_6H_5NH_3^+$ c. $C_6H_5NH_3^+$

The acid with the largest K_a value is the strongest acid. To calculate K_a values for $C_6H_5NH_3^+$ and $CH_3NH_3^+$, use $K_a = K_w/K_b$ where K_b refers to the bases $C_6H_5NH_2$ or CH_3NH_2.

77. $NaOH(aq) \rightarrow Na^+(aq) + OH^-(aq)$; NaOH is a strong base which completely dissociates into Na^+ and OH^-. The initial concentration of NaOH will equal the concentration of OH^- donated by NaOH.

a. $[OH^-] = 0.10 \; M$; pOH $= -\log[OH^-] = -\log(0.10) = 1.00$

pH $= 14.00 - $ pOH $= 14.00 - 1.00 = 13.00$

Note that H_2O is also present, but the amount of OH^- produced by H_2O will be insignificant compared to the $0.10 \; M \; OH^-$ produced from the NaOH.

b.   The $[OH^-]$ concentration donated by the NaOH is $1.0 \times 10^{-10} \; M$. Water by itself donates $1.0 \times 10^{-7} \; M$. In this problem, water is the major OH^- contributor and $[OH^-] = 1.0 \times 10^{-7} \; M$.

pOH $= -\log(1.0 \times 10^{-7}) = 7.00$; pH $= 14.00 - 7.00 = 7.00$

c. $[OH^-] = 2.0 \; M$; pOH $= -\log(2.0) = -0.30$; pH $= 14.00 - (-0.30) = 14.30$

78.   a. $Ca(OH)_2 \rightarrow Ca^{2+} + 2 \; OH^-$; $Ca(OH)_2$ is a strong base and dissociates completely.

$[OH^-] = 2(0.00040) = 8.0 \times 10^{-4} \; M$; pOH $= -\log [OH^-] = 3.10$; pH $= 14.00 - $ pOH $= 10.90$

b. $\dfrac{25 \text{ g KOH}}{L} \times \dfrac{1 \text{ mol KOH}}{56.11 \text{ g KOH}} = 0.45$ mol KOH/L

KOH is a strong base, so $[OH^-] = 0.45\ M$; pOH = -log (0.45) = 0.35; pH = 13.65

c. $\dfrac{150.0\ \text{g NaOH}}{L} \times \dfrac{1\ \text{mol}}{40.00\ \text{g}} = 3.750\ M$; NaOH is a strong base, so $[OH^-] = 3.750\ M$.

pOH = $-$log (3.750) = -0.5740 and pH = 14.0000 $-$ (-0.5740) = 14.5740

Although we are justified in calculating the answer to four decimal places, in reality pH values are generally measured to two decimal places, sometimes three.

79.   a. Major species: K^+, OH^-, H_2O (KOH is a strong base.)

$[OH^-] = 0.015\ M$, pOH = $-$log (0.015) = 1.82; pH = 14.00 $-$ pOH = 12.18

b. Major species: Ba^{2+}, OH^-, H_2O; $Ba(OH)_2(aq) \rightarrow Ba^{2+}(aq) + 2\ OH^-(aq)$; Since each mol of the strong base $Ba(OH)_2$ dissolves in water to produce two mol OH^-, then $[OH^-] = 2(0.015\ M) = 0.030\ M$.

pOH = $-$log (0.030) = 1.52; pH = 14.00 $-$ 1.52 = 12.48

80.   a. Major species: Na^+, Li^+, OH^-, H_2O (NaOH and LiOH are both strong bases.)

$[OH^-] = 0.050 + 0.050 = 0.100\ M$; pOH = 1.000; pH = 13.000

b. Major species: Ca^{2+}, Rb^+, OH^-, H_2O; Both $Ca(OH)_2$ and RbOH are strong bases and $Ca(OH)_2$ donates 2 mol OH^- per mol $Ca(OH)_2$.

$[OH^-] = 2(0.0010) + 0.020 = 0.022\ M$; pOH = $-$log (0.022) = 1.66; pH = 12.34

81.   pOH = 14.00 $-$ 11.56 = 2.44; $[OH^-] = [KOH] = 10^{-2.44} = 3.6 \times 10^{-3}\ M$

$0.8000\ \text{L} \times \dfrac{3.6 \times 10^{-3}\ \text{mol KOH}}{L} \times \dfrac{56.11\ \text{g KOH}}{\text{mol KOH}} = 0.16\ \text{g KOH}$

82.   pH = 10.50; pOH = 14.00 $-$ 10.50 = 3.50; $[OH^-] = 10^{-3.50} = 3.2 \times 10^{-4}\ M$

$Sr(OH)_2(aq) \rightarrow Sr^{2+}(aq) + 2\ OH^-(aq)$; $Sr(OH)_2$ donates two mol OH^- per mol $Sr(OH)_2$.

$[Sr(OH)_2] = \dfrac{3.2 \times 10^{-4}\ \text{mol OH} -}{L} \times \left(\dfrac{1\ \text{mol Sr(OH)}_2}{2\ \text{mol OH}^-} \right) = 1.6 \times 10^{-4}\ M\ Sr(OH)_2$

A $1.6 \times 10^{-4}\ M$ $Sr(OH)_2$ solution will produce a pH = 10.50 solution.

83. NH_3 is a weak base with $K_b = 1.8 \times 10^{-5}$. The major species present will be NH_3 and H_2O ($K_b = K_w = 1.0 \times 10^{-14}$). Since NH_3 has a much larger K_b value compared to H_2O, NH_3 is the stronger base present and will be the major producer of OH^-. To determine the amount of OH^- produced from NH_3, we must perform an equilibrium calculation.

$$NH_3(aq) \ + \ H_2O(l) \ \rightleftharpoons \ NH_4^+(aq) \ + \ OH^-(aq)$$

Initial   0.150 M 0   ~0
             x mol/L NH_3 reacts with H_2O to reach equilibrium
Change $-x$ $\rightarrow$ $+x$ $+x$
Equil. $0.150 - x$ x x

$$K_b = 1.8 \times 10^{-5} = \frac{[NH_4^+][OH^-]}{[NH_3]} = \frac{x^2}{0.150 - x} \approx \frac{x^2}{0.150} \quad \text{(assuming } x \ll 0.150)$$

$x = [OH^-] = 1.6 \times 10^{-3} M$; Check assumptions: x is 1.1% of 0.150 so the assumption $0.150 - x \approx$ 0.150 is valid by the 5% rule. Also, the contribution of OH^- from water will be insignificant (which will usually be the case). Finishing the problem, $pOH = -\log [OH^-] = -\log (1.6 \times 10^{-3} M)$ = 2.80; $pH = 14.00 - pOH = 14.00 - 2.80 = 11.20$.

84.   Major species: H_2NNH_2 ($K_b = 3.0 \times 10^{-6}$) and H_2O ($K_b = K_w = 1.0 \times 10^{-14}$); The weak base H_2NNH_2 will dominate OH^- production. We must perform a weak base equilibrium calculation.

$$H_2NNH_2 \ + \ H_2O \ \rightleftharpoons \ H_2NNH_3^+ \ + \ OH^- \quad K_b = 3.0 \times 10^{-6}$$

Initial   2.0 M 0   ~0
             x mol/L H_2NNH_2 reacts with H_2O to reach equilibrium
Change $-x$ $\rightarrow$ $+x$ $+x$
Equil. $2.0 - x$ x x

$$K_b = 3.0 \times 10^{-6} = \frac{[H_2NNH_3^+][OH^-]}{[H_2NNH_2]} = \frac{x^2}{2.0 - x} \approx \frac{x^2}{2.0} \quad \text{(assuming } x \ll 2.0)$$

$x = [OH^-] = 2.4 \times 10^{-3} M$; $pOH = 2.62$; $pH = 11.38$ Assumptions good (x is 0.12% of 2.0).

$[H_2NNH_3^+] = 2.4 \times 10^{-3} M$; $[H_2NNH_2] = 2.0 M$; $[H^+] = 10^{-11.38} = 4.2 \times 10^{-12} M$

85.   These are solutions of weak bases in water. We must solve the equilibrium weak base problem.

a. $(C_2H_5)_3N \ + \ H_2O \ \rightleftharpoons \ (C_2H_5)_3NH^+ + \ OH^- \quad K_b = 4.0 \times 10^{-4}$

Initial   0.20 M 0   ~0
             x mol/L of $(C_2H_5)_3N$ reacts with H_2O to reach equilibrium
Change $-x$ $\rightarrow$ $+x$ $+x$
Equil. $0.20 - x$ x x

$$K_b = 4.0 \times 10^{-4} = \frac{[(C_2H_5)_3NH^+][OH^-]}{[(C_2H_5)_3N]} = \frac{x^2}{0.20 - x} \approx \frac{x^2}{0.20} , \ x = [OH^-] = 8.9 \times 10^{-3} M$$

Assumptions good (x is 4.5% of 0.20). $[OH^-] = 8.9 \times 10^{-3} M$

$$[H^+] = \frac{K_w}{[OH^-]} = \frac{1.0 \times 10^{-14}}{8.9 \times 10^{-3}} = 1.1 \times 10^{-12} M; \ pH = 11.96$$

b. $HONH_2 + H_2O \rightleftharpoons HONH_3^+ + OH^-$ $K_b = 1.1 \times 10^{-8}$

Initial	0.20 M	0	~0
Equil.	0.20 − x	x	x

$K_b = 1.1 \times 10^{-8} = \dfrac{x^2}{0.20 - x} \approx \dfrac{x^2}{0.20}$, $x = [OH^-] = 4.7 \times 10^{-5} M$; Assumptions good.

$[H^+] = 2.1 \times 10^{-10} M$; pH = 9.68

86.   These are solutions of weak bases in water.

a. $C_6H_5NH_2 + H_2O \rightleftharpoons C_6H_5NH_3^+ + OH^-$ $K_b = 3.8 \times 10^{-10}$

Initial	0.20 M	0	~0
	x mol/L of $C_6H_5NH_2$ reacts with H_2O to reach equilibrium		
Change	−x $\rightarrow$	+x	+x
Equil.	0.20 − x	x	x

$3.8 \times 10^{-10} = \dfrac{x^2}{0.20 - x} \approx \dfrac{x^2}{0.20}$, $x = [OH^-] = 8.7 \times 10^{-6} M$; Assumptions good.

$[H^+] = K_w/[OH^-] = 1.1 \times 10^{-9} M$; pH = 8.96

b. $CH_3NH_2 + H_2O \rightleftharpoons CH_3NH_3^+ + OH^-$ $K_b = 4.38 \times 10^{-4}$

Initial	0.20 M	0	~0
Equil.	0.20 − x	x	x

$K_b = 4.38 \times 10^{-4} = \dfrac{x^2}{0.20 - x} \approx \dfrac{x^2}{0.20}$, $x = 9.4 \times 10^{-3} M$; Assumptions good.

$[OH^-] = 9.4 \times 10^{-3} M$; $[H^+] = K_w/[OH^-] = 1.1 \times 10^{-12} M$; pH = 11.96

87.   This is a solution of a weak base in water. We must solve the weak base equilibrium problem.

                    $C_2H_5NH_2 + H_2O \rightleftharpoons C_2H_5NH_3^+ + OH^-$ $K_b = 5.6 \times 10^{-4}$

Initial	0.20 M	0	~0
	x mol/L $C_2H_5NH_2$ reacts with H_2O to reach equilibrium		
Change	−x $\rightarrow$	+x	+x
Equil.	0.20 − x	x	x

$K_b = \dfrac{[C_2H_5NH_3^+][OH^-]}{[C_2H_5NH_2]} = \dfrac{x^2}{0.20 - x} \approx \dfrac{x^2}{0.20}$ (assuming $x \ll 0.20$)

$x = 1.1 \times 10^{-2}$; Checking assumption: $\dfrac{1.1 \times 10^{-2}}{0.20} \times 100 = 5.5\%$

Assumption fails the 5% rule. We must solve exactly using either the quadratic equation or the method of successive approximations (see Appendix 1.4 of the text). Using successive approximations and carrying extra significant figures:

$$\frac{x^2}{0.20-0.011} = \frac{x^2}{0.189} = 5.6 \times 10^{-4}, \ \ x = 1.0 \times 10^{-2} \, M \ \ \text{(consistent answer)}$$

$$x = [OH^-] = 1.0 \times 10^{-2} \, M; \ \ [H^+] = \frac{K_w}{[OH^-]} = \frac{1.0 \times 10^{-14}}{1.0 \times 10^{-2}} = 1.0 \times 10^{-12} \, M; \ \ pH = 12.00$$

88. $$(C_2H_5)_2NH \ + \ H_2O \ \rightleftharpoons \ (C_2H_5)_2NH_2^+ \ + \ OH^- \ \ \ \ K_b = 1.3 \times 10^{-3}$$

Initial	0.050 M		0	~0

x mol/L $(C_2H_5)_2NH$ reacts with H_2O to reach equilibrium

Change	$-x$	$\rightarrow$	$+x$	$+x$
Equil.	$0.050 - x$		x	x

$$K_b = 1.3 \times 10^{-3} = \frac{[(C_2H_5)_2NH_2^+][OH^-]}{[(C_2H_5)_2NH]} = \frac{x^2}{0.050-x} \approx \frac{x^2}{0.050}$$

$x = 8.1 \times 10^{-3}$;   Assumption is bad (x is 16% of 0.20).

Using successive approximations:

$$1.3 \times 10^{-3} = \frac{x^2}{0.050 - 0.081}, \ \ x = 7.4 \times 10^{-3}$$

$$1.3 \times 10^{-3} = \frac{x^2}{0.050 - 0.074}, \ \ x = 7.4 \times 10^{-3} \ \text{(consistent answer)}$$

$$[OH^-] = x = 7.4 \times 10^{-3} \, M; \ \ [H^+] = K_w/[OH^-] = 1.4 \times 10^{-12} \, M; \ \ pH = 11.85$$

89.   To solve for percent ionization, just solve the weak base equilibrium problem.

a. $$NH_3 \ + \ H_2O \ \rightleftharpoons \ NH_4^+ \ + \ OH^- \ \ \ \ K_b = 1.8 \times 10^{-5}$$

Initial	0.10 M	0	~0
Equil.	0.10 $- x$	x	x

$$K_b = 1.8 \times 10^{-5} = \frac{x^2}{0.10-x} \approx \frac{x^2}{0.10} \ , \ \ x = [OH^-] = 1.3 \times 10^{-3} \, M; \ \ \text{Assumptions good.}$$

$$\text{Percent ionization} = \frac{[OH^-]}{[NH_3]_0} \times 100 = \frac{1.3 \times 10^{-3} \, M}{0.10 \, M} \times 100 = 1.3\%$$

b. $$NH_3 \ + \ H_2O \ \rightleftharpoons \ NH_4^+ \ + \ OH^-$$

Initial	0.010 M	0	~0
Equil.	0.010 $- x$	x	x

$$1.8 \times 10^{-5} = \frac{x^2}{0.010 - x} \approx \frac{x^2}{0.010}, \quad x = [OH^-] = 4.2 \times 10^{-4} \, M; \text{Assumptions good.}$$

$$\text{Percent ionization} = \frac{4.2 \times 10^{-4}}{0.010} \times 100 = 4.2\%$$

Note: For the same base, the percent ionization increases as the initial concentration of base decreases.

90. $C_5H_5N + H_2O \rightleftharpoons C_5H_5N^+ + OH^-$ $K_b = 1.7 \times 10^{-9}$

Initial   0.10 M 0   ~0
Equil.   0.10 – x x x

$$K_b = 1.7 \times 10^{-9} = \frac{x^2}{0.10 - x} \approx \frac{x^2}{0.10}, \quad x = [C_5H_5N] = 1.3 \times 10^{-5} \, M; \quad \text{Assumptions good.}$$

$$\%C_5H_5N \text{ reacted} = \frac{1.3 \times 10^{-5} \, M}{0.10 \, M} \times 100 = 1.3 \times 10^{-2} \%$$

91.   Let cod = codeine, $C_{18}H_{21}NO_3$; using the K_b reaction to solve:

                  cod + H_2O $\rightleftharpoons$ codH$^+$ +   OH$^-$

Initial $1.7 \times 10^{-3} M$ 0   ~0
               x mol/L codeine reacts with H_2O to reach equilibrium
Change $-x$ $\rightarrow$ $+x$ $+x$
Equil. $1.7 \times 10^{-3} - x$ x x

$$K_b = \frac{x^2}{1.7 \times 10^{-3} - x}; \quad pH = 9.59; \quad \text{so: pOH} = 14.00 - 9.59 = 4.41.$$

$$[OH^-] = x = 10^{-4.41} = 3.9 \times 10^{-5} M; \quad K_b = \frac{(3.9 \times 10^{-5})^2}{1.7 \times 10^{-3} - 3.9 \times 10^{-5}} = 9.2 \times 10^{-7}$$

92. $HONH_2 + H_2O \rightleftharpoons HONH_3^+ + OH^-$ $K_b = 1.1 \times 10^{-8}$

Initial   I   0   ~0   I = $[HONH_2]_0$
Equil.   I – x x x

$$K_b = 1.1 \times 10^{-8} = \frac{x^2}{I - x} \; ; \quad \text{From problem: pH} = 10.00, \text{ so pOH} = 4.00, \text{ and}$$

$$x = [OH^-] = 1.0 \times 10^{-4} \, M$$

$$1.1 \times 10^{-8} = \frac{(1.0 \times 10^{-4})^2}{I - 1.0 \times 10^{-4}}, \quad I = 0.91 \, M$$

$$\text{mass } HONH_2 = 0.2500 \, L \times \frac{0.91 \, \text{mol } HONH_2}{L} \times \frac{33.03 \, \text{g } HONH_2}{\text{mol } HONH_2} = 7.5 \, \text{g } HONH_2$$

Polyprotic Acids

93. $H_2SO_3(aq) \rightleftharpoons HSO_3^-(aq) + H^+(aq)$ $K_{a_1} = \dfrac{[HSO_3^-][H^+]}{[H_2SO_3]}$

$HSO_3^-(aq) \rightleftharpoons SO_3^{2-}(aq) + H^+(aq)$ $K_{a_2} = \dfrac{[SO_3^{2-}][H^+]}{[HSO_3^-]}$

94. $H_3C_6H_5O_7(aq) \rightleftharpoons H_2C_6H_5O_7^-(aq) + H^+(aq)$ $K_{a_1} = \dfrac{[H_2C_6H_5O_7^-][H^+]}{[H_3C_6H_5O_7]}$

$H_2C_6H_5O_7^-(aq) \rightleftharpoons HC_6H_5O_7^{2-}(aq) + H^+(aq)$ $K_{a_2} = \dfrac{[HC_6H_5O_7^{2-}][H^+]}{[H_2C_6H_5O_7^-]}$

$HC_6H_5O_7^{2-}(aq) \rightleftharpoons C_6H_5O_7^{3-}(aq) + H^+(aq)$ $K_{a_3} = \dfrac{[C_6H_5O_7^{3-}][H^+]}{[HC_6H_5O_7^{2-}]}$

95.   In both these polyprotic acid problems, the dominate equilibrium is the K_{a_1} reaction. The amount of H^+ produced from the subsequent K_a reactions will be minimal since they are all have much smaller K_a values.

a. $H_3PO_4 \quad \rightleftharpoons \quad H^+ \quad + \quad H_2PO_4^- \qquad K_{a_1} = 7.5 \times 10^{-3}$

Initial	0.10 M	~0	0

x mol/L H_3PO_4 dissociates to reach equilibrium

Change	$-x$	$\rightarrow$ $+x$	$+x$
Equil.	0.10 $- x$	x	x

$K_{a_1} = 7.5 \times 10^{-3} = \dfrac{[H^+][H_2PO_4^-]}{[H_3PO_4]} = \dfrac{x^2}{0.10 - x} \approx \dfrac{x^2}{0.10}$, $x = 2.7 \times 10^{-2}$

Assumption is bad (x is 27% of 0.10). Using successive approximations:

$\dfrac{x^2}{0.10 - 0.027} = 7.5 \times 10^{-3}$, $x = 2.3 \times 10^{-2}$; $\dfrac{x^2}{0.10} = 7.5 \times 10^{-3}$, $x = 2.4 \times 10^{-2}$ (consistent answer)

$x = [H^+] = 2.4 \times 10^{-2}\ M$; pH = -log $(2.4 \times 10^{-2}) = 1.62$

b. $H_2CO_3 \quad \rightleftharpoons \quad H^+ \quad + \quad HCO_3^- \qquad K_{a_1} = 4.3 \times 10^{-7}$

Initial	0.10 M	~0	0
Equil.	0.10 $- x$	x	x

$K_{a_1} = 4.3 \times 10^{-7} = \dfrac{[H^+][HCO_3^-]}{[H_2CO_3]} = \dfrac{x^2}{0.10 - x} \approx \dfrac{x^2}{0.10}$

$x = [H^+] = 2.1 \times 10^{-4}\ M$; pH = 3.68; Assumptions good.

96.   The reactions are:

$$H_3AsO_4 \rightleftharpoons H^+ + H_2AsO_4^- \qquad K_{a_1} = 5 \times 10^{-3}$$

$$H_2AsO_4^- \rightleftharpoons H^+ + HAsO_4^{2-} \qquad K_{a_2} = 8 \times 10^{-8}$$

$$HAsO_4^{2-} \rightleftharpoons H^+ + AsO_4^{3-} \qquad K_{a_3} = 6 \times 10^{-10}$$

We will deal with the reactions in order of importance, beginning with the largest K_a, K_{a_1}.

$$H_3AsO_4 \quad \rightleftharpoons \quad H^+ \quad + \quad H_2AsO_4^- \qquad K_{a_1} = 5 \times 10^{-3} = \frac{[H^+][H_2AsO_4^-]}{[H_3AsO_4]}$$

Initial   0.20 M ~0   0
Equil.   0.20 – x x x

$$5 \times 10^{-3} = \frac{x^2}{0.20 - x}, \ x = 2.9 \times 10^{-2} = 3 \times 10^{-2} M \quad \text{(By using successive approximations or the quadratic formula.)}$$

$[H^+] = [H_2AsO_4^-] = 3 \times 10^{-2} M;\ [H_3AsO_4] = 0.20 - 0.03 = 0.17\ M$

Because $K_{a_2} = \dfrac{[H^+][HAsO_4^{2-}]}{[H_2AsO_4^-]} = 8 \times 10^{-8}$ is much smaller than the K_{a_1} value, very little of

$H_2AsO_4^-$ (and $HAsO_4^{2-}$) dissociates compared to H_3AsO_4. Therefore, $[H^+]$ and $[H_2AsO_4^-]$ will not change significantly by the K_{a_2} reaction. Using the previously calculated concentrations of H^+ and $H_2AsO_4^-$ to calculate the concentration of $HAsO_4^{2-}$:

$$8 \times 10^{-8} = \frac{(3 \times 10^{-2})[HAsO_4^{2-}]}{3 \times 10^{-2}}, \ [HAsO_4^{2-}] = 8 \times 10^{-8} M$$

Assumption that the K_{a2} reaction does not change $[H^+]$ and $[HAsO_4^-]$ is good. We repeat the process using K_{a_3} to get $[AsO_4^{3-}]$.

$$K_{a_3} = 6 \times 10^{-10} = \frac{[H^+][AsO_4^{3-}]}{[HAsO_4^{2-}]} = \frac{(3 \times 10^{-2})[AsO_4^{3-}]}{(8 \times 10^{-8})}$$

$[AsO_4^{3-}] = 1.6 \times 10^{-15} \approx 2 \times 10^{-15} M$ Assumption good.

So in 0.20 M analytical concentration of H_3AsO_4:

$[H_3AsO_4] = 0.17\ M;\ [H^+] = [H_2AsO_4^-] = 3 \times 10^{-2}\ M$

$[HAsO_4^{2-}] = 8 \times 10^{-8} M;\ [AsO_4^{3-}] = 2 \times 10^{-15} M$

$[OH^-] = K_w/[H^+] = 3 \times 10^{-13} M$

97.   The dominant H^+ producer is the strong acid H_2SO_4. A 2.0 M H_2SO_4 solution produces 2.0 M HSO_4^- and 2.0 M H^+. However, HSO_4^- is a weak acid which could also add H^+ to the solution.

$$HSO_4^- \rightleftharpoons H^+ + SO_4^{2-}$$

Initial	2.0 M	2.0 M	0

x mol/L HSO_4^- dissociates to reach equilibrium

Change	$-x$	$\rightarrow$	$+x$	$+x$
Equil.	$2.0 - x$		$2.0 + x$	x

$$K_{a_2} = 1.2 \times 10^{-2} = \frac{[H^+][SO_4^{2-}]}{[HSO_4^-]} = \frac{(2.0 + x)(x)}{2.0 - x} \approx \frac{2.0\,(x)}{2.0}, \quad x = 1.2 \times 10^{-2}$$

Because x is 0.60% of 2.0, the assumption is valid by the 5% rule. The amount of additional H^+ from HSO_4^- is 1.2×10^{-2}. The total amount of H^+ present is:

$$[H^+] = 2.0 + 1.2 \times 10^{-2} = 2.0\ M; \quad pH = -\log(2.0) = -0.30$$

Note: In this problem, H^+ from HSO_4^- could have been ignored. However, this is not always the case, especially in more dilute solutions of H_2SO_4.

98.   For H_2SO_4, the first dissociation occurs to completion. The hydrogen sulfate ion, HSO_4^-, is a weak acid with $K_{a_2} = 1.2 \times 10^{-2}$. We will consider this equilibrium for additional H^+ production:

$$HSO_4^- \rightleftharpoons H^+ + SO_4^{2-}$$

Initial	0.0050 M	0.0050 M	0

x mol/L HSO_4^- dissociates to reach equilibrium

Change	$-x$	$\rightarrow$	$+x$	$+x$
Equil.	$0.0050 - x$		$0.0050 + x$	x

$$K_{a_2} = 0.012 = \frac{(0.0050 + x)(x)}{(0.0050 - x)} \approx x, \quad x = 0.012; \text{ Assumption is horrible (240\% error).}$$

Using the quadratic formula:

$$6.0 \times 10^{-5} - 0.012\,x = x^2 + 0.0050\,x, \quad x^2 + 0.017\,x - 6.0 \times 10^{-5} = 0$$

$$x = \frac{-0.017 \pm (2.9 \times 10^{-4} + 2.4 \times 10^{-4})^{1/2}}{2} = \frac{-0.017 \pm 0.023}{2}, \quad x = 3.0 \times 10^{-3}\,M$$

$$[H^+] = 0.0050 + x = 0.0050 + 0.0030 = 0.0080\ M; \quad pH = 2.10$$

Note: We had to consider both H_2SO_4 and HSO_4^- for H^+ production in this problem.

Acid-Base Properties of Salts

99.   One difficult aspect of acid-base chemistry is recognizing what types of species are present in solution, i.e., whether a species is a strong acid, strong base, weak acid, weak base or a neutral

species. Below are some ideas and generalizations to keep in mind that will help in recognizing types of species present.

a. Memorize the following strong acids: HCl, HBr, HI, HNO$_3$, HClO$_4$ and H$_2$SO$_4$

b. Memorize the following strong bases: LiOH, NaOH, KOH, RbOH, Ca(OH)$_2$, Sr(OH)$_2$ and Ba(OH)$_2$

c. All weak acids have a K$_a$ value less than 1 but greater than K$_w$. Some weak acids are in Table 14.2 of the text. All weak bases have a K$_b$ value less than 1 but greater than K$_w$. Some weak bases are in Table 14.3 of the text.

d. All conjugate bases of weak acids are weak bases, i.e., all have a K$_b$ value less than 1 but greater than K$_w$. Some examples of these are the conjugate bases of the weak acids in Table 14.2 of the text.

e. All conjugate acids of weak bases are weak acids, i.e., all have a K$_a$ value less than 1 but greater than K$_w$. Some examples of these are the conjugate acids of the weak bases in Table 14.3 of the text.

f. Alkali metal ions (Li$^+$, Na$^+$, K$^+$, Rb$^+$, Cs$^+$) and heavier alkaline earth metal ions (Ca^{2+}, Sr^{2+}, Ba^{2+}) have no acidic or basic properties in water.

g. All conjugate bases of strong acids (Cl$^-$, Br$^-$, I$^-$, NO$_3^-$, ClO$_4^-$, HSO$_4^-$) have no basic properties in water (K$_b$ << K$_w$) and only HSO$_4^-$ has any acidic properties in water.

Let's apply these ideas to this problem to see what type of species are present. The letters in parenthesis is/are the generalization(s) above which identifies the species.

KOH: strong base (b)

KCl: neutral; K$^+$ and Cl$^-$ have no acidic/basic properties (f and g).

KCN: CN$^-$ is a weak base, K$_b$ = 1.0 × 10^{-14}/6.2 × 10^{-10} = 1.6 × 10^{-5} (c and d). Ignore K$^+$ (f).

NH$_4$Cl: NH$_4^+$ is a weak acid, K$_a$ = 5.6 × 10^{-10} (c and e). Ignore Cl$^-$ (g).

HCl: strong acid (a)

The most acidic solution will be the strong acid followed by the weak acid. The most basic solution will be the strong base followed by the weak base. The KCl solution will be between the acidic and basic solutions at pH = 7.00.

Most acidic → most basic: HCl > NH$_4$Cl > KCl > KCN > KOH

100.   See Exercise 14.99 for some generalizations on acid-base properties of salts. The letters in parenthesis is/are the generalization(s) listed in Exercise 14.99 which identifies the species.

CaBr$_2$:   neutral; Ca^{2+} and Br$^-$ have no acidic/basic properties (f and g).

KNO$_2$:   NO$_2^-$ is a weak base, K$_b$ = 1.0 × 10^{-14}/4.0 × 10^{-4} = 2.5 × 10^{-11} (c and d). Ignore K$^+$ (f).

HClO$_4$:   strong acid (a)

HNO$_2$:   weak acid, K$_a$ = 4.0 × 10^{-4} (c)

HONH$_3$ClO$_4$: HONH$_3^+$ is a weak acid, K$_a$ = 1.0 × 10^{-14}/1.1 × 10^{-8} = 9.1 × 10^{-7} (c and e). Ignore ClO$_4^-$ (g). Note that HNO$_2$ has a larger K$_a$ value than HONH$_3^+$, so HNO$_2$ is a stronger weak acid than HONH$_3^+$.

Using the information above (identity and K$_a$ or K$_b$ values), the ordering is:

most acidic → most basic: HClO$_4$ > HNO$_2$ > HONH$_3$ClO$_4$ > CaBr$_2$ > KNO$_2$

101.   From the K_a values, acetic acid is a stronger acid than hypochlorous acid. Conversely, the conjugate base of acetic acid, $C_2H_3O_2^-$, will be a weaker base than the conjugate base of hypochlorous acid, OCl^-. Thus, the hypochlorite ion, OCl^-, is a stronger base than the acetate ion, $C_2H_3O_2^-$. In general, the stronger the acid, the weaker the conjugate base. This statement comes from the relationship $K_w = K_a \times K_b$, which holds for all conjugate acid-base pairs.

102.   Since NH_3 is a weaker base (smaller K_b value) than CH_3NH_2, the conjugate acid of NH_3 will be a stronger acid than the conjugate acid of CH_3NH_2. Thus, NH_4^+ is a stronger acid than $CH_3NH_3^+$.

103. $NaN_3 \rightarrow Na^+ + N_3^-$; Azide, N_3^-, is a weak base since it is the conjugate base of a weak acid. All conjugate bases of weak acids are weak bases ($K_w < K_b < 1$). Ignore Na^+.

$$N_3^- + H_2O \rightleftharpoons HN_3 + OH^- \qquad K_b = \frac{K_w}{K_a} = \frac{1.0 \times 10^{-14}}{1.9 \times 10^{-5}} = 5.3 \times 10^{-10}$$

Initial	0.010 M	0	~0
	x mol/L of N_3^- reacts with H_2O to reach equilibrium		
Change	$-x$ $\rightarrow$	$+x$	$+x$
Equil.	0.010 $- x$	x	x

$$K_b = 5.3 \times 10^{-10} = \frac{[HN_3][OH^-]}{[N_3^-]} = \frac{x^2}{0.010 - x} \approx \frac{x^2}{0.010} \quad \text{(assuming } x \ll 0.010\text{)}$$

$$x = [OH^-] = 2.3 \times 10^{-6} \, M; \quad [H^+] = \frac{1.0 \times 10^{-14}}{2.3 \times 10^{-6}} = 4.3 \times 10^{-9} \, M \quad \text{Assumptions good.}$$

$[HN_3] = [OH^-] = 2.3 \times 10^{-6} \, M; \quad [Na^+] = 0.010 \, M; \quad [N_3^-] = 0.010 - 2.3 \times 10^{-6} = 0.010 \, M$

104. $C_2H_5NH_3Cl \rightarrow C_2H_5NH_3^+ + Cl^-$; $C_2H_5NH_3^+$ is the conjugate acid of the weak base $C_2H_5NH_2$ ($K_b = 5.6 \times 10^{-4}$). As is true for all conjugate acids of weak bases, $C_2H_5NH_3^+$ is a weak acid. Cl^- has no basic (or acidic) properties. Ignore Cl^-. Solving the weak acid problem:

$$C_2H_5NH_3^+ \rightleftharpoons C_2H_5NH_2 + H^+ \qquad K_a = K_w/5.6 \times 10^{-4} = 1.8 \times 10^{-11}$$

Initial	0.25 M	0	~0
	x mol/L $C_2H_5NH_3^+$ dissociates to reach equilibrium		
Change	$-x$ $\rightarrow$	$+x$	$+x$
Equil.	0.25 $- x$	x	x

$$K_a = 1.8 \times 10^{-11} = \frac{[C_2H_5NH_2][H^+]}{[C_2H_5NH_3^+]} = \frac{x^2}{0.25 - x} \approx \frac{x^2}{0.25} \quad \text{(assuming } x \ll 0.25\text{)}$$

$x = [H^+] = 2.1 \times 10^{-6} \, M; \quad pH = 5.68; \quad$ Assumptions good.

$[C_2H_5NH_2] = [H^+] = 2.1 \times 10^{-6} \, M; \quad [C_2H_5NH_3^+] = 0.25 \, M; \quad [Cl^-] = 0.25 \, M$

$[OH^-] = K_w/[H^+] = 4.8 \times 10^{-9} \, M$

105. a. $CH_3NH_3Cl \rightarrow CH_3NH_3^+ + Cl^-$: $CH_3NH_3^+$ is a weak acid. Cl^- is the conjugate base of a strong acid. Cl^- has no basic (or acidic) properties.

$$CH_3NH_3^+ \rightleftharpoons CH_3NH_2 + H^+ \quad K_a = \frac{[CH_3NH_2][H^+]}{[CH_3NH_3^+]} = \frac{K_w}{K_b} = \frac{1.00 \times 10^{-14}}{4.38 \times 10^{-4}} = 2.28 \times 10^{-11}$$

	$CH_3NH_3^+$	$\rightleftharpoons$	CH_3NH_2	$+$	H^+
Initial	0.10 M		0		~0

x mol/L $CH_3NH_3^+$ dissociates to reach equilibrium

Change	$-x$	$\rightarrow$	$+x$	$+x$
Equil.	$0.10 - x$		x	x

$$K_a = 2.28 \times 10^{-11} = \frac{x^2}{0.10 - x} \approx \frac{x^2}{0.10} \quad \text{(assuming } x << 0.10\text{)}$$

$x = [H^+] = 1.5 \times 10^{-6}\ M$; pH = 5.82   Assumptions good.

b. $NaCN \rightarrow Na^+ + CN^-$: CN^- is a weak base. Na^+ has no acidic (or basic) properties.

$$CN^- + H_2O \rightleftharpoons HCN + OH^- \quad K_b = \frac{K_w}{K_a} = \frac{1.0 \times 10^{-14}}{6.2 \times 10^{-10}} = 1.6 \times 10^{-5}$$

	CN^-	$+$	H_2O	$\rightleftharpoons$	HCN	$+$	OH^-
Initial	0.050 M				0		~0

x mol/L CN^- reacts with H_2O to reach equilibrium

Change	$-x$	$\rightarrow$	$+x$	$+x$
Equil.	$0.050 - x$		x	x

$$K_b = 1.6 \times 10^{-5} = \frac{[HCN][OH^-]}{[CN^-]} = \frac{x^2}{0.050 - x} \approx \frac{x^2}{0.050}$$

$x = [OH^-] = 8.9 \times 10^{-4}\ M$; pOH = 3.05; pH = 10.95 Assumptions good.

106. a. $KNO_2 \rightarrow K^+ + NO_2^-$: NO_2^- is a weak base. Ignore K^+.

$$NO_2^- + H_2O \rightleftharpoons HNO_2 + OH^- \quad K_b = \frac{K_w}{K_a} = \frac{1.0 \times 10^{-14}}{4.0 \times 10^{-4}} = 2.5 \times 10^{-11}$$

	NO_2^-	$+$	H_2O	$\rightleftharpoons$	HNO_2	$+$	OH^-
Initial	0.12 M				0		~0
Equil.	$0.12 - x$				x		x

$$K_b = 2.5 \times 10^{-11} = \frac{[OH^-][HNO_2]}{[NO_2^-]} = \frac{x^2}{0.12 - x} \approx \frac{x^2}{0.12}$$

$x = [OH^-] = 1.7 \times 10^{-6}\ M$; pOH = 5.77; pH = 8.23   Assumptions good.

b. $NaOCl \rightarrow Na^+ + OCl^-$: OCl^- is a weak base. Ignore Na^+.

$$OCl^- + H_2O \rightleftharpoons HOCl + OH^- \qquad K_b = \frac{K_w}{K_a} = \frac{1.0 \times 10^{-14}}{3.5 \times 10^{-8}} = 2.9 \times 10^{-7}$$

Initial   0.45 *M*   0   ~0
Equil.   0.45 – *x*   *x*   *x*

$$K_b = 2.9 \times 10^{-7} = \frac{[HOCl][OH^-]}{[OCl^-]} = \frac{x^2}{0.45 - x} \approx \frac{x^2}{0.45}$$

$x = [OH^-] = 3.6 \times 10^{-4}\,M$; pOH = 3.44; pH = 10.56   Assumptions good.

c. $NH_4ClO_4 \rightarrow NH_4^+ + ClO_4^-$: NH_4^+ is a weak acid. ClO_4^- is the conjugate base of a strong acid. ClO_4^- has no basic (or acidic) properties.

$$NH_4^+ \rightleftharpoons NH_3 + H^+ \qquad K_a = \frac{K_w}{K_b} = \frac{1.0 \times 10^{-14}}{1.8 \times 10^{-5}} = 5.6 \times 10^{-10}$$

Initial   0.40 *M*   0   ~0
Equil.   0.40 – *x*   *x*   *x*

$$K_a = 5.6 \times 10^{-10} = \frac{[NH_3][H^+]}{[NH_4^+]} = \frac{x^2}{0.40 - x} \approx \frac{x^2}{0.40}$$

$x = [H^+] = 1.5 \times 10^{-5}\,M$; pH = 4.82;   Assumptions good.

107.   All these salts contain Na^+, which has no acidic/basic properties, and a conjugate base of a weak acid (except for NaCl where Cl^- is a neutral species.).   All conjugate bases of weak acids are weak bases because the K_b values for these species are between 1 and K_w. To identify the species, we will use the data given to determine the K_b value for the weak conjugate base. From the K_b value and data in Table 14.2 of the text, we can identify the conjugate base present by calculating the K_a value for the weak acid. We will use A^- as an abbreviation for the weak conjugate base.

$$A^- + H_2O \rightleftharpoons HA + OH^-$$

Initial   0.100 mol/1.00 L   0   ~0
             x mol/L A^- reacts with H_2O to reach equilibrium
Change   –*x* $\rightarrow$ +*x*   +*x*
Equil.   0.100 – *x*   *x*   *x*

$$K_b = \frac{[HA][OH^-]}{[A^-]} = \frac{x^2}{0.100 - x};\ \ \text{From the problem, pH} = 8.07:$$

pOH = 14.00 – 8.07 = 5.93; $[OH^-] = x = 10^{-5.93} = 1.2 \times 10^{-6}\,M$

$$K_b = \frac{(1.2 \times 10^{-6})^2}{0.100 - 1.2 \times 10^{-6}} = 1.4 \times 10^{-11} = K_b \text{ value for the conjugate base of a weak acid.}$$

The K_a value for the weak acid equals K_w/K_b: $K_a = \frac{1.0 \times 10^{-14}}{1.4 \times 10^{-11}} = 7.1 \times 10^{-4}$

From Table 14.2 of the text, this K_a value is closest to HF. Therefore, the unknown salt is NaF.

108. $BHCl \rightarrow BH^+ + Cl^-$; Cl^- is the conjugate base of the strong acid HCl, so Cl^- has no acidic/basic properties. BH^+ is a weak acid since it is the conjugate acid of a weak base, B. Determining the K_a value for BH^+:

	BH^+	$\rightleftharpoons$	B	+	H^+
Initial	0.10 M		0		~0
	x mol/L BH^+ dissociates to reach equilibrium				
Change	$-x$	$\rightarrow$	$+x$		$+x$
Equil.	$0.10 - x$		x		x

$K_a = \dfrac{[B][H^+]}{[BH^+]} = \dfrac{x^2}{0.10 - x}$; From the problem, pH = 5.82:

$[H^+] = x = 10^{-5.82} = 1.5 \times 10^{-6} M$; $K_a = \dfrac{(1.5 \times 10^{-6})^2}{0.10 - 1.5 \times 10^{-6}} = 2.3 \times 10^{-11}$

K_b for the base, $B = K_w/K_a = 1.0 \times 10^{-14}/2.3 \times 10^{-11} = 4.3 \times 10^{-4}$.

From Table 14.3 of the text, this K_b value is closest to that for CH_3NH_2, so the unknown salt is CH_3NH_3Cl.

109.   Major species present: $Al(H_2O)_6^{3+}$ ($K_a = 1.4 \times 10^{-5}$), NO_3^- (neutral) and H_2O ($K_w = 1.0 \times 10^{-14}$); $Al(H_2O)_6^{3+}$ is a stronger acid than water so it will be the dominant H^+ producer.

	$Al(H_2O)_6^{3+}$	$\rightleftharpoons$	$Al(H_2O)_5(OH)^{2+}+$		H^+
Initial	0.050 M		0		~0
	x mol/L $Al(H_2O)_6^{3+}$ dissociates to reach equilibrium				
Change	$-x$	$\rightarrow$	$+x$		$+x$
Equil.	$0.050 - x$		x		x

$K_a = 1.4 \times 10^{-5} = \dfrac{[Al(H_2O)_5(OH)^{2+}][H^+]}{[Al(H_2O)_6^{3+}]} = \dfrac{x^2}{0.050 - x} \approx \dfrac{x^2}{0.050}$

$x = 8.4 \times 10^{-4} M = [H^+]$; pH $= -\log(8.4 \times 10^{-4}) = 3.08$; Assumptions good.

110.   Major species: $Co(H_2O)_6^{3+}$ ($K_a = 1.0 \times 10^{-5}$), Cl^- (neutral) and H_2O ($K_w = 1.0 \times 10^{-14}$); $Co(H_2O)_6^{3+}$ will determine the pH since it is a stronger acid than water. Solving the weak acid problem in the usual manner:

$$Co(H_2O)_6^{3+} \rightleftharpoons Co(H_2O)_5(OH)^{2+} + H^+ \quad K_a = 1.0 \times 10^{-5}$$

Initial	0.10 M	0	~0
Equil.	0.10 $-$ x	x	x

$$K_a = 1.0 \times 10^{-5} = \frac{x^2}{0.10 - x} \approx \frac{x^2}{0.10}, \quad x = [H^+] = 1.0 \times 10^{-3} M$$

pH $= -\log(1.0 \times 10^{-3}) = 3.00$; Assumptions good.

111.   Reference Table 14.6 of the text and the solution to Exercise 14.99 for some generalizations on acid-base properties of salts.

a. $NaNO_3 \rightarrow Na^+ + NO_3^-$ neutral; Neither species has any acidic/basic properties.

b. $NaNO_2 \rightarrow Na^+ + NO_2^-$ basic; NO_2^- is a weak base and Na^+ has no effect on pH.

$$NO_2^- + H_2O \rightleftharpoons HNO_2 + OH^- \quad K_b = \frac{K_w}{K_{a,\,HNO_2}} = \frac{1.0 \times 10^{-14}}{4.0 \times 10^{-4}} = 2.5 \times 10^{-11}$$

c. $C_5H_5NHClO_4 \rightarrow C_5H_5NH^+ + ClO_4^-$ acidic; $C_5H_5NH^+$ is a weak acid and ClO_4^- has no effect on pH.

$$C_5H_5NH^+ \rightleftharpoons H^+ + C_5H_5N \quad K_a = \frac{K_w}{K_{b,\,C_5H_5N}} = \frac{1.0 \times 10^{-14}}{1.7 \times 10^{-9}} = 5.9 \times 10^{-6}$$

d. $NH_4NO_2 \rightarrow NH_4^+ + NO_2^-$ acidic; NH_4^+ is a weak acid ($K_a = 5.6 \times 10^{-10}$) and NO_2^- is a weak base ($K_b = 2.5 \times 10^{-11}$). Because $K_{a,\,NH_4^+} > K_{b,\,NO_2^-}$, the solution is acidic.

$$NH_4^+ \rightleftharpoons H^+ + NH_3 \quad K_a = 5.6 \times 10^{-10}; \quad NO_2^- + H_2O \rightleftharpoons HNO_2 + OH^- \quad K_b = 2.5 \times 10^{-11}$$

e. $KOCl \rightarrow K^+ + OCl^-$ basic; OCl^- is a weak base and K^+ has no effect on pH.

$$OCl^- + H_2O \rightleftharpoons HOCl + OH^- \quad K_b = \frac{K_w}{K_{a,\,HOCl}} = \frac{1.0 \times 10^{-14}}{3.5 \times 10^{-8}} = 2.9 \times 10^{-7}$$

f. $NH_4OCl \rightarrow NH_4^+ + OCl^-$ basic; NH_4^+ is a weak acid and OCl^- is a weak base. Because $K_{b,\,OCl^-} > K_{a,\,NH_4^+}$, the solution is basic.

$$NH_4^+ \rightleftharpoons NH_3 + H^+ \quad K_a = 5.6 \times 10^{-10}; \quad OCl^- + H_2O \rightleftharpoons HOCl + OH^- \quad K_b = 2.9 \times 10^{-7}$$

112.   a. $KCl \rightarrow K^+ + Cl^-$ neutral; K^+ and Cl^- have no effect on pH.

b. $NH_4C_2H_3O_2 \rightarrow NH_4^+ + C_2H_3O_2^-$ neutral; NH_4^+ is a weak acid and $C_2H_3O_2^-$ is a weak base.

Because $K_{a,\,NH_4^+} = K_{b,\,C_2H_3O_2^-}$, pH = 7.00.

$$NH_4^+ \rightleftharpoons NH_3 + H^+ \quad K_a = \frac{K_w}{K_{b,\,NH_3}} = \frac{1.0 \times 10^{-14}}{1.8 \times 10^{-5}} = 5.6 \times 10^{-10}$$

$$C_2H_3O_2^- + H_2O \rightleftharpoons HC_2H_3O_2 + OH^- \quad K_b = \frac{K_w}{K_{b,\,HC_2H_3O_2}} = \frac{1.0 \times 10^{-14}}{1.8 \times 10^{-5}} = 5.6 \times 10^{-10}$$

c. $CH_3NH_3Cl \rightarrow CH_3NH_3^+ + Cl^-$ acidic; $CH_3NH_3^+$ is a weak acid and Cl^- has no effect on pH.

$$CH_3NH_3^+ \rightleftharpoons H^+ + CH_3NH_2 \quad K_a = \frac{K_w}{K_{b,\,CH_3NH_2}} = \frac{1.00 \times 10^{-14}}{4.38 \times 10^{-4}} = 2.28 \times 10^{-11}$$

d. $KF \rightarrow K^+ + F^-$ basic; F^- is a weak base and K^+ has no effect on pH.

$$F^- + H_2O \rightleftharpoons HF + OH^- \quad K_b = \frac{K_w}{K_{a,\,HF}} = \frac{1.0 \times 10^{-14}}{7.2 \times 10^{-4}} = 1.4 \times 10^{-11}$$

e. $NH_4F \rightarrow NH_4^+ + F^-$ acidic; NH_4^+ is a weak acid and F^- is a weak base. Because $K_{a,\,NH_4^+} > K_{b,\,F^-}$, the solution is acidic.

$$NH_4^+ \rightleftharpoons H^+ + NH_3 \quad K_a = 5.6 \times 10^{-10}; \quad F^- + H_2O \rightleftharpoons HF + OH^- \quad K_b = 1.4 \times 10^{-11}$$

f. $CH_3NH_3CN \rightarrow CH_3NH_3^+ + CN^-$ basic; $CH_3NH_3^+$ is a weak acid and CN^- is a weak base. Because $K_{b,\,CN^-} > K_{a,\,CH_3NH_3^+}$, the solution is basic.

$$CH_3NH_3^+ \rightleftharpoons H^+ + CH_3NH_2 \quad K_a = 2.28 \times 10^{-11}$$

$$CN^- + H_2O \rightleftharpoons HCN + OH^- \quad K_b = \frac{K_w}{K_{a,\,HCN}} = \frac{1.0 \times 10^{-14}}{6.2 \times 10^{-10}} = 1.6 \times 10^{-5}$$

Relationships Between Structure and Strengths of Acids and Bases

113.   a. $HIO_3 < HBrO_3$; As the electronegativity of the central atom increases, acid strength increases.

b. $HNO_2 < HNO_3$; As the number of oxygen atoms attached to the central nitrogen atom increases, acid strength increases.

c. $HOI < HOCl$; Same reasoning as in a.

d. $H_3PO_3 < H_3PO_4$; Same reasoning as in b.

114.   a. $BrO_3^- < IO_3^-$; These are the conjugate bases of the acids in Exercise 14.113a. Since $HBrO_3$ is the stronger acid, the conjugate base of $HBrO_3$ (BrO_3^-) will be the weaker base. IO_3^- will be the stronger base since HIO_3 is the weaker acid.

       b. $NO_3^- < NO_2^-$; These are the conjugate bases of the acids in Exercise 14.113b. Conjugate base strength is inversely related to acid strength.

       c. $OCl^- < OI^-$. These are the conjugate bases of the acids in Exercise 14.113c.

115.   a. $H_2O < H_2S < H_2Se$; As the strength of the H–X bond decreases, acid strength increases.

       b. $CH_3CO_2H < FCH_2CO_2H < F_2CHCO_2H < F_3CCO_2H$; As the electronegativity of neighboring atoms increases, acid strength increases.

       c. $NH_4^+ < HONH_3^+$; Same reason as in b.

       d. $NH_4^+ < PH_4^+$; Same reason as in a.

116.   In general, the stronger the acid, the weaker the conjugate base.

       a. $SeH^- < SH^- < OH^-$; These are the conjugate bases of the acids in Exercise 14.115a. The ordering of the base strength is the opposite of the acids.

       b. $PH_3 < NH_3$ (See Exercise 14.115d.)

       c. $HONH_2 < NH_3$ (See Exercise 14.115c.)

117.   In general, metal oxides form basic solutions when dissolved in water and nonmetal oxides form acidic solutions in water.

       a.   basic; $CaO(s) + H_2O(l) \rightarrow Ca(OH)_2(aq)$; $Ca(OH)_2$ is a strong base.

       b.   acidic; $SO_2(g) + H_2O(l) \rightarrow H_2SO_3(aq)$; H_2SO_3 is a weak diprotic acid.

       c.   acidic; $Cl_2O(g) + H_2O(l) \rightarrow 2\ HOCl(aq)$; HOCl is a weak acid.

118   a.   basic; $Li_2O(s) + H_2O(l) \rightarrow 2\ LiOH(aq)$; LiOH is a strong base.

       b.   acidic; $CO_2(g) + H_2O(l) \rightarrow H_2CO_3(aq)$; H_2CO_3 is a weak diprotic acid.

       c.   basic; $SrO(s) + H_2O(l) \rightarrow Sr(OH)_2(aq)$; $Sr(OH)_2$ is a strong base.

Lewis Acids and Bases

119.   A Lewis base is an electron pair donor, and a Lewis acid is an electron pair acceptor.

       a. $B(OH)_3$, acid; H_2O, base   b. Ag^+, acid; NH_3, base   c. BF_3, acid; F^-, base

120.   a. Fe^{3+}, acid; H_2O, base   b. H_2O, acid; CN^-, base   c. HgI_2, acid; I^-, base

121. $Al(OH)_3(s) + 3\ H^+(aq) \rightarrow Al^{3+}(aq) + 3\ H_2O(l)$ (Brønsted-Lowry base, H^+ acceptor)

        $Al(OH)_3(s) + OH^-(aq) \rightarrow Al(OH)_4^-(aq)$ (Lewis acid, electron pair acceptor)

122. $Zn(OH)_2(s) + 2\ H^+(aq) \rightarrow Zn^{2+}(aq) + 2\ H_2O(l)$ (Brønsted-Lowry base)

        $Zn(OH)_2(s) + 2\ OH^-(aq) \rightarrow Zn(OH)_4^{2-}(aq)$ (Lewis acid)

123. Fe^{3+} should be the stronger Lewis acid. Fe^{3+} is smaller and has a greater positive charge. Because of this, Fe^{3+} will be more strongly attracted to lone pairs of electrons as compared to Fe^{2+}.

124.   The Lewis structures for the reactants and products are:

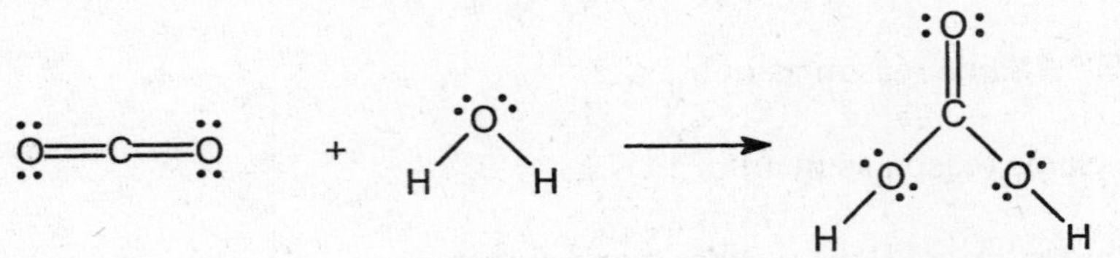

        In this reaction, H_2O donates a pair of electrons to carbon in CO_2, which is followed by a proton shift to form H_2CO_3. H_2O is the Lewis base, and CO_2 is the Lewis acid.

Additional Exercises

125.   At pH = 2.000, $[H^+] = 10^{-2.000} = 1.00 \times 10^{-2}\ M$; At pH = 4.000, $[H^+] = 10^{-4.000} = 1.00 \times 10^{-4}\ M$

        $$\text{mol } H^+ \text{ present} = 0.0100\ L \times \frac{0.0100\ \text{mol } H^+}{L} = 1.00 \times 10^{-4}\ \text{mol } H^+$$

        Let V = total volume of solution at pH = 4.000:

        $$1.00 \times 10^{-4}\ \text{mol/L} = \frac{1.00 \times 10^{-4}\ \text{mol } H^+}{V},\ \ V = 1.00\ L$$

        Volume of water added = 1.00 L − 0.0100 L = 0.99 L = 990 mL

126.   Conjugate acid-base pairs differ by an H^+ in the formula. Pairs in parts a, c, and d are conjugate acid-base pairs. For part b, HSO_4^- is the conjugate base of H_2SO_4. In addition, HSO_4^- is the conjugate acid of SO_4^{2-}

127.   a.   The initial concentrations are halved since equal volumes of the two solutions are mixed.

	$HC_2H_3O_2$	$\rightleftharpoons$	H^+	+	$C_2H_3O_2^-$
Initial	0.100 M		$5.00 \times 10^{-4}\ M$		0
Equil.	0.100 − x		$5.00 \times 10^{-4} + x$		x

$$K_a = 1.8 \times 10^{-5} = \frac{x(5.00 \times 10^{-4} + x)}{(0.100 - x)} \approx \frac{x(5.00 \times 10^{-4})}{(0.100)}$$

$x = 3.6 \times 10^{-3}$; Assumption is horrible. Using the quadratic formula:

$$x^2 + 5.18 \times 10^{-4}\,x - 1.8 \times 10^{-6} = 0$$

$$x = 1.1 \times 10^{-3}\,M;\ [H^+] = 5.00 \times 10^{-4} + x = 1.6 \times 10^{-3}\,M;\ pH = 2.80$$

b. $x = [C_2H_3O_2^-] = 1.1 \times 10^{-3}\,M$

128.   Let HSac = saccharin and I = $[HSac]_o$.

$$HSac \quad \rightleftharpoons \quad H^+ \quad + \quad S_{sac}^- \qquad\qquad K_a = 10^{-11.70} = 2.0 \times 10^{-12}$$

Initial	I	~0	0
Equil.	I - x	x	x

$$K_a = 2.0 \times 10^{-12} = \frac{x^2}{I - x};\ x = [H^+] = 10^{-5.75} = 1.8 \times 10^{-6}\,M$$

$$2.0 \times 10^{-12} = \frac{(1.8 \times 10^{-6})^2}{I - 1.8 \times 10^{-6}},\ \ I = 1.6\,M = [HSac]_o.$$

$$100.0\ g\ HC_7H_4NSO_3 \times \frac{1\,mol}{183.19\,g} \times \frac{1\,L}{1.6\,mol} \times \frac{1000\,mL}{L} = 340\ mL$$

129.   The light bulb is bright because a strong electrolyte is present, i.e., a solute is present that dissolves to produce a lot of ions in solution. The pH meter value of 4.6 indicates that a weak acid is present. (If a strong acid were present, the pH would be close to zero.) Of the possible substances, only HCl (strong acid), NaOH (strong base) and NH_4Cl are strong electrolytes. Of these three substances, only NH_4Cl contains a weak acid (the HCl solution would have a pH close to zero and the NaOH solution would have a pH close to 14.0). NH_4Cl dissociates into NH_4^+ and Cl^- ions when dissolved in water. Cl^- is the conjugate base of a strong acid, so it has no basic (or acidic properties) in water. NH_4^+, however, is the conjugate acid of the weak base NH_3, so NH_4^+ is a weak acid and would produce a solution with a pH = 4.6 when the concentration is ~1 M.

130. $CaO(s) + H_2O(l) \rightarrow Ca(OH)_2(aq);\ Ca(OH)_2(aq) \rightarrow Ca^{2+}(aq) + 2\,OH^-(aq)$

$$[OH^-] = \frac{0.25\,g\ CaO \times \dfrac{1\,mol\ CaO}{56.08\,g} \times \dfrac{1\,mol\ Ca(OH)_2}{1\,mol\ CaO} \times \dfrac{2\,mol\ OH^-}{mol\ Ca(OH)_2}}{1.5\,L} = 5.9 \times 10^{-3}$$

$$[OH^-] = 5.9 \times 10^{-3}\,M$$

$$pOH = -\log(5.9 \times 10^{-3}) = 2.23,\ pH = 14.00 - 2.23 = 11.77$$

131.   HBz $\rightleftharpoons$ H$^+$ +   Bz$^-$ HBz = C$_6$H$_5$CO$_2$H

Initial   C   ~0   0   C = [HBz]$_o$ = concentration of HBz
                     x mol/L HBz dissociates to reach equilibrium   that dissolves to give saturated
Change $-x$ $\rightarrow$ $+x$ $+x$ solution.
Equil.   C $- x$ x x

$$K_a = \frac{[H^+][Bz^-]}{[HBz]} = 6.4 \times 10^{-5} = \frac{x^2}{C-x} \text{ , where } x = [H^+]$$

$$6.4 \times 10^{-5} = \frac{[H^+]^2}{C-[H^+]}; \quad pH = 2.80; \quad [H^+] = 10^{-2.80} = 1.6 \times 10^{-3} M$$

$$C - 1.6 \times 10^{-3} = \frac{(1.6 \times 10^{-3})^2}{6.4 \times 10^{-5}} = 4.0 \times 10^{-2}, \quad C = 4.0 \times 10^{-2} + 1.6 \times 10^{-3} = 4.2 \times 10^{-2} M$$

The molar solubility of C$_6$H$_5$CO$_2$H is 4.2×10^{-2} mol/L.

132.   Because K$_{a_2}$ for H$_2$S is so small, we can ignore the H$^+$ contribution from the K$_{a_2}$ reaction.

                     H$_2$S $\rightleftharpoons$ H$^+$ HS$^-$ K$_{a_1}$ = 1.0×10^{-7}

Initial   0.10 M ~0   0
Equil.   0.10 $- x$ x x

$$K_{a_1} = 1.0 \times 10^{-7} = \frac{x^2}{0.10-x} \approx \frac{x^2}{0.10}, \quad x = [H^+] = 1.0 \times 10^{-4}; \quad \text{Assumptions good.}$$

$$pH = -\log(1.0 \times 10^{-4}) = 4.00$$

Use the K$_{a_2}$ reaction to determine [S$_2^-$].

                     HS$^-$ $\rightleftharpoons$ H$^+$ +   S^{2-}
Initial 1.0×10^{-4} M 1.0×10^{-4} M 0
Equil. $1.0 \times 10^{-4} - x$ $1.0 \times 10^{-4} + x$ x

$$K_{a_2} = 1.0 \times 10^{-19} = \frac{(1.0 \times 10^{-4} + x)x}{(1.0 \times 10^{-4} - x)} \approx \frac{1.0 \times 10^{-4}\,x}{1.0 \times 10^{-4}}$$

$x = [S^{2-}] = 1.0 \times 10^{-19}$ M;   Assumptions good.

133.   For H$_2$C$_6$H$_6$O$_6$. K$_{a_1}$ = 7.9×10^{-5} and K$_{a_2}$ = 1.6×10^{-12}. Because K$_{a_1}$ $\gg$ K$_{a_2}$, the amount of H$^+$
         produced by the K$_{a_2}$ reaction will be negligible.

$$[H_2C_6H_6O_6]_o = \frac{0.500\,g \times \dfrac{1\,mol\,H_2C_6H_6O_6}{176.12\,g}}{0.2000\,L} = 0.0142\,M$$

$$H_2C_6H_6O_6(aq) \rightleftharpoons HC_6H_6O_6{}^-(aq) + H^+(aq) \qquad K_{a_1} = 7.9 \times 10^{-5}$$

Initial	$0.0142\,M$	0	~ 0
Equil.	$0.0142 - x$	x	x

$$K_{a_1} = 7.9 \times 10^{-5} = \frac{x^2}{0.0142 - x} \approx \frac{x^2}{0.0142}, \quad x = 1.1 \times 10^{-3}; \quad \text{Assumption fails the 5\% rule.}$$

Solving by the method of successive approximations:

$$7.9 \times 10^{-5} = \frac{x^2}{0.0142 - 1.1 \times 10^{-3}}, \quad x = 1.0 \times 10^{-3}\,M \ \ \text{(consistent answer)}$$

Since H^+ produced by the K_{a_2} reaction will be negligible, $[H^+] = 1.0 \times 10^{-3}$ and pH = 3.00.

134. $[H^+]_o = 1.0 \times 10^{-2} + 1.0 \times 10^{-2} = 2.0 \times 10^{-2}\,M$ from the strong acids HCl and H_2SO_4.

$HSO_4{}^-$ is a good weak acid ($K_a = 0.012$). However, HCN is a poor weak acid ($K_a = 6.2 \times 10^{-10}$) and can be ignored. Calculating the H^+ contribution from $HSO_4{}^-$:

$$HSO_4{}^- \rightleftharpoons H^+ + SO_4{}^{2-} \qquad K_a = 0.012$$

Initial	$0.010\,M$	$0.020\,M$	0
Equil.	$0.010 - x$	$0.020 + x$	x

$$K_a = \frac{x\,(0.020 + x)}{(0.010 - x)} = 0.012 \approx \frac{x\,(0.020)}{(0.010)}, \quad x = 0.0060; \quad \text{Assumption poor (60\% error).}$$

Using the quadratic formula: $x^2 + 0.032\,x - 1.2 \times 10^{-4} = 0$, $x = 3.4 \times 10^{-3}\,M$

$[H^+] = 0.020 + x = 0.020 + 3.4 \times 10^{-3} = 0.023\,M$; pH = 1.64

135.   For this problem we will abbreviate $CH_2{=}CHCO_2H$ as Hacr and $CH_2{=}CHCO_2{}^-$ as acr$^-$.

   a.   Solving the weak acid problem:

$$Hacr \rightleftharpoons H^+ + acr^- \qquad K_a = 5.6 \times 10^{-5}$$

Initial	$0.10\,M$	~ 0	0
Equil.	$0.10 - x$	x	x

$$\frac{x^2}{0.10 - x} = 5.6 \times 10^{-5} \approx \frac{x^2}{0.10}, \quad x = [H^+] = 2.4 \times 10^{-3}\,M; \quad pH = 2.62; \quad \text{Assumptions good.}$$

b. % dissociation $= \dfrac{[H^+]}{[Hacr]_0} \times 100 = \dfrac{2.4 \times 10^{-3}}{0.10} \times 100 = 2.4\%$

c. acr^- is a weak base and the major source of OH^- in this solution.

$$acr^- \ + \ H_2O \ \rightleftharpoons \ Hacr \ + \ OH^- \quad K_b = \dfrac{K_w}{K_a} = \dfrac{1.0 \times 10^{-14}}{5.6 \times 10^{-5}}$$

Initial   0.050 M 0   ~0 $K_b = 1.8 \times 10^{-10}$
Equil.   0.050 – x x x

$$K_b = \dfrac{[Hacr][OH^-]}{[acr^-]} = 1.8 \times 10^{-10} = \dfrac{x^2}{0.050 - x} \approx \dfrac{x^2}{0.050}$$

$x = [OH^-] = 3.0 \times 10^{-6} \ M; \ pOH = 5.52; \ pH = 8.48$ Assumptions good.

136.   From the pH, $C_7H_4ClO_2^-$ is a weak base. Use the weak base data to determine K_b for $C_7H_4ClO_2^-$ (which we will abbreviate as CB^-).

$$CB^- \ + \ H_2O \ \rightleftharpoons \ HCB \ + \ OH^-$$

Initial   0.20 M 0   ~0
Equil.   0.20 – x x x

Because pH = 8.65, pOH = 5.35 and $[OH^-] = 10^{-5.35} = 4.5 \times 10^{-6} \ M = x$.

$$K_b = \dfrac{[HCB][OH^-]}{[CB^-]} = \dfrac{x^2}{0.20 - x} = \dfrac{(4.5 \times 10^{-6})^2}{0.20 - 4.5 \times 10^{-6}} = 1.0 \times 10^{-10}$$

Since CB^- is a weak base, HCB, chlorobenzoic acid, is a weak acid. Solving the weak acid problem:

$$HCB \ \rightleftharpoons \ H^+ \ + \ CB^-$$

Initial   0.20 M ~0   0
Equil.   0.20 – x x x

$$K_a = \dfrac{K_w}{K_b} = \dfrac{1.0 \times 10^{-14}}{5.6 \times 10^{-10}} = 1.0 \times 10^{-4} = \dfrac{x^2}{0.20 - x} \approx \dfrac{x^2}{0.20}$$

$x = [H^+] = 4.5 \times 10^{-3} M; \ pH = 2.35$ Assumptions good.

137.   a. $Fe(H_2O)_6^{3+} + H_2O \ \rightleftharpoons \ Fe(H_2O)_5(OH)^{2+} + \ H_3O^+$

Initial   0.10 M 0   ~0
Equil.   0.10 – x x x

$$K_a = \frac{[Fe(H_2O)_5(OH)^{2+}][H_3O^+]}{[Fe(H_2O)_6^{3+}]} = 6.0 \times 10^{-3} = \frac{x^2}{0.10 - x} \approx \frac{x^2}{0.10}$$

$x = 2.4 \times 10^{-2}$; Assumption is poor (x is 24% of 0.10). Using successive approximations:

$$\frac{x^2}{0.10 - 0.024} = 6.0 \times 10^{-3}, \ x = 0.021$$

$$\frac{x^2}{0.10 - 0.021} = 6.0 \times 10^{-3}, \ x = 0.022; \quad \frac{x^2}{0.10 - 0.022} = 6.0 \times 10^{-3}, \ x = 0.022$$

$x = [H^+] = 0.022 \ M; \ pH = 1.66$

b. Because of the lower charge, Fe^{2+}(aq) will not be as strong an acid as Fe^{3+}(aq). A solution of iron(II) nitrate will be less acidic (have a higher pH) than a solution with the same concentration of iron(III) nitrate.

138.   See generalizations in Exercise 14.99.

a. HI: strong acid; HF: weak acid ($K_a = 7.2 \times 10^{-4}$)

   NaF: F^- is the conjugate base of the weak acid HF so F^- is a weak base. The K_b value for $F^- = K_w/K_{a, HF} = 1.4 \times 10^{-11}$. Na^+ has no acidic or basic properties.

   NaI: neutral (pH = 7.0); Na^+ and I^- have no acidic/basic properties.

   To place in order of increasing pH, we place the compounds from most acidic (lowest pH) to most basic (highest pH). Increasing pH: HI < HF < NaI < NaF.

b. NH₄Br: NH_4^+ is a weak acid ($K_a = 5.6 \times 10^{-10}$) and Br^- is a neutral species.
   HBr: strong acid
   KBr: neutral; K^+ and Br^- have no acidic/basic properties
   NH₃: weak base, $K_b = 1.8 \times 10^{-5}$

   Increasing pH: HBr < NH₄Br < KBr < NH₃
                   most   most
                   acidic   basic

c. C₆H₅NH₃NO₃: $C_6H_5NH_3^+$ is a weak acid ($K_w / K_{b, C_6H_5NH_2} = 1.0 \times 10^{-14}/3.8 \times 10^{-10}$ $= 2.6 \times 10^{-5}$) and NO_3^- is a neutral species.

   NaNO₃: neutral; Na^+ and NO_3^- have no acidic/basic properties.
   NaOH: strong base
   HOC₆H₅: weak acid ($K_a = 1.6 \times 10^{-10}$)
   KOC₆H₅: $OC_6H_5^-$ is a weak base ($K_b = K_w / K_{a, HOC_6H_5} = 6.3 \times 10^{-5}$) and K^+ is a neutral species.
   C₆H₅NH₂: weak base ($K_b = 3.8 \times 10^{-10}$)
   HNO₃: strong acid

This is a little more difficult than the previous parts of this problem because two weak acids and two weak bases are present. Between the weak acids, $C_6H_5NH_3^+$ is a stronger weak acid than HOC_6H_5 because the K_a value for $C_6H_5NH_3^+$ is larger than the K_a value for HOC_6H_5. Between the two weak bases, because the K_b value for $OC_6H_5^-$ is larger than the K_b value for $C_6H_5NH_2$, $OC_6H_5^-$ is a stronger weak base than $C_6H_5NH_2$.

Increasing pH: $HNO_3 < C_6H_5NH_3NO_3 < HOC_6H_5 < NaNO_3 < C_6H_5NH_2 < KOC_6H_5 < NaOH$
  most   most
  acidic   basic

139.   The solution is acidic from $HSO_4^- \rightleftharpoons H^+ + SO_4^{2-}$. Solving the weak acid problem:

$$HSO_4^- \quad \rightleftharpoons \quad H^+ \quad + \quad SO_4^{2-} \qquad K_a = 1.2 \times 10^{-2}$$

Initial   0.10 M   ~0   0
Equil.   0.10 – x   x   x

$$1.2 \times 10^{-2} = \frac{[H^+][SO_4^{2-}]}{[HSO_4^-]} = \frac{x^2}{0.10 - x} \approx \frac{x^2}{0.10} \ , \quad x = 0.035$$

Assumption is not good (x is 35% of 0.10). Using successive approximations:

$$\frac{x^2}{0.10 - x} = \frac{x^2}{0.10 - 0.035} = 1.2 \times 10^{-2}, \ x = 0.028$$

$$\frac{x^2}{0.10 - 0.028} = 1.2 \times 10^{-2}, \ x = 0.029; \quad \frac{x^2}{0.10 - 0.029} = 1.2 \times 10^{-2}, \ x = 0.029$$

$x = [H^+] = 0.029 \ M; \ pH = 1.54$

140.   The relevant reactions are:

$$H_2CO_3 \rightleftharpoons H^+ + HCO_3^- \quad K_{a_1} = 4.3 \times 10^{-7}; \quad HCO_3^- \rightleftharpoons H^+ + CO_3^{2-} \quad K_{a_2} = 5.6 \times 10^{-11}$$

Initially, we deal only with the first reaction (because $K_{a_1} \gg K_{a_2}$) and then let these results control values of the concentrations in the second reaction.

$$H_2CO_3 \quad \rightleftharpoons \quad H^+ \quad + \quad HCO_3^-$$

Initial   0.010 M   ~0   0
Equil.   0.010 – x   x   x

$$K_{a_1} = 4.3 \times 10^{-7} = \frac{[H^+][HCO_3^-]}{[H_2CO_3]} = \frac{x^2}{0.010 - x} \approx \frac{x^2}{0.010}$$

$x = 6.6 \times 10^{-5} \ M = [H^+] = [HCO_3^-] \ ; \quad$ Assumptions good.

$$HCO_3^- \quad \rightleftharpoons \quad H^+ \quad + \quad CO_3^{2-}$$

Initial $6.6 \times 10^{-5} M$ $6.6 \times 10^{-5} M$ 0

Equil. $6.6 \times 10^{-5} - y$ $6.6 \times 10^{-5} + y$ y

If y is small, then $[H^+] = [HCO_3^-]$ and $K_{a_2} = 5.6 \times 10^{-11} = \dfrac{[H^+][CO_3^{2-}]}{[HCO_3^-]} \approx y$

$y = [CO_3^{2-}] = 5.6 \times 10^{-11} M$;   Assumptions good.

The amount of H^+ from the second dissociation is $5.6 \times 10^{-11} M$ or:

$$\frac{5.6 \times 10^{-11}}{6.6 \times 10^{-5}} \times 100 = 8.5 \times 10^{-5} \% \ H^+ \ \text{from the second dissociation}$$

This result justifies our treating the equilibria separately. If the second dissociation contributed a significant amount of H^+, then we would have to treat both equilibria simultaneously. The reaction that occurs when acid is added to a solution of HCO_3^- is:

$$HCO_3^-(aq) + H^+(aq) \rightarrow H_2CO_3(aq) \rightarrow H_2O(l) + CO_2(g)$$

The bubbles are $CO_2(g)$ and are formed by the breakdown of unstable H_2CO_3 molecules. We should write $H_2O(l) + CO_2(aq)$ or $CO_2(aq)$ for what we call carbonic acid. It is for convenience, however, that we write $H_2CO_3(aq)$.

141. a. In the lungs, there is a lot of O_2 and the equilibrium favors $Hb(O_2)_4$. In the cells, there is a deficiency of O_2, and the equilibrium favors HbH_4^{4+}.

b. CO_2 is a weak acid, $CO_2 + H_2O \rightleftharpoons HCO_3^- + H^+$. Removing CO_2 essentially decreases H^+. $Hb(O_2)_4$ is then favored and O_2 is not released by hemoglobin in the cells. Breathing into a paper bag increases CO_2 in the blood, thus increasing H^+, which shifts the reaction left.

c. CO_2 builds up in the blood and it becomes too acidic, driving the equilibrium to the left. Hemoglobin can't bind O_2 as strongly in the lungs. Bicarbonate ion acts as a base in water and neutralizes the excess acidity.

142. a. $NH_3 + H_3O^+ \rightleftharpoons NH_4^+ + H_2O$

$$K_{eq} = \frac{[NH_4^+]}{[NH_3][H^+]} = \frac{1}{K_a \ \text{for} \ NH_4^+} = \frac{K_b \ \text{for} \ NH_3}{K_w} = \frac{1.8 \times 10^{-5}}{1.0 \times 10^{-14}} = 1.8 \times 10^9$$

b. $NO_2^- + H_3O^+ \rightleftharpoons HNO_2 + H_2O \quad K_{eq} = \dfrac{[HNO_2]}{[NO_2^-][H^+]} = \dfrac{1}{K_a \ \text{for} \ HNO_2} = \dfrac{1}{4.0 \times 10^{-4}}$

$$= 2.5 \times 10^3$$

c. $NH_4^+ + OH^- \rightleftharpoons NH_3 + H_2O \quad K_{eq} = \dfrac{1}{K_b \ \text{for} \ NH_3} = \dfrac{1}{1.8 \times 10^{-5}} = 5.6 \times 10^4$

d. $HNO_2 + OH^- \rightleftharpoons H_2O + NO_2^-$

$$K_{eq} = \frac{[NO_2^-]}{[HNO_2][OH^-]} \times \frac{[H^+]}{[H^+]} = \frac{K_a \text{ for } HNO_2}{K_w} = \frac{4.0 \times 10^{-4}}{1.0 \times 10^{-14}} = 4.0 \times 10^{10}$$

143.   a. H_2SO_3 b. $HClO_3$ c. H_3PO_3

NaOH and KOH are soluble ionic compounds composed of Na^+ and K^+ cations and OH^- anions. All soluble ionic compounds dissolve to form the ions from which they are formed. In oxyacids, the compounds are all covalent compounds in which electrons are shared to form bonds (unlike ionic compounds). When these compounds are dissolved in water, the covalent bond between oxygen and hydrogen breaks to form H^+ ions.

Challenge Problems

144.   The pH of this solution is not 8.00 because water will donate a significant amount of H^+ from the autoionization of water. You can't add an acid to water and get a basic pH. The pertinent reactions are:

$H_2O \rightleftharpoons H^+ + OH^-$ $K_w = [H^+][OH^-] = 1.0 \times 10^{-14}$

$HCl \rightarrow H^+ + Cl^-$ K_a is very large, so we assume that only the forward reaction occurs.

In any solution, the overall net positive charge must equal the overall net negative charge (called the charge balance). For this problem:

[positive charge] = [negative charge], so $[H^+] = [OH^-] + [Cl^-]$

From K_w, $[OH^-] = K_w/[H^+]$, and from $1.0 \times 10^{-8} M$ HCl, $[Cl^-] = 1.0 \times 10^{-8} M$. Substituting into the charge balance equation:

$$[H^+] = \frac{1.0 \times 10^{-14}}{[H^+]} + 1.0 \times 10^{-8}, \quad [H^+]^2 - 1.0 \times 10^{-8} [H^+] - 1.0 \times 10^{-14} = 0$$

Using the quadratic formula to solve:

$$[H^+] \frac{-(-1.0 \times 10^{-8}) \pm [(-1.0 \times 10^{-8})^2 - 4(1)(-1.0 \times 10^{-14})]^{1/2}}{2(1)}, \quad [H^+] = 1.1 \times 10^{-7} M$$

$pH = -\log(1.1 \times 10^{-7}) = 6.96$

145.   Since this is a very dilute solution of NaOH, we must worry about the amount of OH^- donated from the autoionization of water.

$NaOH \rightarrow Na^+ + OH^-$

$H_2O \rightleftharpoons H^+ + OH^-$ $K_w = [H^+][OH^-] = 1.0 \times 10^{-14}$

This solution, like all solutions, must be charge balanced, that is [positive charge] = [negative charge]. For this problem, the charge balance equation is:

$$[Na^+] + [H^+] = [OH^-], \text{ where } [Na^+] = 1.0 \times 10^{-7} \, M \text{ and } [H^+] = \frac{K_w}{[OH^-]}$$

Substituting into the charge balance equation:

$$1.0 \times 10^{-7} + \frac{1.0 \times 10^{-14}}{[OH^-]} = [OH^-], \quad [OH^-]^2 - 1.0 \times 10^{-7} \, [OH^-] - 1.0 \times 10^{-14} = 0$$

Using the quadratic formula to solve:

$$[OH^-] = \frac{-(-1.0 \times 10^{-7}) \pm [(-1.0 \times 10^{-7})^2 - 4(1)(-1.0 \times 10^{-14})]^{1/2}}{2(1)}$$

$$[OH^-] = 1.6 \times 10^{-7} \, M; \quad pOH = -\log (1.6 \times 10^{-7}) = 6.80; \quad pH = 7.20$$

146. $Ca(OH)_2 \, (s) \rightarrow Ca^{2+}(aq) + 2 \, OH^-(aq)$

This is a very dilute solution of $Ca(OH)_2$ so we can't ignore the OH^- contribution from H_2O. From the dissociation of $Ca(OH)_2$ alone, $2[Ca^{2+}] = [OH^-]$. Including H_2O autoionization to H^+ and OH^-, the overall charge balance is:

$2[Ca^{2+}] + [H^+] = [OH^-]$

$2(3.0 \times 10^{-7} \, M) + K_w/[OH^-] = [OH^-], \quad [OH^-]^2 = 6.0 \times 10^{-7} \, [OH^-] + K_w$

$[OH^-]^2 - 6.0 \times 10^{-7} \, [OH^-] - 1.0 \times 10^{-14} = 0$;   Using quadratic formula: $[OH^-] = 6.2 \times 10^{-7} \, M$

147.

	HA	$\rightleftharpoons$	H^+	+	A^-	$K_a = 1.00 \times 10^{-6}$
Initial	C		~0		0	C = [HA]$_0$; For pH = 4.000,
Equil.	C - 1.00 $\times 10^{-4}$		1.00 $\times 10^{-4}$		1.00 $\times 10^{-4}$	x = [H$^+$] = 1.00 $\times 10^{-4} \, M$

$$K_a = \frac{(1.00 \times 10^{-4})^2}{C - 1.00 \times 10^{-4}} = 1.00 \times 10^{-6}; \quad \text{Solving: } C = 0.0101 \, M$$

The solution initially contains $50.0 \times 10^{-3} \, L \times 0.0101 \, mol/L = 5.05 \times 10^{-4}$ mol HA. We then dilute to a total volume, V, in liters. The resulting pH = 5.000, so $[H^+] = 1.00 \times 10^{-5}$. In the typical weak acid problem, x = [H$^+$], so:

	HA	$\rightleftharpoons$	H^+	+	A^-
Initial	5.05 $\times 10^{-4}$ mol/V		~0		0
Equil.	5.05 $\times 10^{-4}$ /V - 1.00 $\times 10^{-5}$		1.00 $\times 10^{-5}$		1.00 $\times 10^{-5}$

$$K_a = \frac{(1.00 \times 10^{-5})^2}{5.05 \times 10^{-4}\,/\,V - 1.00 \times 10^{-5}} = 1.00 \times 10^{-6}, \quad 1.00 \times 10^{-4} = 5.05 \times 10^{-4}\,/\,V - 1.00 \times 10^{-5}$$

V = 4.59 L; 50.0 mL are present initially, so we need to add 4540 mL of water.

148.

	HBrO	$\rightleftharpoons$	H⁺	+	BrO⁻	$K_a = 2 \times 10^{-9}$
Initial	$1.0 \times 10^{-6}\ M$		~0		0	

x mol/L HBrO dissociates to reach equilibrium

Change	$-x$	$\rightarrow$	$+x$		$+x$
Equil.	$1.0 \times 10^{-6} - x$		x		x

$$K_a = 2 \times 10^{-9} = \frac{x^2}{1.0 \times 10^{-6} - x} \approx \frac{x^2}{1.0 \times 10^{-6}}; \quad x = [H^+] = 4 \times 10^{-8}\ M;\ pH = 7.4$$

Let's check the assumptions. This answer is impossible! We can't add a small amount of an acid to a water and get a basic solution. The highest possible pH for an acid in water is 7.0. In the correct solution, we would have to take into account the autoionization of water.

149. Major species present are H_2O, $C_5H_5NH^+$ ($K_a = K_w/K_b(C_5H_5N) = 1.0 \times 10^{-14}/1.7 \times 10^{-9} = 5.9 \times 10^{-6}$) and F^- ($K_b = K_w/K_a(HF) = 1.0 \times 10^{-14}/7.2 \times 10^{-4} = 1.4 \times 10^{-11}$). The reaction to consider is the best acid present ($C_5H_5NH^+$) reacting with the best base present (F^-). Solving for the equilibrium concentrations:

	$C_5H_5NH^+$(aq)	+	F^-(aq)	$\rightleftharpoons$	C_5H_5N(aq)	+	HF(aq)
Initial	0.200 M		0.200 M		0		0
Change	$-x$		$-x$	$\rightarrow$	$+x$		$+x$
Equil.	$0.200 - x$		$0.200 - x$		x		x

$$K = K_{a,\,C_5H_5NH^+} \times \frac{1}{K_{a,\,HF}} = 5.9 \times 10^{-6}\ (1/7.2 \times 10^{-4}) = 8.2 \times 10^{-3}$$

$$K = \frac{[C_5H_5N][HF]}{[C_5H_5NH^+][F^-]} = 8.2 \times 10^{-3} = \frac{x^2}{(0.200 - x)^2}; \quad \text{Taking the square root of both sides:}$$

$$0.091 = \frac{x}{0.200 - x}, \quad x = 0.018 - 0.091\,x, \quad x = 0.016\ M$$

From the setup to the problem, $x = [C_5H_5N] = [HF] = 0.016\ M$ and $0.200 - x = 0.200 - 0.016 = 0.184\ M = [C_5H_5NH^+] = [F^-]$. To solve for the [H⁺], we can use either the K_a equilibrium for $C_5H_5NH^+$ or the K_a equilibrium for HF. Using $C_5H_5NH^+$ data:

$$K_{a,\,C_5H_5NH^+} = 5.9 \times 10^{-6} = \frac{[C_5H_5N][H^+]}{[C_5H_5NH^+]} = \frac{(0.016)[H^+]}{(0.184)}, \quad [H^+] = 6.8 \times 10^{-5}\ M$$

$$pH = -\log(6.8 \times 10^{-5}) = 4.17$$

As one would expect, because the K_a for the weak acid is larger than the K_b for the weak base, a solution of this salt should be acidic.

150.   Major species: NH_4^+, OCl^-, and H_2O; K_a for $NH_4^+ = 1.0 \times 10^{-14}/1.8 \times 10^{-5} = 5.6 \times 10^{-10}$ and K_b for $OCl^- = 1.0 \times 10^{-14}/3.5 \times 10^{-8} = 2.9 \times 10^{-7}$.

Because OCl^- is a better base than NH_4^+ is an acid, the solution will be basic. The dominant equilibrium is the best acid (NH_4^+) reacting with the best base (OCl^-) present.

$$NH_4^+ \quad + \quad OCl^- \quad \rightleftharpoons \quad NH_3 \quad + \quad HOCl$$

Initial	0.50 M	0.50 M	0	0
Change	$-x$	$-x$ $\rightarrow$	$+x$	$+x$
Equil.	$0.50 - x$	$0.50 - x$	x	x

$$K = K_{a,\,NH_4} \times \frac{1}{K_{a,\,HOCl}} = 5.6 \times 10^{-10}/3.5 \times 10^{-8} = 0.016$$

$$K = 0.016 = \frac{[NH_3][HOCl]}{[NH_4^+][OCl^-]} = \frac{x(x)}{(0.50 - x)(0.50 - x)}$$

$$\frac{x^2}{(0.50 - x)^2} = 0.016, \quad \frac{x}{0.50 - x} = (0.016)^{1/2} = 0.13, \quad x = 0.058 \, M$$

To solve for the H^+, use any pertinent K_a or K_b value. Using K_a for NH_4^+:

$$K_{a,\,NH_4^+} = 5.6 \times 10^{-10} = \frac{[NH_3][H^+]}{[NH_4^+]} = \frac{(0.058)[H^+]}{0.50 - 0.058}, \quad [H^+] = 4.3 \times 10^{-9} \, M, \quad pH = 8.37$$

151.   Since NH_3 is so concentrated, we need to calculate the OH^- contribution from the weak base NH_3.

$$NH_3 \quad + \quad \rightleftharpoons \quad NH_4^+ \quad + \quad OH^- \qquad K_b = 1.8 \times 10^{-5}$$

Initial	15.0 M	0	0.0100 M	(Assume no volume change.)
Equil.	$15.0 - x$	x	$0.0100 + x$	

$$K_b = 1.8 \times 10^{-5} = \frac{x(0.0100 + x)}{15.0 - x} \approx \frac{x(0.0100)}{15.0}, \quad x = 0.027; \text{ Assumption is horrible}$$
$$(x \text{ is } 270\% \text{ of } 0.0100).$$

Using the quadratic formula:

$$1.8 \times 10^{-5}(15.0 - x) = 0.0100\,x + x^2, \quad x^2 + 0.0100\,x - 2.7 \times 10^{-4} = 0$$

$$x = 1.2 \times 10^{-2}, \quad [OH^-] = 1.2 \times 10^{-2} + 0.0100 = 0.022 \, M$$

152. For 0.0010% dissociation: $[NH_4^+] = 1.0 \times 10^{-5} (0.050) = 5.0 \times 10^{-7} M$

$$NH_3 + H_2O \rightleftharpoons NH_4^+ + OH^- \quad K_b = \frac{(5.0 \times 10^{-7})[OH^-]}{0.050 - 5.0 \times 10^{-7}} = 1.8 \times 10^{-5}$$

Solving: $[OH^-] = 1.8 M$; Assuming no volume change:

$$1.0 \, L \times \frac{1.8 \, \text{mol NaOH}}{L} \times \frac{40.00 \, \text{g NaOH}}{\text{mol NaOH}} = 72 \, \text{g of NaOH}$$

153. $$\text{Molar mass} = \frac{dRT}{P} = \frac{\dfrac{5.11 \, g}{L} \times \dfrac{0.08206 \, L \, atm}{\text{mol K}} \times 298 \, K}{1.00 \, atm} = 125 \, \text{g/mol}$$

$$[HA]_o = \frac{1.50 \, g \times \dfrac{1 \, \text{mol}}{125 \, g}}{0.100 \, L} = 0.120 \, M; \quad pH = 1.80, \quad [H^+] = 10^{-1.80} = 1.6 \times 10^{-2} \, M$$

$$\begin{array}{ccccc} & HA & \rightleftharpoons & H^+ & + & A^- \end{array}$$

Equil. $\quad 0.120 - x \qquad x \qquad x \qquad\qquad x = [H^+] = 1.6 \times 10^{-2} \, M$

$$K_a = \frac{[H^+][A^-]}{[HA]} = \frac{(1.6 \times 10^{-2})^2}{0.120 - 0.016} = 2.5 \times 10^{-3}$$

154. $$HC_2H_3O_2 \rightleftharpoons H^+ + C_2H_3O_2^- \qquad K_a = 1.8 \times 10^{-5}$$

Initial $\quad 1.00 \, M \qquad\quad 0 \qquad\quad 0$
Equil. $\quad 1.00 - x \qquad\quad x \qquad\quad x$

$$1.8 \times 10^{-5} = \frac{x^2}{1.00 - x} \approx \frac{x^2}{1.00}, \quad x = [H^+] = 4.24 \times 10^{-3} \, M \text{ (using one extra sig fig)}$$

$pH = -\log (4.24 \times 10^{-3}) = 2.37$ Assumptions good.

We want to double the pH to $2(2.37) = 4.74$ by addition of the strong base NaOH. As is true with all strong bases, they are great at accepting protons. In fact, they are so good that we can assume strong bases accept protons 100% of the time. The best acid present will react with the strong base. This is $HC_2H_3O_2$. The initial reaction that occurs when strong base is added is:

$$HC_2H_3O_2 + OH^- \rightarrow C_2H_3O_2^- + OH^-$$

Note that this reaction has the net effect of converting $HC_2H_3O_2$ into its conjugate base, $C_2H_3O_2^-$.

For a pH = 4.74, let's calculate the ratio of $[C_2H_3O_2^-] / HC_2H_3O_2]$ necessary to achieve this pH.

$$HC_2H_3O_2 \rightleftharpoons H^+ + C_2H_3O_2^- \quad K_a = \frac{[H^+][C_2H_3O_2^-]}{[HC_2H_3O_2]}$$

When pH = 4.74, $[H^+] = 10^{-4.74} = 1.8 \times 10^{-5}$.

$$K_a = 1.8 \times 10^{-5} = \frac{1.8 \times 10^{-5}[C_2H_3O_2^-]}{[HC_2H_3O_2]}, \quad \frac{[C_2H_3O_2^-]}{[HC_2H_3O_2]} = 1.0$$

So for a solution having pH = 4.74, we need to have equal concentrations (equal moles) of $C_2H_3O_2^-$ and $HC_2H_3O_2$. Therefore, we need to add an amount of NaOH that will convert one-half of the $HC_2H_3O_2$ into $C_2H_3O_2^-$. This amount is 0.50 M NaOH.

$$HC_2H_3O_2 \;+\; OH^- \;\rightarrow\; C_2H_3O_2^- \;+\; H_2O$$

Initial	1.00 M	0.50 M	0
Change	−0.50	−0.50	+0.50
After	0.50 M	0	0.50 M
completion			

From the above stoichiometry problem, adding enough NaOH(s) to produce a 0.50 M OH^- solution will convert one-half of the $HC_2H_3O_2$ into $C_2H_3O_2^-$ resulting in a solution with pH = 4.74.

$$\text{mass NaOH} = 1.0 \text{ L} \times \frac{0.500 \text{ mol NaOH}}{\text{L}} \times \frac{40.00 \text{ g NaOH}}{\text{L}} = 20.0 \text{ g NaOH}$$

155. PO_4^{3-} is the conjugate base of HPO_4^{2-}. The K_a value for HPO_4^{2-} is $K_{a_3} = 4.8 \times 10^{-13}$.

$$PO_4^{3-}(aq) + H_2O(l) \rightleftharpoons HPO_4^{2-}(aq) + OH^-(aq) \quad K_b = \frac{K_w}{K_{a_3}} = \frac{1.0 \times 10^{-14}}{4.8 \times 10^{-13}} = 0.021$$

HPO_4^{2-} is the conjugate base of $H_2PO_4^-$ $(K_{a_2} = 6.2 \times 10^{-8})$.

$$HPO_4^{2-} + H_2O \rightleftharpoons H_2PO_4^- + OH^- \quad K_b = \frac{K_w}{K_{a_1}} = \frac{1.0 \times 10^{-14}}{6.2 \times 10^{-8}} = 1.6 \times 10^{-7}$$

$H_2PO_4^-$ is the conjugate base of H_3PO_4 $(K_{a_1} = 7.5 \times 10^{-3})$.

$$H_2PO_4^- + H_2O \rightleftharpoons H_3PO_4 + OH^- \quad K_b = \frac{K_w}{K_{a_1}} = \frac{1.0 \times 10^{-14}}{7.5 \times 10^{-3}} = 1.3 \times 10^{-12}$$

From the K_b values, PO_4^{3-} is the strongest base. This is expected because PO_4^{3-} is the conjugate base of the weakest acid (HPO_4^{2-}).

156.   Major species: Na^+, PO_4^{3-} (a weak base), H_2O; From the K_b values calculated in Exercise 14.155, the dominant producer of OH^- is the K_b reaction for PO_4^{3-}. We can ignore the contribution of OH^- from the K_b reactions for HPO_4^{2-} and $H_2PO_4^-$. From Exercise 14.155, K_b for PO_4^{3-} = 0.021.

$$PO_4^{3-} + H_2O \rightleftharpoons HPO_4^{2-} + OH^- \qquad K_b = 0.021$$

	PO_4^{3-}		HPO_4^{2-}	OH^-
Initial	0.10 M		0	~0
Equil.	0.10 − x		x	x

$K_b = 0.021 = \dfrac{x^2}{0.10 - x}$; Because K_b is so large, the 5% assumption will not hold. Solving using

the quadratic equation:

$$x^2 + 0.021\,x - 0.0021 = 0, \quad x = [OH^-] = 3.7 \times 10^{-2}\,M, \quad pOH = 1.43, \quad pH = 12.57$$

157. a. $NH_4(HCO_3) \rightarrow NH_4^+ + HCO_3^-$

K_a for $NH_4^+ = \dfrac{1.0 \times 10^{-14}}{1.8 \times 10^{-5}} = 5.6 \times 10^{-10}$; K_b for $HCO_3^- = \dfrac{K_w}{K_{a_1}} = \dfrac{1.0 \times 10^{-14}}{4.3 \times 10^{-7}} = 2.3 \times 10^{-8}$

Solution is basic because HCO_3^- is a stronger base than NH_4^+ is as an acid. The acidic properties of HCO_3^- were ignored because K_{a_2} is very small (5.6×10^{-11}).

b. $NaH_2PO_4 \rightarrow Na^+ + H_2PO_4^-$; Ignore Na^+.

K_{a_2} for $H_2PO_4^- = 6.2 \times 10^{-8}$; K_b for $H_2PO_4^- = \dfrac{K_w}{K_{a_1}} = \dfrac{1.0 \times 10^{-14}}{7.5 \times 10^{-3}} = 1.3 \times 10^{-12}$

Solution is acidic because $K_a > K_b$.

c. $Na_2HPO_4 \rightarrow 2\,Na^+ + HPO_4^{2-}$; Ignore Na^+.

K_{a_3} for $HPO_4^{2-} = 4.8 \times 10^{-13}$; K_b for $HPO_4^{2-} = \dfrac{K_w}{K_{a_2}} = \dfrac{1.0 \times 10^{-14}}{6.2 \times 10^{-8}} = 1.6 \times 10^{-7}$

Solution is basic because $K_b > K_a$.

d. $NH_4(H_2PO_4) \rightarrow NH_4^+ + H_2PO_4^-$

NH_4^+ is weak acid and $H_2PO_4^-$ is also acidic (see b). Solution with both ions present will be acidic.

e. $NH_4(HCO_2) \rightarrow NH_4^+ + HCO_2^-$; From Appendix 5, K_a for $HCO_2H = 1.8 \times 10^{-4}$.

K_a for $NH_4^+ = 5.6 \times 10^{-10}$; K_b for $HCO_2^- = \dfrac{K_w}{K_a} = \dfrac{1.0 \times 10^{-14}}{1.8 \times 10^{-4}} = 5.6 \times 10^{-11}$

Solution is acidic because NH_4^+ is a stronger acid than HCO_2^- is as a base.

158.   a. $HCO_3^- + HCO_3^- \rightleftharpoons H_2CO_3 + CO_3^{2-}$

$$K_{eq} = \frac{[H_2CO_3][CO_3^{2-}]}{[HCO_3^-][HCO_3^-]} \times \frac{[H^+]}{[H^+]} = \frac{K_{a_2}}{K_{a_1}} = \frac{5.6 \times 10^{-11}}{4.3 \times 10^{-7}} = 1.3 \times 10^{-4}$$

b. $[H_2CO_3] = [CO_3^{2-}]$ since the reaction in part a is the principle equilibrium reaction.

c. $H_2CO_3 \rightleftharpoons 2\,H^+ + CO_3^{2-}$ $K_{eq} = \dfrac{[H^+]^2[CO_3^{2-}]}{[H_2CO_3]} = K_{a_1} \times K_{a_2}$

Because, $[H_2CO_3] = [CO_3^{2-}]$ from part b, $[H^+]^2 = K_{a_1} \times K_{a_2}$.

$[H^+] = (K_{a_1} \times K_{a_2})^{1/2}$ or $pH = \dfrac{pK_{a_1} + pK_{a_2}}{2}$

d. $[H^+] = [(4.3 \times 10^{-7}) \times (5.6 \times 10^{-11})]^{1/2}$, $[H^+] = 4.9 \times 10^{-9}\,M$; $pH = 8.31$

159.   Molality $= m = \dfrac{0.100\,g \times \dfrac{1\,mol}{100.0\,g}}{0.5000\,kg} = 2.00 \times 10^{-3}\,mol/kg \approx 2.00 \times mol/L$ (dilute solution)

$\Delta T_f = iK_f m$, $0.0056°C = i(1.86°C/molal)(2.00 \times 10^{-3}\,molal)$, $i = 1.5$

If $i = 1.0$, the percent dissociation of the acid $= 0\%$ and if $i = 2.0$, the percent dissociation of the acid $= 100\%$. Since $i = 1.5$, the weak acid is 50.% dissociated.

$$HA \rightleftharpoons H^+ + A^- \qquad K_a = \frac{[H^+][A^-]}{[HA]}$$

Because the weak acid is 50.% dissociated:

$[H^+] = [A^-] = [HA]_o \times 0.50 = 2.00 \times 10^{-3}\,M \times 0.50 = 1.0 \times 10^{-3}\,M$

$[HA] = [HA]_o -$ amount HA reacted $= 2.00 \times 10^{-3}\,M - 1.0 \times 10^{-3}\,M = 1.0 \times 10^{-3}\,M$

$$K_a = \frac{[H^+][A^-]}{[HA]} = \frac{(1.0 \times 10^{-3})(1.0 \times 10^{-3})}{1.0 \times 10^{-3}} = 1.0 \times 10^{-3}$$

160.   a.   Assuming no ion association between SO_4^{2-} (aq) and Fe^{3+}(aq), then $i = 5$ for $Fe_2(SO_4)_3$.

$\pi = iMRT = 5(0.0500\,mol/L)(0.08206\,L\,atm/K \cdot mol)(298\,K) = 6.11\,atm$

b. $Fe_2(SO_4)_3(aq) \rightarrow 2\,Fe^{3+}(aq) + 3\,SO_4^{2-}(aq)$

Under ideal circumstances, 2/5 of π calculated above results from Fe^{3+} and 3/5 results from SO_4^{2-}. The contribution to π from SO_4^{2-} is $3/5 \times 6.11$ atm = 3.67 atm. Because SO_4^{2-} is assumed unchanged in solution, the SO_4^{2-} contribution in the actual solution will also be 3.67 atm. The contribution to the actual osmotic pressure from the $Fe(H_2O)_6^{3+}$ dissociation reaction is $6.73 - 3.67 = 3.06$ atm.

The initial concentration of $Fe(H_2O)_6^{2+}$ is $2(0.0500) = 0.100$ M. The set-up for the weak acid problem is:

$$Fe(H_2O)_6^{3+} \rightleftharpoons H^+ + Fe(OH)(H_2O)_5^{2+} \qquad K_a = \frac{[H^+][Fe(OH)(H_2O)_5^{2+}]}{[Fe(H_2O)_6^{3+}]}$$

Initial   0.100 M ~0   0
          x mol/L of $Fe(H_2O)_6^{3+}$ reacts to reach equilibrium
Equil.   0.100 − x x x

$$\pi = iMRT; \text{ Total ion concentration} = iM = \frac{\pi}{RT} = \frac{3.06 \text{ atm}}{0.8206 \text{ L atm/ K} \bullet \text{mol} (298)} = 0.125 \ M$$

$$0.125 \ M = 0.100 - x + x + x = 0.100 + x, \ x = 0.025 \ M$$

$$K_a = \frac{[H^+][Fe(OH)(H_2O)_5^{2+}]}{[Fe(H_2O)_6^{3+}]} = \frac{x^2}{0.100 - x} = \frac{(0.025)^2}{(0.100 - 0.025)} = \frac{(0.025)^2}{0.075}, \ K_a = 8.3 \times 10^{-3}$$

Integrative Problems

161. $$[IO^-] = \frac{2.14 \text{ g NaIO} \times \dfrac{1 \text{ mol NaIO}}{165.89 \text{ g}} \times \dfrac{1 \text{ mol IO}^-}{\text{mol NaIO}}}{1.25 \text{ L}} = 1.03 \times 10^{-2} \ M \ IO^-$$

$$IO^- + H_2O \rightleftharpoons HIO + OH^- \qquad K_b = \frac{[HIO][OH^-]}{[IO^-]}$$

Initial $1.03 \times 10^{-2} M$ 0   ~0
Equil. $1.03 \times 10^{-2} - x$ x x

$$K_b = \frac{x^2}{1.03 \times 10^{-2} - x}; \text{ From the problem, pOH} = 14.00 - 11.32 = 2.68$$

$$[OH^-] = 10^{-2.68} = 2.1 \times 10^{-3} M = x; \quad K_b = \frac{(2.1 \times 10^{-3})^2}{1.03 \times 10^{-2} - 2.1 \times 10^{-3}} = 5.4 \times 10^{-4}$$

162. $$10.0 \text{ g NaOCN} \times \frac{1 \text{ mol}}{65.01 \text{ g}} = 0.154 \text{ mol NaOCN}$$

$$10.0 \text{ g H}_2\text{C}_2\text{O}_4 \times \frac{1 \text{ mol}}{90.04 \text{ g}} = 0.111 \text{ mol H}_2\text{C}_2\text{O}_4$$

$$\frac{\text{mol NaOCN}}{\text{mol H}_2\text{SO}_4}\text{ (actual)} = \frac{0.154 \text{ mol}}{0.111 \text{ mol}} = 1.39$$

The balanced reaction requires a larger 2:1 mole ratio. Therefore, NaOCN in the numerator is limiting. Since there is a 2:2 mol correspondence between mole NaOCN reacted and mole HNCO produced, 0.154 mol of HNCO will be produced.

$$\text{HNCO} \rightleftharpoons \text{H}^+ + \text{NCO}^- \qquad K_a = 1.2 \times 10^{-4}$$

Initial	0.154 mol/0.100 L	~0	0
Equil.	1.54 − x	x	x

$$K_a = 1.2 \times 10^{-4} = \frac{x^2}{1.54 - x} \approx \frac{x^2}{1.54}, \quad x = [\text{H}^+] = 1.4 \times 10^{-2} \, M$$

$$\text{pH} = -\log(1.4 \times 10^{-2}) = 1.85; \quad \text{Assumptions good.}$$

163. $$\frac{30.0 \text{ mg papH}^+\text{Cl}^-}{\text{mL soln}} \times \frac{1000 \text{ mL}}{\text{L}} \times \frac{1 \text{ g}}{1000 \text{ mg}} \times \frac{1 \text{ mol papH}^+\text{Cl}^-}{378.85 \text{ g}} \times \frac{1 \text{ mol papH}^+}{\text{mol papH}^+\text{Cl}^-} = 0.0792 \, M$$

$$\text{papH}^+ \rightleftharpoons \text{pap} + \text{H}^+ \qquad K_a = \frac{K_w}{K_{b,\text{pap}}} = \frac{2.1 \times 10^{-14}}{8.33 \times 10^{-9}} = 2.5 \times 10^{-6}$$

Initial	0.0792 M	0	~0
Equil.	0.0792 − x	x	x

$$K_a = 2.5 \times 10^{-6} = \frac{x^2}{0.0792 - x} \approx \frac{x^2}{0.0792}, \quad x = [\text{H}^+] = 4.4 \times 10^{-4} \, M$$

$$\text{pH} = -\log(4.4 \times 10^{-4}) = 3.36; \quad \text{Assumptions good.}$$

Marathon Problems

164. To determine the pH of solution A, the K_a value for HX must be determined. Use solution B to determine K_b for X^-, which can then be used to calculate K_a for HX ($K_a = K_w/K_b$).

Solution B:

$$X^- + H_2O \rightleftharpoons HX + OH^- \qquad K_b = \frac{[HX][OH^-]}{[X^-]}$$

Initial	0.0500 M	0	~0
Change	−x →	+x	+x
Equil.	0.0500 − x	x	x

$K_b = \dfrac{x^2}{0.0500 - x}$;   From the problem, pH = 10.02, so pOH = 3.98 and $[OH^-] = x = 10^{-3.98}$

$K_b = \dfrac{(10^{-3.98})^2}{0.0500 - 10^{-3.98}} = 2.2 \times 10^{-7}$

Solution A:

$H_{a,HX} = K_w / K_{b,X^-} = 1.0 \times 10^{-14} / 2.2 \times 10^{-7} = 4.5 \times 10^{-8}$

$$HX \quad \rightleftharpoons \quad H^+ \quad + \quad X^- \qquad K_a = 4.5 \times 10^{-8} = \dfrac{[H^+][X^-]}{[HX]}$$

	HX		H^+	X^-
Initial	0.100 M		~0	0
Change	$-x$	$\rightarrow$	$+x$	$+x$
Equil.	0.100 $- x$		x	x

$K_a = 4.5 \times 10^{-8} = \dfrac{x^2}{0.100 - x} \approx \dfrac{x^2}{0.100}$, $x = [H^+] = 6.7 \times 10^{-5}\,M$

Assumptions good (x is 6.7×10^{-2} % of 0.100);   pH = 4.17

Solution C:

Major species: HX ($K_a = 4.5 \times 10^{-8}$), Na^+, OH^-; The OH^- from the strong base is exceptional at accepting protons. OH^- will react with the best acid present (HX) and we can assume that OH^- will react to completion with HX, i.e., until one (or both) of the reactants runs out. Since we have added one volume of substance to another, we have diluted both solutions from their initial concentrations. What hasn't changed is the moles of each reactant. So let's work with moles of each reactant initially.

mol HX = 0.0500 L $\times \dfrac{0.100 \text{ mol HX}}{L} = 5.00 \times 10^{-3}$ mol HX

mol OH^- = 0.0150 L $\times \dfrac{0.250 \text{ mol NaOH}}{L} \times \dfrac{1 \text{ mol } OH^-}{\text{mol NaOH}} = 3.75 \times 10^{-3}$ mol OH^-

Now let's determine what is remaining in solution after OH^- reacts completely with HX. Note that OH^- is the limiting reagent.

	HX	+	OH^-	$\rightarrow$	X^-	+	H_2O
Initial	5.00×10^{-3} mol		3.75×10^{-3} mol		0		–
Change	-3.75×10^{-3}		-3.75×10^{-3}	$\rightarrow$	$+3.75 \times 10^{-3}$		$+3.75 \times 10^{-3}$
After completion	1.25×10^{-3} mol		0		3.75×10^{-3} mol		–

After reaction, the solution contains HX, X^-, Na^+ and H_2O. The Na^+ (like most +1 metal ions) has no effect on the pH of water. However, HX is a weak acid and its conjugate base, X^-, is a weak base. Since both K_a and K_b reactions refer to these species, we could use either reaction to solve for the pH; we will use the K_b reaction. To solve the equilibrium problem using the K_b reaction, we need to convert to concentration units since K_b is in concentration units of mol/L.

$$[HX] = \frac{1.25 \times 10^{-3} \text{ mol}}{(0.0500 + 0.0150) \text{ L}} = 0.0192 \; M; \quad [X^-] = \frac{3.75 \times 10^{-3} \text{ mol}}{0.0650 \text{ L}} = 0.0577 \; M$$

$[OH^-] = 0$ (We reacted all of it to completion.)

$$X^- \quad + \quad H_2O \quad \rightleftharpoons \quad HX \quad + \quad OH^- \qquad K_b = 2.2 \times 10^{-7}$$

Initial	0.0577 M		0.0192 M	0
	x mol/L of X^- reacts to reach equilibrium			
Change	$-x$	$\rightarrow$	$+x$	$+x$
Equil.	$0.0577 - x$		$0.0192 + x$	x

$$K_b = 2.2 \times 10^{-7} = \frac{(0.0192 + x)(x)}{(0.0577 - x)} \approx \frac{(0.0192) \, x}{(0.0577)} \quad \text{(assuming } x \text{ is} \ll 0.0192)$$

$$x = [OH^-] = \frac{2.2 \times 10^{-7} \, (0.0577)}{0.0192} = 6.6 \times 10^{-7} \; M \quad \text{Assumptions great (} x \text{ is } 3.4 \times 10^{-3} \text{ \% of } 0.0192).$$

$[OH^-] = 6.6 \times 10^{-7} \; M$, pOH = 6.18, pH = 14.00 − 6.18 = 7.82 = pH of solution C

The combination is 4−17−7−82.

165.   a.   Strongest acid from group I = HCl;   Weakest base from group II = $NaNO_2$

0.20 M HCl + 0.20 M $NaNO_2$; Major species = H^+, Cl^-, Na^+, NO_2^-, H_2O; Let the added protons from H^+ react completely with the best base present, NO_2^-. Since strong acids are great at what they do (donate protons), assume the H^+ reacts to completion.

$$H^+ \quad + \quad NO_2^- \quad \rightarrow \quad HNO_2$$

Initial	0.10 M	0.10 M	0	(Molarities are halved due to dilution.)
After	0	0	0.10 M	

$$HNO_2 \quad \rightleftharpoons \quad H^+ \quad + \quad NO_2^-$$

Initial	0.10 M	0	0
Change	$-x$	$+x$	$+x$
Equil.	$0.10 - x$	x	x

$$\frac{x^2}{0.10-x} = 4.0 \times 10^{-4}; \quad \text{Solving: } x = [H^+] = 6.3 \times 10^{-3} M, \text{ pH} = 2.20$$

b. Weakest acid from group I $= (C_2H_5)_3NHCl$; Best base from group II $=$ KOI

$$OI^- + (C_2H_5)_3NH^+ \rightleftharpoons HOI + (C_2H_5)_3N$$

Initial	0.10 M	0.10 M	0	0
Equil.	0.10 − x	0.10 − x	x	x

$$K = \frac{K_a \text{ for } (C_2H_5)_3NH^+}{K_a \text{ for HOI}} = \frac{1.0 \times 10^{-14}}{4.0 \times 10^{-4}} \times \frac{1}{2 \times 10^{-11}} = 1.25 \text{ (carrying extra sig fig)}$$

$$\frac{x^2}{(0.10-x)^2} = 1.25, \quad \frac{x}{0.10-x} = 1.12, \quad x = 0.053; \quad [HOI] = 0.053 \ M \text{ and } [OI^-] = 0.047 \ M$$

(extra sig fig)

$$HOI \rightleftharpoons H^+ + OI^- \quad K_a = 2 \times 10^{-11}; \text{ Solve for } H^+ \text{ and pH:}$$

$$2 \times 10^{-11} = \frac{[H^+](0.047 \ M)}{(0.053 \ M)}, \quad [H^+] = 2.3 \times 10^{-11} \ M, \text{ pH} = 10.64 = 10.6$$

c. K_a for $(C_2H_5)_3NH^+ = \dfrac{1.0 \times 10^{-14}}{4.0 \times 10^{-4}} = 2.5 \times 10^{-11}$; K_b for $NO_2^- = \dfrac{1.0 \times 10^{-14}}{4.0 \times 10^{-4}} = 2.5 \times 10^{-11}$

Because $K_a = K_b$, mixing $(C_2H_5)_3NHCl$ with $NaNO_2$ will result in a solution with pH = 7.00. We suggest you prove it by doing a calculation similar to that done in part b.

CHAPTER FIFTEEN

APPLICATIONS OF AQUEOUS EQUILIBRIA

For Review

1. A common ion is an ion that appears in an equilibrium reaction but came from a source other than that reaction. Addition of a common ion (H^+ or NO_2^-) to the reaction $HNO_2 \rightleftharpoons H^+ + NO_2^-$ will drive the equilibrium to the left as predicted by LeChatelier's principle.

    When a weak acid solution has some of the conjugate base added from an outside source, this solution is called a buffer. Similarly, a weak base solution with its conjugate acid added from an outside source would also be classified as a buffer.

2. A buffer solution is one that resists a change in its pH when either hydroxide ions or protons (H^+) are added. Any solution that contains a weak acid and its conjugate base or a weak base and its conjugate acid is classified as a buffer. The pH of a buffer depends on the [base]/[acid] ratio. When H^+ is added to a buffer, the weak base component of the buffer reacts with the H^+ and forms the acid component of the buffer. Even though the concentrations of the acid and base component of the buffer change some, the ratio of [base]/[acid] does not change that much. This translates into a pH that doesn't change much. When OH^- is added to a buffer, the weak acid component is converted into the base component of the buffer. Again, the [base]/[acid] does not change a lot (unless a large quantity of OH^- is added), so the pH does not change much.

    The concentrations of weak acid and weak base do not have to be equal in a buffer. As long as there are both a weak acid and a weak base present, the solution will be buffered. If the concentrations are the same, the buffer will have the same capacity towards added H^+ and added OH^-. Also, buffers with equal concentrations of weak acid and conjugate base have $pH = pK_a$.

    Because both the weak acid and conjugate base are major spelcies present, both equilibriums that refer to these species must hold true. That is, the K_a equilibrium must hold because the weak acid is present, and the K_b equilibrium for the conjugate base must hold true because the conjugate base is a major species. Both the K_a and K_b equilibrium have the acid and conjugate base concentrations in their expressions. The same equilibrium concentrations of the acid and conjugate base must satisfy both equilibriums. In addition, the [H^+] and [OH^-] concentrations must be related through the K_w constant. This leads to the same pH answer whether the K_a or K_b equilibrium is used.

    The third method to solve a buffer problem is to use the Henderson-Hasselbalch equation. The equation is:

    $$pH = pK_a + \log\frac{[\text{base}]}{[\text{acid}]}$$

where the base is the conjugate base of the weak acid present or the acid is the conjugate acid of the weak base present. The equation takes into account the normal assumptions made for buffers. Specifically, it is assumed that the initial concentration of the acid and base component of the buffer equal the equilibrium concentrations. For any decent buffer, this will always hold true.

3. Whenever strong acid is added to a solution, always react the H^+ from the strong acid with the best base present in solution. The best base has the largest K_b value. For a buffer, this will be the conjugate base (A^-) of the acid component of the buffer. The H^+ reacts with the conjugate base, A^-, to produce the acid, HA. The assumption for this reaction is that because strong acids are great at what they do, they are assumed to donate the proton to the conjugate base 100% of the time. That is, the reaction is assumed to go to completion. Completion is when a reaction goes until one or both of the reactants runs out. This reaction is assumed to be a stoichiometry problem like those we solved in Chapter 3.

Whenever a strong base is added to a buffer, the OH^- ions react with the best acid present. This reaction is also assumed to go to completion. In a buffer, the best acid present is the acid component of the buffer (HA). The OH^- rips a proton away from the acid to produce the conjugate base of the acid (A^-) and H_2O. Again, we know strong bases are great at accepting protons, so we assume this reaction goes to completion. It is assumed to be a stoichiometry problem like the ones we solved in Chapter 3.

When [HA] = [A^-] (or [BH^+] = [B]) for a buffer, the pH of the solution is equal to the pK_a value for the acid component of the buffer (pH = pK_a because [H^+] = K_a). A best buffer has equal concentrations of the acid and base component so it is equally efficient at absorbing H^+ or OH^-. For a pH = 4.00 buffer, we would choose the acid component having a K_a close to $10^{-4.00} = 1.0 \times 10^{-4}$ (pH = pK_a for a best buffer). For a pH = 10.00 buffer, we would want the acid component of the buffer to have a K_a close to $10^{-10.00} = 1.0 \times 10^{-10}$. Of course, we can have a buffer solution made from a weak base and its conjugate acid. For a pH = 10.00 buffer, our conjugate acid should have $K_a \approx 1.0 \times 10^{-10}$ which translates into a K_b value of the base close to 1.0×10^{-4} ($K_b = K_w/K_a$ for conjugate acid-base pairs).

The capacity of a buffer is a measure of how much strong acid or strong base the buffer can neutralize. All the buffers listed have the same pH (= pK_a = 4.74) because they all have a 1:1 concentration ratio between the weak acid and the conjugate base. The 1.0 M buffer has the greatest capacity; the 0.01 M buffer the least capacity. In general, the larger the concentrations of weak acid and conjugate base, the greater the buffer capacity, i.e., the more strong acid or strong base that can be neutralized with little pH change.

4. Let's review the strong acid-strong base titration using the example (case study) covered in section 15.4 of the text. The example used was the titration of 50.0 mL of 0.200 M HNO_3 titrated by 0.100 M NaOH. See Figure 15.1 for the titration curve. The important points are:

a. Initially, before any strong base has been added. Major species: H^+, NO_3^-, and H_2O. To determine the pH, determine the [H^+] in solution after the strong acid has completely dissociated as we always do for strong acid problems.

b. After some strong base has been added, up to the equilivance point. For our example, this is from just after 0.00 mL NaOH added up to just before 100.0 mL NaOH added. Major species before any reaction: H^+, NO_3^-, Na^+, OH^-, and H_2O. Na^+ and NO_3^- have no acidic or basic properties. In this region, the OH^- from the strong base reacts with some of the H^+ from the strong acid to produce water ($H^+ + OH^- \rightarrow H_2O$). As is always the case when something strong reacts, we assume the reaction goes to completion. Major species after reaction: H^+, NO_3^-, Na^+, and H_2O: To determine the pH of the solution, we first determine how much of the H^+ is neutralized by the OH^-. Then we determine the excess $[H^+]$ and take the –log of this quantity to determine pH. From 0.1 mL to 99.9 mL NaOH added, the excess H^+ from the strong acid determines the pH.

c. The equivalence point (100.0 mL NaOH added). Major species before reaction: H^+, NO_3^-, Na^+, OH^-, and H_2O. Here, we have added just enough OH^- to neutralize all of the H^+ from the strong acid (moles OH^- added = moles H^+ present). After the stoichiometry reaction ($H^+ + OH^- \rightarrow H_2O$), both H^+ and OH^- have run out (this is the definition of the equivalence point). Major species after reaction: Na^+, NO_3^-, and H_2O. All we have in solution are some ions with no acidic or basic properties (NO_3^- and Na^+ in H_2O). The pH = 7.00 at the equivalence point of a strong acid by a strong base.

d. Past the equivalence point (volume of NaOH added > 100.0 mL). Major species before reaction H^+, NO_3^-, Na^+, OH^-, and H_2O. After the stoichiometry reaction goes to completion ($H^+ + OH^- \rightarrow H_2O$), we have excess OH^- present. Major species after reaction: OH^-, Na^+, NO_3^-, and H_2O. We determine the excess $[OH^-]$ and convert this into the pH. After the equivalence point, the excess OH^- from the strong base determines the pH.

See Figure 15.2 for a titration curve of a strong base by a strong acid. The stoichiometry problem is still the same, $H^+ + OH^- \rightarrow H_2O$, but what is in excess after this reaction goes to completion is reverse of the strong acid-strong base titration. The pH up to just before the equivalence point is determined by the excess OH^- present. At the equivalence point, pH = 7.00 because we have added just enough H^+ from the strong acid to react with all of the OH^- from the strong base (mole base present = mole acid added). Past the equivalence point, the pH is determined by the excess H^+ present. As can be seen from Figures 15.1 and 15.2, both strong by strong titrations have pH = 7.00 at the equivalence point, but the curves are the reverse of each other before and after the equivalence point.

5. In section 15.4, the case study for the weak acid-strong base titration is the titration of 50.0 mL of 0.10 M $HC_2H_3O_2$ by 0.10 M NaOH. See Figure 15.3 for the titration curve.

As soon as some NaOH has been added to the weak acid, OH^- reacts with the best acid present. This is the weak acid titrated ($HC_2H_3O_2$ in our problem). The reaction is: $OH^- + HC_2H_3O_2 \rightarrow H_2O + C_2H_3O_2^-$. Because something strong is reacting, we assume the reaction goes to completion. This is the stoichiometry part of a titration problem. To solve for the pH, we see what is in solution after the stoichiometry problem and decide how to proceed. The various parts to the titration are:

a. Initially, before any OH^- has been added. The major species present is the weak acid, $HC_2H_3O_2$, and water. We would use the K_a reaction for the weak acid and solve the equilibrium problem to determine the pH.

b. Just past the start of the titration up to just before the equivalence point (0.1 mL to 49.9 mL NaOH added). In this region, the major species present after the OH^- reacts to completion are $HC_2H_3O_2$, $C_2H_3O_2^-$, Na^+, and water. We have a buffer solution because both a weak acid and a conjugate base are present. We can solve the equilibrium buffer problem using the K_a reaction for $HC_2H_3O_2$, the K_b reaction for $C_2H_3O_2^-$, or the Henderson-Hasselbalch equation. A special point in the buffer region is the halfway point to equivalence. At this point (25.0 mL of NaOH added), exactly one-half of the weak acid has been converted into its conjugate base. At this point, we have [weak acid] = [conjugate base] so that pH = pK_a. For the $HC_2H_3O_2$ titration, the pH at 25.0 mL NaOH added is $-\log (1.8 \times 10^{-5}) = 4.74$; the pH is acidic at the halfway point to equivalence. However, other weak acid-strong base titrations could have basic pH values at the halfway point. This just indicates that the weak acid has $K_a < 1 \times 10^{-7}$, which is fine.

c. The equivalence point (50.0 mL NaOH added). Here we have added just enough OH^- to convert all of the weak acid into its conjugate base. In our example, the major species present are $C_2H_3O_2^-$, Na^+, and H_2O. Because the conjugate base of a weak acid is a weak base, we will have a basic pH (pH > 7.0) at the equivalence point. To calculate the pH, we write out the K_b reaction for the conjugate base and then set-up and solve the equilibrium problem. For our example, we would write out the K_b reaction for $C_2H_3O_2^-$.

d. Past the equivalence point (V > 50.0 mL). Here we added an excess of OH^-. After the stoichiometry part of the problem, the major species are OH^-, $C_2H_3O_2^-$, H_2O, and Na^+. We have two bases present, the excess OH^- and the weak conjugate base. The excess OH^- dominates the solution and thus determines the pH. We can ignore the OH^- contribution from the weak conjugate base.

See the titration curve after Figure 15.3 that compares and contrasts strong acid-strong base titrations to weak acid-strong base titration. The two curves have the same pH only after the equivalence point where the excess strong base added determines the pH. The strong acid titration is acidic at every point before the equivalence point, has a pH = 7.0 at the equivalence point, and is basic at every point after the equivalence point. The weak acid titration is much more complicated because we cannot ignore the basic properties of the conjugate base of the weak acid; we could ingore the conjugate base in the strong acid titration because it had no basic properties. In the weak acid titration, we start off acidic (pH < 7.0), but where it goes from there depends on the strength of the weak acid titrated. At the halfway point where pH = pK_a, the pH may be acidic or basic depending on the K_a value of the weak acid. At the equivalence, the pH must be basic. This is due to the presence of the weak conjugate base. Past the equivalence point, the strong acid and weak acid titrations both have their pH determined by the excess OH^- added.

6. The case study of a weak base-strong acid titration in section 15.4 is the titration of 100.0 mL of 0.050 M NH_3 by 0.10 M HCl. The titration curve is in Figure 15.5.

As HCl is added, the H^+ from the strong acid reacts with the best base present, NH_3. Because something strong is reacted, we assume the reaction goes to completion. The reaction used for the stoichiometry part of the problem is: $H^+ + NH_3 \rightarrow NH_4^+$. Note that the effect of this reaction is to convert the weak base into its conjugate acid. The various parts to a weak base-strong acid titration are:

a.   Initially before any strong acid is added. We have a weak base in water. Write out the K_b reaction for the weak base, set-up the ICE table, and then solve.

b.   From 0.1 mL HCl added to just gefore the equivalence point (49.9 mL HCl added). The major species present in this region are NH_3, NH_4^+, Cl^-, and water. We have a weak base and its conjugate acid present at the same time; we have a buffer. Solve the buffer problem using the K_a reaction for NH_4^+, the K_b reaction for NH_3, or the Henderson-Hasselbalch equation. The special point in the buffer region of the titration is the halfway point to equivalence. Here, $[NH_3] = [NH_4^+]$, so $pH = pK_a = -\log(5.6 \times 10^{-10}) = 9.25$. For this titration, the pH is basic at the halfway point. However, if the K_a for the weak acid component of the buffer has a $K_a > 1 \times 10^{-7}$, (K_b for the base $< 1 \times 10^{-7}$) then the pH will be acidic at the halfway point. This is fine. In this review question, it is asked what is the K_b value for the weak base where the halfway point to equivalence has $pH = 6.0$ (which is acidic). Be-cause $pH = pK_a$ at this point, $pK_a = 6.0$ so $pK_b = 14.00 - 6.0 = 8.0$; $K_b = 10^{-8.0} = 1.0 \times 10^{-8}$.

c.   The equivalence point (50.0 mL HCl added). Here, just enough H^+ has been added to convert all of the NH_3 into NH_4^+. The major species present are NH_4^+, Cl^- and H_2O. The only important species present is NH_4^+, a weak acid. This is always the case in a weak base-strong acid titration. Because a weak acid is always present at the equivalence point, the pH is always acidic ($pH < 7.0$). To solve for the pH, write down the K_a reaction for the conjugate acid and then determine K_a ($= K_w/K_b$). Fill in the ICE table for the problem, and then solve to determine pH.

d.   Past the equivalence point ($V > 50.0$ mL HCl added). The excess strong acid added determines the pH. The major species present for our example would be H^+ (excess), NH_4^+, Cl^-, and H_2O. We have two acids present, but NH_4^+ is a weak acid. Its H^+ contribution will be negligible compared to the excess H^+ added from the strong acid. The pH is determined by the molarity of the excess H^+.

Examine Figures 15.2 and 15.5 to compare and contrast a strong base-strong acid titration with a weak base-strong acid titration. The points in common are only after the equivalence point where excess strong acid determines the pH. The two titrations before and at the equivalence point are very different. This is because the conjugate acid of a weak base is a weak acid, whereas, when a strong base dissolves in water, only OH^- is important; the cation in the strong base is garbage (has no acidic/basic properties). There is no conjugate acid to worry about.

For a strong base-strong acid titration, the excess OH^- from the strong base determines the pH from the initial point all the way up to the equivaldnce point. At the equivalence point, the added H^+ has reacted with all of the OH^- and $pH = 7.0$. For a weak base-strong acid, we initially have a weak base problem to solve in order to calculate the pH. After H^+ has been added, some of the weak base is converted into its conjugate acid and we have buffer solutions to solve in order to calculate the pH. At the equivalence point, we have a weak acid problem to solve. Here, all of the weak base has been converted into its conjugate acid by the added H^+.

7.   An acid-base indicator marks the end point of a titration by changing color. Acid-base indicators are weak acids themselves. We abbreviate the acid form of an indicator as HIn and the conjugate base form as In^-. The reason there is a color change with indicators is that the HIn form has one color associated with it while the In^- form has a different color associated with it. Which form dominates in solution and dictates the color is determined by the pH of the solution. The related quilibrium is: $HIn \rightleftharpoons H^+ + In^-$. In a very acidic solution, there are lots of H^+ ions present which drives the indicator equilibrium to the left. The HIn form dominates and the color of the solution is the color due to the HIn form. In a very basic solution, H^+ has been removed from solution. This drives the indicator equilibrium to the right and the In^- form dominates. In very basic solutions, the solution takes on the color of the In^- form. In between very acidic and very basic solutions, there is a range of pH values where the solution has significant amounts of both the HIn and In^- forms present. This is where the color change occurs and we want this pH to be close to the stoichiometric point of the titration. The pH that the color change occurs is determined by the K_a of the indicator.

Equivalence point: when enough titrant has been added to react exactly with the substance in the solution being titrated. Endpoint: indicator changes color. We want the indicator to tell us when we have reached the equivalence point. We can detect the end point visually and assume it is the equivalence point for doing stoichiometric calculations. They don't have to be as close as 0.01 pH units since, at the equivalence point, the pH is changing very rapidly with added titrant. The range over which an indicator changes color only needs to be close to the pH of the equivalence point.

The two forms of an indicator are different colors. The HIn form has one color and the In^- form has another color. To see only one color, that form must be in an approximately ten-fold excess or greater over the other form. When the ratio of the two forms is less than 10, both colors are present. To go from $[HIn]/[In^-] = 10$ to $[HIn]/[In^-] = 0.1$ requires a change of 2 pH units (a 100-fold decrease in $[H^+]$) as the indicator changes from the HIn color to the In^- color.

From Figure 15.8, thymol blue has three colors associated with it: organge, yellow, and blue. In order for this to happen, thymol blue must be a diprotic acid. The H_2In form has the orange color, the HIn^- form has the yellow color, and the In^{2-} form has the blue color associated with it. Thymol blue cannot be monoprotic; monoprotic indicators only have two colors associated with them (either the HIn color or the In^- color).

8. K_{sp} refers to the equilibrium reaction where a salt (ionic compound) dissolves into its ions to form a saturated solution: For example, consider $Ca_3(PO_4)_2(s)$. The K_{sp} reaction and K_{sp} expression are:

$$Ca_3(PO_4)_2(s) \rightleftharpoons 3\,Ca^{2+}(aq) + 2\,PO_4^{3-}(aq) \qquad K_{sp} = [Ca^{2+}]^3[PO_4^{3-}]^2$$

K_{sp} is just an equilibrium constant (called the solubility product constant) that refers to a specific equilibrium reaction. That reaction is always a solid salt dissolving into its ions. Because the ionic compound is a solid, it is not included in the K_{sp} expression.

The solubility of a salt is the maximum amount of that salt that will dissolve per liter of solution. We determine solubility by solving a typical equilibrium problem using the K_{sp} reaction. We define our solubility (usually called s) as the maximum amount of the salt that will dissolve, then fill in our ICE table and solve. The two unknowns in the equilibrium problem are the K_{sp} value and the solubility. You are given one of the unknowns and asked to solve for the other. See Sample Exercises 15.12-14.14 for example calculations. In Sample Exercise 15.12 and 15.13, you are given the solubility of the salt and asked to calculate K_{sp} for the ionic compound. In Sample Exercise 15.14, you are given the K_{sp} value for a salt and asked to calculate the solubility. In both types of problem, set-up the ICE table in order to solve.

If the number of ions in the two salts is the same, the K_{sp}'s can be compared directly to determine relative solubilities, i.e., 1:1 electrolytes (1 cation:1 anion) can be compared to each other; 2:1 electrolyes can be compared to each other, etc. If the number of ions is the same, the salt with the largest K_{sp} value has the largest molar solubility. If the number of ions are different be-tween two salts, then you must actually calculate the solubility of each salt to see which is more or less soluble.

A common ion is when either the cation or anion of the salt in question is added from an outside source. For example, a common ion for the salt CaF_2 would be if F^- (or Ca^{2+}) was added to solution by dissolving NaF [or $Ca(NO_3)_2$]. When a common ion is present, not as much of the salt dissolves (as predicted by LeChatelier's Principle), so the solubility decreases. This decrease in solubility is called the common ion effect.

Salts whose anions have basic properties have their solubiities increase as the solution becomes more acidic. Some examples are CaF_2, $Ca_3(PO_4)_2$, $CaCO_3$, and $Fe(OH)_3$. In all of these cases, the anion has basic properties and reacts with H^+ in acidic solutions. This removes one of the ions from the equilibrium so more salt dissolves to repenish the ion concentrations (as predicted by LeChatelier's Principle). In our example, F^-, PO_4^{3-}, and CO_3^{2-} are all conjugate bases of weak acids so they are all weak bases. In $Fe(OH)_3$, OH^- is a strong base.

For salts with no pH solubility, the ions in the salt must not have any acidic or basic proper-ties. Examples of these salts have anions that are the conjugate bases of strong acids so they are worthless bases. Examples of these types of salts are $AgCl$, $PbBr_2$, and Hg_2I_2. The solubility of these salts do not depend on pH because Cl^-, Br^-, and I^- have no basic (or acidic) properties.

9.   Q and K_{sp} have the same expression; the difference is the type of concentrations used. K_{sp} always uses equilibrium concentrations for the ions. Q, however, uses initial concentrations of the ions given in a problem. The purpose of Q is to see if a reaction is at equilibrium. If Q = K_{sp}, then the salt is at equilibrium with ion concentrations given in the problem. If Q ≠ K_{sp}, then the reaction is not at equilibrium; these concentrations must change in order for the salt

to get to equilibrium with its ions. If $Q > K_{sp}$, the ion concentrations are too large. The K_{sp} reaction shifts left to reduce the ion concentrations and to eventually get to equilibrium. If $Q < K_{sp}$, the K_{sp} reaction shifts right to produce more ions in order to get to equilibrium.

Selective precipitation is a way to separate out ions in an aqueous mixture. One way this is done is to add a reagent that precipitates with only one of the ions in the mixture. That ion is removed by forming the prcipitate. Another way to selectively precipitate out some ions in a mixture is to choose a reagent that forms a precipitate with all of the ions in the mixture. The key is that each salt has a different solubility with the ion in common. We add the common ion slowly until a precipitate starts to form. The first precipitate to form will be the least soluble precipitate. After precipitation of the first is complete, we filter off the solution and continue adding more of the common ion until precipitation of the next least soluble salt is complete. This process is continued until all of the ions have been pricipitated out of solution.

For the 0.10 M Mg^{2+}, Ca^{2+}, and Ba^{2+}, adding F^- (NaF) slowly will separate the ions due to their solubility differences with these ions. The first compound to precipitate is the least soluble CaF_2 compound (it has the smallest K_{sp} value, 4.0×10^{-11}). After all of the CaF_2 has precipitated and been removed, we continue adding F^- until the second least soluble flouride has precipitated. This is MgF_2 with the intermediate K_{sp} value (6.4×10^{-9}). Finally, the only ion left in solution is Ba^{2+} which is precipitated out by adding more NaF. BaF_2 precipitates last because it is the most soluble fluoride salt in the mixture ($K_{sp} = 2.4 \times 10^{-5}$).

For the Ag^+, Pb^{2+}, Sr^{2+} mixture, because the phosphate salt of these ions do not all have the same number of ions, we cannot just compare K_{sp} values to deduce the order of precipitation. This would work for $Pb_3(PO_4)_2$, $K_{sp} = 1 \times 10^{-54}$ and $Sr_3(PO_4)_2$, $K_{sp} = 1 \times 10^{-31}$ because these contain the same number of ions (5). However, $Ag_3PO_4(s)$ only contains 4 ions per formula unit. We must calculate the $[PO_4^{3-}]$ necessary to start precipitation. We do this by setting $Q = K_{sp}$ and determining the $[PO_4^{3-}]$ necessary for this to happen. Any $[PO_4^{3-}]$ greater than this calculated concentration will cause $Q > K_{sp}$ and precipitation of the salt. A sample calculation is:

$$Sr_3(PO_4)_2 \;\rightleftharpoons\; 3\,Sr^{2+}(aq) + 2\,PO_4^{3-}(aq) \qquad K_{sp} = 1 \times 10^{-31}$$

$$Q = 1 \times 10^{-31} = [Sr^{2+}]^3[PO_4^{3-}]^2 = (1.0\,M)^3\,[PO_4^{3-}]^2, \;\; [PO_4^{3-}] = 3 \times 10^{-16}\,M$$

When the $[PO_4^{3-}] > 3 \times 10^{-16}\,M$, precipitation of $Sr_3(PO_4)_2$ will occur.

Doing similar calculations with the other two salts leads to the answers:

$Ag_3PO_4(s)$ will precipitate when $[PO_4^{3-}] > 1.8 \times 10^{-18}\,M$.

$Pb_3(PO_4)_2(s)$ will precipitate when $[PO_4^{3-}] > 1 \times 10^{-27}\,M$.

From the calculations, $Pb_3(PO_4)_2(s)$ needs the smallest $[PO_4^{3-}]$ to precipitate, so it precipitates first as we add K_3PO_4. The next salt to precipitate is $Ag_3PO_4(s)$, and $Sr_3(PO_4)_2(s)$ is last to precipitate because it requires the largest $[PO_4^{3-}]$.

10.   A complex ion is a charged species consisting of a metal ion surrounded by ligands. A ligand is a molecule or ion having a lone pair of electrons that can be donated to an empty orbital on the metal ion to form a covalent bond. A ligand is a Lewis base (electron pair donor).

$$Cu^{2+}(aq) + NH_3(aq) \rightleftharpoons Cu(NH_3)^{2+}(aq) \qquad K_1 \approx 1 \times 10^3$$

$$Cu(NH_3)^{2+}(aq) + NH_3(aq) \rightleftharpoons Cu(NH_3)_2{}^{2+}(aq) \qquad K_2 \approx 1 \times 10^4$$

$$Cu(NH_3)_2{}^{2+}(aq) + NH_3(aq) \rightleftharpoons Cu(NH_3)_3{}^{2+}(aq) \qquad K_3 \approx 1 \times 10^3$$

$$Cu(NH_3)_3{}^{2+}(aq) + NH_3(aq) \rightleftharpoons Cu(NH_3)_4{}^{2+}(aq) \qquad K_4 \approx 1 \times 10^3$$

Because the K values are much greater than one, all of these reactions lie far to the right (products are mostly present at equilibrium). So most of the Cu^{2+} in a solution of NH_3 will be converted into $Cu(NH_3)_4{}^{2+}$. Therefore, the $[Cu(NH_3)_4{}^{2+}]$ will be much larger than the $[Cu^{2+}]$ at equilibrium.

$$Cu(OH)_2(s) \rightleftharpoons Cu^{2+}(aq) + 2\,OH^-(aq)$$

As NH_3 is added, it removes Cu^{2+} from the above K_{sp} equilibrium for $Cu(OH)_2$. It removes Cu^{2+} by reacting with it to form $Cu(NH_3)_4{}^{2+}$ mostly. As Cu^{2+} is removed, more of the $Cu(OH)_2(s)$ will dissolve to replenish the Cu^{2+}. This process continues until equilibrium is reached or until all of the $Cu(OH)_2$ dissolves.

$$H^+(aq) + NH_3(aq) \rightarrow NH_4{}^+(aq)$$

The added H^+ from the strong acid reacts with the weak base NH_3 to form $NH_4{}^+$. As NH_3 is removed from solution, the complex ion equilibrium will shift left to produce more NH_3. This has the effect of also producing more Cu^{2+}. Eventually enough Cu^{2+} will be produced to react with OH^- to form $Cu(OH)_2(s)$.

The general effect of common ion formation is to increase the solubility of salts that contain cations which form common ions.

Questions

13.   When an acid dissociates or when a salt dissolves, ions are produced. A common ion effect is observed when one of the product ions in a particular equilibrium is added from an outside source. For a weak acid dissociating to its conjugate base and H^+, the common ion would be the conjugate base; this would be added by dissolving a soluble salt of the conjugate base into the acid solution. The presence of the conjugate base from an outside source shifts the equilibrium to the left so less acid dissociates. For the K_{sp} reaction of a salt dissolving into its respective ions, a common ion would be one of the ions in the salt added from an outside source. When a common ion is present, the K_{sp} equilibrium shifts to the left resulting in less of the salt dissolving into its ions.

14. $pH = pK_a + \log \dfrac{[base]}{[acid]}$; When [acid] > [base], then $\dfrac{[base]}{[acid]} < 1$ and $\log\left(\dfrac{[base]}{[acid]}\right) < 0$.

From the Henderson-Hasselbalch equation, if the log term is negative, then $pH < pK_a$. When one has more acid than base in a buffer, the pH will be on the acidic side of the pK_a value, i.e., the pH is at a value lower than the pK_a value. When one has more base than acid in a buffer ([conjugate base] > [weak acid]), then the log term in the Henderson-Hasselbalch equation is positive resulting in $pH > pK_a$. When one has more base than acid in a buffer, the pH is on the basic side of the pK_a value, i.e., the pH is at a value greater than the pK_a value. The other scenario you can run across in a buffer is when [acid] = [base]. Here, the log term is equal to zero and $pH = pK_a$.

15.   The more weak acid and conjugate base present, the more H^+ and/or OH^- that can be absorbed by the buffer without significant pH change. When the concentrations of weak acid and conjugate base are equal (so that $pH = pK_a$), the buffer system is equally efficient at absorbing either H^+ or OH^-. If the buffer is overloaded with weak acid or with conjugate base, then the buffer is not equally efficient at absorbing either H^+ or OH^-.

16.   Titration i is a strong acid titrated by a strong base. The pH is very acidic until just before the equivalence point; at the equivalence point, pH = 7.00; and past the equivalence the pH is very basic. Titration ii is a strong base titrated by a strong acid. Here the pH is very basic until just before the equivalence point; at the equivalence point, pH = 7.00; and past the equivalence point the pH is very acidic. Titration iii is a weak base titrated by a strong acid. The pH starts out basic because a weak base is present. However, the pH will not be as basic as in Titration ii where a strong base is titrated. The pH drops as HCl is added, then at the halfway point to equivalence, $pH = pK_a$. Because $K_b = 4.4 \times 10^{-4}$ for CH_3NH_2, $CH_3NH_3^+$ has $K_a = K_w/K_b = 2.3 \times 10^{-11}$ and $pK_a = 10.64$. So at the halfway point to equivalence for this weak base-strong acid titration, pH = 10.64. The pH continues to drop as HCl is added; then at the equivalence point the pH is acidic (pH < 7.00) because the only important major species present is a weak acid (the conjugate acid of the weak base). Past the equivalence point the pH becomes more acidic as excess HCl is added. Titration iv is a weak acid titrated by a strong base. The pH starts off acidic, but not nearly as acidic as the strong acid titration (i). The pH increases as NaOH is added, then at the halfway point to equivalence, $pH = pK_a$ for $HF = -\log(7.2 \times 10^{-4}) = 3.14$. The pH continues to increase past the halfway point, then at the equivalence point the pH is basic (pH > 7.0) because the only important major species present is a weak base (the conjugate base of the weak acid). Past the equivalence point, the pH becomes more basic as excess NaOH is added.

a.   All require the same volume of titrant to reach the equivalence point. At the equivalence point for all of these titrations, moles acid = moles base ($M_A V_A = M_B V_B$). Because all of the molarities and volumes are the same in the titrations, the volume of titrant will be the same (50.0 mL titrant added to reach equivalence point).

b.   Increasing initial pH: i < iv < iii < ii; The strong acid titration has the lowest pH, the weak acid titration is next, followed by the weak base titration, with the strong base titration having the highest pH.

c.   i < iv < iii < ii. The strong acid-titration has the lowest pH at the halfway point to equivalence and the strong base titration has the highest halfway point pH. For the weak acid titration, $pH = pK_a = 3.14$, and for the weak base titration, $pH = pK_a = 10.64$.

d.   Equivalence point pH: iii < ii = i < iv; The strong by strong titrations have pH = 7.00 at the equivalence point. The weak base titration has an acidic pH at the equivalence point and a weak acid titration has a basic equivalence point pH.

The only different answer when the weak acid and weak base are changed would be for part c. This is for the halfway point to equivalence where pH = pK_a.

HOC_6H_5; $K_a = 1.6 \times 10^{-10}$, $pK_a = -\log(1.6 \times 10^{-10}) = 9.80$

$C_5H_5NH^+$, $K_a = \dfrac{K_w}{K_{b,\,C_5H_5N}} = \dfrac{1.0 \times 10^{-14}}{1.7 \times 10^{-9}} = 5.9 \times 10^{-6}$, $pK_a = 5.23$

From the pK_a values, the correct ordering at the halfway point to equivalence would be: i < iii < iv < ii. Note that for the weak base-strong acid titration using C_5H_5N, the pH is acidic at the halfway point to equivalence, while the weak acid-strong base titration using HOC_6H_5 is basic at the halfway point to equivalence. This is fine; this will always happen when the weak base titrated has a $K_b < 1 \times 10^{-7}$ (so K_a of the conjugate acid is greater than 1×10^{-7}) and when the weak acid titrated has a $K_a < 1 \times 10^{-7}$ (so K_b of the conjugate base is greater than 1×10^{-7}).

17.   The three key points to emphasize in your sketch are the initial pH, pH at the halfway point to equivalence, and the pH at the equivalence point. For all of the weak bases titrated, pH = pK_a at the halfway point to equivalence (50.0 mL HCl added) because [weak base] = [conjugate acid] at this point. Here, the weak base with $K_b = 10^{-5}$ has a pH = 9.0 at the halfway point and the weak base with $K_b = 10^{-10}$ has a pH = 4.0 at the halfway point to equivalence. For the initial pH, the strong base has the highest pH (most basic), while the weakest base has the lowest pH (least basic). At the equivalence point (100.0 mL HCl added), the strong base titration has pH = 7.0. The weak bases titrated have acidic pHs because the conjugate acids of the weak bases titrated are the major species present. The weakest base has the strongest conjugate acid so its pH will be lowest (most acidic) at the equivalence point.

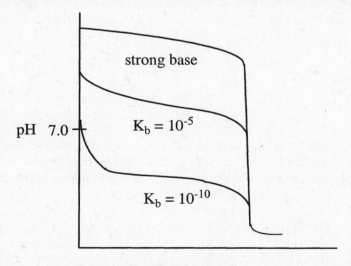

Volume HCl added (mL)

18. $HIn \rightleftharpoons H^+ + In^-$ $K_a = \dfrac{[H^+][In^-]}{[HIn]}$

Indicators are weak acids themselves. The special property they have is that the acid form of the indicator (HIn) has one distinct color, while the conjugate base form (In⁻) has a different distinct color. Which form dominates and thus determines the color of the solution is determined by the pH. An indicator is chosen in order to match the pH of the color change at about the pH of the equivalence point.

19.   i.   This is the result when you have a salt that breaks up into two ions. Examples of these salts (but not all) could be $AgCl$, $SrSO_4$, $BaCrO_4$, and $ZnCO_3$.

ii.   This is the result when you have a salt that breaks up into three ions, either two cations and one anion or one cation and two anions. Some examples are SrF_2, Hg_2I_2, and Ag_2SO_4.

iii.   This is the result when you have a salt that breaks up into four ions, either three cations and one anion (Ag_3PO_4) or one cation and three anions (ignoring the hydroxides, there are no examples of this type of salt in Table 15.4).

iv.   This is the result when you have a salt that breaks up into five ions, either three cations and two anions [$Sr_3(PO_4)_2$] or two cations and three anions (no examples of this type of salt are in Table 15.4).

20.   Some people would automatically think that an increase in temperature would increase the solubility of a salt. This is not always the case as some salts show a decrease in solubility as temperature increases. The two major methods used to increase solubility of a salt both involve removing one of the ions in the salt by reaction. If the salt has an ion with basic properties, adding H^+ will increase the solubility of the salt because the added H^+ will react with the basic ion, thus removing it from solution. More salt dissolves in order to to make up for the lost ion. Some examples of salts with basic ions are AgF, $CaCO_3$, and $Al(OH)_3$. The other way to remove an ion is to form a complex ion. For example, the Ag^+ ion in silver salts forms the complex ion $Ag(NH_3)_2^+$ as ammonia is added. Silver salts increase their solubility as NH_3 is added because the Ag^+ ion is removed through complex ion formation.

Exercises

Buffers

21.   When strong acid or strong base is added to a bicarbonate/carbonate mixture, the strong acid/base is neutralized. The reaction goes to completion, resulting in the strong acid/base being replaced with a weak acid/base, which results in a new buffer solution. The reactions are:

$$H^+(aq) + CO_3^{2-}(aq) \rightarrow HCO_3^-(aq); \quad OH^- + HCO_3^-(aq) \rightarrow CO_3^{2-}(aq) + H_2O(l)$$

22.   Similar to the HCO_3^-/CO_3^{2-} buffer discussed in Exercise 21, the $HONH_3^+/HONH_2$ buffer absorbs added OH^- and H^+ in the same fashion.

$$HONH_2(aq) + H^+(aq) \rightarrow HONH_3^+(aq)$$

$$HONH_3^+(aq) + OH^-(aq) \rightarrow HONH_2(aq) + H_2O(l)$$

23.   a.   This is a weak acid problem. Let $HC_3H_5O_2$ = HOPr and $C_3H_5O_2^-$ = OPr$^-$.

	HOPr	$\rightleftharpoons$	H$^+$	+	OPr$^-$	$K_a = 1.3 \times 10^{-5}$
Initial	0.100 M		~0		0	
	x mol/L HOPr dissociates to reach equilibrium					
Change	$-x$	$\rightarrow$	$+x$		$+x$	
Equil.	0.100 $- x$		x		x	

$$K_a = 1.3 \times 10^{-5} = \frac{[H^+][OPr^-]}{[HOPr]} = \frac{x^2}{0.100 - x} \approx \frac{x^2}{0.100}$$

$$x = [H^+] = 1.1 \times 10^{-3}\,M; \quad pH = 2.96 \qquad \text{Assumptions good by the 5\% rule.}$$

b.   This is a weak base problem (Na$^+$ has no acidic/basic properties).

	OPr$^-$	+	H$_2$O	$\rightleftharpoons$	HOPr	+	OH$^-$	$K_b = \dfrac{K_w}{K_a} = 7.7 \times 10^{-10}$
Initial	0.100 M				0		~0	
	x mol/L OPr$^-$ reacts with H$_2$O to reach equilibrium							
Change	$-x$			$\rightarrow$	$+x$		$+x$	
Equil.	0.100 $- x$				x		x	

$$K_b = 7.7 \times 10^{-10} = \frac{[HOPr][OH^-]}{[OPr^-]} = \frac{x^2}{0.100 - x} \approx \frac{x^2}{0.100}$$

$$x = [OH^-] = 8.8 \times 10^{-6}\,M; \quad pOH = 5.06; \quad pH = 8.94 \quad \text{Assumptions good.}$$

c.   pure H$_2$O, $[H^+] = [OH^-] = 1.0 \times 10^{-7}\,M$; pH = 7.00

d.   This solution contains a weak acid and its conjugate base. This is a buffer solution. We will solve for the pH using the weak acid equilibrium reaction.

	HOPr	$\rightleftharpoons$	H$^+$	+	OPr$^-$	$K_a = 1.3 \times 10^{-5}$
Initial	0.100 M		~0		0.100 M	
	x mol/L HOPr dissociates to reach equilibrium					
Change	$-x$	$\rightarrow$	$+x$		$+x$	
Equil.	0.100 $- x$		x		0.100 $+ x$	

$$1.3 \times 10^{-5} = \frac{(0.100 + x)(x)}{0.100 - x} \approx \frac{(0.100)(x)}{0.100} = x = [H^+]$$

$$[H^+] = 1.3 \times 10^{-5}\,M; \quad pH = 4.89 \quad \text{Assumptions good.}$$

Alternatively, we can use the Henderson-Hasselbalch equation to calculate the pH of buffer solutions.

$$pH = pK_a + \log\frac{[Base]}{[Acid]} = pK_a + \log\frac{(0.100)}{(0.100)} = -\log(1.3 \times 10^{-5}) = 4.89$$

The Henderson-Hasselbalch equation will be valid when an assumption of the type $0.1 + x \approx 0.1$ that we just made in this problem is valid. From a practical standpoint, this will almost always be true for useful buffer solutions. If the assumption is not valid, the solution will have such a low buffering capacity that it will be of no use to control the pH. Note: The Henderson-Hasselbalch equation can <u>only</u> be used to solve for the pH of buffer solutions.

24.   a. Weak base problem:

$$HONH_2 \; + \; H_2O \; \rightleftharpoons \; HONH_3^+ \; + \; OH^- \qquad K_b = 1.1 \times 10^{-8}$$

Initial	0.100 M	0	~0

x mol/L $HONH_2$ reacts with H_2O to reach equilibrium

Change	$-x$	$\rightarrow$	$+x$	$+x$
Equil.	$0.100 - x$		x	x

$$K_b = 1.1 \times 10^{-8} = \frac{x^2}{0.100 - x} \approx \frac{x^2}{0.100}$$

$x = [OH^-] = 3.3 \times 10^{-5}\,M$; pOH = 4.48; pH = 9.52   Assumptions good.

b. Weak acid problem (Cl^- has no acidic/basic properties);

$$HONH_3^+ \; \rightleftharpoons \; HONH_2 \; + \; H^+$$

Initial	0.100 M	0	~0

x mol/L $HONH_3^+$ dissociates to reach equilibrium

Change	$-x$	$\rightarrow$	$+x$	$+x$
Equil.	$0.100 - x$		x	x

$$K_a = \frac{K_w}{K_b} = 9.1 \times 10^{-7} = \frac{[HONH_2][H^+]}{[HONH_3^+]} = \frac{x^2}{0.100 - x} \approx \frac{x^2}{0.100}$$

$x = [H^+] = 3.0 \times 10^{-4}\,M$; pH = 3.52   Assumptions good.

c. Pure H_2O, pH = 7.00

d. Buffer solution where $pK_a = -\log(9.1 \times 10^{-7}) = 6.04$. Using the Henderson-Hasselbalch equation:

$$pH = pK_a + \log\frac{[Base]}{[Acid]} = 6.04 + \log\frac{[HONH_2]}{[HONH_3^+]} = 6.04 + \log\frac{(0.100)}{(0.100)} = 6.04$$

25. $0.100\ M\ HC_3H_5O_2$: percent dissociation $= \dfrac{[H^+]}{[HC_3H_5O_2]_0} \times 100 = \dfrac{1.1\times10^{-3}\ M}{0.100\ M} = 1.1\%$

$0.100\ M\ HC_3H_5O_2 + 0.100\ M\ NaC_3H_5O_2$: % dissociation $= \dfrac{1.3\times10^{-5}}{0.100} \times 100 = 1.3 \times 10^{-2}\ \%$

The percent dissociation of the acid decreases from 1.1% to $1.3 \times 10^{-2}\ \%$ when $C_3H_5O_2^-$ is present. This is known as the common ion effect. The presence of the conjugate base of the weak acid inhibits the acid dissociation reaction.

26. $0.100\ M\ HONH_2$: percent ionization $\dfrac{[OH^-]}{[HONH_2]_0} \times 100 = \dfrac{3.3\times10^{-5}\ M}{0.100\ M} \times 100$

$$= 3.3 \times 10^{-2}\ \%$$

$0.100\ M\ HONH_2 + 0.100\ M\ HONH_3^+$: % ionization $= \dfrac{1.1\times10^{-8}}{0.100} \times 100 = 1.1 \times 10^{-5}\ \%$

The percent ionization decreases by a factor of 3000. The presence of the conjugate acid of the weak base inhibits the weak base reaction with water. This is known as the common ion effect.

27.   a.   We have a weak acid ($HOPr = HC_3H_5O_2$) and a strong acid (HCl) present. The amount of H^+ donated by the weak acid will be negligible as compared to the $0.020\ M\ H^+$ from the strong acid. To prove it let's consider the weak acid equilibrium reaction:

	HOPr	⇌	H^+	+	OPr^-	$K_a = 1.3 \times 10^{-5}$

Initial	$0.100\ M$		$0.020\ M$		0

x mol/L HOPr dissociates to reach equilibrium

Change	$-x$	→	$+x$	$+x$
Equil.	$0.100 - x$		$0.020 + x$	x

$$K_a = 1.3 \times 10^{-5} = \frac{(0.020 + x)(x)}{0.100 - x} \approx \frac{(0.020)(x)}{0.100}\ ,\quad x = 6.5 \times 10^{-5}\ M$$

$[H^+] = 0.020 + x = 0.020\ M$; pH = 1.70 Assumptions good ($x = 6.5 \times 10^{-5}$ which is $<< 0.020$).

b.   Added H^+ reacts completely with the best base present, OPr^-. Since all species present are in the same volume of solution, we can use molarity units to do the stoichiometry part of the problem (instead of moles). The stoichiometry problem is:

	OPr^-	+	H^+	→	HOPr

Before	$0.100\ M$		$0.020\ M$		0	
Change	-0.020		-0.020	→	$+0.020$	Reacts completely
After	0.080		0		$0.020\ M$	

After reaction, a weak acid, HOPr , and its conjugate base, OPr⁻, are present. This is a buffer solution. Using the Henderson-Hasselbalch equation where $pK_a = -\log(1.3 \times 10^{-5})$ = 4.89:

$$pH = pK_a + \log\frac{[Base]}{[Acid]} = 4.89 + \log\frac{(0.080)}{(0.020)} = 5.49 \qquad \text{Assumptions good.}$$

c.   This is a strong acid problem. $[H^+] = 0.020\ M$; pH = 1.70

d.   Added H^+ reacts completely with the best base present, OPr⁻.

	OPr⁻	+	H^+	→	HOPr	
Before	0.100 M		0.020 M		0.100 M	
Change	−0.020		−0.020	→	+0.020	Reacts completely
After	0.080		0		0.120	

A buffer solution results (weak acid + conjugate base). Using the Henderson-Hasselbalch equation:

$$pH = pK_a + \frac{[Base]}{[Acid]} = 4.89 + \log\frac{(0.080)}{(0.120)} = 4.71$$

28.   a.   Added H^+ reacts completely with $HONH_2$ (the best base present) to form $HONH_3^+$.

	$HONH_2$	+	H^+	→	$HONH_3^+$	
Before	0.100 M		0.020 M		0	
Change	−0.020		−0.020	→	+0.020	Reacts completely
After	0.080		0		0.020	

After this reaction, a buffer solution exists, i.e., a weak acid ($HONH_3^+$) and its conjugate base ($HONH_2$) are present at the same time. Using the Henderson-Hasselbalch equation to solve for the pH where $pK_a = -\log(K_w/K_b) = 6.04$:

$$pH = pK_a + \log\frac{[Base]}{[Acid]} = 6.04 + \log\frac{(0.080)}{(0.020)} = 6.04 + 0.60 = 6.64$$

b.   We have a weak acid and a strong acid present at the same time. The H^+ contribution from the weak acid, $HONH_3^+$, will be negligible. So, we have to consider only the H^+ from HCl. $[H^+] = 0.020\ M$; pH = 1.70

c.   This is a strong acid in water. $[H^+] = 0.020\ M$; pH = 1.70

d.   Major species: H_2O, Cl^-, $HONH_2$, $HONH_3^+$, H^+

H^+ will react completely with $HONH_2$, the best base present.

$$\text{HONH}_2 \quad + \quad \text{H}^+ \quad \rightarrow \quad \text{HONH}_3^+$$

Before	0.100 M	0.020 M	0.100 M
Change	−0.020	−0.020 $\rightarrow$	+0.020 Reacts completely
After	0.080	0	0.120

A buffer solution results after reaction. Using the Henderson-Hasselbalch equation:

$$pH = 6.04 + \log \frac{[\text{HONH}_2]}{[\text{HONH}_3^+]} = 6.04 + \log \frac{(0.080)}{(0.120)} = 6.04 - 0.18 = 5.86$$

29.   a. OH^- will react completely with the best acid present, HOPr.

$$\text{HOPr} \quad + \quad \text{OH}^- \quad \rightarrow \quad \text{OPr}^- + \text{H}_2\text{O}$$

Before	0.100 M	0.020 M	0
Change	−0.020	−0.020 $\rightarrow$	+0.020 Reacts completely
After	0.080	0	0.020

A buffer solution results after the reaction. Using the Henderson-Hasselbalch equation:

$$pH = pK_a + \log \frac{[\text{Base}]}{[\text{Acid}]} = 4.89 + \log \frac{(0.020)}{(0.080)} = 4.29$$

b.   We have a weak base and a strong base present at the same time. The amount of OH^- added by the weak base will be negligible compared to the 0.020 M OH^- from the strong base. To prove it, let's consider the weak base equilibrium:

$$\text{OPr}^- + \text{H}_2\text{O} \quad \rightleftharpoons \quad \text{HOPr} \quad + \quad \text{OH}^- \qquad K_b = 7.7 \times 10^{-10}$$

Initial	0.100 M	0	0.020 M

x mol/L OPr$^-$ reacts with H_2O to reach equilibrium

Change	−x $\rightarrow$	+x	+x
Equil.	0.100 − x	x	0.020 + x

$$K_b = 7.7 \times 10^{-10} = \frac{(x)(0.020 + x)}{0.100 - x} \approx \frac{(x)(0.020)}{0.100}, \quad x = 3.9 \times 10^{-9} \, M$$

$[\text{OH}^-] = 0.020 + x = 0.020 \, M$; pOH = 1.70; pH = 12.30   Assumptions good.

c.   This is a strong base in water. $[\text{OH}^-] = 0.020 \, M$; pOH = 1.70; pH = 12.30

d. OH^- will react completely with HOPr, the best acid present.

$$\text{HOPr} \quad + \quad \text{OH}^- \quad \rightarrow \quad \text{OPr}^- \quad + \quad \text{H}_2\text{O}$$

Before	0.100 M	0.020 M	0.100 M
Change	−0.020	−0.020 $\rightarrow$	+0.020 Reacts completely
After	0.080	0	0.120

Using the Henderson-Hasselbalch equation to solve for the pH of the resulting buffer solution:

$$pH = pK_a + \log\frac{[Base]}{[Acid]} = 4.89 + \frac{(0.120)}{(0.080)} = 5.07$$

30.   a.   We have a weak base and a strong base present at the same time. The OH^- contribution from the weak base, $HONH_2$, will be negligible. Consider only the added strong base as the primary source of OH^-.

         $[OH^-] = 0.020\ M$; $pOH = 1.70$; $pH = 12.30$

   b.   Added strong base will react to completion with the best acid present, $HONH_3^+$.

$$OH^- \quad + \quad HONH_3^+ \quad \rightarrow \quad HONH_2 \quad + \quad H_2O$$

	OH⁻	HONH₃⁺	HONH₂	
Before	0.020 M	0.100 M	0	
Change	−0.020	−0.020 →	+0.020	Reacts completely
After	0	0.080	0.020	

The resulting solution is a buffer (a weak acid and its conjugate base). Using the Henderson-Hasselbalch equation:

$$pH = 6.04 + \log\frac{(0.020)}{(0.080)} = 6.04 - 0.60 = 5.44$$

   c.   This is a strong base in water. $[OH^-] = 0.020\ M$; $pOH = 1.70$; $pH = 12.30$

   d.   Major species: H_2O, Cl^-, Na^+, $HONH_2$, $HONH_3^+$, OH^-

Again, the added strong base reacts completely with the best acid present, $HONH_3^+$.

$$HONH_3^+ \quad + \quad OH^- \quad \rightarrow \quad HONH_2 \quad + \quad H_2O$$

	HONH₃⁺	OH⁻	HONH₂	
Before	0.100 M	0.020 M	0.100 M	
Change	−0.020	−0.020 →	+0.020	Reacts completely
After	0.080	0	0.120	

A buffer solution results. Using the Henderson-Hasselbalch equation:

$$pH = 6.04 + \log\frac{[HONH_2]}{[HONH_3^+]} = 6.04 + \log\frac{(0.120)}{(0.080)} = 6.04 + 0.18 = 6.22$$

31.   Consider all of the results to Exercises 15.23, 15.27, and 15.29:

Solution	Initial pH	after added acid	after added base
a	2.96	1.70	4.29
b	8.94	5.49	12.30
c	7.00	1.70	12.30
d	4.89	4.71	5.07

The solution in Exercise 15.23d is a buffer; it contains both a weak acid ($HC_3H_5O_2$) and a weak base ($C_3H_5O_2^-$). Solution d shows the greatest resistance to changes in pH when either strong acid or strong base is added; this is the primary property of buffers.

32.   Consider all of the results to Exercises 15.24, 15.28, and 15.30.

Solution	Initial pH	after added acid	after added base
a	9.52	6.64	12.30
b	3.52	1.70	5.44
c	7.00	1.70	12.30
d	6.04	5.86	6.22

The solution in Exercise 15.24d is a buffer; it shows the greatest resistance to a change in pH when strong acid or base is added. The solution in Exercise 15.24d contains a weak acid ($HONH_3^+$) and a weak base ($HONH_2$), which constitutes a buffer solution.

33.   Major species: HNO_2, NO_2^- and Na^+. Na^+ has no acidic or basic properties. One appropriate equilibrium reaction you can use is the K_a reaction of HNO_2 which contains both HNO_2 and NO_2^-. However, you could also use the K_b reaction for NO_2^- and come up with the same answer. Solving the equilibrium problem (called a buffer problem):

$$HNO_2 \quad\rightleftharpoons\quad NO_2^- \quad + \quad H^+$$

Initial	1.00 M		1.00 M	~0

x mol/L HNO_2 dissociates to reach equilibrium

Change	$-x$	$\rightarrow$	$+x$	$+x$
Equil.	$1.00 - x$		$1.00 + x$	x

$$K_a = 4.0 \times 10^{-4} = \frac{[NO_2^-][H^+]}{[HNO_2]} = \frac{(1.00 + x)(x)}{1.00 - x} \approx \frac{(1.00)(x)}{1.00} \quad \text{(assuming } x << 1.00\text{)}$$

$x = 4.0 \times 10^{-4}\ M = [H^+]$;   Assumptions good ($x$ is 4.0×10^{-2} % of 1.00).

$$pH = -\log(4.0 \times 10^{-4}) = 3.40$$

Note: We would get the same answer using the Henderson-Hasselbalch equation. Use whichever method you prefer.

34.   Major species: HF, F^- and K^+ (no acidic/basic properties). We will use the K_a reaction of HF which contains both HF and F^- to solve the equilibrium problem.

$$HF \quad\rightleftharpoons\quad F^- \quad + \quad H^+$$

Initial	0.60 M		1.00 M	~0

x mol/L HF dissociates to reach equilibrium

Change	$-x$	$\rightarrow$	$+x$	$+x$
Equil.	$0.60 - x$		$1.00 + x$	x

$$K_a = 7.2 \times 10^{-4} = \frac{[F^-][H^+]}{[HF]} = \frac{(1.00 + x)(x)}{0.60 - x} \approx \frac{(1.00)(x)}{0.60} \quad \text{(assuming } x \ll 0.60)$$

$$x = [H^+] = 0.60 \times (7.2 \times 10^{-4}) = 4.3 \times 10^{-4} \, M; \text{ Assumptions good } (x \text{ is } 7.2 \times 10^{-2} \%$$
$$\text{of } 0.60).$$

$$pH = -\log(4.3 \times 10^{-4}) = 3.37$$

35.   Major species after NaOH added: HNO_2, NO_2^-, Na^+ and OH^-. The OH^- from the strong base will react with the best acid present (HNO_2). Any reaction involving a strong base is assumed to go to completion. Since all species present are in the same volume of solution, we can use molarity units to do the stoichiometry part of the problem (instead of moles). The stoichiometry problem is:

	OH$^-$	+	HNO$_2$	$\rightarrow$	NO$_2^-$	+ H$_2$O	
Before	0.10 mol/1.00 L		1.00 M		1.00 M		
Change	-0.10 M		-0.10 M	$\rightarrow$	$+0.10$ M		Reacts completely
After	0		0.90		1.10		

After all the OH^- reacts, we are left with a solution containing a weak acid (HNO_2) and its conjugate base (NO_2^-). This is what we call a buffer problem. We will solve this buffer problem using the K_a equilibrium reaction.

	HNO$_2$	$\rightleftharpoons$	NO$_2^-$	+	H$^+$
Initial	0.90 M		1.10 M		~0
	x mol/L HNO$_2$ dissociates to reach equilibrium				
Change	$-x$	$\rightarrow$	$+x$		$+x$
Equil.	$0.90 - x$		$1.10 + x$		x

$$K_a = 4.0 \times 10^{-4} = \frac{(1.10 + x)(x)}{0.90 - x} \approx \frac{(1.10)(x)}{0.90} , \quad x = [H^+] = 3.3 \times 10^{-4} \, M; \quad pH = 3.48;$$
$$\text{Assumptions good.}$$

Note: The added NaOH to this buffer solution changes the pH only from 3.40 to 3.48. If the NaOH were added to 1.0 L of pure water, the pH would change from 7.00 to 13.00.

Major species after HCl added: HNO_2, NO_2^-, H^+, Na^+, Cl^-; The added H^+ from the strong acid will react completely with the best base present (NO_2^-,).

	H$^+$	+	NO$_2^-$	$\rightarrow$	HNO$_2$	
Before	$\dfrac{0.20 \text{ mol}}{1.00 \text{ L}}$		1.00 M		1.00 M	
Change	-0.20 M		-0.20 M	$\rightarrow$	$+0.20$ M	Reacts completely
After	0		0.80		1.20	

After all the H^+ has reacted, we have a buffer solution (a solution containing a weak acid and its conjugate base). Solving the buffer problem:

$$\begin{array}{ccccc} & HNO_2 & \rightleftharpoons & NO_2^- & + & H^+ \end{array}$$

Initial	1.20 M	0.80 M	0
Equil.	1.20 - x	0.80 + x	+x

$$K_a = 4.0 \times 10^{-4} = \frac{(0.80 + x)(x)}{1.20 - x} \approx \frac{0.80)(x)}{1.20} \ , \ x = [H^+] = 6.0 \times 10^{-4}\,M; \ \ pH = 3.22;$$

Assumptions good.

Note: The added HCl to this buffer solution changes the pH only from 3.40 to 3.22. If the HCl were added to 1.0 L of pure water, the pH would change from 7.00 to 0.70.

36.   When NaOH is added, the OH$^-$ reacts completely with the best acid present, HF.

$$\begin{array}{ccccccc} OH^- & + & HF & \rightarrow & F^- & + & H_2O \end{array}$$

Before	$\dfrac{0.10\ mol}{1.00\ L}$	0.60 M	1.00 M	
Change	-0.10 M	-0.10 M $\rightarrow$	+0.10 M	Reacts completely
After	0	0.50	1.10	

We now have a new buffer problem. Solving the equilibrium part of the problem:

$$\begin{array}{ccccc} HF & \rightleftharpoons & F^- & + & H^+ \end{array}$$

Initial	0.50 M	1.10 M	0
Equil.	0.50 - x	1.10 + x	x

$$K_a = 7.2 \times 10^{-4} = \frac{(1.10 + x)(x)}{0.50 - x} \approx \frac{1.10(x)}{0.50} \ , \ x = [H^+] = 3.3 \times 10^{-4}\,M$$

pH = 3.48;   Assumptions good.

When HCl is added, H$^+$ reacts to completion with the best base (F$^-$) present.

$$\begin{array}{ccccc} H^+ & + & F^- & \rightarrow & HF \end{array}$$

Before	0.20 M	1.00 M	0.60 M
After	0	0.80 M	0.80 M

After reaction, we have a buffer problem:

$$\begin{array}{ccccc} HF & \rightleftharpoons & F^- & + & H^+ \end{array}$$

Initial	0.80 M	0.80 M	0
Equil.	0.80 - x	0.80 + x	x

$$K_a = 7.2 \times 10^{-4} = \frac{(0.80 + x)(x)}{0.80 - x} \approx x, \ x = [H^+] = 7.2 \times 10^{-4}\,M; \ \ pH = 3.14;$$

Assumptions good.

37. $[HC_7H_5O_2] = \dfrac{21.5 \text{ g } HC_7H_5O_2 \times \dfrac{1 \text{ mol } HC_7H_5O_2}{122.12 \text{ g}}}{0.2000 \text{ L}} = 0.880 \ M$

$[C_7H_5O_2^-] = \dfrac{37.7 \text{ g } NaC_7H_5O_2 \times \dfrac{1 \text{ mol } NaC_7H_5O_2}{144.10 \text{ g}} \times \dfrac{1 \text{ mol } C_7H_5O_2^-}{\text{mol } NaC_7H_5O_2}}{0.2000 \text{ L}} = 1.31 \ M$

We have a buffer solution since we have both a weak acid and its conjugate base present at the same time. One can use the K_a reaction or the K_b reaction to solve. We will use the K_a reaction for the acid component of the buffer.

$$HC_7H_5O_2 \ \rightleftharpoons \ H^+ \ + \ C_7H_5O_2^-$$

Initial   0.880 M ~0   1.31 M
                  x mol/L of $HC_7H_5O_2$ dissociates to reach equilibrium
Change $-x$ $\rightarrow$ $+x$ $+x$
Equil. $0.880 - x$ x $1.31 + x$

$K_a = 6.4 \times 10^{-5} = \dfrac{x(1.31 + x)}{0.880 - x} \approx \dfrac{x(1.31)}{0.880}, \ \ x = [H^+] = 4.3 \times 10^{-5} M$

$pH = -\log(4.3 \times 10^{-5}) = 4.37;$ Assumptions good.

Alternatively, we can use the Henderson-Hasselbalch equation to calculate the pH of buffer solutions.

$pH = pK_a + \log\dfrac{[\text{Base}]}{[\text{Acid}]} = pK_a + \log\dfrac{[C_7H_5O_2^-]}{[HC_7H_5O_2]}$

$pH = -\log(6.4 \times 10^{-5}) + \log\left(\dfrac{1.31}{0.880}\right) = 4.19 + 0.173 = 4.36$

Within round-off error, this is the same answer we calculated solving the equilibrium problem using the K_a reaction.

The Henderson-Hasselbalch equation will be valid when an assumption of the type $1.31 + x \approx 1.31$ that we just made in this problem is valid. From a practical standpoint, this will almost always be true for useful buffer solutions. If the assumption is not valid, the solution will have such a low buffering capacity that it will be of no use to control the pH. Note: The Henderson-Hasselbalch equation can only be used to solve for the pH of buffer solutions.

38. $50.0 \text{ g } NH_4Cl \times \dfrac{1 \text{ mol } NH_4Cl}{53.49 \text{ g } NH_4Cl} = 0.935 \text{ mol } NH_4Cl$ added to 1.00 L; $[NH_4^+] = 0.935 \ M$

$pH = pK_a + \log\dfrac{[NH_3]}{[NH_4^+]} = -\log(5.6 \times 10^{-10}) + \log\left(\dfrac{0.75}{0.935}\right) = 9.25 - 0.096 = 9.15$

39. $[H^+]$ added $= \dfrac{0.010 \text{ mol}}{0.25 \text{ L}} = 0.040 \ M$; The added H^+ reacts completely with NH_3 to form NH_4^+.

a. NH_3 $+$ H^+ $\rightarrow$ NH_4^+

Before	0.050 M		0.040 M		0.15 M
Change	-0.040		-0.040	$\rightarrow$	$+0.040$ Reacts completely
After	0.010		0		0.19

A buffer solution still exists after H^+ reacts completely. Using the Henderson-Hasselbalch equation:

$$pH = pK_a + \log\frac{[NH_3]}{[NH_4^+]} = -\log(5.6 \times 10^{-10}) + \log\left(\frac{0.010}{0.19}\right) = 9.25 + (-1.28) = 7.97$$

b. NH_3 $+$ H^+ $\rightarrow$ NH_4^+

Before	0.50 M		0.040 M		1.50 M
Change	-0.040		-0.040	$\rightarrow$	$+0.040$ Reacts completely
After	0.46		0		1.54

A buffer solution still exists. $pH = pK_a + \log\dfrac{[NH_3]}{[NH_4^+]} = 9.25 + \log\left(\dfrac{0.46}{1.54}\right) = 8.73$

The two buffers differ in their capacity and not in pH (both buffers had an initial pH = 8.77). Solution b has the greater capacity because it has the largest concentration of weak acid and conjugate base. Buffers with greater capacities will be able to absorb more H^+ or OH^- added.

40.   a. pK_b for $C_6H_5NH_2 = -\log(3.8 \times 10^{-4}) = 9.42$; pK_a for $C_6H_5NH_3^+ = 14.00 - 9.42 = 4.58$

$$pH = pK_a + \frac{[C_6H_5NH_2]}{[C_6H_5NH_3^+]}, \ \ 4.20 = 4.58 + \log\frac{0.50 \ M}{[C_6H_5NH_3^+]}$$

$$-0.38 = \log\frac{0.50 \ M}{[C_6H_5NH_3^+]}, \ \ [C_6H_5NH_3^+] = [C_6H_5NH_3Cl] = 1.2 \ M$$

b. $4.0 \text{ g NaOH} \times \dfrac{1 \text{ mol NaOH}}{40.00 \text{ g}} \times \dfrac{1 \text{ mol OH}^-}{\text{mol NaOH}} = 0.10 \text{ mol OH}^-$, $[OH^-] = \dfrac{0.10 \text{ mol}}{1.0 \text{ L}} = 0.10 \ M$

              $C_6H_5NH_3^+$ $+$ OH^- $\rightarrow$ $C_6H_5NH_2$ $+$ H_2O

Before	1.2 M		0.10 M		0.50 M
Change	-0.10		-0.10	$\rightarrow$	$+0.10$
After	1.1		0		0.60

A buffer solution exists. $pH = 4.58 + \log\left(\dfrac{0.60}{1.1}\right) = 4.32$

41. $pH = pK_a + \log \dfrac{[C_2H_3O_2^-]}{[HC_2H_3O_2]}$; $pK_a = -\log(1.8 \times 10^{-5}) = 4.74$

Since the buffer components, $C_2H_3O_2^-$ and $HC_2H_3O_2$, are both in the same volume of water, the concentration ratio of $[C_2H_3O_2^-]/[HC_2H_3O_2]$ will equal the mol ratio of mol $C_2H_3O_2^-$/mol $HC_2H_3O_2$.

$5.00 = 4.74 + \log \dfrac{mol\ C_2H_3O_2^-}{mol\ HC_2H_3O_2}$; $mol\ HC_2H_3O_2 = 0.5000\ L \times \dfrac{0.200\ mol}{L} = 0.100\ mol$

$0.26 = \log \dfrac{mol\ C_2H_3O_2^-}{0.100\ mol}$, $\dfrac{mol\ C_2H_3O_2^-}{0.100} = 10^{0.26} = 1.8$, $mol\ C_2H_3O_2^- = 0.18\ mol$

mass $NaC_2H_3O_2 = 0.18\ mol\ NaC_2H_3O_2 \times \dfrac{82.03\ g}{mol} = 15\ g\ NaC_2H_3O_2$

42. $pH = pK_a + \log \dfrac{[NO_2^-]}{[HNO_2]}$, $3.55 = \log(4.0 \times 10^{-4}) + \log \dfrac{[NO_2^-]}{[HNO_2]}$

$3.55 = 3.40 + \log \dfrac{[NO_2^-]}{[HNO_2]}$, $\dfrac{[NO_2^-]}{[HNO_2]} = 10^{0.15} = 1.4$

Let x = volume (L) HNO_2 solution needed, then $1.00 - x$ = volume of $NaNO_2$ solution needed to form this buffer solution.

$$\dfrac{[NO_2^-]}{[HNO_2]} = 1.4 = \dfrac{(1.00 - x) \times \dfrac{0.50\ mol\ NaNO_2}{L}}{x \times \dfrac{0.50\ mol\ HNO_2}{L}} = \dfrac{0.50 - 0.50x}{0.50x}$$

$0.70\ x = 0.50 - 0.50\ x$, $1.20\ x = 0.50$, $x = 0.42\ L$

We need 0.42 L of 0.50 M HNO_2 and $1.00 - 0.42 = 0.58$ L of 0.50 M $NaNO_2$ to form a pH = 3.55 buffer solution.

43. $C_5H_5NH^+ \rightleftharpoons H^+ + C_5H_5N$ $K_a = \dfrac{K_w}{K_b} = \dfrac{1.0 \times 10^{-14}}{1.7 \times 10^{-9}} = 5.9 \times 10^{-6}$; $pK_a = -\log(5.9 \times 10^{-6})$
$= 5.23$

We will use the Henderson-Hasselbalch equation to calculate the concentration ratio necessary for each buffer.

$pH = pK_a + \log \dfrac{[Base]}{[Acid]}$, $pH = 5.23 + \log \dfrac{[C_5H_5N]}{[C_5H_5NH^+]}$

a. $4.50 = 5.23 + \log \dfrac{[C_5H_5N]}{[C_5H_5NH^+]}$ b. $5.00 = 5.23 + \log \dfrac{[C_5H_5N]}{[C_5H_5NH^+]}$

$\log \dfrac{[C_5H_5N]}{[C_5H_5NH^+]} = -0.73$ $\log \dfrac{[C_5H_5N]}{[C_5H_5NH^+]} = -0.23$

$\dfrac{[C_5H_5N]}{[C_5H_5NH^+]} = 10^{-0.73} = 0.19$ $\dfrac{[C_5H_5N]}{[C_5H_5NH^+]} = 10^{-0.23} = 0.59$

c. $5.23 = 5.23 + \log \dfrac{[C_5H_5N]}{[C_5H_5NH^+]}$ d. $5.50 = 5.23 + \log \dfrac{[C_5H_5N]}{[C_5H_5NH^+]}$

$\dfrac{[C_5H_5N]}{[C_5H_5NH^+]} = 10^{0.0} = 1.0$ $\dfrac{[C_5H_5N]}{[C_5H_5NH^+]} = 10^{0.27} = 1.9$

44.   a. $pH = pK_a + \log \dfrac{[Base]}{[Acid]}$, $pK_a = -\log(4.3 \times 10^{-7}) = 6.37$, $7.40 = 6.37 + \log \dfrac{[HCO_3^-]}{[H_2CO_3]}$

$\dfrac{[HCO_3^-]}{[H_2CO_3]} = 10^{1.03} = 11$; $\dfrac{[H_2CO_3]}{[HCO_3^-]} = \dfrac{[CO_2]}{[HCO_3^-]} = \dfrac{1}{11} = 0.091$

b. $7.15 = -\log(6.2 \times 10^{-8}) + \log \dfrac{[HPO_4^{2-}]}{[H_2PO_4^-]}$, $7.15 = 7.21 + \log \dfrac{[HPO_4^{2-}]}{[H_2PO_4^-]}$

$\dfrac{[HPO_4^{2-}]}{[H_2PO_4^-]} = 10^{-0.06} = 0.9$, $\dfrac{[HPO_4^{2-}]}{[H_2PO_4^-]} = \dfrac{1}{0.9} = 1.1 \approx 1$

c.   A best buffer has approximately equal concentrations of weak acid and conjugate base so that pH $\approx$ pK$_a$ for a best buffer.   The pK$_a$ value for a $H_3PO_4/H_2PO_4^-$ buffer is $-\log(7.5 \times 10^{-3}) = 2.12$.   A pH of 7.1 is too high for a $H_3PO_4/H_2PO_4^-$ buffer to be effective. At this high pH, there would be so little H_3PO_4 present that we could hardly consider it a buffer. This solution would not be effective in resisting pH changes, especially when a strong base is added.

45.   A best buffer has large and equal quantities of weak acid and conjugate base. For a best

buffer, [acid] = [base], so $pH = pK_a + \log \dfrac{[Base]}{[Acid]} = pK_a + 0 = pK_a$ $(pH = pK_a)$.

The best acid choice for a pH = 7.00 buffer would be the weak acid with a pK$_a$ close to 7.0 or $K_a \approx 1 \times 10^{-7}$. HOCl is the best choice in Table 14.2 ($K_a = 3.5 \times 10^{-8}$; pK$_a = 7.46$). To make this buffer, we need to calculate the [base]/[acid] ratio.

$$7.00 = 7.46 + \log \frac{[\text{Base}]}{[\text{Acid}]}, \quad \frac{[\text{OCl}^-]}{[\text{HOCl}]} = 10^{-0.46} = 0.35$$

Any OCl$^-$/HOCl buffer in a concentration ratio of 0.35:1 will have a pH = 7.00. One possibility is [NaOCl] = 0.35 M and [HOCl] = 1.0 M.

46.   For a pH = 5.00 buffer, we want an acid with a pK$_a$ close to 5.0. For a conjugate acid-base pair, 14.00 = pK$_a$ + pK$_b$. So for a pH = 5.00 buffer, we want the base to have a pK$_b$ close to 14.0 − 5.0 = 9.0 or a K$_b$ close to 1×10^{-9}. The best choice in Table 14.3 is pyridine, C$_5$H$_5$N, with K$_b$ = 1.7 × 10^{-9}.

$$pH = pK_a + \log \frac{[\text{Base}]}{[\text{Acid}]}; \quad pK_a = \frac{K_w}{K_b} = \frac{1.0 \times 10^{-14}}{1.7 \times 10^{-9}} = 5.9 \times 10^{-6}$$

$$5.00 = -\log(5.9 \times 10^{-6}) + \log \frac{[\text{Base}]}{[\text{Acid}]}, \quad \frac{[\text{C}_5\text{H}_5\text{N}]}{[\text{C}_5\text{H}_5\text{N}^+]} = 10^{-0.23} = 0.59$$

There are several possibilities for this buffer. One possibility is a solution of [C$_5$H$_5$N] = 0.59 M and [C$_5$H$_5$NHCl] = 1.0 M. The pH of this solution will be 5.00 because the base to acid concentration ratio is 0.59:1.

47.   The reaction OH$^-$ + CH$_3$NH$_3^+$ → CH$_3$NH$_2$ + H$_2$O goes to completion for solutions a, c and d (no reaction occurs between the species in solution because both species are bases). After the OH$^-$ reacts completely, there must be both CH$_3$NH$_3^+$ and CH$_3$NH$_2$ in solution for it to be a buffer. The important components of each solution (after the OH$^-$ reacts completely) is/are:

a.   0.05 M CH$_3$NH$_2$ (no CH$_3$NH$_3^+$ remains, no buffer)

b.   0.05 M OH$^-$ and 0.1 M CH$_3$NH$_2$ (two bases present, no buffer)

c.   0.05 M OH$^-$ and 0.05 M CH$_3$NH$_2$ (too much OH$^-$ added, no CH$_3$NH$_3^+$ remains, no buffer)

d.   0.05 M CH$_3$NH$_2$ and 0.05 M CH$_3$NH$_3^+$ (a buffer solution results)

Only the combination in mixture d results in a buffer. Note that the concentrations are halved from the initial values. This is because equal volumes of two solutions were added together, which halves the concentrations.

48.   a.   No; A solution of a strong acid (HNO$_3$) and its conjugate base (NO$_3^-$) is not generally considered a buffer solution.

b.   No; Two acids are present (HNO$_3$ and HF), so it is not a buffer solution.

c.   H$^+$ reacts completely with F$^-$. Since equal volumes are mixed, the initial concentrations in the mixture are 0.10 M HNO$_3$ and 0.20 M NaF.

$$H^+ \quad + \quad F^- \quad \rightarrow \quad HF$$

Before	0.10 M	0.20 M	0	
Change	-0.10	-0.10	$\rightarrow$ +0.10	Reacts completely
After	0	0.10	0.10	

After H^+ reacts completely, a buffer solution results, i.e., a weak acid (HF) and its conjugate base (F^-) are both present in solution in large quantities.

d. No; A strong acid (HNO_3) and a strong base (NaOH) do not form buffer solutions. They will neutralize each other to form H_2O.

49. Added OH^- converts $HC_2H_3O_2$ into $C_2H_3O_2^-$: $HC_2H_3O_2 + OH^- \rightarrow C_2H_3O_2^- + H_2O$

From this reaction, the moles of $C_2H_3O_2^-$ produced <u>equal</u> the moles of OH^- added. Also, the total concentration of acetic acid plus acetate ion must equal 2.0 M (assuming no volume change on addition of NaOH). Summarizing for each solution:

$$[C_2H_3O_2^-] + [HC_2H_3O_2] = 2.0 \ M \text{ and } [C_2H_3O_2^-] \text{ produced} = [OH^-] \text{ added}$$

a. $pH = pK_a + \log\dfrac{[C_2H_3O_2^-]}{[HC_2H_3O_2]}$; For $pH = pK_a$, $\log\dfrac{[C_2H_3O_2^-]}{[HC_2H_3O_2]} = 0$

Therefore, $\dfrac{[C_2H_3O_2^-]}{[HC_2H_3O_2]} = 1.0$ and $[C_2H_3O_2^-] = [HC_2H_3O_2]$

Because $[C_2H_3O_2^-] + [HC_2H_3O_2] = 2.0 \ M$, $[C_2H_3O_2^-] = [HC_2H_3O_2] = 1.0 \ M = [OH^-]$ added.

To produce a 1.0 M $C_2H_3O_2^-$ solution, we need to add 1.0 mol of NaOH to 1.0 L of the 2.0 M $HC_2H_3O_2$ solution. The resultant solution will have $pH = pK_a = 4.74$.

b. $4.00 = 4.74 + \log\dfrac{[C_2H_3O_2^-]}{[HC_2H_3O_2]}$, $\dfrac{[C_2H_3O_2^-]}{[HC_2H_3O_2]} = 10^{-0.74} = 0.18$

$[C_2H_3O_2^-] = 0.18 \ [HC_2H_3O_2]$ or $[HC_2H_3O_2] = 5.6 \ [C_2H_3O_2^-]$; Because $[C_2H_3O_2^-] + [HC_2H_3O_2] = 2.0 \ M$, then:

$$[C_2H_3O_2^-] + 5.6 \ [C_2H_3O_2^-] = 2.0 \ M, \ [C_2H_3O_2^-] = \frac{2.0}{6.6} = 0.30 \ M = [OH^-] \text{ added}$$

We need to add 0.30 mol of NaOH to 1.0 L of 2.0 M $HC_2H_3O_2$ solution to produce a buffer solution with $pH = 4.00$.

c. $5.00 = 4.74 + \log \dfrac{[C_2H_3O_2^-]}{[HC_2H_3O_2]}, \quad \dfrac{[C_2H_3O_2^-]}{[HC_2H_3O_2]} = 10^{0.26} = 1.8$

1.8 $[HC_2H_3O_2] = [C_2H_3O_2^-]$ or $[HC_2H_3O_2] = 0.56\ [C_2H_3O_2^-]$; Because $[HC_2H_3O_2] + [C_2H_3O_2^-] = 2.0\ M$, then:

$1.56\ [C_2H_3O_2^-] = 2.0\ M,\ \ [C_2H_3O_2^-] = 1.3\ M = [OH^-]$ added

We need to add 1.3 mol of NaOH to 1.0 L of 2.0 M $HC_2H_3O_2$ to produce a buffer solution with pH = 5.00.

50.   When H^+ is added, it converts $C_2H_3O_2^-$ into $HC_2H_3O_2$: $C_2H_3O_2^- + H^+ \rightarrow HC_2H_3O_2$. From this reaction, the moles of $HC_2H_3O_2$ produced must equal the moles of H^+ added and the total concentration of acetate ion + acetic acid must equal 1.0 M (assuming no volume change). Summarizing for each solution:

$[C_2H_3O_2^-] + [HC_2H_3O_2] = 1.0\ M$ and $[HC_2H_3O_2] = [H^+]$ added

a. $pH = pK_a + \log \dfrac{[C_2H_3O_2^-]}{[HC_2H_3O_2]}$; For pH = pK_a, $[C_2H_3O_2^-] = [HC_2H_3O_2]$.

For this to be true, $[C_2H_3O_2^-] = [HC_2H_3O_2] = 0.50\ M = [H^+]$ added, which means that 0.50 mol of HCl must be added to 1.0 L of the initial solution to produce a solution with pH = pK_a.

b. $4.20 = 4.74 + \log \dfrac{[C_2H_3O_2^-]}{[HC_2H_3O_2]}, \quad \dfrac{[C_2H_3O_2^-]}{[HC_2H_3O_2]} = 10^{-0.54} = 0.29$

$[C_2H_3O_2^-] = 0.29\ [HC_2H_3O_2]$; $0.29\ [HC_2H_3O_2] + [HC_2H_3O_2] = 1.0\ M$

$[HC_2H_3O_2] = 0.78\ M = [H^+]$ added

0.78 mol of HCl must be added to produce a solution with pH = 4.20.

c. $5.00 = 4.74 + \log \dfrac{[C_2H_3O_2^-]}{[HC_2H_3O_2]}, \quad \dfrac{[C_2H_3O_2^-]}{[HC_2H_3O_2]} = 10^{0.26} = 1.8$

$[C_2H_3O_2^-] = 1.8\ [HC_2H_3O_2]$; $1.8\ [HC_2H_3O_2] + [HC_2H_3O_2] = 1.0\ M$

$[HC_2H_3O_2] = 0.36\ M = [H^+]$ added

0.36 mol of HCl must be added to produce a solution with pH = 5.00.

Acid-Base Titrations

51.

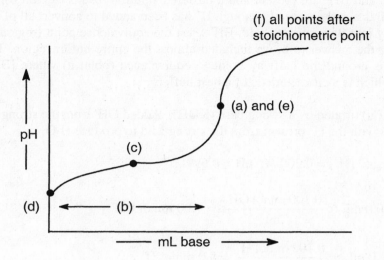

HA + OH$^-$ → A$^-$ + H$_2$O; Added OH$^-$ from the strong base converts the weak acid, HA, into its conjugate base, A$^-$. Initially, before any OH$^-$ is added (point d), HA is the dominant species present. After OH$^-$ is added, both HA and A$^-$ are present and a buffer solution results (region b). At the equivalence point (points a and e), exactly enough OH$^-$ has been added to convert all of the weak acid, HA, into its conjugate base, A$^-$. Past the equivalence point (region f), excess OH$^-$ is present. For the answer to part b, we included almost the entire buffer region. The maximum buffer region (or the region which is the best buffer solution) is around the halfway point to equivalence (point c). At this point, enough OH$^-$ has been added to convert exactly one-half of the weak acid present initially into its conjugate base so [HA] = [A$^-$] and pH = pK$_a$. A best buffer has about equal concentrations of weak acid and conjugate base present.

52.

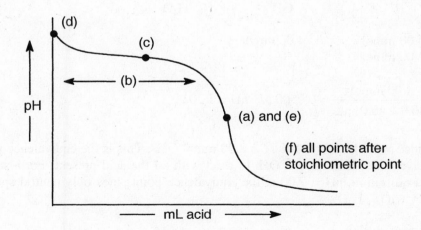

$B + H^+ \rightarrow BH^+$; Added H^+ from the strong acid converts the weak base, B, into its conjugate acid, BH^+. Initially, before any H^+ is added (point d), B is the dominant species present. After H^+ is added, both B and BH^+ are present and a buffered solution results (region b). At the equivalence point (points a and e), exactly enough H^+ has been added to convert all of the weak base present initially into its conjugate acid, BH^+. Past the equivalence point (region f), excess H^+ is present. For the answer to b, we included almost the entire buffer region. The maximum buffer region is around the halfway point to equivalence (point c) where $[B] = [BH^+]$. Here, $pH = pK_a$ which is a characteristic of a best buffer.

53.   This is a strong acid ($HClO_4$) titrated by a strong base (KOH). Added OH^- from the strong base will react completely with the H^+ present from the strong acid to produce H_2O.

a.   Only strong acid present. $[H^+] = 0.200\ M$; $pH = 0.699$

b.   mmol OH^- added $= 10.0\ mL \times \dfrac{0.100\ mmol\ OH^-}{mL} = 1.00\ mmol\ OH^-$

mmol H^+ present $= 40.0\ mL \times \dfrac{0.100\ mmol\ H^+}{mL} = 8.0\ mmol\ H^+$

Note: The units mmoles are usually easier numbers to work with. The units for molarity are moles/L but are also equal to mmoles/mL.

$$H^+ \quad + \quad OH- \quad \rightarrow \quad H_2O$$

Before	8.00 mmol	1.00 mmol	
Change	−1.00 mmol	−1.00 mmol	Reacts completely
After	7.00 mmol	0	

The excess H^+ determines pH. $[H^+]_{excess} = \dfrac{7.00\ mmol\ H^+}{40.0\ mL + 10.0\ mL} = 0.140\ M$; $pH = 0.854$

c.   mmol OH^- added $= 40.0\ mL \times 0.100\ M = 4.00\ mmol\ OH^-$

$$H^+ \quad + \quad OH^- \quad \rightarrow \quad H_2O$$

Before	8.00 mmol	4.00 mmol	
After	4.00 mmol	0	

$[H^+]_{excess} = \dfrac{4.00\ mmol}{(40.0 + 40.0)\ mL} = 0.0500\ M$; $pH = 1.301$

d.   mmol OH^- added $= 80.0\ mL \times 0.100\ M = 8.00\ mmol\ OH^-$; This is the equivalence point because we have added just enough OH^- to react with all the acid present. For a strong acid-strong base titration, $pH = 7.00$ at the equivalence point since only neutral species are present (K^+, ClO_4^-, H_2O).

e.   mmol OH^- added $= 100.0\ mL \times 0.100\ M = 10.0\ mmol\ OH^-$

$$H^+ \quad + \quad OH^- \quad \rightarrow \quad H_2O$$

Before	8.00 mmol	10.0 mmol
After	0	2.0 mmol

Past the equivalence point, the pH is determined by the excess OH^- present.

$$[OH^-]_{excess} = \frac{2.0 \text{ mmol}}{(40.0 + 100.0) \text{ mL}} = 0.014 \ M; \ pOH = 1.85; \ pH = 12.15$$

54.   This is a strong base, $Ba(OH)_2$, titrated by a strong acid, HCl. The added strong acid will neutralize the OH^- from the strong base. As is always the case when a strong acid and/or strong base reacts, the reaction is assumed to go to completion.

a.   Only a strong base is present, but it breaks up into two moles of OH^- ions for every mole of $Ba(OH)_2$. $[OH^-] = 2 \times 0.100 \ M = 0.200 \ M; \ pOH = 0.699; \ pH = 13.301$

b. $\text{mmol } OH^- \text{ present} = 80.0 \text{ mL} \times \dfrac{0.100 \text{ mmol } Ba(OH)_2}{\text{mL}} \times \dfrac{2 \text{ mmol } OH^-}{\text{mmol } Ba(OH)_2}$

$$= 16.0 \text{ mmol } OH^-$$

$$\text{mmol } H^+ \text{ added} = 20.0 \text{ mL} \times \frac{0.400 \text{ mmol } H^+}{\text{mL}} = 8.00 \text{ mmol } H^+$$

$$OH^- \quad + \quad H^+ \quad \rightarrow \quad H_2O$$

Before	16.0 mmol	8.00 mmol	
Change	−8.00 mmol	−8.00 mmol	Reacts completely
After	8.0 mmol	0	

$$[OH^-]_{excess} = \frac{8.0 \text{ mmol } OH^-}{80.0 + 20.0 \text{ mL}} = 0.080 \ M; \ pOH = 1.10; \ pH = 12.90$$

c. $\text{mmol } H^+ \text{ added} = 30.0 \text{ mL} \times 0.400 \ M = 12.0 \text{ mmol } H^+$

$$OH^- \quad + \quad H^+ \quad \rightarrow \quad H_2O$$

Before	16.0 mmol	12.0 mmol
After	4.0 mmol	0

$$[OH^-]_{excess} = \frac{4.0 \text{ mmol } OH^-}{(80.0 + 30.0) \text{ mL}} = 0.036 \ M; \ pOH = 1.44; \ pH = 12.56$$

d. $\text{mmol } H^+ \text{ added} = 40.0 \text{ mL} \times 0.400 \ M = 16.0 \text{ mmol } H^+$; This is the equivalence point. Because the H^+ will exactly neutralize the OH^- from the strong base, all we have in solution is Ba^{2+}, Cl^- and H_2O. All are neutral species, so pH = 7.00.

e. $\text{mmol } H^+ \text{ added} = 80.0 \text{ mL} \times 0.400 \ M = 32.0 \text{ mmol } H^+$

$$OH^- \quad + \quad H^+ \quad \rightarrow \quad H_2O$$

Before   16.0 mmol   32.0 mmol
After   0   16.0 mmol

$$[H^+]_{excess} = \frac{16.0 \text{ mmol}}{(80.0 + 80.0) \text{ mL}} = 0.100 \, M; \quad pH = 1.000$$

55.   This is a weak acid ($HC_2H_3O_2$) titrated by a strong base (KOH).

a.   Only a weak acid is present. Solving the weak acid problem:

$$HC_2H_3O_2 \quad \rightleftharpoons \quad H^+ \quad + \quad C_2H_3O_2^-$$

Initial   0.200 M ~0   0
               x mol/L $HC_2H_3O_2$ dissociates to reach equilibrium
Change $-x$ $\rightarrow$ $+x$ $+x$
Equil. $0.200 - x$ x x

$$K_a = 1.8 \times 10^{-5} = \frac{x^2}{0.200 - x} = \frac{x^2}{0.200} \, , \quad x = [H^+] = 1.9 \times 10^{-3} M; \quad pH = 2.72;$$

Assumptions good.

b.   The added OH^- will react completely with the best acid present, $HC_2H_3O_2$.

$$mmol \; HC_2H_3O_2 \; present = 100.0 \text{ mL} \times \frac{0.200 \text{ mmol } HC_2H_3O_2}{mL} = 20.0 \text{ mmol } HC_2H_3O_2$$

$$mmol \; OH^- \; added = 50.0 \text{ mL} \times \frac{0.100 \text{ mmol } OH^-}{mL} = 5.00 \text{ mmol } OH^-$$

$$HC_2H_3O_2 \quad + \quad OH^- \quad \rightarrow \quad C_2H_3O_2^- \; + \; H_2O$$

Before   20.0 mmol   5.00 mmol   0
Change   −5.00 mmol   −5.00 $\rightarrow$ +5.00 mmol   Reacts completely
After   15.0 mmol   0   5.00 mmol

After reaction of all the strong base, we will have a buffered solution containing a weak acid ($HC_2H_3O_2$) and its conjugate base ($C_2H_3O_2^-$). We will use the Henderson-Hasselbalch equation to solve for the pH of this buffer.

$$pH = pK_a + \log\frac{[C_2H_3O_2^-]}{[HC_2H_3O_2]} = -\log(1.8 \times 10^{-5}) + \log\left(\frac{5.00 \text{ mmol}/V_T}{15.0 \text{ mmol}/V_T}\right)$$

where V_T = total volume

$$pH = 4.74 + \log\left(\frac{5.00}{15.0}\right) = 4.74 + (-0.477) = 4.26$$

Note that the total volume cancels in the Henderson-Hasselbalch equation. For the [base]/ [acid] term, the mole (or mmole) ratio equals the concentration ratio because the components of the buffer are always in the same volume of solution.

c.   mmol OH^- added = 100.0 mL × 0.100 mmol OH^-/mL = 10.0 mmol OH^-; The same amount (20.0 mmol) of $HC_2H_3O_2$ is present as before (it never changes). As before, let the OH^- react to completion, then see what remains in solution after the reaction.

$$HC_2H_3O_2 \quad + \quad OH^- \quad \rightarrow \quad C_2H_3O_2^- \quad + \quad H_2O$$

Before	20.0 mmol	10.0 mmol	0
After	10.0 mmol	0	10.0 mmol

A buffered solution results after the reaction. Because $[C_2H_3O_2^-] = [HC_2H_3O_2] = 10.0$ mmol/ total volume, pH = pK_a. This is always true at the halfway point to equivalence for a weak acid/strong base titration, pH = pK_a.

$$pH = -\log(1.8 \times 10^{-5}) = 4.74$$

d.   mmol OH^- added = 150.0 mL × 0.100 M = 15.0 mmol OH^-. Added OH^- reacts completely with the weak acid.

$$HC_2H_3O_2 \quad + \quad OH^- \quad \rightarrow \quad C_2H_3O_2^- \quad + \quad H_2O$$

Before	20.0 mmol	15.0 mmol	0
After	5.0 mmol	0	15.0 mmol

We have a buffered solution after all the OH^- reacts to completion. Using the Henderson-Hasselbalch equation:

$$pH = 4.74 + \log\frac{[C_2H_3O_2^-]}{[HC_2H_3O_2]} = 4.74 + \log\left(\frac{15.00 \text{ mmol}}{5.0 \text{ mmol}}\right) \quad \text{(Total volume cancels, so we can use mmol ratios.)}$$

$$pH = 4.74 + 0.48 = 5.22$$

e.   mmol OH^- added = 200.00 mL × 0.100 M = 20.0 mmol OH^-; As before, let the added OH^- react to completion with the weak acid, then see what is in solution after this reaction.

$$HC_2H_3O_2 \quad + \quad OH^- \quad \rightarrow \quad C_2H_3O_2^- \quad + \quad H_2O$$

Before	20.0 mmol	20.0 mmol	0
After	0	0	20.0 mmol

This is the equivalence point. Enough OH^- has been added to exactly neutralize all the weak acid present initially. All that remains that affects the pH at the equivalence point is the conjugate base of the weak acid, $C_2H_3O_2^-$. This is a weak base equilibrium problem because the conjugate bases of all weak acids are weak bases themselves.

$$C_2H_3O_2^- + H_2O \rightleftharpoons HC_2H_3O_2 + OH^- \qquad K_b = \frac{K_w}{K_a} = \frac{1.0 \times 10^{-14}}{1.8 \times 10^{-5}}$$

Initial	20.0 mmol/300.0 mL	0	0	$K_b = 5.6 \times 10^{-10}$

x mol/L $C_2H_3O_2^-$ reacts with H_2O to reach equilibrium

Change	$-x$	$\rightarrow$	$+x$	$+x$
Equil.	$0.0667 - x$		x	x

$$K_b = 5.6 \times 10^{-10} = \frac{x^2}{0.0667 - x} \approx \frac{x^2}{0.0667}, \quad x = [OH^-] = 6.1 \times 10^{-6} \, M$$

pOH = 5.21; pH = 8.79; Assumptions good.

Note: the pH at the equivalence point for a weak acid-strong base will always be greater than 7.0. This is because a weak base will always be the only major species present having any acidic or basic properties.

f.   mmol OH^- added = 250.0 mL $\times$ 0.100 M = 25.0 mmol OH^-

$$HC_2H_3O_2 \quad + \quad OH^- \quad \rightarrow \quad C_2H_3O_2^- \quad + \quad H_2O$$

Before	20.0 mmol	25.0 mmol	0
After	0	5.0 mmol	20.0 mmol

After the titration reaction, we will have a solution containing excess OH^- and a weak base, $C_2H_3O_2^-$. When a strong base and a weak base are both present, assume the amount of OH^- added from the weak base will be minimal, i.e., the pH past the equivalence point will be determined by the amount of excess strong base.

$$[OH^-]_{excess} = \frac{5.0 \text{ mmol}}{100.0 \text{ mL} + 250.0 \text{ mL}} = 0.014 \, M; \quad pOH = 1.85; \quad pH = 12.15$$

56.   This is a weak base (H_2NNH_2) titrated by a strong acid (HNO_3). To calculate the pH at the various points, let the strong acid react completely with the weak base present, then see what is in solution.

a.   Only a weak base is present. Solve the weak base equilibrium problem.

$$H_2NNH_2 + H_2O \rightleftharpoons H_2NNH_3^+ + OH^-$$

Initial	0.100 M	0	~0
Equil.	$0.100 - x$	x	x

$$K_b = 3.0 \times 10^{-6} = \frac{x^2}{0.100 - x} \approx \frac{x^2}{0.100}, \quad x = [OH^-] = 5.5 \times 10^{-4} \, M$$

pOH = 3.26; pH = 10.74; Assumptions good.

b.   mmol H_2NNH_2 present $= 100.0$ mL $\times \dfrac{0.100 \text{ mmol } H_2NNH_2}{\text{mL}} = 10.0$ mmol H_2NNH_2

mmol H^+ added $= 20.0$ mL $\times \dfrac{0.200 \text{ mmol } H^+}{\text{mL}} = 4.00$ mmol H^+

Let the H^+ from the strong acid react to completion with the best base present (H_2NNH_2).

	H_2NNH_2	+	H^+	$\rightarrow$	$H_2NNH_3^+$	
Before	10.0 mmol		4.00 mmol		0	
Change	-4.00 mmol		-4.00 mmol	$\rightarrow$	$+4.00$ mmol	Reacts completely
After	6.0 mmol		0		4.00 mmol	

A buffered solution results after the titration reaction. Solving using the Henderson-Hasselbalch equation:

$$pH = pK_a + \log \frac{[\text{Base}]}{[\text{Acid}]}, \quad K_a = \frac{K_w}{K_b} = \frac{1.0 \times 10^{-14}}{3.0 \times 10^{-6}} = 3.3 \times 10^{-9}$$

$$pH = -\log (3.3 \times 10^{-9}) + \log \left(\frac{6.0 \text{ mmol} / V_T}{4.00 \text{ mmol} / V_T} \right) \quad \text{where } V_T = \text{total volume,}$$

which cancels

$$pH = 8.48 + \log (1.5) = 8.48 + 0.18 = 8.66$$

c.   mmol H^+ added $= 25.0$ mL $\times 0.200\ M = 5.00$ mmol H^+

	H_2NNH_2	+	H^+	$\rightarrow$	$H_2NNH_3^+$
Before	10.0 mmol		5.00 mmol		0
After	5.0 mmol		0		5.00 mmol

This is the halfway point to equivalence where $[H_2NNH_3^+] = [H_2NNH_2]$. At this point, $pH = pK_a$ (which is characteristic of the halfway point for any weak base/strong acid titration).

$$pH = -\log (3.3 \times 10^{-9}) = 8.48$$

d.   mmol H^+ added $= 40.0$ mL $\times 0.200\ M = 8.00$ mmol H^+

	H_2NNH_2	+	H^+	$\rightarrow$	$H_2NNH_3^+$
Before	10.0 mmol		8.00 mmol		0
After	2.0 mmol		0		8.00 mmol

A buffer solution results.

$$pH = pK_a + \log \frac{[\text{Base}]}{[\text{Acid}]} = 8.48 + \log\left(\frac{2.0\,\text{mmol}/V_T}{8.00\,\text{mmol}/V_T}\right) = 8.48 + (-0.60) = 7.88$$

e.   mmol H^+ added = 50.0 mL × 0.200 M = 10.0 mmol H^+. This is the equivalence point where just enough H^+ has been added to react with all of the weak base present.

	H_2NNH_2	+	H^+	→	$H_2NNH_3^+$

	H_2NNH_2	H^+	$H_2NNH_3^+$
Before	10.0 mmol	10.0 mmol	0
After	0	0	10.0 mmol

As is always the case in a weak base/strong acid titration, the pH at the equivalence point is acidic because only a weak acid ($H_2NNH_3^+$) is present (conjugate acids of all weak bases are weak acids themselves). Solving the weak acid equilibrium problem:

	$H_2NNH_3^+$	⇌	H^+	+	H_2NNH_2

	$H_2NNH_3^+$	H^+	H_2NNH_2
Initial	10.0 mmol/150.0 mL	0	0
Equil.	0.0667 − x	x	x

$$K_a = 3.3 \times 10^{-9} = \frac{x^2}{0.0667 - x} \approx \frac{x^2}{0.0667}, \quad x = [H^+] = 1.5 \times 10^{-5}\,M$$

pH = 4.82; Assumptions good.

f.   mmol H^+ added = 100.0 mL × 0.200 M = 20.0 mmol H^+

	H_2NNH_2	+	H^+	→	$H_2NNH_3^+$

	H_2NNH_2	H^+	$H_2NNH_3^+$
Before	10.0 mmol	20.0 mmol	0
After	0	10.0 mmol	10.0 mmol

Two acids are present past the equivalence point, but the excess H^+ will determine the pH of the solution since $H_2NNH_3^+$ is a weak acid. Whenever two acids are present, the stronger acid usually determines the pH.

$$[H^+]_{\text{excess}} = \frac{10.0\,\text{mmol}}{100.0\,\text{mL} + 100.0\,\text{mL}} = 0.0500\,M; \ \ pH = 1.301$$

57.   We will do sample calculations for the various parts of the titration. All results are summarized in Table 15.1 at the end of Exercise 15.60.

At the beginning of the titration, only the weak acid $HC_3H_5O_3$ is present.

$$\text{HLac} \quad \rightleftharpoons \quad \text{H}^+ \quad + \quad \text{Lac}^- \qquad K_a = 10^{-3.86} = 1.4 \times 10^{-4}$$

$$\text{HLac} = \text{HC}_3\text{H}_5\text{O}_3$$

Initial   0.100 M   ~0   0 $\text{Lac}^- = \text{C}_3\text{H}_5\text{O}_3^-$

x mol/L HLac dissociates to reach equilibrium

Change $-x$ $\rightarrow$ $+x$ $+x$

Equil. $0.100 - x$ x x

$$1.4 \times 10^{-4} = \frac{x^2}{0.100 - x} \approx \frac{x^2}{0.100}, \quad x = [\text{H}^+] = 3.7 \times 10^{-3} M; \quad \text{pH} = 2.43 \quad \text{Assumptions good.}$$

Up to the stoichiometric point, we calculate the pH using the Henderson-Hasselbalch equation because we have buffer solutions that result after the OH⁻ from the strong base reacts completely with the best acid present, HLac. This is the buffer region. For example, at 4.0 mL of NaOH added:

$$\text{initial mmol HLac present} = 25.0 \text{ mL} \times \frac{0.100 \text{ mmol}}{\text{mL}} = 2.50 \text{ mmol HLac}$$

$$\text{mmol OH}^- \text{ added} = 4.0 \text{ mL} \times \frac{0.100 \text{ mmol}}{\text{mL}} = 0.40 \text{ mmol OH}^-$$

Note: The units mmol are usually easier numbers to work with. The units for molarity are moles/L but are also equal to mmoles/mL.

The 0.40 mmol added OH⁻ convert 0.40 mmoles HLac to 0.40 mmoles Lac⁻ according to the equation:

$$\text{HLac} + \text{OH}^- \rightarrow \text{Lac}^- + \text{H}_2\text{O} \qquad \text{Reacts completely}$$

mmol HLac remaining = 2.50 - 0.40 = 2.10 mmol; mmol Lac⁻ produced = 0.40 mmol

We have a buffer solution. Using the Henderson-Hasselbalch equation where $pK_a = 3.86$:

$$\text{pH} = pK_a + \log\frac{[\text{Lac}^-]}{[\text{HLac}]} = 3.86 + \log\frac{(0.40)}{(2.10)} \qquad \text{(Total volume cancels, so we can use the mole or mmole ratio.)}$$

$$\text{pH} = 3.86 - 0.72 = 3.14$$

Other points in the buffer region are calculated in a similar fashion. Perform a stoichiometry problem first, followed by a buffer problem. The buffer region includes all points up to 24.9 mL OH⁻ added.

At the stoichiometric (equivalence) point (25.0 mL OH⁻ added), we have added enough OH⁻ to convert all of the HLac (2.50 mmol) into its conjugate base, Lac⁻. All that is present is a weak base. To determine the pH, we perform a weak base calculation.

$$[Lac^-]_o = \frac{2.50 \text{ mmol}}{25.0 \text{ mL} + 25.0 \text{ mL}} = 0.0500 \ M$$

$$Lac^- + H_2O \rightleftharpoons HLac + OH^- \qquad K_b = \frac{1.0 \times 10^{-14}}{1.4 \times 10^{-4}} = 7.1 \times 10^{-11}$$

Initial	0.0500 M	0	0

x mol/L Lac$^-$ reacts with H_2O to reach equilibrium

Change	$-x$	$\rightarrow$	$+x$	$+x$
Equil.	0.0500 $-x$		x	x

$$K_b = \frac{x^2}{0.0500 - x} \approx \frac{x^2}{0.0500} = 7.1 \times 10^{-11}$$

$x = [OH^-] = 1.9 \times 10^{-6} \ M$; pOH = 5.72; pH = 8.28   Assumptions good.

Past the stoichiometric point, we have added more than 2.50 mmol of NaOH. The pH will be determined by the excess OH$^-$ ion present. An example of this calculation follows.

At 25.1 mL: OH$^-$ added = 25.1 mL $\times \dfrac{0.100 \text{ mmol}}{\text{mL}} = 2.51$ mmol OH$^-$

2.50 mmol OH$^-$ neutralizes all the weak acid present. The remainder is excess OH$^-$.

[OH$^-$]$_{excess}$ = 2.51 $-$ 2.50 = 0.01 mmol

$$[OH^-]_{excess} = \frac{0.01 \text{ mmol}}{(25.0 + 25.1 \text{ mL})} = 2 \times 10^{-4} \ M; \ \ pOH = 3.7; \ \ pH = 10.3$$

All results are listed in Table 15.1 at the end of the solution to Exercise 15.60.

58.   Results for all points are summarized in Table 15.1 at the end of the solution to Exercise 15.60. At the beginning of the titration, we have a weak acid problem:

$$HOPr \rightleftharpoons H^+ + OPr^- \qquad\qquad HOPr = HC_3H_5O_2$$
$$OPr^- = C_3H_5O_2^-$$

Initial	0.100 M	~0	0

x mol/L HOPr acid dissociates to reach equilibrium

Change	$-x$	$\rightarrow$	$+x$	$+x$
Equil.	0.100 $-x$		x	x

$$K_a = \frac{[H^+][OPr^-]}{[HOPr]} = 1.3 \times 10^{-5} = \frac{x^2}{0.100 - x} \approx \frac{x^2}{0.100}$$

$x = [H^+] = 1.1 \times 10^{-3} M$; pH = 2.96   Assumptions good.

The buffer region is from 4.0 $-$ 24.9 mL of OH$^-$ added. We will do a sample calculation at 24.0 mL OH$^-$ added.

$$\text{initial mmol HOPr present} = 25.0 \text{ mL} \times \frac{0.100 \text{ mmol}}{\text{mL}} = 2.50 \text{ mmol HOPr}$$

$$\text{mmol OH}^- \text{ added} = 24.0 \text{ mL} \times \frac{0.100 \text{ mmol}}{\text{mL}} = 2.40 \text{ mmol OH}^-$$

The added strong base converts HOPr into OPr$^-$.

	HOPr	+	OH$^-$	$\rightarrow$	OPr$^-$	+	H$_2$O	
Before	2.50 mmol		2.40 mmol		0			
Change	-2.40		-2.40	$\rightarrow$	$+2.40$			Reacts completely
After	0.10 mmol		0		2.40 mmol			

A buffer solution results. Using the Henderson-Hasselbalch equation where pK$_a$ = $-\log(1.3 \times 10^{-5}) = 4.89$:

$$\text{pH} = \text{pK}_a + \log \frac{[\text{Base}]}{[\text{Acid}]} = 4.89 + \log \frac{[\text{OPr}^-]}{[\text{HOPr}]}$$

$$\text{pH} = 4.89 + \log \frac{(2.40)}{(0.10)} = 4.89 + 1.38 = 6.27 \text{ (Volume cancels, so we can use the mole or mmole ratio.)}$$

All points in the buffer region, 4.0 mL to 24.9 mL, are calculated this way. See Table 15.1 at the end of Exercise 15.60 for all the results.

25.0 mL NaOH added: This is the equivalence point where just enough OH$^-$ (2.50 mmol) has been added to react with all of the weak acid present (also 2.50 mmol). The only major species present with any acidic or basic properties is OPr$^-$, the conjugate base of the weak acid HOPr. The pH will be basic at the equivalence because OPr$^-$ is a weak base (as is true for all conjugate bases of weak acids). Solving the weak base problem:

	OPr$^-$	+	H$_2$O	$\rightleftharpoons$	OH$^-$	+	HOPr$^-$
Initial	$\dfrac{2.50 \text{ mmol}}{50.0 \text{ mL}} = 0.0500 \, M$				0		0

x mol/L OPr$^-$ reacts with H$_2$O to reach equilibrium

	OPr$^-$			$\rightarrow$	OH$^-$		HOPr$^-$
Change	$-x$			$\rightarrow$	$+x$		$+x$
Equil.	$0.0500 - x$				x		x

$$\text{K}_b = \frac{[\text{OH}^-][\text{HOPr}]}{[\text{OPr}^-]} = \frac{\text{K}_w}{\text{K}_a} = 7.7 \times 10^{-10} = \frac{x^2}{0.0500 - x} \approx \frac{x^2}{0.0500}$$

$x = 6.2 \times 10^{-6} \, M = [\text{OH}^-]$, pOH = 5.21, pH = 8.79 Assumptions good.

Beyond the stoichiometric point, the pH is determined by the excess strong base added. The results are the same as those in Exercise 15.57 (see Table 15.1).

For example at 26.0 mL NaOH added:

$$[OH^-] = \frac{2.60 \text{ mmol} - 2.50 \text{ mmol}}{(25.0 + 26.0) \text{ mL}} = 2.0 \times 10^{-3} M; \quad pOH = 2.70; \quad pH = 11.30$$

59.   At beginning of the titration, only the weak base NH_3 is present. As always, solve for the pH using the K_b reaction for NH_3.

$$NH_3 + H_2O \rightleftharpoons NH_4^+ + OH^- \quad K_b = 1.8 \times 10^{-5}$$

Initial   0.100 M   0   ~0
Equil.   0.100 − x   x   x

$$K_b = \frac{x^2}{0.100 - x} \approx \frac{x^2}{0.100} = 1.8 \times 10^{-5}$$

$x = [OH^-] = 1.3 \times 10^{-3} M; \quad pOH = 2.89; \quad pH = 11.11$ Assumptions good.

In the buffer region (4.0 − 24.9 mL), we can use the Henderson-Hasselbalch equation:

$$K_a = \frac{1.0 \times 10^{-14}}{1.8 \times 10^{-5}} = 5.6 \times 10^{-10}; \quad pK_a = 9.25; \quad pH = 9.25 + \log\frac{[NH_3]}{[NH_4^+]}$$

We must determine the amounts of NH_3 and NH_4^+ present after the added H^+ reacts completely with the NH_3. For example, after 8.0 mL HCl are added:

$$\text{initial mmol } NH_3 \text{ present} = 25.0 \text{ mL} \times \frac{0.100 \text{ mmol}}{mL} = 2.50 \text{ mmol } NH_3$$

$$\text{mmol } H^+ \text{ added} = 8.0 \text{ mL} \times \frac{0.100 \text{ mmol}}{mL} = 0.80 \text{ mmol } H^+$$

Added H^+ reacts with NH_3 to completion: $NH_3 + H^+ \rightarrow NH_4^+$

mmol NH_3 remaining = 2.50 − 0.80 = 1.70 mmol; mmol NH_4^+ produced = 0.80 mmol

$$pH = 9.25 + \log\frac{1.70}{0.80} = 9.58$$ (Mole or mmole ratios can be used since the total volume cancels.)

Other points in the buffer region are calculated in similar fashion. Results are summarized in Table 15.1 at the end of Exercise 15.60.

At the stoichiometric point (25.0 mL H^+ added), just enough HCl has been added to convert all of the weak base (NH_3) into its conjugate acid (NH_4^+). Because all conjugate acids of weak bases are weak acids themselves, perform a weak acid calculation to determine the pH. $[NH_4^+]_o = 2.50$ mmol/50.0 mL = 0.0500 M

$$NH_4^+ \quad \rightleftharpoons \quad H^+ \quad + \quad NH_3 \qquad K_a = 5.6 \times 10^{-10}$$

Initial	0.0500 M	0	0
Equil.	0.0500 − x	x	x

$$5.6 \times 10^{-10} = \frac{x^2}{0.0500 - x} \approx \frac{x^2}{0.0500}, \; x = [H^+] = 5.3 \times 10^{-6} \, M; \; pH = 5.28 \quad \text{Assumptions good.}$$

Beyond the stoichiometric point, the pH is determined by the excess H^+. For example, at 28.0 mL of H^+ added:

$$\text{mmol } H^+ \text{ added} = 28.0 \text{ mL} \times \frac{0.100 \text{ mmol}}{\text{mL}} = 2.80 \text{ mmol } H^+$$

$$\text{Excess mmol } H^+ = 2.80 \text{ mmol} - 2.50 \text{ mmol} = 0.30 \text{ mmol excess } H^+$$

$$[H^+]_{excess} = \frac{0.30 \text{ mmol}}{(25.0 + 28.0) \text{ mL}} = 5.7 \times 10^{-3} \, M; \; pH = 2.24$$

All results are summarized in Table 15.1.

60.   Initially, a weak base problem:

$$py \quad + \quad H_2O \quad \rightleftharpoons \quad Hpy^+ \quad + \quad OH^- \qquad py \text{ is pyridine}$$

Initial	0.100 M		0	~0
Equil.	0.100 − x		x	x

$$K_b = \frac{[Hpy^+][OH^-]}{[py]} = \frac{x^2}{0.100 - x} = \frac{x^2}{0.100} = 1.7 \times 10^{-9}$$

$$x = [OH^-] = 1.3 \times 10^{-5} \, M; \; pOH = 4.89; \; pH = 9.11 \quad \text{Assumptions good.}$$

Buffer region (4.0 − 24.5 mL): Added H^+ reacts completely with py: $py + H^+ \rightarrow Hpy^+$. Determine the moles (or mmoles) of py and Hpy^+ after the reaction, and then use the Henderson-Hasselbalch equation to solve for the pH.

$$K_a = \frac{K_w}{K_b} = \frac{1.0 \times 10^{-14}}{1.7 \times 10^{-9}} = 5.9 \times 10^{-6}; \; pK_a = 5.23; \; pH = 5.23 + \log \frac{[py]}{[Hpy^+]}$$

Results in the buffer region are summarized in Table 15.1 that follows this problem. See Exercise 15.59 for a similar sample calculation.

At the stoichiometric point (25.0 mL H^+ added), this is a weak acid problem since just enough H^+ has been added to convert all of the weak base into its conjugate acid. The initial concentration of $Hpy^+ = 0.0500 \, M$.

$$Hpy^+ \quad \rightleftharpoons \quad py \quad + \quad H^+ \quad K_a = 5.9 \times 10^{-6}$$

Initial	0.0500 M	0	0
Equil.	0.0500 − x	x	x

$$5.9 \times 10^{-6} = \frac{x^2}{0.0500 - x} = \frac{x^2}{0.0500}, \ x = [H^+] = 5.4 \times 10^{-4} \ M; \ pH = 3.27 \quad \text{Assumptions good.}$$

Beyond the equivalence point, the pH determination is made by calculating the concentration of excess H^+. See Exercise 15.59 for an example. All results are summarized in Table 15.1.

Table 15.1: Summary of pH Results for Exercises 15.57 - 15.60 (Graph follows)

Titrant mL	Exercise 15.57	Exercise 15.58	Exercise 15.59	Exercise 15.60
0.0	2.43	2.96	11.11	9.11
4.0	3.14	4.17	9.97	5.95
8.0	3.53	4.56	9.58	5.56
12.5	3.86	4.89	9.25	5.23
20.0	4.46	5.49	8.65	4.63
24.0	5.24	6.27	7.87	3.85
24.5	5.6	6.6	7.6	3.5
24.9	6.3	7.3	6.9	−
25.0	8.28	8.79	5.28	3.27
25.1	10.3	10.3	3.7	−
26.0	11.30	11.30	2.71	2.71
28.0	11.75	11.75	2.24	2.24
30.0	11.96	11.96	2.04	2.04

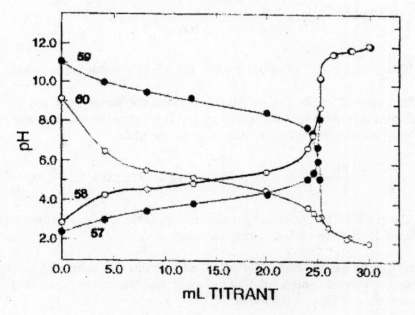

61.   a.   This is a weak acid/strong base titration. At the halfway point to equivalence, [weak acid] = [conjugate base], so pH = pK$_a$ (always true for a weak acid/strong base titration).

pH = $-\log (6.4 \times 10^{-5}) = 4.19$

mmol $HC_7H_5O_2$ present = 100. mL $\times$ 0.10 M = 10. mmol $HC_7H_5O_2$. For the equivalence point, 10. mmol of OH^- must be added. The volume of OH^- added to reach the equivalence point is:

$$10.\text{ mmol } OH^- \times \frac{1\,\text{mL}}{0.10\,\text{mmol } OH^-} = 1.0 \times 10^2 \text{ mL } OH^-$$

At the equivalence point, 10. mmol of $HC_7H_5O_2$ is neutralized by 10. mmol of OH^- to produce 10. mmol of $C_7H_5O_2^-$. This is a weak base. The total volume of the solution is 100.0 mL + 1.0 $\times$ 10^2 mL = 2.0 $\times$ 10^2 mL. Solving the weak base equilibrium problem:

$$C_7H_5O_2^- + H_2O \rightleftharpoons HC_7H_5O_2 + OH^- \qquad K_b = \frac{K_w}{K_a} = \frac{1.0 \times 10^{-14}}{6.4 \times 10^{-5}}$$

Initial   10. mmol/2.0 $\times$ 10^2 mL   0   0 K_b = 1.6 $\times$ 10^{-10}
Equil.   0.050 $- x$ x x

$$K_b = 1.6 \times 10^{-10} = \frac{x^2}{0.050 - x} \approx \frac{x^2}{0.050}, \quad x = [OH^-] = 2.8 \times 10^{-6} M$$

pOH = 5.55; pH = 8.45   Assumptions good.

   b.   At the halfway point to equivalence for a weak base/strong acid titration, pH = pK$_a$ since [weak base] = [conjugate acid].

$$K_a = \frac{K_w}{K_b} = \frac{1.0 \times 10^{-14}}{5.6 \times 10^{-4}} = 1.8 \times 10^{-11}; \quad pH = pK_a = -\log (1.8 \times 10^{-11}) = 10.74$$

For the equivalence point (mmol acid added = mmol base present):

mmol $C_2H_5NH_2$ present = 100.0 mL $\times$ 0.10 M = 10. mmol $C_2H_5NH_2$

$$\text{mL } HNO_3 \text{ added} = 10.\text{ mmol } H^+ \times \frac{1\,\text{mL}}{0.20\,\text{mmol}} = 50.\text{ mL } H^+$$

The strong acid added completely converts the weak base into its conjugate acid. Therefore, at the equivalence point, $[C_2H_5NH_3^+]_0$ = 10. mmol/(100.0 + 50.) mL = 0.067 M. Solving the weak acid equilibrium problem:

$$C_2H_5NH_3^+ \rightleftharpoons H^+ + C_2H_5NH_2$$

Initial   0.067 M 0   0
Equil.   0.067 $- x$ x x

$$K_a = 1.8 \times 10^{-11} = \frac{x^2}{0.067 - x} \approx \frac{x^2}{0.067}, \quad x = [H^+] = 1.1 \times 10^{-6} \, M$$

pH = 5.96; Assumption good.

c. In a strong acid/strong base titration, the halfway point has no special significance other than exactly one-half of the original amount of acid present has been neutralized.

mmol H^+ present = 100.0 mL $\times$ 0.50 M = 50. mmol H^+

$$\text{mL OH}^- \text{ added} = 25 \text{ mmol OH}^- \times \frac{1 \, \text{mL}}{0.25 \, \text{mmol}} = 1.0 \times 10^2 \text{ mL OH}^-$$

$$H^+ \quad + \quad OH^- \rightarrow \quad H_2O$$

Before	50. mmol	25 mmol
After	25 mmol	0

$$[H^+]_{excess} = \frac{25 \, \text{mmol}}{(100.0 + 1.0 \times 10^2) \, \text{mL}} = 0.13 \, M; \quad pH = 0.89$$

At the equivalence point of a strong acid/strong base titration, only neutral species are present (Na^+, Cl^-, H_2O), so the pH = 7.00.

62.   50.0 mL $\times$ 1.0 M = 50. mmol CH_3NH_2 present initially; $CH_3NH_2 + H^+ \rightarrow CH_3NH_3^+$

a. 50.0 mL $\times$ 0.50 M = 25. mmol HCl added. The added H^+ will convert half of the CH_3NH_2 into $CH_3NH_3^+$. This is the halfway point to equivalence where $[CH_3NH_2]$ = $[CH_3NH_3^+]$.

$$pH = pK_a + \log \frac{[CH_3NH_2]}{[CH_3NH_3^+]} = pK_a; \quad K_a = \frac{1.0 \times 10^{-14}}{4.4 \times 10^{-4}} = 2.3 \times 10^{-11}$$

$$pH = pK_a = -\log (2.3 \times 10^{-11}) = 10.64$$

b. It will take 100. mL of HCl solution to reach the stoichiometric (equivalence) point. Here the added H^+ will convert all of the CH_3NH_2 into its conjugate acid, $CH_3NH_3^+$.

$$[CH_3NH_3^+]_o = \frac{50. \, \text{mmol}}{150. \, \text{mL}} = 0.33 \, M$$

$$CH_3NH_3^+ \quad \rightleftharpoons \quad H^+ \quad + \quad CH_3NH_2 \qquad K_a = \frac{K_w}{K_b} = 2.3 \times 10^{-11}$$

Initial	0.33 M	0	0
Equil.	0.33 – x	x	x

$$2.3 \times 10^{-11} = \frac{x^2}{0.33 - x} \approx \frac{x^2}{0.33}, \quad x = [H^+] = 2.8 \times 10^{-6} \, M; \quad pH = 5.55 \quad \text{Assumptions good.}$$

63. $75.0 \text{ mL} \times \dfrac{0.10 \text{ mmol}}{\text{mL}} = 7.5 \text{ mmol HA}; \quad 30.0 \text{ mL} \times \dfrac{0.10 \text{ mmol}}{\text{mL}} = 3.0 \text{ mmol OH}^- \text{ added}$

The added strong base reacts to completion with the weak acid to form the conjugate base of the weak acid and H_2O.

$$HA \quad + \quad OH^- \quad \rightarrow \quad A^- \quad + \quad H_2O$$

	HA	OH⁻	A⁻
Before	7.5 mmol	3.0 mmol	0
After	4.5 mmol	0	3.0 mmol

A buffer results after the OH^- reacts to completion. Using the Henderson-Hasselbalch equation:

$$pH = pK_a + \log\frac{[A^-]}{[HA]}, \quad 5.50 = pK_a + \log\left(\frac{3.0 \text{ mmol}/105.0 \text{ mmol}}{4.5 \text{ mmol}/105.0 \text{ mmol}}\right)$$

$$pK_a = 5.50 - \log(3.0/4.5) = 5.50 - (-0.18) = 5.68; \quad K_a = 10^{-5.68} = 2.1 \times 10^{-6}$$

64.   a.   500.0 mL of HCl added represents the halfway point to equivalence. At the halfway point to equivalence in a weak base/strong acid titration, $pH = pK_a$. So, $pH = pK_a = 5.00$ and $K_a = 1.0 \times 10^{-5}$. Because $K_a = 1.0 \times 10^{-5}$ for the acid, K_b for the conjugate base, A^-, equals 1.0×10^{-9} ($K_a \times K_b = K_w = 1.0 \times 10^{-14}$).

b.   Added H^+ converts A^- into HA. At the equivalence point, only HA is present. The moles of HA present equal the moles of H^+ added (= 1.00 L $\times$ 0.100 mol/L = 0.100 mol). The concentration of HA at the equivalence point is:

$$[HA]_o = \frac{0.100 \text{ mol}}{1.10 \text{ L}} = 0.0909 \ M$$

Solving the weak acid equilibrium problem:

$$HA \quad \rightleftharpoons \quad H^+ \quad + \quad A^- \qquad K_a = 1.0 \times 10^{-5}$$

	HA	H⁺	A⁻
Initial	0.0909 M	0	0
Equil.	0.0909 – x	x	x

$$1.0 \times 10^{-5} = \frac{x^2}{0.0909 - x} \approx \frac{x^2}{0.0909}$$

$x = 9.5 \times 10^{-4} \ M = [H^+]; \quad pH = 3.02$ Assumption good.

Indicators

65. $HIn \rightleftharpoons In^- + H^+$ $K_a = \dfrac{[In^-][H^+]}{[HIn]} = 1.0 \times 10^{-9}$

a.   In a very acid solution, the HIn form dominates, so the solution will be yellow.

b.   The color change occurs when the concentration of the more dominant form is approximately ten times as great as the less dominant form of the indicator.

$\dfrac{[HIn]}{[In^-]} = \dfrac{10}{1};$ $K_a = 1.0 \times 10^{-9} = \left(\dfrac{1}{10}\right)[H^+],$ $[H^+] = 1 \times 10^{-8}\,M;$ pH = 8.0 at color change

c.   This is way past the equivalence point (100.0 mL OH⁻ added), so the solution is very basic and the In⁻ form of the indicator dominates. The solution will be blue.

66.   The color of the indicator will change over the approximate range of $pH = pK_a \pm 1 = 5.3 \pm 1$. Therefore, the useful pH range of methyl red where it changes color would be about: 4.3 (red) - 6.3 (yellow). Note that at pH < 4.3, the HIn form of the indicator dominates, and the color of the solution is the color of HIn (red). At pH > 6.3, the In⁻ form of the indicator dominates, and the color of the solution is the color of In⁻ (yellow). In titrating a weak acid with a strong base, we start off with an acidic solution with pH < 4.3 so the color would change from red to orange at pH ~ 4.3. In titrating a weak base with a strong acid, the color change would be from yellow to orange at pH ~ 6.3. Only a weak base/strong acid titration would have an acidic pH at the equivalence point, so only in this type of titration would the color change of methyl red indicate the approximate endpoint.

67.   At the equivalence point, P^{2-} is the major species. It is a weak base because it is the conjugate base of a weak acid.

$$P^{2-} \quad + \quad H_2O \quad \rightleftharpoons \quad HP^- \quad + \quad OH^-$$

Initial $\dfrac{0.5\,g}{0.1\,L} \times \dfrac{1\,mol}{204.22\,g} = 0.024\,M$ \qquad 0 \qquad\qquad 0 \qquad (carry extra sig. fig.)

Equil. $0.024 - x$ \qquad\qquad\qquad\qquad\qquad x \qquad\qquad x

$K_b = \dfrac{[HP^-][OH^-]}{[P^{2-}]} = \dfrac{K_w}{K_a} = \dfrac{1.0 \times 10^{-14}}{10^{-5.51}},$ $3.2 \times 10^{-9} = \dfrac{x^2}{0.024 - x} \approx \dfrac{x^2}{0.024}$

$x = [OH^-] = 8.8 \times 10^{-6}\,M;$ pOH = 5.1;   pH = 8.9   Assumptions good.

Phenolphthalein would be a suitable indicator for this titration because it changes color at pH ~9.

68. $HIn \rightleftharpoons In^- + H^+$ $K_a = \dfrac{[In^-][H^+]}{[HIn]} = 10^{-3.00}$

At 7.00% conversion of HIn into In⁻, [In⁻]/[HIn] = 7.00/93.00.

$$K_a = 1.0 \times 10^{-3} = \frac{[In^-]}{[HIn]} \times [H^+] = \frac{7.00}{93.00} \times [H^+], \quad [H^+] = 1.3 \times 10^{-2}\, M, \quad pH = 1.89$$

The color of the base form will start to show when the pH is increased to 1.89.

69. When choosing an indicator, we want the color change of the indicator to occur approximately at the pH of the equivalence point. Since the pH generally changes very rapidly at the equivalence point, we don't have to be exact. This is especially true for strong acid/strong base titrations. Some choices where color change occurs at about the pH of the equivalence point are:

Exercise	pH at eq. pt.	Indicator
15.53	7.00	bromthymol blue or phenol red
15.55	8.79	o-cresolphthalein or phenolphthalein

70.

Exercise	pH at eq. pt.	Indicator
15.54	7.00	bromthymol blue or phenol red
15.56	4.82	bromcresol green

71.

Exercise	pH at eq. pt.	Indicator
15.57	8.28	phenolphthalein
15.59	5.28	bromcresol green

72.

Exercise	pH at eq. pt.	Indicator
15.58	8.79	phenolphthalein
15.60	3.27	2,4-dinitrophenol

The titration in 15.60 is not feasible. The pH break at the equivalence point is too small.

73. pH > 5 for bromcresol green to be blue. pH < 8 for thymol blue to be yellow. The pH is between 5 and 8.

74. a. yellow   b. green (Both yellow and blue forms are present.)   c. yellow   d. blue

Solubility Equilibria

75. a. $AgC_2H_3O_2(s) \rightleftharpoons Ag^+(aq) + C_2H_3O_2^-(aq)$ $K_{sp} = [Ag^+]\,[C_2H_3O_2^-]$

   b. $Al(OH)_3(s) \rightleftharpoons Al^{3+}(aq) + 3\, OH^-(aq)$ $K_{sp} = [Al^{3+}]\,[OH^-]^3$

   c. $Ca_3(PO_4)_2(s) \rightleftharpoons 3\, Ca^{2+}(aq) + 2\, PO_4^{3-}(aq)$ $K_{sp} = [Ca^{2+}]^3\,[PO_4^{3-}]^2$

76.   a. $Ag_2CO_3(s) \rightleftharpoons 2\,Ag^+(aq) + CO_3^{2-}(aq)$ $K_{sp} = [Ag^+]^2\,[CO_3^{2-}]$

       b. $Ce(IO_3)_3(s) \rightleftharpoons Ce^{3+}(aq) + 3\,IO_3^-(aq)$ $K_{sp} = [Ce^{3+}]\,[IO_3^-]^3$

       c. $BaF_2(s) \rightleftharpoons Ba^{2+}(aq) + 2\,F^-(aq)$ $K_{sp} = [Ba^{2+}]\,[F^-]^2$

77.   In our setup, s = solubility of the ionic solid in mol/L. This is defined as the maximum amount of a salt which can dissolve. Because solids do not appear in the K_{sp} expression, we do not need to worry about their initial and equilibrium amounts.

       a.

	$CaC_2O_4(s)$	$\rightleftharpoons$	$Ca^{2+}(aq)$	$+$	$C_2O_4^{2-}(aq)$
Initial			0		0
	s mol/L of $CaC_2O_4(s)$ dissolves to reach equilibrium				
Change	$-s$	$\rightarrow$	$+s$		$+s$
Equil.			s		s

From the problem, $s = \dfrac{6.1\times10^{-3}\,g}{L} \times \dfrac{1\,mol\,CaC_2O_4}{128.10\,g} = 4.8 \times 10^{-5}\,mol/L.$

$K_{sp} = [Ca^{2+}]\,[C_2O_4^{2-}] = (s)(s) = s^2,\ K_{sp} = (4.8\times10^{-5})^2 = 2.3 \times 10^{-9}$

       b.

	$BiI_3(s)$	$\rightleftharpoons$	$Bi^{3+}(aq)$	$+$	$3\,I^-(aq)$
Initial			0		0
	s mol/L of $BiI_3(s)$ dissolves to reach equilibrium				
Change	$-s$	$\rightarrow$	$+s$		$+3s$
Equil.			s		$3s$

$K_{sp} = [Bi^{3+}]\,[I^-]^3 = (s)(3s)^3 = 27\,s^4,\ K_{sp} = 27(1.32\times10^{-5})^4 = 8.20 \times 10^{-19}$

78.   a.

	$Pb_3(PO_4)_2(s)$	$\rightleftharpoons$	$3\,Pb^{2+}(aq)$	$+$	$2\,PO_4^{3-}(aq)$
Initial			0		0
	s mol/L of $Pb_3(PO_4)_2(s)$ dissolves to reach equilibrium = molar solubility				
Change	$-s$	$\rightarrow$	$+3s$		$+2s$
Equil.			$3s$		$2s$

$K_{sp} = [Pb^{2+}]^3\,[PO_4^{3-}]^2 = (3s)^3(2s)^2 = 108\,s^5,\ K_{sp} = 108(6.2 \times 10^{-12})^5 = 9.9 \times 10^{-55}$

       b.

	$Li_2CO_3(s)$	$\rightleftharpoons$	$2\,Li^+(aq)$	$+$	$CO_3^{2-}(aq)$
Initial	s = solubility (mol/L)		0		0
Equil.			$2s$		s

$K_{sp} = [Li^+]^2\,[CO_3^{2-}] = (2s)^2(s) = 4s^3,\ K_{sp} = 4(7.4\times10^{-2})^3 = 1.6 \times 10^{-3}$

79.

$$PbBr_2(s) \rightleftharpoons Pb^{2+}(aq) + 2\,Br^-(aq)$$

Initial		0	0

s mol/L of $PbBr_2(s)$ dissolves to reach equilibrium

Change	$-s$	$\rightarrow$	$+s$	$+2s$
Equil.			s	$2s$

From the problem, $s = [Pb^{2+}] = 2.14 \times 10^{-2}\, M$. So:

$$K_{sp} = [Pb^{2+}][Br^-]^2 = s(2s)^2 = 4s^3,\ K_{sp} = 4(2.14 \times 10^{-2})^3 = 3.92 \times 10^{-5}$$

80.

$$Ag_2C_2O_4(s) \rightleftharpoons 2\,Ag^+(aq) + C_2O_4^{2-}(aq)$$

Initial	s = solubility (mol/L)	0	0
Equil.		$2s$	s

From problem, $[Ag^+] = 2s = 2.2 \times 10^{-4}\, M$, $s = 1.1 \times 10^{-4}\, M$

$$K_{sp} = [Ag^+]^2\,[C_2O_4^{2-}] = (2s)^2(s) = 4s^3 = 4(1.1 \times 10^{-4})^3 = 5.3 \times 10^{-12}$$

81.   In our setups, s = solubility in mol/L. Because solids do not appear in the K_{sp} expression, we do not need to worry about their initial or equilibrium amounts.

a.

$$Ag_3PO_4(s) \rightleftharpoons 3\,Ag^+(aq) + PO_4^{3-}(aq)$$

Initial	0	0

s mol/L of $Ag_3PO_4(s)$ dissolves to reach equilibrium

Change	$-s$	$\rightarrow$	$+3s$	$+s$
Equil.			$3s$	s

$$K_{sp} = 1.8 \times 10^{-18} = [Ag^+]^3\,[PO_4^{3-}] = (3s)^3(s) = 27\,s^4$$

$$27\,s^4 = 1.8 \times 10^{-18},\ s = (6.7 \times 10^{-20})^{1/4} = 1.6 \times 10^{-5}\,\text{mol/L} = \text{molar solubility}$$

b.

$$CaCO_3(s) \rightleftharpoons Ca^{2+}(aq) + CO_3^{2-}(aq)$$

Initial	s = solubility (mol/L)	0	0
Equil.		s	s

$$K_{sp} = 8.7 \times 10^{-9} = [Ca^{2+}][CO_3^{2-}] = s^2,\ s = 9.3 \times 10^{-5}\,\text{mol/L}$$

c.

$$Hg_2Cl_2(s) \rightleftharpoons Hg_2^{2+}(aq) + 2\,Cl^-(aq)$$

Initial	s = solubility (mol/L)	0	0
Equil.		s	$2s$

$$K_{sp} = 1.1 \times 10^{-18} = [Hg_2^{2+}][Cl^-]^2 = (s)(2s)^2 = 4s^3,\ s = 6.5 \times 10^{-7}\,\text{mol/L}$$

82.   a. $PbI_2(s)$ $\rightleftharpoons$ $Pb^{2+}(aq)$ + $2\,I^-(aq)$

Initial s = solubility (mol/L)   0   0
Equil. s $2s$

$K_{sp} = 1.4 \times 10^{-8} = [Pb^{2+}][I^-]^2 = s(2s)^2 = 4s^3$

$s = (1.4 \times 10^{-8}/4)^{1/3} = 1.5 \times 10^{-3}\,mol/L$ = molar solubility

b. $CdCO_3(s)$ $\rightleftharpoons$ $Cd^{2+}(aq)$ + $CO_3^{2-}(aq)$

Initial s = solubility (mol/L)   0   0
Equil. s s

$K_{sp} = 5.2 \times 10^{-12} = [Cd^{2+}][CO_3^{2-}] = s^2$, $s = 2.3 \times 10^{-6}\,mol/L$

c. $Sr_3(PO_4)_2(s)$ $\rightleftharpoons$ $3\,Sr^{2+}(aq)$ + $2\,PO_4^{3-}(aq)$

Initial s = solubility (mol/L)   0   0
Equil. $3s$ $2s$

$K_{sp} = 1 \times 10^{-31} = [Sr^{2+}]^3[PO_4^{3-}]^2 = (3s)^3(2s)^2 = 108\,s^5$, $s = 2 \times 10^{-7}\,mol/L$

83. $M_2X_3(s)$ $\rightleftharpoons$ $2\,M^{3+}(aq)$ + $3\,X^{2-}(aq)$ $K_{sp} = [M^{3+}]^2[X^{2-}]^3$

Initial s = solubility (mol/L)   0   0
               s mol/L of $M_2X_3(s)$ dissolves to reach equilibrium
Change $-s$ $+2s$ $+3s$
Equil. $2s$ $3s$

$K_{sp} = (2s)^2(3s)^3 = 108\,s^5$; $s = \dfrac{3.60 \times 10^{-7}\,g}{L} \times \dfrac{1\,mol\,M_2X_3}{288\,g} = 1.25 \times 10^{-9}\,mol/L$

$K_{sp} = 108\,(1.25 \times 10^{-9})^5 = 3.30 \times 10^{-43}$

84.   mol Ag^+ added = $0.200\,L \times \dfrac{0.24\,mol\,AgNO_3}{L} \times \dfrac{1\,mol\,Ag^+}{mol\,AgNO_3} = 0.048\,mol\,Ag^+$

The added Ag^+ will react with the halogen ions to form a precipitate. Because the K_{sp} values are small, we can assume these precipitation reactions go to completion. The order of precipitation will be AgI(s) first (the least soluble compound since K_{sp} is the smallest), followed by AgBr(s), with AgCl(s) forming last [AgCl(s) is the most soluble compound listed since it has the largest K_{sp}].

Let the Ag^+ react with I^- to completion.

$$Ag^+(aq) + I^-(aq) \rightarrow AgI(s) \qquad K = 1/K_{sp} \gg 1$$

Before	0.048 mol	0.018 mol	0
Change	-0.018	-0.018	+0.018
After	0.030 mol	0	0.018 mol

I^- is limiting.

Let the Ag^+ remaining react next with Br^- to completion.

$$Ag^+(aq) + Br^-(aq) \rightarrow AgBr(s) \qquad K = 1/K_{sp} \gg 1$$

Before	0.030 mol	0.018 mol	0
Change	-0.018	-0.018	+0.018
After	0.012 mol	0	0.018 mol

Br^- is limiting.

Finally, let the remaining Ag^+ react with Cl^- to completion.

$$Ag^+(aq) + Cl^-(aq) \rightarrow AgCl(s) \qquad K = 1/K_{sp} \gg 1$$

Before	0.012 mol	0.018 mol	0
Change	-0.012	-0.012	+0.012
After	0	0.006 mol	0.012 mol

Ag^+ is limiting.

Some of the AgCl will redissolve to produce some Ag^+ ions; we can't have $[Ag^+] = 0$ M. Calculating how much AgCl(s) redissolves:

$$AgCl(s) \rightarrow Ag^+(aq) + Cl^-(aq) \qquad K_{sp} = 1.6 \times 10^{-10}$$

Initial	s = solubility (mol/L)	0	0.006 mol/0.200 L = 0.03 M
	s mol/L of AgCl dissolves to reach equilibrium		
Change	-s	$\rightarrow$ +s	+s
Equil.		s	0.03 + s

$K_{sp} = 1.6 \times 10^{-10} = [Ag^+][Cl^-] = s(0.03 + s) \approx 0.03\,s$

$s = 5 \times 10^{-9}$ mol/L; The assumption that $0.03 + s \approx 0.03$ is good.

mol AgCl present = 0.012 mol $- 5 \times 10^{-9}$ mol = 0.012 mol

mass AgCl present = 0.012 mol AgCl $\times \dfrac{143.4 \text{ g}}{\text{mol AgCl}} = 1.7$ g AgCl

$[Ag^+] = s = 5 \times 10^{-9}$ mol/L

85.   Let s = solubility of $Co(OH)_3$ in mol/L. Note: Since solids do not appear in the K_{sp} expression, we do not need to worry about their initial or equilibrium amounts.

$$Co(OH)_3(s) \quad \rightleftharpoons \quad Co^{3+}(aq) \quad + \quad 3\,OH^-(aq)$$

Initial   0 $1.0 \times 10^{-7}\,M$ from water

s mol/L of $Co(OH)_3(s)$ dissolves to reach equilibrium = molar solubility

Change $-s$ $\rightarrow$ $+s$ $+3s$

Equil. s $1.0 \times 10^{-7} + 3s$

$$K_{sp} = 2.5 \times 10^{-43} = [Co^{3+}][OH^-]^3 = (s)(1.0 \times 10^{-7} + 3s)^3 \approx s(1.0 \times 10^{-7})^3$$

$$s = \frac{2.5 \times 10^{-43}}{1.0 \times 10^{-21}} = 2.5 \times 10^{-22}\,mol/L; \quad \text{Assumption good } (1.0 \times 10^{-7} + 3s \approx 1.0 \times 10^{-7}).$$

86. $$Cd(OH)_2(s) \quad \rightleftharpoons \quad Cd^{2+}(aq) \quad + \quad 2\,OH^-(aq) \qquad K_{sp} = 5.9 \times 10^{-15}$$

Initial s = solubility (mol/L)   0 $1.0 \times 10^{-7}\,M$

Equil. s $1.0 \times 10^{-7} + 2s$

$$K_{sp} = [Cd^{2+}][OH^-]^2 = s(1.0 \times 10^{-7} + 2s)^2; \quad \text{Assume that } 1.0 \times 10^{-7} + 2s \approx 2s, \text{ then:}$$

$$K_{sp} = 5.9 \times 10^{-15} = s(2s)^2 = 4s^3, \quad s = 1.1 \times 10^{-5}\,mol/L$$

Assumption is good (1.0×10^{-7} is 0.4% of $2s$). Molar solubility = $1.1 \times 10^{-5}\,mol/L$

87.   a.   Both solids dissolve to produce 3 ions in solution, so we can compare the values of K_{sp} to determine relative molar solubility. Because the K_{sp} for CaF_2 is smaller, $CaF_2(s)$ is less soluble (in mol/L).

b.   We must calculate molar solubilities since each salt yields a different number of ions when it dissolves.

$$Ca_3(PO_4)_2(s) \quad \rightleftharpoons \quad 3\,Ca^{2+}(aq) \quad + \quad 2\,PO_4^{3-}(aq) \qquad K_{sp} = 1.3 \times 10^{-32}$$

Initial s = solubility (mol/L)   0   0

Equil. $3s$ $2s$

$$K_{sp} = [Ca^{2+}]^3[PO_4^{3-}]^2 = (3s)^3(2s)^2 = 108\,s^5, \quad s = (1.3 \times 10^{-32}/108)^{1/5} = 1.6 \times 10^{-7}\,mol/L$$

$$FePO_4(s) \quad \rightleftharpoons \quad Fe^{3+}(aq) \quad + \quad PO_4^{3-}(aq) \qquad K_{sp} = 1.0 \times 10^{-22}$$

Initial s = solubility (mol/L)   0   0

Equil. s s

$$K_{sp} = [Fe^{3+}][PO_4^{3-}] = s^2, \quad s = \sqrt{1.0 \times 10^{-22}} = 1.0 \times 10^{-11}\,mol/L$$

The molar solubility of $FePO_4$ is smaller, so $FePO_4$ is less soluble (in mol/L).

88.   a. $FeC_2O_4(s) \rightleftharpoons Fe^{2+}(aq) + C_2O_4{}^{2-}(aq)$

      Equil. s = solubility (mol/L) s s

      $K_{sp} = 2.1 \times 10^{-7} = [Fe^{2+}][C_2O_4{}^{2-}] = s^2$, $s = 4.6 \times 10^{-4}$ mol/L

                           $Cu(IO_4)_2(s) \rightleftharpoons Cu^{2+}(aq) + 2 IO_4{}^-(aq)$

      Equil. s $2s$

      $K_{sp} = 1.4 \times 10^{-7} = [Cu^{2+}][IO_4{}^-]^2 = s(2s)^2 = 4s^3$, $s = (1.4 \times 10^{-7}/4)^{1/3} = 3.3 \times 10^{-3}$ mol/L

      By comparing calculated molar solubilities, $FeC_2O_4(s)$ is less soluble (in mol/L).

   b. Each salt produces 3 ions in solution, so we can compare K_{sp} values to determine relative molar solubilities. Therefore, $Mn(OH)_2(s)$ will be less soluble (in mol/L) because it has a smaller K_{sp} value.

89.   a. $Fe(OH)_3(s) \rightleftharpoons Fe^{3+}(aq) + 3 OH^-(aq)$

      Initial   0 $1 \times 10^{-7} M$ from water

      s mol/L of $Fe(OH)_3(s)$ dissolves to reach equilibrium = molar solubility

      Change $-s$ $\rightarrow$ $+s$ $+3s$
      Equil. s $1 \times 10^{-7} + 3s$

      $K_{sp} = 4 \times 10^{-38} = [Fe^{3+}][OH^-]^3 = (s)(1 \times 10^{-7} + 3s)^3 \approx s(1 \times 10^{-7})^3$

      $s = 4 \times 10^{-17}$ mol/L   Assumption good $(3s << 1 \times 10^{-7})$.

   b. $Fe(OH)_3(s) \rightleftharpoons Fe^{3+}(aq) + 3 OH^-(aq)$ pH = 5.0, $[OH^-] = 1 \times 10^{-9} M$

      Initial   0 $1 \times 10^{-9} M$ (buffered)

      s mol/L dissolves to reach equilibrium

      Change $-s$ $\rightarrow$ $+s$ $-$ (assume no pH change in buffer)
      Equil. s 1×10^{-9}

      $K_{sp} = 4 \times 10^{-38} = [Fe^{3+}][OH^-]^3 = (s)(1 \times 10^{-9})^3$, $s = 4 \times 10^{-11}$ mol/L = molar solubility

   c. $Fe(OH)_3(s) \rightleftharpoons Fe^{3+}(aq) + 3 OH^-(aq)$ pH = 11.0 so $[OH^-] = 1 \times 10^{-3} M$

      Initial   0   0.001 M (buffered)

      s mol/L dissolves to reach equilibrium

      Change $-s$ $\rightarrow$ $+s$ $-$ (assume no pH change)
      Equil. s 0.001

      $K_{sp} = 4 \times 10^{-38} = [Fe^{3+}][OH^-]^3 = (s)(0.001)^3$, $s = 4 \times 10^{-29}$ mol/L = molar solubility

      Note: As $[OH^-]$ increases, solubility decreases. This is the common ion effect.

90.   a. $Ag_2SO_4(s)$ $\rightleftharpoons$ $2\,Ag^+(aq)$ + $SO_4^{2-}(aq)$

Initial s = solubility (mol/L)   0   0
Equil. $2s$ s

$K_{sp} = 1.2 \times 10^{-5} = [Ag^+]^2\,[SO_4^{2-}] = (2s)^2 s = 4s^3, \; s = 1.4 \times 10^{-2}\,mol/L$

b. $Ag_2SO_4(s)$ $\rightleftharpoons$ $2\,Ag^+(aq)$ + $SO_4^{2-}(aq)$

Initial s = solubility (mol/L)   0.10 M 0
Equil.   0.10 + $2s$ s

$K_{sp} = 1.2 \times 10^{-5} = (0.10 + 2s)^2 (s) \approx (0.10)^2 (s), \; s = 1.2 \times 10^{-3}\,mol/L;$ Assumption good.

c. $Ag_2SO_4(s)$ $\rightleftharpoons$ $2\,Ag^+(aq)$ + $SO_4^{2-}\,(aq)$

Initial s = solubility (mol/L)   0   0.20 M
Equil $2s$ 0.20 + s

$1.2 \times 10^{-5} = (2s)^2 (0.20 + s) \approx 4s^2 (0.20), \; s = 3.9 \times 10^{-3}\,mol/L;$ Assumption good.

Note: Comparing the solubilities of parts b and c to that of part a illustrates that the solubility of a salt decreases when a common ion is present.

91. $Ca_3(PO_4)_2(s)$ $\rightleftharpoons$ $3\,Ca^{2+}(aq)$ + $2\,PO_4^{3-}(aq)$

Initial   0   0.20 M
               s mol/L of $Ca_3(PO_4)_2(s)$ dissolves to reach equilibrium
Change $-s$ $\rightarrow$ $+3s$ $+2s$
Equil. $3s$ 0.20 + $2s$

$K_{sp} = 1.3 \times 10^{-32} = [Ca^{2+}]^3\,[PO_4^{3-}]^2 = (3s)^3 (0.20 + 2s)^2$

Assuming $0.20 + 2s \approx 0.20$: $1.3 \times 10^{-32} = (3s)^3 (0.20)^2 = 27\,s^3 (0.040)$

s = molar solubility = $2.3 \times 10^{-11}\,mol/L;$ Assumption good.

92. $Ce(IO_3)_3(s)$ $\rightleftharpoons$ $Ce^{3+}(aq)$ + $3\,IO_3^-\,(aq)$

Initial s = solubility (mol/L)   0   0.20 M
Equil. s 0.20 + $3s$

$K_{sp} = [Ce^{3+}]\,[IO_3^-]^3 = s(0.20 + 3s)^3$

From the problem, $s = 4.4 \times 10^{-8}\,mol/L;$ Solving for K_{sp}:

$K_{sp} = (4.4 \times 10^{-8}) \times [0.20 + 3(4.4 \times 10^{-8})]^3 = 3.5 \times 10^{-10}$

93.
$$\text{ZnS(s)} \quad \rightleftharpoons \quad \text{Zn}^{2+} + \text{S}^{2-} \qquad K_{sp} = [\text{Zn}^{2+}][\text{S}^{2-}]$$

Initial s = solubility (mol/L)   0.050 M 0
Equil.   0.050 + s s

$K_{sp} = 2.5 \times 10^{-22} = (0.050 + s)(s) \approx 0.050\ s, \quad s = 5.0 \times 10^{-21}$ mol/L;   Assumptions good.

mass ZnS that dissolves $= 0.3000\ \text{L} \times \dfrac{5.0 \times 10^{-21}\ \text{mol ZnS}}{\text{L}} \times \dfrac{97.45\ \text{g ZnS}}{\text{mol}} = 1.5 \times 10^{-19}$ g

94. For 99% of the Mg^{2+} to be removed, we need at equilibrium, $[\text{Mg}^{2+}] = 0.01(0.052\ M)$. Using the K_{sp} equilibrium constant, calculate the $[\text{OH}^-]$ required to reach this reduced $[\text{Mg}^{2+}]$.

$$\text{Mg(OH)}_2(s) \rightleftharpoons \text{Mg}^{2+}(aq) + 2\ \text{OH}^-\ (aq) \qquad K_{sp} = 8.9 \times 10^{-12}$$

$8.9 \times 10^{-12} = [\text{Mg}^{2+}][\text{OH}^-]^2 = [0.01(0.052\ M)]\ [\text{OH}^-]^2, \quad [\text{OH}^-] = 1.3 \times 10^{-4}\ M$ (extra sig fig)

pOH $= -\log(1.3 \times 10^{-4}) = 3.89$;   pH = 10.11;   At a pH = 10.1, 99% of the Mg^{2+} in seawater will be removed as $\text{Mg(OH)}_2(s)$.

95. If the anion in the salt can act as a base in water, the solubility of the salt will increase as the solution becomes more acidic. Added H^+ will react with the base, forming the conjugate acid. As the basic anion is removed, more of the salt will dissolve to replenish the basic anion. The salts with basic anions are Ag_3PO_4, CaCO_3, CdCO_3 and $\text{Sr}_3(\text{PO}_4)_2$. Hg_2Cl_2 and PbI_2 do not have any pH dependence since Cl^- and I^- are terrible bases (the conjugate bases of strong acids).

$$\text{Ag}_3\text{PO}_4(s) + \text{H}^+(aq) \rightarrow 3\ \text{Ag}^+(aq) + \text{HPO}_4{}^{2-}(aq) \xrightarrow{\text{excess H}^+} 3\ \text{Ag}^+(aq) + \text{H}_3\text{PO}_4(aq)$$

$$\text{CaCO}_3(s) + \text{H}^+ \rightarrow \text{Ca}^{2+} + \text{HCO}_3^- \xrightarrow{\text{excess H}^+} \text{Ca}^{2+} + \text{H}_2\text{CO}_3\ [\text{H}_2\text{O}(l) + \text{CO}_2(g)]$$

$$\text{CdCO}_3(s) + \text{H}^+ \rightarrow \text{Cd}^{2+} + \text{HCO}_3^- \xrightarrow{\text{excess H}^+} \text{Cd}^{2+} + \text{H}_2\text{CO}_3\ [\text{H}_2\text{O}(l) + \text{CO}_2(g)]$$

$$\text{Sr}_3(\text{PO}_4)_2(s) + 2\ \text{H}^+ \rightarrow 3\ \text{Sr}^{2+} + 2\ \text{HPO}_4{}^{2-} \xrightarrow{\text{excess H}^+} 3\ \text{Sr}^{2+} + 2\ \text{H}_3\text{PO}_4$$

96.   a. AgF   b. Pb(OH)_2 c. $\text{Sr(NO}_2)_2$ d. Ni(CN)_2

All the above salts have anions that are bases. The anions of the other choices are conjugate bases of strong acids. They have no basic properties in water and, therefore, do not have solubilities which depend on pH.

97.   Potentially, $BaSO_4(s)$ could form if Q is greater than K_{sp}.

$$BaSO_4(s) \rightleftharpoons Ba^{2+}(aq) + SO_4^{2-}(aq) \quad K_{sp} = 1.5 \times 10^{-9}$$

To calculate Q, we need the initial concentrations of Ba^{2+} and SO_4^{2-}.

$$[Ba^{2+}]_o = \frac{\text{mmoles } Ba^{2+}}{\text{total mL solution}} = \frac{75.0 \text{ mL} \times \dfrac{0.020 \text{ mmoles } Ba^{2+}}{\text{mL}}}{75.0 \text{ mL} + 125 \text{ mL}} = 0.0075 \ M$$

$$[SO_4^{2-}]_o = \frac{\text{mmoles } SO_4^{2-}}{\text{total mL solution}} = \frac{125 \text{ mL} \times \dfrac{0.040 \text{ mmoles } SO_4^{2-}}{\text{mL}}}{200. \text{ mL}} = 0.025 \ M$$

$$Q = [Ba^{2+}]_o[SO_4^{2-}]_o = (0.0075 \ M)(0.025 \ M) = 1.9 \times 10^{-4}$$

$Q > K_{sp} \ (1.5 \times 10^{-9})$ so $BaSO_4(s)$ will form.

98.   The formation of $Mg(OH)_2(s)$ is the only possible precipitate. $Mg(OH)_2(s)$ will form if Q > K_{sp}.

$$Mg(OH)_2(s) \rightleftharpoons Mg^{2+}(aq) + 2 \ OH^-(aq) \quad K_{sp} = [Mg^{2+}][OH^-]^2 = 8.9 \times 10^{-12}$$

$$[Mg^{2+}]_o = \frac{100.0 \text{ mL} \times 4.0 \times 10^{-4} \text{ mmol } Mg^{2+} / \text{mL}}{100.0 \text{ mL} + 100.0 \text{ mL}} = 2.0 \times 10^{-4} \ M$$

$$[OH^-]_o = \frac{100.0 \text{ mL} \times 2.0 \times 10^{-4} \text{ mmol } OH^- / \text{mL}}{200.0 \text{ mL}} = 1.0 \times 10^{-4} \ M$$

$$Q = [Mg^{2+}]_o[OH^-]_0^2 = (2.0 \times 10^{-4} \ M)(1.0 \times 10^{-4})^2 = 2.0 \times 10^{-12}$$

Since $Q < K_{sp}$, then $Mg(OH)_2(s)$ will not precipitate, so no precipitate forms.

99.   The concentrations of ions are large, so Q will be greater than K_{sp} and $BaC_2O_4(s)$ will form. To solve this problem, we will assume that the precipitation reaction goes to completion; then we will solve an equilibrium problem to get the actual ion concentrations. This makes the math reasonable.

$$100. \text{ mL} \times \frac{0.200 \text{ mmol } K_2C_2O_4}{\text{mL}} = 20.0 \text{ mmol } K_2C_2O_4$$

$$150. \text{ mL} \times \frac{0.250 \text{ mmol } BaBr_2}{\text{mL}} = 37.5 \text{ mmol } BaBr_2$$

$$Ba^{2+}(aq) \quad + \quad C_2O_4^{2-}(aq) \quad \rightarrow \quad BaC_2O_4(s) \qquad K = 1/K_{sp} \gg 1$$

Before	37.5 mmol	20.0 mmol	0	
Change	−20.0	−20.0	$\rightarrow$ +20.0	Reacts completely (K is large)
After	17.5	0	20.0	

New initial concentrations (after complete precipitation) are:

$$[Ba^{2+}] = \frac{17.5 \text{ mmol}}{250. \text{ mL}} = 7.00 \times 10^{-2} \ M; \ \ [C_2O_4^{2-}] = 0 \ M$$

$$[K^+] = \frac{2(20.0 \text{ mmol})}{250. \text{ mL}} = 0.160 \ M; \ \ [Br^-] = \frac{2(37.5 \text{ mmol})}{250. \text{ mL}} = 0.300 \ M$$

For K^+ and Br^-, these are also the final concentrations. We can't have $0 \ M \ C_2O_4^{2-}$. For Ba^{2+} and $C_2O_4^{2-}$, we need to perform an equilibrium calculation.

$$BaC_2O_4(s) \quad \rightleftharpoons \quad Ba^{2+}(aq) \quad + \quad C_2O_4^{2-}(aq) \qquad K_{sp} = 2.3 \times 10^{-8}$$

Initial	0.0700 M	0
	s mol/L of $BaC_2O_4(s)$ dissolves to reach equilibrium	
Equil.	0.0700 + s	s

$$K_{sp} = 2.3 \times 10^{-8} = [Ba^{2+}] \ [C_2O_4^{2-}] = (0.0700 + s)(s) \approx 0.0700 \ s$$

$$s = [C_2O_4^{2-}] = 3.3 \times 10^{-7} \text{ mol/L}; \ \ [Ba^{2+}] = 0.0700 \ M; \ \ \text{Assumption good } (s \ll 0.0700).$$

100.   50.0 mL × 0.10 M = 5.0 mmol Pb^{2+}; 50.0 mL × 1.0 M = 50. mmol Cl^-. For this solution, Q > K_{sp}, so $PbCl_2$ precipitates. Assume precipitation of $PbCl_2(s)$ is complete. 5.0 mmol Pb^{2+} requires 10. mmol of Cl^- for complete precipitation, which leaves 40. mmol Cl^- in excess. Now, let some of the $PbCl_2(s)$ redissolve to establish equilibrium

$$PbCl_2(s) \quad \rightleftharpoons \quad Pb^{2+}(aq) \quad + \quad 2 \ Cl^-(aq)$$

Initial	0	$\dfrac{40. \text{ mmol}}{100.0 \text{ mL}} = 0.40 \ M$
	s mol/L of $PbCl_2(s)$ dissolves to reach equilibrium	
Equil.	s	0.40 + 2s

$$K_{sp} = [Pb^{2+}] \ [Cl^-]^2, \ \ 1.6 \times 10^{-5} = s(0.40 + 2s)^2 \approx s(0.40)^2$$

$$s = 1.0 \times 10^{-4} \text{ mol/L}; \ \ \text{Assumption good.}$$

At equilibrium: $[Pb^{2+}] = s = 1.0 \times 10^{-4}$ mol/L; $[Cl^-] = 0.40 + 2s, \ \ 0.40 + 2(1.0 \times 10^{-4})$
$$= 0.40 \ M$$

101. $Ag_3PO_4(s) \rightleftharpoons 3\ Ag^+(aq) + PO_4^{3-}(aq)$; When Q is greater than K_{sp}, precipitation will occur. We will calculate the $[Ag^+]_o$ necessary for $Q = K_{sp}$. Any $[Ag^+]_o$ greater than this calculated number will cause precipitation of $Ag_3PO_4(s)$. In this problem, $[PO_4^{3-}]_o = [Na_3PO_4]_o = 1.0 \times 10^{-5}\ M$.

$K_{sp} = 1.8 \times 10^{-18}$; $Q = 1.8 \times 10^{-18} = [Ag^+]_o^3\ [PO_4^{3-}]_o = [Ag^+]_o^3\ (1.0 \times 10^{-5}\ M)$

$$[Ag^+]_o = \left(\frac{1.8 \times 10^{-18}}{1.0 \times 10^{-5}}\right)^{1/3}, \quad [Ag^+]_o = 5.6 \times 10^{-5}\ M$$

When $[Ag^+]_o = [AgNO_3]_o$ is greater than $5.6 \times 10^{-5}\ M$, precipitation of $Ag_3PO_4(s)$ will occur.

102.   From Table 15.4, K_{sp} for $NiCO_3 = 1.4 \times 10^{-7}$ and K_{sp} for $CuCO_3 = 2.5 \times 10^{-10}$. From the K_{sp} values, $CuCO_3$ will precipitate first since it has the smaller K_{sp} value and will be the least soluble. For $CuCO_3(s)$, precipitation begins when:

$$[CO_3^{2-}] = \frac{K_{sp,\,CuCO_3}}{[Cu^{2+}]} = \frac{2.5 \times 10^{-10}}{0.25\ M} = 1.0 \times 10^{-9}\ M\ CO_3^{2-}$$

For $NiCO_3(s)$ to precipitate:

$$[CO_3^{2-}] = \frac{K_{sp,\,NiCO_3}}{[Ni^{2+}]} = \frac{1.4 \times 10^{-7}}{0.25\ M} = 5.6 \times 10^{-7}\ M\ CO_3^{2-}$$

Determining the $[Cu^{2+}]$ when $NiCO_3(s)$ begins to precipitate:

$$[Cu^{2+}] = \frac{K_{sp,\,CuCO_3}}{[CO_3^{2-}]} = \frac{2.5 \times 10^{-10}}{5.6 \times 10^{-7}\ M} = 4.5 \times 10^{-4}\ M\ Cu^{2+}$$

For successful separation, 1% Cu^{2+} or less of the initial amount of Cu^{2+} (0.25 M) must be present before $NiCO_3(s)$ begins to precipitate. The percent of Cu^{2+} present when $NiCO_3(s)$ begins to precipitate is:

$$\frac{4.5 \times 10^{-4}\ M}{0.25\ M} \times 100 = 0.18\%\ Cu^{2+}$$

Since less than 1% of the initial amount of Cu^{2+} remains, the metals can be separated through slow addition of $Na_2CO_3(aq)$.

Complex Ion Equilibria

103.   a.

$Ni^{2+} + CN^- \rightleftharpoons NiCN^+$	K_1
$NiCN^+ + CN^- \rightleftharpoons Ni(CN)_2$	K_2
$Ni(CN)_2 + CN^- \rightleftharpoons Ni(CN)_3^-$	K_3
$Ni(CN)_3^- + CN^- \rightleftharpoons Ni(CN)_4^{2-}$	K_4

$Ni^{2+} + 4\ CN^- \rightleftharpoons Ni(CN)_4^{2-}$ $\qquad\qquad K_f = K_1K_2K_3K_4$

Note: The various K's are included for your information. Each NH_3 adds with a corresponding K value associated with that reaction. The overall formation constant, K_f, for the overall reaction is equal to the product of all the stepwise K values.

b.
$$V^{3+} + C_2O_4^{2-} \rightleftharpoons VC_2O_4^{+} \qquad K_1$$
$$VC_2O_4^{+} + C_2O_4^{2-} \rightleftharpoons V(C_2O_4)_2^{-} \qquad K_2$$
$$V(C_2O_4)_2^{-} + C_2O_4^{2-} \rightleftharpoons V(C_2O_3)^{3-} \qquad K_2$$

$$\overline{V^{3+} + 3\,C_2O_4^{2-} \rightleftharpoons V(C_2O_4)_3^{3-} \qquad K_f = K_1K_2K_3}$$

104. a.
$$Co^{3+} + F^{-} \rightleftharpoons CoF^{2+} \qquad K_1$$
$$CoF^{2+} + F^{-} \rightleftharpoons CoF_2^{+} \qquad K_2$$
$$CoF_2^{+} + F^{-} \rightleftharpoons CoF_3 \qquad K_3$$
$$CoF_3 + F^{-} \rightleftharpoons CoF_4^{-} \qquad K_4$$
$$CoF_4^{-} + F^{-} \rightleftharpoons CoF_5^{2-} \qquad K_5$$
$$CoF_5^{2-} + F^{-} \rightleftharpoons CoF_6^{3-} \qquad K_6$$

$$\overline{Co^{3+} + 6\,F^{-} \rightleftharpoons CoF_6^{3-} \qquad K_f = K_1K_2K_3K_4K_5K_6}$$

b.
$$Zn^{2+} + NH_3 \rightleftharpoons ZnNH_3^{2+} \qquad K_1$$
$$ZnNH_3^{2+} + NH_3 \rightleftharpoons Zn(NH_3)_2^{2+} \qquad K_2$$
$$Zn(NH_3)_2^{2+} + NH_3 \rightleftharpoons Zn(NH_3)_3^{2+} \qquad K_3$$
$$Zn(NH_3)_3^{2+} + NH_3 \rightleftharpoons Zn(NH_3)_4^{2+} \qquad K_4$$

$$\overline{Zn^{2+} + 4\,NH_3 \rightleftharpoons Zn(NH_3)_4^{2+} \qquad K_f = K_1K_2K_3K_4}$$

105.
$$Mn^{2+} + C_2O_4^{2-} \rightleftharpoons MnC_2O_4 \qquad K_1 = 7.9 \times 10^3$$
$$MnC_2O_4 + C_2O_4^{2-} \rightleftharpoons Mn(C_2O_4)_2^{2-} \qquad K_2 = 7.9 \times 10^1$$

$$\overline{Mn^{2+}(aq) + 2\,C_2O_4^{2-}(aq) \rightleftharpoons Mn(C_2O_4)_2^{2-}(aq) \qquad K_f = K_1K_2 = 6.2 \times 10^5}$$

106. $Fe^{3+}(aq) + 6\,CN^{-}(aq) \rightleftharpoons Fe(CN)_6^{3-} \qquad K = \dfrac{[Fe(CN)_6^{3-}]}{[Fe^{3+}][CN^{-}]^6}$

$$K = \frac{1.5 \times 10^{-3}}{(8.5 \times 10^{-40})(0.11)^6} = 1.0 \times 10^{42}$$

107. $Hg^{2+}(aq) + 2\,I^{-}(aq) \rightarrow HgI_2(s); \quad HgI_2(s) + 2\,I^{-}(aq) \rightarrow HgI_4^{2-}(aq)$
                        orange ppt   soluble complex ion

108. $Ag^{+}(aq) + Cl^{-}(aq) \rightleftharpoons AgCl(s)$, white ppt.; $AgCl(s) + 2\,NH_3(aq) \rightleftharpoons Ag(NH_3)_2^{+}(aq) +$
                                                                                                                     $Cl^{-}(aq)$

$Ag(NH_3)_2^{+}(aq) + Br^{-}(aq) \rightleftharpoons AgBr(s) + 2\,NH_3(aq)$, pale yellow ppt.

$AgBr(s) + 2\,S_2O_3^{2-}(aq) \rightleftharpoons Ag(S_2O_3)_2^{3-}(aq) + Br^{-}(aq)$

$Ag(S_2O_3)_2^{3-}(aq) + I^-(aq) \rightleftharpoons AgI(s) + 2\ S_2O_3^{2-}(aq)$, yellow ppt.

The least soluble salt (smallest K_{sp} value) must be AgI because it forms in the presence of Cl^- and Br^-. The most soluble salt (largest K_{sp} value) must be AgCl since it forms initially, but never reforms. The order of K_{sp} values are: K_{sp} (AgCl) > K_{sp} (AgBr) > K_{sp} (AgI)

109.   The formation constant for HgI_4^{2-} is an extremely large number. Because of this, we will let the Hg^{2+} and I^- ions present initially react to completion, and then solve an equilibrium problem to determine the Hg^{2+} concentration.

$$Hg^{2+}\quad +\quad 4\ I^-\quad \rightleftharpoons \quad HgI_4^{2-}\qquad K = 1.0 \times 10^{30}$$

Before	0.010 M	0.78 M	0
Change	−0.010	−0.040 $\rightarrow$	+0.010	Reacts completely (K large)
After	0	0.74	0.010	New initial

x mol/L HgI_4^{2-} dissociates to reach equilibrium

Change	+x	+4x $\leftarrow$	−x
Equil.	x	0.74 + 4x	0.010 − x

$K = 1.0 \times 10^{30} = \dfrac{[HgI_4^{2-}]}{[Hg^{2+}][I^-]^4} = \dfrac{(0.010 - x)}{(x)\,(0.74 + 4x)^4}$; Making normal assumptions:

$1.0 \times 10^{30} = \dfrac{(0.010)}{(x)\,(0.74)^4}$, $x = [Hg^{2+}] = 3.3 \times 10^{-32}\ M$;   Assumptions good.

Note: 3.3×10^{-32} mol/L corresponds to one Hg^{2+} ion per 5×10^7 L. It is very reasonable to approach this problem in two steps. The reaction does essentially go to completion.

110. $[X^-]_0 = 5.00\ M$ and $[Cu^+]_0 = 1.0 \times 10^{-3}\ M$ because equal volumes of each reagent are mixed.

Because the K values are much greater than 1, assume the reaction goes completely to CuX_3^{2-}, and then solve an equilibrium problem.

$$Cu^+\quad +\quad 3\ X^-\quad \rightleftharpoons \quad CuX_3^{2-}\qquad K = K_1 \times K_2 \times K_3$$
$$= 1.0 \times 10^9$$

Before	$1.0 \times 10^{-3}\ M$	5.00 M	0
After	0	$5.00 - 3(10^{-3}) \approx 5.00$	1.0×10^{-3}	Reacts completely
Equil.	x	5.00 + 3x	$1.0 \times 10^{-3} - x$

$K = \dfrac{(1.0 \times 10^{-3} - x)}{(x)\,(5.00 + 3x)^3} = 1.0 \times 10^9 \approx \dfrac{1.0 \times 10^{-3}}{(x)\,(5.00)^3}$, $x = [Cu^+] = 8.0 \times 10^{-15}\ M$

Assumptions good.

$[CuX_3^{2-}] = 1.0 \times 10^{-3} - 8.0 \times 10^{-15} = 1.0 \times 10^{-3}\ M$

$K_3 = \dfrac{[CuX_3^{2-}]}{[CuX_2^-][X^-]} = 1.0 \times 10^3 = \dfrac{(1.0 \times 10^{-3})}{[CuX_2^-]\,(5.00)}$, $[CuX_2^-] = 2.0 \times 10^{-7}\ M$

Summarizing:

$$[CuX_3^{2-}] = 1.0 \times 10^{-3} \, M \quad \text{(answer a)}$$
$$[CuX_2^-] \; = 2.0 \times 10^{-7} \, M \quad \text{(answer b)}$$
$$[Cu^{2+}] \; = 8.0 \times 10^{-15} \, M \quad \text{(answer c)}$$

111. a. $AgI(s) \rightleftharpoons Ag^+(aq) + I^-(aq) \quad K_{sp} = [Ag^+][I^-] = 1.5 \times 10^{-16}$

Initial s = solubility (mol/L)   0   0
Equil. s s

$$K_{sp} = 1.5 \times 10^{-16} = s^2, \; s = 1.2 \times 10^{-8} \, \text{mol/L}$$

b. $AgI(s) \rightleftharpoons Ag^+ + I^- \qquad\qquad K_{sp} = 1.5 \times 10^{-16}$

$Ag^+ + 2\,NH_3 \rightleftharpoons Ag(NH_3)_2^+ \qquad\qquad K_f = 1.7 \times 10^7$

$AgI(s) + 2\,NH_3(aq) \rightleftharpoons Ag(NH_3)_2^+(aq) + I^-(aq) \qquad K = K_{sp} \times K_f = 2.6 \times 10^{-9}$

             $AgI(s) + 2\,NH_3 \rightleftharpoons Ag(NH_3)_2^+ + I^-$

Initial   3.0 M 0   0
             s mol/L of AgBr(s) dissolves to reach equilibrium = molar solubility
Equil.   3.0 − 2s s s

$$K = \frac{[Ag(NH_3)_2^+][I^-]}{[NH_3]^2} = \frac{s^2}{(3.0 - 2s)^2} = 2.6 \times 10^{-9} \approx \frac{s^2}{(3.0)^2}, \; s = 1.5 \times 10^{-4} \, \text{mol/L}$$

Assumption good.

c. The presence of NH_3 increases the solubility of AgI. Added NH_3 removes Ag^+ from solution by forming the complex ion, $Ag(NH_3)_2^+$. As Ag^+ is removed, more AgI(s) will dissolve to replenish the Ag^+ concentration.

112. $AgBr(s) \rightleftharpoons Ag^+ + Br^- \qquad\qquad K_{sp} = 5.0 \times 10^{-13}$

$Ag^+ + 2\,S_2O_3^{2-} \rightleftharpoons Ag(S_2O_3)_2^{3-} \qquad\qquad K_f = 2.9 \times 10^{13}$

$AgBr(s) + 2\,S_2O_3^{2-} \rightleftharpoons Ag(S_2O_3)_2^{3-} + Br^- \qquad K = K_{sp} \times K_f = 14.5 \quad \text{(Carry extra sig. figs.)}$

          $AgBr(s) + 2\,S_2O_3^{2-} \rightleftharpoons Ag(S_2O_3)_2^{3-} + Br^-$

Initial   0.500 M 0   0
          s mol/L AgBr(s) dissolves to reach equilibrium
Change   −s −2s →   +s +s
Equil.   0.500 − 2s s s

$$K = \frac{s^2}{(0.500 - 2s)^2} = 14.5; \text{ Taking the square root of both sides:}$$

$$\frac{s}{0.500 - 2s} = 3.81, \ s = 1.91 - 7.62 \, s, \ s = 0.222 \text{ mol/L}$$

$$1.00 \text{ L} \times \frac{0.222 \text{ mol AgBr}}{\text{L}} \times \frac{187.8 \text{ g AgBr}}{\text{mol AgBr}} = 41.7 \text{ g AgBr} = 42 \text{ g AgBr}$$

113. $AgCl(s) \rightleftharpoons Ag^+ + Cl^-$ $K_{sp} = 1.6 \times 10^{-10}$

          $Ag^+ + 2 NH_3 \rightleftharpoons Ag(NH_3)_2^+$ $K_f = 1.7 \times 10^7$

$AgCl(s) + 2 NH_3 \rightleftharpoons Ag(NH_3)_2^+(aq) + Cl^-(aq)$ $K = K_{sp} \times K_f = 2.7 \times 10^{-3}$

	$AgCl(s) + 2NH_3 \rightleftharpoons$	$Ag(NH_3)_2^+$	$+ Cl^-$
Initial		$1.0 \, M$	0	0

s mol/L of AgCl(s) dissolves to reach equilibrium = molar solubility

| Equil. | | $1.0 - 2s \rightleftharpoons$ | s | s |

$$K = 2.7 \times 10^{-3} = \frac{[Ag(NH_3)_2^+][Cl^-]}{[NH_3]^2} = \frac{s^2}{(1.0 - 2s)^2}, \text{ Taking the square root:}$$

$$\frac{s}{1.0 - 2s} = (2.7 \times 10^{-3})^{1/2} = 5.2 \times 10^{-2}, \ s = 4.7 \times 10^{-2} \text{ mol/L}$$

In pure water, the solubility of AgCl(s) is $(1.6 \times 10^{-10})^{1/2} = 1.3 \times 10^{-5}$ mol/L. Notice how the presence of NH_3 increases the solubility of AgCl(s) by over a factor of 3500.

114.   a. $CuCl(s) \rightleftharpoons Cu^+ + Cl^-$

Initial	s = solubility (mol/L)	0	0
Equil.		s	s

$$K_{sp} = 1.2 \times 10^{-6} = [Cu^+][Cl^-] = s^2, \ s = 1.1 \times 10^{-3} \text{ mol/L}$$

b. Cu^+ forms the complex ion $CuCl_2^-$ in the presence of Cl^-. We will consider both the K_{sp} reaction and the complex ion reaction at the same time.

$CuCl(s) \rightleftharpoons Cu^+(aq) + Cl^-(aq)$ $K_{sp} = 1.2 \times 10^{-6}$

$Cu^+(aq) + 2 Cl^-(aq) \rightleftharpoons CuCl_2^-(aq)$ $K_f = 8.7 \times 10^4$

$CuCl(s) + Cl^-(aq) \rightleftharpoons CuCl_2^-(aq)$ $K = K_{sp} \times K_f = 0.10$

$$CuCl(s) + Cl^- \rightleftharpoons CuCl_2^-$$

Initial	0.10 M	0
Equil.	0.10 $-$ s	s where s = solubility of CuCl(s) in mol/L

$$K = 0.10 = \frac{[CuCl_2^-]}{[Cl^-]} = \frac{s}{0.10 - s}, \quad 1.0 \times 10^{-2} - 0.10\,s = s, \quad s = 9.1 \times 10^{-3}\,mol/L$$

115. Test tube 1: added Cl^- reacts with Ag^+ to form a silver chloride precipitate. The net ionic equation is $Ag^+(aq) + Cl^-(aq) \rightarrow AgCl(s)$. Test tube 2: added NH_3 reacts with Ag^+ ions to form a soluble complex ion, $Ag(NH_3)_2^+$. As this complex ion forms, Ag^+ is removed from the solution, which causes the AgCl(s) to dissolve. When enough NH_3 is added, all of the silver chloride precipitate will dissolve. The equation is $AgCl(s) + 2\,NH_3(aq) \rightarrow Ag(NH_3)_2^+(aq) + Cl^-$ (aq). Test tube 3: added H^+ reacts with the weak base, NH_3, to form NH_4^+. As NH_3 is removed from the $Ag(NH_3)_2^+$ complex ion, Ag^+ ions are released to solution and can then react with Cl^- to reform AgCl(s). The equations are $Ag(NH_3)_2^+(aq) + 2\,H^+(aq) \rightarrow Ag^+(aq) + 2\,NH_4^+(aq)$ and $Ag^+(aq) + Cl^-$ (aq) $\rightarrow$ AgCl(s).

116. In NH_3, Cu^{2+} forms the soluble complex ion, $Cu(NH_3)_4^{2+}$. This increases the solubility of $Cu(OH)_2(s)$ because added NH_3 removes Cu^{2+} from the equilibrium causing more $Cu(OH)_2(s)$ to dissolve. In HNO_3, H^+ removes OH^- from the K_{sp} equilibrium causing more $Cu(OH)_2(s)$ to dissolve. Any salt with basic anions will be more soluble in an acid solution. $AgC_2H_3O_2(s)$ will be more soluble in either NH_3 or HNO_3. This is because Ag^+ forms the complex ion $Ag(NH_3)_2^+$, and $C_2H_3O_2^-$ is a weak base, so it will react with added H^+. AgCl(s) will be more soluble only in NH_3 due to $Ag(NH_3)_2^+$ formation. In acid, Cl^- is a horrible base, so it doesn't react with added H^+. AgCl(s) will not be more soluble in HNO_3.

Additional Exercises

117. $NH_3 + H_2O \rightleftharpoons NH_4^+ + OH^- \quad K_b = \dfrac{[NH_4^+][OH^-]}{[NH_3]}$; Taking the $-\log$ of the K_b expression:

$$-\log K_b = -\log [OH^-] - \log\frac{[NH_4^+]}{[NH_3]}, \quad -\log [OH^-] = -\log K_b + \log\frac{[NH_4^+]}{[NH_3]}$$

$$pOH = pK_b + \log\frac{[NH_4^+]}{[NH_3]} \quad \text{or} \quad pOH = pK_b + \log\frac{[Acid]}{[Base]}$$

118. a. $pH = pK_a = -\log (6.4 \times 10^{-5}) = 4.19$ since $[HBz] = [Bz^-]$ where $HBz = C_6H_5CO_2H$ and $[Bz^-] = C_6H_5CO_2^-$.

b. $[Bz^-]$ will increase to 0.120 M, and $[HBz]$ will decrease to 0.080 M after OH^- reacts completely with HBz. The Henderson-Hasselbalch equation is derived from the K_a equilibrium reaction. It assumes that the initial concentrations of HBz and Bz^- will equal the equilibrium concentrations. This assumption will hold here.

$$pH = pK_a + \log\frac{[Bz^-]}{[HBz]}, \quad pH = 4.19 + \log\frac{(0.120)}{(0.080)} = 4.37$$

c. $Bz^- + H_2O \rightleftharpoons HBz + OH^-$

Initial	0.120 M	0.080 M	0
Equil.	0.120 – x	0.080 + x	x

$$K_b = \frac{K_w}{K_a} = \frac{1.0 \times 10^{-14}}{6.4 \times 10^{-5}} = \frac{(0.080 + x)(x)}{(0.120 - x)} \approx \frac{(0.080)(x)}{0.120}$$

$x = [OH^-] = 2.34 \times 10^{-10}\ M$ (carrying extra sig. figs.); Assumptions good.

pOH = 9.63; pH = 4.37

d. We get the same answer. Both equilibria involve the two major species, benzoic acid and benzoate anion. Both equilibria must hold true. K_b is related to K_a by K_w and $[OH^-]$ is related to $[H^+]$ by K_w, so all constants are interrelated.

119. a. $C_2H_5NH_3^+ \rightleftharpoons H^+ + C_2H_5NH_2$ $K_a = \dfrac{K_w}{K_b} = \dfrac{1.0 \times 10^{-14}}{5.6 \times 10^{-4}} = 1.8 \times 10^{-11}$; p$K_a$ = 10.74

$$pH = pK_a + \log\frac{[C_2H_5NH_2]}{[C_2H_5NH_3^+]} = 10.74 + \log\frac{0.10}{0.20} = 10.74 - 0.30 = 10.44$$

b. $C_2H_5NH_3^+ + OH^- \rightleftharpoons C_2H_5NH_2$; After 0.050 M OH$^-$ reacts to completion (converting $C_2H_5NH_3^+$ into $C_2H_5NH_2$), a buffer solution still exists where $[C_2H_5NH_3^+] = [C_2H_5NH_2] = 0.15\ M$. Here pH = p$K_a$ + log 1.0 = 10.74 (pH = pK_a).

120. $pH = pK_a + \log\dfrac{[C_2H_3O_2^-]}{[HC_2H_3O_2]}$, $4.00 = -\log(1.8 \times 10^{-5}) + \log\dfrac{[C_2H_3O_2^-]}{[HC_2H_3O_2]}$

$\dfrac{[C_2H_3O_2^-]}{[HC_2H_3O_2]} = 0.18$; This is also equal to the mole ratio between $C_2H_3O_2^-$ and $HC_2H_3O_2$.

Let x = volume of 1.00 M $HC_2H_3O_2$ and y = volume of 1.00 M $NaC_2H_3O_2$

$x + y = 1.00$ L, $x = 1.00 - y$

x (1.0 mol/L) = mol $HC_2H_3O_2$; y (1.00 mol/L) = mol $NaC_2H_3O_2$ = mol $C_2H_3O_2^-$

So, $\dfrac{y}{x} = 0.18$ or $\dfrac{y}{1.00 - y} = 0.18$; Solving: $y = 0.15$ L so $x = 1.00 - 0.15 = 0.85$ L

We need 850 mL of 1.00 M $HC_2H_3O_2$ and 150 mL of 1.00 M $NaC_2H_3O_2$ to produce a buffer solution at pH = 4.00.

121.   A best buffer is when pH $\approx$ pK$_a$;   these solutions have about equal concentrations of weak acid and conjugate base. Therefore, choose combinations that yield a buffer where pH $\approx$ pK$_a$, i.e., look for acids whose pK$_a$ is closest to the pH.

   a.   Potassium fluoride + HCl will yield a buffer consisting of HF (pK$_a$ = 3.14) and F$^-$.

   b.   Benzoic acid + NaOH will yield a buffer consisting of benzoic acid (pK$_a$ = 4.19) and benzoate anion.

   c.   Sodium acetate + acetic acid (pK$_a$ = 4.74) is the best choice for pH = 5.0 buffer since acetic acid has a pK$_a$ value closest to 5.0.

   d.   HOCl and NaOH: This is the best choice to produce a conjugate acid/base pair with pH = 7.0. This mixture would yield a buffer consisting of HOCl (pK$_a$ = 7.46) and OCl$^-$. Actually, the best choice for a pH = 7.0 buffer is an equimolar mixture of ammonium chloride and sodium acetate. NH$_4^+$ is a weak acid (K$_a$ = 5.6 $\times$ 10^{-10}) and C$_2$H$_3$O$_2^-$ is a weak base (K$_b$ = 5.6 $\times$ 10^{-10}). A mixture of the two will give a buffer at pH = 7.0 beccause the weak acid and weak base are the same strengths (K$_a$ for NH$_4^+$ = K$_b$ for C$_2$H$_3$O$_2^-$). NH$_4$C$_2$H$_3$O$_2$ is commercially available, and its solutions are used for pH = 7.0 buffers.

   e.   Ammonium chloride + NaOH will yield a buffer consisting of NH$_4^+$ (pK$_a$ = 9.26) and NH$_3$.

122.   a.   The optimum pH for a buffer is when pH = pK$_a$. At this pH, a buffer will have equal neutralization capacity for both added acid and base. As shown below, the pK$_a$ for TRISH$^+$ is about 8, so the optimal buffer pH is about 8.

$$K_b = 1.19 \times 10^{-6}\,;\ \ K_a = K_w/K_b = 8.40 \times 10^{-9}\,;\ \ pK_a = -\log(8.40 \times 10^{-9}) = 8.076$$

   b. $pH = pK_a + \log \dfrac{[TRIS]}{[TRISH^+]}$, $7.00 = 8.076 + \log \dfrac{[TRIS]}{[TRISH^+]}$

$$\frac{[TRIS]}{[TRISH^+]} = 10^{-1.08} = 0.083 \quad (\text{at pH} = 7.00)$$

$$9.00 = 8.076 + \log \frac{[TRIS]}{[TRISH^+]}, \quad \frac{[TRIS]}{[TRISH^+]} = 10^{0.92} = 8.3 \quad (\text{at pH} = 9.00)$$

   c. $\dfrac{50.0\,\text{g TRIS}}{2.0\,\text{L}} \times \dfrac{1\,\text{mol}}{121.14\,\text{g}} = 0.206\,M = 0.21\,M = [TRIS]$

$$\frac{65.0\,\text{g TRISHCl}}{2.0\,\text{L}} \times \frac{1\,\text{mol}}{157.60\,\text{g}} = 0.206\,M = 0.21\,M = [TRISHCl] = [TRISH^+]$$

$$pH = pK_a + \log\frac{[TRIS]}{[TRISH^+]} = 8.076 + \log\frac{(0.21)}{(0.21)} = 8.08$$

The amount of H^+ added from HCl is: $0.50 \times 10^{-3}\,L \times \dfrac{12\ mol}{L} = 6.0 \times 10^{-3}\,mol\ H^+$

The H^+ from HCl will convert TRIS into $TRISH^+$. The reaction is:

	TRIS	+	H^+	$\rightarrow$	$TRISH^+$	
Before	0.21 M		$\dfrac{6.0 \times 10^{-3}}{0.2005} = 0.030\,M$		0.21 M	
Change	−0.030		−0.030	$\rightarrow$	+0.030	Reacts completely
After	0.18		0		0.24	

Now use the Henderson-Hasselbalch equation to solve the buffer problem.

$$pH = 8.076 + \log\frac{(0.18)}{(0.24)} = 7.95$$

123.   a. $HC_2H_3O_2 + OH^- \rightleftharpoons C_2H_3O_2^- + H_2O$

$$K_{eq} = \frac{[C_2H_3O_2^-]}{[HC_2H_3O_2][OH^-]} \times \frac{[H^+]}{[H^+]} = \frac{K_{a,HC_2H_3O_2}}{K_w} = \frac{1.8 \times 10^{-5}}{1.0 \times 10^{-14}} = 1.8 \times 10^9$$

b. $C_2H_3O_2^- + H^+ \rightleftharpoons HC_2H_3O_2$ $K_{eq} = \dfrac{[HC_2H_3O_2]}{[H^+][C_2H_3O_2^-]} = \dfrac{1}{K_{a,HC_2H_3O_2}} = 5.6 \times 10^4$

c. $HCl + NaOH \rightarrow NaCl + H_2O$

Net ionic equation is: $H^+ + OH^- \rightleftharpoons H_2O$; $K_{eq} = \dfrac{1}{K_w} = 1.0 \times 10^{14}$

124.   a.   Because all acids are the same initial concentration, the pH curve with the highest pH at 0 mL of NaOH added will correspond to the titration of the weakest acid. This is pH curve f.

b.   The pH curve with the lowest pH at 0 mL of NaOH added will correspond to the titration of the strongest acid. This is pH curve a.

The best point to look at to differentiate a strong acid from a weak acid titration (if initial concentrations are not known) is the equivalence point pH. If the pH = 7.00, the acid titrated is a strong acid; if the pH is greater than 7.00, the acid titrated is a weak acid.

c.   For a weak acid-strong base titration, the pH at the halfway point to equivalence is equal to the pK_a value. The pH curve, which represents the titration of an acid with $K_a = 1.0 \times 10^{-6}$, will have a pH $= -\log(1 \times 10^{-6}) = 6.0$ at the halfway point. The equivalence

point, from the plots, occurs at 50 mL NaOH added, so the halfway point is 25 mL. Plot
d has a pH ~6.0 at 25 mL of NaOH added, so the acid titrated in this pH curve (plot d)
has K_a ~1 ×10^{-6} .

125.   In the final solution: $[H^+] = 10^{-2.15} = 7.1 \times 10^{-3}\,M$

Beginning mmol HCl = 500.0 mL × 0.200 mmol/mL = 100. mmol HCl

Amount of HCl that reacts with NaOH = 1.50×10^{-2} mmol/mL × V

$$\frac{7.1 \times 10^{-3}\,\text{mmol}}{\text{mL}} = \frac{\text{final mmol H}^+}{\text{total volume}} = \frac{1.00 - 0.0150\,\text{V}}{500.0 + \text{V}}$$

$3.6 + 7.1 \times 10^{-3}\,\text{V} = 100. - 1.50 \times 10^{-2}\,\text{V},\ 2.21 \times 10^{-2}\,\text{V} = 100. - 3.6$

$V = 4.36 \times 10^3\,\text{mL} = 4.36\,\text{L} = 4.4\,\text{L NaOH}$

126.   For a titration of a strong acid with a strong base, the added OH$^-$ reacts completely with the
H$^+$ present. To determine the pH, we calculate the concentration of excess H$^+$ or OH$^-$ after
the neutralization reaction and then calculate the pH.

0 mL: $[H^+] = 0.100\,M$ from HNO$_3$; pH = 1.000

4.0 mL: initial mmol H$^+$ present = 25.0 mL × $\dfrac{0.100\,\text{mmol H}^+}{\text{mL}}$ = 2.50 mmol H$^+$

mmol OH$^-$ added = 4.0 mL × $\dfrac{0.100\,\text{mmol OH}^-}{\text{mL}}$ = 0.40 mmol OH$^-$

0.40 mmol OH$^-$ reacts completely with 0.40 mmol H$^+$: OH$^-$ + H$^+$ → H$_2$O

$[H^+]_{\text{excess}} = \dfrac{(2.50 - 0.40)\,\text{mmol}}{(25.0 + 4.0)\,\text{mL}} = 7.24 \times 10^{-2}\,M$; pH = 1.140

We follow the same procedure for the remaining calculations.

8.0 mL: $[H^+]_{\text{excess}} = \dfrac{(2.50 - 0.80)\,\text{mmol}}{33.0\,\text{mL}} = 5.15 \times 10^{-2}\,M$; pH = 1.288

12.5 mL: $[H^+]_{\text{excess}} = \dfrac{(2.50 - 1.25)\,\text{mmol}}{37.5\,\text{mL}} = 3.33 \times 10^{-2}\,M$; pH = 1.478

20.0 mL: $[H^+]_{\text{excess}} = \dfrac{(2.50 - 2.00)\,\text{mmol}}{45.0\,\text{mL}} = 1.1 \times 10^{-2}\,M$; pH = 1.96

24.0 mL: $[H^+]_{\text{excess}} = \dfrac{(2.50 - 2.40)\,\text{mmol}}{49.0\,\text{mL}} = 2.0 \times 10^{-3}\,M$; pH = 2.70

24.5 mL: $[H^+]_{excess} = \dfrac{(2.50 - 2.45)\ mmol}{49.5\ mL} = 1 \times 10^{-3}\ M;\ pH = 3.0$

24.9 mL: $[H^+]_{excess} = \dfrac{(2.50 - 2.49)\ mmol}{49.9\ mL} = 2 \times 10^{-4}\ M;\ pH = 3.7$

25.0 mL: Equivalence point; We have a neutral solution because there is no excess H^+ or OH^- remaining after the neutralization reaction. pH = 7.00

25.1 mL: base in excess, $[OH^-]_{excess} = \dfrac{(2.51 - 2.50)\ mmol}{50.1\ mL} = 2 \times 10^{-4}\ M;\ pOH = 3.7;$
pH = 10.3

26.0 mL: $[OH^-]_{excess} = \dfrac{(2.60 - 2.50)\ mmol}{51.0\ mL} = 2.0 \times 10^{-3}\ M;\ pOH = 2.70;\ pH = 11.30$

28.0 mL: $[OH^-]_{excess} = \dfrac{(2.80 - 2.50)\ mmol}{53.0\ mL} = 5.7 \times 10^{-3}\ M;\ pOH = 2.24;\ pH = 11.76$

30.0 mL: $[OH^-]_{excess} = \dfrac{(3.00 - 2.50)\ mmol}{55.0\ mL} = 9.1 \times 10^{-3}\ M;\ pOH = 2.04;\ pH = 11.96$

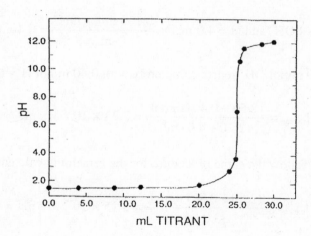

127. $HA + OH^- \rightarrow A^- + H_2O$ where HA = acetylsalicylic acid (assuming a monoprotic acid)

mmol HA present = $27.36\ mL\ OH^- \times \dfrac{0.5106\ mmol\ OH^-}{mL\ OH^-} \times \dfrac{1\ mmol\ HA}{mmol\ OH^-} = 13.97\ mmol$
HA

Molar mass of HA = $\dfrac{grams}{mol} \times \dfrac{2.51\ g\ HA}{13.97 \times 10^{-3}\ mol\ HA} = 180.\ g/mol$

To determine the K_a value, use the pH data. After complete neutralization of acetylsalicylic acid by OH$^-$, we have 13.97 mmol of OH$^-$ produced from the neutralization reaction. A$^-$ will react completely with the added H$^+$ and reform acetylsalicylic acid, HA.

$$\text{mmol H}^+ \text{ added} = 13.68 \text{ mL} \times \frac{0.5106 \text{ mmol H}^+}{\text{mL}} = 6.985 \text{ mmol H}^+$$

$$\text{A}^- \quad + \quad \text{H}^+ \quad \rightarrow \quad \text{HA}$$

Before	13.97 mmol	6.985 mmol	0	
Change	$^-$6.985	$^-$6.985	$\rightarrow$ +6.985	Reacts completely
After	6.985 mmol	0	6.985 mmol	

We have back titrated this solution to the halfway point to equivalence where pH = pK_a (assuming HA is a weak acid). We know this because after H$^+$ reacts completely, equal mmol of HA and A$^-$ are present, which only occurs at the halfway point to equivalence. Assuming acetylsalicylic acid is a weak monoprotic acid, then pH = pK_a = 3.48. $K_a = 10^{-3.48} = 3.3 \times 10^{-4}$

128. $$\text{NaOH added} = 50.0 \text{ mL} \times \frac{0.500 \text{ mmol}}{\text{mL}} = 25.0 \text{ mmol NaOH}$$

$$\text{NaOH left unreacted} = 31.92 \text{ mL HCl} \times \frac{0.289 \text{ mmol}}{\text{mL}} \times \frac{1 \text{ mmol NaOH}}{\text{mmol HCl}}$$
$$= 9.22 \text{ mmol NaOH}$$

NaOH reacted with aspirin = 25.0 $-$ 9.22 = 15.8 mmol NaOH

$$15.8 \text{ mmol NaOH} \times \frac{1 \text{ mmol aspirin}}{2 \text{ mmol NaOH}} \times \frac{180.2 \text{ mg}}{\text{mmol}} = 1420 \text{ mg} = 1.42 \text{ g aspirin}$$

$$\text{Purity} = \frac{1.42 \text{ g}}{1.427 \text{ g}} \times 100 = 99.5\%$$

Here, a strong base is titrated by a strong acid, so the equivalence point will be at pH = 7.0. However, the acetate ion is present and we want our indicator to turn color before the acetate starts to be titrated. Thus, an indicator that turns color at a higher pH would be best. Cresol red seems to be the best choice from Figure 15.8. Its color change occurs at about 9.0 and it has a color change that can be seen easily (unlike phenolphthalein and others that change color at pH ~9.0). Because strong base-strong acid titrations have a huge change in pH at the equivalence point, having a indicator that turns color at a pH greater than 7.0 will not add significant error.

129. $\text{HC}_2\text{H}_3\text{O}_2 \rightleftharpoons \text{H}^+ + \text{C}_2\text{H}_3\text{O}_2^-$; Let C_o = initial concentration of $\text{HC}_2\text{H}_3\text{O}_2$

From normal weak acid setup where x = [H$^+$]:

$$K_a = 1.8 \times 10^{-5} = \frac{[\text{H}^+][\text{C}_2\text{H}_3\text{O}_2^-]}{[\text{HC}_2\text{H}_3\text{O}_2]} = \frac{[\text{H}^+]^2}{C_o - [\text{H}^+]}$$

$$[H^+] = 10^{-2.68} = 2.1 \times 10^{-3} M; \quad 1.8 \times 10^{-5} = \frac{(2.1 \times 10^{-3})^2}{C_0 - 2.1 \times 10^{-3}}, \quad C_0 = 0.25 \, M$$

25.0 mL × 0.25 mmol/mL = 6.3 mmol $HC_2H_3O_2$; Need 6.3 mol KOH to reach equivalence point.

6.3 mmol KOH = V_{KOH} × 0.0975 mmol/mL, V_{KOH} = 65 mL

130.   mol acid = 0.210 g × $\dfrac{1 \, \text{mol}}{192 \, \text{g}}$ = 0.00109 mol

mol OH^- added = 0.0305 L × $\dfrac{0.108 \, \text{mol NaOH}}{\text{L}}$ × $\dfrac{1 \, \text{mol OH}^-}{\text{mol NaOH}}$ = 0.00329 mol OH^-

$\dfrac{\text{mol OH}^-}{\text{mol acid}} = \dfrac{0.00329}{0.00109} = 3.02$

The acid is triprotic (H_3A) because 3 mol of OH^- are required to react with 1 mol of the acid, i.e., the acid must have 3 mol H^+ in the formula to react with 3 mol of OH^-.

131.   50.0 mL × 0.100 M = 5.00 mmol NaOH initially

at pH = 10.50, pOH = 3.50, $[OH^-]$ = $10^{-3.50}$ = 3.2 × 10^{-4} M

mmol OH^- remaining = 3.2 × 10^{-4} mmol/mL × 73.75 mL = 2.4 × 10^{-2} mmol

mmol OH^- that reacted = 5.00 − 0.024 = 4.98 mmol

Because the weak acid is monoprotic, 23.75 mL of the weak acid solution contains 4.98 mmol HA.

$[HA]_o = \dfrac{4.98 \, \text{mmol}}{23.75 \, \text{mL}} = 0.210 \, M$

132.   HA + OH^- → A^- + H_2O; It takes 25.0 mL of 0.100 M NaOH to reach the equivalence point where mmol HA = mmol OH^- = 25.0 mL (0.100 M) = 2.50 mmol. At the equivalence point, some HCl is added. The H^+ from the strong acid reacts to completion with the best base present, A^-.

	H^+	+	A^-	→	HA
Before	13.0 mL × 0.100 M		2.5 mmol		0
Change	−1.3 mmol		−1.3 mmol		+1.3 mmol
After	0		1.2 mmol		1.3 mmol

A buffer solution is present after the H^+ has reacted completely.

$$pH = pK_a + \log \frac{[A^-]}{[HA]}, \quad 4.7 = pK_a + \log\left(\frac{1.2 \, \text{mmol} / V_T}{1.3 \, \text{mmol} / V_T}\right)$$

Because the log term will be negative $[\log(1.2/1.3) = -0.035)]$, the pK_a value of the acid must be greater than 4.7.

133. a.
$$Cu(OH)_2 \rightleftharpoons Cu^{2+} + 2\ OH^- \qquad\qquad K_{sp} = 1.6 \times 10^{-19}$$
$$Cu^{2+} + 4\ NH_3 \rightleftharpoons Cu(NH_3)_4{}^{2+} \qquad\qquad K_f = 1.0 \times 10^{13}$$

$$Cu(OH)_2(s) + 4\ NH_3(aq) \rightleftharpoons Cu(NH_3)_4{}^{2+}(aq) + 2\ OH^-(aq) \quad K = K_{sp}K_f = 1.6 \times 10^{-6}$$

b.
$$Cu(OH)_2(s)\ +\ 4\ NH_3 \rightleftharpoons Cu(NH_3)_4{}^{2+}\ +\ 2\ OH^- \qquad K = 1.6 \times 10^{-6}$$

Initial	5.0 M	0	0.0095 M

s mol/L $Cu(OH)_2$ dissolves to reach equilibrium

Equil.	5.0 − 4s	s	0.0095 + 2s

$$K = 1.6 \times 10^{-6} = \frac{[Cu(NH_3)_4^{2+}][OH^-]^2}{[NH_3]^4} = \frac{s(0.0095 + 2s)^2}{(5.0 - 4s)^4}$$

If s is small: $1.6 \times 10^{-6} = \dfrac{s(0.0095)^2}{(5.0)^4}$, $s = 11.$ mol/L

Assumptions are horrible. We will solve the problem by successive approximations.

$$s_{calc} = \frac{1.6 \times 10^{-6}\ (5.0 - 4s_{guess})^4}{(0.0095 + 2s_{guess})^2},\ \text{The results from six trials are:}$$

s_{guess}:   0.10, 0.050, 0.060, 0.055, 0.056

s_{calc}: 1.6×10^{-2}, 0.071, 0.049, 0.058, 0.056

Thus, the solubility of $Cu(OH)_2$ is 0.056 mol/L in 5.0 M NH_3.

134.
$$Ba(OH)_2(s) \rightleftharpoons Ba^{2+}(aq) + 2\ OH^-(aq) \quad K_{sp} = [Ba^{2+}][OH^-]^2 = 5.0 \times 10^{-3}$$

Initial	s = solubility (mol/L)	0	~0
Equil.		s	2s

$K_{sp} = 5.0 \times 10^{-3} = s(2s)^2 = 4s^3$, $s = 0.11$ mol/L; Assumption good.

$[OH^-] = 2s = 2(0.11) = 0.22$ mol/L; pOH = 0.66, pH = 13.34

$$Sr(OH)_2(s) \rightleftharpoons Sr^{2+}(aq) + 2\ OH^-(aq) \quad K_{sp} = [Sr^{2+}][OH^-]^2 = 3.2 \times 10^{-4}$$

Equil.		s	2s

$K_{sp} = 3.2 \times 10^{-4} = 4s^3$, $s = 0.043$ mol/L; Asssumption good.

$[OH^-] = 2(0.043) = 0.086\ M$; pOH = 1.07, pH = 12.93

$$Ca(OH)_2(s) \rightleftharpoons Ca^{2+}(aq) + 2\,OH^-(aq) \qquad K_{sp} = [Ca^{2+}][OH^-]^2 = 1.3 \times 10^{-6}$$

Equil. s $2s$

$K_{sp} = 1.3 \times 10^{-6} = 4s^3$, $s = 6.9 \times 10^{-3}$ mol/L; Assumption good.

$[OH^-] = 2(6.9 \times 10^{-3}) = 1.4 \times 10^{-2}$ mol/L; pOH = 1.85, pH = 12.15

135. $$Ca_5(PO_4)_3OH(s) \rightleftharpoons 5\,Ca^{2+} + 3\,PO_4^{3-} + OH^-$$

Initial	s = solubility (mol/L)	0	0	1.0×10^{-7} from water
Equil.		$5s$	$3s$	$s + 1.0 \times 10^{-7} \approx s$

$$K_{sp} = 6.8 \times 10^{-37} = [Ca^{2+}]^5 [PO_4^{3-}]^3 [OH^-] = (5s)^5(3s)^3(s)$$

$6.8 \times 10^{-37} = (3125)(27)s^9$, $s = 2.7 \times 10^{-5}$ mol/L;   Assumption is good.

The solubility of hydroxyapatite will increase as the solution gets more acidic because both phosphate and hydroxide can react with H^+.

$$Ca_5(PO_4)_3F(s) \rightleftharpoons 5\,Ca^{2+} + 3\,PO_4^{3-} + F^-$$

Initial	s = solubility (mol/L)	0	0	0
Equil.		$5s$	$3s$	s

$K_{sp} = 1 \times 10^{-60} = (5s)^5(3s)^3(s) = (3125)(27)s^9$, $s = 6 \times 10^{-8}$ mol/L

The hydroxyapatite in tooth enamel is converted to the less soluble fluorapatite by fluoride-treated water. The less soluble fluorapatite is more difficult to remove, making teeth less susceptible to decay.

136. $K_{sp} = 6.4 \times 10^{-9} = [Mg^{2+}][F^-]^2$, $6.4 \times 10^{-9} = (0.00375 - y)(0.0625 - 2y)^2$

This is a cubic equation. No simplifying assumptions can be made since y is relatively large. Solving cubic equations is difficult unless you have a graphing calculator. However, if you don't have a graphing calculator, one way to solve this problem is to make the simplifying assumption to run the precipitation reaction to completion. This assumption is made because of the very small value for K, indicating that the ion concentrations are very small. Once this assumption is made, the problem becomes much easier to solve.

137.   a. $$Pb(OH)_2(s) \rightleftharpoons Pb^{2+}(aq) + 2\,OH^-(aq)$$

Initial	s = solubility (mol/L)	0	1.0×10^{-7} M from water
Equil.		s	$1.0 \times 10^{-7} + 2s$

$$K_{sp} = 1.2 \times 10^{-15} = [Pb^{2+}][OH^-]^2 = s(1.0 \times 10^{-7} + 2s)^2 \approx s(2s^2) = 4s^3$$

$s = [Pb^{2+}] = 6.7 \times 10^{-6}\,M$; Assumption to ignore OH^- from water is good by the 5% rule.

b. $Pb(OH)_2(s) \rightleftharpoons Pb^{2+}(aq) \quad + \quad 2\,OH^-(aq)$

Initial		0	0.10 M

pH = 13.00, $[OH^-] = 0.10\,M$

s mol/L $Pb(OH)_2(s)$ dissolves to reach equilibrium

Equil. s 0.10   (buffered solution)

$1.2 \times 10^{-15} = (s)(0.10)^2$, $s = [Pb^{2+}] = 1.2 \times 10^{-13}\,M$

c. We need to calculate the Pb^{2+} concentration in equilibrium with $EDTA^{4-}$. Because K is large for the formation of $PbEDTA^{2-}$, let the reaction go to completion; then solve an equilibrium problem to get the Pb^{2+} concentration.

$$Pb^{2+} \quad + \quad EDTA^{4-} \quad \rightleftharpoons \quad PbEDTA^{2-} \qquad K = 1.1 \times 10^{18}$$

Before   0.010 M 0.050 M 0

0.010 mol/L Pb^{2+} reacts completely (large K)

Change -0.010 -0.010 $\rightarrow$ $+0.010$ Reacts completely

After   0   0.040   0.010   New initial

x mol/L $PbEDTA^{2-}$ dissociates to reach equilibrium

Equil. x 0.040 + x 0.010 − x

$1.1 \times 10^{18} = \dfrac{(0.010 - x)}{(x)(0.040 + x)} \approx \dfrac{(0.010)}{(x)(0.040)}$, $x = [Pb^{2+}] = 2.3 \times 10^{-19}\,M$;   Assumptions good.

Now calculate the solubility quotient for $Pb(OH)_2$ to see if precipitation occurs. The concentration of OH^- is 0.10 M because we have a solution buffered at pH = 13.00.

$$Q = [Pb^{2+}]_0 [OH^-]_0^2 = (2.3 \times 10^{-19})(0.10)^2 = 2.3 \times 10^{-21} < K_{sp}\,(1.2 \times 10^{-15})$$

$Pb(OH)_2(s)$ will not form since Q is less than K_{sp}.

Challenge Problems

138.   At 4.0 mL NaOH added: $\left|\dfrac{\Delta pH}{\Delta mL}\right| = \left|\dfrac{2.43 - 3.14}{0 - 4.0}\right| = 0.18$

The other points are calculated in a similar fashion. The results are summarized and plotted below. As can be seen from the plot, the advantage of this approach is that it is much easier to accurately determine the location of the equivalence point.

mL	pH	$|\Delta pH/\Delta mL|$
0	2.43	–
4.0	3.14	0.18
8.0	3.53	0.098
12.5	3.86	0.073
20.0	4.46	0.080
24.0	5.24	0.20
24.5	5.6	0.7
24.9	6.3	2
25.0	8.28	20
25.1	10.3	20
26.0	11.30	1
28.0	11.75	0.23
30.0	11.96	0.11

139.   mmol $HC_3H_5O_2$ present initially = $45.0 \text{ mL} \times \dfrac{0.750 \text{ mmol}}{\text{mL}} = 33.8$ mmol $HC_3H_5O_2$

mmol $C_3H_5O_2^-$ present initially = $55.0 \text{ mL} \times \dfrac{0.700 \text{ mmol}}{\text{mL}} = 38.5$ mmol $C_3H_5O_2^-$

The initial pH of the buffer is:

$$pH = pK_a + \log \frac{[C_3H_5O_2^-]}{[HC_3H_5O_2]} = -\log (1.3 \times 10^{-5}) + \log \frac{\dfrac{38.5 \text{ mmol}}{100.0 \text{ mL}}}{\dfrac{33.8 \text{ mmol}}{100.0 \text{ mL}}}$$

$$pH = 4.89 + \log \frac{38.5}{33.8} = 4.95$$

Note: Because the buffer components are in the same volume of solution, we can use the mol (or mmol) ratio in the Henderson-Hasselbalch equation to solve for pH instead of using the concentration ratio of $[C_3H_5O_2^-]/[HC_3H_5O_2]$. The total volume always cancels for buffer solutions.

When NaOH is added, the pH will increase, and the added OH^- will convert $HC_3H_5O_2$ into $C_3H_5O_2^-$. The pH after addition of OH^- increases by 2.5%, so the resulting pH is:

4.95 + 0.025 (4.95) = 5.07

At this pH, a buffer solution still exists and the mmol ratio between $C_3H_5O_2^-$ and $HC_3H_5O_2$ is:

$$pH = pK_a + \log \frac{\text{mmol } C_3H_5O_2^-}{\text{mmol } HC_3H_5O_2}, \quad 5.07 = 4.89 + \log \frac{\text{mmol } C_3H_5O_2^-}{\text{mmol } HC_3H_5O_2}$$

$$\frac{\text{mmol } C_3H_5O_2^-}{\text{mmol } HC_3H_5O_2} = 10^{0.18} = 1.5$$

Let x = mmol OH^- added to increase pH to 5.07. Because OH^- will essentially react to completion with $HC_3H_5O_2$, the setup for the problem using mmol is:

$$HC_3H_5O_2 \quad + \quad OH^- \quad \rightarrow \quad C_3H_5O_2^- + H_2O$$

	$HC_3H_5O_2$	OH^-		$C_3H_5O_2^-$	
Before	33.8 mmol	x mmol		38.5 mmol	
Change	$-x$	$-x$	$\rightarrow$	$+x$	Reacts completely
After	$33.8 - x$	0		$38.5 + x$	

Solving for x:

$$\frac{\text{mmol } C_3H_5O_2^-}{\text{mmol } HC_3H_5O_2} = 1.5 = \frac{38.5 + x}{33.8 - x}, \quad 1.5\,(33.8 - x) = 38.5 + x$$

$x = 4.9$ mmol OH^- added

The volume of NaOH necessary to raise the pH by 2.5% is:

$$4.9 \text{ mmol NaOH} \times \frac{1 \text{ mL}}{0.10 \text{ mmol NaOH}} = 49 \text{ mL}$$

49 mL of 0.10 M NaOH must be added to increase the pH by 2.5%.

140. $0.400 \text{ mol/L} \times V_{NH_3} = \text{mol } NH_3 = \text{mol } NH_4^+$ after reaction with HCl at the equiv. point.

At the equivalence point: $[NH_4^+]_o = \dfrac{\text{mol } NH_4^+}{\text{total volume}} = \dfrac{0.400 \times V_{NH_3}}{1.50 \times V_{NH_3}} = 0.267\ M$

$$NH_4^+ \quad \rightleftharpoons \quad H^+ \quad + \quad NH_3$$

	NH_4^+	H^+	NH_3
Initial	0.267 M	0	0
Equil.	0.267 – x	x	x

$$K_a = \frac{K_w}{K_b} = \frac{1.0 \times 10^{-14}}{1.8 \times 10^{-5}} = 5.6 \times 10^{-10} = \frac{x^2}{0.267 - x} \approx \frac{x^2}{0.267}$$

$x = [H^+] = 1.2 \times 10^{-5}\ M$; pH = 4.92;   Assumption good.

141. For HOCl, $K_a = 3.5 \times 10^{-8}$ and $pK_a = -\log(3.5 \times 10^{-8}) = 7.46$; This will be a buffer solution since the pH is close to the pK_a value.

$$pH = pK_a + \log\frac{[OCl^-]}{[HOCl]}, \quad 8.00 = 7.46 + \log\frac{[OCl^-]}{[HOCl]}, \quad \frac{[OCl^-]}{[HOCl]} = 10^{0.54} = 3.5$$

$1.00 \text{ L} \times 0.0500\ M = 0.0500 \text{ mol HOCl}$ initially. Added OH^- converts HOCl into OCl^-. The total moles of OCl^- and HOCl must equal 0.0500 mol. Solving where n = moles:

$n_{OCl^-} + n_{HOCl} = 0.0500$ and $n_{OCl^-} = 3.5\, n_{HOCl}$

$4.5\, n_{HOCl} = 0.0500$, $n_{HOCl} = 0.011$ mol; $n_{OCl^-} = 0.039$ mol

We need to add 0.039 mol NaOH to produce 0.039 mol OCl^-.

0.039 mol $OH^- = V \times 0.0100\, M$, $V = 3.9$ L NaOH

142. 50.0 mL $\times 0.100\, M = 5.00$ mmol H_2SO_4; 30.0 mL $\times 0.100\, M = 3.00$ mmol HOCl

25.0 mL $\times 0.200\, M = 5.00$ mmol NaOH; 10.0 mL $\times 0.150\, M = 1.50$ mmol KOH

25.0 mL $\times 0.100\, M = 2.50$ mmol $Ba(OH)_2 = 5.00$ mmol OH^-

We've added 11.50 mmol OH^- total.

Let the OH^- react with the best acid present. This is H_2SO_4, which is a diprotic acid. For H_2SO_4, $K_{a_1} \gg 1$ and $K_{a_2} = 1.2 \times 10^{-2}$. The reaction is:

  10.00 mmol $OH^- + 5.00$ mmol $H_2SO_4 \rightarrow 10.00$ mmol $H_2O + 5.00$ mmol SO_4^{2-}

OH^- still remains, and it reacts with the next best acid, HOCl ($K_a = 3.5 \times 10^{-8}$). The remaining 1.50 mmol OH^- will convert 1.50 mmol HOCl into 1.50 mmol OCl^-, resulting in a solution containing 1.50 mmol OCl^- and (3.00 – 1.50 =) 1.50 mmol HOCl. Major species at this point: HOCl, OCl^-, SO_4^{2-}, H_2O plus cations that don't affect pH. SO_4^{2-} is an extremely weak base ($K_b = 8.3 \times 10^{-13}$). We have a buffer solution where the major equilibrium affecting pH is: $HOCl \rightleftharpoons H^+ + OCl^-$. Because $[HOCl] = [OCl^-]$:

  $[H^+] = K_a = 3.5 \times 10^{-8}\, M$; $pH = 7.46$ Assumptions good.

143. The first titration plot (from 0-100.0 mL) corresponds to the titration of H_2A by OH^-. The reaction is $H_2A + OH^- \rightarrow HA^- + H_2O$. After all of the H_2A has been reacted, the second titration (from 100.0 – 200.0 mL) corresponds to the titration of HA^- by OH^-. The reaction is $HA^- + OH^- \rightarrow A^{2-} + H_2O$.

a. At 100.0 mL of NaOH, just enough OH^- has been added to react completely with all of the H_2A present (mol OH^- added = mol H_2A present initially). From the balanced equation, the mol of HA^- produced will equal the mol of H_2A present initially. Because mol HA^- present at 100.0 mL OH^- added equals the mol of H_2A present initially, exactly 100.0 mL more of NaOH must be added to react with all of the HA^-. The volume of NaOH added to reach the second equivalence point equals 100.0 mL + 100.0 mL = 200.0 mL.

b. $H_2A + OH^- \rightarrow HA^- + H_2O$ is the reaction occurring from 0-100.0 mL NaOH added.

  i. No reaction has taken place, so H_2A and H_2O are the major species.

ii. Adding OH^- converts H_2A into HA^-. The major species up to 100.0 mL NaOH added are H_2A, HA^-, H_2O, and Na^+.

iii. At 100.0 mL NaOH added, mol of OH^- = mol H_2A, so all of the H_2A present initially has been converted into HA^-. The major species are HA^-, H_2O, and Na^+.

iv. Between 100.0 and 200.0 mL NaOH added, the OH^- converts HA^- into A^{2-}. The major species are HA^-, A^{2-}, H_2O, and Na^+.

v.   At the second equivalence point (200.0 mL), just enough OH^- has been added to convert all of the HA^- into A^{2-}. The major species are A^{2-}, H_2O, and Na^+.

vi. Past 200.0 mL NaOH added, excess OH^- is present. The major species are OH^-, A^{2-}, H_2O, and Na^+.

c. 50.0 mL of NaOH added correspond to the first halfway point to equivalence. Exactly one-half of the H_2A present initially has been converted into its conjugate base HA^-, so $[H_2A] = [HA^-]$ in this buffer solution.

$$H_2A \rightleftharpoons HA^- + H^+ \qquad K_{a_1} = \frac{[HA^-][H^+]}{[H_2A]}$$

When $[HA^-] = [H_2A]$, then $K_{a_1} = [H^+]$ or $pK_{a_1} = pH$.

Here, pH = 4.0 so $K_{a_1} = 4.0$ and $K_{a_1} = 10^{-4.0} = 1 \times 10^{-4}$.

150.0 mL of NaOH added correspond to the second halfway point to equivalence where $[HA^-] = [A^{2-}]$ in this buffer solution.

$$HA^- \rightleftharpoons A^{2-} + H^+ \qquad K_{a_2} = \frac{[A^{2-}][H^+]}{[HA^-]}$$

When $[A^{2-}] = [HA^-]$, then $K_{a_2} = [H^+]$ or $pK_{a_2} = pH$.

Here, pH = 8.0 so $pK_{a_2} = 8.0$ and $K_{a_2} = 10^{-8.0} = 1 \times 10^{-8}$.

144. a. Na^+ is present in all solutions. The added H^+ from HCl reacts completely with CO_3^{2-} to convert it into HCO_3^- (points A-C). After all of the CO_3^{2-} is reacted (after point C, the first equivalence point), then H^+ reacts completely with the next best base present, HCO_3^- (points C-E). Point E represents the second equivalence point. The major species present at the various points after H^+ reacts completely follow.

A. CO_3^{2-}, H_2O B. CO_3^{2-}, HCO_3^-, H_2O, Cl^-

C. HCO_3^-, H_2O, Cl^- D. HCO_3^-, CO_2 (H_2CO_3), H_2O, Cl^-

E. CO_2 (H_2CO_3), H_2O, Cl^- F. H^+ (excess), CO_2 (H_2CO_3), H_2O, Cl^-

b. $H_2CO_3 \rightleftharpoons HCO_3^- + H^+$ $K_{a_1} = 4.3 \times 10^{-7}$

$HCO_3^- \rightleftharpoons CO_3^{2-} + H^+$ $K_{a_2} = 5.6 \times 10^{-11}$

The first titration reaction occurring between points A-C is:

$H^+ + CO_3^{2-} \rightarrow HCO_3^-$

At point B, enough H^+ has been added to convert one-half of the CO_3^{2-} into its conjugate. At this halfway point to equivalence, $[CO_3^{2-}] = [HCO_3^-]$. For this buffer solution, $pH = pK_{a_2} = -\log(5.6 \times 10^{-11}) = 10.25$.

The second titration reaction occurring between points C-E is:

$H^+ + HCO_3^- \rightarrow H_2CO_3$

Point D is the second half-way point to equivalence where $[HCO_3^-] = [H_2CO_3]$. Here, $pH = pK_{a_1} = -\log(4.3 \times 10^{-7}) = 6.37$.

145.   An indicator changes color at $pH \approx pK_a \pm 1$. The results from each indicator tells us something about the pH. The conclusions are summarized below:

Results from	pH
bromphenol blue	$\geq \sim 5.0$
bromcresol purple	$\leq \sim 5.0$
bromcresol green *	$pH \sim pK_a \sim 4.8$
alizarin	$\leq \sim 5.5$

*For bromcresol green, the resultant color is green.
This is a combination of the extremes (yellow and blue).
This occurs when $pH \sim pK_a$ of the indicator.

From the indicator results, the pH of the solution is about 5.0. We solve for K_a by setting up the typical weak acid problem.

$$HX \rightleftharpoons H^+ + X^-$$

	HX	H⁺	X⁻
Initial	$1.0\,M$	~ 0	0
Equil.	$1.0 - x$	x	x

$K_a = \dfrac{[H^+][X^-]}{[HX]} = \dfrac{x^2}{1.0 - x}$; Because $pH \sim 5.0$, $[H^+] = x \approx 1 \times 10^{-5}\,M$.

$K_a \approx \dfrac{(1 \times 10^{-5})^2}{1.0 - 1 \times 10^{-5}} \approx 1 \times 10^{-10}$

146.
$$Ag^+ + NH_3 \rightleftharpoons AgNH_3^+ \qquad K_1 = 2.1 \times 10^3$$
$$AgNH_3^+ + NH_3 \rightleftharpoons Ag(NH_3)_2^+ \qquad K_2 = 8.2 \times 10^3$$

$$Ag^+ + 2\,NH_3 \rightleftharpoons Ag(NH_3)_2^+ \qquad K = K_1K_2 = 1.7 \times 10^7$$

The initial concentrations are halved because equal volumes of the two solutions are mixed. Let the reaction go to completion since K is large, then solve an equilibrium problem.

$$Ag^+ \quad + \quad 2\,NH_3 \quad \rightleftharpoons \quad Ag(NH_3)_2^+$$

Before	0.20 M	2.0 M	0
After	0	1.6	0.20
Equil.	x	$1.6 + 2x$	$0.20 - x$

$$K = 1.7 \times 10^7 = \frac{[Ag(NH_3)_2^+]}{[Ag^+][NH_3]^2} = \frac{0.20 - x}{x(1.6 + 2x)^2} \approx \frac{0.20}{x(1.6)^2}, \quad x = 4.6 \times 10^{-9}\,M;$$

Assumptions good.

$$[Ag^+] = x = 4.6 \times 10^{-9}\,M; \quad [NH_3] = 1.6\,M; \quad [Ag(NH_3)_2^+] = 0.20\,M$$

Use either the K_1 or K_2 equilibrium expression to calculate $[AgNH_3^+]$.

$$AgNH_3^+ + NH_3 \rightleftharpoons Ag(NH_3)_2^+ \qquad K_2 = 8.2 \times 10^3$$

$$8.2 \times 10^3 = \frac{[Ag(NH_3)_2^+]}{[AgNH_3^+][NH_3]} = \frac{0.20}{[AgNH_3^+](1.6)}, \quad [AgNH_3^+] = 1.5 \times 10^{-5}\,M$$

147. $\quad K_{sp} = [Ni^{2+}][S^{2-}] = 3 \times 10^{-21}$

$$H_2S \rightleftharpoons H^+ + HS^- \qquad K_{a_1} = 1.0 \times 10^{-7}$$
$$HS^- \rightleftharpoons H^+ + S^{2-} \qquad K_{a_2} = 1 \times 10^{-19}$$

$$H_2S \rightleftharpoons 2\,H^+ + S^{2-} \qquad K = K_{a_1} \times K_{a_2} = 1 \times 10^{-26} = \frac{[H^+]^2[S^{2-}]}{[H_2S]}$$

Because K is very small, only a tiny fraction of the H_2S will react. At equilibrium, $[H_2S] = 0.10\,M$ and $[H^+] = 1 \times 10^{-3}$.

$$[S^{2-}] = \frac{K[H_2S]}{[H^+]^2} = \frac{1 \times 10^{-26}(0.10)}{(1 \times 10^{-3})^2} = 1 \times 10^{-21}\,M$$

$$NiS(s) \rightleftharpoons Ni^{2+}(aq) + S^{2-}(aq) \qquad K_{sp} = 3.0 \times 10^{-21}$$

Precipitation of NiS will occur when $Q > K_{sp}$. We will calculate $[Ni^{2+}]$ for $Q = K_{sp}$.

$$Q = K_{sp} = [Ni^{2+}][S^{2-}] = 3.0 \times 10^{-21}, \quad [Ni^{2+}] = \frac{3.0 \times 10^{-21}}{1 \times 10^{-21}} = 3\,M$$

148. $MX \rightleftharpoons M^+ + X^-$; $\Delta T = K_f m$, $m = \dfrac{\Delta T}{K_f} = \dfrac{0.028°C}{1.86°C/molal} = 0.015$ mol/kg

$\dfrac{0.015 \text{ mol}}{\text{kg}} \times \dfrac{1 \text{ kg}}{1000 \text{ g}} \times 250 \text{ g} = 0.00375$ mol total solute particles (carrying extra sig fig)

0.0375 mol = mol M^+ + mol X^-, mol M^+ = mol X^- = $0.0375/2$

Because the density of the solution is 1.0 g/mL, 250 g = 250 mL of solution.

$[M^+] = \dfrac{(0.00375/2) \text{ mol } M^+}{0.25 \text{ L}} = 7.5 \times 10^{-3} \ M$, $[X^-] = \dfrac{(0.00375/2) \text{ mol } X^-}{0.25 \text{ L}} = 7.5 \times 10^{-3} \ M$

$K_{sp} = [M^+][X^-] = (7.5 \times 10^{-3})^2 = 5.6 \times 10^{-5}$

149.   a. $\qquad\qquad SrF_2(s) \ \rightleftharpoons \ Sr^{2+}(aq) \ + \ 2\,F^-(aq)$

Initial $\qquad\qquad\qquad\qquad\quad 0 \qquad\qquad\quad 0$
$\qquad\qquad$ s mol/L SrF_2 dissolves to reach equilibrium
Equil. $\qquad\qquad\qquad\qquad\quad s \qquad\qquad\quad 2s$

$[Sr^{2+}][F^-]^2 = K_{sp} = 7.9 \times 10^{-10} = 4s^3$, $s = 5.8 \times 10^{-4}$ mol/L

b.   Greater, because some of the F^- would react with water:

$F^- + H_2O \rightleftharpoons HF + OH^- \qquad K_b = \dfrac{K_w}{K_a(HF)} = 1.4 \times 10^{-11}$

This lowers the concentration of F^-, forcing more SrF_2 to dissolve.

c. $SrF_2(s) \rightleftharpoons Sr^{2+} + 2\,F^- \quad K_{sp} = 7.9 \times 10^{-10} = [Sr^{2+}][F^-]^2$

Let s = solubility = $[Sr^{2+}]$, then $2s$ = total F^- concentration.

Because F^- is a weak base, some of the F^- is converted into HF. Therefore:

total F^- concentration = $2s = [F^-] + [HF]$.

$HF \rightleftharpoons H^+ + F^- \quad K_a = 7.2 \times 10^{-4} = \dfrac{[H^+][F^-]}{[HF]} = \dfrac{1.0 \times 10^{-2}[F^-]}{[HF]}$ (pH = 2.00 buffer)

$7.2 \times 10^{-2} = \dfrac{[F^-]}{[HF]}$, $[HF] = 14\,[F^-]$; Solving:

$[Sr^{2+}] = s$; $2s = [F^-] + [HF] = [F^-] + 14\,[F^-]$, $2s = 15\,[F^-]$, $[F^-] = 2s/15$

$7.9 \times 10^{-10} = [Sr^{2+}][F^-]^2 = (s)\left(\dfrac{2s}{15}\right)^2$, $s = 3.5 \times 10^{-3}$ mol/L

150.
$$M_3X_2(s) \rightarrow 3\ M^{2+}(aq) + 2\ X^{3-}(aq) \qquad K_{sp} = [M^{2+}]^3[X^{3-}]^2$$

Initial	s = solubility (mol/L)	0	0
Equil.		$3s$	$2s$

$$K_{sp} = (3s)^3(2s)^2 = 108\ s^5; \quad \text{Total ion concentration} = 3s + 2s = 5s$$

$$\pi = iMRT, \quad iM = \text{total ion concentration} = \frac{\pi}{RT} = \frac{2.64 \times 10^{-2}\ \text{atm}}{0.08206\ \text{L atm/K} \bullet \text{mol} \times 298\ \text{K}}$$

$$= 1.08 \times 10^{-3}\ \text{mol/L}$$

$$5s = 1.08 \times 10^{-3}\ \text{mol/L}, \quad s = 2.16 \times 10^{-4}\ \text{mol/L}; \quad K_{sp} = 108\ s^5 = 108(2.16 \times 10^{-4})^5$$

$$K_{sp} = 5.08 \times 10^{-17}$$

Integrative Problems

151.
$$\text{pH} = pK_a + \log \frac{[C_7H_4O_2F^-]}{[C_7H_5O_2F]} = 2.90 + \log\left(\frac{55.0\ \text{mL} \times 0.472\ M / V_T}{75.0\ \text{mL} \times 0.275\ M / V_T}\right)$$

$$\text{pH} = 2.90 + \log\left(\frac{26.0}{20.6}\right) = 2.90 + 0.101 = 3.00$$

152.   M: $[Xe]6s^2 4f^{14} 5d^{10}$; This is mercury, Hg. Because X^- has 54 electrons, X has 53 protons and is iodine, I. The identity of Q = Hg_2I_2.

$$[I^-]_0 = \frac{1.98\ \text{g NaI} \times \dfrac{1\ \text{mol NaI}}{149.9\ \text{g}} \times \dfrac{1\ \text{mol I}^-}{\text{mol NaI}}}{0.150\ \text{L}} = 0.0881\ \text{mol/L}$$

$$Hg_2I_2(s) \rightleftharpoons Hg_2^{2+} + 2\ I^- \qquad K_{sp} = 4.5 \times 10^{-29}$$

Initial	s = solubility (mol/L)	0	0.0881 M
Equil.		s	0.0881 + $2s$

$$K_{sp} = 4.5 \times 10^{-29} = [Hg_2^{2+}][I^-]^2 = s(0.0881 + 2s)^2 \approx s(0.0881)^2$$

$$s = 5.8 \times 10^{-27}\ \text{mol/L}; \quad \text{Assumption good.}$$

153.   The added OH^- from the strong base reacts to completion with the best acid present, HF. To determine the pH, see what is in solution after the OH^- reacts to completion.

$$OH^- \text{ added} = 38.7\ \text{g soln} \times \frac{1.50\ \text{g NaOH}}{100.0\ \text{g soln}} \times \frac{1\ \text{mol NaOH}}{40.00\ \text{g}} \times \frac{1\ \text{mol OH}^-}{\text{mol NaOH}} = 0.0145\ \text{mol OH}^-$$

For the 0.174 m HF solution, if we had exactly 1 kg of H_2O, then the solution would contain 0.174 mol HF.

$$0.174 \text{ mol HF} \times \frac{20.01 \text{ g}}{\text{mol HF}} = 3.48 \text{ g HF}$$

mass of solution = 1000.00 g H_2O + 3.48 g HF = 1003.48 g

$$\text{volume of solution} = 1003.48 \text{ g} \times \frac{1 \text{ mL}}{1.10 \text{ g}} = 912 \text{ mL}$$

$$\text{mol HF} = 250. \text{ mL} \times \frac{0.174 \text{ mol HF}}{912 \text{ mL}} = 4.77 \times 10^{-2} \text{ mol HF}$$

$$\text{OH}^- \quad + \quad \text{HF} \quad \rightarrow \quad \text{F}^- \quad + \quad H_2O$$

	OH⁻	HF	F⁻
Before	0.0145 mol	0.0477 mol	0
Change	−0.0145	−0.0145	+0.0145
After	0	0.0332 mol	0.0145 mol

After reaction, a buffer solution results containing HF, a weak acid, and F⁻, its conjugate base. Let V_T = total volume of solution.

$$\text{pH} = \text{p}K_a + \log\frac{[\text{F}^-]}{[\text{HF}]} = -\log(7.2 \times 10^{-4}) + \log\left(\frac{0.0145/V_T}{0.0332/V_T}\right)$$

$$\text{pH} = 3.14 + \log\left(\frac{0.0145}{0.0332}\right) = 3.14 + (-0.360), \ \text{pH} = 2.78$$

Marathon Problem

154. a. Because $K_{a_1} \gg K_{a_2}$, the amount of H^+ contributed by the K_{a_2} reaction will be negligible. The $[H^+]$ donated by the K_{a_1} reaction is $10^{-2.06} = 8.7 \times 10^{-3} \, M \, H^+$.

$$H_2A \quad \rightleftharpoons \quad H^+ \quad + \quad HA^- \qquad K_{a_1} = 5.90 \times 10^{-2}$$

	H_2A	H^+	HA^-
Initial	$[H_2A]_o$	~0	0
Equil.	$[H_2A]_o - x$	x	x

$[H_2A]_o$ = initial concentration

$$K_{a_1} = 5.90 \times 10^{-2} = \frac{x^2}{[H_2A]_0 - x} = \frac{(8.7 \times 10^{-3})^2}{[H_2A]_0 - 8.7 \times 10^{-3}}, \quad [H_2A]_0 = 1.0 \times 10^{-2} \, M$$

$$\text{mol } H_2A \text{ present initially} = 0.250 \text{ L} \times \frac{1 \times 10^{-2} \text{ mol } H_2A}{\text{L}} = 2.5 \times 10^{-3} \text{ mol } H_2A$$

$$\text{molar mass } H_2A = \frac{0.225 \text{ g } H_2A}{2.5 \times 10^{-3} \text{ mol } H_2A} = 90. \text{ g/mol}$$

b. $H_2A + 2\ OH^- \rightarrow A^{2-} + H_2O$; At the second equivalence point, the added OH^- has converted all the H_2A into A^{2-}; so A^{2-} is the major species present that determines the pH. The mmol of A^{2-} present at the equivalence point equals the mmol of H_2A present initially (2.5 mmol) and the mmol of OH^- added to reach the second equivalence point is 2(2.5 mmol) = 5.0 mmol OH^- added. The only information we need now in order to calculate the K_{a_2} value is the volume of $Ca(OH)_2$ added in order to reach the second equivalent point. We will use the K_{sp} value for $Ca(OH)_2$ to help solve for the volume of $Ca(OH)_2$ added.

$$Ca(OH)_2(s) \quad \rightleftharpoons \quad Ca^{2+} \ + \ 2OH^- \quad K_{sp} = 1.3 \times 10^{-6} = [Ca^{2+}]\,[OH^-]^2$$

Initial	s = solubility (mol/L)	0	~0
Equil.		s	$2s$

$K_{sp} = 1.3 \times 10^{-6} = (s)\,(2s)^2 = 4s^3,\ \ s = 6.9 \times 10^{-3}\,M\ Ca(OH)_2$;   Assumptions good.

The volume of $Ca(OH)_2$ required to deliver 5.0 mmol OH^- (the amount of OH^- necessary to reach the second equivalence point) is:

$$5.0\ \text{mmol}\ OH^- \times \frac{1\ \text{mmol}\ Ca(OH)_2}{2\ \text{mmol}\ OH^-} \times \frac{1\ \text{mL}}{6.9 \times 10^{-3}\ \text{mmol}\ Ca(OH)_2}$$

$$= 362\ \text{mL} = 360\ \text{mL}\ Ca(OH)_2$$

At the second equivalence point, the total volume of solution is:

250. mL + 360 mL = 610 mL

Now we can solve for K_{a_2} using the pH data at the second equivalence point. The only species present which has any effect on pH is the weak base, A^{2-}, so the set-up to the problem requires the K_b reaction for A^{2-}.

$$A^{2-} \ + \ H_2O \ \rightleftharpoons HA^- \ + \ OH^- \qquad K_b = \frac{K_w}{K_{a_2}} = \frac{1.0 \times 10^{-14}}{K_{a_2}}$$

Initial	$\dfrac{2.5\ \text{mmol}}{610\ \text{mL}}$	0	0
Equil.	$4.1 \times 10^{-3}\,M - x$	x	x

$$K_b = \frac{1.0 \times 10^{-14}}{K_{a_2}} = \frac{x^2}{4.1 \times 10^{-3} - x}$$

From the problem, pH = 7.96, so $OH^- = 10^{-6.04} = 9.1 \times 10^{-7}\,M = x$.

$$K_b = \frac{1.0 \times 10^{-14}}{K_{a_2}} = \frac{(9.1 \times 10^{-7})^2}{4.1 \times 10^{-3} - 9.1 \times 10^{-7}} = 2.0 \times 10^{-10},\ \ K_{a_2} = 5.0 \times 10^{-5}$$

Note: The amount of OH^- donated by the weak base HA^- will be negligible since the K_b value for A^{2-} is more than a 1000 times larger than the K_b value for HA^-.

CHAPTER SIXTEEN

SPONTANEITY, ENTROPY, AND FREE ENERGY

For Review

1.   a.   A spontaneous process is one that occurs without any outside intervention.

        b.   Entropy is a measure of disorder or randomness.

        c.   Positional probability is a type of probability that depends on the number of arrangements in space that yield a particular state.

        d.   The system is the portion of the universe in which we are interested.

        e.   The surroundings are everything else in the universe besides the system.

        f.   The universe is everything; universe = system + surroundings.

2.   Second law of thermodynamics: in any spontaneous process, there is always an increase in the entropy of the universe. $\Delta S_{univ} = \Delta S_{sys} + \Delta S_{surr}$; When both ΔS_{sys} and ΔS_{surr} are positive, ΔS_{univ} must be positive (so process is spontaneous). ΔS_{univ} is always negative (so process is nonspontaneous) when both ΔS_{sys} and ΔS_{surr} are negative. When the signs of ΔS_{sys} are opposite of each other [(ΔS_{sys} (+), ΔS_{surr} (−) or vice versa], the process may or may not be spontaneous.

3. ΔS_{surr} is primarily determined by heat flow. This heat flow into or out of the surroundings comes from the heat flow out of or into the system. In an exothermic process ($\Delta H < 0$), heat flows into the surroundings from the system. The heat flow into the surroundings increases the random motions in the surroundings and increases the entropy of the surroundings ($\Delta S_{surr} > 0$). This is a favorable driving force for spontaneity. In an endothermic reaction ($\Delta H > 0$), heat is transferred from the surroundings into the system. This heat flow out of the surroundings decreases the random motions in the surroundings and decreases the entropy of the surroundings ($\Delta S_{surr} < 0$). This is unfavorable. The magnitude of ΔS_{surr} also depends on the temperature. The relationship is inverse; at low temperatures, a specific amount of heat exchange makes a larger percent change in the surroundings than the same amount of heat flow at a higher temperature. The negative sign in the $\Delta S_{surr} = -\Delta H/T$ equation is necessary to get the signs correct. For an exothermic reaction where ΔH is negative, this increases ΔS_{surr} so the negative sign converts the negative ΔH value into a positive quantity. For an endothermic process where ΔH is positive, the sign of ΔS_{surr} is negative and the negative sign converts the positive ΔH value into a negative quantity.

4. $\Delta S_{univ} = -\Delta G/T$ (at constant T and P); When ΔG is negative ($\Delta S_{univ} > 0$), the process is spontaneous. When ΔG is positive ($\Delta S_{univ} < 0$), the process in nonspontaneous (the reverse process is spontaneous). When $\Delta G = 0$, the process is at equilibrium.

$\Delta G = \Delta H - T\Delta S$; See Table 16.5 for the four possible sign conventions and the temperature dependence for these sign combinations. When the signs for ΔH and ΔS are both the same, then temperature determines if the process is spontaneous. When ΔH is positive (unfavorable) and ΔS is positive (favorable), high temperatures are needed so the favorable ΔS term dominates making the process spontaneous ($\Delta G < 0$). When ΔH is negative (favorable) and ΔS is negative (unfavorable), low temperatures are needed so the favorable ΔH term dominates making the process spontaneous ($\Delta G < 0$). Note that if ΔG is positive for a process, then the reverse process has a negative ΔG value and is spontaneous.

At the phase change temperature (melting point or boiling point), two phases are in equilibrium with each other so $\Delta G = 0$. The $\Delta G = \Delta H - T\Delta S$ equation reduces to $\Delta H = T\Delta S$ at the phase change temperature. For the s $\rightarrow$ l phase change, ΔG is negative above the freezing point because the process is spontaneous (as we know). For the l $\rightarrow$ g phase change, the sign of ΔG is positive below the boiling point as the process is nonspontaneous (as we know).

5.   Third law of thermodynamics: the entropy of a perfect crystal at 0 K is zero. Standard entropy values ($S°$) represent the increase in entropy that occurs when a substance is heated from 0 K to 298 K at 1 atm pressure. The equation to calculate $\Delta S°$ for a reaction using the standard entropy values is: $\Delta S°_{rxn} = \Sigma n_p S°_{products} - \Sigma n_r S°_{reactants}$

This equation works because entropy is a state function of the system (it is not pathway-dependent). Because of this, one can manipulate chemical reactions with known $\Delta S°$ values to determine $\Delta S°$ for a different reaction. The entropy change for a different reaction equals the sum of the entropy changes for the reactions added together that yield the different reaction. This is utilizing Hess's law. The superscript° indicates conditions where T = 25°C and P = 1 atm.

To predict signs for gas phase reactions, you need to realize that the gaseous state represents a hugely more disordered state as compared to the solid and liquid states. Gases dominate sign predictions for reactions. Those reactions that show an increase in the number of moles of gas as reactants are converted to products have an increase in disorder which translates into a positive $\Delta S°$ value. $\Delta S°$ values are negative when there is a decrease in the moles of gas as reactants are converted into products. When the moles of gaseous reactants and products are equal, $\Delta S°$ is usually difficult to predict for chemical reactions. However, predicting signs for phase changes can be done by realizing the solid state is the most ordered phase (lowest $S°$ values), the liquid state is a slightly more disordered phase than the solid state, with the gaseous state being the most disordered phase by a large margin ($S°_{solid} < S°_{liquid} \ll S°_{gas}$). Another process involving condensed phases whose sign is also easy to predict (usually) is the dissolution of a solute in a solvent. Here, the mixed up solution state is usually the more disordered state as compared to the solute and solvent separately.

6.   Standard free energy change: the change in free energy that will occur for one unit of reaction if the reactants in their standard states are converted to products in their standard state. The

standard free energy of formation (ΔG_f^o) of a substance is the change in free energy that accompanies the formation of 1 mole of that substance from its constituent elements with all reactants and products in their standard states. The equation that manipulates ΔG_f^o values to determining $\Delta G_{reaction}^o$ is: $\Delta G^\circ = \Sigma n_p \Delta n_{f\,(products)}^o - \Sigma n_r \Delta G_{f\,(reactants)}^o$.

Because ΔG° is a state function (path independent), chemical reactions with known ΔG° values can be manipulated to determine ΔG° for a different reaction. ΔG° for the different reaction is the sum of ΔG° for all the steps (reactions) added together to get the different reaction. This is Hess's law.

Another way to determine ΔG° for a reaction is to utilize the $\Delta G^\circ = \Delta H^\circ - T\Delta S^\circ$ equation. Here, you need to know ΔH°, ΔS°, and the temperature, then you can use the above equation to calculate ΔG°.

Of the functions ΔG°, ΔH°, and ΔS°, ΔG° has the greatest dependence on temperature. The temperature is usually assumed to be 25°C. However, if other temperatures are used in a reaction, we can estimate ΔG° at that different temperature by assuming ΔH° and ΔS° are temperature independent (which is not always the best assumption). We calculate ΔH° and ΔS° values for a reaction using Appendix 4 data, then use the different temperature in the $\Delta G^\circ = \Delta H^\circ - T\Delta S^\circ$ equation to determine (estimate) ΔG° at that different temperature.

7.   No; When using ΔG_f^o values in Appendix 4, we have specified a temperature of 25°C. Further, if gases or solutions are involved, we have specified partial pressures of 1 atm and solute concentrations of 1 molar. At other temperatures and compositions, the reaction may not be spontaneous. A negative ΔG° value means the reaction is spontaneous under <u>standard conditions</u>.

The free energy and pressure relationship is $G = G^\circ + RT \ln (P)$. The RT ln P term corrects for nonstandard pressures (or concentrations if solutes are involved in the reaction). The standard pressure for a gas is 1 atm and the standard concentration for solutes is 1 M. The equation to calculate ΔG for a reaction at nonstandard conditions is: $\Delta G = \Delta G^\circ + RT \ln Q$ where Q is the reaction quotient determined at the nonstandard pressures and/or concentrations of the gases and/or solutes in the reaction. The reaction quotient has the exact same form as the equilibrium constant K. The difference is that the partial pressures or concentrations used may or may not be the equilibrium concentrations.

All reactions want to minimize their free energy. This is the driving force for any process. As long as ΔG is a negative, the process occurs. The equilibrium position represents the lowest total free energy available to any particular reaction system. Once equilibrium is reached, the system cannot minimize its free energy anymore. Converting from reactants to products or products to reactants will increase the total free energy of the system which reactions do not want to do.

8.   At equilibrium, $\Delta G = 0$ and Q = K (the reaction quotient equals the equilibrium constant value). From the $\Delta G^\circ = -RT \ln K$ equation, when a reaction has K < 1, the ln K term is negative, giving a positive ΔG° value. When K > 1, the ln K term is positive so ΔG° is negative. When $\Delta G^\circ = 0$, this tell us that K for the process is equal to one (K = 1) because ln 1 = 0.

The sign of ΔG (positive or negative) tells us which reaction is spontaneous (the forward or reverse reaction). If $\Delta G < 0$, then the forward reaction is spontaneous and if $\Delta G > 0$, then the reverse reaction is spontaneous. If $\Delta G = 0$, then the reaction is at equilibrium (neither the forward or reverse reactions are spontaneous). $\Delta G°$ gives the equilibrium position by determining K for a reaction utilizing the equation $\Delta G° = -RT \ln K$. $\Delta G°$ can only be used to predict spontaneity when all reactants and products are present at standard pressures of 1 atm and/or standard concentrations of 1 M.

9.   A negative ΔG value does not guarantee that a reaction will occur. It does say that it can occur (is spontaneous), but whether it will occur also depends on how fast the reaction is (depends on the kinetics). A process with a negative ΔG may not occur because it is too slow. The example used in the text is the conversion of diamonds into graphite. Thermodynamics says the reaction can occur ($\Delta G > 0$), but the reaction is so slow that it doesn't occur.

The rate of a reaction is directly related to temperature. As temperature increases, the rate of a reaction increases. Spontaneity, however, does not necessarily have a direct relationship to temperature. The temperature dependence of spontaneity depends on the signs of ΔH and ΔS (see Table 16.5 of the text). For example, when ΔH and ΔS are both negative, the reaction becomes more favorable thermodynamically (ΔG becomes more negative) with decreasing temperature. This is just the opposite of the kinetics dependence on temperature. Other sign combinations of ΔH and ΔS have different spontaneity temperature dependence.

10. $w_{max} = \Delta G$; When ΔG is negative, the magnitude of ΔG is equal to the maximum possible useful work obtainable from the process (at constant T and P). When ΔG is positive, the magnitude of ΔG is equal to the minimum amount of work that must be expended to make the process spontaneous. Due to waste energy (heat) in any real process, the amount of useful work obtainable from a spontaneous process is always less than w_{max}, and for a non-spontaneous reaction, an amount of work greater than w_{max} must be applied to make the process spontaneous.

Reversible process: a cyclic process carried out by a hypothetical pathway, which leaves the universe the same as it was before. No real process is reversible.

Questions

7.   Living organisms need an external source of energy to carry out these processes. Green plants use the energy from sunlight to produce glucose from carbon dioxide and water by photosynthesis. In the human body, the energy released from the metabolism of glucose helps drive the synthesis of proteins. For all processes combined, ΔS_{univ} must be greater than zero (2nd law).

8.   Dispersion increases the entropy of the universe because the more widely something is dispersed, the greater the disorder. We must do work to overcome this disorder. In terms of the 2nd law, it would be more advantageous to prevent contamination of the environment rather than to clean it up later. As a substance disperses, we have a much larger area that must be decontaminated.

9.   It appears that the sum of the two processes has no net change. This is not so. By the second law of thermodynamics, ΔS_{univ} must have increased even though it looks as if we have gone through a cyclic process.

10.   The introduction of mistakes is an effect of entropy. The purpose of redundant information is to provide a control to check the "correctness" of the transmitted information.

11.   As a process occurs, ΔS_{univ} will increase; ΔS_{univ} cannot decrease. Time, like ΔS_{univ}, only goes in one direction.

12.   This reaction is kinetically slow but thermodynamically favorable ($\Delta G < 0$). Thermodynamics only tells us if a reaction can occur. To answer the question will it occur, one also needs to consider the kinetics (speed of reaction). The ultraviolet light provides the activation energy for this slow reaction to occur.

13.   Possible arrangements for one molecule:

1 way   1 way

Both are equally probable.

Possible arrangements for two molecules:

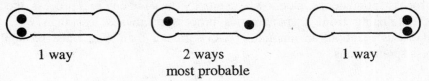

1 way   2 ways   1 way
                      most probable

Possible arrangement for three molecules:

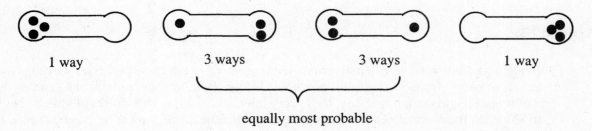

1 way   3 ways   3 ways   1 way

equally most probable

14. $\Delta S_{surr} = -\Delta H/T$; Heat flow ($\Delta H$) into or out of the system dictates ΔS_{surr}. If heat flows into the surroundings, the random motions of the surroundings increase and the entropy of the surroundings increase. The opposite is true when heat flows from the surroundings into the system (an endothermic reaction). Although the driving force described here really results from the change in entropy of the surroundings, it is often described in terms of energy. Nature tends to seek the lowest possible energy.

15.   Note that these substances are not in the solid state, but are in the aqueous state; water molecules are also present. There is an apparent increase in ordering when these ions are placed in water as compared to the separated state. The hydrating water molecules must be in a highly ordered arrangement when surrounding these anions.

16. $\Delta G° = -RT\ln K = \Delta H° - T\Delta S°$; $HX(aq) \rightleftharpoons H^+(aq) + X^-(aq)$ K_a reaction;   The value of K_a for HF is less than one while the other hydrogen halide acids have $K_a > 1$. In terms of $\Delta G°$, HF must have a positive $\Delta G°_{rxn}$ value while the other H-X acids have $\Delta G_{rxn} < 0$. The reason for the sign change in the K_a value between HF versus HCl, HBr, and HI is entropy. ΔS for the dissociation of HF is very large and negative. There is a high degree of ordering that occurs as the water molecules associate (hydrogen bond) with the small F^- ions. The entropy of hydration strongly opposes HF dissociating in water, so much so that it overwhelms the favorable hydration energy making HF a weak acid.

17.   One can determine $\Delta S°$ and $\Delta H°$ for the reaction using the standard entropies and standard enthalpies of formation in Appendix 4, then use the equation $\Delta G° = \Delta H° - T\Delta S°$. One can also use the standard free energies of formation in Appendix 4. And finally, one can use Hess's law to calculate $\Delta G°$. Here, reactions having known $\Delta G°$ values are manipulated to determine $\Delta G°$ for a different reaction.

        For temperatures other than 25°C, $\Delta G°$ is estimated using the $\Delta G° = \Delta H° - T\Delta S°$ equation. The assumptions made are that the $\Delta H°$ and $\Delta S°$ values determined from Appendix 4 data are temperature independent. We use the same $\Delta H°$ and $\Delta S°$ values as determined when T = 25°C, then plug in the new temperature in Kelvin into the equation to estimate $\Delta G°$ at the new temperature.

18.   The sign of ΔG tells us if a reaction is spontaneous or not at whatever concentrations are present (at constant T and P). The magnitude of ΔG equals w_{max}. When $\Delta G < 0$, the magnitude tells us how much work, in theory, could be harnessed from the reaction. When $\Delta G > 0$, the magnitude tells us the minimum amount of work that must be supplied to make the reaction occur. $\Delta G°$ gives us the same information only when the concentrations for all reactants and products are at standard conditions (1 atm for gases, 1 *M* for solute). These conditions rarely occur.

        $\Delta G° = -RT\ln K$;   From this equation, one can calculate K for a reaction if $\Delta G°$ is known at that temperature. Therefore, $\Delta G°$ gives the equilibrium position for a reaction. To determine K at a temperature other than 25°C, one needs to know $\Delta G°$ at that temperature. We assume $\Delta H°$ and $\Delta S°$ are temperature independent and use the equation $\Delta G° = \Delta H° - T\Delta S°$ to estimate $\Delta G°$ at the different temperature. For K = 1, we want $\Delta G° = 0$, which occurs when $\Delta H° = T\Delta S°$. Again, assume $\Delta H°$ and $\Delta S°$ are temperature independent, then solve for T ($=\Delta H°/\Delta S°$). At this temperature, K = 1 because $\Delta G° = 0$. This only works for reactions where the signs of $\Delta H°$ and $\Delta S°$ are the same (either both positive or both negative). When the signs are opposite, K will always be greater than one (when $\Delta H°$ is negative and $\Delta S°$ is positive) or K will always be less than one (when $\Delta H°$ is positive and $\Delta S°$ is negative). When the signs of $\Delta H°$ and $\Delta S°$ are opposite, K can never equal one.

Exercises

Spontaneity, Entropy, and the Second Law of Thermodynamics: Free Energy

19.   a, b and c; From our own experiences, salt water, colored water and rust form without any outside intervention. A bedroom, however, spontaneously gets cluttered. It takes an outside energy source to clean a bedroom.

20.   c and d; It takes an outside energy source to build a house and to launch and keep a satellite in orbit.

21.   We draw all of the possible arrangements of the two particles in the three levels.

```
2 kJ     __     __     x      __      x      xx
1 kJ     __      x     __     xx      x      __
0 kJ     xx      x      x      __     __      __

Total E =   0 kJ    1 kJ    2 kJ    2 kJ    3 kJ    4 kJ
```

The most likely total energy is 2 kJ.

22.
```
2 kJ    __   __   AB   __   __   B    A    B    A
1 kJ    __   AB   __   B    A    __   __   A    B
0 kJ    AB   __   __   A    B    A    B    __   __

E_T =   0 kJ  2 kJ  4 kJ  1 kJ  1 kJ  2 kJ  2 kJ  3 kJ  3 kJ
```

The most likely total energy is 2 kJ.

23.   a. H_2 at 100°C and 0.5 atm; Higher temperature and lower pressure means greater volume and hence, greater positional probability.

b. N_2 at STP has the greater volume.

c. $H_2O(l)$ is more positional probability than $H_2O(s)$.

24.   Of the three phases (solid, liquid, and gas), solids are most ordered and gases are most disordered. Thus, a , b, and f (melting, sublimation, and boiling) involve an increase in the entropy of the system since going from a solid to a liquid or a solid to a gas or a liquid to a gas increases disorder. For freezing (process c), a substance goes from the more disordered liquid state to the more ordered solid state, hence, entropy decreases. Process d (mixing) involves an increase in disorder (entropy) while separation increases order (decreases the entropy of the system). So of all the processes, a, b, d, and f result in an increase in the entropy of the system.

25.   a.   To boil a liquid requires heat. Hence, this is an endothermic process. All endothermic processes decrease the entropy of the surroundings (ΔS_{surr} is negative).

b. This is an exothermic process. Heat is released when gas molecules slow down enough to form the solid. In exothermic processes, the entropy of the surroundings increases (ΔS_{surr} is positive).

26. a. $\Delta S_{surr} = \dfrac{-\Delta H}{T} = \dfrac{-(-2221\,kJ)}{298\,K} = 7.45\,kJ/K = 7.45 \times 10^3\,J/K$

b. $\Delta S_{surr} = \dfrac{-\Delta H}{T} = \dfrac{-112\,kJ}{298\,K} = -0.376\,kJ/K = -376\,J/K$

27. $\Delta G = \Delta H - T\Delta S$; When ΔG is negative, then the process will be spontaneous.

a. $\Delta G = \Delta H - T\Delta S = 25 \times 10^3\,J - (300.\,K)(5.0\,J/K) = 24,000\,J$, Not spontaneous

b. $\Delta G = 25,000\,J - (300.\,K)(100.\,J/K) = -5000\,J$, Spontaneous

c. Without calculating ΔG, we know this reaction will be spontaneous at all temperatures. ΔH is negative and ΔS is positive ($-T\Delta S < 0$). ΔG will always be less than zero with these sign combinations for ΔH and ΔS.

d. $\Delta G = -1.0 \times 10^4\,J - (200.\,K)(-40.\,J/K) = -2000\,J$, Spontaneous

28. $\Delta G = \Delta H - T\Delta S$; A process is spontaneous when $\Delta G < 0$. For the following, assume ΔH and ΔS are temperature independent.

a. When ΔH and ΔS are both negative, ΔG will be negative below a certain temperature where the favorable ΔH term dominates. When $\Delta G = 0$, then $\Delta H = T\Delta S$. Solving for this temperature:

$$T = \frac{\Delta H}{\Delta S} = \frac{-18,000\,J}{-60.\,J/K} = 3.0 \times 10^2\,K$$

At $T < 3.0 \times 10^2\,K$, this process will be spontaneous ($\Delta G < 0$).

b. When ΔH and ΔS are both positive, ΔG will be negative above a certain temperature where the favorable ΔS term dominates.

$$T = \frac{\Delta H}{\Delta S} = \frac{18,000\,J}{60.\,J/K} = 3.0 \times 10^2\,K$$

At $T > 3.0 \times 10^2\,K$, this process will be spontaneous ($\Delta G < 0$).

c. When ΔH is positive and ΔS is negative, this process can never be spontaneous at any temperature because ΔG can never be negative.

d. When ΔH is negative and ΔS is positive, this process is spontaneous at all temperatures because ΔG will always be negative.

29.   At the boiling point, $\Delta G = 0$ so $\Delta H = T\Delta S$.

$$\Delta S = \frac{\Delta H}{T} = \frac{27.5 \text{ kJ/mol}}{(273+35) \text{ K}} = 8.93 \times 10^{-2} \text{ kJ/K}\cdot\text{mol} = 89.3 \text{ J/K}\cdot\text{mol}$$

30.   At the boiling point, $\Delta G = 0$ so $\Delta H = T\Delta S$. $T = \frac{\Delta H}{\Delta S} = \frac{58.51 \times 10^3 \text{ J/mol}}{92.92 \text{ J/K}\cdot\text{mol}} = 629.7 \text{ K}$

31.   a. $NH_3(s) \rightarrow NH_3(l)$; $\Delta G = \Delta H - T\Delta S = 5650 \text{ J/mol} - 200. \text{ K } (28.9 \text{ J/K}\cdot\text{mol})$

$\Delta G = 5650 \text{ J/mol} - 5780 \text{ J/mol} = T = =- 130 \text{ J/mol}$

Yes, NH_3 will melt because $\Delta G < 0$ at this temperature.

   b.   At the melting point, $\Delta G = 0$ so $T = \frac{\Delta H}{\Delta S} = \frac{5650 \text{ J/mol}}{28.9 \text{ J/K}\cdot\text{mol}} = 196 \text{ K}$.

32. $C_2H_5OH(l) \rightarrow C_2H_5OH(g)$; At the boiling point, $\Delta G = 0$ and $\Delta S_{univ} = 0$. For the vaporization process, ΔS is a positive value while ΔH is a negative value. To calculate ΔS_{sys}, we will determine ΔS_{surr} from ΔH and the temperature, then $\Delta S_{sys} = -\Delta S_{surr}$ for a system at equilibrium.

$$\Delta S_{surr} = \frac{-\Delta H}{T} = \frac{38.7 \times 10^3 \text{ J/mol}}{351 \text{ K}} = -110. \text{ J/K}\cdot\text{mol}$$

$$\Delta S_{sys} = -\Delta S_{surr} = -(-110.) = 110. \text{ J/K}\cdot\text{ mol}$$

Chemical Reactions: Entropy Changes and Free Energy

33.   a.   Decrease in disorder; $\Delta S°(-)$ b.   Increase in disorder; $\Delta S°(+)$

   c.   Decrease in disorder ($\Delta n < 0$); $\Delta S°(-)$ d.   Increase in disorder ($\Delta n > 0$); $\Delta S°(+)$

For c and d, concentrate on the gaseous products and reactants. When there are more gaseous product molecules than gaseous reactant molecules ($\Delta n > 0$), then $\Delta S°$ will be positive (disorder increases). When Δn is negative, then $\Delta S°$ is negative (disorder decreases or order increases).

34.   a.   Decrease in disorder ($\Delta n < 0$); $\Delta S°(-)$ b.   Decrease in disorder ($\Delta n < 0$); $\Delta S°(-)$

   c.   Increase in disorder; $\Delta S°(+)$ d.   Increase in disorder; $\Delta S°(+)$

35.   a. $C_{graphite}(s)$; Diamond has a more ordered structure than graphite.

   b. $C_2H_5OH(g)$; The gaseous state is more disordered than the liquid state.

   c. $CO_2(g)$; The gaseous state is more disordered than the solid state.

36.   a.   He (10 K); S = 0 at 0 K   b. N_2O; More complicated molecule

c. $H_2O(l)$:   The liquid state is more disordered than the solid state.

37.   a. $2 H_2S(g) + SO_2(g) \rightarrow 3 S_{rhombic}(s) + 2 H_2O(g)$; Because there are more molecules of reactant gases as compared to product molecules of gas ($\Delta n = 2 - 3 < 0$), $\Delta S°$ will be negative.

$$\Delta S° = \sum n_p S°_{products} - \sum n_r S°_{reactants}$$

$\Delta S° = [3 \text{ mol } S_{rhombic}(s) (32 \text{ J/K}\bullet mol) + 2 \text{ mol } H_2O(g) (189 \text{ J/K}\bullet mol)]$

$- [2 \text{ mol } H_2S(g) (206 \text{ J/K}\bullet mol) + 1 \text{ mol } SO_2(g) (248 \text{ J/K}\bullet mol)]$

$\Delta S° = 474 \text{ J/K} - 660. \text{ J/K} = -186 \text{ J/K}$

b. $2 SO_3(g) \rightarrow 2 SO_2(g) + O_2(g)$; Because Δn of gases is positive ($\Delta n = 3 - 2$), $\Delta S°$ will be positive.

$\Delta S = 2 \text{ mol}(248 \text{ J/K}\bullet mol) + 1 \text{ mol}(205 \text{ J/K}\bullet mol) - [2 \text{ mol}(257 \text{ J/K}\bullet mol)] = 187 \text{ J/K}$

c. $Fe_2O_3(s) + 3 H_2(g) \rightarrow 2 Fe(s) + 3 H_2O(g)$; Because Δn of gases = 0 ($\Delta n = 3 - 3$), we can't easily predict if $\Delta S°$ will be positive or negative.

$\Delta S = 2 \text{ mol}(27 \text{ J/K}\bullet mol) + 3 \text{ mol}(189 \text{ J/K}\bullet mol) -$

$[1 \text{ mol}(90. \text{ J/K}\bullet mol) + 3 \text{ mol } (141 \text{ J/K}\bullet mol)] = 138 \text{ J/K}$

38.   a. $H_2(g) + 1/2 O_2(g) \rightarrow H_2O(l)$; Since Δn of gases is negative, then $\Delta S°$ will be negative.

$\Delta S° = 1 \text{ mol } H_2O(l) (70. \text{ J/K}\bullet mol) -$

$[1 \text{ mol } H_2(g) (131 \text{ J/K}\bullet mol) + 1/2 \text{ mol } O_2(g) (205 \text{ J/K}\bullet mol)]$

$\Delta S° = 70. \text{ J/K} - 234 \text{ J/K} = -164 \text{ J/K}$

b. $2 CH_3OH(g) + 3 O_2(g) \rightarrow 2 CO_2(g) + 4 H_2O(g)$; Because Δn of gases is positive, $\Delta S°$ will be positive.

$[2 \text{ mol } (214 \text{ J/K}\bullet mol) + 4 \text{ mol } (189 \text{ J/K}\bullet mol)] -$

$[2 \text{ mol } (240. \text{ J/K}\bullet mol) + 3 \text{ mol } (205 \text{ J/K}\bullet mol)] = 89 \text{ J/K}$

c. $HCl(g) \rightarrow H^+(aq) + Cl^-(aq)$; The gaseous state dominates predictions of $\Delta S°$. Here the gaseous state is more disordered than the ions in solution so $\Delta S°$ will be negative.

$\Delta S° = 1 \text{ mol } H^+(0) + 1 \text{ mol } Cl^-(57 \text{ J/K}\bullet mol) - 1 \text{ mol } HCl(187 \text{ J/K}\bullet mol) = -130. \text{ J/K}$

39. $C_2H_2(g) + 4 F_2(g) \rightarrow 2 CF_4(g) + H_2(g)$; $\Delta S° = 2S°_{CF_4} + S°_{H_2} - [S°_{C_2H_2} + 4S°_{F_2}]$

-358 J/K $= (2 \text{ mol}) S°_{CF_4} + 131$ J/K $- [201$ J/K $+ 4(203$ J/K$)]$, $S°_{CF_4} = 262$ J/K•mol

40. -144 J/K $= (2 \text{ mol}) S°_{AlBr_3} - [2(28 \text{ J/K}) + 3(152 \text{ J/K})]$, $S°_{AlBr_3} = 184$ J/K•mol

41.   a. $S_{rhombic} \rightarrow S_{monoclinic}$; This phase transition is spontaneous ($\Delta G < 0$) at temperatures above 95°C. $\Delta G = \Delta H - T\Delta S$; For ΔG to be negative only above a certain temperature, then ΔH is positive and ΔS is positive (see Table 16.5 of text).

b.   Because ΔS is positive, $S_{rhombic}$ is the more ordered crystalline structure.

42.   Enthalpy is not favorable, so ΔS must provide the driving force for the change. Thus, ΔS is positive. There is an increase in disorder, so the original enzyme has the more ordered structure.

43.   a.   When a bond is formed, energy is released so ΔH is negative. There are more reactant molecules of gas than product molecules of gas ($\Delta n < 0$), so ΔS will be negative.

b. $\Delta G = \Delta H - T\Delta S$; For this reaction to be spontaneous ($\Delta G < 0$), the favorable enthalpy term must dominate. The reaction will be spontaneous at low temperatures where the ΔH term dominates.

44.   Because there are more product gas molecules than reactant gas molecules ($\Delta n > 0$), ΔS will be positive. From the signs of ΔH and ΔS, this reaction is spontaneous at all temperatures. It will cost money to heat the reaction mixture. Because there is no thermodynamic reason to do this, the purpose of the elevated temperature must be to increase the rate of the reaction, i.e., kinetic reasons.

45   a.

	$CH_4(g)$	+ $2 O_2(g)$	$\rightarrow$ $CO_2(g)$	+ $2 H_2O(g)$
$\Delta H°_f$	-75 kJ/mol	0	-393.5	-242
$\Delta G°_f$	-51 kJ/mol	0	-394	-229 Data from Appendix 4
$S°$	186 J/K•mol	205	214	189

$\Delta H° = \sum n_p \Delta H°_{f, \text{products}} - \sum n_r \Delta H°_{f, \text{reactants}}$; $\Delta S° = \sum n_p S°_{\text{products}} - \sum n_r S°_{\text{reactants}}$

$\Delta H° = 2 \text{ mol}(-242 \text{ kJ/mol}) + 1 \text{ mol}(-393.5 \text{ kJ/mol}) - [1 \text{ mol}(-75 \text{ kJ/mol})] = -803$ kJ

$\Delta S° = 2 \text{ mol}(189 \text{ J/K·mol}) + 1 \text{ mol}(214 \text{ J/K•mol})$

$- [1 \text{ mol}(186 \text{ J/K•mol}) + 2 \text{ mol}(205 \text{ J/K•mol})] = -4$ J/K

There are two ways to get $\Delta G°$. We can use $\Delta G° = \Delta H° - T\Delta S°$ (be careful of units):

$$\Delta G° = \Delta H° - T\Delta S° = -803 \times 10^3 \text{ J} - (298 \text{ K})(-4 \text{ J/K}) = -8.018 \times 10^5 \text{ J} = -802 \text{ kJ}$$

or we can use $\Delta G_f°$ values where $\Delta G° = \sum n_p \Delta G_{f, \text{products}}° - \sum n_r \Delta G_{f, \text{reactants}}°$:

$$\Delta G° = 2 \text{ mol}(-229 \text{ kJ/mol}) + 1 \text{ mol}(-394 \text{ kJ/mol}) - [1 \text{ mol}(-51 \text{ kJ/mol})]$$

$$\Delta G° = -801 \text{ kJ} \text{ (Answers are the same within round off error.)}$$

b.
$$6 \, CO_2(g) \quad + \quad 6 \, H_2O(l) \quad \rightarrow \quad C_6H_{12}O_6(s) \quad + \quad 6 \, O_2(g)$$

$\Delta H_f°$	−393.5 kJ/mol	−286	−1275	0
$S°$	214 J/K•mol	70.	212	205

$$\Delta H° = -1275 - [6(-286) + 6(-393.5)] = 2802 \text{ kJ}$$

$$\Delta S° = 6(205) + 212 - [6(214) + 6(70.)] = -262 \text{ J/K}$$

$$\Delta G° = 2802 \text{ kJ} - (298 \text{ K})(-0.262 \text{ kJ/K}) = 2880. \text{ kJ}$$

c.
$$P_4O_{10}(s) \quad + \quad 6 \, H_2O(l) \quad \rightarrow \quad 4 \, H_3PO_4(s)$$

$\Delta H_f°$ (kJ/mol)	−2984	−286	−1279
$S°$ (J/K•mol)	229	70.	110.

$$\Delta H° = 4 \text{ mol}(-1279 \text{ kJ/mol}) - [1 \text{ mol}(-2984 \text{ kJ/mol}) + 6 \text{ mol}(-286 \text{ kJ/mol})] = -416 \text{ kJ}$$

$$\Delta S° = 4(110.) - [229 + 6(70.)] = -209 \text{ J/K}$$

$$\Delta G° = \Delta H° - T\Delta S° = -416 \text{ kJ} - (298 \text{ K})(-0.209 \text{ kJ/K}) = -354 \text{ kJ}$$

d.
$$HCl(g) \quad + \quad NH_3(g) \quad \rightarrow \quad NH_4Cl(s)$$

$\Delta H_f°$ (kJ/mol)	−92	−46	−314
$S°$ (J/K•mol)	187	193	96

$$\Delta H° = -314 - [-92 - 46] = -176 \text{ kJ}; \quad \Delta S° = 96 - [187 + 193] = -284 \text{ J/K}$$

$$\Delta G° = \Delta H° - T\Delta S° = -176 \text{ kJ} - (298 \text{ K})(-0.284 \text{ kJ/K}) = -91 \text{ kJ}$$

46.   a. $\Delta H° = 2(-46 \text{ kJ}) = -92 \text{ kJ}$; $\Delta S° = 2(193 \text{ J/K}) - [3(131 \text{ J/K}) + 192 \text{ J/K}] = -199 \text{ J/K}$

$$\Delta G° = \Delta H° - T\Delta S° = -92 \text{ kJ} - 298 \text{ K}(-0.199 \text{ kJ/K}) = -33 \text{ kJ}$$

    b. $\Delta G°$ is negative, so this reaction is spontaneous at standard conditions.

    c. $\Delta G° = 0$ when $T = \dfrac{\Delta H°}{\Delta S°} = \dfrac{-92 \text{ kJ}}{-0.199 \text{ kJ/K}} = 460 \text{ K}$

At $T < 460$ K and standard pressures (1 atm), the favorable $\Delta H°$ term dominates and the reaction is spontaneous ($\Delta G° < 0$).

47. $\Delta G° = -58.03 \text{ kJ} - (298 \text{ K})(-0.1766 \text{ kJ/K}) = -5.40 \text{ kJ}$

$$\Delta G° = 0 = \Delta H° - T\Delta S°, \quad T = \frac{\Delta H°}{\Delta S°} = \frac{-58.03 \text{ kJ}}{-0.1766 \text{ kJ/K}} = 328.6 \text{ K}$$

$\Delta G°$ is negative below 328.6 K where the favorable $\Delta H°$ term dominates.

48. $H_2O(l) \rightarrow H_2O(g)$; $\Delta G° = 0$ at the boiling point of water at 1 atm and 100.°C.

$$\Delta H° = T\Delta S°, \quad \Delta S° = \frac{\Delta H°}{T} = \frac{40.6 \times 10^3 \text{ J/mol}}{373 \text{ K}} = 109 \text{ J/K} \bullet \text{mol}$$

At 90.°C: $\Delta G° = \Delta H° - T\Delta S° = 40.6 \text{ kJ/mol} - (363 \text{ K})(0.109 \text{ kJ/K} \bullet \text{mol}) = 1.0 \text{ kJ/mol}$

As expected, $\Delta G° > 0$ at temperatures below the boiling point of water at 1 atm (process is nonspontaneous).

At 110.°C: $\Delta G° = \Delta H° - T\Delta S° = 40.6 \text{ kJ/mol} - (383 \text{ K})(0.109 \text{ J/K} \bullet \text{mol}) = -1.1 \text{ kJ/mol}$

When $\Delta G° < 0$, the boiling of water is spontaneous at 1 atm and $T > 100.$°C (as expected).

49. $CH_4(g) + CO_2(g) \rightarrow CH_3CO_2H(l)$

$\Delta H° = -484 - [-75 + (-393.5)] = -16 \text{ kJ}$; $\Delta S° = 160 - [186 + 214] = -240. \text{ J/K}$

$\Delta G° = \Delta H° - T\Delta S° = -16 \text{ kJ} - (298 \text{ K})(-0.240 \text{ kJ/K}) = 56 \text{ kJ}$

This reaction is spontaneous only at temperatures below $T = \Delta H°/\Delta S° = 67$ K (where the favorable $\Delta H°$ term will dominate giving a negative $\Delta G°$ value). This is not practical. Substances will be in condensed phases and rates will be very slow at this extremely low temperature.

$CH_3OH(g) + CO(g) \rightarrow CH_3CO_2H(l)$

$\Delta H° = -484 - [-110.5 + (-201)] = -173 \text{ kJ}$; $\Delta S° = 160 - [198 + 240.] = -278 \text{ J/K}$

$\Delta G° = -173$ kJ $- (298$ K$)(-0.278$ kJ/K$) = -90.$ kJ

This reaction also has a favorable enthalpy and an unfavorable entropy term. This reaction is spontaneous at temperatures below T $= \Delta H°/\Delta S° = 622$ K. The reaction of CH_3OH and CO will be preferred. It is spontaneous at high enough temperatures that the rates of reaction should be reasonable.

50. $C_2H_4(g) + H_2O(g) \rightarrow CH_3CH_2OH(l)$

$\Delta H° = -278 - (52 - 242) = -88$ kJ; $\Delta S° = 161 - (219 + 189) = -247$ J/K

When $\Delta G° = 0$, $\Delta H° = T\Delta S°$, $T = \dfrac{\Delta H°}{\Delta S°} = \dfrac{-88 \times 10^3 \text{ J}}{-247 \text{ J/K}} = 360$ K

Because the signs of $\Delta H°$ and $\Delta S°$ are both negative, this reaction will be spontaneous at temperatures below 360 K (where the favorable $\Delta H°$ term will dominate).

$C_2H_6(g) + H_2O(g) \rightarrow CH_3CH_2OH(l) + H_2(g)$

$\Delta H° = -278 - (-84.7 - 242) = 49$ kJ; $\Delta S° = 131 + 161 - (229.5 + 189) = -127$ J/K

This reaction can never be spontaneous because of the signs of $\Delta H°$ and $\Delta S°$.

Thus the reaction $C_2H_4(g) + H_2O(g) \rightarrow C_2H_5OH(l)$ would be preferred.

51. $CH_4(g) \rightarrow 2 H_2(g) + C(s)$ $\Delta G° = -(-51$ kJ$)$

   $2 H_2(g) + O_2(g) \rightarrow 2 H_2O(l)$ $\Delta G° = -2(237$ kJ$)$

    $C(s) + O_2(g) \rightarrow CO_2(g)$ $\Delta G° = -394$ kJ

   $CH_4(g) + 2 O_2(g) \rightarrow 2 H_2O(l) + CO_2(g)$ $\Delta G° = -817$ kJ

52. $6 C(s) + 6 O_2(g) \rightarrow 6 CO_2(g)$ $\Delta G° = 6(-394$ kJ$)$

  $3 H_2(g) + 3/2 O_2(g) \rightarrow 3 H_2O(l)$ $\Delta G° = 3(-237$ kJ$)$

$6 CO_2(g) + 3 H_2O(l) \rightarrow C_6H_6(l) + 15/2 O_2(g)$ $\Delta G° = -1/2 (-6399$ kJ$)$

   $6 C(s) + 3 H_2(g) \rightarrow C_6H_6(l)$ $\Delta G° = 125$ kJ

53. $\Delta G° = \sum n_p \Delta G°_{f,\text{products}} - \sum n_r \Delta G°_{f,\text{reactants}}$, -374 kJ $= -1105$ kJ $- \Delta G°_{f, SF_4}$

$\Delta G°_{f, SF_4} = -731$ kJ/mol

54. $-5490.$ kJ $= 8(-394$ kJ$) + 10(-237$ kJ$) - 2\Delta G°_{f, C_4H_{10}}$, $\Delta G°_{f, C_4H_{10}} = -16$ kJ/mol

55. $\Delta G° = \sum n_p \Delta G°_{f, \text{products}} - \sum n_r \Delta G°_{f, \text{reactants}}$

$\Delta G° = [-57.37 \text{ kJ} + (-68.85 \text{ kJ}) + 3(-95.30 \text{ kJ})] - [3(0) + 2(-50.72 \text{ kJ})] = -310.68 \text{ kJ}$

For a temperature change from 25°C to ~20°C (room temperature), the magnitude of $\Delta G°$ will not change much. Therefore, $\Delta G°$ will be a negative value at room temperature (~20°C), so the reaction will be spontaneous.

56.   a. $\Delta G° = 2(-270. \text{ kJ}) - 2(-502 \text{ kJ}) = 464 \text{ kJ}$

b.   Because $\Delta G°$ is positive, this reaction is not spontaneous at standard conditions at 298 K.

c. $\Delta G° = \Delta H° - T\Delta S°, \ \Delta H° = \Delta G° + T\Delta S° = 464 \text{ kJ} + 298 \text{ K}(0.179 \text{ kJ/K}) = 517 \text{ kJ}$

We need to solve for the temperature when $\Delta G° = 0$:

$$\Delta G° = 0 = \Delta H° - T\Delta S°, \ T = \frac{\Delta H°}{\Delta S°} = \frac{517 \text{ kJ}}{0.179 \text{ kJ/K}} = 2890 \text{ K}$$

This reaction will be spontaneous at standard conditions ($\Delta G° < 0$) when T > 2890 K. Here the favorable entropy term will dominate.

Free Energy: Pressure Dependence and Equilibrium

57. $\Delta G = \Delta G° + RT \ln Q$; For this reaction: $\Delta G = \Delta G° + RT \ln \dfrac{P_{NO_2} \times P_{O_2}}{P_{NO} \times P_{O_3}}$

$\Delta G° = 1 \text{ mol}(52 \text{ kJ/mol}) + 1 \text{ mol}(0) - [1 \text{ mol}(87 \text{ kJ/mol}) + 1 \text{ mol}(163 \text{ kJ/mol})] = -198 \text{ kJ}$

$\Delta G = -198 \text{ kJ} + \dfrac{8.3145 \text{ J/K} \bullet \text{mol}}{1000 \text{ J/kJ}}(298 \text{ K}) \ln \dfrac{(1.00 \times 10^{-7})(1.00 \times 10^{-3})}{(1.00 \times 10^{-6})(1.00 \times 10^{-6})}$

$\Delta G = -198 \text{ kJ} + 9.69 \text{ kJ} = -188 \text{ kJ}$

58. $\Delta G° = 3(0) + 2(-229) - [2(-34) + 1(-300.)] = -90. \text{ kJ}$

$\Delta G = \Delta G° + RT \ln \dfrac{P_{H_2O}^2}{P_{H_2S}^2 \times P_{SO_2}} = -90. \text{ kJ} + \dfrac{(8.3145)(298)}{1000} \text{ kJ} \left[\ln \dfrac{(0.030)^2}{(1.0 \times 10^{-4})(0.010)} \right]$

$\Delta G = -90. \text{ kJ} + 39.7 \text{ kJ} = -50. \text{ kJ}$

59. $\Delta G = \Delta G° + RT \ln Q = \Delta G° + RT \ln \dfrac{P_{N_2O_4}}{P_{NO_2}^2}$

$\Delta G° = 1 \text{ mol}(98 \text{ kJ/mol}) - 2 \text{ mol}(52 \text{ kJ/mol}) = -6 \text{ kJ}$

a. These are standard conditions so $\Delta G = \Delta G°$ because $Q = 1$ and $\ln Q = 0$. Because $\Delta G°$ is negative, the forward reaction is spontaneous. The reaction shifts right to reach equilibrium.

b. $\Delta G = -6 \times 10^3 \text{ J} + 8.3145 \text{ J/K} \cdot \text{mol (298 K) } \ln \dfrac{0.50}{(0.21)^2}$

$\Delta G = -6 \times 10^3 \text{ J} + 6.0 \times 10^3 \text{ J} = 0$

Because $\Delta G = 0$, this reaction is at equilibrium (no shift).

c. $\Delta G = -6 \times 10^3 \text{ J} + 8.3145 \text{ J/K} \cdot \text{mol (298 K) } \ln \dfrac{1.6}{(0.29)^2}$

$\Delta G = -6 \times 10^3 \text{ J} + 7.3 \times 10^3 \text{ J} = 1.3 \times 10^3 \text{ J} = 1 \times 10^3 \text{ J}$

Because ΔG is positive, the reverse reaction is spontaneous, and the reaction shifts to the left to reach equilibrium.

60. a. $\Delta G = \Delta G° + RT \ln \dfrac{P_{NH_3}^2}{P_{N_2} \times P_{H_2}^2}$; $\quad \Delta G° = 2\Delta G°_{f, NH_3} = 2(-17) = -34 \text{ kJ}$

$\Delta G = -34 \text{ kJ} + \dfrac{(8.3145 \text{ J/K} \bullet \text{mol})(298 \text{ K})}{1000 \text{ J/kJ}} \ln \dfrac{(50.)^2}{(200.)(200.)^3}$

$\Delta G = -34 \text{ kJ} - 33 \text{ kJ} = -67 \text{ kJ}$

b. $\Delta G = -34 \text{ kJ} \dfrac{(8.3145 \text{ J/K} \bullet \text{mol})(298 \text{ K})}{1000 \text{ J/kJ}} \ln \dfrac{(200.)^2}{(200.)(600.)^3}$

$\Delta G = -34 \text{ kJ} - 34.4 \text{ kJ} = -68 \text{ kJ}$

61. At 25.0°C: $\Delta G° = \Delta H° - T\Delta S° = -58.03 \times 10^3 \text{ J/mol} - (298.2 \text{ K})(-176.6 \text{ J/K} \cdot \text{mol})$

$= -5.37 \times 10^3 \text{ J/mol}$

$\Delta G° = -RT \ln K, \;\; \ln K = \dfrac{-\Delta G°}{RT} = \exp\left(\dfrac{-(-5.37 \; 10^3 \text{ J/mol})}{(8.3145 \text{ J/K} \bullet \text{mol})(298.2 \text{ K})}\right) = 2.166$

$K = e^{2.166} = 8.72$

At 100.0°C: $\Delta G° = -58.03 \times 10^3 \text{ J/mol} - (373.2 \text{ K})(-176.6 \text{ J/K} \cdot \text{mol}) = 7.88 \times 10^3 \text{ J/mol}$

$\ln K = \dfrac{-(7.88 \times 10^3 \text{ J/mol})}{(8.3145 \text{ J/K} \bullet \text{mol})(373.2 \text{ K})} = -2.540, \;\; K = e^{-2.540} = 0.0789$

Note: When determining exponents, we will round off after the calculation is complete. This helps eliminate excessive round off error.

62.   a. $\Delta H° = 2 \text{ mol}(-92 \text{ kJ/mol}) - [1 \text{ mol}(0) + 1 \text{ mol}(0)] = -184 \text{ kJ}$

$\Delta S° = 2 \text{ mol}(187 \text{ J/K·mol}) - [1 \text{ mol}(131 \text{ J/K·mol}) + 1 \text{ mol}(223 \text{ J/K·mol})] = 20. \text{ J/K}$

$\Delta G° = \Delta H° - T\Delta S° = -184 \times 10^3 \text{ J} - 298 \text{ K} (20. \text{ J/K}) = -1.90 \times 10^5 \text{ J} = -190. \text{ kJ}$

$\Delta G° = -RT \ln K, \ \ln K = \dfrac{-\Delta G°}{RT} = \dfrac{-(-1.90 \times 10^5 \text{ J})}{8.3145 \text{ J/K} \bullet \text{mol}(298 \text{ K})} = 76.683$

$K = e^{76.683} = 2.01 \times 10^{33}$

b.   These are standard conditions so $\Delta G = \Delta G° = -190. \text{ kJ}$. When ΔG is negative, the forward reaction is spontaneous so the reaction shifts right to reach equilibrium.

63.   When reactions are added together, the equilibrium constants are multiplied together to determine the K value for the final reaction.

$H_2(g) + O_2(g) \rightleftharpoons H_2O_2(g)$ $\qquad\qquad K = 2.3 \times 10^6$
$\qquad H_2O(g) \rightleftharpoons H_2(g) + 1/2 O_2(g)$ $\qquad K = (1.8 \times 10^{37})^{-1/2}$
_____

$H_2O(g) + 1/2 O_2(g) \rightleftharpoons H_2O_2(g)$ $\qquad\qquad K = 2.3 \times 10^6 (1.8 \times 10^{-37})^{-1/2} = 5.4 \times 10^{-13}$

$\Delta G° = -RT \ln K = -8.3145 \text{ J/K·mol} (600. \text{ K}) \ln(5.4 \times 10^{-13}) = 1.4 \times 10^5 \text{ J/mol} = 140 \text{ kJ/mol}$

64.   a.

	$\Delta H_f°$ (kJ/mol)	$S°$ (J/K·mol)
$NH_3(g)$	−46	193
$O_2(g)$	0	205
$NO(g)$	90.	211
$H_2O(g)$	−242	189
$NO_2(g)$	34	240.
$HNO_3(l)$	−174	156
$H_2O(l)$	−286	70.

$4 \ NH_3(g) + 5 \ O_2(g) \rightarrow 4 \ NO(g) + 6 \ H_2O(g)$

$\Delta H° = 6(-242) + 4(90.) - [4(-46)] = -908 \text{ kJ}$

$\Delta S° = 4(211) + 6(189) - [4(193) + 5(205)] = 181 \text{ J/K}$

$\Delta G° = -908 \text{ kJ} - 298 \text{ K} (0.181 \text{ kJ/K}) = -962 \text{ kJ}$

$\Delta G° = -RT \ln K, \ \ln K = \dfrac{-\Delta G°}{RT} = \left(\dfrac{-(-962 \times 10^3 \text{ J})}{8.3145 \text{ J/K} \bullet \text{mol} \times 298 \text{ K}} \right) = 388$

$\ln K = 2.303 \log K, \ \log K = 168, \ K = 10^{168}$ (an extremely large number)

$2 \ NO(g) + O_2(g) \rightarrow 2 \ NO_2(g)$

$\Delta H° = 2(34) - [2(90.)] = -112 \text{ kJ}; \ \Delta S° = 2(240.) - [2(211) + (205)] = -147 \text{ J/K}$

$\Delta G° = -112$ kJ $- (298$ K$)(-0.147$ kJ/K$) = -68$ kJ

$$K = \exp\frac{-\Delta G°}{RT} = \exp\left(\frac{-(-68{,}000 \text{ J})}{8.3145 \text{ J/K} \bullet \text{mol} (298 \text{ K})}\right) = e^{27.44} = 8.3 \times 10^{11}$$

Note: When determining exponents, we will round off after the calculation is complete.

$3 NO_2(g) + H_2O(l) \rightarrow 2 HNO_3(l) + NO(g)$

$\Delta H° = 2(-174) + (90.) - [3(34) + (-286)] = -74$ kJ

$\Delta S° = 2(156) + (211) - [3(240.) + (70.)] = -267$ J/K

$\Delta G° = -74$ kJ $- (298$ K$)(-0.267$ kJ/K$) = 6$ kJ

$$K = \exp\frac{-\Delta G°}{RT} = \exp\left(\frac{-6000 \text{ J}}{8.3145 \text{ J/K} \bullet \text{mol} (298 \text{ K})}\right) = e^{-2.4} = 9 \times 10^{-2}$$

b. $\Delta G° = -RT \ln K$; T $= 825°C = (825 + 273)$ K $= 1098$ K; We must determine $\Delta G°$ at 1098 K.

$$\Delta G°_{1098} = \Delta H° - T\Delta S° = -908 \text{ kJ} - (1098 \text{ K})(0.181 \text{ kJ/K}) = -1107 \text{ kJ}$$

$$K = \exp\frac{-\Delta G°}{RT} = \exp\left(\frac{-(-1.107 \times 10^6 \text{ J})}{8.3145 \text{ J/K} \bullet \text{mol} (1098 \text{ K})}\right) = e^{121.258} = 4.589 \times 10^{52}$$

c.   There is no thermodynamic reason for the elevated temperature because $\Delta H°$ is negative and $\Delta S°$ is positive. Thus, the purpose for the high temperature must be to increase the rate of the reaction.

65. $$K = \frac{P^2_{NF_3}}{P_{N_2} \times P^3_{F_2}} = \frac{(0.48)^2}{0.021(0.063)^3} = 4.4 \times 10^4$$

$\Delta G°_{800} = -RT \ln K = -8.3145$ J/K$\bullet$mol $(800.$ K$) \ln (4.4 \times 10^4) = -7.1 \times 10^4$ J/mol $=$
$$-71 \text{ kJ/mol}$$

66. $2 SO_2(g) + O_2(g) \rightarrow 2 SO_3(g)$; $\Delta G° = 2(-371$ kJ$) - [2(-300.$ kJ$)] = -142$ kJ

$$\Delta G° = -RT \ln K, \quad \ln K = \frac{-\Delta G°}{RT} = \frac{-(-142.000 \text{ J})}{8.3145 \text{ J/K} \bullet \text{mol} (298 \text{ K})} = 57.311$$

$K = e^{57.311} = 7.76 \times 10^{24}$

$$K = 7.76 \times 10^{24} = \frac{P^2_{SO_3}}{P^2_{SO_2} \times P_{O_2}} = \frac{(2.0)^2}{P^2_{SO_2} \times (0.50)}, \quad P_{SO_2} = 1.0 \times 10^{-12} \text{ atm}$$

From the negative value of $\Delta G°$, this reaction is spontaneous at standard conditions. There are more molecules of reactant gases than product gases, so $\Delta S°$ will be negative (unfavorable). Therefore, this reaction must be exothermic ($\Delta H° < 0$). When $\Delta H°$ and $\Delta S°$ are both negative, the reaction will be spontaneous at relatively low temperatures where the favorable $\Delta H°$ term dominates.

67. The equation $\ln K = \dfrac{-\Delta H°}{R}\left(\dfrac{1}{T}\right) + \dfrac{\Delta S°}{R}$ is in the form of a straight line equation

($y = mx + b$). A graph of $\ln K$ vs. $1/T$ will yield a straight line with slope $= m = -\Delta H°/R$ and a y-intercept $= b = \Delta S°/R$.

From the plot:

$$\text{slope} = \frac{\Delta y}{\Delta x} = \frac{0 - 40.}{3.0 \times 10^{-3}\ K^{-1} - 0} = -1.3 \times 10^4\ K$$

$$-1.3 \times 10^4\ K = -\Delta H°/R,\ \ \Delta H° = 1.3 \times 10^4\ K \times 8.3145\ J/K\bullet mol\ = 1.1 \times 10^5\ J/mol$$

$$\text{y-intercept} = 40. = \Delta S°/R,\ \ \Delta S° = 40. \times 8.3145\ J/K\bullet mol = 330\ J/K\bullet mol$$

As seen here, when $\Delta H°$ is positive, the slope of the $\ln K$ vs. $1/T$ plot is negative. When $\Delta H°$ is negative as in an exothermic process, then the slope of the $\ln K$ vs. $1/T$ plot will be positive (slope $= -\Delta H°/R$).

68. The $\ln K$ vs. $1/T$ plot gives a straight line with slope $= -\Delta H°/R$ and y-intercept $= \Delta S°/R$.

$$1.352 \times 10^4\ K = -\Delta H°/R,\ \ \Delta H° = -(8.3145\ J/\ K\bullet mol)\ (1.352 \times 10^4\ K)$$

$$\Delta H° = -1.124 \times 10^5\ J/mol = -112.4\ kJ/mol$$

$$-14.51 = \Delta S°/R,\ \ \Delta S° = (-14.51)(8.3145\ J/\ K\bullet mol) = -120.6\ J\ /\ K\bullet mol$$

Note that the signs for $\Delta H°$ and $\Delta S°$ make sense. When a bond forms, $\Delta H° < 0$ and $\Delta S° < 0$.

Additional Exercises

69. From Appendix 4, $S° = 198\ J/K\bullet mol$ for $CO(g)$ and $S° = 27\ J/K\bullet mol$ for $Fe(s)$.

Let $S_l° = S°$ for $Fe(CO)_5(l)$ and $S_g° = S°$ for $Fe(CO)_5(g)$.

$$\Delta S° = -677\ J/K = 1\ mol(S_l°) - [1\ mol\ (27\ J/K\bullet mol) + 5\ mol(198\ J/\ K\bullet mol]$$

$$S_l° = 340.\ J/K\bullet mol$$

$$\Delta S° = 107\ J/K = 1\ mol\ (S_g°) - 1\ mol\ (340.\ J/K\bullet mol)$$

$$S_g° = S°\ for\ Fe(CO)_5(g) = 447\ J/K\bullet mol$$

70.   When an ionic solid dissolves, one would expect the disorder of the system to increase, so ΔS_{sys} is positive. Because temperature increased as the solid dissolved, this is an exothermic process and ΔS_{surr} is positive ($\Delta S_{surr} = -\Delta H/T$). Because the solid did dissolve, the dissolving process is spontaneous, so ΔS_{univ} is positive.

71. ΔS will be negative because 2 mol of gaseous reactants form 1 mol of gaseous product. For ΔG to be negative, ΔH must be negative (exothermic). For exothermic reactions, K decreases as T increases. Therefore, the ratio of the partial pressure of PCl_5 to the partial pressure of PCl_3 will decrease when T is raised.

72.   At boiling point, $\Delta G = 0$ so $\Delta S = \dfrac{\Delta H_{vap}}{T}$; For methane: $\Delta S = \dfrac{8.20 \times 10^3 \text{ J/mol}}{112 \text{ K}}$

$$= 73.2 \text{ J/mol}\bullet\text{K}$$

For hexane: $\Delta S = \dfrac{28.9 \times 10^3 \text{ J/mol}}{342 \text{ K}} = 84.5 \text{ J/mol}\bullet\text{K}$

$V_{met} = \dfrac{nRT}{P} = \dfrac{1.00 \text{ mol} (0.08206)(112 \text{ K})}{1.00 \text{ atm}} = 9.19 \text{ L}$; $V_{hex} = \dfrac{nRT}{P} = R(342 \text{ K}) = 28.1 \text{ L}$

Hexane has the larger molar volume at the boiling point so hexane should have the larger entropy. As the volume of a gas increases, positional disorder increases.

73.   solid I $\rightarrow$ solid II; Equilibrium occurs when $\Delta G = 0$.

$\Delta G = \Delta H - T\Delta S$, $\Delta H = T\Delta S$, $T = \Delta H/\Delta S = \dfrac{-743.1 \text{ J/mol}}{-17.0 \text{ J/K}\bullet\text{mol}} = 43.7 \text{ K} = -229.5°\text{C}$

74.   a. $\Delta G° = -RT \ln K = -(8.3145 \text{ J/K}\bullet\text{mol})(298 \text{ K}) \ln 0.090 = 6.0 \times 10^3 \text{ J/mol} = 6.0 \text{ kJ/mol}$

       b.   H–O–H + Cl–O–Cl $\rightarrow$ 2 H–O–Cl

            On each side of the reaction there are 2 H–O bonds and 2 O–Cl bonds. Both sides have the same number and type of bonds. Thus, $\Delta H \approx \Delta H° \approx 0$.

       c. $\Delta G° = \Delta H° - T\Delta S°$, $\Delta S° = \dfrac{\Delta H° - \Delta G°}{T} = \dfrac{0 - 6.0 \times 10^3 \text{ J}}{298 \text{ K}} = -20. \text{ J/K}$

       d.   For $H_2O(g)$, $\Delta H_f° = -242 \text{ kJ/mol}$ and $S° = 189 \text{ J/K}\bullet\text{mol}$

            $\Delta H° = 0 = 2\Delta H_{f,HOCl}° - [1 \text{ mol}(-242 \text{ kJ/mol}) + 1 \text{ mol}(80.3 \text{ J/K/mol})]$, $\Delta H_{f,HOCl}°$

$$= -81 \text{ kJ/mol}$$

            $-20. \text{ J/K} = 2S_{HOCl}° - [1 \text{ mol}(189 \text{ J/K}\bullet\text{mol}) + 1 \text{ mol}(266.1 \text{ J/K}\cdot\text{mol})]$, $S_{HOCl}°$

$$= 218 \text{ J/K}\bullet\text{mol}$$

e.   Assuming $\Delta H°$ and $\Delta S°$ are T independent: $\Delta G°_{500} = 0 - (500.\ K)(-20.\ J/K) = 1.0 \times 10^4\ J$

$$\Delta G° = -RT \ln K, \quad K = \exp\left(\frac{-\Delta G°}{RT}\right) = \exp\left(\frac{-1.0 \times 10^4}{(8.3145)(500.)}\right) = e^{-2.41} = 0.090$$

f. $\Delta G = \Delta G° + RT \ln \dfrac{P^2_{HOCl}}{P_{H_2O} \times P_{Cl_2O}}$; From part a, $\Delta G° = 6.0$ kJ/mol.

We should express all P's in atm. However, we perform the pressure conversion the same number of times in the numerator and denominator, so the factors of 760 torr/atm will all cancel. Thus, we can use the pressures in units of torr.

$$\Delta G = \frac{6.0\ kJ/mol + (8.3145\ J/K \bullet mol)(298\ K)}{1000\ J/kJ} \ln\left(\frac{(0.10)^2}{(18)(2.0)}\right) = 6.0 - 20. = -14\ kJ/mol$$

75. $HgbO_2 \qquad \rightarrow \quad Hgb + O_2 \qquad \Delta G° = -(-70\ kJ)$
          $Hgb + CO \rightarrow HgbCO \qquad\qquad \Delta G° = -80\ kJ$

          $HgbO_2 + CO \rightarrow HgbCO + O_2 \qquad \Delta G° = -10\ kJ$

$$\Delta G° = -RT \ln K, \quad K = \exp\left(\frac{-\Delta G°}{RT}\right) = \exp\left(\frac{-(-10 \times 10^3\ J)}{8.3145\ J/K \bullet mol\ (298\ K)}\right) = 60$$

76. $Ba(NO_3)_2(s) \rightleftharpoons Ba^{2+}(aq) + 2\ NO_3^-(aq) \quad K = K_{sp};\quad \Delta G° = -561 + 2(-109) - (-797) = 18\ kJ$

$$\Delta G° = -RT \ln K_{sp}, \quad \ln K_{sp} = \frac{-\Delta G°}{RT} = \frac{-18,000\ J}{8.3145\ J/K \bullet mol\ (298\ K)} = -7.26, \quad K_{sp} = e^{-7.26}$$

$$= 7.0 \times 10^{-4}$$

77. $HF(aq) \rightleftharpoons H^+(aq) + F^-(aq);\quad \Delta G = \Delta G° + RT \ln \dfrac{[H^+][F^-]}{[HF]}$

$\Delta G° = -RT \ln K = -(8.3145\ J/K\bullet mol)\ (298\ K) \ln (7.2 \times 10^{-4}) = 1.8 \times 10^4\ J/mol$

a.   The concentrations are all at standard conditions so $\Delta G = \Delta G = 1.8 \times 10^4\ J/mol$ ($Q = 1.0$ and $\ln Q = 0$). Because $\Delta G°$ is positive, the reaction shifts left to reach equilibrium.

b. $\Delta G = 1.8 \times 10^4\ J/mol + (8.3145\ J/K\bullet mol)\ (298\ K) \ln \dfrac{(2.7 \times 10^{-2})^2}{0.98}$

    $\Delta G = 1.8 \times 10^4\ J/mol - 1.8 \times 10^4\ J/mol = 0$

    $\Delta G = 0$, so the reaction is at equilibrium (no shift).

c. $\Delta G = 1.8 \times 10^4 \text{ J/mol} + 8.3145 \, (298 \text{ K}) \ln \dfrac{(1.0 \times 10^{-5})^2}{1.0 \times 10^{-5}} = -1.1 \times 10^4 \text{ J/mol};$ shifts right

d. $\Delta G = 1.8 \times 10^4 + 8.3145 \, (298) \ln \dfrac{7.2 \times 10^{-4} \, (0.27)}{0.27} = 1.8 \times 10^4 - 1.8 \times 10^4 = 0;$

at equilibrium

e. $\Delta G = 1.8 \times 10^4 + 8.3145 \, (298) \ln \dfrac{1.0 \times 10^{-3} \, (0.67)}{0.52} = 2 \times 10^3 \text{ J/mol};$ shifts left

78. $K^+ \text{ (blood)} \rightleftharpoons K^+ \text{ (muscle)}$ $\Delta G^\circ = 0;$ $\Delta G = RT \ln \left(\dfrac{[K^+]_m}{[K^+]_b} \right);$ $\Delta G = w_{max}$

$\Delta G = \dfrac{8.3145 \text{ J}}{\text{K mol}} \, (310. \text{ K}) \ln \left(\dfrac{0.15}{0.0050} \right),$ $\Delta G = 8.8 \times 10^3 \text{ J/mol} = 8.8 \text{ kJ/mol}$

At least 8.8 kJ of work must be applied.

Other ions will have to be transported in order to maintain electroneutrality. Either anions must be transported into the cells, or cations (Na^+) in the cell must be transported to the blood. The latter is what happens: [Na^+] in blood is greater than [Na^+] in cells as a result of this pumping.

79.   a. $\Delta G^\circ = -RT \ln K,$ $K = \exp(-\Delta G^\circ / RT)$ $= \exp \left(\dfrac{-(-30,500 \text{ J})}{8.3145 \text{ J} / \text{K} \bullet \text{mol} \times 298 \text{ K}} \right) = 2.22 \times 10^5$

b. $C_6H_{12}O_6(s) + 6 \, O_2(g) \rightarrow 6 \, CO_2(g) + 6 \, H_2O(l)$

$\Delta G^\circ = 6 \text{ mol}(-394 \text{ kJ/mol}) + 6 \text{ mol}(-237 \text{ kJ/mol}) - 1 \text{ mol}(-911 \text{ kJ/mol}) = -2875 \text{ kJ}$

$\dfrac{2875 \text{ kJ}}{\text{mol glucose}} \times \dfrac{1 \text{ mol ATP}}{30.5 \text{ kJ}} = \dfrac{94.3 \text{ mol ATP}}{\text{mol glucose}};$ 94.3 molecules ATP/molecule glucose

This is an overstatement. The assumption that all of the free energy goes into this reaction is false. Actually only 38 moles of ATP are produced by metabolism of one mole of glucose.

c.   From Exercise 17.78, $\Delta G = 8.8$ kJ in order to transport 1.0 mol K^+ from the blood to the muscle cells.

$8.8 \text{ kJ} \times \dfrac{1 \text{ mol ATP}}{30.5 \text{ kJ}} = 0.29 \text{ mol ATP}$

80.   a. $\Delta G^\circ = -RT \ln K$

$\ln K = \dfrac{-\Delta G^\circ}{RT} = \dfrac{-14,000 \text{ J}}{(8.3145 \text{ J} / \text{K} \bullet \text{mol})(298 \text{ K})} = -5.65,$ $K = e^{-5.65} = 3.5 \times 10^{-3}$

b.

$$\text{Glutamic acid} + NH_3 \; \rightarrow \; \text{Glutamine} + H_2O \qquad \Delta G° = 14 \text{ kJ}$$

$$ATP + H_2O \; \rightarrow \; ADP + H_2PO_4^- \qquad \Delta G° = -30.5 \text{ kJ}$$

$$\text{Glutamic acid} + ATP + NH_3 \; \rightarrow \; \text{Glutamine} + ADP + H_2PO_4^- \qquad \Delta G° = 14 - 30.5$$

$$= -17 \text{ kJ}$$

$$\ln K = \frac{-\Delta G°}{RT} = \frac{-(-17,000 \text{ J})}{8.3145 \text{ J}/\text{K} \bullet \text{mol } (298 \text{ K})} = 6.86, \; K = e^{6.86} = 9.5 \times 10^2$$

81. ΔS is more favorable for reaction two than for reaction one, resulting in $K_2 > K_1$. In reaction one, seven particles in solution are forming one particle. In reaction two, four particles form one particle which results in a smaller decrease in disorder than for reaction one.

82.   A graph of ln K vs. 1/T will yield a straight line with slope equal to $-\Delta H°/R$ and y-intercept equal to $\Delta S°/R$.

Temp (°C)	T(K)	1000/T (K^{-1})	K_w	ln K_w
0	273	3.66	1.14×10^{-15}	-34.408
25	298	3.36	1.00×10^{-14}	-32.236
35	308	3.25	2.09×10^{-14}	-31.499
40.	313	3.19	2.92×10^{-14}	-31.165
50.	323	3.10	5.47×10^{-14}	-30.537

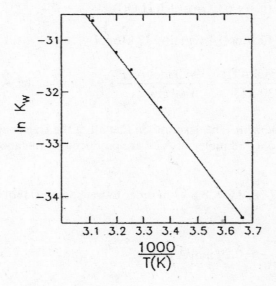

The straight line equation (from a calculator) is: $\ln K = -6.91 \times 10^3 \left(\dfrac{1}{T}\right) - 9.09$

$$\text{Slope} = -6.91 \times 10^3 \text{ K} = \frac{-\Delta H°}{R}, \; \Delta H° = - \, (-6.91 \times 10^3 \text{ K} \times 8.3145 \text{ J}/\text{K} \bullet \text{mol})$$

$$= 5.75 \times 10^4 \text{ J/mol}$$

y-intercept $= -9.09 = \dfrac{\Delta S^{\circ}}{R}$, $\Delta S^{\circ} = -9.09 \times 8.3145$ J/K•mol $= -75.6$ J/K•mol

83. $\Delta G^{\circ} = -RT \ln K$; When $K = 1.00$, $\Delta G^{\circ} = 0$ since $\ln 1.00 = 0$. $\Delta G^{\circ} = 0 = \Delta H^{\circ} - T\Delta S^{\circ}$

$\Delta H^{\circ} = 3(-242$ kJ$) - [-826$ kJ$] = 100.$ kJ; $\Delta S^{\circ} = [2(27$ J/K$) + 3(189$ J/K$)] -$
$$[90.\text{ J/K} + 3(131\text{ J/K})] = 138\text{ J/K}$$

$\Delta H^{\circ} = T\Delta S^{\circ}$, $T = \dfrac{\Delta H^{\circ}}{\Delta S^{\circ}} = \dfrac{100.\text{ kJ}}{0.138\text{ kJ / K}} = 725$ K

Challenge Problems

84. The liquid water will evaporate at first and eventually an equilibrium will be reached (physical equilibrium).

  • Because evaporation is an endothermic process, ΔH is positive.
  • Because $H_2O(g)$ is more disordered (greater positional probability), ΔS is positive.
  • The water will become cooler (the higher energy water molecules leave), thus ΔT_{water} will be negative.
  • The vessel is insulated ($q = 0$), so $\Delta S_{surr} = 0$.
  • Because the process occurs, it is spontaneous, so ΔS_{univ} is positive.

85. $3\,O_2(g) \rightleftharpoons 2\,O_3(g)$; $\Delta H^{\circ} = 2(143$ kJ$) = 286$ kJ; $\Delta G^{\circ} = 2(163$ kJ$) = 326$ kJ

$\ln K = \dfrac{-\Delta G^{\circ}}{RT} = \dfrac{-326 \times 10^3\text{ J}}{(8.3145\text{ J / K} \bullet \text{mol})(298\text{ K})} = -131.573$, $K = e^{-131.573} = 7.22 \times 10^{-58}$

We need the value of K at 230. K. From Section 16.8 of the text:

$\ln K = \dfrac{-\Delta G^{\circ}}{RT} + \dfrac{\Delta S^{\circ}}{R}$

For two sets of K and T:

$\ln K_1 = \dfrac{-\Delta H^{\circ}}{R}\left(\dfrac{1}{T_1}\right) + \dfrac{\Delta S}{R}$; $\ln K_2 = \dfrac{-\Delta H^{\circ}}{R}\left(\dfrac{1}{T_2}\right) + \dfrac{\Delta S^{\circ}}{R}$

Subtracting the first expression from the second:

$\ln K_2 - \ln K_1 = \dfrac{\Delta H^{\circ}}{R}\left(\dfrac{1}{T_1} - \dfrac{1}{T_2}\right)$ or $\ln \dfrac{K_2}{K_1} = \dfrac{\Delta H^{\circ}}{R}\left(\dfrac{1}{T_1} - \dfrac{1}{T_2}\right)$

Let $K_2 = 7.22 \times 10^{-58}$, $T_2 = 298$ K; $K_1 = K_{230}$, $T_1 = 230.$ K; $\Delta H^{\circ} = 286 \times 10^3$ J

$$\ln \frac{7.22 \times 10^{-58}}{K_{230}} = \frac{286 \times 10^3}{8.3145} \left(\frac{1}{230.} - \frac{1}{298} \right) = 34.13$$

$$\frac{7.22 \times 10^{-58}}{K_{230}} = e^{34.13} = 6.6 \times 10^{14}, \quad K_{230} = 1.1 \times 10^{-72}$$

$$K_{230} = 1.1 \times 10^{-72} = \frac{P_{O_3}^2}{P_{O_3}^3} = \frac{P_{O_3}^2}{(1.0 \times 10^{-3} \text{ atm})^3}, \quad P_{O_3} = 3.3 \times 10^{-41} \text{ atm}$$

The volume occupied by one molecule of ozone is:

$$V = \frac{nRT}{P} = \frac{(1/6.022 \times 10^{23} \text{ mol})(0.08206 \text{ L atm}/\text{mol} \bullet \text{K})(230. \text{ K})}{(3.3 \times 10^{-41} \text{ atm})} = 9.5 \times 10^{17} \text{ L}$$

Equilibrium is probably not maintained under these conditions. When only two ozone molecules are in a volume of 9.5×10^{17} L, the reaction is not at equilibrium. Under these conditions, $Q > K$ and the reaction shifts left. But with only 2 ozone molecules in this huge volume, it is extremely unlikely that they will collide with each other. At these conditions, the concentration of ozone is not large enough to maintain equilibrium.

86.   Arrangement I and V: $S = k \ln W$; $W = 1$; $S = k \ln 1 = 0$

Arrangement II and IV: $W = 4$; $S = k \ln 4 = 1.38 \times 10^{-23}$ J/K $\ln 4$, $S = 1.91 \times 10^{-23}$ J/K

Arrangement III: $W = 6$; $S = k \ln 6 = 2.47 \times 10^{-23}$ J/K

87.   a.   From the plot, the activation energy of the reverse reaction is $E_a + (-\Delta G^\circ) = E_a - \Delta G^\circ$
      (ΔG° is a negative number as drawn in the diagram).

$$k_f = A \exp\left(\frac{-E_a}{RT} \right) \text{ and } k_r = A \exp\left(\frac{-(E_a - \Delta G^\circ)}{RT} \right), \quad \frac{k_f}{k_r} = \frac{A \exp\left(\dfrac{-E_a}{RT} \right)}{A \exp\left(\dfrac{-(E_a - \Delta G^\circ)}{RT} \right)}$$

If the A factors are equal: $\dfrac{k_f}{k_r} = \exp\left(\dfrac{-E_a}{RT} + \dfrac{(E_a - \Delta G^\circ)}{RT} \right) = \exp\left(\dfrac{-\Delta G^\circ}{RT} \right)$

From $\Delta G^\circ = -RT \ln K$, $K = \exp\left(\dfrac{-\Delta G^\circ}{RT} \right)$; Because K and $\dfrac{k_f}{k_r}$ are both equal to the

same expression, $K = \dfrac{k_f}{k_r}$.

b.   A catalyst will lower the activation energy for both the forward and reverse reaction (but not change $\Delta G°$). Therefore, a catalyst must increase the rate of both the forward and reverse reactions.

88.   At equilibrium:

$$P_{H_2} = \frac{nRT}{V} = \frac{\left(\dfrac{1.10 \times 10^{13} \text{ molecules}}{6.022 \times 10^{23} \text{ molecules/mol}}\right)\left(\dfrac{0.08206 \text{ L atm}}{\text{mol K}}\right)(298 \text{ K})}{1.00 \text{ L}}$$

$$P_{H_2} = 4.47 \times 10^{-10} \text{ atm}$$

The pressure of H_2 decreased from 1.00 atm to 4.47×10^{-10} atm. Essentially all of the H_2 and Br_2 has reacted. Therefore, $P_{HBr} = 2.00$ atm because there is a 2:1 mole ratio between HBr and H_2 in the balanced equation. Because we began with equal moles of H_2 and Br_2, we will have equal moles of H_2 and Br_2 at equilibrium. Therefore, $P_{H_2} = P_{Br_2} = 4.47 \times 10^{-10}$ atm.

$$K = \frac{P_{HBr}^2}{P_{H_2} \times P_{Br_2}} = \frac{(2.00)^2}{(4.47 \times 10^{-10})^2} = 2.00 \times 10^{19}; \quad \text{Assumptions good.}$$

$$\Delta G° = -RT \ln K = -(8.3145 \text{ J/K•mol})(298 \text{ K}) \ln (2.00 \times 10^{19}) = -1.10 \times 10^5 \text{ J/mol}$$

$$\Delta S° = \frac{\Delta H° - \Delta G°}{T} = \frac{-103,800 \text{ J/mol} - (-1.0 \times 10^5 \text{ J/mol})}{298 \text{ K}} = 20 \text{ J/K•mol}$$

89.   a. $\Delta G° = G_B° - G_A° = 11{,}718 - 8996 = 2722 \text{ J}$

$$K = \exp\left(\frac{-\Delta G°}{RT}\right) = \exp\left(\frac{-2722 \text{ J}}{(8.3145 \text{ J/K • mol})(298 \text{ K})}\right) = 0.333$$

b.   When Q = 1.00 > K, the reaction shifts left. Let x = atm of B(g) which reacts to reach equilibrium.

$$A(g) \rightleftharpoons B(g)$$

Initial	1.00 atm	1.00 atm
Equil.	1.00 + x	1.00 − x

$$K = \frac{P_B}{P_A} = \frac{1.00 - x}{1.00 + x} = 0.333, \quad 1.00 - x = 0.333 + 0.333\,x, \quad x = 0.50 \text{ atm}$$

$P_B = 1.00 - 0.50 = 0.50$ atm; $P_A = 1.00 + 0.50 = 1.50$ atm

c. $\Delta G = \Delta G° + RT \ln Q = \Delta G° + RT \ln (P_B/P_A)$

$\Delta G = 2722 \text{ J} + (8.3145)(298) \ln (0.50/1.50) = 2722 \text{ J} - 2722 \text{ J} = 0$ (carrying extra
sig. figs.)

90. From Exercise 16.67, $\ln K = \dfrac{-\Delta H^\circ}{RT} + \dfrac{\Delta S^\circ}{R}$. For K at two temperatures T_1 and T_2, the equation can be manipulated to give (see Exercise 16.77): $\ln\dfrac{K_2}{K_1} = \dfrac{\Delta H^\circ}{R}\left(\dfrac{1}{T_1} - \dfrac{1}{T_2}\right)$

$$\ln\left(\frac{3.25 \times 10^{-2}}{8.84}\right) = \frac{\Delta H^\circ}{8.3145\,\text{J}/\text{K} \bullet \text{mol}}\left(\frac{1}{298\,\text{K}} - \frac{1}{348\,\text{K}}\right)$$

$-5.61 = (5.8 \times 10^{-5}\,\text{mol/J})\,(\Delta H^\circ),\ \ \Delta H^\circ = -9.7 \times 10^4\,\text{J/mol}$

For $K = 8.84$ at $T = 25°C$:

$$\ln 8.84 = \frac{-(-9.7 \times 10^4\,\text{J}/\text{mol})}{(8.3145\,\text{J}/\text{K} \bullet \text{mol})\,(298\,\text{K})} + \frac{\Delta S^\circ}{8.3145\,\text{J}/\text{K} \bullet \text{mol}},\ \ \frac{\Delta S^\circ}{8.3145} = -37$$

$\Delta S^\circ = -310\,\text{J/K} \bullet \text{mol}$

We get the same value for ΔS° using $K = 3.25 \times 10^{-2}$ at $T = 348\,\text{K}$ data.

$\Delta G^\circ = -RT \ln K$; When $K = 1.00$, then $\Delta G^\circ = 0$ since $\ln 1.00 = 0$. Assuming ΔH° and ΔS° do not depend on temperature:

$$\Delta G^\circ = 0 = \Delta H^\circ - T\Delta S^\circ,\ \ \Delta H^\circ = T\Delta S^\circ,\ \ T = \frac{\Delta H^\circ}{\Delta S^\circ} = \frac{-9.7 \times 10^4\,\text{J}/\text{mol}}{-310\,\text{J}/\text{K} \bullet \text{mol}} = 310\,\text{K}$$

91. $K = P_{CO_2}$; To insure Ag_2CO_3 from decomposing, P_{CO_2} should be greater than K.

From Exercise 16.67, $\ln K = \dfrac{\Delta H^\circ}{RT} + \dfrac{\Delta S^\circ}{R}$. For two conditions of K and T, the equation is:

$$\ln\frac{K_2}{K_1} = \frac{\Delta H^\circ}{R}\left(\frac{1}{T_1} + \frac{1}{T_2}\right)$$

Let $T_1 = 25°C = 298\,\text{K}$, $K_1 = 6.23 \times 10^{-3}\,\text{torr}$; $T_2 = 110.°C = 383\,\text{K}$, $K_2 = ?$

$$\ln\frac{K_2}{6.23 \times 10^{-3}\,\text{torr}} = \frac{79.14 \times 10^3\,\text{J}/\text{mol}}{8.3145\,\text{J}/\text{K} \bullet \text{mol}}\left(\frac{1}{298\,\text{K}} - \frac{1}{383\,\text{K}}\right)$$

$$\ln\frac{K_2}{6.23 \times 10^{-3}} = 7.1,\ \ \frac{K_2}{6.23 \times 10^{-3}} = e^{7.1} = 1.2 \times 10^3,\ \ K_2 = 7.5\,\text{torr}$$

To prevent decomposition of Ag_2CO_3, the partial pressure of CO_2 should be greater than 7.5 torr.

92.   From the problem, $\chi^L_{C_6H_6} = \chi^L_{CCl_4} = 0.500$. We need the pure vapor pressures (P^o) in order to
        calculate the vapor pressure of the solution. Using the thermodynamic data:

$$C_6H_6(l) \rightleftharpoons C_6H_6(g) \quad K = P_{C_6H_6} = P^o_{C_6H_6} \quad \text{at } 25°C$$

$$\Delta G^o_{rxn} = \Delta G^o_{f,C_6H_6(g)} - \Delta G^o_{f,C_6H_6(l)} = 129.66 \text{ kJ/mol} - 124.50 \text{ kJ/mol} = 5.16 \text{ kJ/mol}$$

$$\Delta G^o = -RT \ln K, \quad \ln K = \frac{-\Delta G^o}{RT} = \exp \frac{-5.16 \times 10^3 \text{ J/mol}}{(8.3145 \text{ J/K} \bullet \text{mol})(298 \text{ K})} = -2.08$$

$$K = P^o_{C_6H_6} = e^{-2.08} = 0.125 \text{ atm}$$

For CCl₄: $\Delta G^o_{rxn} = \Delta G^o_{f,CCl_4(g)} - \Delta G^o_{f,CCl_4(l)} = -60.59 \text{ kJ/mol} - (-65.21 \text{ kJ/mol})$
$$= 4.62 \text{ kJ/mol}$$

$$K = P^o_{CCl_4} = \exp\left(\frac{-\Delta G^o}{RT}\right) = \exp\left(\frac{-4620 \text{ J/mol}}{8.3145 \text{ J/K} \bullet \text{mol} \times 298 \text{ K}}\right) = 0.155 \text{ atm}$$

$$P_{C_6H_6} = \chi^L_{C_6H_6} P^o_{C_6H_6} = 0.500 \, (0.125 \text{ atm}) = 0.0625 \text{ atm}; \quad P_{CCl_4} = 0.500 \, (0.155 \text{ atm})$$
$$= 0.0775 \text{ atm}$$

$$\chi^V_{C_6H_6} = \frac{P_{C_6H_6}}{P_{tot}} = \frac{0.0625 \text{ atm}}{0.0625 \text{ atm} + 0.0775 \text{ atm}} = \frac{0.0625}{0.1400} = 0.446$$

$$\chi^V_{CCl_4} = 1.000 - 0.446 = 0.554$$

93.   Use the thermodynamic data to calculate the boiling point of the solvent.

At boiling point: $\Delta G = 0 = \Delta H - T\Delta S, \quad T = \dfrac{\Delta H}{\Delta S} = \dfrac{33.90 \times 10^3 \text{ J/mol}}{95.95 \text{ J/K} \bullet \text{mol}} = 353.3 \text{ K}$

$$\Delta T = K_b m, \quad (355.4 \text{ K} - 353.3 \text{ K}) = 2.5 \text{ K kg/mol} \, (m), \quad m = \frac{2.1}{2.5} = 0.84 \text{ mol/kg}$$

$$\text{mass solvent} = 150. \text{ mL} \times \frac{0.879 \text{ g}}{\text{mL}} \times \frac{1 \text{ kg}}{1000 \text{ g}} = 0.132 \text{ kg}$$

$$\text{mass solute} = 0.132 \text{ kg solvent} \times \frac{0.84 \text{ mol solute}}{\text{kg solvent}} \times \frac{142 \text{ g}}{\text{mol}} = 15.7 \text{ g} = 16 \text{ g solute}$$

94. $\Delta S_{surr} = -\Delta H/T = -q_P/T$

q = heat loss by hot water = moles × molar heat capacity × ΔT

$$q = 1.00 \times 10^3 \text{ g } H_2O \times \frac{1 \text{ mol } H_2O}{18.02 \text{ g}} \times \frac{75.4 \text{ J}}{K \bullet mol} \times (298.2 - 363.2) = -2.72 \times 10^5 \text{ J}$$

$$\Delta S_{surr} = \frac{-(-2.72 \times 10^5 \text{ J})}{298.2 \text{ K}} = 912 \text{ J/K}$$

95. $\qquad\qquad HX \rightleftharpoons H^+ + X^- \qquad K_a = \dfrac{[H^+][X^-]}{[HX]}$

Initial	0.10 M	~0	0
Equil.	0.10 – x	x	x

From problem, $x = [H^+] = 10^{-5.83} = 1.5 \times 10^{-6}$; $K_a = \dfrac{(1.5 \times 10^{-6})^2}{0.10 - 1.5 \times 10^{-6}} = 2.3 \times 10^{-11}$

$\Delta G° = -RT \ln K = -8.3145 \text{ J/K} \bullet mol \ (298 \text{ K}) \ln(2.3 \times 10^{-11}) = 6.1 \times 10^4 \text{ J/mol} = 61 \text{ kJ/mol}$

96. $NaCl(s) \rightleftharpoons Na^+(aq) + Cl^-(aq) \qquad K = K_{sp} = [Na^+][Cl^-]$

$\Delta G° = [(-262 \text{ kJ}) + (-131 \text{ kJ})] - (-384 \text{ kJ}) = -9 \text{ kJ} = -9000 \text{ J}$

$$\Delta G° = = -RT \ln K_{sp}, \ K_{sp} = \exp\left[\frac{-(-9000 \text{ J})}{8.3145 \text{ J}/K \bullet mol \times 298 \text{ K}}\right] = 38 = 40$$

$\qquad\qquad NaCl(s) \rightleftharpoons Na^+(aq) + Cl^-(aq) \qquad K_{sp} = 40$

Initial	s = solubility (mol/L)	0	0
Equil.		s	s

$K_{sp} = 40 = s(s)$, $s = (40)^{1/2} = 6.3 = 6 \ M = [Cl^-]$

Integrative Problems

97.   Because the partial pressure of C(g) decreased, the net change that occurs for this reaction to reach equilibrium is for products to convert to reactants.

$$A(g) + 2 B(g) \rightleftharpoons C(g)$$

Initial	0.100 atm	0.100 atm		0.100 atm
Change	+x	+2x	←	−x
Equil.	0.100 + x	0.100 + 2x		0.100 – x

From the problem, $P_C = 0.040$ atm $= 0.100 - x$, $x = 0.060$ atm

The equilibrium partial pressures are: $P_A = 0.100 + x = 0.100 + 0.060 = 0.160$ atm, $P_B = 0.100 + 2((0.60)) = 0.220$ atm, and $P_C = 0.040$ atm

$$K = \frac{0.040}{0.160(0.220)^2} = 5.2$$

$\Delta G° = -RT \ln K = -8.3145$ J/K•mol (298 K) $\ln 5.2 = -4.1 \times 10^3$ J/mol $= -4.1$ kJ/mol

98. $\Delta G° = \Delta H° - T\Delta S° = -28.0 \times 10^3$ J $- 298$ K$(-175$ J/K$) = 24,200$ J

$$\Delta G° = -RT \ln K, \quad \ln K = \frac{-\Delta G°}{RT} = \frac{-24,000 \text{ J}}{8.3145 \text{ J/K} \bullet \text{mol} \times 298 \text{ K}} = -9.767$$

$K = e^{-9.767} = 5.73 \times 10^{-5}$

$$\text{B} \quad + \quad \text{H}_2\text{O} \quad \rightleftharpoons \quad \text{BH}^+ \quad + \quad \text{OH}^- \qquad K = K_b = 5.73 \times 10^{-5}$$

	B		BH$^+$	OH$^-$
Initial	0.125 M		0	~0
Change	$-x$		$+x$	$+x$
Equil.	$0.125 - x$		x	x

$$K_b = 5.73 \times 10^{-5} = \frac{[\text{BH}^+][\text{OH}^-]}{[\text{B}]} = \frac{x^2}{0.125 - x} \approx \frac{x^2}{0.125}, \quad x = [\text{OH}^-] = 2.68 \times 10^{-3} M$$

$\text{pH} = -\log(2.68 \times 10^{-3}) = 2.572$; $\text{pOH} = 14.000 - 2.572 = 11.428$; Assumptions good

Marathon Problem

99.   a. $\Delta S°$ will be negative because there is a decrease in the number of moles of gas.

b.   Because $\Delta S°$ is negative, $\Delta H°$ must be negative for the reaction to be spontaneous at some temperatures. Therefore, ΔS_{surr} is positive.

c. $\text{Ni(s)} + 4\,\text{CO(g)} \rightleftharpoons \text{Ni(CO)}_4\text{(g)}$

$\Delta H° = -607 - [4(-110.5)] = -165$ kJ; $\Delta S° = 417 - [4(198) + (30.)] = -405$ J/K

d. $\Delta G° = 0 = \Delta H° - T\Delta S°$, $T = \dfrac{\Delta H°}{\Delta S°} = \dfrac{-165 \times 10^3 \text{ J}}{-405 \text{ J/K}} = 407$ K or 134°C

e. $T = 50.°\text{C} + 273 = 323$ K

$$\Delta G^{\circ}_{323} = -165 \text{ kJ} - (323 \text{ K})(-0.405 \text{ kJ/K}) = -34 \text{ kJ}$$

$$\ln K = \frac{-\Delta G^{\circ}}{RT} = \frac{-(-34,000 \text{ J})}{8.3145 \text{ J} / \text{K} \bullet \text{mol} (323 \text{ K})} = 12.66, \ K = e^{12.66} = 3.1 \times 10^{5}$$

f. $T = 227^{\circ}C + 273 = 500. \text{ K}$

$$\Delta G^{\circ}_{500} = -165 \text{ kJ} - (500. \text{ K})(-0.405 \text{ kJ/K}) = 38 \text{ kJ}$$

$$\ln K = \frac{-38,000 \text{ J}}{(8.3145 \text{ J} / \text{K} \bullet \text{mol})(500. \text{ K})} = -9.14, \ K = e^{-9.14} = 1.1 \times 10^{-4}$$

g.   The temperature change causes the value of the equilibrium constant to change from a large value favoring formation of $Ni(CO)_4$ to a small value favoring the decomposition of $Ni(CO)_4$ into pure Ni and CO. This is exactly what is wanted in order to purify a nickel sample.

h. $Ni(CO)_4(l) \rightleftharpoons Ni(CO)_4(g) \qquad K = P_{Ni(CO)_4}$

At $42^{\circ}C$ (the boiling point): $\Delta G^{\circ} = 0 = \Delta H^{\circ} - T\Delta S^{\circ}$

$$\Delta S^{\circ} = \frac{\Delta H^{\circ}}{T} = \frac{29.0 \times 10^{3} \text{ J}}{315 \text{ K}} = 92.1 \text{ J/K}$$

At $152^{\circ}C$: $\Delta G^{\circ}_{152} = \Delta H^{\circ} - T\Delta S^{\circ} = 29.0 \times 10^{3} \text{ J} - 425 \text{ K} (92.1 \text{ J/K}) = -10,100 \text{ J}$

$$\Delta G^{\circ} = -RT \ln K, \ \ln K = \frac{-(-10,100 \text{ J})}{8.3145 \text{ J} / \text{K} \bullet \text{mol}(425 \text{ K})} = 2.858, \ K_p = e^{2.858} = 17.4$$

A maximum pressure of 17.4 atm can be attained before $Ni(CO)_4(g)$ will liquify.

CHAPTER SEVENTEEN

ELECTROCHEMISTRY

For Review

1. Electrochemistry is the study of the interchange of chemical and electrical energy. A redox (oxidation-reduction) reaction is a reaction in which one or more electrons are transferred. In a galvanic cell, a spontaneous redox reaction occurs which produces an electric current. In an electrolytic cell, electricity is used to force a nonspontaneous redox reaction to occur.

2. Before we answer the question, here are four important terms relating to redox reactions and galvanic cells.

    a. Cathode: The electrode at which reduction occurs.

    b. Anode: The electrode at which oxidation occurs.

    c. Oxidation half-reaction: The half-reaction in which electrons are products. In a galvanic cell, the oxidation half-reaction always occurs at the anode.

    d. Reduction half-reaction: The half-reaction in which electrons are reactants. In a galvanic cell, the reduction half-reaction always occurs at the cathode.

    See Figures 17.2 and 17.3 for designs of galvanic cells. The electrode compartment in which reduction occurs is called the cathode and the electrode compartment in which oxidation occurs is called the anode. These compartments have electrodes (a solid surface) immersed in a solution. For a standard cell, the solution contains the reactant and product solutes and gases that are in the balanced half-reactions. The solute concentrations are all 1 M and gas partial pressures are all 1 atm for a standard cell. The electrodes are connected via a wire and a salt-bridge connects the two solutions.

    The purpose of the electrodes is to provide a solid surface for electron transfer to occur in the two compartments. Electrons always flow from the anode (where they are produced) to the cathode (where they are reactants). The salt bridge allows counter ions to flow into the two cell compartments to maintain electrical neutrality. Without a salt bridge, no sustained electron flow can occur. In the salt bridge, anions flow into the anode to replenish the loss of negative charge as electrons are lost; cations flow into the cathode to balance the negative charge as electrons are transferred into the cathode. The "pull" or driving force on the electrons is called the cell potential (E_{cell}) or the electromotive force. The unit of electrical potential is the volt (V) which is defined as 1 joule of work per coulomb of charge transferred. It is the cell potential that can be used to do useful work. We harness the spontaneous redox reaction to produce a cell potential which can do useful work.

3. The zero point for standard reduction potentials ($E°$) is the standard hydrogen electrode. The half-reaction is: $2 H^+ + 2 e^- \rightarrow H_2$. This half-reaction is assigned a standard potential of zero, and all other reduction half-reactions are measured relative to this zero point. Substances less easily reduced than H^+ have negative standard reduction potentials ($E° < 0$), while substances more easily reduced than H^+ have positive standard reduction potentials ($E° > 0$). The species most easily reduced has the most positive $E°$ value; this is F_2. The least easily reduced species is Li^+ with the most negative $E°$ value.

When a reduction half-reaction is reversed to obtain an oxidation half-reaction, the sign of the reduction potential is reversed to give the potential for the oxidation half-reaction ($E°_{ox} = -E_{red}$). The species oxidized are on the product side of the reduction half-reactions listed in Table 17.1. Li will have the most positive oxidation potential [$E°_{ox} = -E_{red} = -(-3.05 V) = 3.05 V$], so Li is the most easily oxidized of the species. The species most easily oxidized is the best reducing agent. The worst reducing agent is F^- because it has the most negative oxidation potential ($E°_{ox} = -2.87 V$).

For a spontaneous reaction at standard conditions, $E°_{cell}$ must be positive ($E°_{cell} = E°_{red} + E°_{ox} > 0$). For any two half-reactions, there is only one way to manipulate them to come up with a positive $E°_{cell}$ (a spontaneous reaction). Because the half-reactions do not depend on how many times the reaction occurs, half-reactions are an intensive property. This means that the value of $E°_{red}$ or $E°_{ox}$ is not changed when the half-reactions are multiplied by integers to get the electrons to cross off.

The line notation of the standard galvanic cell illustrated in Figure 17.5 would be:

$Zn(s) \mid Zn^{2+}(aq) \parallel H_2(g) \mid H^+(aq) \mid Pt$ or

$Zn(s) \mid Zn^{2+}(1.0\ M) \parallel H_2(1.0\ atm) \mid H^+(1.0\ M) \mid Pt$

The double line represents the salt-bridge separating the anode and cathode compartments. To the left of the double line are the pertinent anode compartment contents and to the right are the pertinent cathode compartment contents. At each end, the electrodes are listed; to the inside, the solution contents are listed. A single line is used to separate the contents of each compartment whenever there is a phase change. Here in the cathode compartment, a single line is used to separate $H_2(g)$ from $H^+(aq)$ and to separate $H^+(aq)$ from Pt (the electrode). When concentrations and partial pressures are not listed, they are assumed to be standard (1.0 M for solutes and 1.0 atm for gases). For cells having nonstandard concentrations and pressures, we always include the actual concentrations and pressures in the line notation instead of the phases.

4. $\Delta G° = -nFE°$; $\Delta G°$ is the standard free energy change for the overall balanced reaction, n is the number of electrons transferred in the overall balanced reaction, F is called the Faraday constant (1 F = 96,485 coulombs of charge transferred per mole of electrons), and $E°$ is the standard cell potential for the reaction. For a spontaneous redox reaction, $E°_{cell}$ is positive while $\Delta G°_{rxn}$ is negative. The negative sign is necessary to convert the positive $E°_{cell}$ value for a spontaneous reaction into a negative $\Delta G°_{rxn}$. The superscript ° indicates standard conditions. These are T = 25°C, solute concentrations of 1.0 M, and gas partial pressures of

1.0 atm. Note that n is necessary in order to convert the intensive property E° into the extensive property, ΔG°.

5. $E = E° - \dfrac{RT}{nF} \ln Q$; At 25°C, the Nernst equation is: $E = E° - \dfrac{0.0591}{n} \log Q$

Nonstandard conditions are when solutes are not all 1.0 M and/or partial pressures of gases are not all 1.0 atm. Nonstandard conditions also occur when T ≠ 25°C, For most problem solving, T = 25°C is usually assumed, hence the second version of the Nernst equation is most often used.

E = cell potential at the conditions of the cell; E° = standard cell potential; n = number of electrons transferred in the overall reaction, and Q is the reaction quotient determined at the concentrations and partial pressures of the cell contents.

At equilibrium, E = 0 and Q = K. At 25°C, E° = (0.0591/n) log K. The standard cell potential allows calculation of the equilibrium constant for a reaction. When K < 1, the log K term is negative, so $E°_{cell}$ is negative and ΔG° is positive. When K > 1, the log K term is positive, so $E°_{cell}$ is positive and ΔG° is negative.

From the equation E° = (0.0591/n) log K, the value of E° allows calculation of the equilibrium constant K. We say that E° gives the equilibrium position for a reaction. E is the actual cell potential at the conditions of the cell reaction. If E is positive, then the cell reaction is spontaneous as written (the forward reaction can be used to make a galvanic cell to produce a voltage). If E is negative, the forward reaction is not spontaneous at the conditions of cell, but the reverse reaction is spontaneous. The reverse reaction can be used to form a galvanic cell. E° can only be used to determine spontaneity when all reactants and products are at standard conditions (T = 25°C, [ ] = 1.0 M, P = 1.0 atm).

6.   Concentration cell: a galvanic cell in which both compartments contain the same components, but at different concentrations. All concentration cells have $E°_{cell}$ = 0 because both compartments contain the same contents. The driving force for the cell is the different ion concentrations at the anode and cathode. The cell produces a voltage as long as the ion concentrations are different. Equilibrium for a concentration cell is reached (E = 0) when the ion concentrations in the two compartments are equal.

The net reaction in a concentration cell is:

M^{a+}(cathode, x M) → M^{a+} (anode, y M) $E°_{cell}$ = 0

and the Nernst equation is:

$$E = E° - \frac{0.0591}{n} \log Q = -\frac{0.0591}{a} \log \frac{[M^{a+} \text{ (anode)}]}{[M^{a+} \text{ (cathode)}]}$$ where a is the number of electrons transferred.

To register a potential (E > 0), the log Q term must be a negative value. This occurs when M^{a+}(cathode) > M^{a+}(anode). The higher ion concentration is always at the cathode and the lower ion concentration is always at the anode. The magnitude of the cell potential depends on the magnitude of the differences in ion concentrations between the anode and cathode. The larger the difference in ion concentrations, the more negative the log Q term and the more positive the cell potential. Thus, as the difference in ion concentrations between the anode and cathode compartments increase, the cell potential increases. This can be accomplished by decreasing the ion concentration at the anode and/or by increasing the ion concentration at the cathode.

When NaCl is added to the anode compartment, Ag^+ reacts with Cl^- to form AgCl(s). Adding Cl^-, lowers the Ag^+ concentration which causes an increase in the cell potential. To determine K_{sp} for AgCl ($K_{sp} = [Ag^+][Cl^-]$), we must know the equilibrium Ag^+ and Cl^- concentrations. Here, $[Cl^-]$ is given and we use the Nernst equation to calculate the $[Ag^+]$ at the anode.

7.   As a battery discharges, E_{cell} decreases, eventually reaching zero. A charged battery is not at equilibrium. At equilibrium, $E_{cell} = 0$ and $\Delta G = 0$. We get no work out of an equilibrium system. A battery is useful to us because it can do work as it approaches equilibrium.

Both fuel cells and batteries are galvanic cells that produce cell potentials to do useful work. However, fuel cells, unlike batteries, have the reactants continuously supplied and can produce a current indefinitely.

The overall reaction in the hydrogen-oxygen fuel cell is $2\,H_2(g) + O_2(g) \rightarrow 2\,H_2O(l)$. The half-reactions are:

$$4\,e^- + O_2 + 2\,H_2O \rightarrow 4\,OH^- \qquad \text{cathode}$$

$$2\,H_2 + 4\,OH^- \rightarrow 4\,H_2O + 4\,e^- \qquad \text{anode}$$

Utilizing the standard potentials in Table 17.1, $E^\circ_{cell} = 0.40\,V + 0.83\,V = 1.23\,V$ for the hydrogen-oxygen fuel cell. As with all fuel cells, the $H_2(g)$ and $O_2(g)$ reactants are continuously supplied. See Figure 17.16 for a schematic of this fuel cell.

8.   The corrosion of a metal can be viewed as the process of returning metals to their natural state. The natural state of metals is to have positive oxidation numbers. This corrosion is the oxidation of a pure metal (oxidation number = 0) into its ions. For corrosion of iron to take place, you must have:

a.   exposed iron surface – a reactant

b. $O_2(g)$ – a reactant

c. $H_2O(l)$ – a reactant, but also provides a medium for ion flow (it provides the salt bridge)

d.   ions – to complete the salt bridge

Because water is a reactant and acts as a salt bridge for corrosion, cars do not rust in dry air climates, while corrosion is a big problem in humid climates. Salting roads in the winter also increases the severity of corrosion. The dissolution of the salt into ions on the surface of a metal increases the conductivity of the aqueous solution and accelerates the corrosion process.

Some of the ways metals (iron) are protected from corrosion are listed below.

a. Paint: Covers the metal surface so no contact occurs between the metal and air. This only works as long as the painted surface is not scratched.

b. Durable oxide coatings: Covers the metal surface so no contact occurs between the metal and air.

c. Galvanizing: Coating steel with zinc; Zn forms an effective oxide coating over steel; also, zinc is more easily oxidized than the iron in the steel.

d. Sacrificial metal: Attaching a more easily oxidized metal to an iron surface; the more active metal is preferentially oxidized instead of iron.

e. Alloying: Adding chromium and nickel to steel; the added Cr and Ni form oxide coatings on the steel surface.

f. Cathodic protection: A more easily oxidized metal is placed in electrical contact with the metal we are trying to protect. It is oxidized in preference to the protected metal. The protected metal becomes the cathode electrode, thus, cathodic protection.

9.   An electrolytic cell uses electrical energy to produce a chemical change. The process of electrolysis involves forcing a current through a cell to produce a chemical change for which the cell potential is negative. Electrical work is used to force a nonspontaneous reaction to occur.

The units for current are amperes (A) which equal 1 coulomb of charge per sec.

current (A) × time (s) = coulombs of charge passed

We use Faraday's constant (F = 96,485 coulombs of charge per mole) to convert coulombs of charge passed into moles of electrons passed. The half-reaction gives the mole ratio between moles of electrons and moles of metal produced (or plated out). Plating means depositing the neutral metal on the electrode by reducing the metal ions in solution.

In electrolysis, as with any redox reaction, the reaction that occurs first is the one most favored thermodynamically. The reduction reaction most favored thermodynamically has the largest, most positive E^o_{red} value. The oxidation reaction most likely to occur is the one with the largest, most positive E^o_{ox} value. Note that for electrolytic cells that $E^o_{cell} < 0$, so the E^o_{red} and E^o_{ox} values are commonly negative. The half-reactions that occur first as a current is applied are the ones with the least negative potentials (which are the most positive potentials). To predict the cathode half-reaction, write down the half-reaction and E^o_{red} value for all species present that can be reduced. The cathode reaction that occurs has the least negative (most positive) E^o_{red} value. The same thing is done for the anode; write down everything present that can be oxidized; the species oxidized has the least negative (most positive) E^o_{ox} value. Note that we commonly assume standard conditions when predicting which half-reactions occur, so we can use the standard potentials in Table 17.1.

When molten salts are electrolyzed, there is only one species present that can be oxidized (the anion in simple salts) and there is only one species that can be reduced (the cation in simple salts). When H_2O is present as is the case when aqueous solutions are electrolyzed, we must consider the oxidation and reduction of water as potential reactions that can occur. When water is present, more reactions can take place, making predictions more difficult.

When the voltage required to force a chemical reaction to occur is larger than expected, this is called overvoltage. The amount of overvoltage necessary to force a reaction to occur varies with the type of substance present. Because of this, $E°$ values must be used cautiously when predicting the half-reactions that occur.

10.   Electrolysis is used to produce many pure metals and pure elements for commercial use. It also is used to purify metals as well as to plate out thin coatings on substances to provide protection from corrosion and to beautify objects. Another application of electrolysis is the charging of batteries.

When aqueous NaCl is electrolyzed, water, with its less negative reduction potential is preferentially reduced over Na^+ ions. Thus, the presence of water doesn't allow Na^+ ions to be reduced to Na. In molten NaCl, water is not present, so Na^+ can be reduced to Na.

Purification by electrolysis is called electrorefining. See the text for a discussion of the electrorefining of copper. Electrorefining is possible because of the selectivity of electrode reactions. The anode is made up of the impure metal. A potential is applied so just the metal of interest and all more easily oxidized metals are oxidized at the anode. The metal of interest is the only metal plated at the cathode due to the careful control of the potential applied. The metal ions that could plate out at the cathode in preference to the metal we are purifying will not be in solution, because these metals were not oxidized at the anode.

Review of Oxidation - Reduction Reactions

13.   Oxidation: increase in oxidation number; loss of electrons

Reduction: decrease in oxidation number; gain of electrons

14.   See Table 4.2 in Chapter 4 of the text for rules for assigning oxidation numbers.

a. H (+1), O (-2), N (+5)   b. Cl (-1), Cu (+2)

c. O (0)   d. H (+1), O (-1)

e. H(+1), O (-2), C (0)   f. Ag (0)

g. Pb (+2), O (−2), S (+6)   h. O (−2), Pb (+4)

i. Na (+1), O (−2), C (+3)   j. O (−2), C (+4)

k. $(NH_4)_2Ce(SO_4)_3$ contains NH_4^+ ions and SO_4^{2-} ions. Thus, cerium exists as the Ce^{4+} ion.
    H (+1), N (−3), Ce (+4), S (+6), O (−2)

l. O (−2), Cr (+3)

15.   The species oxidized shows an increase in oxidation numbers and is called the reducing agent.   The species reduced shows a decrease in oxidation numbers and is called the oxidizing agent. The pertinent oxidation numbers are listed by the substance oxidized and the substance reduced.

	Redox?	Ox. Agent	Red. Agent	Substance Oxidized	Substance Reduced
a.	Yes	H_2O	CH_4	CH_4 (C, −4 → +2)	H_2O (H, +1 → 0)
b.	Yes	$AgNO_3$	Cu	Cu (0 → +2)	$AgNO_3$ (Ag, +1 → 0)
c.	Yes	HCl	Zn	Zn (0 → +2)	HCl (H, +1 → 0)

d. No; There is no change in any of the oxidation numbers.

16.   See Chapter 4.10 of the text for rules on balancing oxidation-reduction reactions.

a. $Cr \rightarrow Cr^{3+} + 3\ e^-$

$$NO_3^- \rightarrow NO$$
$$4\ H^+ + NO_3^- \rightarrow NO + 2\ H_2O$$
$$3\ e^- + 4\ H^+ + NO_3^- \rightarrow NO + 2\ H_2O$$

$$Cr \rightarrow Cr^{3+} + 3\ e^-$$
$$3\ e^- + 4\ H^+ + NO_3^- \rightarrow NO + 2\ H_2O$$
_____

$$4\ H^+(aq) + NO_3^-(aq) + Cr(s) \rightarrow Cr^{3+}(aq) + NO(g) + 2\ H_2O(l)$$

b. $(Al \rightarrow Al^{3+} + 3\ e^-) \times 5$

$$MnO_4^- \rightarrow Mn^{2+}$$
$$8\ H^+ + MnO_4^- \rightarrow Mn^{2+} + 4\ H_2O$$
$$(5\ e^- + 8\ H^+ + MnO_4^- \rightarrow Mn^{2+} + 4\ H_2O) \times 3$$

$$5\ Al \rightarrow 5\ Al^{3+} + 15\ e^-$$
$$15\ e^- + 24\ H^+ + 3\ MnO_4^- \rightarrow 3\ Mn^{2+} + 12\ H_2O$$
_____

$$24\ H^+(aq) + 3\ MnO_4^-(aq) + 5\ Al(s) \rightarrow 5\ Al^{3+}(aq) + 3\ Mn^{2+}(aq) + 12\ H_2O(l)$$

c. $(Ce^{4+} + e^- \rightarrow Ce^{3+}) \times 6$

$$CH_3OH \rightarrow CO_2$$
$$H_2O + CH_3OH \rightarrow CO_2 + 6\,H^+$$
$$H_2O + CH_3OH \rightarrow CO_2 + 6\,H^+ + 6\,e^-$$

$$6\,Ce^{4+} + 6\,e^- \rightarrow 6\,Ce^{3+}$$
$$H_2O + CH_3OH \rightarrow CO_2 + 6\,H^+ + 6\,e^-$$

$$H_2O(l) + CH_3OH(aq) + 6\,Ce^{4+}(aq) \rightarrow 6\,Ce^{3+}(aq) + CO_2(g) + 6\,H^+(aq)$$

d.

$$PO_3^{3-} \rightarrow PO_4^{3-}$$
$$(H_2O + PO_3^{3-} \rightarrow PO_4^{3-} + 2\,H^+ + 2\,e^-) \times 3$$

$$MnO_4^- \rightarrow MnO_2$$
$$(3\,e^- + 4\,H^+ + MnO_4^- \rightarrow MnO_2 + 2\,H_2O) \times 2$$

$$3\,H_2O + 3\,PO_3^{3-} \rightarrow 3\,PO_4^{3-} + 6\,H^+ + 6\,e^-$$
$$6\,e^- + 8\,H^+ + 2\,MnO_4^- \rightarrow 2\,MnO_2 + 4\,H_2O$$

$$2\,H^+ + 2\,MnO_4^- + 3\,PO_3^{3-} \rightarrow 3\,PO_4^{3-} + 2\,MnO_2 + H_2O$$

Now convert to a basic solution by adding 2 OH$^-$ to <u>both</u> sides. $2\,H^+ + 2\,OH^- \rightarrow 2\,H_2O$ on the reactant side. After converting H$^+$ to OH$^-$, simplify the overall equation by crossing off one H_2O on each side of the reaction. The overall balanced equation is:

$$H_2O(l) + 2\,MnO_4^-(aq) + 3\,PO_3^{3-}(aq) \rightarrow 3\,PO_4^{3-}(aq) + 2\,MnO_2(s) + 2\,OH^-(aq)$$

e.

$$Mg \rightarrow Mg(OH)_2$$
$$2\,H_2O + Mg \rightarrow Mg(OH)_2 + 2\,H^+ + 2\,e^-$$

$$OCl^- \rightarrow Cl^-$$
$$2\,e^- + 2\,H^+ + OCl^- \rightarrow Cl^- + H_2O$$

$$2\,H_2O + Mg \rightarrow Mg(OH)_2 + 2\,H^+ + 2\,e^-$$
$$2\,e^- + 2\,H^+ + OCl^- \rightarrow Cl^- + H_2O$$

$$OCl^-(aq) + H_2O(l) + Mg(s) \rightarrow Mg(OH)_2(s) + Cl^-(aq)$$

The final overall reaction does not contain H$^+$, so we are done.

f.

$$H_2CO \rightarrow HCO_3^-$$
$$2\,H_2O + H_2CO \rightarrow HCO_3^- + 5\,H^+ + 4\,e^-$$

$$Ag(NH_3)_2^+ \rightarrow Ag + 2\,NH_3$$
$$(e^- + Ag(NH_3)_2^+ \rightarrow Ag + 2\,NH_3) \times 4$$

$$2\,H_2O + H_2CO \rightarrow HCO_3^- + 5\,H^+ + 4\,e^-$$
$$4\,e^- + 4\,Ag(NH_3)_2^+ \rightarrow 4\,Ag + 8\,NH_3$$

$$4\,Ag(NH_3)_2^+ + 2\,H_2O + H_2CO \rightarrow HCO_3^- + 5\,H^+ + 4\,Ag + 8\,NH_3$$

Convert to a basic solution by adding 5 OH$^-$ to both sides (5 H$^+$ + 5 OH$^-$ → 5 H$_2$O). Then, cross off 2 H$_2$O on both sides, which gives the overall balanced equation:

$$5\,OH^-(aq) + 4\,Ag(NH_3)_2^+(aq) + H_2CO(aq) \rightarrow HCO_3^-(aq) + 3\,H_2O(l) + 4\,Ag(s) +$$

$$8\,NH_3(aq)$$

Questions

17.   Magnesium is an alkaline earth metal; Mg will oxidize to Mg^{2+}. The oxidation state of hydrogen in HCl is +1. To be reduced, the oxidation state of H must decrease. The obvious choice for the hydrogen product is $H_2(g)$ where hydrogen has a zero oxidation state. The balanced reaction is: $Mg(s) + 2HCl(aq) \rightarrow MgCl_2(aq) + H_2(g)$. Mg goes from the 0 to the +2 oxidation state by losing two electrons. Each H atom goes from the +1 to the 0 oxidation state by gaining one electron. Since there are two H atoms in the balanced equation, then a total of two electrons are gained by the H atoms. Hence, two electrons are transferred in the balanced reaction. When the electrons are transferred directly from Mg to H^+, no work is obtained. In order to harness this reaction to do useful work, we must control the flow of electrons through a wire. This is accomplished by making a galvanic cell which separates the reduction reaction from the oxidation reaction in order to control the flow of electrons through a wire to produce a voltage.

18.   Galvanic cells use spontaneous redox reactions to produce a voltage. The key is to have an overall positive E°_{cell} value when manipulating the half-reactions. For any two half-reactions, the half-reaction with the most positive reduction potential will always be the cathode reaction. For negative potentials, this will be the half-reaction with the standard reduction potential closest to zero. The remaining half-reaction (the one with the most negative E°_{red}) will be reversed and become the anode half-reaction ($E_{ox} = - E^\circ_{red}$). This combination will always yield a positive overall standard cell potential which can be used to run a galvanic cell.

19.   An extensive property is one that depends directly on the amount of substance. The free energy change for a reaction depends on whether 1 mol of product is produced or 2 mol of product is produced or 1 million mol of product is produced. This is not the case for cell potentials which do not depend on the amount of substance. The equation that relates ΔG to E is $\Delta G = -nFE$. It is the n term that converts the intensive property E into the extensive property ΔG. n is the number of moles of electrons transferred in the balanced reaction that ΔG is associated with.

20. $$E = E^\circ_{cell} - \frac{0.0591}{n} \log Q$$

A concentration cell has the same anode and cathode contents; thus, $E^\circ_{cell} = 0$ for a concentration cell. No matter which half-reaction you choose, the opposite half-reaction is occurring in the other cell. The driving force to produce a voltage is the $-\log Q$ term in the Nernst equation. Q is determined by the concentration of ions in the anode and cathode compartments. The larger the difference in concentrations, the larger the $-\log Q$ term and the larger the voltage produced. Therefore, the driving force for concentration cells is the difference in ion concentrations between the cathode and anode compartments. When the ion concentrations are equal, $Q = 1$ and $\log Q = 0$, and no voltage is produced.

21.   A potential hazard when jump starting a car is the possibility for the electrolysis of $H_2O(l)$ to occur. When $H_2O(l)$ is electrolyzed, the products are the explosive gas mixture of $H_2(g)$ and $O_2(g)$. A spark produced during jump starting a car could ignite any $H_2(g)$ and $O_2(g)$ produced. Grounding the jumper cable far from the battery minimizes the risk of a spark nearby the battery where $H_2(g)$ and $O_2(g)$ could be collecting.

22.   Metals corrode because they oxidize easily. Referencing Table 17.1, most metals are associated with negative standard reduction potentials. This means the reverse reactions, the oxidation half-reactions, have positive oxidation potentials indicating they oxidize fairly easily. Another key point is that the reduction of O_2 (which is a reactant in corrosion processes) has a more positive E^o_{red} than most of the metals (for O_2, $E^o_{red} = 0.40$ V). This means that when O_2 is coupled with most metals, the reaction will be spontaneous since $E^o_{cell} > 0$, so corrosion occurs.

The noble metals (Ag, Au, and Pt) all have standard reduction potentials greater than that of O_2. Therefore, O_2 is not capable of oxidizing these metals at standard conditions.

Note: the standard reduction potential for $Pt \rightarrow Pt^{2+} + 2 e^-$ is not in Table 17.1. As expected, its reduction potential is greater than that of O_2 ($E^o_{Pt} = 1.19$ V).

23.   You need to know the identity of the metal so you know which molar mass to use. You need to know the oxidation state of the metal ion in the salt so the mol of electrons transferred can be determined. And finally, you need to know the amount of current and the time the current was passed through the electrolytic cell. If you know these four quantities, then the mass of metal plated out can be calculated.

24.   Aluminum is found in nature as an oxide. Aluminum has a great affinity for oxygen so it is extremely difficult to reduce the Al^{3+} ions in the oxide to pure metal. One potential way is to try to dissolve the aluminum oxide in water in order to free up the ions. Even if aluminum ions would go into solution, water would be preferentially reduced in an electrolytic cell. Another way to mobilize the ions is to melt the aluminum oxide. This is not practical because of the very high melting point of aluminum oxide.

The key discovery was finding a solvent that would not be more easily reduced than Al^{3+} ions (as water is). The solvent discovered by Hall and Heroult (separately) was Na_3AlF_6. A mixture of Al_2O_3 and Na_3AlF_6 has a melting point much lower than that of pure Al_2O_3. Therefore, Al^{3+} ion mobility is easier to achieve, making it possible to reduce Al^{3+} to Al.

Exercises

Galvanic Cells, Cell Potentials, Standard Reduction Potentials, and Free Energy

25.   A typical galvanic cell diagram is:

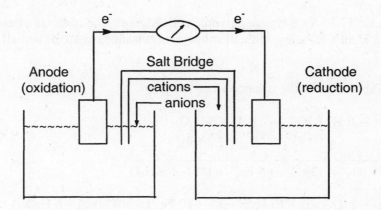

The diagram for all cells will look like this. The contents of each half-cell compartment will be identified for each reaction, with all solute concentrations at 1.0 M and all gases at 1.0 atm. For Exercises 17.25 and 17.26, the flow of ions through the salt bridge was not asked for in the questions.   If asked, however, cations always flow into the cathode compartment, and anions always flow into the anode compartment. This is required to keep each compartment electrically neutral.

a.   Table 17.1 of the text lists balanced reduction half-reactions for many substances. For this overall reaction, we need the Cl_2 to Cl^- reduction half-reaction and the Cr^{3+} to $Cr_2O_7^{2-}$ oxidation half-reaction. Manipulating these two half-reactions gives the overall balanced equation.

$$(Cl_2 + 2\ e^- \rightarrow 2\ Cl^-) \times 3$$
$$7\ H_2O + 2\ Cr^{3+} \rightarrow Cr_2O_7^{2-} + 14\ H^+ + 6\ e^-$$

$$7\ H_2O(l) + 2\ Cr^{3+}(aq) + 3\ Cl_2(g) \rightarrow Cr_2O_7^{2-}\ (aq) + 6\ Cl^-(aq) + 14\ H^+(aq)$$

The contents of each compartment are:

Cathode: Pt electrode; Cl_2 bubbled into solution, Cl^- in solution

Anode: Pt electrode; Cr^{3+}, H^+, and $Cr_2O_7^{2-}$ in solution

We need a nonreactive metal to use as the electrode in each case, since all the reactants and products are in solution. Pt is a common choice. Another possibility is graphite.

b. $Cu^{2+} + 2\,e^- \rightarrow Cu$

$Mg \rightarrow Mg^{2+} + 2e^-$

$Cu^{2+}(aq) + Mg(s) \rightarrow Cu(s) + Mg^{2+}(aq)$

Cathode: Cu electrode; Cu^{2+} in solution; Anode: Mg electrode; Mg^{2+} in solution

26.   Reference Exercise 17.25 for a typical galvanic cell diagram. The contents of each half-cell compartment are identified below with all solute concentrations at 1.0 M and all gases at 1.0 atm.

a.   Reference Table 17.1 for the balanced half-reactions.

$$5\,e^- + 6\,H^+ + IO_3^- \rightarrow 1/2\,I_2 + 3\,H_2O$$
$$(Fe^{2+} \rightarrow Fe^{3+} + e^-) \times 5$$

$$6\,H^+ + IO_3^- + 5\,Fe^{2+} \rightarrow 5\,Fe^{3+} + 1/2\,I_2 + 3\,H_2O$$

or $12\,H^+(aq) + 2\,IO_3^-(aq) + 10\,Fe^{2+}(aq) \rightarrow 10\,Fe^{3+}(aq) + I_2(aq) + 6\,H_2O(l)$

Cathode: Pt electrode; IO_3^-, I_2 and H_2SO_4 (H^+ source) in solution.

Note: $I_2(s)$ would make a poor electrode since it sublimes.

Anode: Pt electrode; Fe^{2+} and Fe^{3+} in solution

b. $(Ag^+ + e^- \rightarrow Ag) \times 2$

$Zn \rightarrow Zn^{2+} + 2\,e^-$

$Zn(s) + 2\,Ag^+(aq) \rightarrow 2\,Ag(s) + Zn^{2+}(aq)$

Cathode: Ag electrode; Ag^+ in solution; Anode: Zn electrode; Zn^{2+} in solution

27.   To determine E° for the overall cell reaction, we must add the standard reduction potential to the standard oxidation potential ($E^o_{cell} = E^o_{red} + E^o_{ox}$). Reference Table 17.1 for values of standard reduction potentials. Remember that $E^o_{ox} = -E^o_{red}$ and that standard potentials are not multiplied by the integer used to obtain the overall balanced equation.

25a. $E^o_{cell} = E^o_{Cl_2 \rightarrow Cl^-} + E^o_{Cr^{3+} \rightarrow Cr_2O_7^{2-}} = 1.36\ V + (-1.33\ V) = 0.03\ V$

25b. $E^o_{cell} = E^o_{Cu^{2+} \rightarrow Cu} + E^o_{Mg \rightarrow Mg^{2+}} = 0.34\ V + 2.37\ V = 2.71\ V$

28.   26a. $E^o_{cell} = E^o_{IO_3^- \rightarrow I_2} + E^o_{Fe^{2+} \rightarrow Fe^{3+}} = 1.20\ V + (-0.77\ V) = 0.43\ V$

26b. $E^o_{cell} = E^o_{Ag^+ \rightarrow Ag} + E^o_{Zn \rightarrow Zn^{2+}} = 0.80\ V + 0.76\ V = 1.56\ V$

29.   Reference Exercise 17.25 for a typical galvanic cell design. The contents of each half-cell compartment are identified below with all solute concentrations at 1.0 M and all gases at 1.0 atm. For each pair of half-reactions, the half-reaction with the largest (most positive) standard reduction potential will be the cathode reaction, and the half-reaction with the smallest (most negative) reduction potential will be reversed to become the anode reaction. Only this combination gives a spontaneous overall reaction, i.e., a reaction with a positive overall standard cell potential. Note that in a galvanic cell as illustrated in Exercise 17.25, the cations in the salt bridge migrate to the cathode, and the anions migrate to the anode.

a. $Cl_2 + 2 e^- \rightarrow 2 Cl^-$ $E° = 1.36$ V
            $2 Br^- \rightarrow Br_2 + 2 e^-$ $-E° = -1.09$ V

        _____

        $Cl_2(g) + 2 Br^-(aq) \rightarrow Br_2(aq) + 2 Cl^-(aq)$ $E°_{cell} = 0.27$ V

        The contents of each compartment are:

            Cathode: Pt electrode; $Cl_2(g)$ bubbled in, Cl^- in solution

            Anode: Pt electrode; Br_2 and Br^- in solution

b. $(2 e^- + 2 H^+ + IO_4^- \rightarrow IO_3^- + H_2O) \times 5$ $E° = 1.60$ V
                      $(4 H_2O + Mn^{2+} \rightarrow MnO_4^- + 8 H^+ + 5 e^-) \times 2$ $-E° = -1.51$ V

        _____

        $10 H^+ + 5 IO_4^- + 8 H_2O + 2 Mn^{2+} \rightarrow 5 IO_3^- + 5 H_2O + 2 MnO_4^- + 16 H^+$ $E°_{cell} = 0.09$ V

        This simplifies to:

            $H_2O(l) + 5 IO_4^-(aq) + 2 Mn^{2+}(aq) \rightarrow 5 IO_3^-(aq) + 2 MnO_4^-(aq) + 6 H^+(aq)$

                                                                              $E°_{cell} = 0.09$ V

        Cathode: Pt electrode; IO_4^-, IO_3^-, and H_2SO_4 (as a source of H^+) in solution

        Anode: Pt electrode; Mn^{2+}, MnO_4^- and H_2SO_4 in solution

30.   Reference Exercise 17.25 for a typical galvanic cell design. The contents of each half-cell compartment are identified below, with all solute concentrations at 1.0 M and all gases at 1.0 atm.

a. $H_2O_2 + 2 H^+ + 2 e^- \rightarrow 2 H_2O$ $E° = 1.78$ V
            $H_2O_2 \rightarrow O_2 + 2 H^+ + 2 e^-$ $-E° = -0.68$ V

        _____

            $2 H_2O_2(aq) \rightarrow 2 H_2O(l) + O_2(g)$ $E°_{cell} = 1.10$ V

        Cathode: Pt electrode; H_2O_2 and H^+ in solution

        Anode: Pt electrode; $O_2(g)$ bubbled in, H_2O_2 and H^+ in solution

b.

$$(Fe^{3+} + 3\,e^- \rightarrow Fe) \times 2 \qquad\qquad E° = -0.036\ V$$
$$(Mn \rightarrow Mn^{2+} + 2\,e^-) \times 3 \qquad -E° = \ \ 1.18\ V$$

$$2\ Fe^{3+}(aq) + 3\ Mn(s) \rightarrow 2\ Fe(s) + 3\ Mn^{2+}(aq) \qquad E°_{cell} = \ 1.14\ V$$

Cathode: Fe electrode; Fe^{3+} in solution; Anode: Mn electrode; Mn^{2+} in solution

31.   In standard line notation, the anode is listed first and the cathode is listed last. A double line separates the two compartments. By convention, the electrodes are on the ends with all solutes and gases towards the middle. A single line is used to indicate a phase change. We also included all concentrations.

25a. $Pt\,|\,Cr^{3+}\,(1.0\ M),\ Cr_2O_7^{2-}\,(1.0\ M),\ H^+\,(1.0\ M)\,\|\,Cl_2\,(1.0\ atm)\,|\,Cl^-\,(1.0\ M)\,|\,Pt$

25b. $Mg\,|\,Mg^{2+}\,(1.0\ M)\,\|\,Cu^{2+}\,(1.0\ M)\,|\,Cu$

29a. $Pt\,|\,Br^-\,(1.0\ M),\ Br_2\,(1.0\ M)\,\|\,Cl_2\,(1.0\ atm)\,|\,Cl^-\,(1.0\ M)\,|\,Pt$

29b. $Pt\,|\,Mn^{2+}\,(1.0\ M),\ MnO_4^-\,(1.0\ M),\ H^+\,(1.0\ M)\,\|\,IO_4^-\,(1.0\ M),\ H^+\,(1.0\ M),$
$$IO_3^-\,(1.0\ M)\,|\,Pt$$

32.   26a. $Pt\,|\,Fe^{2+}\,(1.0\ M),\ Fe^{3+}\,(1.0\ M)\,\|\,IO_3^-\,(1.0\ M),\ H^+\,(1.0\ M),\ I_2\,(1.0\ M)\,|\,Pt$

26b. $Zn\,|\,Zn^{2+}\,(1.0\ M)\,\|\,Ag^+\,(1.0\ M)\,|\,Ag$

30a. $Pt\,|\,H_2O_2\,(1.0\ M),\ H^+\,(1.0\ M)\,|\,O_2\,(1.0\ atm)\,\|\,H_2O_2\,(1.0\ M),\ H^+\,(1.0\ M)\,|\,Pt$

30b. $Mn\,|\,Mn^{2+}\,(1.0\ M)\,\|\,Fe^{3+}\,(1.0\ M)\,|\,Fe$

33.   Locate the pertinent half-reactions in Table 17.1, and then figure which combination will give a positive standard cell potential. In all cases, the anode compartment contains the species with the smallest standard reduction potential. For part a, the copper compartment is the anode, and in part b, the cadmium compartment is the anode.

a.

$$Au^{3+} + 3\,e^- \rightarrow Au \qquad\qquad\qquad E° = 1.50\ V$$
$$(Cu^+ \rightarrow Cu^{2+} + e^-) \times 3 \qquad -E° = -0.16\ V$$

$$Au^{3+}(aq) + 3\ Cu^+(aq) \rightarrow Au(s) + 3\ Cu^{2+}(aq) \qquad E°_{cell} = 1.34\ V$$

b.

$$(VO_2^+ + 2\,H^+ + e^- \rightarrow VO^{2+} + H_2O) \times 2 \qquad E° = 1.00\ V$$
$$Cd \rightarrow Cd^{2+} + 2e^- \qquad\qquad -E° = 0.40\ V$$

$$2\ VO_2^+(aq) + 4\ H^+(aq) + Cd(s) \rightarrow 2\ VO^{2+}(aq) + 2\ H_2O(l) + Cd^{2+}(aq) \quad E°_{cell} = 1.40\ V$$

34.   a.

$$(H_2O_2 + 2\,H^+ + 2\,e^- \rightarrow 2\ H_2O) \times 3 \qquad E° = 1.78\ V$$
$$2\ Cr^{3+} + 7\ H_2O \rightarrow Cr_2O_7^{2-} + 14\ H^+ + 6\,e^- \qquad -E° = -1.33\ V$$

$$3\ H_2O_2(aq) + 2\ Cr^{3+}(aq) + H_2O(l) \rightarrow Cr_2O_7^{2-}(aq) + 8\ H^+(aq) \qquad E°_{cell} = 0.45\ V$$

b. $(2 H^+ + 2 e^- \rightarrow H_2) \times 3$ $E° = 0.00$ V
      $(Al \rightarrow Al^{3+} + 3 e^-) \times 2$ $-E° = 1.66$ V

_____

$6 H^+(aq) + 2 Al(s) \rightarrow 3 H_2(g) + 2 Al^{3+}(aq)$ $E°_{cell} = 1.66$ V

35. a. $(5 e^- + 8 H^+ + MnO_4^- \rightarrow Mn^{2+} + 4 H_2O) \times 2$ $E° = 1.51$ V
           $(2 I^- \rightarrow I_2 + 2 e^-) \times 5$ $-E° = -0.54$ V

_____

$16 H^+(aq) + 2 MnO_4^-(aq) + 10 I^-(aq) \rightarrow 5 I_2(aq) + 2 Mn^{2+}(aq) + 8 H_2O(l)$ $E°_{cell} = 0.97$ V

This reaction is spontaneous at standard conditions because $E°_{cell} > 0$.

b. $(5 e^- + 8 H^+ + MnO_4^- \rightarrow Mn^{2+} + 4 H_2O) \times 2$ $E° = 1.51$ V
      $(2 F^- \rightarrow F_2 + 2 e^-) \times 5$ $-E° = -2.87$ V

_____

$16 H^+(aq) + 2 MnO_4^-(aq) + 10 F^-(aq) \rightarrow 5 F_2(aq) + 2 Mn^{2+}(aq) + 8 H_2O(l)$ $E°_{cell} = -1.36$ V

This reaction is not spontaneous at standard conditions because $E°_{cell} < 0$.

36. a. $H_2 \rightarrow 2H^+ + 2 e^-$ $E° = 0.00$ V
           $H_2 + 2 e^- \rightarrow 2H^-$ $-E° = -2.23$ V

_____

$2H_2(g) \rightarrow 2H^+(aq) + 2 H^-(aq)$ $E°_{cell} = -2.23$ V   Not spontaneous

b. $Au^{3+} + 3 e^- \rightarrow Au$ $E° = 1.50$ V
      $(Ag \rightarrow Ag^+ + e^-) \times 3$ $-E° = -0.80$ V

_____

$Au^{3+}(aq) + 3 Ag(s) \rightarrow Au(s) + 3 Ag^+(aq)$ $E°_{cell} = 0.70$ V

                                                                        Spontaneous

37. $Cl_2 + 2 e^- \rightarrow 2 Cl^-$ $E° = 1.36$ V
            $(ClO_2^- \rightarrow ClO_2 + e^-) \times 2$ $-E° = -0.954$ V

_____

$2 ClO_2^-(aq) + Cl_2(g) \rightarrow 2 ClO_2(aq) + 2 Cl^-(aq)$ $E°_{cell} = 0.41$ V $= 0.41$ J/C

$\Delta G° = -nFE°_{cell} = -(2$ mol $e^-)(96,485$ C/mol $e^-)(0.41$ J/C$) = -7.9 \times 10^4$ J $= -79$ kJ

38. a. $(4 H^+ + NO_3^- + 3 e^- \rightarrow NO + 2 H_2O) \times 2$ $E° = 0.96$ V
           $(Mn \rightarrow Mn^{2+} + 2 e^-) \times 3$ $-E° = 1.18$ V

_____

$3 Mn(s) + 8 H^+(aq) + 2 NO_3^-(aq) \rightarrow 2 NO(g) + 4 H_2O(l) + 3 Mn^{2+}(aq)$ $E°_{cell} = 2.14$ V

      $(2 e^- + 2 H^+ + IO_4^- \rightarrow IO_3^- + H_2O) \times 5$ $E° = 1.60$ V
      $(Mn^{2+} + 4 H_2O \rightarrow MnO_4^- + 8 H^+ + 5 e^-) \times 2$ $-E° = -1.51$ V

_____

$5 IO_4^-(aq) + 2 Mn^{2+}(aq) + 3 H_2O(l) \rightarrow 5 IO_3^-(aq) + 2 MnO_4^-(aq) + 6 H^+(aq)$ $E°_{cell} = 0.09$ V

b. Nitric acid oxidation (see above for E_{cell}^o):

$$\Delta G^o = -nFE_{cell}^o - (6 \text{ mol e}^-)(96,485 \text{ C/mol e}^-)(2.14 \text{ J/C}) = -1.24 \times 10^6 \text{ J} = -1240 \text{ kJ}$$

Periodate oxidation (see above for E_{cell}^o):

$$\Delta G^o = -(10 \text{ mol e}^-)(96,485 \text{ C/mol e}^-)(0.09 \text{ J/C})(1 \text{ kJ}/1000 \text{ J}) = -90 \text{ kJ}$$

39. Because the cells are at standard conditions, $w_{max} = \Delta G = \Delta G^o = -nFE_{cell}^o$. See Exercise 17.33 for the balanced overall equations and for E_{cell}^o.

33a. $w_{max} = -(3 \text{ mol e}^-)(96,485 \text{ C/mol e}^-)(1.34 \text{ J/C}) = -3.88 \times 10^5 \text{ J} = -388 \text{ kJ}$

33b. $w_{max} = -(2 \text{ mol e}^-)(96,485 \text{ C/mol e}^-)(1.40 \text{ J/C}) = -2.70 \times 10^5 \text{ J} = -270. \text{ kJ}$

40. Because the cells are at standard conditions, $w_{max} = \Delta G = \Delta G^o = -nFE_{cell}^o$. See Exercise 17.34 for the balanced overall equations and for E_{cell}^o.

34a. $w_{max} = -(6 \text{ mol e}^-)(96,485 \text{ C/mol e}^-)(0.45 \text{ J/C}) = -2.6 \times 10^5 \text{ J} = -260 \text{ kJ}$

34b. $w_{max} = -(6 \text{ mol e}^-)(96,485 \text{ C/mol e}^-)(1.66 \text{ J/C}) = -9.61 \times 10^5 \text{ J} = -961 \text{ kJ}$

41. $CH_3OH(l) + 3/2 \, O_2(g) \rightarrow CO_2(g) + 2 \, H_2O(l)$ $\Delta G^o = 2(-237) + (-394) - [-166] = -702 \text{ kJ}$

The balanced half-reactions are:

$$H_2O + CH_3OH \rightarrow CO_2 + 6 \, H^+ + 6 \, e^- \text{ and } O_2 + 4 \, H^+ + 4 \, e^- \rightarrow 2 \, H_2O$$

For 3/2 mol O_2, 6 moles of electrons will be transferred (n = 6).

$$\Delta G^o = -nFE^o, \ E^o = \frac{-\Delta G^o}{nF} = \frac{-(-702,000 \text{ J})}{(6 \text{ mole e}^-)(96,485 \text{ C}/\text{mol e}^-)} = 1.21 \text{ J/C} = 1.21 \text{ V}$$

42. $Fe^{2+} + 2 \, e^- \rightarrow Fe$ $E^o = -0.44 \text{ V} = -0.44 \text{ J/C}$

$$\Delta G^o = -nFE^o = -(2 \text{ mol e}^-)(96,485 \text{ C/mol e}^-)(-0.44 \text{ J/C})(1 \text{ kJ}/1000 \text{ J}) = 85 \text{ kJ}$$

$85 \text{ kJ} = 0 - [\Delta G_{f, Fe^{2+}}^o + 0]$, $\Delta G_{f, Fe^{2+}}^o = -85 \text{ kJ}$

We can get $\Delta G_{f, Fe^{3+}}^o$ two ways. Consider: $Fe^{3+} + e^- \rightarrow Fe^{2+}$ $E^o = 0.77 \text{ V}$

$$\Delta G^o = -(1 \text{ mol e})(96,485 \text{ C/mol e}^-)(0.77 \text{ J/C}) = -74,300 \text{ J} = -74 \text{ kJ}$$

$Fe^{2+} \rightarrow Fe^{3+} + e^-$ $\Delta G^o = 74 \text{ kJ}$
$Fe \rightarrow Fe^{2+} + 2 \, e^-$ $\Delta G^o = -85 \text{ kJ}$

$Fe \rightarrow Fe^{3+} + 3 \, e^-$ $\Delta G^o = -11 \text{ kJ}$, $\Delta G_{f, Fe^{3+}}^o = -11 \text{ kJ/mol}$

or consider: $Fe^{3+} + 3\,e^- \rightarrow Fe$ $E° = -0.036$ V

$\Delta G° = -(3 \text{ mol } e^-)(96,485 \text{ C/mol } e^-)(-0.036 \text{ J/C}) = 10,400 \text{ J} \approx 10. \text{ kJ}$

$10. \text{ kJ} = 0 - [\Delta G°_{f,Fe^{3+}} + 0]$, $\Delta G°_{f,Fe^{3+}} = -10. \text{ kJ/mol}$; Round-off error explains the 1 kJ

discrepancy.

43.   Good oxidizing agents are easily reduced. Oxidizing agents are on the left side of the reduction half-reactions listed in Table 17.1. We look for the largest, most positive standard reduction potentials to correspond to the best oxidizing agents. The ordering from worst to best oxidizing agents is:

	K^+	<	H_2O	<	Cd^{2+}	<	I_2	<	$AuCl_4^-$	<	IO_3^-
$E°(V)$	-2.87		-0.83		-0.40		0.54		0.99		1.20

44.   Good reducing agents are easily oxidized. The reducing agents are on the right side of the reduction half-reactions listed in Table 17.1. The best reducing agents have the most negative standard reduction potentials ($E°$) or the most positive standard oxidation potentials, $E°_{ox}$ ($= -E°$). The ordering from worst to best reducing agents is:

	F^-	<	H_2O	<	I_2	<	Cu^+	<	H^-	<	K
$-E°(V)$	-2.92		-1.23		-1.20		-0.16		2.23		2.92

45.   a. $2\,H^+ + 2\,e^- \rightarrow H_2$ $E° = 0.00$ V; $Cu \rightarrow Cu^{2+} + 2\,e^-$ $-E° = -0.34$ V

$E°_{cell} = -0.34$ V; No, H^+ cannot oxidize Cu to Cu^{2+} at standard conditions ($E°_{cell} < 0$).

b. $Fe^{3+} + e^- \rightarrow Fe^{2+}$ $E° = 0.77$ V; $2\,I^- \rightarrow I_2 + 2\,e^-$ $-E° = -0.54$ V

$E°_{cell} = 0.77 - 0.54 = 0.23$ V; Yes, Fe^{3+} can oxidize I^- to I_2.

c. $H_2 \rightarrow 2\,H^+ + 2\,e^-$ $-E° = 0.00$ V; $Ag^+ + e^- \rightarrow Ag$ $E° = 0.80$ V

$E°_{cell} = 0.80$ V; Yes, H_2 can reduce Ag^+ to Ag at standard conditions ($E°_{cell} > 0$).

d. $Fe^{2+} \rightarrow Fe^{3+} + e^-$ $-E° = -0.77$ V; $Cr^{3+} + e^- \rightarrow Cr^{2+}$ $E° = -0.50$ V

$E°_{cell} = -0.50 - 0.77 = -1.27$ V; No, Fe^{2+} cannot reduce Cr^{3+} to Cr^{2+} at standard conditions.

46. $Cl_2 + 2\,e^- \rightarrow 2\,Cl^-$ $E° = 1.36$ V $Ag^+ + e^- \rightarrow Ag$ $E° = 0.80$ V

$Pb^{2+} + 2\,e^- \rightarrow Pb$ $E° = -0.13$ V $Zn^{2+} + 2\,e^- \rightarrow Zn$ $E° = -0.76$ V

$Na^+ + e^- \rightarrow Na$ $E° = -2.71$ V

a.   Oxidizing agents (species reduced) are on the left side of the above reduction half-reactions. Of the species available, Ag^+ would be the best oxidizing agent since it has the largest $E°$ value. Note that Cl_2 is a better oxidizing agent than Ag^+, but it is not one of the choices listed.

b.   Reducing agents (species oxidized) are on the right side of the reduction half-reactions. Of the species available, Zn would be the best reducing agent since it has the largest $-E°$ value.

c. $SO_4^{2-} + 4 H^+ + 2 e^- \rightarrow H_2SO_3 + H_2O$ $E° = 0.20$ V; SO_4^{2-} can oxidize Pb and Zn at standard conditions. When SO_4^{2-} is coupled with these reagents, $E_{cell}^°$ is positive.

d. $Al \rightarrow Al^{3+} + 3 e^-$ $-E° = 1.66$ V; Al can reduce Ag^+ and Zn^{2+} at standard conditions since $E_{cell}^° > 0$.

47.   a. $2 Br^- \rightarrow Br_2 + 2 e^-$ $-E° = -1.09$ V; $2 Cl^- \rightarrow Cl_2 + 2 e^-$ $-E° = -1.36$ V; $E° > 1.09$ V to oxidize Br^-; $E° < 1.36$ V to not oxidize Cl^-; $Cr_2O_7^{2-}$, O_2, MnO_2, and IO_3^- are all possible since when all of these oxidizing agents are coupled with Br^-, $E_{cell}^° > 0$, and when coupled with Cl^-, $E_{cell}^° < 0$ (assuming standard conditions).

b. $Mn \rightarrow Mn^{2+} + 2 e^-$ $-E° = 1.18$; $Ni \rightarrow Ni^{2+} + 2 e^-$ $-E° = 0.23$ V; Any oxidizing agent with -0.23 V $> E° > -1.18$ V will work. $PbSO_4$, Cd^{2+}, Fe^{2+}, Cr^{3+}, Zn^{2+} and H_2O will be able to oxidize Mn but not Ni (assuming standard conditions).

48.   a. $Cu^{2+} + 2 e^- \rightarrow Cu$ $E° = 0.34$ V; $Cu^{2+} + e^- \rightarrow Cu^+$ $E° = 0.16$ V;   To reduce Cu^{2+} to Cu but not reduce Cu^{2+} to Cu^+, the reducing agent must have a standard oxidation potential $E_{ox}^° = -E°$) between -0.34 V and -0.16 V (so $E_{cell}^°$ is positive only for the Cu^{2+} to Cu reduction). The reducing agents (species oxidized) are on the right side of the half-reactions in Table 17.1. The reagents at standard conditions which have $E_{ox}^°$ (=$-E°$) between -0.34 V and -0.16 V are Ag (in 1.0 M Cl^-) and H_2SO_3.

b. $Br_2 + 2 e^- \rightarrow 2 Br^-$ $E° = 1.09$ V; $I_2 + 2 e^- \rightarrow 2 I^-$ $E° = 0.54$ V; From Table 17.1, VO^{2+}, Au (in 1.0 M Cl^-), NO, ClO_2^-, Hg_2^{2+}, Ag, Hg, Fe^{2+}, H_2O_2 and MnO_4^- are all capable at standard conditions of reducing Br_2 to Br^- but not reducing I_2 to I^-. When these reagents are coupled with Br_2, $E_{cell}^° > 0$, and when coupled with I_2, $E_{cell}^° < 0$.

49. $ClO^- + H_2O + 2 e^- \rightarrow 2 OH^- + Cl^-$ $E° = 0.90$ V
           $2 NH_3 + 2 OH^- \rightarrow N_2H_4 + 2 H_2O + 2 e^-$ $-E° = 0.10$ V
           _____

           $ClO^-(aq) + 2 NH_3(aq) \rightarrow Cl^-(aq) + N_2H_4(aq) + H_2O(l)$ $E_{cell}^° = 1.00$ V

Because $E_{cell}^°$ is positive for this reaction, at standard conditions ClO^- can spontaneously oxidize NH_3 to the somewhat toxic N_2H_4.

50. $Tl^{3+} + 2 e^- \rightarrow Tl^+$ $E° = 1.25$ V
               $3 I^- \rightarrow I_3^- + 2 e^-$ $-E° = -0.55$ V
           _____

           $Tl^{3+} + 3 I^- \rightarrow Tl^+ + I_3^-$ $E_{cell}^° = 0.70$ V

In solution, Tl^{3+} can oxidize I^- to I_3^-. Thus, we expect TlI_3 to be thallium(I) triiodide.

The Nernst Equation

51.
$$H_2O_2 + 2\ H^+ + 2\ e^- \rightarrow 2\ H_2O \qquad\qquad E^\circ = 1.78\ V$$
$$(Ag \rightarrow Ag^+ + e^-) \times 2 \qquad\qquad -E^\circ = -0.80\ V$$

$$H_2O_2(aq) + 2\ H^+(aq) + 2\ Ag(s) \rightarrow 2\ H_2O(l) + 2\ Ag^+(aq) \qquad E^\circ_{cell} = 0.98\ V$$

a. A galvanic cell is based on spontaneous redox reactions. At standard conditions, this reaction produces a voltage of 0.98 V. Any change in concentration that increases the tendency of the forward reaction to occur will increase the cell potential. Conversely, any change in concentration that decreases the tendency of the forward reaction to occur (increases the tendency of the reverse reaction to occur) will decrease the cell potential. Using Le Chatelier's principle, increasing the reactant concentrations of H_2O_2 and H^+ from 1.0 M to 2.0 M will drive the forward reaction further to right (will further increase the tendency of the forward reaction to occur). Therefore, E_{cell} will be greater than E°_{cell}.

b. Here, we decreased the reactant concentration of H^+ and increased the product concentration of Ag^+ from the standard conditions. This decreases the tendency of the forward reaction to occur which will decrease E_{cell} as compared to E°_{cell} ($E_{cell} < E^\circ_{cell}$).

52. The concentrations of Fe^{2+} in the two compartments are now 0.01 M and 1×10^{-7} M. The driving force for this reaction is to equalize the Fe^{2+} concentrations in the two compartments. This occurs if the compartment with 1×10^{-7} M Fe^{2+} becomes the anode (Fe will be oxidized to Fe^{2+}) and the compartment with the 0.01 M Fe^{2+} becomes the cathode (Fe^{2+} will be reduced to Fe). Electron flow, as always for galvanic cells, goes from the anode to the cathode, so electron flow will go from the right compartment ($[Fe^{2+}] = 1 \times 10^{-7} M$) to the left compartment ($[Fe^{2+}] = 0.01\ M$).

53. For concentration cells, the driving force for the reaction is the difference in ion concentrations between the anode and cathode. In order to equalize the ion concentrations, the anode always has the smaller ion concentration. The general setup for this concentration cell is:

Cathode: $Ag^+(x\ M) + e^- \rightarrow Ag$ $\qquad\qquad E^\circ = 0.80\ V$
Anode: $Ag \rightarrow Ag^+ (y\ M) + e^-$ $\qquad\qquad -E^\circ = -0.80\ V$

$$Ag^+(\text{cathode},\ x\ M) \rightarrow Ag^+\ (\text{anode},\ y\ M) \qquad E^\circ_{cell} = 0.00\ V$$

$$E_{cell} = E^\circ_{cell} - \frac{0.0591}{n} \log Q = \frac{-0.0591}{1} \log \frac{[Ag^+]_{anode}}{[Ag^+]_{cathode}}$$

For each concentration cell, we will calculate the cell potential using the above equation. Remember that the anode always has the smaller ion concentration.

a. Both compartments are at standard conditions ($[Ag^+] = 1.0\ M$), so $E_{cell} = E^\circ_{cell} = 0$ V. No voltage is produced since no reaction occurs. Concentration cells only produce a voltage when the ion concentrations are not equal.

b. Cathode = 2.0 M Ag^+; Anode = 1.0 M Ag^+; Electron flow is always from the anode to the cathode, so electrons flow to the right in the diagram.

$$E_{cell} = \frac{-0.0591}{n} \log \frac{[Ag^+]_{anode}}{[Ag^+]_{cathode}} = \frac{-0.0591}{1} \log \frac{1.0}{2.0} = 0.018 \text{ V}$$

c. Cathode = 1.0 M Ag^+; Anode = 0.10 M Ag^+; Electrons flow to the left in the diagram.

$$E_{cell} = \frac{-0.0591}{n} \log \frac{[Ag^+]_{anode}}{[Ag^+]_{cathode}} = \frac{-0.0591}{1} \log \frac{0.10}{1.0} = 0.059 \text{ V}$$

d. Cathode = 1.0 M Ag^+; Anode = 4.0×10^{-5} M Ag^+; Electrons flow to the left in the diagram.

$$E_{cell} = \frac{-0.0591}{n} \log \frac{4.0 \times 10^{-5}}{1.0} = 0.26 \text{ V}$$

e. The ion concentrations are the same, thus $\log ([Ag^+]_{anode}/[Ag^+]_{cathode}) = \log (1.0) = 0$ and $E_{cell} = 0$. No electron flow occurs.

54.   As is the case for all concentration cells, $E^\circ_{cell} = 0$, and the smaller ion concentration is always in the anode compartment. The general Nernst equation for the Ni | $Ni^{2+}(x\ M)$ || $Ni^{2+}(y\ M)$ | Ni concentration cell is:

$$E_{cell} = E^\circ_{cell} - \frac{0.0591}{n} \log Q = \frac{-0.0591}{2} \log \frac{[Ni^{2+}]_{anode}}{[Ni^{2+}]_{cathode}}$$

a. Both compartments are at standard conditions ($[Ni^{2+}] = 1.0$ M), and $E_{cell} = E^\circ_{cell} = 0$ V. No electron flow occurs.

b. Cathode = 2.0 M Ni^{2+}; Anode = 1.0 M Ni^{2+}; Electron flow is always from the anode to the cathode, so electrons flow to the right in the diagram.

$$E_{cell} = \frac{-0.0591}{2} \log \frac{[Ni^{2+}]_{anode}}{[Ni^{2+}]_{cathode}} = \frac{-0.0591}{2} \log \frac{1.0}{2.0} = 8.9 \times 10^{-3} \text{ V}$$

c. Cathode = 1.0 M Ni^{2+}; Anode = 0.10 M Ni^{2+}; Electrons flow to the left in the diagram.

$$E_{cell} = \frac{-0.0591}{2} \log \frac{0.10}{1.0} = 0.030 \text{ V}$$

d. Cathode = 1.0 M Ni^{2+}; Anode = 4.0×10^{-5} M Ni^{2+}; Electrons flow to the left in the diagram.

$$E_{cell} = \frac{-0.0591}{2} \log \frac{4.0 \times 10^{-5}}{1.0} = 0.13 \text{ V}$$

e.   Because both concentrations are equal, log (2.5/2.5) = log 1.0 = 0 and E_{cell} = 0.   No electron flow occurs.

55.   n = 2 for this reaction (lead goes from Pb → Pb^{2+} in $PbSO_4$).

$$E = E° - \frac{-0.0591}{2}\log \frac{1}{[H^+]^2[HSO_4^-]^2} = 2.04\text{ V} - \frac{-0.0591}{2}\log \frac{1}{(4.5)^2(4.5)^2}$$

E = 2.04 V + 0.077 V = 2.12 V

56. $Cr_2O_7^{2-} + 14\,H^+ + 6\,e^- \rightarrow 2\,Cr^{3+} + 7\,H_2O$ E° = 1.33 V
         $(Al \rightarrow Al^{3+} + 3\,e^-) \times 2$ −E° = 1.66

$Cr_2O_7^{2-} + 14\,H^+ + 2\,Al \rightarrow 2\,Al^{3+} + 2\,Cr^{3+} + 7\,H_2O$ $E°_{cell}$ = 2.99 V

$$E = E° - \frac{0.0591}{n}\log Q, \quad E = 2.99\text{ V} - \frac{0.0591}{6}\log \frac{[Al^{3+}]^2[Cr^{3+}]^2}{[Cr_2O_7^{2-}][H^+]^{14}}$$

$$3.01 = 2.99 - \frac{0.0591}{n}\log Q \frac{(0.30)^2(0.15)^2}{(0.55)[H^+]^{14}}, \quad \frac{-6(0.02)}{0.0591} = \log\left(\frac{3.7\times10^{-3}}{[H^+]^{14}}\right)$$

$$\frac{3.7\times10^{-3}}{[H^+]^{14}} = 10^{-2.0} = 0.01, \quad [H^+]^{14} = 0.37, \quad [H^+] = 0.93 = 0.9\ M, \quad \text{pH} = -\log(0.9) = 0.05$$

57. $Cu^{2+} + 2\,e^- \rightarrow Cu$ E° = 0.34 V
         $Zn \rightarrow Zn^{2+} + 2\,e^-$ −E° = 0.76 V

$Cu^{2+}(aq) + Zn(s) \rightarrow Zn^{2+}(aq) + Cu(s)$ $E°_{cell}$ = 1.10 V

Because Zn^{2+} is a product in the reaction, the Zn^{2+} concentration increases from 1.00 M to 1.20 M.   This means that the reactant concentration of Cu^{2+} must decrease from 1.00 M to 0.80 M (from the 1:1 mol ratio in the balanced reaction).

$$E_{cell} = E°_{cell} - \frac{0.0591}{n}\log Q = 1.10\text{ V} - \frac{0.0591}{2}\log \frac{[Zn^{2+}]}{[Cu^{2+}]}$$

$$E_{cell} = 1.10\text{ V} - \frac{0.0591}{2}\log \frac{1.20}{0.80} = 1.10\text{ V} - 0.0052\text{ V} = 1.09\text{ V}$$

58. $(Pb^{2+} + 2\,e^- \rightarrow Pb) \times 3$ E° = −0.13 V
         $(Al \rightarrow Al^{3+} + 3\,e^-) \times 2$ −E° = 1.66 V

$3\,Pb^{2+}(aq) + 2\,Al(s) \rightarrow 3\,Pb(s) + 2\,Al^{3+}(aq)$ $E°_{cell}$ = 1.53 V

From the balanced reaction, when the Al^{3+} has increased by 0.60 mol/L (Al^{3+} is a product in the spontaneous reaction), then the Pb^{2+} concentration has decreased by 3/2 (0.60 mol/L) = 0.90 M.

$$E_{cell} = 1.53 \text{ V} - \frac{0.0591}{6} \log \frac{[Al^{3+}]^2}{[Pb^{2+}]^3} = 1.53 - \frac{0.0591}{6} \log \frac{(1.60)^2}{(0.10)^3}$$

$$E_{cell} = 1.53 \text{ V} - 0.034 \text{ V} = 1.50 \text{ V}$$

59. $Cu^{2+}(aq) + H_2(g) \rightarrow 2 H^+(aq) + Cu(s)$ $E^o_{cell} = 0.34 \text{ V} - 0.00 \text{ V} = 0.34 \text{ V}$; n = 2 mol electrons

$$P_{H_2} = 1.0 \text{ atm and } [H^+] = 1.0 \ M: \ E_{cell} = E^o_{cell} - \frac{0.0591}{n} \log \frac{1}{[Cu^{2+}]}$$

a. $E_{cell} = 0.34 \text{ V} - \dfrac{0.0591}{2} \log \dfrac{1}{2.5 \times 10^{-4}} = 0.34 \text{ V} - 0.11 \text{V} = 0.23 \text{ V}$

b. $0.195 \text{ V} = 0.34 \text{ V} - \dfrac{0.0591}{2} \log \dfrac{1}{[Cu^{2+}]}$, $\log \dfrac{1}{[Cu^{2+}]} = 4.91$, $[Cu^{2+}] = 10^{-4.91}$

$$= 1.2 \times 10^{-5} \ M$$

Note: When determining exponents, we will carry extra significant figures.

60. $3 Ni^{2+}(aq) + 2 Al(s) \rightarrow 2 Al^{3+}(aq) + 3 Ni(s)$ $E^o_{cell} = -0.23 + 1.66 = 1.43 \text{ V}$;
n = 6 mol electrons for this reaction.

a. $E_{cell} = 1.43 \text{ V} - \dfrac{0.0591}{6} \log \dfrac{[Al^{3+}]^2}{[Ni^{2+}]^3} = 1.43 - \dfrac{0.0591}{6} \log \dfrac{(7.2 \times 10^{-3})^2}{(1.0)^3}$

$$E_{cell} = 1.43 \text{ V} - (-0.042 \text{ V}) = 1.47 \text{ V}$$

b. $1.62 \text{ V} = 1.43 \text{ V} - \dfrac{0.0591}{6} \log \dfrac{[Al^{3+}]^2}{(1.0)^3}$, $\log [Al^{3+}]^2 = -19.29$

$$[Al^{3+}]^2 = 10^{-19.29}, \ [Al^{3+}] = 2.3 \times 10^{-10} \ M$$

61. $Cu^{2+}(aq) + H_2(g) \rightarrow 2 H^+(aq) + Cu(s)$ $E^o_{cell} = 0.34 \text{ V} - 0.00 \text{ V} = 0.34 \text{ V}$; n = 2

$$P_{H_2} = 1.0 \text{ atm and } [H^+] = 1.0 \ M: \ E_{cell} = E^o_{cell} - \frac{0.0591}{2} \log \frac{1}{[Cu^{2+}]}$$

Use the K_{sp} expression to calculate the Cu^{2+} concentration in the cell.

$Cu(OH)_2(s) \rightleftharpoons Cu^{2+}(aq) + 2 OH^-(aq)$ $K_{sp} = 1.6 \times 10^{-19} = [Cu^{2+}][OH^-]^2$

From problem, $[OH^-] = 0.10 \ M$, so: $[Cu^{2+}] = \dfrac{1.6 \times 10^{-19}}{(0.10)^2} = 1.6 \times 10^{-17} \ M$

$$E_{cell} = E^o_{cell} - \frac{0.0591}{2} \log \frac{1}{[Cu^{2+}]} = 0.34 \text{ V} - \frac{0.0591}{2} \log \frac{1}{1.6 \times 10^{-17}} = 0.34 - 0.50 = -0.16 \text{ V}$$

Because $E_{cell} < 0$, the forward reaction is not spontaneous, but the reverse reaction is spontaneous. The Cu electrode becomes the anode and $E_{cell} = 0.16$ V for the reverse reaction. The cell reaction is: $2 H^+(aq) + Cu(s) \rightarrow Cu^{2+}(aq) + H_2(g)$.

62. $3 Ni^{2+}(aq) + 2 Al(s) \rightarrow 2 Al^{3+}(aq) + 3 Ni(s)$ $E^\circ_{cell} = -0.23$ V $+ 1.66$ V $= 1.43$ V; n $= 6$

$$E_{cell} = E^\circ_{cell} - \frac{0.0591}{n} \log \frac{[Al^{3+}]^2}{[Ni^{2+}]^3}, \quad 1.82 \text{ V} = 1.43 \text{ V} - \frac{0.0591}{6} \log \frac{[Al^{3+}]^2}{(1.0)^3}$$

$$\log [Al^{3+}]^2 = -39.59, \quad [Al^{3+}]^2 = 10^{-39.59}, \quad [Al^{3+}] = 1.6 \times 10^{-20} M$$

$Al(OH)_3(s) \rightleftharpoons Al^{3+}(aq) + 3 OH^-(aq)$ $K_{sp} = [Al^{3+}] [OH^-]^3$; From the problem, $[OH^-]$ $= 1.0 \times 10^{-4} M$.

$$K_{sp} = (1.6 \times 10^{-20}) (1.0 \times 10^{-4})^3 = 1.6 \times 10^{-32}$$

63.   Cathode: $M^{2+} + 2e^- \rightarrow M(s)$ $E^\circ = -0.31$ V
        Anode: $M(s) \rightarrow M^{2+} + 2e^-$ $-E^\circ = 0.31$ V
        _____

                M^{2+} (cathode) $\rightarrow M^{2+}$ (anode) $E^\circ_{cell} = 0.00$ V

$$E_{cell} = 0.44 \text{ V} = 0.00 \text{ V} - \frac{0.0591}{2} \log \frac{[M^{2+}]_{anode}}{[M^{2+}]_{cathode}}, \quad 0.44 = -\frac{0.0591}{2} \log \frac{[M^{2+}]_{anode}}{1.0}$$

$$\log [M^{2+}]_{anode} = -\frac{2(0.44)}{0.0591} = -14.89, \quad [M^{2+}]_{anode} = 1.3 \times 10^{-15} M$$

Because we started with equal numbers of moles of SO_4^{2-} and M^{2+}, $[M^{2+}] = [SO_4^{2-}]$ at equilibrium.

$$K_{sp} = [M^{2+}][SO_4^{2-}] = (1.3 \times 10^{-15})^2 = 1.7 \times 10^{-30}$$

64.   a. Ag^+ (x M, anode) $\rightarrow Ag^+$ (0.10 M, cathode); For the silver concentration cell, $E^\circ = 0.00$ (as is always the case for concentration cells) and n $= 1$.

$$E = 0.76 \text{ V} = 0.00 - \frac{0.0591}{1} \log \frac{[Ag^+]_{anode}}{[Ag^+]_{cathode}}$$

$$0.76 = -0.0591 \log \frac{[Ag^+]_{anode}}{0.10}, \quad \frac{[Ag^+]_{anode}}{0.10} = 10^{-12.86}, \quad [Ag^+]_{anode} = 1.4 \times 10^{-14} M$$

        b. $Ag^+(aq) + 2 S_2O_3^{2-}(aq) \rightleftharpoons Ag(S_2O_3)_2^{3-}(aq)$

$$K = \frac{[Ag(S_2O_3)_2^{3-}]}{[Ag^+][S_2O_3^{2-}]^2} = \frac{1.0 \times 10^{-3}}{1.4 \times 10^{-14} (0.050)^2} = 2.9 \times 10^{13}$$

65.   See Exercises 17.25, 17.27, and 17.29 for balanced reactions and standard cell potentials. Balanced reactions are necessary to determine n, the moles of electrons transferred.

25a. $7\ H_2O + 2\ Cr^{3+} + 3\ Cl_2 \rightarrow Cr_2O_7^{2-} + 6\ Cl^- + 14\ H^+$ $E^o_{cell} = 0.03\ V = 0.03\ J/C$

$\Delta G^o = -nFE^o_{cell} = -(6\ mol\ e^-)(96{,}485\ C/mol\ e^-)(0.03\ J/C) = -1.7 \times 10^4\ J = -20\ kJ$

$E_{cell} = E^o_{cell} - \dfrac{0.0591}{n}\ \log Q$: At equilibrium, $E_{cell} = 0$ and $Q = K$, so:

$E^o_{cell} = \dfrac{0.0591}{n}\ \log K,\ \ \log K = \dfrac{nE^o}{0.0591} = \dfrac{6(0.03)}{0.0591} = 3.05,\ \ K = 10^{3.05} = 1 \times 10^3$

Note: When determining exponents, we will round off to the correct number of significant figures after the calculation is complete in order to help eliminate excessive round-off error.

25b. $\Delta G^o = -(2\ mol\ e^-)(96{,}485\ C/mol\ e^-)(2.71\ J/C) = -5.23 \times 10^5\ J = -523\ kJ$

$\log K = \dfrac{2(2.71)}{0.0591} = 91.709,\ \ K = 5.12 \times 10^{91}$

29a. $\Delta G^o = -(2\ mol\ e^-)(96{,}485\ C/mol^-)(0.27\ J/C) = -5.21 \times 10^4\ J = -52\ kJ$

$\log K = \dfrac{2(0.27)}{0.0591} = 9.14,\ \ K = 1.4 \times 10^9$

29b. $\Delta G^o = -(10\ mol\ e^-)(96{,}485\ C/mol\ e^-)(0.09\ J/C) = -8.7 \times 10^4\ J = -90\ kJ$

$\log K = \dfrac{10(0.09)}{0.0591} = 15.23,\ \ K = 2 \times 10^{15}$

66. $\Delta G^o = -nFE^o_{cell};\ \ E^o_{cell} = \dfrac{0.0591}{n}\ \log K,\ \ \log K = \dfrac{nE^o}{0.0591}$

26a. $\Delta G^o = -(10\ mol\ e^-)(96{,}485\ C/mol\ e^-)(0.43\ J/C) = -4.1 \times 10^5\ J = -410\ kJ$

$\log K = \dfrac{10(0.43)}{0.0591} = 72.76,\ \ K = 10^{72.76} = 5.8 \times 10^{72}$

26b. $\Delta G^o = -(2\ mol\ e^-)(96{,}485\ C/mol\ e^-)(1.56\ J/C) = -3.01 \times 10^5\ J = -301\ kJ$

$\log K = \dfrac{2(1.56)}{0.0591} = 52.792,\ \ K = 6.19 \times 10^{52}$

30a. $\Delta G^\circ = -(2 \text{ mol}^-)(96,485 \text{ C/mol e}^-)(1.10 \text{ J/C}) = -2.12 \times 10^5 \text{ J} = -212 \text{ kJ}$

$$\log K = \frac{2(1.10)}{0.0591} = 37.225, \ K = 1.68 \times 10^{37}$$

30b. $\Delta G^\circ = -(6 \text{ mol e}^-)(96,485 \text{ C/mol e}^-)(1.14 \text{ J/C}) = -6.60 \times 10^5 \text{ J} = -660. \text{ kJ}$

$$\log K = \frac{6(1.14)}{0.0591} = 115.736, \ K = 5.45 \times 10^{115}$$

67. $Cu^{2+} + 2 e^- \rightarrow Cu$ $E^\circ = 0.34 \text{ V}$

       $Fe \rightarrow Fe^{2+} + 2 e^-$ $-E^\circ = 0.44 \text{ V}$

    $Fe + Cu^{2+} \rightarrow Cu + Fe^{2+}$ $E^\circ_{cell} = 0.78 \text{ V}$

For this reaction, $K = \dfrac{[Fe^{2+}]}{[Cu^{2+}]}$, so let's solve for K to determine the equilibrium ion ratio.

$$E^\circ = \frac{0.0591}{n} \log K, \ \log K = \frac{2(0.78)}{0.0591} = 26.40, \ K = \frac{[Fe^{2+}]}{[Cu^{2+}]} = 10^{26.40} = 2.5 \times 10^{26}$$

68. $Ni^{2+} + 2 e^- \rightarrow Ni$ $E^\circ = -0.23 \text{ V}$

       $Sn \rightarrow Sn^{2+} + 2 e^-$ $-E^\circ = 0.14 \text{ V}$

    $Ni^{+2+} + Sn \rightarrow Sn^{2+} + Ni$ $E^\circ_{cell} = -0.09 \text{ V}$

Let's calculate the ion ratio when this reaction is at equilibrium ($E_{cell} = 0$).

$$E^\circ = \frac{0.0591}{n} \log K, \ -0.09 = \frac{0.0591}{2} \log \frac{[Sn^{2+}]}{[Ni^{2+}]}$$

$$\frac{[Sn^{2+}]}{[Ni^{2+}]} = 10^{2(-0.09)/0.0591} = 9 \times 10^{-4}$$

The reaction is at equilibrium when the $[Sn^{2+}]/[Ni^{2+}]$ ratio is equal to 9×10^{-4}. A reaction shifts to the right (which is what we want in order to produce a voltage) when $Q < K_{sp}$. The minimum ratio necessary to make this reaction spontaneous is a $[Sn^{2+}]/[Ni^{2+}]$ ratio just less than 9×10^{-4}. Only when the ratio is below 9×10^{-4} will E_{cell} be positive.

69.   a.   Possible reaction: $I_2(s) + 2 Cl^-(aq) \rightarrow 2 I^-(aq) + Cl_2(g)$ $E^\circ_{cell} = 0.54 \text{ V} - 1.36 \text{ V}$

                                                            $= -0.82 \text{ V}$

This reaction is not spontaneous at standard conditions because $E^\circ_{cell} < 0$. No reaction occurs.

b.   Possible reaction: $Cl_2(g) + 2 I^-(aq) \rightarrow I_2(s) + 2 Cl^-(aq)$ $E^\circ_{cell} = 0.82 \text{ V}$; This reaction is spontaneous at standard conditions because $E^\circ_{cell} > 0$. The reaction will occur.

$$Cl_2(g) + 2\, I^-(aq) \rightarrow I_2(s) + 2\, Cl^-(aq) \qquad E^\circ_{cell} = 0.82\ V = 0.82\ J/C$$

$$\Delta G^\circ = -nFE^\circ_{cell} = -(2\ mol\ e^-)(96{,}485\ C/mol\ e^-)(0.82\ J/C) = -1.6 \times 10^5\ J = -160\ kJ$$

$$E^\circ = \frac{0.0591}{n} \log K, \ \log K = \frac{nE^\circ}{0.0591} = \frac{2(0.82)}{0.0591} = 27.75, \ K = 10^{27.75} = 5.6 \times 10^{27}$$

c. Possible reaction: $2\ Ag(s) + Cu^{2+}(aq) \rightarrow Cu(s) + 2\ Ag^+(aq)$ $E^\circ_{cell} = -0.46\ V$; No reaction occurs.

d. Fe^{2+} can be oxidized or reduced. The other species present are H^+, SO_4^{2-}, H_2O, and O_2 from air. Only O_2 in the presence of H^+ has a large enough standard reduction potential to oxidize Fe^{2+} to Fe^{3+} (resulting in $E^\circ_{cell} > 0$). All other combinations, including the possible reduction of Fe^{2+}, give negative cell potentials. The spontaneous reaction is:

$$Fe^{2+}(aq) + 4\ H^+(aq) + O_2(g) \rightarrow 4\ Fe^{3+}(aq) + 2\ H_2O(l) \quad E^\circ_{cell} = 1.23 - 0.77 = 0.46\ V$$

$$\Delta G^\circ = -nFE^\circ_{cell} = -(4\ mol\ e^-)(96{,}485\ C/mol\ e^-)(0.46\ J/C)(1\ kJ/1000\ J) = -180\ kJ$$

$$\log K = \frac{4(0.46)}{0.0591} = 31.13, \ K = 1.3 \times 10^{31}$$

70. a. $Cu^+ + e^- \rightarrow Cu$ $\qquad\qquad\qquad$ $E^\circ = 0.52\ V$
$\qquad\quad$ $Cu^+ \rightarrow Cu^{2+} + e^-$ $\qquad\qquad\quad$ $-E^\circ = -0.16\ V$

$\qquad\quad$ $2\ Cu^+(aq) \rightarrow Cu^{2+}(aq) + Cu(s)$ $\qquad$ $E^\circ_{cell} = 0.36\ V$; Spontaneous

$$\Delta G^\circ = -nFE^\circ_{cell} = -(1\ mol\ e^-)(96{,}485\ C/mol\ e^-)(0.36\ J/C) = -34{,}700\ J = -35\ kJ$$

$$E^\circ_{cell} = \frac{0.0591}{n} \log K, \ \log K = \frac{nE^\circ}{0.0591} = \frac{1(0.36)}{0.0591} = 6.09, \ K = 10^{6.09} = 1.2 \times 10^6$$

b. $Fe^{2+} + 2\ e^- \rightarrow Fe$ $\qquad\qquad\qquad$ $E^\circ = -0.44\ V$
$\qquad\quad$ $(Fe^{2+} \rightarrow Fe^{3+} + e^-) \times 2$ $\qquad\quad$ $-E^\circ = -0.77\ V$

$\qquad\quad$ $3\ Fe^{2+}(aq) \rightarrow 2\ Fe^{3+}(aq) + Fe(s)$ $\qquad$ $E^\circ_{cell} = -1.21\ V$; Not spontaneous

c. $HClO_2 + 2\ H^+ + 2\ e^- \rightarrow HClO + H_2O$ $\qquad\qquad$ $E^\circ = 1.65\ V$
$\qquad$ $HClO_2 + H_2O \rightarrow ClO_3^- + 3\ H^+ + 2\ e^-$ $\qquad\quad$ $-E^\circ = -1.21\ V$

$\qquad\quad$ $2\ HClO_2(aq) \rightarrow ClO_3^-(aq) + H^+(aq) + HClO(aq)$ $\quad$ $E^\circ_{cell} = 0.44\ V$; Spontaneous

$$\Delta G^\circ = -nFE^\circ_{cell} = -(2\ mol\ e^-)(96{,}485\ C/mol\ e^-)(0.44\ J/C) = -84{,}900\ J = -85\ kJ$$

$$\log K = \frac{nE^\circ}{0.0591} = \frac{2(0.44)}{0.0591} = 14.89, \ K = 7.8 \times 10^{14}$$

71. a.
$$Au^{3+} + 3\,e^- \rightarrow Au \qquad\qquad E° = 1.50\ V$$
$$(Tl \rightarrow Tl^+ + e^-) \times 3 \qquad -E° = 0.34\ V$$

$$Au^{3+}(aq) + 3\,Tl(s) \rightarrow Au(s) + 3\,Tl^+(aq) \qquad E°_{cell} = 1.84\ V$$

b. $\Delta G° = -nFE°_{cell} = -(3\ mol\ e^-)(96{,}485\ C/mol\ e^-)(1.84\ J/C) = -5.33 \times 10^5\ J = -533\ kJ$

$$\log K = \frac{nE°}{0.0591} = \frac{3(1.84)}{0.0591} = 93.401,\ \ K = 10^{93.401} = 2.52 \times 10^{93}$$

c. $E°_{cell} = 1.84\ V - \dfrac{0.0591}{3}\log\dfrac{[Tl^+]^3}{[Au^{3+}]} = 1.84 - \dfrac{0.0591}{3}\log\dfrac{(1.0\times10^{-4})^3}{1.0\times10^{-2}}$

$E°_{cell} = 1.84 - (-0.20) = 2.04\ V$

72.
$$(Cr^{2+} \rightarrow Cr^{3+} + e^-) \times 2$$
$$Co^{2+} + 2\,e^- \rightarrow Co$$

$$2\,Cr^{2+} + Co^{2+} \rightarrow 2\,Cr^{3+} + Co$$

$$E°_{cell} = \frac{0.0591}{n}\log K = \frac{0.0591}{2}\log(2.79 \times 10^7) = 0.220\ V$$

$$E = E° - \frac{0.0591}{n}\log\frac{[Cr^{3+}]^2}{[Cr^{2+}]^2[Co^{2+}]} = 0.220\ V - \frac{0.0591}{2}\log\frac{(2.0)^2}{(0.30)^2(0.20)} = 0.151\ V$$

$\Delta G = -nFE = -(2\ mol\ e^-)(96{,}485\ C/mol\ e^-)(0.151\ J/C) = -2.91 \times 10^4\ J = -29.1\ kJ$

73. The K_{sp} reaction is: $FeS(s) \rightleftharpoons Fe^{2+}(aq) + S^{2-}(aq)$ $K = K_{sp}$. Manipulate the given equations so when added together we get the K_{sp} reaction. Then we can use the value of $E°_{cell}$ for the reaction to determine K_{sp}.

$$FeS + 2\,e^- \rightarrow Fe + S^{2-} \qquad\qquad E° = -1.01\ V$$
$$Fe \rightarrow Fe^{2+} + 2\,e^- \qquad\qquad -E° = \ \ 0.44\ V$$

$$Fe(s) \rightarrow Fe^{2+}(aq) + S^{2-}(aq) \qquad E°_{cell} = -0.57\ V$$

$$\log K_{sp} = \frac{nE°}{0.0591} = \frac{2(-0.57)}{0.0591} = -19.29,\ \ K_{sp} = 10^{-19.29} = 5.1 \times 10^{-20}$$

74.
$$Al^{3+} + 3\,e^- \rightarrow Al \qquad\qquad E° = -1.66\ V$$
$$Al + 6\,F^- \rightarrow AlF_6^{3-} + 3\,e^- \qquad -E° = \ \ 2.07\ V$$

$$Al^{3+}(aq) + 6\,F^-(aq) \rightarrow AlF_6^{3-}(aq) \qquad E°_{cell} = \ 0.41\ V \quad K = ?$$

$$\log K = \frac{nE°}{0.0591} = \frac{3(0.41)}{0.0591} = 20.81, \ K = 10^{20.81} = 6.5 \times 10^{20}$$

75. NO_3^- is a spectator ion. The reaction that occurs is Ag^+ reacting with Zn.

$$\begin{array}{ll} (Ag^+ + e^- \rightarrow Ag) \times 2 & E° = 0.80 \text{ V} \\ Zn \rightarrow Zn^{2+} + 2 \ e^- & -E° = 0.76 \text{ V} \end{array}$$

$$\begin{array}{ll} \overline{2 \ Ag^+ + Zn \rightarrow 2 \ Ag + Zn^{2+}} & E°_{cell} = 1.56 \text{ V} \end{array}$$

$$\log K = \frac{nE}{0.0591} = \frac{2(1.56)}{0.0591}, \ K = 10^{52.792} = 6.19 \times 10^{52}$$

76. $$\begin{array}{ll} CuI + e^- \rightarrow Cu + I^- & E°_{CuI} = ? \\ Cu \rightarrow Cu^+ + e^- & -E° = -0.52 \text{ V} \end{array}$$

$$\begin{array}{ll} \overline{CuI(s) \rightarrow Cu^+(aq) + I^-(aq)} & E°_{cell} = E°_{CuI} - 0.52 \text{ V} \end{array}$$

For this overall reaction, $K = K_{sp} = 1.1 \times 10^{-12}$:

$$E°_{cell} = \frac{0.0591}{n} \log K_{sp} = \frac{0.0591}{1} \log (1.1 \times 10^{-12}) = -0.71 \text{ V}$$

$$E°_{cell} = -0.71 \text{ V} = E°_{CuI} - 0.52, \ E°_{CuI} = -0.19 \text{ V}$$

Electrolysis

77.   a. $Al^{3+} + 3 \ e^- \rightarrow Al$; 3 mol e^- are needed to produce 1 mol Al from Al^{3+}.

$$1.0 \times 10^3 \text{ g Al} \times \frac{1 \text{ mol Al}}{26.98 \text{ g Al}} \times \frac{3 \text{ mol } e^-}{\text{mol Al}} \times \frac{96{,}485 \text{ C}}{\text{mol } e^-} \times \frac{1 \text{ s}}{100.0 \text{ C}} = 1.07 \times 10^5 \text{ s}$$

$$= 30. \text{ hours}$$

b. $$1.0 \text{ g Ni} \times \frac{1 \text{ mol Ni}}{58.69 \text{ g Ni}} \times \frac{2 \text{ mol } e^-}{\text{mol Ni}} \times \frac{96{,}485 \text{ C}}{\text{mol } e^-} \times \frac{1 \text{ s}}{100.0 \text{ C}} = 33 \text{ s}$$

c. $$5.0 \text{ mol Ag} \times \frac{1 \text{ mol } e^-}{\text{mol Ag}} \times \frac{96{,}485 \text{ C}}{\text{mol } e^-} \times \frac{1 \text{ s}}{100.0 \text{ C}} = 4.8 \times 10^3 \text{ s} = 1.3 \text{ hours}$$

78.   The oxidation state of bismuth in BiO^+ is +3 because oxygen has a -2 oxidation state in this ion.   Therefore, 3 moles of electrons are required to reduce the bismuth in BiO^+ to Bi(s).

$$10.0 \text{ g Bi} \times \frac{1 \text{ mol Bi}}{209.0 \text{ g Bi}} \times \frac{3 \text{ mol } e^-}{\text{mol Bi}} \times \frac{96{,}485 \text{ C}}{\text{mol } e^-} \times \frac{1 \text{ s}}{25.0 \text{ C}} = 554 \text{ s} = 9.23 \text{ min}$$

79. $15 \text{ A} = \dfrac{15 \text{ C}}{\text{s}} \times \dfrac{60 \text{ s}}{\text{min}} \times \dfrac{60 \text{ min}}{\text{h}} = 5.4 \times 10^4 \text{ C of charge passed in 1 hour}$

a. $5.4 \times 10^4 \text{ C} \times \dfrac{1 \text{ mol e}^-}{96,485 \text{ C}} \times \dfrac{1 \text{ mol Co}}{2 \text{ mol e}^-} \times \dfrac{58.93 \text{ g Co}}{\text{mol Co}} = 16 \text{ g Co}$

b. $5.4 \times 10^4 \text{ C} \times \dfrac{1 \text{ mol e}^-}{96,485 \text{ C}} \times \dfrac{1 \text{ mol Hf}}{4 \text{ mol e}^-} \times \dfrac{178.5 \text{ g Hf}}{\text{mol Hf}} = 25 \text{ g Hf}$

c. $2 \text{ I}^- \rightarrow \text{I}_2 + 2 \text{ e}^-$; $5.4 \times 10^4 \text{ C} \times \dfrac{1 \text{ mol e}^-}{96,485 \text{ C}} \times \dfrac{1 \text{ mol I}_2}{2 \text{ mol e}^-} \times \dfrac{253.8 \text{ g I}_2}{\text{mol I}_2} = 71 \text{ g I}_2$

d. $\text{CrO}_3(\text{l}) \rightarrow \text{Cr}^{6+} + 3 \text{ O}^{2-}$; 6 mol e$^-$ are needed to produce 1 mol Cr from molten CrO_3.

$5.4 \times 10^4 \text{ C} \times \dfrac{1 \text{ mol e}^-}{96,485 \text{ C}} \times \dfrac{1 \text{ mol Cr}}{6 \text{ mol e}^-} \times \dfrac{52.00 \text{ g Cr}}{\text{mol Cr}} = 4.9 \text{ g Cr}$

80.   Al is in the +3 oxidation in Al_2O_3, so 3 mol e$^-$ are needed to convert Al^{3+} into Al(s).

$2.00 \text{ h} \times \dfrac{60 \text{ min}}{\text{h}} \times \dfrac{60 \text{ s}}{\text{min}} \times \dfrac{1.00 \times 10^6 \text{ C}}{\text{s}} \times \dfrac{1 \text{ mol e}^-}{96,485 \text{ C}} \times \dfrac{1 \text{ mol Al}}{3 \text{ mol e}^-} \times \dfrac{26.98 \text{ g Al}}{\text{mol Al}} = 6.71 \times 10^5 \text{ g}$

81. $74.1 \text{ s} \times \dfrac{2.00 \text{ C}}{\text{s}} \times \dfrac{1 \text{ mol e}^-}{96,485 \text{ C}} \times \dfrac{1 \text{ mol M}}{3 \text{ mol e}^-} = 5.12 \times 10^{-4} \text{ mol M where M = unknown metal}$

Molar mass $= \dfrac{0.107 \text{ g M}}{5.12 \times 10^{-4} \text{ mol M}} = \dfrac{209 \text{ g}}{\text{mol}}$; The element is bismuth.

82.   Alkaline earth metals form +2 ions, so 2 mol of e$^-$ are transferred to form the metal, M.

mol M $= 748 \text{ s} \times \dfrac{5.00 \text{ C}}{\text{s}} \times \dfrac{1 \text{ mol e}^-}{96,485 \text{ C}} \times \dfrac{1 \text{ mol M}}{2 \text{ mol e}^-} \times \dfrac{1 \text{ mol e}^-}{96,485 \text{ C}} = 1.94 \times 10^{-2} \text{ mol M}$

molar mass of M $= \dfrac{0.471 \text{ g M}}{1.94 \times 10^{-2} \text{ mol M}} = 24.3 \text{ g/mol}$; MgCl_2 was electrolyzed.

83. F_2 is produced at the anode: $2 \text{ F}^- \rightarrow \text{F}_2 + 2 \text{ e}^-$

$2.00 \text{ h} \times \dfrac{60 \text{ min}}{\text{h}} \times \dfrac{60 \text{ s}}{\text{min}} \times \dfrac{10.0 \text{ C}}{\text{s}} \times \dfrac{1 \text{ mol e}^-}{96,485 \text{ C}} = 0.746 \text{ mol e}^-$

$0.746 \text{ mol e}^- \times \dfrac{1 \text{ mol F}_2}{2 \text{ mol e}^-} = 0.373 \text{ mol F}_2$; $PV = nRT$, $V = \dfrac{nRT}{P}$

$$\frac{(0.373 \text{ mol})(0.08206 \text{ L} \bullet \text{atm}/\text{K} \bullet \text{mol})(298 \text{ K})}{1.00 \text{ atm}} = 9.12 \text{ L F}_2$$

K is produced at the cathode: $K^+ + e^- \rightarrow K$

$$0.746 \text{ mol } e^- \times \frac{1 \text{ mol K}}{\text{mol } e^-} \times \frac{39.10 \text{ g K}}{\text{mol K}} = 29.2 \text{ g K}$$

84.   The half-reactions for the electrolysis of water are:

$$(2 \text{ e}^- + 2 \text{ H}_2\text{O} \rightarrow \text{H}_2 + 2 \text{ OH}^-) \times 2$$
$$2 \text{ H}_2\text{O} \rightarrow 4 \text{ H}^+ + \text{O}_2 + 4 \text{ e}^-$$

$$\overline{\hspace{5cm}}$$

$$2 \text{ H}_2\text{O}(l) \rightarrow 2 \text{ H}_2(g) + \text{O}_2(g) \qquad$$ Note: $4 \text{ H}^+ + 4 \text{ OH}^- \rightarrow 4 \text{ H}_2\text{O}$ and n $= 4$ for this reaction as it is written.

$$15.0 \text{ min} \times \frac{60 \text{ s}}{\text{min}} \times \frac{2.50 \text{ C}}{\text{s}} \times \frac{1 \text{ mol } e^-}{96{,}485 \text{ C}} \times \frac{2 \text{ mol H}_2}{4 \text{ mol } e^-} = 1.17 \times 10^{-2} \text{ mol H}_2$$

At STP, 1 mole of an ideal gas occupies a volume of 22.42 L (see Chapter 5 of the text).

$$1.17 \times 10^{-2} \text{ mol H}_2 \times \frac{22.42 \text{ L}}{\text{mol H}_2} = 0.262 \text{ L} = 262 \text{ mL H}_2$$

$$1.17 \times 10^{-2} \text{ mol H}_2 \times \frac{1 \text{ mol O}_2}{2 \text{ mol H}_2} \times \frac{22.42 \text{ L}}{\text{mol O}_2} = 0.131 \text{ L} = 131 \text{ mL O}_2$$

85. $$\frac{150. \times 10^3 \text{ g C}_6\text{H}_8\text{N}_2}{\text{h}} \times \frac{1 \text{ h}}{60 \text{ min}} \times \frac{1 \text{ min}}{60 \text{ s}} \times \frac{1 \text{ mol C}_6\text{H}_8\text{N}_2}{108.14 \text{ g C}_6\text{H}_8\text{N}_2} \times \frac{2 \text{ mol } e^-}{\text{mol C}_6\text{H}_8\text{N}_2} \times \frac{96{,}485 \text{ C}}{\text{mol } e^-}$$

$$= 7.44 \times 10^4 \text{ C/s or a current of } 7.44 \times 10^4 \text{ A}$$

86. $Al^{3+} + 3 \text{ e}^- \rightarrow Al$; 3 mol e^- are needed to produce Al from Al^{3+}

$$2000 \text{ lb Al} \times \frac{453.6 \text{ g}}{\text{lb}} \times \frac{1 \text{ mol Al}}{26.98 \text{ g}} \times \frac{3 \text{ mol } e^-}{\text{mol Al}} \times \frac{96{,}485 \text{ C}}{\text{mol } e^-} = 1 \times 10^{10} \text{ C of electricity needed}$$

$$\frac{1 \times 10^{10} \text{ C}}{24 \text{ h}} \times \frac{1 \text{ h}}{60 \text{ min}} \times \frac{1 \text{ min}}{60 \text{ s}} = 1 \times 10^5 \text{ C/s} = 1 \times 10^5 \text{ A}$$

87. $$2.30 \text{ min} \times \frac{60 \text{ s}}{\text{min}} = 138 \text{ s}; \quad 138 \text{ s} \times \frac{2.00 \text{ C}}{\text{s}} \times \frac{1 \text{ mol } e^-}{96{,}485 \text{ C}} \times \frac{1 \text{ mol Ag}}{\text{mol } e^-} = 2.86 \times 10^{-3} \text{ mol Ag}$$

$$[Ag^+] = 2.86 \times 10^{-3} \text{ mol Ag}^+/0.250 \text{ L} = 1.14 \times 10^{-2} \text{ } M$$

88. $0.50 \text{ L} \times 0.010 \text{ mol Pt}^{4+}/\text{L} = 5.0 \times 10^{-3} \text{ mol Pt}^{4+}$

To plate out 99% of the Pt^{4+}, we will produce $0.99 \times 5.0 \times 10^{-3} \text{ mol Pt}$.

$$0.99 \times 5.0 \times 10^{-3} \text{ mol Pt} \times \frac{4 \text{ mol e}^-}{\text{mol Pt}} \times \frac{96,485 \text{ C}}{\text{mol e}^-} \times \frac{1 \text{ s}}{4.00 \text{ C}} \times \frac{1 \text{ mol Ag}}{\text{mol e}^-} = 480 \text{ s}$$

89. $Au^{3+} + 3 \text{ e}^- \rightarrow Au \qquad E° = 1.50 \text{ V} \qquad Ni^{2+} + 2 \text{ e}^- \rightarrow Ni \qquad E° = -0.23 \text{ V}$

$Ag^+ + \text{e}^- \rightarrow Ag \qquad E° = 0.80 \text{ V} \qquad Cd^{2+} + 2 \text{ e}^- \rightarrow Cd \qquad E° = -0.40 \text{ V}$

$2 H_2O + 2e^- \rightarrow H_2 + 2 OH^- \qquad E° = -0.83 \text{ V}$

Au(s) will plate out first since it has the most positive reduction potential, followed by Ag(s), which is followed by Ni(s), and finally Cd(s) will plate out last since it has the most negative reduction potential of the metals listed. Water will not interfere with the plating process.

90. To begin plating out Pd:

$$E = 0.62 - \frac{0.0591}{2} \log \frac{[Cl^-]^4}{[PdCl_4{}^{2-}]} = 0.62 - \frac{0.0591}{2} \log \frac{(1.0)^4}{0.020}$$

$$E = 0.62 \text{ V} - 0.050 \text{ V} = 0.57 \text{ V}$$

When 99% of Pd has plated out, $[PdCl_4^-] = \dfrac{0.020}{100} = 0.00020 \; M$.

$$E = 0.62 - \frac{0.0591}{2} \log \frac{(1.0)^4}{2.0 \times 10^{-4}} = 0.62 \text{ V} - 0.11 \text{V} = 0.51 \text{ V}$$

To begin Pt plating: $E = 0.73 \text{ V} - \dfrac{0.0591}{2} \log \dfrac{(1.0)^4}{0.020} = 0.73 - 0.050 = 0.68 \text{ V}$

When 99% of Pt plated: $E = 0.73 - \dfrac{0.0591}{2} \log \dfrac{(1.0)^4}{2.0 \times 10^{-4}} = 0.73 - 0.11 = 0.62 \text{ V}$

To begin Ir plating: $E = 0.77 \text{ V} - \dfrac{0.0591}{3} \log \dfrac{(1.0)^4}{0.020} = 0.77 - 0.033 = 0.74 \text{ V}$

When 99% of Ir plated: $E = 0.77 - \dfrac{0.0591}{3} \log \dfrac{(1.0)^4}{2.0 \times 10^{-4}} = 0.77 - 0.073 = 0.70 \text{ V}$

Yes, because the range of potentials for plating out each metal do not overlap, we should be able to separate the three metals. The exact potential to apply depends on the oxidation reaction. The order of plating will be Ir(s) first, followed by Pt(s) and finally Pd(s) as the potential is gradually increased.

91.   Reduction occurs at the cathode, and oxidation occurs at the anode. First, determine all the species present, then look up pertinent reduction and/or oxidation potentials in Table 17.1 for all these species. The cathode reaction will be the reaction with the most positive reduction potential, and the anode reaction will be the reaction with the most positive oxidation potential.

a.   Species present: Ni^{2+} and Br^-; Ni^{2+} can be reduced to Ni, and Br^- can be oxidized to Br_2 (from Table 17.1). The reactions are:

Cathode: $Ni^{2+} + 2e^- \rightarrow Ni$ $E° = -0.23$ V
Anode: $2\,Br^- \rightarrow Br_2 + 2\,e^-$ $-E° = -1.09$ V

b.   Species present: Al^{3+} and F^-; Al^{3+} can be reduced, and F^- can be oxidized. The reactions are:

Cathode: $Al^{3+} + 3\,e^- \rightarrow Al$ $E° = -1.66$ V
Anode: $2\,F^- \rightarrow F_2 + 2\,e^-$ $-E° = -2.87$ V

c.   Species present: Mn^{2+} and I^-; Mn^{2+} can be reduced, and I^- can be oxidized. The reactions are:

Cathode: $Mn^{2+} + 2\,e^- \rightarrow Mn$ $E° = -1.18$ V
Anode: $2\,I^- \rightarrow I_2 + 2\,e^-$ $-E° = -0.54$ V

92.   These are all in aqueous solutions, so we must also consider the reduction and oxidation of H_2O in addition to the potential redox reactions of the ions present. For the cathode reaction, the species with the most positive reduction potential will be reduced, and for the anode reaction, the species with the most positive oxidation potential will be oxidized.

a.   Species present: Ni^{2+}, Br^- and H_2O. Possible cathode reactions are:

$Ni^{2+} + 2e^- \rightarrow Ni$ $E° = -0.23$ V
$2\,H_2O + 2\,e^- \rightarrow H_2 + 2\,OH^-$ $E° = -0.83$ V

Because it is easier to reduce Ni^{2+} than H_2O (assuming standard conditions), Ni^{2+} will be reduced by the above cathode reaction.

Possible anode reactions are:

$2\,Br^- \rightarrow Br_2 + 2\,e^-$ $-E° = -1.09$ V
$2\,H_2O \rightarrow O_2 + 4\,H^+ + 4\,e^-$ $-E° = -1.23$ V

Because Br^- is easier to oxidize than H_2O (assuming standard conditions), Br^- will be oxidized by the above anode reaction.

b.   Species present: Al^{3+}, F^- and H_2O; Al^{3+} and H_2O can be reduced. The reduction potentials are $E° = -1.66$ V for Al^{3+} and $E° = -0.83$ V for H_2O (assuming standard conditions). H_2O will be reduced at the cathode ($2\,H_2O + 2\,e^- \rightarrow H_2 + 2\,OH^-$).

F^- and H_2O can be oxidized. The oxidation potentials are $-E° = -2.87$ V for F^- and $-E° = -1.23$ V for H_2O (assuming standard conditions). From the potentials, we would predict H_2O to be oxidized at the anode ($2\ H_2O \rightarrow O_2 + 4\ H^+ + 4\ e^-$).

c.   Species present: Mn^{2+}, I^- and H_2O; Mn^{2+} and H_2O can be reduced. The possible cathode reactions are:

$$Mn^{2+} + 2\ e^- \rightarrow Mn \qquad\qquad E° = -1.18 \text{ V}$$
$$2\ H_2O + 2\ e^- \rightarrow H_2 + 2\ OH^- \qquad E° = -0.83 \text{ V}$$

Reduction of H_2O will occur at the cathode since $E°_{H_2O}$ is most positive.

I^- and H_2O can be oxidized. The possible anode reactions are:

$$2\ I^- \rightarrow I_2 + 2\ e^- \qquad\qquad -E° = -0.54 \text{ V}$$
$$2\ H_2O \rightarrow O_2 + 4\ H^+ + 4\ e^- \qquad -E° = -1.23 \text{ V}$$

Oxidation of I^- will occur at the anode since $-E°_{I^-}$ is most positive.

Additional Exercises

93.   The half-reaction for the SCE is:

$$Hg_2Cl_2 + 2\ e^- \rightarrow 2\ Hg + 2\ Cl^- \qquad E_{SCE} = 0.242 \text{ V}$$

For a spontaneous reaction to occur, E_{cell} must be positive. Using the standard reduction potentials in Table 17.1 and the given the SCE potential, deduce which combination will produce a positive overall cell potential.

a. $Cu^{2+} + 2\ e^- \rightarrow Cu \qquad E° = 0.34$ V

$E_{cell} = 0.34 - 0.242 = 0.10$ V; SCE is the anode.

b. $Fe^{3+} + e^- \rightarrow Fe^{2+} \qquad E° = 0.77$ V

$E_{cell} = 0.77 - 0.242 = 0.53$ V; SCE is the anode.

c. $AgCl + e^- \rightarrow Ag + Cl^- \quad E° = 0.22$ V

$E_{cell} = 0.242 - 0.22 = 0.02$ V; SCE is the cathode.

d. $Al^{3+} + 3\ e^- \rightarrow Al \qquad E° = -1.66$ V

$E_{cell} = 0.242 + 1.66 = 1.90$ V; SCE is the cathode.

e. $Ni^{2+} + 2\ e^- \rightarrow Ni \qquad E° = -0.23$ V

$E_{cell} = 0.242 + 0.23 = 0.47$ V; SCE is the cathode.

94.   The potential oxidizing agents are NO_3^- and H^+. Hydrogen ion cannot oxidize Pt under either condition. Nitrate cannot oxidize Pt unless there is Cl^- in the solution. Aqua regia has both Cl^- and NO_3^-. The overall reaction is:

$$(NO_3^- + 4\,H^+ + 3\,e^- \rightarrow NO + 2\,H_2O) \times 2 \qquad E° = 0.96\ V$$
$$(4\,Cl^- + \ Pt \rightarrow PtCl_4^{2-} + 2\,e^-) \times 3 \qquad -E° = -0.755\ V$$

$$12\,Cl^-(aq) + 3\,Pt(s) + 2\,NO_3^-(aq) + 8\,H^+(aq) \rightarrow 3\,PtCl_4^{2-}(aq) + 2\,NO(g) + 4\,H_2O(l)$$
$$E°_{cell} = 0.21\ V$$

95. $2\,Ag^+(aq) + Cu(s) \rightarrow Cu^{2+}(aq) + 2\,Ag(s)$ $E°_{cell} = 0.80 - 0.34\ V = 0.46\ V$; A galvanic cell produces a voltage as the forward reaction occurs. Any stress that increases the tendency of the forward reaction to occur will increase the cell potential, while a stress that decreases the tendency of the forward reaction to occur will decrease the cell potential.

a.   Added Cu^{2+} (a product ion) will decrease the tendency of the forward reaction to occur, which will decrease the cell potential.

b.   Added NH_3 removes Cu^{2+} in the form of $Cu(NH_3)_4^{2+}$. Removal of a product ion will increase the tendency of the forward reaction to occur, which will increase the cell potential.

c.   Added Cl^- removes Ag^+ in the form of $AgCl(s)$. Removal of a reactant ion will decrease the tendency of the forward reaction to occur, which will decrease the cell potential.

d. $Q_1 = \dfrac{[Cu^{2+}]_o}{[Ag^+]_o^2}$; As the volume of solution is doubled, each concentration is halved.

$$Q_2 = \dfrac{1/2[Cu^{2+}]_o}{(1/2[Ag^+]_o)^2} = \dfrac{[Cu^{2+}]_o}{[Ag^+]_o^2} = 2\,Q_1$$

The reaction quotient is doubled as the concentrations are halved. Because reactions are spontaneous when $Q < K$ and because Q increases when the solution volume doubles, the reaction is closer to equilibrium, which will decrease the cell potential.

e.   Because $Ag(s)$ is not a reactant in this spontaneous reaction, and because solids do not appear in the reaction quotient expressions, replacing the silver electrode with a platinum electrode will have no effect on the cell potential.

96. $$(Al^{3+} + 3\,e^- \rightarrow Al) \times 2 \qquad E° = -1.66\ V$$
$$(M \rightarrow M^{2+} + 2\,e^-) \times 3 \qquad -E° = ?$$

$$3\,M(s) + 2\,Al^{3+}(aq) \rightarrow 2\,Al(s) + 3\,M^{2+}(aq) \qquad E°_{cell} = -E° - 1.66\ V$$

$\Delta G° = -nFE°_{cell}$, $\ -411 \times 10^3\ J = -(6\ mol\ e^-)(96{,}485\ C/mol\ e^-)\,E°_{cell}$, $\ E°_{cell} = 0.71\ V$

$E°_{cell} = -E° - 1.66\ V = 0.71\ V$, $-E° = 2.37$ or $E° = -2.37$

From Table 17.1, the reduction potential for $Mg^{2+} + 2\,e^- \rightarrow Mg$ is -2.37 V, which fits the data. Hence, the metal is magnesium.

97.   a. $\Delta G° = \sum n_p \Delta G°_{f,\,products} - \sum n_r \Delta G°_{f,\,reactants} = 2(-480.) + 3(86) - [3(-40.)] = -582$ kJ

From oxidation numbers, $n = 6$. $\Delta G° = -nFE°$, $E° = \dfrac{-\Delta G°}{nF} = \dfrac{-(-582,000\text{ J})}{6(96,485)\text{ C}} = 1.01$ V

$\log K = \dfrac{nE°}{0.0591} = \dfrac{6(1.01)}{0.0591} = 102.538$, $K = 10^{102.538} = 3.45 \times 10^{102}$

   b.
$$2\,e^- + Ag_2S \rightarrow 2\,Ag + S^{2-}) \times 3 \qquad\qquad E°_{Ag_2S} = \;?$$
$$(Al \rightarrow Al^{3+} + 3\,e^-) \times 2 \qquad\qquad -E° = 1.66\text{ V}$$

$3\,Ag_2S(s) + 2\,Al(s) \rightarrow 6\,Ag(s) + 3\,S^{2-}(aq) + 2\,Al^{3+}(aq) \qquad E°_{cell} = 1.01\text{ V} = E°_{Ag_2S} + 1.66\text{V}$

$E°_{Ag_2S} = 1.01\text{ V} - 1.66\text{ V} = -0.65$ V

98. $Zn \rightarrow Zn^{2+} + 2\,e^-$ $-E° = 0.76$ V; $Fe \rightarrow Fe^{2+} + 2\,e^-$ $-E° = 0.44$ V

It is easier to oxidize Zn than Fe, so the Zn would be preferentially oxidized, protecting the iron of the *Monitor's* hull.

99.   Aluminum has the ability to form a durable oxide coating over its surface. Once the HCl dissolves this oxide coating, Al is exposed to H^+ and is easily oxidized to Al^{3+}, i.e., the Al foil disappears after the oxide coating is dissolved.

100.   Only statement e is true. The attached metals that are more easily oxidized than iron are called sacrificial metals. For statement a, corrosion is a spontaneous process, like the ones harnessed to make galvanic cells. For statement b, corrosion of steel is the oxidation of iron coupled with the reduction of oxygen. For statement c, cars rust more easily in high moisture areas (the humid areas) because water is a reactant in the reduction half-reaction as well as providing a medium for ion migration (a salt bridge of sorts). For statement d, salting roads adds ions to the corrosion process, which increases the conductivity of the aqueous solution and, in turn, accelerates corrosion.

101.   Consider the strongest oxidizing agent combined with the strongest reducing agent from Table 17.1:

$$F_2 + 2\,e^- \rightarrow 2\,F^- \qquad\qquad E° = 2.87\text{ V}$$
$$(Li \rightarrow Li^+ + e^-) \times 2 \qquad\qquad -E° = 3.05\text{ V}$$

$F_2(g) + 2\,Li(s) \rightarrow 2\,Li^+(aq) + 2\,F^-(aq) \qquad E°_{cell} = 5.92$ V

The claim is impossible. The strongest oxidizing agent and strongest reducing agent when combined only give an $E°_{cell}$ value of about 6 V.

102. $2 H_2(g) + O_2(g) \rightarrow 2 H_2O(l)$; Oxygen goes from the zero oxidation state to the -2 oxidation state in H_2O. Because two moles of O are in the balanced reaction, n = 4 moles of electrons transferred.

    a. $E^\circ_{cell} = \dfrac{0.0591}{n} \log K = \dfrac{0.0591}{4} \log (1.28 \times 10^{83})$, $E^\circ_{cell} = 1.23$ V

    $\Delta G^\circ = -nFE^\circ_{cell} = -(4 \text{ mol e}^-)(96{,}485 \text{ C/mol e}^-)(1.23 \text{ J/C}) = -4.75 \times 10^5 \text{ J} = -475 \text{ kJ}$

    b. Because the moles of gas decrease as reactants are converted into products, ΔS° will be negative (unfavorable). Because the value of ΔG° is negative, ΔH° must be negative to override the unfavorable ΔS° ($\Delta G^\circ = \Delta H^\circ - T\Delta S^\circ$).

    c. $\Delta G = w_{max} = \Delta H - T\Delta S$. Because ΔS is negative, as T increases, ΔG becomes more positive (closer to zero). Therefore, w_{max} will decrease as T increases.

103. $O_2 + 2 H_2O + 4 e^- \rightarrow 4 OH^-$ $E^\circ = 0.40$ V
       $(H_2 + 2 OH^- \rightarrow 2 H_2O + 2 e^-) \times 2$ $-E^\circ = 0.83$ V

            $2 H_2(g) + O_2(g) \rightarrow 2 H_2O(l)$ $E^\circ_{cell} = 1.23$ V $= 1.23$ J/C

Because standard conditions are assumed, $w_{max} = \Delta G^\circ$ for 2 mol H_2O produced.

$\Delta G^\circ = -nFE^\circ_{cell} = -(4 \text{ mol e}^-)(96{,}485 \text{ C/mol e}^-)(1.23 \text{ J/C}) = -475{,}000 \text{ J} = -475 \text{ kJ}$

For 1.00×10^3 g H_2O produced, w_{max} is:

$$1.00 \times 10^3 \text{ g } H_2O \times \frac{1 \text{ mol } H_2O}{18.02 \text{ g } H_2O} \times \frac{-475 \text{ kJ}}{2 \text{ mol } H_2O} = -13{,}200 \text{ kJ} = w_{max}$$

The work done can be no larger than the free energy change. The best that could happen is that all of the free energy released would go into doing work, but this does not occur in any real process because there is always waste energy in a real process. Fuel cells are more efficient in converting chemical energy into electrical energy; they are also less massive. The major disadvantage is that they are expensive. In addition, $H_2(g)$ and $O_2(g)$ are an explosive mixture if ignited; much more so than fossil fuels.

104.   Cadmium goes from the zero oxidation state to the $+2$ oxidation state in $Cd(OH)_2$. Because one mol of Cd appears in the balanced reaction, n = 2 mol electrons transferred. At standard conditions:

    $w_{max} = \Delta G^\circ = -nFE^\circ$, $w_{max} = -(2 \text{ mol e}^-)(96{,}485 \text{ C/mol e}^-)(1.10 \text{ J/C}) = -2.12 \times 10^5 \text{ J}$

                                                $= -212 \text{ kJ}$

105. $(CO + O^{2-} \rightarrow CO_2 + 2 e^-) \times 2$

       $O_2 + 4 e^- \rightarrow 2 O^{2-}$

       ———————————————

       $2 CO + O_2 \rightarrow 2 CO_2$

$$\Delta G = -nFE, \quad E = \frac{-\Delta G^\circ}{nF} = \frac{-(-380 \times 10^3 \text{ J})}{(4 \text{ mol e}^-)(96{,}485 \text{ C/mol e}^-)} = 0.98 \text{ V}$$

106.   For C_2H_5OH, H has a +1 oxidation state and O has a −2 oxidiation state. This dictates a −2 oxidation state for C. For CO_2, O has a −2 oxidiation state so carbon has a +4 oxidiation state. Six moles of electrons are transferred per mole of carbon oxidized (C goes from −2 $\rightarrow$ +4). Two moles of carbon are in the balanced reaction, so n = 12.

$$w_{max} = -1320 \text{ kJ} = \Delta G = -nFE, \quad -1320 \times 10^3 \text{ J} = -nFE = -(12 \text{ mol e}^-)(96{,}485 \text{ C/mol e}^-)E$$

$$E = 1.14 \text{ J/C} = 1.14 \text{ V}$$

107.   The oxidation state of gold in $Au(CN)_2^-$ is +1. Each mole of gold produced requires 1 mole of electrons gained (+1 $\rightarrow$ 0). The only oxygen containing reactant is H_2O. Each mole of oxygen goes from −2 $\rightarrow$ 0 oxidation states as H_2O is converted into O_2. One mole of O_2 contains 2 moles O, so 4 moles of electrons are lost when 1 mole O_2 is formed. In order to balance the electrons, we need 4.00 moles of gold for every mole of O_2 produced or 0.250 moles O_2 for every 1.00 mole of gold formed.

108.   In the electrolysis of aqueous sodium chloride, H_2O is reduced in preference to Na^+, and Cl^- is oxidized in preference to H_2O. The anode reaction is $2 Cl^- \rightarrow Cl_2 + 2 e^-$, and the cathode reaction is $2 H_2O + 2 e^- \rightarrow H_2 + 2 OH^-$. The overall reaction is:

       $2 H_2O(l) + 2 Cl^-(aq) \rightarrow Cl_2(g) + H_2(g) + 2 OH^-(aq)$.

From the 1:1 mol ratio between Cl_2 and H_2 in the overall balanced reaction, if 257 L of $Cl_2(g)$ are produced, then 257 L of $H_2(g)$ will also be produced because moles and volume of gas are directly proportional at constant T and P (see Chapter 5 of text).

109. $\text{mol e}^- = 50.0 \text{ min} \times \dfrac{60 \text{ s}}{\text{min}} \times \dfrac{2.50 \text{ C}}{\text{s}} \times \dfrac{1 \text{ mol e}^-}{96{,}485 \text{ C}} = 7.77 \times 10^{-2} \text{ mol e}^-$

       $\text{mol Ru} = 2.618 \text{ g Ru} \times \dfrac{1 \text{ mol Ru}}{101.1 \text{ g Ru}} = 2.590 \times 10^{-2} \text{ mol Ru}$

       $\dfrac{\text{mol e}^-}{\text{mol Ru}} = \dfrac{7.77 \times 10^{-2} \text{ mol e}^-}{2.590 \times 10^{-2} \text{ mol Ru}} = 3.00$; The charge on the ruthenium ions is +3.

                                   $(Ru^{3+} + 3 e^- \rightarrow Ru)$

110. $15 \text{ kWh} = \dfrac{15000 \text{ J h}}{\text{s}} \times \dfrac{60 \text{ s}}{\text{min}} \times \dfrac{60 \text{ min}}{\text{h}} = 5.4 \times 10^7 \text{ J or } 5.4 \times 10^4 \text{ kJ}$ (Hall process)

To melt 1.0 kg Al requires: 1.0×10^3 g Al $\times \dfrac{1 \text{ mol Al}}{26.98 \text{ g}} \times \dfrac{10.7 \text{ kJ}}{\text{mol Al}} = 4.0 \times 10^2$ kJ

It is feasible to recycle Al by melting the metal because, in theory, it takes less than 1% of the energy required to produce the same amount of Al by the Hall process.

Challenge Problems

111. $\Delta G° = -nFE° = \Delta H° - T\Delta S°$, $E° = \dfrac{T\Delta S°}{nF} - \dfrac{\Delta H°}{nF}$

If we graph E° vs. T we should get a straight line (y = mx + b). The slope of the line is equal to $\Delta S°/nF$, and the y-intercept is equal to $-\Delta H°/nF$. From the equation above, E° will have a small temperature dependence when $\Delta S°$ is close to zero.

112.   a.   We can calculate $\Delta G°$ from $\Delta G° = \Delta H° - T\Delta S°$ and then E° from $\Delta G° = -nFE°$; or we can use the equation derived in Exercise 17.111. For this reaction, n = 2 (from oxidation states).

$$E°_{-20} = \frac{T\Delta S° - \Delta H°}{nF} = \frac{(253 \text{ K})(263.5 \text{ J/K}) + 315.9 \times 10^3 \text{ J}}{(2 \text{ mol e}^-)(96,485 \text{ C/mol e}^-)} = 1.98 \text{ J/C} = 1.98 \text{ V}$$

b. $E_{-20} = E_{-20} - \dfrac{RT}{nF} \ln Q = 1.98 \text{ V} - \dfrac{RT}{nF} \ln \dfrac{1}{[H^+]^2[HSO_4^-]^2}$

$$E_{-20} = 1.98 \text{ V} - \frac{(8.3145 \text{ J/K} \bullet \text{mol})(253 \text{K})}{(2 \text{ mol e}^-)(96,485 \text{ C/mol e}^-)} \ln \frac{1}{(4.5)^2(4.5)^2} = 1.98 \text{ V} + 0.066 \text{ V}$$

$$= 2.05 \text{ V}$$

c.   From Exercise 17.55, E = 2.12 V at 25°C. As the temperature decreases, the cell potential decreases. Also, oil becomes more viscous at lower temperatures, which adds to the difficulty of starting an engine on a cold day. The combination of these two factors results in batteries failing more often on cold days than on warm days.

113. $(Ag^+ + e^- \rightarrow Ag) \times 2$ $E° = 0.80 \text{ V}$
              $Pb \rightarrow Pb^{2+} + 2 e^-$ $-E° = -(-0.13)$

          _____

         $2 Ag^+ + Pb \rightarrow 2 Ag + Pb^{2+}$ $E°_{cell} = 0.93 \text{ V}$

$E = E° - \dfrac{0.0591}{n} \log \dfrac{[Pb^{2+}]}{[Ag^+]^2}$, $0.83 \text{ V} = 0.93 \text{ V} - \dfrac{0.0591}{n} \log \dfrac{(1.8)}{[Ag^+]^2}$

$\log \dfrac{(1.8)}{[Ag^+]^2} = \dfrac{0.10(2)}{0.0591} = 3.4$, $\dfrac{(1.8)}{[Ag^+]^2} = 10^{3.4}$, $[Ag^+] = 0.027 \ M$

$$Ag_2SO_4(s) \;\rightleftharpoons\; 2\,Ag^+(aq) \;+\; SO_4^{2-}(aq) \quad K_{sp} = [Ag^+]^2[SO_4^{2-}]$$

Initial s = solubility (mol/L)   0   0
Equil.   2s s

From problem: $2s = 0.027\,M,\;\; s = 0.027/2$

$$K_{sp} = (2s)^2(s) = (0.027)^2(0.027/2) = 9.8 \times 10^{-6}$$

114.   a. $Zn(s) + Cu^{2+}(aq) \rightarrow Zn^{2+}(aq) + Cu(s)$ $E^{\circ}_{cell} = 1.10\ V$; $E_{cell} = 1.10\ V - \dfrac{0.0591}{2}\log\dfrac{[Zn^{2+}]}{[Cu^{2+}]}$

$$E_{cell} = 1.10\ V - \frac{0.0591}{2}\log\frac{0.10}{2.50} = 1.10\ V + 0.041\ V = 1.14\ V$$

b. $10.0\ h \times \dfrac{60\ min}{h} \times \dfrac{60\ s}{min} \times \dfrac{10.0\ C}{s} \times \dfrac{1\ mol\ e^-}{96{,}485\ C} \times \dfrac{1\ mol\ Cu}{2\ mol\ e^-} = 1.87\ mol\ Cu\ produced$

The Cu^{2+} concentration will decrease by 1.87 mol/L, and the Zn^{2+} concentration will increase by 1.87 mol/L.

$[Cu^{2+}] = 2.50 - 1.87 = 0.63\ M$; $[Zn^{2+}] = 0.10 + 1.87 = 1.97\ M$

$$E_{cell} = 1.10\ V - \frac{0.0591}{2}\log\frac{0.97}{0.63} = 1.10\ V - 0.015\ V = 1.09\ V$$

c. $1.87\ mol\ Zn\ consumed \times \dfrac{65.38\ g\ Zn}{mol\ Zn} = 122\ g\ Zn$; Mass of electrode = 200. − 122

$$= 78\ g\ Zn$$

$1.87\ mol\ Cu\ formed \times \dfrac{63.55\ g\ Cu}{mol\ Cu} = 119\ g\ Cu$; Mass of electrode = 200. + 119

$$= 319\ g\ Cu$$

d.   Three things could possibly cause this battery to go dead:

1.   All of the Zn is consumed.
2.   All of the Cu^{2+} is consumed.
3.   Equilibrium is reached ($E_{cell} = 0$).

We began with 2.50 mol Cu^{2+} and 200. g Zn × 1 mol Zn/65.38 g Zn = 3.06 mol Zn. Cu^{2+} is the limiting reagent and will run out first. To react all the Cu^{2+} requires:

$$2.50\ mol\ Cu^{2+} \times \frac{2\ mol\ e^-}{mol\ Cu^{2+}} \times \frac{96{,}485\ C}{mol\ e^-} \times \frac{1\ s}{10.0\ C} \times \frac{1\ h}{3600\ s} = 13.4\ h$$

For equilibrium to be reached: $E = 0 = 1.10 \text{ V} - \dfrac{0.0591}{2}\log\dfrac{[Zn^{2+}]}{[Cu^{2+}]}$

$$\dfrac{[Zn^{2+}]}{[Cu^{2+}]} = K = 10^{2(1.10)/0.0591} = 1.68 \times 10^{37}$$

This is such a large equilibrium constant that virtually all of the Cu^{2+} must react to reach equilibrium. So, the battery will go dead in 13.4 hours.

115. $2 H^+ + 2 e^- \rightarrow H_2$ $E° = 0.000 \text{ V}$
                       $Fe \rightarrow Fe^{2+} + 2 e^-$ $-E° = -(-0.440V)$

$2 H^+(aq) + Fe(s) \rightarrow H_2(g) + Fe^{2+}(aq)$ $E°_{cell} = 0.440 \text{ V}$

$E_{cell} = E°_{cell} - \dfrac{0.0591}{n}\log Q$, where $n = 2$ and $Q = \dfrac{P_{H_2} \times [Fe^{2+}]}{[H^+]^2}$

To determine K_a for the weak acid, first use the electrochemical data to determine the H^+ concentration in the half-cell containing the weak acid.

$$0.333 \text{ V} = 0.440 \text{ V} - \dfrac{0.0591}{2}\log\dfrac{1.00(1.00\times10^{-3})}{[H^+]^2}$$

$$\dfrac{0.107(2)}{0.0591} = \log\dfrac{1.00\times10^{-3}}{[H^+]^2}, \quad \dfrac{1.00\times10^{-3}}{[H^+]^2} = 10^{3.621} = 4.18 \times 10^3, \quad [H^+] = 4.89 \times 10^{-4} M$$

Now we can solve for the K_a value of the weak acid HA through the normal setup for a weak acid problem.

	HA	$\rightleftharpoons$	H^+ +	A^-	$K_a = \dfrac{[H^+][A^-]}{[HA]}$
Initial	1.00 M		~0	0	
Equil.	1.00 - x		x	x	

$$K_a = \dfrac{x^2}{1.00 - x} \text{ where } x = [H^+] = 4.89 \times 10^{-4} M, \; K_a = \dfrac{(4.89\times10^{-4})^2}{1.00 - 4.89\times10^{-4}} = 2.39 \times 10^{-7}$$

116.   a.   Nonreactive anions are present in each half-cell to balance the cation charges.

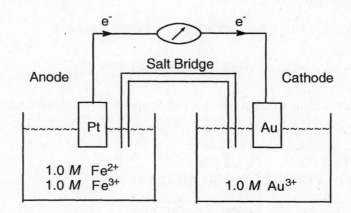

b. $Au^{3+}(aq) + 3\ Fe^{2+}(aq) \rightarrow 3\ Fe^{3+}(aq) + Au(s)$ $E^{o}_{cell} = 1.50 - 0.77 = 0.73\ V$

$$E_{cell} = E^{o}_{cell} - \frac{0.0591}{n} \log Q = 0.73\ V - \frac{0.0591}{3}\ \frac{[Fe^{3+}]^{3}}{[Au^{3+}][Fe^{2+}]^{3}}$$

Because $[Fe^{3+}] = [Fe^{2+}] = 1.0\ M$: $0.31\ V = 0.73\ V - \dfrac{0.0591}{3} \log \dfrac{1}{[Au^{3+}]}$

$$\frac{3(-0.42)}{0.0591} = -\log \frac{1}{[Au^{3+}]},\ \ \log [Au^{3+}] = -21.32,\ \ [Au^{3+}] = 10^{-21.32} = 4.8 \times 10^{-22}\ M$$

$Au^{3+} + 4\ Cl^{-} \rightleftharpoons AuCl_{4}^{-}$; Because the equilibrium Au^{3+} concentration is so small, assume $[AuCl_{4}^{-}] \approx [Au^{3+}]_{o} \approx 1.0\ M$, i.e., assume K is large, so the reaction essentially goes to completion.

$$K = \frac{[AuCl_{4}^{-}]}{[Au^{3+}][Cl^{-}]^{4}} = \frac{1.0}{(4.8 \times 10^{-22})(0.10)^{4}} = 2.1 \times 10^{25};\ \ \text{Assumption good (K is large).}$$

117.   a. $E_{cell} = E_{ref} + 0.05916\ pH,\ \ 0.480\ V = 0.250\ V + 0.05916\ pH$

$$pH = \frac{0.480 - 0.250}{0.05916} = 3.888;\ \ \text{Uncertainty} = \pm 1\ mV = \pm 0.001\ V$$

$$pH_{max} = \frac{0.481 - 0.250}{0.05916} = 3.905;\ \ \ pH_{min} = \frac{0.479 - 0.250}{0.05916} = 3.871$$

If the uncertainty in potential is $\pm 0.001\ V$, the uncertainty in pH is ± 0.017 or about ± 0.02 pH units. For this measurement, $[H^{+}] = 10^{-3.888} = 1.29 \times 10^{-4}\ M$. For an error of +1 mV, $[H^{+}] = 10^{-3.905} = 1.24 \times 10^{-4}\ M$. For an error of -1 mV, $[H^{+}] = 10^{-3.871} = 1.35 \times 10^{-4}\ M$. So, the uncertainty in $[H^{+}]$ is $\pm 0.06 \times 10^{-4}\ M = \pm 6 \times 10^{-6}\ M$.

b. From part a, we will be within ± 0.02 pH units if we measure the potential to the nearest ± 0.001 V (1 mV).

118. a. From Table 17.1: $2 H_2O + 2 e^- \rightarrow H_2 + 2 OH^-$ $E° = -0.83$ V

$E°_{cell} = E°_{H_2O} - E°_{Zr} = -0.83$ V $+ 2.36$ V $= 1.53$ V

Yes, the reduction of H_2O to H_2 by Zr is spontaneous at standard conditions because $E°_{cell} > 0$.

b. $(2 H_2O + 2 e^- \rightarrow H_2 + 2 OH^-) \times 2$
          $Zr + 4 OH^- \rightarrow ZrO_2 \bullet H_2O + H_2O + 4 e^-$
          _____

        $3 H_2O(l) + Zr(s) \rightarrow 2 H_2(g) + ZrO_2 \bullet H_2O(s)$

c. $\Delta G° = -nFE° = -(4$ mol $e^-)(96{,}485$ C/mol $e^-)(1.53$ J/C$) = -5.90 \times 10^5$ J $= -590.$ kJ

$E = E° - \dfrac{0.0591}{n} \log Q$; At equilibrium, E = 0 and Q = K.

$E° = \dfrac{0.0591}{n} \log K$, $\log K = \dfrac{4(1.53)}{0.0591} = 104$, $K \approx 10^{104}$

d. 1.00×10^3 kg Zr $\times \dfrac{1000 \text{ g}}{\text{kg}} \times \dfrac{1 \text{ mol Zr}}{91.22 \text{ g Zr}} \times \dfrac{2 \text{ mol } H_2}{\text{mol Zr}} = 2.19 \times 10^4$ mol H_2

2.19×10^4 mol $H_2 \times \dfrac{2.016 \text{ } H_2}{\text{mol } H_2} = 4.42 \times 10^4$ g H_2

$V = \dfrac{nRT}{P} = \dfrac{2.19 \times 10^4 \text{ mol} \times \dfrac{0.08206 \text{ L atm}}{\text{mol K}} \times 1273 \text{ K}}{1.0 \text{ atm}} = 2.3 \times 10^6$ L H_2

e. Probably yes; Less radioactivity overall was released by venting the H_2 than what would have been released if the H_2 had exploded inside the reactor (as happened at Chernobyl). Neither alternative is pleasant, but venting the radioactive hydrogen is the less unpleasant of the two alternatives.

119. a. $(Ag^+ + e^- \rightarrow Ag) \times 2$ $E° = 0.80$ V
                    $Cu \rightarrow Cu^{2+} + 2 e^-$ $-E° = -0.34$ V
          _____

        $2 Ag^+(aq) + Cu(s) \rightarrow 2 Ag(s) + Cu^{2+}(aq)$ $E°_{cell} = 0.46$ V

$E_{cell} = E°_{cell} - \dfrac{0.0591}{n} \log Q$ where n = 2 and $Q = \dfrac{[Cu^{2+}]}{[Ag^+]^2}$

To calculate E_{cell}, we need to use the K_{sp} data to determine $[Ag^+]$.

$$AgCl(s) \quad \rightleftharpoons \quad Ag^+(aq) \quad + \quad Cl^-(aq) \quad K_{sp} = 1.6 \times 10^{-10}$$

Initial s = solubility (mol/L)   0   0

Equil. s s

$$K_{sp} = 1.6 \times 10^{-10} = [Ag^+][Cl^-] = s^2, \; s = [Ag^+] = 1.3 \times 10^{-5} \, \text{mol/L}$$

$$E_{cell} = 0.46 \, V - \frac{0.0591}{2} \log\frac{2.0}{(1.3 \times 10^{-5})^2} = 0.46 \, V - 0.30 = 0.16 \, V$$

b. $Cu^{2+}(aq) + 4 \, NH_3(aq) \rightleftharpoons Cu(NH_4)_4^{2+}(aq) \quad K = 1.0 \times 10^{13} = \dfrac{[Cu(NH_3)_4^{2+}]}{[Cu^{2+}][NH_3]^4}$

Because K is very large for the formation of $Cu(NH_3)_4^{2+}$, the forward reaction is dominant. At equilibrium, essentially all of the 2.0 M Cu^{2+} will react to form 2.0 M $Cu(NH_3)_4^{2+}$. This reaction requires 8.0 M NH_3 to react with all of the Cu^{2+} in the balanced equation. Therefore, the mol of NH_3 added to 1.0 L solution will be larger than 8.0 mol since some NH_3 must be present at equilibrium. In order to calculate how much NH_3 is present at equilibrium, we need to use the electrochemical data to determine the Cu^{2+} concentration.

$$E_{cell} = E_{cell}^\circ - \frac{0.0591}{n} \log Q, \; 0.52 \, V = 0.46 \, V - \frac{0.0591}{2} \log\frac{[Cu^{2+}]}{(1.3 \times 10^{-5})^2}$$

$$\log\frac{[Cu^{2+}]}{(1.3 \times 10^{-5})^2} = \frac{-0.06(2)}{0.0591} = -2.03, \; \frac{[Cu^{2+}]}{(1.3 \times 10^{-5})^2} = 10^{-2.03} = 9.3 \times 10^{-3}$$

$[Cu^{2+}] = 1.6 \times 10^{-12} = 2 \times 10^{-12} \, M$ (We carried extra significant figures in the

calculation.)

Note: Our assumption that the 2.0 M Cu^{2+} essentially reacts to completion is excellent as only $2 \times 10^{-12} \, M$ Cu^{2+} remains after this reaction. Now we can solve for the equilibrium $[NH_3]$.

$$K = 1.0 \times 10^{13} = \frac{[Cu(NH_3)_4^{2+}]}{[Cu^{2+}][NH_3]^4} = \frac{(2.0)}{(2 \times 10^{-12}) \, [NH_3]^4}, \; [NH_3] = 0.6 \, M$$

Since 1.0 L of solution is present, then 0.6 mol NH_3 remains at equilibrium. The total mol of NH_3 added is 0.6 mol plus the 8.0 mol NH_3 necessary to form 2.0 M $Cu(NH_3)_4^{2+}$. Therefore, $8.0 + 0.6 = 8.6$ mol NH_3 were added.

120.   Standard reduction potentials can only be manipulated and added together when electrons in the reduction half-reaction exactly cancel with the electrons in the oxidation half-reaction. We will solve this problem by applying the equation $\Delta G^\circ = -nFE^\circ$ to the half-reactions. ΔG_f° for $e^- = 0$.

$$M^{3+} + 3 \, e^- \rightarrow M \quad \Delta G^\circ = -nFE^\circ = -3(96,485)(-0.10) = 2.9 \times 10^4 \, J$$

Because M and e^- have $\Delta G_f^\circ = 0$, 2.9×10^4 J $= -\Delta G_{f,\,M^{3+}}^\circ$, $\Delta G_{f,\,M^{3+}}^\circ = -2.9 \times 10^4$ J

$M^{2+} + 2\,e^- \rightarrow M$ $\Delta G^\circ = -nFE^\circ = -2(96,485)(-0.50) = 9.6 \times 10^4$ J

9.6×10^4 J $= -\Delta G_{f,\,M^{2+}}^\circ$, $\Delta G_{f,\,M^{2+}}^\circ = -9.6 \times 10^4$ J

$M^{3+} + e^- \rightarrow M^{2+}$ $\Delta G^\circ = -9.6 \times 10^4$ J $- (-2.9 \times 10^4$ J$) = -6.7 \times 10^4$ J

$E^\circ = \dfrac{-\Delta G^\circ}{nF} = \dfrac{-(-6.7 \times 10^4)}{(1)(96,485)} = 0.69$ V for $M^{3+} + e^- \rightarrow M^{2+}$

121. $2\,Ag^+ + Ni \rightarrow Ni^{2+} + Ag$;   The cell is dead at equilibrium.

$E_{cell}^\circ = 0.80$ V $+ 0.23$ V $= 1.03$ V

$0 = 1.03$ V $- \dfrac{0.0591}{2} \log K$;   Solving: $K = 7.18 \times 10^{34}$

K is very large. Let the forward reaction go to completion.

$2Ag^+ + Ni \rightarrow Ni^{2+} + 2\,Ag$ $K = [Ni^{2+}]/[Ag^+]^2 = 7.18 \times 10^{34}$

Before   1.0 M 1.0 M
After   0 M 1.5 M

Now allow reaction to get back to equilibrium.

$2Ag^+ + Ni \rightleftharpoons \quad Ni^{2+} + Ag$

Initial	0		1.5 M
Change	$+2x$	$\leftarrow$	$-x$
Equil.	$2x$		$1.5 - x$

$K = 7.18 \times 10^{34} = \dfrac{1.5 - x}{(2x)^2} \approx \dfrac{1.5}{(2x)^2}$; Solving: $x = 2.3 \times 10^{-18}$ M. Assumptions good.

$[Ag^+] = 2x = 4.6 \times 10^{-18}\,M$; $[Ni^{2+}] = 1.5 - 2.3 \times 10^{-18}\,M = 1.5\,M$

122.   a. $Ag_2CrO_4(s) + 2\,e^- \rightarrow 2\,Ag(s) + CrO_4^{2-}(aq)$ $E^\circ = 0.446$ V

$Hg_2Cl_2 + 2\,e^- \rightarrow 2\,Hg + 2\,Cl^-$ $E_{SCE} = 0.242$ V

SCE will be the oxidation half-reaction with $E_{cell} = 0.446 - 0.242 = 0.204$ V.

$\Delta G = -nFE_{cell} = -2(96,485)(0.204)J = -3.94 \times 10^4$ J $= -39.4$ kJ

b. In SCE, we assume all concentrations are constant. Therefore, only CrO_4^{2-} appears in the Q expression and it will appear in the numerator since CrO_4^{2-} is produced in the reduction half-reaction. To calculate E_{cell} at nonstandard CrO_4^{2-} concentrations, we use the following equation.

$$E_{cell} = E_{cell}^{o} - \frac{0.0591}{2} \log [CrO_4^{2-}] = 0.204 \text{ V} - \frac{0.0591}{2} \log [CrO_4^{2-}]$$

c. $E_{cell} = 0.204 - \dfrac{0.0591}{2} \log (1.00 \times 10^{-5}) = 0.204 \text{ V} - (-0.148 \text{ V}) = 0.352 \text{ V}$

d. $0.504 \text{ V} = 0.204 \text{ V} - (0.0591/2) \log [CrO_4^{2-}]$

$\log [CrO_4^{2-}] = -10.152, \ [CrO_4^{2-}] = 10^{-10.152} = 7.05 \times 10^{-11} M$

e. $Ag_2CrO_4 + 2 \, e^- \rightarrow 2 \, Ag + CrO_4^{2-} \qquad\qquad E^o = 0.446 \text{ V}$
    $(Ag \rightarrow Ag^+ + e^-) \times 2 \qquad\qquad\qquad -E^o = -0.80 \text{ V}$

   _____

   $Ag_2CrO_4(s) \rightarrow 2 \, Ag^+(aq) + CrO_4^{2-} \, (aq) \qquad E_{cell}^{o} = -0.35 \text{ V} \quad K = K_{sp} = ?$

$$E_{cell}^{o} = \frac{0.0591}{n} \log K_{sp}, \ \log K_{sp} = \frac{(-0.35)(2)}{0.0591} = -11.84, \ K_{sp} = 10^{-11.84} = 1.4 \times 10^{-12}$$

123. a. $E^o = 0$ (concentration cell); $E = 0 - \dfrac{0.0591}{2} \log\left(\dfrac{1.0 \times 10^4}{1.00}\right), \ E = 0.12 \text{ V}$

   b. $Cu^{2+} + 4 \, NH_3 \rightleftharpoons Cu(NH_3)_4^{2+} \quad K_{overall} = K_1 \cdot K_2 \cdot K_3 \cdot K_4 = 1.0 \times 10^{13}$

   Because $K >> 1$, let the reaction go to completion, then solve the back equilibrium problem.

   $$Cu^{2+} \quad + \quad 4 \, NH_3 \quad \rightarrow \quad Cu(NH_3)_4^{2+} \qquad K = 1.0 \times 10^{13}$$

	Cu^{2+}	$4 \, NH_3$	$Cu(NH_3)_4^{2+}$
Before	$1.0 \times 10^{-4} M$	$2.0 \, M$	0
After	0	2.0	1.0×10^{-4}

   Now allow the reaction to reach equilibrium.

   $$Cu^{2+} \quad + \quad 4 \, NH_3 \quad \rightarrow \quad Cu(NH_3)_4^{2+}$$

	Cu^{2+}	$4 \, NH_3$	$Cu(NH_3)_4^{2+}$
Initial	0	$2.0 \, M$	$1.0 \times 10^{-4} M$
Equil.	$+x$	$2.0 + 4x$	$1.0 \times 10^{-4} - x$

$$K = 1.0 \times 10^{13} = \frac{(1.0 \times 10^{-4} - x)}{x(2.0 + 4x)^4} \approx \frac{1.0 \times 10^{-4}}{x(2.0)^4} = 1.0 \times 10^{13}, \ x = [Cu^{2+}] = 6.3 \times 10^{-19} M$$

Assumptions good.

At this Cu^{2+} concentration, the cell potential is:

$$E = 0 - \frac{0.0591}{2} \log\left(\frac{6.3 \times 10^{-19}}{1.00}\right), \quad E = 0.54 \text{ V}$$

124.   a. $3 \times (e^- + 2 H^+ + NO_3^- \rightarrow NO_2 + H_2O)$ $E^\circ = 0.775 \text{ V}$

                              $2 H_2O + NO \rightarrow NO_3^- + 4 H^+ + 3 e^-$ $- E^\circ = -0.957 \text{ V}$

$2 H^+(aq) + 2 NO_3^-(aq) + NO(g) \rightarrow 3 NO_2(g) + H_2O(l)$ $E^\circ_{cell} = -0.182 \text{ V}$ $K = ?$

$$\log K = \frac{nE^\circ}{0.0591} = \frac{3(-0.182)}{0.0591} = -9.239, \quad K = 10^{-9.239} = 5.77 \times 10^{-10}$$

b.   Let C = concentration of $HNO_3 = [H^+] = [NO_3^-]$

$$5.77 \times 10^{-10} = \frac{P_{NO_2}^3}{P_{NO} \times [H^+]^2 \times [NO_3^-]^2} = \frac{P_{NO_2}^3}{P_{NO} \times C^4}$$

If 0.20 mol % NO_2 and $P_{tot} = 1.00$ atm:

$$P_{NO_2} = \frac{0.20 \text{ mol } NO_2}{100. \text{ mol total}} \times 1.00 \text{ atm} = 2.0 \times 10^{-3} \text{ atm}; \quad P_{NO} = 1.00 - 0.0020 = 1.00 \text{ atm}$$

$$5.77 \times 10^{-10} = \frac{(2.0 \times 10^{-3})^3}{(1.00) C^4}, \quad C = 1.9 \text{ } M \text{ } HNO_3$$

Integrative Problems

125.   a. $(In^+ + e^- \rightarrow In) \times 2$ $E^\circ = -0.126 \text{ V}$
            $In^+ \rightarrow In^{3+} + 2 e^-$ $-E^\circ = 0.444 \text{ V}$

            $3 In^+ \rightarrow In^{3+} + 2 In$ $E^\circ_{cell} = 0.318$

$$\log K = \frac{nE^\circ}{0.0591} = \frac{2(0.318)}{0.0591} = 10.761, \quad K = 10^{10.761} = 5.77 \times 10^{10}$$

b. $\Delta G^\circ = -nFE^\circ = -(2 \text{ mol } e^-)(96,485 \text{ C/mol } e^-)(0.318 \text{ J/C}) = -6.14 \times 10^5 \text{ J} = -61.4 \text{ kJ}$

$\Delta G^\circ_{rxn} = -61.4 \text{ kJ} = [2(0) + 1(-97.9 \text{ kJ})] - 3 \Delta G^\circ_{f, In^+}, \quad \Delta G^\circ_{f, In^+} = -12.2 \text{ kJ/mol}$

126. $E^\circ_{cell} = 0.400 \text{ V} - 0.240 \text{ V} = 0.160 \text{ V}; \quad E = E^\circ - \frac{0.0591}{n} \log Q$

$$0.180 = 0.160 - \frac{0.0591}{n} \log(9.32 \times 10^{-3}), \quad 0.020 = \frac{0.120}{n}, \quad n = 6$$

Six moles of electrons are transferred in the overall balanced reaction. We now have to figure out how to get 6 mol e^- into the overall balanced equation. The two possibilities are to have ion charges of +1 and +6 or +2 and +3; only these two combinations yield a 6 when common multiples are determined when adding the reduction half-reaction to the oxidation half-reaction. Because N forms +2 charged ions, M must form for +3 charged ions. The overall cell reaction can now be determined.

$$(M^{3+} + 3\,e^- \rightarrow M) \times 2 \qquad E° = 0.400 \text{ V}$$
$$(N \rightarrow N^{2+} + 2\,e^-) \times 3 \qquad -E° = -0.240 \text{ V}$$

$$\overline{2\,M^{3+} + 3\,N \rightarrow 3\,N^{2+} + 2\,M \qquad E°_{cell} = 0.160 \text{ V}}$$

$$Q = 9.32 \times 10^{-3} = \frac{[N^{2+}]_o^3}{[M^{3+}]_o^2} = \frac{(0.10)^3}{[M^{3+}]^2}, \quad [M^{3+}] = 0.33 \text{ } M$$

$$w_{max} = \Delta G = -nFE = -6(96{,}485)(0.180) = -1.04 \times 10^5 \text{ J} = -104 \text{ kJ}$$

The maximum amount of work this cell could produce is 104 kJ.

127. Chromium(III) nitrate [$Cr(NO_3)_3$] has chromium in the +3 oxidation state.

$$1.15 \text{ g Cr} \times \frac{1 \text{ mol Cr}}{52.00 \text{ g}} \times \frac{3 \text{ mol } e^-}{\text{mol Cr}} \times \frac{96{,}485 \text{ C}}{\text{mol } e^-} = 6.40 \times 10^3 \text{ C of charge}$$

For the Os cell, 6.40×10^3 C of charge was also passed.

$$3.15 \text{ g Os} \times \frac{1 \text{ mol Os}}{190.2 \text{ g}} = 0.0166 \text{ mol Os}; \quad 6.40 \times 10^3 \text{ C} \times \frac{1 \text{ mol } e^-}{96{,}485 \text{ C}} = 0.0663 \text{ mol } e^-$$

$$\frac{\text{mol } e^-}{\text{mol Os}} = \frac{0.0663}{0.0166} = 3.99 \approx 4$$

This salt is composed of Os^{4+} and NO_3^- ions. The compound is $Os(NO_3)_4$, osmium(IV) nitrate.

For the third cell, identify X by determining its molar mass. Two moles of electrons are transferred when X^{2+} is reduced to X.

$$\text{molar mass} = \frac{2.11 \text{ g X}}{6.40 \times 10^3 \text{ C} \times \frac{1 \text{ mol } e^-}{96{,}485 \text{ C}} \times \frac{1 \text{ mol X}}{2 \text{ mol } e^-}} = 63.6 \text{ g/mol}$$

This is copper, Cu. The electron configuration is: $[Ar]4s^1 3d^{10}$.

Marathon Problems

128.   a.

$$Cu^{2+} + 2 e^- \rightarrow Cu \qquad\qquad E° = 0.34 \text{ V}$$
$$V \rightarrow V^{2+} + 2 e^- \qquad\qquad -E° = 1.20 \text{ V}$$

$$Cu^{2+}(aq) + V(s) \rightarrow Cu(s) + V^{2+}(aq) \qquad E°_{cell} = 1.54 \text{ V}$$

$$E_{cell} = E°_{cell} - \frac{0.0591}{n} \log Q \text{ where } n = 2 \text{ and } Q = \frac{[V^{2+}]}{[Cu^{2+}]} = \frac{[V^{2+}]}{1.00\,M}$$

To determine E_{cell}, we must know the initial $[V^{2+}]$, which can be determined from the stoichiometric point data. At the stoichiometric point, mol H_2EDTA^{2-} added = mol V^{2+} present initially.

$$\text{mol } V^{2+} \text{ present initially} = 0.5000 \text{ L} \times \frac{0.0800 \text{ mol } H_2EDTA^{2-}}{L} \times \frac{1 \text{ mol } V^{2+}}{\text{mol } H_2EDTA^{2-}}$$

$$= 0.0400 \text{ mol } V^{2+}$$

$$[V^{2+}]_o = \frac{0.0400 \text{ mol } V^{2+}}{1.00 \text{ L}} = 0.0400\,M$$

$$E_{cell} = 1.54 \text{ V} - \frac{0.0591}{2} \log \frac{0.0400}{1.00} = 1.54 \text{ V} - (-0.0413 \text{ V}) = 1.58 \text{ V}$$

b.   Use the electrochemical data to solve for the equilibrium $[V^{2+}]$.

$$E_{cell} = E°_{cell} - \frac{0.0591}{n} \log \frac{[V^{2+}]}{[Cu^{2+}]}, \quad 1.98 \text{ V} = 1.54 \text{ V} - \frac{0.0591}{2} \log \frac{[V^{2+}]}{1.00\,M}$$

$$[V^{2+}] = 10^{-(0.44)(2)/0.0591} = 1.3 \times 10^{-15}\,M$$

$$H_2EDTA^{2-}(aq) + V^{2+}(aq) \rightleftharpoons VEDTA^{2-}(aq) + 2 H^+(aq) \quad K = \frac{[VEDTA^{2-}][H^+]^2}{[H_2EDTA^{2-}][V^{2+}]}$$

In this titration reaction, equal moles of V^{2+} and H_2EDTA^{2-} are reacted at the stoichiometric point. Therefore, equal moles of both reactants must be present at equilibrium, so $[H_2EDTA^{2-}] = [V^{2+}] = 1.3 \times 10^{-15}\,M$. In addition, because $[V^{2+}]$ at equilibrium is very small as compared to the initial 0.0400 M concentration, the reaction essentially goes to completion. The moles of $VEDTA^{2-}$ produced will equal the moles of V^{2+} reacted (= 0.0400 mol). At equilibrium, $[VEDTA^{2-}] = 0.0400$ mol/(1.00 L + 0.5000 L) = 0.0267 M. Finally, since we have a buffer solution, then the pH is assumed not to change so $[H^+] = 10^{-10.00} = 1.0 \times 10^{-10}\,M$. Calculating K for the reaction:

$$K = \frac{[\text{VEDTA}^{2-}][\text{H}^+]^2}{[\text{H}_2\text{EDTA}^{2-}][\text{V}^{2+}]} = \frac{(0.0267)(1.0 \times 10^{-10})^2}{(1.3 \times 10^{-15})(1.3 \times 10^{-15})} = 1.6 \times 10^8$$

c. At the halfway point, 250.0 mL of $\text{H}_2\text{EDTA}^{2-}$ has been added to 1.00 L of 0.0400 M V^{2+}. Exactly one-half of the 0.0400 mol of V^{2+} present initially has been converted into VEDTA^{2-}. Therefore, 0.0200 mol of V^{2+} remains in $1.00 + 0.2500 = 1.25$ L solution.

$$E_{cell} = 1.54 \text{ V} - \frac{0.0591}{n}\log\frac{[\text{V}^{2+}]}{[\text{Cu}^{2+}]} = 1.54 - \frac{0.0591}{2}\log\frac{(0.0200/1.25)}{1.00}$$

$$E_{cell} = 1.54 - (-0.0531) = 1.59 \text{ V}$$

129. Begin by choosing any reduction potential as 0.00 V. For example, let's assume

$$\text{B}^{2+} + 2\,e^- \rightarrow \text{B} \qquad E° = 0.00 \text{ V}$$

From the data, when B/B^{2+} and E/E^{2+} are together as a cell, $E° = 0.81$ V.

$\text{E}^{2+} + 2\,e^- \rightarrow \text{E}$ must have a potential of -0.81 V or 0.81 V since E may be involved in either the reduction or the oxidation half-reaction. We will arbitrarily choose E to have a potential of -0.81 V.

Setting the reduction potential at -0.81 for E and 0.00 for B, we get the following table of potentials.

$$\text{B}^{2+} + 2\,e^- \rightarrow \text{B} \qquad 0.00 \text{ V}$$

$$\text{E}^{2+} + 2\,e^- \rightarrow \text{E} \qquad -0.81 \text{ V}$$

$$\text{D}^{2+} + 2\,e^- \rightarrow \text{D} \qquad 0.19 \text{ V}$$

$$\text{C}^{2+} + 2\,e^- \rightarrow \text{C} \qquad -0.94 \text{ V}$$

$$\text{A}^{2+} + 2\,e^- \rightarrow \text{A} \qquad -0.53 \text{ V}$$

From largest to smallest:

$$\text{D}^{2+} + 2\,e^- \rightarrow \text{D} \qquad 0.19 \text{ V}$$

$$\text{B}^{2+} + 2\,e^- \rightarrow \text{B} \qquad 0.00 \text{ V}$$

$$\text{A}^{2+} + 2\,e^- \rightarrow \text{A} \qquad -0.53 \text{ V}$$

$$\text{E}^{2+} + 2\,e^- \rightarrow \text{E} \qquad -0.81 \text{ V}$$

$$\text{C}^{2+} + 2\,e^- \rightarrow \text{C} \qquad -0.94 \text{ V}$$

$A^{2+} + 2\,e^- \rightarrow A$ is in the middle. Let's call this 0.00 V. We get:

$$D^{2+} + 2\,e^- \rightarrow D \quad 0.72 \text{ V}$$

$$B^{2+} + 2\,e^- \rightarrow B \quad 0.53 \text{ V}$$

$$A^{2+} + 2\,e^- \rightarrow A \quad 0.00 \text{ V}$$

$$E^{2+} + 2\,e^- \rightarrow E \quad -0.28 \text{ V}$$

$$C^{2+} + 2\,e^- \rightarrow C \quad -0.41 \text{ V}$$

Of course, since the reduction potential of E could have been assumed to 0.81 V instead of -0.81 V, we can also get:

$$C^{2+} + 2\,e^- \rightarrow C \quad 0.41 \text{ V}$$

$$E^{2+} + 2\,e^- \rightarrow E \quad 0.28 \text{ V}$$

$$A^{2+} + 2\,e^- \rightarrow A \quad 0.00 \text{ V}$$

$$B^{2+} + 2\,e^- \rightarrow B \quad -0.53 \text{ V}$$

$$D^{2+} + 2\,e^- \rightarrow D \quad -0.72 \text{ V}$$

One way to determine which table is correct is to add metal C to a solution with D^{2+} and metal D to a solution with C^{2+}. If D comes out of solution, the first table is correct. If C comes out of solution, the second table is correct.

CHAPTER EIGHTEEN

THE NUCLEUS: A CHEMIST'S VIEW

For Review

1.   a.   Thermodynamic stability: the potential energy of a particular nucleus as compared to the sum of the potential energies of its component protons and neutrons.

         b.   Kinetic stability: the probability that a nucleus will undergo decomposition to form a different nucleus.

         c.   Radioactive decay: a spontaneous decomposition of a nucleus to form a different nucleus.

         d.   Beta-particle production: a decay process for radioactive nuclides where an electron is produced; the mass number remains constant and the atomic number changes.

         e.   Alpha-particle production: a common mode of decay for heavy radioactive nuclides where a helium nucleus is produced causing the mass number to change.

         f.   Positron production: a mode of nuclear decay in which a particle is formed having the same mass as an electron but opposite in charge.

         g.   Electron capture: a process in which one of the inner-orbital electrons in an atom is captured by the nucleus.

         h.   Gamma-ray emissions; the production of high-energy photons called gamma rays that frequently accompany nuclear decays and particle reactions.

A is the mass number and is equal to the number of protons plus neutrons in a nuclei; the sum of all the mass number values must be the same on both sides of the equation (A is conserved). Z is the atomic number and is equal to the number of protons in a nucleus; the sum of the atomic number values must also be the same on both sides of the equation (Z is conserved).

2.   The zone of stability is the area encompassing the stable nuclides on a plot of their positions as a function of the number of protons and the number of neutrons in the nucleus. The neutron/proton ratio increases to a number greater than one as elements become heavier. Nuclides with too many neutrons undergo beta-particle production in order to decrease the neutron/proton ratio to a more stable value. Position production, electron capture and alpha-particle production all increase the neutron/proton ratio, so these occur for nuclides having too many protons.

3.   First-order kinetics is where there is a direct relationship between the rate of decay and the number of nuclides in a given sample. The rate law for all radioactive decay is rate = kN. Because of the direct relationship between rate and N, as the number of nuclides is halved, the rate is also halved. The first-order rate law and the integrated first-order rate law are:

$$\text{rate} = kN \text{ and } \ln\left(\frac{N}{N_o}\right) = -kt$$

k is the first-order rate constant, N is the number of nuclides present at some time t, N_o is the initial number of nuclides present at t = 0, and t is the time the decay process has been occurring.

The half-life equation is: $t_{1/2} = \ln 2/k$. The half-life for all radioactive decay is independent of the number of nuclides present; it is a constant. From the half-life equation, $t_{1/2}$ is inversely related to the rate constant, k. As k increases, $t_{1/2}$ decreases and vice versa.

4.   Nuclear transformation: the change of one element into another. Like all nuclear processes, the reaction must be mass number balanced and atomic number balanced. Particle accelerators are devices used to accelerate nuclear particles to very high speeds. Because of the electrostatic repulsion between the target nucleus and a positive ion, accelerators are needed for bombardment of like charged ions in order to overcome the electrostatic repulsion.

5.   Geiger counter: an instrument that measures the rate of radioactive decay based on the ions and electrons produced as a radioactive particle passes through a gas-filled chamber. The instrument takes advantage of the fact that the high-energy particles from radioactive decay processes produce ions when they travel through matter. The formation of ions and electrons by the passage of high-energy particles allows a momentary current to flow. Electronic devices detect the current flow and the number of these events can be counted. This gives the decay rate of the radioactive sample.

Scintillation counter: an instrument that measures radioactive decay by sensing flashes of light produced in a substance by the radiation. Certain substances, such as zinc sulfide, give off light when they are struck by high energy radiation. A photocell senses the flashes of light which is a measure of the number of decay events per unit of time.

Radiotracer: a radioactive nuclide, introduced into an organism for diagnostic purposes, whose pathway can be traced by monitoring its radioactivity. ^{14}C and ^{31}P work well as radiotracers because the molecules in the body contain carbon and/or phosphorus; they will be incorporated into the worker molecules of the body easily, which allows monitoring of the pathways of these worker molecules. ^{131}I works well for thyroid problems because iodine concentrates in the thyroid.

To study chemical equilibrium, a nonradioactive substance can be put in equilibrium with a radioactive substance. The two materials can then be checked to see if all the radioactivity remains in the original material or if it has been scrambled by the equilibrium. The scrambling of the radioactive substance is proof that equilibrium is dynamic.

6.   Plants take in CO_2 in the photosynthesis process, which incorporates carbon, including ^{14}C, into its molecules. As long as the plant is alive, the $^{14}C/^{12}C$ ratio in the plant will equal the

ratio in the atmosphere. When the plant dies, ^{14}C is not replenished as ^{14}C decays by beta-particle production. By measuring the ^{14}C activity today in the artifact and comparing this to the assumed ^{14}C activity when the plant died to make the artifact, an age can be determined for the artifact. The assumptions are that the ^{14}C level in the atmosphere is constant or that the ^{14}C level at the time the plant died can be calculated. A constant ^{14}C level is a pure assumption, and accounting for variation is complicated. Another problem is that some of the material must be destroyed to determine the ^{14}C level.

^{238}U has a half-life of 4.5×10^9 years. In order to be useful, we need a significant number of decay events by ^{238}U to have occurred. With the extremely long half-life of ^{238}U, the period of time required for a significant number of decay events is on the order of 10^8 years. This is the time frame of when the earth was formed. ^{238}U is worthless for aging 10,000 year-old objects or less because a measurable quantity of decay events has not occurred in 10,000 years or less. ^{14}C is good at dating these objects because ^{14}C has a half-life on the order of 10^3 years. ^{14}C is worthless for dating ancient objects because of the relatively short half-life; no discernable amount of ^{14}C will remain after 10^8 years.

7.   Mass defect: the change in mass occurring when a nucleus is formed from its component nucleons.

Binding energy: the energy required to decompose a nucleus into its component nucleons.

The mass defect is determined by summing the masses of the individual neutrons and protons that make up a nuclide and comparing this to the actual mass of the nuclide. The difference in mass is the mass defect. This quantity of mass determines the energy released when a nuclide is formed from its protons and neutrons. This energy is called the binding energy. The equation $\Delta E = \Delta mc^2$ allows conversion of the mass defect into the binding energy. ^{56}Fe, with the largest binding energy per nucleon of any nuclide, is the most stable nuclide. This is because when ^{56}Fe is formed from its protons and neutrons, it has the largest relative mass defect. Therefore, ^{56}Fe is the most stable nuclei because it would require the largest amount of energy per nucleon to decompose the nucleus.

8.   Fission: splitting of a heavy nucleus into two (or more) lighter nuclei.

Fusion: Combining two light nuclei to form a heavier nucleus.

The energy changes for these nuclear processes are typically millions of times larger than those associated with chemical reactions. The fusion of ^{235}U produces about 26 million times more energy than the combustion of methane.

The maximum biding energy per nucleon occurs at Fe. Nuclei smaller than Fe become more stable by fusing to form heavier nuclei closer in mass to Fe. Nuclei larger than Fe form more stable nuclei by splitting to form lighter nuclei closer in mass to Fe. In each process, more stable nuclei are formed. The difference in stability is released as energy.

For fusion reactions, a collision of sufficient energy must occur between two positively charged particles to initiate the reaction. This requires high temperatures. In fission, an electrically neutral neutron collides with the positively charged nucleus. This has a much lower activation energy.

9. ^{235}U splits into lighter elements when it absorbs a neutron; neutrons are also produced in the fission reaction. These neutrons produced can go on to react with other ^{235}U nuclides, thus continuing the reaction. This self-sustaining fission process is called a chain reaction.

In order for a fission process to be self-sustaining, at least one neutron from each fission event must go on to split another nucleus. If, on average, less than one neutron causes another fission event, the process dies out and the reaction is said to be subcritical. A reaction is critical when exactly one neutron from each fission event causes another event to occur. For supercritical reactions, more than one neutron produced causes another fission event to occur. Here, the process escalates rapidly and the heat build up causes a violent explosion. The critical mass is the mass of fissionable material required to produce a self-sustaining chain reaction, not too small and not too large.

Reference Figure 18.14 for a schematic of a nuclear power plant. The energy produced from controlled fission reactions is used to heat water to produce steam to run turbine engines. This is how coal-burning power plants generate energy.

Moderator: slows the neutrons to increase the efficiency of the fission reaction.

Control rods: absorbs neutrons to slow or halt the fission reaction.

Some problems associated with nuclear reactors are radiation exposure to workers, disposal of wastes, nuclear accidents including a meltdown, and potential terrorist targets. Another problem is the supply of ^{235}U, which is not endless. There may not be enough ^{235}U on earth to make fission economically feasible in the long run.

Breeder reactors produce fissionable fuel as the reactor runs. The current breeder reactors convert the abundant ^{238}U isotope (which is nonfissionable) into fissionable plutonium. The reaction involves absorption of a neutron. Breeder reactors, however, have the additional hazard of handling plutonium which flames on contact with air and is very toxic.

10.   Some factors for the biological effects of radiation exposure are:

a.   The energy of the radiation. The higher the energy, the more damage it can cause.

b.   The penetrating ability of radiation. The ability of specific radiation to penetrate human tissue where it can do damage must be considered.

c.   The ionizing ability of the radiation. When biomolecules are ionized, there function is usually disturbed.

d.   The chemical properties of the radiation source. Specifically, can the radioactive substance be readily incorporated into the body, or is the radiation source inert chemically so it passes through the body relatively quickly.

^{90}Sr will be incorporated into the body by replacing calcium in the bones. Once incorporated, ^{90}Sr can cause leukemia and bone cancer. Krypton is chemically inert so it will not be incorporated into the body.

Even though gamma rays penetrate human tissue very deeply, they are very small and cause only occasional ionization of biomolecules. Alpha particles, because they are much more massive, are very effective at causing ionization of biomolecules; these produce a dense trail of damage once they get inside an organism.

Questions

1. Characteristic frequencies of energies emitted in a nuclear reaction suggest that discrete energy levels exist in the nucleus. The extra stability of certain numbers of nucleons and the predominance of nuclei with even numbers of nucleons suggest that the nuclear structure might be described by using quantum numbers.

2. No, coal-fired power plants also pose risks. A partial list of risks is:

Coal	Nuclear
Air pollution	Radiation exposure to workers
Coal mine accidents	Disposal of wastes
Health risks to miners	Meltdown
(black lung disease)	Terrorists
	Public fear

3. β-particle production has the net effect of turning a neutron into a proton. Radioactive nuclei having too many neutrons typically undergo β-particle decay. Positron production has the net effect of turning a proton into a neutron. Nuclei having too many protons typically undergo positron decay.

4. Annihilation is collision of matter and antimatter resulting in the change of particulate matter into electromagnetic radiation.

5. The transuranium elements are the elements having more protons than uranium. They are synthesized by bombarding heavier nuclei with neutrons and positive ions in a particle accelerator.

6. All radioactive decay follows first order kinetics. A sample is analyzed for the ^{176}Lu and ^{176}Hf content, from which the first order rate law can be applied to determine the age of the sample. The reason ^{176}Lu decay is valuable for dating very old objects is the extremely long half-life. Substances formed a long time ago that have short half-lives have virtually no remaining nuclei. On the other hand, ^{176}Lu decay hasn't even approached one half-life when dating 5 billion year old objects.

7. $\Delta E = \Delta mc^2$; The key difference is the mass change when going from reactants to products. In chemical reactions, the mass change is indiscernible. In nuclear processes, the mass change is discernable. It is the conversion of this discernable mass change into energy that results in the huge energies associated with nuclear processes.

8. Effusion is the passage of a gas through a tiny orifice into an evacuated container. Graham's law of effusion says that the effusion of a gas in inversely proportional to the square root of

the mass of its particle. The key to effusion, and to the gaseous diffusion process, is that they are both directly related to the velocity of the gas molecules, which is inversely related to the molar mass. The lighter $^{235}UF_6$ gas molecules have a faster average velocity than the heavier $^{238}UF_6$ gas molecules. The difference in average velocity is used in the gaseous diffusion process to enrich the ^{235}U content in natural uranium.

9. Sr-90 is an alkaline earth metal having chemical properties similar to calcium. Sr-90 can collect in bones replacing some of the calcium. Once embedded inside the human body, β particles can do significant damage. Rn-222 is a noble gas so one would expect Rn to be unreactive and pass through the body quickly; it does. The problem with Rn-222 is the rate at which it produces alpha particles. With a short half-life, the few moments that Rn-222 is in the lungs, a significant number of decay events can occur; each decay event produces an alpha particle which is very effective at causing ionization and can produce a dense trail of damage.

10. The linear model postulates that damage from radiation is proportional to the dose, even at low levels of exposure. Thus any exposure is dangerous. The threshold model, on the other hand, assumes that no significant damage occurs below a certain exposure, called the threshold exposure. A recent study supported the linear model.

Exercises

Radioactive Decay and Nuclear Transformations

11. All nuclear reactions must be charge balanced and mass balanced. To charge balance, balance the sum of the atomic numbers on each side of the reaction, and to mass balance, balance the sum of the mass numbers on each side of the reaction.

   a. $^{51}_{24}Cr + ^{0}_{-1}e \rightarrow ^{51}_{23}V$ b. $^{131}_{53}I \rightarrow ^{0}_{-1}e + ^{131}_{54}Xe$

12. a. $^{32}_{15}P \rightarrow ^{0}_{-1}e + ^{32}_{16}S$ b. $^{235}_{92}U \rightarrow ^{4}_{2}He + ^{231}_{90}Th$

13. a. $^{68}_{31}Ga + ^{0}_{-1}e \rightarrow ^{68}_{30}Zn$ b. $^{62}_{29}Cu \rightarrow ^{0}_{+1}e + ^{62}_{28}Ni$

   c. $^{212}_{87}Fr \rightarrow ^{4}_{2}He + ^{208}_{85}At$ d. $^{129}_{51}Sb \rightarrow ^{0}_{-1}e + ^{129}_{52}Te$

14. a. $^{73}_{31}Ga \rightarrow ^{73}_{32}Ge + ^{0}_{-1}e$ b. $^{192}_{78}Pt \rightarrow ^{188}_{76}Os + ^{4}_{2}He$

   c. $^{205}_{83}Bi \rightarrow ^{205}_{82}Pb + ^{0}_{+1}e$ d. $^{241}_{96}Cm + ^{0}_{-1}e \rightarrow ^{241}_{95}Am$

15. $^{247}_{97}Bk \rightarrow ^{207}_{82}Pb + ? \, ^{4}_{2}He + ^{0}_{-1}e$; The change in mass number (247 – 207 = 40) is due exclusively to the alpha particles. A change in mass number of 40 requires $10 \, ^{4}_{2}He$ particles to be produced. The atomic number only changes by 97 – 82 = 15. The 10 alpha particles change the atomic number by 20, so $5 \, ^{0}_{-1}e$ (5 beta particles) are produced in the decay series of ^{247}Bk to ^{207}Pb.

16.   a. $^{241}_{95}\text{Am} \rightarrow \ ^{4}_{2}\text{He} + \ ^{237}_{93}\text{Np}$

       b. $^{241}_{95}\text{Am} \rightarrow 8\ ^{4}_{2}\text{He} + 4\ ^{0}_{-1}\text{e} + \ ^{209}_{83}\text{Bi}$; The final product is $^{209}_{83}\text{Bi}$.

       c. $^{241}_{95}\text{Am} \rightarrow \ ^{237}_{93}\text{Np} + \alpha \rightarrow \ ^{233}_{91}\text{Pa} + \alpha \rightarrow \ ^{233}_{92}\text{U} + \beta \rightarrow \ ^{229}_{90}\text{Th} + \alpha \rightarrow \ ^{225}_{88}\text{Ra} + \alpha$
       $$\downarrow$$
       $^{213}_{84}\text{Po} + \beta \leftarrow \ ^{213}_{83}\text{Bi} + \alpha \leftarrow \ ^{217}_{85}\text{At} + \alpha \leftarrow \ ^{221}_{87}\text{Fr} + \alpha \leftarrow \ ^{225}_{89}\text{Ac} + \beta$
       $$\downarrow$$
       $^{209}_{82}\text{Pb} + \alpha \rightarrow \ ^{209}_{83}\text{Bi} + \beta$

       The intermediate radionuclides are:
       $^{237}_{93}\text{Np}$, $^{233}_{91}\text{Pa}$, $^{233}_{92}\text{U}$, $^{229}_{90}\text{Th}$, $^{225}_{88}\text{Ra}$, $^{225}_{89}\text{Ac}$, $^{221}_{87}\text{Fr}$, $^{217}_{85}\text{At}$, $^{213}_{83}\text{Bi}$, $^{213}_{84}\text{Po}$, and $^{209}_{82}\text{Pb}$.

17. $^{53}_{26}\text{Fe}$ has too many protons. It will undergo either positron production, electron capture and/or alpha particle production. $^{59}_{26}\text{Fe}$ has too many neutrons and will undergo beta particle production. (See Table 18.2 of the text.)

18.   Reference Table 18.2 of the text for potential radioactive decay processes. ^{17}F and ^{18}F contain too many protons or too few neutrons. Electron capture and positron production are both possible decay mechanisms that increase the neutron to proton ratio. Alpha particle production also increases the neutron to proton ratio, but it is not likely for these light nuclei. ^{21}F contains too many neutrons or too few protons. Beta production lowers the neutron to proton ratio, so we expect ^{21}F to be a β-emitter.

19.   a. $^{249}_{98}\text{Cf} + \ ^{18}_{8}\text{O} \rightarrow \ ^{263}_{106}\text{Sg} + 4\ ^{0}_{1}\text{n}$ b. $^{259}_{104}\text{Rf}$; $^{263}_{106}\text{Sg} \rightarrow \ ^{4}_{2}\text{He} + \ ^{259}_{104}\text{Rf}$

20.   a. $^{240}_{95}\text{Am} + \ ^{4}_{2}\text{He} \rightarrow \ ^{243}_{97}\text{Bk} + \ ^{0}_{1}\text{n}$ b. $^{238}_{92}\text{U} + \ ^{12}_{6}\text{C} \rightarrow \ ^{244}_{98}\text{Cf} + 6\ ^{0}_{1}\text{n}$

       c. $^{249}_{98}\text{Cf} + \ ^{15}_{7}\text{N} \rightarrow \ ^{260}_{105}\text{Db} + 4\ ^{0}_{1}\text{n}$ d. $^{249}_{98}\text{Cf} + \ ^{10}_{5}\text{B} \rightarrow \ ^{257}_{103}\text{Lr} + 2\ ^{0}_{1}\text{n}$

Kinetics of Radioactive Decay

21.   All radioactive decay follows first-order kinetics where $t_{1/2} = (\ln 2)/k$.

$$t_{1/2} = \frac{\ln 2}{k} = \frac{0.693}{1.0 \times 10^{-3}\ \text{h}^{-1}} = 690\ \text{h}$$

22. $k = \dfrac{\ln 2}{t_{1/2}} = \dfrac{0.69315}{432.2\,\text{yr}} \times \dfrac{1\,\text{yr}}{365\,\text{d}} \times \dfrac{1\,\text{d}}{24\,\text{h}} \times \dfrac{1\,\text{h}}{3600\,\text{s}} = 5.086 \times 10^{-11}\ \text{s}^{-1}$

$$\text{Rate} = kN = 5.086 \times 10^{-11}\ s^{-1}\ \times 5.00\ g \times \frac{1\ mol}{241\ g} \times \frac{6.022 \times 10^{23}\ nuclei}{mol}$$

$$= 6.35 \times 10^{11}\ decays/s$$

6.35×10^{11} alpha particles are emitted each second from a 5.00 g ^{241}Am sample.

23.   Kr-81 is most stable because it has the longest half-life while Kr-73 is hottest (least stable) because it has the shortest half-life.

12.5% of each isotope will remain after 3 half-lives:

$$100\% \xrightarrow[t_{1/2}]{} 50\% \xrightarrow[t_{1/2}]{} 25\% \xrightarrow[t_{1/2}]{} 12.5\%$$

For Kr-73: t = 3(27 s) = 81 s;   For Kr-74: t = 3(11.5 min) = 34.5 min

For Kr-76: t = 3(14.8 h) = 44.4 h;   For Kr-81: t = 3(2.1 × 10^5 yr) = 6.3 × 10^5 yr

22. $k = \dfrac{\ln 2}{t_{1/2}} = \dfrac{0.6931}{12.8\ d} \times \dfrac{1\ d}{24\ h} \times \dfrac{1\ h}{3600\ s} = 6.27 \times 10^{-7}\ s^{-1}$

b.   Rate $= kN = 6.27 \times 10^{-7}\ s^{-1}\ \times \left(28.0 \times 10^{-3}\ g\ \times \dfrac{1\ mol}{64.0\ g} \times \dfrac{6.022 \times 10^{23}\ nuclei}{mol} \right)$

Rate $= 1.65 \times 10^{14}$ decays/s

c.   25% of the ^{64}Cu will remain after 2 half-lives (100% decays to 50% after one half-life, which decays to 25% after a second half-life). Hence, 2(12.8 days) = 25.6 days is the time frame for the experiment.

25.   Units for N and N$_o$ are usually the number of nuclei but can also be grams if the units are the same for both N and N$_o$. In this problem m = the mass of ^{32}P that remains.

$$175\ mg\ \ Na_3{}^{32}PO_4 \times \frac{32.0\ mg\ ^{32}P}{165.0\ mg\ Na_3{}^{32}PO_4} = 33.9\ mg\ ^{32}P\ \text{initially};\ \ k = \frac{\ln 2}{t_{1/2}}$$

$$\ln\left(\frac{N}{N_0}\right) = -kt = \frac{-0.6931\,t}{t_{1/2}},\ \ \ln\left(\frac{m}{33.9\ mg}\right) = \frac{-0.6931(35.0\ d)}{14.3\ d};\ \text{Carrying extra sig. figs.:}$$

$\ln(m) = -1.696 + 3.523 = 1.827,\ m = e^{1.827} = 6.22\ mg\ ^{32}P$ remains

26.   a. $0.0100\ Ci \times \dfrac{3.7 \times 10^{10}\ decays/s}{Ci} = 3.7 \times 10^8\ decays/s;\ \ k = \dfrac{\ln 2}{t_{1/2}}$

Rate $= kN,\ \ \dfrac{3.7 \times 10^8\ decays}{s} = \left(\dfrac{0.6931}{2.87\ h} \times \dfrac{1\ h}{3600\ s} \right) \times N,\ N = 5.5 \times 10^{12}$ atoms of ^{38}S

$$5.5 \times 10^{12} \text{ atoms } ^{38}\text{S} \times \frac{1 \text{ mol } ^{38}\text{S}}{6.02 \times 10^{23} \text{ atoms}} \times \frac{1 \text{ mol Na}_2 ^{38}\text{SO}_4}{\text{mol } ^{38}\text{S}} = 9.1 \times 10^{-12} \text{ mol Na}_2 ^{38}\text{SO}_4$$

$$9.1 \times 10^{-12} \text{ mol Na}_2 ^{38}\text{SO}_4 \times \frac{148.0 \text{ g Na}_2 ^{38}\text{SO}_4}{\text{mol Na}_2 ^{38}\text{SO}_4} = 1.3 \times 10^{-9} \text{ g} = 1.3 \text{ ng Na}_2 ^{38}\text{SO}_4$$

b.   99.99% decays, 0.01% left; $\ln\left(\dfrac{0.01}{100}\right) = -kt = \dfrac{-0.6931 t}{2.87 \text{ h}}$, t = 38.1 hours $\approx$ 40 hours

27. $t = 61.0 \text{ yr}; \quad k = \dfrac{\ln 2}{t_{1/2}}; \quad \ln\left(\dfrac{N}{N_0}\right) = -kt = \dfrac{-0.6931 \times 61.0 \text{ yr}}{28.8 \text{ yr}} = -1.47, \quad \left(\dfrac{N}{N_0}\right) = e^{-1.47} = 0.230$

23.0% of the ^{90}Sr remains as of July 16, 2006.

28.   Assuming 2 significant figures in 1/100:

$$\ln(N/N_o) = -kt; \quad N = 0.010 \, N_o; \quad t_{1/2} = (\ln 2)/k$$

$$\ln(0.010) = \frac{-(\ln 2)t}{t_{1/2}} = \frac{-0.693 \, t}{8.1 \, \text{d}}, \quad t = 54 \text{ days}$$

29. $\ln\left(\dfrac{N}{N_0}\right) = -kt = \dfrac{-(\ln 2) \, t}{t_{1/2}}, \quad \ln\left(\dfrac{1.0 \text{ g}}{N_0}\right) = \dfrac{-0.693\left(3.0 \text{ d} \times \dfrac{24 \text{ h}}{\text{d}} \times \dfrac{60 \text{ min}}{\text{h}}\right)}{1.0 \times 10^3 \text{ min}}$

$\ln\left(\dfrac{1.0}{N_0}\right) = -3.0, \quad \dfrac{1.0}{N_0} = e^{-3.0}, \quad N_0 = 20. \text{ g } ^{82}\text{Br needed}$

$$20. \text{ g } ^{82}\text{Br} \times \frac{1 \text{ mol } ^{82}\text{Br}}{82.0 \text{ g}} \times \frac{1 \text{ mol Na}^{82}\text{Br}}{\text{mol } ^{82}\text{Br}} \times \frac{105.0 \text{ g Na}^{82}\text{Br}}{\text{mol Na}^{82}\text{Br}} = 26 \text{ g Na}^{82}\text{Br}$$

30.   Assuming the current year is 2006, t = 60. yr.

$\ln\left(\dfrac{N}{N_0}\right) = -kt = \dfrac{-0.693 \, t}{t_{1/2}}, \quad \ln\left(\dfrac{N}{5.5}\right) = \dfrac{-0.693(60. \text{ yr})}{12.3 \text{ yr}}, \quad N = \dfrac{0.19 \text{ decay events}}{\text{min} \bullet 100. \text{ g water}}$

31. $k = \dfrac{\ln 2}{t_{1/2}}; \quad \ln\left(\dfrac{N}{N_0}\right) = -kt = \dfrac{-0.693 \, t}{t_{1/2}}, \quad \ln\left(\dfrac{N}{13.6}\right) = \dfrac{-0.693 \, (15,000 \text{ yr})}{5730 \text{ yr}} = -1.8$

$\dfrac{N}{13.6} = e^{-1.8} = 0.17, \quad N = 13.6 \times 0.17 = 2.3 \text{ counts per minute per g of C}$

If we had 10. mg C, we would see:

$$10.\ mg \times \frac{1\ g}{1000\ mg} \times \frac{2.3\ counts}{min\ g} = \frac{0.023\ counts}{min}$$

It would take roughly 40 min to see a single disintegration. This is too long to wait, and the background radiation would probably be much greater than the ^{14}C activity. Thus, ^{14}C dating is not practical for very small samples.

32. $\ln\left(\dfrac{N}{N_0}\right) = -kt = \dfrac{-0.6931\,t}{t_{1/2}}, \quad \ln\left(\dfrac{1.2}{13.6}\right) = \dfrac{-0.6931\,t}{5730\ yr}, \quad t = 2.0 \times 10^4\ yr$

33.   Assuming 1.000 g ^{238}U present in a sample, then 0.688 g ^{206}Pb is present. Since 1 mol ^{206}Pb is produced per mol ^{238}U decayed, then:

$$^{238}U\ decayed = 0.688\ g\ Pb \times \frac{1\ mol\ Pb}{206\ g\ Pb} \times \frac{1\ mol\ U}{mol\ Pb} \times \frac{238\ g\ U}{mol\ U} = 0.795\ g\ ^{238}U$$

Original mass ^{238}U present = 1.000 g + 0.795 g = 1.795 g ^{238}U

$$\ln\left(\frac{N}{N_0}\right) = -kt = \frac{-(\ln 2)\,t}{t_{1/2}}, \quad \ln\left(\frac{1.000\ g}{1.795\ g}\right) = \frac{-0.693\,(t)}{4.5 \times 10^9\ yr}, \quad t = 3.8 \times 10^9\ yr$$

34.   a.   The decay of ^{40}K is not the sole source of ^{40}Ca.

      b.   Decay of ^{40}K is the sole source of ^{40}Ar and that no ^{40}Ar is lost over the years.

      c. $\dfrac{0.95\ g\ ^{40}Ar}{1.00\ g\ ^{40}K}$ = current mass ratio

          0.95 g of ^{40}K decayed to ^{40}Ar. 0.95 g of ^{40}K is only 10.7% of the total ^{40}K that decayed, or:

          0.107 (m) = 0.95 g,   m = 8.9 g = total mass of ^{40}K that decayed

          Mass of ^{40}K when the rock was formed was 1.00 g + 8.9 g = 9.9 g.

$$\ln\left(\frac{1.00\ g\ ^{40}K}{9.9\ g\ ^{40}K}\right) = -kt = \frac{-(\ln 2)\,t}{t_{1/2}} = \frac{-0.6931\,t}{1.27 \times 10^9\ yr}, \quad t = 4.2 \times 10^9\ years\ old$$

      d.   If some ^{40}Ar escaped, then the measured ratio of $^{40}Ar/^{40}K$ is less than it should be. We would calculate the age of the rock to be less than it actually is.

Energy Changes in Nuclear Reactions

35. $\Delta E = \Delta m c^2, \ \Delta m = \dfrac{\Delta E}{c^2} = \dfrac{3.9 \times 10^{23} \text{ kg m}^2/\text{s}^2}{(3.00 \times 10^8 \text{ m/s})^2} = 4.3 \times 10^6 \text{ kg}$

The sun loses 4.3×10^6 kg of mass each second. Note: $1 \text{ J} = 1 \text{ kg m}^2/\text{s}^2$

36. $\dfrac{1.8 \times 10^{14} \text{ kJ}}{\text{s}} \times \dfrac{1000 \text{ J}}{\text{kJ}} \times \dfrac{3600 \text{ s}}{\text{h}} \times \dfrac{24 \text{ h}}{\text{day}} = 1.6 \times 10^{22} \text{ J/day}$

$\Delta E = \Delta m c^2, \ \Delta m = \dfrac{\Delta E}{c^2} = \dfrac{1.6 \times 10^{22} \text{ J}}{(3.00 \times 10^8 \text{ m/s})^2} = 1.8 \times 10^5$ kg of solar material provides 1 day
of solar energy to the earth.

$1.6 \times 10^{22} \text{ J} \times \dfrac{1 \text{ kJ}}{1000 \text{ J}} \times \dfrac{1 \text{ g}}{32 \text{ kJ}} \times \dfrac{1 \text{ kg}}{1000 \text{ g}} = 5.0 \times 10^{14}$ kg of coal is needed to provide the same
amount of energy.

37.   We need to determine the mass defect, Δm, between the mass of the nucleus and the mass of the individual parts that make up the nucleus. Once Δm is known, we can then calculate ΔE (the binding energy) using $E = mc^2$. Note: $1 \text{ J} = 1 \text{ kg m}^2/\text{s}^2$.

For $^{232}_{94}\text{Pu}$ (94 e, 94 p, 138 n):

mass of ^{232}Pu nucleus $= 3.85285 \times 10^{-22}$ g – mass of 94 electrons

mass of ^{232}Pu nucleus $= 3.85285 \times 10^{-22}$ g – $94(9.10939 \times 10^{-28})$ g $= 3.85199 \times 10^{-22}$ g

$\Delta m = 3.85199 \times 10^{-22}$ g – (mass of 94 protons + mass of 138 neutrons)

$\Delta m = 3.85199 \times 10^{-22}$ g – $[94(1.67262 \times 10^{-24}) + 138(1.67493 \times 10^{-24})]$ g
$= -3.168 \times 10^{-24}$ g

For 1 mol of nuclei: $\Delta m = -3.168 \times 10^{-24}$ g/nuclei $\times 6.0221 \times 10^{23}$ nuclei/mol
$= -1.908$ g/mol

$\Delta E = \Delta m c^2 = (-1.908 \times 10^{-3} \text{ kg/mol})(2.9979 \times 10^8 \text{ m/s})^2 = -1.715 \times 10^{14} = \text{J/mol}$

For $^{231}_{91}\text{Pa}$ (91 e, 91 p, 140 n):

mass of ^{231}Pa nucleus $= 3.83616 \times 10^{-22}$ g - $91(9.10939 \times 10^{-28})$ g $= 3.83533 \times 10^{-22}$ g

$\Delta m = 3.83533 \times 10^{-22}$ g - $[91(1.67262 \times 10^{-24}) + 140(1.67493 \times 10^{-24})]$ g
$= -3.166 \times 10^{-24}$ g

$$\Delta E = \Delta mc^2 = \frac{-3.166 \times 10^{-27} \text{ kg}}{\text{nuclei}} \times \frac{6.0221 \times 10^{23} \text{ nuclei}}{\text{mol}} \times \left(\frac{2.9979 \times 10^8 \text{ m}}{\text{s}} \right)^2$$

$$= -1.714 \times 10^{14} \text{ J/mol}$$

38. From the back page of the text, the mass of a proton = 1.00728 amu, the mass of a neutron = 1.00866 amu, and the mass of an electron = 5.486×10^{-4} amu.

Mass of nucleus = mass of atom - mass of electrons = 55.9349 - 26(0.0005486)
$$= 55.9206 \text{ amu}$$

$$26\,^1_1\text{H} + 30\,^1_0\text{n} \rightarrow \,^{56}_{26}\text{Fe}; \quad \Delta m = 55.9206 \text{ amu} - [26(1.00728) + 30(1.00866)] \text{ amu}$$
$$= -0.5285 \text{ amu}$$

$$\Delta E = \Delta mc^2 = -0.5285 \text{ amu} \times \frac{1.6605 \times 10^{-27} \text{ kg}}{\text{amu}} \times (2.9979 \times 10^8 \text{ m/s})^2 = -7.887 \times 10^{-11} \text{ J}$$

$$\frac{\text{binding energy}}{\text{nucleon}} = \frac{7.887 \times 10^{-11} \text{ J}}{56 \text{ nuleons}} = 1.408 \times 10^{-12} \text{ J/nucleon}$$

39. Let m_e = mass of electron; For ^{12}C (6e, 6p, 6n): mass defect = Δm = mass of ^{12}C nucleus – [mass of 6 protons + mass of 6 neutrons]. Note: the atomic masses of the elements given include the mass of the electrons.

$$\Delta m = 12.0000 \text{ amu} - 6 \, m_e - [6(1.00782 - m_e) + 6(1.00866)]; \quad \text{Mass of electrons cancel.}$$

$$\Delta m = 12.0000 - [6(1.00782) + 6(1.00866)] = -0.0989 \text{ amu}$$

$$\Delta E = \Delta mc^2 = -0.0989 \text{ amu} \times \frac{1.6605 \times 10^{-27} \text{ kg}}{\text{amu}} \times (2.9979 \times 10^8 \text{ m/s})^2 = -1.48 \times 10^{-11} \text{ J}$$

$$\frac{\text{BE}}{\text{nucleon}} = \frac{1.48 \times 10^{-11} \text{ J}}{12 \text{ nucleons}} = 1.23 \times 10^{-12} \text{ J/nucleon}$$

For ^{235}U (92e, 92p, 143n):

$$\Delta m = 235.0439 - 92 \, m_e - [92(1.00782 - m_e) + 143(1.00866)] = -1.9139 \text{ amu}$$

$$\Delta E = \Delta mc^2 = -1.9139 \text{ amu} \times \frac{1.66054 \times 10^{-27} \text{ kg}}{\text{amu}} \times (2.99792 \times 10^8 \text{ m/s})^2$$
$$= -2.8563 \times 10^{-10} \text{ J}$$

$$\frac{\text{BE}}{\text{nucleon}} = \frac{2.8563 \times 10^{-10} \text{ J}}{235 \text{ nucleons}} = 1.2154 \times 10^{-12} \text{ J/nucleon}$$

Because ^{56}Fe is the most stable known nucleus, the binding energy per nucleon for ^{56}Fe (1.408×10^{-12} J/nucleon) will be larger than that for ^{12}C or ^{235}U (see Figure 18.9 of the text).

40.   For $_1^2$H: mass defect = Δm = mass of $_1^2$H nucleus − mass of proton − mass of neutron; Let's determine the mass defect in a slightly different way than in Exercise 18.39. Instead of using the atomic mass of H−1, we will use the mass of the electron and the mass of the proton seperately. The mass of the ^{2}H nucleus will equal the atomic mass of ^{2}H minus the mass of the electron in a ^{2}H atom. From the back of the text, the pertinent masses are: $m_e = 5.49 \times 10^{-4}$ amu, $m_p = 1.00728$ amu, $m_n = 1.00866$ amu.

$$\Delta m = 2.01410 \text{ amu} - 0.000549 \text{ amu} - [1.00728 \text{ amu} + 1.00866 \text{ amu}] = -2.39 \times 10^{-3} \text{ amu}$$

$$\Delta E = \Delta mc^2 = -2.39 \times 10^{-3} \text{ amu} \times \frac{1.6605 \times 10^{-27} \text{ kg}}{\text{amu}} \times (2.998 \times 10^8 \text{ m/s})^2$$

$$= -3.57 \times 10^{-13} \text{ J}$$

$$\frac{\text{BE}}{\text{nucleon}} = \frac{3.57 \times 10^{-13} \text{ J}}{2 \text{ nucleons}} = 1.79 \times 10^{-13} \text{ J/nucleon}$$

For $_1^3$H, $\Delta m = 3.01605 - 0.000549 - [1.00728 + 2(1.00866)] = -9.10 \times 10^{-3}$ amu

$$\Delta E = -9.10 \times 10^{-3} \text{ amu} \times \frac{1.6605 \times 10^{-27} \text{ kg}}{\text{amu}} \times (2.998 \times 10^8 \text{ m/s})^2 = -1.36 \times 10^{-12} \text{ J}$$

$$\frac{\text{BE}}{\text{nucleon}} = \frac{1.36 \times 10^{-12} \text{ J}}{3 \text{ nucleons}} = 4.53 \times 10^{-13} \text{ J/nucleon}$$

41.   Let m_{Li} = mass of ^{6}Li nucleus; A ^{6}Li nucleus has 3p and 3n.

−0.03434 amu = m_{Li} − $(3m_p + 3m_n)$ = m_{Li} −[3(1.00728 amu) + 3(1.00866 amu)]

m_{Li} = 6.01348 amu

mass of ^{6}Li atom = 6.01348 amu + 3 m_e = 6.01348 + 3(5.49 × 10^{-4} amu) = 6.01513 amu
(includes mass of 3 e$^-$)

42.   binding energy = $\dfrac{1.326 \times 10^{-12} \text{ J}}{\text{nucleon}} \times 27$ nucleons = 3.580×10^{-11} J for each ^{27}Mg nucleus

$$\Delta E = \Delta mc^2, \quad \Delta m = \frac{\Delta E}{c^2} = \frac{-3.580 \times 10^{-11} \text{ J}}{(2.9979 \times 10^8 \text{ m/s})^2} = -3.983 \ 10^{-28} \text{ kg}$$

$$\Delta m = -3.983 \ 10^{-28} \text{ kg} \times \frac{1 \text{ amu}}{1.6605 \times 10^{-27} \text{ kg}} = -0.2399 \text{ amu}$$

Let m_{Mg} = mass of ^{27}Mg nucleus; A ^{27}Mg nucleus has 12 p and 15 n.

-0.2399 amu $= m_{Mg} - [12\ m_p + 15\ m_n] = m_{Mg} - [2(1.00728\ \text{amu}) + 15(1.00866\ \text{amu})]$

$m_{Mg} = 26.9764$ amu

mass of ^{27}Mg atom $= 26.9764\ \text{amu} + 12\ m_e,\ 26.9764 + 12(5.49\times 10^{-4}\ \text{amu}) = 26.9830$ amu (includes mass of 12 e⁻)

43. $^1_1H + ^1_1H \rightarrow\ ^2_1H + ^0_{+1}e;\ \ \Delta m = (2.01410\ \text{amu} - m_e + m_e) - 2(1.00782\ \text{amu} - m_e)$

$\Delta m = 2.01410 - 2(1.00782) + 2(0.000549) = -4.4 \times 10^{-4}$ amu for two protons reacting

When two mol of protons undergo fusion, $\Delta m = -4.4 \times 10^{-4}$ g.

$\Delta E = \Delta mc^2 = -4.4 \times 10^{-7}\ \text{kg} \times (3.00 \times 10^8\ \text{m/s})^2 = -4.0 \times 10^{10}$ J

$$\frac{-4.0 \times 10^{10}\ \text{J}}{2\ \text{mol protons}} \times \frac{1\ \text{mol}}{1.01\ \text{g}} = -2.0 \times 10^{10}\ \text{J/g of hydrogen nuclei}$$

44. $^2_1H + ^3_1H \rightarrow\ ^4_2H + ^0_1n;$ Using atomic masses, the masses of the electrons cancel when determining Δm for this nuclear reaction.

$\Delta m = [4.00260 + 1.00866 - (2.01410 + 3.01605)]\ \text{amu} = -1.889 \times 10^{-2}$ amu

For the production of one mol of ^4_2H: $\Delta m = -1.889 \times 10^{-2}\ \text{g} = -1.889 \times 10^{-5}\ \text{kg}$

$\Delta E = \Delta mc^2 = -1.889 \times 10^{-5}\ \text{kg} \times (2.9979 \times 10^8\ \text{m/s})^2 = -1.698 \times 10^{12}$ J/mol

For 1 nucleus of ^4_2H: $\dfrac{-1.698 \times 10^{12}\ \text{J}}{\text{mol}} \times \dfrac{1\ \text{mol}}{6.0221 \times 10^{23}\ \text{nuclei}} = -2.820 \times 10^{-12}\ \text{J/nucleus}$

Detection, Uses, and Health Effects of Radiation

45.   The Geiger-Müller tube has a certain response time. After the gas in the tube ionizes to produce a "count," some time must elapse for the gas to return to an electrically neutral state. The response of the tube levels off because at high activities, radioactive particles are entering the tube faster than the tube can respond to them.

46.   Not all of the emitted radiation enters the Geiger-Müller tube. The fraction of radiation entering the tube must be constant.

47.   All evolved oxygen in O_2 comes from water and not from carbon dioxide.

48.   Water is produced in this reaction by removing an OH group from one substance and H from the other substance. There are two ways to do this:

i. $CH_3\overset{\displaystyle O}{\overset{\|}{C}}\!-\!\!\boxed{OH \; + \; H}\!-\!^{18}OCH_3 \longrightarrow CH_3\overset{\displaystyle O}{\overset{\|}{C}}\!-\!^{18}OCH_3 \; + \; HO\!-\!H$

ii. $CH_3\overset{\displaystyle O}{\overset{\|}{C}}O\!-\!\!\boxed{H \; + \; H\,^{18}O}\!-\!CH_3 \longrightarrow CH_3\overset{\displaystyle O}{\overset{\|}{C}}O\!-\!CH_3 \; + \; H\!-\!^{18}OH$

Because the water produced is not radioactive, methyl acetate forms by the first reaction in which all the oxygen-18 ends up in methyl acetate.

49. $^{235}_{92}U \; + \; ^{1}_{0}n \; \rightarrow \; ^{144}_{58}Ce \; + \; ^{90}_{38}Sr \; + \; ? \; ^{1}_{0}n \; + \; ? \; ^{0}_{-1}e;$ To balance the atomic number, we need 4 β-particles and to balance the mass number, we need 2 neutrons.

50.   So $\; ^{238}_{92}U \; + \; ^{1}_{0}n \; \rightarrow \; ^{239}_{92}U \; \rightarrow \; ^{0}_{-1}e \; + \; ^{239}_{93}Np \; \rightarrow \; ^{0}_{-1}e \; + \; ^{239}_{94}Pu$

Plutonium-239 is the fissionable material in breeder reactors.

51.   Release of Sr is probably more harmful. Xe is chemically unreactive. Strontium is in the same family as calcium and could be absorbed and concentrated in the body in a fashion similar to Ca. This puts the radioactive Sr in the bones; red blood cells are produced in bone marrow. Xe would not be readily incorporated into the body.

The chemical properties determine where a radioactive material may be concentrated in the body or how easily it may be excreted. The length of time of exposure and what is exposed to radiation significantly affects the health hazard. (See exercise 18.52 for a specific example.)

52.   i) and ii) mean that Pu is not a significant threat outside the body. Our skin is sufficient to keep out the α particles. If Pu gets inside the body, it is easily oxidized to Pu^{4+} (iv), which is chemically similar to Fe^{3+} (iii). Thus, Pu^{4+} will concentrate in tissues where Fe^{3+} is found. One of these is the bone marrow where red blood cells are produced. Once inside the body, α particles cause considerable damage.

Additional Exercises

53.   The most abundant isotope is generally the most stable isotope. The periodic table predicts that the most stable isotopes for exercises a - d are ^{39}K, ^{56}Fe, ^{23}Na and ^{204}Tl. (Reference Table 18.2 of the text for potential decay processes.)

a.   Unstable; ^{45}K has too many neutrons and will undergo beta particle production.

b.   Stable

c. Unstable; ^{20}Na has too few neutrons and will most likely undergo electron capture or positron production. Alpha particle production makes too severe of a change to be a likely decay process for the relatively light ^{20}Na nuclei. Alpha particle production usually occurs for heavy nuclei.

d. Unstable; ^{194}Tl has too few neutrons and will undergo electron capture, positron production and/or alpha particle production.

54. $t_{1/2} = 5730$ yr; $k = (\ln 2)/t_{1/2}$; $\ln (N/N_o) = -kt$; $\ln\dfrac{15.1}{15.3} = \dfrac{-(\ln 2)t}{5730 \text{ yr}}$, $t = 109$ yr

No; From ^{14}C dating, the painting was produced during the late 1800s.

55. The third-life will be the time required for the number of nuclides to reach one-third of the original value ($N_0/3$).

$$\ln\left(\frac{N}{N_0}\right) = -kt = \frac{-0.6931\,t}{t_{1/2}}, \quad \ln\left(\frac{1}{3}\right) = \frac{-0.6931\,t}{31.4 \text{ yr}}, \quad t = 49.8 \text{ yr}$$

The third-life of this nuclide is 49.8 yr.

56. $\ln(N/N_o) = -kt$; $k = (\ln 2)/t_{1/2}$; $N = 0.001 \times N_o$

$$\ln\left(\frac{0.001 \times N_0}{N_0}\right) = \frac{-(\ln 2)\,t}{24{,}100 \text{ yr}}, \quad \ln 0.001 = -2.88 \times 10^{-5}\,t, \quad t = 2 \times 10^5 \text{ yr} = 200{,}000 \text{ yr}$$

57. $\ln\left(\dfrac{N}{N_0}\right) = -kt = \dfrac{-(\ln 2)\,t}{12.3 \text{ yr}}, \quad \ln\left(\dfrac{0.17 \times N_0}{N_0}\right) = -5.64 \times 10^{-2}\,t, \quad t = 31.4$ yr

It takes 31.4 yr for the tritium to decay to 17% of the original amount. Hence, the watch stopped fluorescing enough to be read in 1975 (1944 + 31.4).

58. $\Delta m = -2(5.486 \times 10^{-4} \text{ amu}) = -1.097 \times 10^{-3} \text{ amu}$

$$\Delta E = \Delta mc^2 = -1.097 \times 10^{-3} \text{ amu} \times \frac{1.6605 \times 10^{-27} \text{ kg}}{\text{amu}} \times (2.9979 \times 10^8 \text{ m/s})^2$$

$$= -1.637 \times 10^{-13} \text{ J}$$

$E_{photon} = 1/2(1.637 \times 10^{-13} \text{ J}) = 8.185 \times 10^{-14} \text{ J} = hc/\lambda$

$$\lambda = \frac{hc}{E} = \frac{6.6261 \times 10^{-34} \text{ J s} \times 2.9979 \times 10^8 \text{ m/s}}{8.185 \times 10^{-14} \text{ J}} = 2.427 \times 10^{-12} \text{ m} = 2.427 \times 10^{-3} \text{ nm}$$

59. $20{,}000$ ton TNT $\times \dfrac{4 \times 10^9 \text{ J}}{\text{ton TNT}} \times \dfrac{1 \text{ mol } ^{235}\text{U}}{2 \times 10^{13} \text{ J}} \times \dfrac{235 \text{ g } ^{235}\text{U}}{\text{mol } ^{235}\text{U}} = 940 \text{ g } ^{235}\text{U} \approx 900 \text{ g } ^{235}\text{U}$

This assumes that all of the ^{235}U undergoes fission.

60.   In order to sustain a nuclear chain reaction, the neutrons produced by the fission must be contained within the fissionable material so that they can go on to cause other fissions. The fissionable material must be closely packed together to ensure that neutrons are not lost to the outside. The critical mass is the mass of material in which exactly one neutron from each fission event causes another fission event so that the process sustains itself. A supercritical situation occurs when more than one neutron from each fission event causes another fission event. In this case, the process rapidly escalates and the heat build up causes a violent explosion.

61.   Mass of nucleus = atomic mass − mass of electron = 2.01410 amu − 0.000549 amu

$$= 2.01355 \text{ amu}$$

$$u_{rms} = \left(\frac{3\,RT}{M}\right)^{1/2} = \left(\frac{3(8.3145\,\text{J}/\text{K} \bullet \text{mol})\,(4 \times 10^7\,\text{K})}{2.01355\,\text{g}\,(1\,\text{kg}/1000\,\text{g})}\right)^{1/2} = 7 \times 10^5\,\text{m/s}$$

$$KE_{avg} = \frac{1}{2}mu^2 = \frac{1}{2}\left(2.01355\,\text{amu} \times \frac{1.66 \times 10^{-27}\,\text{kg}}{\text{amu}}\right)(7 \times 10^5\,\text{m/s})^2 = 8 \times 10^{-16}\,\text{J/nuclei}$$

We could have used $KE_{ave} = (3/2)RT$ to determine the same average kinetic energy.

Challenge Problems

62.   total activity injected = 3.7×10^3 cps

activity withdrawn = 20. cps/0.20 mL = 1.0×10^2 cps/mL

Assuming no significant decay occurs, then the volume of the animal's blood multiplied by 1.0×10^2 cps/mL blood withdrawn must equal the total activity injected.

$$V \times \frac{1.0 \times 10^2\,\text{cps}}{\text{mL}} = 3.7 \times 10^3\,\text{cps},\ \ V = 37\,\text{mL}$$

63.   Assuming that the radionuclide is long lived enough such that no significant decay occurs during the time of the experiment, the total counts of radioactivity injected are:

$$0.10\,\text{mL} \times \frac{5.0 \times 10^3\,\text{cpm}}{\text{mL}} = 5.0 \times 10^2\,\text{cpm}$$

Assuming that the total activity is uniformly distributed only in the rat's blood, the blood volume is:

$$V \times \frac{48\,\text{cpm}}{\text{mL}} = 5.0 \times 10^2\,\text{cpm},\ \ V = 10.4\,\text{mL} = 10.\,\text{mL}$$

64.   a.   From Table 17.1: $2\,H_2O + 2\,e^- \rightarrow H_2 + 2\,OH^-$ $E° = -0.83$ V

$$E°_{cell} = E°_{H_2O} - E°_{Zr} = -0.83\,\text{V} + 2.36\,\text{V} = 1.53\,\text{V}$$

Yes, the reduction of H_2O to H_2 by Zr is spontaneous at standard conditions since $E^{\circ}_{cell} > 0$.

b. $(2\ H_2O + 2\ e^- \rightarrow H_2 + 2\ OH^-) \times 2$
     $Zr + 4\ OH^- \rightarrow ZrO_2 \cdot H_2O + H_2O + 4\ e^-$

   _____

   $3\ H_2O(l) + Zr(s) \rightarrow 2\ H_2(g) + ZrO_2 \cdot H_2O(s)$

c. $\Delta G^{\circ} = -nFE^{\circ} = -\ (4\ \text{mol}\ e^-)(96{,}485\ \text{C/mol}\ e^-)(1.53\ \text{J/C}) = -5.90 \times 10^5\ \text{J} = -590.\ \text{kJ}$

   $E = E^{\circ} - \dfrac{0.0591}{n} \log Q;\ \ \text{At equilibrium, E = 0 and Q = K.}$

   $E^{\circ} = \dfrac{0.0591}{n} \log K,\ \ \log K = \dfrac{4(1.53)}{0.0591} = 104,\ \ K \approx 10^{104}$

d. $1.00 \times 10^3\ \text{kg Zr} \times \dfrac{1000\ \text{g}}{\text{kg}} \times \dfrac{1\ \text{mol Zr}}{91.22\ \text{g Zr}} \times \dfrac{2\ \text{mol}\ H_2}{\text{mol Zr}} = 2.19 \times 10^4\ \text{mol}\ H_2$

   $2.19 \times 10^4\ \text{mol}\ H_2 \times \dfrac{2.016\ \text{g}\ H_2}{\text{mol}\ H_2} = 4.42 \times 10^4\ \text{g}\ H_2$

   $V = \dfrac{nRT}{P} \times \dfrac{(2.19 \times 10^4\ \text{mol})(0.08206\ \text{L atm/mol} \cdot \text{K})(1273\ \text{K})}{1.0\ \text{atm}} = 2.3 \times 10^6\ \text{L}\ H_2$

e.   Probably yes; Less radioactivity overall was released by venting the H_2 than what would have been released if the H_2 had exploded inside the reactor (as happened at Chernobyl). Neither alternative is pleasant, but venting the radioactive hydrogen is the less unpleasant of the two alternatives.

65.   a. ^{12}C; It takes part in the first step of the reaction but is regenerated in the last step. ^{12}C is not consumed, so it is not a reactant.

   b. ^{13}N, ^{13}C, ^{14}N, ^{15}O, and ^{15}N are the intermediates.

   c. $4\ {}^{1}_{1}H \rightarrow\ {}^{4}_{2}H\ +\ 2\ {}^{0}_{+1}e\ ;\ \ \Delta m = 4.00260\ \text{amu} - 2\ m_e + 2\ m_e - [4(1.00782\ \text{amu} - m_e)]$

   $\Delta m = 4.00260 - 4(1.00782) + 4(0.000549) = -0.02648\ \text{amu for 4 protons reacting}$

   For 4 mol of protons, $\Delta m = -0.02648$ g and ΔE for the reaction is:

   $\Delta E = \Delta mc^2 = -2.648 \times 10^{-5}\ \text{kg} \times (2.9979 \times 10^8\ \text{m/s})^2 = -2.380 \times 10^{12}\ \text{J}$

   For 1 mol of protons reacting: $\dfrac{-2.380 \times 10^{12}\ \text{J}}{4\ \text{mol}\ {}^{1}\text{H}} = -5.950 \times 10^{11}\ \text{J/mol}\ {}^{1}\text{H}$

66. a. $^{238}_{92}U \rightarrow \, ^{222}_{86}Rn + ? \, ^{4}_{2}He + ? \, ^{0}_{-1}e$;   To account for the mass number change, 4 alpha particles are needed.   To balance the number of protons, 2 beta particles are needed.

$^{222}_{86}Rn \rightarrow \, ^{4}_{2}He + \, ^{218}_{84}Po$;   Polonium-218 is produced when ^{222}Rn decays.

b. Alpha particles cause significant ionization damage when inside a living organism. Because the half-life of ^{222}Rn is relatively short, a significant number of alpha particles will be produced when ^{222}Rn is present (even for a short period of time) in the lungs.

c. $^{222}_{86}Rn \rightarrow \, ^{4}_{2}He + \, ^{218}_{84}Po$; $^{218}_{84}Po \rightarrow \, ^{4}_{2}He + \, ^{214}_{82}Pb$;;   Polonium-218 is produced when radon-222 decays. ^{218}Po is a more potent alpha particle producer since it has a much shorter half-life than ^{222}Rn. In addition, ^{218}Po is a solid, so it can get trapped in the lung tissue once it is produced. Once trapped, the alpha particles produced from polonium-218 (with its very short half-life) can cause significant ionization damage.

d. Rate = kN;   rate = $\dfrac{4.0 \, pCi}{L} \times \dfrac{1 \times 10^{-12} \, Ci}{pCi} \times \dfrac{3.7 \times 10^{10} \, decays/sec}{Ci} = 0.15$ decays/sec•L

$k = \dfrac{\ln 2}{t_{1/2}} = \dfrac{0.6391}{3.82 \, d} \times \dfrac{1 \, d}{24 \, hr} \times \dfrac{1 \, hr}{3600 \, s} = 2.10 \times 10^{-6} \, s^{-1}$

$N = \dfrac{rate}{K} = \dfrac{0.15 \, decays/sec•L}{2.10 \times 10^{-6} \, s^{-1}} = 7.1 \times 10^{4} \, ^{222}Rn$ atoms/L

$\dfrac{7.1 \times 10^{4} \, ^{222}Rn \, atoms}{L} \times \dfrac{1 \, mol \, ^{222}Rn}{6.02 \times 10^{23} \, atoms} = 1.2 \times 10^{-19} \, mol \, ^{222}Rn/L$

67. mol $I^{-} = \dfrac{33 \, counts}{min} \times \dfrac{1 \, mol \, I • min}{5.0 \times 10^{11} \, counts} = 6.6 \times 10^{-11}$ mol I^{-}

$[I^{-}] = \dfrac{6.6 \times 10^{-11} \, mol \, I^{-}}{0.150 \, L} = 4.4 \times 10^{-10}$ mol/L

$Hg_2I_2(s) \rightarrow \qquad Hg_2^{2+}(aq) \quad + \quad 2 \, I^{-}(aq) \qquad K_{sp} = [Hg_2^{2+}][I^{-}]^2$

Initial s = solubility (mol/L)   0 $\qquad\qquad$ 0
Equil. $\qquad\qquad\qquad\qquad$ s $\qquad\qquad$ $2s$

From the problem, $2s = 4.4 \times 10^{-10}$ mol/L, $s = 2.2 \times 10^{-10}$ mol/L .

$K_{sp} = (s)(2s)^2 = (2.2 \times 10^{-10})(4.4 \times 10^{-10})^2 = 4.3 \times 10^{-29}$

68. $^{2}_{1}H + \, ^{2}_{1}H \rightarrow \, ^{4}_{2}He$;   Q for $^{2}_{1}H = 1.6 \times 10^{-19}$ C;   Mass of deuterium = 2 amu

$$E = \frac{9.0 \times 10^9 \text{ J} \bullet \text{m/C}^2 (Q_1 Q_2)}{r} = \frac{9.0 \times 10^9 \text{ J} \bullet \text{m/C}^2 (1.6 \times 10^{-19} \text{ C})^2}{2 \times 10^{-15} \text{ m}}$$

$$= 1 \times 10^{-13} \text{ J per alpha particle}$$

$KE = 1/2 \; mv^2; \; 1 \times 10^{-13} \text{ J} = 1/2 (2 \text{ amu} \times 1.66 \times 10^{-27} \text{ kg/amu}) v^2, \; v = 8 \times 10^6 \text{ m/s}$

From the kinetic molecular theory discussed in Chapter 5:

$$u_{rms} = \left(\frac{3 \, RT}{M} \right)^{1/2} \text{ where M = molar mass in kg} = 2 \times 10^{-3} \text{ kg/mol for deuterium}$$

$$8 \times 10^6 \text{ m/s} = \left(\frac{3(8.3145 \text{ J/K} \bullet \text{mol})(T)}{2 \times 10^{-3} \text{ kg}} \right)^{1/2}, \quad T = 5 \times 10^9 \text{ K}$$

Integrative Problems

69. $^{249}_{97}\text{Bk} + ^{22}_{10}\text{Ne} \rightarrow ^{267}_{107}\text{Bh} + ?$; This equation is charge balanced, but it is not mass balanced. The products are off by 4 mass units. The only possibility to account for the 4 mass units is to have 4 neutrons produced. The balanced equation is:

$$^{249}_{97}\text{Bk} + ^{22}_{10}\text{Ne} \rightarrow ^{267}_{107}\text{Bh} + 4\,^1_0\text{n}$$

$$\ln\left(\frac{N}{N_0} \right) = -kt = \frac{-0.6931 \, t}{t_{1/2}}, \quad \ln\left(\frac{11}{199} \right) = \frac{-0.6931 \, t}{15.0 \text{ s}}, \quad t = 62.7 \text{ s} \quad \text{(Assuming 11 is exact.)}$$

Bh: $[\text{Rn}]7s^2 5f^{14} 6d^5$ is the expected electron configuration.

70. $^{58}_{26}\text{Fe} + 2\,^1_0\text{n} \rightarrow ^{60}_{27}\text{Co} + ?$; In order to balance the equation, the missing particle has no mass and a charge of -1; this is an electron.

An atom of $^{60}_{27}\text{Co}$ has 27 e, 27 p, and 33 n. The mass defect of the ^{60}Co nucleus is:

$$\Delta m = (59.9338 - 27 \, m_e) - [27(1.00782 - m_e) + 33(1.00866] = -0.5631 \text{ amu}$$

$$\Delta E = \Delta mc^2 = -0.5631 \text{ amu} \times \frac{1.6605 \times 10^{-27} \text{ kg}}{\text{amu}} \times (2.9979 \times 10^8 \text{ m/s})^2 = -8.403 \times 10^{-11} \text{ J}$$

$$\frac{\text{binding energy}}{\text{nucleon}} = \frac{8.403 \times 10^{-11} \text{ J}}{60 \text{ nucleons}} = 1.401 \times 10^{-12} \text{ J/nucleon}$$

The emitted particle was an electron which has a mass of 9.109×10^{-31} kg. The deBroglie wavelength is:

$$\lambda = \frac{h}{mv} = \frac{6.626 \times 10^{-34} \text{ J s}}{9.109 \times 10^{-31} \text{ kg} \times (0.90 \times 2.998 \times 10^8 \text{ m/s})} = 2.7 \times 10^{-12} \text{ m}$$

CHAPTER NINETEEN

THE REPRESENTATIVE ELEMENTS: GROUPS 1A THROUGH 4A

For Review

1.   Oxygen and silicon are the two most abundant elements in the earth's crust, oceans, and atmosphere. Oxygen is found in the atmosphere as O_2, in the oceans in H_2O, and in the earth's crust primarily in silicate and carbonate minerals. Because oxygen is everywhere, it is not too surprising that it is the most abundant element. The second most abundant element, silicon, is found throughout the earth's crust in silica and silicate minerals that form the basis of most sand, rocks, and soils. Again, it is not too surprising that silicon is the second most abundant element, as it is involved in the composition of much of the earth.

The four most abundant elements in the human body are oxygen, carbon, hydrogen, and nitrogen. Not surprisingly, these elements form the basis for all biologically important molecules in the human body. They should be abundant.

2.   Hydrogen forms many compounds in which the oxidation state is +1, as do the Group 1A elements. For example, H_2SO_4 and HCl compare to Na_2SO_4 and NaCl. On the other hand, hydrogen forms diatomic H_2 molecules and is a nonmetal, while the Group 1A elements are metals. Hydrogen also forms compounds with a -1 oxidation state, which is not characteristic of Group 1A metals, e.g., NaH.

3.   Alkali metals have a ns^1 valence shell electron configuration. Alkali metals lose this valence electron with relative ease to form M^+ cations when in ionic compounds. They all are easily oxidized. Therefore, in order to prepare the pure metals, alkali metals must be produced in the absence of materials (H_2O, O_2) that are capable of oxidizing them. The method of preparation is electrochemical processes, specifically, electrolysis of molten chloride salts and reduction of alkali salts with Mg and H_2. In all production methods, H_2O and O_2 must be absent.

One would predict the alkali metal oxides to all have the M_2O formula. However, only lithium does this in the presence of excess oxygen gas. Two other types of oxides can form with alkali metals, hence, making prediction of the oxide formula difficult. The two other oxides formed are peroxides, M_2O_2, and superoxides, MO_2. In peroxides, certain alkali metals form an ionic compound with the peroxide anion, O_2^{2-}. In superoxides, certain alkali metals form an ionic compound with the superoxide anion, O_2^-.

A reaction in self-contained breathing apparatuses is: $4 KO_2(s) + 2 CO_2(g) \rightarrow 2 K_2CO_3(s) + 3 O_2(g)$; Potassium superoxide reacts with exhaled CO_2 to produce O_2, which then can be breathed.

The formulas of the compounds between alkali metals and other nonmetals are much easier to predict. From Table 19.6, MF, M_2S, M_3N (Li only), MH, and MOH are the predicted formulas when alkali metals react with F_2, S, N_2, H_2, and H_2O, respectively. These formulas exhibit the typical oxidation states as predicted by the periodic table.

4.   The two major industrial uses of hydrogen are ammonia (NH_3) production and hydrogenation of vegetable oils.

The three types of hydrides are ionic, covalent, and metallic (or interstitial). The ionic and covalent hydrides are true compounds obeying the law of definite proportions and differ from each other in the type of bonding. The interstitial hydrides are more like solid solutions of hydrogen with a transition metal and do not obey the law of definite proportions.

5.   Alkaline earth metals have ns^2 for valence electron configurations. They are all very reactive, losing their two valence electrons to nonmetals to form ionic compounds containing M^{2+} cations. Alkaline earth metals, like alkali metals, are easily oxidized. Their preparation as pure metals must be done in the absence of O_2 and H_2O. The method of preparation is electrolysis of molten alkaline earth halides.

The alkaline earth ions that give water the hard designation are Ca^{2+} and Mg^{2+}. These ions interfere with the action of detergents and form unwanted precipitates with soaps. Large scale water softeners remove Ca^{2+} by precipitating out the calcium ions as $CaCO_3$. In homes, Ca^{2+} and Mg^{2+} (plus other cations) are removed by ion exchange. See Figure 19.7 for a schematic of a typical cation exchange resin.

6.   Table 19.8 summarizes the formulas of alkaline earth metals with typical nonmetals. With a rare exception or two, there aren't many surprises. The typical formulas are MF_2, MO, MS, M_3N_2, MH_2, and $M(OH)_2$, when alkaline earth metals are reacted with F_2, O_2, S, N_2, H_2, and H_2O, respectively.

7.   The valence electron configuration of Group 3A elements is ns^2np^1. The lightest Group 3A element, boron, is a nonmetal as most of its compounds are covalent. Aluminum, although commonly thought of as a metal, does have some nonmetallic properties as its bonds to other nonmetals have significant covalent character. The other Group 3A elements have typical metal characteristics; its compounds formed with nonmetals are ionic. From this discussion, metallic character increases as the Group 3A elements get larger.

As discussed above, boron is a nonmetal in both properties and compounds formed. However aluminum has physical properties of metals like high thermal and electrical conductivities and a lustrous appearance. The compounds of aluminum with other nonmetals, however, do have some nonmetallic properties as the bonds have significant covalent character.

An amphoteric substance is one that can behave as either an acid or as a base. Al_2O_3 dissolves in both acidic and basic solutions. The reactions are:

$$Al_2O_3(s) + 6\ H^+(aq) \rightarrow\ 2Al^{3+}(aq) + 3\ H_2O(l)$$

$$Al_2O_3(s) + 2\ OH^-(aq) + 3\ H_2O(l) \rightarrow\ 2\ Al(OH)_4^-(aq)$$

8.   The formulas that aluminum form with nonmetals (as well as the formulas of other heavier Group 3A elements) are summarized in Table 19.10. The compounds formed between aluminum and F_2, O_2, S, and N_2 follow what would be predicted for ionic compounds containing Al^{3+}. However, there is some covalent character in these compounds. The formulas are AlF_3, Al_2O_3, Al_2S_3, and AlN.

9.   The valence electron configuration of Group 4A elements is ns^2np^2. The two most important elements on earth are both Group 4A elements. They are carbon, found in all biologically important molecules, and silicon, found in most of the compounds that make up the earth's crust. They are important because they are so prevalent in compounds necessary for life and the geologic world.

        As with Group 3A, Group 4A shows an increase in metallic character as the elements get heavier. Carbon is a typical nonmetal, silicon and germanium have properties of both metals and nonmetals so they are classified as semimetals, while tin and lead have typical metallic characteristics.

        Carbon forms strong covalent bonds with itself as well as with other nonmetals like H, O, N, and P. Carbon also forms π bonds. Silicon, on the other hand, forms a very strong single bond with oxygen and does not form π bonds. Silicon would rather have Si–O bonds than any other type of bond, including multiple bonds. This is unlike carbon.

        The two major allotropic forms of carbon are graphite and diamond. See Section 10.5 for their structures and a description of their properties.

10.   Germanium is a relatively rare element and is classified as a semimetal. Its main uses are in the manufacture of semiconductors. Tin is a metal and is used to form alloys with other metals. Some alloys containing tin are bronze, solder, and pewter. Tin's major current use is as a protective coating for steel which helps prevent the corrosion of iron in steel. Lead is a metal, but has a relatively low melting point. Lead is very toxic and the use of lead paints and lead additives to gasoline are not allowed in the United States. The major use of lead is for electrodes in the lead storage battery used in automobiles.

        Ge forms GeF_4 when reacted with F_2 and forms GeO_2 when reacted with O_2. Both these compounds have Ge in the predicted +4 oxidation state as determined from its position in the periodic table. However, the fluorine compound is strictly covalent in nature, while the oxygen compound has more ionic character.

Questions

1.   The gravity of the earth is not strong enough to keep the light H_2 molecules in the atmosphere.

2.   The small size of the Li^+ cation results in a much greater attraction to water. The attraction to water is not as great for the other alkali metal ions. Thus, lithium salts tend to absorb water.

3.   The acidity decreases. Solutions of Be^{2+} are acidic, while solutions of the other M^{2+} ions are neutral.

4.   Compounds called boranes have three-centered bonds. Three-centered bonds occur when a single H atom forms bridging bonds between two boron atoms. The bonds have two electrons bonding all three atoms together. The bond is electron deficient, and makes boranes very reactive.

5.   In graphite, planes of carbon atoms slide easily along each other. In addition, graphite is not volatile. The lubricant will not be lost when used in a high-vacuum environment.

6.   Quartz: crystalline, has long range order; the structure is an ordered arrangement of 12-membered rings, each containing six Si and six O atoms.

Amorphous SiO_2: no long range order; irregular arrangement that contains many different ring sizes. See Chapter 10.5 of the text.

7.   Group 3A elements have one fewer valence electron than Si or Ge. A p-type semiconductor would form.

8.   Size decreases from left to right and increases going down the periodic table. So, going one element right and one element down would result in a similar size for the two elements diagonal to each other. The ionization energies will be similar for the diagonal elements since the periodic trends also oppose each other. Electron affinities are harder to predict, but atoms with similar size and ionization energy should also have similar electron affinities.

9.   For groups 1A-3A, the small size of H (as compared to Li), Be (as compared to Mg), and B (as compared to Al) seems to be the reason why these elements have nonmetallic properties, while others in the groups 1A-3A are strictly metallic. The small size of H, Be, and B also causes these species to polarize the electron cloud in nonmetals, thus forcing a sharing of electrons when bonding occurs. For groups 4A-6A, a major difference between the first and second members of a group is the ability to form π bonds. The smaller elements form stable π bonds, while the larger elements are not capable of good overlap between parallel p orbitals and, in turn, do not form strong π bonds. For group 7A, the small size of F as compared to Cl is used to explain the low electron affinity of F and the weakness of the F–F bond.

10.   Counting over in the periodic table, the next alkali metal will be element 119. It will be located under Fr. One would expect the physical properties of element 119 to follow the trends shown in Table 19.4. Element 119 should have the smallest ionization energy, the most negative standard reduction potential, the largest radius and the smallest melting point of all the alkali metals listed in Table 19.4. It should also be radioactive like Fr.

11.   Solids have stronger intermolecular forces than liquids. In order to maximize the hydrogen bonding in the solid phase, ice is forced into an open structure. This open structure is why $H_2O(s)$ is less dense than $H_2O(l)$.

12.   Beryllium has a small size and a large electronegativity as compared to the other alkaline earth metals. The electronegativity of Be is so high that it does not readily give up electrons to nonmetals as is the case for the other alkaline earth metals. Instead, Be has significant covalent character in its bonds; it prefers to share valence electrons rather than give them up to form ionic bonds.

Exercises

Group 1A Elements

13.   a. $\Delta H° = -110.5 - [-75 + (-242)] = 207$ kJ; $\Delta S° = 198 + 3(131) - [186 + 189] = 216$ J/K

      b. $\Delta G° = \Delta H° - T\Delta S°$; $\Delta G° = 0$ when $T = \dfrac{\Delta H°}{\Delta S°} = \dfrac{207 \times 10^3 \text{ J}}{216 \text{ J/K}} = 958$ K

           At T > 958 K and standard pressures, the favorable $\Delta S°$ term dominates, and the reaction is spontaneous ($\Delta G° < 0$).

14.   a. $\Delta H° = 2(-46$ kJ$) = -92$ kJ; $\Delta S° = 2(193$ J/K$) - [3(131$ J/K$) + 192$ J/K$] = -199$ J/K;

           $\Delta G° = \Delta H° - T\Delta S° = -92$ kJ $- 298$ K$(-0.199$ kJ/K$) = -33$ kJ

      b.   Because $\Delta G°$ is negative, this reaction is spontaneous at standard conditions.

      c. $\Delta G° = 0$ when $T = \dfrac{\Delta H°}{\Delta S°} = \dfrac{-92 \text{ kJ}}{-0.199 \text{ kJ/K}} = 460$ K

           At T < 460 K and standard pressures, the favorable $\Delta H°$ term dominates and the reaction is spontaneous ($\Delta G° < 0$).

15.   a.   lithium oxide   b.   potassium superoxide   c.   sodium peroxide

16.   a. Li_3N b. K_2CO_3 c.   RbOH   d.   NaH

17.   a. $Li_2O(s) + H_2O(l) \rightarrow 2\,LiOH(aq)$ b. $Na_2O_2(s) + 2\,H_2O(l) \rightarrow 2\,NaOH(aq) + H_2O_2(aq)$

      c. $LiH(s) + H_2O(l) \rightarrow H_2(g) + LiOH(aq)$

      d. $2\,KO_2(s) + 2H_2O(l) \rightarrow 2\,KOH(aq) + O_2(g) + H_2O_2(aq)$

18. $4\,Li(s) + O_2(g) \rightarrow 2\,Li_2O(s)$

      $16\,Li(s) + S_8(s) \rightarrow 8\,Li_2S(s)$; $2\,Li(s) + Cl_2(g) \rightarrow 2\,LiCl(s)$

      $12\,Li(s) + P_4(s) \rightarrow 4\,Li_3P(s)$; $2\,Li(s) + H_2(g) \rightarrow 2\,LiH(s)$

      $2\,Li(s) + 2\,H_2O(l) \rightarrow 2\,LiOH(aq) + H_2(g)$; $2\,Li(s) + 2\,HCl(aq) \rightarrow 2\,LiCl(aq) + H_2(g)$

19. $2\,Li(s) + 2\,C_2H_2(g) \rightarrow 2\,LiC_2H(s) + H_2(g)$; This is an oxidation-reduction reaction.

20.   We need another reactant beside NaCl(aq) because oxygen and hydrogen are in some of the products. The obvious choice is H_2O.

           $2\,NaCl(aq) + 2\,H_2O(l) \rightarrow Cl_2(g) + H_2(g) + 2\,NaOH(aq)$

      Note that hydrogen is reduced and chlorine is oxidized in this electrolysis process.

Group 2A Elements

21.   a. magnesium carbonate   b. barium sulfate   c. strontium hydroxide

22.   a. Ca_3N_2 b. $BeCl_2$ c. BaH_2

23. $CaCO_3(s) + H_2SO_4(aq) \rightarrow CaSO_4(aq) + H_2O(l) + CO_2(g)$

24. $2\ Sr(s) + O_2(g) \rightarrow 2\ SrO(s);\ \ 8\ Sr(s) + S_8(s) \rightarrow 8\ SrS(s)$

$Sr(s) + Cl_2(g) \rightarrow SrCl_2(s);\ \ 6\ Sr(s) + P_4(s) \rightarrow 2\ Sr_3P_2(s)$

$Sr(s) + H_2(g) \rightarrow SrH_2(s);\ \ Sr(s) + 2\ H_2O(l) \rightarrow Sr(OH)_2(aq) + H_2(g)$

$Sr(s) + 2\ HCl(aq) \rightarrow SrCl_2(aq) + H_2(g)$

25.   In the gas phase, linear molecules would exist.

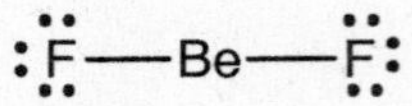

In the solid state, BeF_2 has the following extended structure:

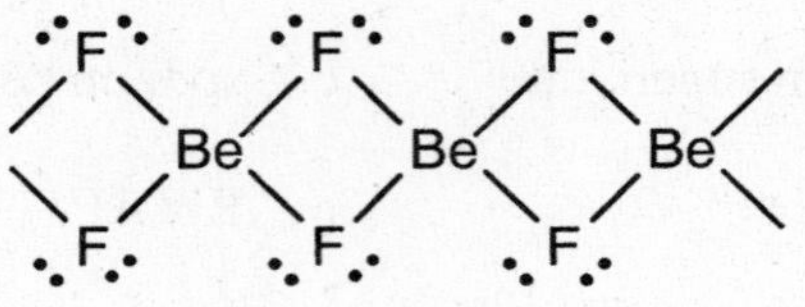

26. $BeCl_2$, with only four valence electrons, needs four more electrons to satisfy the octet rule. NH_3 has a lone pair of electrons on the N atom. Therefore, $BeCl_2$ will react with two NH_3 molecules in order to achieve the octet rule, making $BeCl_2(NH_3)_2$ the likely product in excess ammonia. $BeCl_2(NH_3)_2$ has $2 + 2(7) + 2(5) + 6(1) = 32$ valence electrons.

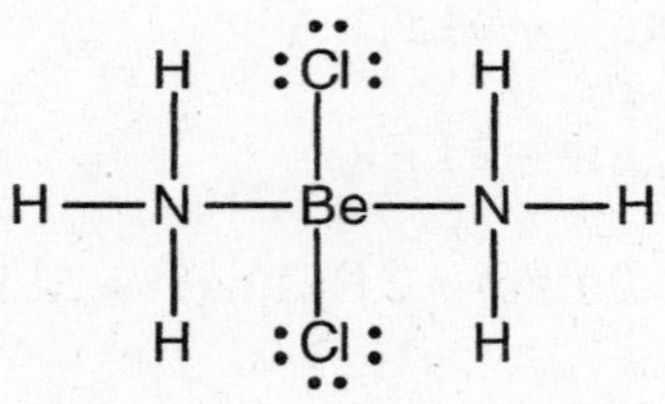

27. $\dfrac{1\ mg\ F^-}{L} \times \dfrac{1\ g}{1000\ mg} \times \dfrac{1\ mol\ F^-}{19.00\ g\ F^-} = 5.3 \times 10^{-5}\ M\ F^- = 5 \times 10^{-5}\ M\ F^-$

$CaF_2(s) \rightleftharpoons Ca^{2+}(aq) + 2\ F^-(aq)\ \ \ K_{sp} = [Ca^{2+}][\ F^-]^2 = 4.0 \times 10^{-11}$; Precipitation will occur when $Q > K_{sp}$. Let's calculate $[Ca^{2+}]$ so that $Q = K_{sp}$.

$Q = 4.0 \times 10^{-11} = [Ca^{2+}]_o[F^-]_o^2 = [Ca^{2+}]_o(5 \times 10^{-5})^2, \quad [Ca^{2+}]_o = 2 \times 10^{-2} M$

$CaF_2(s)$ will precipitate when $[Ca^{2+}]_o > 2 \times 10^{-2} M$. Therefore, hard water should have a calcium ion concentration of less than $2 \times 10^{-2} M$ in order to avoid $CaF_2(s)$ formation.

28. $CaCO_3(s) \quad \rightleftharpoons \quad Ca^{2+}(aq) \ + \ CO_3^{2-}(aq)$

Initial s = solubility (mol/L)   0   0
Equil. s s

$K_{sp} = 8.7 \times 10^{-9} = [Ca^{2+}][CO_3^{2-}] = s^2, \ s = 9.3 \times 10^{-5}$ mol/L

29. $Ba^{2+} + 2 e^- \rightarrow Ba$; $6.00 \text{ hr} \times \dfrac{60 \text{ min}}{h} \times \dfrac{60 \text{ s}}{\min} \times \dfrac{2.50 \times 10^5 \text{ C}}{s} \times \dfrac{1 \text{ mol } e^-}{96,485 \text{ C}} \times \dfrac{1 \text{ mol Ba}}{2 \text{ mol } e^-}$

$$\times \frac{137.3 \text{ g Ba}}{\text{mol Ba}} = 3.84 \times 10^6 \text{ g Ba}$$

30.   Alkaline earth metals form +2 charged ions so 2 mol of e^- are transferred to form the metal, M.

$\text{mol M} = 748 \text{ s} \times \dfrac{5.00 \text{ C}}{s} \times \dfrac{1 \text{ mol } e^-}{96,485 \text{ C}} \times \dfrac{1 \text{ mol M}}{2 \text{ mol } e^-} = 1.94 \times 10^{-2} \text{ mol M}$

$\text{molar mass of M} = \dfrac{0.471 \text{ g M}}{1.94 \times 10^{-2} \text{ mol M}} = 24.3 \text{ g/mol};$ $MgCl_2$ was electrolyzed.

Group 3A Elements

31.   a. AlN b. GaF_3 c. Ga_2S_3

32. Tl_2O_3, thallium(III) oxide; Tl_2O, thallium(I) oxide; $InCl_3$, indium(III) chloride; $InCl$, indium(I) chloride

33. $B_2H_6(g) + 3 O_2(g) \rightarrow 2 B(OH)_3(s)$

34. $B_2O_3(s) + 3 Mg(s) \rightarrow 3 MgO(s) + 2 B(s)$

35. $Ga_2O_3(s) + 6 H^+(aq) \rightarrow 2 Ga^{3+}(aq) + 3 H_2O(l)$

$Ga_2O_3(s) + 2 OH^-(aq) + 3 H_2O(l) \rightarrow 2 Ga(OH)_4^-(aq)$

$In_2O_3(s) + 6 H^+(aq) \rightarrow 2 In^{3+}(aq) + 3 H_2O(l);$ $In_2O_3(s) + OH^-(aq) \rightarrow$ no reaction

36. $Al(OH)_3(s) + 3 H^+(aq) \rightarrow Al^{3+}(aq) + 3 H_2O(l)$

$Al(OH)_3(s) + OH^-(aq) \rightarrow Al(OH)_4^-(aq)$

37. $2 \, Ga(s) + 3 \, F_2(g) \rightarrow 2 \, GaF_3(s); \; 4 \, Ga(s) + 3 \, O_2(g) \rightarrow 2 \, Ga_2O_3(s)$

    $16 \, Ga(s) + 3 \, S_8(s) \rightarrow 8 \, Ga_2S_3(s); \; 2 \, Ga(s) + N_2(g) \rightarrow 2 \, GaN(s)$

    Note: GaN would be predicted, but in practice, this reaction does not occur.

    $2 \, Ga(s) + 6 \, HCl(aq) \rightarrow 2 \, GaCl_3(aq) + 3 \, H_2(g)$

38. $2 \, Al(s) + 2 \, NaOH(aq) + 6 \, H_2O(l) \rightarrow \; 2 \, Al(OH)_4^-(aq) + 2 \, Na^+(aq) + 3 \, H_2(g)$

Group 4A Elements

39. $CF_4, \; 4 + 4(7) = 32 \; e^-$ $GeF_4, \; 4 + 4(7) = 32 \; e^-$ $GeF_6^{2-}, \; 4 + 6(7) + 2 = 48 \; e^-$

                      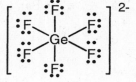

    tetrahedral; 109.5°; sp^3 tetrahedral; 109.5°; sp^3 octahedral; 90°; d^2sp^3

    In order to form CF_6^{2-}, carbon would have to expand its octet of electrons. Carbon compounds do not expand their octet because of the small atomic size of carbon and because no low energy d-orbitals are available for carbon to accommodate the extra electrons.

40. CS_2 has $4 + 2(6) = 16$ valence electrons. C_3S_2 has $3(4) + 2(6) = 24$ valence electrons.

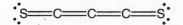

    $\ddot{S}\!=\!\!=\!\!C\!=\!\!=\!\ddot{S}$ linear; $\ddot{S}\!=\!\!=\!\!C\!=\!\!=\!\!C\!=\!\!=\!\!C\!=\!\!=\!\ddot{S}$ linear

41.   a. $SiO_2(s) + 2 \, C(s) \rightarrow Si(s) + 2 \, CO(g)$

    b. $SiCl_4(l) + 2 \, Mg(s) \rightarrow Si(s) + 2 \, MgCl_2(s)$

    c. $Na_2SiF_6(s) + 4 \, Na(s) \rightarrow Si(s) + 6 \, NaF(s)$

42. $Sn(s) + 2 \, Cl_2(g) \rightarrow SnCl_4(s); \; Sn(s) + O_2(g) \rightarrow SnO_2(s)$

    $Sn(s) + 2 \, HCl(aq) \rightarrow SnCl_2(aq) + H_2(g)$

43.   Lead is very toxic. As the temperature of the water increases, the solubility of lead increases. Drinking hot tap water from pipes containing lead solder could result in higher lead concentrations in the body.

44. $Pb(OH)_2(s)$ $\rightleftharpoons$ Pb^{2+} + $2\,OH^-$ $K_{sp} = 1.2 \times 10^{-15} = [Pb^{2+}][OH^-]^2$

Initial s = solubility (mol/L)   0 $1.0 \times 10^{-7}\,M$
Equil. s $1.0 \times 10^{-7} + 2s \approx 2s$

$K_{sp} = (s)(2s)^2 = 1.2 \times 10^{-15}$, $4s^3 = 1.2 \times 10^{-15}$, $s = 6.7 \times 10^{-6}$ mol/L; Assumption good.

$Pb(OH)_2(s)$ is more soluble in acidic solutions. Added H^+ reacts with OH^- to form H_2O. As OH^- is removed through this reaction, more $Pb(OH)_2(s)$ will dissolve to replenish the OH^-.

45. $C_6H_{12}O_6(aq) \rightarrow 2\,C_2H_5OH(aq) + 2\,CO_2(g)$

46. $Sn(s) + 2F_2(g) \rightarrow SnF_4(s)$, tin(IV) fluoride; $Sn(s) + F_2(g) \rightarrow SnF_2(s)$, tin(II) fluoride

47.   The π electrons are free to move in graphite, thus giving it greater conductivity (lower resistance). The electrons in graphite have the greatest mobility within sheets of carbon atoms, resulting in a lower resistance in the plane of the sheets (basal plane). Electrons in diamond are not mobile (high resistance). The structure of diamond is uniform in all directions; thus, resistivity has no directional dependence in diamond.

48.   SiC would have a covalent network structure similar to diamond.

Additional Exercises

49.   Heat released = 0.250 g Na $\times \dfrac{1\,mol}{22.99\,g} \times \dfrac{368\,kJ}{2\,mol} = 2.00$ kJ

To melt 50.0 g of ice requires: 50.0 g ice $\times \dfrac{1\,mol\,H_2O}{18.02\,g} \times \dfrac{6.02\,kJ}{mol} = 16.7$ kJ

The reaction doesn't release enough heat to melt all of the ice. The temperature will remain at 0°C.

50.   If Be^{3+}, the formula is $Be(C_5H_7O_2)_3$ and molar mass $\approx 13.5 + 15(12) + 21(1) + 6(16)$ = 311 g/mol.

If Be^{2+}, the formula is $Be(C_5H_7O_2)_2$ and molar mass $\approx 9.0 + 10(12) + 14(1) + 4(16)$ = 207 g/mol.

Data Set I (molar mass = dRT/P and d = mass/V):

$$\text{molar mass} = \frac{\text{mass} \times RT}{PV} = \frac{0.2022\,g \times \dfrac{0.08206\,L\,atm}{mol\,K} \times 286\,K}{\left(765.2\,torr \times \dfrac{1\,atm}{760\,torr}\right) \times 22.6 \times 10^{-3}\,L} = 209\,g/mol$$

Data Set II:

$$\text{molar mass} = \frac{\text{mass} \times RT}{PV} = \frac{0.2224 \text{ g} \times \dfrac{0.08206 \text{ L atm}}{\text{mol K}} \times 290. \text{ K}}{\left(764.6 \text{ torr} \times \dfrac{1 \text{ atm}}{760 \text{ torr}}\right) \times 26.0 \times 10^{-3} \text{ L}} = 202 \text{ g/mol}$$

These results are close to the expected value of 207 g/mol for $Be(C_5H_7O_2)_2$. Thus, we conclude from these data that beryllium is a divalent element with an atomic mass of 9.0 amu.

51. $$15 \text{ kWh} = \frac{15000 \text{ J h}}{\text{s}} \times \frac{60 \text{ s}}{\text{min}} \times \frac{60 \text{ min}}{\text{h}} = 5.4 \times 10^7 \text{ J or } 5.4 \times 10^4 \text{ kJ}   \text{(Hall process)}$$

To melt 1.0 kg Al requires: $$1.0 \times 10^3 \text{ g Al} \times \frac{1 \text{ mol Al}}{26.98 \text{ g}} \times \frac{10.7 \text{ kJ}}{\text{mol Al}} = 4.0 \times 10^2 \text{ kJ}$$

It is feasible to recycle Al by melting the metal because, in theory, it takes less than 1% of the energy required to produce the same amount of Al by the Hall process.

52.   Borazine ($B_3N_3H_6$) has $3(3) + 3(5) + 6(1) = 30$ valence electrons. The possible resonance structures are similar to those of benzene, C_6H_6.

53. $$HgbO_2 \rightarrow Hgb + O_2 \qquad \Delta G° = -(-70 \text{ kJ})$$
$$Hgb + CO \rightarrow HgbCO \qquad \Delta G° = -80 \text{ kJ}$$

$$HgbO_2 + CO \rightarrow HgbCO + O_2 \qquad \Delta G° = -10 \text{ kJ}$$

$$\Delta G° = -RT \ln K, \ K = \exp\left(\frac{-\Delta G°}{RT}\right) = \exp\left(\frac{-(-10 \times 10^3 \text{ J})}{8.3145 \text{ J/K} \bullet \text{mol (298 K)}}\right) = 60$$

54.   CO, $4 + 6 = 10 \text{ e}^-$; CO_2, $4 + 2(6) = 16 \text{ e}^-$; C_3O_2, $3(4) + 2(6) = 24 \text{ e}^-$

There is no molecular structure for the diatomic CO molecule. The carbon in CO is sp hybridized. CO_2 is a linear molecule, and the central carbon atom is sp hybridized. C_3O_2 is a linear molecule with all of the central carbon atoms exhibiting sp hybridization.

55.   n = 2 for this reaction (lead goes from Pb → Pb^{2+} in $PbSO_4$).

$$E = E° - \frac{-0.0591}{2}\log \frac{1}{[H^+]^2[HSO_4^-]^2} = 2.04 \text{ V} - \frac{-0.0591}{2}\log \frac{1}{(4.5)^2(4.5)^2}$$

E = 2.04 V + 0.077 V = 2.12 V

56.   For 589.0 nm: $\nu = \dfrac{c}{\lambda} = \dfrac{2.9979 \times 10^8 \, \text{m/s}}{589.0 \times 10^{-9} \, \text{m}} = 5.090 \times 10^{14} \, \text{s}^{-1}$

E = hν = 6.6261 × 10^{-34} J s × 5.090 × 10^{14} s^{-1} = 3.373 × 10^{-19} J

For 589.6 nm: ν = c/λ = 5.085 × $10^{14}$$s^{-1}$;   E = h$\nu$ = 3.369 × 10^{-19} J

The energies in kJ/mol are:

$$3.373 \times 10^{-19} \text{ J} \times \frac{1 \, \text{kJ}}{1000 \, \text{J}} \times \frac{6.0221 \times 10^{23}}{\text{mol}} = 203.1 \text{ kJ/mol}$$

$$3.369 \times 10^{-19} \text{ J} \times \frac{1 \, \text{kJ}}{1000 \, \text{J}} \times \frac{6.0221 \times 10^{23}}{\text{mol}} = 202.9 \text{ kJ/mol}$$

57.   Strontium and calcium are both alkaline earth metals, so they have similar chemical properties. Because milk is a good source of calcium, strontium could replace some calcium in milk without much difficulty.

58.   The Be^{2+} ion is a Lewis acid and has a strong affinity for the lone pairs of electrons on oxygen in water. Thus, the compound is not dehydrated easily. The ion in solution is $Be(H_2O)_4^{2+}$. The acidic solution results from the reaction: $Be(H_2O)_4^{2+}(aq) \rightleftharpoons$ $Be(H_2O)_3(OH)^+(aq) + H^+(aq)$

59.   The "inert pair effect" refers to the difficulty of removing the pair of s electrons from some of the elements in the fifth and sixth periods of the periodic table. As a result, multiple oxidation states are exhibited for the heavier elements of Groups 3A and 4A. In^+, In^{3+}, Tl^+ and Tl^{3+} oxidation states are all important to the chemistry of In and Tl.

60.   Element 113 would fall below Tl in the periodic table. Element 113: $[Rn] \, 7s^2 5f^{14} 6d^{10} 7p^1$.

61.   Major species present: $Al(H_2O)_6^{3+}$ (K_a = 1.4 × 10^{-5}), NO_3^- (neutral) and H_2O; K_w = 1.0 × 10^{-14}. $Al(H_2O)_6^{3+}$ is a stronger acid than water so it will be the dominant H^+ producer.

	$Al(H_2O)_6^{3+}$	$\rightleftharpoons$	$Al(H_2O)_5(OH)^{2+}$	+	H^+
Initial	0.050 M		0		~0
	x mol/L $Al(H_2O)_6^{3+}$ dissociates to reach equilibrium				
Change	−x	→	+x		+x
Equil.	0.050 − x		x		x

$$K_a = 1.4 \times 10^{-5} = \frac{[Al(H_2O)_5(OH)^{2+}][H^+]}{[Al(H_2O)_6{}^{3+}]} = \frac{x^2}{0.050-x} \approx \frac{x^2}{0.050}$$

$x = 8.4 \times 10^{-4} \, M = [H^+];$ $pH = -\log(8.4 \times 10^{-4}) = 3.08;$ Assumptions good.

62. $Tl^{3+} + 2\,e^- \rightarrow Tl^+$ $E° = 1.25 \, V$
          $3\,I^- \rightarrow I_3^- + 2\,e^-$ $-E° = -0.55 \, V$
          _____
          $Tl^{3+} + 3\,I^- \rightarrow Tl^+ + I_3^-$ $E°_{cell} = 0.70 \, V$

In solution, Tl^{3+} can oxidize I^- to I_3^-. Thus, we expect TlI_3 to be thallium(I) triiodide.

63.   Ga(I): $[Ar]4s^2 3d^{10}$, no unpaired e^-; Ga(III): $[Ar]3d^{10}$, no unpaired e^-

Ga(II): $[Ar]4s^1 3d^{10}$, 1 unpaired e^-; Note: s electrons are lost before the d electrons.

If the compound contained Ga(II), it would be paramagnetic, and if the compound contained Ga(I) and Ga(III), it would be diamagnetic. This can be determined easily by measuring the mass of a sample in the presence and in the absence of a magnetic field. Paramagnetic compounds will have an apparent increase in mass in a magnetic field.

64.   a.   Out of 100.0 g of compound there are:

$$44.4 \text{ g Ca} \times \frac{1 \text{ mol}}{40.08 \text{ g}} = 1.11 \text{ mol Ca}; \quad 20.0 \text{ g Al} \times \frac{1 \text{ mol}}{26.98 \text{ g}} = 0.741 \text{ mol Al}$$

$$35.6 \text{ g O} \times \frac{1 \text{ mol}}{16.00 \text{ g}} = 2.23 \text{ mol O}$$

$$\frac{1.11}{0.741} = 1.50; \quad \frac{0.741}{0.741} = 1.00; \quad \frac{2.23}{0.741} = 3.01; \quad \text{Empirical formula is } Ca_3Al_2O_6.$$

b. $Ca_9Al_6O_{18}$

c.   There are covalent bonds between Al and O atoms in the $Al_6O_{18}{}^{18-}$ anion; sp^3 hybrid orbitals on aluminum overlap with sp^3 hybrid orbitals on oxygen to form the sigma bonds.

65. $$750. \text{ mL grape juice} \times \frac{12 \text{ mL } C_2H_5OH}{100. \text{ mL juice}} \times \frac{0.79 \text{ g } C_2H_5OH}{\text{mL}} \times \frac{1 \text{ mol } C_2H_5OH}{46.07 \text{ g}}$$

$$\times \frac{2 \text{ mol } CO_2}{1 \text{ mol } C_2H_5OH} = 1.54 \text{ mol } CO_2 \quad \text{(carry extra significant figure)}$$

$1.54 \text{ mol } CO_2 = \text{total mol } CO_2 = \text{mol } CO_2(g) + \text{mol } CO_2(aq) = n_g + n_{aq}$

$$P_{CO_2} = \frac{n_g RT}{V} = \frac{n_g \left(\dfrac{0.08206 \text{ L atm}}{\text{mol K}} \right)(298 \text{ K})}{7.5 \times 10^{-3} \text{ L}} = 326 \, n_g$$

$$P_{CO_2} = \frac{C}{k} = \frac{\dfrac{n_{aq}}{0.750 \text{ L}}}{\dfrac{3.1 \times 10^{-2} \text{ mol}}{\text{L atm}}} = 43.0 \, n_{aq}$$

$P_{CO_2} = 326 \, n_g = 43.0 \, n_{aq}$ and from above, $n_{aq} = 1.54 - n_g$; Solving:

$326 \, n_g = 43.0(1.54 - n_g)$, $369 \, n_g = 66.2$, $n_g = 0.18$ mol

$P_{CO_2} = 326(0.18) = 59$ atm in gas phase

$$C = k \, P_{CO_2} = \frac{3.1 \times 10^{-2} \text{ mol}}{\text{L atm}} \times 59 \text{ atm} = 1.8 \text{ mol } CO_2/\text{L in wine}$$

66. Pb_3O_4: We assign –2 for the oxidation state of O. The sum of the oxidation states of Pb must be +8. We get this if two of the lead atoms are Pb(II) and one is Pb(IV). Therefore, the mole ratio of lead(II) to lead(IV) is 2:1.

67. $Pb(NO_3)_2(aq) + H_3AsO_4(aq) \rightarrow PbHAsO_4(s) + 2 \, HNO_3(aq)$

Note: The insecticide used is $PbHAsO_4$ and is commonly called lead arsenate. This is not the correct name, however. Correctly, lead arsenate would be $Pb_3(AsO_4)_2$ and $PbHAsO_4$ should be named lead hydrogen arsenate.

Challenge Problems

68.   Table 19.2 lists the mass percents of various elements in the human body. If we consider the mass percents through sulfur, that will cover 99.5% of the body mass which is fine for a reasonable estimate. In our calculation, we assumed an average human mass of 150 lb = 68,000 g.

mol O = 0.650 × 68,000 g × 1 mol O/16.00 g O = 2760 mol
mol C = 0.180 × 68,000 g × 1 mol C/12.01 g C = 1020 mol
mol H = 0.100 × 68,000 g × 1 mol H/1.008 g H = 6750 mol
mol N = 0.030 × 68,000 g × 1 mol N/14.01 g N = 150 mol
mol Ca = 0.014 × 68,000 g × 1 mol Ca/40.08 g Ca = 24 mol
mol P = 0.010 × 68,000 g × 1 mol P/30.97 g P = 22 mol
mol Mg = 0.0050 × 68,000 g × 1 mol Mg/24.31 g Mg = 14 mol
mol K = 0.0034 × 68,000 g × 1 mol K/39.10 g K = 5.9 mol
mol S = 0.0026 × 68,000 g × 1 mol S/32.07 g S = 5.5 mol

Total mol elements in 150 lb body = 10,750 mol atoms

$$10{,}750 \text{ mol atoms} \times \frac{6.022 \times 10^{23} \text{ atoms}}{\text{mol atoms}} = 6.474 \times 10^{27} \text{ atoms} \approx 6.5 \times 10^{27} \text{ atoms}$$

69.   The reaction is: $X(s) + 2H_2O(l) \longrightarrow H_2(g) + X(OH)_2(aq)$

$$\text{mol X} = \text{mol H}_2 = \frac{PV}{RT} = \frac{1.00 \text{ atm} \times 6.10 \text{ L}}{\dfrac{0.08206 \text{ L atm}}{\text{K mol}} \times 298 \text{ K}} = 0.249 \text{ mol}$$

$$\text{molar mass X} = \frac{10.00 \text{ g X}}{0.249 \text{ mol X}} = 40.2 \text{ g/mol}; \text{ X is Ca.}$$

$Ca(s) + 2 H_2O(l) \rightarrow H_2(g) + Ca(OH)_2(aq); Ca(OH)_2$ is a strong base.

$$[OH^-] = \frac{10.00 \text{ g Ca} \times \dfrac{1 \text{ mol Ca}}{40.08 \text{ g}} \times \dfrac{1 \text{ mol Ca(OH)}_2}{\text{mol Ca}} \times \dfrac{2 \text{ mol OH}^-}{\text{mol Ca(OH)}_2}}{10.0 \text{ L}} = 0.0499 \text{ } M$$

$pOH = -\log(0.0499) = 1.302, pH = 14.000 - 1.302 = 12.698$

70.   GaAs can be either ^{69}GaAs or ^{71}GaAs. The mass spectrum for GaAs will have 2 peaks at 144 (= 69 + 75) and 146 (= 71 + 75) with intensities in the ratio of 60:40 or 3:2.

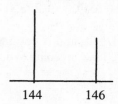

Ga$_2$As$_2$ can be ^{69}Ga$_2$As$_2$, ^{69}Ga^{71}GaAs$_2$, or ^{71}Ga$_2$As$_2$. The mass spectrum will have 3 peaks at 288, 290, and 292 with intensities in the ratio of 36:48:16 or 9:12:4. We get this ratio from the following probability table:

	^{69}Ga (0.60)	^{71}Ga (0.40)
^{69}Ga (0.60)	0.36	0.24
^{71}Ga (0.40)	0.24	0.16

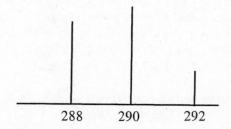

71. $CO_2(g) + H_2O(l) \rightarrow H_2CO_3(aq)$; $H_2CO_3(aq)$ is a diprotic acid with $K_{a_1} = 4.3 \times 10^{-7}$ and $K_{a_2} = 5.6 \times 10^{-11}$. Because $K_{a_1} \gg K_{a_2}$, the H^+ contribution from the K_{a_2} reaction will be insignificant.

$$H_2CO_3 \rightleftharpoons H^+ + HCO_3^-$$

Initial	0.50 mol/1.0 L	~0	0
Change	$-x$	$+x$	$+x$
Equil.	0.50 M - x	x	x

$$K_{a_1} = 4.3 \times 10^{-7} = \frac{x^2}{0.50 - x} \approx \frac{x^2}{0.50}, \quad x = [H^+] = 4.6 \times 10^{-4} \ M; \quad \text{Assumptions good.}$$

$$pH = -\log(4.6 \times 10^{-4}) = 3.34$$

$$HCO_3^- \rightleftharpoons H^+ + CO_3^{2-}$$

Initial	$4.6 \times 10^{-4} \ M$	$4.6 \times 10^{-4} \ M$	0
Change	$-x$	$+x$	$+x$
Equil.	$4.6 \times 10^{-4} - x$	$4.6 \times 10^{-4} + x$	x

$$K_{a_2} = 5.6 \times 10^{-11} = \frac{(4.6 \times 10^{-4} + x)x}{4.6 \times 10^{-4} - x} \approx \frac{4.6 \times 10^{-4} x}{4.6 \times 10^{-4}} = x$$

$$x = [CO_3^{2-}] = 5.6 \times 10^{-11} \ M; \quad \text{Assumptions good.}$$

72.   a. K^+ (blood) $\rightleftharpoons$ K^+ (muscle) $\Delta G^\circ = 0$; $\Delta G = RT \ln\left(\dfrac{[K^+]_m}{[K^+]_b}\right)$; $\Delta G = w_{max}$

$$\Delta G = \frac{8.3145 \ J}{K \ mol} (310. \ K) \ln\left(\frac{0.15}{0.0050}\right), \quad \Delta G = 8.8 \times 10^3 \ J/mol = 8.8 \ kJ/mol$$

At least 8.8 kJ of work must be applied to transport 1 mol K^+.

b.   Other ions will have to be transported in order to maintain electroneutrality. Either anions must be transported into the cells, or cations (Na^+) in the cell must be transported to the blood. The latter is what happens: [Na^+] in blood is greater than [Na^+] in cells as a result of this pumping.

c. $\Delta G^\circ = -RT \ln K = -(8.3145 \ J/K \cdot mol)(310. \ K) \ln 1.7 \times 10^5 = -3.1 \times 10^4 \ J/mol$
$$= -31 \ kJ/mol$$

The hydrolysis of ATP (at standard conditions) provides 31 kJ/mol of energy to do work. We need 8.8 kJ of work to transport 1.0 mol of K^+.

$$8.8 \ kJ \times \frac{1 \ mol \ ATP}{31 \ kJ} = 0.28 \ mol \ ATP \text{ must be hydrolyzed.}$$

73. $$Pb^{2+} \quad + \quad H_2EDTA^{2-} \quad \rightleftharpoons \quad PbEDTA^{2-} \quad + \quad 2\,H^+$$

Before	0.0010 M	0.050 M	0	$1.0 \times 10^{-6}\,M$	(buffer, [H$^+$] constant)
Change	-0.0010	-0.0010	$\rightarrow$ +0.0010	No change	Reacts completely
After	0	0.049	0.0010	1.0×10^{-6}	New initial conditions

x mol/L PbEDTA^{2-} dissociates to reach equilibrium

Change	$+x$	$+x$	$\leftarrow$ $-x$		
Equil.	x	$0.049 + x$	$0.0010 - x$	1.0×10^{-6}	(buffer)

$$K = 1.0 \times 10^{23} = \frac{[PbEDTA^{2-}][H^+]^2}{[Pb^{2+}][H_2EDTA^{2-}]} = \frac{(0.0010 - x)(1.0 \times 10^{-6})^2}{(x)(0.049 + x)}$$

$$1.0 \times 10^{23} \approx \frac{(0.0010)(1.0 \times 10^{-12})}{(x)(0.049)} \quad x = [Pb^{2+}] = 2.0 \times 10^{-37}\,M; \quad \text{Assumptions good.}$$

74. $SiCl_4(l) + 2\,H_2O(l) \rightarrow SiO_2(s) + 4\,H^+(aq) + 4\,Cl^-(aq)$

$\Delta H° = -911 + 4(0) + 4(-167) - [-687 + 2(-286)] = -320.\ kJ$

$\Delta S° = 42 + 4(0) + 4(57) - [240. + 2(70.)] = -110.\ J/K; \quad \Delta G° = \Delta H° - T\Delta S°$

$\Delta G° = 0$ when $T = \Delta H°/\Delta S° = -320. \times 10^3\ J/(-110.\ J/K) = 2910\ K$

Due to the favorable $\Delta H°$ term , this reaction is spontaneous at temperatures below 2910 K.

The corresponding reaction for CCl$_4$ is:

$CCl_4(l) + 2\,H_2O(l) \rightarrow CO_2(g) + 4\,H^+(aq) + 4\,Cl^-(aq)$

$\Delta H° = -393.5 + 4(0) + 4(-167) - [-135 + 2(-286)] = -355\ kJ$

$\Delta S° = 214 + 4(0) + 4(57) - [216 + 2(70.)] = 86\ J/K$

Thermodynamics predict that this reaction would be spontaneous at any temperature.

The answer must lie with kinetics. SiCl$_4$ reacts because an activated complex can form by a water molecule attaching to silicon in SiCl$_4$. The activated complex requires silicon to form a fifth bond. Silicon has low energy 3d orbitals available to expand the octet. Carbon will not break the octet rule; therefore, CCl$_4$ cannot form this activated complex. CCl$_4$ and H$_2$O require a different pathway to get to products. The different pathway has a higher activation energy and, in turn, the reaction is much slower. (See Exercise 19.75.)

75. Carbon cannot form the fifth bond necessary for the transition state because of the small atomic size of carbon and because carbon doesn't have low energy d orbitals available to expand the octet.

76.   White tin is stable at normal temperatures. Gray tin is stable at temperatures below 13.2°C. Thus for the phase change: Sn(gray) → Sn(white), ΔG is (−) at T > 13.2°C and ΔG is (+) at T < 13.2°C. This is only possible if ΔH is (+) and ΔS is (+). Thus, gray tin has the more ordered structure.

77. $PbX_4 \rightarrow PbX_2 + X_2$; From the equation, mol PbX_4 = mol PbX_2. Let x = molar mass of the halogen. Setting up an equation where mol PbX_4 = mol PbX_2:

$$\frac{25.00 \text{ g}}{207.2 + 4x} = \frac{16.12 \text{ g}}{207.2 + 2x} ; \quad \text{Solving, } x = 127.1; \text{ The halogen is iodine, I.}$$

Integrative Exercises

78. 1.75×10^8 g pitchblende $\times \dfrac{1 \text{ metric ton}}{1.0 \times 10^6 \text{ g}} \times \dfrac{1.0 \text{ g Ra}}{7.0 \text{ metric tons}} \times \dfrac{1 \text{ mol Ra}}{226 \text{ g Ra}}$

$$\times \frac{6.022 \times 10^{23} \text{ atoms Ra}}{\text{mol Ra}} = 6.7 \times 10^{22} \text{ atoms Ra}$$

Radioactive decay follows first order kinetics.

$$\ln\left(\frac{N}{N_0}\right) = -kt = \frac{-(\ln 2)t}{t_{1/2}}; \quad \ln\left(\frac{N}{15.0 \text{ mg}}\right) = \frac{-0.6931\,(100.\text{ yr})}{1.60 \times 10^3 \text{ yr}}, \text{ N} = 14.4 \text{ mg Ra}$$

$$14.4 \times 10^{-3} \text{ g Ra} \times \frac{1 \text{ mol Ra}}{226 \text{ g Ra}} \times \frac{6.022 \times 10^{23} \text{ atoms Ra}}{\text{mol Ra}} = 3.84 \times 10^{19} \text{ atoms Ra}$$

79.   a. $\text{mol In(CH}_3)_3 = \dfrac{PV}{RT} = \dfrac{2.00 \text{ atm} \times 2.56 \text{ L}}{0.08206 \text{ L atm}/\text{K} \bullet \text{mol} \times 900.\text{ K}} = 0.0693 \text{ mol}$

$$\text{mol PH}_3 = \frac{PV}{RT} = \frac{3.00 \text{ atm} \times 1.38 \text{ L}}{0.08206 \text{ L atm}/\text{K} \bullet \text{mol} \times 900.\text{ K}} = 0.0561 \text{ mol}$$

Because the reaction requires a 1:1 mole ratio between these reactants, the reactant with the small number of moles (PH_3) is limiting.

$$0.0561 \text{ mol PH}_3 \times \frac{1 \text{ mol InP}}{\text{mol PH}_3} \times \frac{145.8 \text{ g InP}}{\text{mol InP}} = 8.18 \text{ g InP}$$

The actual yield of InP is: 0.87×8.18 g = 7.1 g InP

b. $\lambda = \dfrac{hc}{E} = \dfrac{6.626 \times 10^{-34} \text{ J s} \times 2.998 \times 10^8 \text{ m/s}}{2.03 \times 10^{-19} \text{ J}} = 9.79 \times 10^{-7} \text{ m} = 979 \text{ nm}$

From the Figure 7.2 of the text, visible light has wavelengths between 4×10^{-7} m and 7×10^{-7} m. Therefore, this wavelength is not visible to humans; it is in the infrared region of the electromagnetic radiation spectrum.

c. $[Kr]5s^2 4d^{10} 5p^4$ is the electron configuration for tellurium, Te. Because Te has more valence electrons than P, this would form an n-type semiconductor (n-type doping).

80.   a. SnF_3^-: $4 + 3(7) + 1 = 26 \text{ e}^-$; Assuming covalent bonding:

trigonal pyramid; sp^3 hybridization

b. $4 \text{ NaF(aq)} + 3 \text{ SnF}_2(\text{aq}) \rightarrow \text{Na}_4\text{Sn}_3\text{F}_{10}(\text{s})$

c. $\text{mol NaF} = 0.0350 \text{ L} \times \dfrac{1.25 \text{ mol NaF}}{\text{L}} = 4.38 \times 10^{-2} \text{ mol}$

$\text{mol SnF}_2 = 0.0155 \text{ L} \times \dfrac{1.48 \text{ mol SnF}_2}{\text{L}} = 2.29 \times 10^{-2} \text{ mol}$

$\dfrac{\text{mol NaF}}{\text{mol SnF}_2} \text{(actual)} = \dfrac{4.38 \times 10^{-2} \text{ mol}}{2.29 \times 10^{-2} \text{ mol}} = 1.91$

The balanced equation requires a 4:3 (= 1.33) mol ratio between NaF and SnF_2. Because actual > theoretical, the denominator (SnF_2) is limiting.

$2.29 \times 10^{-2} \text{ mol SnF}_2 \times \dfrac{1 \text{ mol Na}_4\text{Sn}_3\text{F}_{10}}{3 \text{ mol SnF}_2} \times \dfrac{638.1 \text{ g}}{\text{mol}} = 4.87 \text{ g Na}_4\text{Sn}_3\text{F}_{10}$

Marathon Problem

81.   The answer to the clues are: (1) BeO is amphoteric; (2) NaN$_3$ is the compound used in airbags; (3) Fr is radioactive; (4) Na has the least negative E° value (the symbol in reverse is an); (5) K$_2$O is potash; (6) Only Li forms Li$_3$N; (7) In is the first group 3A element to form stable +1 and +3 ions in its compounds (the second letter of the symbol is n).

Inserting the symbols into the blanks gives Ben Franklin for the name of the American scientist.

CHAPTER TWENTY
THE REPRESENTATIVE ELEMENTS:
GROUPS 5A THROUGH 8A

For Review

1. Group 5A: ns^2np^3; As with groups IIIA and IVA, metallic character increases going down a group. Nitrogen is strictly a nonmetal in properties, while bismuth, the heaviest Group 5A element, has mostly metallic physical properties. The trend of increasing metallic character going down the group is due in part to the decrease in electronegativity. Nitrogen, with its high electronegativity, forms covalent compounds as nonmetals do. Bismuth and antimony, with much lower electronegativities, exhibit ionic character in most of their compounds. Bismuth and antimony exist as +3 metal cations in these ionic compounds.

    NH_3, $5 + 3(1) = 8\ e^-$

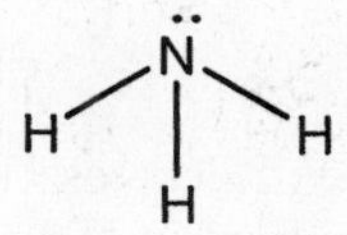

    trigonal pyramid; sp^3

    $AsCl_5$, $5 + 5(7) = 40\ e^-$

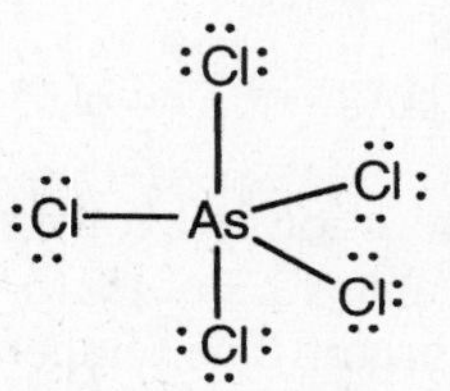

    trigonal bipyramid; dsp^3

    PF_6^-, $5 + 6(7) + 1 = 48\ e^-$

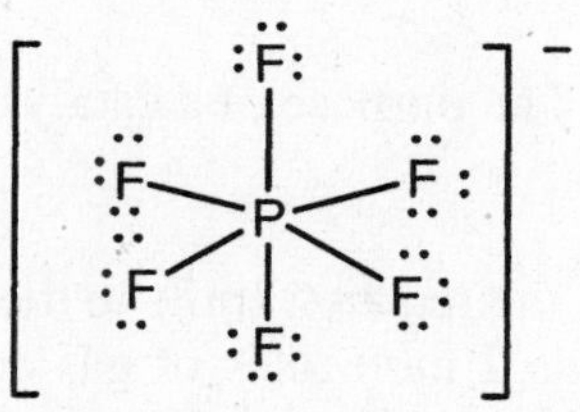

    Octahedral; d^2sp^3

    Nitrogen does not have low energy d orbitals it can use to expand its octet. Both NF_5 and NCl_6^- would require nitrogen to have more than 8 valence electrons around it; this never happens.

2. N: $1s^22s^22p^5$; The extremes of the oxidation states for N can be rationalized by examining the electron configuration of N. Nitrogen is three electrons short of the stable Ne electron configuration of $1s^22s^22p^6$. Having an oxidation state of −3 makes sense. The +5 oxidation state corresponds to N "losing" its 5 valence electrons. In compounds with oxygen, the N−O bonds are polar covalent, with N having the partial positive end of the bond dipole. In the

751

bonds are polar covalent, with N having the partial positive end of the bond dipole. In the world of oxidation states, electrons in polar covalent bonds are assigned to the more electronegative atom; this is oxygen in N–O bonds. N can form enough bonds to oxygen to give it a +5 oxidation state. This loosely corresponds to losing all of the valence electrons.

NH_3: fertilizers, weak base properties, can form hydrogen bonds; N_2H_4: rocket propellant, blowing agent in manufacture of plastics, can form hydrogen bonds; NH_2OH: weak base properties, can form hydrogen bonds; N_2: makes up 78% of air, very stable compound with a very strong triple bond, is inert chemically; N_2O: laughing gas, propellant in aerosol cans, effect on earth's temperature being studied; NO: toxic when inhaled, may play a role in regulating blood pressure and blood clotting, one of the few odd electron species that forms; N_2O_3, least common of nitrogen oxides, a blue liquid that readily dissociates into NO(g) and NO_2(g); NO_2: another odd electron species, dimerizes to form N_2O_4, plays a role in smog production; HNO_3: important industrial chemical, used to form nitrogen-based explosives, strong acid and a very strong oxidizing agent.

3. Hydrazine also can hydrogen bond because it has covalent N–H bonds as well as having a lone pair of electrons on each N. The high boiling point for hydrazine's relatively small size supports this.

$N_2(g) + 3 H_2(g) \rightleftharpoons 2 NH_3(g) + heat$

a. This reaction is exothermic, so an increase in temperature will decrease the value of K (see Table 13.3 of text.) This has the effect of lowering the amount of NH_3(g) produced at equilibrium. The temperature increase, therefore, must be for kinetics reasons. When the temperature increases, the reaction reaches equilibrium much faster. At low temperatures, this reaction is very slow, too slow to be of any use.

b. As NH_3(g) is removed, the reaction shifts right to produce more NH_3(g).

c. A catalyst has no effect on the equilibrium position. The purpose of a catalyst is to speed up a reaction so it reaches equilibrium quicker.

d. When the pressure of reactants and products is high, the reaction shifts to the side that has fewer gas molecules. Since the product side contains 2 molecules of gas compared to 4 molecules of gas on the reactant side, the reaction shifts right to products at high pressures of reactants and products. Also, a high pressure indicates that reactants are present in large quanties. The more reactants present, the further right the reaction shifts.

The pollution provides nitrogen and phosphorous nutrients so the algae can grow. The algae consume oxygen, causing fish to die.

4. White phosphorus consists of discrete tetrahedral P_4 molecules. The bond angles in the P_4 tetrahedrons are only 60°, which makes P_4 very reactive, especially towards oxygen. Red and black phosphorus are covalent network solids. In red phosphorus, the P_4 tetrahedra are bonded to each other in chains, making them less reactive than white phosphorus. They need a source of energy to react with oxygen, such as when one strikes a match. Black phosphorus is crystalline, with the P atoms tightly bonded to each other in the crystal, and is fairly unreactive towards oxygen.

Even though phosphine and ammonia have identical Lewis structures, the bond angles of PH_3 are only 94°, well below the predicted tetrahedral bond angles of 109.5°. PH_3 is an unusual exception to the VSEPR model.

The acidic hydrogens in the oxyacids of phosporus all are bonded to oxygen. The hydrogens bonded directly to phosphorus are not acidic. H_3PO_4 has three oxygen bonded hydrogens, and it is a triprotic acid. H_3PO_3 has only two of the hydrogens bonded to oxygen and it is a diprotic acid. The third oxyacid of phosphorus, H_3PO_2, has only one of the hydrogens bonded to an oxygen; it is a monoprotic acid.

5.   Group 6A: ns^2np^4; As expected from the trend in other groups, oxygen has properties which are purely nonmetal. Polonium, on the other hand, has some metallic properties. The most significant property differences are radioactivity and toxicity. Polonium is only composed of radioactive isotopes, unlike oxygen, and polonium is highly toxic, unlike oxygen.

The two allotropic forms of oxygen are O_2 and O_3.

O_2, $2(6) = 12 \text{ e}^-$ O_3, $3(6) = 18 \text{ e}^-$

The MO electron configuration of O_2 has two unpaired electrons in the degenerate pi antibonding (π^*_{2p}) orbitals. A substance with unpaired electrons is paramagnetic (see Figure 9.40). Ozone has a V-shape molecular structure with bond angles of 117°, slightly less than the predicted 120° trigonal planar bond angle.

In the upper atmosphere, O_3 acts as a filter for UV radiation:

$$O_3 \xrightarrow{h\nu} O_2 + O$$

O_3 is also a powerful oxidizing agent. It irritates the lungs and eyes, and, at high concentration, it is toxic. The smell of a "fresh spring day" is O_3 formed during lightning discharges. Toxic materials don't necessarily smell bad. For example, HCN smells like almonds.

6.   Both rhombic and monoclinic sulfur exist in S_8 rings. The difference between the two is that the S_8 rings are stacked together differently giving different solid structures.

Oxygen forms strong π bonds and, because of this, exists in nature as O_2 molecules. Sulfur forms much stronger sigma bonds than π bonds. Therefore, elemental sulfur is found in nature singly bonded to other sulfur atoms. We assume SO doesn't form because of the difference in ability of oxygen and sulfur to form π bonds. Sulfur forms relatively weak π bonds as compared to oxygen.

$SO_2(aq) + H_2O(l) \rightarrow H_2SO_3(aq)$; $SO_3(aq) + H_2O(l) \rightarrow H_2SO_4(aq)$; SO_2 and SO_3 dissolve in water to form the acids H_2SO_3 and H_2SO_4, respectively. Figures 20.18 and 20.19 show the Lewis structures for SO_2 and SO_3. The molecular structure of SO_2 is bent with a 119° bond angle (close to the predicted 120° trigonal planar geometry). The molecular structure of SO_3

is trigonal planar with 120° bond angles. Both SO_2 and SO_3 exhibit resonance. Both sulfurs in SO_2 and SO_3 are sp^2 hybridized. To explain the equal bond lengths that occur in SO_2 and SO_3, the molecular orbital model assumes that the π electrons are delocalized over the entire surface of the molecule. The orbitals that form the delocalized π bonding system are unhybridized p atomic orbitals from the sulfurs and oxygens in each molecule. When all of the p atomic orbitals overlap together, there is a cloud of electron density above and below the entire surface of the molecule. Because the π electrons are delocalized over the entire surface of the molecule in SO_2 and SO_3, all of the S–O bonds in each molecule are equivalent.

A dehydrating agent is one that has a high affinity for water. Sulfuric acid grabs water whenever it can. When it reacts with sugar ($C_{12}H_{22}O_{11}$) it removes the hydrogen and oxygen in a 2:1 ratio even though there are no H_2O molecules in sugar. H_2SO_4 is indeed a powerful dehydrating agent.

7.   Group 7A: ns^2np^5; The diatomic halogens (X_2) are nonpolar, so they only exibit London dispersion intermolecular forces. The strength of LD forces increases with size. The boiling points and melting points steadily increase from F_2 to I_2 because the strength of the intermolecular forces are increasing.

Fluorine is the most reactive of the halogens because it is the most electronegative atom and the bond in the F_2 molecule is very weak.

One reason is that the H – F bond is stronger than the other hydrohalides, making it more difficult to form H^+ and F^-. The main reason HF is a weak acid is entropy. When F^- (aq) forms from the dissociation of HF, there is a high degree of ordering that takes place as water molecules hydrate this small ion. Entropy is considerably more unfavorable for the formation of hydrated F^- than for the formation of the other hydrated halides. The result of the more unfavorable $\Delta S°$ term is a positive $\Delta G°$ value, which leads to a K_a value less than one.

HF exhibits the relatively strong hydrogen bonding intermolecular forces, unlike the other hydrogen halides. HF has a high boiling point due to its ability to form these hydrogen bonding interactions.

The halide ion is the –1 charged ion that halogens form when in ionic compounds. As can be seen from the positive standard reduction potentials in Table 20.6, the halogens energetically favor the X^- form over the X_2 form. Because the reduction potentials are so large, this give an indication of the relative ease to which halogens will grab electrons to form the halide ion. In general, the halogens are highly reactive; that is why halogens exist as cations in various minerals and in seawater as opposed to free elements in nature.

Some compounds of chlorine exhibiting the –1 to +7 oxidation state are: HCl(–1), HOCl (+1), $HClO_2$ (+3), $HClO_3$ (+5), and $HClO_4$ (+7). Note that these are all acids. HCl is a strong acid, and of the oxyacids, only $HClO_4$ is a strong acid. The oxyacid strength increases as the number of oxygens in the formula increase. Therefore, the order of the oxyacids from weakest to strongest acid is $HOCl < HClO_2 < HClO_3 < HClO_4$.

8.   Most of the compounds in Table 20.11 have the following molecular structures, bond angles, and hybridization. Examples found in Table 20.11 are listed for each.

trigonal planar: $120°$, sp^2, e.g., BX_3

V-shape: $< 109.5°$, sp^3, e.g., OF_2, OCl_2, OBr_2, SF_2, SCl_2, $SeCl_2$

trigonal pyramid: $< 109.5°$, sp^3, e.g., NX_3, PX_3, AsF_3, SbF_3

tetrahedral: $109.5°$, sp^3, e.g., BF_4^-, CX_4, SiF_4, $SiCl_4$, GeF_4, $GeCl_4$

T-shape: $90°$, dsp^3, e.g., ClF_3, BrF_3, ICl_3, IF_3

see-saw: $90°$ and $\sim 120°$, dsp^3, e.g., SF_4, SCl_4, SeF_4, $SeCl_4$, $SeBr_4$, $TeBr_4$, $TeCl_4$, $TeBr_4$, TeI_4

trigonal bipyramid: $90°$ and $120°$, dsp^3, e.g., PF_5, PCl_5, PBr_5, AsF_5, SbF_5

square pyramid: $90°$, d^2sp^3, e.g., ClF_5, BrF_5, IF_5

octahedral: $90°$, d^2sp^3, e.g., SiF_6^{2-}, GeF_6^{2-}, SF_6, SeF_6, TeF_6

ICl, IBr, BrF, BrCl, and ClF have no molecular structure or bond angles. The predicted hybridization for each halogen is sp^3. N_2F_4 is trigonal pyramid about both nitrogens, with $< 109.5°$ bond angles and sp^3 hybridization. O_2F_2, S_2Cl_2, S_2F_2, and S_2Cl_2 is V-shape about both central oxygens or sulfurs with $< 109.5°$ bond angles and sp^3 hybridization.

Some of the compounds in Table 20.11 are exceptions to the octet rule, like ICl_3. The row three halogens (Cl) and heavier (Br and I) have low lying empty d-orbitals available to expand their octet when they have to. Fluorine, with its valence electrons in the n = 2 level, does not have low energy d-orbitals available to expand its octet. When F is the central atom, its compounds always obeys the octet rule.

9.   The noble gases have filled s and p valence orbitals (ns^2np^6 = valence electron configuration). They don't need to react like other representative elements in order to achieve the stable ns^2np^6 configuration. Noble gases are unreactive because they do not want to lose their stable valence electron configuration.

Noble gases exist as free atoms in nature. They only exhibit London dispersion forces in the condensed phases. Because LD forces increase with size, as the noble gas gets bigger, the strength of the intermolecular forces get stronger leading to higher melting and boiling points.

Helium is unreactive and doesn't combine with any other elements. It is a very light gas and would easily escape the earth's gravitational pull as the planet was formed.

In Mendeleev's time, none of the noble gases were known. Since an entire family was missing, no gaps seemed to appear in the periodic arrangement. Mendeleev had no evidence to predict the existence of such a family. The heavier members of the noble gases are not really inert. Xe and Kr have been shown to react and form compounds with other elements.

10. XeF_2: $180°$, dsp^3; XeO_2F_2: $\sim 90°$ and $\sim 120°$, dsp^3; XeO_3: $< 109.5°$, sp^3; XeO_4: $109.5°$, sp^3; XeF_4: $90°$, d^2sp^3; XeO_3F_2: $90°$ and $120°$, dsp^3; XeO_2F_4, $90°$, d^2sp^3

Questions

1.   This is due to nitrogen's ability to form strong π bonds whereas heavier group 5A elements do not form strong π bonds. Therefore, P_2, As_2, and Sb_2 do not form since two π bonds are required to form these diatomic substances.

2.   Nitrogen fixation is the process of transforming N_2 to other nitrogen-containing compounds. Some examples are:

$$N_2(g) + 3 H_2(g) \rightarrow 2 NH_3(g)$$

$$N_2(g) + O_2(g) \rightarrow 2 NO(g)$$

$$N_2(g) + 2 O_2(g) \rightarrow 2 NO_2(g)$$

3.   There are medical studies that have shown an inverse relationship between the incidence of cancer and the selenium levels in soil. The foods grown in these soils and eventually digested are assumed to somehow furnish protection from cancer. Selenium is also involved in the activity of vitamin E and certain enzymes in the human body. In addition, selenium deficiency has been shown to be connected to the occurrence of congestive heart failure.

4.   Chlorine is a good oxidizing agent. Similarly, ozone is a good oxidizing agent. After chlorine reacts, residues of chloro compounds are left behind. Long term exposure to some chloro compounds may cause cancer. Ozone would not break down and form harmful substances. The major problem with ozone is that because virtually no ozone is left behind after initial treatment, the water supply is not protected against recontamination. In contrast, for chlorination, significant residual chlorine remains after treatment, thus reducing (eliminating) the risk of recontamination.

5.   +6 oxidation state: SO_4^{2-}, SO_3, SF_6
      +4 oxidation state: SO_3^{2-}, SO_2, SF_4
      +2 oxidation state: SCl_2
       0 oxidation state: S_8 and all other elemental forms of sulfur
      –2 oxidation state: H_2S, Na_2S

6. sp^3 hybridization: HBr, $1 + 7 = 8\ e^-$ IBr, $7 + 7 = 14\ e^-$

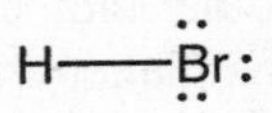

Diatomic molecules don't have a molecular structure because they have no bond angles.

dsp^3 hybridization: BrF_3, $7 + 3(7) = 28\ e^-$

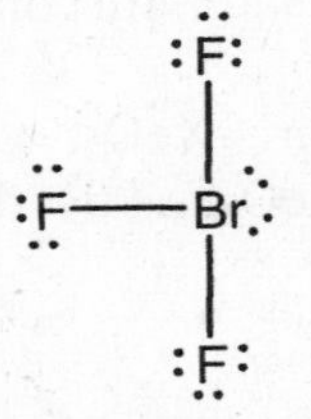

T-shaped

d^2sp^3 hybridization: BrF_5, $7 + 5(7) = 42\ e^-$

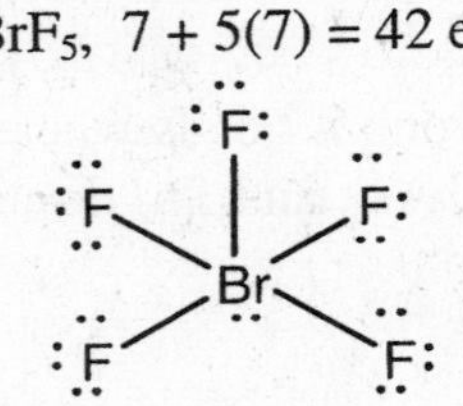

square pyramid

7.   a. $H_2(g) + Cl_2(g) \rightarrow 2\ HCl(g)$; this reaction produces a lot of energy which can be used in a cannon apparatus to send a stopper across the room. To initiate this extremely slow reaction, light of specific wavelengths is needed. This is the purpose of lighting the magnesium strip. When magnesium is oxidized to MgO, an intense white light is produced. Some of the wavelengths of this light can break Cl–Cl bonds and get the reaction started.

      b. Br_2 is brown. The disappearance of the brown color indicates that all of the Br_2 has reacted with the alkene (no free Br_2 is remaining).

      c. $2\ Al(s) + 3\ I_2(s) \rightarrow 2\ AlI_3(s)$; This is a highly exothermic reaction, hence the sparks that accompany this reaction. The purple smoke is excess $I_2(s)$ being vaporized [the purple smoke is $I_2(g)$].

8.   One would expect RnF_2 and RnF_4 to form in fashion similar to XeF_2 and XeF_4. The chemistry of radon is difficult to study because radon isotopes are all radioactive. The hazards of dealing with radioactive materials are immense.

Exercises

Group 5A Elements

9. NO_4^{3-}

Both NO_4^{3-} and PO_4^{3-} have 32 valence electrons, so both have similar Lewis structures. From the Lewis structure for NO_4^{3-}, the central N atom has a tetrahedral arrangement of electron pairs. N is small. There is probably not enough room for all 4 oxygen atoms around N. P is larger, thus, PO_4^{3-} is stable.

PO_3^-

PO_3^- and NO_3^- each have 24 valence electrons so both have similar Lewis structures. From the Lewis structure for PO_3^-, PO_3^- has a trigonal planar arrangement of electron pairs about the central P atom (two single bonds and one double bond). P=O bonds are not particularly stable, while N=O bonds are stable. Thus, NO_3^- is stable.

10.   a. PF_5;   N is too small and doesn't have low energy d-orbitals to expand its octet to form NF_5.

       b. AsF_5;   I is too large to fit 5 atoms of I around As.

       c. NF_3;   N is too small for three large bromine atoms to fit around it.

11.   a.   NO: $\%N = \dfrac{14.01\,\text{g N}}{30.01\,\text{g NO}} \times 100 = 46.68\%\,\text{N}$

      b. NO_2: $\%N = \dfrac{14.01\,\text{g N}}{46.01\,\text{g NO}_2} \times 100 = 30.45\%\,\text{N}$

      c. N_2O_4: $\%N = \dfrac{28.02\,\text{g N}}{92.02\,\text{g N}_2\text{O}_4} \times 100 = 30.45\%\,\text{N}$

      d. N_2O: $\%N = \dfrac{28.02\,\text{g N}}{44.02\,\text{g N}_2\text{O}_4} \times 100 = 63.65\%\,\text{N}$

The order from lowest to highest mass percentage of nitrogen is: $NO_2 = N_2O_4 < NO < N_2O$.

12. $1.0 \times 10^6\,\text{kg HNO}_3 \times \dfrac{1000\,\text{g HNO}_3}{\text{kg HNO}_3} \times \dfrac{1\,\text{mol HNO}_3}{63.02\,\text{g HNO}_3} = 1.6 \times 10^7\,\text{mol HNO}_3$

We need to get the relationship between moles of HNO_3 and moles of NH_3. We have to use all 3 equations.

$$\dfrac{2\,\text{mol HNO}_3}{3\,\text{mol NO}_2} \times \dfrac{2\,\text{mol NO}_2}{2\,\text{mol NO}} \times \dfrac{4\,\text{mol NO}}{4\,\text{mol NH}_3} = \dfrac{16\,\text{mol HNO}_3}{24\,\text{mol NH}_3}$$

Thus, we can produce 16 mol HNO_3 for every 24 mol NH_3 we begin with:

$$1.6 \times 10^7\,\text{mol HNO}_3 \times \dfrac{24\,\text{mol NH}_3}{16\,\text{mol HNO}_3} \times \dfrac{17.03\,\text{g NH}_3}{\text{mol NH}_3} = 4.1 \times 10^8\,\text{g or } 4.1 \times 10^5\,\text{kg}$$

This is an oversimplified answer. In practice, the NO produced in the third step is recycled back continuously into the process in the second step. If this is taken into consideration, then the conversion factor between mol NH_3 and mol HNO_3 turns out to be 1:1, i.e., 1 mol of NH_3 produces 1 mol of HNO_3. Taking into consideration that NO is recycled back gives an answer of 2.7×10^5 kg NH_3 reacted.

13.   a. $NH_4NO_3(s) \xrightarrow{\text{heat}} N_2O(g) + 2\,H_2O(g)$

      b. $2\,N_2O_5(g) \rightarrow 4\,NO_2(g) + O_2(g)$

      c. $2\,K_3P(s) + 6\,H_2O(l) \rightarrow 2\,PH_3(g) + 6\,KOH(aq)$

      d. $PBr_3(l) + 3\,H_2O(l) \rightarrow H_3PO_3(aq) + 3\,HBr(aq)$

      e. $2\,NH_3(aq) + NaOCl(aq) \rightarrow N_2H_4(aq) + NaCl(aq) + H_2O(l)$

14. $4 As(s) + 3 O_2(g) \rightarrow As_4O_6(s); 4 As(s) + 5 O_2(g) \rightarrow As_4O_{10}(s)$

        $As_4O_6(s) + 6 H_2O(l) \rightarrow 4 H_3AsO_3(aq); As_4O_{10}(s) + 6 H_2O(l) \rightarrow 4 H_3AsO_4(aq)$

15.   Unbalanced equation:

        $CaF_2 \bullet 3Ca_3(PO_4)_2(s) + H_2SO_4(aq) \rightarrow H_3PO_4(aq) + HF(aq) + CaSO_4 \bullet 2H_2O(s)$

        Balancing Ca^{2+}, F^-, and PO_4^{3-}:

        $CaF_2 \bullet 3Ca_3(PO_4)_2(s) + H_2SO_4(aq) \rightarrow 6 H_3PO_4(aq) + 2 HF(aq) + 10 CaSO_4 \bullet 2H_2O(s)$

        On the right hand side, there are 20 extra hydrogen atoms, 10 extra sulfates, and 20 extra water molecules. We can balance the hydrogen and sulfate with 10 sulfuric acid molecules. The extra waters came from the water in the sulfuric acid solution. The balanced equation is:

        $CaF_2 \bullet 3Ca_3(PO_4)_2(s) + 10 H_2SO_4(aq) + 20 H_2O(l) \rightarrow$

        $\qquad\qquad\qquad 6 H_3PO_4(aq) + 2 HF(aq) + 10 CaSO_4 \bullet 2H_2O(s)$

16.   a. NO_2, $5 + 2(6) = 17 e^-$ N_2O_4, $2(5) + 4(6) = 34 e^-$

        plus other resonance structures   plus other resonance structures

        b. BH_3, $3 + 3(1) = 6 e^-$ NH_3, $5 + 3(1) = 8 e^-$

        BF_3NH_3, $6 + 8 = 14 e^-$

        In reaction a, NO_2 has an odd number of electrons, so it is impossible to satisfy the octet rule. By dimerizing to form N_2O_4, the odd electron on two NO_2 molecules can pair up, giving a species whose Lewis structure can satisfy the octet rule. In general, odd electron species are very reactive. In reaction b, BH_3 is electron deficient. Boron has only six electrons around it. By forming BH_3NH_3, the boron atom satisfies the octet rule by accepting a lone pair of electrons from NH_3 to form a fourth bond.

17. $2 NaN_3(s) \rightarrow 2 Na(s) + 3 N_2(g)$

$$n_{N_2} = \frac{PV}{RT} = \frac{1.00\, atm \times 70.0\, L}{\dfrac{0.08206\, L\, atm}{mol\, K} \times 273\, K} = 3.12\, mol\, N_2 \text{ needed to fill air bag.}$$

mol NaN_3 reacted $= 3.12\, mol\, N_2 \times \dfrac{2\, mol\, NaN_3}{3\, mol\, N_2} = 2.08\, mol\, NaN_3$

18.   For ammonia (in one minute):

$$n_{NH_3} = \frac{PV}{RT} = \frac{90.\, atm \times 500.\, L}{\dfrac{0.08206\, L\, atm}{mol\, K} \times 496\, K} = 1.1 \times 10^3\, mol\, NH_3$$

NH_3 flows into the reactor at a rate of 1.1×10^3 mol/min.

For CO_2 (in one minute):

$$n_{CO_2} = \frac{PV}{RT} = \frac{45\, atm \times 600.\, L}{\dfrac{0.08206\, L\, atm}{mol\, K} \times 496\, K} = 6.6 \times 10^2\, mol\, CO_2$$

CO_2 flows into the reactor at 6.6×10^2 mol/min.

To react completely with 1.1×10^3 mol NH_3/min, we need:

$$\frac{1.1 \times 10^3\, NH_3}{min} \times \frac{1\, mol\, CO_2}{2\, mol\, NH_3} = 5.5 \times 10^2\, mol\, CO_2/min$$

Because 660 mol CO_2/min are present, ammonia is the limiting reagent.

$$\frac{1.1 \times 10^3\, NH_3}{min} \times \frac{1\, mol\, urea}{2\, mol\, NH_3} \times \frac{60.06\, g\, urea}{mol\, urea} = 3.3 \times 10^4\, g\, urea/min$$

19.

Bonds broken: Bonds formed:

1 N–N (160. kJ/mol)   1 N≡ N (941 kJ/mol)

4 N–H (391 kJ/mol)   2 × 2 O–H (467 kJ/mol)

1 O=O (495 kJ/mol)

$\Delta H = 160. + 4(391) + 495 - [941 + 4(467)] = 2219\, kJ - 2809\, kJ = -590.\, kJ$

20. $5 \, N_2O_4(l) + 4 \, N_2H_3CH_3(l) \rightarrow 12 \, H_2O(g) + 9 \, N_2(g) + 4 \, CO_2(g)$

$$\Delta H^\circ = \left[12 \, mol\left(\frac{-242 \, kJ}{mol} \right) + 4 \, mol\left(\frac{-393.5 \, kJ}{mol} \right) \right] - \left[5 \, mol\left(\frac{-20. \, kJ}{mol} \right) + 4 \, mol\left(\frac{54 \, kJ}{mol} \right) \right]$$

$$= -4594 \, kJ$$

Using bond energies, $\Delta H = -5.0 \times 10^3$ kJ (from Sample Exercise 20.2). When using bond energies to calculate ΔH, the enthalpy change is assumed to be due only to the difference in bond strength between reactants and products. Bond energies generally give a very good estimate for ΔH for gas phase reactions. However, when solids and liquids are present, ΔH estimates from bond energy differences are not as good. This is because the difference in the strength of the intermolecular forces between reactants and products is not considered when using bond energies. Here, the reactants are in the liquid phase. The loss in strength of the intermolecular forces as the liquid reactants are converted to the gaseous products was not considered when using bond energies in Sample Exercise 20.2; hence, the large difference between the two calculated ΔH values.

21. $1/2 \, N_2(g) + 1/2 \, O_2(g) \rightarrow NO(g)$ $\Delta G^\circ = \Delta G^\circ_{f, NO} = 87$ kJ/mol; By definition, ΔG°_f for a compound equals the free energy change that would accompany the formation of 1 mol of that compound from its elements in their standard states. NO (and some other oxides of nitrogen) have weaker bonds as compared to the triple bond of N_2 and the double bond of O_2. Because of this, NO (and some other oxides of nitrogen) have higher (positive) standard free energies of formation as compared to the relatively stable N_2 and O_2 molecules.

22. $\Delta H^\circ = 2(90. \, kJ) - [0 + 0] = 180. \, kJ$; $\Delta S^\circ = 2(211 \, J/K) - [192 + 205] = 25 \, J/K$

$\Delta G^\circ = 2(87 \, kJ) - [0] = 174 \, kJ$

At the high temperatures in automobile engines, the reaction $N_2 + O_2 \rightarrow 2 \, NO$ becomes spontaneous since the favorable ΔS° term will become dominate. In the atmosphere, even though $2 \, NO \rightarrow N_2 + O_2$ is spontaneous at the cooler temperatures of the atmosphere, it doesn't occur because the rate is slow. Therefore, higher concentrations of NO are present in the atmosphere as compared to what is predicted by thermodynamics.

23.   MO model:

NO^+: $(\sigma_{2s})^2(\sigma_{2s}*)^2(\pi_{2p})^4(\sigma_{2p})^2$, Bond order = (8 – 2)/2 = 3, 0 unpaired e^- (diamagnetic)

NO: $(\sigma_{2s})^2(\sigma_{2s}*)^2(\pi_{2p})^4(\sigma_{2p})^2(\pi_{2p}*)^1$, B.O. = 2.5, 1 unpaired e^- (paramagnetic)

NO^-: $(\sigma_{2s})^2(\sigma_{2s}*)^2(\pi_{2p})^4(\sigma_{2p})^2(\pi_{2p}*)^2$, B.O. = 2, 2 unpaired e^- (paramagnetic)

Lewis structures: NO^+: $\left[\; :N\equiv O: \;\right]^+$

NO: $\cdot\overset{\cdot\cdot}{N}=\overset{\cdot\cdot}{O}:\quad\longleftrightarrow\quad :\overset{\cdot\cdot}{N}=\overset{\cdot}{O}:\quad\longleftrightarrow\quad \cdot\overset{\cdot\cdot}{N}=\overset{\cdot}{O}\cdot$

NO^-: $\left[\; :\overset{\cdot\cdot}{N}=\overset{\cdot\cdot}{O}: \;\right]^-$

The two models give the same results only for NO^+ (a triple bond with no unpaired electrons). Lewis structures are not adequate for NO and NO^-. The MO model gives a better representation for all three species. For NO, Lewis structures are poor for odd electron species. For NO^-, both models predict a double bond, but only the MO model correctly predicts that NO^- is paramagnetic.

24. For $NCl_3 \rightarrow NCl_2 + Cl$, only the N–Cl bond is broken. For $O=N-Cl \rightarrow NO + Cl$, the NO bond gets stronger (bond order increases from 2.0 to 2.5) when the N–Cl bond is broken. This makes ΔH for the reaction smaller than just the energy necessary to break the N–Cl bond.

25. a. $H_3PO_4 > H_3PO_3$; The strongest acid has the most oxygen atoms.

b. $H_3PO_4 > H_2PO_4^- > HPO_4^{2-}$; Acid strength decreases as protons are removed.

26. TSP = Na_3PO_4; PO_4^{3-} is the conjugate base of the weak acid HPO_4^{2-} ($K_a = 4.8 \times 10^{-13}$). All conjugate bases of weak acids are effective bases ($K_b = K_w/K_a = 1.0 \times 10^{-14}/4.8 \times 10^{-13} = 2.1 \times 10^{-2}$). The weak base reaction of PO_4^{3-} with H_2O is: $PO_4^{3-} + H_2O \rightleftharpoons HPO_4^{2-} + OH^-$ $K_b = 2.1 \times 10^{-2}$.

27. The acidic protons are attached to oxygen.

$H_4P_2O_6$ (50 valence e^-): $H_4P_2O_5$ (44 valence e^-):

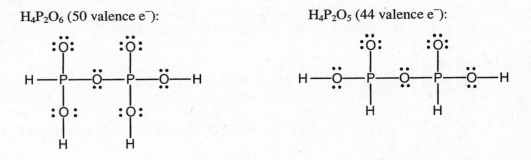

28.   a. SbF_5, 40 valence e^- HSO_3F, 32 valence e^- $H_2SO_3F^+$, 32 valence e^-

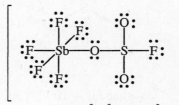

          dsp^3 sp^3 sp^3

              F_5SbOSO_2FH, 72 valence e^- $F_5SbOSO_2F^-$, 72 valence e^-

                  Sb: d^2sp^3; S: sp^3 Sb: d^2sp^3; S: sp^3

       b.   The active protonating species is $H_2SO_3F^+$, the species with two OH bonds.

Group 6A Elements

29. $O=O-O \rightarrow O=O + O$

       Break O–O bond: $\Delta H = \dfrac{146\,kJ}{mol} \times \dfrac{1\,mol}{6.022 \times 10^{23}} = 2.42 \times 10^{-22}\,kJ = 2.42 \times 10^{-19}\,J$

       A photon of light must contain at least $2.42 \times 10^{-19}\,J$ to break one O–O bond.

       $E_{photon} = \dfrac{hc}{\lambda}$, $\lambda = \dfrac{(6.626 \times 10^{-34}\,J\,s)(2.998 \times 10^8\,m/s)}{2.42 \times 10^{-19}\,J} = 8.21 \times 10^{-7}\,m = 821\,nm$

30.   From Figure 7.2 in the text, light from violet to green will work.

31.   a. $2\,SO_2(g) + O_2(g) \rightarrow 2\,SO_3(g)$ b. $SO_3(g) + H_2O(l) \rightarrow H_2SO_4(aq)$

       c. $2\,Na_2S_2O_3(aq) + I_2(aq) \rightarrow Na_2S_4O_6(aq) + 2\,NaI(aq)$

       d. $Cu(s) + 2\,H_2SO_4(aq) \rightarrow CuSO_4(aq) + 2\,H_2O(l) + SO_2(aq)$

32. $H_2SeO_4(aq) + 3\,SO_2(g) \rightarrow Se(s) + 3\,SO_3(g) + H_2O(l)$

33.   a. SO_3^{2-}, $6 + 3(6) + 2 = 26$ e^- b. O_3, $3(6) = 18$ e^-

trigonal pyramid; $\approx 109.5°$; sp^3 V-shaped; $\approx 120°$; sp^2

c. SCl_2, $6 + 2(7) = 20$ e^- d. $SeBr_4$, $6 + 4(7) = 34$ e^-

V-shaped; $\approx 109.5°$; sp^3 see-saw; $a \approx 120°$, $b \approx 90°$; dsp^3

e. TeF_6, $6 + 6(7) = 48$ e^-

octahedral; $90°$; d^2sp^3

34. S_2N_2 has $2(6) + 2(5) = 22$ valence electrons.

35. $1.50 \text{ g BaO}_2 \times \dfrac{1 \text{ mol BaO}_2}{169.3 \text{ g BaO}_2} = 8.86 \times 10^{-3} \text{ mol BaO}_2$

$25.0 \text{ mL} \times \dfrac{0.0272 \text{ g HCl}}{\text{mL}} \times \dfrac{1 \text{ mol HCl}}{36.46 \text{ HCl}} = 1.87 \times 10^{-2} \text{ mol HCl}$

The required mole ratio from the balanced reaction is 2 mol HCl to 1 mol BaO_2. The actual ratio is:

$\dfrac{1.87 \times 10^{-2} \text{ mol HCl}}{8.86 \times 10^{-3} \text{ mol BaO}_2} = 2.11$

Because the actual mole ratio is larger than the required mole ratio, the denominator (BaO_2) is the limiting reagent.

$$8.86 \times 10^{-3} \text{ mol BaO}_2 \times \frac{1 \text{ mol H}_2\text{O}_2}{\text{mol BaO}_2} \times \frac{34.02 \text{ g H}_2\text{O}_2}{\text{mol H}_2\text{O}_2} = 0.301 \text{ g H}_2\text{O}_2$$

The amount of HCl reacted is:

$$8.86 \times 10^{-3} \text{ mol BaO}_2 \times \frac{2 \text{ mol HCl}}{\text{mol BaO}_2} = 1.77 \times 10^{-2} \text{ mol HCl}$$

excess mol HCl = 1.87×10^{-2} mol − 1.77×10^{-2} mol = 1.0×10^{-3} mol HCl

mass of excess HCl = 1.0×10^{-3} mol HCl $\times \dfrac{36.46 \text{ g HCl}}{\text{mol HCl}} = 3.6 \times 10^{-2}$ g HCl

36. $1.00 \text{ L} \times \dfrac{0.200 \text{ mol Na}_2\text{S}_2\text{O}_3}{\text{L}} \times \dfrac{1 \text{ mol AgBr}}{2 \text{ mol Na}_2\text{S}_2\text{O}_3} \times \dfrac{187.8 \text{ mol AgBr}}{\text{mol AgBr}} = 18.8 \text{ g AgBr}$

Group 7A Elements

37. O_2F_2 has 2(6) + 2(7) = 26 valence e^-; From the following Lewis structure, each oxygen atom has a tetrahedral arrangement of electron pairs. Therefore, bond angles ≈ 109.5° and each O is sp^3 hybridized.

$$:\!\overset{..}{\underset{..}{F}}\!\!-\!\!\overset{..}{\underset{..}{O}}\!\!-\!\!\overset{..}{\underset{..}{O}}\!\!-\!\!\overset{..}{\underset{..}{F}}\!:$$

Formal Charge	0	0	0	0
Oxid. Number	-1	+1	+1	-1

Oxidation numbers are more useful. We are forced to assign +1 as the oxidation number for oxygen. Oxygen is very electronegative, and +1 is not a stable oxidation state for this element.

38.   a. CCl_2F_2, 4 + 2(7) + 2(7) = 32 e^- b. $HClO_4$, 1 + 7 + 4(6) = 32 e^-

tetrahedral; 109.5°; sp^3

About Cl: tetrahedral; 109.5°; sp^3
About O: V-shaped; ≈ 109.5°; sp^3

c. ICl_3, $7 + 3(7) = 28$ e^-
d. BrF_5, $7 + 5(7) = 42$ e^-

T-shaped; $\approx 90°$; dsp^3
square pyramid; $\approx 90°$; d^2sp^3

39. a. $BaCl_2(s) + H_2SO_4(aq) \rightarrow BaSO_4(s) + 2\ HCl(g)$

b. $BrF(s) + H_2O(l) \rightarrow HF(aq) + HOBr(aq)$

c. $SiO_2(s) + 4\ HF(aq) \rightarrow SiF_4(g) + 2\ H_2O(l)$

40. a. $F_2 + H_2O \rightarrow HOF + HF$; $2\ HOF \rightarrow 2\ HF + O_2$; $3\ HOF + H_2O \rightarrow 3\ HF + H_2O_2 + O_2$; $HOF + H_2O \rightarrow HF + H_2O_2$ (dilute acid)

In dilute base, HOF exists as OF^- and HF exists as F^-. The balanced reaction is:

$$(2e^- + H_2O + OF^- \rightarrow F^- + 2\ OH^-) \times 2$$
$$4\ OH^- \rightarrow O_2 + 2\ H_2O + 4e^-$$

$$\overline{2\ OF^- \rightarrow O_2 + 2\ F^-}$$

b. HOF: Assign +1 to H and –1 to F. The oxidation state of oxygen is then zero. Oxygen is very electronegative. A zero oxidation state is not very stable since oxygen is a very good oxidizing agent.

41.
$$ClO^- + H_2O + 2\ e^- \rightarrow 2\ OH^- + Cl^- \qquad E° = 0.90\ V$$
$$2\ NH_3 + 2\ OH^- \rightarrow N_2H_4 + 2\ H_2O + 2\ e^- \qquad -E° = 0.10\ V$$

$$\overline{ClO^-(aq) + 2\ NH_3(aq) \rightarrow Cl^-(aq) + N_2H_4(aq) + H_2O(l) \qquad E°_{cell} = 1.00\ V}$$

Because $E°_{cell}$ is positive for this reaction, ClO^-, at standard conditions, can spontaneously oxidize NH_3 to the somewhat toxic N_2H_4.

42. A disproportion reaction is an oxidation-reduction reaction in which one species will act as both the oxidizing agent and reducing agent. The species reacts with itself, forming products with higher and lower oxidation states. For example, $2\ Cu^+ \rightarrow Cu + Cu^{2+}$ is a disproportion reaction.

$HClO_2$ will disproportionate at standard conditions because $E°_{cell} > 0$:

$$HClO_2 + 2\ H^+ + 2\ e^- \rightarrow HClO + H_2O \qquad E° = 1.65\ V$$
$$HClO_2 + H_2O \rightarrow ClO_3^- + 3\ H^+ + 2\ e^- \qquad -E° = -1.21\ V$$

$$\overline{2\ HClO_2(aq) \rightarrow HClO(aq) + ClO_3^-(aq) + H^+(aq) \qquad E°_{cell} = 0.44\ V}$$

Group 8A Elements

43.   Xe has one more valence electron than I. Thus, the isoelectric species will have I plus one
       extra electron substituted for Xe, giving a species with a net minus one charge.

       a. IO_4^- b. IO_3^- c. IF_2^- d. IF_4^- e. IF_6^-

44.   a. KrF_2, $8 + 2(7) = 22$ e^- b. KrF_4, $8 + 4(7) = 36$ e^-

       linear; 180°; dsp^3 square planar; 90°; d^2sp^3

       c. XeO_2F_2, $8 + 2(6) + 2(7) = 34$ e^-

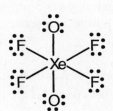   or   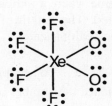   or

       All are: see-saw; $\approx 90°$ and $\approx 120°$; dsp^3

       d. XeO_2F_4, $8 + 2(6) + 4(7) = 48$ e^-

       All are: octahedral; 90°; d^2sp^3

45. XeF_2 can react with oxygen and water to produce explosive xenon oxides and oxyfluorides,
       and react with water to form HF.

46. 10.0 m $\times$ 10.0 m $\times$ 10.0 m $= 1.00 \times 10^3$ m^3; From Table 20.12, volume % Ar = 0.9%.

       $$1.00 \times 10^3 \text{ m}^3 \times \left(\frac{10 \text{ dm}}{\text{m}}\right)^3 \times \frac{1 \text{ L}}{\text{dm}^3} \times \frac{0.9 \text{ L Ar}}{100 \text{ L air}} = 9 \times 10^3 \text{ L of Ar in the room}$$

$$PV = nRT, \quad n = \frac{PV}{RT} = \frac{(1.0 \text{ atm})(9 \times 10^3 \text{ L})}{(0.08206 \text{ L atm/mol} \cdot \text{K})(298 \text{ K})} = 4 \times 10^2 \text{ mol Ar}$$

$$4 \times 10^2 \text{ mol Ar} \times \frac{39.95 \text{ g}}{\text{mol}} = 2 \times 10^4 \text{ g Ar in the room}$$

$$4 \times 10^2 \text{ mol Ar} \times \frac{6.022 \times 10^{23} \text{ atoms}}{\text{mol}} = 2 \times 10^{26} \text{ atoms Ar in the room}$$

A 2 L breath contains: $\quad 2 \text{ L air} \times \dfrac{0.9 \text{ L Ar}}{100 \text{ L air}} = 2 \times 10^{-2} \text{ L Ar}$

$$n = \frac{PV}{RT} = \frac{(1.0 \text{ atm})(2 \times 10^{-2} \text{ L})}{(0.08206 \text{ L atm/mol} \cdot \text{K})(298 \text{ K})} = 8 \times 10^{-4} \text{ mol Ar}$$

$$8 \times 10^{-4} \text{ mol Ar} \times \frac{6.022 \times 10^{23} \text{ atoms}}{\text{mol}} = 5 \times 10^{20} \text{ atoms of Ar in a 2 L breath}$$

Because Ar and Rn are both noble gases, both species will be relatively unreactive. However, all nuclei of Rn are radioactive, unlike most nuclei of Ar. It is the radioactive decay products of Rn that can cause biological damage when inhaled.

47.   Release of Sr is probably more harmful. Xe is chemically unreactive. Strontium is in the same family as calcium and could be absorbed and concentrated in the body in a fashion similar to Ca. This puts the radioactive Sr in the bones, and red blood cells are produced in bone marrow. Xe would not be readily incorporated into the body.

The chemical properties determine where a radioactive material may concentrate in the body or how easily it may be excreted. The length of time of exposure and what is exposed to radiation significantly affects the health hazard.

48.   a. $^{238}_{92}\text{U} \rightarrow {}^{222}_{86}\text{Rn} + ? \; {}^{4}_{2}\text{He} + ? \; {}^{0}_{-1}\text{e}$;   To account for the mass number change, 4 alpha particles are needed. To balance the number of protons, 2 beta particles are needed.

$^{222}_{86}\text{Rn} \rightarrow {}^{4}_{2}\text{He} + {}^{218}_{84}\text{Po}$;   Polonium-218 is produced when ^{222}Rn decays.

b.   Alpha particles cause significant ionization damage when inside a living organism. Because the half-life of ^{222}Rn is relatively short, a significant number of alpha particles will be produced when ^{222}Rn is present (even for a short period of time) in the lungs.

Additional Exercises

49.   As the halogen atoms get larger, it becomes more difficult to fit three halogen atoms around the small nitrogen atom, and the NX_3 molecule becomes less stable.

50.   a.   The Lewis structures for NNO and NON are:

$$:\ddot{N}=N=\ddot{O}: \longleftrightarrow :N\equiv N-\ddot{\underset{\cdot\cdot}{O}}: \longleftrightarrow :\ddot{\underset{\cdot\cdot}{N}}-N\equiv O:$$

$$:\ddot{N}=O=\ddot{N}: \longleftrightarrow :N\equiv O-\ddot{\underset{\cdot\cdot}{N}}: \longleftrightarrow :\ddot{\underset{\cdot\cdot}{N}}-O\equiv N:$$

The NNO structure is correct. From the Lewis structures, we would predict both NNO and NON to be linear. However, we would predict NNO to be polar and NON to be nonpolar. Since experiments show N_2O to be polar, NNO is the correct structure.

b. Formal charge = number of valence electrons of atoms – [(number of lone pair electrons) + 1/2 (number of shared electrons)].

$$:\ddot{N}=N=\ddot{O}: \longleftrightarrow :N\equiv N-\ddot{\underset{\cdot\cdot}{O}}: \longleftrightarrow :\ddot{\underset{\cdot\cdot}{N}}-N\equiv O:$$
$$\;\;-1\quad+1\quad 0 \qquad\qquad 0\quad +1\quad -1 \qquad\qquad -2\quad +1\quad +1$$

The formal charges for the atoms in the various resonance structures are below each atom. The central N is sp hybridized in all of the resonance structures. We can probably ignore the third resonance structure on the basis of the relatively large formal charges compared to the first two resonance structures.

c. The sp hybrid orbitals on the center N overlap with atomic orbitals (or hybrid orbitals) on the other two atoms to form the two sigma bonds. The remaining two unhybridized p orbitals on the center N overlap with two p orbitals on the peripheral N to form the two π bonds.

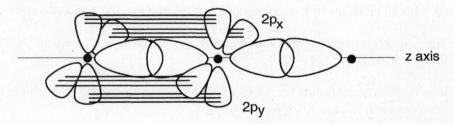

51.   OCN– has $6 + 4 + 5 + 1 = 16$ valence electrons.

$$\left[:\ddot{O}=C=\ddot{\underset{\cdot}{N}}:\right]^{-} \longleftrightarrow \left[:\ddot{\underset{\cdot\cdot}{O}}-C\equiv N:\right]^{-} \longleftrightarrow \left[:O\equiv C-\ddot{\underset{\cdot\cdot}{N}}:\right]^{-}$$

Formal
charge   0   0   -1   -1   0   0   +1   0   -2

Only the first two resonance structures should be important. The third places a positive formal charge on the most electronegative atom in the ion and a -2 formal charge on N.

CNO⁻:

$$\left[:\ddot{C}=N=\ddot{\underset{\cdot}{O}}:\right]^{-} \longleftrightarrow \left[:C\equiv N-\ddot{\underset{\cdot\cdot}{O}}:\right]^{-} \longleftrightarrow \left[:\ddot{\underset{\cdot\cdot}{C}}-N\equiv O:\right]^{-}$$

Formal
charge   -2   +1   0   -1   +1   -1   -3   +1   +1

All of the resonance structures for fulminate (CNO^-) involve greater formal charges than in cyanate (OCN^-), making fulminate more reactive (less stable).

52.   a.

$$(2e^- + NaBiO_3 \rightarrow BiO_3^{3-} + Na^+) \times 5$$
$$(4\ H_2O + Mn^{2+} \rightarrow MnO_4^- + 8\ H^+ + 5e^-) \times 2$$

$$8\ H_2O(l) + 2Mn^{2+}(aq) + 5\ NaBiO_3(s) \rightarrow 2\ MnO_4^-(aq) + 16\ H^+(aq) + 5\ BiO_3^{3-}(aq)$$
$$+ 5\ Na^+(aq)$$

b.   Bismuthate exists as a covalent network solid: $(BiO_3^-)_x$.

53. 1.0×10^4 kg waste $\times \dfrac{3.0\text{ kg }NH_4^+}{100\text{ kg waste}} \times \dfrac{1000\text{ g}}{\text{kg}} \times \dfrac{1\text{ mol }NH_4^+}{18.04\text{ g }NH_4^+} \times \dfrac{1\text{ mol }C_5H_7O_2N}{55\text{ mol }NH_4^+}$

$\times \dfrac{113.12\text{ g }C_5H_7O_2N}{\text{mol }C_5H_7O_2N} = 3.4 \times 10^4$ g tissue if all NH_4^+ converted

Since only 95% of the NH_4^+ ions react:

mass of tissue = $(0.95)\ (3.4 \times 10^4\text{ g}) = 3.2 \times 10^4$ g or 32 kg bacterial tissue

54.   This element is in the oxygen family as all oxygen family members have ns^2np^4 valence electron configurations.

a.   As with all elements of the oxygen family, this element has 6 valence electrons.

b.   The nonmetals in the oxygen family are O, S, Se and Te, which are all possible identities for the element.

c.   Ions in the oxygen family are –2 charged in ionic compounds. Li_2X would be the formula between Li^+ and X^{2-} ions.

d.   In general, radii increase from right to left across the periodic table and increase going down a family. From this trend, the radius of the unknown element must be smaller than the Ba radius.

e.   The ioniation energy trend is the opposite of the radii trend indicated in the previous answer. From this trend, the unknown element will have a smaller ionization energy than fluorine.

55. TeF_5^- has $6 + 5(7) + 1 = 42$ valence electrons

The lone pair of electrons around Te exerts a stronger repulsion than the bonding pairs, pushing the four square planar F's away from the lone pair and thus reducing the bond angles between the axial F atom and the square planar F atoms.

56.   a. $AgCl(s) \xrightarrow{h\nu} Ag(s) + Cl$; The reactive chlorine atom is trapped in the crystal. When light is removed, Cl reacts with silver atoms to reform AgCl, i.e., the reverse reaction occurs. In pure AgCl, the Cl atoms escape, making the reverse reaction impossible.

b.   Over time, chlorine is lost and the dark silver metal is permanent.

57.   As temperature increases, the value of K decreases. This is consistent with an exothermic reaction. In an exothermic reaction, heat is a product and an increase in temperature shifts the equilibrium to the reactant side (as well as lowering the value of K).

58. $7.15 = -\log(6.2 \times 10^{-8}) + \log\dfrac{[HPO_4^{2-}]}{[H_2PO_4^-]}$, $7.15 = 7.21 + \log\dfrac{[HPO_4^{2-}]}{[H_2PO_4^-]}$

$\dfrac{[HPO_4^{2-}]}{[H_2PO_4^-]} = 10^{-0.06} = 0.9$, $\dfrac{[HPO_4^{2-}]}{[H_2PO_4^-]} = \dfrac{1}{0.9} = 1.1 \approx 1$

A best buffer has approximately equal concentrations of weak acid and conjugate base so that $pH \approx pK_a$ for a best buffer.   The pK_a value for a $H_3PO_4/H_2PO_4^-$ buffer is $-\log(7.5 \times 10^{-3}) = 2.12$. A pH of 7.1 is too high for a $H_3PO_4/H_2PO_4^-$ buffer to be effective. At this high a pH, there would be so little H_3PO_4 present that we could hardly consider it a buffer. This solution would not be effective in resisting pH changes, especially when a strong base is added.

59. $MgSO_4(s) \rightarrow Mg^{2+}(aq) + SO_4^{2-}(aq)$; $NH_4NO_3(s) \rightarrow NH_4^+(aq) + NO_3^-(aq)$

Note that the dissolution of $MgSO_4$ used in hot packs is an exothermic process, and the dissolution of NH_4NO_3 in cold packs is an endothermic process.

60.   Strong acids have a $K_a \gg 1$ and weak acids have $K_a < 1$. Table 14.2 in the text lists some K_a values for weak acids. K_a values for strong acids are hard to determine so they are not listed in the text. However, there are only a few common strong acids, so if you memorize the strong acids, then all other acids will be weak acids. The strong acids to memorize are HCl, HBr, HI, HNO_3, $HClO_4$ and H_2SO_4.

a. $HClO_4$ is a strong acid.

b.   HOCl is a weak acid ($K_a = 3.5 \times 10^{-8}$).

c. H_2SO_4 is a strong acid.

d. H_2SO_3 is a weak diprotic acid with K_{a1} and K_{a2} values less than one.

61. EO_3^- is the formula of the ion. The Lewis structure has 26 valence electrons. Let x = number of valence electrons of element E.

$26 = x + 3(6) + 1$, $x = 7$ valence electrons

Element E is a halogen because halogens have 7 valence electrons. Some possible identities are F, Cl, Br and I. The EO_3^- ion has a trigonal pyramid molecular structure with bond angles $\approx 109.5°$.

62.   The formula is EF_2O^{2-} and the Lewis structure has 28 valence electrons.

$$28 = x + 2(7) + 6 + 2, \quad x = 6 \text{ valence electrons for element E}$$

Element E must belong to the group 6A elements since E has 6 valence electrons. E must also be a row 3 or heavier element since this ion has more than 8 electrons around the central E atom (row 2 elements never have more than 8 electrons around them). Some possible identities for E are S, Se and Te. The ion has a T-shaped molecular structure with bond angles of $\approx 90°$.

63. $8 \text{ corners} \times \dfrac{1/8 \text{ Xe}}{\text{corner}} + 1 \text{ Xe inside cell} = 2 \text{ Xe}; \quad 8 \text{ edges} \times \dfrac{1/4 \text{ F}}{\text{edge}} + 2 \text{ F inside cell} = 4 \text{ F}$

Empirical formula is XeF_2. This is also the molecular formula.

Challenge Problems

64.   In order to form a π bond, the d and p orbitals must overlap "side to side" instead of "head to head" as in sigma bonds. A representation of the "side to side" overlap follows. For a bonding orbital to form, the phases of the lobes must match (positive to positive and negative to negative).

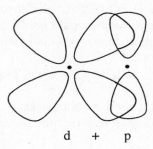

d   +   p

65.   For the reaction:

$$\text{O=N—N=O} \longrightarrow NO_2 + NO$$

the activation energy must in some way involve breaking a nitrogen-nitrogen single bond. For the reaction:

$$\text{O=N—N=O} \longrightarrow O_2 + N_2O$$

at some point nitrogen-oxygen bonds must be broken. N–N single bonds (160. kJ/mol) are weaker than N–O single bonds (201 kJ/mol). In addition, resonance structures indicate that there is more double bond character in the N–O bonds than in the N–N bond. Thus, NO_2 and NO are preferred by kinetics because of the lower activation energy.

66. $Mg^{2+} + P_3O_{10}^{5-} \rightleftharpoons MgP_3O_{10}^{3-}$ $K = 4.0 \times 10^8$

$$[Mg^{2+}]_o = \frac{50. \times 10^{-3}\,g}{L} \times \frac{1\,mol}{24.31\,g} = 2.1 \times 10^{-3}\,M$$

$$[P_3O_{10}^{5-}]_o = \frac{40.\,g\,Na_5P_3O_{10}}{L} \times \frac{1\,mol}{367.86\,g} = 0.11\,M$$

Assume the reaction goes to completion because K is large. Then solve the back equilibrium problem to determine the small amount of Mg^{2+} present.

$$Mg^{2+} \quad + \quad P_3O_{10}^{5-} \quad \rightleftharpoons \quad MgP_3O_{10}^{3-}$$

Before	$2.1 \times 10^{-3}\,M$	$0.11\,M$	0
Change	-2.1×10^{-3}	-2.1×10^{-3} $\rightarrow$	$+2.1 \times 10^{-3}$ React completely
After	0	0.11	2.1×10^{-3} New initial condition

x mol/L $MgP_3O_{10}^{3-}$ dissociates to reach equilibrium

Change	$+x$	$+x$ $\leftarrow$	$-x$
Equil.	x	$0.11 + x$	$2.1 \times 10^{-3} - x$

$$K = 4.0 \times 10^8 = \frac{[MgP_3O_{10}^{3-}]}{[Mg^{2+}][P_3O_{10}^{5-}]} = \frac{2.1 \times 10^{-3} - x}{x(0.11 + x)} \quad (\text{assume } x \ll 2.1 \times 10^{-3})$$

$$4.0 \times 10^8 \approx \frac{2.1 \times 10^{-3}}{x(0.11)}, \quad x = [Mg^{2+}] = 4.8 \times 10^{-11}\,M; \quad \text{Assumptions good.}$$

67.   a.   NO is the catalyst. NO is present in the first step of the mechanism on the reactant side, but it is not a reactant because it is regenerated in the second step and does not appear in the overall balanced equation.

   b. NO_2 is an intermediate. Intermediates also never appear in the overall balanced equation. In a mechanism, intermediates always appear first on the product side while catalysts always appear first on the reactant side.

   c. $k = A \exp(-E_a/RT)$; $\dfrac{k_{cat}}{k_{un}} = \dfrac{A \exp[-E_a(cat)/RT]}{A \exp[-E_a(cat)/RT]} = \exp\left(\dfrac{E_a(un) - E_a(cat)}{RT}\right)$

$$\frac{k_{cat}}{k_{un}} = \exp\left(\frac{2100 \text{ J/mol}}{8.3145 \text{ J/K} \bullet \text{mol} \times 298 \text{ K}}\right) = e^{0.85} = 2.3$$

The catalyzed reaction is approximately 2.3 times faster than the uncatalyzed reaction at 25°C.

d. The mechanism for the chlorine-catalyzed destruction of ozone is:

$$O_3(g) + Cl(g) \rightarrow O_2(g) + ClO(g) \quad \text{slow}$$
$$ClO(g) + O(g) \rightarrow O_2(g) + Cl(g) \quad \text{fast}$$

$$O_3(g) + O(g) \rightarrow 2 \ O_2(g)$$

e. Because the chlorine atom-catalyzed reaction has a lower activation energy, the Cl catalyzed rate is faster. Hence, Cl is a more effective catalyst. Using the activation energy, we can estimate the efficiency that Cl atoms destroy ozone as compared to NO molecules.

$$\text{At 25°C: } \frac{k_{Cl}}{k_{NO}} = \exp\left(\frac{-E_a(Cl)}{RT} + \frac{E_a(NO)}{RT}\right) = \exp\left(\frac{(-2100 + 11{,}900) \text{ J/mol}}{(8.3145 \times 298) \text{ J/mol}}\right)$$
$$= e^{3.96} = 52$$

At 25°C, the Cl–catalyzed reaction is roughly 52 times faster (more efficient) than the NO–catalyzed reaction, assuming the frequency factor A is the same for each reaction and assuming similar rate laws.

68. $3 \ O_2(g) \rightleftharpoons 2 \ O_3(g)$; $\Delta H° = 2(143 \text{ kJ}) = 286 \text{ kJ}$; $\Delta G° = 2(163 \text{ kJ}) = 326 \text{ kJ}$

$$\ln K = \frac{-\Delta G°}{RT} = \frac{-326 \times 10^3 \text{ J}}{8.3145 \text{ J/K} \bullet \text{mol} \times 298 \text{ K}} = -131.573, \ K = e^{-131.573} = 7.22 \times 10^{-58}$$

Note: We carried extra significant figures for the K calculation.

We need the value of K at 230. K. From Section 16.8 of the text: $\ln K = \dfrac{-\Delta H°}{RT} = \dfrac{\Delta S°}{R}$
For two sets of K and T:

$$\ln K_1 = \frac{-\Delta H°}{R}\left(\frac{1}{T_1}\right) + \frac{\Delta S°}{R}; \ \ln K_2 = \frac{-\Delta H°}{R}\left(\frac{1}{T_2}\right) + \frac{\Delta S°}{R}$$

Subtracting the first expression from the second:

$$\ln K_2 - \ln K_1 = \frac{\Delta H°}{R}\left(\frac{1}{T_1} + \frac{1}{T_2}\right) \text{ or } \ln\frac{K_2}{K_1} = \frac{\Delta H°}{R}\left(\frac{1}{T_1} - \frac{1}{T_2}\right)$$

Let $K_2 = 7.22 \times 10^{-58}$, $T_2 = 298$; $K_1 = K_{230}$, $T_1 = 230.$ K; $\Delta H^\circ = 286 \times 10^3$ J

$$\ln \frac{7.22 \times 10^{-58}}{K_{230}} = \frac{286 \times 10^3}{8.3145}\left(\frac{1}{230.} - \frac{1}{298}\right) = 34.13 \text{ (Carrying extra sig. figs.)}$$

$$\frac{7.22 \times 10^{-58}}{K_{230}} = e^{34.13} = 6.6 \times 10^{14}, \ K_{230} = 1.1 \times 10^{-72}$$

$$K_{230} = 1.1 \times 10^{-72} = \frac{P_{O_3}^2}{P_{O_2}^3} = \frac{P_{O_3}^2}{(1.0 \times 10^{-3})^3}, \quad P_{O_3} = 3.3 \times 10^{-41} \text{ atm}$$

The volume occupied by one molecule of ozone is:

$$V = \frac{nRT}{P} = \frac{(1/6.022 \times 10^{23} \text{ mol}) \times 0.08206 \text{ L atm/mol} \cdot \text{K} \times 230. \text{ K}}{3.3 \times 10^{-41} \text{ atm}}, \ V = 9.5 \times 10^{17} \text{ L}$$

Equilibrium is probably not maintained under these conditions. When only two ozone molecules are in a volume of 9.5×10^{17} L, the reaction is not at equilibrium. Under these conditions, $Q > K$ and the reaction shifts left. But with only 2 ozone molecules in this huge volume, it is extremely unlikely that they will collide with each other. In these conditions, the concentration of ozone is not large enough to maintain equilibrium.

69. $NH_3 + NH_3 \rightleftharpoons NH_4^+ + NH_2^-$ $K = [NH_4^+][NH_2^-] = 1.8 \times 10^{-12}$

NH_3 is the solvent, so it is not included in the K expression. In a neutral solution of ammonia:

$$[NH_4^+] = [NH_2^-]; \ 1.8 \times 10^{-12} = [NH_4^+]^2, \ [NH_4^+] = 1.3 \times 10^{-6} \ M = [NH_2^-]$$

We could abbreviate this autoionization as: $NH_3 \rightleftharpoons H^+ + NH_2^-$, where $[H^+] = [NH_4^+]$.

This abbreviation is synonomous to the abbreviation of the autoionization of water ($H_2O \rightleftharpoons H^+ + OH^-$). So: $pH = pNH_4^+ = -\log(1.3 \times 10^{-6}) = 5.89$.

70.   Let's consider a reaction between $3.00 \ x$ mol N_2 and $3.00 \ x$ mol H_2 (equimolar).

$$N_2(g) \quad + \quad 3 H_2(g) \quad \rightarrow \quad 2 NH_3(g)$$

	$N_2(g)$	$3 H_2(g)$	$2 NH_3(g)$
Before	$3.00 \ x$ mol	$3.00 \ x$ mol	0
Change	$-1.00 \ x$ mol	$-3.00 \ x$ mol	$+2.00 \ x$ mol
Equil.	$2.00 \ x$ mol	0	$2.00 \ x$ mol

When an equimolar mixture is reacted, the number of moles of gas present decreases from $6.00 \ x$ moles initially to $4.00 \ x$ moles after completion.

a. The total pressure in the piston apparatus is a constant 1.00 atm. After the reaction, we have 2.00 x moesl N_2 and 2.00 x moles NH_3. One-half of the moles of gas present are NH_3 molecules, so one-half of the total pressure is due to the NH_3 molecules. P_{NH_3} = 0.500 atm.

b. $\chi_{NH_3} = \dfrac{\text{mol } NH_3}{\text{total mol}} = \dfrac{2.00 \text{ mol } x}{(2.00\, x + 2.00\, x)\text{ mol}} = 0.500$

c. At constant P and T, volume is directly proportional to n. Because n decreased from 6.00 x moles to 4.00 x moles, the volume will decrease by the same factor.

$V_{final} = 15.0 \text{ L } (4/6) = 10.0 \text{ L}$

71. Let n_{SO_2} = initial mol SO_2 present. The reaction is summarized in the following table (O_2 is in excess).

$$2\, SO_2 \quad + \quad O_2(g) \quad \rightarrow \quad 2\, SO_3(g)$$

Initial	n_{SO_2}	2.00 mol	0
Change	$-n_{SO_2}$	$-n_{SO_2}/2$	$+n_{SO_2}$
Final	0	$2.00 - n_{SO_2}/2$	n_{SO_2}

d = mass/volume; Let d_i = initial density of gas mixture and d_f = final density of gas mixture after reaction. Because mass is conserved in a chemical reaction, $mass_i = mass_f$.

$$\frac{d_f}{d_i} = \frac{mass_f/V_f}{mass_i/V_i} = \frac{V_i}{V_f}$$

At constant P and T, $V \propto n$, so: $\dfrac{d_f}{d_i} = \dfrac{V_i}{V_f} = \dfrac{n_i}{n_f}$; Setting up an equation:

$$\frac{d_f}{d_i} = \frac{0.8471\,g/L}{0.8000\,g/L} = 1.059, \quad 1.059 = \frac{n_i}{n_f} = \frac{n_{SO_2} + 2.00}{(2.00 - n_{SO_2}/2) + n_{SO_2}} = \frac{n_{SO_2} + 2.00}{2.00 + n_{SO_2}/2}$$

Solving: $n_{SO_2} = 0.25$ mol; so, 0.25 moles of SO_3 formed

0.25 mol $SO_3 \times \dfrac{80.07\text{ g}}{\text{mol}} = 20.\text{ g } SO_3$

72. $$Ca(IO_3)_2(s) \quad \rightleftharpoons \quad Ca^{2+}(aq) \; + \; 2\, IO_3^{-}(aq) \qquad\qquad K_{sp} = [Ca^{2+}][\, IO_3^{-}]^2$$

Initial	s = solubility (mol/L)	0	0	
Equil.		s	$2s$	$K_{sp} = s(2s)^2 = 4s^3$

$$\text{mol IO}_3^- \text{ present} = 0.0149 \text{ L} \times \frac{0.100 \text{ mol S}_2\text{O}_3^{2-}}{\text{mol}} \times \frac{1 \text{ mol I}_2}{2 \text{ mol S}_2\text{O}_3^{2-}} \times \frac{1 \text{ mol IO}_3^-}{3 \text{ mol I}_2}$$

$$= 2.48 \times 10^{-4} \text{ mol IO}_3^-$$

$$[\text{IO}_3^-] = \frac{2.48 \times 10^{-4} \text{ mol}}{0.0100 \text{ L}} = 2.48 \times 10^{-2} \; M = 2s, \; s = 1.24 \times 10^{-2} \; M$$

$$K_{sp} = 4s^3 = 4(1.24 \times 10^{-2})^3 = 7.63 \times 10^{-6}$$

Integrative Problems

73.   a. $-307 \text{ kJ} = [-1136 + x] - [(-254 \text{ kJ}) + 3(-96 \text{ kJ})], \; x = \Delta H^\circ_{f, \text{NI}_3} = 287 \text{ kJ/mol}$

b. $\text{IF}_2^+, \; 7 + 2(7) - 1 = 20 \text{ e}^-$ $\text{BF}_4^-, \; 3 + 4(7) + 1 = 32 \text{ e}^-$

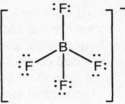

V-shaped; sp^3 tetrahedral; sp^3

74.   a.   Because the hydroxide ion has a -1 charge, Te has a $+6$ oxidation state.

b. $\text{mol Te} = (0.545 \text{ cm})^3 \times \dfrac{6.240 \text{ g}}{\text{cm}^3} \times \dfrac{1 \text{ mol Te}}{127.6} = 7.92 \times 10^{-3} \text{ mol Te}$

$$\text{mol F}_2 = n = \frac{PV}{RT} = \frac{1.06 \text{ atm} \times 2.34 \text{ L}}{0.08206 \text{ L atm} / \text{K} \bullet \text{mol} \times 298 \text{ K}} = 0.101 \text{ mol F}_2$$

$$\frac{\text{mol F}_2}{\text{mol Te}} \text{(actual)} = \frac{0.101 \text{ mol}}{7.92 \times 10^{-3} \text{ mol}} = 12.8$$

The balanced reaction requires a 3:1 mol ratio of F_2 to Te. Because actual > theoretical, the denominator (Te) is limiting. Assuming 115 mL of solution:

$$[\text{TeF}_6]_0 = \frac{7.92 \times 10^{-3} \text{ mol Te} \times \dfrac{1 \text{ mol TeF}_6}{\text{mol Te}}}{0.115 \text{ L}} = 6.89 \times 10^{-2} \; M$$

Because $K_{a_1} > K_{a_2}$, the amount of protons produced by the K_{a_2} reaction will be insignificant.

$$Te(OH)_6 \rightleftharpoons Te(OH)_5O^- + H^+ \qquad K_{a_1} = 10^{-7.68} = 2.1 \times 10^{-8}$$

	$Te(OH)_6$	$Te(OH)_5O^-$	H^+
Initial	0.0689 M	0	~0
Equil.	0.0689 $-x$	x	x

$$K_{a_1} = 2.1 \times 10^{-8} = \frac{x^2}{0.0689 - x} \approx \frac{x^2}{0.0689}, \quad x = [H^+] = 3.8 \times 10^{-5} \ M$$

$$pH = -\log(3.8 \times 10^{-5}) = 4.42; \quad \text{Assumptions good.}$$

Marathon Problem

75.   The answers to the clues are:

(1) H$\underline{I}$ has the second highest boiling point; (2) H$\underline{F}$ is the weak hydrogen halide acid; (3) $\underline{He}$ was first discovered from the sun's emission spectrum; (4) Both Bi and Sb form MOCl precipitates. For a message that makes sense, $\underline{Bi}$ is the correct choice; (5) $\underline{Te}$ is a semiconductor; (6) $\underline{S}$ has both rhombic and monoclinic solid forms; (7) $\underline{Cl}_2$ is a yellow-green gas and Cl$^-$ forms the indicated precipitates; (8) $\underline{O}$ is the most abundant element in and near the earth's crust; (9) $\underline{Se}$ appears to furnish some form of protection against cancer; (10) Kr forms compounds. The symbol in reverse order is $\underline{rk}$; (11) $\underline{As}$ forms As$_4$ molecules; (12) $\underline{N}_2$ is a major inert component of air and N is often found in fertilizers and explosives.

Filling in the blank spaces with the answers to the clues, the message is "If he bites, close ranks."

CHAPTER TWENTY-ONE

TRANSITION METALS AND COORDINATION CHEMISTRY

For Review

1. Chromium ($[Ar]:4s^03d^5$) and copper $[Ar]:4s^13d^{10}$) have electron configurations which are different from that predicted from the periodic table. Other exceptions to the predicted filling order are transition metal ions. These all lose the s electrons before they lose the d electrons. In neutral atoms, the ns and (n−1)d orbitals are very close in energy, with the ns orbitals slightly lower in energy. However, for transition metal ions, there is an apparent shifting of energies between the ns and (n−1)d orbitals. For transition metal ions, the energy of the (n−1)d orbitals are significantly less than that of the ns electrons. So when transition metal ions form, the highest energy electrons are removed, which are the ns electrons. For example, Mn^{2+} has the electron configuration $[Ar]:4s^03d^5$ and not $[Ar]:4s^23d^3$.

   Most transition metals have unfilled d orbitals, which creates a large number of other electrons that can be removed. Stable ions of the representative metals are determined by how many s and p valence electrons can be removed. In general, representative metals lose all of the s and p valence electrons to form their stable ions. Transition metals generally lose the s electron(s) to form +1 and +2 ions, but they can also lose some (or all) of the d electrons to form other oxidation states as well.

2. a. Coordination compound: a compound composed of a complex ion (see b) and counterions (see c) sufficient to give no net charge.

   b. Complex ion: a charged species consisting of a metal ion surrounded by ligands (see e).

   c. Counterions: anions or cations that balance the charge on a complex ion in a coordination compound.

   d. Coordination number: the number of bonds formed between the metal ion and the ligands (see e) in a complex ion.

   e. Ligand: Species that donates a pair of electrons to form a covalent bond to a metal ion. Ligands act as Lewis bases (electron pair donors).

   f. Chelate: Ligand that can form more than one bond to a metal ion.

   g. Bidentate: Ligand that forms two bonds to a metal ion.

   Because transition metals form bonds to species that donate lone pairs of electrons, transition metals are Lewis acids (electron pair acceptors). The Lewis bases in coordination compounds are the ligands, all of which have an unshared pair of electrons to donate. The coordinate covalent bond between the ligand and the transition metal just indicates that both electrons in the bond originally came from one of the atoms in the bond. Here, the electrons in the bond come from the ligand.

3. Linear geometry (180° bond angles) is observed when the coordination number is 2. Tetrahedral geometry (109.5° bond angles) or square planar geometry (90° bond angles) is observed when the coordination number is 4. Octahedral geometry (90° bond angles) is observed when the coordination number is 6.

    For the following complex ions, see Table 21.13 if you don't know the formula, the charge, or the number of bonds the ligands form.

    a. $Ag(CN)_2^-$; Ag^+: $[Kr]4d^{10}$

    b. $Cu(H_2O)_4^+$; Cu^+: $[Ar]3d^{10}$

    c. $Mn(C_2O_4)^{2-}$; Mn^{2+}: $[Ar]3d^5$

    d. $Pt(NH_3)_4^{2+}$; Pt^{2+}: $[Xe]4f^{14}5d^8$

    e. $Fe(EDTA)^-$; Fe^{3+}: $[Ar]3d^5$; Note: EDTA has an overall 4– charge and is a six coordinate ligand.

    f. $Co(Cl)_6^{4-}$; Co^{2+}: $[Ar]3d^7$

    g. $Cr(en)_3^{3+}$ where en = ethylenediane ($NH_2CH_2CH_2NH_2$); Cr^{3+}: $[Ar]3d^3$

4. See section 21.3 for a nice summary of the nomenclature rules.

    a. The correct name is tetraamminecopper(II) chloride. The complex ion is named incorrectly in several ways.

    b. The correct name is bis(ethylenediamine)nickel(II) sulfate. The ethylenediamine ligands are neutral and sulfate has a 2– charge. Therefore, Ni^{2+} is present, not Ni^{4+}.

    c. The correct name is potassium diaquatetrachlorochromate(III). Because the complex ion is an anion, the –ate suffix ending is added to the name of the metal. Also, the ligands were not in alphabetical order (a in aqua comes before c in chloro).

    d. The correct name is sodium tetracyanooxalatocobaltate(II). The only error is that tetra should be omitted in front of sodium. That four sodium ions are needed to balance charge is deduced from the name of the complex ion.

5. a. Isomers: species with the same formulas but different properties; they are different compounds. See the text for examples of the following types of isomers.

    b. Structural isomers: isomers that have one or more bonds that are different.

    c. Steroisomers: isomers that contain the same bonds but differ in how the atoms are arranged in space.

    d. Coordination isomers: structural isomers that differ in the atoms that make up the complex ion.

    e. Linkage isomers: structural isomers that differ in how one or more ligands are attached to the transition metal.

    f. Geometric isomers: (cis-trans isomerism); steroisomers that differ in the positions of atoms with respect to a rigid ring, bond, or each other.

g. Optical isomers: steroisomers tbat are nonsuperimposable mirror images of each other; that is, they are different in the same way that our left and right hands are different.

The trans form of $Cr(en)Cl_2$ is not optically active, but the the cis form is optically active. See Figure 21.17 for illustrations showing the cis and trans forms for a similar compound; shown also is the optical activity of the cis form. The only difference between the complex in this question, and the complex in Figure 21.17, is that Cr^{2+} has replaced Co^{2+}. Note that not all cis isomers are optically active. For example, the cis isomer of $Cr(NH_3)_4Cl_2$ is not optically active because the mirror image is superimposable (prove it to yourself).

In Figure 21.17, a plane of symmetry exists through the square planar orientation of the two en ligands. Other planes of symmetry also exist in the trans isomer. In the cis isomer in Figure 21.17, no plane of symmetry exists, so this cis form is optically active (as we know).

6. The crystal field model focuses on the energies of the d orbitals and what happens to the energies of these d orbitals as negative point charges (the ligands) approach (and repel) the electrons in the d orbitals. For octahedral geometry, six ligands are bonded to the metal ion. Because of the different orientations of the d orbitals, not all d orbitals are affected the same when six negative point charges (ligands) approach the metal ion along the x, y, and z axis. It turns out that the d_{xy}, d_{xz}, and d_{zy} orbitals are all destabilized by the same amount from the octahedrally arranged point charges, as are the $d_{x^2-y^2}$ and d_{z^2} orbitals. These are the two sets that the d orbitals split into. The d_{xy}, d_{xz}, and d_{yz} set is called the t_{2g} set, while the $d_{x^2-y^2}$ and d_{z^2} set is called the e_g set.

Another major point for the octahedral crystal field diagram is that the e_g set of orbitals is destabilized more than the t_{2g} set. This is because the t_{2g} orbital set (d_{xy}, d_{xz}, and d_{zy}) points between the point charges while the e_g orbital set ($d_{x^2-y^2}$ and d_{z^2}) points directly at the point charges. Hence, there is more destabilization in the e_g orbital set, and they are at a higher energy.

a. Weak field ligand: ligand that will give complex ions with the maximum number of unpaired electrons.

b. Strong-field ligand: ligand that will give complex ions with the minimum number of unpaired electrons.

c. Low-spin complex: complex ion with a minimum number of unpaired electrons (low-spin = strong-field).

d. High-spin complex: complex ion with a maximum number of unpaired electrons (high-spin = weak-field).

In both cobalt complex ions, Co^{3+} exists which is a d^6 ion (6 d electrons are present). The difference in magnetic properties is that $Co(NH_3)_6^{3+}$ is a strong-field (low-spin) complex having a relatively large Δ, while CoF_6^{3-} is a weak-field (high-spin) complex having a relatively small Δ. The electron configurations for Co^{3+} in a strong field vs. a weak field is shown in Figure 21.22. The strong-field d^6 ion is diamagnetic because all electrons are paired. This is the diagram for $Co(NH_3)_6^{3+}$. The weak field d^6 ion is paramagnetic because it has unpaired electrons (4 total). This is the diagram for CoF_6^{3-}.

Looking at Figure 21.22, d^1, d^2, and d^3 metal ions would all have the same number of unpaired electrons. This won't happen again until we get all the way up to d^8, d^9, and d^{10} metal ions (prove it to yourself that d^4, d^5, d^6, and d^7 metal ions have a different d orbital electron configurations depending on a strong-field or a weak-field). V^{3+} is a d^2 ion (2 unpaired electrons in the t_{2g} set). It has the same diagram no matter how strong the field strength. The same is true for the d^8 Ni^{2+} ion (filled t_{2g} set and half-filled e_g set). However, Ru^{2+}, a d^6 ion, will have different diagrams depending on a strong-field or a weak-field. If a weak-field is present, then there are four unpaired electrons. In the strong-field case, all six d electrons are in the t_{2g} set and all are paired (no unpaired electrons).

7.   The valence d electrons for the metal ion in the complex ion are placed into the octahedral crystal field diagram. If electrons are all paired, then the complex is predicted to be diamagnetic. If there are unpaired electrons, then the complex is predicted to be paramagnetic.

Color results by the absorption of specific wavelengths of light. The d-orbital splitting, Δ, is on the order of the energies of visible light. The complex ion absorbs the wavelength of light that has energy equal to the d-orbital splitting, Δ. The color we detect for the substance is not the color of light absorbed. We detect (see) the complementary color to that color of light absorbed. See Table 21.16 for observed colors of substances given the color of light absorbed.

From Table 21.16, if a complex appears yellow then it absorbs blue light on the order of λ ~450 nm. Therefore, $Cr(NH_3)_6^{3+}$ absorbs blue light.

The spectrochemical series places ligands in order of their ability to split the d-orbitals. The strongest field ligands (large Δ) are on one side of the series with the weakest field ligands (small Δ) on the other side. The series was developed from studies of the light absorbed by many octahedral complexes. From the color of light absorbed, one can determine the d-orbital splitting. Strong-field ligands absorb higher energy light (violet light, for example, with λ ~400 nm), while weak-field ligands absorb lower energy light (red light, for example, with λ ~650 nm).

The higher the charge on the metal ion, the larger the d-orlbital splitting. Thus, the Co^{3+} complex ion [$Co(NH_3)_6^{3+}$], would absorb higher energy (shorter wavelength) light than a Co^{2+} complex ion (assuming the ligands are the same).

Cu^{2+}: $[Ar]3d^9$; Cu^+: $[Ar]3d^{10}$; Cu(II) is d^9 and Cu(I) is d^{10}. Color is a result of the electron transfer between split d orbitals. This cannot occur for the filled d orbitals in Cu(I). Cd^{2+}, like Cu^+, is also d^{10}. We would not expect $Cd(NH_3)_4Cl_2$ to be colored because the d orbitals are filled in this Cd^{2+} complex.

Sc^{3+} has no electrons in d orbitals. Ti^{3+} and V^{3+} have d electrons present. Color of transition metal complexes results from electron transfer between split d orbitals. If no d electrons are present, no electron transfer can occur, and the compounds are not colored.

8.   The crystal field diagrams are different because the geometries of where the ligands point is different. The tetrahedrally oriented ligands point differently in relationship to the d-orbitals than do the octahedrally oriented ligands. Plus, we have more ligands in an octahedral complex.

See Figure 21.27 for the tetrahedral crystal field diagram. Notice that the orbitals are reverse of that in the octahedral crystal field diagram. The degenerate d_{z^2} and $d_{x^2-y^2}$ are at a lower energy than the degenerate d_{xy}, d_{xz}, and d_{yz} orbitals. Again, the reason for this is that tetrahedral ligands are oriented differently than octahedral field ligands so the interactions with specifically oriented d-orbitals are different. Also notice that the difference in magnitude of the d-orbital splitting for the two geometries. The d-orbital splitting in tetrahedral complexes is less than one-half the d-orbital splitting in octahedral complexes. There are no known ligands powerful enough to produce the strong-field case, hence all tetrahedral complexes are weak-field or high spin.

See Figure 21.28 for the descriptions of the square planar and linear crystal field diagrams. Each is unique which is not surprising. The ligands for any specific geometry will point differently relative to the orientations of the five d-orbitals. Different interactions result giving different crystal field diagrams.

9.   Each hemoglobin molecule can bind four O_2 molecules. It is an Fe^{2+} ion in hemoglobin that binds an individual O_2 molecule, and each hemoglobin molecule has four of these Fe^{2+} binding sites. The Fe^{2+} ion at the binding site is six-coordinate. Five of the coordination sites come from nitrogens in the hemoglobin molecule. The sixth site is available to attach an O_2 molecule. When the O_2 molecule is released, H_2O takes up the sixth position around the Fe^{2+} ion. O_2 is a strong field ligand, unlike H_2O, so in the lungs, O_2 readily replaces the H_2O ligand. With four sites, each hemoglobin molecule has a total of four O_2 molecules attached when saturated with O_2 from the lungs. In the cells, O_2 is released by the hemoglobin and the O_2 site is replaced by H_2O. The oxygen binding is pH dependent, so changes in pH in the cells as compared to blood, causes the release of O_2 (see Exercise 21.72). Once the O_2 is released and replaced by H_2O, the hemoglobin molecules return to the lungs to replenish with the O_2.

CN^- and CO form much stronger complexes with Fe(II) than O_2. Thus, O_2 is not transported by hemoglobin in the presence of CN^- or CO because the binding sites prefer the toxic CN^- and CO ligands.

10.   The definitions follow. See section 21.8 for examples.

a.   Roasting: converting sulfide minerals to oxides by heating in air below their melting points.

b.   Smelting: reducing metal ions to the free metal.

c.   Flotation: separation of mineral particles in an ore from the unwanted impurities. This process depends on the greater wetability of the mineral particles as compared to the unwanted impurities.

d.   Leaching: the extraction of metals from ores using aqueous chemical solutions.

e.   Gangue: the impurities (such as clay, sand, or rock) in an ore.

Advantages of hydrometallurgy: cheap energy cost; less air pollution; Disadvantages of hydrometallurgy: chemicals used in hydrometallurgy are expensive and sometimes toxic.

In zone refining, a bar of impure metal travels through a heater. The impurities present are more soluble in the molten metal than in the solid metal. As the molten zone moves down a metal, the impurities are swept along with the liquid, leaving behind relatively pure metal.

Questions

5. $Fe_2O_3(s) + 6\ H_2C_2O_4(aq) \rightarrow 2\ Fe(C_2O_4)_3^{3-}(aq) + 3\ H_2O(l) + 6\ H^+(aq)$; The oxalate anion forms a soluble complex ion with iron in rust (Fe_2O_3), which allows rust stains to be removed.

6.   Only the Cr^{3+} ion can form four different compounds with H_2O ligands and Cl^- ions. The Cr^{2+} ion could form only three different compounds while the Cr^{4+} ion could form five different compounds.

The Cl^- ions that form precipitates with Ag^+ are the counter ions, not the ligands in the complex ion. The four compounds and mol AgCl precipitate that would form with 1 mol of compound are:

Compound	mol AgCl(s)
$[Cr(H_2O)_6]Cl_3$	3 mol
$[Cr(H_2O)_5Cl]Cl_2$	2 mol
$[Cr(H_2O)_4Cl_2]Cl$	1 mol
$[Cr(H_2O)_3Cl_3]$	0 mol

7.

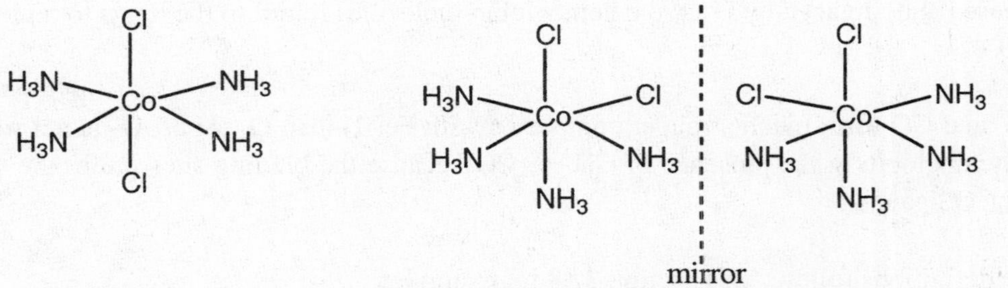

trans
(mirror image is
superimposable)

cis

The mirror image of the cis
isomer is also superimposable.

No; both the trans or the cis forms of $Co(NH_3)_4Cl_2^+$ have mirror images that are superimposable. For the cis form, the mirror image only needs a 90° rotation to produce the original structure. Hence, neither the trans nor cis forms are optically active.

8.   The transition metal ion must form octahedral complex ions; only with the octahedral geometry are two different arrangements of d electrons possible in the split d orbitals. These two arrangements depend on whether a weak field or strong field is present. For four unpaired electrons, the two possible weak field cases are for transition metal ions with $3d^4$ or $3d^6$ electron configurations:

Of these two, only d^6 ions have no unpaired electron in the strong field case.

Therefore, the transition metal ion has a $3d^6$ arrangement of electrons. Two possible metal ions that are $3d^6$ are Fe^{2+} and Co^{3+}. Thus, one of these ions is present in the four coordination compounds and each of these complex ions has a coordination number of 6.

The colors of the compounds are related to the magnitude of Δ (the d-orbital splitting value). The weak field compounds will have the smallest Δ, so the λ of light absorbed will be longest. Using Table 21.16, the green solution (absorbs 650 nm light) and the blue solution (absorbs 600 nm light) absorb the longest wavelength light; these solutions contain the complex ions which are the weak field cases with four unpaired electrons. The red solution (absorbs 490 nm light) and yellow solution (absorbs 450 nm light) contain the two strong field case complex ions because they absorb the shortest wavelength (highest energy) light. These complex ions are diamagnetic.

9.   a. $CoCl_4^{2-}$; Co^{2+}: $4s^03d^7$; All tetrahedral complexes are a weak field (high-spin).

$CoCl_4^{2-}$ is an example of a weak-field case having three unpaired electrons.

small Δ

b. $Co(CN)_6^{3-}$: Co^{3+} : $4s^03d^6$; Because CN^- is a strong-field ligand, $Co(CN)_6^{3-}$ will be a strong-field case (low-spin case).

↕   ↕   ↕

CN⁻ is a strong field ligand so $Co(CN)_6^{3-}$ will be a low-spin case having zero unpaired electrons.

large Δ

10. a. The coordination compound has the formula $[Co(H_2O)_6]Cl_2$. The complex ion is $Co(H_2O)_6^{2+}$ and the counter ions are the Cl^- ions. The geometry would be octahedral and the electron configuration of Co^{2+} is $[Ar]3d^7$.

   b. The coordination compound is $Na_3[Ag(S_2O_3)_2]$. The compound consists of Na^+ counter-ions and the $Ag(S_2O_3)_2^{3-}$ complex ion. The complex ion is linear and the electron configuration of Ag^+ is: $[Kr]4d^{10}$.

   c. The two coordination compounds are $Pt(NH_3)_2Cl_2$ and K_2PtCl_4. For $Pt(NH_3)_2Cl_2$ we need four ligands for a square planar geometry. Since only four species are attached to Pt, then there are no counterions. The complex is $Pt(NH_3)_2Cl_2$. Because chlorines each have a -1 charge, the platinum must be +2. The electron configuration for Pt^{2+} is: $[Xe]\,4f^{14}5d^8$. Note that there are two possible arrangements for the Cl^- and NH_3 ligands. From the name of the compounds, the cis isomer is the one discussed in the problem.

cis   trans

For the K_2PtCl_4 coordination compound, K^+ are the counterions and $PtCl_4^{2-}$ is the square planar complex ion. Platinum is also in the +2 oxidation state with a $[Xe]4f^{14}5d^8$ electron configuration.

   d. The reactant coordination compound is $[Cu(NH_3)_4]Cl_2$. The complex ion is $Cu(NH_3)_4^{2+}$, and the counterions are Cl^- ions. The complex ion is tetrahedral (given in the question) and the electron configuration of Cu^{2+} is: $[Ar]3d^9$. The product coordination compound is $[Cu(NH_3)_4]Cl$. The complex ion is $Cu(NH_3)_4^+$ with Cl^- counterions. The complex ion is tetrahedral, and the electron configuration of Cu^+ is: $[Ar]3d^{10}$.

11. At high altitudes, the oxygen content of air is lower, so less oxyhemoglobin is formed which diminishes the transport of oxygen in the blood. A serious illness called high-altitude sickness can result from the decrease of O_2 in the blood. High-altitude acclimatization is the phenomenom that occurs in the human body in response to the lower amounts of oxyhemoglobin in the blood. This response is to produce more hemoglobin, and, hence, increase the oxyhemoglobin in the blood. High-altitude acclimatization takes several weeks to take hold for people moving from lower altitudes to higher altitudes.

12. Metals are easily oxidized by oxygen and other substances to form the metal cations. Because of this, metals are found in nature combined with nonmetals such as oxygen, sulfur, and the

halogens. These compounds are called ores. To recover and use the metals, we must separate them from their ores and reduce the metal ions. Then, because most metals are unsuitable for use in the pure state, we must form alloys with the metals in order to form materials having desirable properties.

Exercises

Transition Metals and Coordination Compounds

13.   a.   Ni: $[Ar]4s^2 3d^8$ b.   Cd: $[Kr]5s^2 4d^{10}$

      c.   Zr: $[Kr]5s^2 4d^2$ d.   Os: $[Xe]6s^2 4f^{14} 5d^6$

14.   Transition metal ions lose the s electrons before the d electrons.

      a. Ni^{2+}: $[Ar]3d^8$ b. Cd^{2+}: $[Kr]4d^{10}$

      c. Zr^{3+}: $[Kr]4d^1$; Zr^{4+}: $[Kr]$ d. Os^{2+}: $[Xe]4f^{14} 5d^6$; Os^{3+}: $[Xe]4f^{14} 5d^5$

15.   Transition metal ions lose the s electrons before the d electrons.

a. Ti: $[Ar]4s^2 3d^2$	b. Re: $[Xe]6s^2 4f^{14} 5d^5$	c. Ir: $[Xe]6s^2 4f^{14} 5d^7$
Ti^{2+}: $[Ar]3d^2$	Re^{2+}: $[Xe]4f^{14} 5d^5$	Ir^{2+}: $[Xe]4f^{14} 5d^7$
Ti^{4+}: $[Ar]$ or $[Ne]3s^2 3p^6$	Re^{3+}: $[Xe]4f^{14} 5d^4$	Ir^{3+}: $[Xe]4f^{14} 5d^6$

16.   Cr and Cu are exceptions to the normal filling order of electrons.

a. Cr: $[Ar]4s^1 3d^5$	b. Cu: $[Ar]4s^1 3d^{10}$	c. V: $[Ar]4s^2 3d^3$
Cr^{2+}: $[Ar]3d^4$	Cu^+: $[Ar]3d^{10}$	V^{2+}: $[Ar]3d^3$
Cr^{3+}: $[Ar]3d^3$	Cu^{2+}: $[Ar]3d^9$	V^{3+}: $[Ar]3d^2$

17.   a.   With K^+ and CN^- ions present, iron has a +3 charge. Fe^{3+}: $[Ar]3d^5$

      b.   With a Cl^- ion and neutral NH_3 molecules present, silver has a +1 charge. Ag^+: $[Kr] 4d^{10}$

      c.   With Br^- ions and neutral H_2O molecules present, nickel has a +2 charge. Ni^{2+}: $[Ar]3d^8$

      d.   With NO_2^- ions, an I^- ion, and neutral H_2O molecules present, chromium has a +3 charge. Cr^{3+}: $[Ar]3d^3$

18.   a.   With NH_4^+ ions, Cl^- ions, and neutral H_2O molecules present, iron has a +2 charge. Fe^{2+}: $[Ar]3d^6$

b. With I^- ions and neutral NH_3 and $NH_2CH_2CH_2NH_2$ molecules present, cobalt has a +2 charge. Co^{2+}: $[Ar]3d^7$

c. With Na^+ and F^- ions present, tantalum has a +5 charge. Ta^{5+}: $[Xe]4f^{14}$ (expected)

d. Each platinum complex ion must have an overall charge if the two complex ions are counterions to each. Knowing that platinum forms +2 and +4 charged ions, we can deduce that the six coordinate complex ion has a +4 charged platinum ion and the four coordinate complex ion has a +2 charged ion. With I^- ions and neutral NH_3 molecules present, the two complex ions are $[Pt(NH_3)_4I_2]^{2+}$ and $[PtI_4]^{2-}$.

Pt^{2+}: $[Xe]4f^{14}5d^8$; Pt^{4+}: $[Xe]4f^{14}5d^6$

19. a. molybdenum(IV) sulfide; molybdenum(VI) oxide

b. MoS_2, +4; MoO_3, +6; $(NH_4)_2Mo_2O_7$, +6; $(NH_4)_6Mo_7O_{24} \cdot 4\ H_2O$, +6

20. Fe_2O_3: iron has a +3 oxidation state; Fe_3O_4: iron has a +8/3 oxidation state. The three iron ions in Fe_3O_4 must have a total charge of +8. The only combination that works is to have two Fe^{3+} ions and one Fe^{2+} ion per formula unit. This makes sense from the other formula for magnetite, $FeO \cdot Fe_2O_3$. FeO has an Fe^{2+} ion and Fe_2O_3 has two Fe^{3+} ions.

21. The lanthanide elements are located just before the 5d transition metals. The lanthanide contraction is the steady decrease in the atomic radii of the lanthanide elements when going from left to right across the periodic table. As a result of the lanthanide contraction, the sizes of the 4d and 5d elements are very similar (see the following Exercise). This leads to a greater similarity in the chemistry of the 4d and 5d elements in a given vertical group.

22. Size also decreases going across a period. Sc & Ti and Y & Zr are adjacent elements. There are 14 elements (the lanthanides) between La and Hf, making Hf considerably smaller.

23. $CoCl_2(s) + 6\ H_2O(g) \rightleftharpoons CoCl_2 \cdot 6\ H_2O(s)$;   If rain were imminent, there would be a lot of water vapor in the air causing the reaction to shift to the right. The indicator would take on the color of $CoCl_2 \cdot 6\ H_2O$, pink.

24. $H^+ + OH^- \rightarrow H_2O$; Sodium hydroxide (NaOH) will react with the H^+ on the product side of the reaction. This effectively removes H^+ from the equilibrium, which will shift the reaction to the right to produce more H^+ and CrO_4^{2-}. As more CrO_4^{2-} is produced, the solution turns yellow.

25. Test tube 1: added Cl^- reacts with Ag^+ to form a silver chloride precipitate. The net ionic equation is $Ag^+(aq) + Cl^-(aq) \rightarrow AgCl(s)$. Test tube 2: added NH_3 reacts with Ag^+ ions to form the soluble complex ion $Ag(NH_3)_2^+$. As this complex ion forms, Ag^+ is removed from solution, which causes the AgCl(s) to dissolve. When enough NH_3 is added, all of the silver chloride precipitate will dissolve. The equation is $AgCl(s) + 2\ NH_3(aq) \rightarrow Ag(NH_3)_2^+(aq) + Cl^-(aq)$. Test tube 3: added H^+ reacts with the weak base NH_3 to form NH_4^+. As NH_3 is removed from the $Ag(NH_3)_2^+$ complex ion equilibrium, Ag^+ ions are released to the solution which can then react with Cl^- to reform AgCl(s).   The equations are $Ag(NH_3)_2^+(aq) + 2\ H^+(aq) \rightarrow Ag^+(aq) + 2\ NH_4^+(aq)$ and $Ag^+(aq) + Cl^-(aq) \rightarrow AgCl(s)$.

26. CN^- is a weak base, so OH^- ions are present that lead to precipitation of $Ni(OH)_2(s)$. As excess CN^- is added, the $Ni(CN)_4^{2-}$ complex ion forms. The two reactions are:

$Ni^{2+}(aq) + 2\ OH^-(aq) \rightarrow Ni(OH)_2(s)$; The precipitate is $Ni(OH)_2(s)$.

$Ni(OH)_2(s) + 4\ CN^-(aq) \rightarrow Ni(CN)_4^{2-}(aq) + 2\ OH^-(aq)$; $Ni(CN)_4^{2-}$ is a soluble species.

27.   Because each compound contains an octahedral complex ion, the formulas for the compounds are $[Co(NH_3)_6]I_3$, $[Pt(NH_3)_4I_2]I_2$, $Na_2[PtI_6]$ and $[Cr(NH_3)_4I_2]I$. Note that in some cases, the I^- ions are ligands bound to the transition metal ion as required for a coordination number of 6, while in other cases the I^- ions are counterions required to balance the charge of the complex ion. The $AgNO_3$ solution will only precipitate the I^- counterions and will not precipitate the I^- ligands. Therefore, 3 moles of AgI will precipitate per mole of $[Co(NH_3)_6]I_3$, 2 moles of AgI will precipitate per mole of $[Pt(NH_3)_4I_2]I_2$, 0 moles of AgI will precipitate per mole of $Na_2[PtI_6]$, and 1 mole of AgI will precipitate per mole of $[Cr(NH_3)_4I_2]I$.

28. $BaCl_2$ gives no precipitate, so SO_4^{2-} must be in the coordination sphere ($BaSO_4$ is insoluble). A precipitate with $AgNO_3$ means the Cl^- is not in the coordination sphere. Because there are only four ammonia molecules in the coordination sphere, SO_4^{2-} must be acting as a bidentate ligand. The structure is:

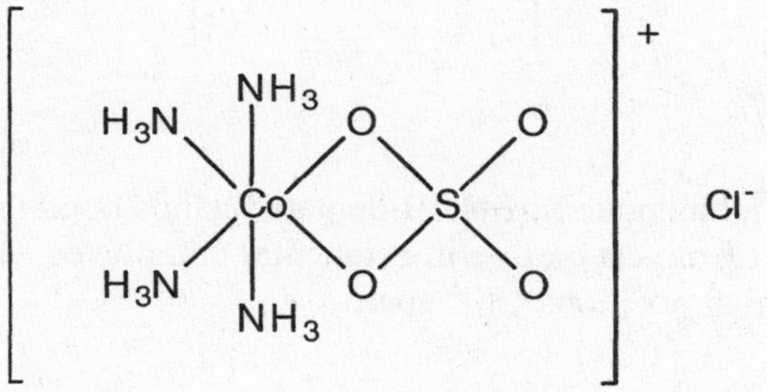

29.   To determine the oxidation state of the metal, you must know the charges of the various common ligands (see Table 21.13 of the text).

a.   pentaamminechlororuthenium(III) ion
b.   hexacyanoferrate(II) ion
c.   tris(ethylenediamine)manganese(II) ion
d.   pentaamminenitrocobalt(III) ion

30.   a.   tetracyanonicklate(II) ion
b.   tetraamminedichlorochromium(III) ion
c.   tris(oxalato)ferrate(III) ion
d.   tetraaquadithiocyanatocobalt(III) ion

31.   a.   hexaamminecobalt(II) chloride
b.   hexaaquacobalt(III) iodide
c.   potassium tetrachloroplatinate(II)
d.   potassium hexachloroplatinate(II)
e.   pentaamminechlorocobalt(III) chloride
f.   triamminetrinitrocobalt(III)

32.   a.   pentaaquabromochromium(III) bromide
b.   sodium hexacyanocobaltate(III)
c.   bis(ethylenediamine)dinitroiron(III) chloride
d.   tetraamminediiodoplatinum(IV) tetraiodoplatinate(II)

33. a. $K_2[CoCl_4]$

b. $[Pt(H_2O)(CO)_3]Br_2$

c. $Na_3[Fe(CN)_2(C_2O_4)_2]$

d. $[Cr(NH_3)_3Cl(H_2NCH_2CH_2NH_2)]I_2$

34. a. $FeCl_4^-$

b. $[Ru(NH_3)_5H_2O]^{3+}$

c. $[Cr(CO)_4(OH)_2]^+$

d. $[Pt(NH_3)Cl_3]^-$

35. a.

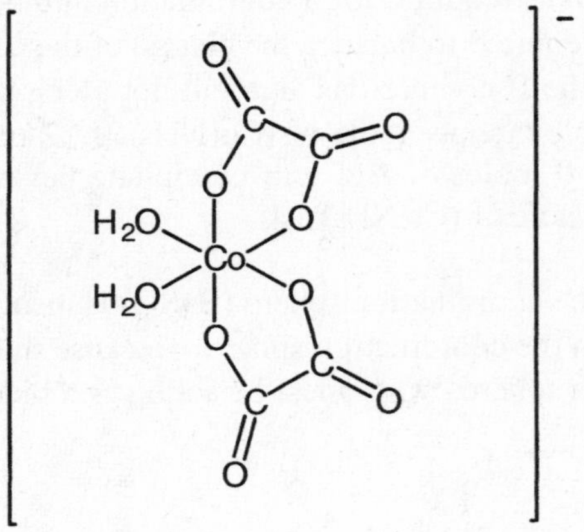

cis 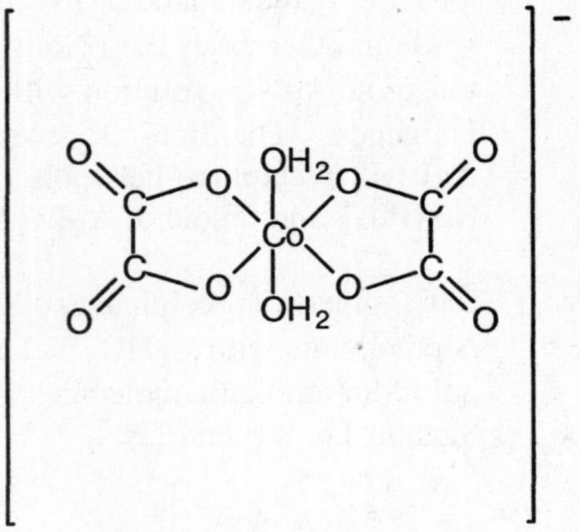   trans

Note: $C_2O_4^{2-}$ is a bidentate ligand. Bidentate ligands bond to the metal at two positions that are 90° apart from each other in octahedral complexes. Bidentate ligands do not bond to the metal at positions 180° apart.

b.

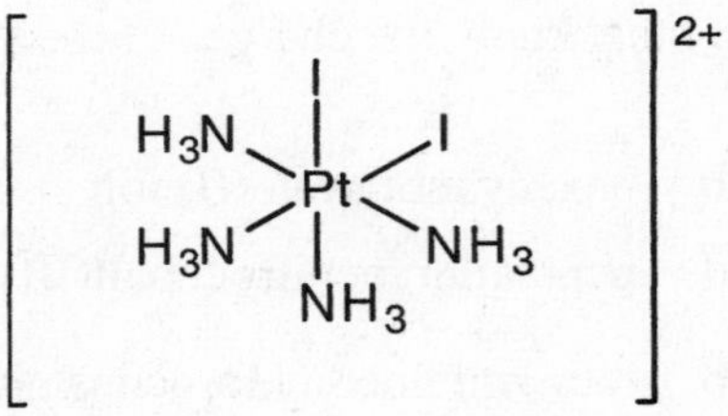

cis 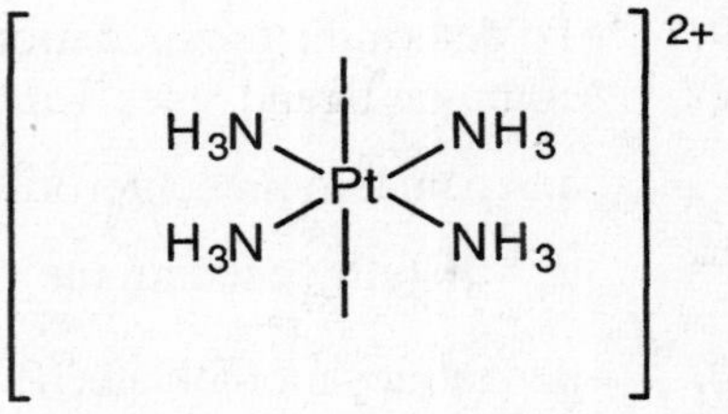   trans

c.

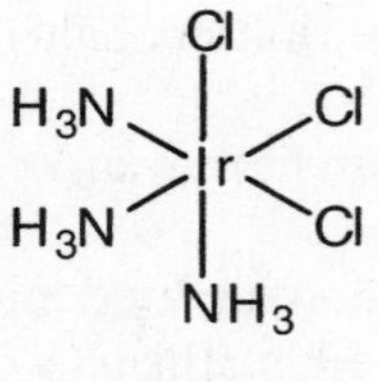

cis 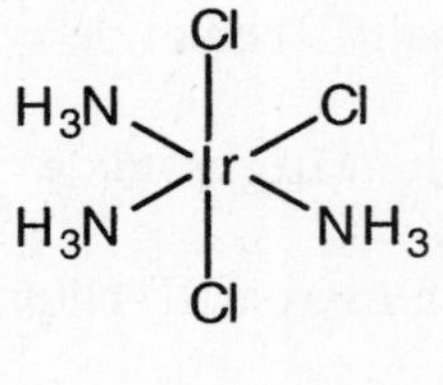   trans

d.

Note: N⌒N is an abbreviation for the bidentate ligand ethylenediamine ($H_2NCH_2CH_2NH_2$).

36.   a.   b.

c.   d.

e.

37.

M = transition metal ion

and

38.   M = transition metal ion

39.   Linkage isomers differ in the way the ligand bonds to the metal. SCN⁻ can bond through the sulfur or through the nitrogen atom. NO_2^- can bond through the nitrogen or through the oxygen atom. OCN⁻ can bond through the oxygen or through the nitrogen atom. N_3^-, $NH_2CH_2CH_2NH_2$ and I⁻ are not capable of linkage isomerism.

40.

41.   Similar to the molecules discussed in Figures 21.16 and 21.17 of the text, $Cr(acac)_3$ and cis-$Cr(acac)_2(H_2O)_2$ are optically active.   The mirror images of these two complexes are nonsuperimposable. There is a plane of symmetry in trans-$Cr(acac)_2(H_2O)_2$, so it is not optically active. A molecule with a plane of symmetry is never optically active because the mirror images are always superimposable. A plane of symmetry is a plane through a molecule where one side reflects the other side of the molecule.

42.   There are five geometrical isomers (labeled i-v). Only isomer v, where the CN⁻, Br⁻ and H₂O ligands are cis to each other, is optically active. The nonsuperimposable mirror image is shown for isomer v.

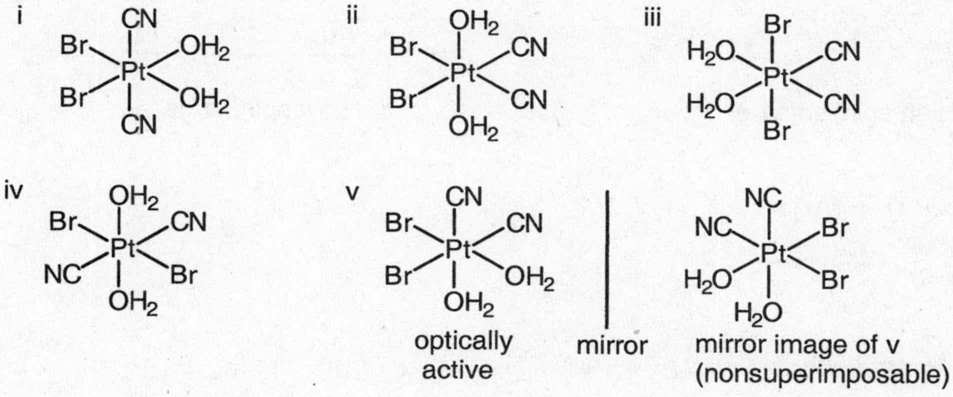

i

Br—Pt—OH₂ with CN top, OH₂ right, CN bottom

ii

Br—Pt—CN with OH₂ top, CN right, OH₂ bottom

iii

H₂O—Pt—CN with Br top, CN right, Br bottom

iv

Br—Pt—CN with OH₂ top, NC left, Br right, OH₂ bottom

v

Br—Pt—CN with CN top, OH₂ right, OH₂ bottom (Br left)

optically
active

mirror

NC—Pt—Br with NC top, Br right, H₂O left, H₂O bottom

mirror image of v
(nonsuperimposable)

Bonding, Color, and Magnetism in Coordination Compounds

43.   a. Fe^{2+}: $[Ar]3d^6$

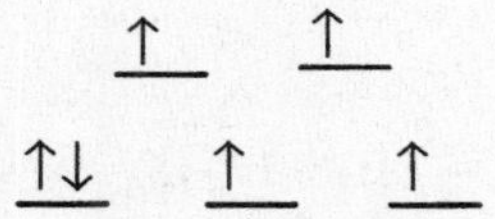

↑   ↑

↑↓   ↑   ↑

High spin, small Δ

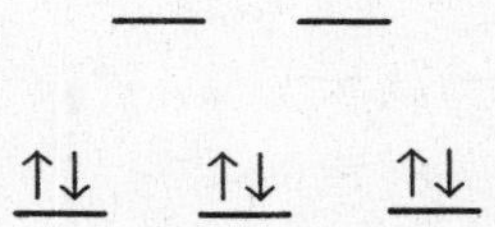

—   —

↑↓   ↑↓   ↑↓

Low spin, large Δ

b. Fe^{3+}: $[Ar]3d^5$

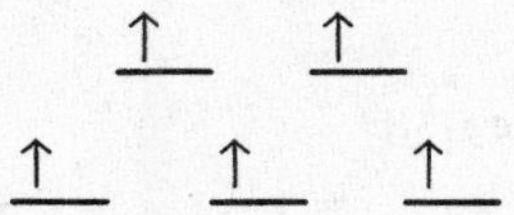

↑   ↑

↑   ↑   ↑

High spin, small Δ

c. Ni^{2+}: $[Ar]3d^8$

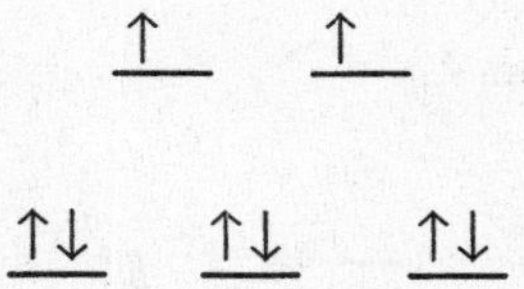

↑   ↑

↑↓   ↑↓   ↑↓

44.   a. Zn^{2+}: $[Ar]3d^{10}$

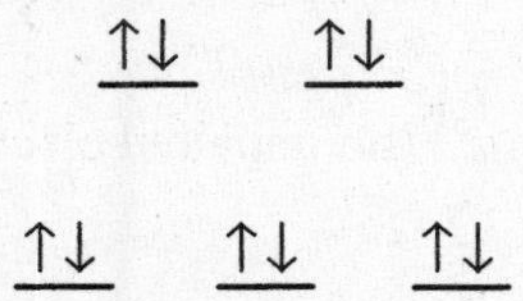

↑↓   ↑↓

↑↓   ↑↓   ↑↓

b. Co^{2+}: $[Ar]3d^7$

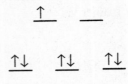

High spin, small Δ Low spin, large Δ

c. Ti^{3+}: $[Ar]3d^1$

45.   Because fluorine has a -1 charge as a ligand, chromium has a +2 oxidation state in CrF_6^{4-}. The electron configuration of Cr^{2+} is: $[Ar]3d^4$. For four unpaired electrons, this must be a weak-field (high-spin) case where the splitting of the d-orbitals is small and the number of unpaired electrons is maximized. The crystal field diagram for this ion is:

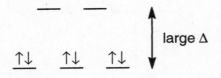

small Δ

46. NH_3 and H_2O are neutral ligands, so the oxidation states of the metals are Co^{3+} and Fe^{2+}. Both have six d electrons ($[Ar]3d^6$). To explain the magnetic properties, we must have a strong-field for $Co(NH_3)_6^{3+}$ and a weak-field for $Fe(H_2O)_6^{2+}$.

Co^{3+}: $[Ar]3d^6$ Fe^{2+}: $[Ar]3d^6$

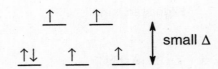

large Δ small Δ

Only this splitting of d-orbitals gives a diamagnetic $Co(NH_3)_6^{3+}$ (no unpaired electrons) and a paramagnetic $Fe(H_2O)_6^{2+}$ (unpaired electrons present).

47.   To determine the crystal field diagrams, you need to determine the oxidation state of the transition metal, which can only be determined if you know the charges of the ligands (see Table 21.13). The electron configurations and the crystal field diagrams follow.

a. Ru^{2+}: [Kr]$4d^6$, no unpaired e^- b. Ni^{2+}: [Ar]$3d^8$, 2 unpaired e^-

—   —

                                         ↑   ↑

↑↓   ↑↓   ↑↓   ↑↓   ↑↓   ↑↓

Low spin, large Δ

c. V^{3+}: [Ar]$3d^2$, 2 unpaired e^-

—   —   —

↑   ↑   —

Note: Ni^{2+} must have 2 unpaired electrons, whether high-spin or low-spin, and V^{3+} must have 2 unpaired electrons, whether high-spin or low-spin.

48.   In both compounds, iron is in the +3 oxidation state with an electron configuration of [Ar]$3d^5$. Fe^{3+} complexes have one unpaired electron when a strong-field case and five unpaired electrons when a weak-field case. $Fe(CN)_6^{2-}$ is a strong-field case and $Fe(SCN)_6^{3-}$ is a weak-field case. Therefore, cyanide, CN^-, is a stronger field ligand than thiocyanate, SCN^-.

49.   All have octahedral Co^{3+} ions so the difference in d orbital splitting and the wavelength of light absorbed only depends on the ligands. From the spectrochemical series, the order of the ligands from strongest to weakest field is CN^- > en > H_2O > I^-. The strongest field ligand produces the greatest d-orbital splitting (Δ) and will absorb light having the smallest wavelength. The weakest field ligand produces the smallest Δ and absorbs light having the longest wavelength. The order is

$$Co(CN)_6^{3-} < Co(en)_3^{3+} < Co(H_2O)_6^{3+} < CoI_6^{3-}$$
shortest λ longest λ
absorbed   absorbed

50.   Replacement of water ligands by ammonia ligands resulted in shorter wavelengths of light being absorbed. Energy and wavelength are inversely related, so the presence of the NH_3 ligands resulted in a larger d-orbital splitting (larger Δ). Therefore, NH_3 is a stronger field ligand than H_2O.

51.   From Table 21.16 of the text, the violet complex ion absorbs yellow-green light ($\lambda \sim 570$ nm), the yellow complex ion absorbs blue light ($\lambda \sim 450$ nm), and the green complex ion absorbs red light ($\lambda \sim 650$ nm). The spectrochemical series shows that NH_3 is a stronger-field ligand than H_2O which is a stronger-field ligand than Cl^-. Therefore, $Cr(NH_3)_6^{3+}$ will have the largest d-orbital splitting and will absorb the lowest wavelength electromagnetic radiation (λ

~ 450 nm) since energy and wavelength are inversely related (λ = hc/E). Thus, the yellow solution contains the $Cr(NH_3)_6^{3+}$ complex ion. Similarly, we would expect the $Cr(H_2O)_4Cl_2^+$ complex ion to have the smallest d-orbital splitting since it contains the weakest-field ligands. The green solution with the longest wavelength of absorbed light contains the $Cr(H_2O)_4Cl_2^+$ complex ion. This leaves the violet solution, which contains the $Cr(H_2O)_6^{3+}$ complex ion. This makes sense as we would expect $Cr(H_2O)_6^{3+}$ to absorb light of a wavelength between that of $Cr(NH_3)_6^{3+}$ and $Cr(H_2O)_4Cl_2^+$.

52.   All these complex ions contain Co^{3+} bound to different ligands, so the difference in d-orbital splitting for each complex ion is due to the difference in ligands. The spectrochemical series indicates that CN^- is a stronger field ligand than NH_3 which is a stronger field ligand than F^-. Therefore, $Co(CN)_6^{3-}$ will have the largest d-orbital splitting and will absorb the lowest wavelength electromagnetic radiation (λ = 290 nm) since energy and wavelength are inversely related (λ = hc/E). $Co(NH_3)_6^{3+}$ will absorb 440 nm electromagnetic radiation while CoF_6^{3-} will absorb the longest wavelength electromagnetic radiation (λ = 770 nm) since F^- is the weakest field ligand present.

53. $CoBr_6^{4-}$ has an octahedral structure, and $CoBr_4^{2-}$ has a tetrahedral structure (as do most Co^{2+} complexes with four ligands). Coordination complexes absorb electromagnetic radiation (EMR) of energy equal to the energy difference between the split d-orbitals. Because the tetrahedral d-orbital splitting is less than one-half of the octahedral d-orbital splitting, tetrahedral complexes will absorb lower energy EMR, which corresponds to longer wavelength EMR (E = hc/λ). Therefore, $CoBr_6^{2-}$ will absorb EMR having a wavelength shorter than 3.4×10^{-6} m.

54. Co^{2+}: $[Ar]3d^7$; The corresponding d-orbital splitting diagram for tetrahedral Co^{2+} complexes is:

$$\underline{\uparrow} \qquad \underline{\uparrow} \qquad \underline{\uparrow}$$

$$\underline{\uparrow\downarrow} \qquad \underline{\uparrow\downarrow}$$

All tetrahedral complexes are high-spin since the d-orbital splitting is small. Ions with 2 or 7 d electrons should give the most stable tetrahedral complexes since they have the greatest number of electrons in the lower energy orbitals compared to the number of electrons in the higher energy orbitals.

55.   Because the ligands are Cl^-, iron is in the +3 oxidation state. Fe^{3+}: $[Ar]3d^5$

$$\underline{\uparrow} \qquad \underline{\uparrow} \qquad \underline{\uparrow}$$

$$\underline{\uparrow} \qquad \underline{\uparrow}$$

Since all tetrahedral complexes are high-spin, there are 5 unpaired electrons in $FeCl_4^-$.

56.   Pd is in the +2 oxidation state in $PdCl_4^{2-}$; Pd^{2+}: $[Kr]4d^8$. If $PdCl_4^{2-}$ were a tetrahedral complex, then it would have 2 unpaired electrons and would be paramagnetic (see diagram below). Instead, $PdCl_4^{2-}$ has a square planar molecular structure with the d-orbital splitting

diagram also shown below. Note that all electrons are paired in the square planar diagram; this explains the diamagnetic properties of $PdCl_4^{2-}$.

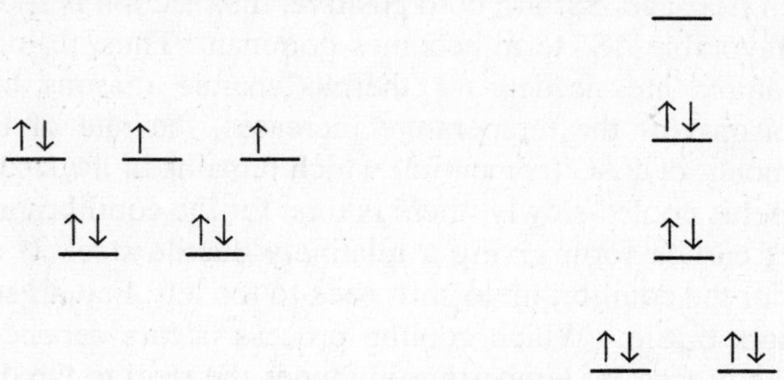

$\overline{}$

$\uparrow\downarrow$ $\uparrow$ $\uparrow$ $\qquad\qquad\qquad$ $\uparrow\downarrow$

$\uparrow\downarrow$ $\uparrow\downarrow$ $\qquad\qquad\qquad$ $\uparrow\downarrow$

$\qquad\qquad\qquad\qquad$ $\uparrow\downarrow$ $\uparrow\downarrow$

tetrahedral d^8 $\qquad\qquad\qquad\qquad$ square planar d^8

Metallurgy

57.   a.   To avoid fractions, let's first calculate ΔH for the reaction:

$$6\ FeO(s) + 6\ CO(g) \rightarrow 6\ Fe(s) + 6\ CO_2(g)$$

$6\ FeO + 2\ CO_2 \rightarrow 2\ Fe_3O_4 + 2\ CO$	$\Delta H° = -2(18\ kJ)$
$2\ Fe_3O_4 + CO_2 \rightarrow 3\ Fe_2O_3 + CO$	$\Delta H° = -(-39\ kJ)$
$3\ Fe_2O_3 + 9\ CO \rightarrow 6\ Fe + 9\ CO_2$	$\Delta H° = 3(-23\ kJ)$

$6\ FeO(s) + 6\ CO(g) \rightarrow 6\ Fe(s) + 6\ CO_2(g)$ $\qquad$ $\Delta H° = -66\ kJ$

So for: $FeO(s) + CO(g) \rightarrow Fe(s) + CO_2(g)$ $\qquad$ $\Delta H° = \dfrac{-66\ kJ}{6} = -11\ kJ$

b. $\Delta H° = 2(-110.5\ kJ) - [-393.5\ kJ + 0] = 172.5\ kJ$

$\Delta S° = 2(198\ J/K) - [214\ J/K + 6\ J/K] = 176\ J/K$

$\Delta G° = \Delta H° - T\Delta S°$, $\Delta G° = 0$ when $T = \dfrac{\Delta H°}{\Delta S°} = \dfrac{172.5\ kJ}{0.176\ kJ/K} = 980.\ K$

Due to the favorable $\Delta S°$ term, this reaction is spontaneous at $T > 980.\ K$. From Figure 21.36 of the text, this reaction takes place in the blast furnace at temperatures greater than 980. K as required by thermodynamics.

58. $3 Fe + C \rightarrow Fe_3C$; $\Delta H° = 21 - [3(0) + 0] = 21$ kJ; $\Delta S° = 108 - [3(27) + 6] = 21$ J/K

$\Delta G° = \Delta H° \; T\Delta S°$; When $\Delta H°$ and $\Delta S°$ are both positive, the reaction is spontaneous at high temperatures where the favorable $\Delta S°$ term becomes dominant. Thus, to incorporate carbon into steel, high temperatures are needed for thermodynamic reasons but will also be beneficial for kinetic reasons (as the temperature increases, the rate of the reaction will increase). The relative amount of Fe_3C (cementite) which remains in the steel depends on the cooling process. If the steel is cooled slowly, there is time for the equilibrium to shift back to the left; small crystals of carbon form giving a relatively ductile steel. If cooling is rapid, there is not enough time for the equilibrium to shift back to the left; Fe_3C is still present in the steel, and the steel is more brittle. Which cooling process occurs depends on the desired properties of the steel. The process of tempering fine tunes the steel to the desired properties by repeated heating and cooling.

59.   Review section 4.10 for balancing reactions in basic solution by the half-reaction method.

$$(2 CN^- + Ag \rightarrow Ag(CN)^{2-} + e^-) \times 4$$
$$4 e^- + O_2 + 4 H^+ \rightarrow 2 H_2O$$

$$\overline{8 CN^- + 4 Ag + O_2 + 4 H^+ \rightarrow 4 Ag(CN)_2^- + 2 H_2O}$$

Adding 4 OH^- to both sides and crossing off 2 H_2O on both sides of the equation gives the balanced equation:

$$8 CN^-(aq) + 4 Ag(s) + O_2(g) + 2 H_2O(l) \rightarrow 4 Ag(CN)_2^-(aq) + 4 OH^-(aq)$$

60. $Mn + HNO_3 \rightarrow Mn^{2+} + NO_2$

$$Mn \rightarrow Mn^{2+} + 2 e^- \qquad\qquad HNO_3 \rightarrow NO_2$$
$$HNO_3 \rightarrow NO_2 + H_2O$$
$$(e^- + H^+ + HNO_3 \rightarrow NO_2 + H_2O) \times 2$$

$$Mn \rightarrow Mn^{2+} + 2 e^-$$
$$2 e^- + 2 H^+ + 2 HNO_3 \rightarrow 2 NO_2 + 2 H_2O$$

$$\overline{2 H^+(aq) + Mn(s) + 2 HNO_3(aq) \rightarrow Mn^{2+}(aq) + 2 NO_2(g) + 2 H_2O(l)}$$

$Mn^{2+} + IO_4^- \rightarrow MnO_4^- + IO_3^-$

$$(4 H_2O + Mn^{2+} \rightarrow MnO_4^- + 8 H^+ + 5 e^-) \times 2 \qquad (2 e^- + 2 H^+ + IO_4^- \rightarrow IO_3^- + H_2O) \times 5$$

$$8 H_2O + 2 Mn^{2+} \rightarrow 2 MnO_4^- + 16 H^+ + 10 e^-$$
$$10 e^- + 10 H^+ + 5 IO_4^- \rightarrow 5 IO_3^- + 5 H_2O$$

$$\overline{3 H_2O(l) + 2 Mn^{2+}(aq) + 5 IO_4^-(aq) \rightarrow 2 MnO_4^-(aq) + 5 IO_3^-(aq) + 6 H^+(aq)}$$

Additional Exercises

61.   i. $0.0203 \text{ g CrO}_3 \times \dfrac{52.00 \text{ g Cr}}{100.0 \text{ g CrO}_3} = 0.0106 \text{ g Cr};$ $\% \text{ Cr} = \dfrac{0.0106}{0.105} \times 100 = 10.1\% \text{ Cr}$

ii. $32.93 \times 10^{-3} \text{L HCl} \times \dfrac{0.100 \text{ mol HCl}}{\text{L}} \times \dfrac{1 \text{ mol NH}_3}{\text{mol HCl}} \times \dfrac{17.03 \text{ g NH}_3}{\text{mol}} = 0.0561 \text{ g NH}_3$

$\% \text{ NH}_3 = \dfrac{0.0561 \text{ g}}{0.341 \text{ g}} \times 100 = 16.5\% \text{ NH}_3$

iii. $73.53\% \text{ I} + 16.5\% \text{ NH}_3 + 10.1\% \text{ Cr} = 100.1\%;$ The compound must be composed of only Cr, NH_3, and I.

Out of 100.00 g of compound:

$10.1 \text{ g Cr} \times \dfrac{1 \text{ mol}}{52.00 \text{ g}} = 0.194$ $\dfrac{0.194}{0.194} = 1.00$

$16.5 \text{ g NH}_3 \times \dfrac{1 \text{ mol}}{17.03 \text{ g}} = 0.969$ $\dfrac{0.969}{0.194} = 4.99$

$73.53 \text{ g I} \times \dfrac{1 \text{ mol}}{126.9 \text{ g}} = 0.5794$ $\dfrac{0.5794}{0.194} = 2.99$

$\text{Cr(NH}_3)_5\text{I}_3$ is the empirical formula. Cr(III) forms octahedral complexes. So, compound A is made of the octahedral $[\text{Cr(NH}_3)_5\text{I}]^{2+}$ complex ion and two I^- counter ions; the formula is $[\text{Cr(NH}_3)_5\text{I}]\text{I}_2$. Let's check this proposed formula using the freezing point data.

iv. $\Delta T_f = iK_f m;$ For $[\text{Cr(NH}_3)_5\text{I}]\text{I}_2$, $i = 3.0$ (assuming complete dissociation).

$m = \dfrac{0.601 \text{ g complex}}{1.000 \times 10^{-2} \text{ kg H}_2\text{O}} \times \dfrac{1 \text{ mol complex}}{517.9 \text{ g complex}} = 0.116 \text{ molal}$

$\Delta T_f = 3.0 \times 1.86°\text{C/molal} \times 0.116 \text{ molal} = 0.65°\text{C}$

Because ΔT_f is close to the measured value, this is consistent with the formula $[\text{Cr(NH}_3)_5\text{I}]\text{I}_2$.

62. $0.308 \text{ g AgCl} \times \dfrac{35.45 \text{ g Cl}}{143.4 \text{ g AgCl}} = 0.0761 \text{ g Cl};$ $\% \text{Cl} = \dfrac{0.0761 \text{ g}}{0.256 \text{ g}} \times 100 = 29.7\% \text{ Cl}$

Cobalt(III) oxide, Co_2O_3: $2(58.93) + 3(16.00) = 165.86 \text{ g/mol}$

$0.145 \text{ g Co}_2\text{O}_3 \times \dfrac{117.86 \text{ g Co}}{165.86 \text{ g Co}_2\text{O}_3} = 0.103 \text{ g Co};$ $\% \text{Co} = \dfrac{0.103 \text{ g}}{0.416 \text{ g}} \times 100 = 24.8\% \text{ Co}$

The remainder, $100.0 - (29.7 + 24.8) = 45.5\%$, is water.

Out of 100.0 g of compound, there are:

$$24.8 \text{ g Co} \times \frac{1 \text{ mol Co}}{58.93 \text{ g Co}} = 0.421 \text{ mol Co}; \quad 29.7 \text{ g Cl} \times \frac{1 \text{ mol Cl}}{35.45 \text{ g Cl}} = 0.838 \text{ mol Cl}$$

$$45.5 \text{ g H}_2\text{O} \times \frac{1 \text{ mol}}{18.02 \text{ g H}_2\text{O}} = 2.52 \text{ mol H}_2\text{O}$$

Dividing all results by 0.421, we get $CoCl_2 \cdot 6H_2O$ for the formula. The oxidation state of cobalt is +2 because the chloride counterions have a -1 charge each. Because the waters are the ligands, the formula of the compound is $[Co(H_2O)_6]Cl_2$.

63. $Hg^{2+}(aq) + 2\ I^-(aq) \rightarrow HgI_2(s)$, orange ppt.; $HgI_2(s) + 2\ I^-(aq) \rightarrow HgI_4^{2-}(aq)$,

soluble complex ion

Hg^{2+} is a d^{10} ion. Color is the result of electron transfer between split d orbitals. This cannot occur for the filled d orbitals in Hg^{2+}. Therefore, we would not expect Hg^{2+} complex ions to form colored solutions.

64. a. Copper is both oxidized and reduced in this reaction, so, yes, this reaction is an oxidation-reduction reaction. The oxidation state of copper in $[Cu(NH_3)_4]Cl_2$ is +2, the oxidation state of copper in Cu is zero, and the oxidation state of copper in $[Cu(NH_3)_4]Cl$ is +1.

   b. Total mass of copper used:

$$10,000 \text{ boards} \times \frac{(8.0 \text{ cm} \times 16.0 \text{ cm} \times 0.060 \text{ cm})}{\text{board}} \times \frac{8.96 \text{ g}}{\text{cm}^3} = 6.9 \times 10^5 \text{ g Cu}$$

Amount of Cu to be recovered = $0.80 \times 6.9 \times 10^5$ g = 5.5×10^5 g Cu

$$5.5 \times 10^5 \text{ g Cu} \times \frac{1 \text{ mol Cu}}{63.55 \text{ g Cu}} \times \frac{1 \text{ mol } [Cu(NH_3)_4]Cl_2}{\text{mol Cu}} \times \frac{202.59 \text{ g } [Cu(NH_3)_4]Cl_2}{\text{mol } [Cu(NH_3)_4]Cl_2}$$

$$= 1.8 \times 10^6 \text{ g } [Cu(NH_3)_4]Cl_2$$

$$5.5 \times 10^5 \text{ g Cu} \times \frac{1 \text{ mol Cu}}{63.55 \text{ g Cu}} \times \frac{4 \text{ mol NH}_3}{\text{mol Cu}} \times \frac{17.03 \text{ g NH}_3}{\text{mol NH}_3} = 5.9 \times 10^5 \text{ g NH}_3$$

65. a. 2; Forms bonds through the lone pairs on the two oxygen atoms.

   b. 3; Forms bonds through the lone pairs on the three nitrogen atoms.

   c. 4; Forms bonds through the two nitrogen atoms and the two oxygen atoms.

   d. 4; Forms bonds through the four nitrogen atoms.

66. a. In the following structures, we omitted the 4 NH_3 ligands coordinated to the outside cobalt atoms.

mirror

b. All are Co(III). The three "ligands" each contain 2 OH$^-$ and 4 NH$_3$ groups. If each cobalt is in the +3 oxidation state, then each ligand has a +1 overall charge. The +3 charge from the three ligands, along with the +3 charge of the central cobalt atom, gives the overall complex a +6 charge. This is balanced by the −6 charge of the six Cl$^-$ ions.

c. Co^{3+}: [Ar]3d^6; There are zero unpaired electrons if a low-spin (strong-field) case.

67.   a. Ru(phen)$_3$$^{2+}$ exhibits optical isomerism [similar to Co(en)$_3$$^{3+}$ in Figure 21.16 of the text].

b. Ru^{2+}: [Kr]4d^6; Since there are no unpaired electrons, Ru^{2+} is a strong-field (low-spin) case.

68.   a. Be(tfa)$_2$ exhibits optical isomerism. A representation for the tetrahedral optical isomers are:

mirror

Note: The dotted line indicates a bond pointing into the plane of the paper, and the wedge indicates a bond pointing out of the plane of the paper.

b. Square planar $Cu(tfa)_2$ molecules exhibit geometric isomerism. In one geometric isomer, the CF_3 groups are cis to each other and in the other isomer, the CF_3 groups are trans.

cis   trans

69.   Octahedral Cr^{2+} complexes should be used. Cr^{2+}: $[Ar]3d^4$; High-spin (weak-field) Cr^{2+} complexes have 4 unpaired electrons and low-spin (strong-field) Cr^{2+} complexes have 2 unpaired electrons. Ni^{2+}: $[Ar]3d^8$; Octahedral Ni^{2+} complexes will always have 2 unpaired electrons, whether high or low-spin. Therefore, Ni^{2+} complexes cannot be used to distinguish weak from strong-field ligands by examining magnetic properties. Alternatively, the ligand field strengths can be measured using visible spectra. Either Cr^{2+} or Ni^{2+} complexes can be used for this method.

70.   a. $Fe(H_2O)_6^{3+} + H_2O \rightleftharpoons Fe(H_2O)_5(OH)^{2+} + H_3O^+$

Initial	0.10 M	0	~0
Equil.	0.10 – x	x	x

$$K_a = \frac{[Fe(H_2O)_5(OH)^{2+}][H_3O^+]}{[Fe(H_2O)_6^{3+}]} = 6.0 \times 10^{-3} = \frac{x^2}{0.10 - x} \approx \frac{x^2}{0.10}$$

$x = 2.4 \times 10^{-2}$; Assumption is poor (x is 24% of 0.10). Using successive approximations:

$$\frac{x^2}{0.10 - 0.024} = 6.0 \times 10^{-3}, \ x = 0.021$$

$$\frac{x^2}{0.10 - 0.021} = 6.0 \times 10^{-3}, \ x = 0.022; \quad \frac{x^2}{0.10 - 0.022} = 6.0 \times 10^{-3}, \ x = 0.022$$

$$x = [H^+] = 0.022 \ M; \ \ pH = 1.66$$

b. Because of the lower charge, Fe^{2+}(aq) will not be as strong an acid as Fe^{3+}(aq). A solution of iron(II) nitrate will be less acidic (have a higher pH) than a solution with the same concentration of iron(III) nitrate.

71. We need to calculate the Pb^{2+} concentration in equilibrium with $EDTA^{4-}$. Since K is large for the formation of $PbEDTA^{2-}$, let the reaction go to completion; then solve an equilibrium problem to get the Pb^{2+} concentration.

$$Pb^{2+} \quad + \quad EDTA^{4-} \ \rightleftharpoons \ PbEDTA^{2-} \quad K = 1.1 \times 10^{18}$$

Before	0.010 M	0.050 M	0

0.010 mol/L Pb^{2+} reacts completely (large K)

Change	−0.010	−0.010	→ +0.010	Reacts completely
After	0	0.040	0.010	New initial condition

x mol/L $PbEDTA^{2-}$ dissociates to reach equilibrium

Equil.	x	0.040 + x	0.010 - x

$$1.1 \times 10^{18} = \frac{(0.10 - x)}{(x)(0.040 + x)} \approx \frac{(0.10)}{x(0.040)}, \ x = [Pb^{2+}] = 2.3 \times 10^{-19} \ M; \ \ \text{Assumptions good.}$$

Now calculate the solubility quotient for $Pb(OH)_2$ to see if precipitation occurs. The concentration of OH^- is 0.10 M because we have a solution buffered at pH = 13.00.

$$Q = [Pb^{2+}]_o [OH^-]_o^{\ 2} = (2.3 \times 10^{-19})(0.10)^2 = 2.3 \times 10^{-21} < K_{sp} \ (1.2 \times 10^{-15})$$

$Pb(OH)_2$(s) will not form because Q is less than K_{sp}.

72. a. In the lungs, there is a lot of O_2, and the equilibrium favors $Hb(O_2)_4$. In the cells, there is a deficiency of O_2, and the equilibrium favors HbH_4^{4+}.

b. CO_2 is a weak acid, $CO_2 + H_2O \rightleftharpoons HCO_3^- + H^+$. Removing CO_2 essentially decreases H^+. $Hb(O_2)_4$ is then favored, and O_2 is not released by hemoglobin in the cells. Breathing into a paper bag increases $[CO_2]$ in the blood, thus increasing $[H^+]$ which shifts the reaction left.

c. CO_2 builds up in the blood, and it becomes too acidic, driving the equilibrium to the left. Hemoglobin can't bind O_2 as strongly in the lungs. Bicarbonate ion acts as a base in water and neutralizes the excess acidity.

73.
$$HbO_2 \rightarrow Hb + O_2 \qquad \Delta G° = -(-70 \text{ kJ})$$
$$Hb + CO \rightarrow HbCO \qquad \Delta G° = -80 \text{ kJ}$$

$$HbO_2 + CO \rightarrow HbCO + O_2 \qquad \Delta G° = -10 \text{ kJ}$$

$$\Delta G° = -RT \ln K, \quad K = \exp\left(\frac{-\Delta G°}{RT}\right) = \exp\left(\frac{-(-10 \times 10^3 \text{ J})}{(8.3145 \text{ J/K} \cdot \text{mol})(298 \text{ kJ})}\right) = 60$$

74.

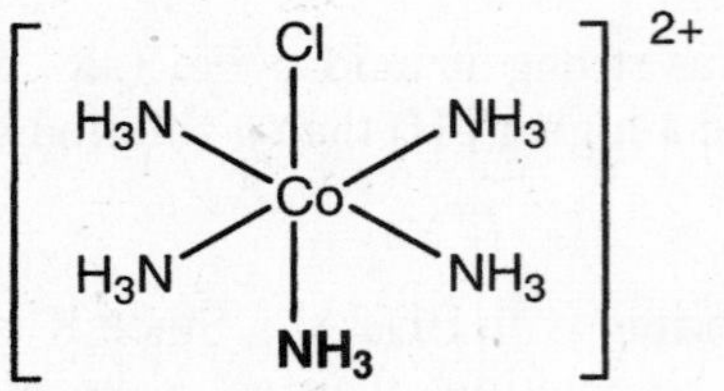

To form the trans isomer, Cl^- would replace the NH_3 ligand that is bold in the structure above. If any of the other four NH_3 molecules are replaced by Cl^-, the cis isomer results. Therefore, the expected ratio of the cis:trans isomer in the product is 4:1.

Challenge Problems

75. $Ni^{2+} = d^8$; If ligands A and B produced very similar crystal fields, the trans-$[NiA_2B_4]^{2+}$ complex ion would give the following octahedral crystal field diagram for a d^8 ion:

This is paramagnetic.

Because it is given that the complex ion is diamagnetic, the A and B ligands must produce different crystal fields giving a unique d-orbital splitting diagram that would result in a diamagnetic species.

76.   a. $\Delta S°$ will be negative because there is a decrease in the number of moles of gas.

b.   Because $\Delta S°$ is negative, $\Delta H°$ must be negative for the reaction to be spontaneous at some temperatures. Therefore, ΔS_{surr} is positive.

c. $Ni(s) + 4 CO(g) \rightleftharpoons Ni(CO)_4(g)$

$\Delta H° = -607 - [4(-110.5)] = -165 \text{ kJ}$; $\Delta S° = 417 - [4(198) + (30.)] = -405 \text{ J/K}$

d. $\Delta G° = 0 = \Delta H° - T\Delta S°$, $T = \dfrac{\Delta H°}{\Delta S°} = \dfrac{-165 \times 10^3 \text{ J}}{-405 \text{ J/K}} = 407 \text{ K or } 134°C$

e. $T = 50.°C + 273 = 323 \text{ K}$

$$\Delta G^{\circ}_{323} = -165 \text{ kJ} - (323 \text{ K})(-0.405 \text{ kJ/K}) = -34 \text{ kJ}$$

$$\ln K = \frac{-\Delta G^{\circ}}{RT} = \frac{-(-34,000 \text{ J})}{(8.3145 \text{ J}/\text{K} \bullet \text{mol})(323 \text{ K})} = 12.66, \ K = e^{12.66} = 3.1 \times 10^5$$

f. $T = 227°C + 273 = 500. \text{ K}$

$$\Delta G^{\circ}_{500} = -165 \text{ kJ} - (500. \text{ K})(-0.405 \text{ kJ/K}) = 38 \text{ kJ}$$

$$\ln K = \frac{-38,000 \text{ J}}{(8.145)(500.)} = -9.14, \ K = e^{-9.14} = 1.1 \times 10^{-4}$$

g.   The temperature change causes the value of the equilibrium constant to change from a large value favoring formation of $Ni(CO)_4$ to a small value favoring the decomposition of $Ni(CO)_4$ into pure Ni and CO. This is exactly what is wanted in order to purify a nickel sample.

77.   a.   Consider the following electrochemical cell:

$$Co^{3+} + e^- \rightarrow Co^{2+} \qquad\qquad E^{\circ} = 1.82 \text{ V}$$
$$Co(en)_3^{2+} \rightarrow Co(en)_3^{3+} + e^- \qquad -E^{\circ} = ?$$

$$\overline{Co^{3+} + Co(en)_3^{2+} \rightarrow Co^{2+} + Co(en)_3^{3+} \qquad E^{\circ}_{cell} = 1.82 - E^{\circ}}$$

The equilibrium constant for this overall reaction is:

$$Co^{3+} + 3 \text{ en} \rightarrow Co(en)_3^{3+} \qquad\qquad K_1 = 2.0 \times 10^{47}$$
$$Co(en)_3^{2+} \rightarrow Co^{2+} + 3 \text{ en} \qquad\qquad K_2 = 1/1.5 \times 10^{12}$$

$$\overline{Co^{3+} + Co(en)_3^{2+} \rightarrow Co(en)_3^{3+} + Co^{2+} \qquad K = K_1 K_2 = \frac{2.0 \times 10^{47}}{1.5 \times 10^{12}} = 1.3 \times 10^{35}}$$

From the Nernst equation for the overall reaction:

$$E^{\circ}_{cell} = \frac{0.0591}{n} \log K = \frac{0.0591}{1} \log(1.3 \times 10^{35}), \ \log(1.3 \times 10^{35}), \ E^{\circ}_{cell} = 2.08 \text{ V}$$

$$E^{\circ}_{cell} = 1.82 - E^{\circ} = 2.08 \text{ V}, \ E^{\circ} = 1.82 \text{ V} - 2.08 \text{ V} = -0.26 \text{ V}$$

b.   The stronger oxidizing agent will be the more easily reduced species and will have the more positive standard reduction potential. From the reduction potentials, Co^{3+} ($E^{\circ} = 1.82$ V) is a much stronger oxidizing agent than $Co(en)_3^{3+}$ ($E^{\circ} = -0.26$ V).

c.   In aqueous solution, Co^{3+} forms the hydrated transition metal complex, $Co(H_2O)_6^{3+}$. In both complexes, $Co(H_2O)_6^{3+}$ and $Co(en)_3^{3+}$, cobalt exists as Co^{3+} which has 6 d electrons.

Assuming a strong-field case for each complex ion, the d-orbital splitting diagram for each is:

—   — e_g

$\uparrow\downarrow$ $\uparrow\downarrow$ $\uparrow\downarrow$ t_{2g}

When each complex gains an electron, the electron enters a higher energy e_g orbital. Since en is a stronger field ligand than H_2O, the d-orbital splitting is larger for $Co(en)_3^{3+}$, and it takes more energy to add an electron to $Co(en)_3^{3+}$ than to $Co(H_2O)_6^{3+}$. Therefore, it is more favorable for $Co(H_2O)_6^{3+}$ to gain an electron than for $Co(en)_3^{3+}$ to gain an electron.

$$\underset{II}{}\quad\underset{III}{}\qquad\qquad\underset{III}{}\quad\underset{II}{}$$

78. $(H_2O)_5Cr-Cl-Co(NH_3)_5 \rightarrow (H_2O)_5Cr-Cl-Co(NH_3)_5 \rightarrow Cr(H_2O)_5Cl^{2+} + Co(II)$ complex

Yes; After the oxidation, the ligands on Cr(III) won't exchange. Since Cl$^-$ is in the coordination sphere, it must have formed a bond to Cr(II) before the electron transfer occurred (as proposed through the formation of the intermediate).

79.   No; In all three cases, six bonds are formed between Ni^{2+} and nitrogen, so ΔH values should be similar. $\Delta S°$ for formation of the complex ion is most negative for 6 NH_3 molecules reacting with a metal ion (7 independent species become 1). For penten reacting with a metal ion, 2 independent species become 1, so $\Delta S°$ is least negative of all three of the reactions. Thus, the chelate effect occurs because the more bonds a chelating agent can form to the metal, the more favorable $\Delta S°$ is for the formation of the complex ion and the larger the formation constant.

80.

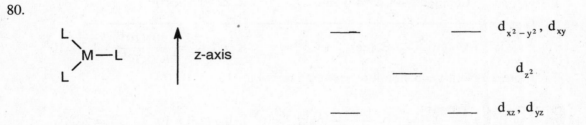

The $d_{x^2-y^2}$ and d_{xy} orbitals are in the plane of the three ligands and should be destabilized the most. The amount of destabilization should be about equal when all the possible interactions are considered. The d_{z^2} orbital has some electron density in the xy plane (the doughnut) and should be destabilized a lesser amount as compared to the $d_{x^2-y^2}$ and d_{xy} orbitals. The d_{xz} and d_{yz} orbitals have no electron density in the plane and should be lowest in energy.

81.

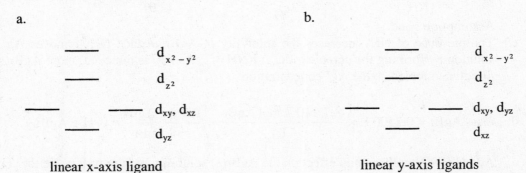

The d_{z^2} orbital will be destabilized much more than in the trigonal planar case (see Exercise 21.80). The d_{z^2} orbital has electron density on the z-axis directed at the two axial ligands. The $d_{x^2-y^2}$ and d_{xy} orbitals are in the plane of the three trigonal planar ligands and should be destabilized a lesser amount as compared to the d_{z^2} orbital; only a portion of the electron density in the $d_{x^2-y^2}$ and d_{xy} orbitals is directed at the ligands. The d_{xz} and d_{yz} orbitals will be destabilized the least since the electron density is directed between the ligands.

82.   For a linear complex ion with ligands on the x-axis, the $d_{x^2-y^2}$ will be destabilized the most with the lobes pointing directly at the ligands. The d_{yz} orbital has the fewest interactions with x-axis ligands so it is destabilized the least. The d_{xy} and d_{xz} orbitals will have similar destabilization, but will have more interactions with x-axis ligands than the d_{xy} orbital. Finally, the d_{z^2} orbital with the doughnut of electron density in the xy plane will probably be destabilized more than the d_{xy} and d_{xz} orbitals, but will have nowhere near the amount of destabilization that occurs with the $d_{x^2-y^2}$ orbital. The only difference that would occur in the diagram if the ligands were on the y-axis is the relative positions of the d_{xy}, d_{xz}, and d_{yz} orbirals. The d_{xz} will have the smallest destabilization of all of these orbitals while the d_{xy} and d_{yz} orbitals will be degenerate since we expect both to be destabilized equivalently from y-axis ligands. The d-orbital splitting diagrams are:

a.   b.

——	$d_{x^2-y^2}$	
——	d_{z^2}	
—— ——	d_{xy}, d_{xz}	
——	d_{yz}	

linear x-axis ligand

——	$d_{x^2-y^2}$	
——	d_{z^2}	
—— ——	d_{xy}, d_{yz}	
——	d_{xz}	

linear y-axis ligands

83.   The coordinate system for trans-$[Ni(NH_3)_2(CN)_4]^{2-}$ is shown below. Because CN^- produces a much stronger crystal field, it will dominate the d-orbital splitting. From the coordinate system, the CN^- ligands are in a square planar arrangement. Therefore, the diagram will most resemble the square planar diagram. Note that the relative position of d_{z^2} orbital is hard to predict; it could switch positions with the d_{xy} orbital.

84.   a. $AgBr(s) \rightleftharpoons Ag^+(aq) + Br^-(aq)$ $K_{sp} = [Ag^+][Br^-] = 5.0 \times 10^{-13}$

Initial s = solubility (mol/L)   0   0
Equil. s s

$K_{sp} = 5.0 \times 10^{-13} = s^2$, $s = 7.1 \times 10^{-7}$ mol/L

b. $AgBr(s) \rightleftharpoons Ag^+ + Br^-$ $K_{sp} = 5.0 \times 10^{-13}$
             $Ag^+ + 2\,NH_3 \rightleftharpoons Ag(NH_3)_2^+$ $K_f = 1.7 \times 10^7$

$AgBr(s) + 2\,NH_3(aq) \rightleftharpoons Ag(NH_3)_2^+(aq) + Br^-(aq)$ $K = K_{sp} \times K_f = 8.5 \times 10^{-6}$

           $AgBr(s) + 2\,NH_3 \rightleftharpoons Ag(NH_3)_2^+ + Br^-$

Initial   3.0 M 0   0
                s mol/L of AgBr(s) dissolves to reach equilibrium = molar solubility
Equil. $3.0 - 2s$ s s

$$K = \frac{[Ag(NH_3)_2^+][Br^-]}{[NH_3]^2} = \frac{s^2}{(3.0 - 2s)^2} = 8.5 \times 10^{-6} \approx \frac{s^2}{(3.0)^2}, \; s = 8.7 \times 10^{-3}\,\text{mol/L}$$

Assumption good.

c.   The presence of NH_3 increases the solubility of AgBr. Added NH_3 removes Ag^+ from solution by forming the complex ion, $Ag(NH_3)_2^+$. As Ag^+ is removed, more AgBr(s) will dissolve to replenish the Ag^+ concentration.

d.   mass AgBr $= 0.2500\,\text{L} \times \dfrac{8.7 \times 10^{-3}\,\text{mol AgBr}}{\text{L}} \times \dfrac{187.8\,\text{g AgBr}}{\text{mol AgBr}} = 0.41$ g AgBr

e.   Added HNO_3 will have no effect on the AgBr(s) solubility in pure water. Neither H^+ nor NO_3^- react with Ag^+ or Br^- ions. Br^- is the conjugate base of the strong acid HBr, so it is a terrible base. However, added HNO_3 will reduce the solubility of AgBr(s) in the ammonia solution. NH_3 is a weak base ($K_b = 1.8 \times 10^{-5}$). Added H^+ will react with NH_3 to form NH_4^+. As NH_3 is removed, a smaller amount of the $Ag(NH_3)_2^+$ complex ion will form, resulting in a smaller amount of AgBr(s) that will dissolve.

Integrative Problems

85. a. Because O is in the -2 oxidation state, iron must be in the $+6$ oxidation state. Fe^{6+}: $[Ar]3d^2$.

b. Using the half-reaction method of balancing redox reactions, the balanced equation is:

$$10\ H^+(aq) + 2\ FeO_4^{2-}(aq) + 2\ NH_3(aq) \rightarrow 2\ Fe^{3+}(aq) + N_2(g) + 8\ H_2O(l)$$

$$0.0250\ L \times \frac{0.243\ mol}{L} = 6.08 \times 10^{-3}\ mol\ FeO_4^{2-}$$

$$0.0550\ L \times \frac{1.45\ mol}{L} = 7.98 \times 10^{-2}\ mol\ NH_3$$

$$\frac{mol\ NH_3}{mol\ FeO_4^{2-}} = \frac{7.98 \times 10^{-2}\ mol}{6.08 \times 10^{-3}\ mol} = 13.1$$

The actual mole ratio is larger than the theoretical ratio of 1:1, so FeO_4^{2-} is limiting.

$$V_{N_2} = \frac{nRT}{P} = \frac{(6.08 \times 10^{-3}\ mol\ FeO_4^{2-}) \times \dfrac{1\ mol\ N_2}{2\ mol\ FeO_4^{2-}} \times \dfrac{0.08206\ L\ atm}{K\ mol} \times 298\ K}{1.50\ atm}$$

$$V_{N_2} = 0.0496\ L = 49.6\ mL\ N_2$$

86. a. $\lambda = \dfrac{hc}{E} = \dfrac{6.626 \times 10^{-34}\ J\ s \times 2.998 \times 10^8\ m/s}{1.75 \times 10^4\ cm^{-1} \times \dfrac{1.986 \times 10^{-23}\ J}{cm^{-1}}} = 5.72 \times 10^{-7}\ m = 572\ nm$

b. There are three resonance structures for NCS^-. From a formal charge standpoint, the following resonance structure is best.

$$\left[:N\equiv C - \ddot{\underset{\displaystyle \cdot\cdot}{S}}: \right]^-$$

The N in this resonance structure is sp hybridized. Because the sp hybrid orbitals are 180° apart, one would expect that when the lone pair in an sp hybrid orbital on N is donated to the Cr^{3+} ion, the 180° bond angle would stay intact between Cr, N, C, and S.

Similar to $Co(en)_2Cl_2^+$ discussed in Figures 21.16 and 21.17 of the text, $[Co(en)_2(NCS)_2]^+$ would exhibit cis/trans isomerism (geometric isomerism) and only the cis form would exhibit optical isomerism. For $[Co(en)_2(NCS)_2]^+$, NCS^- just replaces the Cl^- ions in the isomers drawn in Figures 21.16 and 21.17. The trans isomer would not exhibit optical isomerism.

Marathon Problem

87. $CrCl_3 \cdot 6H_2O$ contains nine possible ligands; only six of which are used to form the octahedral complex ion. The three species not present in the complex ion will either be counterions to balance the charge of the complex ion and/or waters of hydration. The number of counterions for each compound can be determined from the silver chloride precipitate data and the number of waters of hydration can be determined from the dehydration data. In all experiments, the ligands in the complex ion do not react.

Compound I:

$$\text{mol } CrCl_3 \cdot 6H_2O = 0.27 \text{ g} \times \frac{1 \text{ mol}}{266.45} = 1.0 \times 10^{-3} \text{ mol } CrCl_3 \cdot 6H_2O$$

$$\text{mol waters of hydration} = 0.036 \text{ g } H_2O \times \frac{1 \text{ mol}}{18.02 \text{ g}} = 2.0 \times 10^{-3} \text{ mol } H_2O$$

$$\frac{\text{mol waters of hydration}}{\text{mol compound}} = \frac{2.0 \times 10^{-3} \text{ mol}}{1.0 \times 10^{-3} \text{ mol}} = 2.0$$

In compound I, two of the H_2O molecules are waters of hydration so the other four water molecules are present in the complex ion as ligands. Therefore, the formula for compound I must be $[Cr(H_2O)_4Cl_2]Cl \cdot 2H_2O$. Two of the Cl^- ions are present as ligands in the octahedral complex ion and one Cl^- ion is present as a counterion. From the following calculations, this compound yields 1430 mg AgCl. This agrees with the precipitate data in the problem.

$$\text{mol } Cl^- \text{ from compound I} = 0.1000 \text{ L} \times \frac{0.100 \text{ mol } [Cr(H_2O)_4Cl_2]Cl \cdot 2H_2O}{L}$$

$$\times \frac{1 \text{ mol } Cl^-}{\text{mol } [Cr(H_2O)_4Cl_2]Cl \cdot 2H_2O} = 0.0100 \text{ mol } Cl^-$$

$$\text{mass AgCl produced} = 0.0100 \text{ mol } Cl^- \times \frac{1 \text{ mol AgCl}}{\text{mol } Cl^-} \times \frac{143.4 \text{ g AgCl}}{\text{mol AgCl}} = 1.43 \text{ g}$$

$$= 1430 \text{ mg AgCl}$$

Compound II:

$$\frac{\text{mol waters of hydration}}{\text{mol compound}} = \frac{0.018 \text{ g } H_2O \times \dfrac{1 \text{ mol}}{18.02 \text{ g}}}{1.0 \times 10^{-3} \text{ mol compound}} = 1.0$$

The formula for compound II must be $[Cr(H_2O)_5Cl]Cl_2 \cdot H_2O$. The 2870 mg AgCl precipitate data refers to this compound. For 0.0100 mol of compound II, 0.0200 mol Cl^- are present as counterions:

$$\text{mass AgCl produced} = 0.0200 \text{ mol Cl}^- \times \frac{1 \text{ mol AgCl}}{\text{mol Cl}^-} \times \frac{143.4 \text{ g}}{\text{mol}} = 2.87 \text{ g} = 2870 \text{ mg AgCl}$$

Compound III:

This compound has no mass loss on dehydration so there are no waters of hydration present. The formula for compound III must be $[Cr(H_2O)_6]Cl_3$. 0.0100 mol of this compound produces 4300 mg of AgCl(s) when treated with $AgNO_3$.

$$0.0300 \text{ mol Cl}^- \times \frac{1 \text{ mol AgCl}}{\text{mol Cl}^-} \times \frac{143.4 \text{ g AgCl}}{\text{mol AgCl}} = 4.30 \text{ g} = 4.30 \times 10^3 \text{ mg AgCl}$$

The structural formulas for the compounds are:

Compound I:

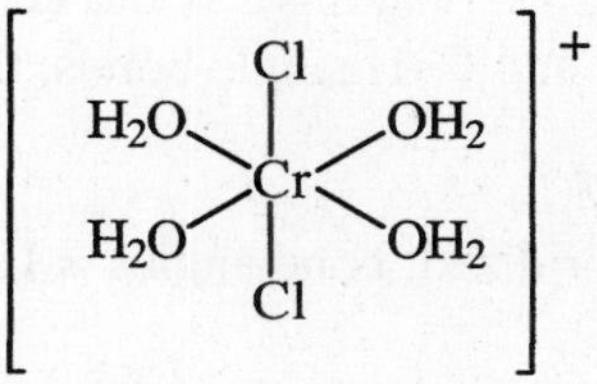

$$\left[\begin{array}{c} Cl \\ H_2O \diagdown \ \ \big| \ \ \diagup OH_2 \\ Cr \\ H_2O \diagup \ \ \big| \ \ \diagdown OH_2 \\ Cl \end{array} \right]^+ \ Cl \bullet 2\,H_2O \quad \text{or} \quad \left[\begin{array}{c} Cl \\ H_2O \diagdown \ \ \big| \ \ \diagup Cl \\ Cr \\ H_2O \diagup \ \ \big| \ \ \diagdown OH_2 \\ OH_2 \end{array} \right]^+ \ Cl \bullet 2\,H_2O$$

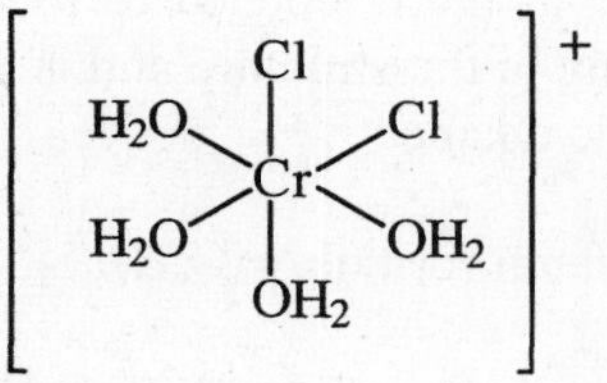

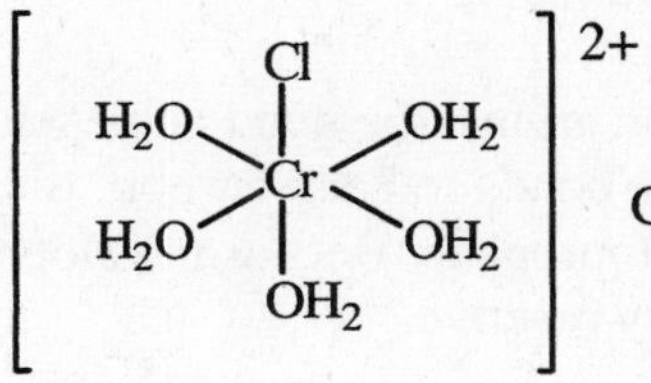

Compound II: Compound III:

$$\left[\begin{array}{c} Cl \\ H_2O \diagdown \ \ \big| \ \ \diagup OH_2 \\ Cr \\ H_2O \diagup \ \ \big| \ \ \diagdown OH_2 \\ OH_2 \end{array} \right]^{2+} \ Cl_2 \bullet H_2O \qquad \left[\begin{array}{c} OH_2 \\ H_2O \diagdown \ \ \big| \ \ \diagup OH_2 \\ Cr \\ H_2O \diagup \ \ \big| \ \ \diagdown OH_2 \\ OH_2 \end{array} \right]^{3+} \ Cl_3$$

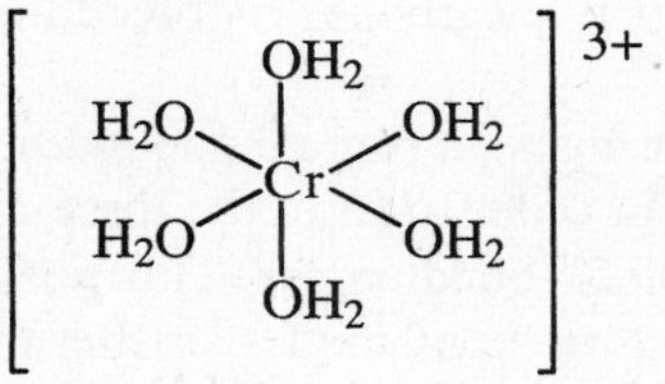

From Table 20.16 of the text, the violet compound will be the one that absorbs light with the shortest wavelength (highest energy). This should be compound III. H_2O is a stronger field ligand than Cl^-; compound III with the most coordinated H_2O molecules will have the largest d-orbital splitting and will absorb the higher energy light.

The magnetic properties would be the same for all three compounds. Cr^{3+} is a d^3 ion. With only three electrons present, all Cr^{3+} complexes will have three unpaired electrons, whether strong field or weak field. If Cr^{2+} was present with the d^4 configuration, then the magnetic properties might be different for the complexes and could be worth examining.

CHAPTER TWENTY-TWO

ORGANIC AND BIOLOGICAL MOLECULES

For Review

1. A hydrocarbon is a compound composed of only carbon and hydrogen. A saturated hydrocarbon has only carbon-carbon single bonds in the molecule. An unsaturated hydrocarbon has one or more carbon-carbon multiple bonds, but may also contain carbon-carbon single bonds.

    An alkane is a saturated hydrocarbon composed of only C–C and C–H single bonds. Each carbon in an alkane is bonded to four other atoms (either C or H atoms). If the compound contains a ring in the structure and is composed of only C–C and C–H single bonds, then it is called a cyclic alkane.

    Alkanes: general formula = C_nH_{2n+2}; all carbons are sp^3 hybridized; bond angles = $109.5°$

    Cyclic alkanes: general formula C_nH_{2n} (if only one ring is present in the compound); all carbons are sp^3 hybridized; prefers $109.5°$ bond angles, but rings with three carbons or four carbons or five carbons are forced into bond angles less than $109.5°$.

    In cyclopropane, a ring compound made up of three carbon atoms, the bond angles are forced into $60°$ in order to form the three-carbon ring. With four bonds to each carbon, the carbons prefer $109.5°$ bond angles. This just can't happen for cyclopropane. Because cyclopropane is forced to form bond angles smaller than it prefers, it is very reactive.

    The same is true for cyclobutane. Cyclobutane is composed of a four-carbon ring. In order to form a ring compound with four carbons, the carbons in the ring are forced to form $90°$ bond angles; this is much smaller than the preferred $109.5°$ bond angles.

    Cyclopentane (five-carbon rings) also has bond angles slightly smaller than $109.5°$, but they are very close ($108°$), so cyclopentane is much more stable than cyclopropane or cyclobutane. For rings having six or more carbons, the observed bonds are all $109.5°$.

    Straight chain hydrocarbons just indicates that there is one chain of consecutively bonded C-atoms in the molecule. They are not in a straight line which infers $180°$ bond angles. The bond angles are the predicted $109.5°$.

    To determine the number of hydrogens bonded to the carbons in cyclic alkanes (or any alkane where they may have been omitted), just remember that each carbon has four bonds. In cycloalkanes, only the C–C bonds are shown. It is assumed you know that the remaining bonds on each carbon are C–H bonds. The number of C–H bonds is that number required to give the carbon four total bonds.

2.   Alkenes are unsaturated hydrocarbons that contain a carbon-carbon double bond. Carbon-carbon single bonds may also be present. Alkynes are unsaturated hydrocarbons that contain a carbon-carbon triple bond.

Alkenes: C_nH_{2n} is the general formula. The carbon atoms in the C=C bond exhibit 120° bond angles. The double-bonded carbon atoms are sp^2 hybridized. The three sp^2 hybrid orbitals form three sigma bonds to the attached atoms. The unhybridized p atomic orbital on each sp^2 hybridized carbon overlap side to side to form the π bond in the double bond. Because the p orbitals must overlap parallel to each other, there is no rotation in the double bond (this is true whenever π bonds are present). See Figure 22.7 for the bonding in the simplest alkene, C_2H_4.

Alkynes: C_nH_{2n-2} is the general formula. The carbon atoms in the C≡C bond exhibit 180° bond angles. The triple bonded carbons are sp hybridized. The two sp hybrid orbitals go to form the two sigma bonds to the attached atoms. The two unhybridized p atomic orbitals overlap with two unhybridized p atomic orbitals on the other carbon in the triple bond, forming two π bonds. If the z-axis is the internuclear axis, then one π bond would form by parallel overlap of p_y orbitals on each carbon and the other π bond would form by parallel overlap of p_x orbitals. As is the case with alkenes, alkynes have restricted rotation due to the π bonds. See Figure 22.10 for the bonding in the simplest alkyne, C_2H_2.

Any time a multiple bond or a ring structure is added to a hydrocarbon, two hydrogens are lost from the general formula. The general formula for a hydrocarbon having one double bond and one ring structure would lose four hydrogens from the alkane general formula. The general formula would be C_nH_{2n-2}.

3.   Aromatic hydrocarbons are a special class of unsaturated hydrocarbons based on the benzene ring. Benzene has the formula C_6H_6. It is a planar molecule (all atoms are in the same plane). The bonding in benzene is discussed in detail in section 9.5 of the text. Figures 9.46, 9.47, and 9.48 detail the bonding in benzene.

C_6H_6, has 6(4) + 6(1) = 30 valence electrons. The two resonance Lewis structures for benzene are:

These are abbreviated as:

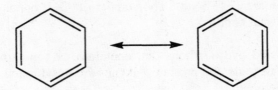

Each carbon in benzene is attached to three other atoms; it exhibits trigonal planar geometry with 120° bond angles. Each carbon is sp^2 hybridized. The sp^2 hybrid orbitals go to form the three sigma bonds to each carbon. The unhybridized p atomic orbital on each carbon overlap side to side with unhybridized p orbitals on adjacent carbons to form the π bonds. All six of the carbons in the six-membered ring have one unhybridized p atomic orbital. All six of the unhybridized p orbitals ovlerlap side to side to give a ring of electron density above and below the six-membered ring of benzene.

The six π electrons in the π bonds in benzene can roam about above and below the entire ring surface; these π electrons are delocalized. This is important because all six carbon-carbon bonds in benzene are equivalent in length and strength. The Lewis structures say something different (three of the bonds are single and three of the bonds are double). This is not correct. To explain the equivalent bonds, the π bonds can't be situated between two carbon atoms as is the case in alkenes and alkynes; that is, the π bonds can't be localized. Instead, the six π electrons can roam about over a much larger area; they are delocalized over the entire surface of the molecule. All this is implied in the following shorthand notation for benzene.

4.   A short summary of the nomenclature rules for alkanes, alkenes, and alkynes follow. See the text for details.

a.   Memorize the base names of C_1–C_{10} carbon chains (see Table 22.1). When the C_1–C_{10} carbon chains are named as a substituent, change the –ane suffix to–yl.

b.   Memorize the additional substituent groups in Table 22.2.

c.   Names are based on the longest continuous carbon chain in the molecule. Alkanes use the suffix –ane, alkenes end in –ene, and alkynes end in –yne.

d.   To indicate the position of a branch or substituent, number the longest chain of carbons consecutively in order to give the lowest numbers to the substituents or branches. Identify the number of the carbon that the substituent is bonded to by writing the number in front of the name of the substituent.

e.   Name substituents in alphabetical order.

f.   Use a prefix (di–, tri–, tetra–, etc.) to indicate the number of a substituent if more than one is present. Note that if, for example, three methyl substituent groups are bonded to carbons on the longest chain, use the tri-prefix but also include three numbers indicating the positions of the methyl groups on the longest chain. Also note that prefixes like di–, tri–, tetra–, etc. are ignored when naming substituent groups in alphabetical order.

g.   A cyclic hydrocarbon is designated by the prefix cyclo–.

h.   For alkenes and alkynes, the position of the double or triple bond is indicated with a number placed directly in front of the base name of the longest chain. If more than one multiple bonds is present, the number of multiple bonds is indicted in the base name using the prefix di–, tri–, tetra–, etc., but also a number for the position of each multiple bond is indicated in front of the base name. When numbering the longest chain, if double or triple bonds are present, give the multiple bonds the lowest number possible (not the substitutent groups).

This is a start. As you will find out, there are many interesting situations that can come up which aren't covered by these rules. We will discuss them as they come up.

For aromatic nomenclature rules, reference section 22.3.

The errors in the names are discussed below.

a.   The longest chain gives the base name.

b.   The suffix –ane indicates only alkanes. Alkenes and alkynes have different suffixes as do other "types" of organic compounds.

c.   Smallest numbers are used to indicate the position of substituents.

d.   Numbers are required to indicate the positions of double or triple bonds.

e.   Multiple bonds (double or triple) get the lowest number.

f.   The term ortho– in benzene nomenclature indicates substituents in the benzene ring bonded to C–1 and C–2. The term meta– describes C–1 and C–3 substituent groups while para– is used for C–1 and C– substituent groups.

5.   See Table 22.4 for the types of bonds and atoms in the functional groups listed in a-h of this question. Examples are also listed in Table 22.4.

a.   Halohydrocarbons: name the halogens as substituents, adding o to the end of the name of the halogen. Assuming no multiple bonds, all carbons and the halogens are sp^3 hybridized because the bond angles are all 109.5°.

b.   Alcohols: –ol suffix; the oxygen is sp^3 hybridized because the preldicted bond angle about O is 109.5°.

c. Ethers: name the two R-groups bonded to O as substituent groups (in alphabetical order), and then end the name in ether. These are the common nomenclature rules for ethers. The oxygen in an ether is sp^3 hybridized due to the predicted 109.5° bond angle.

d. Aldehydes: –al suffix; the carbon doubly bonded to oxygen is sp^2 hybridized because this carbon exhibits 120° bond angles. The oxygen in the double bond is also sp^2 hybridized because it has three effective pairs of electrons around it (two lone pairs and the bonded carbon atom).

e. Ketones: –one suffix; the carbon doubly bonded to oxygen is sp^2 hybridized because the bond angles about this carbon are 120°. The O in the double bond is sp^2 hybridized.

f. Carboxylic acids: –oic acid is added to the end of the base name; the carbon doubly bonded to oxygen is sp^2 hybridized (120° bond angles) and the oxygen with two single bonds is sp^3 hybridized (predicted 109.5° bond angles). The oxygen in the double bond is sp^2 hybridized.

g. Esters: the alcohol part of ester is named as a substituent using the –yl suffix; the carboxylic acid part of the ester gives the base name using the suffix –oate. In the common nomenclature rules, the carboxylic acid part is named using common names for the carboxyclic acid ending in the suffix –ate. The bonding and bond angles are the same as discussed previously with carboxylic acids.

h. Amines: similar to ethers, the R-groups are named as substituent groups (in alphabetical order), and then end the name in amine (common rules). The nitrogen in amines is sp^3 hybridized due to predicted 109.5 ° bond angles.

The difference between a primary, secondary, and tertiary alcohol is the number of R-groups (other carbons) that are bonded to the carbon with the OH group. Primary: 1 R-group; secondary: 2 R-groups; tertiary: 3 R-groups.

A number is required to indicate the location of a functional group only when that functional group can be present in more than one position in the longest chain. Hydrohalogens, alcohols, and ketones require a number. The aldeyde group must be on C–1 in the longest chain, and the carboxylic acid group must also be on C–1; no numbers are used for aldehyde and carboxylic acid nomenclature. In addition, no numbers are used for nomenclature of simple ethers, simple esters, and simple amines.

carboxylic acid   aldehyde

:O: :O:

‖   ‖

R——C——Ö——H   R——C——H

RCOOH   RCHO

The R designation may be a hydrogen, but is usually a hydrocarbon fragment. The major point in the R-group designation is that if the R-group is a hydrocarbon fragment, then the first atom in the R-group is a carbon atom. What the R-group has after the first carbon is not important to the functional group designation.

6.   Resonance: All atoms are in the same position. Only the positions of π electrons are
          different.

          Isomerism: Atoms are in different locations in space.

          Isomers are distinctly different substances. Resonance is the use of more than one Lewis
          structure to describe the bonding in a single compound. Resonance structures are **not** isomers.

          Structural isomers: Same formula but different bonding, either in the kinds of bonds present
          or the way in which the bonds connect atoms to each other.

          Geometrical isomers: Same formula and same bonds, but differ in the arrangement of atoms
          in space about a rigid bond or ring.

          To distinguish isomers from molecules that differ by rotations about some bonds, name them.
          If two structures have different names, they are different isomers (different compounds). If
          the two structures have the same name, then they are the same compound. The two com-
          pounds may look different, but if they have the same names, they are the same compounds
          that only differ by some rotations about single bonds in the molecule.

          Two isomers of C_4H_8 are:

          $H_2C = CHCH_2CH_3$

          1-butene   cyclobutane (2 hydrogens
                                      are bonded to each carbon)

          For cis-trans isomerism (geometric isomerism), you must have at least two carbons with
          restricted rotation (double bond or ring) that each have two different groups bonded to it. The
          cis isomer will generally have the largest groups bonded to the two carbons with restricted
          rotation on the same side of the double bond or ring. The trans isomer generally has the
          largest groups bonded to the two carbons with restricted rotation on opposite sides of the
          double bond or ring.

          For alcohols and ethers, consider the formula C_3H_8O. An alcohol and an ether that have this
          formula are:

          OH
          |
          $CH_3CH_2CH_2$ $CH_3 — O — CH_2CH_3$

          alcohol   ether

          For aldehydes and ketones, consider the formula C_4H_8O. An aldehyde and a ketone that have
          this formula are:

$$O$$
$$\parallel$$
$$CH_3CH_2CH_2CH$$

aldehyde

$$O$$
$$\parallel$$
$$CH_3CH_2CCH_3$$

ketone

Esters are structural isomers of carboxylic acids. An ester and a carboxylic acid having the formula $C_2H_4O_2$ are:

$$O$$
$$\parallel$$
$$CH_3COH$$

carboxylic acid

$$O$$
$$\parallel$$
$$CH_3\!-\!\!O\!-\!\!CH$$

ester

Optical isomers: The same formula and the same bonds, but the compounds are nonsuperimposable mirror images of each other. The key to identifying optical isomerism in organic compounds is to look for a tetrahedral carbon atom with four different substituents attached. When four different groups are bonded to a carbon atom, then a nonsuperimposable mirror image does exist.

1–bromo–1–chloroethane

1–bromo–2–chloroethane

$$\begin{array}{c} Cl \\ | \\ Br\!-\!\!\overset{*}{C}\!-\!\!CH_3 \\ | \\ H \end{array}$$

$$\begin{array}{cc} H & Cl \\ | & | \\ Br\!-\!\!C\!-\!\!C\!-\!\!H \\ | & | \\ H & H \end{array}$$

The carbon with the asterisk has 4 different groups bonded to it (1–Br; 2–Cl; 3–CH₃; 4–H). This compound has a nonsuperimposable mirror image.

Neither of the two carbons have four different groups bonded to it The mirror image of this molecule will be superimposable (it does not exhibit optical isomerism).

7. Hydrocarbons only have nonpolar C–C and C–H bonds; they are always nonpolar compounds having only London dispersion forces. The strength of the London dispersion (LD) forces is related to size (molar mass). The larger the compound, the stronger the LD forces. Because n-heptane (C_7H_{16}) is a larger molecule than n-butane (C_4H_{10}), n-heptane has the stronger LD forces holding the molecule together in the liquid phase and will have a higher boiling point.

Another factor affecting the strength of intermolecular forces is the shape of the molecule. The strength of LD forces also depends on the surface area contact among neighboring molecules. As branching increases, there is less surface area contact among neighboring molecules, leading to weaker LD forces and lower boiling points.

All the function groups in Table 22.4 have a very electronegative atom bonded to the carbon chain in the compound. This creates bond dipoles in the molecule leading to a polar molecule which exhibits additional dipole-dipole forces. Most of the functional groups have carbon-oxygen polar bonds leading to a polar molecule. In halohydrocarbons, the polar bond is C–X where X is a halogen. In amines, the polar bond is C–N. Note that CF_4, even though it has 4 polar C–F bonds, is nonpolar. The bond dipoles are situated about carbon so they all cancel each other out. This type of situation is atypical in hydrocarbons.

Alcohols, carboxylic acids and amines exibit a special type of dipole force. That force is the relatively strong hydrogen-bonding interaction. These compounds have an O–H or N–H bond, which is a requirement for H–bonding.

Reference the isomers of C_3H_8O in Review question 6. The alcohol can H–bond, the ether cannot (no O–H bonds exist in the ether). Because the alcohol has the ability to H–bond, it will have a significantly higher boiling point than the ether.

The same holds true for carboxylic acids and esters which are structural isomers. Even though the isomers have the same formula, the bonds are arranged differently. In a carboxylic acid, there is an O–H bond, so it can H–bond. The ester does not have an O–H bond. Therefore, carboxylic acids boil at a higher temperature than same size esters.

$CH_3CH_2CH_3$	CH_3CH_2OH	$CH_3\overset{\displaystyle O}{\overset{\|}{C}}H$	$H\!-\!\overset{\displaystyle O}{\overset{\|}{C}}\!-\!OH$
LD only	LD + H-bonding	LD + dipole	LD + H-bonding + dipole

Because these compounds are about the same size (molar mass: 44-46 g/mol), they all have about the same strength LD forces. However, three of the compounds have additional intermolecular forces, hence they boil at a higher (and different) temperature than the nonpolar $CH_3CH_2CH_3$. Among the polar compounds; the two compounds which H–bond will have higher boiling points than the aldehyde. Between the two compounds which can H–bond, the carboxylic acid wins out because it has additional dipole forces from the polar C=O bond. The alcohol does not have this. The order of boiling points is:

$$CH_3CH_2CH_3 < CH_3CHO < CH_3CH_2OH < HCOOH$$
lowest boiling point   highest boiling point

8.   Substitution: An atom or group is replaced by another atom or group.

e.g., H in benzene is replaced by Cl. $C_6H_6 + Cl_2 \xrightarrow{\text{catalyst}} C_6H_5Cl + HCl$

Addition: Atoms or groups are added to a molecule.

e.g., Cl_2 adds to ethene. $CH_2=CH_2 + Cl_2 \rightarrow CH_2Cl - CH_2Cl$

To react Cl_2 with an alkane, ultraviolet light must be present to catalyze the reaction. To react Cl_2 with benzene, a special iron catalyst is needed. Its formula is $FeCl_3$. For both of these hydrocarbons, if no catalyst is present, there is no reaction. This is not the case for reacting Cl_2 with alkenes or alkynes. In these two functional groups, the π electrons situated above and below the carbon-carbon bond are easily attacked by substances that are attracted to the negative charge of the π electrons. . Hence, the π bonds in alkenes and alkynes are why these are more reactive. Note that even though benzene has π electrons, it does not want to disrupt the delocalized π bonding. When Cl_2 reacts with benzene, it is the C–H bond that changes, not the π bonding.

A combustion reaction just means reacting something with oxygen (O_2) gas. For organic compounds made up of C, H, and perhaps O, the assumed products are $CO_2(g)$ and $H_2O(g)$.

a. $CH_2=CH_2 + H_2O \xrightarrow{H^+}$

b. $CH_3CH_2 \xrightarrow{oxidation} CH_3CH \xrightarrow{oxidation} CH_3C-OH$ (with OH and O groups shown)

c. $CH_3CHCH_3 \xrightarrow{oxidation} CH_3CCH_3$ (with OH and O groups shown)

d. $CH_3-O-H + HO-CCH_3 \xrightarrow{H^+} CH_3-O-CCH_3 + H_2O$

9.   a.   Addition polymer: a polymer that forms by adding monomer units together (usually by reacting double bonds). Teflon, polyvinyl chloride and polyethylene are examples of addition polymers.

b.   Condensation polymer: a polymer that forms when two monomers combine by eliminating a small molecule (usually H_2O or HCl). Nylon and Dacron are examples of condensation polymers.

c.   Copolymer: a polymer formed from more than one type of monomer. Nylon and Dacron are copolymers.

d.   Homopolymer: a polymer formed from the polymerization of only one type of monomer. Polyethylene, Teflon, and polystyrene are examples of homopolymers.

e. Polyester: a condensation polymer whose monomers link together by formation of the ester functional group.

$$\text{amide} = \quad R\!-\!\!-\!\!-\!\!\overset{\displaystyle \overset{O}{\|}}{C}\!-\!\!-\!\!-\!\!\overset{\displaystyle \overset{H}{|}}{N}\!-\!\!-\!\!-R'$$

f. Polyamide: a condensation polymer whose monomers link together by formation of the amide functional group. Nylon is a polyamide as are proteins in the human body.

$$\text{amide} = \quad R\!-\!\!-\!\!-\!\!\overset{\displaystyle \overset{O}{\|}}{C}\!-\!\!-\!\!-\!\!\overset{\displaystyle \overset{H}{|}}{N}\!-\!\!-\!\!-R$$

A thermoplastic polymer can be remelted; a thermoset polymer cannot be softened once it is formed.

The physical properties depend on the strengths of the intermolecular forces among adjacent polymer chains. These forces are affected by chain length and extent of branching: longer chains = stronger intermolecular forces; branched chains = weaker intermolecular forces.

Crosslinking makes a polymer more rigid by bonding adjacent polymer chains together.

The regular arrangement of the methyl groups in the isotactic chains allows adjacent polymer chains to pack together very closely. This leads to stronger intermolecular forces among chains as compared to atactic polypropylene where the packing of polymer chains is not as efficient.

Polyvinyl chloride contains some polar C–Cl bonds compared to only nonpolar C–H bonds in polyethylene. The stronger intermolecular forces would be found in polyvinyl chloride since there are dipole-dipole forces present in PVC that are not present in polyethylene.

10. These questions are meant to guide you as you read section 22.6 on Natural Polymers. The three specific natural polymers discussed are proteins, carbohydrates, and nucleic acids, all of which are essential polymers found and utilized by our bodies. Read the questions to familiarize yourself with the important terms and concepts covered in section 22.6, and then review the Natural Polymer section to help you answer these questions.

Questions

1.   a. 1-sec-butylpropane   b. 4-methylhexane

$$CH_3CH\overset{\overset{\displaystyle CH_2CH_2CH_3}{|}}{}CH_2CH_3$$

$$CH_3CH_2CH_2CH\overset{\overset{\displaystyle CH_3}{|}}{}CH_2CH_3$$

3-methylhexane is correct.   3-methylhexane is correct.

c. 2-ethylpentane

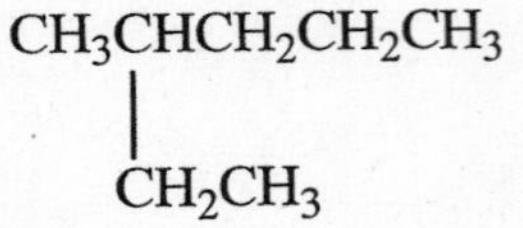

$$CH_3CHCH_2CH_2CH_3$$
$$|$$
$$CH_2CH_3$$

3-methylhexane is correct.

d. 1-ethyl-1-methylbutane

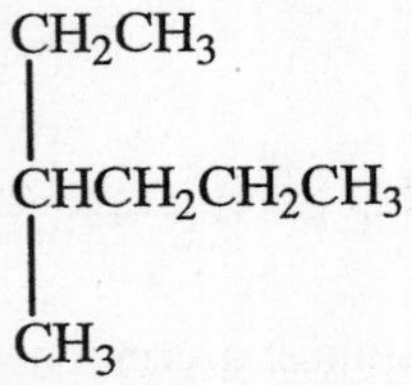

$$CH_2CH_3$$
$$|$$
$$CHCH_2CH_2CH_3$$
$$|$$
$$CH_3$$

3-methylhexane is correct.

e. 3-methylhexane

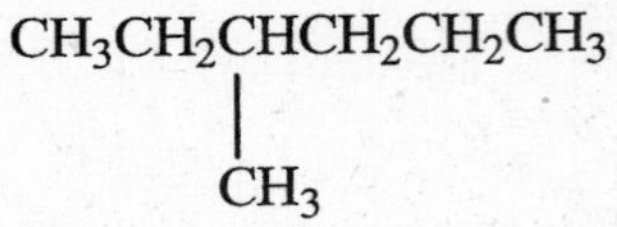

$$CH_3CH_2CHCH_2CH_2CH_3$$
$$|$$
$$CH_3$$

f. 4-ethylpentane

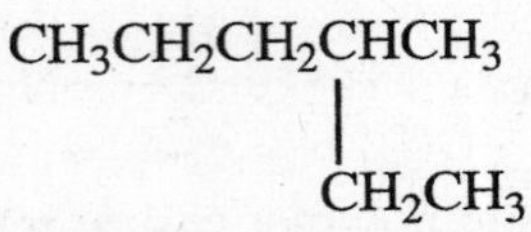

$$CH_3CH_2CH_2CHCH_3$$
$$|$$
$$CH_2CH_3$$

3-methylhexane is correct.

All six of these compounds are the same. They only differ from each other by rotations about one or more carbon-carbon single bonds. Only one isomer of C_7H_{16} is present in all of these names, 3-methylhexane.

2.   a. C_6H_{12} can exhibit structural, geometric, and optical isomerism. Two structural isomers (of many) are:

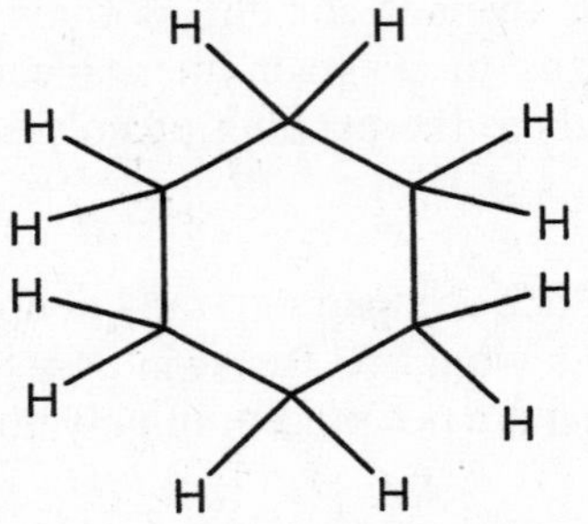

cyclohexane

$$CH_2=CHCH_2CH_2CH_2CH_3$$

1-hexene

The structural isomer 2-hexene (plus others) exhibits geometric isomerism.

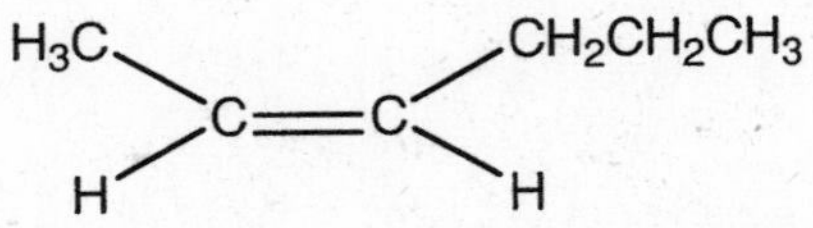

cis

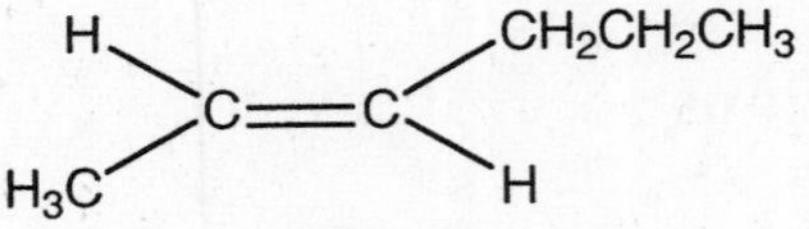

trans

The structural isomer 3-methyl-1-pentene exhibits optical isomerism (the asterisk marks the chiral carbon).

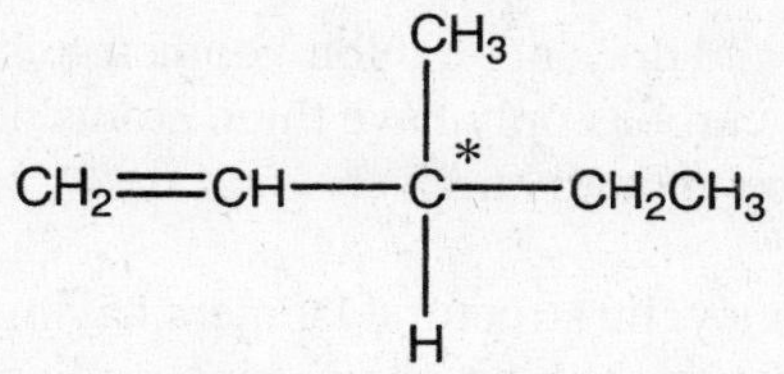

$$CH_2\!\!=\!\!CH\!\!-\!\!\overset{\displaystyle CH_3}{\underset{\displaystyle H}{\overset{|}{\underset{|}{C^*}}}}\!\!-\!\!CH_2CH_3$$

Optical isomerism is also possible with some of the cyclobutane and cyclopropane structural isomers.

b. $C_5H_{12}O$ can exhibit structural and optical isomerism. Two structural isomers (of many) are:

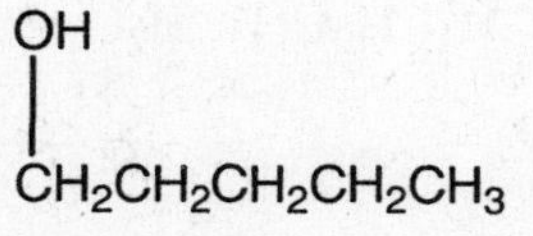

$$\overset{\displaystyle OH}{\underset{}{\overset{|}{}}}$$
$$CH_2CH_2CH_2CH_2CH_3 \qquad\qquad CH_3\!\!-\!\!O\!\!-\!\!CH_2CH_2CH_2CH_3$$

1-pentanol 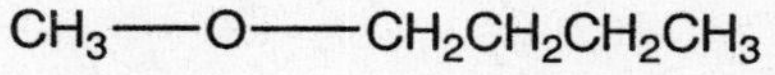   butyl methyl ether

Two of the optically active isomers having a $C_5H_{12}O$ formula are:

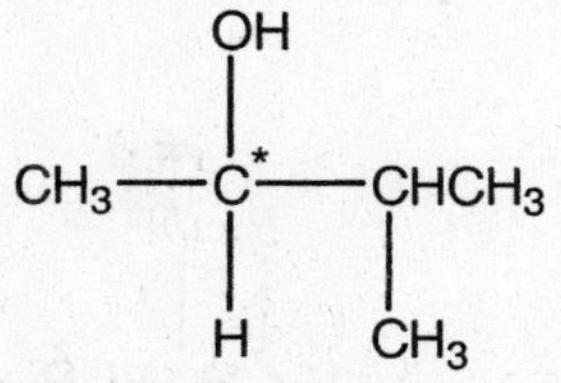

$$CH_3\!\!-\!\!\overset{\displaystyle OH}{\underset{\displaystyle H}{\overset{|}{\underset{|}{C^*}}}}\!\!-\!\!\overset{}{\underset{\displaystyle CH_3}{\overset{}{\underset{|}{CH}}}}CH_3 \qquad\qquad CH_3\!\!-\!\!\overset{\displaystyle OH}{\underset{\displaystyle H}{\overset{|}{\underset{|}{C^*}}}}\!\!-\!\!CH_2CH_2CH_3$$

3-methyl-2-butanol 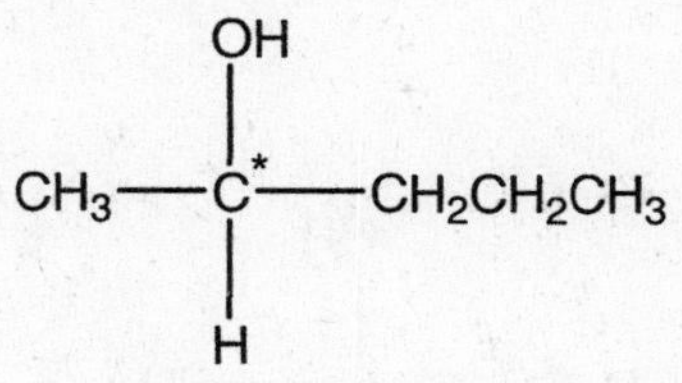   2-pentanol

No isomers of $C_5H_{12}O$ exhibit geometric isomerism because no double bonds or ring structures are possible with 12 hydrogens present.

c. We will assume the structure having the $C_6H_4Br_2$ formula is a benzene ring derivative. $C_6H_4Br_2$ exhibits structural isomerism only. Two structural isomers of $C_6H_4Br_2$ are:

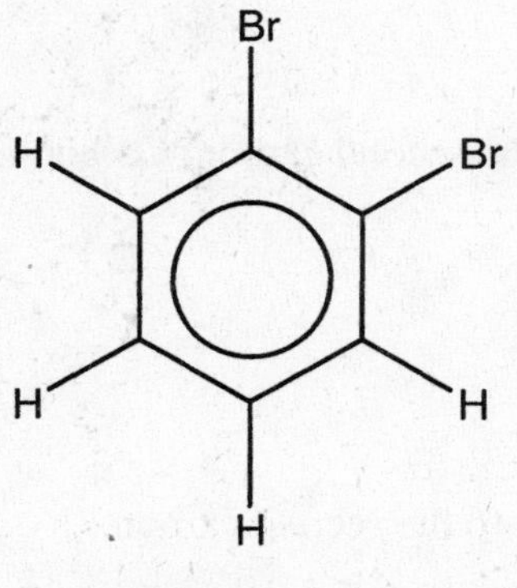

o-dibromobenzene
or 1,2-dibromobenzene   m-dibromobenzene
or 1,3-dibromobenzene

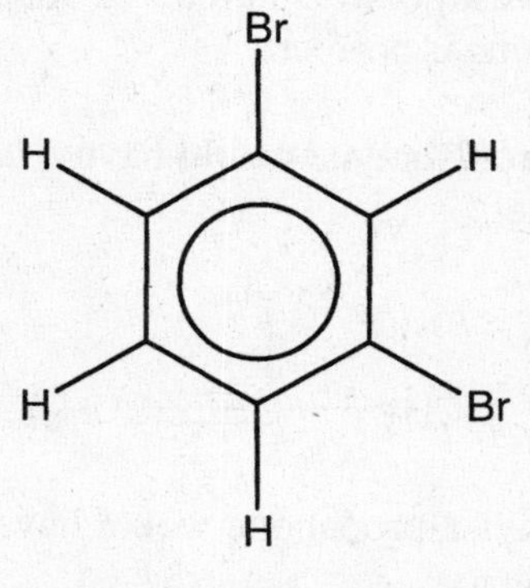

The benzene ring is planar and does not exhibit geometric isomerism. It also does not exhibit optical activity. All carbons only have three atoms bonded to them; it is impossible for benzene to be optically active.

Note: there are possible noncyclic structural isomers having the formula $C_6H_4Br_2$. These noncyclic isomers can, in theory, exhibit geometrical and optical isomerism. But they are beyond the introduction to organic chemistry given in this text.

3. a.

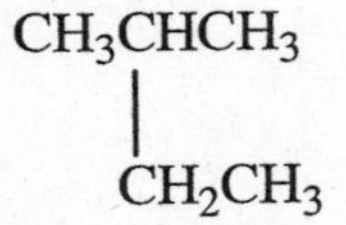

CH₃CHCH₃
  |
  CH₂CH₃

The longest chain is 4 carbons long. The correct name is 2-methylbutane.

b.

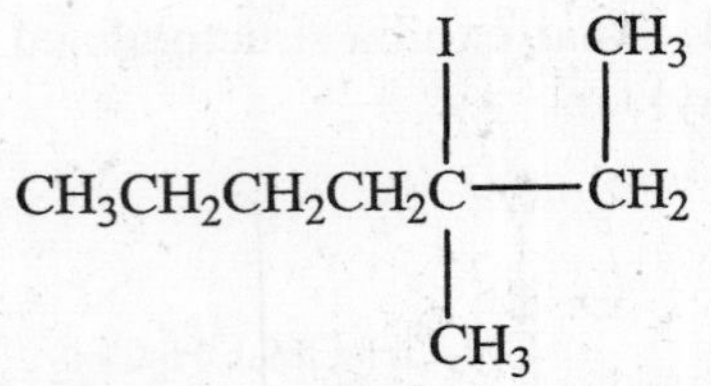

          I   CH₃
          | |
CH₃CH₂CH₂CH₂C——CH₂
          |
          CH₃

The longest chain is 7 carbons long and we would start the numbering system at the other end for lowest possible numbers. The correct name is 3-iodo-3-methyl-heptane.

c.

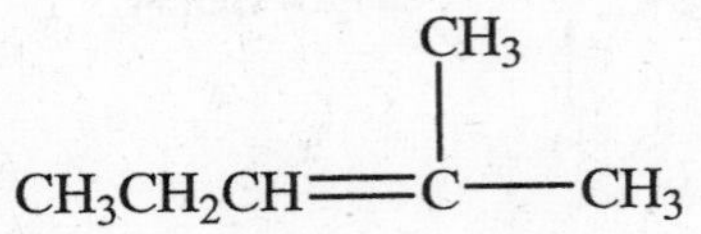

                CH₃
                |
CH₃CH₂CH═══C——CH₃

This compound cannot exhibit cis–trans isomerism since one of the double bonded carbons has the same two groups (CH₃) attached. The numbering system should also start at the other end to give the double bond the lowest possible number. 2-methyl-2-pentene is correct.

d.

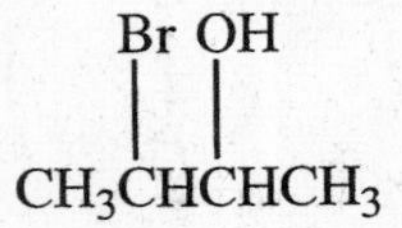

Br OH
 | |
CH₃CHCHCH₃

The OH functional group gets the lowest number. 3-bromo-2-butanol is correct.

4. a. 2-chloro-2-butyne would have 5 bonds to the second carbon. Carbon never expands its octet.

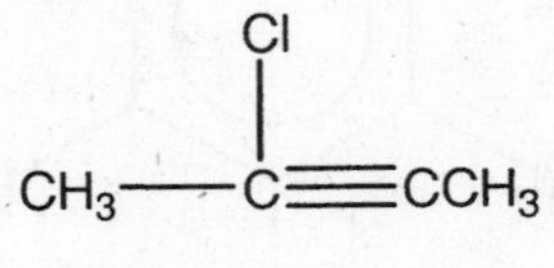

              Cl
              |
CH₃——C≡≡≡CCH₃

b. 2-methyl-2-propanone would have 5 bonds to the second carbon.

              O
              ‖
CH₃——C——CH₃
              |
              CH₃

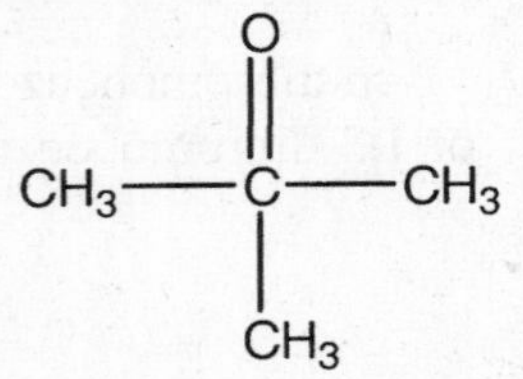

c. Carbon-1 in 1,1-dimethylbenzene would have 5 bonds.

d. You cannot have an aldehyde functional group off a middle carbon in a chain. Aldehyde groups:

can only be at the beginning and/or the end of a chain of carbon atoms.

e. You cannot have a carboxylic acid group off a middle carbon in a chain. Carboxylic groups:

must be at the beginning and/or the end of a chain of carbon atoms.

f. In cyclobutanol, the 1 and 5 positions refer to the same carbon atom. 5,5-dibromo-1-cyclobutanol would have five bonds to carbon-1. This is impossible; carbon never expands its octet.

5.   Hydrocarbons are nonpolar substances exhibiting only London dispersion forces. Size and shape are the two most important structural features relating to the strength of London dispersion forces. For size, the bigger the molecule (the larger the molar mass), the stronger the London dispersion forces and the higher the boiling point. For shape, the more branching present in a compound, the weaker the London dispersion forces and the lower the boiling point.

6.   In order to hydrogen bond, the compound must have at least one N–H, O–H or H–F covalent bond in the compound. In Table 22.4, alcohols and carboxylic acids have an O-H covalent bond so they can hydrogen bond. In addition, primary and secondary amines have at least one N-H covalent bond so they can hydrogen bond.

CH_2CF_2 cannot form hydrogen bonds because it has no hydrogens covalently bonded to the fluorine atoms.

7. The amide functional group is: 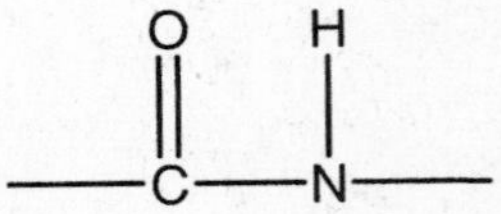

When the amine end of one amino acid reacts with the carboxylic acid end of another amino acid, the two amino acids link together by forming an amide functional group. A polypeptide has many amino acids linked together, with each linkage made by the formation of an amide functional group. Because all linkages result in the presence of the amide functional group, the resulting polymer is called a polyamide. The correct order of strength is:

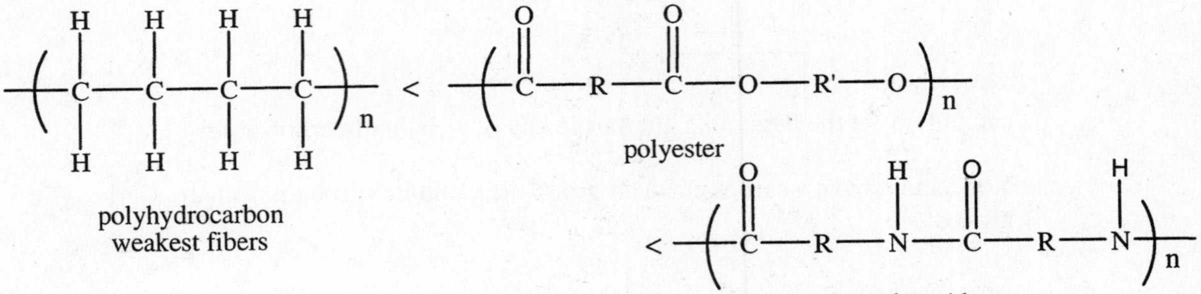

polyhydrocarbon
weakest fibers

polyamide
strongest fibers

The difference in strength is related to the types of intermolecular forces present. All of these types of polymers have London dispersion forces. However, the polar ester group in polyesters and the polar amide group in polya mides give rise to additional dipole forces. The polyamide has the ability to form relatively strong hydrogen bonding interactions, hence why it would form the strongest fibers.

8. a. 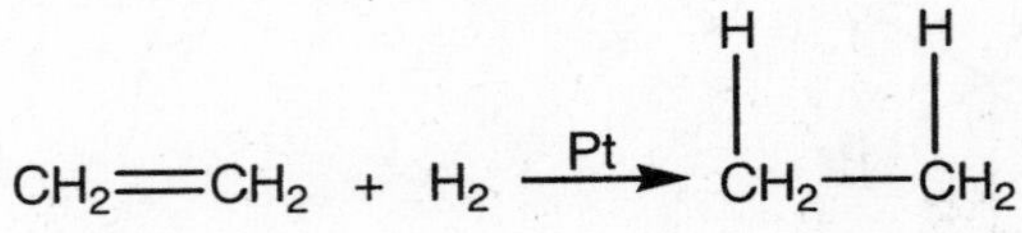

ethene ethane

b. 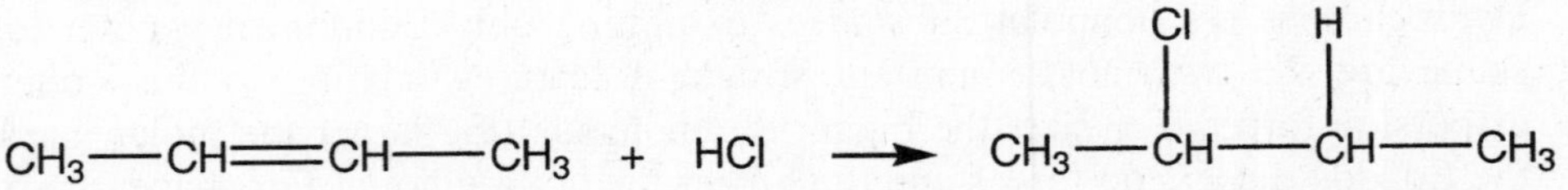

2-butene (cis or trans) 2-chlorobutane

c. 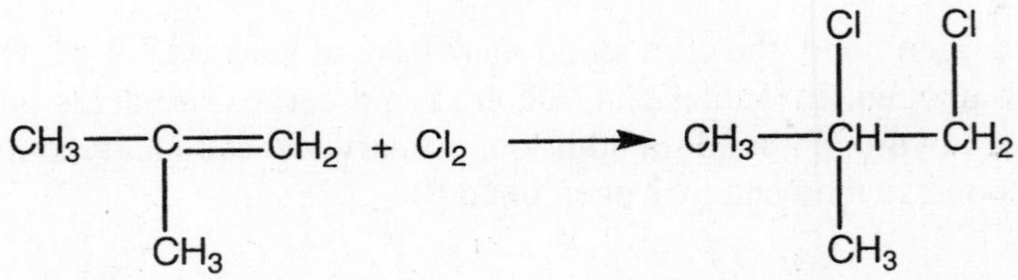

2-methyl-1-propene (or 2-methylpropene)

1,2-dichloro-2-methylpropane

d.

$$H-C\equiv C-H \ + \ 2\,Br_2 \ \longrightarrow \ \begin{array}{c} Br \quad Br \\ | \quad\quad | \\ HC-CH \\ | \quad\quad | \\ Br \quad Br \end{array}$$

ethyne   1,1,2,2-tetrabromoethane

or

$$H-C=C-H \ + \ Br_2 \ \longrightarrow \ \begin{array}{c} Br \quad Br \\ | \quad\quad | \\ HC-CH \\ | \quad\quad | \\ Br \quad Br \end{array}$$

1,2-dibromoethene   1,1,2,2-tetrabromoethane

e.

benzene $+ \ Cl_2 \ \xrightarrow{\ FeCl_3\ }$ chlorobenzene

f. $CH_3CH_3 \ \xrightarrow[500°C]{Cr_2O_3} \ CH_2{=}CH_2 \ + \ H_2$

ethane   ethene

or $\begin{array}{c} OH \quad\ H \\ | \quad\quad | \\ CH_2-CH_2 \end{array} \ \xrightarrow{\ H^+\ } \ CH_2{=}CH_2 \ + \ H_2O$

ethanol   ethene

This reaction is not explicitly discussed in the text. This is the reverse of the reaction used to produce alcohols. This reaction is reversible. Which organic substance dominates is determined by LeChatelier's principle. For example, if the alcohol is wanted, then water is removed as reactants are converted to products, driving the reaction to produce more water (and more alcohol).

9.   a. $CH_2\!=\!CH_2$ + H_2O $\xrightarrow{H^+}$ $CH_2\!-\!CH_2$ (with OH and H substituents)   1° alcohol

b. $CH_2CH\!=\!CH_2$ + H_2O $\xrightarrow{H^+}$ $CH_2CH\!-\!CH_2$ (with OH and H substituents)   2° alcohol
major product

c. $CH_3C\!=\!CH_2$ (with CH_3 branch) + H_2O $\xrightarrow{H^+}$ $CH_3C\!-\!CH_2$ (with OH, H, and CH_3 substituents)   3° alcohol
major product

d. CH_3CH_2OH $\xrightarrow{oxidation}$ $CH_3\overset{O}{\overset{\|}{C}}H$ aldehyde

e. $CH_3\overset{OH}{\overset{|}{C}}HCH_3$ $\xrightarrow{oxidation}$ $CH_3\overset{O}{\overset{\|}{C}}CH_3$ ketone

f. $CH_3CH_2CH_2OH$ $\xrightarrow{oxidation}$ $CH_3CH_2\overset{O}{\overset{\|}{C}}\!-\!OH$ carboxylic acid

or

$CH_3CH_2\overset{O}{\overset{\|}{C}}H$ $\xrightarrow{oxidation}$ $CH_3CH_2\overset{O}{\overset{\|}{C}}\!-\!OH$

g. CH_3OH + $HO\overset{O}{\overset{\|}{C}}CH_3$ $\xrightarrow{H^+}$ $CH_3\!-\!O\!-\!\overset{O}{\overset{\|}{C}}CH_3$ + H_2O ester

10.   Polystyrene is an addition polymer formed from the monomer styrene.

n CH$_2$══CH ⟶ ─(─CH$_2$CHCH$_2$CH─)$_n$─

a.   Syndiotactic polystyrene has all of the benzene ring side groups aligned on alternate sides of the chain. This ordered alignment of the side groups allows individual polymer chains of polystyrene to pack together efficiently, maximizing the London dispersion forces. Stronger London dispersion forces translates into stronger polymers.

b.   By copolymerizing with butadiene, double bonds exist in the carbon backbone of the polymer. These double bonds can react with sulfur to form crosslinks (bonds) between individual polymer chains. The crosslinked polymer is stronger.

c.   The longer the chain of polystyrene, the stronger the London dispersion forces between polymer chains.

d.   In linear (vs. branched) polystyrene, chains pack together more efficiently resulting in stronger London dispersion forces.

11.   a.   A polyester forms when an alcohol functional group reacts with a carboxylic acid functional group. The monomer for a homopolymer polyester must have an alcohol functional group and a carboxylic acid functional group present in the structure.

b.   A polyamide forms when an amine functional group reacts with a carboxylic acid functional group. For a copolymer polyamide, one monomer would have at least two amine functional groups present and the other monomer would have at least two carboxylic acid functional groups present. For polymerization to occur, each monomer must have two reactive functional groups present.

c.   To form an addition polymer, a carbon-carbon double bond must be present. To form a polyester, the monomer would need the alcohol and carboxylic acid functional groups present. To form a polyamide, the monomer would need the amine and carboxylic acid functional groups present. The two possibilities are for the monomer to have a carbon-carbon double bond, an alcohol functional group, and a carboxylic acid functional group present, or to have a carbon-carbon double bond, an amine functional group, and a carboxylic acid functional group present.

12.   Proteins are polymers made up of monomer units called amino acids. One of the functions of proteins is to provide structural integrity and strength for many types of tissues. In addition, proteins transport and store oxygen and nutrients, catalyze many reactions in the body, fight invasion by foreign objects, participate in the body's many regulatory systems, and transport electrons in the process of metabolizing nutrients.

Carbohydrate polymers, such as starch and cellulose, are composed of the monomer units called monosaccharides or simple sugars. Carbohydrates serve as a food source for most organisms.

Nucleic acids are polymers made up of monomer units called nucleotides. Nucleic acids store and transmit genetic information, and are also responsible for the synthesis of various proteins needed by a cell to carry out its life functions.

Exercises

Hydrocarbons

13.   i.

$$CH_3 — CH_2 — CH_2 — CH_2 — CH_2 — CH_3$$

ii.

$$
\begin{array}{c}
CH_3 \\
| \\
CH_3 — CH — CH_2 — CH_2 — CH_3
\end{array}
$$

iii.   iv.

$$
\begin{array}{c}
CH_3 \\
| \\
CH_3 — CH_2 — CH — CH_2 — CH_3
\end{array}
\qquad
\begin{array}{c}
CH_3 \\
| \\
CH_3 — C — CH_2 — CH_3 \\
| \\
CH_3
\end{array}
$$

v.

$$
\begin{array}{c}
CH_3 \quad CH_3 \\
| \qquad | \\
CH_3 — CH — CH — CH_3
\end{array}
$$

All other possibilities are identical to one of these five compounds.

14.   See Exercise 22.13 for the structures. The names of structures i - v respectively, are: hexane (or n-hexane), 2-methylpentane, 3-methylpentane, 2,2-dimethylbutane and 2,3-dimethylbutane.

15.   A difficult task in this problem is recognizing different compounds from compounds that differ by rotations about one or more C–C bonds (called conformations). The best way to distinguish different compounds from conformations is to name them. Different name = different compound; same name = same compound, so it is not an isomer, but instead, is a conformation.

a.

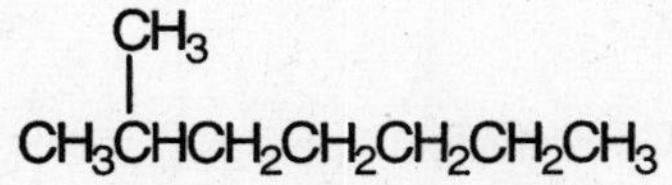

$$CH_3CHCH_2CH_2CH_2CH_2CH_3$$ with CH_3 above first CH

2-methylheptane

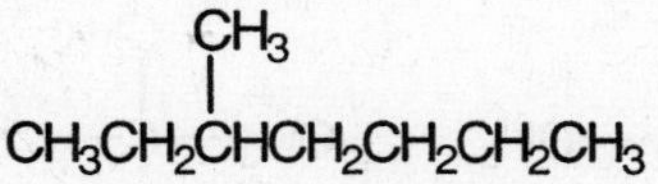

$$CH_3CH_2CHCH_2CH_2CH_2CH_3$$ with CH_3 above

3-methylheptane

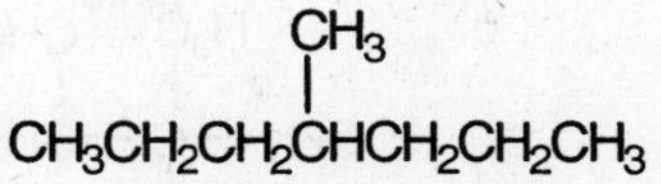

$$CH_3CH_2CH_2CHCH_2CH_2CH_3$$ with CH_3 above

4-methylheptane

b.

$$CH_3-C-C-CH_3$$ with CH_3 CH_3 above and CH_3 CH_3 below

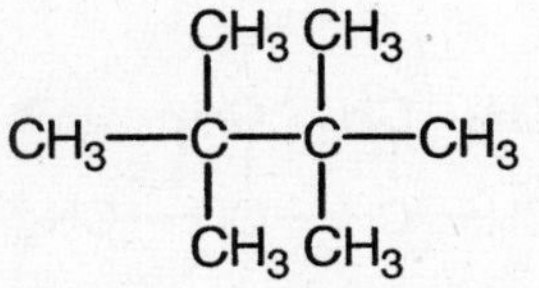

2,2,3,3-tetramethylbutane

16.   a.

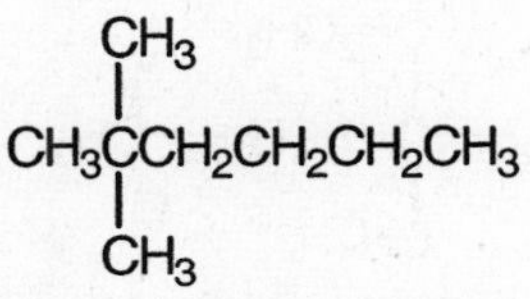

$$CH_3CCH_2CH_2CH_2CH_3$$ with CH_3 above and CH_3 below

2,2-dimethylhexane

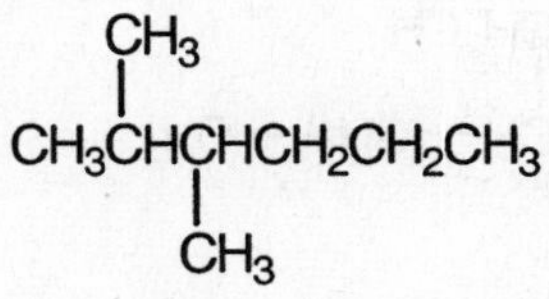

$$CH_3CHCHCH_2CH_2CH_3$$ with CH_3 above and CH_3 below

2,3-dimethylhexane

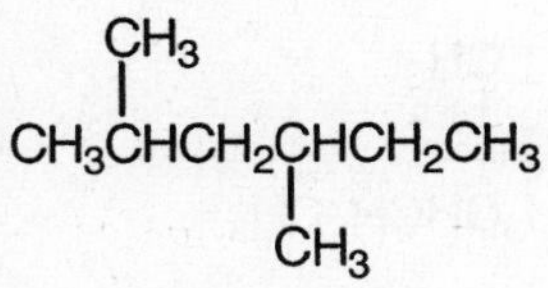

$$CH_3CHCH_2CHCH_2CH_3$$ with CH_3 above and CH_3 below

2,4-dimethylhexane

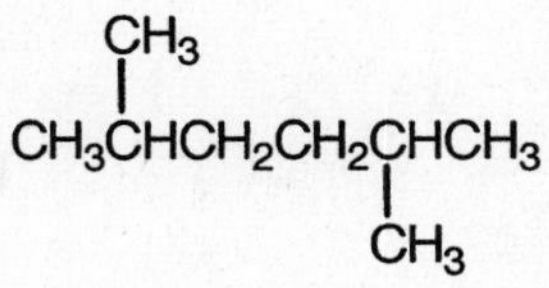

$$CH_3CHCH_2CH_2CHCH_3$$ with CH_3 above and CH_3 below

2,5-dimethylhexane

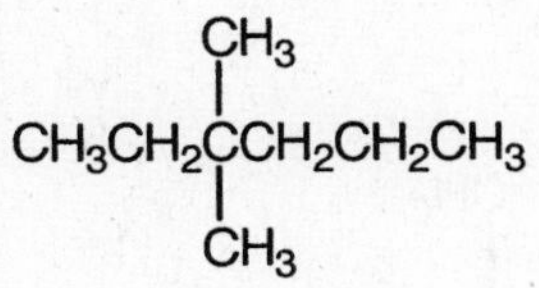

$$CH_3CH_2CCH_2CH_2CH_3$$ with CH_3 above and CH_3 below

3,3-dimethylhexane

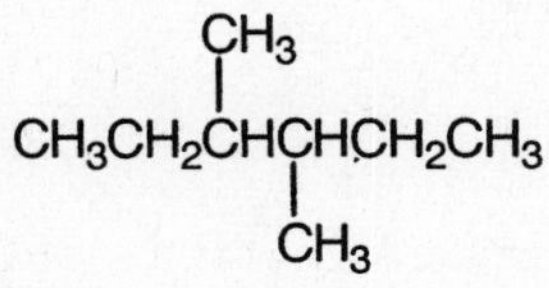

$$CH_3CH_2CHCHCH_2CH_3$$ with CH_3 above and CH_3 below

3,4-dimethylhexane

$$CH_3CH_2CHCH_2CH_2CH_3$$ with CH_2CH_3 above

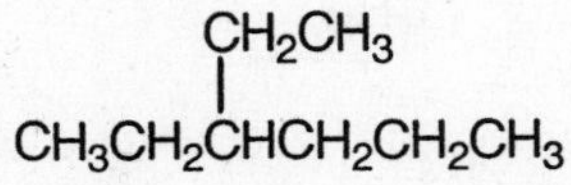

3-ethylhexane

b.

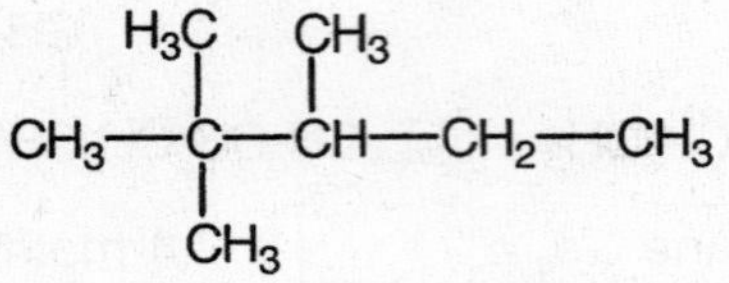

H3C   CH3
CH3—C—CH—CH2—CH3
       |
       CH3

2,2,3-trimethylpentane

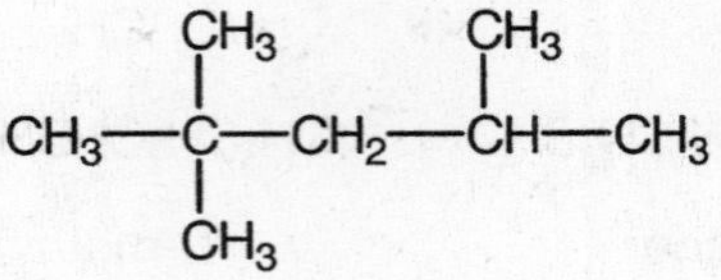

CH3   CH3
CH3—C—CH2—CH—CH3
     |
     CH3

2,2,4-trimethylpentane

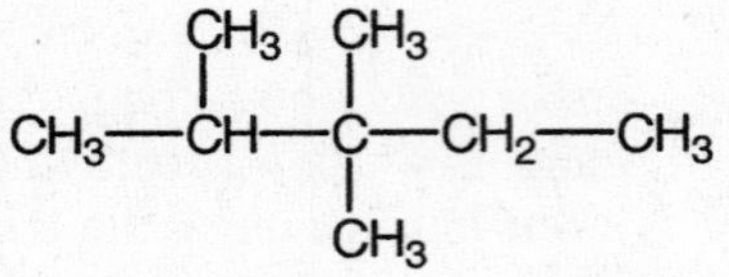

CH3   CH3
CH3—CH—C—CH2—CH3
        |
        CH3

2,3,3-trimethylpentane

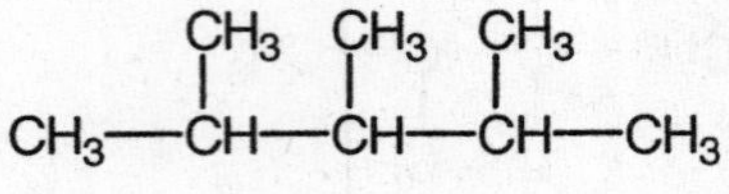

CH3   CH3   CH3
CH3—CH—CH—CH—CH3

2,3,4-trimethylpentane

CH3   CH2CH3
CH3—CH—CH—CH2—CH3

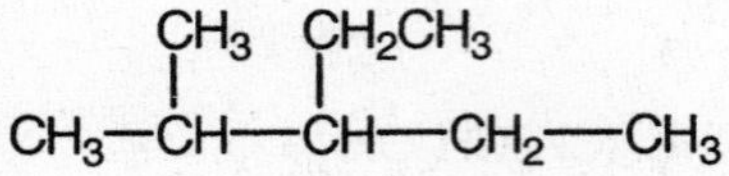

3-ethyl-2-methylpentane

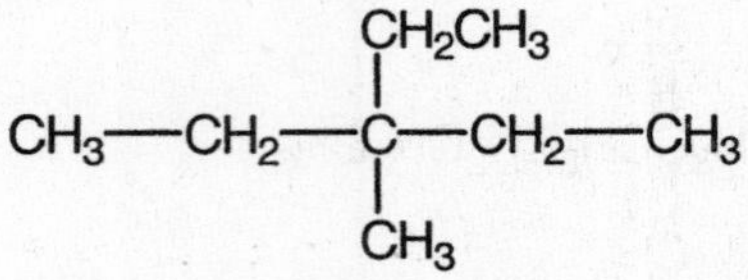

CH2CH3
CH3—CH2—C—CH2—CH3
         |
         CH3

3-ethyl-3-methylpentane

17. a.
CH3
|
CH3CHCH3

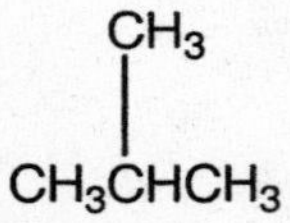

b.
CH3
|
CH3CHCH2CH3

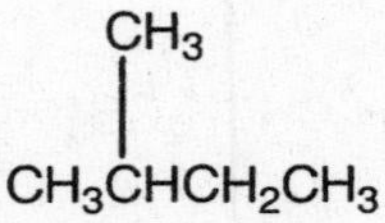

c.
CH3
|
CH3CHCH2CH2CH3

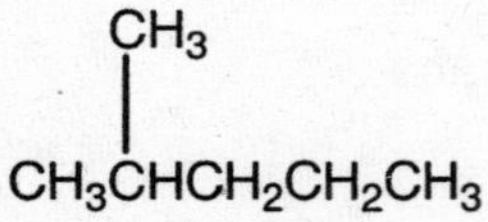

d.
CH3
|
CH3CHCH2CH2CH2CH3

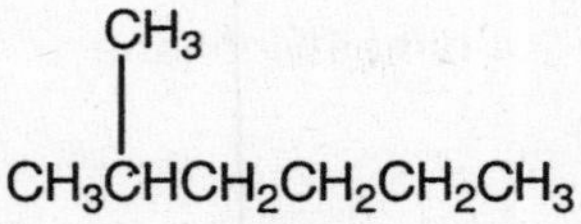

18. a.
CH3
|
CH3CCH2CH2CH2CH2CH3
|
CH3

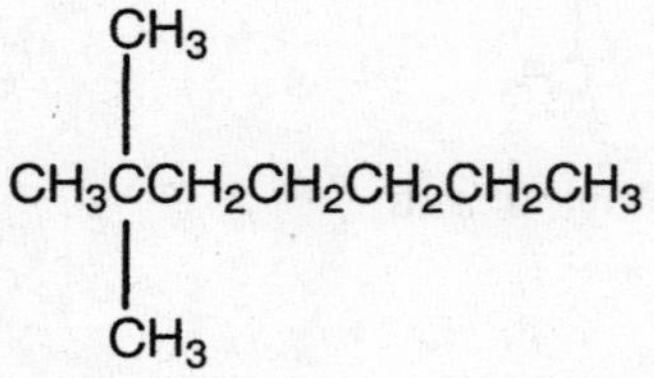

b.
CH3
|
CH3CHCHCH2CH2CH2CH3
      |
      CH3

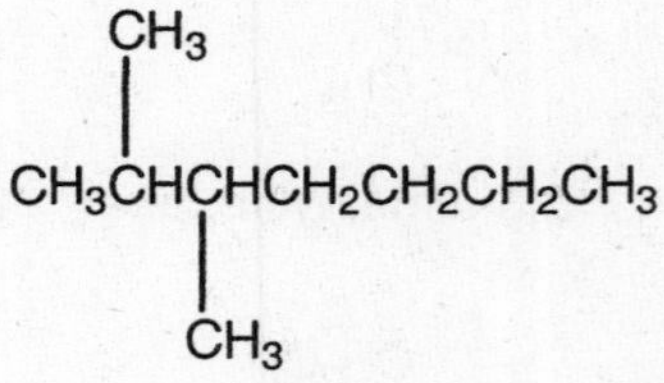

c.
CH3
|
CH3CH2CCH2CH2CH2CH3
|
CH3

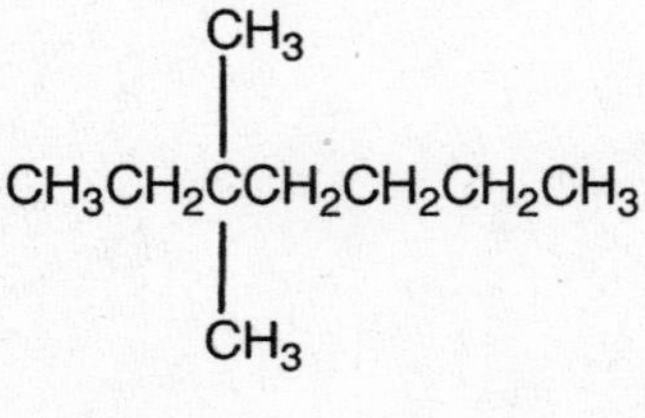

d.
CH3
|
CH3CHCH2CHCH2CH2CH3
           |
           CH3

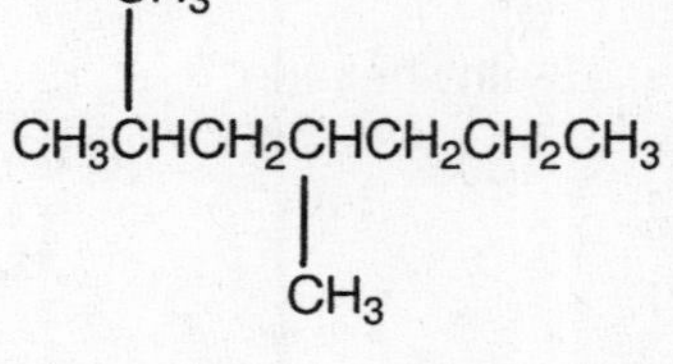

19.   a.

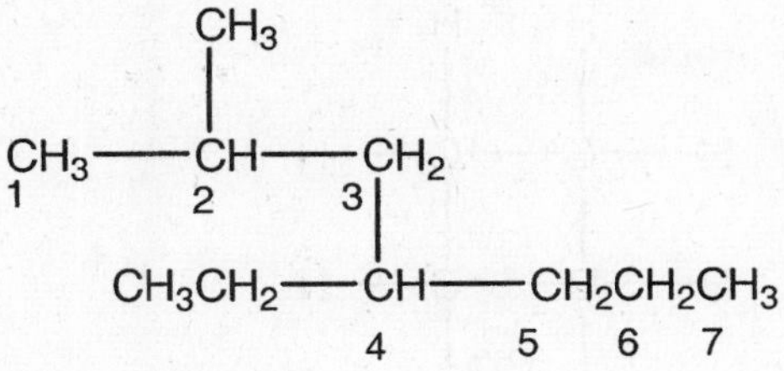

CH3
|
CH3——CH——CH2
 1   2   3
      CH3CH2——CH——CH2CH2CH3
             4   5   6   7

b.

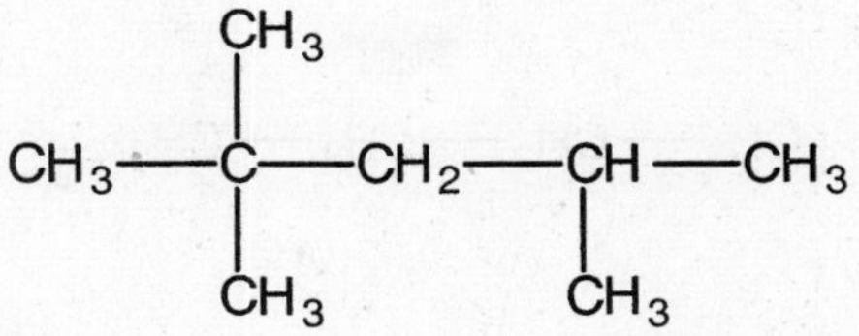

CH3
|
CH3——C——CH2——CH——CH3
      | |
      CH3   CH3

c.

CH3
|
CH3——C——CH3
 1   2
      CH3CHCH2CH2CH3
        3   4   5   6

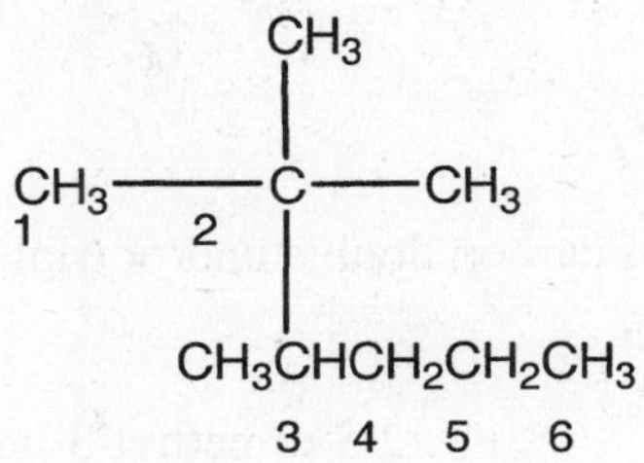

d.   For 3-isobutylhexane, the longest
      chain is 7 carbons long. The correct
      name is 4-ethyl-2-methylheptane. For
      2-tert-butylpentane, the longest chain
      is 6 carbons long. The correct name is
      2,2,3-trimethylhexane.

20.

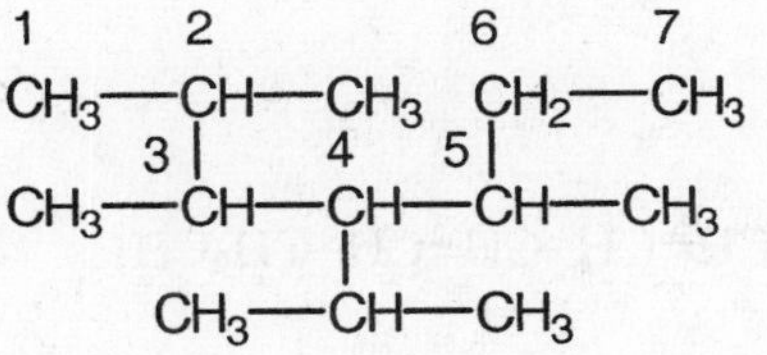

1   2   6   7
CH3——CH——CH3 CH2——CH3
    3 | 4   5 |
CH3——CH——CH——CH——CH3
    CH3——CH——CH3

4-isopropyl-2,3,5-trimethylheptane

21.   a. 2,2,4-trimethylhexane   b. 5-methylnonane   c. 2,2,4,4-tetramethylpentane

       d. 3-ethyl-3-methyloctane

       Note: For alkanes, always identify the longest carbon chain for the base name first, then
       number the carbons to give the lowest overall numbers for the substituent groups.

22.   The hydrogen atoms in ring compounds are commonly omitted. In organic compounds,
       carbon atoms satisfy the octet rule of electrons by forming four bonds to other atoms.
       Therefore, add C-H bonds to the carbon atoms in the ring in order to give each C atom four
       bonds. You can also determine the formula of these cycloalkanes by using the general formula
       C_nH_{2n}.

       a. isopropylcyclobutane; C_7H_{14} b. 1-tert-butyl-3-methylcyclopentane; $C_{10}H_{20}$

       c. 1,3-dimethyl-2-propylcyclohexane; $C_{11}H_{22}$

23.

$$CH_3\!\!-\!\!CH_2\!\!-\!\!CH_2\!\!-\!\!CH_3$$

Each carbon is bonded to four other carbon and/or hydrogen atoms in a saturated hydrocarbon (only single bonds are present).

24. $CH_2\!\!=\!\!CH_2$ $HC\!\!\equiv\!\!C\!\!-\!\!CH\!\!=\!\!CH_2$

An unsaturated hydrocarbon has at least one carbon-carbon double and/or triple bond in the structure.

25.   a. 1-butene   b. 4-methyl-2-hexene   c. 2,5-dimethyl-3-heptene

Note: The multiple bond is assigned the lowest number possible.

26.   a. 2,3-dimethyl-2-butene   b. 4-methyl-2-hexyne

c. 2,3-dimethyl-1-pentene

27.   a. $CH_3\!\!-\!\!CH_2\!\!-\!\!CH\!\!=\!\!CH\!\!-\!\!CH_2\!\!-\!\!CH_3$ b. $CH_3\!\!-\!\!CH\!\!=\!\!CH\!\!-\!\!CH\!\!=\!\!CH\!\!-\!\!CH_2CH_3$
c.

$$CH_3\!\!-\!\!\underset{\underset{\displaystyle CH_3}{|}}{CH}\!\!-\!\!CH\!\!=\!\!CH\!\!-\!\!CH_2CH_2CH_2CH_3$$

28.

a. $HC\!\!\equiv\!\!C\!\!-\!\!CH_2\!\!-\!\!\underset{\underset{\displaystyle CH_3}{|}}{CH}\!\!-\!\!CH_3$ b. $H_2C\!\!=\!\!C\!\!-\!\!\underset{\underset{\displaystyle CH_3}{|}}{\overset{\overset{\displaystyle CH_3\;CH_3}{|\quad|}}{C}}\!\!-\!\!CH_2CH_2CH_3$

c. $CH_3CH_2\!\!-\!\!\underset{\underset{\displaystyle CH_2CH_3}{|}}{CH}\!\!-\!\!CH\!\!=\!\!CH\!\!-\!\!CH_2CH_2CH_2CH_2CH_3$

29.   a.

b.

c.

d.

30.   isopropylbenzene or 2-phenylpropane

31.   a.   1,3-dichlorobutane   b.   1,1,1-trichlorobutane

       c.   2,3-dichloro-2,4-dimethylhexane   d.   1,2-difluoroethane

32.   a.   3-chloro-l-butene   b.   1-ethyl-3-methycyclopentene

       c.   3-chloro-4-propylcyclopentene   d.   1,2,4-trimethylcyclohexane

       e.   2-bromotoluene (or 1-bromo-2-methylbenzene) f.   1-bromo-2-methylcyclohexane

       g.   4-bromo-3-methylcyclohexene

       Note: If the location of the double bond is not given in the name, it is assumed to be located
       between C_1 and C_2. Also, when the base name can be numbered in equivalent ways, give the
       first substituent group the lowest number, e.g., for part f, 1-bromo-2-methylcyclohexane is
       preferred to 2-bromo-1-methycyclohexane.

Isomerism

33. CH_2Cl–CH_2Cl, 1-2-dichloroethane: There is free rotation about the C–C single bond that
       doesn't lead to different compounds. $CHCl=CHCl$, 1,2-dichloroethene: There is no rota-tion
       about the C=C double bond. This creates the cis and trans isomers, which are different
       compounds.

34.   a.   All of these structures have the formula C_5H_8. The compounds with the same physical properties will be the compounds that are identical to each other, i.e., compounds that only differ by rotations of C–C single bonds. To recognize identical compounds, name them. The names of the compounds are:

i.   trans-1,3-pentadiene   ii.   cis-1,3-pentadiene

iii.   cis-1,3-pentadiene   iv.   2-methyl-1,3-butadiene

Compounds ii and iii are identical compounds, so they would have the same physical properties.

b.   Compound i is a trans isomer because the bulkiest groups off the $C_3=C_4$ double bond are on opposite sides of the double bond.

c.   Compound iv does not have carbon atoms in a double bond that each have two different groups attached. Compound iv does not exhibit cis-trans isomerism.

35.   To exhibit cis-trans isomerism, each carbon in the double bond must have two structurally different groups bonded to it. In Exercise 22.25, this occurs for compounds b and c. The cis isomer has the bulkiest groups on the same side of the double bond while the trans isomer has the bulkiest groups on opposite sides of the double bond. The cis and trans isomers for 25b and 25c are:

25 b.

cis   trans

25 c.

cis   trans

Similarly, all the compounds in Exercise 22.27 exhibit *cis-trans* isomerism.

In compound a of Exercise 22.25, the first carbon in the double bond does not contain two different groups.   The first carbon in the double bond contains two H atoms. To illustrate that this compound does not exhibit *cis-trans* isomerism, let's look at the potential *cis-trans* isomers.

These are the same compounds; they only differ by a simple rotation of the molecule. Therefore, they are not isomers of each other, but instead are the same compound.

36.   In Exercise 22.26, none of the compounds can exhibit *cis-trans* isomerism since none of the carbons with the multiple bond have two different groups bonded to each. In Exercise 22.28, only 3-ethyl-4-decene can exhibit *cis-trans* isomerism since the fourth and fifth carbons each have two different groups bonded to the carbon atoms with the double bond.

37. C_5H_{10} has the general formula for alkenes, C_nH_{2n}. To distinguish the different isomers from each other, we will name them. Each isomer must have a different name.

$$CH_2\!\!=\!\!CHCH_2CH_2CH_3 \qquad\qquad CH_3CH\!\!=\!\!CHCH_2CH_3$$

1-pentene   2-pentene

$$CH_2\!\!=\!\!\underset{\underset{CH_3}{|}}{C}CH_2CH_3 \qquad\qquad CH_3\underset{\underset{CH_3}{|}}{C}\!\!=\!\!CHCH_3$$

2-methyl-1-butene   2-methyl-2-butene

$$CH_3\underset{\underset{CH_3}{|}}{C}HCH\!\!=\!\!CH_2$$

3-methyl-1-butene

38.   Only 2-pentene exhibits cis-trans isomerism. The isomers are:

cis   trans

The other isomers of C_5H_{10} do not contain carbons in the double bonds that each have two different groups attached.

39.   To help distinguish the different isomers, we will name them.

cis-1-chloro-1-propene   trans-1-chloro-1-propene

2-chloro-1-propene   3-chloro-1-propene   chlorocyclopropane

40.   HCBrCl–CH=CH$_2$

The cyclic isomers of bromochloropropene (C_3H_4BrCl) are:

trans   cis

41.

42.   The *cis* isomer has the CH_3 groups on the same side of the ring. The *trans* isomer has the CH_3 groups on opposite sides of the ring.

cis   trans

The cyclic structural and geometric isomers of C_4H_7F are:

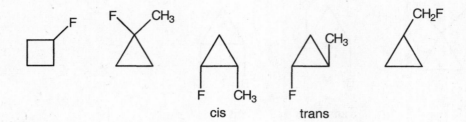

cis   trans

43.

a. H_3C―C=C―$CH_2CH_2CH_3$ with H, H below

b. H_3C―C=C―H with H, CH_3 below

c. H_3C―C=C―CH_2CH_3 with Cl, Cl below

44.   a.   cis-1-bromo-1-propene   b.   cis-4-ethyl-3-methyl-3-heptene

c.   trans-1,4-diiodo-2-propyl-1-pentene

Note: In general, cis-trans designations refer to the relative positions of the largest groups. In compound b, the largest group off the first carbon in the double bond is CH_2CH_3, and the largest group off the second carbon in the double bond is $CH_2CH_2CH_3$. Because their relative placement is on the same side of the double bond, this is the cis isomer.

45.   a.

CH_3^*―CH_2^*―CH_2^*―CH_2―CH_3

There are three different types of hydrogens in n-pentane (see asterisks). Thus there are three monochloro isomers of n-pentane (1-chloropentane, 2-chloropentane and 3-chloropentane).

b.

CH_3^*―CH^*―CH_2^*―CH_3^* with CH_3 above the CH

There are four different types of hydrogens in 2-methylbutane, so four monochloro isomers of 2-methylbutane are possible.

c.

CH_3^*―CH^*―CH_2^*―CH―CH_3 with CH_3 above each CH

There are three different types of hydrogens, so three monochloro isomers are possible.

d.

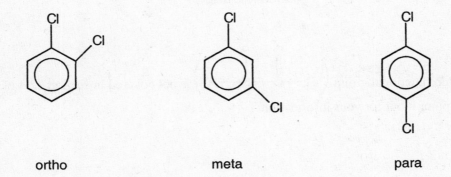

There are four different types of hydrogens, so four monochloro isomers are possible.

46.   a.

ortho   meta   para

b. There are three trichlorobenzenes (1,2,3-trichlorobenzene, 1,2,4-trichlorobenzene and 1,3,5-trichlorobenzene).

c. The meta isomer will be very difficult to synthesize.

d. 1,3,5-trichlorobenzene will be the most difficult to synthesize since all Cl groups are meta to each other in this compound.

Functional Groups

47.   Reference Table 22.5 for the common functional groups.

    a. ketone   b. aldehyde   c. carboxylic acid   d. amine

48.   a.   b.

c.

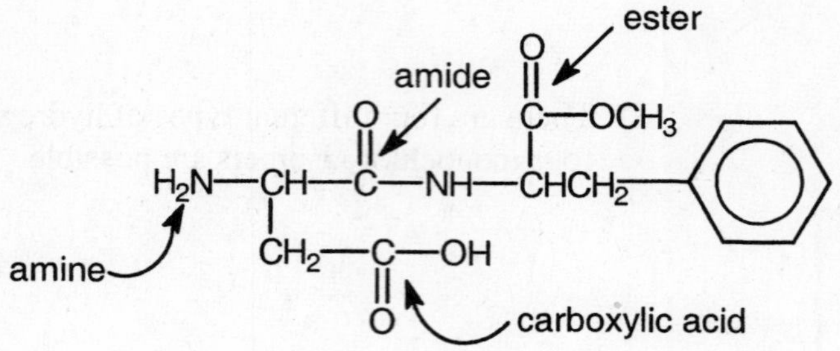

Note: the amide functional group $\left(R\!-\!\overset{\overset{\textstyle O}{\|}}{C}\!-\!\overset{\overset{\textstyle R'}{|}}{N}\!-\!R'' \right)$ is not covered in section 22.4 of the text. We point it out for your information.

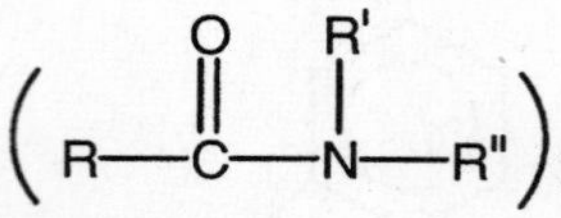

49.   a.

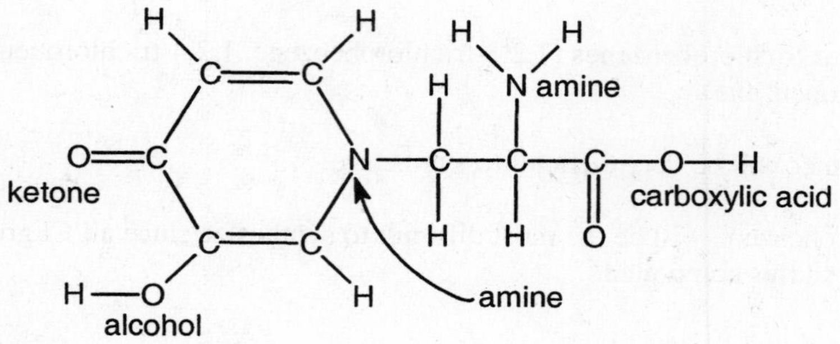

b.   5 carbons in the ring and the carbon in $-CO_2H$: sp^2; the other two carbons: sp^3

c.   24 sigma bonds; 4 pi bonds

50.   Hydrogen atoms are usually omitted from ring structures. In organic compounds, the carbon atoms form four bonds. With this in mind, the following structure has the missing hydrogen atoms included in order to give each carbon atom the four bond requirement.

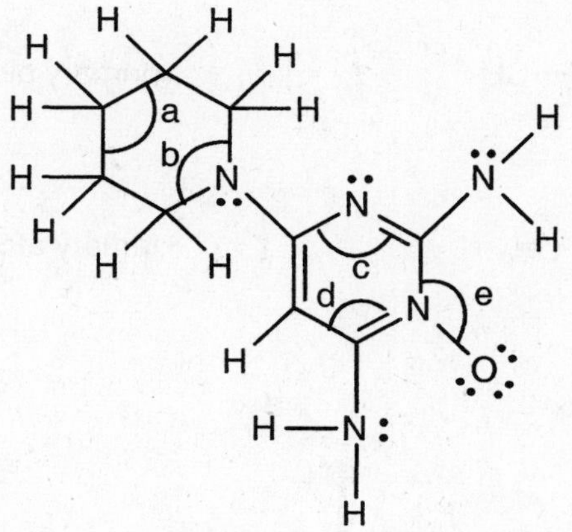

a. Minoxidil would be more soluble in acidic solution. The nitrogens with lone pairs can be protonated, forming a water soluble cation.

b. The two nitrogens in the ring with double bonds are sp^2 hybridized. The other three N's are sp^3 hybridized.

c. The five carbon atoms in the ring with one nitrogen are all sp^3 hybridized. The four carbon atoms in the other ring with double bonds are all sp^2 hybridized.

d. Angles a and b $\approx$ 109.5°; Angles c, d, and e $\approx$ 120°

e. 31 sigma bonds

f. 3 pi bonds

51. a. 3-chloro-1-butanol: Because the carbon containing the OH group is bonded to just 1 other carbon (1 R group), this is a primary alcohol.

b. 3-methyl-3-hexanol; Because the carbon containing the OH group is bonded to three other carbons (3 R groups), this is a tertiary alcohol.

c. 2-methylcyclopentanol; Secondary alcohol (2 R groups bonded to carbon containing the OH group); Note: In ring compounds, the alcohol group is assumed to be bonded to C_1, so the number designation is commonly omitted for the alcohol group.

52.

a.

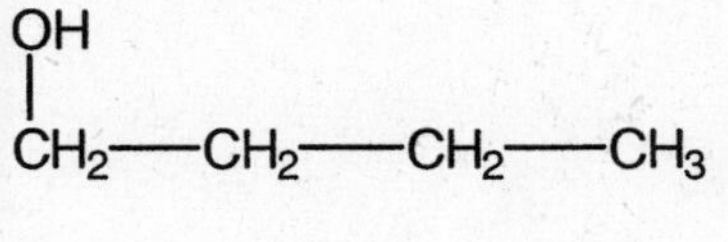

primary alcohol

b.

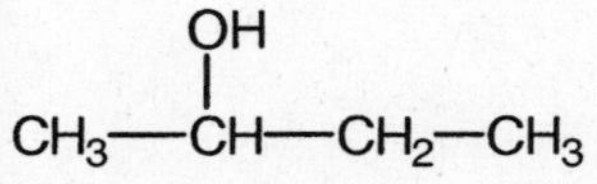

secondary alcohol

c. CH_2—CH—CH_2—CH_3 primary alcohol

(with OH on CH_2 and CH_3 on CH)

d. CH_3—C—CH_2—CH_3 tertiary alcohol

(with CH_3 above and OH below the central C)

53.

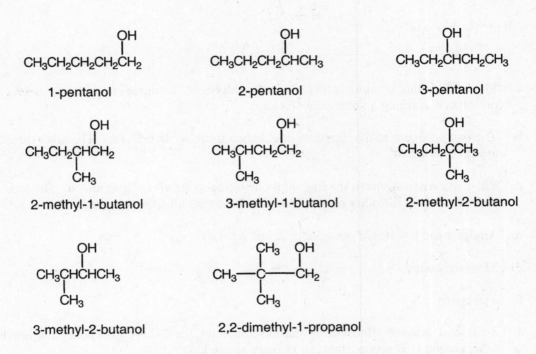

$CH_3CH_2CH_2CH_2CH_2$ (OH)

1-pentanol

$CH_3CH_2CH_2CHCH_3$ (OH)

2-pentanol

$CH_3CH_2CHCH_2CH_3$ (OH)

3-pentanol

$CH_3CH_2CHCH_2$ (OH, CH_3)

2-methyl-1-butanol

$CH_3CHCH_2CH_2$ (OH, CH_3)

3-methyl-1-butanol

$CH_3CH_2CCH_3$ (OH, CH_3)

2-methyl-2-butanol

$CH_3CHCHCH_3$ (OH, CH_3)

3-methyl-2-butanol

CH_3—C—CH_2 (CH_3, OH, CH_3)

2,2-dimethyl-1-propanol

There are six isomeric ethers with formula $C_5H_{12}O$. The structures follow.

CH_3—O—$CH_2CH_2CH_2CH_3$

CH_3—O—$CHCH_2CH_3$ (CH_3)

CH_3—O—CH_2CHCH_3 (CH_3)

CH_3—O—C—CH_3 (CH_3, CH_3)

CH_3CH_2—O—$CH_2CH_2CH_3$

CH_3CH_2—O—CH (CH_3, CH_3)

54.   There are four aldehydes and three ketones with formula $C_5H_{10}O$. The structures follow.

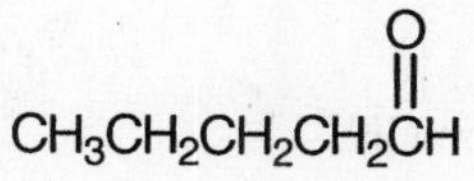

$$CH_3CH_2CH_2CH_2CH \overset{O}{\overset{\|}{}}$$

pentanal

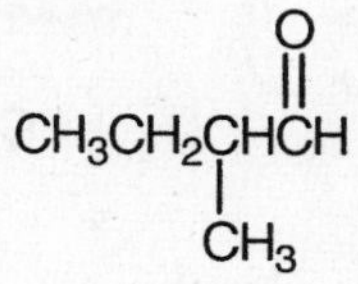

$$CH_3CH_2CHCH \overset{O}{\overset{\|}{}} \quad (CH_3)$$

2-methylbutanal

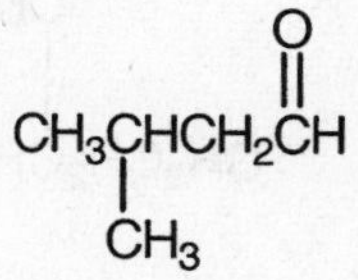

$$CH_3CHCH_2CH \overset{O}{\overset{\|}{}} \quad (CH_3)$$

3-methylbutanal

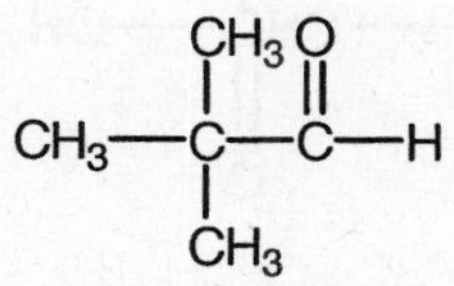

$$CH_3-\underset{CH_3}{\overset{CH_3}{C}}-\overset{O}{\overset{\|}{C}}-H$$

2,2-dimethylpropanal

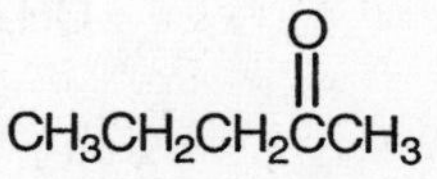

$$CH_3CH_2CH_2\overset{O}{\overset{\|}{C}}CH_3$$

2-pentanone

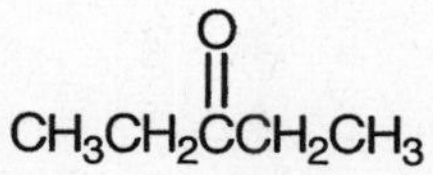

$$CH_3CH_2\overset{O}{\overset{\|}{C}}CH_2CH_3$$

3-pentanone

$$CH_3CHCCH_3 \overset{O}{\overset{\|}{}} \quad (CH_3)$$

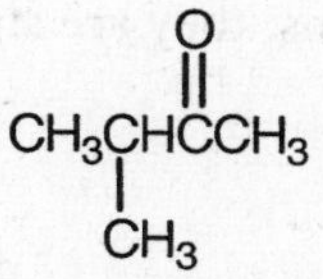

3-methyl-2-butanone

55.   a.   4,5-dichloro-3-hexanone   b.   2,3-dimethylpentanal

        c.   3-methylbenzaldehyde or m-methylbenzaldehyde

56.   a.   b.

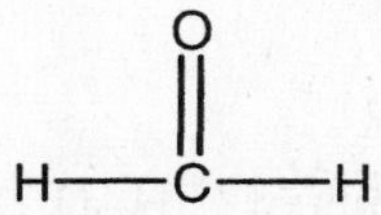

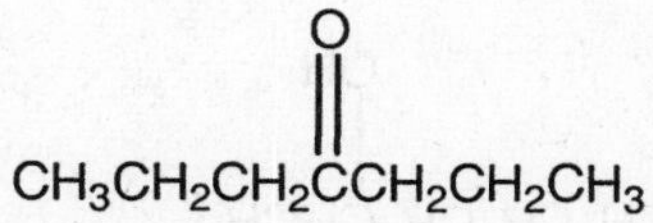

$$H-\overset{O}{\overset{\|}{C}}-H$$

$$CH_3CH_2CH_2\overset{O}{\overset{\|}{C}}CH_2CH_2CH_3$$

        c. 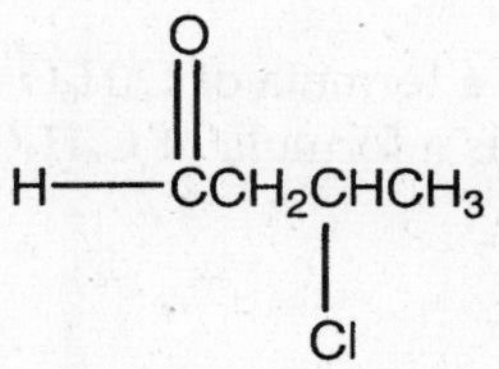   d.

$$H-\overset{O}{\overset{\|}{C}}CH_2\underset{Cl}{CH}CH_3$$

$$CH_3\overset{O}{\overset{\|}{C}}CH_2CH_2\underset{CH_3}{\overset{CH_3}{C}}CH_3$$

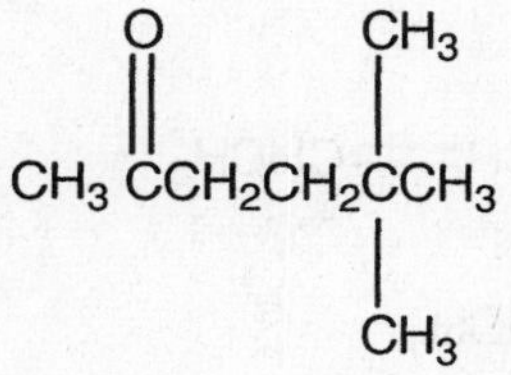

57.   a.   4-chlorobenzoic acid or p-chlorobenzoic acid

        b.   3-ethyl-2-methylhexanoic acid

        c.   methanoic acid (common name = formic acid)

58. a.

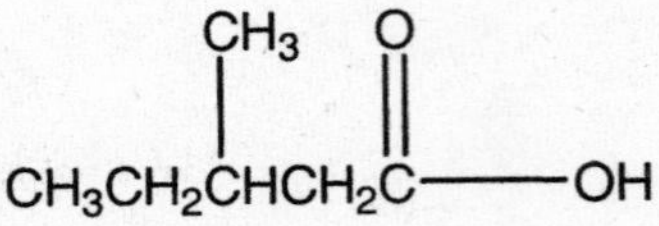

$$CH_3CH_2CHCH_2C{-}OH$$

with CH_3 group and O (double bond) on the carbonyl carbon

b.

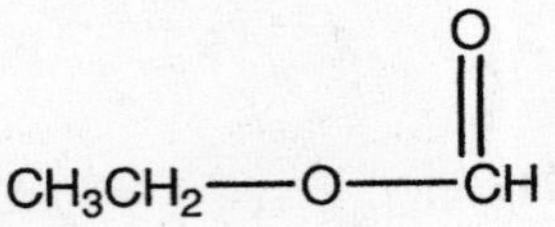

$$CH_3CH_2{-}O{-}CH$$

with O (double bond) above CH

c.

$$C{-}OCH_3$$

with O (double bond) above C, and a benzene ring below C

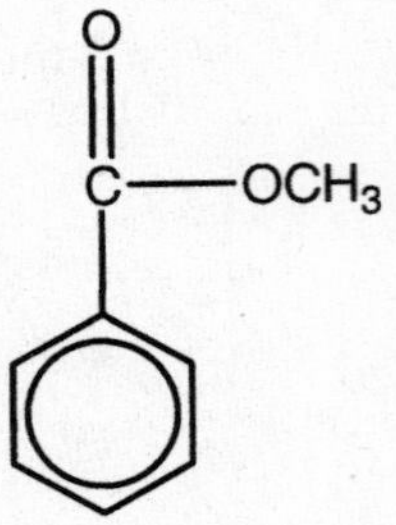

d.

$$CH_3CH_2CH{-}CH{-}CHC{-}OH$$

with CH_3 groups above the first CH and the CHC carbon, Cl below the middle CH, and O (double bond) below the C

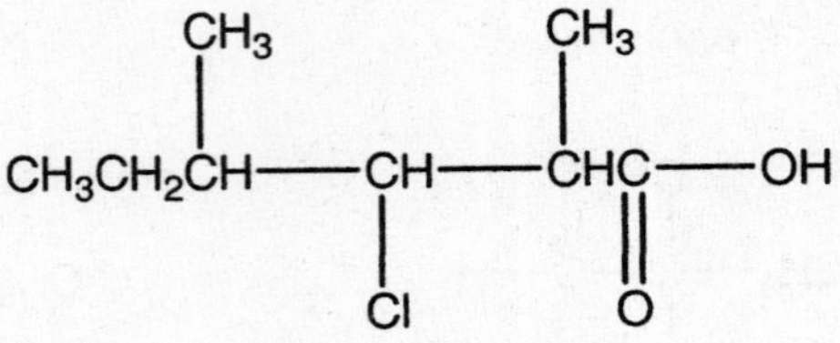

59.   Only statement d is false. The other statements refer to compounds having the same formula but different attachment of atoms; they are structural isomers.

a.

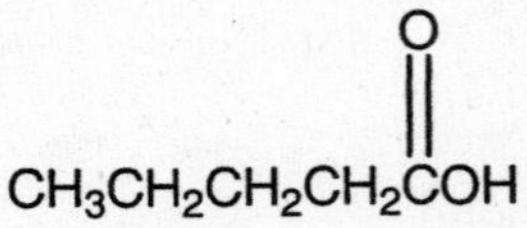

$$CH_3CH_2CH_2CH_2COH$$

with O (double bond) above the C

Both have a formula of $C_5H_{10}O_2$.

b.

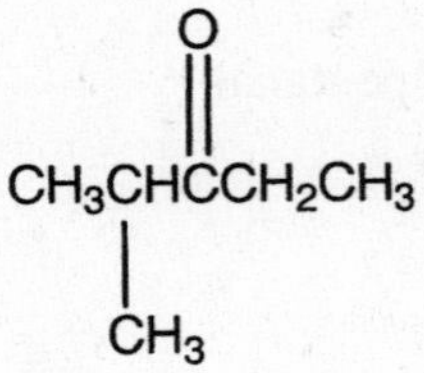

$$CH_3CHCCH_2CH_3$$

with O (double bond) above the middle C and CH_3 below the first CH

Both have a formula of $C_6H_{12}O$.

c.

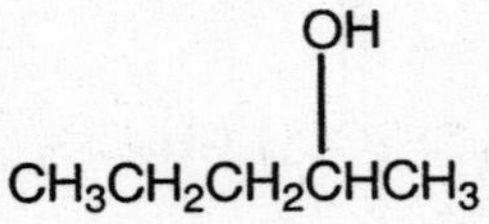

$$CH_3CH_2CH_2CHCH_3$$

with OH above the CH

Both have a formula of $C_5H_{12}O$.

d.

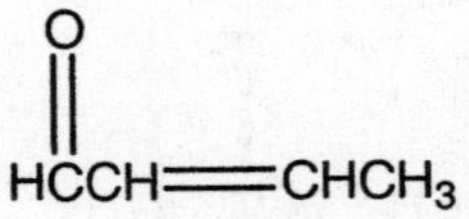

$$HCCH{=}CHCH_3$$

with O (double bond) above the first HC

2-butenal has a formula of C_4H_6O while the alcohol has a formula of C_4H_8O.

e.

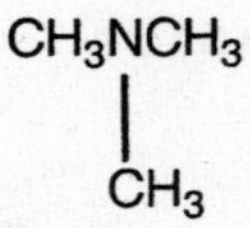

$$CH_3NCH_3$$

with CH_3 below the N

Both have a formula of C_3H_9N.

60.

a.   trans-2-butene: [structure: CH_3 and H on left carbon, double bond to right carbon with H and CH_3]   , formula = C_4H_8

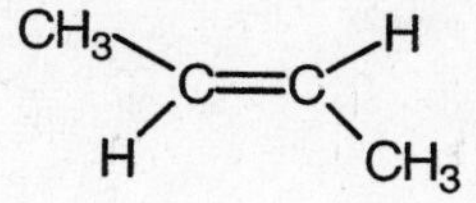

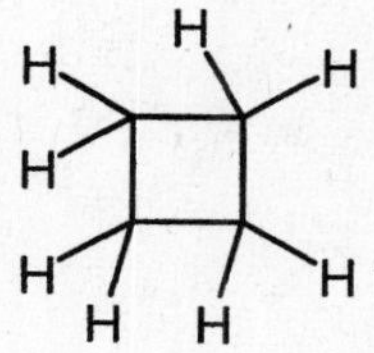

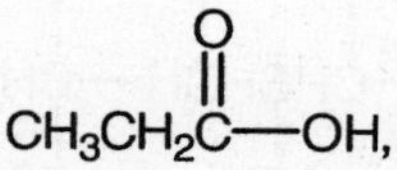

[two cyclic structures shown: cyclobutane ring with H atoms   or   cyclopropane ring with CH_3 and H atoms]

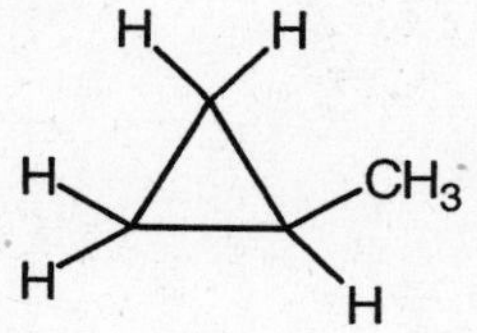

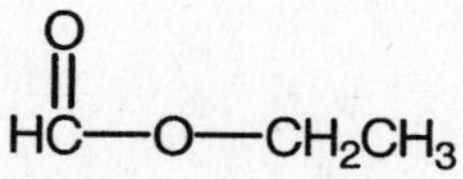

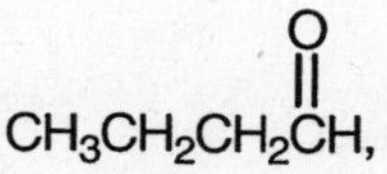

b.   propanoic acid: $CH_3CH_2\overset{O}{\overset{\|}{C}}$—OH,   formula = $C_3H_6O_2$

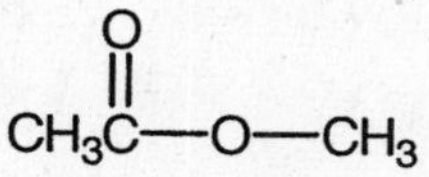

$CH_3\overset{O}{\overset{\|}{C}}$—O—$CH_3$ or $H\overset{O}{\overset{\|}{C}}$—O—$CH_2CH_3$

c.   butanal: $CH_3CH_2CH_2\overset{O}{\overset{\|}{C}}H$,   formula = C_4H_8O

$CH_3CH_2\overset{O}{\overset{\|}{C}}CH_3$

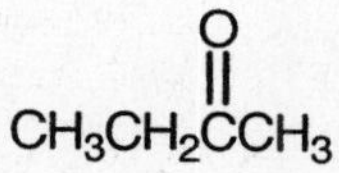

d.   butylamine: $CH_3CH_2CH_2CH_2NH_2$,   formula = $C_4H_{11}N$:

A secondary amine has two R groups bonded to N.

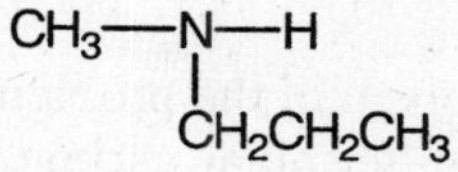

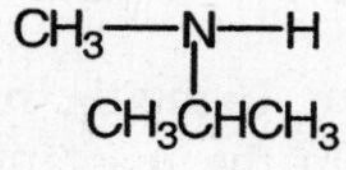

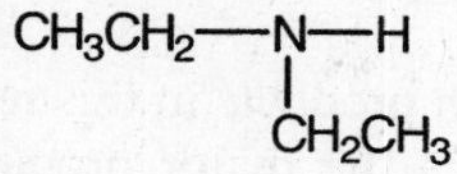

CH_3—N—H CH_3—N—H CH_3CH_2—N—H
        | | |
$CH_2CH_2CH_3$ CH_3CHCH_3 CH_2CH_3

e.   A tertiary amine has three R groups bonded to N. (See answer d for structure of butylamine.)

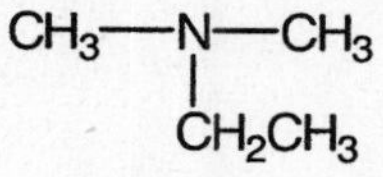

CH_3—N—CH_3
        |
CH_2CH_3

f.   2-methyl-2-propanol: $CH_3\overset{CH_3}{\underset{OH}{\overset{|}{\underset{|}{C}}}}CH_3$,   formula = $C_4H_{10}O$

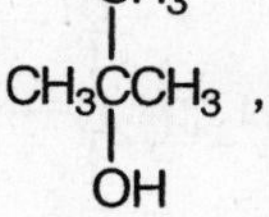

CH_3—O—$CH_2CH_2CH_3$ 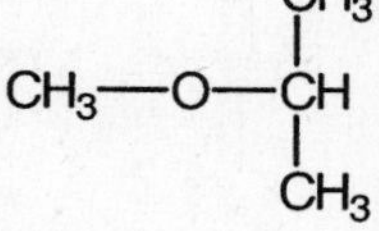 CH_3—O—$\overset{CH_3}{\underset{CH_3}{\overset{|}{\underset{|}{CH}}}}$ CH_3CH_2—O—CH_2CH_3

g.   A secondary alcohol has two R groups attached to the carbon bonded to the OH group. (See answer f for the structure of 2-methyl-2-propanol.)

$$
\begin{array}{c}
OH \\
| \\
CH_3CHCH_2CH_3
\end{array}
$$

Reactions of Organic Compounds

61.

a.
$$
\begin{array}{cc}
H & H \\
| & | \\
CH_3CH & -CHCH_3
\end{array}
$$

b.
$$
\begin{array}{cccc}
Cl & Cl & Cl & Cl \\
| & | & | & | \\
CH_2- & CHCHCH- & CH \\
& | & | \\
& CH_3 & CH_3
\end{array}
$$

c.   —Cl + HCl

d. $C_4H_8(g) + 6\,O_2(g) \rightarrow 4\,CO_2(g) + 4\,H_2O(g)$

62.   a.   The two possible products for the addition of HOH to this alkene are:

$$
\begin{array}{cc}
OH & H \\
| & | \\
CH_3CH_2CH & -CH_2
\end{array}
\qquad\qquad
\begin{array}{cc}
H & OH \\
| & | \\
CH_3CH_2CH & -CH_2
\end{array}
$$

major product   minor product

We would get both products in this reaction. Using the rule given in the problem, the first compound listed is the major product. In the reactant, the terminal carbon has more hydrogens bonded to it (2 vs. 1), so H forms a bond to this carbon, and OH forms a bond to the other carbon in the double bond for the major product. We will list only the major product for the remaining parts to this problem.

b.   c.

$$
\begin{array}{cc}
Br & H \\
| & | \\
CH_3CH_2CH & -CH_2
\end{array}
\qquad\qquad
\begin{array}{cc}
Br & H \\
| & | \\
CH_3CH_2C & -CH \\
| & | \\
Br & H
\end{array}
$$

d.

e.

63.

ortho   para

To substitute for the benzene ring hydrogens, an iron(III) catalyst must be present. Without this special iron catalyst, the benzene ring hydrogens are unreactive. To substi-tute for an alkane hydrogen, light must be present. For toluene, the light-catalyzed reaction substitutes a chlorine for a hydrogen in the methyl group attached to the benzene ring.

64.   When $CH_2=CH_2$ reacts with HCl, there is only one possible product, chloroethane. When Cl_2 is reacted with CH_3CH_3 (in the presence of light), there are six possible products because any number of the six hydrogens in ethane can be substituted for by Cl. The light-catalyzed substitution reaction is very difficult to control, hence, it is not a very efficient method of producing monochlorinated alkanes.

65.   Primary alcohols (a, d and f) are oxidized to aldehydes, which can be oxidized further to carboxylic acids. Secondary alcohols (b, e and f) are oxidized to ketones, and tertiary alcohols (c and f) do not undergo this type of oxidation reaction. Note that compound f contains a primary, secondary and tertiary alcohol. For the primary alcohols (a, d and f), we listed both the aldehyde and the carboxylic acid as possible products.

a. 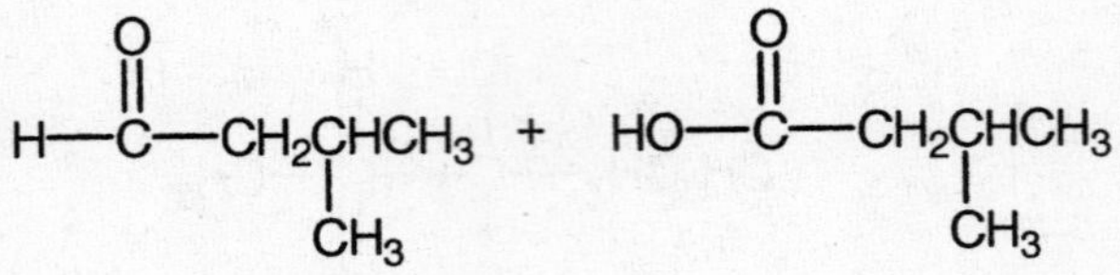
$$H-\overset{\overset{\displaystyle O}{\|}}{C}-CH_2\underset{\underset{\displaystyle CH_3}{|}}{C}HCH_3 \quad + \quad HO-\overset{\overset{\displaystyle O}{\|}}{C}-CH_2\underset{\underset{\displaystyle CH_3}{|}}{C}HCH_3$$

b. 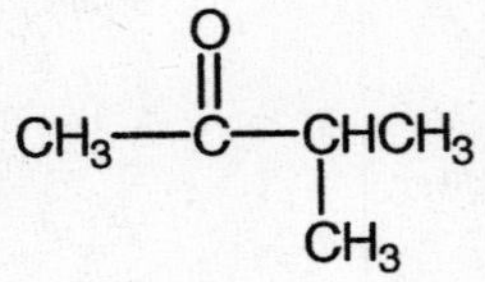
$$CH_3-\overset{\overset{\displaystyle O}{\|}}{C}-\underset{\underset{\displaystyle CH_3}{|}}{C}HCH_3$$

c.   No reaction

d. 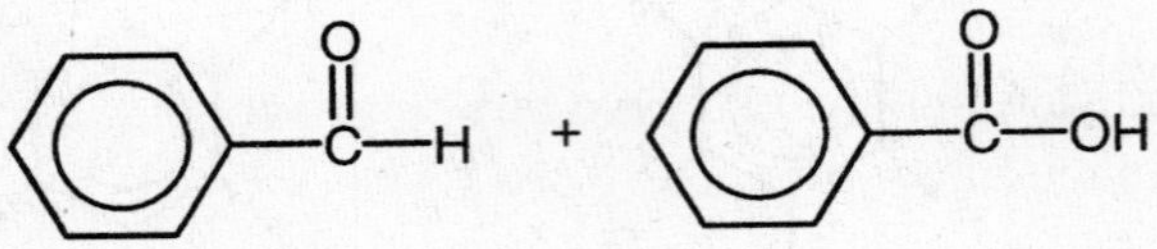
benzaldehyde + benzoic acid

e. 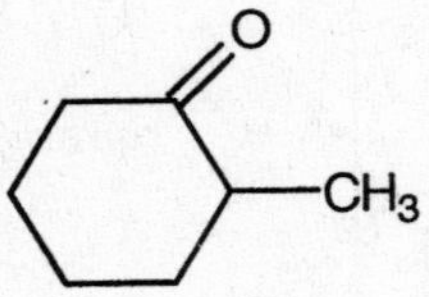
2-methylcyclohexanone

f. 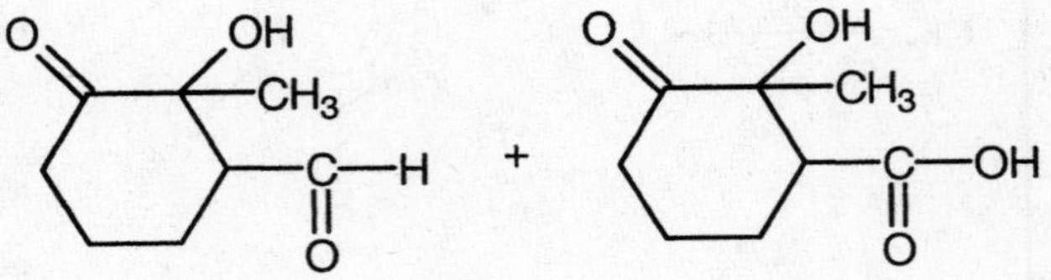
+

66.   a. 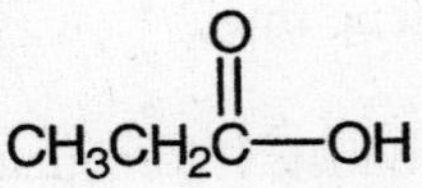   b.

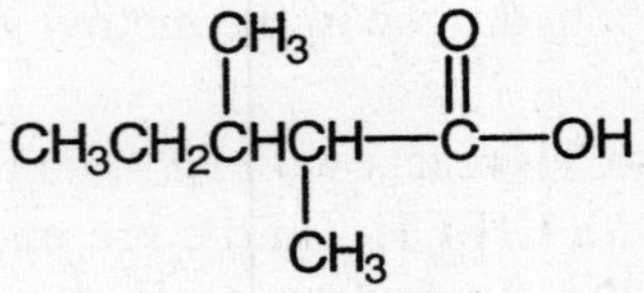

$$CH_3CH_2\overset{\overset{\displaystyle O}{\|}}{C}-OH$$

$$CH_3CH_2\underset{\underset{\displaystyle CH_3}{|}}{\overset{\overset{\displaystyle CH_3}{|}}{C}}H\overset{\overset{\displaystyle O}{\|}}{C}-OH$$

c.

$$CH_3CH_2\underset{\text{(benzene ring)}}{}\overset{\overset{\displaystyle O}{\|}}{C}-OH$$

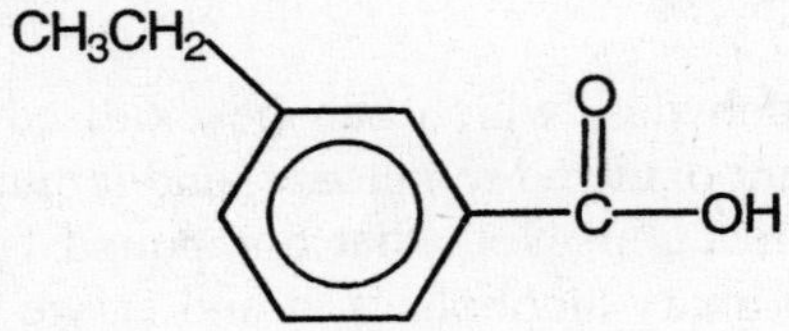

67.   a. $CH_3CH=CH_2 + Br_2 \rightarrow CH_3CHBrCH_2Br$ (Addition reaction of Br_2 with propene)

b.

$$CH_3 - \underset{\underset{\displaystyle OH}{|}}{CH} - CH_3 \xrightarrow{\text{oxidation}} CH_3 - \underset{\underset{\displaystyle }{\overset{\displaystyle O}{\|}}}{C} - CH_3$$

Oxidation of 2-propanol yields acetone (2-propanone).

c.

$$CH_2 = \underset{\overset{\displaystyle CH_3}{|}}{C} - CH_3 + H_2O \xrightarrow{H^+} CH_2 - \underset{\underset{\displaystyle OH}{|}}{\overset{\overset{\displaystyle CH_3}{|}}{C}} - CH_3$$
$$\underset{\displaystyle H}{|}$$

Addition of H_2O to 2-methylpropene would yield tert-butyl alcohol
(2-methyl-2-propanol) as the major product.

d. $CH_3CH_2CH_2OH \xrightarrow{KMnO_4} CH_3CH_2\overset{\overset{\displaystyle O}{\|}}{C} - OH$

Oxidation of 1-propanol would eventually yield propanoic acid.
Propanal is produced first in this reaction and is then oxidized
to propanoic acid.

68.   a. $CH_2 = CHCH_2CH_3$ will react with Cl_2 without any catalyst present. $CH_3CH_2CH_2CH_3$ only
reacts with Cl_2 when ultraviolet light is present.

b. $CH_3CH_2CH_2\overset{\overset{\displaystyle O}{\|}}{C}OH$ is an acid, so this compound should react positively with a base
like $NaHCO_3$. The other compound is a ketone, which will not react with a base.

c. $CH_3CH_2CH_2OH$ can be oxidized with $KMnO_4$ to propanoic acid. 2-propanone
(a ketone) will not react with $KMnO_4$.

d. $CH_3CH_2NH_2$ is an amine, so it behaves as a base in water. Dissolution of some of this
base in water will produce a solution with a basic pH. The ether, CH_3OCH_3, will not
produce a basic pH when dissolved in water.

69. Reaction of a carboxylic acid with an alcohol can produce these esters.

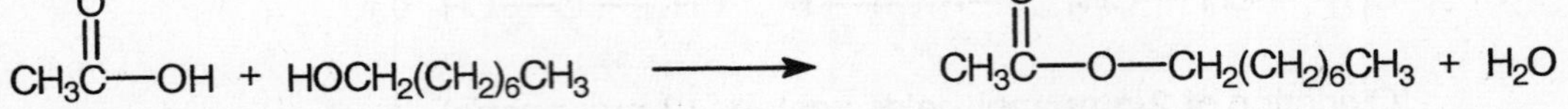

$$CH_3\overset{\overset{O}{\|}}{C}-OH + HOCH_2(CH_2)_6CH_3 \longrightarrow CH_3\overset{\overset{O}{\|}}{C}-O-CH_2(CH_2)_6CH_3 + H_2O$$

ethanoic acid   octanol   n-octylacetate

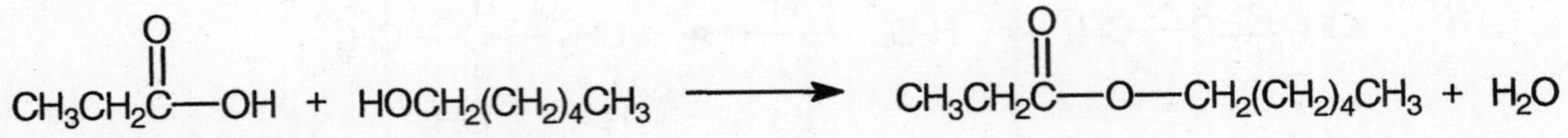

(acetic acid)

$$CH_3CH_2\overset{\overset{O}{\|}}{C}-OH + HOCH_2(CH_2)_4CH_3 \longrightarrow CH_3CH_2\overset{\overset{O}{\|}}{C}-O-CH_2(CH_2)_4CH_3 + H_2O$$

propanoic acid   hexanol

70.

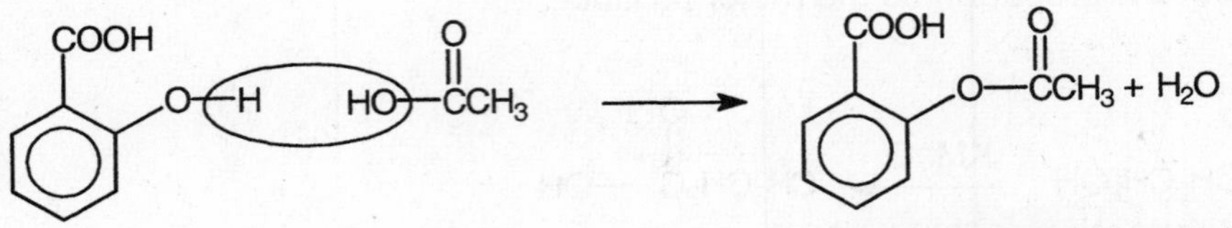

acetylsalicylic acid (aspirin)

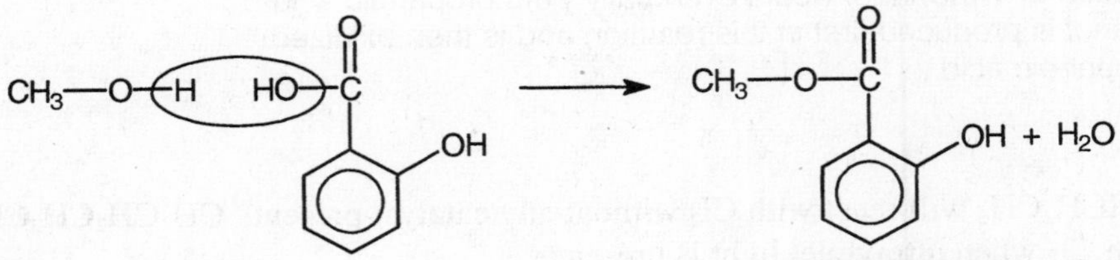

methyl salicylate

Polymers

71. The backbone of the polymer contains only carbon atoms, which indicates that Kel-F is an addition polymer. The smallest repeating unit of the polymer and the monomer used to produce this polymer are:

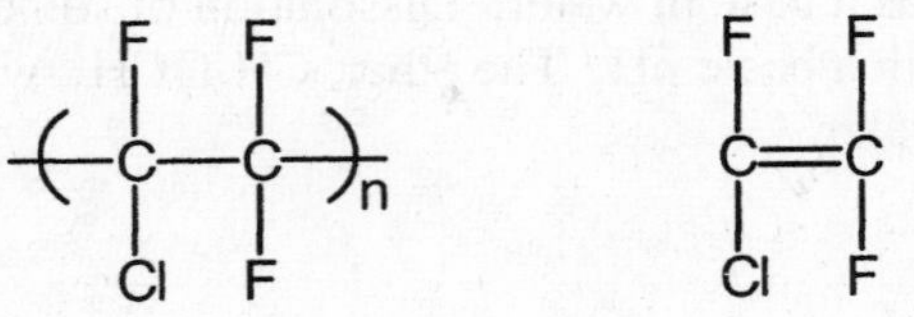

Note: Condensation polymers generally have O or N atoms in the backbone of the polymer.

72.   a.

repeating unit: monomer: $CHF{=}CH_2$

$$\left(\!\!-CHF\!-\!CH_2\!-\!\right)_n$$

b.

repeating unit: $\left(\!\!-OCH_2CH_2\overset{\displaystyle O}{\overset{\|}{C}}\!\!-\right)_n$ monomer: $HO{-}CH_2CH_2{-}CO_2H$

c.

repeating unit:

$$\left(\!\!-\overset{H}{\underset{}{N}}\!-\!CH_2CH_2\!-\!\overset{H}{\underset{}{N}}\!-\!\overset{\displaystyle O}{\overset{\|}{C}}\!-\!CH_2CH_2\!-\!\overset{\displaystyle O}{\overset{\|}{C}}\!\!-\right)_n$$

copolymer of: $H_2NCH_2CH_2NH_2$
and $HO_2CCH_2CH_2CO_2H$

d. monomer:

$$CH_3\!-\!C{=}CH_2$$

e. monomer:

$$CH{=}CH$$
$$CH_3$$

f.   monomer: $CClF{=}CF_2$

g.   copolymer of:

$HOCH_2\!-\!\bigcirc\!-\!CH_2OH$ and $HO_2C\!-\!\bigcirc\!-\!CO_2H$

Addition polymers: a, d, e and f; Condensation polymers: b, c and g; Copolymer: c and g

73.

Super glue is an addition polymer formed by reaction of the C=C bond in methyl cyanoacrylate.

74. a. 2-methyl-1,3-butadiene

b.

cis-polyisoprene (natural rubber)

trans-polyisoprene (gutta percha)

75. H_2O is eliminated when Kevlar forms. Two repeating units of Kevlar are:

76.   This condensation polymer forms by elimination of water. The ester functional group repeats, hence the term, polyester.

77.   This is a condensation polymer where two molecules of H_2O form when the monomers link together.

78.

79.   Divinylbenzene has two reactive double bonds that are both used when divinylbenzene inserts itself into two adjacent polymer chains. The chains cannot move past each other because the crosslinks bond adjacent polymer chains together, making the polymer more rigid.

80.   a.

b.

81   a. The polymer formed using 1,2-diaminoethane will exhibit relatively strong hydrogen
          bonding interactions between adjacent polymer chains. Hydrogen bonding is not present
          in the ethylene glycol polymer (a polyester polymer forms), so the 1,2-diaminoethane
          polymer will be stronger.

      b. The presence of rigid groups (benzene rings or multiple bonds) makes the polymer stiffer.
          Hence, the monomer with the benzene ring will produce the more rigid polymer.

      c. Polyacetylene will have a double bond in the carbon backbone of the polymer.

          The presence of the double bond in polyacetylene will make polyacetylene a more rigid
          polymer than polyethylene. Polyethylene doesn't have C=C bonds in the backbone of the
          polymer (the double bonds in the monomers react to form the polymer).

82.   At low temperatures, the polymer is coiled into balls. The forces between poly(lauryl
      methacrylate) and oil molecules will be minimal, and the effect on viscosity will be minimal.
      At higher temperatures, the chains of the polymer will unwind and become tangled with the oil
      molecules, increasing the viscosity of the oil. Thus, the presence of the polymer counteracts
      the temperature effect, and the viscosity of the oil remains relatively constant.

Natural Polymers

83.   a. Serine, tyrosine and threonine contain the -OH functional group in the R group.

      b. Aspartic acid and glutamic acid contain the -COOH functional group in the R group.

c.   An amine group has a nitrogen bonded to other carbon and/or hydrogen atoms. Histidine, lysine, arginine and tryptophan contain the amine functional group in the R group.

d.   The amide functional group is:

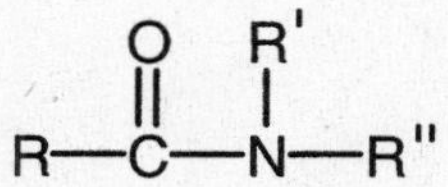

This functional group is formed when individual amino acids bond together to form the peptide linkage. Glutamine and asparagine have the amide functional group in the R group.

84.   Crystalline amino acids exist as zwitterions, $^{+}H_3NCRHCOO^{-}$, held together by ionic forces. The ionic interparticle forces are strong. Before the temperature gets high enough to melt the solid, the amino acid decomposes.

85.   a.   Aspartic acid and phenylalanine make up aspartame.

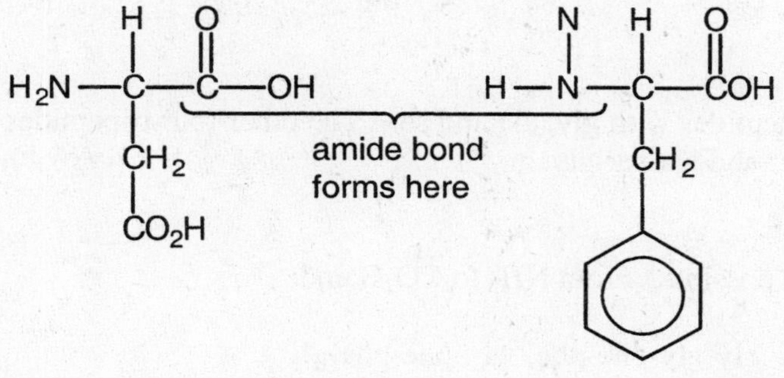

b.   Aspartame contains the methyl ester of phenylalanine. This ester can hydrolyze to form methanol:

$$R-CO_2CH_3 + H_2O \rightleftharpoons RCO_2H + HOCH_3$$

86.

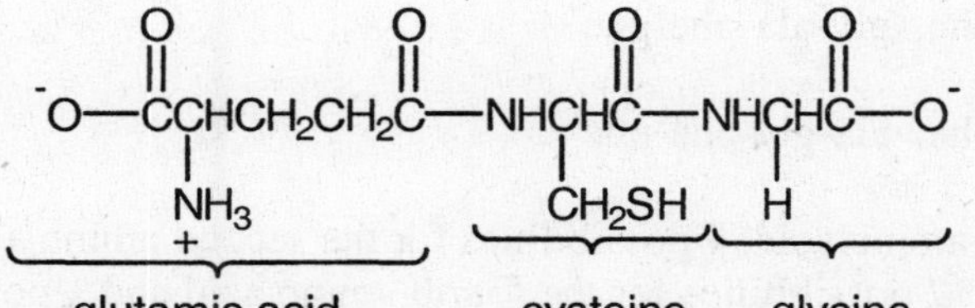

Glutamic acid, cysteine and glycine are the three amino acids in glutathione. Glutamic acid uses the -COOH functional group in the R group to bond to cysteine instead of the carboxylic acid group bonded to the α-carbon. The cysteine-glycine bond is the typical peptide linkage.

87.

ser - ala   ala - ser

88.

gly   ala   ser   ser   ala   gly

There are six possible tripeptides with gly, ala and ser. The other four tripeptides are gly-ser-ala, ser-gly-ala, ala-gly-ser and ala-ser-gly.

89.   a.   Six tetrapeptides are possible. From NH_2 to CO_2H end:

phe-phe-gly-gly, gly-gly-phe-phe, gly-phe-phe-gly,

phe-gly-gly-phe, phe-gly-phe-gly, gly-phe-gly-phe

b.   Twelve tetrapeptides are possible. From NH_2 to CO_2H end:

phe-phe-gly-ala, phe-phe-ala-gly, phe-gly-phe-ala,

phe-gly-ala-phe, phe-ala-phe-gly, phe-ala-gly-phe,

gly-phe-phe-ala, gly-phe-ala-phe, gly-ala-phe-phe

ala-phe-phe-gly, ala-phe-gly-phe, ala-gly-phe-phe

90.   There are 5 possibilities for the first amino acid, 4 possibilities for the second amino acid, 3 possibilities for the third amino acid, 2 possibilities for the fourth amino acid and 1 possibility for the last amino acid. The number of possible sequences is:

$5 \times 4 \times 3 \times 2 \times 1 = 5! = 120$ different pentapeptides

91.   a. Ionic: Need NH_2 on side chain of one amino acid with CO_2H on side chain of the other
             amino acid. The possibilities are:

             NH_2 on side chain = His, Lys or Arg; CO_2H on side chain = Asp or Glu

         b. Hydrogen bonding: Need N–H or O–H bond present in side chain. The hydrogen
                                bonding interaction occurs between the X– H bond and a carbonyl
                                group from any amino acid.

             X–H · · · · · · · O = C (carbonyl group)

                 Ser Asn   Any amino acid
                 Glu Thr
                 Tyr Asp
                 His Gln
                 Arg Lys

         c. Covalent: Cys–Cys (forms a disulfide linkage)

         d. London dispersion: All amino acids with nonpolar R groups. They are:

             Gly, Ala, Pro, Phe, Ile, Trp, Met, Leu and Val

         e. Dipole-dipole: Need side chain with OH group. Tyr, Thr and Ser all could form this
             specific dipole-dipole force with each other since all contain an OH group in the side
             chain.

92.   Reference Exercise 22.91 for a more detailed discussion of these various interactions.

         a. Covalent   b. Hydrogen bonding

         c. Ionic   d. London dispersion

93.   Glutamic acid: $R = -CH_2CH_2CO_2H$; Valine: $R = -CH(CH_3)_2$; A polar side chain is replaced
         by a nonpolar side chain. This could affect the tertiary structure of hemoglobin and the ability
         of hemoglobin to bind oxygen.

94.   Glutamic acid: $R = -CH_2CH_2COOH$; Glutamine: $R = -CH_2CH_2CONH_2$; The R groups only
         differ by OH vs NH_2. Both of these groups are capable of forming hydrogen bonding
         interactions, so the change in intermolecular forces is minimal. Thus, this change is not
         critical because the secondary and tertiary structures of hemoglobin should not be greatly
         affected.

95.   See Figures 22.29 and 22.30 of the text for examples of the cyclization process.

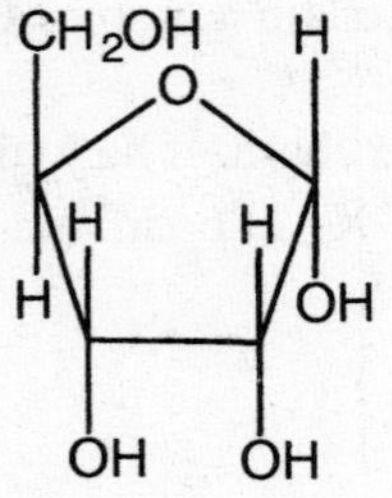

D-Ribose

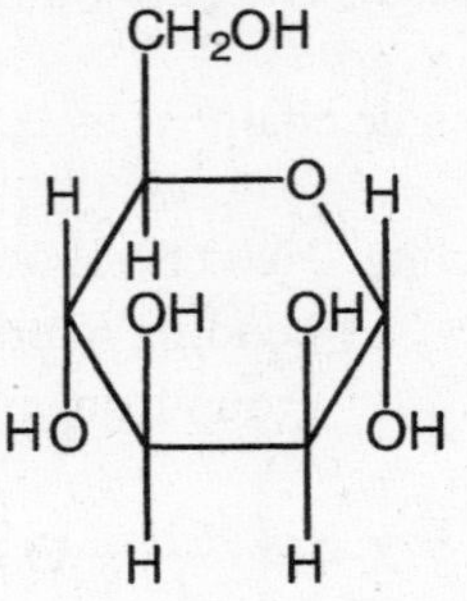

D-Mannose

96.   The chiral carbon atoms are marked with asterisks. A chiral carbon atom has four different substituent groups attached.

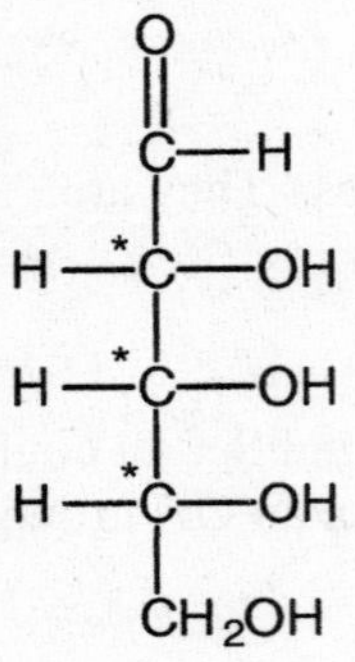

D-Ribose

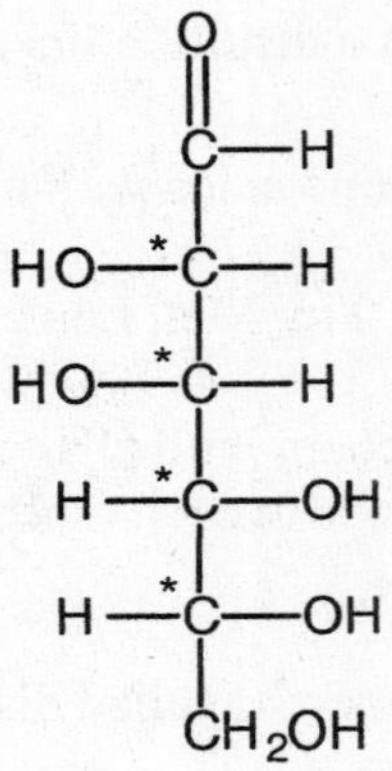

D-Mannose

97.   The aldohexoses contain 6 carbons and the aldehyde functional group. Glucose, mannose and galactose are aldohexoses. Ribose and arabinose are aldopentoses since they contain 5 carbons with the aldehyde functional group. The ketohexose (6 carbons + ketone functional group) is fructose and the ketopentose (5 carbons + ketone functional group) is ribulose.

98.   This is an example of Le Chatelier's principle at work. For the equilibrium reactions among the various forms of glucose, reference Figure 22.30 of the text. The chemical tests involve reaction of the aldehyde group found only in the open-chain structure. As the aldehyde group is reacted, the equilibrium between the cyclic forms of glucose and the open-chain structure will shift to produce more of the open-chain structure. This process continues until either the glucose or the chemicals used in the tests run out.

99.   The α and β forms of glucose differ in the orientation of a hydroxy group on one specific carbon in the cyclic forms (see Figure 22.30 of the text). Starch is a polymer composed of only α-D-glucose, and cellulose is a polymer composed of only β-D-glucose.

100. Humans do not possess the necessary enzymes to break the β-glycosidic linkages found in cellulose. Cows, however, do possess the necessary enzymes to break down cellulose into the β-D-glucose monomers and, therefore, can derive nutrition from cellulose.

101. A chiral carbon has four different groups attached to it. A compound with a chiral carbon is optically active. Isoleucine and threonine contain more than the one chiral carbon atom (see asterisks).

isoleucine   threonine

102. There is no chiral carbon atom in glycine since it contains no carbon atoms with four different groups bonded to it.

103. Only one of the isomers is optically active. The chiral carbon in this optically active isomer is marked with an asterisk.

104.

The compound has four chiral carbon atoms. The fourth group bonded to the three chiral carbon atoms in the ring is a hydrogen atom.

105. The complimentary base pairs in DNA are cytosine (C) and guanine (G), and thymine (T) and adenine (A). The complimentary sequence is: C-C-A-G-A-T-A-T-G

106. For each letter, there are 4 choices; A, T, G, or C. Hence, the total number of codons is $4 \times 4 \times 4 = 64$.

107.   Uracil will hydrogen bond to adenine.

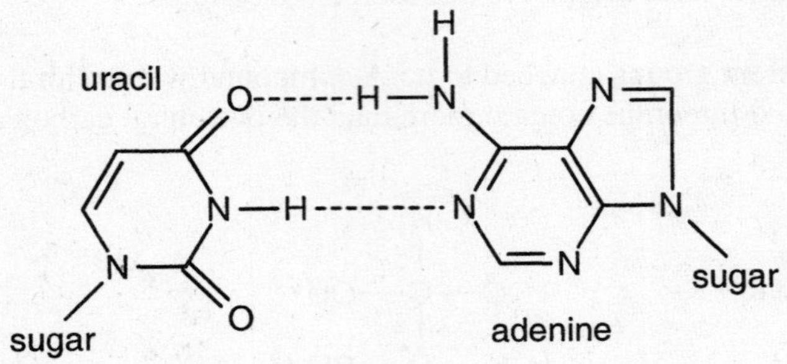

108.   The tautomer could hydrogen bond to guanine, forming a G–T base pair instead of A–T.

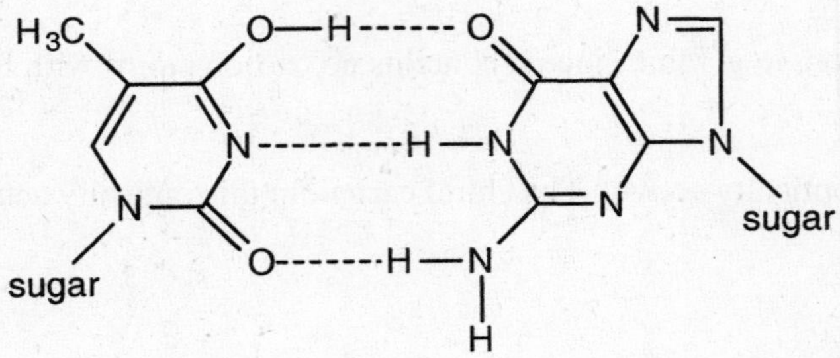

109.   Base pair:

RNA   DNA

A . . . . T

G C

C . . . . G

U . . . . A

a.   Glu: CTT, CTC   Val: CAA, CAG, CAT, CAC

Met: TAC   Trp: ACC

Phe: AAA, AAG   Asp: CTA, CTG

b.   DNA sequence for trp-glu-phe-met:

ACC –CTT –AAA –TAC
    or   or
    CTC   AAG

c. Due to glu and phe, there is a possibility of four different DNA sequences. They are:

ACC–CTT–AAA–TAC or ACC–CTC–AAA–TAC or

ACC–CTT–AAG–TAC or ACC–CTC–AAG –TAC

d.

T—A—C—C—T—G—A—A—G

met   asp   phe

e.   TAC–CTA–AAG; TAC–CTA–AAA; TAC–CTG–AAA

110.   In sickle cell anemia, glutamic acid is replaced by valine. DNA codons: Glu: CTT, CTC; Val: CAA, CAG, CAT, CAC; Replacing the middle T with an A in the code for Glu will code for Val.

CTT → CAT or CTC → CAC
Glu   Val   Glu   Val

Additional Exercises

111.   We omitted the hydrogens for clarity. The number of hydrogens bonded to each carbon is the number necessary to form four bonds.

a.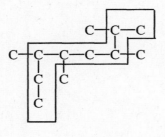

b.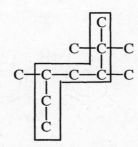

2,3,5,6-tetramethyloctane   2,2,3,5-tetramethylheptane

c.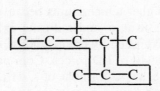

d.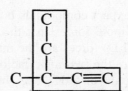

2,3,4-trimethylhexane   3-methyl-1-pentyne

112   a. Only one monochlorination product can form (1-chloro-2,2-dimethylpropane). The other possibilities differ from this compound by a simple rotation, so they are not different compounds.

$$CH_3 - \underset{\underset{CH_3}{|}}{\overset{\overset{CH_3}{|}}{C}} - \underset{Cl}{CH_2}$$

b. Three different monochlorination products are possible (ignoring cis-trans isomers).

c. Two different monochlorination products are possible (the other possibilities differ by a simple rotation of one of these two compounds).

113.

There are many possibilities for isomers. Any structure with four chlorines replacing four hydrogens in any four of the numbered positions would be an isomer, i.e., 1,2,3,4-tetra-chloro-dibenzo-p-dioxin is a possible isomer.

114.   We would expect compounds b and d to boil at the higher temperatures because they exhibit additional dipole forces that the nonpolar compounds in a, c, and e do not exhibit. London dispersion (LD) forces are the intermolecular forces exhibited by compounds a, c, and e. Size and shape are the two main factors that affect the strength of LD forces. Com-pounds a and e have a formula of C_5H_{12} and the bigger compound c has a formula of C_6H_{14}. The smaller compounds in a and e will boil at the two lowest boiling points. Between a and e, compound a has a more elongated structure which leads to stronger LD forces; compound a boils at 36°C and compound e boils at 9.5°C.

115.   The isomers are:

$$CH_3 \!-\! O \!-\! CH_3 \qquad\qquad CH_3CH_2OH$$

   dimethyl ether, $-23\,°C$ ethanol, $78.5\,°C$

Ethanol, with its ability to form the relatively strong hydrogen bonding interactions, boils at the higher temperature.

116.   The isomers are:

boils at lowest temperature
(no H-bonding)

With the exception of the first isomer, the other isomers can form the relatively strong hydrogen bonding interactions. The isomers which can hydrogen bond will boil at higher temperatures.

117.   Alcohols consist of two parts, the polar OH group and the nonpolar hydrocarbon chain attached to the OH group. As the length of the nonpolar hydrocarbon chain increases, the solubility of the alcohol decreases in water, a very polar solvent. In methyl alcohol (methanol), the polar OH group overrides the effect of the nonpolar CH_3 group, and methyl alcohol is soluble in water. In stearyl alcohol, the molecule consists mostly of the long nonpolar hydrocarbon chain, so it is insoluble in water.

118. $CH_3CH_2CH_2CH_2CH_2CH_2CH_2COOH + OH^- \rightarrow CH_3\!-\!(CH_2)_6\!-\!COO^- + H_2O$; Octanoic acid is more soluble in 1 M NaOH. Added OH^- will remove the acidic proton from octanoic acid, creating a charged species. As is the case with any substance with an overall charge, solubility in water increases. When morphine is reacted with H^+, the amine group is protonated, creating a positive charge on morphine ($R_3N + H^+ \longrightarrow R_3\overset{+}{N}H$). By treating morphine with HCl, an ionic compound results which is more soluble in water and in the blood stream than the neutral covalent form of morphine.

119.   The structures, the types of intermolecular forces exerted, and the boiling points for the compounds are:

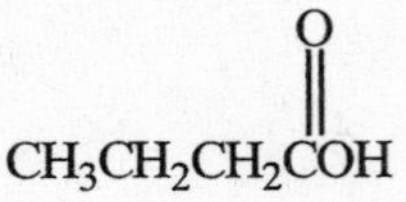

$CH_3CH_2CH_2\overset{\displaystyle O}{\overset{\|}{C}}OH$

butanoic acid, 164 °C
LD + dipole + H bonding

$CH_3CH_2CH_2CH_2CH_2OH$

1-pentanol, 137 °C
LD + H bonding

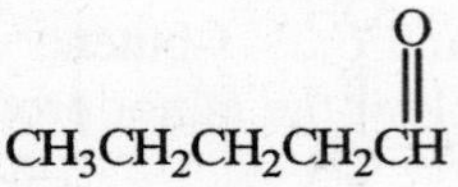

$CH_3CH_2CH_2CH_2\overset{\displaystyle O}{\overset{\|}{C}}H$

pentanal, 103 °C
LD + dipole

$CH_3CH_2CH_2CH_2CH_2CH_3$

n-hexane, 69 °C
LD only

All these compounds have about the same molar mass. Therefore, the London dispersion (LD) forces in each are about the same. The other types of forces determine the boiling point order. Since butanoic acid and 1-pentanol both exhibit hydrogen bonding inter-actions, these two compounds will have the two highest boiling points. Butanoic acid has the highest boiling point since it exhibits H bonding along with dipole-dipole forces due to the polar C=O bond.

120.   Water is produced in this reaction by removing an OH group from one substance and H from the other substance. There are two ways to do this:

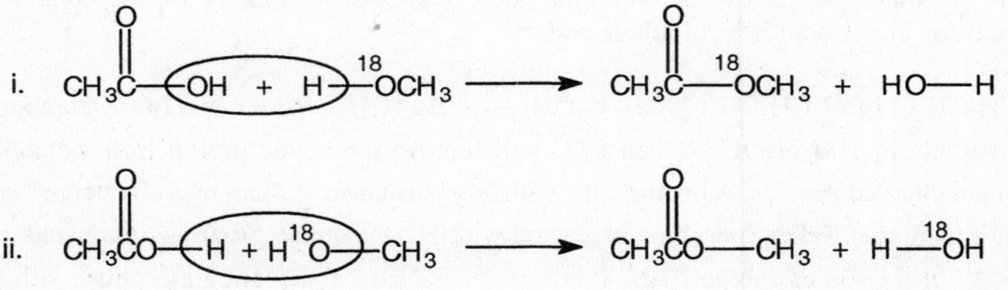

i. $CH_3\overset{\displaystyle O}{\overset{\|}{C}}-(OH + H)-\overset{18}{O}CH_3 \longrightarrow CH_3\overset{\displaystyle O}{\overset{\|}{C}}-\overset{18}{O}CH_3 + HO-H$

ii. $CH_3\overset{\displaystyle O}{\overset{\|}{C}}O-(H + H^{18}O)-CH_3 \longrightarrow CH_3\overset{\displaystyle O}{\overset{\|}{C}}O-CH_3 + H-\overset{18}{O}H$

Because the water produced is not radioactive, methyl acetate forms by the first reaction where all the oxygen-18 ends up in methyl acetate.

121. $85.63 \text{ g C} \times \dfrac{1 \text{ mol C}}{12.01 \text{ g C}} = 7.130 \text{ mol C}; \quad 14.37 \text{ g H} \times \dfrac{1 \text{ mol H}}{1.008 \text{ g H}} = 14.26 \text{ mol H}$

Because the mol H to mol C ratio is 2:1 (14.26/7.130 = 2.000), the empirical formula is CH_2. The empirical formula mass ≈ 12 + 2(1) = 14. Since 4 × 14 = 56 puts the molar mass between 50 and 60, the molecular formula is C_4H_8.   The isomers of C_4H_8 are:

$$CH_2\!\!=\!\!CHCH_2CH_3 \qquad CH_3CH\!\!=\!\!CHCH_3 \qquad \overset{\displaystyle CH_3}{\overset{|}{CH\!\!=\!\!CHCH_3}}$$

1-butene   2-butene   2-methyl-1-propene

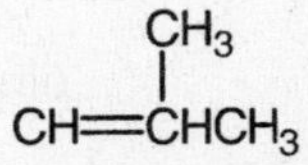

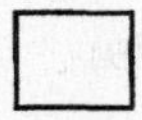

cyclobutane 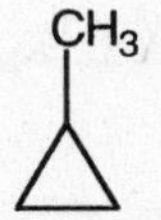   methylcyclopropane

Only the alkenes will react with H_2O to produce alcohols, and only 1-butene will produce a secondary alcohol for the major product and a primary alcohol for the minor product.

$$CH_2\!\!=\!\!CHCH_2CH_3 + H_2O \longrightarrow \overset{H\quad OH}{\overset{|\quad\ |}{CH_2\!\!-\!\!CHCH_2CH_3}}$$

2° alcohol, major product

$$CH_2\!\!=\!\!CHCH_2CH_3 + H_2O \longrightarrow \overset{OH\quad H}{\overset{|\quad\ |}{CH_2\!\!-\!\!CHCH_2CH_3}}$$

1° alcohol, minor product

2-butene will produce only a secondary alcohol when reacted with H_2O, and 2-methyl-1-propene will produce a tertiary alcohol as the major product and a primary alcohol as the minor product.

122. B_2H_6, $2(3) + 6(1) = 12$ e⁻ C_2H_6, $2(4) + 6(1) = 14$ e⁻

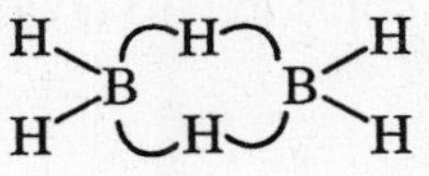

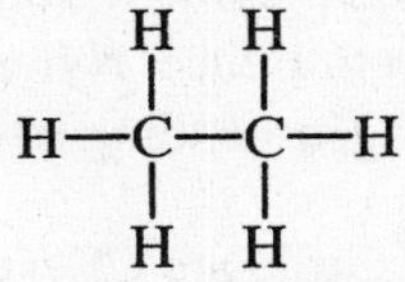

B_2H_6 has three centered bonds. In these bonds, a single pair of electrons is used to bond all three atoms together. Because these three centered bonds are extremely electron-deficient, they are highly reactive. C_2H_6 has two more valence electrons than B_2H_6 and does not require three-centered bonds to attach the atoms together. C_2H_6 is much more stable.

123. $KMnO_4$ will oxidize primary alcohols to aldehydes and then to carboxylic acids. Secondary alcohols are oxidized to ketones by $KMnO_4$. Tertiary alcohols and ethers are not oxidized by $KMnO_4$.

The three isomers and their reactions with $KMnO_4$ are:

$$CH_3 \underline{\quad} O \underline{\quad} CH_2CH_3 \xrightarrow{KMnO_4} \text{no reaction}$$

ether

$$\underset{\text{2° alcohol}}{CH_3 \underline{\quad} \overset{\overset{\displaystyle OH}{|}}{CH} \underline{\quad} CH_3} \xrightarrow{KMnO_4} \underset{\text{2-propanone (acetone)}}{CH_3 \underline{\quad} \overset{\overset{\displaystyle O}{\|}}{C} \underline{\quad} CH_3}$$

$$\underset{\text{1° alcohol}}{CH_3CH_2CH_2} \xrightarrow{KMnO_4} \underset{\text{propanal}}{CH_3CH_2\overset{\overset{\displaystyle O}{\|}}{CH}} \xrightarrow{KMnO_4} \underset{\text{propanoic acid}}{CH_3CH_2\overset{\overset{\displaystyle O}{\|}}{C} \underline{\quad} OH}$$

The products of the reactions with excess $KMnO_4$ are 2-propanone and propanoic acid.

124.   When addition polymerization of monomers with C=C bonds occurs, the backbone of the polymer chain consists of only carbon atoms. Because the backbone contains oxygen atoms, this is not an addition polymer; it is a condensation polymer. Because the ester functional group is present, we have a polyester condensation polymer. To form an ester functional group, we need the carboxylic acid and alcohol functional groups present in the monomers. From the structure of the polymer, we have a copolymer formed by the following monomers.

125.   In nylon, hydrogen-bonding interactions occur due to the presence of N–H bonds in the polymer. For a given polymer chain length, there are more N–H groups in Nylon-46 as compared to Nylon-6. Hence, Nylon-46 forms a stronger polymer compared to Nylon-6 due to the increased hydrogen-bonding interactions.

126.   The monomers for nitrile are CH_2=CHCN (acrylonitrile) and CH_2=CHCH=CH_2 (butadiene). The structure of polymer nitrile is:

127.   a.

b.   Repeating unit:

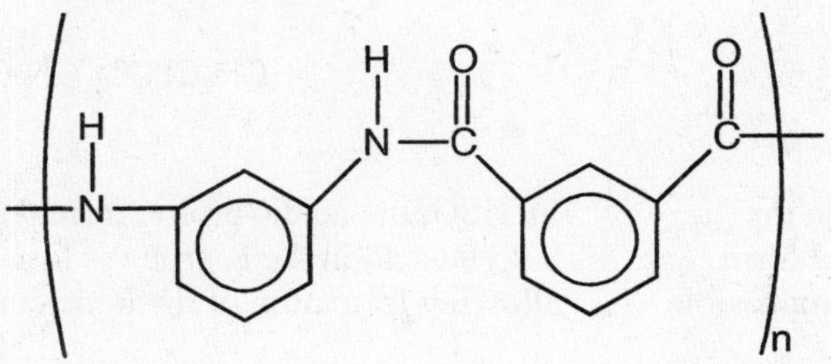

The two polymers differ in the substitution pattern on the benzene rings. The Kevlar chain is straighter, and there is more efficient hydrogen bonding between Kevlar chains than between Nomex chains.

128.   Polyacrylonitrile:

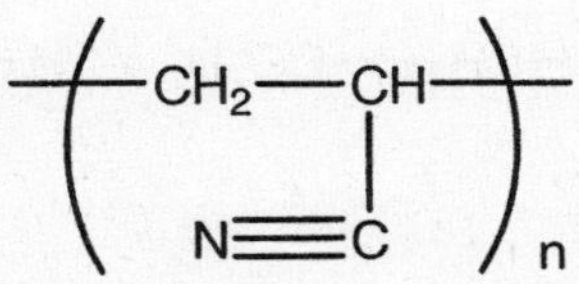

The CN triple bond is very strong and will not easily break in the combustion process. A likely combustion product is the toxic gas hydrogen cyanide, HCN(g).

129.   a.   The bond angles in the ring are about 60°. VSEPR predicts bond angles close to 109°. The bonding electrons are closer together than they prefer, resulting in strong electron-electron repulsions. Thus, ethylene oxide is unstable (reactive).

b.   The ring opens up during polymerization; the monomers link together through the formation of O–C bonds.

$$\left(\text{O—CH}_2\text{CH}_2\text{—O—CH}_2\text{CH}_2\text{—O—CH}_2\text{CH}_2\right)_n$$

130.

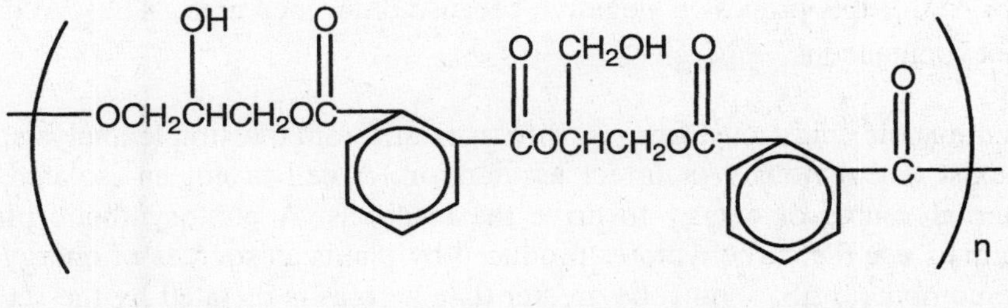

Two linkages are possible with glycerol. A possible repeating unit with both types of linkages is shown above. With either linkage, there are unreacted OH groups on the polymer chains. These can react with the acid groups of phthalic acid to form crosslinks among various polymer chains.

131.   Glutamic acid: Monosodium glutamate:

$$H_2N —CH —CO_2H$$
$$\qquad\qquad |$$
$$\qquad CH_2CH_2CO_2H$$

$$H_2N —CH —CO_2H$$
$$\qquad\qquad |$$
$$\qquad CH_2CH_2CO_2^- Na^+$$

One of the two acidic protons in the carboxylic acid groups is lost to form MSG. Which proton is lost is impossible for you to predict.

In MSG, the acidic proton from the carboxylic acid in the R group is lost, allowing formation of the ionic compound.

132. a.

$$H_2N——CH_2——CO_2H \ + \ H_2N——CH_2——CO_2H \ \rightleftharpoons$$

$$\qquad\qquad\qquad\qquad O$$
$$\qquad\qquad\qquad\qquad \|$$
$$H_2N——CH_2——C——N——CH_2——CO_2H \ + \ H——O——H$$
$$\qquad\qquad\qquad\qquad\quad |$$
$$\qquad\qquad\qquad\qquad\quad H$$

Bonds broken: Bonds formed:

1 C–O (358 kJ/mol)   1 C–N (305 kJ/mol)

1 H–N (391 kJ/mol)   1 H–O (467 kJ/mol)

$$\Delta H \ = 358 + 391 - (305 + 467) = -23 \ kJ$$

b. ΔS for this process is negative (unfavorable) because order increases (disorder decreases).

c. $\Delta G = \Delta H - T\Delta S$; ΔG is positive because of the unfavorable entropy change. The reaction is not spontaneous.

133. $\Delta G = \Delta H - T\Delta S$; For the reaction, we break a P–O and O–H bond and form a P–O and O–H bond, so $\Delta H \approx 0$. ΔS for this process is negative because order increases. Thus, $\Delta G > 0$ and the reaction is not spontaneous.

134.   Both proteins and nucleic acids must form for life to exist. From the simple analysis, it looks as if life can't exist, an obviously incorrect assumption. A cell is not an isolated system. There is an external source of energy to drive the reactions. A photosynthetic plant uses sunlight, and animals use the carbohydrates produced by plants as sources of energy. When all processes are combined, ΔS_{univ} must be greater than zero as is dictated by the second law of thermodynamics.

135.   Alanine can be thought of as a diprotic acid. The first proton to leave comes from the carboxylic acid end with $K_a = 4.5 \times 10^{-3}$. The second proton to leave comes from the protonated amine end (K_a for $R-NH_3^+ = K_w/K_b = 1.0 \times 10^{-14}/7.4 \times 10^{-5} = 1.4 \times 10^{-10}$).

In 1.0 M H^+, both the carboxylic acid and the amine end will be protonated since H^+ is in excess. The protonated form of alanine is below. In 1.0 M OH^-, the dibasic form of alanine will be present because the excess OH^- will remove all acidic protons from alanine. The dibasic form of alanine follows.

1.0 M H+ :   protonated form   1.0 M OH⁻ :   dibasic form

136.   The number of approximate base pairs in a DNA molecule is:

$$\frac{4.5 \times 10^9 \text{ g/mol}}{600 \text{ g/mol}} = 8 \times 10^6 \text{ base pairs}$$

The approximate number of complete turns in a DNA molecule is:

$$8 \times 10^6 \text{ base pairs} \times \frac{0.34 \text{ nm}}{\text{base pair}} \times \frac{1 \text{ turn}}{3.4 \text{ nm}} = 8 \times 10^5 \text{ turns}$$

137.   For denaturation, heat is added so it is an endothermic process. Because the highly ordered secondary structure is disrupted, entropy (disorder) will increase. Thus, ΔH and ΔS are both positive for protein denaturation.

138.   a. $^+H_3NCH_2COO^- + H_2O \rightleftharpoons H_2NCH_2CO_2^- + H_3O^+$

$$K_{eq} = K_a\,(-NH_3^+) = \frac{K_w}{K_b(-NH_2)} = \frac{1.0 \times 10^{-14}}{6.0 \times 10^{-5}} = 1.7 \times 10^{-10}$$

b. $H_2NCH_2CO_2^- + H_2O \rightleftharpoons H_2NCH_2CO_2H + OH^-$

$$K_{eq} = K_b\,(-CO_2^-) = \frac{K_w}{K_a(-CO_2H)} = \frac{1.0 \times 10^{-14}}{4.3 \times 10^{-3}} = 2.3 \times 10^{-12}$$

c. $^+H_3NCH_2CO_2H \rightleftharpoons 2\,H^+ + H_2NCH_2CO_2^-$

$$K_{eq} = K_a(-CO_2H) \times K_a(-NH_3^+) = (4.3 \times 10^{-3})(1.7 \times 10^{-10}) = 7.3 \times 10^{-13}$$

Challenge Problems

139.   For the reaction:

$$^+H_3NCH_2CO_2H \rightleftharpoons 2\,H^+ + H_2NCH_2CO_2^-\quad K_{eq} = 7.3 \times 10^{-13} = K_a\,(\text{-}CO_2H) \times K_a\,(\text{-}NH_3^+)$$

$$7.3 \times 10^{-13} = \frac{[H^+]^2[H_2NCH_2CO_2^-]}{[^+H_3NCH_2CO_2H]} = [H^+]^2,\quad [H^+] = (7.3 \times 10^{-13})^{1/2}$$

$$[H^+] = 8.5 \times 10^{-7}\,M;\quad pH = -\log[H^+] = 6.07 = \text{isoelectric point}$$

140.   a. The new amino acid is most similar to methionine due to its $-CH_2CH_2SCH_3$ R group.

b. The new amino acid replaces methionine. The structure of the tetrapeptide is:

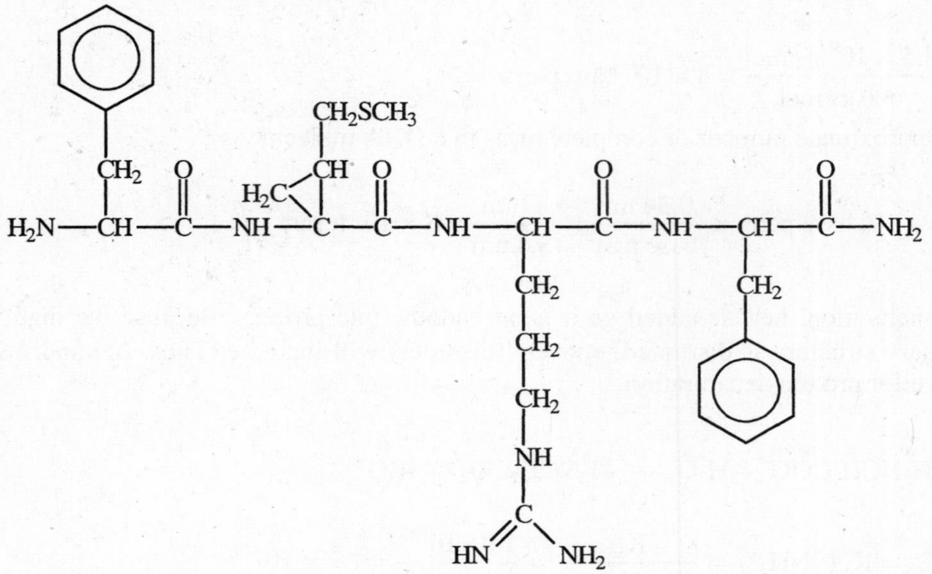

c. The chiral carbons are indicated with an asterisk.

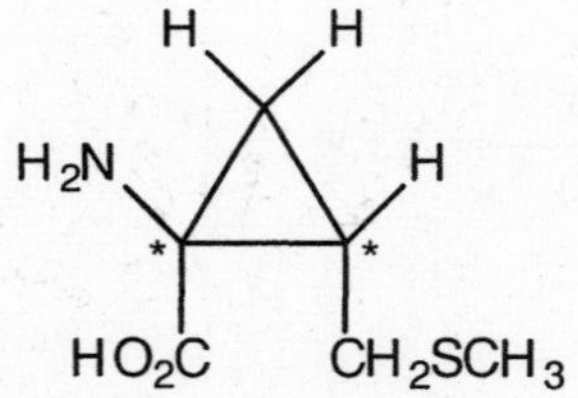

141.   a. Even though this form of tartaric acid contains 2 chiral carbon atoms (see asterisks in the following structure), the mirror image of this form of tartaric acid is superim-posable. Therefore, it is not optically active. An easier way to identify optical activity in molecules with two or more chiral carbon atoms is to look for a plane of symmetry in the molecule. If a molecule has a plane of symmetry, then it is never optically active. A plane of

symmetry is a plane that bisects the molecule where one side exactly reflects on the other side.

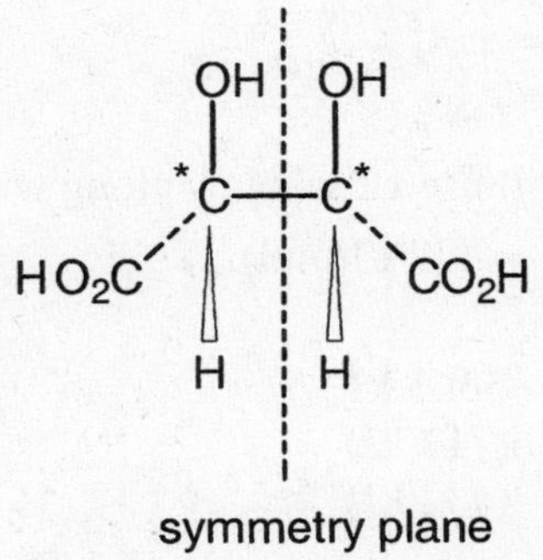

symmetry plane

b. The optically active forms of tartaric acid have no plane of symmetry. The structures of the optically active forms of tartaric acid are:

mirror

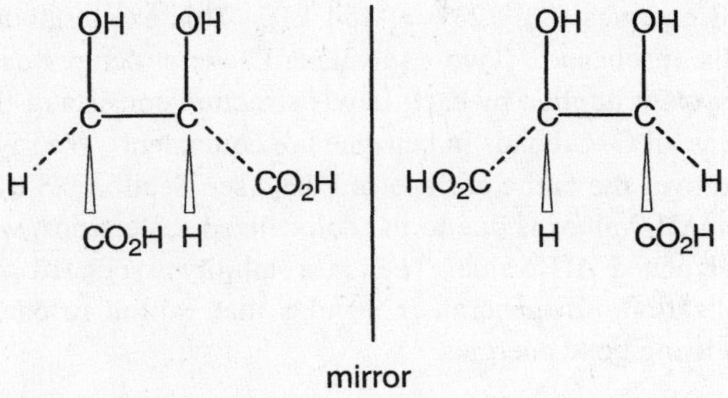

These two forms of tartaric acid are nonsuperimposable.

142.   One of the resonance structures for benzene is:

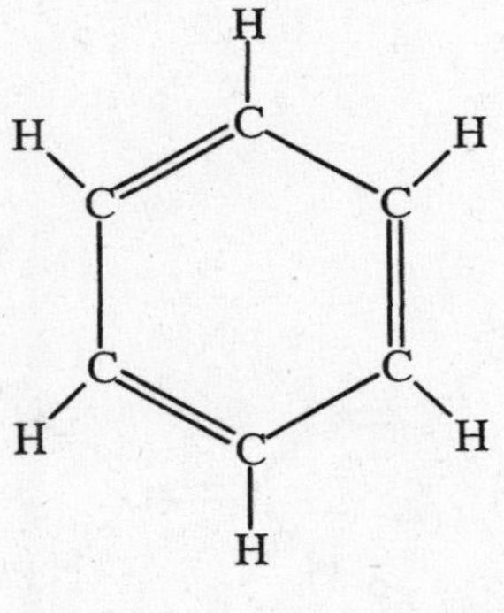

To break $C_6H_6(g)$ into $C(g)$ and $H(g)$ requires breaking 6 C–H bonds, 3 C=C bonds and 3 C–C bonds:

$$C_6H_6(g) \rightarrow 6\ C(g) + 6\ H(g) \quad \Delta H = 6\ D_{C-H} + 3\ D_{C=C} + 3\ D_{C-C}$$

$$\Delta H = 6(413\ kJ) + 3(614\ kJ) + 3(347\ kJ) = 5361\ kJ$$

The question asks for ΔH_f° for $C_6H_6(g)$, which is ΔH for the reaction:

$$6\ C(s) + 3\ H_2(g) \rightarrow C_6H_6(g) \quad \Delta H = \Delta H_{f,\,C_6H_6(g)}^\circ$$

To calculate ΔH for this reaction, we will use Hess's law along with the ΔH_f° value for $C(g)$ and the bond energy value for H_2 ($D_{H_2} = 432$ kJ/mol).

$$
\begin{array}{ll}
6\ C(g) + 6\ H(g) \rightarrow C_6H_6(g) & \Delta H_1 = -5361 \text{ kJ} \\
6\ C(s) \rightarrow 6\ C(g) & \Delta H_2 = 6(717 \text{ kJ}) \\
3\ H_2(g) \rightarrow 6\ H(g) & \Delta H_3 = 3(432 \text{ kJ})
\end{array}
$$

$$6\ C(s) + 3\ H_2(g) \rightarrow C_6H_6(g)\ \ \Delta H = \Delta H_1 + \Delta H_2 + \Delta H_3 = 237 \text{ kJ}; \ \ \Delta H_{f,\,C_6H_6(g)}^\circ = 237 \text{ kJ/mol}$$

The experimental ΔH_f° for $C_6H_6(g)$ is more stable (lower in energy) by 154 kJ as compared to ΔH_f° calculated from bond energies ($83 - 237 = -154$ kJ). This extra stability is related to benzene's ability to exhibit resonance. Two equivalent Lewis structures can be drawn for benzene. The π bonding system implied by each Lewis structure consists of three localized π bonds. This is not correct as all C–C bonds in benzene are equivalent. We say the π electrons in benzene are delocalized over the entire surface of C_6H_6 (see Section 9.5 of the text). The large discrepancy between ΔH_f° values is due to the delocalized π electrons, whose effect was not accounted for in the calculated ΔH_f° value. The extra stability associated with benzene can be called resonance stabilization. In general, molecules that exhibit resonance are usually more stable than predicted using bond energies.

143.

144.

cis-2-cis-4-hexadienoic acid

trans-2-cis-4-hexadienoic acid

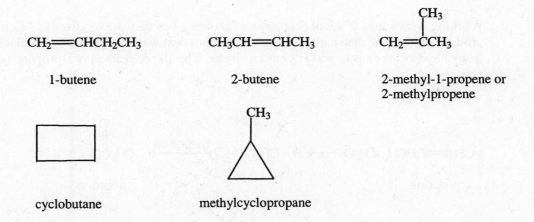

cis-2-trans-4-hexadienoic acid   trans-2-trans-4-hexadienoic acid

145.   a.   The three structural isomers of C_5H_{12} are:

CH$_3$CH$_2$CH$_2$CH$_2$CH$_3$ CH$_3$CHCH$_2$CH$_3$ CH$_3$—C—CH$_3$
                                                    | |
                                                   CH$_3$ CH$_3$ (top: CH$_3$, bottom: CH$_3$)

        n-pentane   2-methylbutane   2,2-dimethylpropane

n-pentane will form three different monochlorination products: 1-chloropentane, 2-chloropentane and 3-chloropentane (the other possible monochlorination products differ by a simple rotation of the molecule; they are not different products from the ones listed). 2-2,dimethylpropane will only form one monochlorination product: 1-chloro-2,2-dimethylpropane. 2-methylbutane is the isomer of C_5H_{12} that forms four different monochlorination products: 1-chloro-2-methylbutane, 2-chloro-2-methyl-butane, 3-chloro-2-methylbutane (or we could name this compound 2-chloro-3-methylbutane), and 1-chloro-3-methylbutane.

    b.   The isomers of C_4H_8 are:

                                                                            CH$_3$
                                                                             |
CH$_2$=CHCH$_2$CH$_3$ CH$_3$CH=CHCH$_3$ CH$_2$=CCH$_3$

        1-butene   2-butene   2-methyl-1-propene or
                                                                        2-methylpropene

                                        CH$_3$

        cyclobutane   methylcyclopropane

The cyclic structures will not react with H_2O; only the alkenes will add H_2O to the double bond. From Exercise 22.62, the major product of the reaction of 1-butene and H_2O is 2-butanol (a 2° alcohol). 2-butanol is also the major (and only) product when 2-butene and

H_2O react.   2-methylpropene forms 2-methyl-2-propanol as the major product when reacted with H_2O; this product is a tertiary alcohol. Therefore, the C_4H_8 isomer is 2-methylpropene.

2-methyl-2-propanol
(a 3° alcohol, 3 R
groups)

c. The structure of 1-chloro-1-methylcyclohexane is:

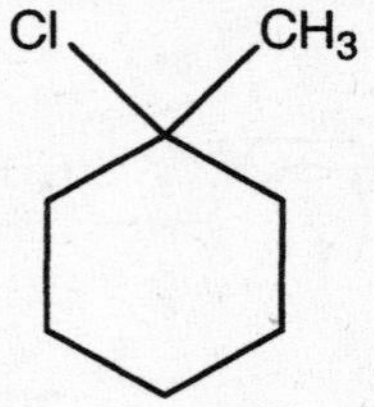

The addition reaction of HCl with an alkene is a likely choice for this reaction (see Exercise 22.62). The two isomers of C_7H_{12} that produce 1-chloro-1-methylcyclohexane as the major product are:

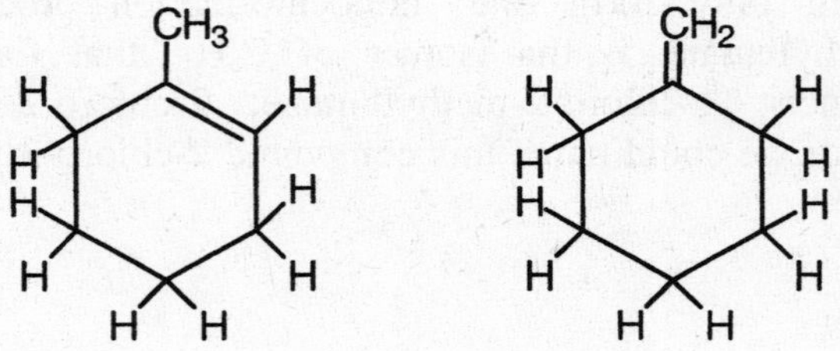

d. Working backwards, 2° alcohols produce ketones when they are oxidized (1° alco-hols produce aldehydes, then carboxylic acids). The easiest way to produce the 2° alcohol from a hydrocarbon is to add H_2O to an alkene. The alkene reacted is 1-propene (or propene).

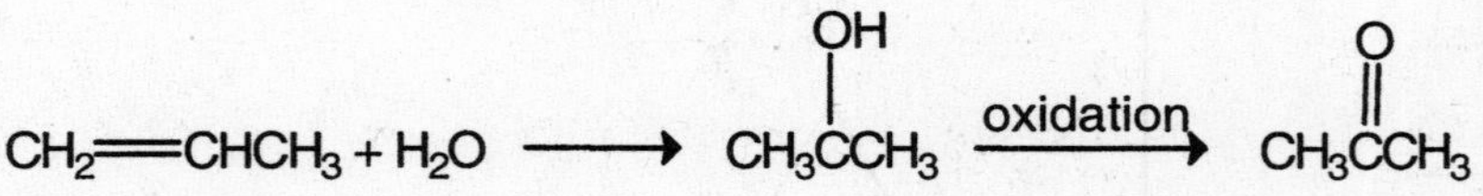

propene   acetone

e. The $C_5H_{12}O$ formula has too many hydrogens to be anything other than an alcohol (or an unreactive ether). 1° alcohols are first oxidized to aldehydes, then to carboxylic acids. Therefore, we want a 1° alcohol. The 1° alcohols with formula $C_5H_{12}O$ are:

1-pentanol   2-methyl-1-butanol   3-methyl-1-butanol   2,2-dimethyl-1-propanol

There are other alcohols with formula $C_5H_{12}O$, but they are all 2° or 3° alcohols, which do not produce carboxylic acids when oxidized.

146.   a.

b.   Condensation; HCl is eliminated when the polymer bonds form.

147.

148.   a.

acrylonitrile   butadiene   styrene

The structure of ABS plastic assuming a 1:1:1 mol ratio is:

Note: Butadiene does not polymerize in a linear fashion in ABS plastic (unlike other butadiene polymers). There is no way for you to be able to predict this.

b. Only acrylonitrile contains nitrogen. If we have 100.00 g of polymer:

$$8.80 \text{ g N} \times \frac{1 \text{ mol } C_3H_3N}{14.01 \text{ g N}} = \frac{53.06 \text{ g } C_3H_3N}{1 \text{ mol } C_3H_3 \text{ N}} = 33.3 \text{ g } C_3H_3N$$

$$\% \ C_3H_3N = \frac{33.3 \text{ g } C_3H_3N}{100.00 \text{ g polymer}} = 33.3\% \ C_3H_3N$$

Br_2 adds to double bonds of alkenes (benzene's delocalized π bonds in the styrene monomer will not react with Br_2 unless a special catalyst is present). Only butadiene in the polymer has a reactive double bond. From the polymer structure in part a, butadiene will react in a 1:1 mol ratio with Br_2.

$$0.605 \text{ g } Br_2 \times \frac{1 \text{ mol } Br_2}{159.8 \text{ g } Br_2} \times \frac{1 \text{ mol } C_4H_6}{\text{mol } Br_2} \times \frac{54.09 \text{ g } C_4H_6}{\text{mol } C_4H_6} = 0.205 \text{ g } C_4H_6$$

$$\% \ C_4H_6 = \frac{0.205 \text{ g}}{1.20 \text{ g}} \times 100 = 17.1\% \ C_4H_6$$

% styrene (C_8H_8) = 100.0 − 33.3 − 17.1 = 49.6% C_8H_8.

c. If we have 100.0 g of polymer:

$$33.3 \text{ g } C_3H_3N \times \frac{1 \text{ mol } C_3H_3N}{53.06 \text{ g}} = 0.628 \text{ mol } C_3H_3N$$

$$17.1 \text{ g } C_4H_6 \times \frac{1 \text{ mol } C_4H_6}{54.09 \text{ g } C_4H_6} = 0.316 \text{ mol } C_4H_6$$

$$49.6 \text{ g } C_8H_8 \times \frac{1 \text{ mol } C_8H_8}{104.14 \text{ g } C_8H_8} = 0.476 \text{ mol } C_8H_8$$

Dividing by 0.316: $\dfrac{0.628}{0.316} = 1.99$; $\dfrac{0.316}{0.316} = 1.00$; $\dfrac{0.476}{0.316} = 1.51$

This is close to a mol ratio of 4:2:3.   Thus, there are 4 acrylonitrile to 2 butadiene to 3 styrene molecules in this polymer sample; or $(A_4B_2S_3)_n$.

149.   a.   The temperature of the rubber band increases when it is stretched.

b.   Exothermic because heat is released.

c.   As the chains are stretched, they line up more closely together, resulting in stronger London dispersion forces between the chains.   Heat is released as the strength of the intermolecular forces increases.

d.   Stretching is not spontaneous so, ΔG is positive. $\Delta G = \Delta H - T\Delta S$;   Since ΔH is negative then ΔS must be negative in order to give a positive ΔG.

e.

unstretched   stretched

The structure of the stretched polymer is more ordered (lower S).

150.   a.

step 1:   1-butanol

$$CH_2=CHCH_2CH_3 + H_2O$$
1-butene

step 2: $CH_2=CHCH_2CH_3 + H_2 \xrightarrow{Pt} CH_3CH_2CH_2CH_3$
1-butene   butane

b.

step 1:

$$CH_2(OH)-CHCH_2CH_3 \xrightarrow{H^+} CH_2=CHCH_2CH_3 + H_2O$$

1-butanol   1-butene

step 2:

$$CH_2=CHCH_2CH_3 + H_2O \xrightarrow{H^+} CH_2(H)-CH(OH)CH_2CH_3$$

1-butene   2-butanol (major product)

step 3:

$$CH_3-CH(OH)CH_2CH_3 \xrightarrow{\text{oxidation}} CH_3-C(O)-CH_2CH_3$$

2-butanol   2-butanone

151. 4.2×10^{-3} g $K_2CrO_7 \times \dfrac{1 \text{ mol } K_2Cr_2O_7}{294.20 \text{ g}} \times \dfrac{1 \text{ mol } Cr_2O_7^{2-}}{\text{mol } K_2Cr_2O_7} \times \dfrac{3 \text{ mol } C_2H_5OH}{2 \text{ mol } Cr_2O_7^{2-}}$

$$= 2.1 \times 10^{-5} \text{ mol } C_2H_5OH$$

$$n_{\text{breath}} = \frac{PV}{RT} = \frac{\left(750. \text{ mm Hg} \times \dfrac{1 \text{ atm}}{760 \text{ mm Hg}}\right) \times 0.500 \text{ L}}{\dfrac{0.08206 \text{ L atm}}{\text{K mol}} \times 303 \text{ K}} = 0.0198 \text{ mol breath}$$

mol % $C_2H_5OH = \dfrac{2.1 \times 10^{-5} \text{ mol } C_2H_5OH}{0.0198 \text{ mol total}} \times 100 = 0.11\%$ alcohol

152. Assuming 1.000 L of the hydrocarbon (C_xH_y), then the volume of products will be 4.000 L and the mass of products ($H_2O + CO_2$) will be:

1.391 g/L × 4.000 L = 5.564 g products

moles $C_xH_y = n_{C_xH_y} = \dfrac{PV}{RT} = \dfrac{0.959 \text{ atm} \times 1.000 \text{ L}}{\dfrac{0.08206 \text{ L atm}}{\text{K mol}} \times 298 \text{ K}} = 0.0392$ mol

moles products $= n_p = \dfrac{PV}{RT} = \dfrac{1.51 \text{ atm} \times 4.000 \text{ L}}{\dfrac{0.08206 \text{ L atm}}{\text{K mol}} \times 375 \text{ K}} = 0.196$ mol

C_xH_y + oxygen $\rightarrow$ x CO_2 + y/2 H_2O;   Setting up two equations:

0.0392x + 0.0392(y/2) = 0.196 (mol of products)

0.0392x(44.01 g/mol) + 0.0392(y/2)(18.02 g/mol) = 5.564 g (mass of products)

Solving: x = 2 and y = 6, so the formula of the hydrocarbon is C_2H_6.

153.   The five chiral carbons are marked with an asterisk.

Each of these five carbons have four different groups bonded to it. The fourth bond that is not shown for any of the five chiral carbons is a C–H bond.

Integrative Problems

154.   a.   0.5063 g CO_2 $\times$ $\dfrac{1\,\text{mol } CO_2}{44.01\,\text{g}}$ $\times$ $\dfrac{1\,\text{mol C}}{\text{mol } CO_2}$ $\times$ $\dfrac{12.01\,\text{g C}}{\text{mol C}}$ = 0.1382 g C

mass %C = $\dfrac{0.1382\,\text{g C}}{0.1450\,\text{g compound}}$ $\times$ 100 = 95.31%

%H = 100.00 – 95.31 = 4.69%H

Assuming 100.00 g compound:

95.31 g C $\times$ $\dfrac{1\,\text{mol C}}{12.01\,\text{g C}}$ = 7.936 mol C/4.653 = 1.706 mol C

4.69 g H $\times$ $\dfrac{1\,\text{mol H}}{1.008\,\text{g H}}$ = 4.653 mol H/4.653 = 1 mol H

Multiplying by 10 gives the empirical formula $C_{17}H_{10}$.

b.   mol helicene = 0.0125 kg $\times$ $\dfrac{0.0175\,\text{mol helicene}}{\text{kg solvent}}$ = 2.19 $\times$ 10^{-4} mol helicene

$$\text{molar mass} = \frac{0.0938 \text{ g}}{2.19 \times 10^{-4} \text{ mol}} = 428 \text{ g/mol}$$

Empirical formula mass $\approx 17(12) + 10(1) = 214$ g/mol

Because $\dfrac{428}{214} = 2.00$, the molecular formula is $(C_{17}H_{10}) \times 2 = C_{34}H_{20}$

c. $C_{34}H_{20}(s) + 39 \text{ O}_2(g) \rightarrow 34 \text{ CO}_2(g) + 10 \text{ H}_2O(l)$

155. a. Zn^{2+} has the $[Ar]3d^{10}$ electron configuration and zinc does form +2 charged ions.

$$\text{mass \%Zn} = \frac{\text{mass of 1 mol Zn}}{\text{mass of 1 mol CH}_3\text{CH}_2\text{ZnBr}} \times 100 = \frac{65.38 \text{ g}}{174.34 \text{ g}} \times 100 = 37.50\% \text{ Zn}$$

b. The reaction is:

The hybridization changes from sp^2 to sp^3.

c. 3,4-dimethyl-3-hexanol

Marathon Problems

156. a. urea, ammonium cyanate   b. saturated   c. tetrahedral
      d. straight-chain or normal   e. bonds   f. –ane
      g. longest   h. number   i. combustion
      j. substitution   k. addition   l. hydrogenation
      m. aromatic   n. functional   o. primary
      p. carbon monoxide   q. fermentation   r. carbonyl
      s. oxidation   t. carboxyl   u. esters, alcohol

157. a. statement (17)   b. statement (13)   c. statement (15)
      d. statement (12)   e. statement (8)   f. statement (9)
      g. statement (16)   h. statement (2)   i. statement (4)
      j. statement (10)   k. statement (11)   l. statement (7)
      m. statement (14)   n. statement (3)   o. statement (6)
      p. statement (1)   q. statement (5)

158. a. deoxyribonucleic acid   b. nucleotides   c. ribose
      d. ester   e. complentary   f. thymine, guanine
      g. gene   h. transfer, messenger i. DNA